Stressors and the Adjustment Disorders

WILEY SERIES IN GENERAL AND CLINICAL PSYCHIATRY

Series Chair
MAURICE R. GREEN, M.D.
New York University
Medical School

The Broad Scope of Ego Function Assessment
Edited by Leopold Bellak and Lisa A. Goldsmith

The Psychological Experience of Surgery
Edited by Richard S. Blacher

Presentations of Depression: Depressive Symptoms in Medical and Other
Psychiatric Disorders
Edited by Oliver G. Cameron

Clinical Guidelines in Cross-Cultural Mental Health
Edited by Lillian Comas-Diaz and Ezra E. H. Griffith

Sleep Disorders: Diagnosis and Treatment (Second Edition)
Edited by Robert L. Williams, Ismet Karacan and Constance A. Moore

Multiple Personality Disorder: Diagnosis, Clinical Features, and Treatment
Colin A. Ross

Stressors and the Adjustment Disorders
Edited by Joseph D. Noshpitz and R. Dean Coddington

STRESSORS AND THE ADJUSTMENT DISORDERS

Edited by

Joseph D. Noshpitz
R. Dean Coddington

A Wiley-Interscience Publication

JOHN WILEY & SONS

New York · Chichester · Brisbane · Toronto · Singapore

Library of Congress Cataloging-in-Publication Data:

Stressors and the adjustment disorders / edited by Joseph D. Noshpitz
    and R. Dean Coddington.
        p.   cm. — (Wiley series in General and Clinical Psychiatry)
    Includes bibliographical references.
    ISBN 0-471-62186-2
    1. Adjustment disorders.   2. Stress (Psychology)   I. Noshpitz,
Joseph D.   II. Coddington, R. Dean, 1924-   .   III. Series.
    [DNLM: 1. Adjustment Disorders.   2. Stress, Psychological.   WM
171 S915]
RC455.4.S87S78   1990
616.9′8—dc20
DNLM/DLC
for Library of Congress   89-25065

Printed in the United States of America

10 9 8 7 6 5 4 3 2 1

Contributors

PAUL L. ADAMS, MD
Emeritus Professor of Child
    Psychiatry
The University of Texas Medical
    Branch at Galveston
Galveston, Texas
Private Practice, Louisville,
    Kentucky

CARL P. ADATTO, MD
Clinical Professor Emeritus
Louisiana State University
    School of Medicine
Training and Supervising Analyst
    Emeritus
New Orleans Psychoanalytic
    Institute
New Orleans, Louisiana

RANSOM J. ARTHUR, MD
Professor of Psychiatry and
    Behavioral Sciences, Emeritus
UCLA School of Medicine
Los Angeles, California

IRVING N. BERLIN, MD
Professor of Psychiatry and
    Pediatrics
University of New Mexico
Senior Consultant, Division of
    Child and Adolescent
    Psychiatry
The Children's Psychiatric
    Hospital
Albuquerque, New Mexico

NORMAN R. BERNSTEIN, MD
Professor of Psychiatry, Harvard
    University
Staff Psychiatrist, Massachusetts
    General Hospital
Boston, Massachusetts
Clinical Associate, University of
    Chicago Medical School
Chicago, Illinois

STELLA CHESS, MD
Professor of Child Psychiatry
New York University Medical
    Center
New York, New York

RICHARD F. DALTON, MD
Associate Professor of Psychiatry
and Pediatrics
Tulane University School of
Medicine
New Orleans, Louisiana

BRUCE L. DANTO, MD
Lt. Col. U.S.A.R., Retired
Special Forces
Fort Bragg, North Carolina
Private Practice, Fullerton,
California

BRUCE P. DOHRENWEND, PhD
Professor, Department of
Psychology
Columbia University
Chief, Department of Social
Psychiatry
New York State Psychiatric
Institute
New York, New York

GORDON K. FARLEY, MD
Clinical Director, Division of
Child Psychiatry
University of Colorado Health
Sciences Center
Denver, Colorado

SHERMAN C. FEINSTEIN, MD
Editor in Chief
Annals of the American Society
for Adolescent Psychiatry
Clinical Professor of Psychiatry
Pritzker School of Medicine
Highland Park, Illinois

RICHARD A. GARDNER, MD
Clinical Professor of Child
Psychiatry

Columbia University, College of
Physicians and Surgeons
New York, New York

ELLEN GERRITY, PhD
Assistant Research Professor of
Psychiatry and Behavioral
Sciences
George Washington University
School of Medicine
Washington, District of
Columbia

RAPHAEL S. GOOD, MD
Professor of Clinical Psychiatry
and Obstetrics-Gynecology
University of Miami School of
Medicine
Miami, Florida

MARTIN HARROW, PhD
Professor of Psychiatry
Pritzker School of Medicine
University of Chicago
Director, Clinical Psychiatry
Michael Reese Hospital
Chicago, Illinois

SEYMOUR L. HALLECK, MD
Residency Training Program
Department of Psychiatry
The North Carolina Memorial
Hospital
University of North Carolina
Chapel Hill, North Carolina

JAMES R. HENRY, MD, PhD
Research Professor
Department of Psychiatry,
School of Medicine
Loma Linda University
Loma Linda, California

MARC HERTZMAN, MD
Director, Pain and Physical
   Symptom Treatment Program
Department of Psychiatry and
   Behavioral Sciences
The George Washington
   University Medical Center
Washington, District of
   Columbia

JOSEPH H. HERZBERG, MD
Professor of Community
   Psychiatry
School of Medicine in New
   Orleans
Louisiana State University
New Orleans, Louisiana

BARRY IVKER, PhD
Department of Psychiatry
Louisiana State University
   Medical Center
New Orleans, Louisiana

JERRY W. JOHNSON, MPA
Director of Administration and
   Senior Associate
The Will Menninger Center for
   Applied Behavioral Sciences
The Menninger Clinic
Topeka, Kansas

CHARLES KEITH, MD
Training Director, Division of
   Child and Adolescent
   Psychiatry
Associate Professor of Psychiatry
Duke University Medical Center
Durham, North Carolina

RANDY KETTERING, PhD
Department of Psychiatry
Good Shepherd Hospital

Barrington, Illinois
Private Practice, Schaumburg,
   Illinois

GILBERT W. KLIMAN, MD
Director of Preventative and
   Forensic Services
Psychological Trauma Center
St. Mary's Hospital and Medical
   Center
San Francisco, California

REGINA P. LEDERMAN, PhD
Professor and Associate Dean of
   Academic Affairs
School of Nursing
University of Texas Medical
   Branch
Galveston, Texas

HOYLE LEIGH, MD
Professor of Psychiatry
Yale University School of
   Medicine
New Haven, Connecticut

BRUCE G. LINK, PhD
Associate Professor of Clinical
   Public Health (Epidemiology)
Social Psychiatry Research Unit
Columbia University
New York, New York

MARY LYSTAD, PhD
Chief, Emergency Services
   Branch
Department of Health and
   Human Services
National Institute of Mental
   Health
Rockville, Maryland

GERALD G. MCKENNA, MD
Associate Clinical Professor of
  Psychiatry
John A. Burns School of
  Medicine
University of Hawaii at Manoa
Lihue, Hawaii

CAROL C. NADELSON, MD
Professor and Vice Chairman for
  Academic Affairs
Director of Training and
  Education
Department of Psychiatry
Tufts–New England Medical
  Center Hospitals
Boston, Massachussetts

JOSEPH D. NOSHPITZ, MD
Clinical Professor of Psychiatry
  and Behavioral Science
George Washington University
Washington, District of
  Columbia

MALKAH T. NOTMAN, MD
Director of Academic Affairs
Cambridge Hospital
Clinical Professor of Psychiatry
Harvard Medical School
Cambridge, Massachussetts

HOWARD J. OSOFSKY, MD, PhD
Professor and Head
Department of Psychiatry
Louisiana State University
  Medical Center
New Orleans, Louisiana

DANE G. PRUGH, MD
Emeritus Professor of Psychiatry
  and Pediatrics

University of Colorado School of
  Medicine
Denver, Colorado
Clinical Professor of Psychiatry
  and Pediatrics
University of California Irvine
  Medical School
Pomona, California

LILLIAN H. ROBINSON, MD
Emeritus Professor of Psychiatry
  and Pediatrics
Tulane University School of
  Medicine
New Orleans, Louisiana

JUSTIN O. SCHECHTER, MD
Clinical Assistant Professor of
  Psychiatry
New York Medical College
Director of Outpatient
  Department of Psychiatry
  Division
Stanford Hospital
Stanford, Connecticut

JON A. SHAW, MD
Professor of Psychiatry
Uniformed Services
University of the Health Sciences
F. Edward Herbert School of
  Medicine
Bethesda, Maryland

PATRICK E. SHROUT, PhD
Associate Professor of Clinical
  Public Health
Social Psychiatry Research Unit
Columbia University College of
  Physicians and Surgeons
New York, New York

ANDREW E. SKODOL, MD
Associate Clinical Professor of
  Psychiatry
Social Psychiatry Research Unit
Columbia University College of
  Physicians and Surgeons
New York, New York

BERTRAM SLAFF, MD
Associate Clinical Professor of
  Psychiatry
Mt. Sinai School of Medicine
City University of New York
New York, New York

BRANDT F. STEELE, MD
Professor of Psychiatry Emeritus
University of Colorado School of
  Medicine
Psychiatrist, C. H. Kemp
  National Center for Prevention
  and Treatment of Child Abuse
  and Neglect
Training Analyst
Denver Institute for
  Psychoanalysis
Denver, Colorado

PETER STEINGLASS, MD
Professor of Psychiatry and
  Behavioral Sciences
George Washington University
  School of Medicine
Washington, District of
  Columbia

MICHAEL H. STONE, MD
Professor of Clinical Psychiatry
Columbia College of Physicians
  and Surgeons
New York, New York

GLENN SWOGGER, JR., MD
Senior Associate
The Will Menninger Center for
  Applied Behavioral Sciences
The Menninger Center
Topeka, Kansas

WILLIAM C. SZE, PhD
Department of Psychiatry
Louisiana State University
  Medical Center
New Orleans, Louisiana

TROY L. THOMPSON II, MD
Professor and Chairman
Department of Psychiatry
Jefferson Medical College
Philadelphia, Pennsylvania

MOLLIE M. WALLICK, PhD
Professor of Psychiatry
Louisiana State University
  School of Medicine
New Orleans, Louisiana

THOMAS G. WEBSTER, MD
Professor Emeritus of Psychiatry
  and Behavioral Sciences and
  Child Health and Development
George Washington University
  Medical Center
Washington, D.C.

SIDNEY WERKMAN, MD
Professor of Psychiatry
University of Colorado Health
  Sciences Center
Denver, Colorado

DAVID D. YOUNGS, MD
Staff Surgeon
Department of Gynecology and
  Psychiatry
Cleveland Clinic Foundation
Cleveland, Ohio

Series Preface

This series of books is addressed to psychiatrists, mental health specialists, and other serious students of the behavioral sciences. It is inspired by the genius of Adolf Meyer, who introduced psychobiology to psychiatry and charted the course, recently reformulated by George L. Engel, of the biopsychosocial model. Each book may consider the importance of any level of human behavioral interaction—community, family, interpersonal, individual, psychological, psychoanalytic, physiological, biochemical, and genetic or constitutional. Each level is respected on its own terms; no book in this series will fall victim to the fallacy of reductionism.

All aspects of psychiatric disorders, including theoretical, empirical, and therapeutic, are considered. Specific research studies, with their practical applications, are also included. It is our intention that the books in this series be comprehensive, thorough, rigorous, systematic, and original.

MAURICE R. GREEN

New York University Medical Center
New York, New York

Preface

The history of this book begins with the annals of the Task Force on Psychiatric Therapies of the American Psychiatric Association. Dr. Byram Karasu was entrusted with the creation and direction of that major APA project, and he turned to psychiatrists all over the country to help in its achievement. Among other aspects of the undertaking, it was decided to address the various syndromes individually and to render an account of the treatment methods currently in use. The many colleagues who joined Dr. Karasu in carrying out this project convened panels of experts on each of the several major categories of psychiatric illness. These panels then accomplished the actual writing of the text.

The two Editors of the present volume were recruited for this taskforce and were given the mission of producing a work on the treatment of the Adjustment Disorders. In considering how best to carry out this commission, we offered Dr. Karasu two options: a more focused effort dealing with the treatment aspects as such, and a more global approach directed toward an overall consideration of human stress response, with the Adjustment Disorders as the prime example of how people do indeed deal with stress. Ultimately, it was decided to do both. Accordingly, we embarked on the larger project and included, within its structure, the direct study of the treatment of Adjustment Disorders.

With this, the invitations were sent out to the various authors who were to comprise the Panel on the Adjustment Disorders, explaining the project and asking their help in writing the several chapters. This turned out to be a complex undertaking. In the nature of things, the varieties of stress and the many sources of stress are not neatly enfolded within the psychiatric diagnostic or treatment realms, and it was no mean effort to find authors who were expert in the wide variety of stress areas under consideration. It is said of Beethoven that he would write impossible parts for the French horn and then find impossible horn players to perform them. Our problem was somewhat similar; we sought authors who could write about such matters as the impact of business reverses or the loss of an ideal or the experience of being kidnapped as sources of stress. These, it turns out, are not to be had for the asking. In fact, some ideas simply could not be realized; within the available time frame, no authors could be found for the assigned topics. Some assignments fell by the wayside for other reasons; anyone who tries to put together a multi-authored work knows the hazards and the complex human situations that befall such a project. Nonetheless, we persevered, and the work got under way.

The papers began coming in for our review. After going over each one in some detail, we then exchanged views, sometimes differing but usually agreeing. One of us (R.D.C.) assumed the tasks of putting together the suggestions that had arisen out of the editorial exchanges and of corresponding with the several authors about suggested changes. In time, the present volume took shape.

Meanwhile, it came time to arrange for the preparation of the APA's Task Force volume. The appropriate materials were culled from the larger array of papers (about stress and stress responses) and formed into a coherent statement about the nature and treatment of the Adjustment Disorders and were sent on to Dr. Karasu for inclusion in the report of the APA's Task Force. Once that work had been accomplished, we turned our energies toward the more global essay on stress responses, which was then prepared for publication and is presented here.

As noted, this was conceived as a study of the human adjustment to stress, where it is assumed that the initial response is usually in the form of an Adjustment Disorder. It was evident from the outset (nor did the APA peer reviewers fail to observe) that other kinds of reaction patterns are described within the psychiatric framework, for example, the PostTraumatic Stress Disorder. The issue of boundaries, of distinguishing the Adjustment Disorders from other possible syndromes, remains rather an undecided question. It is difficult to draw such a distinction because the chief defining characteristic of the Adjustment Disorder is not what it *looks like* clinically so much as *when* it occurs—and how long it lasts. Time will have to unravel some of these questions, and we can do no more at this point than to present the views of the many experts who have contributed to this volume.

In any case, it is evident that the role of stress reactions is of primary importance to modern psychiatric thinking, and that the patterning and the underlying mechanisms of such responses are major sites for future research. The present work is not a research enterprise: It is rather an attempt to make a clinical statement about the sources of stress, the forms of stress response, and the current array of treatment possibilities. We hope that it will heighten the sensitivity of the field to the powerful potential of many everyday situations to engender distress. We are also hopeful that it will add to the skill data base of the professional reader who comes in contact with these disturbing clinical problems and that it will offer useful suggestions about how best to alleviate the pain accompanying these disorders.

JOSEPH D. NOSHPITZ, MD
R. DEAN CODDINGTON, MD

Washington, DC
July 1990

Contents

**SECTION ONE   THE NATURE OF STRESS AND
THE NATURE OF ADJUSTMENT DISORDERS**   **1**

1 The Nature of Stress: Problems of Measurement   **3**
   Andrew E. Skodol, MD
   Bruce P. Dohrenwend, PhD
   Bruce G. Link, PhD
   Patrick E. Shrout, PhD

SECTION TWO   TYPES OF STRESSORS   **21**

A   STRESS ARISING FROM OBJECT LOSS

2 Object Loss Due to Death of Parent or Sibling   **23**
   Richard A. Gardner, MD

3 Childhood Stress Due to Parental Divorce   **43**
   Richard A. Gardner, MD

B   STRESS ARISING FROM ILLNESS

**4 Illness as a Source of Stress: Acute Illness, Chronic Illness,
   and Surgical Procedures**   **60**
   Dane G. Prugh, MD
   Troy L. Thompson II, MD

5 Illness as Stress: Accidents and Toxic Ingestions   **143**
   Justin O. Schechter, MD
   Hoyle Leigh, MD

6 Pain as Stress: Relationships to Treatment   160
   Marc Hertzman, MD

C DEVELOPMENTAL SOURCES OF STRESS

7 Birth-Related Reactions as Sources of Stress   176
   Raphael S. Good, MD
   Regina P. Lederman, PhD
   Howard J. Osofsky, MD, PhD
   David D. Youngs, MD

8 Developmental Sources of Stress: The First through the Fifth
   Year of Life   189
   Mollie M. Wallick, PhD

9 Developmental Sources of Stress: Latency   217
   Joseph D. Noshpitz, MD

10 Developmental Sources of Stress: Puberty   238
   Bertram Slaff, MD

D STRESS ARISING FROM NATURAL DISASTERS

11 Flood, Tornado, and Hurricane   247
   Mary Lystad, PhD

12 Fire   260
   Norman R. Bernstein, MD

E STRESS ARISING FROM HUMAN VIOLENCE

13 Human-Engendered Bodily Trauma: Rape and Spouse
   Beating   278
   Carol C. Nadelson, MD
   Malkah T. Notman, MD

14 Stress Experienced by Robbery Victims, Hostages,
   Kidnapping Victims, and Prisoners of War   294
   Bruce L. Danto, MD

15 Child Abuse: Its Nature and Treatment   315
    Brandt F. Steele, MD

16 Assault by Fellow Citizens   327
    Charles Keith, MD

17 Stress Engendered by Military Action on Military and
    Civilian Populations   340
    Jon A. Shaw, MD

          F   STRESS ENGENDERED BY SOCIAL TRAUMA

18 Prejudice and Exclusion as Social Traumata   362
    Paul L. Adams, MD

19 The Psychological Impact of Being Accused of, Investigated
    for, or Tried for Malfeasance   392
    Seymour L. Halleck, MD

20 Forced Displacement to a New Environment   399
    Peter Steinglass, MD
    Ellen Gerrity, PhD

21 Geographic Change as a Stressor: Developmental Perspectives   418
    Gordon K. Farley, MD
    Sidney Werkman, MD

22 Loss of an Ideal   432
    Michael H. Stone, MD

23 Economic Trauma: A Public Health Problem   447
    Joseph H. Herzberg, MD

SECTION THREE   VULNERABILITIES   455

24 Pathogenesis of the Adjustment Disorders: Vulnerabilities due
    to Temperamental Factors   457
    Stella Chess, MD

25 Stress, Neuroendocrine Patterns, and Emotional Response   477
    James P. Henry, MD, PhD

SECTION FOUR   PROTECTIVE FACTORS:
EGO STRENGTHS   497

26 Family and Extended Family as Ego Supports   499
      Lillian H. Robinson, MD
      Richard F. Dalton, MD

27 Ego Strength and Coping Capacity: Friend and Social Group
    Affiliation   510
      William C. Sze, PhD

28 Ego Strength and Coping Capacity: Large Group Affiliation   521
      William C. Sze, PhD
      Barry Ivker, PhD

SECTION FIVE   THE ADJUSTMENT DISORDER
SYNDROME   535

29 Disturbances of Conduct Following Stress   537
      Charles Keith, MD

30 Psychological Responses to Stress: Work and Academic
    Inhibition and Withdrawal   547
      Jerry W. Johnson, MPA
      Glenn Swogger, Jr., MD

31 Adjustment Reactions: The Psychotic Syndrome   559
      Sherman C. Feinstein, MD
      Randy Kettering, PhD
      Martin Harrow, PhD

32 Stress, Adjustment Disorders, and Treatment Interventions in
    Mental Retardation   569
      Thomas G. Webster, MD

SECTION SIX   PREVENTION AND INTERVENTION   587

33 Toward Preventive Intervention in Early Childhood:
    Object Loss   589
      Gilbert W. Kliman, MD

**34 The Impact of Life Stress in Infancy, Childhood, and
     Adolescence**   **600**
     Irving N. Berlin, MD

35 Stress Prevention in Adults   **616**
     Gerald J. McKenna, MD
     Ransom J. Arthur, MD

36 Treatment for Stress-Related Disorders   **630**
     Joseph D. Noshpitz, MD

37 Individual Psychotherapy in Adjustment Disorders   **651**
     Carl P. Adatto, MD

     Author Index   **661**

     Subject Index   **684**

Stressors and the Adjustment Disorders

The Nature of Stress and the Nature of Adjustment Disorders

It is reasonable to begin a book about stress and the Adjustment Disorders with a brief overview of the definitional problems involved. Many distinctions have now been drawn, such as the difference between a stressor and a precipitant. Oddly enough, one separation the field has not yet accomplished is that between a disorder and a reaction. Throughout the editing of this work it has been remarkable how many colleagues continue to refer to the syndrome as Adjustment Reaction rather than Adjustment Disorder, the form offered in the *Diagnostic and Statistical Manual of Mental Disorders* (DSM-III). It is perhaps no surprise that a discipline reared in the essentially Meyerian tradition of the reaction-types and reinforced by the DSM-II utilization of the same language (which in effect made it canonical) should have some trouble abandoning the vocabulary that expressed so perfectly the philosophy of the master. Nonetheless, the impact of DSM-III has been powerful. In many other realms it has quite displaced all previous formulations—but not this one.

In any case, precise definitions and some understanding of the problems of measurement of stress as well as the reactions and disturbances that come in its wake are necessary components of any effort to grasp the function and utility of these concepts. These then are the issues the authors address in Section One; They are basic to what is to follow.

The Nature of Stress: Problems of Measurement

ANDREW E. SKODOL, MD
BRUCE P. DOHRENWEND, PhD
BRUCE G. LINK, PhD
PATRICK E. SHROUT, PhD

Determining the role of stress in the development of mental disorders has been the subject of considerable research by social scientists. This research has shown that the evaluation of stress is not a straightforward task and that numerous theoretical and practical problems are associated with its measurement.

The essential feature that characterizes an Adjustment Disorder according to the *Diagnostic and Statistical Manual on Mental Disorders* (DSM-III, DSM-III-R; American Psychiatric Association, 1980, 1987) is a maladaptive reaction to an identifiable psychosocial stressor. The maladaptive nature of the reaction is indicated either by symptoms in excess of an expectable reaction to the stressor, or by evidence of associated social or occupational impairment. An Adjustment Disorder is not considered part of a pattern of overreaction to stress nor an exacerbation of another Axis I disorder. The criteria of DSM-III stated that, under ordinary circumstances, when the stressor ceased, the disorder was expected to remit; or, if the stressor continued, the disorder ended when the individual adapted to its presence. The criteria of DSM-III-R require that the maladaptive reaction persist for no longer than 6 months following the stressor. Therefore, in the diagnosis of Adjustment Disorders by the DSM-III systems, the assessment of the occurrence of psychosocial stressors becomes important as a prelude to their treatment.

ASSESSING STRESS WITH DSM-III AXIS IV

In the innovative DSM-III multiaxial system, psychosocial stressors were to be evaluated as to their importance in the development or exacerbation of any current mental disorder; the occurrence of such stressors was then indicated on Axis IV, Severity of Psychosocial Stressors. Axis IV provided a 7-point rating scale of severity, as well as a suggestion that the specific stressors themselves be noted. As a guide to making Axis IV severity ratings, DSM-III included a table that displayed the numerical ratings, the associated term used to describe the levels of severity, and a few chosen examples of the kinds of stressors that might be associated with each level for both an adult patient and a child or adolescent. DSM-III did not include an exhaustive list of types of psychosocial stressors, but gave additional stressors for consideration in various areas of life, without the recommended corresponding severity ratings. The rationale for including in DSM-III an axis for assessing psychosocial stressors was to try to add predictive validity to the Axis I diagnosis. It was assumed that an individual's prognosis might be better if a disorder developed from severe stress rather than after no—or only minimal—stress.

Conventions for Axis IV Ratings

Numerous conventions were introduced in DSM-III for making the Axis IV severity ratings. These conventions reflected many assumptions about the nature of stress and its relationship to the occurrence of mental disorders. They also raised several important issues concerning the measurement of stress. According to DSM-III the rating should be based on the clinician's judgment of the stress that a theoretically "average" person would experience under similar circumstances and not on the reaction of a particular person who might be especially vulnerable. DSM-III stated that the rating should include a consideration of the amount of change that resulted from the stressor, the degree to which the event was desired and under the individual's control, and the summed effect of a number of stressors, if they occurred jointly. In most cases, DSM-III said, the stressor would have occurred in the year preceding the development or exacerbation of the mental disorder, but it did allow for noting and rating stressors that had occurred prior to that time, especially in the case of very severe or catastrophic events. Each of these statements has been difficult to operationalize in actual practice, and each poses an interesting, and in some cases unanswered, theoretical question about stress measurement.

Theoretical Critiques of DSM-III Axis IV

There have been numerous reactions, both positive and negative, to the inno-vation of including Axis IV in DSM-III. These have been reviewed in detail by Williams (1985a), and will only be briefly summarized here. Frances and Cooper (1981) and Roth (1983) have questioned the decision to base the Axis IV severity rating on the stress that an average person would experience rather than on a patient's particular vulnerability; they feel that the patient's state would be more clinically meaningful. Their approach would result, however, in a rating that would merely echo the psychiatric diagnosis, because the severity of the patient's response to the stressor would already be reflected in the Axis I or II diagnosis.

The value of making a single global rating on Axis IV has also been questioned by Kendell (1983) and by Rutter and Shaffer (1980). Particularly problematic in this approach, they point out, is the assumption that all psychosocial stressors differ from one another only quantitatively. The evidence, however, suggests that chronic, ongoing stressors exert an effect that is quite different from that of a single, stressful life event. As discussed later in this chapter, systems for rating the severity of stressful life events have evolved more rapidly than have systems for rating the severity of ongoing stressful life circumstances.

Other critiques of the DSM-III approach have addressed two additional issues. One is the absence of a complete listing of stressors and their severity ratings; the other is the presence of a presumed etiologic relationship of Axis IV to Axis I and Axis II diagnoses in an otherwise atheoretical diagnostic system. All of the preceding criticisms lend themselves to empirical testing; the following section reviews em-pirical studies of DSM-III's Severity of Psychosocial Stressors axis.

Empirical Studies of DSM-III Axis IV

Empirical studies evaluating the practical use and usefulness of DSM-III Axis IV suggested that Axis IV ratings had limited reliability and uncertain validity. In the DSM-III field trials (Spitzer & Forman, 1979), Axis IV severity ratings were found to have just adequate reliability (ICC = 0.62 for joint interviews and 0.58 for test-retest evaluations). No reliability coefficients were reported for the listing of the corresponding psychosocial stressors. In two studies of DSM-III multiaxial diagnosis in children, Mezzich, Mezzich, and Coffman (1985) reported poor reli-ability (ICC = 0.25) for Axis IV severity ratings and Russell, Cantwell, Mattison, and Will (1979) reported only modest agreement for the stressors. Rey and col-leagues (Rey, Plapp, Stewart, Richards, & Bashir, 1987) reported an ICC of 0.44 for Axis IV ratings made on adolescents. They pointed to the complex instructions for making the ratings, including the requirement that the stressor contribute to the development or exacerbation of the current mental disorder, as sources of unreli-ability (Rey, Stewart, Plapp, Bashir, & Richards, 1988).

Six studies have addressed the validity of Axis IV. In a study of Axis IV ratings made during evaluations at a walk-in clinic, Mezzich, Evanczuk, Mathias, & Coffman (1984) found a 0.12 correlation between the Axis IV rating and the decision to admit for inpatient treatment. Gordon, Jardiolin, & Gordon (1985) developed a "strain ratio," based on the ratio of the Axis IV score and an inverted Axis V score; they found that higher strain ratios were associated with longer hospital stays. Zimmerman, Pfohl, Stangl, & Coryell (1985) described "construct validity" for Axis IV in a sample of 130 depressed inpatients. Higher Axis IV ratings were found to be associated with specific kinds of events, fewer abnormal dexamethasone suppression tests (DSTs), higher rates of familial alcoholism, greater frequency of personality disorder, and greater likelihood of suicide attempt. Zimmerman, Pfohl, Coryell, and Stangl (1987) went on to show, however, that Axis IV ratings did not have predictive validity, as suggested by DSM-III, because higher ratings (more stress) were not associated with better outcomes for depressed patients 6 months after hospitalization. Schrader, Gordon, & Harcourt (1986) identified the judgment of the etiologic significance of the stressor as a major difficulty in implementing Axis IV assessments.

In our own study of the use of Axis IV in both an inpatient and an outpatient setting, we found that ratings were made that conformed to both clinical sense and previous research on the relationship of stress to mental disorder. For example, patients with major depression had higher ratings than those with schizophrenia, and higher ratings were associated with first episodes than with repeat (Skodol and Shrout, 1989b). We found good correspondence (Skodol & Shrout, 1988) between the Axis IV severity ratings and severity ratings (expressed as change weights) developed for the Life Events Inventory of the Psychiatric Epidemiology Research Interview (PERI) (Dohrenwerd, Krasnoff, Askenasy, & Dohrenwend, 1978). An independent life events interview also was more likely to confirm events listed by clinicians on Axis IV if these events were severe than if they were mild (Skodol & Shrout, 1989a). For instance, a family death, a rape, or a serious physical illness was confirmed by the standardized life events assessment more often than an argument with a friend or a job promotion. The discrepancies between the two methods for measuring stress were due to the different conventions employed by each, underscoring that the method used may significantly influence both the information obtained and the conclusions drawn about the relationship of stress to mental disorder. The reasons for the discrepancies suggested a number of problems with the DSM-III Axis IV approach.

For example, the convention that the clinician should not rate an event that had occurred but was judged not to "have been a significant contributor to the development or exacerbation of the current disorder" (American Psychiatric Association, 1980, p. 26) was one reason for discrepancies between Axis IV ratings and PERI interview results. This etiologic judgment called for by Axis IV seemed to lead to error because of the limitations in a clinician's ability to know how relevant a particular event was in the course of a patient's disorder; this situation often becomes clearer over time or with comparative analyses on the basis of more complete data.

An example of how this convention influenced Axis IV ratings is illustrated in the following case vignette:

K.A. was a 33-year-old man who presented to the outpatient psychiatry clinic for lithium management, following a job-related move to a new city. His second marriage had ended in divorce 10 months previously, because of constant fighting. Following the divorce, the patient decided to accept the new job opportunity, because he felt few ties to his previous home. The clinical assessment revealed a diagnosis of Bipolar Disorder of 8 years' duration and a long-standing Mixed Personality Disorder. Because the patient had no current exacerbation of his mental disorders and the divorce, new job, and move were thought to be more the result of his problems than the cause, the clinician gave a rating of 1-None on Axis IV. The life events interview reported that all three events had occurred.

In addition, this particular Axis IV convention was likely to bias stressor ratings toward lower, less significant values among patients with chronic mental disorders, such as schizophrenia, for whom the role of stress is, according to conventional wisdom, judged to be less significant. A consequent neglect of stressful events in treatment planning may result.

The DSM-III instruction to have the Axis IV severity rating "reflect the summed effect of all the psychosocial stressors that are listed" (American Psychiatric Association, 1980, p. 27) was not adequate to guide clinical practice. Clinicians made their overall ratings based on the severity of the first-listed (and presumably most severe) stressor and generally ignored additional stressors for the purpose of the rating. An example of this situation is the following:

P. G. was a 24-year-old single woman who presented to the psychiatry clinic with a major depressive episode of 4 months' duration. During the year preceding the onset of the disorder, she had given birth to her first child and had been diagnosed as having systemic lupus erythematosus. The clinician gave her a rating of a 5-Severe on Axis IV, presumably on the basis of her severe physical disorder.

The birth of this patient's out-of-wedlock child, which was also listed, undoubtedly made her situation even more stressful, but there are no clear guidelines in DSM-III regarding how much to increase the severity rating on Axis IV to take into account such additional stressors.

Another reason that DSM-III stressors did not correspond exactly with those elicited by PERI was that the DSM-III definition of a stressor was broader and included chronic strains that are not traditionally considered to be life events. These stressful life circumstances included such situations as "being a single mother," or "chronic unemployment." Current theoretical models in stress research generally consider these as ongoing social situations that may contribute to the development of mental disorders quite independently from life events (see later section on theoretical models); indeed, most researchers assume that their effects are quite different (Williams, 1985b). What is more, although DSM-III allowed for the inclusion of these stressful situations in assigning the Axis IV ratings, there were no specific guidelines for making the ratings. DSM-III examples of stressors and their corresponding ratings were almost exclusively traditional life event categories.

Thus, the introduction of a formalized system for routinely rating life stress in the multiaxial evaluation system of DSM-III may have represented a step forward in the process of measuring stress in relation to mental disorder; nonetheless, many problems with its use existed. An opportunity came to attempt to deal with some of the problems and criticisms in the 1987 revision of DSM-III, which introduced changes into the Axis IV format as stated in DSM-III-R.

REVISING AXIS IV FOR DSM-III-R

Some of those who worked on the revision of DSM-III believed that the relatively scanty research generated by the multiaxial system was evidence enough for an overhaul (Williams, 1987). Others, like ourselves (Skodol and Shrout, 1988), believed that the changes should be motivated by empirical data.

Because critics of DSM-III had suggested separating consideration of acute events from chronic, enduring circumstances in making severity ratings, and our studies revealed that etiologically significant stressors are sometimes not acutely occurring, discrete events, the multiaxial advisory committee to the Work Group to Revise DSM-III-R made a major change. In DSM-III-R, separate rating scales with examples of each type of stressor for both adults and for children and adolescents have been devised.

Because of the difficulties several groups had encountered with judging the etiologic significance of the stressors being rated, consideration was given to eliminating the etiologic requirement for listing and rating stressors on Axis IV. Instead, the description of the relationship of the stressor to the disorder was expanded to emphasize that the stressor may have contributed to (1) the development of a new mental disorder, (2) the recurrence of a prior mental disorder, or (3) the exacerbation of an already existing mental disorder (e.g., divorce occurring during a major depressive episode or during the course of chronic schizophrenia). This broader definition is intended to reduce the possibility that a potentially relevant stressor will be overlooked.

Some investigators have suggested listing only severe stressors, simplifying the rating scale by including fewer levels of severity, or eliminating the severity rating altogether (Rey et al., 1988), because severity appears to increase the reliability of the ratings and the ratings are based primarily on the most severe stressor. Our own data provided some support for these suggestions because more severe stressors were more likely to be independently verified. Greater emphasis on severe stressors is reflected in DSM-III-R, which now states, "When more than one stressor is present, the severity rating will generally be that of the most severe stressor" (American Psychiatric Association, 1987, p. 19). DSM-III-R, however, continues to assert, "In the case of multiple severe or extreme stressors, a higher rating should be considered" (p. 19). Furthermore, the rating scales have been abbreviated to 6 points by eliminating the point for "minimal," which was judged clinically insignificant and undoubtedly unreliable.

It is unclear whether Axis IV in DSM-III-R is actually an improvement over the DSM-III version. It is fair to say that the new Axis IV has a somewhat firmer empirical foundation than the original, but some have found it now overly complex and others have predicted that it will confuse clinicians and inhibit research (Rey, Stewart, & Plapp, 1988). Many of the most difficult problems in measuring stress remain to be resolved before achieving an adequate measurement system. In order to chart current progress, it is necessary to consider other developments in the field of stress measurement research.

HISTORY OF STRESS MEASUREMENT

Many data suggest that environmentally induced stress can cause adverse changes in health, including mental health; the strongest and most convincing evidence comes from studies of extreme situations. For humans, such situations include the occurrence of natural or man-made disasters or prolonged exposure to combat during war. The relationship of extreme stressors to adverse health changes is evident both from their temporal priority and from their occurrence being clearly outside the control of the subject. In particular, such health changes cannot be caused by the insidious onset of the health problems or personal characteristics of the subject that might have a predisposing effect. The objective magnitude of extreme stressors can usually be readily measured in terms of, for example, the casualty rate of a military unit during combat or the voltage of an electric shock administered in a stress experiment with animals.

Because most people do not experience such extreme stressors, the relatively high rates of mental disorders found in community populations, if they are in fact related to environmentally induced stress, must be in response to stressors that occur more frequently in the general population (B. P. Dohrenwend, 1983; Dohrenwend & de Figueiredo, 1983). Such more common stressful life events might include divorce, loss of a job, or death of a loved one. However, an event like divorce or loss of job may or may not be independent of the personal dispositions or behavior of the subjects. Hence, for such events, the magnitude of the event is less clear-cut, and an interpretation of its relationship to adverse health changes is more problematic. Moreover, the relationship of these more common life events to adverse health changes is much weaker than that for extreme situations (Rabkin & Struening, 1976).

One approach to measuring the magnitude of these more usual stressful events has been to get subjective ratings of the events. Researchers obtain these data from the individuals whose stress experiences in relationship to their psychopathology are being studied (Grant, Gerst, & Yager, 1976). Unfortunately, such ratings are almost certainly not independent of the personal dispositions and behavior of the subjects, including the disposition to or actual presence of psychopathology. The use of subjective ratings, therefore, is virtually guaranteed to confound the relationship between stressful events and psychopathology. For example, not unexpectedly, psychiatric patients rate such events as more stressful than do nonpatients (Grant et al., 1976; Schless, Schwartz, Goetz, & Mendels, 1974), just as a person who has experienced a life event or series of life events followed by a heart attack is likely to rate such events as more stressful than a person who has survived a similar sequence of events without a heart attack (Theorell, 1974).

This is not to say that subjective appraisals of the magnitude of the life events an individual experiences are useless. In a prospective study, it may be possible to learn something from them about vulnerability, provided there are objective measures as well. If the study is retrospective, researchers can learn something about rationalization or "effort after meaning" (Brown, 1974, p. 223). These matters should not be confused, however, with adequate measurement of the objective stress to which the individual has been exposed (B. P. Dohrenwend, 1979).

Two Methods for Measuring Objective Life Event Stress

Historically, the two methods for measuring objective life event stress have been (1) the use of judges to rate the severity of lists of life events, and (2) the rating by researchers of the contextual threat attributed to a particular event. The former, earlier, approach is typified by the work of Holmes and Rahe (1967) and the later, more recent, work by Brown and Harris (1978). Neither approach has been without problems.

The first approach involves life event lists and standardized questions that elicit the occurrence of specific life events, with corresponding magnitude scores, over a given time period. This approach has been criticized by Brown (1981). His most telling criticism is that the single score for each event on the life event list equates all the events that occur within that life event category with respect to their severity and therefore their magnitude, regardless of the context in which they occur. Thus, this method does not allow for potential variability in the impact of, for example, the death of a loved one, depending on whether it occurred suddenly and unexpectedly, or after a prolonged illness that had been far more stressful in its early stages.

The contextual threat approach assesses the event as it occurs within the particular life circumstances of a subject, thereby overcoming the previously mentioned limitation of the list method (Tennant, Smith, Bebbington, & Hurry, 1979). Tennant, Bebbington, and Hurry (1981), however, have pointed out that by including features of an individual's social situation, and even personality attributes, in the stressful life event measure, Brown has artificially produced an association between life events and other antecedent conditions that would not necessarily be found empirically; thus he overestimates the causal role of life events in illness. When several constructs are mixed, as they are in Brown's approach, one cannot isolate which aspects of the life stress process are causal.

RECENT DEVELOPMENTS IN MEASURING LIFE EVENT STRESS

A measurement approach is needed that can take into account intraevent variability but also keep other components of the life stress process operationally distinct. We have been involved in a number of recent developments in research on methods for measuring life event stress that represent advances along this line. These include methods to assess variability within life event categories, the concept that the co-occurrence of certain kinds of events may be critical to the life event stress process, and the development of alternative theoretical models that can take into consideration relationships between recent life events and other factors important in the stress process.

Assessing Variability within Life Event Categories

In order to improve on currently available techniques, several theoretically important aspects of life events need to be measured more rigorously. Although previous work has touched on the importance of these concepts for measuring intraevent variability, our work is designed to measure each aspect by taking the particular circumstances surrounding an event into account. These are the independence of the event, the amount of change resulting, the positive versus negative valence, the degree of anticipation possible, and the degree of control over the occurrence of the event.

The claim that life events play an unambiguous causal role in the life stress process rests on the independence of such events from the health outcomes and from the predispositions to such outcomes. Establishing whether this independence exists is a central task in the study of the role of environmentally induced stress. One of the most widely held explanations of the characteristics of life events that makes them stressful is that their occurrence results in changes in the usual activities of an individual. Indeed, the severity ratings of the traditional life events checklists are based on this premise (Holmes & Rahe, 1967). As described earlier, however, it is probably not valid to assume that all events of a particular type result in the same amount of change; more refined ways are needed of measuring change that may vary within a category.

Another plausible explanation for what makes events stressful is the negative quality of the event. Some events, such as a married couple's having a planned baby, cause a large amount of change but are basically desirable. This event would not be as stressful as a basically negative event that caused an equal amount of change. Other important aspects may be the degree to which an individual is able to anticipate an event (even if it is negative and may result in considerable change), and the degree to which the occurrence of an event is inside or outside an individual's control. Each factor makes the stressfulness of a particular event in a particular case variable; to determine when an event is stressful, it may be necessary to measure each of these dimensions in every case.

Independence of Occurrence of Events. The approach to measuring life event stress described in this chapter uses the ratings developed and described by B. S. Dohrenwend et al. (1978) as a starting point for assessing independence. In their research, judgments were made of the likely independence of events from an individual's psychological condition: "Death of a spouse" was rated as independent, whereas "fired" was judged to be possibly dependent. We call these ratings, based on event categories, "normative ratings." Our work is designed to refine these ratings by collecting verbatim descriptions of exactly what happened surrounding the occurrence of an event. When there is strong evidence to suggest that the independence hypothesis (even though based on the previous work) is incorrect, the normative hypothesis can be rejected. Thus, the event category "assaulted" is rated as independent by Dohrenwend et al. If, however, the verbatim description includes evidence that the respondent had been drinking, became verbally abusive, and ended up in a barroom fight, we then reject the normative judgment and rate this particular event as possibly dependent.

Desirability of Changes. Again using the descriptions of the occurrence of events by respondents, we attempt to rate whether the changes that accompany an event are mainly positive, mainly negative, or mixed positive and negative.

Amount of Change. Ratings of amount of change are made on a 4-point scale, ranging from an "extremely large amount of change" to "a little change."

Control. This is a rating of the extent to which a respondent's behavior brought about the event as opposed to the event's being determined by external circumstances. Such a rating can be made both for the effect of the subject's behavior on the occurrence of the immediate event, and for the effect of the behavior on the sequence of events leading up to the specific event in question. Thus, an event such as being fired might in itself be outside the control of the individual; however, the events leading up to the firing, such as poor performance on the job, can be very much influenced by the individual. This rating is made on a 5-point scale ranging from "0 = completely determined by external circumstances" to "4 = completely determined by respondent's behavior."

Other Ratings. It is useful to rate events on several other dimensions. These include whether the event leads to physical exhaustion, is life threatening, or involves altruism.

Empirical Data on Qualitative Ratings of Life Events

Dohrenwend et al. (1987) have reported data on the variability within life event categories in a sample of community respondents. For 10 severe, negative events, they found variability in a number of factors: the amount of change resulting; the desirability of the change; and the amount the individual's behavior influenced the immediate occurrence of the event, the sequence leading up to the event, and the occurrence of changes following the event. For example, for the event "serious illness started or got worse," an extremely large amount of change was noted for some respondents (8.6%), little change for others (11.4%), and no change for still others (20.0%). Of the respondents who experienced the event "stopped working not retirement" 40.5% had complete control over the occurrence of the event, but 18.9% had no control whatsoever. The authors conclude that any scheme designed to capture the nature of stressful life events that ignores variability will be inadequate.

Future directions for research in this area include the development of specific probes to elicit the precise information needed to make the ratings of interest and a list of possible changes resulting from events. With the help of such an array, respondents will have maximally useful stimuli with which to provide the needed information. Work on each of these procedures is under way in our department at Columbia University. Finally, a crucial question remains: Do life events rated according to these kinds of variable characteristics show a stronger relationship to the development of mental disorders than life events rated according to traditional measures? In our most recent analyses (Shrout, Link, Dohrenwend, Skodol, Stueve, & Mirotznik, 1989) we have found that patients with major depression, as compared to community controls, were almost three times as likely to have experienced a recent, negative life event that was judged to be independent of the person's psychological condition and more than minimally disruptive.

Importance of Specific Combinations of Events

There is little doubt that extreme degrees of stressful events, such as natural disasters and man-made calamities like war, can produce many varieties of severe psychopathology in previously normal persons (Dohrenwend, 1979; Dohrenwend & Egri, 1981). Such extreme situations are rare, however, and play little or no role in the occurrence and distribution of psychopathology in the epidemiological studies that have implicated life events in the etiology of mental disorders (Dohrenwend, et al., 1980). It is possible, though, that when more commonly occurring and less extreme life events accumulate over brief periods of time, they may expose persons to severe stress. Thus, it would not be the occurrence of any one particular event that would put a person at greater risk for an adverse health outcome, but rather the occurrence of several different kinds of events close together in a brief period of time that would be significant. Three specific kinds of events may have an especially pathogenic effect when they happen together: fateful loss events (such as the death of loved ones) that are outside the person's control; events that exhaust the individual physically (such as those involving life-threatening physical illnesses and injuries); and other events that are likely to disrupt social supports (such as change of jobs or marital separation) (Dohrenwend, 1979). Referred to as a pathogenic triad, this combination of events may approximate the stress conditions of extreme situations.

Results from an Ongoing Case-Control Study. We currently have a retrospective case-control study investigating the occurrence of episodes of depression and schizophrenia in adult subjects in New York City (B. P. Dohrenwend, 1986; Dohrenwend, Shrout, Link, Martin, & Skodol, 1986). The subjects consist of 121 persons diagnosed by DSM-III as having major depression, and 65 persons with DSM-III diagnoses of schizophrenia, schizophreniform disorder, and other nonaffective psychoses. They have been matched against 197 well controls from a community sample that has been screened to eliminate cases of severe psychopathology. In this study, we recorded the occurrence of recent life events in the 1-year period prior to the episode of disorder for the depressed cases and the cases with schizophreniclike disorder, and we contrasted this with the 1-year period prior to the interview for the controls. We have examined events in each of the three elements of the pathogenic triad.

The following were considered fateful loss events: death of child, death of spouse, inability to get treatment for an illness or injury, loss of home through fire or other disaster, medical determination of inability to have children, death of family member other than spouse or child, miscarriage or stillbirth, death of close friend, reduction in wages or salary without a demotion, assault, failure to get an expected wage or salary increase, and lay-off. Based on a simple count of whether these events were reported to be present or absent, and with demographic variables controlled, we found a significantly higher rate of fateful loss events for major depressives than for controls. No similar increase was found for those with schizophrenic disorders.

In both the major depressive group and the schizophrenic group, the number of physical illnesses and injuries reported was higher than in the controls. This finding also held true with the relevant demographic variables controlled.

The events considered likely to disrupt usual social supports were the following: divorce, imprisonment, marital infidelity, separation of a married couple, retirement, extended period of stopping work (not retirement), getting fired, breakup of a friendship, person moving out of household, and broken engagement. In this instance, higher rates for these events were reported by both major depressives and those with schizophreniclike disorders as compared with controls. These differences held for both first episode and repeat episode cases, which were represented in the samples. Thus, the results have implications for both onset and recurrences of the two types of disorders. Moreover, the relationship was evident for only these three types, the pathogenic triad events. There was no relationship for the total number of events. One conclusion that can be drawn is that when measuring life event stress, it may be important to measure the amount of stress associated with certain events occurring over a given time period, rather than of all events that occurred.

Models for the Relationship of Stress to Psychopathology

Only some of those exposed to the more usual kinds of life events discussed here actually develop episodes of various types of psychiatric disorder (B. P. Dohrenwend & B. S. Dohrenwend, 1981; B. S. Dohrenwend & B. P. Dohrenwend, 1981c; Dohrenwend & Egri, 1981). Within the framework of social science research, conceptualization of the life stress process has been broadened in order to try to account for this state of affairs. Currently, this process can be thought of as having three major social and psychological components: recent life events (ranging from extreme to more usual occurrences), personal dispositions (including personality traits, genetic vulnerability, and the personality residuals of remote events), and ongoing social situations (including the availability of social supports). In addition to the accurate measurement of these three components, the key problem is to understand how they interact to bring about their effects. Dohrenwend and Dohrenwend (1981a, 1981b, 1981c) have described five alternative models of possible relationships among these components. They are referred to as *victimization, vulnerability, additive burden, chronic burden,* and event *proneness;* they are diagrammed in Figure 1.1.

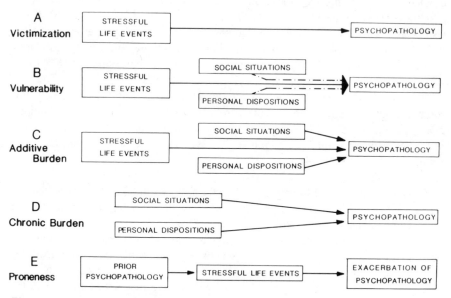

Figure 1.1 Five hypotheses about the life stress process.

Victimization. The victimization hypothesis suggests that the accumulation of stressful life events causes psychopathology. The pathogenic triad of concomitant events and conditions involving physical exhaustion, loss of social support, and fateful negative events (as described earlier) would be one example of a victimization paradigm. According to this model the other two aspects of the life event process, that is, the personal dispositions and the ongoing social situations, would play a minimal role. In sum, then, the model asserts that if enough stress was experienced, adverse health changes would occur.

Vulnerability. The vulnerability hypothesis proposes that the preexisting personal dispositions and social conditions moderate the causal relationship between stressful life events and psychopathology. This model has been advanced by various researchers in discussions of the etiology of schizophrenia and major depression (Brown & Harris, 1978; Zubin & Spring, 1977). In this model, certain personal dispositions such as adaptive coping skills might mitigate against the development of psychopathology in the face of stressful life events, whereas others such as genetic predisposition might enhance the pathogenic effect. Similarly, some social situations would be protective whereas others would make the person more susceptible.

Additive Burden. This hypothesis differs from the vulnerability hypothesis in that, rather than moderating the impact of stressful life events, personal dispositions and social conditions make independent causal contributions to the occurrence of psychopathology. This hypothesis has received empirical support in a study of psychosocial symptoms by Andrews, Tennant, Hewson, and Vaillant (1978). It has also been proposed by Tennent and Bebbington (1978) as offering a better fit than does the vulnerability hypothesis in explaining the findings of Brown and Harris (1978) in their study of social factors in the etiology of depression.

Chronic Burden. The chronic burden hypothesis denies any role to recent life events, proposing instead that stable personal dispositions and social conditions alone cause adverse health changes. This hypothesis has been offered as an explanation of changes in children's psychological symptom patterns (Gersten, Langner, Eisenberg, & Orzek, 1974).

Proneness. This final hypothesis raises the issue of the direction of the causal relation between life events and psychopathology. It states that the presence of a mental disorder leads to stressful life events, which, in turn, exacerbate the disorder. This hypothesis has received empirical support in a study of chronic patients (Fontana, Marcus, Noel, & Rakusin, 1972), but not in a recent study of neurotic disorders (Tennant & Andrews, 1978).

The following case serves to illustrate how the five models might explain the development of psychopathology in a particular patient.

H.S. was a 35-year-old, recently divorced female with borderline intellectual functioning, who was admitted to the hospital for an exacerbation of a chronic schizoaffective disorder. She was the mother of four children and lived on public assistance. Family history was positive for schizophrenia and major depression among her siblings. The patient had not only been divorced 6 months prior to admission, but had also experienced worsening of her chronic hypertension, and had had one of her children hospitalized for disturbed behavior.

According to the victimization hypothesis, the accumulation of stressors, that is, the physical illness, the divorce, and the separation from her child would lead to the current episode. The vulnerability hypothesis would consider the low socioeconomic status, the positive family history, and the borderline intellectual functioning to be necessary predisposing elements making her susceptible to the stressful life events. The additive burden model would argue for equivalent contributions of the events, the social situation, and the personal liabilities in the exacerbation of the disorder. The chronic burden hypothesis would minimize the role of the events, stressing instead that, in the light of the chronic handicaps of this patient, exacerbations of her disorder were inevitable and the events were mere chance occurrences. Under the proneness hypothesis, the importance of schizoaffective disorder as a cause of the divorce, the child's problems, and possibly the poor social conditions would be emphasized. One must remember that these hypotheses are neither exhaustive nor mutually exclusive. They provide a framework, however, for attempting to advance understanding of the relationship of life stress and psychopathology.

SUMMARY

A host of important measurement issues underlie an understanding of the relationship of stress to psychopathology. In this chapter, we have described the current state of stress measurement for clinical purposes, as represented by both DSM-III and DSM-III-R formulations and research findings. We have outlined several of the problems in stress measurement, focusing specifically on the problems of measuring stressful life events. Similar, sometimes even more complex, problems exist in the measurement of the other two components of the life stress process, personal dispositions and social situations. The chapter therefore includes a review of several new developments in stress measurement. It concludes with a discussion of models for a potential understanding of the crucial relationships between the various aspects of the life stress process.

In the future, it will be important to pay careful attention to measurement problems that have made the results from many previous studies on stress and psychopathology difficult to interpret. Especially important will be continued efforts to avoid confounding with one another the various measures of events, personal dispositions, enduring social situations, and psychopathology.

REFERENCES

American Psychiatric Association. (1980). *Diagnostic and statistical manual of mental disorders* (3rd ed.). Washington, DC: Author.

American Psychiatric Association. *Diagnostic and statistical manual of mental disorders* (1987). (3rd ed.-Rev.) Washington, DC: Author.

Andrews, G., Tennant, C., Hewson, D. M., & Vaillant, G. E. (1978). Life event stress, social support, coping style, and risk of psychological impairment. *Journal of Nervous and Mental Disease, 166,* 307–317.

Brown, G. W. (1974). Meaning, measurement, and stress of life events. In B. S. Dohrenwend & B. P. Dohrenwend (Eds.), *Stressful life events: Their nature and effects* (pp. 217-243). New York: Wiley.

Brown, G. (1981). Life events, psychiatric disorder and physical illness. *Journal of Psychosomatic Research, 25,* 461–473.

Brown, G., & Harris, T. (1978). *Social origins of depression: A study of psychiatric disorder in women.* New York: The Free Press.

Dohrenwend, B. P. (1979) Stressful life events and psychopathology: Some issues of theory and method. In J. F. Barrett, R. M. Rose, & G. L. Klerman (Eds.), *Stress and mental disorder* (pp. 1–15). New York: Raven Press.

Dohrenwend, B. P. (1983). The epidemiology of mental disorder. In D. Mechanic (Ed.), *Handbook of health, health care, and the health professions* (pp. 157–194). New York: The Free Press.

Dohrenwend, B. P. (1986). Social stress and psychopathology. In M. Kessler & S. E. Goldston (Eds.), *A decade of progress in primary prevention* (pp. 87–114). Hanover, NH: University Press of New England.

Dohrenwend, B. P., & Dohrenwend, B. S. (1981). Socioenvironmental factors, stress and psychopathology. Part 1: Quasi-experimental evidence on social causation-social selection issue posed by class differences. *American Journal of Community Psychology, 9,* 129–146.

Dohrenwend, B. P., Dohrenwend, B. S., Gould, M., Link, B., Neugebauer, R., & Wunsch-Hitzig, R. (1980). *Mental illness in the United States: Epidemiological estimates.* New York: Praeger.

Dohrenwend, B. P., & Egri, G. (1981). Recent stressful life events and episodes of schizophrenia. *Schizophrenia Bulletin 7,* 12–23.

Dohrenwend, B. P., & de Figueiredo, J. M. (1983). Remote and recent life events and psychopathology. In D. F. Ricks & B. S. Dohrenwend (Eds.), *Origins of psychopathology: Problems in research and public policy* (pp. 91–106). New York: Cambridge University Press.

Dohrenwend, B. P., Link, B., Kern, R., Shrout, P., & Markowitz, J. (1987). Measuring life events: The problem of variability within event categories. In B. Cooper (Ed.), *Psychiatric epidemiology: Progress and prospects* (pp. 103–119). England: Croom Helm.

Dohrenwend, B. P., Shrout, P. E., Link, B., Martin, J., & Skodol, A. E. (1986). Overview and initial results from a risk factor study of depression and schizophrenia. In J. E. Barrett (Ed.), *Mental disorders in the community: Progress and challenge* (pp. 184–215). New York: Guilford Press.

Dohrenwend, B. S., & Dohrenwend, B. P. (1981a). Life stress and illness: Formulation of the issues. In B. S. Dohrenwend & B. P. Dohrenwend (Eds.), *Stressful life events and their contexts* (pp. 1–27). New York: PRODIST (Neal Watson Academic Publications).

Dohrenwend, B. S., & Dohrenwend, B. P. (1981b). Life stress and psychopathology. In D. A. Regier & G. Allen (Eds.), *Risk factor research in the major mental disorders* (pp. 131–141). (National Institute of Mental Health, DHHS Pub. No. ADM 81-1086). Washington, DC: U.S. Government Printing Office.

Dohrenwend, B. S., & Dohrenwend, B. P. (1981c). Socioenvironmental factors, stress and psychopathology. Part 2: Hypotheses about stress processes linking social class to various types of psychopathology. *American Journal of Community Psychology 9*, 146–159.

Dohrenwend, B. S., Krasnoff, L., Askenasy, A., & Dohrenwend, B. P. (1978). Exemplification of a method for scaling life events: The PERI life events scale. *Journal of Health & Social Behavior, 19*, 205–229.

Fontana, A. F., Marcus, J. L., Noel, B., & Rakusin, J. M. (1972). Prehospitalization coping styles of psychiatric patients: The goal-directedness of life events. *Journal of Nervous and Mental Disease, 155*, 311–321.

Frances, A., & Cooper, A. M. (1981). Descriptive and dynamic psychiatry: A perspective on DSM-III. *American Journal of Psychiatry, 138*, 1198–1202.

Gersten, J. C., Langner, T. S., Eisenberg, J. G., & Orzek, L. (1974). Child behavior and life events: Undesirable change or change per se? In B. S. Dohrenwend & B. P. Dohrenwend (Eds.), *Stressful life events: Their nature and effects* (pp. 159–170). New York: Wiley.

Gordon, R. E., Jardiolin, P., & Gordon, K. K. (1985). Predicting length of hospital stay of psychiatric patients. *American Journal of Psychiatry, 142*, 235–237.

Grant, I., Gerst, M., & Yager, J. (1976). Scaling of life events by psychiatric patients and normals. *Journal of Psychosomatic Research, 20*, 141–149.

Holmes, T. H., & Rahe, R. H. (1967). The social readjustment rating scale. *Journal of Psychosomatic Research, 11*, 213–218.

Kendell, R. E. (1983). DSM-III: A major advance in psychiatric nosology. R. L. Spitzer, J. B. W. Williams, & A. E. Skodol (Eds.), *International Perspectives on DSM-III* (pp. 55–68). Washington, DC: American Psychiatric Press.

Mezzich, J. E., Evanczuk, K. J., Mathias, R. J., & Coffman, G. A. (1984). Admission decisions and multiaxial diagnosis. *Archives of General Psychiatry, 41*, 1001–1004.

Mezzich, A. C., Mezzich, J. E., & Coffman, G. A. (1985). Reliability of DSM-III vs. DSM-II in child psychopathology. *Journal of American Academy of Child Psychiatry, 24*, 273–280.

Rabkin, J., & Struening, E. (1976). Life events, stress and illness. *Science, 194*, 1013–1020.

Rey, J. M., Plapp, J. M., Stewart, G. W., Richards, I., & Bashir, M. (1987). Reliability of the psychosocial axes of the DSM-III in an adolescent population. *British Journal of Psychiatry, 150*, 228–234.

Rey, J. M., Stewart, G. W., & Plapp, J. M. (1988). In reply to Skodol, A. E., & Shrout, P. E.: Axis IV of DSM-III. *American Journal of Psychiatry, 145*, 1046–1047.

Rey, J. M., Stewart, G. W., Plapp, J. M., Bashir, M. R., & Richards, I. N. (1988). DSM-III axis IV revisited. *American Journal of Psychiatry, 145*, 286–292.

Roth, M. (1983). The achievements and limitations of DSM-III. In R. L. Spitzer, J. B. W. Williams, & A. E. Skodol (Eds.), *International perspectives on DSM-III* (pp. 91–105). Washington, DC: American Psychiatric Press.

Russell, A. T., Cantwell, D. P., Mattison, R., & Will, L. (1979). A comparison of DSM-II and DSM-III in the diagnosis of childhood psychiatric disorders. III. Multiaxial features. *Archives of General Psychiatry, 36*, 1223–1226.

Rutter, M., & Shaffer, D. (1980). DSM-III: A step forward or back in terms of the classification of child psychiatric disorders? *Journal of the American Academy of Child Psychiatry, 19,* 371–394.

Schless, A. P., Schwartz, L., Goetz, C., & Mendels, J. (1974). How depressives view the significance of life events. *British Journal of Psychiatry, 125,* 406–410.

Schrader, G., Gordon, M., & Harcourt, R. (1986). The usefulness of DSM-III axis IV and axis V assessments. *American Journal of Psychiatry, 143,* 904–907.

Shrout, P. E., Link, B. G., Dohrenwend, B. P., Skodol, A. E., Stueve, A., & Mirotznik, J. (1989). Characterizing life events as risk factors for depression: The role of fateful loss events. *Journal of Abnormal Psychology, 98,* 460–467.

Skodol, A. E., & Shrout, P. E. (1988). Axis IV of DSM-III. *American Journal of Psychiatry, 145,* 1046.

Skodol, A. E., & Shrout, P. E. (1989a). Use of DSM-III axis IV in clinical practice: Rating etiologically significant stressors. *American Journal of Psychiatry, 146,* 61–66.

Skodol, A. E., & Shrout, P. E. (1989b). Use of DSM-III axis IV in clinical practice: Rating the severity of psychosocial stressors. *Psychiatry Research, 30,* 201–211.

Spitzer, R. L., & Forman, J. B. W. (1979). DSM-III field trials: II. Initial experience with the multiaxial system. *American Journal of Psychiatry, 136,* 818–820.

Tennant, C., & Andrews, G. (1978). The pathogenic quality of life event stress in neurotic impairment. *Archives of General Psychiatry, 35,* 859–863.

Tennant, C., & Bebbington P. (1978). The social causation of depression: A critique of the work of Brown and his colleagues. *Psychological Medicine, 8,* 565–575.

Tennant, C., Bebbington, P., & Hurry, J. (1981). The role of life events in depressive illness: Is there a substantial causal relation? *Psychological Medicine, 11,* 379–389.

Tennant, C., Smith, A., Bebbington, P., & Hurry, J. (1979). The contextual threat of life events: The concept and its reliability. *Psychological Medicine, 9,* 525–528.

Theorell, T. (1974). Life events before and after the onset of a premature myocardial infarction. In B. B. Dohrenwend & B. P. Dohrenwend (Eds.), *Stressful life events: Their nature and effects* (pp. 101–117). New York: Wiley.

Williams, J. B. W. (1985a). The multiaxial system of DSM-III: Where did it come from and where should it go? I. Its origins and critiques. *Archives of General Psychiatry, 42,* 175–180.

Williams, J. B. W. (1985b). The multiaxial system of DSM-III: Where did it come from and where should it go? II. Empirical studies, innovations, and recommendations. *Archives of General Psychiatry, 42,* 181–186.

Williams, J. B. W. (1987). Multiaxial diagnosis. In A. E. Skodol & R. L. Spitzer (Eds.), *An annotated bibliography of DSM-III* (pp. 31–36). Washington, DC: American Psychiatric Press.

Zimmerman, M., Pfohl, B., Coryell, W., & Stangl, D. (1987). The prognostic validity of DSM-III axis IV in depressed inpatients. *American Journal of Psychiatry, 144,* 102–106.

Zimmerman, M., Pfohl, B., Stangl, D., & Coryell, W. (1985). The validity of DSM-III axis IV (Severity of Psychosocial Stressors). *American Journal of Psychiatry, 142,* 1437–1441.

Zubin, J., & Spring, B. (1977). Vulnerability: A new view of schizophrenia. *Journal of Abnormal Psychology, 86,* 103–126.

Types of Stressors

A major goal of the present work has been to indicate the nature of the stress engendered by the everyday as well as by the exceptional moments in life. In a sense, the heart of this effort is contained in the chapters in Section Two. What we sought to do was to compile a list of the major sources of human stress; the chapter titles reflect the outcome. The result represents the distillation of a great deal of clinical experience and some intense soul-searching. We pondered a variety of human situations in order to derive an appropriate list. Some of the sources of stress considered were self-evident, such as childhood separation experiences, illness, surgery, accidents, ingestions, and pain. Such topics need no justification for their inclusion in any list of human stressors. These experiences have been and continue to be the subject of intense and ever-widening research. Indeed, the sheer quality of effort that has gone into their study is extraordinary, making one wonder if the lessons learned thus far are being applied as widely as they should be.

A less obvious source of stress is the nature of development itself. This is probably more apparent to the child psychiatrist than to colleagues who work with adults. In our day, however, there is a strong tendency for all psychiatry to become developmental. More and more practitioners are becoming aware that development continues to produce stages and changes all through the adult years. In childhood, however, and especially into the adolescent years, the rate of change of body size, endocrine activation, and intellectual unfolding—and the often tempestuous character of these transformations—make the very processes of growth a sometimes striking source of endogenous stress. When combined with the inevitable social expectancies and responses that the child's developmental progress evokes, the internal and external challenges can be powerful indeed. The tension states thus brought into being and the impact of the child's attempted resolutions, such as becoming a runaway, can radically alter his or her future developmental prospects.

Albeit episodic, another realm appropriate for inclusion under this rubric is the array of disasters that so often have an impact on the lives of people. Fire is probably the commonest of this group; but the effects of floods and catastrophic storms create a recurrent tale that the American public encounters every year (and one that surely is even more disastrous elsewhere in the world). Large numbers of people are affected; even more to the point, the adequately trained mental health practitioner can provide a great deal of help. It seems safe to say that practitioners are not likely to get this preparation from the average training program.

One of the pervasive concerns dwelling within the American consciousness is an underlying fear of physical assault. This occurs both in the home and in the street; it is common in both realms. Rape, spouse beating, kidnapping, the taking of hostages, child abuse, and mugging are only some of the kinds of assault that send a chill up the back of the average citizen. These fears have considerable effect on the mental health of the individuals involved; a whole study of victimology is growing up around the phenomena. But along with these peacetime fears, many people also feel the impact of war. It has been calculated that something in the neighborhood of 40 armed conflicts are currently being waged at various sites throughout the world. Not infrequently, in one form or another, these events impinge on the awareness and the experience of Americans. All in all, an enormous amount of human stress is experienced around these many varieties of physical assault. The muggings and rapes are everyday occurrences; scarcely a family in America has not felt their presence directly. Waves of refugees from widespread armed conflicts are spreading over national borders everywhere in the world, and Americans are coming to grips with their own Vietnam veterans as well as with the loss of U.S. Marines in the Middle East. War is real and ubiquitous. Hence the material we have garnered considers some of its aspects.

A less obvious but not less important begetter of psychic pain can best be called "social trauma." Such traumas are all too often taken for granted by the culture, and their significance is glossed over or overlooked (or, perhaps more accurately, regarded as the fair wear and tear of daily living). This minimization of their impact carries with it a high price. Thus, the emotional cost of being accused of malfeasance, regardless of outcome, can be life changing in its impact. The loss of an ideal through deception or a failure in trust has been the stuff with which novelists have worked, but the stress value of such events is incalculable. In this fashion the chapter titles that deal with social traumata tell a grim series of stories that do not seem to attract much attention from the culture in general or the mental health establishment in particular. They should.

CHAPTER 2

Object Loss Due to Death of Parent or Sibling

RICHARD A. GARDNER, MD

The death of a parent is one of the greatest traumas that can befall a child. If it occurs early in life, it will leave an indelible trace on the total course of a child's life. Although the loss of a sibling is not as traumatic, it too can play a significant role in the child's subsequent development. This chapter will present the factors that play a role in determining a child's mode of adjustment to these traumas. Preventive and therapeutic aspects of such adjustment are also discussed.

PARENTAL DEATH

Early Life Exposures to Death

A child's initial contact with death usually comes through exposure to dead insects or other wild creatures, and pets. Furman (1974) states that children as young as 2 years of age can appreciate the irreversibility of the death of an animal. These experiences permit the child to observe firsthand that the dead animal does not move spontaneously and cannot be brought back to life (Kliman, 1968). Parents do well not to protect their children from such exposures. The parent who surreptitiously replaces a dead hamster or goldfish with an identical live one is doing the child a disservice. It is preferable to help the child encounter the loss, express sorrow over the death of the pet, assist in the burial ritual, and dispose of the animal in a special way (Fraiberg, 1959). Parents who protect their children from knowledge of the death of a friend or relative are also doing them a disservice. The parents are depriving their children of exposures that bring death into their scheme of things, help to some degree to desensitize them, and thus serve to lessen the traumatic effect of a loved one's death.

Anticipatory Mourning

If the parent is suffering from a terminal illness and is coping by means of denial mechanisms, this situation must be respected. Reasonable attempts must be made to protect such a parent from hearing statements about his or her inevitable demise. Because children are notoriously unreliable regarding such disclosure, it is often judicious to withhold such information from the child or to tell the child only what is being told the patient. If the parent is willing to discuss the matter, then the child may have the opportunity to adjust slowly to the parent's death. This is far and away the preferable course because it provides the child with the opportunity for anticipatory mourning and desensitization (Gardner, 1971; Furman, 1974).

The Mourning Process in Children

The term *mourning* refers to the series of psychological responses that an individual utilizes in the attempt to deal with the death of a meaningful person. Many investigators have addressed the question of whether children can mourn, and, if so, at what age they develop the capacity. Most agree that in order for children to mourn, they must be old enough to differentiate themselves from the dead person. Children below the age of 6 months are still psychologically fused with their caretaking figures and do not distinguish among them with total clarity. Accordingly, they are not considered capable of experiencing their loss. Such children may suffer distress, however, when there is a change in the quality of the care they are receiving, especially if this is in the direction of deterioration (Nagera, 1970). Anna Freud (1952) holds that the capacity for differentiation takes place during the second half of the first year of life. Sigmund Freud (1917/1953) believed that for mourning to occur, the child must first accept that the loved one no longer exists. Without such a realization the child cannot withdraw libidinal energy from the lost person and invest it in others. Nagera (1970) holds that children cannot mourn until they can appreciate death's irreversibility.

In addition to the developmental factors that determine when and whether a child can mourn, environmental factors are also important. Children brought up in homes where they are protected from exposure to death are less likely to recognize its full impact. In addition, a child generally goes through a two-stage process in appreciating the full significance of death. The first stage involves the child's realization that death can occur to others; the second, that he or she will ultimately suffer the same fate. There may be a gap of months and even years between these two phases of recognition. Many authors who write about the age at which children can appreciate death do not make these distinctions; sometimes they fail to consider the environmental influences. Hence the wide variety of opinions in the literature regarding the age at which children exhibit the capacity to mourn.

Facilitating Healthy Mourning

Children who are preoccupied with fears that they themselves might die cannot mourn effectively. If they are greatly concerned that they may no longer be provided with food, clothing, shelter, and the other necessities of life, these fears too compromise their capacity to mourn. Accordingly, at the time of parental death, therapists and parents should assure children that these eventualities are unlikely.

A common error the surviving parent makes it to tell the child that the departed parent is enjoying a blissful existence in heaven. If this is indeed the parent's bona fide belief, then it may provide some reassurance. If the parent has no such conviction, however, then it is not likely to mollify the child; the troubled youngster is all too likely to sense the parent's lack of conviction. Indeed, such a fabrication will engender distrust of the surviving parent just at the time when the child can least afford any compromise in the remaining relationship. Some parents provide long theological and philosophical explanations in an attempt to avoid direct discussion of the painful reality. Such evasiveness engenders not only distrust but confusion as well. The parents should tell the child exactly what his or her view is regarding the afterlife, even if the view is that the parent does not know, or is dubious.

The Question of Whether the Child Should Attend the Funeral

A common parental concern is that it is psychologically detrimental for the child to attend the funeral. This is most often untrue. There are many good reasons why the child should be invited to attend both the services and the burial. It can provide the child with highly meaningful firsthand information about death. Children learn best from the mastery of concrete experiences, and the funeral (as morbid as it may be) can most effectively provide such an experience. In addition, the child's encounter with the expression of emotion that usually occurs at a funeral will facilitate the child's own emotional expression, which is so vital to the healthy mourning process. If the parent fears that the child may disrupt the services, arrangements should be made for a nonfamily member to accompany the child in order to remove him or her if the need arises.

The Grieving Process

Grieving, more than anything else, provides a piecemeal desensitization to the trauma of the loss. Each time the child thinks about the lost parent and expresses the painful feelings associated with such thoughts, the pain becomes a little more bearable. The process also allows for a slow and continual release of the emotions evoked by the loss. Suppression and repression of such expression is one of the most common causes of untoward psychological reactions to parental loss.

The therapist can give parents a number of useful suggestions to facilitate the mourning process. Some parents, for example, would remove from the home all the property of the deceased in the belief that this will help the child forget the lost parent. This is misguided benevolence. In fact, the parent does better to provide the child with treasured possessions, photographs, and other memorabilia of the deceased parent because these help catalyze the grief reaction. The parent should be helped to appreciate that the child's repeated questions about the deceased parent serve a useful function. Reiteration is part of the working-through process and provides for desensitization. Squelching these questions interferes with the healthy grieving process. Furthermore, such questions can help the child correct cognitive distortions about the parent's death. In therapy the child may exhibit preoccupation with a particular story, the central theme of which deals in some way with the death motif. Therapists should have the highest regard for such stories because they serve symbolically to facilitate the mourning process.

Anger Reactions

Frustration produces anger, and the death of a parent is a significant source of frustration. After all, the parent is without question a child's most treasured possession. Therapists should advise parents that such anger is inevitable and that it would be psychologically detrimental to make the child feel guilty over its expression. The guilt reaction is likely to occur because there is a strong taboo against speaking ill of a recently deceased person, especially a parent. Although a child may recognize that the parent did not wish to die, the youngster still suffers the frustrations and resentments attendant on the parent's death. When not permitted expression, the anger may be revealed in a variety of ways. It may be acted out (Arnstein, 1962), released in nightmares (Gardner, 1973), expressed symbolically, as by soiling (Chethik, 1970), or projected onto others such as the surviving parent (Scharl, 1961).

Spontaneous Identification with the Dead Parent

One of the primitive mechanisms utilized in compensating for the loss is the psychological incorporation of the deceased parent (Furman, 1974). It is as if the child were saying: "My mommy is not really dead; I have her here inside of me."

Seven of the 18 bereaved children studied by Kliman (1968) manifested such incorporation via identification with parental mannerisms, behavior, and areas of interest. Indeed, so accurate are the imitations that sometimes the identification process is almost uncanny. Occasionally the child's play reveals this process of acquisition. Such identification can have either positive or negative effects; in large measure this depends on the traits selected and their value. When the identification involves the acquisition of a parent's talent or skill, the enhanced competence can contribute to the child's coping with the deprivation suffered from the parental loss.

The Formation of a Substitute Relationship

The mourning process does not simply serve to release the feelings evoked by the parent's death. Its ultimate purpose is to free the individual and enable him or her to form attachments with others, thereby facilitating the continuation of meaningful living. Therapists and parents must work together in helping children reach this goal. However, it is unreasonable to set as the goal total detachment from the deceased parent—even if that were possible. The memories of the lost parent may serve a child well, both at the time of the death and subsequently. In particular, the memories of the parent's affection are reassuring and contribute to the child's feelings of self-worth. The advice and teachings of the deceased parent may remain with the child throughout his or her life and contribute to healthy superego development. If the attachment warrants this persistence, the parent's healthy and desirable personality traits will continue to be incorporated into the child's psychic structure, supporting a healthy pattern of development. These lingering involvements notwithstanding, the most desirable outcome for the mourning child is to develop meaningful relationships with substitutes. This is the most predictable way to avoid the development of untoward psychological reactions to the loss (Gardner, 1978). A child sometimes feels disloyal over affectionate feelings for a surrogate. Therapists and parents should help to alleviate this guilt by reassuring the child that such feelings are normal, predictable, and healthy (Kliman, 1968).

Pathological Reactions to Parental Death Resulting from the Failure to Mourn Successfully

The death of a parent does not necessarily cause a child to develop psychopathology, but it does increase the risk of untoward psychological reactions. It is important to differentiate between psychopathology resulting from the failure to have a successful mourning experience and that arising from the deprivation caused by the absence of a parent. This section considers the outcome of failed mourning, including the reactions that generally appear immediately after the death of a parent. The following section is devoted to reactions to parental loss. These are likely to exhibit themselves months and even years after the event.

Denial. Denial is one of the most primitive of the mental mechanisms, and it is not surprising that children resort to it so readily. This in part explains why children generally react less intensely than adults to the death of a loved one. Furthermore, children often use play as a vehicle for working through their reaction and thus appear to be responding with even less pain. Moreover, children are more prone to avoid painful feelings than are adults, and this may contribute to the child's seemingly pain-free reaction. Twelve of the 18 children studied by Kliman (1968) denied the parental death for periods as long as a week. The most common factor contributing to a child's utilization of denial is parental denial, in particular, the failure on the part of the surviving parent to be completely honest with the child regarding the death of the lost parent (Brown, 1968). Inevitably, such a pattern of denial interferes significantly with the initiation of the mourning process.

Repression and Suppression of Emotional Response. Central to the mourning process is the expression of feelings of grief. Any process that consciously suppresses or unconsciously represses the child's emotions is likely to interfere with mourning. Familial and cultural influences may play a significant role in producing such inhibitions. Some families and cultures view the expression of feelings as primitive or improper and admire persons who deal with pain with stoicism and composure. A child may, for example, observe mother being admired for not "breaking down" following the death of her husband; she may even be complimented on "how well she's taking it." Such a mother serves as a model for the child's inhibition of emotional response, and her well-meaning friends and relatives merely entrench the pattern for both mother and child. The child, however, may be exposed to more direct messages that instill emotional inhibition: "Boys don't cry," "See how brave you can be," and "See how grown-up you can be by not crying like a baby." Overprotective parents often operate on the principle that every precaution should be utilized to prevent their child from experiencing pain. Such a parent may inhibit expressions of grief to avoid upsetting the child, who may then inhibit his or her own emotional reactions via identification with the parent. Furthermore, children in this situation may recognize that their emotional expression will cause parental discomfort, and the youngsters accordingly strive even more strongly to inhibit themselves. Therapists need to try to help such parents realize that their inhibition is a disservice to their children as well as to themselves.

The Regressive Reaction. Regression is a common reaction to parental death, especially in younger children. They may become more infantile, demand more food and attention, want more cuddling, revert to baby talk, become enuretic, and so on. When it is transient, such regression should be considered normal. Because it provides the child with reassurance that love, guidance, and protection will still be forthcoming, the surviving parent can be encouraged to indulge it to some degree. When, however, the regression becomes excessively deep, the child may not proceed along his or her proper "developmental track" and instead remains fixated at earlier levels. In extreme cases intellectual and social functioning may also become impaired. Such children are obviously in need of treatment. In many cases the regressive reaction is probably the result of other factors, and not simply a reaction to the parent's death (Shambaugh, 1961). Thus it may be the result of inordinate parental overprotection following the death. Conversely, it may be a reaction to the pressures on the child to become excessively mature and to take on the increased demands and responsibilities resulting from the parental death. A certain amount of adult responsibility sometimes is warranted and in fact can be healthy. It is excessive demands for such maturity that may evoke the regressive reaction.

Guilt Reactions. In the complex broil of events surrounding a parent's death, many factors can cause children to feel guilty. Again, parental attitudes play a significant role in determining whether children experience a guilt reaction. The therapist should strive to counsel parents who comport themselves in a fashion that encourages guilt because such behavior can add an enormous burden to the bereaved child's difficulties. One common reaction that most if not all people have to the death of a loved one is "There, but for the grace of God, go I." This reaction is especially common when the death has been caused by an accident. Healthy adults come to realize that such feelings are normal, but children may not. Children who exhibit this kind of guilt have to be helped to appreciate that this particular reaction is normal and that they are not wicked for having such thoughts.

Mention has been made that children generally do not react to death as intensely as do adults. Children who observe the painful reactions of adults may come to feel guilty because they are not experiencing a similar degree of pain. And parental comments may entrench such guilt: "How can you kids be laughing and playing? Your father died only yesterday." The clear implication here is that the child has not loved deeply enough. Therapists must help such children and their parents understand that most children do not react to death in the same way as do adults, and that the child who exhibits occasional levity or playfulness during the mourning period is not necessarily impaired in affection for the deceased parent.

During early development, children tend to consider themselves to be the cause of many phenomena around them (Piaget, 1954). Accordingly, it is not uncommon for young children to believe a parent's death is the result of their occasional wish that the parent go away and/or die. Such children may even fear that the dead parent's ghost is ever hovering over them in order to wreak vengeance. It is necessary to help such children learn that all children have angry thoughts and feelings toward their parents and that these frequently take the form of death wishes. The youngsters need to recognize that thoughts or wishes cannot affect the real world. In addition, providing children with specific information about the causes of the parent's death can help alleviate such guilt.

Most children feel angry at the dead parent for having abandoned them. At the same time, they usually feel that such anger represents some deficiency in their love and may thereby feel guilty over it. Again, these children have to appreciate that such angry feelings are normal and do not represent a betrayal of the deceased parent. Indeed, their anger is understandable in that they have been deprived of one of their most treasured possessions.

In the process of disciplining, parents may produce guilt with comments such as these: "What would your father think if he were alive today and found out what you have done?" "Your mother will never rest peacefully in her grave as long as you continue being bad," and "Your mother would roll over in her grave if she knew what you said today." Instilling in a child the belief that the spirit of the dead parent is somehow still hovering about, still observing, still reaching, and that it is pained by the child's behavior may be a very effective way of getting a child to comply with parental requests and demands, but it is also one of the most predictable ways of producing pathological guilt. It is a cruel disciplinary measure, and the therapist does well to discourage parents from utilizing it.

Yet another form of guilt may manifest itself at the time of a parent's death. Some children may become obsessed with thoughts such as "He died because I didn't treat him well. I was bad and that upset him and made him sick. It's my fault. If I had been a better child he would still be alive." Such guilt is basically different from the aforementioned types of guilt reactions. Although it is associated with feelings of self-criticism, it is basically an attempt to gain control in a situation over which the child realistically has no control. Implicit in the guilt reaction is the child's belief that he or she could have prevented the death by being "good." (Gardner, 1969a, 1969b, 1970, 1971). Such children need help to differentiate between those things in life that they can control and those that they cannot. They have to learn to accept events over which they have no control and to strive to change those things that they can control. Within the context of such discussions, a therapist must help these children resign themselves to their realistic limitations in such situations. At the same time, such vulnerable youngsters can be given the reassurance and solace of knowing that there are others in the world who will provide them with at least some of the affection previously supplied by the deceased parent.

Whatever the origin of the guilt, children may attempt to assuage it by eliciting punishment. And antisocial behavior is one way that the child may try in order to achieve this. Some children become accident-prone to reduce guilt, as though each accident provided an increment of guilt-alleviating punishment. Others become obsessed with feelings of unworthiness and self-denigration for the most minor indiscretions. Here, there is a displacement from the feelings of guilt related to the aforementioned factors to the present misdeeds. Additional literature elsewhere (Gardner, 1977) elaborates on the guilt mechanisms associated with parental death and the therapeutic approaches to their amelioration.

Depression. Sigmund Freud (1917) differentiated between mourning and melancholia. He considered mourning to be the normal healthy reaction to death, and melancholia to be a pathological response. Freud hypothesized that melancholia developed when the bereaved person failed to decathect libido from the internal image of the lost object. He considered the self-denigration often seen in depression to be a result of redirecting the anger felt toward the deceased against oneself. Melancholia (depression) then occurs when the mourning has not taken its normal course. In her exhaustive study of bereaved children, Furman (1974) did not find an invariable relationship between depression and inhibited anger. She found that those children who became inordinatedly depressed often had suffered concomitant losses. Furthermore, she could not find any particular factor (inhibited anger or other) that had predictive value in determining which children would become depressed following parental death. It is clear, however, that there are children who do become depressed and who exhibit apathy, loss of appetite, and impaired interest in the world about them. Such a child does not become desensitized to the painful affects associated with the loss of the parent. In extreme cases the child may attempt suicide. Furman (1974) considers identification elements to be present in these instances, as well as efforts to reunite with the dead parent. One of Furman's patients, in attempting suicide, ingested the same kind of pills her mother had used in her own suicidal attempt. In this case, of course, both the identification and the reunion elements were present.

The reactions discussed in this section are likely to impede mourning; they thereby deprive the afflicted children of the salutary relief that comes from the mourning process. It is likely that some children can profit from a belated mourning and others may not. In a case described elsewhere (Gardner, 1971) a 4-year-old girl whose brother had died 6 months earlier came for evaluation. Her parents had not told her the circumstances surrounding her brother's death, and she was thus deprived of a mourning experience. When she was first brought for treatment, she presented with a constellation of phobic symptoms, all of which appeared to be related to her failure to have worked through her reactions to her brother's death. Her parents were advised to provide her with detailed information about the event and to take out of storage various memorabilia related to her brother, which they had been hiding, and give these to her. In addition, the parent's encouraged her to discuss her brother and ask questions, and they answered every question honestly and accurately. The patient then underwent a belated mourning experience, and her symptoms cleared. However, the symptomatology did not clear simply from the mourning, but also from the dispelling of the fears engendered by her ignorance of the circumstances of her brother's death. For other patients, such a belated mourning experience is not possible. Over time, the pent-up emotions contribute to the development of other forms of psychopathology for which the mere mourning experience is not likely to be the key therapeutic factor. Rather, the other elements contributing to the pathology must be understood and worked through. The next section considers these additional psychopathological reactions.

Pathological Reactions to Parental Death Resulting from Deprivation and Other Untoward Effects of the Loss

In all of the 18 children studied by Kliman (1968), within 1 month of bereavement, new symptoms had appeared. The most common symptoms observed were separation anxiety, fearfulness, insomnia, and eating disturbances. Many children developed a significant loss of trust. After all, if one parent can abandon a child, can the other really be trusted? Behaviors may develop that represent symbolically a search for the lost parent (Wolfenstein, 1969). For example, the child may become materialistic and even steal—the acquired object symbolizing the lost parent. Another associated pathological reaction is splitting: The child's ambivalence for the lost parent may be split, with the positive feelings remaining attached to the dead parent and the negative ones being directed toward the surviving parent or surrogate.

Idealization of the deceased parent is common. Eulogies tend to idealize the deceased and this tradition can contribute to the distortion. In our society, which does not consider it proper to speak ill of the dead, a child may further develop a notion that the dead parent was perfect or close to it. Children do best when they grow up in a home where they come to appreciate that their parents are mixtures of both assets and liabilities. Without such experiences children may become perfectionistic from continuously comparing themselves unfavorably with the perfect parent. After the perfect parent is deceased, there is no opportunity for reality experiences to correct their distortions. Also, they may have difficulty relating to others because they are forever comparing the idealized dead parent with the mere human beings they encounter. This can produce difficulties in the dating period and in relationships with peers, employers, employees, and spouses; it may even contribute to subsequent divorce. Accordingly, therapists should advise surviving parents to avoid such idealization and to describe the dead parent in honest and balanced terms. On occasion, such idealization may serve as a reaction formation against unconscious angry feelings that the child harbors toward the deceased parent but is too guilty to express. Therapists should strive to help such children feel less guilty over their angry feelings and thus have less need to resort to pathological defenses.

Many younger children develop strong shame reactions over the death of a parent. Such a child becomes mortified in school if the teacher goes around the class asking each child what his or her parents do for a living. Children have been known to lie under such circumstances and to describe a living parent with a particular occupation, rather than to admit publicly that they are not like the other children who have two parents. These children may also actually fill out the name of the parent on a questionnaire rather than write that the parent is dead. Many children feel this difference between themselves and their peers acutely. This may contribute to feelings of lowered self-worth as they ever compare themselves unfavorably with others. These feelings may become especially painful when other children relate happy events in school on the days following Mother's Day and Father's Day.

However, in reaction to feelings of inferiority engendered by the loss, some of these children overcompensate by becoming superachievers. In later life this may contribute significantly to successes in their fields of endeavor. Wakerman (1984) has written an excellent study of the effects on girls of the death of a father, both in childhood and in subsequent years.

Another common reaction is that of overdependency on the surviving parent. If this is indulged by the surviving parent or if, in response, the surviving parent becomes overprotective, then this adaptation is likely to become entrenched. If perpetuated, the youngster remains immature and fails to develop at the same rate as his or her peers. In extreme cases the youngster continues to dwell in the home with the surviving parent after reaching adulthood, and the two then live in a kind of symbiotic relationship. The adaptation is even more likely if the surviving parent tended to parentalize the deceased spouse. As the child grows older, he or she too becomes parentalized and depended on, eventually becoming a psychological parent to his or her own parent. And when the surviving parent dies, the child (now adult) may develop a serious psychiatric disturbance, even requiring hospitalization. Such a person has never become equipped to function independently in the world.

Individuals who have lost a parent in childhood are likely to be more insecure and distrustful in their relationships with others. Having been abandoned by one of the most important people in their lives, they tend to distrust not only the remaining spouse but all others whom they may encounter. This combination of insecurity and lack of trust can significantly compromise their relationships. They are ever expecting rejection and have a reduced capacity to deal with the inevitable slights to which all individuals are exposed from time to time in their lives. This sense of distrust may make it difficult for them to involve themselves in meaningful relationsihps. And the insecurity and dependency may in themselves be alienating, thus reducing the likelihood of developing a trusting relationship. Some individuals who have lost a parent in childhood find themselves compulsively gravitating toward people who will abandon them. It is as if rejection and abandonment have become the model for their relationships, and thereafter, they feel uncomfortable and even strange with individuals who are not likely to reject and abandon them. A process of selection follows in which they choose people with high potential for abandonment and thus self fulfill their prophecy of being rejected.

The younger the child at the time of the parental death, the longer the period of potential deprivation of parental affection, and the greater the likelihood for the development of untoward reactions to the parental loss. This pathology, however, is likely to be avoided if the remaining parent provides adequate affection, care, guidance, and protection. And, if the surviving parent provides a surrogate for the child, then the likelihood of the development of pathological reactions is reduced even further. Birtchnell (1971) found that the death of the same-sexed parent was associated with an unfavorable long-term outcome for the same-sexed child. However, the presence of an older sibling of the same sex as the dead parent tended to alleviate somewhat the untoward effects of the loss, as though the older sibling took over the place of the dead parent. The psychiatric literature is replete with articles describing the relationship between parental loss and the subsequent development of psychopathology. A wide variety of untoward psychological reactions have been described, the most common being schizophrenia, juvenile delinquency, psychopathy, alcoholism, depression, and suicide. Bowlby (1952) and Kliman (1968) have provided excellent reviews of the literature on this relationship.

SIBLING DEATH

Although the psychological trauma following the death of a sibling is not generally as severe as from the death of a parent, it is still a formidable form of stress and has not received the attention it deserves in the psychiatric literature. Compared to the number of articles on parental loss, I have found relatively few on the subject of sibling loss. In part this reflects the relative rarity of this calamity in recent years. Up until the early part of this century, however, the death of a sibling was a commonplace phenomenon. So ravaged were children by a wide variety of diseases that many parents would have twice as many children as they ultimately hoped to raise because they anticipated that approximately half of them would not survive the early years. Although advances in medicine have caused sibling death to be much less common, this still does not warrant the paucity of studies on this subject.

Preparing Brothers and Sisters for an Impending Sibling Loss

As noted earlier, children's knowledge of the impending loss of a parent may present a risk with regard to the dying parent's utilization of denial mechanisms. In the nature of things, the same problem is present when a dying child is using denial mechanisms; the likelihood that they will be respected by the surviving siblings is small. Accordingly, under such circumstances, it is often preferable for the siblings to receive only the same information that is being provided to the sick child. However, if the child is aware of his or her impending death, knowledge of it can prove salutary for the siblings. It provides them with the opportunity for anticipatory mourning, and this improves their capacity for dealing optimally with the siblings death. Furthermore, unmentionable subjects generally produce more anxiety, delusion's, and distortions than do painful subjects that are openly discussed.

Discussions with the healthy siblings about the impending death should take place within the family context both with and without the presence of the dying child. In this tragic situation, such shared grieving can be a cohesive force of great power. The desensitization then takes place within a supportive atmosphere. The open discussion thus provided is likely to reduce the possibility that the surviving children will harbor cognitive distortions. Pakes (1973) points out that when a child is not told about the death of the sibling and there is a family conspiracy of silence, the child generally fantasizes things that are far worse. One of these could include the fear of the impending death of a parent.

Kübler-Ross (1978) suggests telling children that a dying loved one is like a butterfly leaving a cocoon. When the child draws such a picture, it confirms to her that her advice has proven useful. I believe this may be injudicious advice. She is strengthening the belief that there is definitely some existence after death. Even Kübler-Ross does not know whether there is an afterlife. I would be uncomfortable using such an image and prefer a more neutral position. This would apply especially to therapists who basically do not share such a belief. The resort to such duplicity could compromise the therapist–patient relationship.

One could argue that a close relationship between the dying and surviving siblings can be a source of support for the dying child. For the surviving child, however, the loss becomes devastating when the "best friend" dies. Rosen (1986) describes a situation in which a sister had not recovered, even after the passage of many years, from the death of her brother, to whom she was extremely close and who was indeed her best friend. However, where siblings have meaningful involvements with others, they are better prepared to cope. Upon the death of the brother or sister, they are more likely to find compensatory gratifications. Thus in Rosen's case, this girl appeared to lack meaningful involvements with others and thus suffered grievously from the loss of her brother.

An important question is whether it is preferable for the sick child to die at home or in the hospital. Rolsky (1983) points out that one of the advantages of the sibling's dying at home is that the brothers and sisters will observe directly the reality of death. This tends to dispel the morbid fantasies that could be engendered by the sibling's dying in the hospital. In addition, it keeps the dying child in closer contact with the parents, and this is also salutary. Binger, Ablin, Kushner, and Perin (1983) point out that the practice of confining death to the hospital is a recent trend, and one that may not be in the dying patient's best interests. It deprives the patient of the close family ties that can be so supportive. Furthermore, siblings who are not permitted to visit the hospital are denied anticipatory grief reactions and many concrete experiences that can help them work through their responses. Binger et al. found that when siblings assisted in the home care of the terminally ill brother or sister, it was therapeutic for both. It was reassuring for the siblings to see the parents caring for the dying child; it meant that love and affection was present in the home for all the children. Kübler-Ross (1978) considers the common rule in most hospitals forbidding visits with dying patients by children under 14 to be an unfortunate practice. The assumption is that visiting dying patients is psychologically traumatic for children, but she believes the youngsters are thereby deprived of an important experience that can help them deal better with death.

Rosen (1986) points out that where a child is suffering sibling loss, the extended family will generally view the parents as needing more support than the child. This is especially likely for the child whose denial may be interpreted by adults to mean that the sibling warrants less attention. Such an interpretation is regrettable because it deprives the sibling of important support at a crucial time.

The Guilt Reactions of Children Associated with the Death of a Sibling

It is important to remember that the term *guilt* serves as an overarching rubric under which various subvarieties of guilt may manifest themselves. In order to reduce confusion and communication errors, it would probably be preferable that specific terms be utilized to designate the different kinds of guilt.

Psychological guilt (as opposed to legal guilt) generally refers to the feeling of lowered self-worth associated with thoughts, feelings, or acts that are usually considered reprehensible. People with weak superego development do not feel much guilt. Thus, guilt may take the form of a surviving child's feeling responsible for the death of the sibling. In the overwhelming majority of cases such guilt is unwarranted because the surviving child played no role in bringing about the sibling's demise. However, there are situations in which the surviving child may indeed have participated and where the guilt is appropriate. Cohn (1971) describes the case of a boy who died in a fire that both he and his brother had started. The surviving brother developed symptoms of guilt, compulsive eating, fire setting, and hitting and biting himself. In therapy he described his feelings of guilt and claimed responsibility for his brother's death. The therapist repeatedly emphasized that the boy had not really wanted his brother to die and that the brother's death was an accident. These differentiations helped alleviate this child's guilt. Such an outcome, however, is rare. Most often this kind of guilt involves delusional elements and distortions of thinking.

A variety of factors in sibling death situations cause guilt related to hostility. At times all children feel rivalry with and even hateful feelings toward their siblings. Because of harboring occasional death wishes, surviving children may feel particularly guilty when a sibling dies. Rogers (1967) claimed that older siblings who lost younger siblings were more likely to feel guilty; in the nature of things, they had indeed wished the death of the younger sibling, especially at the time of the sibling's birth. Or the child may feel guilty over the angry feelings that arose in the course of normal sibling rivalries. Wishing that a sibling would die is not an uncommon thought in the course of children's growth. The surviving siblings may be angry over the restrictions on their lives caused by the sickness of the terminal sibling. They may even have wished that that child were already dead so that the restrictions would be lifted. The well child may be angry at the dying sibling because he or she is receiving extra attention. Again, there may be anger at being abandoned by the deceased sibling. Rosenblatt (1969) describes the case of a young boy whose sister died during an asthmatic attack. He subsequently developed fears that he too would die. He believed that the feelings that he would die were punishments for the anger he felt toward her because she had abandoned him. Nor does the death itself bring all this to an end. Following the death, the child may be jealous of the parents' grief over the deceased sibling. In both cases there may be guilt concerning the angry and jealous feelings.

Children who feel guilt about their hostility must be helped to understand that they did not bring about the death of the sibling and that such thoughts are normal. The therapist must repeatedly emphasize that thoughts cannot harm and cannot make an event occur. Only actions can bring about an event. In play therapy one can emphasize that no matter how hard one wishes for something to take place, that alone will not make it happen. The therapist can point out that one cannot control the natural elements such as rain, wind, and snow. These can be differentiated from things that one can control, for example, homework, fighting with a sibling, and watching television. Doll play can help impress these important differentiations upon the child.

Guilt may also be present over the child's feelings of relief and even happiness that it is the sibling and not the surviving child who is going to die. This is related to the universal "There, but for the grace of God, go I" phenomenon. Therapists should help children realize that such thoughts are natural.

Surviving siblings often receive extra attention and indulgence from parents and relatives. This usually stems from the desire to ensure that the surviving sibling will not suffer the same fate. Some children feel guilty that they are now given this special attention because it would not have been provided if the sibling had lived.

The aforementioned guilt reactions are different in quality from the kind of guilt that is linked to the need to control. In the latter instance there is less a sense of self-criticism than there is an attempt to control the uncontrollable. If the child brought about the sibling's death, the notion is implicit that the child has control over death, rather than that death is the product of forces over which the child has no control. The child who believes that his or her misbehavior, that is, being "bad," caused the sibling's death, can logically think that being "good" will undo the heinous crime. Such children may then become very well-behaved, start doing chores around the house, are cooperative and obedient, and refrain from disruptive behavior. Although the attempt here is not to undo the death, it serves the purpose of preventing the death of others. Elsewhere in the literature (Gardner, 1969a, 1969b, 1970), this guilt mechanism is discussed in detail.

Dealing with and Preventing Untoward Psychological Reactions to a Sibling's Death

Rosen (1986) discusses the effects of friends and extended family on children's reactions to sibling loss. One type of advice to the child on the part of these outsiders is "Be strong for your parents." This places a great burden on the children because it inhibits expression of their own grief reactions. Such children feel suddenly catapulted into an adult role where they are to be supportive and parentlike with their parents. Another response of outsiders is silence, where the assumption is made that the surviving siblings have had no reaction to the loss. This too prevents the catalysis of mourning responses. Rosen describes one child's teacher who told the other children in the class not to talk about the death of the surviving child's sibling. Children, too, out of their embarrassment and discomfort, may avoid talking about the death to the surviving sibling.

Some families deal with the sibling loss by destroying all the dead child's possessions and never mentioning his or her name again. Most of the children in Rosen's study wanted to keep some souvenir of the dead sibling. Many did so in spite of parental wishes to the contrary. This suggests powerful natural forces in children that work toward facilitation of the mourning process. The same was true of children whose parents did not wish to mention the name of the deceased child. The children, in contrast, insisted on doing so. This approach of erasing all traces of the dead child is an unfortunate and psychologically detrimental practice. It deprives the child of the physical memorabilia, cognitive reiteration, and emotional catharsis necessary for mourning and working through. Like all conspiracies of silence, it is generally misguided. Although designed to protect the parents and the surviving siblings from pain, it results in another kind of pain related to the failure to express the thoughts and feelings necessary for working through the trauma. By intention, such a taboo is supposed to help the survivors go on with the business of living; in fact, it lessens the likelihood of their doing so by squelching the mourning process. People are in a better position to go on with their lives *after* they have mourned and have been allowed desensitization.

In the case of a child whose parents withheld any details regarding an older brother's death, the sister was told that he had gone to heaven, but she did not participate in any of the events surrounding the funeral and burial. Later on the child came to treatment with symptoms of severe separation anxiety. Whereas previously she had visited the homes of friends and had gone to school without difficulty, she now refused to do so. She would even hide in the closet when a stranger came to the door of the house. It was clear that this child feared that at any moment she might be plucked off the surface of the earth. The parents were encouraged to provide her with the details of her brother's death and to take her to visit the actual site of his burial. Following these disclosures she experienced a dramatic alleviation of her symptoms (Gardner, 1971). Lewis and Lewis (1983) recommend that the dead child's room not be given to a sibling until after the mourning process is over. At that point, the decision is more likely to be made on a rational basis and will be less affected by the grief of the loss. Application of the principles described in this example can be salutary. They provide concrete evidence of exactly what has happened, facilitate the mourning process, reduce distortions that may be wreathed about the death, and, although painful, ultimately result in the child's suffering far less grief.

Rosen (1985) describes the good behavior of the surviving child as a way of reducing parental grief. The older the child, the greater the probability that this reaction will occur. Out of sympathy for the parent's pain, the child tries to assuage their grief by being good. Rosen found that many of these children have a sense of responsibility for the parents and want to make up to them for the loss they have incurred. Another factor may also be operative here. Such children may be utilizing the parents as a source of vicarious solace for themselves. By assuaging the parent's grief, they are ameliorating their own. It is as if they project themselves into their parents and ease the grief of the projected self.

Many people tend to avoid the surviving siblings. A probable factor in such avoidance is the fear of the child's anger. Aggression must be controlled in a civilized society, and people generally want to stay away from a "time bomb." There is a general sense that the sibling of a child who has died must be quite angry, and people want to avoid the expression of this anger. This, of course, can be a source of deprivation for the youngsters so regarded.

Rosen and Cohn (1981) point out that the surviving siblings may suffer a double loss: the dead sibling and the grieving parents. The latter are often so preoccupied with their grief that they may not attend properly to the child. Of course, under these circumstances the loss of the parent is temporary. Furthermore, the parents may become depressed, and this too deprives the surviving children of proper attention and affection. Cobb (1956) describes surviving siblings as being prone to overreact to minor illnesses. Considering that their deceased sibling's fatal illness may have begun with minor symptoms, this is all too understandable. Antisocial acting out may also manifest itself. I had a patient whose older brother suffered from Gilles de la Tourette syndrome and whose younger brother had leukemia. Naturally, the parents were significantly preoccupied with the illnesses of their oldest and youngest children. The middle child was one of the most severely obstructionistic and antisocial children I have seen. These reactions were clearly related to the attention this child's siblings were receiving.

Rosen (1986) describes what she calls "fate-provoking" behavior following the death of a sibling. One teenager had a sibling who had died in a diving accident; the survivor on a number of occasions dove into the same swimming pool. It was apparently a counterphobic way of gaining assurance that one need not be killed under these circumstances. It served to assuage her death fears. Another patient described by Rosen insisted on walking down the same street where her sibling had been hit by a car. The sibling of one of my patients had fallen off a cliff and died. The patient insisted on playing with her friends at the cliff's edge and even on dancing there at night under somewhat precarious conditions. This behavior was judged to represent an attempt to prove their own invulnerability to the same catastrophe. Therapists do well to differentiate between relatively innocuous counterphobic maneuvers and ones that are truly dangerous.

Long-Term Sequelae to the Death of a Sibling

Krell and Rabkin (1979) describe three types of children who have survived sibling death: (1) The "haunted child" is one whose family has been silent regarding the circumstances of the sibling's death. The child becomes distrustful, ever fearful of his or her own death. (2) The "bound child" is overprotected by the family, who tries to guard the child against any catastrophe. The child becomes overdependent and thereafter views the world as dangerous. (3) The "resurrected child" results when the parents attempt to resurrect or replace the lost child with one of the siblings. The parents relate to this child at both the "real" and the "illusory" level. Siblings born after the death are especially likely to be viewed as resurrections of the deceased child. One parental reaction to such a child may be to place enormous demands on that child to achieve to a significant degree. I have found no studies on this subject but personal experience leads me to this conclusion; in studies of high achievers this factor might prove to be an important one.

Rosen (1986) describes how the death of a sibling in childhood may result in the surviving sibling, as an adult, becoming overprotective and oversolicitous of his or her own children. She believes that such overprotectiveness is a derivative of the childhood loss. This stems not only from a general fear of childhood death but from the utilization of the child as substitute for a sibling who may have been lost many years previously.

REFERENCES

Arnstein, H. S. (1962). *What to tell your child*. New York: Pocket Books.

Binger, C. M., Ablin, A. R., Kushner, J. H., & Perin, G. A. (1983). Terminal phase of childhood cancer: Home care of the dying. In J. J. Schowalter, P. R. Patterson, M. Tallmer, A. H. Kutscher, S. V. Gullo, & D. Peretz (Eds.), *The child and death*. (pp. 156–179). New York: Columbia University Press.

Birtchnell, J. (1971). Early parent death in relation to size and construction of sibship in psychiatric patients and general population controls. *Acta Psychiatrica Scandinavica, 47,* 250–270.

Bowlby, J. (1952). Maternal care and mental health. Geneva, Switzerland: World Health Organization.

Brown, F. (1968). Bereavement and lack of a parent in childhood. In E. Miller (Ed.), *Foundations of Child Psychiatry* (pp. 435–455). London: Pergamon Press.

Chethik, M. (1970). The impact of object loss on a six-year-old. *American Journal of Child Psychiatry, 9,* 709–711.

Cobb, B. (1956). Psychological impact of long illness and death of a child on the family circle. *Journal of Pediatrics, 49,* 746–751.

Cohn, F. W. (1971). *Mark and the paint brush: How art therapy helped one little boy*. Austin, TX: Howg Foundation for Mental Health.

Fraiberg, S. H. (1959). *The magic years*. New York: Scribner's.

Freud, A. (1952). The mutual influences in the development of ego and id. In R. S. Eissler, A. Freud, H. Hartmann, & E. Kris (Eds.), *Psychoanalytic study of the child* (Vol. 7, pp. 42–50). New York: International Universities Press.

Freud, S. (1953). Mourning and melancholia, in *Collected Papers* (Vol. 4, pp. 152–170). New York: Basic Books. (Original work published 1917)

Furman, E. (1974). *A child's parent dies*. New Haven: Yale University Press.

Gardner, R. A. (1969a). Guilt, Job, and J. B. *Medical Opinion and Review, 5*(2), 146–155.

Gardner, R. A. (1969b). The guilt reaction of parents of children with severe physical disease. *American Journal of Psychiatry, 126*(5), 82–90.

Gardner, R. A. (1970). The use of guilt as a defense against anxiety. *The Psychoanalytic Review, 57,* 124–128.

Gardner, R. A. (1971). Therapeutic communication with children: The mutual storytelling technique. Northvale, NJ: Jason Aronson.

Gardner, R. A. (1973). *Understanding children—A parents guide to child rearing.* Cresskill, NJ: Creative Therapeutics.

Gardner, R. A. (1977). Children's guilt reactions to parental death: Psychodynamics and therapeutic management. *Hiroshima Forum for Psychology, 4,* 45–50.

Gardner, R. A. (1978). *The boys and girls book about one-parent families.* New York: Putnam. (Paperback ed. published by Bantam, 1983)

Kliman, G. (1968). *Psychological emergencies of childhood.* New York: Grune & Stratton.

Krell, R., & Rabkin, L. (1979). The effects of sibling death on the surviving child: A family perspective. *Journal of Family Processes, 18,* 471–477.

Kübler-Ross, E. (1978). Helping parents teach their children about death and life. In L. E. Arnold (Ed.), *Helping parents help their children* (pp. 270–278). New York: Brunner/Mazel.

Lewis, M., & Lewis, D. O. (1983). Dying children and their families. In J. J. Schowalter, P. R. Patterson, M. Tallmer, A. H. Kutscher, S. V. Gallo, & D. Peretz (Eds.), *The child and death* (pp. 137–155). New York: Columbia University Press.

Nagera, H. (1970). Children's reaction to the death of important objects. In R. S. Eissler, A. Freud, H. Hartmann, M. Kris, & S. Lustman (Eds.), *Psychoanalytic study of the child* (Vol. 25, pp. 360–400). New York: International Universities Press.

Pakes, E. H. (1973). Care for the care givers. In J. J. Schowalter, P. R. Patterson, M. Tallmer, A. H. Kutscher, S. V. Gallo, & D. Peretz (Eds.), *The child and death* (pp. 250–265). New York: Columbia University Press.

Piaget, J. (1954). *The Construction of Reality in the Child.* New York: Basic books.

Rogers, R. (1967). Children's reaction to sibling death. *Psychosomatic medicine: Proceedings of the First International Congress of the Academy of Psychosomatic Medicine, Palma de Mallorca, Spain, Sept. 12–16, 1966.* Amsterdam, NY: Excerpta Medica Foundation.

Rolsky, J. T. (1983). Helping a child with leukemia to die at home. In J. J. Schowalter, P. R. Patterson, M. Tallmer, A. H. Kutscher, S. V. Gallo, & D. Peretz (Eds.), *The child and death* (pp. 180–186). New York: Columbia University Press.

Rosen, H. (1985). Prohibitions against mourning in childhood sibling loss. *OMEGA: Journal of Death and Dying, 15*(4), 307–316.

Rosen, H. (1986). *Unspoken grief: Coping with childhood sibling loss.* Lexington, MA: D. C. Heath.

Rosen, H., & Cohn, H. L. (1981). Children's reactions to sibling loss. *Clinical Social Work Journal, 9,* 211–218. New York: Human Sciences Press.

Rosenblatt, B. (1969). A young boy's reaction to the death of a sister. *Journal of Child Psychiatry, 8,* 321–335.

Scharl, A. E. (1961). Regression and restitution in object loss. In R. S. Eissler, A. Freud, H. Hartman, & M. Kris (Eds.), *Psychoanalytic study of the child* (Vol. 16, pp. 471–480). New York: International Universities Press.

Shambaugh, B. (1961). A study of loss reactions in a seven-year-old. In R. S. Eissler, A.

Freud, H. Hartman, & M. Kris (Eds.), *Psychoanalytic study of the child* (Vol. 16, pp. 510–522). New York: International Universities Press.

Wakerman, E. (1984). *Father loss: Daughters discuss the man that got away*. Garden City: New York: Doubleday.

Wolfenstein, M. (1969). Loss, rage, and repetition. In R. S. Eissler, A. Freud, H. Hartmann, M. Kris, & S. Lustman (Eds.), *Psychoanalytic study of the child* (Vol. 24, pp. 432–460). New York: International Universities Press.

Childhood Stress Due to Parental Divorce

RICHARD A. GARDNER, MD

Of the various forms of object loss that a child may suffer, the death of a parent probably produces the most serious psychological sequelae (Gardner, 1979a). The loss of a parent following parental divorce, although less traumatic, may also cause significant distress. Stresses so engendered may play a significant role in the child's subsequent development. This chapter describes the kinds of stresses and the kinds of adjustment reactions, both healthy and pathological, that may result from parental divorce.

SOURCES OF STRESS IN DIVORCE

Absence of One Parent from the Home

The absence of a parent from the home is one of the obvious stresses created by the divorce situation. The younger the child at the time of the separation, the greater the likelihood that the child will be affected by the absence of a parent. Obviously, two caretaking adults can provide much more input than one. Often, the problem of diminished caretaking availability is compounded because the remaining parent may have to work outside the home in order to deal with the extra financial burdens attendant on the divorce. This results in even greater deprivation for the child. Also, children who are the same sex as the absent parent are likely to experience interference in the identification process. The two sexes have different personality patterns and roles in life, and in order to adjust well in society, children have to learn what these differences are and how to relate to persons of both sexes. The child who grows up with one parent is deprived of the opportunity for growth experiences with both sexes. Many children view the absent parent as an "abandoner." One possible result of such a reaction is to distrust that parent and, by extension, to grow up distrusting the whole class of individuals who are the same sex as the absent parent.

Children's Involvement in the Parental Conflict

The greater the children's involvement in the parental conflict, the greater the likelihood that psychopathology will develop. In fact, one of the most important determinants of whether children of divorce will develop psychological disturbance is the degree to which they are exposed to and/or embroiled in such parental conflicts. This is true before, during, and after the separation. Parents whom I see in pre-separation counseling often ask about the likelihood of their children developing psychiatric disturbances. I generally answer that I cannot predict the future, but that the main determinants will be their own behavior. If they are able to avoid involving the children in their conflict, then the children are less likely to suffer. This is especially likely to occur after the separation when animosity tends to intensify (especially if protracted litigation is occurring). During that period, the greater the parental capacity for good communication and cooperation, the less the likelihood of the children developing psychiatric disturbances. Moreover, the more attentive, reliable, and involved the absent parent is, the lower the probability that children will suffer the stresses that bring about maladaptive adjustment reactions.

Telling Children about the Separation

The way parents tell children about an impending separation may be an important determinant of whether psychopathology will develop. First, generally it is advisable that the parents be together when they tell their children. In this way they both establish for themselves the reputations of being accessible to discuss the pertinent issues. More than that, the parents should be available for ongoing communication at any point thereafter. In the context of this ongoing communicative relationship, they can offer the children the most meaningful input.

At this point, a common source of stress for children is the failure of the parents to be reasonably honest regarding the main reasons for the separation. Many parents, often with the most benevolent intentions, withhold vital information from the children, making it impossible for them to deal adequately with the separation stresses. For parents to say to a child that they no longer love each other provides little useful information. Obviously, if one or both have decided to separate, there must be some significant deficiency in the parents' loving feelings. Some parents justify their lack of information with the rationalization that the children are not old enough to understand. It is no surprise then that in these situations, children fantasize that they themselves were responsible for the divorce. Having been given no substantive information regarding the cause, the children may turn to themselves in order to provide an explanation. Another reason children develop the notion that the divorce was their fault relates to the need to control what is basically an uncontrollable situation. Intrinsic to the idea "It's my fault" is the concept of control (Gardner, 1970b, 1979a).

This is not to suggest revealing every single detail of the parents' private lives but merely discussing with the children the major issues that brought about the separation, at a level commensurate with their maturity. This would include such subjects as alcoholism, drug addiction, and the presence of a third party who might have played a significant role in the separation. Some parents object that it is psychologically detrimental if the children hear one parent criticize the other. This position, although well-meaning, is unrealistic and not in the children's best interests. First, it is basically dishonest. In order to have initiated the separation, at least one of the parents must have had significant dissatisfactions with the other. Often enough, both have significant criticisms of each other. If the parents strictly follow the counsel of not criticizing one another, then the child can only wonder why the parents are getting divorced. Therapists need to help parents present their criticisms in the most objective and benevolent manner. It is evident that at the time of the separation this may be extremely difficult, if not impossible. However, the drawbacks of presenting the criticisms in this highly emotional atmosphere are far less than the consequences of withholding them entirely. Over time, a greater element of objectivity may develop, and therapy can often help parents reach this goal. If, however, the parents have decided that certain issues should not be discussed with the children, then, to the extent that these subjects come up, the parents do well to tell the children honestly that certain things will not be discussed at that point and are best left for the future. Although there is some withholding here, at least there is no duplicity.

Ideally, wherever possible, children should be told about 3 or 4 weeks prior to the time of the separation. A longer lead time may contribute to the development of denial mechanisms (which are in any case likely to develop). Shorter notice (for example, as the parent leaves the home) deprives them of the opportunity to work through some of their anticipatory reactions. During this 3- or 4-week period the parent who is going to leave the home should have the children visit his or her new domicile, install a telephone, and assure the children that communication will be easily available. An actual visit to the new home can also be useful in that it concretizes the situation and reduces at least one source of abandonment anxiety.

Parental Attitudes toward the Children's Emotional Reactions

An important determinant of whether the children develop untoward psychological reactions to the stresses of the divorce is their freedom to express their feelings appropriately. If this is to occur, the parents themselves must serve as good models for such emotional expression. Parents who feel that they should not tell the children about the divorce until they can do it in a calm and collected manner are probably misguided. It is better for the children if the parents reveal their feelings of grief, resentment, and disillusionment concerning the separation. By doing so, the parents serve as good models for the children's expression of their own feelings. It should be self-evident that wild hysteria, histrionics, and violent rage outbursts are not useful. Rather, what is suggested here is a more moderate and reasonable expression of feelings. Where parents tend to respond with exaggerated reactions, therapy can often help to reduce them to healthier levels.

An important response that parents need to encourage at the time of the separation is the direct expression of the children's grief. Overall, the grief response to parental divorce is generally more circumscribed and less formidable than that occurring after the death of a parent (Gardner, 1979a). In both situations, however, the child must be given the opportunity to grieve. Grieving allows for a piecemeal desensitization to the trauma. Each time the child thinks about the painful event it becomes a little more bearable. Grieving is also cathartic in that each time the person expresses the painful emotions they become less painful. Some parents suppress the process with comments such as, "Big boys and girls don't cry" and "He's [She's] taking it like a man (woman)." Parents do far better if they facilitate children's emotional reactions by serving as models for their expression and by encouraging the children's verbal expression of their thoughts and feelings.

The child's suppression (conscious) and repression (unconscious) of feelings can also contribute to the development of other maladaptive reactions. The failure to express the anger that inevitably arises in the course of divorce proceedings may contribute to the development of depression and anger-inhibition problems. In a more complex way such suppressed anger may in turn lead to the emergence of obsessive-compulsive symptomatology. When the parents do not discuss in detail and correct the child's misconceptions about what may occur following the separation, the child may begin to manifest evidences of tension such as tics and a wide variety of psychosomatic symptoms.

Reconciliation Preoccupations

In the weeks and months following the separation it is normal for children to harbor hopes that their parents will reconcile. With the exception of situations involving significantly harsh treatment and/or rejection by the departing parent, children can be expected to entertain fantasies of reconciliation. Generally, as children come to appreciate the futility of these hopes, they gradually dissipate.

However, when such preoccupations persist for many months and even years after the separation, then other processes are generally operative. Such fantasies occur most commonly when one of the parents still harbors hopes of reconciliation. For example, in one instance a child asks the mother whether the parents will ever get back together again, and the mother responds, "Absolutely not." In another case, the mother replies, "Well maybe, but I don't think it's likely." The second response perpetuates the normal reconciliation preoccupation because it provides hope for parental reunion. No matter how small the hope and how remote the possibility, as long as the parent communicates it to the child (even subtly), reconciliation fantasies are likely to be perpetuated. There are many ways of saying "never." When expressed with certainty, the child gets the message; when stated with hesitation or with a lack of conviction, the child gets the opposite message.

There are other ways in which parents may contribute to reconciliation preoccupations in their children. Albeit legally divorced, some parents are still psychologically married, and they may continue to provide their children with hopes that there will be a reunion. Paradoxically, the psychological marriage may manifest itself entirely by means of malevolent interaction. The opposite of love is not hate, but indifference. Although children may not consciously appreciate this, they recognize at some level that the ongoing hostile encounters between their parents represent a kind of relationship that is closer to reunion than complete indifference to one another would be. Some children may even foment fights between the parents because they recognize that such animosity provides more "togetherness" than would be the case without such conflicts.

Another way in which parents may contribute to the development of reconciliation fantasies in their children is by having too warm and benevolent a relationship following the separation. It is certainly desirable for divorced parents to communicate well with each other and to cooperate in those areas that benefit the children. However, if the parents go beyond this and maintain various other kinds of friendly involvement, this too can engender fantasies of reconciliation. Obviously, it is impossible to get accurate statistics on the frequency of sexual relationships between previously separated and divorced couples. Based on my clinical experiences, the figures may be higher than is generally imagined. Although with rare exceptions, children are not witness to such encounters, the youngsters do observe the variety of benevolent involvements that usually precede sexual relations. In this situation, reconciliation preoccupations are inevitable. Moreover, to the extent that the children have a justifiable basis for their anticipations, they should probably not be considered inappropriate.

Protracted Litigation

Prior to World War I, fathers were generally considered the preferable custodial parent (Derdeyn, 1976; Ramos, 1979). The prevailing notion was that it was unfair to ask fathers to support children who were living with their mothers. Following the passage of the child labor laws, children became an economic liability rather than an asset and fathers quickly became more receptive to mothers' being viewed as the preferable custodial parent. Accordingly, from the 1920s to the mid-1970s, under the "tender years presumption" mothers were generally considered the preferable custodial parent. The rationale was that, by virtue of being female, mothers were intrinsically superior to fathers in respect to parenting capacity. During this period, the only way a man could hope to gain custody was to prove to the court that his wife as grossly deficient as a mother because of such disorders as drug addiction, chronic alcoholism, psychosis, and blatant promiscuity.

In the mid-1970s men began to complain that the tender years presumption was sexist, and the courts agreed. As a result, men began to litigate for custody, and many were successful. The positions of mothers became increasingly precarious with the result that brainwashing of the children became more common. Interestingly, children began to contribute their own scenarios to the denigration of their fathers. Around 1980 the concept of joint custody became increasingly popular (Gardner, 1982). The notion here was that it was denigrating for the visiting father to have the children only a small percentage of the time and to be a "second-class citizen" when it came to making important decisions in their lives. With the heightened popularity of the joint custodial concept, mothers' positions became even more precarious, which caused even more brainwashing and even more deprecations of fathers by their children. These developments have created a burgeoning of child custody litigation that has reached epidemic proportions (Gardner, 1985, 1986, 1989). In addition, the phenomenon of children's preoccupation with hatred of their fathers—as the result of maternal brainwashing and the children's own contributions to the obsessive denigration of their fathers—has also reached epidemic proportions. This phenomenon is now so common that it warrants a name, and I have recommended the term *parental alienation syndrome* (Gardner, 1985, 1986, 1987a, 1987b, 1989). Because this syndrome has emerged so recently, there is little in the literature on it at present. However, in traveling and lecturing throughout the country, I am receiving reports of it with increasing frequency.

The most common cause of this disorder is protracted custody litigation. Typically, the obsession with hatred becomes so great that the child never says anything positive about the father. The hatred of the father extends to his extended family as well, to the point where loving cousins, aunts, uncles, and grandparents are totally rejected. The child rejects all recollections of past pleasurable experiences with the father, and when he or she is confronted with them, there is denial that they were indeed enjoyable. The child expresses the most crass profanities, yet appears to be guiltless, especially when the mother is present. The litany of complaints has about it an artificial quality, and one can often detect the mother's terminology throughout the child's diatribes. These are willingly given to anyone who will ask for them: psychiatrists, psychologists, judges, lawyers, and so on. This behavioral pattern is presently one of the most common forms of child psychopathology, and it is a direct result of protracted custody litigation.

CHILDREN'S REACTIONS TO DIVORCE AT VARIOUS DEVELOPMENTAL LEVELS

A question sometimes raised is whether there are specific developmental levels at which children are particularly vulnerable to parental separation. More specifically, are there certain ages at which children are more likely to suffer untoward psychological sequelae? I believe that the younger the children are at the time of the separation, the greater the likelihood that they will be traumatized by this event. The younger the child the longer will be the period during which he or she will be deprived of the absent parent and all the benefits to be derived therefrom. This involves a lessened likelihood of identification and modeling as well as less opportunity to learn to relate to people of the same sex as the absent parent. Furthermore, younger children are less capable of understanding what is happening than are older ones, and the confusions and distortions that arise from such failure to understand can also contribute to the development of maladaptive reactions. Younger children are far more dependent and beholden to parents than are older children. This dependency in turn is associated with a sense of helplessness and importance that can contribute to psychopathology. Adolescents are far more autonomous and independent and are thereby much less vulnerable to the development of psychopathological reactions to the divorce. Within the context of these generalizations, there are specific reactions that may occur at particular age levels.

Infancy

As mentioned, children generally view divorce as an abandonment. Even though a parent may attempt to reassure a child that it is the spouse who is being left and not the children, such reassurances may not be successful. This is certainly the case for very young children who suffer the deprivation of a parent after a bond has been established (especially after the age of 12 months or thereabouts); as they experience it, the parent simply has disappeared. The parent's absence may then be reacted to as if it were a formidable rejection, and this may contribute to the child's loss of what Erikson (1963) refers to as *basic trust*. Hetherington (1973) found that girls who grew up in homes without fathers were far less trusting of adult males than were those who grew up in homes with fathers. Such impairments in trust can be engendered by the parents' failure to be reasonably honest with the children about the reasons for the separation. Or, if a child is not told about the separation, with the rationalization that he or she is too young to understand, then that child may similarly lose trust in the parent(s) withholding this vital information. Parents are commonly instructed that children of divorce should always be reassured that the absent parent loves them, lest they suffer the psychologically devastating effects of being rejected by a parent. There are caring parents who subscribe to this in situations when there is absolutely no evidence of any love or affection by the departed parent. Under such circumstances the children will ultimately come to appreciate the duplicity, and this too can contribute to feelings of distrust. A child exposed to one parent's vilification of the other may come to distrust the denigrated parent.

The Preschool Period

Classical Freudian analysts often warn parents about children's vulnerability to untoward psychological reactions to divorce if the separation takes place during the oedipal period. As discussed elsewhere (Gardner 1968, 1971, 1973), it does not seem likely that the failure to resolve the Oedipus complex is at the root of all psychoneurotic processes. Rather, those children who manifest symptoms that appear to emerge from the oedipal paradigm do so because of specific factors in the environment conducive to the development of such symptomatology, such as parental titillation and/or actual castration threats. The proponents of oedipal theory warn parents that if the father, for example, leaves the home during this period, a boy may entertain fantasies that the father has left because of the boy's wishes that he do so. Similar warnings are given about the girl whose mother may leave the home. Accordingly, parents contemplating divorce are advised to wait until after the child has passed through this presumably crucial phase.

The same theory holds that the oedipal preoccupations reappear in the early adolescent period. Accordingly, if parents were to follow such advice, they would have to delay their plans to separate until the youngest same-sexed child of the departing parent was past early adolescence. This would be a heavy price to pay for compliance with a theory to which only a small fraction of all mental health professionals subscribe. The additional psychological stress that such compliance would cause the parents might very well result in the children suffering more grief than they would have felt if the parent had left. Furthermore, the advice suggests that the parents forestall or modify their plans to separate because the child may distort the departing parent's true intention. Rather than having the parents attempt to correct the distortion—to help the child appreciate that the parent is not leaving because of some wish on the child's part, but rather because of serious deficiencies in the relationship—the parent is advised to stay. This is a poor principle to follow, whether it be in therapy or in life. It is far better to do what one considers to be justifiable and to take one's chances with regard to the distortions and misinterpretations that may arise in others' minds over the act. To do otherwise is to be at the mercy of every delusion that others may have about one's actions.

Children in the preschool period, however, may be more vulnerable to the separation than children of grade school age. The attachment needs of children during this phase of life are so great that they may suffer intensely from the removal of a parent from the home. Furthermore, because they have less opportunity for involvement with surrogate parents, especially teachers, they are less capable of compensating for the loss. In addition, they are more dependent on the parent because they require more care than school-age children. These factors may place children in the preschool period at higher risk for the development of psycho-pathology than are children of school age.

Freud believed that at the end of the oedipal period there is rapid superego development because oedipal resolution involves, in part, the child's identifying with the same-sexed parent's superego dictates against incest. Such identification is accelerated by the boy's castration anxiety. By identifying with his father's dictates against incest, the boy protects himself from the retaliation he anticipates from his father. In the process of such incorporation, other values (derived from society) are also acquired by the child. It seems likely to me that the preschool period is indeed a time of rapid superego development, but not as a consequence of the resolution of the Oedipus complex. Rather, during this period the child, for the first time spends increasingly more time out of the house in places such as nursery school and the homes of other children. In order to adjust within these new environments, the child must rapidly learn "the rules" of the authorities in such settings because not to do so would result in significant alienation from these important figures. This need, more than anything else, results in the child's rapid acquisition of important information related to superego dictates. Although both parents participate in the child's superego development by direct instruction and by modeling, there is good reason to believe that (in our society) fathers are more likely to be the primary conveyors of such dictates. This in part relates to the general view of the father as the supreme authority in the home (a cultural legacy that still persists, sexual egalitarianism notwithstanding).

Another factor that may contribute to an impairment in superego development is the child's identification with the warring parents. Despite their relatively civilized behavior with others, many parents involved in custody conflicts exhibit various kinds of psychopathic behavior in their relationships with one another. Such conflicts can contribute to children developing psychopathic trends themselves. This is es-pecially the case when the children are used as weapons in parental conflicts; the youngsters may be taught antisocial behavior directly and even rewarded for it. When custody litigation is protracted, parents are likely to be even more vicious and less guilty over the expression of their litigation-engendered sadism.

In their intensive study of children's reactions to parental divorce, Wallerstein and Kelly (1980) found that during the preschool period children commonly react to the separation with a variety of fantasies, for example, that they are being replaced by another family elsewhere, that the mother asked the father to leave (rather than his initiating the departure), that the family will come back together again, and that the abandoning parent will be retrieved. In addition, they exhibit significant denial mechanisms, fear of catastrophe, confusion, and regression.

Elementary School Level

In the early elementary school period children have reached a point where they wish to expand their horizons and engage in a wide variety of activities outside the home. They may be hampered in this respect by the absence of a parent who, prior to the separation, would have been available for such activities. Their dependency cravings, then, become intensified and the frustrations formidable. The anger they feel over such rejection and abandonment, however, may often be inhibited lest they see even less of the absent parent. Intense loyalty conflicts often manifest themselves as the children say to each parent what they believe that parent wants to hear at the time. Youngsters do this out of their fear of losing the parents' affection. For similar reasons, when they do express anger, it is more often toward the custodial than the visiting parent. The visiting parent has already established for him- or herself the reputation of being an abandoner, and they fear alienating that parent even further, lest there be total rejection.

These clinical observations are supported by the studies of Wallerstein and Kelly (1980) who found that young children in the school-age period (ages 6–8 years), exhibited grief, disorganized fear, feelings of deprivation, yearning for the departed parent, inhibition of hostility toward the departed parent, anger at the custodial parent, fantasies of responsibility in reconciliation, and loyalty conflicts.

In my experience, older elementary schoolchildren become more comfortable about the expression of their hostility. It is in this period, especially, that one sees significant antisocial acting out at home, in the neighborhood, and in school. The anger they feel toward the parents (especially the one who has left the home) is displaced onto any available target, especially the custodial parent. They may join forces with one of the warring parents and cause significant trouble for the other. Wallerstein and Kelly (1980) describe the following reactions among such children: overt anger (the most striking symptom of children at this period of development), somatic symptoms, alignment with one parent against the other (more common at this age level than at any other), identification with the lost parent, attempts to control the parents (for example intefering with the mother's dating), and attempts to coerce the parents into reconciliation.

Adolescence

If the divorce takes place during the adolescent period, it is far less likely to be psychologically traumatic than if it occurs at younger ages. This is especially the case if the home was relatively stable during the earlier phases of the child's development. But even if the home was somewhat unstable, adolescents, being more autonomous and less dependent on the parents, are more capable of functioning for themselves during this time. Older adolescents often have available transportation providing even greater mobility and autonomy. In the sexual realm, however, adolescents may have particular difficulty. Jealous rivalry with a dating parent is common, and the problem may become intensified if the parent has some pathological need to be rivalrous with the child in this area. Such rivalry may result in sexual acting out and even competition with the parent for his or her dates. The parent who is injudicious enough to expose the children to a parade of lovers (without in any way exposing the children to sexual activities per se) is likely to engender strong feelings of resentment and rivalry. It is reasonable for a boy in such a situation to conclude that every male in the world—with the exception of himself—is a potential candidate for sexual experiences with his mother. And the girl with a father who exposes her to many lovers may react similarly. This cannot but be humiliating, titillating, and a source of the kinds of conflicts that produce psychopathological adjustments.

Such sexual tensions are most likely to arise within the stepfamily home, especially if the stepparent is significantly younger than the natural parent and of opposite sex to the adolescent. Hormones know nothing of incest taboos. In the original family, sexual feelings between parents and children tend to get reduced by the ongoing familiarity and desensitization to one another that inevitably result when people live together over a long period. In the stepfamily there has been no period for such desensitization. Rather, the stepparent and stepchild are quite novel to one another—a situation that may engender strong sexual fantasies. Sometimes these attractions are covered up by means of violent arguments, and the resulting alienation serves to keep the individuals at a safe distance from one another (Gardner, 1979b).

Adult Life

Later in their lives, because of their unfortunate experiences, children of divorce may very well be less likely to marry. They are also more likely to divorce because they model themselves after their parents. The distrust engendered by the original abandonment may result in ongoing feelings of lack of faith in one's spouse. Some children may react in adult life by involving the spouse in a way that attempts to rectify early childhood traumas. For example, they may become overpossessive of the spouse in order to compensate symbolically for the deprivations suffered in childhood from one of the parents. Or they may displace onto the spouse the hostilities and feelings of vengence engendered in childhood toward their parents. Kubie (1956) considered this to be an important factor in the development of a wide variety of marital conflicts; he described this desire as an attempt to "wipe out an old pain or pay off an old score" (p. 23).

Children of divorce may grow up to view all relationships as flimsy and transient, and to expect their own marriages to be similarly unstable. Late adolescents and young adults in divorced homes may marry and leave their own homes early in order to remove themselves from the unhappiness in their households. Such marriages are often misguided and unstable. Or the young adult may marry and leave home prematurely because of a bad relationship with a stepparent. Sometimes, the marriage partner is sought as a maternal or paternal figure, rather than as a peer. Such marriages too are not likely to be stable.

RESOURCES THAT CHILDREN MAY USE TO HELP THEM COPE

The most important resources that children may use in order to cope with the divorce are the parents themselves, and the most important determinant of whether youngsters can in fact draw on these resources, is the way that their parents deal with their children at the time of family disruptions. If the parent who is out of the home continues to involve him- or herself with love, affection, guidance, protection, interest, and a wide variety of other manifestations of parental commitment, then the children are likely to cope well with the divorce. The reverse is true if the absent parent does not provide such involvement. If, on the other hand, the parents embroil the children in their conflict, especially in the litigation, then it is quite likely that the children will develop untoward psychological reactions and will not be able to cope adequately with the situation. This outcome is especially common where there is litigation over custody (Gardner, 1986). Elsewhere, I have described in detail the wide variety of ways in which parents can contribute to their children's coping successfully with their divorce (Gardner, 1976, 1977).

The presence of parental surrogates can be useful. If either or both of the parents involve themselves meaningfully with new partners, then it is important that these partners strive to develop a good relationship with the children. Where they can do so, this new relationship can be quite therapeutic. The child need not view the attachment to these surrogates as a source of conflict. One can love both a parent and a stepparent; it need not be "either–or," it can be "both–and." Grandparents, as well, can often provide meaningful support although this is more likely to take place if they have studiously avoided taking sides during the divorce proceedings and thereafter. Teachers can be of considerable help. A teacher spends 5 to 6 hours a day with a child. Although often not available for significant input, the teacher can serve both as a role model and as a person who can provide the child with occasional meaningful counseling. Many schools have group meetings for children of divorce. To be sure, the school personnel who conduct such groups do not generally have all the necessary family information to make such therapy optimal; nonetheless they can still provide a useful service for these children. In such groups, children of divorce feel less different from others and can share common experiences. They can also provide each other with advice and recommendations. Churches too often provide such groups. Organizations such as Parents Without Partners can be useful; there the children can involve themselves with other children of divorce in social situations, and they can also have experiences with parental surrogates who need not be individual partners with the parents.

Certain bibliotherapeutic techniques are useful in helping children cope with the divorce situation. These books (Gardner, 1970a, 1978, 1981) provide children with information and advice that can prove useful. The books are designed to be read by the children themselves as well as with parents and stepparents. This provides the fringe benefit of improving family relationships, for those involved can then work together toward the common goal of alleviating the child's difficulties.

THE COMMON ADJUSTMENT REACTIONS TO DIVORCE

In this context, the term *adjustment reactions* refers to the maladaptive responses that children may exhibit in the face of divorce. The many sources of stress in divorce described earlier are conducive to the development of such untoward conditions. There are a wide variety of such patterns of reaction; space permits only brief mention of a few of the more common ones.

Anger Reactions

Because they suffer deprivations when they lose a parent from the home, children of divorce are generally angry. If the children are embroiled in the ongoing parental conflict, or merely exposed to it to any significant degree, this too is likely to provoke resentment. Some children handle their anger by suppressing or repressing it. Indeed, when involved in divorce, children are particularly prone to the development of anger-inhibition problems. They may fear that expressing anger toward the parent who has left the home will result in their seeing even less of that parent. They may fear expressing anger to the remaining parent, lest that parent abandon them as well—after all, if one parent can abandon them why not the other? Common symptomatic manifestations of anger repression are depression, inhibition of self-assertion, psychosomatic complaints, self-flagellation and denigration, and guilt over the expression of hostility.

More commonly, however, these children deal with their anger by acting out. Often the custodial parent gets the brunt of the anger; as noted, the child is afraid that expressing it directly toward the absent parent will cause even further alienation. Because of vengeful gratifications that the absent parent may enjoy from it, he or she may then overtly or covertly support the expression of the child's anger toward the other. Directing anger against school authorities is also quite common. School personnel may be viewed as even safer targets because the child regards them as dispensable. So great is the need to express the hostility that the child does not recognize the self-destructiveness of such acting out. Behavioral problems may become intensified by the impairments in superego development that often develop in the context of divorce. If the child, at early critical stages in development, observes the parents guiltlessly enacting their own anger toward one another, it is less likely that the child's own superego development will proceed along normal lines.

Guilt Reactions

Guilt here refers to the feeling of low self-esteem that people experience when they have memories of deeds, or merely thoughts and feelings, that they have been taught are wrong by significant figures in their environment. Such patterns are especially likely to appear during childhood. Children of divorce may feel very guilty over the anger they experience toward their parents as a result of the separation. Many factors arise in the course of a divorce that predictably cause children to be angry, and those who have been brought up in homes where they have been made to feel guilty about their anger are likely to exhibit such guilt. Parents do well to help such children appreciate that their angry reactions are normal and that there are healthy ways to redirect the anger. Among other things, the youngsters often find themselves in a loyalty conflict. If they side with the mother, then their father may be angry at them. And if they side with the father, then it may provoke their mother. In such situations it is common for children to lie. They say to each parent whatever they anticipate will ingratiate them with that parent at that moment. Some children come to feel guilty over their lying, adding an extra burden of guilt to their other difficulties.

One form of guilt reaction commonly exhibited by these children is the feeling that the divorce was their fault. It is not uncommon for a child to say, for example, "I know, Daddy, that you're leaving because I was bad. I promise I'll never be bad. I'll always be good. I'll listen to you when you tell me to stop television. I promise I'll never hit my sister again." Although the term *guilt* is used to describe this phenomenon, these comments often have less to do with guilt than to do with the need to control. Implicit in saying "It's my fault" is the notion of control. The child caught up in divorce feels totally helpless and can achieve no sense of mastery over this uncontrollable event in his or her life. By creating the delusion that the divorce was brought about by the child's own actions, he or she gains a specious sense of control (Gardner, 1970b). The child then believes that merely by refraining from performing the acts that presumably brought about the divorce in the first place, reconciliation can be effected. Accordingly, parental reassurances that it was not the child's fault are not likely to be effective. Rather, such children have to be helped to differentiate between those things they can control and those they cannot, and to adjust to the uncontrollable in ways not involving delusions.

Low Self-Esteem

A number of factors in the divorce situation can contribute to the development of low self-esteem in children. One relates to the actual rejection or abandonment experienced when one of the parents leaves the home. A child may conclude that if he or she was really lovable (of high worth), then the parent would not have left. If the child lives in a community where divorce is unusual and is subjected to taunts and teasing by other children, then this too may lower feelings of self-worth. Fortunately, such ridicule is far less common today than in past years. The economic hardship often associated with divorce may change the family's lifestyle and require a wide variety of privations that contribute to low self-worth. The aforementioned guilt reactions have an intrinsic esteem-lowering element. The separation inevitably gives rise to feelings of insecurity that further reduce the sense of self-worth. A parent who has been an important source of protection and guidance is no longer so readily available. The child may be asked to bear new burdens and to face challenges that he or she feels incapable of handling, and this can lower self-confidence. Sometimes the child is used as a scapegoat. A rejected mother may take out her hostility on her child, diminishing the child's self-esteem. The parent who uses the child as a surrogate spouse will become dependent on and try to obtain advice and support from the child. This is likely to reduce the child's self-worth because he or she cannot live up to such demands.

Children of divorce are likely to exhibit a wide variety of other adjustment reactions that may be alleviated through the use of specific therapeutic approaches (Gardner, 1976).

THERAPEUTIC APPROACHES TO THE ALLEVIATION OF THE ADJUSTMENT REACTIONS TO DIVORCE

In considering the psychotherapeutic approaches to the adjustment reactions to divorce, a few important principles are worthy of emphasis. The criteria that are generally utilized to decide whether a child of divorce needs treatment do not differ from those applied to children in intact homes. These criteria are readily divided into four categories. The first, and the most important, is the child's functioning in school. The school is the most sensitive indicator of the presence of psycho-pathology. It is the most demanding of all the situations in which the child is generally involved, and a considerable degree of integration is necessary for healthy functioning in that context. Accordingly, it may be the first area in which the child's symptomatology becomes evident. The therapist should make inquiries about changes in academic as well as social functioning in the school. Questions should be asked about whether the child is working at the level that the teacher considers to be his or her intellectual capacity. One should inquire about how the child is relating to the teacher, whether he or she is showing proper respect for the teacher's authority, whether there is receptivity to teaching, and whether there are behavior problems in the classroom. Inquiry into the child's relationships with classmates is also important.

The second area relates to the child's functioning in the neighborhood. Here again, a high degree of integration is necessary for successful functioning. Peers will not tolerate the kinds of atypical behavior accepted by parents. If a child both seeks and is sought by friends, and if the friends are age-appropriate and reasonably healthy, then it is not likely that the child is suffering any disturbance in this area.

The third area, and, paradoxically, the least useful in ascertaining whether psy-chopathology is present, is the level of functioning in the home. This is not a particularly sensitive area of inquiry because usually it is here that one finds both the greatest degree of flexibility and the greatest tolerance and denial of deviant behavior. Children normally balk at carrying out household responsibilities, fight with their siblings, do not consistently respect their parents' authority, and otherwise engage in all kinds of irritating and frustrating behavior. Furthermore, with regard to such home behavior, it is difficult to know where the normal level ends and the pathological begins. Accordingly, it is not a sensitive barometer of psychopathology.

The last area of inquiry relates to whether the child exhibits symptoms found in the *Diagnostic and Statistical Manual of Mental Disorders*. Third Edition, Revised (DSM-III-R; American Psychiatric Association, 1987). Generally, if the child is functioning well in the three aforementioned areas, he or she is unlikely to have the kinds of symptoms described in DSM-III-R. However, because there is a possibility of such symptomatology being present, the examiner does well to make the appropriate inquiries.

When utilizing these criteria, it is important for the therapist to recognize that special consideration must be given to children of divorce before deciding whether to initiate treatment. Around the time of separation, children often exhibit transient impairment in any of the four areas. Thus, these children may become depressed, angry, lose interest in their studies, withdraw from friends, lose their appetites, experience difficulty sleeping, or exhibit a wide variety of anger reactions. One should not immediately assume that such a child needs treatment. Only when these symptoms persist more than a few months and show no signs of abating should the therapist consider treatment. However, providing the parents with advice during this period can be therapeutic and may abort the development of symptoms.

The overwhelming majority of children of divorce who need psychotherapy are not likely to be helped by individual treatment. Rather, close work with the parents is necessary, in the form of both individual and joint sessions. The examiner should not accept the excuse from the parents that they don't want to be in the same room with one another; to comply with such a restriction is to deprive the therapist of what is probably the most useful aspect of the therapeutic program. After all, the children are part of a network of interpersonal difficulties involving not only the parents, but new parental surrogates as well (men and women friends, fiancées, stepparents, and grandparents). Even though they may be litigating, the parents should play an active role in the treatment. It is generally useful to inform parents that the longer they continue to fight, the less the likelihood of helping their children. In line with this approach, it is reasonable to say that family therapy is indicated for the vast majority of children of divorce. In addition, there are occasions when stepfamily therapy would be appropriate, that is, a treatment approach including the child, the parents, and the stepparents—all in the room at the same time (Gardner, 1984). At the outset, the adults involved may meet this proposal with incredulity. However, those who can get by their initial reluctance and resistance may find it an extremely useful form of treatment. To be sure at times such therapy breaks down because the animosity is so intense that the therapist may literally fear for the physical well-being of one or more of the participants. This should not be a reason for avoiding what can be one of the most valuable forms of therapy.

REFERENCES

American Psychiatric Association (1987). *Diagnostic and statistical manual of mental disorders* (3rd ed-rev.). Washington, DC: Author.

Derdeyn, A. P. (1976). Child custody contests in historical prospective. *American Journal of Psychiatry, 133,* 1369–1376.

Erikson, E. H. (1963). *Childhood and society.* New York: Norton.

Gardner, R. A. (1968). The mutual storytelling technique: use in alleviating childhood oedipal problems. *Contemporary Psychoanalysis, 4,* 161–177.

Gardner, R. A., (1970a). *The boys and girls book about divorce.* Northvale, NJ: Jason Aronson. (Paperback ed. published by Bantam, 1971)

Gardner, R. A. (1970b). The use of guilt as a defense against anxiety. *Psychoanalytic Review, 57,* 124–136.

Gardner, R. A. (1971). *Therapeutic communication with children: The mutual storytelling technique.* Northvale, NJ: Jason Aronson.

Gardner, R. A. (1973). *Understanding children: A parents guide to child rearing.* Cresskill, NJ: Creative Therapeutics.

Gardner, R. A. (1976). *Psychotherapy with children of divorce.* Northvale, NJ: Jason Aronson.

Gardner, R. A. (1977). *The parents book about divorce.* New York: Doubleday. (Paperback ed. published by Bantam, 1979)

Gardner, R. A. (1978). *The boys and girls book about one-parent families.* New York: Putnam. (Paperback ed. published by Bantam, 1983)

Gardner, R. A. (1979a). Death of a parent. In J. Noshpitz (Ed.), *Basic handbook of child psychiatry* (Vol. IV, pp. 270–283). New York: Basic Books.

Gardner, R. A. (1979b). Intergenerational sexual tensions in second marriages. *Medical Aspects of Human Sexuality, 13*(8), 77ff.

Gardner, R. A. (1981). *The boys and girls book about stepfamilies.* Cresskill, NJ: Creative Therapeutics.

Gardner, R. A. (1982). Joint custody is not for everyone. *Family Advocate, 5*(2), 7ff.

Gardner, R. A. (1984). Counseling children in stepfamilies. *Elementary School Guidance and Counseling, 19,* 40–49.

Gardner, R. A. (1985). Recent developments in child custody litigation. *The Academy Forum, 29*(2), 3–7.

Gardner, R. A. (1986). *Child custody litigation: A guide for parents and mental health professionals.* Cresskill, NJ: Creative Therapeutics.

Gardner, R. A. (1987a). Child custody. In J. Noshpitz (Ed.), *Basic handbook of child psychiatry* (Vol. V, pp. 637–646). New York: Basic Books.

Gardner, R. A. (1987b). *The parental alienation syndrome and the differentiation between fabricated and genuine child sex abuse.* Cresskill, NJ: Creative Therapeutics.

Gardner, R. A. (1989). *Family evaluation in child custody mediation, arbitration, and litigation.* Cresskill, NJ: Creative Therapeutics.

Hetherington, E. M. (1973). Girls without fathers. *Psychology Today, 6*(9), 46–52.

Kubie, L. (1956). Psychoanalysis and marriage: Practical and theoretical issues. In V. W. Eisenstein (Ed.), *Neurotic interaction in marriage* (pp. 10–44). New York: Basic Books.

Ramos, S. (1979). *The complete book of child custody.* New York: Putnam.

Wallerstein, J. S., and Kelly, J. B. (1980). *Surviving the breakup.* New York: Basic Books.

— CHAPTER 4

Illness as a Source of Stress: Acute Illness, Chronic Illness, and Surgical Procedures

DANE G. PRUGH, MD
TROY L. THOMPSON II, MD

INTRODUCTION

Since the dawn of history, the stress of illness has been recognized as a universal human experience. In Western society, the Hippocratic oath epitomizes the healing role of the physician. In the 20th century the remarkable increase in the understanding of the causes and treatment of illness has saved many lives and has significantly lengthened the life span. With the shift in major treatment activities from the home to the hospital, where heroic measures can save lives, there has come, however, a paradoxical increase in the stress of treatment for patients and families.

In this chapter, the nature of the stress of illness and its treatment today will be explored. The definition of stress (Caplan, 1981) and related concepts, such as the nature of coping (Lazarus, Averill, & Opton, 1974), are beyond the scope of this discussion, as are such important and complex topics as what constitutes illness (Engel, 1960; Prugh, 1983) and why certain individuals fall ill and others do not (Antonovsky, 1984; Weiner, 1982).

It is important to emphasize that, in the contemporary view, the biomedical model of disease is no longer adequate. Multiple etiologic factors of physical, psychological, and social nature are involved in predisposing, contributory, pre-cipitating, and perpetuating fashion (Prugh, 1983) in any disease state, constituting the biopsychosocial model of disease (Engel, 1977). This discussion, however, will not consider the weighting of etiological forces in illness. The emphasis here will be on the reactions of the individual, in a family and social context, to the stressful influences of physical illness and its treatment, with their effects on physical well-being and psychological and social functioning. Mental and emotional illnesses of course have stressful effects on the individual, but these will be considered only as they may occur as part of the response to the stress of physical illness.

The social field of illness includes the impact of an individual's illness on the most important social unit—the family. An individual's illness may bring about a family crisis. Families with generally healthy adaptive patterns usually, though not always, respond with temporary restriction in function followed by a return to a preillness level of functioning (Koos, 1946; Lewis & Beavers, 1977). A few families may stabilize at a higher level of functioning, representing a type of "family development" (Koos, 1946). In less well-balanced families, there are disturbed parental patterns of handling siblings or other family members.

In seriously disturbed families, the individual who falls ill may be made a scapegoat for family tensions, may be treated unrealistically as a chronic invalid, or may be handled in other ways that reflect the unconscious tendency of family members to respond to illness in terms of their own or the family's needs rather than those of the patient (Prugh, 1983). Severely dysfunctional families may break down adaptively in response to illness of a family member, with deteriorating relations within the family or alienation from the outside world (Lewis, Beavers, Gossett, & Phillips, 1976), divorce, or family disintegration (Anthony, 1970).

Also important are sociocultural influences. Families from different socioeco-nomic backgrounds may react somewhat differently to illness in family members. Families with limited economic means may face a crisis if a jobholding member, particularly the father, falls ill; help in caring for the acutely sick individual at home is more difficult to obtain, and chronic disability is more threatening.

Differences in sociocultural backgrounds are involved in the reactions of indi-viduals and families to illness, hospitalization, and pain (Reiser, 1980; Zborowski, 1969). Attitudes toward the sick person may vary from society to society. In Western society, the role of a patient is more comfortably assigned to a person who is physically rather than mentally ill (Parsons & Fox, 1952). Families from rural parts of southern Europe may resist the admission of a child to the hospital because they regard it as a death house, to be used only for the terminally ill. Hispanic and

Native American families in the American Southwest may distrust hospitals staffed by Anglo-Americans, preferring to ask the help of their own practitioners of folk medicine (Prugh, 1983).

Zborowski (1969) has pointed out that patients from different ethnic backgrounds may react differently to the experience of pain, with differences in attitudes toward drug acceptance and pain relief. Patients from a Mediterranean background, for example, may express emotionally their responses to pain, communicating to their families in an expected way that they are ill and in need of pain relief, which they can accept, along with the support of the family. Patients from an "Old American" background often maintain stoic attitudes toward pain and attempt to minimize it. They may not reveal how much pain they are experiencing and often pride themselves on their ability to bear up under pain. These examples represent stereotypes, and variations exist, even within cultural subgroups. Difficulties in diagnosis and management can arise, however, in relation to the manner in which the individual experiences and communicates feelings of pain or disability. Thus, awareness of cultural and ethnic differences becomes vital to the physician.

This discussion will utilize a developmental or "life span" approach. The most helpful organizing framework from which to consider the stress of illness over the individual's life span is offered by Erik Erikson (1963, 1968), who extended personality development throughout adult life. He has identified certain psychosocial tasks in development that the individual must master by resolving specific conflicts during each life stage.

The infant's major task is to achieve a basic sense of trust, in the surrounding world by positive resolution of a conflict between the senses of trust and mistrust. Establishment of a sense of autonomy, as opposed to a conflicting sense of shame or doubt, is the task of the early preschool period, whereas the later preschool period calls for the development of a sense of initiative rather than a sense of guilt. The major task for the school-age child is the attainment of a sense of industry and competence, with the conflicting possibility of a sense of inferiority. The adolescent must crystallize a sense of identity, in order to avoid a sense of identity diffusion.

During early adult life or young adulthood, the individual must advance beyond a sense of identity to achieve a sense of intimacy in relationships with other persons, rather than a sense of isolation. In middle adulthood, to avoid a sense of stagnation, the mature individual must achieve a sense of generativity. Finally, after mastering earlier stages, the individual in late adulthood and old age can achieve a sense of integrity and satisfaction with his or her life, rather than facing a sense of despair or disgust.

Erikson suggests some ways in which the parents and other family members influence and are influenced by the individual's developing needs and competencies. Although he does not discuss them directly, it is easy to infer, using Erikson's scheme, the possible effects of stressful life events, such as serious or chronic illness and its attendant treatment, on the individual's development at different stages, in interaction with the family, the broader social network, and society.

Responses to the Stress of Illness

Most responses represent adjustment disorders or at times posttraumatic stress disorders. The stress of illness, however, can precipitate or exacerbate developmental disorders in children and psychoneurotic, personality, or psychotic disorders. Such responses may occur with any illness, although some are seen most often in relation to particular types of illness. Some differences in patterns of response are encountered between reactions to acute illness or injury and those arising from chronic illness or handicap. Although these are largely nonspecific responses, the human organism has a generic type of phasic response to serious or catastrophic illness or injury, involving sequential phases of impact, recoil, and restitution (Prugh & Eckhardt, 1980a). A frequently encountered difficulty is distinguishing reactions to illness or injury from reactions to hospitalization and medical or surgical treatment measures.

This discussion will be devoted somewhat arbitrarily to the categories of reactions to acute illness, chronic illness, and surgical procedures. There is some overlap among the categories and the ways in which acute major illnesses are experienced; in addition, treatment will to some degree affect the type of reaction to any chronic illness or limitation in function that may follow.

ACUTE ILLNESS

The immediate response may vary somewhat according to the organ system originally affected and the corresponding reverberations at the psychological and social levels. Thus the local and systemic effects of acute congestive heart failure may have a more severe temporary effect on the psychological and social functioning of the individual and produce greater anxiety in the family than a simple Colles fracture. Acute illnesses affecting the central nervous system, such as viral encephalitis or a cerebrovascular accident, produce delirium or confusion, as well as possible long-term limitations in function, including diffuse cerebral damage or hemiplegia, in contrast to acute respiratory infections. However, even with complete recovery from any physical effects, a Colles fracture or an acute respiratory infection may precipitate a state of partial or complete incapacitation or even chronic invalidism in an individual with a limited adaptive capacity and an inadequate social network. This may involve unconscious secondary gain that perpetuates psychological pain or weakness, such as may be the case following certain simple surgical operations.

Whether an acute illness has a significantly adverse effect on an individual's adaptation depends on the following factors: (1) *adaptive capacity* (which derives from genetic endowment, constitutional and temperamental characteristics, and the nature of the person's past experience, including experience with disease); (2) *developmental level* (psychosocial responses vary, as do vulnerabilities to different

types of illness, from croup in infancy and rheumatic fever in childhood to myocardial infarction in adulthood and cerebrovascular accident in the elderly); (3) the
nature of the illness or injury, including the organ system affected and any residual
limitation in function; (4) the *type of treatment,* whether medical or surgical, at
home or in the hospital, and the degree of discomfort or other stress involved; (5)
the *nature of the individual's relationships* within the family (parent–child, husband–wife, other) and in his or her social network prior to the illness; and (6) the
meaning of the illness* to the individual and his family (in terms of events occurring
immediately before the illness, with any actual or fantasized connection; previous
experience of the individual or family with illness; effect of the illness on other
family members; and effect on the individual's vocational, social, academic, athletic, or other capacities).

The stage of convalescence from acute illness is a particularly important one,
although it can be difficult to determine exactly when convalescence begins or ends
(Senn, 1945). Certain illnesses by their very nature seem to make convalescence
difficult. For reasons that are unclear, infectious hepatitis and infectious mononu-
cleosis often have depressive effects, and myxedema and Cushing's syndrome have
been said to produce similar depressive reactions (Prugh, 1983). Controlled studies
have shown that loss of morale can lengthen convalescence from influenza (Imboden, Canter, & Cluff, 1961) and brucellosis (Imboden, Cluff, & Canter, 1961)
and that attitudinal factors can affect the speed of healing following an operation
for detached retina (Mason & Smith, 1969). Addiction to tracheostomy has been
described in infants (Jackson, 1963).

Weakness and pain, the latter on a conversion basis, may persist in school-age
children following full recovery from rheumatic fever, as may hypochondriacal
concerns in adolescents, and school phobia may be touched off by acute illness in
individuals who are facing conflict about return to school or work (Prugh, 1983).
It is not uncommon for unconscious secondary gain to temporarily prolong illness
in children and adults who are not seriously disturbed.

Direct Effects of Illness

Certain direct effects of illness can be identified in children and adults. Such
effects may closely resemble or overlap with disturbances in behavior resulting
from psychological or interpersonal sources (Prugh & Eckhardt, 1980b).

These include malaise, discomfort, or pain, which may produce listlessness,
prostration, disturbances in sleep and appetite, and irritability. Restlessness is more
common in children, and hyperactivity often occurs when the illness is milder,
especially in preschool children, although lethargy and withdrawal often occur.

---

*It is noteworthy that, in the *Diagnostic and Statistical Manual of Mental Disorders* (DSM-III; American
Psychiatric Association, 1980), physical illness may be listed as a stressor on Axis III if its impact is
due to its meaning to the individual.

Anorexia and refusal of food may be more marked in younger children, and nightmares and night terrors are common. Older children, adolescents, and adults often experience difficulties in falling asleep. In children, feeding refusal and sleep disturbances may continue as part of a struggle for control between child and parents. Sleep and appetite disturbances may persist in adults who are worried about loss of job time.

In addition to such direct effects, other behavioral responses may occur as reactions to being acutely ill. The overlap with reactions to hospitalization is considerable, especially in the case of children and their families; a later section in this chapter is devoted to hospitalization in this age group.

Behavioral Reactions of Infants, Children, and Adolescents to Acute Illness. A ubiquitous response among children and adolescents is anxiety, related to uncertainty about the effects of illness. This may be free-floating or may be manifested in hyperactivity, sleeplessness, or other behavior disturbances. Anxiety may also produce physiological concomitants of anxiety, such as tachycardia, palpitations, hyperventilation, and diarrhea. These may complicate convalescence or may compound the effects of illness, as in the deleterious effects of anxiety on diminished cardiac function in congestive heart failure (Chambers & Reiser, 1953) or the perpetuation of diarrhea originally arising from a bacterial infection (Prugh, 1983). At times, these physiological concomitants may lead to diagnostic confusion with such conditions as hyperthyroidism and rheumatic fever.

Emotional or behavioral regression is a universal response to illness. It is most striking in older infants and preschool children but occurs also in school-age children and adolescents. In infants and young children, regression may take the form of a return to the bottle; clinging or oppositional behavior; a return of earlier fears; and the temporary giving up of recently learned abilities, such as speech, walking, and bowel and bladder control. In older children this is manifested by the reappearance of more immature behavior, including greater dependence on the parents; demanding or aggressive behavior; limitations in the child's capacity to share with siblings, and difficulties in concentration and learning. Adolescents may also act more immaturely and show increased dependence or at times demanding or aggressive behavior.

In addition to the inherent depressive effects of certain illnesses mentioned earlier, and those of certain drugs, depression is a frequent response to illness. Separation from parents during hospitalization may produce depression in older infants and young children. Depression may result from restriction of activity in older children and adolescents, as may feelings of helplessness and loss of control. Sleeping and eating difficulties may mask depression in children and adolescents.

Misinterpretation of the meaning of illness is a common phenomenon, especially among young children, related to their more limited capacity for intellectual understanding and their tendencies toward magical or prelogical thinking. Younger preschool children ordinarily view pain or discomfort arising from illness as punishment for real or fantasized transgressions. Older preschool and early school-age children show fears of bodily mutilation related to treatment procedures. Such fears are more intense when sensitive areas, such as the head or the genital organs are involved; fears of harm to the genital organs are also related to issues of sexual differentiation and psychosexual development. Older children and even adolescents may still show fears of bodily mutilation, often compounded by regression.

Conversion disorders are often seen in school-age children and adolescents. Transient, mild-to-moderate conversion symptoms frequently occur during convalescence, related to conflicts over dependent needs involving unconscious secondary gain. Often the symptoms of the physical illness are incorporated as memory traces into the conversion symptoms, as in the continuance of pain, headache, or weakness (Engel, 1967a). At times other symptoms, such as syncope or disturbances in gait, may appear with a symbolic significance. Most such disorders disappear within a few days or weeks, but they may continue in individuals with limited adaptive capacities and marked conflict about returning to full independence.

Older school-age children and adolescents may develop dissociative reactions; these include amnesia, pseudodelirious states, somnambulism, and fugue states. They may compound an actual delirium, often of subclinical nature. Catatonic reactions unrelated to psychosis may be seen temporarily in normal or mildly disturbed children if the circumstances are sufficiently stressful (Prugh, 1983).

Perceptual-motor lags are seen in children following viral or other infections of the central nervous system, particularly if delirium was present, even following complete recovery from any apparent neurological damage. They may also occur following systemic illness, such as pneumonia or high fevers from any cause, regardless of whether delirium was apparent (Prugh, 1983). Perceptual-motor lags may persist for several weeks or months; they may cause temporary difficulties in learning that, if unrecognized, may lead to chronic learning problems related to resistance to learning or other behavioral disturbances.

Reactions of Infants, Children, and Adolescents to Hospitalization. Over many years, the effects of hospitalization have been studied carefully in this age group, distinguished as far as possible from the effects of illness itself. Today short-term hospitalization, involving several days to 2 weeks, is frequently a part of the treatment of acute illness. Short-term hospitalization may of course shade over into long-term hospitalization, a matter of some weeks to several months. Long-term hospitalization has in the past been used for patients with chronic illness, but this is far less frequent today. Patients with acute major or catastrophic illness or with accidents or burns, however, many of whom would not have survived in the past,

---

*In this discussion, the focus will be on reactions to the psychological stresses of hospitalization. Space is not available for attention to physical stresses, admittedly with psychological reverberations, encountered during hospitalization, such as accidents in children (Cooke, 1967) and drug reactions in children and adults (Boston Collaborative Drug Surveillance Program, 1972).

may now experience long-term hospitalization. The bulk of this discussion will deal with the effects of short-term hospitalization.

Because it involves separation from home and family and often painful treatment, hospitalization may cause a variety of reactions in children (Petrillo & Sanger, 1972; Prugh, 1983; Vernon, Foley, Sipowitz, & Schulman, 1965). In addition to the type of illness, the nature of the reaction depends on the child's age and developmental level; adaptive capacity; quality of parent–child relationships; meaning of the illness to child and family, and other factors mentioned earlier in relation to acute illness. The circumstances under which the separation takes place and the actual nature of the hospital experience assume somewhat greater importance than in adults, because of children's special vulnerabilities.

All children show at least some temporary response to the experience of hospitalization. Such reactions take different forms at different developmental levels, but severe reactions are more intense and prolonged in young children and previously disturbed children.

In infants and children under the age of 4 years, reactions to hospitalization involve principally responses to separation from the mother or the principal caretaker. Separation, anxiety, regression, and depression are often seen in the hospital and following discharge, as are fears, disturbances in sleep and appetite, and continuing problems with the development of trust and autonomy (Vernon, Schulman, & Foley, 1966).

Robertson (1968) has described a sequential type of response with phases of protest, despair, and detachment. In long-continued separations without adequate parent–substitute relationships, the detachment can become chronic and severe, with the picture of "hospitalism" (Spitz, 1951), leading to serious and lasting effects on emotional and intellectual development and increased vulnerability to infection. Long-term hospitalization today usually does not produce such serious effects, but shallow social relationships and distortions in development can occur during "reverse isolation" for infants and young children with severe combined immune deficiencies (Dalton, 1981).

For children from the age of 4 years to the early school-age period, the psychological meaning of the illness and its treatment during hospitalization have greater significance than the actual separation from the parents, although this remains important. Fears of bodily mutilation are characteristic as is the tendency at this stage to misinterpret painful treatment procedures as punishment (A. Freud, 1952). Anxiety, regression, and depression are seen following discharge, along with nightmares, phobias, and lasting difficulties with the development of a sense of initiative.

School-age children can better comprehend the reality of the hospital experience, and separation is less threatening. They may still show fears of punishment, however, in the context of regression, and are vulnerable to anxiety over the functioning of certain organs and to the fear of loss of bodily mastery and control (Jessner, 1959). Depression, withdrawal, fears, and school problems are often seen, with continuing feelings of inadequacy and inferiority. In adolescents, concerns about body image predominate (Kaufman, 1972), and realistic fears of death are evident. The need to depend on others can threaten the adolescent's shaky sense of identity, and behavior problems, related in part to difficulties in acceptance of authority, may interfere with cooperation with treatment programs (Schowalter, 1977).

Reactions of parents to the experience of hospitalization for a child involve guilt or self-blame over the child's illness and fears of judgment by hospital staff. Parents often feel unwanted or left out, and some may show rivalry with nurses and physicians. Some may project their own guilt onto the hospital staff, and a few may exhibit massive denial of the child's illness, with difficulties in acceptance of recommended treatment. Parents of acutely ill infants in neonatal intensive care units, who have not yet begun to interact with their infant, tend to feel bewildered by the technological equipment. Their feelings of helplessness, fear, and guilt may not be noted by the busy hospital staff, and problems may be experienced in parental bonding with the infant (Klaus & Kennell, 1976), as well as, in certain cases of recovery from near death, with the "vulnerable child syndrome" (Green & Solnit, 1964). Siblings of hospitalized children may show anxiety, regression, rivalry, and guilt, among other responses (Prugh, 1983).

Although some reactions of the types described are virtually universal, the majority of children adapt successfully to short-term hospitalization, exhibiting self-limited reactions that ordinarily subside after at most a few weeks. However, the incidence of continuing emotionally deleterious reactions to hospitalization in childhood has ranged, on follow-up studies, from 5% to 15% (Prugh, 1983; Vernon et al., 1966).

Young children are especially vulnerable. A long-term controlled study (Douglas, 1975) indicates that more than one hospital admission between the ages of 6 months and 4 years of age is associated with an increased risk of continuing behavior disturbance throughout childhood and often difficulties in learning in adolescence. Another large-scale study (Quinton & Rutter, 1976) found that, although one hospital admission in early childhood was not necessarily traumatic, a second admission markedly increased the risk of continued emotional problems; multiple hospital admissions under the age of 4 years were associated with both emotional and conduct disturbance in later childhood, a finding supported in a controlled study by Mrazek (1984). Other delayed effects of more than one hospitalization have included enuresis in adolescence (Douglas, 1973) and the occurrence of depression and chronic pain in adult life (Pilowsky, Bassett, Begg, & Thomas, 1982).

Children with chronic family difficulties, particularly in lower socioeconomic groups, are more likely to have experienced early multiple hospital admissions, but Quinton and Rutter (1976) found that children without chronic family difficulties still responded to multiple early admissions with an increased incidence of later emotional disturbance. Thus a significant risk exists in childhood of emotionally traumatic responses of a continuing nature to hospitalizations, requiring careful thought about the indications for hospitalizations and warranting the use of preventive measures and alternatives to hospitalization.

In addition to stresses for children and parents involved in hospitalization, there are stresses for hospital staff, including physicians, nurses, and others, on pediatric units (Beardslee & DeMaso, 1982; Maloney & Ange, 1982). Heavy workloads, rapid changes in medical technology, anxiety over performance, and concern over seriously ill and dying patients and their families are among these, leading at times to high rates of burnout, especially for nursing staff.

In dealing with the stress of hospitalization, it is possible to take steps to bring elements of the child's life span into the hospital. Provisions for the maintenance of the tie between the child and the family can include planning for the parents' visits, overnight stay, and participation in the child's care (Azarnoff, 1984). "Child life activity programs," based on grouping according to age, provide for the child's recreational and educational needs (Plank, 1971; Thompson & Stanford, 1981). Preparation of children for potentially distressing treatment procedures can be planned and carried out by physicians and nurses, with the help of parents and other professionals (Eckhardt & Prugh, 1978). Where indicated, psychiatric consultation and brief, supportive psychotherapy can be offered for children and/or parents.

Group meetings on pediatric wards have been shown to be of therapeutic value for children (Frank, 1978) and for adolescents (Schowalter & Ford, 1970).

For the past 40 years, the prevention of deleterious reactions to hospitalization has received special attention. Long ago a controlled study showed that flexible daily visiting is of preventive value (Prugh, Staub, Sands, Kirschbaum, & Lenihan, 1953), and today unrestricted ("open") visiting by parents is considered optimal practice (Azarnoff & Hardgrove, 1981). Controlled studies have shown that for infants and children under 4 years of age, overnight stay ("living in") by parents is the only truly effective preventive measure (Brain & Maclay, 1968; Fagin, 1966; Mahaffy, 1965). Recently, in some hospitals, mothers of newborns in intensive care, especially if they are breast-feeding, have been encouraged to live in, with fathers and grandparents visiting (Garrow, 1981). Visiting by siblings rounds out the family-oriented approach (Azarnoff, 1984a).

Parental participation in the routine care of the child and during certain treatment procedures, with support and teaching by the nurse, is now regarded as a valuable preventive measure (Hardgrove & Dawson, 1972). Planned "care-by-parent" units, originated in Great Britain, are now available in some children's hospitals (Caldwell, 1981). Preparation of children and parents for hospital admission is considered vital (Azarnoff, 1984b). Individual preparation is best, often in play sessions where the child's questions are answered; but group tours of hospital areas, puppet shows on the ward, booklets, and other methods can be helpful (Azarnoff & Flegal, 1975). Controlled studies have shown that special psychological preparation for cardiac catheterization and similar medical procedures effectively reduces anxiety (Cassel & Paul, 1967).

Evidence is available that psychosocial interventions can reduce the length of hospitalization for children thereby accruing significant cost benefits. Minde and Maler (1968) employed realistic explanations of illness and treatment and nonstructured play sessions for a group of school-age children who were hospitalized for a variety of illnesses; interviews with parents were also offered. In comparison with a control group, the children who received these brief periods of intensive counseling were less anxious following the hospital experience, and the length of their hospitalization was significantly shorter. These same investigators reviewed an earlier controlled investigation by Prugh and his colleagues of the effects of daily visiting compared with weekly visiting and pointed out that the length of hospitalization for the experimental (daily visiting) group was significantly reduced, a finding inadvertently not reported originally (Prugh et al., 1953). Another group (Houts, Turbett, Arnold, & Kruse, 1985) of investigators estimated that nearly 10% of the days spent in a children's hospital by a group of children with varying illnesses would have been preventable if psychiatric treatment had been offered to patients with psychopathology, who appear frequently on pediatric wards but are often not seen in psychiatric or psychological consultation (Stocking, Rothney, Grosser, & Goodwin, 1972).

Alternatives to hospitalization include pediatric home care, developed in Great Britain; young children show less anxiety and regression with this approach (Shrand, 1965). A movement to care for chronically ill patients at home is now underway in this country, using well-trained medical and nursing teams, but the responsibilities are too great for parents of children with acute serious illness. Motel-like facilities adjacent to the hospital (Green, 1965) can make possible outpatient study and day treatment for many children who do not actually require admission; there are not as yet many of these facilities, however. Facilities for overnight stay by children and parents in emergency rooms would allow observation and treatment that could prevent hospitalization (Prugh, 1983). These are still rare today.

Special training of staff and modifications in hospital wards, clinics, and emergency rooms are necessary to implement optimal arrangements for overnight stay in the hospital by parents, care-by-parent units, age grouping, recreational and educational programs, motel units, emergency overnight stay, and other preventive measures. Most children's hospitals and university pediatric programs have made some internal physical changes in these directions. Recommendations for ideal architectural planning for new pediatric hospitals have been made in Great Britain (Great Britain Ministry of Health, 1964) and in this country (Prugh, 1983; Shore, 1966). Virtually no such pediatric hospital units have been built recently in the United States, although some recommendations have occasionally been followed (Ack, 1981; Wallinga, 1982). In addition, nearly 90% of the 4,500,000 children hospitalized each year receive care in general hospitals (Azarnoff & Hardgrove, 1981), many of which do not have separate pediatric units (Prugh & Jordan, 1975).

In helping pediatric hospital staff to cope with stress, regular staff meetings on pediatric wards have been helpful (Beardslee & DeMaso, 1982). Such multidisciplinary groups, supported by the ward leadership and conducted by the consulting child psychiatrist, focus on work-related concerns of the staff, with some emphasis on feelings evoked by patients and parents. A similar approach, involving weekly meetings with staff nurses on high-stress pediatric wards, has resulted in a marked decrease in burnout rates (Maloney & Ange, 1982).

Reactions of Adults to Acute Illness and Hospitalization. In addition to the direct effects of illness, mentioned earlier, adults show behavioral responses to acute illness that bear some similarity to and some differences from the responses described for the childhood age group. Anxiety, with its physiological concomitants, is of course frequently encountered. Regression in adults occurs to a lesser degree than in children; ordinarily it involves the appearance of demanding, dependent, or aggressive behavior. Depression is often seen, related to concerns about illness or fear of being displaced at work, and may compound convalescence through difficulties in regaining strength and independence. Sleeping and eating difficulties may mask depression, as may lethargy or at times overactivity, and relatives may be unaware that patients are depressed.

In adults, conversion disorders are also seen, related to convalescence or admixed with physical disorders, such as epilepsy. As with older children and adolescents, conversion disorders are most frequent in individuals with hysterical personality disorders but may occur in other personality pictures, including healthy personalities. Dissociative reactions in adults occur largely in individuals with chronic personality disorders, most often hysterical, but they may also afflict healthier individuals who become ill under especially stressful circumstances. Misinterpretation will be described later in this chapter.

With adult patients, reactions to hospitalization have rarely been studied separately from reactions to illness. In general, the variables described in relation to children, including the nature and meaning of the illness, its treatment, and the patient's previous adaptive capacity and relationships with others, apply to adults as well.

Strain and Grossman (1975a) have described certain basic stresses of acute illness and hospitalization, including (1) a basic threat to narcissistic integrity, arising from the adult's loss of control over his or her body or routines, coupled with fears of death; (2) fear of strangers; (3) separation anxiety, without key persons and supports in his or her familiar environment;* (4) fear of loss of love and approval from family and friends because of increased dependence; (5) fear of permanent loss of control of developmentally achieved functions, triggered by temporary inability to control emotions, motor functions, speech, bowels, or bladder; (6) fear of loss of or injury to body parts, particularly the eyes, head, and genitals, in the context of regression, symbolism, displacement, and reawakened childhood fantasies; and (7)

---

*Elderly patients are particularly vulnerable. They may develop "catastrophic reactions" (Goldstein, 1952), involving overwhelming anxiety, depression, or aggression in response to separation from their normal environment and routine.

guilt and fear of retaliation, based on the regressive fantasy that illness and hospitalization represent punishment for previous sins of omission or commission, with the corollary concept, for some patients, of cure as forgiveness.

As Strain and Grossman point out, the fear of pain, a prominent source of stress, cuts across all of the preceding categories. Threats to the integrity of patients become more acute with pain. They may view inability to deal with pain as further evidence of general loss of control of previously mastered mental functions or may fear that weakness in the face of pain may cost them the love and approval of important persons. On the other hand, certain "pain-prone" patients, described by Engel (1959), tend unconsciously to use pain and illness behavior as a means of communicating with others. Chronic pain as stress is outside the focus of this discussion, except as it may operate, particularly during convalescence, in the context of unconscious secondary gain.

Certain basic patterns of response to acute illness and hospitalization have been delineated in adult patients by Kahana and Bibring (1964). These include patterns of being overly dependent, demanding, dramatic, long-suffering, querulous, and aloof; they suggest personality types that may require special management. Such patterns may occur in combinations and may change; for example, a patient in pain on admission, who may appear guarded or querulous, can become overly demanding and dependent after receiving initial medical care.

Patients may not be equally vulnerable to all the categories of stress. Some patients may experience separation as a welcome release, not a loss. Patients with strong dependent needs may not experience illness and hospitalization as a threat to physical and emotional integrity. Feelings of anxiety, loss of self-esteem, guilt, and helplessness, may, if especially intense, lead some patients to employ massive denial or other inappropriate defense mechanisms. The physiological concomitants of anxiety, mentioned earlier, may put additional strain on an already damaged system, such as the cardiovascular system, with the secondary consequences compounding the psychological stress. The outcome of the illness and hospitalization, in terms of realistic effects on the patient's capacity to function in life, is a vital consideration.

Strain and Grossman also point out that regression to earlier modes of behavior, with the appearance of more primitive and less reality-oriented defenses, conflicts, modes of thinking, and relationships with others, is not pathological in itself. Regression represents a normal response, allowing for a regrouping of forces, and thus can have both adaptive and maladaptive features. They emphasize that the prerequisites for successful adaptation to illness and hospitalization include the patient's ability to (1) regress adequately and appropriately in the service of recovery (which may be exceedingly difficult for some individuals); (2) maintain adequate defenses against the stresses evoked by the experience; (3) access feelings and fantasies, and communicate needs; and (4) establish basic trust in his or her medical caretakers. All of these requirements presuppose the services of empathic and flexible physicians and nurses.

Reactions of family members to the acute illness and hospitalization of a patient have been less fully studied in adults than in children. Lewis and Beavers (1977) have stated that the family of the hospitalized adult patient is often the most neglected component of the medical treatment system. Although various studies suggest that family variables are important in the course and outcome of illness, Lewis and Beavers indicate that often staff in general hospitals pay little attention to the needs of the family. This may be especially true in intensive care units, where rigid rules often limit visits to a few minutes only every several hours. The staff may have no contact with the family at other times, with little attempt to help them deal with the illness and no awareness that certain families may have a calming and supportive effect on the patient (Lewis, 1976). Of course, certain hospitals are most attentive to the patient's need for visits from family, which may be lifesaving, and to the reactions of the family to the patient's illness. Often, however, the family is frightened and intimidated by strange people, strict rules, and ambiguous expectations (Lewis & Beavers, 1977). Difficulty can arise when the family is seen as an unnecessary interference rather than as a potentially valuable ally, and no therapeutic alliance is formed.

The patient's response to his or her surroundings and treatment program can be importantly influenced by the nature of the relationship between the family and the hospital staff, and well-informed family members can serve as a vital liaison between physician, staff, and patient, as Lewis and Beavers have emphasized. Conversely, confused, frightened family members, receiving little information or respect, can have difficulty finding a role to play, and hostile, dependent, passive, or obstructionist behavior can result. Thus, the family's reaction to a serious illness in a family member is directly influenced by the quality and amount of support they receive from the hospital staff.

Families vary greatly in their attitudes toward illness and in the degree of closeness offered to a family member. Some families tend to see illness as a type of immoral evasion of family responsibilities, treating the patient in a fashion that only adds to the problems of an already lonely and threatening hospital setting. Some families may unconsciously reinforce the patient's pattern of denial or overdependence, or may oppose healthy regressive tendencies. Other families can accept the illness and the attendant threat of loss in a way that effectively reduces the patient's anxiety, guilt, and despair, with, at times, positive effects on his or her response to treatment (Lewis & Beavers, 1977).

Families also vary in their capacity to accept the expression of unpleasant or painful feelings from the sick member, sometimes resulting in the patient's depression or prolonged illness. Different individuals have varying family roles, and inevitably there is some degree of role change when a person becomes acutely ill. The ability of the patient and the family to accept an alteration in the role of the ill member can be an important influence on recovery (Lewis & Beavers, 1977). Parsons and Fox (1952) have indicated that the family's stress has a different quality, depending on whether the ill member is a father, mother, or adolescent child. Also the response may be more intense if the sick person has played a special role within the family, at times causing difficulties in role resumption and even invalidism after recovery and return to the family (Koos, 1946; Lewis & Beavers, 1977).

In a recent family interactional study, Lewis, Beavers, and their colleagues described a continuum of family competence ranging from "healthy" through "midrange dysfunction" to "severely disturbed," based on four specific variables. These include (1) the overt power structure of the family or its pattern of interpersonal influence; (2) the degree to which the family encourages autonomous functioning; (3) the feeling tone and mood of the family; and (4) the family's ability, functioning as a group, to negotiate and solve problems (Lewis, Beavers, Gossett, & Phillips, 1976). All of these variables can be assessed clinically in rough fashion by the physician, with the help of the consulting psychiatrist. Exact predictions of family behavior are difficult, however. The degree and quality of the family's response to illness in one member thus appear to be associated with its general level of competence (Koos, 1946), as well as with the nature and meaning of the illness and its outcome; the sick person's role in the family and individual style of adaptation; the family's capacity to deal with ambiguity and the threat of loss; and the amount and quality of support by the hospital staff (Lewis & Beavers, 1977).

A significant proportion of adults who develop acute illness have some degree of adverse psychological reactions (Dubovsky & Weissberg, 1982; Nemiah, 1961). Lipowski (1967) has found that 30% to 60% of medical or surgical inpatients show a psychological response that is strong enough to significantly impair their treatment or require its significant modification.

Many of the principles discussed in relation to children apply to the management of adult reactions to acute illness and hospitalization. Freer and more flexible hospital visiting policies are vital, as are activity programs geared to the needs of the individual patient. Preparation for potentially distressing procedures, such as cardiac catheterization and coronary cineangiography (Finesilver, 1978) is important. Support for patients is imperative, with active psychotherapeutic measures utilized where appropriate (Karasu, 1979). Supportive work with families, individual and group in nature, is often indicated, including brief psychotherapeutic intervention with families who show maladaptive patterns or limited competence in response to illness. Alternatives to hospitalization, where possible, including day treatment and home care, should be employed.

In addition to the stresses of illness for the patient and his or her family, there are also stresses on the physician, including anxiety about performance and competence in handling the complicated problems of serious acute illness. Physicians today are hard pressed to keep up with the rapid changes in medical technology and the details of new pharmacotherapeutic agents. Patients' patterns of response to illness, varying considerably and changing with the phase of illness, may be confusing, and the physician's response to certain anxious and fearful patients may lead to the prescription of higher doses of medication, longer hospital stays, and more frequent readmissions (Kinsman, Dahlem, & Spector, 1977). The patient who does not get better may threaten the physician's sense of narcissistic integrity, arousing frustration and anger, compounded by guilt (Strain & Grossman, 1975a). This is particularly true with seriously ill patients in intensive care units. Staff support groups (Eisendrath, 1981), in which the liaison psychiatrist can play a central role, can reduce stress on physicians, nurses, and other staff personnel.

Special Types of Stress Involved in Acute Illness and Its Treatment

Review of the specific types of stresses experienced by patients affected by a wide variety of acute illnesses, from serious respiratory infections to meningitis, is not possible within the scope of this chapter. Instead, the discussion will include the specific reactions of children and adults to catastrophic illness or injury; delirium, a disorder experienced frequently by children and adults; and myocardial infarction, a serious disorder of adults. Finally, the stresses of intensive care units will be discussed, together with some of the moral and ethical issues raised by the care of patients in such units.

Reactions to Catastrophic Illness or Injury

In addition to the general patterns of response to illness and hospitalization already described in children and adults, studies have suggested that sequential phases of response to catastrophic illness or injury are characteristic of the human organism, with some variations among children, adolescents, and adults. Phasic responses of this nature have been described in adolescents and adults with spinal cord injuries (Wittkower, 1947); school-age children, adolescents, and adults with serious burns (Hamburg, Hamburg, & DeGoza, 1953; Ravenscroft, 1982); school-age children, adolescents, and adults with respiratory poliomyelitis (Prugh & Tagiuri, 1954), and adults with myocardial infarction (Cassem & Hackett, 1971). Somewhat similar responses have been described in adults reacting to the diagnosis of cancer and other fatal diseases (Kübler-Ross, 1969; Shands, 1955), in parents responding to the birth of a severely defective infant (Drotar, Baskiewicz, Irvin, Kennell, & Klaus, 1975; Solnit & Stark, 1961), and in children and adults in response to civilian or military disaster (Cobb & Lindemann, 1943; Silber et al., 1956).

Such sequential phases have seemed to several investigators (Kimball, 1977b; Krystal, 1969; Prugh & Tagiuri, 1954) to resemble the "work of mourning," that is, the stages in handling grief over the death of a loved person, described by Sigmund Freud (1925/1961) and elaborated by Lindemann (1944). The timetable for the phases of response to catastrophic illness or injury, like that of griefwork, involves at least several months. Although complete recovery may occur, many acute major illnesses result in some degree of chronic disability.

The adaptive process evoked in the reactions of older children and adolescents to catastrophic illness or injury involves characteristic sequential phases that can be categorized as *impact, recoil,* and *restitution* (Prugh & Tagiuri, 1954). *Impact* involves feelings of shock and realistic fears of death or "annihilation of the self," often compounded by a state of altered cerebral metabolism leading to delirium. Marked regression, needs for nurturance, and bodily preoccupations are present, as is heavy denial assisted by primitive fantasy. This phase usually lasts for some days to several weeks.

In the *recoil* phase, lessening of denial and regressive self-preoccupation becomes possible. The patient experiences "mourning for the loss of the self that was to be" and attempts to reestablish some control over the environment. Irrational guilt and the misinterpretation of the illness as punishment characteristically arise in this phase, and serious depression can occur. This phase usually lasts for weeks or several months, and can be most trying for parents and hospital staff members. Feelings of grief may recur later, in muted form.

Restitution brings increasing acceptance of the outcome of the illness, the altered self-image, and the implications of an uncertain future. Premorbid personality patterns reappear, involving apprehensiveness, overdependence, or tendencies to push unrealistically for overindependence. Some continuing measure of denial is often necessary for the maintenance of hope.

Parents show parallel sequential phasic responses to catastrophic situations in their children. After the first feelings of shock and anger, parents experience an initial phase of denial and disbelief, as Richmond (1958) has indicated. Although this phase ordinarily lasts a few days to several weeks for most parents, a few may show continuing or massive denial for many weeks or months, usually related to intense unconscious guilt.

In the phase of fear and frustration, denial is less necessary adaptively, and parents experience "mourning for the loss of the child that was to be." Irrational guilt is experienced in this phase, and blame may be projected onto the spouse, with marital difficulties arising, or at times onto the hospital staff. Although this phase is ordinarily accomplished in a few weeks or several months, feelings of grief may recur in muted form for many months, and depression may overwhelm some parents.

The phase of rational inquiry and planning brings parents increasing acceptance of the illness outcome. They are gradually able to accept the child's limitations, to live with some uncertainty about the future, and to help the child achieve appropriate steps toward rehabilitation with as much independence as possible. Again, some measure of denial is usually necessary for the parents to maintain hope.

Responses of adults generally follow the sequential phasic pattern described, with some differences. In the phase of impact, following the initial feelings of shock, fears of death or disability may be initially more intense, reflecting the adult's greater experience and capacities for comprehension. Anger at the fate that has allowed them to face such extremity may also be more intense. Denial may be brief and less massive, except for some individuals with great needs for autonomy and independence or who are especially threatened by dependence. Regression in adults may involve some degree of depersonalization and dissociation; however, because of their more fully established personality structures, adults usually exhibit less sweeping regression. (The earlier observation about the importance of the capacity of the adult to tolerate appropriate regression is still relevant.)

In the phase of recoil, lessening of denial and regression ordinarily comes earlier for adults, with some exceptions. Guilt and the fear that the illness represents punishment are seen. (The word *pain* is derived from Greek and Latin roots meaning "to punish"; Blumenfield & Thompson, 1981). Mourning for the loss of the self, of which the adult has greater cognitive awareness, occurs; the danger of serious depression in this phase is greater in adults. In the phase of restitution, premorbid personality traits often reemerge earlier in adults and may account for some of the shifting personality responses described by Kahana and Bibring (1964). An acceptance of limitations and an uncertain future becomes possible, with more active movement toward rehabilitation; again some denial seems necessary for hope. Responses of family members to acute major illness have been less well studied in adults. In general, they seem to follow the sequential patterns described for parents.

The management of acute major illness should be geared to the patient's progress through the sequential phases, with respect for the timetable described (Prugh & Eckhardt, 1980a). In the phase of impact, acceptance and strong emotional support are vital. No attempt should be made to attack the denial frontally, regardless of the ultimate outlook. During the phase of recoil, an understanding of the mourning process and the patient's need to reestablish some control over the environment can help the staff accept demanding, often seemingly hostile, behavior and avoid taking it personally. Setting some limits on demands, offering choices where possible in management routines, and encouraging self-help efforts in small ways can offset patients' feelings of helplessness. Emotional support must continue; the patient should be encouraged to talk about his or her feelings, particularly those involving the adaptive mourning process and guilt.

Only after successfully negotiating the impact and recoil phases can the patient utilize rehabilitative measures fully and realistically. Firm encouragement is most beneficial to the patient in entering the phase of restitution, with attention to the reemergence of overly anxious, overly dependent, overly independent, or other premorbid personality patterns. A laissez-faire approach can reinforce the patient's feelings of worthlessness, whereas pushing too hard can produce anxiety over failure. Mental health consultation may be helpful in all phases, and supportive psychotherapy may be indicated for depression, conflicts over enforced dependence, or other problems.

In the management of parents' responses, strong emotional support during the denial and disbelief phase is vital. Temptations may arise to help parents face the reality of the situation before they are ready, but such attempts only increase denial. Opportunities to discuss their grief and feelings of guilt, with "absolution" offered whenever possible, must be available during the phase of fear and frustration, before the parents are ready to deal realistically with plans for the future. Parents often do not match each other, step for step, in their passage through these phases. If a parent shows continuing massive denial or significant depression, psychotherapy may be necessary. Marital therapy may be useful if blaming becomes intense. Attention to the emotional needs of siblings is important. The management of responses by members of the family of adult patients, especially the spouse, can follow similar lines.

Delirium

Delirium represents an acute brain syndrome of reversible nature produced by transient disturbances in cerebral metabolism (Engel & Romano, 1959). It is to be distinguished from dementia or, chronic brain syndrome, in which irreversible brain damage occurs. Depending on a variety of factors, the same etiological agent may produce temporary or permanent damage to the brain (Lipowski, 1980).

Engel (1967b) has estimated that 10% to 15% of all adults hospitalized on acute medical and surgical services show delirium in varying degree, sometimes of subclinical nature. Delirium occurs not only in patients with infectious, traumatic, or other disorders directly affecting the central nervous system but also in patients with severe anemia, fever, cardiopulmonary disturbances, acid-base or electrolyte imbalance, systemic infection, and hepatic or renal insufficiency—not to mention in patients suffering from drug reactions or emerging from coma (Strain & Grossman, 1975b).

Similar disorders may cause delirium in children. In addition, delirium may occur during contagious diseases, such as measles and chicken pox, as a result of insulin reactions, and from multiple antiepileptic medications or heavy doses of one or more tranquilizers. Clinicians have often had the impression that children are more apt to respond to fevers and acute respiratory infections with delirious states than are adults (Prugh, Wagonfeld, Jordan, & Metcalf, 1980). Delirium is also seen postoperatively and in patients in intensive care units (Hackett & Cassem, 1977), as well as in patients with burns and head trauma (Ravenscroft, 1982).

Engel (1967a) has emphasized that many adult patients develop irreversible brain damage because their acute reversible brain syndromes have remained undetected and uncorrected for too long a period. This is particularly true among the elderly chronically ill; in one study (Simon & Kahan, 1963), 50% of geriatric patients in one hospital showed an undetected and untreated acute brain syndrome, resulting from dehydration, vitamin deficiency, or other factors, superimposed on their chronic illness. Even when diagnosed, acute brain syndrome in the elderly may be confused with chronic disorders, and patients may unjustifiably be considered hopeless (Strain & Grossman, 1975b).

The transition from an acute to a chronic brain syndrome may involve the interaction between organic and psychological factors. A patient with acute congestive failure may develop delirium, causing anxiety and agitated behavior, which may increase the impaired cardiac function, thus intensifying further the acute brain syndrome. Lasting brain damage or even a fatal outcome may ensue if such a vicious cycle is not interrupted (Strain & Grossman, 1975b). Catastrophic reactions (Goldstein, 1952), involving agitated and even violent behavior, often occur in elderly patients. Even lesser disturbances in cognitive functions may make it difficult for the patient to remember and follow instructions or to cooperate with medical procedures, with resulting confusion and resentment on the part of the staff, especially if the disorder is unrecognized.

Diagnosis of delirious states is often made by the internist or pediatrician, but the aid of the consulting psychiatrist may be necessary. Wildly agitated and confused behavior, with hallucinations and delusions, or semicomatose states are easily recognizable. Less full-blown or subclinical forms may be manifested by withdrawn or bizarre behavior and may be mistaken for a functional psychosis (Kimball, 1977a; Prugh, 1983). The findings of slowing and disorganization on EEG tracings in both adults and children provide definitive diagnosis. Both gross and subclinical forms of delirium are characteristically worse at night.

The patient's delirious response may affect deleteriously the treatment of the underlying disorder, as in children with burns who tear off their dressings (Prugh, 1983). The dynamic content of hallucinations and delusions is related to the patient's psychodynamic conflicts and past experience (Engel, Romano, 1959). Certain patients appear to be delirium-prone (Prugh et al., 1980). In some adults, a history of a previous delirium seems to represent a risk factor (Quinlan, Kimball, & Osborne, 1974).

Treatment of delirium involves most fundamentally the correction of the underlying disturbance in cerebral metabolism. Other measures may be necessary to deal with the disturbance in awareness, which can endanger the patient's welfare, while the underlying cause is being sought and treated. The central problem, with adults and children, is to help patients deal with the misperception of stimuli in the environment, particularly with visual illusions, and with hallucinations and delusions, if present. In general, such a patient should not be isolated from human contact. A special nurse, nurse's aide (for adults), a foster grandmother (for children), or a relative should be in the room at all times, especially at night. By patiently explaining the patient's misperceptions and gently interpreting reality during hallucinations and delusional states, and by providing supportive physical contact, the caretaker can monitor the patient's mental experiences and serve as a link with the external world. Keeping the room well lighted at all times, especially at night, supports the patient's contact with reality. Visiting by familiar figures from the family is most important, especially for children.

If a sedative is required for agitated or uncontrolled behavior, paraldehyde is best for adults and chloral hydrate for children; barbiturates tend to cause confusion and, in young children, paradoxical stimulation. Any sedative should be used sparingly and physical restraint employed only if really necessary. Tranquilizing agents can help excessively anxious patients but can contribute to confusion in children (Prugh, 1983).

Adults and children may be anxious following the resolution of the delirium, fearing involuntary revelation of thoughts or feelings. Some adult patients show marked depression or posttraumatic stress disorders following delirium and may require continuing psychotherapy. Children may show disturbances in EEG patterns for several months, and many exhibit developmental lags in perceptual-motor function that can contribute to educational problems unless recognized and helped (Prugh et al., 1980).

Myocardial Infarction

Among illnesses that affect adults principally, myocardial infarction inspires exceptional fear because of its relative unpredictability, the experience of total helplessness in its onset, and its high mortality rate. Also disturbing are the economic, psychological, social, and even sexual adjustments that may follow (Block, Boyer, & Imes, 1984). The stresses described by Strain and Grossman (1975a) in relation to acute illness and hospitalization are especially pertinent for middle-aged males, who are the most frequently affected. A discussion of the psychophysiological risks in the development of coronary artery disease and the role of stress in the precipitation of myocardial infarction cannot be included here.

It has long been observed that many patients with coronary artery disease use heavy denial in regard to their illnesses. Anecdotal reports abound of individuals with myocardial infarction who have denied and rationalized as indigestion even the crushing substernal pain of an initial attack. Others have shown denial for days following an attack, to the point of suffering a second, sometimes fatal, infarction because of premature resumption of activity even against advice.

One study (Hackett & Cassem, 1977) suggested that patients with myocardial infarction who showed major denial might have lower mortality during the acute phase. Other studies have since called this finding into question. Recently, Dimsdale and Hackett (1982) have concluded that denial may augment or diminish risk and that, if present in heavy measure, it should call for psychiatric consultation. They have pointed out that denial is seen by some as an unconscious psychological defense distinct from or overlapping with repression, by some as a potential coping resource, and by others as related to alexithymia or the inability to put feelings into words. Other workers have drawn the distinction between patients who use denial only during the acute phase and those who deny more chronically; one study (Soloff, 1978) suggests that there is greater morbidity and mortality among chronic postacute deniers. Two other studies offer some hope of using psychosocial data to identify patients who are at high risk for mortality (Bruhn, Chandler, & Wolf, 1969; Garrity & Klein, 1975). To permit preventive intervention, much more research is needed in this area.

Most reports on patients with myocardial infarctions who were admitted to coronary care units (CCUs) during the acute phase, assert that patients are generally reassured by the sight, in open CCUs, of other patients and modern technical equipment (Doehrman, 1977; Hackett, Cassem, & Wishnie, 1968). Other psycho-logic and physiologic evidence indicates, however, that from one third to more than one half of such patients experience some degree of distress, often denied or suppressed (Doehrman, 1977), particularly in those who witness the death of another patient (Bruhn, Thurman, Chandler, & Bruce, 1970). Cassem and Hackett (1971) have described a type of sequential phasic response in patients, involving anxiety during the first several days, compounded by denial. Depression follows, as the impact of the infarction is experienced, and chronic character traits, reemerge within a week or so. Other reports have corroborated this phasic sequence, although the time relationships are still unclear (Doehrman, 1977; Razin, 1982).

Other reactions of more extreme degree have been reported in patients in CCUs, including altered states of consciousness, delirium, and psychotic episodes. Al-though physiologic factors relating to metabolic imbalance, hypoxia, and medication effects may contribute to these reactions, the intensive care environment, with its sensory overstimulation, lack of cues regarding diurnal sequence, and lack of fa-miliar figures and communication, has been considered at least partly responsible, possibly in interaction with metabolic factors (Hackett et al., 1968; Kornfeld, 1971).*

Other stresses deriving from experience in CCUs have been noted. Several studies have described depression and anxiety as well as adverse physiologic changes, such as cardiac arrhythmias and even reinfarction, associated with transfer of patients from CCUs to general medical wards (Hackett et al., 1968; Razin, 1982). In addition, there are stresses for the nursing staff on CCUs (similar to stresses de-scribed in the discussion to follow on intensive care units) (Cassem & Hackett, 1972). Finally, it is possible that the CCU milieu and its various stresses for patients and staff may increase mortality from myocardial infarction (Cassem & Hackett, 1971; Engel, 1976; Dubovsky, Getto, Gross, & Paley, 1977).

Although psychosocial interventions in the acute phase of coronary disease have been frequent, until recently there has been little systematic study of such efforts (Razin, 1982). One partially controlled intervention study of patients' reactions to transfers from a CCU did find fewer adverse psychological and physical changes in those patients who had been systematically prepared for transfer and who were followed during and after hospitalization by a single designated physician and one nurse (Klein, Kliner, Zipes, Troyer, & Wallace, 1968). A study comparing open and closed CCUs that to some extent ameliorated the environmental abnormalities described earlier, suggested that the frequency and intensity of major psychopath-ological reactions in patients can be reduced (Leigh, Hofer, Cooper, & Reiser, 1972).

A recent review (Mumford, Schlesinger, & Glass, 1982) of several controlled studies indicates that significantly shortened hospital stay and reduced later usage

---

*This has recently been attributed to the intensive care syndrome, with similarities to postoperative delirium, both of which are discussed later in this chapter.

of medical treatment are associated with brief supportive psychotherapeutic interventions in patients hospitalized for heart attacks, with significant cost benefits. Two controlled studies, one of the effects of brief individual psychotherapy (Green, 1975) and one involving brief group psychotherapy (Rahe, O'Neal, & Hagan, 1975), support the value of psychosocial intervention during the recovery phase following acute myocardial infarction, with both psychological and physiological benefits.

Some years ago, a clinical, partially controlled study found that the mortality rate from myocardial infarction in patients in a particular CCU was reduced significantly in patients referred for psychiatric consultation (Cassem & Hackett, 1971). In a more recent study (Dubovsky, Getto, Gross, & Paley, 1977), a CCU, in addition to routine psychiatric consultation for the medical staff, offered the nurses, at their request, regular group meetings in which a psychiatrist, over a period of 15 months, led discussions of the psychosocial aspects of patient care. The experimental unit was compared with a control setting in which a staff psychiatrist was available for psychiatric consultation to the medical staff only. Results indicated that the nurses in the experimental unit spent significantly more time with their patients in direct patient care, communicated more effectively, showed greater charting efficiency, and appeared more sensitive to emotional situations with the potential to trigger serious arrhythmias. Also, although the experimental unit had a population of sicker patients at higher risk of death, its mortality rate decreased significantly over the 15-month period, in contrast to the unchanged mortality rate in the control unit. Methodologic problems exist in such studies, involving consultation and changes in ward milieu (Strain & Grossman, 1975a), but the results are promising; further systematic research into the psychosocial aspects of acute care for such patients is urgently needed.

In a recent critical review of psychosocial intervention in the convalescent/rehabilitative phase of treatment for patients with coronary artery disease, Razin (1982) indicates that supportive psychotherapeutic intervention, behavioral interventions (including biofeedback and relaxation techniques), and group therapy are promising, along with methods of mobilizing social support. He also cites several uncontrolled studies suggesting that improvements in rehospitalization rates, return to work, and other aspects of rehabilitation are associated with programs offering medical staff continuity and follow-up.

In regard to problems in returning to work, there seems to be no simple relationship between the extent of tissue damage sustained during the acute phase of infarction and the probability of return to work, nor is the experience of angina necessarily directly related to the degree of cardiac ischemia, according to a recent review (Block et al., 1984). The majority of patients eventually do return to work, but there are cases of postmyocardial infarction invalidism (Klein, Dean, & Willson, 1965) in some chronically unemployable males. Problems frequently occur in resuming physical activity to the extent possible as well as in resuming full sexual activity (Block et al., 1984). Group psychotherapy, largely of a supportive nature, has been helpful in dealing with such convalescent/rehabilitative problems (Bilodeau & Hackett, 1971), with one controlled study reporting a one-year survival rate 10% higher in treated patients than in controls (Ibrahim et al., 1974).

Involvement of and support for family members, especially spouses, is most important for successful participation by patients in all these types of programs (Block et al., 1984).

Finally, the psychosocial aspects of the approach to prevention of coronary artery disease in susceptible individuals seem to have promise (Razin, 1982). All these areas require much further systematic investigation.

Intensive Care Units (ICUs)

Intensive care units of various kinds have multiplied remarkably over the past 25 years. They offer lifesaving care for patients of all ages with potentially fatal illnesses. A new breed of physicians and nurses has been specially trained to treat specific categories of patients, such as those with cardiac, pulmonary, or renal difficulties, those with severe burns, and those undergoing open-heart surgery. These staff members are action oriented, exhibit an independent turn of mind, and can make quick decisions (Hackett & Cassem, 1977).

In such situations, as a social scientist noted some years ago, high levels of uncertainty are endemic, and the staff must employ a variety of defenses to deal with the stresses posed by ambiguity and death (Fox, 1959). Medical personnel who care for critically ill patients tend to show increased attention to technological matters as tension on the ward rises, with very little discussion of patients as persons (Frader, 1979). Medical residents who are new to the units tend to feel overwhelmed by the new technology and to have difficulty in coping with the deaths of patients. Staff members may become impatient with patients who complain, whose pain persists, and who are slow to recover (Hackett & Cassem, 1977). All these staff behaviors may contribute to depersonalization of patient care (Frader, 1979). Thus stresses in intensive care units, as they affect staff members, affect patients and families as well (West, 1975).

Some types of psychopathological responses of patients on intensive care units have already been described earlier in relation to coronary care units. Anxiety and depression, at times compounded by denial, and other emotional and behavioral reactions are frequently encountered, and schizophreniform and other psychotic reactions have been reported (Kiely, 1976). In addition, critical care medicine, in spite of its benefits, has resulted in the recognition of new iatrogenic syndromes involving altered states of consciousness, such as "postcardiotomy delirium" and "dementia dialytica" (Kimball, 1972). They may involve changes in brain metabolism resulting from heavy anesthesia or other effects of medical and surgical procedures, and they may result in brain damage. Many of them, however, clearly involve responses to the intensive care environment. Irritability, confusion, disorientation, agitated behavior, delusions, and hallucinations are progressively involved in what has come to be called "the intensive care unit syndrome" (McKegney, 1966).

This syndrome has been related to the strangeness and at times bizarreness of the intensive care environment, especially for patients admitted for the first time. A number of workers have described its effects (Kornfeld, Zimberg, & Malm, 1965; McKegney, 1966), and they have been summarized by Kimball (1972).

In such units, beds are crowded closely together with little privacy for patients. Overstimulation, often interfering with sleep, results from many unfamiliar sounds and the large numbers of staff, students, and aides involved in caring for the patient; familiar figures may be only occasionally present, at times because of rigid (and brief) visiting periods. Sensory monotony can result from many repetitious sounds, and there is an absence of the usual day–night sequence, with few orienting stimuli. Witnessing serious illness and death in other patients can be disturbing, and intubation or other processes can interfere with communication. In burn units, patients may lie unclothed behind windows in special environments, with relative isolation from others. These factors combine with the physical discomforts of the disease; the sense of helplessness; anxiety over what is happening; sleep deprivation; and the effects of narcotics, sedatives and minor tranquilizers to produce the disturbances in cognitive functioning involved in the intensive care syndrome. In the acute stages, patients may show impulsive behavior related to hallucinations or delusions, at times bringing harm to themselves or others (Kimball, 1972). Somewhat similar patterns have been described in a pediatric intensive care unit (May, 1972).

The sections on hospitalization have dealt with the stressful effects on patients of the lack of close contacts with family members and the reactions of families to being left without a clearly defined role.

As indicated earlier regarding coronary care units, amelioration of some of the anomalies in intensive care environments, for example, by providing room dividers to increase privacy and avoid overstimulation, bears promise for diminishing the intensity and frequency of the intensive care syndrome (Leigh et al., 1972; Razin, 1982). Preparation for transfer to general medical wards can be of value (Klein et al., 1968). Flexible visiting patterns and greater involvement of the family are of vital importance (Lewis & Beavers, 1977). Treatment of altered states of consciousness involves principles discussed in relation to delirium. Any metabolic or pharmacotherapeutic contributants should be dealt with. Patients in the acute, often agitated, stage should not be left alone (Kimball, 1972; Prugh, 1983); nurse's aides can help the adult patient, and foster grandmothers can help the child patient deal with the illusions involved in hallucinations and support reality in delusional states. Relatively small amounts of phenothiazines can be helpful in adults (Kimball, 1977), with some variation in children (Prugh, 1983). Brief supportive forms of psychotherapy are of value (Kimball, 1977; Prugh, 1983). Psychiatric consultation and intervention are important for other disorders encountered in the intensive care setting, such as severe anxiety, depression, or a functional psychotic episode.

In recent years, reports have begun to appear dealing in detail with the emotional stresses experienced by medical, nursing, and other personnel who work on intensive care units offering treatment to adults (Schwartz, Buletti & Hazel, 1974) and children (Schmidt, 1977). Among medical staff, difficulties in coping with the deaths of patients and problems in relating to the families of critically ill or deceased children and adults may combine with fatigue and overwork to produce severe anxiety or depression (Frader, 1979; White, 1969), particularly among physicians in training (Todres, Howell, & Shannon, 1974). For nurses, the psychological impact of patients' illnesses, shortage of staff and overwhelming workloads, excess responsibility, and poor communication between physicians and nurses cause problems (Vreeland & Ellis, 1969). These can lead to depression and anxiety for the nurse, which may make it difficult for her to function at maximum efficiency (Gentry, Foster & Froehling, 1976; Hay & Oken, 1972). Burnout, especially among nurses, has led to high rates of staff turnover, upsetting patients and staff (Edelvich & Brodsky, 1980; Marshall & Kasman, 1980). (Other factors, such as low salaries and poor hospital morale, can of course be involved in high turnover rates.)

The nursing profession has devoted much time and thought to ways of dealing with the psychological hazards of providing care to the critically ill. Steps have been recommended to ensure adequate staffing; group meetings, work breaks, and rotation of staff are among other measures designed to reduce work stress (Frader, 1979; Hay & Oken, 1972; Vreeland & Ellis, 1969). Psychiatric consultation–liaison programs have encouraged regular group meetings on adult (Hay & Oken, 1972) and pediatric units (Rosini, Howell, Todres, & Dorman, 1974), fostering discussion of stressful aspects of work experience, with opportunities for sharing and ventilating frustration, anger, and guilt. These approaches and group consultation conferences, held at the request of the nursing staff in adult (Simon & Whitely, 1977) and pediatric (Drotar, 1976) units have yielded anecdotal reports of success. Recently, one program involving regular group meetings for nurses on two high-stress pediatric units over a 3-year period reduced by half turnover rates ranging from 30% to 50% (Maloney & Ange, 1982). Informal methods of providing emotional support to medical residents working in intensive care units have led to suggestions for a more formalized approach (Frader, 1979).

Certain moral, ethical, interpersonal, legal, and economic considerations in intensive care overlap with issues mentioned later in relation to terminal care (Duff & Campbell, 1973; Frader, 1979). A thorough discussion of these issues is beyond the scope of this chapter. They are mentioned principally because they contribute to the stresses of critical illness, which can come to bear on patients and families as well as on physicians and other caring persons.

Although medical technology is generally beneficial in the care of the critically ill, its use in situations involving poor prognosis for life or quality of life may be at best marginal and at times harmful; suffering and inconvenience for patients and families as well as financial costs are often greatest at times when expected results are least (Duff, 1981). As yet, no generally accepted ethical principles or precepts have emerged that can serve as moral guidelines for action in intensive care settings. Even clinical guidelines based on diagnostic or technical criteria have been difficult to develop (Frader, 1979).

Although physicians have traditionally assumed the dominant role in making decisions about the care of critically ill or dying patients, many have come to feel that patients or their families should make such decisions (Shaw, 1973), and courts have now become involved (Curran, 1976). In addition, the financing of medical care is changing rapidly; governmental bodies, corporations, and third party payers are emerging as influences in cost containment, and it is likely that cost will become a factor in deciding to continue or discontinue life-sustaining care in ambiguous circumstances (Johnson & Thompson, 1984).

Two recent developments will influence the pattern of decisions regarding the use of medical technology in critical care. One, a set of guidelines for deciding care of critically ill or dying patients, was drawn up in 1984 by an interdisciplinary committee in the Department of Pediatrics at Yale University; the committee had a majority of physicians, with several nurses, several social workers, a chaplain, an attorney, and an administrator. In order to ensure the most caring approach to patient care and family support, the guidelines emphasized the values and autonomy of patients and their families in all decision making, with the roles of nurses and social workers as well as those of physicians considered central (Duff, 1979). The guidelines deal with the role of the "responsible physician" in coordinating decisions about care among team members and appropriate consultants, in accordance with the values of the patient and family.

Recommendations were made for classification, with regular reassessment, of critically ill or dying patients, or those with a very poor prognosis, into groups in which (1) maximum therapeutic effort is justified; (2) selective limitation of therapeutic measures is indicated; or (3) discontinuation of life-sustaining therapy is appropriate. (Criteria for such classification were not spelled out.) Provisions were included for parents, patients, or families to seek legal counsel or court assistance to resolve conflicts with medical authorities, with similar recourse by medical authorities if deemed necessary.

The other major development has to do with the care in newborn intensive care nurseries of infants who are critically ill or who have a major birth defect. As a result of the explosive increase in factual and technical knowledge, few physicians today can assess accurately a seriously handicapped infant's diagnosis and particularly his or her prognosis without the help of other specialists.

Differing opinions on how to ensure optimal care for handicapped and critically ill newborns have been expressed in recent years (Diamond, 1981; McLaughlin, 1981). However, the majority of professionals in the field disagreed with the stand taken by the administration in its "Baby Doe Regulation of 1983," with regard to its reporting, investigating, and enforcement policy (Berseth, 1983). As a result, the American Academy of Pediatrics (1983) has proposed alternative advocacy processes. Infant bioethical committees, with representation by different disciplines and by consumers, have already begun to function in hospitals, in an attempt to provide up-to-date factual information to the pediatrician regarding current techniques and prognoses and to identify and discuss ethical issues in individual cases for the benefit of family and medical staff.

Both of these developments are promising, but much further work in these directions and perhaps others is necessary to resolve the issues for the benefit of our society.

CHRONIC ILLNESS

This section cannot deal with the specific stresses faced by individuals with sensory deficits, such as blindness or deafness; motor defects, such as paralysis or marked muscular weakness; or other physical handicaps, whether congenital or acquired. However, any discussion of chronic illness cannot be divorced from the consideration of disability or limitation in function, and there is much overlap in the kinds of problems faced by individuals with so-called chronic handicaps and those with chronic illnesses.

It is estimated that from 6% to 12% of all children in the United States and Great Britain suffer from chronic physical illness, associated with some disability (Pless & Roghmann, 1971; Rutter, Tizard, & Whitemore, 1968). Estimates of chronic illness and disability for adults are comparable, with some increase with age (Eisenberg, Sutkin, & Jansen, 1984).

A chronic illness is one that is protracted (and sometimes exacerbated). It is usually associated with some impairment of physical function, which may in turn exert effects on psychological and social functioning. Some chronic illnesses are permanent, although they may be compatible with a fairly normal life span. Others follow a progressive course and have a fatal outcome. The onset of a chronic illness or disability may be related to an acute or catastrophic illness, as described earlier, or it may be insidious and gradual. The handling of the acute phase of the catastrophic response may in part determine what problems remain if a chronic phase develops (Prugh, 1983). The individual's stage of development, the severity of the illness and its prognosis, and the type of treatment affect the individual's coping and adaptation. The meaning of the illness, the individual's previous adapative capacity, the nature of his or her previous intimate relationships, and the response of the patient's family and social network, however, seem to be more important than the type of illness or limitation in function (Prugh, 1978).

This discussion will employ the developmental framework of Erikson (1963, 1968). The stress of chronic illness at different life stages throughout the life span will be discussed only in broad outline. A judicious, thoughtful, and detailed review of the effects of specific chronic illnesses and disabilities on the child in the family and the adult in the family and social network has been offered recently by Eisenberg et al. (1984).

Reactions of Infants, Children, and Adolescents

Reactions of birth-related stresses, such as family crises precipitated by prematurity (Caplan, 1960) and the birth of a seriously ill or defective infant (Solnit & Stark, 1960) are discussed elsewhere in this volume. However, certain chronic illnesses, such as those caused by infections and respiratory disorders, make their appearance in the neonatal period. Infants with such problems are cared for in neonatal intensive care units (NICs). Today, their lives can often be saved, but the lengthy separation from the mother, the delay in integrating the infant into the family, and other unusual aspects of the experience result in a high risk of lasting problems in the parent–infant relationship (Klaus & Kennell, 1976).

Reactions of children and adolescents to chronic illness bear some similarities to and show some differences from those described in relation to acute illness. In infancy, the response to separation from the parents, if long-term hospitalization is involved, represents the major threat to the developmental task of achieving a sense of trust. For young children in the early preschool period, although separation from the parents is still important, problems in the development of a sense of autonomy can result from immobilization (Mattsson, 1972) or symptoms, such as those of hemophilia, that pose problems in control of activity by parents (Prugh, 1978). Children in the late preschool period experience more intense threats to their bodily integrity and to the development of a sense of initiative from special and painful treatment procedures, often misinterpreted as punishment, although separation is still a problem.

Children in the school-age period, facing the developmental task of achieving a sense of industry, competence, and accomplishment, show bodily concerns, fears of helplessness and loss of control, and conflicts over handling dependence, with a tendency to blame themselves for illness. Many use denial, reaction formation, and isolation of affect in dealing with such concerns. School phobia is common. In adolescence, similar concerns are seen, with added concerns about identity, independence, sexual adjustment, and death. Changes in body image, as the result of immunosuppressive drugs, for example, may produce reactions that interfere with compliance with rehabilitative procedures. If significant disability is present, older children and adolescents must mourn the loss of the self that was to be during the life stage in which the onset occurred—and again at later stages if disability continues (Prugh, 1983).

Chronic illness and disability pose certain general problems for children. The discomfort and the debilitation produced by certain diseases certainly have a direct effect on the child's academic and social functioning as well as the parents' responses. It is necessary to consider the age of the child at the onset of the illness, along with the adaptive mechanisms available at that stage of development and the presence or absence of normal function before the onset. In addition, the degree of variability of the disease is important; diseases characterized by remissions and exacerbations require repeated and often difficult adjustments on the part of the child and family in their ways of living and expectations (Swartz, 1984).

The degree of visibility of any disability may have varying effects. Although visible cosmetic defects are most troubling in many families, for some a hidden metabolic defect may be more mysterious and threatening, without relation to its actual severity (Prugh, 1978). In addition, the degree of disability may have little correlation with the severity of the illness (Eisenberg et al., 1984). Finally, experienced clinicians have observed that depression and helplessness may detrimentally affect the course of a number of diseases, including ultimately fatal ones. Recently, psychosocial factors, including depression and family conflict, have been found to be serious risk factors, along with the severity of disease and other physical factors, in relation to the deaths of children and adolescents with chronic asthma (Mrazek, personal communication, 1985).

Chronic illness can have definite effects on the personality development of the child, depending on the variables mentioned earlier (Blum, 1984; Haggerty, 1984). However, the earlier concept of specific personality disorders arising from specific illnesses seems no longer valid (Prugh, 1983). The personality pictures seen in children with chronic illness or handicap appear to fall along a continuum, ranging from overly dependent, overly anxious, and passive or withdrawn patterns, with strong secondary gains from illness, to overly independent, aggressive modes of behavior, with strong tendencies to deny illness, even to unhealthy extremes. A middle group of children, however, show realistic dependence and acceptance of their limitations, with adequate social patterns and compensatory outlets and with no more denial than is consistent with the maintenance of hope (Mattsson, 1972; Prugh, 1978).

Thus the earlier concept that chronic illness or disability invariably produces psychopathology in children must be revised. Recent studies on childhood chronic illness have tended to focus on the child's adaptation to disability—the chronicity of the condition, its limiting effects, and the child's sense of being different—rather than on the specific disease (Pless & Pinkerton, 1975). In a recent controlled study, Breslau (1985) found that children with chronic illness and certain physical disabilities had a significantly increased risk of psychosocial disorder over normal controls; severity of physical disability had little effect on psychopathology. Following up on an earlier finding (Rutter, Graham, & Yule, 1970), this study confirmed that children with chronic physical disorder involving the brain had a significantly higher risk of psychosocial disturbance than those without brain involvement (cystic fibrosis). (This risk varied directly with the level of any mental retardation involved.) Much more systematic research is needed in this area.

The reactions of parents vary according to the age and stage of development of the child, the meaning of the illness, the nature of parent–child relationships, the quality of the marital relationship, the type of family functioning, and other variables. Whether the onset was catastrophic or gradual, the parents must mourn for the loss of the child that was to be, during the life stage when the onset occurs— and again at later stages, if disability continues (Kornblum & Anderson, 1982; Prugh, 1983). During the course of chronic illness, parental reactions also fall along a continuum, ranging from overanxiety, overprotectiveness, and overindulgence—

often with difficulties in setting limits on the child's demands; to problems in accepting the child's disability—frequently with denial of its extent, projection of guilt onto the medical staff, and occasional isolation or rejection of the child within the family unit. However, a middle group of parents can, after the initial phases of response, accept the child's limitations with reasonable comfort, permit appropriate dependency, and help constructively to exploit the child's capacities and strengths (Prugh, 1978).

A number of clinical reports in the past have indicated that chronic childhood illness can have a strongly negative effect on the parents' marriage (Bruhn, 1977; Magrab & Calcagno, 1978) with a high rate of divorce occurring, particularly in the case of life-threatening illness. More recent systematic studies (Koocher & O'Malley, 1981; Sabbeth & Leventhal, 1984) have indicated that family breakdown or divorce may be little more frequent in the marriages of parents of children with chronic and even fatal illness than in those with healthy children. Increased marital stress has been found, however (Sabbeth & Leventhal, 1984), and controlled studies have reported a high rate of marital disagreement (Barsch, 1968) and significant difficulties in family integration (Crain, Sussman, & Weil, 1966) in families of children with chronic illness.

Such families may have problems in family alignment, role functioning, and conflict resolution (Minuchin, 1974); in isolated "too cohesive" families, the lives of family members revolve almost entirely around the child with chronic illness (Schaffer, 1964). Difficulties in talking with each other or with the child about the diagnosis are frequent in families of children with chronic illness. Indeed, the capacity to maintain open communication about disease-related issues seems to be an important determinant of a family's adaptation to a child's illness (Drotar, Crawford, & Bush, 1984).

Effects on the siblings of chronically ill or handicapped children include anxiety, rivalry, guilt, and academic and behavioral problems (McKeaver, 1983). A recent controlled study showed that the physical as well as emotional health of siblings of children with a nephrotic syndrome was more impaired than that of siblings of healthy children (Vance, Fazan, Satterwhite, & Pless, 1980). Other systematic studies have indicated that the general mental health of siblings in families with chronically ill children is not necessarily impaired; their vulnerability to problems in social adaptation may be enhanced in certain respects, however (Breslau, Weitzman, & Messenger, 1981; Drotar et al., 1984). Further research is necessary in this area, but it is clear that siblings of children with chronic illness are a high-risk group and that more attention should be paid to their needs.

Reactions of Adults

Many of the reactions of adults to chronic illness resemble those already described in relation to older children and adolescents. Reactions to different disorders may vary somewhat, but the general patterns of adaptation are similar. Excellent reviews of the stressful effects of different chronic illnesses are available (Kimball, 1977b; Weiner, 1977).

Whether the onset has been sudden and catastrophic or gradual, the individual must, when the diagnosis is made, go through the initial impact phase, involving shock and anger, followed by denial; this may be easier when sufficient time is available. Continuing or massive denial, often in somewhat narcissistic individuals with strong needs for control and fears of imperfections, can lead to the seeking of expensive and unproven "cures." Multiple diagnostic procedures and sometimes exploratory surgery can be taxing financially for the patient as well as the family and can result in iatrogenic diseases, such as adhesions secondary to surgery, or to polydrug use and at times drug addiction.

As denial lessens, the recoil phase appears, with the patient beginning to realize the long-term implications and to mourn his or her well-functioning body, while struggling with conflicts about dependency. The patient may tend to amplify typical psychological defenses during this phase, as described by Kahana and Bibring (1964). In the restitution phase that follows, the patient can come to accept limitations imposed by the illness, along with the need for dependence on personnel for necessary treatment. The individual can also reassess his or her life and develop priorities for what is most important, sometimes leading to enrichment of life. At the same time, the patient must maintain what might be termed a secondary denial, in order to live with limitations including discomfort, pain, and debilitation, and still maintain some hope.

For adults, the discomfort and debilitation caused by chronic illness can affect the individual's well-being and vocational effectiveness, at times with serious economic consequences. As with children and adolescents, the degree of visibility of the illness or associated disability is important. Many chronic diseases have variable periods of exacerbation that cannot be predicted or controlled, and repeated adjustments are necessary for patients and family. In addition, the underlying physiological damage that occurs is often permanent with a progressive chronic disease, and the adult, with greater experience and awareness, must come to accept a slowly deteriorating condition. (The course and management of chronic, fatal illness are discussed in the later section on cancer.)

Reactions of families to chronic illness in an adult family member may involve anxiety in spouse and children, and at times resentment. Chronic illness may produce problems for the young adult in the development of a "sense of intimacy," with marital problems centering around difficulties in sexual adjustment. For the adult developing a "sense of generativity," role changes for spouses may occur, difficulties in child rearing may result, and problems with vocational and economic dislocation may arise for the ill person. For the older person attempting to develop a "sense of integrity" and satisfaction with his or her life, chronic illness may contribute to feelings of helplessness, disgust, and despair.

It is now clear (Eisenberg et al., 1984) that activity-limiting chronic conditions are disproportionately great among financially disadvantaged people, in part because of poorer health care. Heart disease, cancer, and stroke are the major causes of death in individuals over 45 years of age, with heart disease accounting for the majority.

Stress for physicians and other health professionals arises from sources similar to those involved in acute illness—heavy workloads, the pressure of medical technology, and the like. Because the chronically ill patient typically does not improve markedly in response to medical treatment, however, a sense of frustration and at times a feeling of defeat is often involved, especially for physicians. Countertransference feelings of frustration and anger can lead to errors in diagnosis and inadequate treatment planning for complaining or resistive patients (Bogdanoff, 1961) and for patients who belong to ethnic groups that differ from the physician's (Ordonez-Plaza, Cohen, & Samora, 1968). Negative iatrogenic effects can result from overprescription of drugs, as in children who show behavioral and cognitive impairments as a result of long-term administration of anticonvulsant therapy (Corbett, Trimble, & Nichol, 1985).

Problems in compliance with medical recommendations are of increasing concern. They occur as a result of gaps in communication between physician and patient, emotional blocks, an excess of information, or a language barrier (Prugh, 1983). Recent studies have indicated that people who are socially isolated or do not have available support systems in the family or neighborhood often have trouble complying with medical regimens or may tend to drop out of treatment (Baekeland & Lundwell, 1975). It has been suggested that, in pediatric practice, such problems, including self-medication, may occur when a relationship with the physician is perceived as noncommunicative or nonsupportive (Korsch, 1968; Haggerty & Roghmann, 1972).

In the approach to management of chronic illness, an ongoing relationship with a primary physician is the most central element of care in helping a patient to cope with the stresses of chronic illness (Dubovsky & Weissberg, 1982; Nemiah, 1961; Reiser, 1980). Relationships with nurses and other professionals are important, and the 5 Cs (communication, collaboration, consultation, continuity of contact, and coordination) are vital principles in caring for patients with chronic illness.

If available, hospitalization for chronically ill infants and children can take place in an "extended-care unit" (Burke, 1969; Hughes, 1982); this involves 1- to 3-months' stay, which avoids the constant turnover of short-term acute care pediatric centers. In the rare situations where longer term intensive medical care is necessary, the best approach is a "medical group foster home," a small group-living arrangement with semiprofessional foster parents and available nursing and medical care. It avoids the potentially traumatic experience of long-term hospitalization or institutionalization, with inadequate parent–substitutes and social experience. Such units are unfortunately rare.

In cases of prolonged hospitalization early psychosocial intervention is important (Geist, 1979; Rie, Boverman, Grossman, & Ozoa, 1967), using a family-centered approach (Drotar et al., 1984). This may involve individual support or psychotherapy, behavior therapy, or family therapy, or may draw on the demonstrated effects of regular group meetings for children and adolescents (Hughes, 1982), group work with parents (Hageberg, 1969), or work with groups of siblings (Chintz, 1981). All the other approaches discussed in the section on hospitalization of children apply, including visiting arrangements, preparation for painful procedures, and educational and recreational programs.

In recent years, pediatric home care has been used for children with various types of chronic illness or disability. Such an approach includes home services that monitor infants with apnea, care in the home for infants with tracheostomies, and programs that avoid institutionalization of ventilator-dependent children as well as children with other chronic conditions.

Home care for children with chronic disorders was developed as a more humane approach—an attempt to bring the technology back from the hospital to the home, uniting the child and family. A systematic study of home care for children with chronic illness, in the context of an ambulatory treatment program, found improvement in the satisfaction of the family with the child's care, as well as improvements in children's adjustment and fewer signs of emotional disturbance in the mother (Stein & Jessop, 1984). There can be real stresses for the family in home care (Feinberg, 1985), however, and much support from professional staff is often necessary. Self-help groups, offering peer support derived from groups with similar problems, offer promise for patients and parents (Caplan & Killilea, 1976; Dumont, 1974; Gartner, 1977).

A controlled study has evaluated home care for fatally ill children as being favorable for the child's death at home, if adequate support is available (Lauer, Mulhern, Wallskog, & Camitta, 1983). (Such care may be associated with hospice care and will be discussed more fully in the section on cancer.)

Care for adults with chronic illness follows much the same approach, with a movement away from the hospital toward the community and home care when possible. Rehabilitation centers follow the model developed by Rusk (1964) after World War II, with interdisciplinary programs of optimistic, positive nature that can produce remarkable results (Wright, 1980) and with involvement of psychiatrists or other mental health professionals (Rossberg, 1961) and the use, if necessary, of individual or group psychotherapy (Agle, Baum, & Chester, 1973). Patients with hemiplegia caused by cerebrovascular disease can be rehabilitated in a functionally oriented medical care approach without formal rehabilitation service if adequate attention is given to ambulatory and self-care activities (Feldman, Unterecher, Lloyd, Rusk, & Toole, 1962).

Efforts to deal with stresses for physicians, nurses, and other hospital staff treating patients with chronic illness include regular staff meetings on intensive care units, oncology units, and other pediatric wards (Beardslee & DeMaso, 1982) where the discussion of patient-related issues, with the support of the ward leadership, leads to shared feelings and identification of stressful problems. Similar groups have been helpful on adult wards (Eisendrath, 1981). Reduction of stress in intensive care units was discussed in the section on acute illness.

Approaches to primary prevention include attention to visiting programs in neonatal intensive care units, making it possible for mothers to live in (Garrow, 1981) (and fathers, at times), with encouragement for visiting by grandparents and, with appropriate precautions, for siblings as well (Schwab, 1983). Secondary prevention involves joint planning by educators (mandated by PL 94-142 to identify and refer children with developmental disabilities) and by pediatricians and other health care personnel who see such children early, for cooperative approaches to early case finding and treatment (Frankenburg, 1985). Child psychiatrists and other mental health professionals also have a role to play in both secondary and tertiary prevention (Tanguay, Shaffer, Hamburg, & Powell, 1984), as do nurse practitioners (Brown & Bloom, 1979) and others.

Special Types of Stresses Involved in Chronic Illness and Its Treatment

As with acute illness, it is impossible within the scope of this chapter to review the specific types of stresses experienced by patients with a wide variety of chronic illnesses. Several chronic illnesses have, for differing reasons, acquired more intensely stressful significance. With the increasing control of infectious disease over a number of years, cancer has emerged as a dreaded disease for adults and children. As the life span has increased, older persons and their families have come to fear senile dementia, especially Alzheimer's disease, and very recently individual high-risk groups and the general public have begun to react almost with panic to the threat of acquired immune deficiency syndrome (AIDS). For these reasons, the stressful impact of these diseases will be considered.

Cancer

Cancer, the second most common cause of death, is probably the most feared illness in the United States today. Even though the prognosis for survival has improved to some extent, especially for certain types of cancer, the diagnosis still arouses a special kind of dread in patients and families. The diagnosis of cancer in a child has been described as the "most devastating experience a family can undergo, often with serious implications for the immediate and long-term mental health of all family members" (Adams, 1978).

During the course of cancer, children and adolescents show many of the reactions associated with any chronic illness, including depression, withdrawal, problems in handling dependence, and the frequent development of school phobia. In addition, fears of death or changes in physical appearance caused by the illness or its treatment (e.g., loss of hair) pose special problems, especially for older children and adolescents (Prugh, 1983). Such critically ill children seem to sense the distress of parents and medical staff, and they often experience frightening fantasies, mistrust, guilt, and feelings of isolation when their diagnoses and prognosis are treated as taboo, which has often been the case (O'Malley, Koocher, Foster, & Slavin, 1979).

Reactions of parents to the diagnosis of cancer in a child partake of the sequential phasic responses mentioned earlier in the discussion of catastrophic illness. These involve the initial feelings of shock and anger, followed by a brief period of denial and disbelief. Massive denial may continue in a few parents, leading to shopping for another opinion. Most move into the phase of fear and frustration, dealing with guilt and beginning to mourn in advance. Blaming the other parent and serious depression in one or both parents can occur in this phase. After several months, parents can generally begin to accept the grim reality of the ultimate fatality of the child's illness, living from day to day and doing what is necessary for the child's welfare, but with still some need for hope.

Kaplan and his colleagues see these sequential parental responses as part of a family coping process, related to the family's patterns of communication, mutual support, and cohesion in times of crisis. He includes the need for all family members to deal with the initial feelings of shock and anger, using the coping mechanisms of denial and disbelief, and then to experience a grief period of shared family mourning that brings mutual consolation, support, and relief from guilt. In Kaplan's view, the family mourning should include the fatally ill child. After the child's death, such a family coping process should also involve a final grieving process, which may take some months, with a final acceptance of the loss of the loved one (Kaplan, Smith, and Grobstein, & Fishman, 1977).

Several early studies of families of leukemic children have described a high incidence of emotional disturbances severe enough to interfere with adequate functioning, including unresolved grief reactions, depression, alcoholism, marital discord often leading to divorce, and work and school problems (Binger, Ablin, & Feuerstein, 1969; Kaplan et al., 1977). Other more recent studies have indicated that a maladaptive outcome was less common (Adams, 1978), with little increase in the incidence of divorce (Lansky, Cairns, Wehr, Lowman, & Hassanein, 1978) and even an increase in adaptive emotional resources in some families (Koocher & O'Malley, 1981; Adams, 1978). All studies noted the importance placed by parents on the support received from each other, as well as the need to identify with others in similar situations in order to deal with feelings of isolation and to learn new modes of adaptation. Other problems similar to those of families with chronically ill children have been described (Kellerman, 1981; Spinetta & Deasy-Spinetta, 1981). Siblings have been said to develop adjustment problems not seen prior to the illness, including jealousy, fears, guilt over survival, withdrawal, acting-out behavior, and poor school performance (Cain, Fast, & Erickson, 1971).

In adults, somewhat similar sequential phasic responses to the diagnosis of cancer were described by Kübler-Ross (1969). During the course of illness, patients exhibited depression, anxiety and agitation, feelings of pessimism or hopelessness, withdrawal, and social isolation, and other psychological symptoms (Craig & Abeloff, 1974; Derogatis, Morrow, & Fetting, 1983). Subtle manifestations of an organic brain syndrome in certain cancer patients can be overlooked or misdiagnosed as depression (Levine, Silberfarb, & Lipowski, 1978). Serious depression associated with suicidal ideation does occur, however; in one third of a group of hospitalized patients with advanced cancer, one seventh had suicidal ideation. Cancer patients were better adjusted than a group of hospitalized psychiatric patients, however, and those who were the most depressed had a prior history of depression (Plumb & Holland, 1981). In another study, the experience of living in limbo during long courses of active treatment with cancer was more stressful for patients with chronic cancer than facing death itself (Cohen & Wellisch, 1978). Although reactions of the family to problems of the adult patient with cancer are not mentioned frequently in the literature, they seem to follow a pattern somewhat similar to that of parents, especially in the case of spouses. In one study of homebound cancer patients, misunderstanding of the patient's emotional responses and other impairments in family relationships were present in over one third of the cases (Wellisch, Landsverk, Guidera, Pasnau, & Fawzy, 1983).

Some evidence exists that stress may affect the course of some malignant diseases.* In a predictive study of patients with malignant melanoma, relapse was more frequent among individuals who exhibited significant difficulty in adjustment to the disease and accompanying surgery than among those who did not (Rogentine, 1979). Other studies have suggested that the enhanced tumor growth and metastases sometimes observed clinically after surgery may be a consequence of the associated stress in certain patients (Sklar & Anisman, 1981).

Even following survival from cancer, special problems may remain. By 1982, the age-adjusted rate of survival for all types of cancer patients indicated that, of all patients in the United States who developed cancer during that year, 41% would survive at least 5 years (American Cancer Society, 1981). It is recognized clinically that some adult patients in this increasing population have medical, psychological, social, work, and economic problems even after treatment is complete and no further evidence of disease exists (Schmale, Morrow, & Schmitt, 1983). In a follow-up study of long-term survivors of pediatric cancer, 51% had adjustment problems, and this group had significantly more depression, anxiety, and poor self-esteem (O'Malley, Koocher, Foster, & Slavin, 1979). Those treated in infancy had less intense and persistent developmental disruptions than those treated in middle childhood or adolescence. Although some adult survivors of cancer seem to develop a special zest for life, with a reassessment of life's priorities, a controlled study indicates that, even years after a cancer experience, individual adults often feel vulnerable, with less self-confidence and more general health worries than healthy controls (Schmale et al., 1983).

Considering the psychosocial aspects of management of patients with malignancy, communication of the diagnosis represents a most important first step. In the 1950s and early 1960s, the prevailing attitude among pediatricians was that

---

*The question of the etiologic effects of stress, among other factors, on the development of cancer (Sklar & Anesman, 1981) involves psychophysiologic considerations that are beyond the scope of this discussion.

seriously ill children should be protected from the knowledge that they faced a life-threatening illness, on the assumption that young patients do not worry about or understand death. Until the early 1960s, a guarded approach to discussion of the diagnosis with adult patients was also prevalent (Oken, 1961). In recent years, increasing knowledge about children's understanding of death (Prugh, 1983) has been available, and there has been an increasing interest in thanatology by physicians treating adults, beginning with the work of Kübler-Ross (1969). As surveys in 1961 (Oken) and 1977 (Slavin, O'Malley, Koocher, & Foster, 1982) show, there has been a dramatic shift in physician's attitudes toward a more open approach to disclosure of the diagnosis and prognosis to both children and adults. A recent retrospective study of a large group of long-term survivors of childhood malignancies showed that good psychosocial adjustment was associated with an earlier knowledge of the diagnosis (Slavin et al., 1982).

Although not all questions have been answered, it seems clear today that health care providers who encourage the development of open communication with the families of children (Vernick, 1973) and adults (Holland, 1977) are rendering an important mental health service. Unfortunately, not all families of children and adults with cancer can tolerate comfortably such an open approach, and individual adaptations may have to be made.

In the approach to long-term management of patients with cancer, oncology programs in pediatrics and internal medicine have adopted a multidisciplinary approach (Murphy, 1975). Although individual relationships between patients and physicians and nurses are still central, representatives of a variety of disciplines, including the clergy, can all make significant contributions to the care of the patient and his family, with the coordination and leadership of the physician. Child psychiatrists (Lansky, 1974) and adult psychiatrists (Holland, 1977) increasingly assist their colleagues in the total medical approach to the management of patients with fatal illness, especially cancer, as do psychologists (Murphy, 1975) and social workers (Adams, 1978). Psychiatrists particularly attend team conferences to consider the emotional as well as the physical needs of patients and families, and staff members are encouraged to discuss their feelings of frustration, depression, and, at times, anger.

Group discussions with parents on a regular basis have been helpful (Heffron, Bommelaera, & Masters, 1973), as well as individual psychotherapy for children and parents (Prugh, 1983) and for adult patients and members of their families (Weisman, 1979) as indicated, usually on a supportive basis. Mothers of leukemic children have utilized short-term group therapy (Kartha & Ertel, 1976), and adult patients have used group therapy (Spiegel & Bloom, 1983). An approach to management of advanced cancer involving special techniques of emotional support has produced better psychosocial adjustment to cancer in adults (Carey, 1974).

Radiotherapy represents both a physical and an emotional stress (Forester, Kornfeld, & Fleiss, 1985) with physical symptoms, such as nausea and fatigue, being influenced by psychological factors. Similar physical symptoms (Morrow & Morrell, 1982), as well as affective and cognitive effects (Silberfarb, Philibert, & Levine, 1978) have been found in association with chemotherapy. In a recent controlled study, adult cancer patients undergoing a course of radiotherapy were given weekly psychotherapeutic sessions involving a variety of combinations of supportive therapy with educational, interpretative, and cathartic components. The reduction in both emotional symptoms (apprehension, anxiety, depression, and social withdrawal) and related physical symptoms was statistically significant in the patients receiving psychotherapy, compared with a control group (Forester et al., 1985). Behavioral treatment has been noted recently to be effective in dealing with somewhat similar symptoms associated with chemotherapy (Morrow & Morrell, 1982).

Cancer pain is one of the most pressing problems facing modern society. Moderate to severe pain appears to affect at least one third of cancer patients during the immediate stage of their disease and two thirds or more during the terminal stage (Noyes, 1981). Cancer pain is often undertreated (Marks & Sachar, 1973), frequently because of the physician's concern for the development of tolerance and fear of narcotic addiction. Recent studies in Great Britain indicate that, if given on a regular basis in adequate dosage (not simply as needed) pain control can be achieved, and these dangers do not materialize (Noyes, 1981).

The availability of adequate pain medication usually diminishes anxiety in patients, supports a sense of control, and promotes trust (Poteet & Reich, 1981). Other physical methods, including palliative irradiation and neurosurgery, may help in cancer pain control (Noyes, 1981). Psychological factors frequently complicate cancer pain and its management, and individual psychotherapy can be helpful (Prugh, 1983), as can group therapy (Spiegel & Bloom, 1983). The use of mental imagery, relaxation techniques, and biofeedback all hold some promise (Noyes, 1981). Hypnotherapy has been helpful in children (Gardner & Hinton, 1980; Hilgard & LeBaron, 1979), as has self-hypnosis (LaBaw, Holton, Tewell, & Eccles, 1975), whereas a combination of self-hypnosis and group therapy, in a controlled study (Spiegel & Bloom, 1983), has been effective in reducing pain sensation and suffering in women with metastatic breast carcinoma.

In the management of terminally ill cancer patients, approaches involving emotional and social support have been made explicit (Carey, 1974) in a fashion that can apply to the handling of patients with other types of terminal illness. Narcotic relief of pain can be provided for children (Howell, 1966) and adults (Marks & Sachar, 1973) without fear of addiction. Group therapy has been employed for terminally ill adult cancer patients (Yalom & Greaves, 1977) and hypnosis has been used to control pain in children (Gardner, 1976) and adults (LaBaw, 1969). Techniques of psychological support for the dying child (Burton, 1974; Green, 1967) and adult (Norton, 1963) have been described, including active psychotherapy when indicated (Zuehlke & Watkins, 1975). Parents have been encouraged to participate actively in the care of dying children (Knudson & Natterson, 1960; Vernick & Karon, 1965), thereby gaining help in the process of anticipatory mourning (Friedman, Chodoff, Mason, & Hamburg, 1963). Ways of supporting active grieving by parents and family members, at the time of a child's death (Prugh, 1983) and immediately afterward (Wessel, 1983), have been described that may also help in the prevention of a "replacement child" (Legg & Sherick, 1976; Poznanski, 1972).

Methods of helping children deal with the impact of the death of a sibling have been discussed (Cain et al., 1971), as has a supportive approach to the handling of children's reactions to the death of a parent (Furman, 1974; Zeligs, 1974). Self-help groups have been said to be helpful as an aid to mourning and grief work for bereaved parents (Davidson, 1979; Satterwhite, Bell-Isle, & Conradt, 1978), although one study (Videka-Sherman & Lieberman, 1985) has questioned the effectiveness of such an approach. The topics of family mourning (Hollingsworth & Pasnau, 1977), and coping with death (Schiff, 1977), have received much recent scrutiny, with special attention to the families who experience the sudden infant death syndrome (Bergman, 1974; Friedman, 1974).

Although most of these studies involved hospitalized patients, home care for cancer patients has been used experimentally for over 30 years (Rossman, 1954), and there have been recent discussions of this approach for both children (Lauer & Camitta, 1980) and adults (Malkin, 1975). A comparison study of parental adaptation following a child's death at home or in the hospital revealed more positive adjustment patterns and a more significant guilt reduction in those parents who participated in home care (Lauer et al., 1983). Adequate medical and social support are important for families electing to allow a member to die at home (Krant, 1982).

Hospice programs provide an alternate approach to cancer care for patients or parents. The hospice movement has developed over the past 30 years (Krant, 1978), in part to fill a gap created in hospital services because physicians have been primarily taught to maintain life and to regard death as a failure (Adams, 1984). Hospice programs are interdisciplinary, involving physicians, nurses, psychologists, social workers, and occasionally psychiatrists, as well as representatives of religious organizations and trained volunteers. The unit of care is the patient and family (Adams, 1984), and an attempt is made to meet psychological, social, and spiritual needs as well as to provide symptomatic physical care. The patient's primary care physician oversees treatment (Adams, 1984), but the role of the nurse is pivotal (Greene, 1984) in coordinating of patient care. Hospice programs exist for children (Burne, 1984) and adults (Saunders, 1978), with especially outstanding programs in Great Britain. Acceptance of hospice services has been said to be generally high among seriously ill patients (Rainey, Crane, Breslow, & Ganz, 1984). Care may be terminal, but the emphasis is often on intervals of respite care for families wishing to take dying patients home (Burne, 1984).

One accomplishment of hospice care has been an increased number of patients who die at home rather than in the hospital setting (Adams, 1984). Especially when combined with home care and death in the home, hospice programs can be cost-effective (Adams, 1984).

Some problems still exist in communication and coordination of care between hospital oncology units and hospice programs. In a survey of cancer patients' attitudes toward hospice services, the vast majority expressed a desire for the continuation of involvement of their personal physician during the period of hospice care (Rainey et al., 1984). Although most hospice programs operate in the community setting, recently some have been incorporated into acute hospital settings as special units.

Although the general impression has been that the majority of cancer patients adjust surprisingly well (Weissman, 1979), much has been learned in recent years regarding the reactions of patients and families to the stress of illness with cancer and its attendant treatment, including terminal care when necessary. Based on this new knowledge, a psychosocial approach has done much to alleviate such stresses. In spite of the trends, psychiatrists and other mental health professionals specializing in consultation liaison with oncology patients are still rare throughout the country, and budgetary support for their work is limited. A recent survey in California of cancer patients' psychosocial needs revealed that only 12% of patients indicated the availability of services from a mental health professional (Rainey et al., 1984). If hospitals and other health care agencies are to organize programs that are responsive to these needs, they must commit themselves to strengthening psychosocial resources. Additional research is needed also to ascertain the most effective type of psychological intervention.

Senile Dementia: Alzheimer's Disease

In the increasing group of older people, the onset of certain chronic diseases, such as diabetes, may be milder than in the young, and little disability may be experienced. Cancer occurring in the elderly generally advances more slowly than in younger people. Other disorders, such as osteoarthritis, are more characteristic of old age and may produce considerable disability. Although about 85% of the elderly suffer from at least one chronic condition (Wilder, 1971), often with some limitation of activity, only about 10% to 15% of the population over 65 have major problems in functioning (Bouvier, Atlee, & McVeigh, 1975; Wilder, 1973). Heart disease, cancer, cerebrovascular disease, and respiratory disease are the most potentially stressful physical diseases of the elderly; these limit daily functioning and can eventually result in death. Arthritis and sensory impairments—loss of vision and hearing—limit the activities of over 25% of older adults (Wilder, 1973).

In addition to these disabilities, approximately 4% to 5% of older adults experience some type of damage to the brain that can produce severe and chronic impairment in cognitive functioning (Busse, 1973), with another 5% to 6% experiencing mild to moderate symptoms. Such damage may result from disease processes, such as arteriosclerosis, heart disease, or stroke, or may involve brain cell death from senile dementia, a chronic brain syndrome. Such disorders are in contrast to the normative physiological changes associated with aging in the central nervous system, which do not necessarily result in chronic disabilities (Schienle & Eiler,

1984). Such normative changes may, however, limit an older person's capacity to respond adaptively to stressful situations, as with older adults who seem to be cognitively impaired under stress but appear normal when the stressful circumstances abate (Gaitz & Varner, 1980).

Of the several types of senile dementia, the most common are primary dementia of the Alzheimer's type (SDAT) and multiinfarct dementia (Schneck, Reisberg, & Ferris, 1982). Although cerebral arteriosclerosis was formerly regarded as a major cause of mental deterioration in the elderly, it now appears that this is generally not true. Such deterioration seems to occur in those cases of multiinfarct dementia, in which cerebral softening results from multiple infarctions of brain tissue (Hackinski, Lassen, & Marshall, 1974).

Alzheimer's disease has an insidious onset without focal neurological signs; there is an increased incidence with age, although there may be a presenile onset. Its etiology is unknown, but slow-virus infections, aluminum toxicity, genetic influences, and other factors are being considered (Schneck et al., 1982). Multiinfarct dementia may have an abrupt onset and is encountered most commonly in men, frequently with hypertension, between the ages of 40 to 60 years; it often develops after a series of strokes. Cases involving mixed dementia, with brain pathology characteristic of both Alzheimer's and multiinfarct disorders, have been described.

Strokes—cerebrovascular accidents—may result in multiple and complex behavioral responses, varying with the location of the lesion, the premorbid personality of the patient, and the reactions of the family and the social network (Raskind, 1984). In more severe cases, aphasia, impulsive behavior, and helplessness can lead to frustration and depression. Repeated strokes may result in multiinfarct dementia, with added problems.

Other less common causes of secondary dementia in the elderly include toxic, nutritional, infectious, endocrine, and cerebral disorders, often with the clinical picture of delirium. If diagnosed and treated early, many cases of secondary dementia can be reversed (Schneck et al., 1982). Depression and other psychological disorders, masked as dementia, are often seen in elderly persons. Patients with pseudodementia of depressive origin frequently show a relatively rapid onset; often a history of affective illness is present (Kiloh, 1961). Mixed cases of dementia and depression are frequent, and depression at times may mask physical symptoms, especially in the elderly.

The elderly person with chronic brain syndrome experiences most basically the subjective feeling that he/she is not himself or herself and fears further loss of mental faculties. Other deficits in cognitive and ego functioning include problems in orientation, memory, intellectual capacity, judgment, and stability of mood and impulse control. Regression may take place, with impairments in moral and ethical codes and a breakthrough of repressed sexual and aggressive impulses (Strain & Grossman, 1975b). Chronic illness of various types may result in temporary adjustment disorders, involving depression, anxiety, withdrawal, anger, or changes in conduct, which may evolve into chronic disabilities.

In patients with multiinfarct dementia, the personality of the individual is better preserved than in those with Alzheimer's disease. The Alzheimer patient progresses from a "forgetfulness phase," associated with anxiety, through a "confusional phase," in which denial often replaces the earlier anxiety. The most frightening phase for relatives and friends is the "dementia phase," in which the patient becomes markedly disoriented and may forget or confuse familiar figures. Motor restlessness and shifting thought processes may usher in the onset of psychotic symptoms, such as delusions, hallucinations, paranoid ideation, and severe agitation. Some of these symptoms are related to the severe cognitive deficit. Somatic and neurologic abnormalities may be seen in this stage, with incontinence and abnormal reflexes (Schneck et al., 1982).

In all cases of senile dementia, but especially in Alzheimer's disease, the impact on the family of the patient's behavior can be most stressful. In addition to concern and confusion, disruption of home routines, changes in family roles, social isolation, and increased physical demands on the spouse or other family caregivers are common, with resulting anxiety, guilt, or depression and detrimental effects on the health of family members (Zarit & Zarit, 1984).

In the past, psychiatric hospitalization and nursing home placement have been frequently used for elderly persons with senile dementia, and hospitals and nursing homes were used for patients with stroke and other chronic disabilities. However, this traditional custodial approach to the care of chronically ill elderly persons has real limitations, with little emphasis on restoring or even maintaining function. Nursing homes often have not offered rehabilitation, which can bring about remarkable responses in stroke patients (Rusk, 1964). Some older individuals give up or become withdrawn and may function at a lower level than necessary, with excess disabilities (Zarit & Zarit, 1984). Also the transfer to a nursing home can be stressful for patients and families.

Today, for a variety of reasons, the majority of patients with senile dementia, often with equally severe symptoms, are given home care by supportive relatives, most frequently spouses and children. The same is true for elderly persons with a variety of chronic disabilities. The extended family, rather than fading away, continues to be the most vital support network for older people (Zarit & Zarit, 1984).

Recently, approaches to community care have been developed that assess and treat the patient, while attempting also to relieve some of the stresses on families. Outpatient facilities include clinics for the elderly and senior day-care centers, with some rehabilitation services available in the home. Individual counseling, crisis intervention, behavior therapy, and more formal psychotherapeutic interventions for patients and family members offer hope (Schienle & Eiler, 1984; Zarit & Zarit, 1984). Antidepressant and tranquilizing drugs can be of benefit (Busse & Pfeiffer, 1977). Self-help groups can be supportive to patients and can diminish caretaker anxiety. However, more research is needed to determine the most effective approaches (K. Solomon, 1984), and mental health services for the elderly are still in short supply.

Support for caregivers, with respite care from relatives, friends, or housekeepers can be valuable, although many communities provide limited help from social service agencies. Some communities have recently developed programs specially designed for dementia patients (Mace & Rabins, 1981; Zarit & Zarit, 1984). Family meetings can be most helpful.

Some patients with senile dementia, particularly those in the later phases of Alzheimer's disease, still require acute hospital care or institutional placement because of having severe forms of other disorders. When this is necessary, specific supportive programs can be effective in reducing relocation trauma (Schienle & Eiler, 1984).

Acquired Immune Deficiency Syndrome (AIDS)

Since it was first described in 1979, AIDS, a contagious and often fatal disease, has become a health problem of epidemic proportions and a psychological crisis (Morin & Batchelor, 1984). Although occurring originally in such discrete at-risk groups as sexually active male homosexuals and bisexual men, persons from Haiti, users of intravenous drugs, and hemophiliac patients (Dilley, Ochitill, Perl, & Volberding, 1985), AIDS has been reported in heterosexuals (Nichols & Ostrow, 1984), in children (Oleske, Minnefor, & Cooper, 1983), and in infants of mothers with the disease (Joneas, Delage, & Chad, 1983). Early studies of the psychological impact of AIDS on adult patients have demonstrated anxiety over the implications of the diagnosis, fears of disability or death, depression, and feelings of social isolation, in addition to neurological problems (Nichols & Ostrow, 1984) and the usual problems associated with dealing with a serious and life-threatening illness (Dilley et al., 1985; Nichols & Ostrow, 1984).

As publicity increased about the illness, anxiety and fear mounted, particularly in the gay community and among hemophiliac patients (Nichols & Ostrow, 1984).* As the contagious nature of the disease and its high mortality became manifest, hospital staff members have developed doubts and fears about close contacts with patients, even though no cases of patient-to-staff transmission have been documented (Nichols & Ostrow, 1984; S. L. Solomon, 1984). In some patients, the diagnosis of AIDS has stimulated conflicts over their sexual orientation, with guilt over their life-style and feelings of punishment. The social isolation of patients has been intensified by conflicted responses about their lifestyle on the part of hospital staff, including psychiatrists (Dilley et al., 1985), leading at times to disruption of the therapeutic milieu on psychiatric wards (Polan, Hollerstein, & Amshin, 1985). Staff

---

*Recently school systems have begun to show panic responses regarding readmission of schoolchildren who are AIDS victims, a major city has demurred regarding the setting up of nursing homes, and church attenders have feared to drink from a common communion cup, among other developments. Demands by some for mandatory testing have raised issues related to civil liberties. More recently moral and religious concerns have arisen in some quarters regarding the usage and advertisement of condoms.

members of hospice programs for the terminally ill have experienced similar conflicts (Geis & Fuller, 1985).

In-service training is urgently needed for staff in hospital and hospice programs, as well as expanded research into the psychosocial dimensions of the disease (Coates, Temoshok, & Mandel, 1981; Nichols & Ostrow, 1984). Support groups for AIDS patients, especially from the gay community, have shown much promise (Geis & Fuller, 1985; Nichols & Ostrow, 1984). Education of the entire community in the United States has begun, spearheaded by the efforts of the Surgeon General, C. E. Koop, MD. More widespread educational steps at local levels, with the involvement of health and mental health professionals, are urgently needed to stem the tide of panic.

THE STRESS OF SURGERY

The discussions of reactions to acute and chronic illness and to hospitalization and intensive care include many observations that are pertinent to a discussion of the stresses involved in surgical experience.

Reactions in Childhood

In general, infants and children under four years of age respond more to the separation caused by hospitalization than to the surgical experience itself. However, very young children who are verbal have sufficient understanding to be able to benefit from simple preparation for operation. Late preschool-age children experience anxiety about bodily integrity, and separation anxiety is still present in less marked degree. Mutilation anxiety is characteristic, along with misinterpretation of painful procedures as punishment, and preparation for surgical experience becomes more vital and effective in this age group (A. Freud, 1952).

In school-age children, separation anxiety is muted; mutilation anxiety is still present, although the capacity to comprehend reality is much greater. The reality of death is not conceptualized until the late school-age period. Fears of loss of body mastery and of control of impulses are characteristic of this age period, related to children's fears of potential harm to the integrity of the emerging body image, especially in situations in which they are not in control. Anxiety, panic, denial, depression, overly passive behavior, and regression have been described in the preoperative period. Preparation is extremely important and helpful at this stage (Jessner, 1959).

Adolescents fear losing their rather shaky identity and independence in a new group of peers, with conflicts about submission to adult authority. Undergoing surgery involves anxieties about the integrity of their newly evoked body image, as well as fears of death and damage to body parts. Preparation is vital (Prugh, 1983).

Anesthesia evokes fears of loss of self-control in schoolchildren especially, and children from the late preschool period through adolescence have fears and fantasies about what may be done, under narcosis, to various bodily organs. Children of different developmental levels respond differently to preoperative sedation or basal anesthesia; young preschool children are often paradoxically stimulated, rather than sedated, particularly by barbiturates (Prugh, 1983). At any age, marked anxiety may raise significantly the sedation or anesthetic threshold (Shagass & Naiman, 1955), at the same time reducing the margin of safety in patients with serious cardiorespiratory problems or other debilitating conditions. Studies in children show significant elevations in 24-hour corticosteroid levels during the preoperative period (Knight, Atkins, & Eagle, 1979); the impression exists that there is an inverse relationship between the steroid level and coping effectiveness.

Young preschool children often react adversely to the strangeness of the induction area and the operating room; the absence of the mother is the factor causing the greatest stress. Many children resist being held down. Many fear they will do or say something "bad"; some are afraid they will awaken before the operation is over, whereas others misinterpret the onset of unconsciousness as impending death (Jessner, Blom, & Waldfogel, 1952).

Difficult inductions have been described, involving crying, shouting, or physical resistance, in 14% of children, 4 to 14 years of age (Bothe & Galdston, 1972). In the same study, excited or delirious emergence from anesthesia was described in 13% of children from 3 to 9 years old. In another study, excited or delirious emergence was noted in 8% of children and adolescents from 10 to 17 years of age (Smessaert, Scher, & Artusio, 1960). Children have been said to have a lower incidence of postoperative delirium than adults (Egerton & Kay, 1964); this requires further research.

During the postoperative period vomiting, depression, regression with overly dependent, oppositional, or aggressive behavior, fear of doctors, and even psychotic disorders have also been described in children, in addition to conversion disorders and other complications of convalescence (Prugh, 1983).

Reactions of parents resemble those described earlier in response to their children's illness and hospitalization. Fears of the child's death are more intense because of the known risks in anesthesia and surgery. Difficulties during convalescence may arise from overanxious or overprotective tendencies on the part of the parents. Paradoxical responses occur in certain unhealthy families who have come to need to treat a child with a chronic defect, such as congenital heart disease, as an invalid, and experience difficulty in letting the child change roles following surgery.

Reactions of Adults

Much of the foregoing discussion is pertinent to the reactions of adults to surgical experience. Baudry and Wiener (1975) have pointed out that the stresses for adult surgical patients include (1) fear of death or mutilation or pain; (2) uncertainty about the future; (3) feelings of helplessness and isolation; (4) anxiety provoked by a strange environment; (5) relatively impersonal and unresponsive caretakers, and (6) violation of privacy, with constant intrusion into the core of one's experience—the body. As with children, the stress of the experience is reflected in high levels of adrenal cortical activity in the preoperative state; especially high levels seem to be associated with ineffective coping (Price, Thaler, & Mason, 1957).

The need for prompt or emergency surgery tends to evoke the type of reactions discussed earlier in relationship to the stresses of acute illness, including the fear of loss or injury to bodily parts, which is frequently involved in surgery. The body part in many cases may not be highly invested psychologically; the gallbladder for example, is not highly invested in most adults. Surgery involving the genitals (hysterectomy and mastectomy for females; vasectomy and orchiectomy for males), as well as the face, eyes, and hands, is frequently associated with high psychological stress.

Most major surgery is associated with scarring (Blumenfield & Thompson, 1981; Guerra & Aldrete, 1980). The individual who is highly invested in body appearance may associate a scar with imperfection and develop psychological problems that persist long after surgery, particularly if the scarring involves areas normally visible to other individuals. However, a scar that is hidden from public view can still cause great stress if it is visible to a marital partner or other family members or intimates. Even an almost invisible scar can arouse concerns in individuals (such as children) with a high degree of body narcissism, resulting in serious problems (Belfer, Harrison, Pillemer, & Murray, 1982).

The experience of anesthesia is also a major stress for adults that is sometimes overlooked (Baudry & Wiener, 1975; Guerra & Aldrete, 1980). Some patients may be seriously frightened of the risks of anesthesia, and others have fantasies about what they may do under the anesthetic. It is stressful for many patients to imagine that they may say things, such as secrets about their lives, under anesthesia. Some individuals fear that their "true self" will come out as they are either being induced or coming out of anesthesia, and they are afraid someone will think less of them and betray them to their family or loved ones. Such personal revelations very rarely occur, and it may be quite reassuring to patients to determine if they have such concerns and educate them about this.

Psychological reactions to the surgical experience include anxiety, fear, denial, depression, regression, and occasional psychotic episodes (Baudry & Wiener, 1975). Postsurgical delirium occurs frequently, as will be discussed in a special section. Excessive pain, with increased demand for narcotics, may occur postoperatively. Although such pain may be the result of inadequate analgesia, because of the physician's fear of narcotic addiction (discussed earlier), it may also be intensified by emotional factors (Baudry & Wiener, 1975).

The individual's past history of surgical procedures may also greatly affect the stress of approaching surgery and anesthesia (Baudry & Wiener, 1975). If the patient or a family member or close friend has had a bad experience due to surgery or anesthesia, the stress and anxiety of an approaching surgery will often be greatly increased. Therefore, a history should be taken from each patient in this regard. It is also useful in evaluating preoperative and postoperative stress to ask the patient to explain his or her understanding of what is wrong and what is going to be done to correct it. Sometimes great distortions will be evident in what the patient believes is wrong or thinks will actually occur surgically. Correcting such misconceptions will usually reduce the stress associated with the surgery.

Baudry and Wiener (1975) have indicated certain types of patients who represent a psychological risk, both preoperatively and postoperatively. These include patients with a previous history of psychotic decompensation or other mental illness, with hospitalization or other psychiatric intervention. Patients who refuse to undergo indicated surgery, either by threatening to sign out of the hospital or refusing to sign a consent form, usually are experiencing acute anxiety or panic. Patients whose relationships with the hospital staff are deteriorating and those with magical or unrealistic expectations concerning their operations are also high-risk groups.

Patients who show too much or too little concern in the preoperative period have been studied by Baudry and Wiener (1975) and others. Among patients who show a pathological lack of concern about surgery, the authors include patients who, consciously or unconsciously, expect to die and often do so, even when the operation is a success. Reinhart and Barnes (1972) found that in a group of highly anxious children, patients who were extremely agitated, and at times openly depressed, expected to die during cardiac surgery; these children did actually die during induction of anesthesia or during the operation itself.

Prediction of Surgical Outcome

Kennedy and Bakst (1966) and Kimball (1969; 1977a) were able to establish correlations between preoperative reactions in adults about to undergo open-heart surgery and the outcomes in the operative phase. Mortality was highest in the depressed group, especially among patients who had given up hope about the outcome, and was next highest in the highly anxious group, with no greater risks in either group than others because of physical factors, age, and so on. Apparently the ability to block out fears of possible complications improved the prognosis of such patients, supporting the need for partial suppression of stressful anticipation associated with some (but not too massive) adaptive denial.

In a prospective study of adults scheduled to undergo open-heart surgery, Kilpatrick and colleagues administered a battery of tests, using intellectual, projective, and neuropsychological approaches, with the patients also rated as to the degree of cardiac impairment. Statistical evaluation of these tests enabled the investigators to identify in advance all of the fatalities and nearly 90% of the survivors (Kilpatrick, Miller, Allain, Higgins, & Williams, 1975). In a prospective study of adults undergoing open-heart surgery, depression in the postoperative period was associated with a high risk of death, which could not be explained solely on the basis of worsened cardiac status (Tufo & Ostfeld, 1968).

A predictive study, using personality rating scales, resulted in the prediction of both successful and unsuccessful outcomes in adults undergoing operation for intractable ulcer (Thoroughman, 1964). Finally, Boshes (1961) has offered anecdotal accounts of paradoxical responses to surgery by adult patients who have come to depend on a long-standing mitral defect, with unconscious secondary gains related to chronic reliance on others. In the face of a successful surgical outcome, these patients appear to be catapulted into health, for which they are not ready, and they frequently commit suicide.

Most of the preceding studies are concerned with cardiac surgery. Somewhat similar factors have been found to be involved in patients undergoing other types of surgery. One controlled study indicated that, for surgical procedures in adults in general, high levels of preoperative fear were associated with slower recovery, greater use of analgesia, and more negative emotions (Sime, 1976). Another study showed that the outcome of surgery was strongly affected by patients' expectations (Cassem & Hackett, 1971). Investigation of delay in surgery showed that, in addition to reality factors, such as finances and distances to travel, difference in coping styles of adults, parental anxiety, and sociocultural factors were most often involved (Andrew, 1976).

Psychosocial interventions similar to those discussed in relation to acute illness and hospitalization apply also to the management of patients with reactions to surgical experience.

For children and adolescents, psychiatric consultation may be vital. It can best be employed in the context of a psychiatric consultation-liaison program on a pediatric surgical ward (Geist, 1977), which makes possible many of the related approaches.*

If a child is significantly depressed, extremely anxious, or convinced he or she is going to die, it is wise to postpone the operation and provide psychiatric consultation; at times preparatory psychotherapy is indicated (Danilowicz & Gabriel, 1976). Such distinguished pediatric surgeons as Gross and Swenson have been reluctant to carry out major operations, particularly involving the heart, under such conditions and ask for psychiatric help (Prugh, 1983).

For children who are experiencing postoperative anxiety, regression, depression, or other symptoms, individual psychotherapy, with parent therapy where indicated, can be helpful (Prugh, 1983).

A number of prevention methods have been developed. Vaughn (1957) has shown, in a controlled study, that psychological preparation, involving a single

---

*As mentioned earlier, the vast majority of children are cared for in general hospitals, many of which do not have separate pediatric units, medical or surgical.

preoperative interview, is effective in preventing deleterious emotional reactions to ophthalmic surgery in school-age children. Another controlled study (Skipper, Leonard, & Rhymes, 1968) concentrated preparatory and supportive intervention on the mothers rather than the children. The mothers who received such information and support in caring for their children had significantly less distress and felt more satisfied than did the control mothers, and their children showed less emotional distress, better adaptation, and more rapid recovery from the physical effects of the operation (shorter length of time to first voiding, better fluid intake, and less vomiting) than children in the control group.

Wolfer and Visintainer (1979) carried out a classic study that confirmed and extended these results. Both parents and children facing minor elective surgery were given preparation in advance and emotional support during periods of distress; both children and parents showed less emotional distress and better adaptation in the hospital, and children showed significantly less disturbed behavior following discharge. Booklets and tours of the hospital are helpful but are not a substitute for psychological preparation (Azarnoff, 1984b).

Jackson (1953), an anesthesiologist, long ago showed in a controlled study that personal preparation of the child the day before surgery, with the anesthesiologist going with the child to the operating room on the day of operation, resulted in a significant diminution of the amount of anesthetic necessary and a reduction in postoperative reactions, such as vomiting. A controlled study by Schulman, Foley, and Vernon (1967) showed that their mothers' presence during the anesthetic induction significantly reduced fears, aggressive behavior, and other negative mood responses in preschool children, while not appreciably disturbing the mothers. As a result of such studies, parents are beginning to be with their children in the anesthetic room (Massachusetts Consumer Directory, 1982) and the recovery room (Maylew, 1983; Rousseau, 1967).

In preschool children, for whom psychological preparation for surgical experience is less effective, two controlled studies (Brain & Maclay, 1968; Mahaffy, 1965) showed that, in children undergoing tonsillectomy, those whose mothers stayed with them overnight had better adjustment in the hospital and less emotional disturbance following discharge. In both studies, there were fewer postoperative complications; in one, children admitted with their mothers showed lower temperatures postoperatively, with lower blood pressure and pulse rate, earlier voiding, better fluid intake, and less crying.

In recent years, pediatric hospital surgical units have increased the use of day surgery (Lawrie, 1964). The parents can be present for the child's induction and recovery; the children seem more relaxed, with less crying, and have a smoother induction under those circumstances; and the parents are happier (Rigg, Dunn, & Cameron, 1980). Such day units avoid the potential for trauma of hospitalization, with its risks, and also achieve a not-incidental cost savings.

In the management of reactions of adults to surgical experience, similar considerations apply. Psychiatric consultation is indicated for any of the high-risk groups of patients mentioned, including those with special diagnostic problems. Experienced surgeons generally request consultation for patients who are significantly depressed or highly anxious, who are inappropriately unconcerned, or who fear dying. With such patients, it is wise to postpone their operations, in order to allow time for extended consultation and psychotherapy when necessary (Prugh, 1983). Patients who show the personality reactions described earlier can benefit from special handling, as recommended by Kahana and Bibring (1964).

Social support following surgery has been effective in promoting patient adjustment following mastectomy (Bloom, Ross, & Burnell, 1978). Special emotional support also has been used by nursing staff to reduce the incidence of postoperative vomiting (Dumas & Leonard, 1963).

Reduction of postoperative pain has been achieved by encouragement and instruction by staff members (Egbert, Battit, Welch, & Bartlett, 1964). Hypnosis has also been helpful in reducing pain (Scott, 1976). Adequate analgesia, prescribed regularly rather than only as needed, should be available.

One of the special stresses associated with surgery is postoperative delirium. This syndrome has also been referred to as "postcardiotomy delirium," "bypass psychiatric syndrome," and "postoperative psychosis." It is seen frequently in open-heart surgical ICUs. Its symptoms are somewhat similar to the intensive care unit syndrome, discussed earlier. After a brief lucid interval following the operation, confusion, disorientation or fluctuation in awareness, hallucinations, and delusions are manifest, lasting for some days or longer (Dubin & Field, 1979; Quinlan, Kimball, & Osborne, 1974). Although brain damage may follow some types of surgery (Editorial, 1982) and drugs and metabolic factors may contribute to the syndrome, the environment of the recovery room and in particular of ICUs has been implicated (Dubin & Field, 1979; Hackett & Cassem, 1977), as well as certain personality factors.

Patients who are older, depressed, or have a previous history of postoperative delirium; patients with organic brain syndrome or a history of head injury; those with drug addiction or alcoholism; and those who exhibit marked anxiety, with ineffective denial, appear to be more susceptible to postoperative delirium (Kimball, 1972; Morse, 1976), as are patients with a limited command of English in American hospitals (Titchener & Levine, 1960). Older patients undergoing bilateral cataract operations have a very high incidence of "black patch delirium" (Linn, 1953). The incidence of postoperative delirium has been said to be about 1% to 3% (Hackett & Cassem, 1977) although one study reported it to occur in 1 of 9 persons (Titchener & Levine, 1960).

The management of postoperative delirium involves considerations discussed earlier in relation to delirium; it is necessary to take the condition seriously, as it can contribute to postoperative morbidity and mortality. Prevention of the syndrome has involved changes in recovery room procedures to make it less impersonal and more supportive (Lazarus & Hagens, 1968). The incidence has been reduced significantly by restructuring the ICU experience, with patients treated in side rooms and mobilized fairly rapidly, with monotonous sounds kept to a minimum (Quinlan et al., 1974) and with special attention paid to encouraging visits by family members (Morse, 1976). Hackett and Cassem (1977) have the impression that a preoperative visit by a psychiatrist or other mental health professional may be of value. Preparation for the possibility of postoperative delirium has also been helpful (Weissman & Hackett, 1958), involving the establishment of a specific doctor–patient relationship.

Major factors in preventing stress associated with surgery are the preparation and education of the adult patient prior to the procedure if at all possible. Some preoperative anxiety is normal, and Janis (1958) has referred to the "work of worrying" that must be done before the operation, as an analogy to the work of mourning. Thus if someone explains in a general sense the surgical procedure and the routines that are followed in the operating room and recovery room, it gives the patient a sense of mastery and control by knowing what will happen, rather than fearing the unknown. In addition, before receiving blanket reassurance, the patient should have time to ask questions that may reveal misconceptions and fantasies, which then can be corrected. The person best qualified to prepare the patient for the surgery is of course the surgeon. In practice, however, the task of preparation is often, by default, left to others, or even ignored (Baudry & Wiener, 1975). The next best person is the family physician, if the patient has one, but the nurse can perform this function. In especially difficult cases, the psychiatrist or other mental health professional may have to become involved.

In a less formal fashion, very anxious patients can be given tours of the operating and recovery room areas. If patients are terrified of losing control under general anesthesia, it may be possible to use a spinal or local anesthesia for certain procedures. Also Hackett and Weissman (1960) have the impression that a preoperative visit by a psychiatrist can be helpful, if necessary, in dealing with preoperative fears and misconceptions.

Controlled studies indicate that preparation for surgery is effective with adults (Schmitt & Woolridge, 1973). Patients were prepared in a group led by a nurse the night before surgery, with discussion of their concerns and fears. The experimental group of patients slept better, were less anxious on the morning of surgery, and showed less postoperative urinary retention than a control group. They also required less anesthetic and pain medications, returned more rapidly to oral intake, and were discharged sooner than the controls.

Other studies are corroborative. Mumford et al. (1982) quantitatively reviewed a number of controlled studies of brief supportive interventions with adult patients in relation to surgical operations. Surgical patients who received information or emotional support mastered the crisis of surgery better than patients who had only ordinary care. In addition, on the average, these brief psychological interventions reduced hospitalization approximately 2 days below the control group's average. Thus, as the authors conclude, beyond the intrinsic value of offering humane and considerate care, the evidence is that psychological care can be cost-effective.

In a controlled study of elderly female patients operated for repair of fractured femurs, an experimental group, offered supportive psychotherapy by a liaison psychiatrist, had a 12-day shorter hospital stay, on the average, than a control group. More than twice the number of patients in the experimental group than in the control group returned home, rather than to an institution (Levitan & Kornfeld, 1981).

Special Types of Stress Involved in Surgery

The foregoing material has presented general patterns of response to surgical experience. There are some differences among reactions to different surgical procedures; limitations of space have not permitted their discussion, although some aspects of cardiac surgery have perforce been touched upon. Reviews covering these areas have been offered in relation to children and adolescents (Prugh, 1983; Reinhart & Barnes, 1972; Toker, 1971) and adults (Hackett & Weissman, 1960; Titchener & Levine, 1960). More recently, two multiauthored volumes have appeared, dealing with the psychiatric aspects of general surgery (Howells, 1976) and of obstetrics (Howells, 1972).

The following discussion will consider briefly one major type of specialized surgery, renal transplantation, as well as the surgical approach to burns and certain operations with necessarily mutilating effects, all employed with both adults and children, and the most common surgical experiences of all, limited to children—circumcision and tonsillectomy and adenoidectomy.

Renal Transplantation

The refinement of surgical techniques of organ transplantation and immunologic advances have made it possible to prolong life through the use of transplanted living donor or cadaver organs. Reactions to renal transplantation have been widely studied in children, adolescents, and adults; these cannot be considered separately from the stressful effects of hemodialysis.

Hemodialysis raises all the problems of a serious chronic illness. Younger children show regression, denial, and withdrawal, as well as fear of pain and immobilization (Korsch, Fine, and Francis, 1971). Older children may show denial and withdrawal, milder regression, depression, fears of death, and school phobias. They also exhibit anxiety about changes in their body and delayed growth, as well as frustration and anger at being dependent on "the machine." A few show oppositional or resistive behavior, leading to noncompliance. Adolescents have conflicts related to dependence, fears of sexual inadequacy, and worries about missing school. They experience anxiety and depression, and some have given up and covertly decided to die (Schowalter, Perhott, & Mann, 1973).

Adults face such conflicts over dependence but especially over activity versus passivity (Abram, 1968); depression and certain personality factors seem to be involved in problems of noncompliance (De-Nour & Czaczkes, 1972). Some adults have attempted suicide (Abram, Moore, & Westervelt, 1971), and others have made the decision to no longer live on dialysis (McKegney & Lange, 1971). Azotemia has produced subclinical delirium in children, adolescents, and adults, with concomitant bizarre behavior mistaken for functional psychosis (Prugh, Wagonfeld, Jordan, & Metcalf, 1980).

The parents of a child undergoing chronic dialysis find it difficult not to be overprotective, and a special interdependence often develops between mother and child, with some fathers feeling displaced. Psychotherapy for children and parents as well as adults on dialysis has been effective (Korsch et al., 1971; De-Nour, 1970); hypnosis and modified group therapy have also been helpful.

When renal transplantation is possible, mortality is decreased and longevity increased for some years. The difference in morbidity between patients on chronic dialysis and those who receive transplants is less impressive (Prugh, 1983). With the development of more sophisticated hemodialysis and peritoneal dialysis as well as the advent of home dialysis, which still has problems (Blagg, Hickman, Eschback, & Schribner, 1970), a true choice between chronic dialysis and transplant is now beginning to become possible. Still, many patients on hemodialysis are not eligible for kidney transplant for a variety of reasons, including economic limitations.

Although the quality of life for patients with successful renal transplantation is generally considered superior to that of patients on chronic renal dialysis, complications of surgery, rejection episodes, the side effects of immunosuppressive drugs, and the number of days of hospitalization suggest that the benefits of transplantation for children and adults may be less than originally hoped for (Kimball, 1977b; Prugh, 1983). Anxiety over the wait for the transplant, if it is to come, affects patients and families at all ages. The bilateral nephrectomy preceding the transplantation poses problems related to the loss of body parts, and uncertainty about integrating a new part—from someone else's body, alive or dead—presents additional problems for adults as well as children (Castelnuovo-Tedesco, 1981), along with the fear of rejection. Children are anxious about changes in their bodies and fear rejection by the peer group, whereas parents are worried and tend to be overprotective. Severe anxiety, regression, or depression in children and adolescents may necessitate psychotherapy in the posttransplantation period. Psychotic episodes have been reported in adults, although these are less common in adolescents and rarely occur in children (Prugh, 1983).

The periods before and after transplantation are generally quite stressful for children and adolescents and their families. Siblings may feel pushed aside and resentful, with the appearance of withdrawn or hostile behavior, and significant shifts in family dynamics have been described as a result of the stresses of surgery (Kemph, Berman, & Coppolillo, 1969).

The donor–patient relationship has frequently complicated family responses

(Simmons, 1981). Although most parents, especially mothers, have been regarded as willing donors, many parents have second thoughts and sometimes feel they have been pushed to the decision. Siblings often have conflicts about donorship, and some medical centers will not permit children or adolescents to donate a kidney. These and other conflicts have led certain surgeons to believe that, although the graft results are better when relatives are donors, the psychological difficulties may outweigh the benefits (Paton, 1976). In addition, increased success of cadaver transplant has recently begun to bring about a gradual decline and perhaps an ultimate disappearance of living donors (Paton, 1976).

In the few available long-term studies of the problems encountered by children and their families in adapting to kidney transplantation (Khan, Herndon, & Ahmadian, 1971; Korsch, Francis, & Fine, 1973; Tisza, Dorsett, & Morse, 1976), the major problems of a psychosocial nature were related primarily to fear of rejection and consequences of immunosuppressive therapy (persistent short stature, weight gain, and cushinoid facies). Tisza and her colleagues observed that, even under these trying circumstances, adolescent patients continued to strive toward mastery of the adolescent developmental tasks involved in achieving independence and self-sufficiency, peer-group acceptance, and sexual identity.

In the sole large-scale controlled follow-up study, carried out by Korsch and her colleagues, only 13% of the patients who had a currently functioning graft were not engaged in some meaningful activity. The remaining 87% had returned to their individual and family preillness condition in about a year. The results of personality tests given the transplant recipients were similar to those of a control group of chronically ill children, but the transplant recipients showed significantly more restricted social adaptation and social activities than a group of well children of the same ages (Korsch et al., 1973).

In this study, about one fifth of the cases followed for more than 5 years (mostly adolescent girls with deep-seated social and emotional problems) showed noncompliance involving interruption of immunosuppressive therapy—related to psychosocial conflicts and leading to irreversible reduction in allograft function or allograft failure. In addition, there is room for speculation around individual case reports—though as yet no incontrovertible proof—that immune mechanisms may in certain cases be affected psychophysiologically (Solomon, 1969) by the "giving up, given up" syndrome (Engel and Schmale, 1968).

Problems for staff in interacting with patients and families facing the stresses involved in renal dialysis transplantation are real, and the interdisciplinary nephrology team obviously must include psychiatrists and other mental health professionals (Levy, 1981; Prugh, 1983). Such a comprehensive approach is necessary from the start in evaluating of patients with end-stage renal disease and in planning their treatment program. With this type of approach, it is possible to identify the resources, strengths, and coping mechanisms, as well as the vulnerabilities and problems of children and families before therapeutic intervention is required (Korsch et al., 1973).

The Surgical Approach to Burns

Burns are among the most common types of accidents in children under 2 or 3 years of age. Accidents often occur in relation to a family crisis, and guilt on the part of child and parents is a long-continued feature (Meyer & Redmond, 1963). Martin and her colleagues in England have made important observations on the psychodynamic factors that may lead to serious burn injury (Martin, Lawrie, & Wilkinson, 1968).

The emotional responses of the burned patient involve anxiety, depression, regression, and aggression, in addition to the delirium in the acute phase (Andreasen, Noyes, & Hartford, 1972; Ravenscroft, 1982). In children, food refusal, depression, and negavistic responses to painful therapies, including isolation, surgery, and changes in burn dressings, complicate and impede recovery in many cases. Refusal to eat, depression, and hostility toward hospital staff around grafting procedures have been reported in adults (Andreasen et al., 1972). This is in spite of the technological advances in the surgical approach to burn treatment, such as early excision and grafting, increased ability to prevent infection, and the development of "artificial skin," which have led to major advances in survival rates from serious burn injury, affecting 80,000 adults and children each year (Bernstein, 1983). Serious long-term psychological disturbances, including body image problems (Stoddard, 1982) have been reported in children and adolescents (Bernstein, 1979). Problems in adults have included anxiety, depression, and fear of deformity (Andreasen et al., 1972). Phasic responses of patients and families resemble the responses described earlier in relation to catastrophic illness or injury (Hamburg et al., 1953; Ravenscroft, 1982).

The psychosocial aspects of the treatment of burns can be facilitated by the presence of a child psychiatrist (Bernstein, 1983), an adult psychiatrist (Hackett & Cassem, 1977), or a psychologist (Kavenaugh, 1983) on the burn unit. Treatment of delirium is important (Hackett & Cassem, 1977; Loomis, 1970), with modifications in the approach discussed earlier. Supportive measures, such as overnight stay by parents and the use of foster grandmothers or nurse's aides, are vital (Prugh, 1983). Psychotherapy may be necessary to deal with depression, guilt, or other responses.

Narcotics have been used traditionally for control of burn pain. Hypnosis has been used successfully to deal with the excruciating pain of changing dressings in children (Bernstein, 1965; LaBaw, 1973) and adults (Schafer, 1975; Wakeman & Kaplan, 1978). Behavior contracting has been used to manage pain (Simmons et al., 1978) as have intensive nursing attention, biofeedback, "imagery" techniques, and group therapy (Bernstein, 1983). Recently, an experimental study of two approaches to dressing changes for burned children was carried out; one involved a standard approach emphasizing staff control and patient distraction, whereas the other was an experimental approach involving patient control and focus on the procedure (Kavenaugh, 1983). Results significantly favored the latter.

Seligman (1972) has described emotional reactions of burned children and their parents in a pediatric intensive care unit, whereas Hackett and Cassem (1977) have discussed the problems of adult patients and their families in a burn unit. These have some similarities to the problems described earlier for patients in intensive care units. Psychotherapy is useful for children and adults with depression and for family members.

Facial burns involve special consideration (Bernstein, 1976), and psychiatric consultation can be important. Many adults, though often socially isolated and tending to use denial during periods of stress, do surprisingly well on long-term follow-up (MacGregor, 1979). Research is needed in this area, particularly regarding the influence of reconstructive surgery on the body image of children and adolescents (Belfer et al., 1982).

Operations with Mutilating Effects

Particular problems may arise in regard to operations with necessarily mutilating effects (Earle, 1979), such as amputation. The phasic responses to illness and injury are of course involved; regression and denial are more prominent in younger children. Young children may use denial initially but ultimately must experience some mourning for the lost part of themselves (Healy & Hansen, 1977). School-age children, engaged in developing their body images and finding their place in the peer group, must struggle with feelings of difference and inferiority (Silber, 1960), whereas adolescents must grapple with conflicts over independence, doubts about sexual attractiveness, and fears about the effect of the resulting handicap on vocational and other life aspirations (Wesseling, 1965).

Strenuous and persistent denial at any age, open depression, withdrawal or other reactions may interfere with the acceptance of prosthetic devices or other rehabilitative measures. Guilt about an accident affects most children and adolescents, and the parents' phasic responses and struggle with their guilt may profoundly affect the child's self-attitude (Plank & Horwood, 1961; Prugh, 1983). Children and adolescents with amputations complain of "phantom limb," a poorly understood phenomenon, less often than do adults, most of whom have such experiences (Parkes, 1976).

Other operations with mutilating effects include mastectomy. Women tend to have anxieties about the possible loss of their sexual attractiveness, as well as the danger of cancer, and depression often occurs (Asken, 1975). At present, radical mastectomy is no longer considered routinely necessary in order to prevent the spread of cancer, and procedures such as lumpectomy seem to promote better postoperative adjustment (Steinberg, Juliano, & Wise, 1985). The experience of hysterectomy* faces a woman with the loss of childbearing functions in particular, a loss she may need to mourn, and often with the fear of loss of sexual effectiveness.

---

*Hysterectomy has been said to be the most common operation in adults; many have believed it is performed too frequently.

Depression often occurs postoperatively, with frequent sexual maladjustment, occasional psychosis, and physical complaints (Raphael, 1975).

Common Childhood Operations

Two operations in childhood deserve discussion when considering the stress of surgery. Tonsillectomy and adenoidectomy, after circumcision, is the most common operation performed on children. Although no longer recommended routinely for all children, in the late 1960s it was still being performed on at least 30% to 40% of children in urban areas (sometimes in family groups), of whom probably no more than 2% to 3% actually required the operation (Haggerty, 1968). Bleeding (with occasional deaths), infection, and other complications, including psychological trauma (Jessner et al., 1952; Levy, 1945) can occur.

Haggerty's guidelines for necessary operations and his measured appraisal of the relatively small place for tonsillectomy and adenoidectomy in the treatment of children have been widely noted, particularly by some third-party insurers, and there has been a noticeable decline in the popularity of such operations. In Vermont, for example, tonsillectomies and adenoidectomies decreased by 46% over a period of 5 years in the middle 1970s with the use of feedback and review (Wennberg, 1977). The number of such operations is still unacceptably high, however (Prugh, 1983), and further effort is necessary to diminish their use.

Circumcision, one of the oldest operations on record and the most common operation performed in hospitals in the United States, has recently had questions raised about its necessity (L. Lubchenko, personal communication, 1980). Daniel and his colleagues, along with others, have pointed out that bleeding, scarring, and other complications occur and that certain disorders, such as penile abnormalities and blood dyscrasias, represent contraindications to the operation (Daniel, Bennett, Matzek, & Ward, 1978). They believe the operation should be reserved for the treatment of phimosis only.

Traditionally, pediatricians and parents have had the impression that circumcision is not painful. A recent study, however, has indicated there is significant pain associated with the operation, but that infants in the neonatal period respond to the pain by becoming quiet (Emde, Harmon, Koenig, Metcalf, & Wagonfeld, 1971). Circumcision of older boys incidental to another operation requiring general anesthesia is likely to be emotionally traumatic, and full explanation and preparation are vital if circumcision is indicated in children of preschool age and beyond (Prugh, 1983).

SUMMARY AND CONCLUSIONS

A review of the stress of illness and its treatment today yields results that are both sobering and hopeful. The experience of being ill, particularly in a hospital setting, is significantly stressful for patients of all ages and, especially in cases of serious illness, for the hospital staff as well. Such stress occurs in the face of generally excellent medical and surgical treatment in the United States for all but the poor, who receive too little care too late.

The situation in regard to the hospitalization of children for acute illness has been especially well studied; the stresses include, among other factors, separation from the parents and painful treatments. The evidence is clear that a significant number of child patients (5%–15%) show continuing deleterious emotional reactions to the experience of hospitalization for acute illness, with very young children exposed to multiple admissions being the group at highest risk. Because at least 4,500,000 children are hospitalized each year in the United States, this means, using the lowest figure, that approximately a quarter of a million children each year are in need of some type of mental health service to offset the experience of being treated in a hospital. Unfortunately, national estimates made by the Joint Commission on Mental Health of Children (1970) and the President's Commission on Mental Health (1979) indicate that the majority of children in need of mental health services in the United States do not receive them.

In this instance, hope springs from the current availability of controlled studies showing that preventive psychosocial measures, such as unrestricted visiting arrangements, overnight stay by parents of young children, and psychological preparation of children for certain upsetting medical procedures, are effective in reducing such deleterious reactions. Certain psychosocial interventions can shorten the hospital stay, with resulting cost-effectiveness. Alternatives to hospitalization, such as motel units permitting ambulatory care, home care, and medical foster homes, have been developed.

It is sobering, nevertheless, to realize that the majority of hospitalized children and their families do not receive the benefits of such effective preventive interventions. They are available in children's hospitals; however, the vast majority of children are hospitalized in general hospitals, many of which do not have pediatric units. Of those hospitals with such units, less than half permit unrestricted visiting arrangements or provide any psychological preparation, and most do not have facilities for overnight stay by parents. Few motel units exist as yet; medical foster homes are rare; and home care services are not available on a wide scale. The lack of availability of such preventive psychosocial services could be remedied by planning. The relatively small expense involved in providing them would be more than offset, on a national scale, by the decrease in the expenses involved in the later provision of mental health services—and, more humanely, by the diminution of stress during the hospital experience for millions of children and their families.

Although adults are less vulnerable than children* to the stress of hospitalization for acute illness, the treatment of illness in an intensive care unit, albeit often lifesaving, involves significant stresses for patients and families. Here splendid

*Adults are vulnerable, however, and more attention should be paid in hospitals to their emotional needs, including liberal visits by families and concern for their reactions.

technology seems all too frequently to dehumanize the experience for patients, who tend to develop the troubling and potentially serious intensive care syndrome. This may be related in part to the effects of drugs, but the environment of the intensive care unit seems to be principally involved, with its sensory overstimulation, monotonous sounds, and lack of contact with family and familiar figures. The result is a disturbance in awareness, representing a type of delirium. Special stresses arise on such units not only for patients and families but also for physicians and nurses.

Here too ameliorative measures are available. Studies suggest that taking steps to improve the emotional climate of intensive care units could diminish stress for patients and families and reduce the incidence of the intensive care syndrome. Its management involves considerations in the treatment of delirium, which aims to prevent confusion and help the patient perceive and cling to reality. Special attention has been called to the visiting needs of patients and families. A controlled study supports the impression that not only morbidity but mortality may be reduced for patients on a coronary care unit when nurses on the unit use regular group consultation, led by a psychiatrist.

In addition to helping patients, psychosocial interventions have been effective in diminishing stress for hospital staff in intensive care units. Psychiatrists, psychiatric nurses, and other mental health professionals have used various methods to deal with the problem of staff burnout. Regular group meetings, led by a psychiatrist, with a focus on work stresses, have resulted in a remarkable drop in turnover rates of nursing staff on high-stress pediatric wards. In neonatal intensive care units, ethical and moral issues have arisen regarding the prolongation of life in badly damaged infants. Ethical guidelines and infant bioethical committees are being developed on a multidisciplinary basis, with parents beginning to participate actively in such decisions (American Academy of Pediatrics, 1984).

Outside the intensive care unit, delirium in children and adults results from infectious, toxic, traumatic, and metabolic sources; it may affect 10% to 15% of all hospitalized patients but is often unrecognized in the milder forms. As an acute brain syndrome, it is reversible with treatment of the basic cause. The resulting disturbance in awareness can have serious effects, and it demands special methods of management.

Myocardial infarction is a particularly frightening acute illness. Methods are being developed of identifying patients with myocardial infarction who are at high risk for fatal outcome, and brief individual and group psychotherapy as well as other measures have been shown in controlled studies to be of benefit, psychologically and physically, to hospitalized patients following an attack.

Estimates have been made that 6% to 12% of all children in the United States and Great Britain suffer from serious chronic illness associated with significant disability. Estimates of chronic illness and disability in adults are comparable, with some increase with age. Although some patients and families make remarkable adjustments, the stress of chronic illness has led to psychopathology in children and adults, with problems in functioning at school for many children and difficulties in vocational functioning for adults, with much economic dislocation. Depression is common in both children and adults, and attitudes of hopelessness and giving up can affect detrimentally the course of chronic illnesses, even fatal ones. Considerable stress often results for parents and siblings of child patients and for spouses and children of adult patients with chronic illness. The importance of emotional support from the patient's social network is now clear. It is certain also that activity-limiting conditions are disproportionately great among financially disadvantaged people, in large part because of limited access to health care and inability of patients to have a continuing relationship with a pediatrician or family physician.

Hospitalization tends to be longer for patients with chronic than acute illness, with greater emotional trauma involved for children, especially very young ones. There is now a trend toward shorter hospital stay, however, with the increasing use of extended care or transitional units. A movement back toward care in the community for patients with chronic illness has begun, with the development of home care programs and ambulatory care centers. Community programs, combined with home care and day-care centers, are being developed for elderly patients with chronic illness, as an alternative to nursing homes, which are often custodial. A home care program for children, in a controlled study, provided greater satisfaction for the patient and family, with less stress for the parents, than ordinary hospital care. Behavior techniques have been of value to chronically ill patients. The use of group methods of emotional support is growing, with group discussions or group therapy offered for children, parents, and adult patients. Self-help groups for patients with specific types of chronic illness are increasing.

In a recent investigation (Mumford, Schlesinger, Glass, Patrick, & Cuerdon, 1984), a metaanalysis of 58 controlled studies was carried out, together with an analysis of the claim files over a 5-year period, for a large group of federal employees with a variety of physical illnesses. The findings provided confirmation of earlier studies supporting evidence of the cost-offset effects of outpatient mental health treatment. Outpatient psychotherapy, largely of a supportive and short-term nature, was offered generally to patients who were physically sicker and had more chronic disease, and it was associated with a subsequent statistically significant reduction in the use of other medical services. Such reductions were associated largely with inpatient rather than outpatient services and tended to be larger for persons over 55 years of age. Such cost-effective use of psychotherapy is not widely practiced as yet.*

Of the three major causes of death in persons over 45 years of age, heart disease, cancer, and stroke, *cancer* is generally the most frightening. Radiotherapy and chemotherapy, however helpful, are now recognized as sources of physical and emotional stress. In a controlled study, supportive psychotherapy for patients

---

*At a time, when, as emphasized throughout this review, psychiatric and other mental health services can be shown to contribute significantly to reductions in the costs of medical and surgical care, it is ironic that reimbursements for mental health services are in danger of reduction by third party payers.

undergoing radiotherapy was found to be effective in diminishing emotional stress and some related physical symptoms, such as nausea and fatigue.

Cancer pain is a pressing problem, and today many cancer patients with pain are undertreated because of the fear of narcotic addiction. Recent studies indicate that if medication is given on a regular basis in adequate dosage to achieve pain control, these dangers do not materialize. Various psychosocial interventions, including individual or group psychotherapy, hypnosis, and relaxation techniques have been used with benefit. In a controlled study, a combination of self-hypnosis and group therapy has effectively reduced pain in women with metastatic breast carcinoma.

In the management of cancer patients, greater attention is now paid to the importance of open communication and discussion of diagnoses and prognoses for children and parents, as well as adult patients and families. The importance of support for the grieving process by patients and families is also being recognized more clearly. Home care programs for patients with terminal cancer have become available. One controlled study of parental adaptation to children's deaths at home, compared to those in the hospital, was supportive of terminal home care. Much emotional support from medical and nursing staff can be necessary. Another alternative to hospital care is the hospice program. It can be combined with home care and/or terminal care and has actually enabled more patients to die at home. A recent survey indicates that patients and families are generally quite positive and wish to have their family physicians involved with hospice programs on a cooperative and continuing basis.

In addition to traditional medical treatment, methods of group support have shown value in helping patients with chronic heart disease to lead active lives and may contribute to a reduction in mortality. Multidisciplinary rehabilitation programs for patients suffering from stroke and other chronic disorders have proven remarkably effective, with psychological measures employed as part of comprehensive care.

In recent years, Alzheimer's disease, a form of senile dementia, has been recognized more widely, with a presenile form seen at times. This is a frightening disease for patients and family, with stages progressing from forgetfulness through confusion to disorientation, with neurological complications leading to loss of control of bodily functions, deterioration, and eventual death. Nursing home care is still necessary for many such elderly patients, but recently specialized community programs, with day care and group methods of support for patient and family, have been helpful. The most frightening disease in this country is now AIDS, with community panic increasing rapidly, affecting even medical, dental, and nursing caretakers. Mental health consultation, often on a systems basis, can be helpful, and community education is vital.

Patients undergoing surgery generally have fears of bodily mutilation and of death under anesthesia, although very young children respond more keenly to the separation involved in hospitalization. Preoperative fears or negative expectations influence surgical outcome for the worse, and it has been possible, in a controlled study, to predict most of the failures (and successes) in surgery for gastric ulcer in adults. Significantly depressed or highly anxious patients or those who believe they will die have the highest mortality, especially in cardiac surgery. A controlled study, using psychological tests resulted in the prediction of 90% of the fatalities in a group of patients undergoing open-heart surgery, laying the way open to the use of psychotherapeutic intervention, which can save lives.

A special stress associated with surgery is postoperative delirium, with symptoms somewhat similar to the intensive care unit syndrome. Although drug effects and metabolic factors may be involved, the environment of the recovery room and in particular of surgical ICUs has been implicated as the principal causative factor. Older patients, patients who are depressed or anxious, and those with a previous history of postoperative delirium, organic brain syndrome, drug addiction, or alcoholism appear to be more susceptible to this disorder, as are patients with a limited command of English in American hospitals. Older patients undergoing bilateral cataract operations have a very high incidence of black patch delirium. The estimated incidence of postoperative delirium has ranged from 1% to 10%. Postoperative delirium can contribute significantly to postoperative morbidity and mortality.

The management of this syndrome involves considerations similar to those of delirium in general. Prevention of postoperative delirium has involved changes in recovery room procedure to make it less impersonal and more supportive, and its incidence has been reduced by restructuring the ICU experience. Preparation for the possibility of postoperative delirium has been helpful.

With the development of successful methods for renal transplantation, technical miracles have been possible, with significant prolongation of life. Yet new problems arise, related to the fear of rejection and the effects of immunosuppressive drugs on the body images of children, among other issues. In addition, our society has yet to face realistically that such operations—and other organ transplantations—are and will continue to be tremendously expensive. Currently a national debate is going on as to who will pay for these operations. Dramatic as they are, these heroic approaches to prolonging life in a relatively small number of individuals cut into the costs of care for millions with medical problems as yet to be treated or prevented, raising questions about ethical values (American Academy of Pediatrics, 1984). In spite of progress toward the acceptance of death, especially among the elderly, our society still has difficulty in yielding to its inevitability.

Psychosocial interventions, including psychotherapy, have been of value in dealnig with patients' emotional reactions to surgical experience, including operations with mutilating effects. In the treatment of burns, specialized techniques, such as hypnosis and behavioral techniques, have been helpful in controlling pain. Reconsideration of indications and contraindications has become possible in regard to common operations on children such as tonsillectomy and adenoidectomy, and circumcision.

Other psychosocial interventions by hospital staff, in a controlled study, have reduced postoperative pain and vomiting in a variety of surgical procedures. In a controlled investigation, supportive treatment by a psychiatrist following admission of elderly patients operated on for fractured femurs resulted in a 12-day reduction in hospital stay. Twice as many patients in the treated group returned home, rather than to an institution.

In the approach to prevention, controlled studies indicate that brief psychological preparation of children for surgery can be effective in reducing anxiety and negative emotional responses; special preparation for anesthesia showed that less anesthetic was necessary, with a greater margin of safety, and resulted in fewer postoperative complications. Overnight stay by mothers of young preschool children on surgical units has been associated, in controlled studies, with significantly less emotional disturbance for children, greater satisfaction of mothers, and quicker physical recovery from tonsillectomy and adenoidectomy. The presence of parents at the induction of anesthesia and in the recovery room has been shown to be greatly supportive to children.

Psychological preparation of adults for surgery has resulted, under controlled circumstances, in significant reduction of anxiety, diminution of necessary anesthetic and pain medication, more rapid physical recovery postoperatively, and earlier discharge. A recent review of a number of controlled studies that used hospital days postsurgery as an outcome indicator showed that, on the average, brief psychological intervention, involving information or emotional support, reduced hospitalization approximately 2 days below the control group's average length of stay. Humanity of care and diminution of stress for patients were achieved, and psychological care was cost-effective.

Alternatives to hospitalization for surgery, such as day surgery, do away with the separation from home and family so troubling to young children and, not incidentally, reduce costs.

In spite of the evidence cited in this chapter for the effectiveness of psychiatric and other mental health services in reducing the stress of acute and chronic illness, hospitalization, and surgical experience, as well as achieving cost-effectiveness, such services unfortunately are not reaching a great many patients. Although psychiatric consultation/liaison services are now available in children's hospitals and most major medical centers, and are expanding to smaller private hospitals, health maintenance organizations, and private practice, they still are seriously underutilized (Pasnau, 1987) and are difficult to maintain financially (Hales & Fink, 1982; Levitan & Kornfeld, 1981). Psychiatry must find creative solutions to this important challenge in its relationship with medicine.

It seems clear that the movement of patients away from home care to hospital care, which began with the modern scientific era of medicine and has saved many lives through technological advances, has ironically made the experience of illness more stressful for patients and families. Promising methods for prevention of deleterious emotional responses to treatment of acute illness in the hospital are becoming available, although these interventions are not yet as widely available as they should be, especially for children, who are the most vulnerable. Various psychosocial interventions have resulted in encouraging trends in the direction of shorter hospital stay for medical and surgical patients, with significant cost-effectiveness. Alternatives to hospitalization are slowly becoming available, and a movement is underway to return the care of patients, especially those with chronic illness, to the home and the community whenever feasible.

REFERENCES

Abram, H. S. (1968). The psychiatrist, the treatment of chronic renal failure, and the prolongation of life. *American Journal of Psychiatry, 124,* 1351–1358.

Abram, H. S., Moore, G. L., & Westervelt, F. B., Jr. (1971). Suicidal behavior in chronic dialysis patients. *American Journal of Psychiatry, 127,* 1199–1215.

Ack, M. (1981). Ecology of care. In P. Azarnoff & C. Hardgrove (Eds.), *The family in child health care.* New York: Wiley.

Adams, A. B. (1984). Dilemmas of hospice: A critical look at its problems. *CA—A Cancer Journal for Clinicians, 34,* 183–190.

Adams, M. A. (1978). Helping the parents of children with malignancy. *Journal of Pediatrics, 93,* 734–738.

Agle, D. P., Baum, G. L., & Chester, E. H. (1973). Multidiscipline treatment of chronic pulmonary insufficiency: I. Psychological aspects of rehabilitation. *Psychosomatic Medicine, 35,* 41–49.

American Academy of Pediatrics. (1983). *Proposed rule regarding nondiscrimination on the basis of handicap relating to health care for handicapped infants.* Evanston, IL: American Academy of Pediatrics.

American Academy of Pediatrics. (1984, July). *Policy statement on organ transplantation.* Evanston, IL: American Academy of Pediatrics.

American Cancer Society. (1981). *Cancer figures and facts.* New York: Author.

American Psychiatric Association. (1980). *Diagnostic and statistical manual of mental disorders* (3rd ed.; DSM-III). Washington, DC: Author.

Andreasen, N. J. C., Noyes, R., & Hartford, C. E. (1972). Management of emotional reactions in seriously burned adults. *New England Journal of Medicine, 286,* 65–69.

Andrew, J. M. (1976). Delay in surgery: Patients' motives. In J. G. Howells (Ed.), *Modern perspectives in the psychiatric aspects of surgery* (pp. 77–108). New York: Brunner/Mazel.

Anthony, E. J. (1970). The impact of mental and physical illness on family life. *American Journal of Psychiatry, 127,* 138–146.

Antonovsky, A. (1984). A call for a new question—salutogenesis—and a proposed answer—the sense of coherence. *Child Psychiatry and Human Development, 2,* 1–12.

Asken, M. J. (1975). Psychoemotional aspects of mastectomy: A review of recent literature. *American Journal of Psychiatry, 132,* 56–59.

Azarnoff, P. (1984a). Parents and siblings of pediatric patients. *Current Problems in Pediatrics, 14,* 3–40.

Azarnoff, P. (1984b). Preparing children for the stress of hospitalization. *Resident & Staff Physician, 30,* 56–62.

Azarnoff, P., & Flegal, S. (1975). *A pediatric play program.* Springfield, IL: Charles C. Thomas.

Azarnoff, P., & Hardgrove, C. (Eds.). (1981). *The family in child health care.* New York: Wiley.

Baekeland, F., & Lundwell, L. (1975). Dropping out of treatment: A critical review. *Psychological Bulletin, 82,* 738–754.

Barsch, R. (1968). *The parent of the handicapped child: Study of child-rearing practices.* Chicago: Charles C. Thomas.

Baudry, F. D., & Wiener, A. (1975). The surgical patient. In J. J. Strain & S. Grossman (Eds.), *Psychological care of the medically ill: A primer in liaison psychiatry* (pp. 123–138). New York: Appleton-Century-Crofts.

Beardslee, W. R., & DeMaso, D. R. (1982). Staff groups in a pediatric hospital: Content and coping. *American Journal of Orthopsychiatry, 52,* 712–718.

Belfer, M., Harrison, A., Pillemer, E., & Murray, J. (1982). Appearance and the influence of reconstructive surgery on body image. *Clinics in Plastic Surgery, 9,* 307–317.

Bergman, A. B. (1974). Psychological aspects of sudden unexpected death in infants and children. *Pediatric Clinics of North America, 21,* 115–142.

Bernstein, N. R. (1965). Observations on the use of hypnosis with burned children on a pediatric ward. *International Journal of Clinical and Experimental Hypnosis, 13,* 1–10.

Bernstein, N. R. (1976). *Emotional problems of the facially burned and disfigured.* Boston: Little, Brown.

Bernstein, N. R. (1979). The child with severe burns. In J. D. Call, J. Noshpitz, R. L. Cohen, & I. N. Berlin (Eds.), *Basic handbook of child psychiatry* (Vol. 1). New York: Basic Books.

Bernstein, N. R. (1983). Child psychiatry and burn care. *Journal of the American Academy of Child Psychiatry, 22,* 202–204.

Berseth, C. L. (1983). A neonatologist looks at the Baby Doe rule: Ethical decisions by edict. *Pediatrics, 72,* 428–429.

Bilodeau, C. P., & Hackett, T. P. (1971). Issues raised in a group setting by patients recovering from myocardial infarction. *American Journal of Psychiatry, 128,* 105–110.

Binger, C. M., Ablin, A. R., & Feuerstein, R. C. (1969). Childhood leukemia: Emotional impact on patient and family. *New England Journal of Medicine, 280,* 414–418.

Blagg, C., Hickman, R., Eshback, J., & Schribner, B. (1970). Home dialysis: Six years experience. *New England Journal of Medicine, 283,* 1126–1131.

Block, A., Boyer, S. L., & Imes, C. (1984). Personal impact of myocardial infarction: A model for coping with disability in middle age. In M. G. Eisenberg, L. C. Sutkin, & M. A. Jansen (Eds.), *Chronic illness and disability through the life span: Effects on self and families* (pp. 209–222). New York: Springer.

Bloom, J. R., Ross, R. D., & Burnell, G. M. (1978). The effect of social support on patient adjustment after breast surgery. *Patient Counseling and Health Education, 1,* 50–59.

Blum, R. (Ed.). (1984). *Chronic illness and disabilities in childhood and adolescence.* New York: Greene & Stratton.

Blumenfield, M., & Thompson, T. L., II. (1981). The psychological reactions to physical illness. In R. C. Simons (Ed.), *Understanding human behavior in health and disease* (3rd ed., pp. 48–59). Baltimore: Williams & Wilkins.

Bogdanoff, M. D. (1961). Countertransference as a source of error in medical care. In L. Linn (Ed.), *Frontiers in general hospital psychiatry*. New York: International University Press.

Boshes, B. (1961). The function of the psychiatrist in a general hospital. In L. Linn (Ed.), *Frontiers in general hospital psychiatry*. New York: International University Press.

Boston Collaborative Drug Surveillance Program. (1972). Problems and challenges. *Pediatric Clinics of North America, 19,* 117–133.

Bothe, A., & Galdston, R. (1972). The child's loss of consciousness: A psychiatric view of pediatric anesthesia. *Pediatrics, 50,* 252–263.

Bouvier, L., Atlee, E., & McVeigh, F. (1975). The elderly in America. *Population Bulletin.*

Brain, D., & Maclay, I. (1968). Controlled study of mothers and children in hospitals. *British Medical Journal, 1,* 278–280.

Breslau, N. (1985). Psychiatric disorder in children with physical disabilities. *Journal of the American Academy of Child Psychiatry, 24,* 87–94.

Breslau, N., Weitzman, M., & Messenger, K. (1981). Psychological functioning of siblings of disabled children. *Pediatrics, 67,* 344–353.

Brown, E., & Bloom, J. R. (1979). The nurse practitioner and hypertension control: A pilot study. *Evaluations of Health Professions, 1,* 87–99.

Bruhn, J. G. (1977). Effects of chronic illness on the family. *Journal of Family Practice, 4,* 1057–1060.

Bruhn, J. G., Chandler, B., & Wolf, S. (1969). A psychological study of survivors and nonsurvivors of myocardial infarction. *Psychosomatic Medicine, 31,* 8–19.

Bruhn, J. G., Thurman, A. E., Chandler, B. C., & Bruce, T. A. (1970). Patients' reactions to death in a coronary care unit. *Journal of Psychosomatic Research, 14,* 65–70.

Burke, F. (1969). The pediatric convalescence hospital: The 30 to 90 day extended care unit. *Pediatrics, 43,* 879–885.

Burne, S. R. (1984). A hospice for children in England. *Pediatrics, 73,* 97–98.

Burton, L. (Ed.). (1974). *Care of the child facing death*. London: Routledge & Kegan Paul.

Busse, E. W. (1973). Mental disorders in later life—organic brain syndromes. In E. W. Busse & E. Pfeiffer (Eds.), *Mental illness in later life*. Washington, DC: American Psychiatric Association.

Busse, E. W., & Pfeiffer, E. (Eds.). (1977). *Behavior and adaptation in later life* (2nd ed.). Boston: Little, Brown.

Cain, A. C., Fast, J., & Erickson, M. E. (1971). Children's disturbed reactions to the death of a sibling. *American Journal of Orthopsychiatry, 34,* 141–152.

Caldwell, B. S. (1981). A care-by-parent unit. In P. Azarnoff & C. Hardgrove (Eds.), *The family in child health care*. New York: Wiley.

Caplan, G. (1960). Patterns of parental response to the crisis of premature births. *Psychiatry, 23,* 365–373.

Caplan, G. (1981). Mastery of stress: Psychological aspects. *American Journal of Psychiatry, 138,* 413–420.

Caplan, G., & Killilea, M. (Eds.). (1976). *Support systems and mutual help: Multidisciplinary explorations*. New York: Grune & Stratton.

Carey, R. G. (1974). Emotional adjustment in terminal patients: A quantitative approach. *Journal of Counseling Psychology, 21,* 433–439.

Cassel, S., & Paul, M. H. (1967). The role of puppet therapy on the emotional responses of children hospitalized for cardiac catheterization. *Journal of Pediatrics, 71,* 233–241.

Cassem, N., & Hackett, T. P. (1971). Psychiatric consultation in a coronary care unit. *Annals of Internal Medicine, 75,* 9–14.

Cassem, N., & Hackett, T. P. (1972). Sources of tension for the CCU nurse. *American Journal of Nursing, 72,* 1426–1430.

Castelnuovo-Tedesco, P. (1981). Transplantation: Psychological implications of changes in body images. In N. B. Levy (Ed.), *Psychonephrology: I. Psychological factors in hemodialysis and transplantation* (pp. 219–225). New York: Plenum.

Chambers, W. M., & Reiser, M. F. (1953). Emotional stress in the precipitation of congestive heart failure. *Psychosomatic Medicine, 15,* 38–42.

Chintz, S. P. (1981). Sibling group for brothers and sisters of handicapped children. *Children Today, 10,* 21–28.

Coates, T. J., Temoshok, L., & Mandel, J. (1981). Psychosocial research is essential to understanding and treating AIDS. *American Psychologist, 39,* 1309–1312.

Cobb, S., & Lindemann, E. (1943). Neuropsychiatric observations. *Annals of Surgery, 117,* 814–823.

Cohen, M. M., & Wellisch, D. K. (1978). Living in limbo: Psychosocial intervention in families with a cancer patient. *American Journal of Psychotherapy, 32,* 561–571.

Cooke, R. E. (1967). Effects of hospitalization upon the child. In J. A. Haller, Jr. (Ed.), *The hospitalized child and his family* (pp. 3–17). Baltimore: Johns Hopkins University Press.

Corbett, J., Trimble, M. R., & Nichol, T. C. (1985). Behavioral and cognitive impairments of children with epilepsy: The long-term effects of anticonvulsant therapy. *Journal of the American Academy of Child Psychiatry, 24,* 17–23.

Craig, T. J., & Abeloff, M. D. (1974). Psychiatric symptomatology among hospitalized cancer patients. *American Journal of Psychiatry, 131,* 1323–1327.

Crain, A., Sussman, M., & Weil, W., Jr. (1966). Effects of a diabetic child on marital integration and related measures of family functioning. *Journal of Health and Human Behavior, 7,* 122–127.

Curran, W. J. (1976). The proper and improper concerns of medical law and ethics. *New England Journal of Medicine, 295,* 1057–1060.

Dalton, R. (1981). The assessment and enhancement of development of a child being raised in reverse isolation. *Journal of the American Academy of Child Psychiatry, 20,* 611–622.

Daniel, W. A., Jr., Bennett, D. L., Matzek, M. J., & Ward, M. S. (1978). Diseases of the reproductive system. In: R. A. Hoekleman, S. Blatman, P. A. Brumell, S. B. Friedman, & H. M. Seidel (Eds.), *Principles of pediatrics: Health care of the young.* New York: McGraw-Hill.

Danilowicz, D. A., & Gabriel, H. F. (1976). Responses of children to cardiac surgery. In J. G. Howells (Ed.), *Modern perspectives on the psychiatric aspects of surgery.* New York: Brunner/Mazel.

Davidson, H. (1979). Development of a bereaved parents group. In M. Lieberman & L. Borman (Eds.), *Self help groups for coping with crisis.* San Francisco: Jossey-Bass.

De-Nour, A. K. (1970). Psychotherapy with patients on chronic hemodialysis. *British Journal of Psychiatry, 116,* 207–215.

De-Nour, A. K., & Czaczkes, J. W. (1972). Personality factors in chronic dialysis patients causing non-compliance with medical regimen. *Psychosomatic Medicine, 34,* 333–344.

Derogatis, L. R., Morrow, G. R., & Fetting, J. (1983). The prevalence of psychiatric disease among cancer patients. *Journal of the American Medical Association, 249,* 751–757.

Diamond, E. F. (1981). Letter to the editor. *Pediatrics, 68,* 908.

Dilley, J. W., Ochitill, H. N., Perl, M., & Volberding, P. A. (1985). Findings in psychiatric consultations with patients with acquired immune deficiency syndrome. *American Journal of Psychiatry, 142,* 82–86.

Dimsdale, J. E., & Hackett, T. P. (1982). Effect of denial on cardiac health and psychological assessment. *American Journal of Psychiatry, 139,* 1477–1480.

Doehrman, S. R. (1977). Psychosocial aspects of recovery from coronary heart disease: A review. *Social Science and Medicine, 11,* 199–218.

Douglas, J. W. B. (1973). Early disturbing events and later enuresis. In J. Kolvin, R. C. MacKeith, & S. R. Meadow (Eds.), *Bladder control and enuresis.* London: Heinemann.

Douglas, J. W. B. (1975). Early hospital admissions and later disturbances of behavior and learning. *Developmental Medicine and Child Neurology, 17,* 456–480.

Drotar, D. (1976). Consultation in the intensive care nursing unit. *International Journal of Psychiatric Medicine, 7,* 69–81.

Drotar, D., Baskiewicz, A., Irvin, N., Kennell, J., & Klaus, M. (1975). The adaptation of parents to the birth of an infant with a congenital malformation: A hypothetical model. *Pediatrics, 56,* 710–717.

Drotar, D., Crawford, P., & Bush, M. (1984). The family context of childhood chronic illness: Implications for psychosocial intervention. In M. G. Eisenberg, L. C. Sutkin, & M. A. Jansen (Eds.), *Chronic illness and disability through the life span: Effects on self and family* (pp. 103–133). New York: Springer.

Dubin, W., & Field, H. (1979). Postcardiotomy delirium: A critical view. *Journal of Thoracic and Cardiovascular Surgery, 77,* 586–592.

Dubovsky, S. L., Getto, C. J., Gross, S. A., & Paley, J. A. (1977). Impact on nursing care and mortality: Psychiatrists on the coronary care unit. *Psychosomatics, 18,* 18–27.

Dubovsky, S. L., & Weissberg, M. P. (1982). *Clinical psychiatry in primary care* (2nd ed.). Baltimore: Williams & Wilkins.

Duff, R. S. (1979). Guidelines for deciding care of critically ill or dying patients. *Pediatrics, 64,* 17–23.

Duff, R. S. (1981). Letter to the editor. *Pediatrics, 68,* 908–909.

Duff, R. S., & Campbell, A. G. M. (1973). Moral and ethical dilemmas in the special care nursery. *New England Journal of Medicine, 289,* 890–895.

Dumas, R., & Leonard, R. (1963). The effect of nursing on the incidence of postoperative vomiting. *Nursing Research, 12,* 12–17.

Dumont, M. (1974). Self-help treatment programs. *American Journal of Psychiatry, 131,* 631–635.

Earle, E. (1979). The psychosocial effects of mutilating surgery in children and adolescents. *Psychoanalytic Study of the Child, 34,* 527–546.

Eckhardt, L. O., & Prugh, D. G. (1978). Preparing children for painful medical and surgical procedures. In E. Gellert (Ed.), *Psychosocial aspects of pediatric care.* New York: Grune & Stratton.

Edelvich, J., & Brodsky, A. (1980). *Burn-out: Stages of disillusionment in the helping professions.* New York: Human Science Press.

Editorial. (1982). Brain damage during open-heart surgery. *Thorax, 37,* 873–876.

Egbert, L. W., Battit, G. E., Welch, C. E., & Bartlett, M. K. (1964). Reduction of post-operative pain by encouragement and instruction of patients. *New England Journal of Medicine, 270,* 825–829.

Egerton, N., & Kay, J. H. (1964). Psychological disturbances associated with open heart surgery. *British Journal of Psychiatry, 110,* 433–444.

Eisenberg, M. G., Sutkin, L. C., & Jansen, M. A. (Eds.). (1984). *Chronic illness and disability through the life span.* New York: Springer.

Eisendrath, S. (1981). Psychiatric liaison support groups for general hospital staffs. *Psychosomatics, 22,* 685–694.

Emde, R. N., Harmon, R., Koenig, K., Metcalf, D., & Wagonfeld, S. (1971). Stress and neonatal sleep. *Psychosomatic Medicine, 33,* 491–506.

Engel, G. L. (1959). Psychogenic pain and the pain-prone patient. *American Journal of Medicine, 26,* 800–909.

Engel, G. L. (1960). A unified concept of health and disease. *Perspectives in Biology and Medicine, 3,* 459–472.

Engel, G. L. (1967a). A reconsideration of the role of conversion in somatic disease. *Comprehensive Psychiatry, 9,* 316–322.

Engel, G. L. (1976). Psychological factors in instantaneous cardiac death. *New England Journal of Medicine, 294,* 1165–1170.

Engel, G. L. (1977). The need for a new medical model: A challenge for biomedicine. *Science, 196,* 129–136.

Engel, G. L. (1967b). Delirium. In A. M. Freedman & H. I. Kaplan (Eds.), *Comprehensive textbook of psychiatry* (pp. 711–716). Baltimore: Williams & Wilkins.

Engel, G. L., & Romano, J. (1959). Delirium: A syndrome of cerebral deficiency. *Journal of Chronic Disease, 9,* 260–277.

Engel, G. L., & Schmale, A. (1968). A life setting conducive to illness: The giving up—given up complex. *Annals of Internal Medicine, 69,* 293–305.

Erikson, E. H. (1963). *Childhood and society.* New York: W. W. Norton.

Erikson, E. H. (1968). *Identity and crisis.* New York: W. W. Norton.

Fagin, C. M. (1966). *The effects of maternal attendance during hospitalization on the post-hospital behavior of young children: A comparative study.* Philadelphia: Davis.

Feinberg, E. A. (1985). Family stress in pediatric home care. *Caring, 4,* 38–41.

Feldman, D. J., Unterecher, J., Lloyd, K., Rush, H. A., & Toole, A. (1962). A comparison of functionally oriented medical care and formal rehabilitation in the management of patients with hemiplegia due to cerebrovascular disease. *Journal of Chronic Diseases, 15,* 297–309.

Finesilver, C. (1978). Preparation of adult patients for cardiac catheterization and coronary cineangiography. *International Journal of Nursing Studies, 15,* 211–221.

Forester, B., Kornfeld, D. S., & Fleiss, J. L. (1985). Psychotherapy during radiotherapy: Effects on emotional and physical distress. *American Journal of Psychiatry, 142,* 22–27.

Fox, R. (1959). *Experiment perilous.* Philadelphia: University of Pennsylvania Press.

Frader, J. E. (1979). Difficulties in providing intensive care. *Pediatrics, 64,* 10–16.

Frank, J. (1978). A weekly group meeting for children on a pediatric ward: Therapeutic and practical functions. *International Journal of Psychiatry in Medicine, 8,* 267–283.

Frankenburg, W. K. (1985, May). What can AAP chapters do to improve the development of children with disabilities? *American Academy of Pediatrics News.*

Freud, A. (1952). The role of bodily illness in the mental life of children. *Psychoanalytic Study of the Child, 7,* 69–81.

Freud, S. (1961). Mourning and melancholia. In J. Strachey (Ed. & Trans.), *The standard edition of the complete psychological works of Sigmund Freud* (Vol. 14). London: Hogarth Press. (Original work published 1925)

Friedman, S. B. (1974). Psychological aspects of sudden death in infants and children. *Pediatric Clinics of North America, 21,* 103–114.

Friedman, S. B., Chodoff, P., Mason, J. W., & Hamburg, D. A. (1963). Behavioral observations on parents anticipating the death of a child. *Pediatrics, 32,* 610–625.

Furman, E. (1974). *A child's parent dies: Studies in childhood bereavement.* New Haven: Yale University Press.

Gaitz, C. M., & Varner, R. V. (1980). Adjustment disorders of late life: Stress disorders. In E. W. Busse & D. V. Blager (Eds.), *Handbook of geriatric psychiatry.* New York: VanNostrand, Reinhold.

Gardner, G. G. (1976). Childhood death and human dignity: Hypnotherapy with David. *International Journal of Clinical and Experimental Hypnosis, 24,* 122–139.

Gardner, G. G., & Hinton, R. M. (1980). Hypnosis with children. In *Handbook of hypnosis and psychosomatic medicine.* New York: Elsevier/North Holland.

Garrity, T. F., & Klein, R. F. (1975). Emotional response and clinical severity as early determinants of six month mortality after myocardial infarction. *Heart and Lung, 4,* 730–737.

Garrow, D. H. (1981). Mothers in intensive care. In R. Azarnoff & C. Hardgrove (Eds.), *The family in child health care.* New York: Wiley.

Gartner, A. (1977). *Self help in the human services.* San Francisco: Jossey Press.

Geis, S., & Fuller, R. (1985). The impact of the first gay patient on hospice staff. *Hospice Journal, 1,* 17–36.

Geist, R. (1977). Consultation on a pediatric surgical ward. *American Journal of Orthopsychiatry, 47,* 432–444.

Geist, R. (1979). Onset of chronic illness in children and adolescents: Psychotherapeutic and consultative intervention. *American Journal of Orthopsychiatry, 49,* 4–23.

Gentry, W. D., Foster, S. B., & Froehling, S. (1976). Psychological response to situational stress in intensive and non-intensive nursing. *Heart and Lung, 6,* 793–796.

Goldstein, K. (1952). The effect of brain damage on the personality. *Psychiatry, 15,* 245–250.

Great Britain Ministry of Health. (1964). *Hospital building note No. 23, children's wards.* London: Her Majesty's Stationery Office.

Green, M. (1965). Integration of ambulatory services in a children's hospital: A unifying design. *American Journal of Diseases of Children, 110,* 178–191.

Green, M. (1967). Care of the dying child. In A. B. Bergman & C. J. A. Schulte (Eds.), *Care of the child with cancer. Pediatrics* (Suppl.), *40,* 312–319.

Green, M., & Solnit, A. (1964). Reactions to the threatened loss of a child: A vulnerable child syndrome. *Pediatrics, 34,* 58–67.

Green, W. (1975). Effects of brief psychotherapy during the hospitalization period on the recovery process in heart attacks. *Journal of Consulting & Clinical Psychology, 43,* 223–232.

Greene, P. E. (1984). The pivotal role of the nurse in hospice care. *CA—A Cancer Journal for Clinicians, 34,* 204–205.

Guerra, F., & Aldrete, J. A. (Eds.). (1980). *Emotional and psychological responses to anesthesia and surgery.* New York: Grune & Stratton.

Hackinski, V. C., Lassen, N. A., & Marshall, J. (1974). Multi-infarct dementia: A cause of mental deterioration in the elderly. *Lancet, 2,* 207–210.

Hackett, T. P., & Cassem, N. H. (1977). The psychology of intensive care: Problems and their management. In G. Usdin (Ed.), *Psychiatric medicine* (228–258). New York: Brunner/Mazel.

Hackett, T. P., Cassem, N. H., & Wishnie, H. A. (1968). The coronary care unit: An appraisal of its psychologic hazards. *New England Journal of Medicine, 279,* 1365–1370.

Hackett, T. P., & Weissman, A. D. (1960). Psychiatric management of operative syndromes: I. The therapeutic consultation and the effect of noninterpretative intervention. *Psychosomatic Medicine, 22,* 267–272.

Hageberg, K. (1969). Social casework and group work methods in a children's hospital. *Children, 16,* 4–23.

Haggerty, R. J. (1968). Diagnosis and treatment: Tonsils and adenoids—A problem revisited. *Pediatrics, 41,* 815–823.

Haggerty, R. J. (Ed.). (1984). Chronic disease in children. *Pediatric Clinics of North America, 31,* 1–46.

Haggerty, R. J., & Roghmann, K. L. (1972). Non-compliance and self-medication: Two neglected aspects of pediatric pharmacology. *Pediatric Clinics of North America, 19,* 101–112.

Hales, R., & Fink, P. J. (1982). A modest proposal for consultation-liaison psychiatry in the 1980's. *American Journal of Psychiatry, 139,* 1015–1021.

Hamburg, D., Hamburg, B., & DeGoza, S. (1953). Adaptive problems and mechanisms in the severely burned patient. *Psychiatry, 16,* 1–19.

Hardgrove, C. B., & Dawson, R. B. (1972). *Parents and children in the hospital: The family role in pediatrics.* Boston: Little, Brown.

Hay, D., & Oken, D. (1972). The psychological stresses of intensive care unit nursing. *Psychosomatic Medicine, 34,* 109–118.

Healy, M. H., & Hansen, H. (1977). Psychiatric management of the limb amputation in a preschool child: The illusion of "like me-not me." *Journal of the American Academy of Child Psychiatry, 16,* 684–696.

Heffron, W., Bommelaera, K., & Masters, R. (1973). Group discussions with the parents of leukemic children. *Pediatrics, 52,* 831–842.

Hilgard, J., & LeBaron, S. (1979). *Hypnotherapy of pain in children with cancer.* Los Altos, CA: William Kaufman.

Holland, J. (1977). Psychological aspects of oncology. *Medical Clinics of North America, 64,* 737–747.

Hollingsworth, C. E., & Pasnau, R. O. (Eds.). (1977). *The family in mourning. A seminar in psychiatry monograph.* (M. Greenblatt, Series Ed.). New York: Grune & Stratton.

Houts, C. B., Turbett, J. A., Arnold, L. E., & Kruse, E. (1985). Cost of medical/surgical pediatric hospital days preventable by psychiatric treatment. *Journal of the American Academy of Child Psychiatry, 24,* 227–230.

Howell, D. A. (1966). A child dies. *Journal of Pediatric Surgery, 1,* 2–7.

Howells, J. G. (Ed.). (1972). *Modern perspectives in psycho-obstetrics.* New York: Brunner/Mazel.

Howells, J. G. (Ed.). (1976). *Modern perspectives in the psychiatric aspects of surgery.* New York: Brunner/Mazel.

Hughes, M. C. (1982). Chronically ill children in groups: Recurrent issues and adaptation. *American Journal of Orthopsychiatry, 52,* 704–711.

Ibrahim, M. A., Feldman, J. G., Sultz, H. A., Staimen, M. G., Young, L. V., Dean, D. (1974). Management after myocardial infarction: A controlled trial of the effect of group psychotherapy. *International Journal of Psychological Medicine, 51,* 253–268.

Imboden, J. B., Canter, A., & Cluff, L. E. (1961). Convalescence from influenza. *Archives of Internal Medicine, 103,* 393–396.

Imboden, J. B., Cluff, L. E., & Canter, A. (1961). Brucellosis III. Psychological aspects of delayed convalescence. *Archives of Internal Medicine, 103*, 406–408.

Jackson, B. (1963). Management of the tracheostomy in cases of tetanus neonatorum treated with intermittent positive pressure respiration. *Journal of Laryngology, 77*, 541–544.

Jackson, K. (1953). Psychologic preparation as a method of reducing the emotional trauma of anesthesia in children. *Anesthesiology, 23*, 964–978.

Janis, J. L. (1958). *Psychological stress: Psychoanalytic and behavioral studies of surgical patients.* New York: Wiley.

Jessner, L. (1959). Some observations on children hospitalized during latency. In L. Jessner & E. Pavenstedt (Eds.), *Dynamic psychopathology in childhood* (pp. 257–268). New York: Green & Stratton.

Jessner, L., Blom, G. E., & Waldfogel, S. (1952). Emotional implications of tonsillectomy and adenoidectomy in children. *Psychoanalytic Study of the Child, 7*, 126–157.

Johnson, D. E., & Thompson, T. R. (1984). The "Baby Doe" rule: Is it all bad? *Pediatrics, 73*, 729–730.

Joint Commission on Mental Health of Children. (1970). *Crisis in child mental health: A challenge for the 1970's.* New York: Harper & Row.

Joneas, J. H., Delage, G., & Chad, Z. (1983). Acquired (or congenital) immunodeficiency syndrome in infants born of Haitian mothers. *New England Journal of Medicine, 308*, 843–849.

Kahana, R. J., & Bibring, G. L. (1964). Personality types in medical management. In N. E. Zimberg (Ed.), *Psychiatry and medical practice in a general hospital* (pp. 108–123). New York: International Universities Press.

Kaplan, D. M., Smith, A., Grobstein, R., & Fishman, S. (1977). Family mediation of stress. In R. H. Moss (Ed.), *Coping with physical illness* (pp. 81–96). New York: Plenum.

Karasu, T. B. (1979). Psychotherapy of the medically ill. *American Journal of Psychiatry, 136*, 1–11.

Kartha, M., & Ertel, I. (1976). Short-term group therapy of mothers of leukemic children. *Clinical Pediatrics, 15*, 803–811.

Kaufman, R. (1972). Body image changes in physically ill teenagers. *Journal of the American Academy of Child Psychiatry, 11*, 157–170.

Kavenaugh, C. (1983). Psychological intervention with the severely burned child: Report of an experimental comparison of two approaches and the effect on psychological sequelae. *Journal of the American Academy of Child Psychiatry, 22*, 145–156.

Kellerman, V. (Ed.). (1981). *Psychological aspects of childhood cancer.* Springfield: IL: Charles C. Thomas.

Kemph, J. P., Berman, E., & Coppolillo, H. P. (1969). Kidney transplants and shifts in family dynamics. *American Journal of Psychiatry, 125*, 39–51.

Kennedy, J. A., & Bakst, H. (1966). The influence of emotions on the outcome of cardiac surgery: A predictive study. *Bulletin of the New York Academy of Medicine, 42*, 811–822.

Khan, A. O., Herndon, C. H., & Ahmadian, S. Y. (1971). Social and emotional adaptations of children with transplanted kidneys and chronic hemodialysis. *American Journal of Psychiatry, 127*, 1194–1209.

Kiely, W. F. (1976). Psychiatric syndromes in critically ill patients. *Journal of the American Medical Association, 235*, 2759–2761.

Kiloh, L. G. (1961). Pseudodementia. *Acta Psychiatrica Scandinavica, 37*, 336–351.

Kilpatrick, D. G., Miller, W. C., Allain, A. M., Higgins, M. D., & Williams, L. H. (1975). The use of psychological test data to predict open heart surgery outcome: A prospective study. *Psychosomatic Medicine, 37*, 62–76.

Kimball, C. P. (1969). A predictive study of adjustment to cardiac surgery. *Journal of Thoracic and Cardiovascular Surgery, 58*, 891–902.

Kimball, C. P. (1972). The experience of open heart surgery: III. Toward a definition and understanding of post cardiotomy delirium. *Archives of General Psychiatry, 27*, 57–62.

Kimball, C. P. (1977a). Psychological responses to the experience of open heart surgery. In R. H. Moss (Ed.), *Coping with physical illness* (pp. 113–133). New York: Plenum.

Kimball, C. P. (1977b). Psychosomatic theories and their contributions to chronic illness. In G. Usdin (Ed.), *Psychiatric medicine* (pp. 259–333). New York: Brunner/Mazel.

Kinsman, R. A., Dahlem, N. W., & Spector, S. L. (1977). Observations on subjective symptomatology, coping behavior, and medical decisions in asthma. *Psychosomatic Medicine, 39*, 102–119.

Klaus, M., & Kennell, J. (1976). *Maternal-infant bonding*. St. Louis: C. V. Mosby.

Klein, R. F., Dean, A., & Willson, M. (1965). The physician and postmyocardial infarction invalidism. *Journal of the American Medical Association, 194*, 123–128.

Klein, R. F., Kliner, V. A., Zipes, D. P., Troyer, W. G., & Wallace, A. G. (1968). Transfer from a coronary care unit. *Archives of Internal Medicine, 122*, 104–108.

Knight, R. B., Atkins, A., & Eagle, C. J. (1979). Psychological stress, ego defense, and cortisol production in children hospitalized for elective surgery. *Psychosomatic Medicine, 41*, 40–51.

Knudson, A., & Natterson, J. (1960). Participation of parents in the hospital care of fatally ill children. *Pediatrics, 26*, 482–491.

Koocher, G. P., & O'Malley, J. E. (1981). *The Damocles syndrome: Psychological consequences of surviving childhood cancer*. New York: McGraw-Hill.

Koos, E. L. (1946). *Families in trouble*. New York: Kings Crown Press.

Kornblum, H., & Anderson, B. (1982). "Acceptance" reassessed—a point of view. *Child Psychiatry and Human Development, 12*, 171–178.

Kornfeld, D. S. (1971). Psychiatric problems of an intensive care unit. *Medical Clinics of North America, 55*, 1353–1363.

Kornfeld, D. S., Zimberg, S., & Malm, J. R. (1965). Psychiatric complications of open heart surgery. *New England Journal of Medicine, 272*, 273–292.

Korsch, B. M. (1968). Pediatrician-patient relations. In M. Green & R. J. Haggerty (Eds.), *Ambulatory pediatrics*. Philadelphia: W. B. Saunders.

Korsch, B. M., Fine, R., & Francis, V. (1971). Experiences with children and their families during extended hemodialysis and kidney transplantation. *Pediatric Clinics of North America, 18*, 625–651.

Korsch, B. M., Francis, V., & Fine, R. (1973). Kidney transplantation in children: Psychosocial follow-up study. *Journal of Pediatrics, 88*, 399–414.

Krant, M. J. (1978). The hospice movement. *New England Journal of Medicine, 299*, 546–549.

Krant, M. J. (1982, May). The adult with cancer: In preparation for death. *Resident & Staff Physician*, pp. 89–93.

Krystal, H. (Ed.). (1969). *Massive psychic trauma*. New York: International Universities Press.

Kübler-Ross, E. (1969). *On death and dying*. New York: Macmillan.

LaBaw, W. L. (1969). Terminal hypnosis in lieu of terminal hospitalization: An effective alternative in fortunate cases. *Gerontology Clinics, 11,* 312–324.

LaBaw, W. L. (1973). Adjunctive trance therapy with severely burned children. *International Journal of Child Psychotherapy, 2,* 80–92.

LaBaw, W. L., Holton, C., Tewell, K., & Eccles, D. (1975). The use of self-hypnosis by children with cancer. *American Journal of Clinical Hypnosis, 17,* 233–238.

Lansky, S. B. (1974). Childhood leukemia: The child psychiatrist as a member of the oncology team. *Journal of the American Academy of Child Psychiatry, 13,* 449–508.

Lansky, S. B., Cairns, N., Wehr, J., Lowman, J. T., & Hassanein, R. (1978). Childhood cancer: Parental discord and divorce. *Pediatrics, 62,* 184–188.

Lauer, M. E., & Camitta, B. M. (1980). Home care for dying children: A nursing model. *Journal of Pediatrics, 97,* 1033–1035.

Lauer, M. E., Mulhern, R. K., Wallskog, J. M., & Camitta, B. M. (1983). A comparison study of parental adaptation following a child's death at home or in the hospital. *Pediatrics, 71,* 107–112.

Lawrie, R. (1964). Operating on children as day cases. *Lancet, 2,* 1289–1292.

Lazarus, H. R., & Hagens, J. H. (1968). Prevention of psychosis following open-heart surgery. *American Journal of Psychiatry, 124,* 1190–1195.

Lazarus, R., Averill, J., & Opton E. (1974). The psychology of coping: Issues of research and assessment. In G. Coelho, D. Hamburg, & J. Adams (Eds.), *Coping and adaptation.* New York: Basic Books.

Legg, C., & Sherick, I. (1976). The replacement child: A developmental tragedy. *Child Psychiatry and Human Development, 7,* 113–122.

Leigh, H., Hofer, M. A., Cooper, J., & Reiser, M. F. (1972). A psychological comparison of patients in "open" and "closed" coronary care units. *Journal of Psychosomatic Research, 16,* 449–457.

Levine, P. M., Silberfarb, P. M., & Lipowski, Z. I. (1978). Mental disorders in cancer patients: A study of 100 psychiatric referrals. *Cancer, 42,* 1385–1391.

Levitan, S. J., & Kornfeld, D. S. (1981). Clinical and cost benefits of liaison psychiatry. *American Journal of Psychiatry, 138,* 790–793.

Levy, D. M. (1945). Psychic trauma of operations in children and a note on combat neurosis. *American Journal of Diseases of Children, 69,* 7–21.

Levy, N. B. (Ed.). (1981). *Psychonephrology: I. Psychological factors in hemodialysis and transplantation.* New York: Plenum.

Lewis, J. M. (1976, October 29). *Psychosocial aspects of heart attack.* Paper presented to the American Association of Critical Care Nurses, Beaumont, TX.

Lewis, J. M., & Beavers, W. R. (1977). The family of the patient. In G. Usdin (Ed.), *Psychiatric medicine* (pp. 401–424). New York: Brunner/Mazel.

Lewis, J. M., Beavers, W. R., Gossett, J. T., & Phillips, V. A. (1976). *No single thread: Psychological health in family systems.* New York: Brunner/Mazel.

Lindemann, E. (1944). Symptomatology and management of acute grief. *American Journal of Psychiatry, 101,* 141–152.

Linn, L. (1953). Patterns of behavior disturbance following cataract extraction. *American Journal of Psychiatry, 110,* 281–289.

Lipowski, Z. Z. (1967). Review of consultation psychiatry and psychosocial medicine: II. Clinical aspects. *Psychosomatic Medicine, 29,* 201–204.

Lipowski, Z. Z. (1980). *Delirium: Acute brain failure in man.* Springfield, IL: Charles C. Thomas.

Loomis, W. G. (1970). The management of children's emotional reactions to severe burns. *Clinical Pediatrics, 9,* 362–371.

Mace, N. L., & Rabins, P. V. (1981). *The 36-hour day.* Baltimore: Johns Hopkins University Press.

MacGregor, F. M. (1979). *After plastic surgery: Adaptation and adjustment.* New York: Holt Rinehart, & Winston.

Magrab, P. R., & Calcagno, P. L. (1978). Psychological impact of chronic pediatric conditions. In *Psychological management of pediatric problems.* Baltimore: University Park Press.

Mahaffy, P. (1965). The effects of hospitalization on children admitted for tonsillectomy and adenoidectomy. *Nursing Research, 14,* 12–19.

Malkin, S. (1975). Care of the terminally ill at home. In C. Garfield (Ed.), *Psychological care of the dying patient.* New York: McGraw-Hill.

Maloney, M. J., & Ange, C. (1982). Group consultation with highly stressed medical personnel to avoid burnout. *American Academy of Child Psychiatry, 21,* 481–485.

Marks, R. M., & Sachar, E. J. (1973). Undertreatment of medical in-patients with narcotic analgesics. *Annals of Internal Medicine, 78,* 173–184.

Marshall, R. E., & Kasman, C. (1980). Burnout in the neonatal intensive care unit. *Pediatrics, 65,* 1161–1165.

Martin, H. L., Lawrie, J. H., & Wilkinson, A. H. (1968). The family of the fatally burned child. *Lancet, 2,* 628–629.

Mason, R. C., & Smith, B. R. (1969). Physical healing related to patients' attitudes. *Journal of Religion & Health, 8,* 123–127.

Massachusetts Consumer Directory. (1982). *Children in hospitals.* Needham, MA: Author.

Mattson, A. (1972). Long-term physical illness in childhood: A challenge to psychosocial adaptation. *Pediatrics, 50,* 801–811.

May, J. G. (1972). A psychiatric study of a pediatric intensive care unit. *Clinical Pediatrics, 11,* 76–85.

Maylew, J. F. (1983). Parents in the recovery room. *Anesthesia and Analgesia, 62,* 124–126.

McKeaver, P. (1983). Siblings of chronically ill children: A literature review with implications for research and practice. *American Journal of Orthopsychiatry, 52,* 209–218.

McKegney, F. P. (1966). The intensive care syndrome. *Community Medicine, 30,* 633–636.

McKegney, F. P., & Lange, P. (1971). The decision to no longer live on chronic dialysis. *American Journal of Psychiatry, 128,* 267–278.

McLaughlin, J. F. (1981). Letter to the editor. *Pediatrics, 68,* 907–908.

Meyer, R. J., & Redmond, S. (1963). Accidental injury to the preschool child. *Journal of Pediatrics, 63,* 95–103.

Minde, K., & Maler, L. (1968). Psychiatric counselling on a pediatric medical ward: A controlled study. *Journal of Pediatrics, 72,* 452–460.

Minuchin, S. (1974). *Families and family therapy.* Cambridge, MA: Harvard University Press.

Morin, S. F., & Batchelor, W. F. (1984). Responding to the psychological crisis of AIDS. *Public Health Reports, 99,* 4–9.

Morrow, G. R., & Morrell, C. (1982). Behavioral treatment for the anticipatory nausea and vomiting induced by cancer therapy. *New England Journal of Medicine, 307,* 1476–1480.

Morse, R. M. (1976). Psychiatry and surgical delirium. In J. G. Howells (Ed.), *Modern perspectives in the psychiatric aspects of surgery.* New York: Brunner/Mazel.

Mrazek, D. A. (1984). Effects of hospitalization on early child development. In R. N. Emde

& R. J. Harmon (Eds.), *Continuities and discontinuities in development* (pp. 211–229). New York: Plenum.

Mumford, E., Schlesinger, H. J., & Glass, G. V. (1982). The effect of psychological intervention on recovery from surgery and heart attacks: An analysis of literature. *American Journal of Public Health, 72,* 141–151.

Mumford, E., Schlesinger, H. J., Glass, G. V., Patrick, C., & Cuerdon, C. (1984). A new look at evidence about reduced cost of medical utilization following mental health treatment. *American Journal of Psychiatry, 141,* 1145–1184.

Murphy, M. L. (1975). The multidiscipline team in a cancer center. *Cancer, 35,* 876–881.

Nemiah, J. C. (1961). *Foundations of psychopathology.* New York: Oxford University Press.

Nichols, S. E., & Ostrow, D. G. (Eds.). (1984). *Acquired immune deficiency syndrome.* Washington: DC: American Psychiatric Association.

Norton, J. (1963). Treatment of a dying patient. *Psychoanalytic Study of the Child, 18,* 544–559.

Noyes, R. (1981). Treatment of cancer pain. *Psychosomatic Medicine, 43,* 57–70.

Oken, D. (1961). What to tell cancer patients: A study of medical attitudes. *Journal of the American Medical Association, 175,* 1120–1128.

Oleske, J., Minnefor, A., & Cooper, R. (1983). Immune deficiency syndrome in children. *Journal of the American Medical Association, 249,* 2349–2352.

O'Malley, J., Koocher, G. P., Foster, D. J., & Slavin, L. S. (1979). Psychiatric sequelae of surviving childhood cancer. *American Journal of Orthopsychiatry, 49,* 608–616.

Ordonez-Plaza, A., Cohen, L. M., & Samora, J. (1968). Communication between physicians and patients in outpatient clinics: Social and cultural factors. *Milbank Memorial Fund Quarterly, 56,* 191–203.

Parkes, C. M. (1976). The psychological reaction to loss of a limb: The first year after amputation. In J. Howells (Ed.), *Modern perspectives in the psychiatric aspects of surgery.* New York: Brunner/Mazel.

Parsons, T., & Fox, R. (1952). Illness, therapy and the modern urban American family. *Journal of Social Issues, 8,* 31–44.

Pasnau, R. O. (1987, April). Quoted in *Psychiatric News,* p. 16.

Paton, A. (1976). The ethical objectives of surgery. In J. Howells (Ed.), *Modern perspectives in the psychiatric aspects of surgery.* New York: Brunner/Mazel.

Petrillo, M., & Sanger, S. (1972). *Emotional care of hospitalized children.* Philadelphia: Lippincott.

Pilowsky, I., Bassett, D. L., Begg, M. W., & Thomas, P. G. (1982). Childhood hospitalization and chronic intractable pain in adults. *International Journal of Psychiatry in Medicine, 12,* 75–84.

Plank, E. N. (1971). *Working with children in hospitals* (2nd ed.). Chicago: Year Book Medical Publication.

Plank, E. N., & Horwood, C. (1961). Leg amputation in a four-year old: Reactions of the child, her family, and the staff. *Psychoanalytic Study of the Child, 16,* 405–423.

Pless, I. B., & Pinkerton, P. (1975). *Chronic childhood disorder: Promoting patterns of adjustment.* Chicago: Yearbook Medical Publication.

Pless, I. B., & Roghmann, K. J. (1971). Chronic illness and its consequences: Observations based on three epidemiological surveys. *Pediatrics, 79,* 351–359.

Pless, I. B., & Satterwhite, B. (1975). Chronic illness. In R. J. Haggerty & I. B. Pless (Eds.), *Child health and the community.* New York: Wiley.

Plumb, M., & Holland, J. (1981). Comparative studies of psychological function in patients with advanced cancer: II. Interviewer-rated current and past psychological symptoms. *Psychosomatic Medicine, 43,* 243–253.

Polan, H. J., Hollerstein, D., & Amshin, J. (1985). Impact of AIDS-related cases on an inpatient therapeutic milieu. *Hospital & Community Psychiatry, 36,* 173–176.

Poteet, J. R., & Reich, P. (1981, November). Psychological management of pain in cancer patients. *Resident & Staff Physician,* pp. 99–107.

Poznanski, E. O. (1972). The "replacement child": A saga of unresolved grief. *Journal of Pediatrics, 81,* 1190–1205.

President's Commission on Mental Health. (1979). *Report.* Washington DC: Government Printing Office.

Price, D., Thaler, M., & Mason, J. (1957). Preoperative emotional states and adrenal cortical activity. *Archives of Neurological Psychiatry, 77,* 646–659.

Prugh, D. G. (1978). Why did it happen to us: A psychiatrist explores chronic childhood disability. *The American family* (Unit II, Report 4). Philadelphia: Smith, Kline & French Laboratories.

Prugh, D. G. (1983). *The psychosocial aspects of pediatrics.* Philadelphia: Lea & Febiger.

Prugh, D. G., & Eckhardt, L. O. (1980a). Stages and phases in the responses of children and adolescents to illness and injury. In B. W. Camp (Ed.), *Advances in behavioral pediatrics* (Vol. 1, Greenwich, CN: Jai Press.

Prugh, D. G., & Eckhardt, L. O. (1980b). Children's reactions to illness, hospitalization, and surgery. In H. I. Kaplan, A. Freedman, & B. J. Sadock (Eds.), *Comprehensive textbook of psychiatry* (3rd ed.; Vol. 3, pp. 2766–2774). Baltimore: Williams & Wilkins.

Prugh, D. G., & Jordan, K. (1975). Physical illness and injury: The hospital as a source of emotional disturbance in child and family. In I. Berlin (Ed.), *Advocacy for child mental health.* New York: Brunner/Mazel.

Prugh, D. G., Staub, E., Sands, H. H., Kirschbaum, R. M., & Lenihan, E. A. (1953). A study of the emotional reactions of children and families to illness and hospitalization. *American Journal of Orthopsychiatry, 23,* 78–106.

Prugh, D. G., & Taguiri, C. K. (1954). Emotional aspects of the respirator care of patients with poliomyelitis. *Psychosomatic Medicine, 16,* 104–116.

Prugh, D. G., Wagonfeld, S., Jordan, K., & Metcalf, D. (1980). A clinical study of delirium in children and adolescents. *Psychosomatic Medicine, 42* (Suppl.), 177–195.

Quinlan, D. M., Kimball, C. P., & Osborne, F. (1974). The experience of open heart surgery: IV. Assessment of disorientation and dysphoria following cardiac surgery. *Archives of General Psychiatry, 31,* 241–244.

Quinton, D. M., & Rutter, M. (1976). Early hospital admissions and later disturbances of behavior: An attempted replication of Douglas' findings. *Developmental Medicine and Child Neurology, 18,* 447–459.

Rahe, R. H., O'Neal, T., & Hagan, S. (1975). Brief group therapy following myocardial infarction: Eighteen month follow-up of a controlled trial. *International Journal of Psychiatry in Medicine, 6,* 349–358.

Rainey, L. C., Crane, L. A., Breslow, D. M., & Ganz, P. A. (1984). Cancer patients' attitudes toward hospice services. *CA—A Cancer Journal for Clinicians, 34,* 191–201.

Raphael, B. (1975). Psychiatric aspects of hysterectomy. In J. G. Howells (Ed.), *Modern perspectives in the psychiatric aspects of surgery.* New York: Brunner/Mazel.

Raskind, M. (1984). Stroke. *Medicine & Psychiatry, 2,* 5–8.

Ravenscroft, K. (1982). Psychiatric consultation to the child with acute physical trauma. *American Journal of Orthopsychiatry, 52*, 298–309.

Razin, A. M. (1982). Psychosocial intervention in coronary artery disease: A review. *Psychosomatic Medicine, 44*, 363–387.

Reinhart, J. B., & Barnes, C. (1972). Measurement and management of anxiety of children undergoing open heart surgery. *Pediatrics, 49*, 250–261.

Reiser, D. E. (1980). Reactions to illness. In D. E. Reiser & A. K. Schroder (Eds.), *Patient interviewing: The human dimension* (pp. 59–84). Baltimore: Williams & Wilkins.

Richmond, J. B. (1958). The pediatric patient in illness. In M. H. Hollander (Ed.), *Psychology of medical practice*. Philadelphia: W.B. Saunders.

Rie, H., Boverman, H., Grossman, B., & Ozoa, N. (1967). Immediate and long-term effects of interventions early in prolonged hospitalization. *Pediatrics, 41*, 755–764.

Rigg, J. R. A., Dunn, G. L., & Cameron, G. S. (1980). Pediatric outpatient surgery under general anesthesia. *Anesthesiology & Intensive Care, 8*, 451–453.

Robertson, J. (1968). *Young children in hospitals*. New York: Basic Books.

Rogentine, G. N. (1979). Psychological factors in the prognosis of malignant melanoma. *Psychosomatic Medicine, 41*, 647–655.

Rosini, L. A., Howell, M. D., Todres, J. D., & Dorman, J. (1974). Group meetings in a pediatric intensive care unit. *Pediatrics, 53*, 371–377.

Rossberg, R. H. (1961). Psychiatric aspects of a physical medicine and rehabilitation program in a general hospital. In L. Linn (Ed.), *Frontiers in general hospital psychiatry*. International Universities Press.

Rossman, I. (1954). Treatment of cancer in a home care program. *Journal of the American Medical Association, 156*, 827–830.

Rousseau, O. (1967). Mothers do help in pediatrics. *American Journal of Nursing, 67*, 798–803.

Rusk, H. (1964). *Rehabilitation medicine*. St. Louis: C. V. Mosby.

Rutter, M., Graham, P., & Yule, W. (1970). *A neuropsychiatric study in childhood*. London: Lavenham Press.

Rutter, M., Tizard, J., & Whitlemore, K. (1968). *Handicapped children: A total population prevalence study of educational, physical, and behavioral disorders*. London: Longmans.

Sabbeth, B. F., & Leventhal, J. M. (1984). Marital adjustment to chronic childhood illness: A critique of the literature. *Pediatrics, 73*, 762–767.

Satterwhite, B., Bell-Isle, J., & Conradt, B. (1978). Parent groups as an aid in mourning and grief work. In O. J. Z. Sahler (Ed.), *The child and death*. St. Louis: C. V. Mosby.

Saunders, C. M. (Ed.). (1978). *The management of terminal disease*. London: Edward Arnold.

Schafer, D. W. (1975). Hypnosis used on a burn unit. *International Journal of Clinical & Experimental Hypnosis, 28*, 1–14.

Schaffer, H. R. (1964). The too cohesive family: A form of group pathology. *International Journal of Sociology & Psychiatry, 10*, 266–275.

Schienle, D. R., & Eiler, J. M. (1984). Clinical intervention with older adults. In M. G. Eisenberg, L. C. Sutkin, & M. A. Jansen (Eds.), *Chronic illness and disability through the life span: Effects on self and family* (pp. 245-269). New York: Springer.

Schiff, H. (1977). *The bereaved parents*. New York: Crown.

Schmale, A. H., Morrow, G. R., & Schmitt, M. H. (1983). Well-being of cancer survivors. *Psychosomatic Medicine, 45*, 163–169.

Schmidt, C. (1977). Emotional stress in the NICU. *Perinatology–Neonatology, 1*, 37–46.

Schmitt, F. E., & Woolridge, P. J. (1973). Psychological preparation of surgical patients. *Nursing Research, 22*, 108–116.

Schneck, M. K., Reisberg, B., & Ferris, S. H. (1982). An overview of current concepts of Alzheimer's disease. *American Journal of Psychiatry, 139*, 165–173.

Schowalter, J. E. (1977). Psychological reactions to physical illness and hospitalization in adolescence. *Journal of the American Academy of Child Psychiatry, 16*, 500–516.

Schowalter, J. E., & Ford, R. (1970). Utilization of patient meetings on an adolescent ward. *Psychiatry in Medicine, 1*, 197–206.

Schowalter, J. E., Perhott, J. B., & Mann, M. M. (1973). The adolescent's decision to die. *Pediatrics, 51*, 97–107.

Schulman, J. L., Foley, J., & Vernon, D. (1967). A study of the effect of the mother's presence during anesthesia induction. *Pediatrics, 39*, 111–119.

Schwab, F. (1983). Sibling visiting in a neonatal intensive care unit. *Pediatrics, 71*, 835–841.

Schwartz, G. R., Buletti, J., & Hazel, B. (1974). Psychological and behavioral responses of hospital staff involved in the care of the critically ill. *Critical Care Medicine, 2*, 48–56.

Scott, D. L. (1976). Hypnosis in surgery. In J. G. Howells (Ed.), *Modern perspectives in the psychiatric aspects of surgery*. New York: Brunner/Mazel.

Seligman, R. (1972). Emotional responses of burned children in a pediatric intensive care unit. *Psychiatry in Medicine, 3*, 59–65.

Senn, M. J. E. (1945). Emotional aspects of convalescence. *Child, 10*, 24–29.

Shagass, C., & Naiman, J. (1955). The sedation threshold. *Psychosomatic Medicine, 17*, 480–489.

Shands, H. (1955). An outline of the process of recovery from severe trauma. *Archives of Neurology and Psychiatry, 13*, 403–415.

Shaw, A. (1973). Dilemmas of "informed consent" in children. *New England Journal of Medicine, 289*, 885–892.

Shore, M. F. (Ed.). (1966). *Red is the color of hurting: Planning for children in the hospital*. Bethesda, MD: National Institute of Mental Health.

Shrand, H. (1965). Behavior changes in sick children nursed at home. *Pediatrics, 36*, 604–607.

Silber, E., Bloch, D., & Perry, S. (1956). Some factors in the emotional reaction of children to disaster. *American Journal of Psychiatry, 113*, 416–423.

Silberfarb, P. M., Philibert, D., & Levine, P. M. (1978). Psychosocial aspects of neoplastic disease: Affective and cognitive effects of chemotherapy in cancer patients. *American Journal of Psychiatry, 137*, 597–601.

Siller, J. (1960). Psychological concomitants of amputation in children. *Child Development, 31*, 109–120.

Sime, A. M. (1976). Relationship of preoperative fear, type of coping and information received to recovery from surgery. *Journal of Personality and Social Psychology, 34*, 716–724.

Simmons, R. D., McFadd, A., Frank, H. A., Green, L. C., Malin, R. M., & Morris, J. L. (1978). Behavior contracting in a burn care facility. A strategy for patient participation. *Journal of Trauma, 118*, 257–260.

Simmons, R. G. (1981). Psychological reactions to giving a kidney. In N. D. Levy (Ed.), *Psychonephrology: I. Psychological factors in hemodialysis and transplantation* (pp. 227–245). New York: Plenum.

Simon, A., & Kahan, R. B. (1963). Acute brain syndromes in geriatric patients. *Psychiatric Research Reports, 6,* 8–14.

Simon, I. V., & Whiteley, S. (1977). Psychiatric consultation with NICU nurses: The consultation conference as a working group. *Heart & Lung, 6,* 497–504.

Skipper, J. K., Leonard, R. C., Rhymes, J. (1968). Child hospitalization and social interaction: An experimental study of mother's feelings of distress. *Medical Care, 6,* 496–514.

Sklar, L. S., & Anisman, H. (1981). Stress and cancer. *Psychology Bulletin, 89,* 369–406.

Slavin, L. A., O'Malley, J. E., Koocher, G. P., & Foster, D. J. (1982). Communication of the cancer diagnosis to pediatric patients: Impact on long-term adjustment. *American Journal of Psychiatry, 139,* 179–183.

Smessaert, A., Scher, C. A., & Artusio, J. F. (1960). Observations in the immediate postanesthesia period. II. Mode of recovery. *British Journal of Anesthesiology, 32,* 181–192.

Solnit, A. J., & Stark, M. H. (1961). Mourning and the birth of a defective child. *Psychoanalytic Study of the Child, 16,* 523–531.

Soloff, P. (1978). Denial and rehabilitation of the post-infarction patient. *International Journal of Psychiatry in Medicine, 8,* 125–132.

Solomon, G. F. (1969). Emotional stress, the central nervous system, and immunity. *Annals of the New York Academy of Science, 164,* 335–352.

Solomon, K. (1984). An essay on preventive geropsychiatry. *Journal of Preventive Psychiatry, 2,* 341–359.

Solomon, S. L. (1984). AIDS: Risks of transmission to medical care workers. *Journal of the American Medical Association, 251,* 397–402.

Spiegel, D., & Bloom, J. R. (1983). Group therapy and hypnosis reduce metastatic carcinoma pain. *Psychosomatic Medicine, 45,* 333–339.

Spinetta, J., & Deasy-Spinetta, P. (Eds.). (1981). *Living with childhood cancer.* St. Louis: C. V. Mosby.

Spitz, X. (1951). Hospitalism: An inquiry into the genesis of psychiatric conditions in early childhood. *Psychoanalytic Study of the Child, 2,* 313–347.

Stein, R. E. K., & Jessop, D. J. (1984). Does pediatric home care make a difference for children with chronic illness? Findings from the pediatric ambulatory care treatment study. *Pediatrics, 73,* 845–853.

Steinberg, M. D., Juliano, M. A., & Wise, L. (1985). Psychological outcome of lumpectomy versus mastectomy in the treatment of breast cancer. *American Journal of Psychiatry, 142,* 34–39.

Stocking, M., Rothney, W., Grosser, G., & Goodwin, R. (1972). Psychopathology in the pediatric hospital: Implications for community health. *American Journal of Public Health, 62,* 551–556.

Stoddard, F. (1982). Body image development in the burned child. *Journal of the American Academy of Child Psychiatry, 21,* 502–507.

Strain, J. J., & Grossman, S. (Eds.). (1975a). *Psychological care of the medically ill: A primer in liaison psychiatry.* New York: Appleton-Century-Crofts.

Strain, J. J., & Grossman, S. (Eds.). (1975b). Organic precipitants of psychological dysfunction. In J. J. Strain & S. Grossman (Eds.), *Psychological care of the medically ill: A primer in liaison psychiatry* (pp. 37–51). New York: Appleton-Century-Crofts.

Swartz, D. R. (1984). Dealing with chronic illness in childhood. *Pediatrics in Review, 6,* 67–73.

Tanguay, P. E., Shaffer, D., Hamburg, B. A., & Powell, G. (1984). Prevention and the child psychiatrist. *Journal of Preventive Psychiatry, 2,* 211–227.

Thompson, R., & Stanford, G. (1981). *Child life in hospitals: Theory and practice.* Springfield, IL: Charles C. Thomas.

Thoroughman, J. C. (1964). Psychological factors and predictive surgical success in patients with intractable peptic ulcer. *Psychosomatic Medicine, 26,* 618–629.

Tisza, V. B., Dorsett, P., & Morse, J. (1976). Psychological implications of renal transplant. *Journal of the American Academy of Child Psychiatry, 15,* 709–724.

Titchener, J. L., & Levine, M. (1960). *Surgery as a human experience: The psychodynamics of surgical practice.* New York: Oxford University Press.

Todres, I. D., Howell, M. C., & Shannon, D. C. (1974). Physicians' reactions to training in a pediatric intensive care unit. *Pediatrics, 53,* 375–383.

Toker, E. (1971). Psychiatric aspects of cardiac surgery in a child. *Journal of American Child Psychiatry, 10,* 156–173.

Tufo, H. M., & Ostfeld, A. M. (1968). A prospective study of open-heart surgery (Abstr). *Psychosomatic Medicine, 30,* 552–553.

Vance, J. C., Fazan, L. E., Satterwhite, B., & Pless, I. B. (1980). Effects of nephrotic syndrome on the family: A controlled study. *Pediatrics, 65,* 948–955.

Vaughn, G. F. (1957). Children in hospitals. *Lancet, 1,* 1117–1120.

Vernick, J. (1973). Meaningful communication with the fatally ill child. In J. Anthony & C. Koupernick (Eds.), *The child and his family: The impact of disease and death.* New York: Wiley.

Vernick, J., & Karon, M. (1965). Who's afraid of death on a leukemia ward. *American Journal of the Diseases of Children, 109,* 393–405.

Vernon, D. T. A., Foley, J. M., Sipowitz, R. R., & Schulman, J. F. (1965). *The psychological responses of children to hospitalization and illness.* Springfield, IL: Charles C. Thomas.

Vernon, D. T. A., Schulman, J. S., & Foley, J. M. (1966). Changes in children's behavior after hospitalization. *American Journal of Diseases of Children, 3,* 581–587.

Videka-Sherman, L., & Lieberman, M. (1985). The effects of self-help and psychotherapy intervention on the child loss: The limits of recovery. *American Journal of Orthopsychiatry, 55,* 70–82.

Vreeland, R., & Ellis, G. L. (1969). Stresses on the nurse in an intensive care unit. *Journal of the American Medical Association, 208,* 332–335.

Wakeman, R. J., & Kaplan, J. Z. (1978). An experimental study of hypnosis in painful burns. *American Journal of Clinical Hypnosis, 21,* 3–12.

Wallinga, J. (1982). Human ecology: Primary prevention in pediatrics. *American Journal of Orthopsychiatry, 52,* 141–145.

Weiner, H. (1977). The psychobiology of human disease: An overview. In G. Usdin (Ed.), *Psychiatric Medicine.* New York: Brunner/Mazel.

Weiner, H. (1982). The prospects for psychosomatic medicine: Selected topics. *Psychosomatic Medicine, 44,* 491–517.

Weissman, A. D. (1979). *Coping with cancer.* New York: McGraw-Hill.

Weissman, A. D., & Hackett, T. P. (1958). Psychosis after eye surgery: Establishment of a specific doctor-patient relationship in the prevention and treatment of black patch delirium. *New England Journal of Medicine, 258,* 1284–1291.

Wellisch, D., Landsverk, J., Guidera, K., Pasnau, R. B., & Fawzy, F. (1983). Evaluation of psychosocial problems of the homebound cancer patient: I. Methodology and problem frequencies. *Psychosomatic Medicine, 45,* 11–21.

Wennberg, J. E. (1977). Changes in tonsillectomy rates associated with feedback and review. *Pediatrics, 59,* 821–824.

Wessel, M. (1983). The primary physician and the death of a child in a specialized hospital setting. *Pediatrics, 71,* 443–445.

Wesseling, E. (1965). The adolescent facing amputation. *American Journal of Nursing, 65,* 90–103.

West, N. D. (1975). Stresses associated with ICU's affect patients, families, and staff. *Hospital, 49,* 62–71.

White, L. P. (1969). The self image of the physician and the care of dying patients. *Annals of the New York Academy of Science, 164,* 822–829.

Wilder, C. S. (1971). Chronic conditions and limitations of activity and mobility: United States, July 1965 to June 1967. *Vital Health Statistics* (Series 10, No. 61), Washington, DC: Department of Health, Education & Welfare.

Wilder, C. S. (1973). Limitations of activity due to chronic conditions: United States 1969–1970. *Vital and Health Statistics* (Series 10, No. 80). Washington, DC: Department of Health, Education & Welfare.

Wittkower, E. (1947). Rehabilitation of the limbless: A joint surgical and psychological study. *Occupational Medicine, 28,* 93–101.

Wolfer, J. A., & Visintainer, J. A. (1979). Prehospital psychological preparation for tonsillectomy: Effects on children's and parents' adjustments. *Pediatrics, 64,* 646–655.

Wright, G. N. (1980). *Total rehabilitation.* Boston: Little, Brown.

Yalom, I. D., & Greaves, G. (1977). Group therapy with the terminally ill. *American Journal of Psychiatry, 134,* 396–400.

Zarit, S. H., & Zarit, J. M. (1984). Psychological approaches to families of the elderly. In M. G. Eisenberg, L. C. Sutkin, & M. A. Jansen (Eds.), *Chronic illness and disability through the life span: Effects on self and family* (pp. 269–289). New York: Springer.

Zborowski, M. (1969). *People in pain.* San Francisco: Jossey-Bass.

Zeligs, R. (1974). *Children's experiences with death.* Springfield, IL: Charles C. Thomas.

Zuehlke, T. E., & Watkins, J. T. (1975). The use of psychotherapy for dying patients: An exploratory study. *Journal of Clinical Psychology, 31,* 729–741.

Illness as Stress: Accidents and Toxic Ingestions

JUSTIN O. SCHECHTER, MD
HOYLE LEIGH, MD

THE STRESS OF ILLNESS ON THE HUMAN ORGANISM

The relationship of stress to the individual is complex. A stressful event and the response of the organism to the stress form a dynamic interaction that often eludes complete and precise description. Selye (1976), a pioneer in stress concepts, defined stress as a generalized pathological response to specific noxious stimuli. Selye sees stress as a particular stimulus that disturbs an individual's physiological homeostasis. If the stress is severe enough, the psychological and physiological disturbances can become pathological.

According to Selye (1950), the primary causes of stress derive from two sources: changes in an individual's physical condition and psychological problems. The social readjustment rating scale (Holmes & Rahe, 1967) was devised more than 20 years ago in an attempt to categorize stressful events by the relative amounts of disruption they brought into the life of the individual. Of the 43 life events listed on a scale of zero to 100, personal injury or illness is scored at 53. Most of the identified stressors involves significant changes in a person's environment, and physiological changes then develop that are secondary to the enviromental or psychological stress. In the case of physical injury or illness, there exist primary environmental stress and direct physiologic changes. The individual must deal not only with the primary bodily changes but also with the secondary effects of stress.

To understand the stressful effects of a given illness on a particular individual, one must take into account the individual's cognitive appraisal of the illness and the various coping mechanisms that are called into play. In addition, illness can present in an acute, subacute, or chronic form, each of which requires different coping strategies. In the case of an accident or toxic ingestion, the sudden onset of the illness is quite distinct from the gradual progression of many other conditions such as chronic obstructive pulmonary disease or atherosclerotic cardiovascular illness. It is obvious then, that for a given illness, the repetition, duration, and pacing of the stress contribute to the type of recovery a person will have.

The reaction to a stressful event may have a number of stages that are generally applicable to most events. In his work on stress response syndromes, Horowitz (1974) describes the following stages:

> There is a common pattern to the progression of phases of stress response. With the onset of the stress event, especially if it is sudden and unanticipated, there may be emotional reactions such as crying out or a stunned uncomprehending daze. After these first emotional reactions and physical responses, there may be a period of comparative denial and numbing. Then an oscillatory period commonly emerges in which there are episodes of intrusive ideas or images, attacks of emotions, or compulsive behaviors alternating with continued denial, numbing, and other indications to ward off the implications of the new information. Finally, a phase of "working through" may occur in which there are less intrusive thoughts and less uncontrolled attacks of emotion with greater recognition, conceptualization, stability of mood, and acceptance of the meanings of the event. (p. 769)

Among the many illnesses that afflict individuals, those resulting from accidents and toxic ingestions stress the individual in a unique fashion. They occur in a situation where stress levels are already high (Stuart & Brown, 1981). The event that causes the illness is a symptom of that initial stress. Often the accident or toxic ingestion suddenly and dramatically changes the homeostatic balance and consequently requires the individual and the family to make adjustments that are rapid and of enormous degree. Because of preexisting crisis, these adjustments cause additional stress at a time when the individual and the family are already highly vulnerable.

Although sharing certain common characteristics, accidents and toxic ingestions cause significantly different psychophysiological changes. In the case of accidents, one finds significant traumatic bodily injury and physical disability, whereas ingestions can leave the individual in a state of acute and/or chronic toxicity along with many behavioral effects. Different injuries may produce substantially distinct response patterns (which will be discussed later). In both types of events, however, the spectrum of responses often includes elements of guilt, regression, and diminished self-esteem.

The following sections will present several of the statistics on the types of accidents and toxic ingestions, the causes of these events, and the various adaptive responses to the events.

ACCIDENTS

Descriptive Data

In the age group of 3 to 36 years, accidents are the leading cause of death. Although all types of accidents pervade daily life, many efforts at data collection have focused on motor vehicle and aeronautical events. Of all fatal accidents, 50% are due to automobiles (Joseph & Schwartz, 1980); thus in 1983, there were 411 fatal traffic accidents in the state of Connecticut alone (Connecticut Department of Motor Vehicles, 1984).

The causes of these accidents can be divided into three categories: environmental conditions, mechanical failure, and operator failure. The most common circumstances contributing to automobile accidents were alcohol and speeding. During the period from 1978 through 1982 in Connecticut, the 25- to 29-year age group sustained the most alcohol-related automobile fatalities. In 80% to 90% of motor vehicle accidents, driver failure has been adjudged a major factor. (McFarland & Moore, 1957). In addition to alcohol ingestion and speeding, other common contributing elements include inattention, fatigue, and failure to obey traffic regulations (Connecticut Department of Motor Vehicles, 1984). Clearly then, the state of mind of the driver has a profound impact on the probability of accidents. Rather than being the passive victim of mechanical breakdown or environmental hazard, the driver often actively increases the accident risk through using alcohol or disregarding basic traffic regulations.

The data for aeronautical accidents are similar to those compiled on motor vehicle accidents. In a review of the medical and psychiatric aspects of accident investigation, Yanowitch (1975) notes that biomedical factors account for 80% to 90%, and mechanical failures 10% to 20% of the 600 annual aircraft accidents in the United States. He furthur describes personality variables, coping abilities, and the use of drugs or alcohol as forces that significantly contribute to the biomedical risk of accidents.

Although less widely discussed, incidents in the home form an important subset of accidents; they constitute the second leading cause of accidental death and often involve children (Joseph & Schwartz, 1980). Because of their poorly developed motor skills, inexperience, and lack of awareness, children are highly susceptible to injury. In 1976, accidents were the leading cause of death in children 1 to 4 years of age (Rogers, 1981). Accidental poisonings claim the lives of approximately 500 children annually (Jones, 1969) and contribute heavily to the overall childhood accident mortality. In nonpoisoning-related incidents, lacerations and musculo-skeletal injuries are the most common. Other notable insults include animal bites and head injuries (Marshall, 1964). In the accidents involving children, age and sex are extremely important factors. In 1982 Knudson-Cooper and Leuchtag reported on a study of 330 burned children; they collected data through a series of intensive interviews with the parents of burn victims. The information included a comprehensive social history of the family, an assessment of the child's preburn adjustment, a family life change events inventory, and a detailed description of the burn accident. The authors found that 65% of those affected were boys, and 35% were girls. The age distribution showed a large peak between ages 1 and 2 years and a smaller peak between ages 8 and 10 years. The significance of this age and sex differential will be discussed in the following section.

Etiologies

To date a number of efforts to determine the primary etiologic factors in accidents have resulted in several interesting theories. The relationship between drug and alcohol ingestion and accidents is well known (Bieber, 1979; Selzer & Vinokur, 1974). The abuse of these substances represents a behavior pattern that is, in part, dependent on an individual's personality. In addition, these behaviors may occur in response to transient life stresses.

Historically, the earlier accident research had focused on the specific personality traits of individuals who were accident-prone (accident-prone personality). As early as 1919, Greenwood and Woods (1964) had noted that within a given facility, a minority of workers accounted for the majority of the factory's accidents. This phenomenon sparked the notion that a select group of workers was more likely to have accidents. The concept that certain individuals are more often victims of accidents has been confirmed by several investigators (Alexander, 1959; Dunbar, 1943). The term *accident-prone* gradually emerged to describe this finding (Holt, 1981). Although there is no consensus as to the personality type that is characteristic of accident-prone individuals, several studies have delineated a common personality style (Alkov, Borowski, & Gaynor, 1982; Conger et al., 1959; LeShan, 1952; Tillman & Hobbs, 1949). The most common characteristic is a readiness to act out emotions and feelings. LeShan's work on the dynamics of accident-prone behavior involves a study of 54 accident-prone persons and 25 controls; both groups were given a projective job application form to complete. An analysis of the data on the form showed that members of the accident-prone group shared a number of traits. They tended to have superficial ties with other human beings, manifested tension over their health and bodies, expressed aggression toward authority, and displayed poor planning for the future. Although the use of projective measures alone to identify personality variables is of questionable validity, the identified behavior patterns seemed to confirm the notion that accident-prone individuals are impulsive, activity-oriented, and characterized by low frustration tolerance. In a similar study at the University of Colorado, Conger et al. performed intensive clinical examinations of 10 high-accident and 10 nonaccident subjects. Using tape-recorded interviews, two judges rated the subjects on 13 variables ranging from "underlying hostility" and "castration anxiety" to "friendship patterns." Their results indicated that the accident subjects displayed a diminished capacity to control hostility, were self-centered, and had little ability to tolerate tension. Both LeShan and others (Freud, 1960; Hutcherson & Krueger, 1980; Tabachnick et al., 1966) have also identified the active drive for self-punishment as another common characteristic of the typical accident victim. In extreme cases, it may be difficult to differentiate accidents from suicide. In these cases, depression is often present prior to the accident and, in fact, the accident may represent a means of resolving unconscious intrapsychic conflict (Menninger, 1952). Unfortunately, the circumstances of the accident often deflect attention from the underlying psychic disturbance.

Recent identification of the effects of various life changes on individuals has shifted the emphasis in accident research from the study of the personality traits of accident-prone individuals to the relationship of transient life changes to accidents. Because of the low correlation between personality variables and the occurrence of accidents in identified populations over extended periods of time, accident probability is no longer viewed as a permanent personality characteristic (Forbes, 1939; McGuire, 1976). Studies by Forbes and McGuire have demonstrated that individuals who have a large number of accidents in a given period of time do not continue to be at the same risk during other time periods.

Attempts to correlate a variety of life changes with accidents have resulted in significant associations. Cohort studies by Padilla (1976) and Brown and Davidson (1978) have confirmed that psychosocial stress as well as family psychiatric disease are associated with increased accident rates. Across a variety of populations and accident situations, stressful events appear to be temporally related to the accident event (Holt, 1981; Selzer & Vinokur, 1974; Stuart & Brown, 1981; Whitlock, Stoll, & Reichdahl, 1977). The most potent stressors involve disruption of close personal relationships. Among children, family stress that disturbs the network of social relations in and out of the family is the major contributor to accidents (Husband, 1973; Knudson-Cooper & Leuchtag, 1982). Knudson-Cooper found that the children in her study sample had moved at approximately three times the rate of children in the general population. In male children aged 2 to 3 years the higher incidence of accidents supports the hypothesis that when stressed, action-oriented male children with impaired or developing motor skills are more likely to be accident victims. Any family relocation is likely to involve multiple adjustments including a change of schools and the need to establish new peer relations. The other family members of the studied children had to encounter new jobs and additional financial pressures as well as the need to reestablish their peer relations. Consequently, the circumstance of moving not only created stress for the individual child but threw a variety of burdens on the family unit that produced a setting ripe for the domestic accident.

In addition to general life stressors, more specific psychophysiological changes have also been correlated with accidents. In the 4-day premenstrual period and during the menses, women are at a greater risk of accidental injuries (Dalton, 1960). As discussed previously, drugs and alcohol play a particularly important psychophysiologic role since accident-prone individuals under stress often use these substances for self-medication; this results in significantly impaired motor skill and driving ability (Bieber, 1979; Finch & Smith, 1970; Selzer & Vinokur, 1974; Tabachnick et al., 1966). Among 294 adults seen on the trauma service of a large university hospital, Bieber found that greater than 20% of the treated patients had positive serum alcohol levels. When compared to the nonintoxicated group for the 5 years prior to the index visit, overall these individuals had a greater number of emergency visits, sustained more head injuries, and made greater use of all emergency services.

Selzer and Vinokur (1974) used a self-administered questionnaire to obtain data from 532 male drivers. The questionnaire consisted of a modified Holmes and Rahe life events checklist and focused on the type and number of life changes and adjustments required of these drivers in the previous 12 months. The results confirmed the notion that life changes in current stress levels may play a greater role in traffic accidents than do demographic or personality variables.

Current information in accident research points toward a theory of interaction between personality variables and recent life stresses that results in an increase in the probability of accidents for some individuals. In fact, the accident-prone persons, when stressed, are often likely to abuse substances; consequently, they have a much higher risk of being an accident victim than other individuals (Selzer & Vinokur, 1974).

Biopsychosocial Response

There is a large spectrum of responses to any given accident. Following an accidental event, individuals are often in a depressed, upset, and angry state of mind (Whitlock et al., 1977). The medical staff usually deal only superficially with the patient's frustration in response to the accident and the subsequent medical treatment; this often leaves the patient in a state of considerable conflict. Loss of control and diminished self-esteem can heap further stress on the individual (White & Edwards, 1970). Industrial accidents in particular leave a significant portion of affected workers in conflict over their feelings of passivity and dependence (Nemiah, 1963). A 1967 study of 321 disabled workers and 74 construction industry fatalities revealed that 39% of the disabled workers experienced leisure activity disturbance and disruption in their family life (Fredin, Gerdman, & Thorson, 1974).

Physical disability resulting from accidents fuels an individual's depression, frustration, and helplessness. After several weeks of hospitalization, the patient returns home to cope with what is often a grim new way of life. For example, spinal cord injury is a common occurrence in industrial and motor vehicle accidents. In a review of the syndrome, Stewart (1977) describes the impact well:

> [It] shatters the crystal of human experience in every facet. Social relationships, interpersonal dynamics, and neurological control of functions, seen and unseen, are all affected. Nothing is spared. (p. 541)

A number of coping strategies and defense mechanisms are invoked to deal with the ensuing stressful life change. Because accident victims are often action oriented, they are particularly vulnerable to the physical limitations of their disability. Among these individuals depression, denial, and anger are common findings. (Rothschild, 1970; Wright, 1960). One unfortunate consequence of the victim's resort to these mechanisms is that the medical staff will often have a great deal of difficulty extending the necessary care.

An additional variable has been identified that affects attitudes toward the disabled; it is the context within which the disability occurred (Katz, Shurka, & Florian, 1978). Disabled military veterans often receive more positive evaluations than do individuals involved in civilian accidents. Military-related disability appears to generate a more sympathetic response because war veterans enjoy high social esteem and rarely are direct participants in causing the accident.

The response of medical personnel to the accident victim forms an important component of the initial adaptation period. In the course of managing the acute crisis, medical staff can also provide the patient and his or her family with an important model for future rehabilitation. The family response will continue long after the patient is released from the hospital; it forms the most critical element in the adaptive period. In the nature of things, the sudden accident leaves little time for the family to prepare emotionally for the ensuing disability or loss. In contrast to the death of a patient following a chronic condition, accidents do not allow for any measure of anticipatory grieving, and family members often are left with feelings of guilt or culpability. In their study of 111 cases of childhood drowning and near-drowning, Nixon and Pearn (1977) found that families often undergo a pathological grief response; under such conditions, the grief is frequently suppressed, inhibited, distorted, or absent entirely. The siblings of an accident victim may manifest similar responses. Commonly, it is a sibling who has been left to watch over a younger child when the accident occurs; siblings may thus observe the accident or death and are consequently plagued with feelings of inadequacy or guilt. Of the 111 families studied by Nixon and Pearn, 19% of the parents received psychiatric treatment following the drowning of their child and 24% of the parent-dyads went on to separate. Symptoms that appeared among the parents included increased alcohol use, sleep disorders, and nightmares and anxiety states. After a child's death, a common response (which was also an additional stressor) was the tendency of the family to move from their home—ostensibly to escape from the reminder of the event. Thus, initial and long-term treatment are both necessary in order to ensure full recovery; these are important not only for the victim, but for close family members as well.

Among the often overlooked but increasingly important postaccident stressors are the many issues involving compensation and litigation. The financial stress on the individual and family results from both the high medical expenses and long-term work impairment. The procedures of compensation boards often place the victim and the family in a demeaning and passive position, thus exacerbating the initial feelings of frustration and loss of control (Naftulin, 1970). Patients who are required to undergo repeated medical and psychiatric evaluations in order to assess disability tend to feel that they must maintain symptoms until final monetary rewards are obtained (White, 1970). Consequently, the financial stressors often increase the longevity and intensity of the initial physical stressors.

TOXIC INGESTIONS

Descriptive Data

Poisoning and toxic ingestion represent a serious health problem in the United States. The 1983 Annual Report of the American Association of Poison Control Centers (AAPCC) indicates that during that year, 251,012 human poisoning exposures were reported (Veltri & Litovitz, 1983). Of these exposures 90.8% occurred in the home, with 64% of the victims being under 6 years of age. Most exposures were acute (98.6%) and involved a single substance (92.3%). The vast majority of exposures were accidental (90%); suicide attempts appeared to represent only 5.4% of the cases reported. The most common substances implicated in fatal exposures included tricyclic antidepressants, acetaminophen, ethanol, and aspirin.

Several other investigators have obtained data consistent with the recent AAPCC findings (Dale, & deFonsa, 1976; Jones, 1969; Mahdi, Ali Taha, & Al Rifai, 1983; Marshall, 1964). In the United States, between 500,000 and 2 million children ingest poisons annually. The incidence of ingestions for children aged 15 years or younger is approximately 3.5 per 1,000 per year. Household chemicals and medications are the substances most often implicated.

Adults rarely ingest poisons by accident (Bayer & Rumack, 1983; McIntire & Angle, 1971); studies show that the majority of adults who ingest poisons were under increased stress or were manifesting symptoms of depression prior to the ingestion. In a review of the literature of suicides between 1960 and 1971, Weissman concluded that 70% to 90% of suicide attempts are by drug ingestion (Weissman, 1974).

Etiologies

Like accidents, toxic ingestions tend to occur in individuals who display similar personality traits and are under heightened stress (Glass, 1973). Children most likely to ingest poisons have been described as anxious, hyperactive, and aggressive (Okasha, Osman, & Kamel, 1976; Sibert & Newcombe, 1977). As stated earlier, adults who ingest poisons have been found to be depressed; family stress preceding the ingestion is another consistent finding (Sibert, 1975). Ongoing family discord, relocation of the family home, and distant parent–child relationships contribute to diminished child supervision and increase the possibility of a child's being exposed to toxic substances.

Sobel and Margolis conducted a study of repetitive childhood poisoning. They compared three groups: 20 families of children who had poisoned themselves two or three times, 19 families of children who had a single episode of poison ingestion, and 17 families with no history of child poisoning. Among the significant findings was evidence that parents of poison repeaters were emotionally detached and sexually incompatible. In addition, families of repeated ingestors had limited social activities and poor mother–child relationships, a child who was often the result of an unplanned pregnancy, and parents who were frequently disappointed with the child's sex (Sobel & Margolis, 1965). Another complicating issue is that adults tend to respond to family and environmental stress with drug and alcohol ingestion. Although initially serving to reduce tension, when used chronically these substances may exacerbate underlying stress and impair coping ability. The result may be reduced parental supervision and a greater risk of toxic ingestion in the family.

Biopsychosocial Response

The ingestion of any substance has immediate and direct physiological effects that have an impact on behavior. Changes in performance, motor functioning, arousal, and thought processing are common. Secondary changes occur in mood, emotional reactions, and personality (Bleecker, 1984); these can leave the individual with a sense of hopelessness and depression (Cleary, 1984).

Currently, group exposure to toxic substances has become an ever-increasing threat. Toxic spills, industrial accidents, and nuclear accidents pose significant risks and heap stress on specific communities. Following the Three Mile Island nuclear incident, 1506 people living within 55 miles of the area were surveyed (Cleary, 1984). The results are contained in a report to the President's Commission; they show significant psychological distress and demoralization within the community (Dohrenwend et al., 1981). Because of the large and uncontrollable nature of the toxic accident, individual coping strategies had little effect on the overall level of distress.

Whether toxic ingestion has occurred on an individual or group level, exposed persons must deal with the initial physiological effects, which often require medical treatment or hospitalization. As noted earlier in relation to accidents, the long-term behavioral effects of the ingestion must also be addressed. Successful treatment invariably includes psychosocial counseling to prevent chronic emotional sequelae.

DISCUSSION

A review of the current literature on accidents and toxic ingestions reveals several interesting items. The magnitude of the problems and the number of individuals affected are vast. Yet, there is a striking paucity of information concerning the various response patterns of those who were victims of accidents and toxic ingestions. In fact, the majority of available data are concerned primarily with the events preceding a traumatic accident.

The early investigations were largely retrospective and relied heavily on projective tests of questionable reliability. The goal was to identify the personality factors that may predispose an individual to accidents (the accident-prone personality). The studies of accident-proneness often failed to control for exposure to dangerous situations among the studied populations and therefore contain signficant methodological flaws (Suchman & Scherzer, 1964). Not surprisingly, later studies showed a relatively poor correlation between these personality traits and the incidence of accidents. In time, there was a shift of research emphasis from personality traits to the transient life stressors preceding accidents. Using retrospective self-reports of stressors, these studies showed significant associations between the occurrence of stress and the risk for accidents. In these retrospective studies, however, when the subjects are asked about antecedent stresses following an accident, they may overreport stressors.

Response patterns to accidents and ingestions have only recently been examined and focus primarily on the victim's adaptation. Studies dealing with family response and long-term sequelae are nonexistent.

Few conditions illustrate the dynamic nature of the stress response cycle better than do accidents and toxic ingestions. It is in these particular syndromes that one can best see the interactive qualities of the individual and his or her environment. Accidents and ingestions are firmly integrated into this cycle (see Figure 5.1) and provide a unique opportunity for prevention and treatment. Rarely do accidents or ingestions arise de novo in an individual or within a family system. Rather, one can identify significant life changes or stressors that act initially to disrupt the preexisting homeostasis. These stressors can take many forms including marital discord, financial pressure, family relocation, or job stress. Not all individuals similarly stressed, however, go on to become accident victims or ingest toxic substances. Instead, victims of ingestions or accidents, rather than responding to stress with a medical illness, constitute an identifiable subset of individuals who are action-oriented, aggressive, and easily frustrated. Therefore, it is the combination of stressors plus predisposed individuals that results in the incident. After

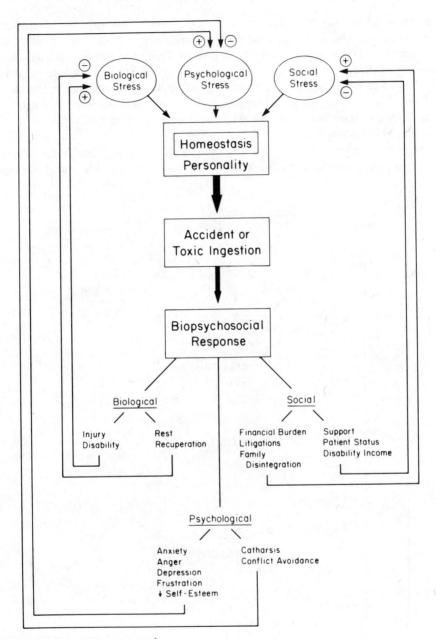

Figure 5.1 The stress response cycle.

the event the sequelae have an impact on many aspects of the individual's personal and social life. The immediate effects of physical injury and disability are followed by longer term financial and interpersonal distress. Frequently, the outcome includes periods of depression, regression, dependency, and diminished self-esteem. Following accidents or ingestions, the individual responses can ultimately take either of two distinct paths. In certain populations, for example, financial and marital difficulties with secondary alcohol abuse can form a combined stress that disrupts existing homeostasis (see Figure 5.2).

The accident that follows can leave a family or individual with depression, injury, or even greater financial burden. Often these new limitations can serve to heap

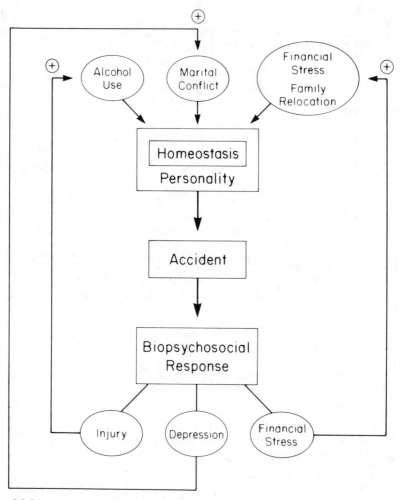

Figure 5.2 Disruption of homeostasis leading to perpetuation of stress.

further stress on an already vulnerable system. This in turn can serve as an additional stimulus that increases the likelihood of further accidents or ingestions. In contrast, and perhaps paradoxically, is the finding that accidents or ingestions may act as stress-reducing phenomena. In such cases (See Figure 5.3) an ingestion and its sequelae may provide an individual with the necessary means to reduce preexisting stress. Instead of elevated stress, victims may experience a cathartic or therapeutic effect (Newson-Smith & Hirsch, 1979). Specifically, the disabled or regressed victim may avoid further environmental stress by having the opportunity to convalesce. Ultimately, the system may be allowed to return to its previous level of homeostasis.

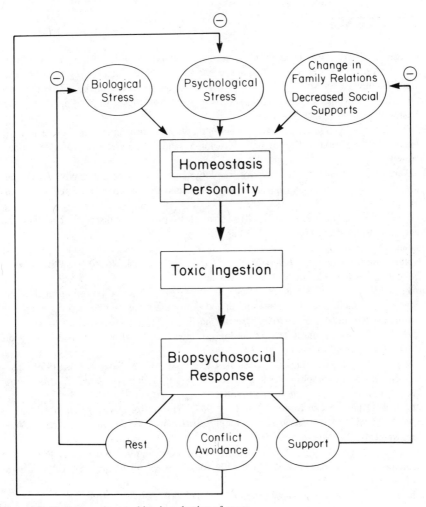

Figure 5.3 Toxic ingestion resulting in reduction of stress.

The determinants of the pathway a given individual will follow have yet to be identified, and they form an interesting topic for further investigation. Most significant, however, is the opportunity for the medical and psychiatric professions to intervene in a process that can ultimately result in stress reduction and healthy adaptation. Early identification of the at-risk population, closely combined medical and psychiatric care in the immediate postaccident/ingestion period, and ongoing psychiatric follow-up for the victim and the involved family after hospital discharge will certainly help to reduce the significant morbidity of accidents and toxic ingestions.

REFERENCES

Alexander, F. (1949). The accident prone individual. *Public Health Reports, 64,* 357–362.

Alkov, R. A., Borowsky, M. S., Gaynor, J. A. (1982). Stress and coping and the U.S. Navy Aircrew Factor Mishap. *Aviation, Space, & Environmental Medicine, 53,* 1112–1115.

Bayer, M. J., & Rumack, B. H. (1983). *Poisoning and overdose.* Rockville, MD: Aspen Systems.

Bieber, M. I. (1979). *The Relationship between alcohol and trauma* (Essay presented to the faculty of the Graduate School of Epidemiology and Public Health). Yale University, New Haven.

Bleecker, M. L. (1984). Clinical neurotoxicology: Detection of neurobehavioral and neurological impairments occuring in the workplace and the environment. *Archives of Environmental Health, 39,* 3, 213–218.

Brown, G. W., & Davidson, S. (1978). Social class, psychiatric disorder of mother and accidents to children. *Lancet, 1,* 378–381.

Calahan, D., Cisin, I. H., & Crossley, H. M. (1969). *American drinking practices: A national study of drinking behavior and attitudes* (Monograph No. 6). New Brunswick: Rutgers University Center of Alcohol Studies.

Calnan, M. W., Dale, J. W., & deFonseka, C. P. (1976). Suspected poisoning in children: Study of the incidence of true poisoning and poisoning scare in a defined population in north east Bristol. *Archives of Disease in Childhood, 51,* 180–185.

Cleary, P. D. (1984, Spring). The psychological impact of the Three Mile Island incident. *Journal of Human Stress,* pp. 28–34.

Conger, J., Gaskill, H., Glad, D., Hassell, L., Rainey, R., & Sawrcz, W. (1959). Psychological and psychophysiological factors in motor vehicle accidents. *Journal of the American Medical Association, 169,* 1581–1587.

Connecticut Department of Motor Vehicles. (1984). Traffic Records Unit, Hartford.

Dalton, K. (1960). Menstruation and accidents. *British Medical Journal, 1,* 1425–1426.

Dohrenwend, B. P., Dohrenwend, B. S., Warheit, G. J., Bartlett, G. S., Goldsteen, R. L., Goldsteen, K., & Martin, J. L. (1981). Stress in the community: A report to the President's Commission on the accident at Three Mile Island, *Annals of the New York Academy of Science,* pp. 159–174.

Dunbar, F. (1943). *Psychosomatic diagnosis.* New York: Harper & Row.

Finch, J., & Smith, J. (1970). *Psychiatric and legal aspects of automobile fatalities*. Springfield, IL: Charles C. Thomas.

Forbes, T. W. (1939). The normal automobile driver as a traffic problem. *Journal of General Psychology, 20,* 471–474.

Fredin, H., Gerdman, P., & Thorson, J. (1974). Industrial accidents in the construction industry. *Scandanavian Journal of Social Medicine, 2,* 67–77.

Freud, S. (1960). The psychopathology of everyday life. In J. Strachey (Ed. & Trans.), *Standard edition of the complete psychological works of Sigmund Freud* (Vol. 6, p. 178). London: Hogarth Press.

Glass, G. S. (1973). Psychedelic drugs, stress, and the ego. *Journal of Nervous and Mental Disease, 156,* 4, 232–241.

Greenwood, M., & Woods, H. (1964). The incidence of industrial accidents upon individuals with special reference to multiple accidents. In W. Haddon, E. Suchman, S. D. Kline (Eds.), *Accident research* (pp. 389–397). New York: Harper and Row.

Holmes, T. H., & Rahe, R. H. (1967). The social readjustment rating scale. *Journal of Psychosomatic Research, 11,* 213–218.

Holt, P. L. (1981). Stressful life events preceding road traffic accidents. *Injury, 13,* 111–115.

Horowitz, M. (1974). Stress response syndromes. *Archives of General Psychiatry, 31,* 768–781.

Husband, P. (1973). The accident-prone child. *The Practitioner, 211,* 335–344.

Hutcherson, R. R., & Krueger, D. W. (1980). Accidents masking suicide attempts. *Journal of Trauma, 20,* 800–801.

Jones, J. C. (1969). Preventing poisoning accidents in children. *Clinical Pediatrics, 8,* 484–491.

Joseph, E. D., & Schwartz, A. H. (1980). Accident proneness. In H. I. Kaplan, A. M. Freedman, & B. J. Sadock (Eds.), *Comprehensive textbook of psychiatry* (3rd ed., pp. 1953–1957). Baltimore: Williams & Wilkins.

Katz, S., Shurka, E., & Florian, V. (1978). The relationship between physical disability, social perception and psychological stress. *Scandanavian Journal of Rehabilitation Medicine, 10,* 109–113.

Knudson-Cooper, M. S., & Leuchtag, A. K. (1982, June). The stress of a family move as a precipitating factor in children's burn accidents. *Journal of Human Stress,* pp. 32–38.

LeShan, L. (1952). Dynamics in accident prone behavior. *Psychiatry, 15,* 73–80.

Mahdi, A. H., Ali Taha, S., & Al Rifai, M. R. (1983). Epidemiology of accidental home poisoning in Riyadh (Saudi Arabia). *Journal of Epidemiology and Community Health, 37,* 291–295.

Marshall, C. L. (1964). *An evaluation of the relationship between poisonings and accidents in childhood.* (Essay presented to the faculty of the Dept. of Epidemiology and Public Health) Yale University.

McFarland, R. A., & Moore, R. C. (1957). Human factors in highway safety: A review and evaluation. *New England Journal of Medicine, 256,* 792–799.

McGuire, F. L. (1976). Personality factors in highway accidents. *Human Factors, 18,* 433–442.

McIntire, M. S., & Angle, C. R. (1971). Is the poisoning accidental? An ever present question beyond the early childhood years. *Clinical Pediatrics, 10,* 414–417.

Menninger, K. A. (1936). Purposive accident as an expression of self-destructive tendencies. *International Journal of Psychoanalysis, 17,* 6–16.

Naftulin, D. H. (1970). The psychological effects of litigation on the industrially injured patients: A research plea. *Industrial Medicine, 39*(4), 26–29.

Nemiah, J. C. (1963). Psychological complications in industrial injuries. *Archives of Environmental Health, 7,* 481–486.

Newson-Smith, J. G. B., & Hirsch, S. R. (1979). Psychiatric symptoms in self-poisoning patients. *Psychological Medicine, 9,* 493–500.

Nixon, J., & Pearn, J. (1977). Emotional sequelae of parents and sibs following the drowning or near-drowning of a child. *Australian and New Zealand Journal of Psychiatry, 11,* 265–268.

Okasha, B., Bishry, Z., Osman, J. M., & Kamel, M. (1976). A psychological study of accident poisoning in Egyptian children. *British Journal of Psychiatry, 129,* 539–543.

Padilla, E. R. Rohsenow, D. J., Bergman, A. B. (1976). Predicting accident frequency in children. *Pediatrics, 58,* 223–226.

Rogers, J. (1981). Recurrent childhood poisoning as a family problem. *Journal of Family Practice, 13,* 337–340.

Rothschild, C. S. (1970). *The sociology and social psychology of disability and rehabilitation.* New York: Random House.

Selye, H. (1950). *The physiology and pathology of exposure to stress.* Montreal: *ACTA.*

Seyle, H. (1976). *The stress of life.* New York: McGraw-Hill.

Selzer, M. L., & Vinokur, A. (1974). Life events, subjective stress and traffic accidents. *American Journal of Psychiatry, 131,* 903–906.

Sibert, J. R., & Newcombe, R. G. (1977). Accidental ingestion of poisons and child personality. *Postgraduate Medical Journal, 53,* 254–256.

Sibert, R. (1975). Stress in families of children who have ingested poisons. *British Medical Journal, 3,* 87–98.

Sobel, R., & Margolis, J. A. (1965). Repetitive poisoning in children: A psychological study. *Pediatrics, 35,* 641–651.

Stewart, T. D. (1977). Spinal cord injury: A role for the psychiatrist. *American Journal of Psychiatry, 134,* 538–541.

Stuart, J. C., & Brown, B. M. (1981). The relationship of stress and coping ability to incidence of diseases and accidents. *Journal of Psychosomatic Research, 25,* 255–260.

Suchman, E., & Scherzer, A. (1964). Accident proneness, in W. Haddon, E. Suchman, & P. Kline (Eds.), *Accident Research* (p. 580). New York: Harper & Row.

Tabachnick, N., Litman, R. E., Oshman, M., Jones, W. L., Cohn, J., Kasper, A., & Moffat, J. (1966). Comparative psychiatric study of accidental suicidal death. *Archives of General Psychiatry, 14,* 60–68.

Tillman, A. W., & Hobbs, G. E. (1949). The accident prone automobile driver. *American Journal of Psychiatry, 105,* 321–331.

Veltri, J. C., & Litovitz, T. L. (1983). *1983 Annual Report of the American Association of Poison Control Centers National Data Collection System.* Washington, DC: Data Collection Committee, AAPCC.

Weissman, M. (1974). The epidemiology of suicide attempts. *Archives of General Psychiatry, 30,* 737–746.

White, R. K., & Edwards, E. T. (1970). Emotional aspects of disability. *South Medical Journal, 63,* 1304–1308.

Whitlock, F. A., Stoll, J. R., & Reichdahl, R. J. (1977). Crisis, life events and accidents, *Australian & New Zealand Journal of Psychiatry, 11,* 127.

Wright, B. A. (1960). *Physical disability: A psychological approach.* New York: Harper & Row.

Yanowitch, R. E. (1975). Medical and psychiatric aspects of accident investigation. *Aviation, Space, and Environmental Medicine, 46,* 1254–1256.

Pain as Stress: Relationships to Treatment

MARC HERTZMAN, MD

Pain may well be the most common and often the most important reported symptom of illness. Pain is described more frequently in association with mental illnesses than it is within the population at large. Despite significant advances in the effort to objectify clinical correlates of pain, patients' subjective experiences continue to be the basis for understanding and treating this condition. Given the current state of the art, this approach is likely to continue for quite some time.

Thus, both the clinical examination of patients and the more basic research on humans in this area must, perforce, rely heavily on patients' self-reports about the nature of their pain. In the last several years, a number of systematic, structured interviews and instruments have been developed to help organize and understand patients' experiences of pain. Perhaps the most widely used is the McGill Pain Questionnaire (Melzack & Torgerson, 1971). Such instruments require that subjects select, from among either statements or adjectives, the words that describe the qualities and rate the severity of the pain being experienced. Such instruments can be employed as part of a comprehensive, individual evaluation; as a means of sequential reporting of progress during the course of treatment; or for research. The intent in this chapter is not to review these instruments, but to point out their usefulness in systematizing the clinical examination.

A DEFINITION OF PAIN

An acceptable definition of pain is the following: "In some respects it is a sensation, in other respects it is an emotional-motivational phenomenon that leads to escape and avoidance behavior," (Weisenberg, 1975, p. 1009). This is a sensible, inclusive set of terms. The distinction, albeit arbitrary, between acute and chronic pain is usually made after 6 months. This cutoff has definite clinical relevance. After an extended period, pain that may have started acutely changes not only in character, but in significance. The neurophysiology of chronic pain may be different from acute pain and nociception. In the chronic situation, not only has the original stimulus long been removed, but the central modulation of pain apperceptions and certainly the patient-related behaviors will have changed significantly (Fordyce & Steger, 1979). So, too, common medications that are clearly indicated in acute pain may, over time, become relatively or absolutely contraindicated. After weeks to months of use, opioids, minor tranquilizers, and other sedatives all lose their efficacy; indeed, by the time the pain becomes chronic, they are generally working against the patient's best interests.

There have also been advances, both theoretical and practical, in the understanding of the neurological and psychological mechanisms that modulate pain perception and transmission. Perhaps the best-known theory is the Gate model, originally proposed by Melzack and Wall (1965). This has been modified over the past two decades to take into account some contradictory, as well as some supportive, evidence (Melzack, 1968). For example, evidence has recently been accumulating that there is an identifiable descending serotonergic pathway, with several centers throughout the central nervous system (CNS) that apparently serve as way stations (Basbaum & Fields, 1978).

Perhaps the most crucial element of the Gate theory is the differential timing of those modulating central efferents that impinge on peripheral reflex arcs. This threshold and, in turn, the receptivity of these tracts, can be raised and lowered. That is to say, the threshold of response to pain can vary and comes to depend on how impulses from indirect efferent pathways modify direct transmission through these major avenues. The gating stipulates that the responsiveness of the large, historically well-defined pain pathways, the spinothalamic tracts, is not a fixed quantity, but rather a variable one (Melzack & Wall, 1965). This model helps to explain how higher centers, including the cerebral cortex, can have an important bearing on how pain is felt and perceived (as well as acted upon). It is useful heuristically in talking with patients and their family members.

"Suffering" is the communication from one human being to another that she/he is in pain. The channels for conveying such information are multiple and often are most critically other than verbal: grimaces; gestures; sometimes more dramatic whole body movements; often, immobility, inaction, or the absence of everyday movements. Although such behaviors may have their origins in recognizable no-ciception, their determinants are clearly more psychological than otherwise. Students of pain problems speak of "pain-related behaviors," which is another—perhaps less judgmental—variant of suffering, a behavioral communication.

SOME EXPERIMENTAL INFERENCES ABOUT PAIN AND STRESS

The rest of this discussion will seek to describe how the relationships between pain and stress can be understood, first experimentally, and then clinically. This background will help provide a rational grounding for the psychiatric therapeutics of pain, which follow.

One may well ask what types of research, basic and clinical, might bear on the question of how stress and pain are related. An extremist position, but one which introduces perhaps a note of healthy skepticism, is that almost no experimental work can truly coincide with clinical situations. This line of argument asserts that volunteers always know that they can stop experimental pain and opt out at any point. Obviously this is different from the plight of the involuntary sufferer, especially in the case of the long-term, chronic patient. For this reason, standard paradigms of pain have severe limitations. One of the most widely used is the cold pressor test, in which continuous exposure to ice water generates a dull, aching pain. This is an example of pain that can be voluntarily terminated. In addition, the subjects—mainly paid college students—are often drawn from different populations than those that include most patients.

Although recently criticized for its insensitivity or possible cruelty, certain work in animals is relevant. The role of endogenous opioidlike peptides, especially the endorphins, has become a matter of intense speculation and their role in pain a focus of active research (Goldstein, 1976). Their effects in cerebrospinal fluid (CSF) appear to be naloxone-reversible, although recently this result has been challenged as insufficient (Gracely, Dubner, Wolskee, & Deeter, 1983). Newborn rats subjected to painful stress, either externally applied or induced through electrical stimulation in a particular brain region (the periaqueductal grey matter), develop more opiate receptors and ligands than do controls (Torda, 1978). This suggests inborn biochemical responses to pain. An older model, that of the "executive monkeys," is well known (Seligman, Maier, & Geer, 1968). In this paradigm, two monkeys are shocked jointly. Only one monkey can terminate the shock but is exposed close at hand to the communications of the other, so that it is quite likely that the executive monkey does infer its control over the shocks delivered to both. If tension and frustration over the pattern are introduced, the executive monkeys develop stress gastrointestinal ulcers at a significant rate (Maier & Jackson, 1979).

The precise physiological mechanisms that modulate pain at the level of the synapse appear quite complex. Adrenergic and especially serotonergic systems are certainly involved in the CNS. One of the best-known chemical modulators of pain neurons is Substance P, which apparently affects depolarization of K+ in peripheral nerves (Katayama & North, 1978). Its primary site of action may be on afferent axons. Hosobuchi (1981) has demonstrated differentially high Substance P levels in chronic back pain patients. They could be lowered by morphine, but this effect proved to be naloxone-reversible. Henry has proposed that either denervation supersensitivity or an overabundance of Substance P may explain the persistance of chronic pain in a number of patients (Henry, 1982).

In speaking of stress and pain, there is often a cart-and-horse problem. That is, it is difficult to know which way the arrow of causality is running: Is it mostly stress causing or augmenting pain; or, is it the reverse? To some extent, animal work can begin to address this question. For example, in a series of experiments with rats, Maier, Drugan, and Grau (1982) determined, "Thus the controllability of the shock or the availability of coping responses determined the antinociceptive reaction which followed" (p. 47). In rats who were able to control their escape from pain, less analgesia to pain occurred.

This work was one of a series of serious efforts to test and modify the "learned helplessness" hypothesis (Seligman et al., 1968). That is, organisms, including humans, conditioned initially to electric shocks that are inescapable, fail to try to escape later, in new situations, when escape is possible. Exposure to inescapable stress, but not that which is escapable, produces persistent analgesia that differs from the immediate, transient analgesic effects. The long-term analgesia appears to be opiate-induced (Maier et al., 1980).

Others have suggested that "whether stress was escapable was not a necessary feature needed to produce the antinociception. Moreover, the magnitude of the antinociception induced by stress was not enhanced in mice that had previously been exposed to stress," (Mah, Suissa, & Anisman, 1980, p. 1160). An example of a possible animal model for pain-related behavior, possibly associated with causalgia, has been proposed (Wiesenfeld & Hallin, 1980). Rats with sciatic nerve sections responded with apparent distress and unusual behaviors only when subjected to the stress of being placed in a cold environment. Neither the injury nor the stressor, cold, was sufficient in and of itself to provoke the responses. Morphine produced antinociception as well, but did not modify the escape response. As volunteer human subjects are progressively trained to anticipate noxious stimuli (in the form of electrical shocks), a number of presumably reflex "vegetative" body mechanisms increase in tone. These include heart and respiratory rates, and even certain peripheral voluntary muscular reflex arcs (Willer, 1980). In sum, although the jury is not yet in, it seems quite possible that control and helplessness/

hopelessness may prove to be basic biopsychological variables that influence the apperception of pain.

As stated earlier, relevant work on pain research has been conducted on human behavior and verbal responses to pain-related variables. For present purposes, the question is, what factors related to pain may be considered stressors? More properly in this chapter, what psychosocial stressors are at work? This discussion will include some stressors that appear to have significant impact on the processes of diagnosis and treatment.

In the realm of therapeutics, the power of suggestion has long been known to play a major role. As a factor vital to understanding pain, however, suggestion has been greatly neglected. In a study with undergraduates, Schweiger and Parducci (1981) claimed to have demonstrated that pain could be induced by informing subjects (incorrectly) that a low voltage current was being passed through the skin of their foreheads. The circumstances clearly were important to the experiment. That is, in order to convey an aura of high technology, the subjects were hooked up to an impressive and frightening array of equipment. Under the same experimental conditions, control subjects with a high frequency of headaches did not have headaches during the experiments; this further reinforced the likelihood that the results were meaningful. The authors refer to this as the "nocebo" effect, the obverse to the use of placebos in research and treatment of pain. This experiment should give workers pause when considering the efficacy of suggestive or technologically oriented pain treatments, such as hypnosis, biofeedback, and even various forms of psychotherapy. There may also be individual differences in responses to information supplied to the subjects about the painful experience. McCaul (1980) has shown that fear level can influence patterns of response, that is, for women low in fear, sensory information acts to reduce stress, but for those with much fear, information raises stress. This has potential treatment implications. In another, more limited study, Turkat and Guise (1983) demonstrated that simply by viewing a movie in which models continued or discontinued to work under certain conditions of painful exposure, naive subjects could be influenced in respect to both their responses to pain and the time that they terminated a task.

Studies of patients who present themselves for treatment of pain are quite relevant. It is well known that the occurrence and meaning of symptoms as recorded in patients may be substantially different from similar data arising in a sample of the general population (taken, say, from door-to-door surveys of symptoms). By way of analogy, psychiatric (nonpain patients) studies of depression suggest a significant frequency of early childhood loss (Roy, 1982). General population statistics do not confirm this, thus distinguishing careseekers from noncareseekers.

Sound epidemiological studies on the incidence and prevalence of pain symptomatology in the general population do not exist. It is quite likely, therefore, that knowledge about human responses to pain is distorted because patients are people who have sought out care for their pain. They may be different from other groups.

Also, healthy college student volunteers for pain experiments may differ significantly from other groups.

Leavitt, Garron, and Bieliauskas (1979) have studied the frequency of occurrence of stressful life events in low back pain. Their subjects were divided into three groups: those with documented organic pathology, those with probable findings, and those without. Each group was administered a modified McGill pain inventory (adjective/descriptor selection list) (Melzack, 1975), and the Holmes and Rahe stress scale (Holmes & Rahe, 1967). The study revealed no relationship between the occurrence of life stressors and back pain. There were, however, complex differences in sensory factors among the groups, which were not easily explainable. Strain (1979) has described a consultation model that takes pain into account as one of the reactions to chronic medical illness. He sets this in a context that considers basic threats to self-esteem and intactness, other basic fears, normal and abnormal psychological development, regression and conflict, and the correspondence among object relations and styles of doctor–patient relationships.

One might well ask what the prevalence of intercurrent psychiatric illness is among pain patients. It is well known that psychiatric patients have high rates of complaints of pain. Hence it would seem likely that pain patients would have unusually high rates of psychiatric illness. This latter point has been confirmed by Reich, Tupin, and Abramowitz (1983). On the other hand, the incidence of depression associated with patients who seek help because of their pain is more controversial. Kramlinger, Swanson, and Maruta (1983) obtained data by using Hamilton Depression rating scales, Minnesota Multiphasic Personality Inventories (MMPIs), and Shipley-Hartford IQ tests. These investigators conclude that patients in a pain program do have high rates of depression (25% "definite" and 39% "probable") but that these depressions are secondary. That is, in almost 90% of cases, with pain treatment, the conditions resolve spontaneously without resort to antidepressant medication. It has even been claimed that based on psychological testing the nature of the depression in chronic pain differs in quality compared to other (particularly psychotic) depressions (Stein, Fruchter, & Trief, 1983). The pain-related depressions were characterized by introjective or self-critical feelings of worthlessness, guilt, and self-devaluation. This stands in contrast to the anaclitic feelings of dependence, helplessness, weakness, and fear of abandonment seen in psychotic depressions. However, the use of such scales in evaluation must be tempered by caution and second thoughts. Rook, Pesch, and Keeler (1981) have suggested that the MMPI does not distinguish between pain with a documented organic basis and pain without such finding. It has also been reported that the MMPI correlates poorly with the Beck Depression Inventory (Doerfler, Tatten, & Hewett, 1983). Moreover, only the motivational-affective (feeling) dimension of the McGill Pain Questionnaire was correlated with MMPI subscales.

Cultural and ethnic influences define and color reports of pain, suffering, and pain-related behavior on the part of both patients and caretakers, including professionals. In work on ethnicity in a Boston community, Zola (1966) described differential responses to pain among indigenous groups, which to a degree, did, indeed, fit their cultural stereotypes. Zborowski (1952) has also done seminal work in this area. In a more recent example, Koopman, Eisenthal, and Stoeckle (1984) found differential age and sex responses to pain and pain reports in Italian-Americans as compared to Anglo-Americans. However, "ethnicity was not found to be significantly related to emotional distress and requests." In a review of cultural influences of nurses' attitudes toward pain (mainly through the work of Davitz and colleagues), Mason (1981) suggests that certain striking differences may be represented in varying cultural backgrounds.

As far as the implications for psychological or even psychotropic medication support are concerned, many questions remain. The importance of specific disease or syndrome entities in the presentation, evaluation, and treatment of pain appears obvious and yet, paradoxically, is not well understood. Thus, some recent workers suggest that the commonalities among disabilities, on the one hand (Stein & Jessop, 1982), and treatment approaches, on the other, are more similar than different across quite different diagnoses associated with pain (Fordyce, 1976). Most of the older literature, however, is more careful to specify the disease entities under consideration. In chronic pain programs, lumbar back disease of unknown cause is easily the most predominant, with other orthopedic illnesses composing the next largest group by far.

Most of the rest of this chapter assumes this preponderance of low back pain. However, it is necessary to recognize the special character of other diagnoses associated with pain. A common example is headache and its many subtypes. When reading about chronic pain treatment programs, it becomes important to know whether headache patients are included in outcome statistics because the treatment of headache by behavioral and other such measures is generally quite successful and can skew the data about back patients. Mersky (1982) has recently reviewed the psychiatric correlates of pain in headache. He makes the point, as have others (Hall, 1982), that so-called tension headaches cannot be demonstrated to have a clear relationship to changes in muscle tension. As contrasted to migraine, apparently this type of headache is not associated with personality type (Martin, 1978). Migraine may be associated with fairly consistent psychological test profiles, such as trait anxiety and the inhibition of expression of feelings (Ziegler, 1978; Price & Blackwell, 1980). This may, indeed, be an example of a psychosomatic profile, an unusual instance where Alexander and French's venerable hypothesis of unique personality organization being associated with specific disease type actually applies.

Although it is beyond the scope of this chapter, a number of serious theoretical models of stress have been proposed that have considerable merit (Cox, 1978). Sternbach's (1966) work has been in the forefront of attempts to operationalize conceptions of stress. In a complex set of measurements, mainly autonomic, Anderse, Stoyva, and Vaughn partially confirmed Sternbach's notions that people respond to stress in stereotypical ways. A central notion of their hypotheses was that recovery would be slow in psychosomatic patients in general; instead, the variability proved rather to be disease-specific. "The phenomenon was consistently observed in the arthritic subjects, absent in hypertensive and tension headache subjects, ambiguous for migraine subjects" (1982, p. 571).

Other examples of disease-specific studies suggest that diagnosis may have to be considered as a major variable. One example is abdominal pain, especially in children. Such pain has been observed in conjunction with stress, such as athletics (Adler, Bongar, & Katz, 1982). It has been suggested that the affected children are subject to childhood depression with great regularity and that specific family dynamics contribute to this (Hughes, 1984). On the other hand, some authors assert that with proper controls, psychological problems are not necessarily more prevalent in this group (McGrath, Goodman, Firestone, Shipman, & Peters, 1983). Christensen and Mortensen (1975) have suggested that in a significant minority of cases, when measured retrospectively with proper controls, or even prospectively, childhood symptoms of chronic abdominal pain persist into adulthood.

The family as a unit is a powerful determinant not only of how pain is experienced by the patient, but of how other family members are affected by one person's disability. Depression and other major psychiatric illnesses are common in pain patients' relatives (Shanfield, Heiman, Cope, & Jones, 1979).

Often spouses are unwittingly aggravating a pain syndrome (Fordyce, 1976). Sexual dysfunction is quite common between spouses in these families. Thus, where family members share a consensus of views about the patient's limitations, the prognosis may be poor. There is some reason to believe that families function better when they continue to be disturbed by the patient's pain, rather than when they have adjusted to it. (Block, Kremer, & Gaylor, 1980; Hertzman, et al., 1985).

In a detailed review, Beck and Siegel (1980) have explored the limitations of studies on pain, anxiety, and stress reduction in childbirth. A number of these studies are efforts at measuring treatment outcome. Katz et al. (1982) studied beta-endorphin levels in the CSF of children being treated for leukemia. Endogenous beta-endorphin is a presumptive pain marker. If it is assumed that pain makes children anxious and that they have symptoms of anxiety along with pain, their anxiety may be an indirect measure of their pain. It turned out that the levels were indeed correlated with anxiety, as rated by the children's nurses. There were also systematic age and sex differences.

In a study of adult cancer patients undergoing chemotherapy, Nerenz, Leventhal, and Love (1982) showed that chronic side effects of the treatment, especially tiredness and pain, were more likely to be correlated with a distress measure than with acute symptoms. Marbach, Richlin, and Lipton (1983) compared patients with facial pain and back pain. They found that those with back pain displayed a significant degree of depression but that this was not true for the facial pain patients, whose level of suffering was related directly to the severity of the pain. In a study of patients with Myofascial Pain Dysfunction Syndrome, Moody et al. (1981) found that the pain patients reported more pain and stress than did other dental patients but that stress and pain reports did not correlate closely with one another. Klepac, Dowling, and Hauge (1982) studied patients who avoid dentists. Within this group they found a preponderance of women, and they were able to differentiate them on the basis of neuroticism, tolerance for pain, and state anxiety. A small number of facial pain patients have been reported to respond to pain by developing a psychosis, which could be relieved by antipsychotic medication and support (Delaney, 1976).

PSYCHOPHARMACOLOGY IN CHRONIC PAIN

The majority of clinic pain patients resort to pain medications, often in great quantities, and with little rationale or consistency. This sets up a counterproductive cycle, in which the response to pain, anxiety, or sleeplessness is to take extra medication. Inadvertantly this reinforces what is sometimes termed *pain-related* or *pain behavior*. These are the visible and verbal communications by the patient to others that he or she is suffering. They include limps and antalgic gaits, grimaces, and other kinesic signals, that signal of "See how disabled I am." For this reason detoxification is usually essential. This is accomplished by placing the patient on regular, expectable, frequent doses. Once this is accomplished, gradual dosage reduction can be carried out.

After detoxification is complete, the choice of psychoactive medications should depend on the outcome of a psychiatric evaluation. Many patients are clinically depressed (Reich et al., 1983). However, in and of itself, this is not a clear indication for antidepressant medication. There is a suggestion from the Mayo Clinic group that as many as 90% or more of these depressions are secondary to chronic pain and remit when pain-specific psychosocial and other biological treatments are instituted (Kramlinger, Swanson, & Maruta, 1983). Where this fails, tricyclics are indicated. Evidence supports the proposition that when used as analgesics, the tricyclics may function by means of mechanisms other than those involved in depression. They are usually prescribed in combination cocktails and may be effective for this purpose at lower doses, typically 75 mg. daily (Pilowsky, Hallett, Bassett, Thomas, & Penhall, 1982). In the absence of a history of previous response to a specific medication or a strong history of first-degree relatives' responses, a serotonergic tricyclic is probably the best first choice, based on research studies (Smoller, personal communication, 1984).

In a small number of cases, electroconvulsive therapy (ECT) may be the treatment of choice. The indications here are basically the same as for ECT generally, a decision-making algorithm for depression. Antipsychotic medication is probably indicated for those patients who respond to pain with psychosis, or in whom withdrawal of medication leads to prolonged and unresolving psychotic symptoms (Delaney, 1976).

Antianxiety agents are relatively contraindicated. In these conditions, most anxiety is secondary to pain or to other causes. In any case, pain patients as a rule, have already tried large amounts of minor tranquilizers, alcohol, and sedatives, all of which tend to induce cross-tolerance. In fact, among clinic pain patients, a previous, prepain history of alcohol and other drug abuse and dependence is quite common.

PSYCHIATRIC MODALITIES OF TREATMENT FOR PAIN

A number of treatments are accepted as helpful for pain sufferers. Most physical treatments are beyond the scope of this chapter, but it is worthwhile to mention a few behavioral methods that make some use of ancillary bioelectronic equipment. Perhaps the first consideration is what combination of treatments is most efficacious. Little work has been completed bearing on this question, and what there is dichotomizes essentially between two poles—unimodality versus multimodality ("total push") programs. Overall, the evidence favors employing a variety of approaches simultaneously. This is not surprising, because if one approach does not work, others may. A multimodality program does not address questions of economy or efficacy and confines itself mainly to what combination works best for which patient. A variety of unimodal treatments have also apparently demonstrated efficacy.

Eclectic psychotherapy, usually dynamically oriented, is one of the most commonly employed treatments for pain symptoms, including chronic pain. Although widely accepted and practiced, its efficacy in chronic pain disorders has unfortunately not been well established. There is strong anecdotal evidence to support its use, and it should be a straightforward matter to design appropriate studies. The basic theoretical position is that if the patient can understand the psychological bases of the pain, then the pain should be alleviated.

A more firmly (but not well) established, systematic therapy for chronic pain is cognitive therapy. Cognitive therapies have the additional advantage of being relatively prescriptive. This facilitates training and provides greater reassurance that practitioners are following the guidelines for the techniques consistently. Although either may stand alone, cognitive therapy is often used in conjunction with behavioral modification. The prototypic model of behavioral modification is the University of Washington program in Seattle, described in many publications (Fordyce & Steger, 1968; Fordyce, 1976).

Although much of the literature has been generated around the management of inpatients, behavioral techniques appear to be adaptable to outpatient populations as well. The central tenet of behavioral modification is that suffering is learned behavior and can therefore be unlearned. This requires a detailed analysis of the components of the pain-related behavior. Often detoxification from very substantial quantities of pain medications is a prerequisite because they are potent reinforcers for pain-related behavior. Dysfunctional activities are carefully quantified, and a graded exercise program with positive reinforcements is then instituted.

The literature on cognitive-behavioral treatments has been reviewed critically and not entirely favorably (Lefebvre, 1979; Linton, 1982; Keefe, 1982). The reviewers do agree that notwithstanding the limitations of previous research operant conditioning does appear promising. Also, they are mildly optimistic about specific techniques, such as relaxation training. These techniques are intended in part to reduce pain but also to increase tolerable activity levels (Linton, 1982).

Turner and Chapman have compiled the several studies of the specific techniques involved in behavioral treatments, and reviewed them critically (Turner & Chapman, 1982). They are quite negative about biofeedback, doubt its efficacy, and favor relaxation, which they regard as at least as effective and more benign. They are grudgingly positive about operant conditioning, at least in selected patients; skeptical about hypnosis; and more positive about cognitive-behavioral approaches.

Acupuncture is an increasingly accepted modality of pain relief. Working with lower back and body chronic pain patients, Toomey, Chia, Mao, and Gregg (1977) compared responders and nonresponders to acupuncture. The nonresponders suffered from greater self-reported stress and were more depressed. They also reported more nonpain illness and appeared to have been sick longer. Interestingly, classical and pain-site-specific acupuncture techniques showed similar results. Travell (1983) has published a number of articles suggesting the importance of identifying and treating ''trigger points'' of pain, either with electrical stimulation or with local anesthesia. Melzack, Stillwell, & Fox (1977) found that trigger points and acupuncture points showed a significant correspondence with several techniques of stimulation.

An ever-growing list of studies of treatment outcome tends to be positive about a number of different programs. Some examples include the following: A four-week, multimodality inpatient program produced gains that were maintained from 12 months (Tyre & Anderson, 1981) to as long as 80 weeks (Newman, Seres, Yospe, & Garlington, 1978). The Washington University and the Mayo Clinic programs have each produced a series of reports indicating that some patients may benefit from multimodality, behaviorally based approaches (Fordyce, 1976; Maruta, Swanson, & Swenson, 1979). Malec, Cayner, and Hervey (1981) have pointed out that the percentage of positive results depends in part on the measures chosen. Generally, the most commonly studied variables are the amount of change in the use of pain medication; degree of alteration in activity levels; and symptom relief. The more variables are combined, the more modest are the results.

Another promising approach, generally used in conjunction with other treatment methods, is family therapy. Khatami and Rush (1982) have produced an intensive, long-term follow-up study of a small group of families. Although the patients were treated with multiple modalities, emphasis was placed on the family component, with promising results. These findings are consistent with other work, notably the review of family studies in chronic pain by Roy (1982). Interesting experimental work by Block (1981) and others (Block et al., 1980) also suggests that, albeit unwittingly, families often tend to reinforce pain behaviors. At the very least, failure to take this into account may handicap treatment unnecessarily.

The rehabilitation process in pain treatment is long and complicated. Vocational rehabilitation is an integral part of this process. Goldberg (1983) has recently reviewed the literature in this light. A number of authors have questioned the apparently negative impact of disability and compensation awards on prognosis and motivation for return to work (Carron, 1982; Hall, 1982). Some results have implied a partially successful effort to get patients into vocational rehabilitation or back to work (Gottlieb, 1977). In a Canadian study, a deliberate effort to put people back to work was built into the program. After this change was instituted, a significantly greater proportion of patients succeeded in resuming their jobs, and a number of patients sustained their gains (Catchlove & Cohen, 1982). For those who cope with stress by becoming ill, there is little research about the levels of reward or types of incentive that may modify the potential disincentives of insurance payment.

CONCLUSION

The evaluation and treatment of pain patients, especially those with chronic illnesses, require intensive examination of psychological and social processes, as well as physiology. In fact, chronic pain is a quintessential example of a condition that requires attention to multiple factors and the cooperation of many disciplines. These patients often appear with intractible symptoms, a history of multiple operations, and little previous reported success in treatment. Inevitably there is a strong temptation to refer such patients on. It is well to keep in mind that the patients themselves may have adopted an overly pessimistic view of their own decline in abilities. For example, patients' self-reports of their own activity levels may be an underestimation as compared to unobtrusive objective observations (Kremer, Block, & Gaylor, 1981). Although efficacy of treatment is not so well established as one might wish with almost any of the methods of treatment available, there is, nonetheless, a wide range of acceptable methods. That patients may fail at some is no bar to the employment of others. Clearly, combination treatments have a significantly greater chance of success than do single methods.

Thus, on the one hand, a healthy skepticism is warranted about any of the treatments in this area. On the other, clinicians are probably well advised to develop a wide-ranging knowledge of behavioral and biological methods, so that they can treat patients with those techniques that stand the best chance of helping their particular problems. The consensus in the literature is that low back pain sufferers are at once the most numerous group of pain patients, those most affected by psychosocial variables, and those most likely to be involved in litigation over compensation. However, another group of roughly equal proportion includes patients with other diagnoses in which the underlying disease itself is an important modifying variable. Psychiatric treatment is appropriate and recommended for both. Where patients cannot accept direct treatment, indirect consultation with other practitioners is still recommended.

REFERENCES

Adler, R., Bongar, B., & Katz, E. R. (1982). Psychogenic abdominal pain and parental pressure in childhood athletics. *Psychosomatics, 23*, 1185–1186.

Anderse, C. D., Stoyva, J. M., & Vaughn, L. F. (1982). A test of delayed recovery following stressful stimulation in four psychosomatic disorders. *Journal of Psychosomatic Research, 26*, 571–580.

Basbaum, A. I., & Fields, H. L. (1978). Endogenous pain control mechanisms: review and hypothesis. *Annals of Neurology, 4*, 451–462.

Beck, N. C., & Siegel, L. G. (1980). Preparation for childbirth and contemporary research on pain, anxiety, and stress reduction: A review and critique. *Psychosomatic Medicine, 42*, 429–445.

Block. A. R. (1981). An investigation of the response of the spouse to chronic pain behavior. *Psychosomatic Medicine, 5*, 415–422.

Block, A. R., Kremer, E. F., & Gaylor, M. (1980). Behavioral treatment of chronic pain: The spouse as a discriminative cue for pain behavior, *Pain, 9*, 243–252.

Carron, H. (1982). Compensation aspects of low back claims. In H. Carron & R. E. McLaughlin (Eds.), *Management of low back pain* (pp. 17–26). Littleton, MA: John Wright-PSG.

Catchlove, R., & Cohen, K. (1982). Effects of a directive return to work approach in the treatment of workman's compensation patients with chronic pain. *Pain, 14*, 181–191.

Christensen, M. F., & Mortensen, O. (1975). Long-term prognosis in children with recurrent abdominal pain. *Archives of Disease in Children, 50*, 110–114.

Cinciripini, P. M., & Floreen, A. (1982). An evaluation of a behavioral program for chronic pain. *Journal of Behavioral Medicine, 5*, 375–389.

Cox, T. (1978). *Stress*. Baltimore: University Park Press.

Delaney, J. F. (1976). Atypical facial pain as a defense against psychosis. *American Journal of Psychiatry, 133*, 1151–1154.

Doerfler, L. A., Tatten, H. A., & Hewett, J. E. (1983). Psychological factors that influence self-reported pain. *Journal of Clinical Psychology, 39*, 22–25.

Fordyce, W. E. (1976). *Behavioral methods for chronic pain and illness*. St. Louis: C. V. Mosby.

Fordyce, W. E., & Steger, J. C. (1979). Chronic pain. In O. F. Pamerleau & J. P. Brady (Eds.), *Behavioral medicine: Theory and practice*. Baltimore: Williams & Wilkins.

Goldberg, R. T. (1983). The social and vocational rehabilitation of persons with chronic pain: A critical evaluation. *Rehabilitation Literature, 43*, 274–283.

Goldstein, A. (1976). Opioid peptides (endorphins) in pituitary and brain. *Science, 193*, 1081–1086.

Gottlieb, H. (1977). Comprehensive rehabilitation of patients having chronic low back pain. *Archives of Physical Medicine & Rehabilitation, 58*, 101–108.

Gracely, R. H., Dubner, R., Wolskee, P. J., & Deeter, W. R. (1983). Placebo and naloxone can alter post-surgical pain by separate mechanisms. *Nature, 306,* 264–265.

Hall, W. (1982). Psychological approaches to the evaluation of chronic pain patients. *Australian & New Zealand Journal of Psychiatry, 16,* 3–9.

Henry, J. L. (1982). Relation of Substance P to pain transmission: Neurophysiological evidence. In R. Porter & M. O'Connor (Eds.), *Substance P in the nervous system.* London: Pitman Books.

Hertzman, M., Williams, J., Sigafoos, A., Hendren, R., Gaarder, K. L., Garfield, R., & Jenkins, R. L. (1985). *The family in chronic pain.* Manuscript submitted for publication, available from authors.

Holmes, T. H. & Rahe, R. H. (1967). The social adjustment rating scale. *Journal of Psychosomatic Research, 11,* 213–218.

Hosobuchi, Y. (1981). Elevated CSF level of substance P in arachnoiditis is reduced by systemic administration of morphine. *Pain Supplement: 257,* 82.

Hughes, M. C. (1984). Recurrent abdominal pain and childhood depression: Clinical observations of 23 children and their families. *American Journal of Orthopsychiatry, 54,* 146–155.

Katayama, Y., & North, R. A. (1978). Does substance P mediate slow synaptic excitation with the myenteric plexus? *Nature, 274,* 387–388.

Katz, E. R., Sharp, B., Kellerman, J., Marston, A. R., Hershman, J. M., & Siegel, S. E. (1982). B-endorphin immunoreactivity and acute behavioral distress in children with leukemia. *Journal of Nervous and Mental Disease, 170,* 72–77.

Keefe, F. J. (1982). Behavioral assessment and treatment of chronic pain: Current status and future directions. *Journal of Consulting and Clinical Psychology, 50,* 896–911.

Khatami, M., & Rush, A. J. (1982). A one-year follow-up of the multi-model treatment for chronic pain. *Pain, 14,* 45–52.

Klepac, R. K., Dowling, J., & Hauge, G. (1982). Characteristics of clients seeking therapy for reduction of dental avoidance: Reactions to pain. *Journal of Behavioral Therapy and Experimental Psychiatry, 13,* 293–300.

Koopman, C., Eisenthal, S., Stoeckle, J. D. (1984). Ethnicity in the reported pain, emotional distress and requests of medical outpatients. *Social Science in Medicine, 18,* 487–490.

Kramlinger, K. G., Swanson, S. W., & Maruta, T. (1983). Are patients with chronic pain depressed? *American Journal of Psychiatry, 140,* 747–749.

Kremer, E. F., Block, A. B., & Gaylor, M. S. (1981). Behavioral approaches to treatment of chronic pain: The inaccuracy of patient self-report measures. *Archives of Physical Medicine & Rehabilitation, 62,* 188–191.

Leavitt, F., Garron, D. C., & Bieliauskas, L. A. (1979). Stressing life events and the experiences of low back pain. *Journal of Psychosomatic Research, 23,* 49–53.

Lefebvre, R. C. (1979). Cognition and the disease process: Genesis, maintenance and treatments. *General Hospital Psychiatry, 1,* 330–337.

Linton, S. J. (1982). A critical review of behavioral treatments for chronic benign pain other than headache. *Journal of Clinical Psychology, 21,* 321–337.

Maier, S. F., Davies, S., Grau, J. W., Jackson, R. L., Morrison, D. H., Moye, T., Madden, J., & Barchas, J. D. (1980). Opiate antagonists and long-term analgesic reaction induced by inescapable shock in rats. *Journal of Comparative Physiology of Psychology, 94,* 1172–1183.

Maier, S. F., Drugan, R. C., & Grau, J. W. (1982). Controlability coping behaviors, and stress-induced analgesia in the rat. *Pain, 12*, 47–56.

Maier, S. F., & Jackson, R. L. (1979). Learned helplessness. All of us were right (and wrong): Inescapable shock has multiple effects. In G. Bower (Ed.), *The phsychology of learning and motivation* (Vol. 13, pp. 155–218). New York: Academic Press.

Mah, C., Suissa, A., & Anisman, H. (1980). Dissociation of antinociception and escape deficits induced by stress in mice. *Journal of Comparative and Physiological Psychology, 94*, 1160–1171.

Malec, J., Cayner, J. J., & Hervey, R. F. (1981). Pain management: Long-term followup of an inpatient program. *Archives of Physical Medicine & Rehabiliation, 62*, 369–372.

Marbach, J. J., Richlin, D. M., & Lipton, J. A. (1983). Illness behavior, depression and anhedonia in myofascial face and back pain patients. *Psychotherapy and Psychosomatics, 39*, 47–54.

Martin, M. J. (1978). Psychogenic factors in headache. *Medical Clinics of North America, 62*, 559–570.

Maruta, T., Swanson, D. W., & Swenson, W. M. (1979). Chronic pain: Which patients may a pain-management program help? *Pain, 7*, 321–329.

Mason, D. J. (1981). An investigation of the influences of selected factors on nurses' inferences of patient suffering. *International Journal of Nursing Studies, 18*, 251–259.

McCaul, K. D. (1980). Sensory information, fear level, and reactions to pain. *Journal of Personality, 48*, 494–504.

McGrath, P. J., Goodman, J. T., Firestone, P., Shipman, R., & Peters, S. (1983). Recurrent abdominal pain: A psychogenic disorder? *Archives of Disease in Childhood, 58*, 888–890.

Melzack, R. (1968). Pain. In D. L. Sills (Ed.), *International encyclopedia of the social sciences* (Vol. 2). New York: Macmillan.

Melzack, R. (1975). The McGill Questionnaire: Major properties and scoring methods. *Pain, 1*, 277–299.

Melzack, R., Stillwell, D. M., & Fox, E. J. (1977). Trigger points and acupuncture points for pain: Correlations and implications. *Pain, 3*, 2–23.

Melzack, R., & Torgerson, W. S. (1971). On the language of pain. *Anesthaesiology, 34*, 50–59.

Melzack, R., & Wall, P. D. (1965). Pain mechanisms: A theory. *Science, 150*, 971–979.

Mersky, H. (1982). Pain and emotion: Their correlation in headache. In M. Critchley (Ed.) *Advances in Neurology*. New York: Raven Press.

Moody, P. M., Calhoun, T. C., Okeson, J. P., & Kemper, J. T. (1981). Stress-pain relationships in MPD syndrome patients and non-MPD syndrome patients. *Journal of Prosthetic Dentistry, 45*, 84–88.

Nerenz, D. R., Leventhal, H., & Love, R. R. (1982). Factors contributing to emotional distress during cancer chemotherapy. *Cancer, 50*, 1020–1027.

Newman, R. I., Seres, J. L., Yospe, L. P., & Garlington, B. (1978). Multidisciplinary treatment of chronic pain: Long-term followup of low-back pain patients. *Pain, 4*, 283–292.

Pilowsky, I., Hallett, E. C., Bassett, D. L., Thomas, P. G., & Penhall, R. K. (1982). A controlled study of amitripyline in the treatment of chronic pain. *Pain, 14*, 169–179.

Price, K. P., & Blackwell, S. (1980). Trait levels of anxiety and psychological response to stress in migraineuers and normal controls. *Journal of Clinical Psychology, 36*, 658–660.

Reich, J., Tupin, J. P., & Abramowitz, S. I. (1983). Psychiatric diagnosis of chronic pain patients. *American Journal of Psychiatry, 140*, 1495–1498.

Rook, J. C., Pesch, R. N., & Keeler, E. C. (1981). Chronic pain and the questionable use of the Minnesota Multiphasic Personality Inventory. *Archives of Physical Medicine & Rehabilitation, 62,* 373–376.

Roy, R. (1982). Marital and family issues in patients with chronic pain. *Psychotherapy and Psychosomatics, 37,* 1–12.

Schweiger, A., & Parducci, A. (1981). Nocebo: The psychologic induction of pain. *Pavlovian Journal of Biological Science, 16,* 140–143.

Seligman, M. E. P., Maier, S. F., & Geer, J. (1968). The alleviation of learned helplessness in the dog. *Journal of Abnormal Psychology, 73,* 256–262.

Shanfield, S. B., Heiman, E. M., Cope, D. N., & Jones, J. R. (1979). Pain and marital relationship: Psychiatric distress. *Pain, 7,* 343–351.

Stein, N., Fruchter, H. J., & Trief, P. (1983). Experiences of depression and illness behavior in patients with intractible chronic pain. *Journal of Clinical Psychology, 39,* 31–33.

Stein, R. E., & Jessop, D. J. (1982). A noncategorical approach to chronic childhood illness. *Public Health Reports, 97,* 354–362.

Sternbach, R. A. (1966). *Principles of psychophysiology: An introductory text and readings.* New York: Academic Press.

Strain, J. J. (1979). Psychological reactions to chronic medical illness. *Psychiatric Quarterly, 51,* 173–183.

Toomey, T. C., Chia, J. N., Mao, W., & Gregg, J. M. (1977). Acupuncture and chronic pain mechanisms: The moderating effects of affect, personality, and stress on response to treatment. *Pain, 3,* 137–145.

Torda, C. (1978). Effects of recurrent postnatal pain-related stressful events on opiate receptor-endogenous ligand system. *Psychoendocrinology, 3,* 85–91.

Travell, J. G. (1983). *Myofascial pain and dysfunction: The trigger point manual.* Baltimore: Williams & Wilkins.

Turkat, I. D., & Guise, B. J. (1983). The effects of vicarious experience and stimulus intensity on pain termination and work avoidance. *Behavioral Research & Therapy, 21,* 241–245.

Turner, J. A., & Chapman, R. C. (1982). Psychological interventions for chronic pain: A review. *Pain, 12,* 1–46.

Tyre, T. E., & Anderson, D. L. (1981). Inpatient management of the chronic pain patient: A one-year followup study. *Journal of Family Practice, 12,* 819–827.

Weisenberg, M. (1975). *Pain: Clinical and experimental perspectives.* St. Louis: C. V. Mosby.

Wiesenfeld, Z., & Hallin, R. G. (1980). Stress-related pain behavior in rats with peripheral nerve injuries. *Pain, 8,* 279–284.

Willer, J. C. (1980). Anticipation of pain-produced stress: Electrophysiological study in man. *Physiology and Behavior, 25,* 49–51.

Zborowski, M. (1952). Cultural components in responses to pain. *Journal of Social Issues, 8,* 16–30.

Ziegler, D. K. (1978). Tension headache. *Medical Clinics of North America, 62,* 495–505.

Zola, I. K. (1966). Culture and symptoms—an analysis of patients' presenting complaints. *American Sociological Revue, 31,* 615.

── *CHAPTER 7* ─────────────────────────

Birth-Related Reactions as Sources of Stress

RAPHAEL S. GOOD, MD
REGINA P. LEDERMAN, PhD
HOWARD J. OSOFSKY, MD, PhD
DAVID D. YOUNGS, MD

INTRODUCTION

Within the context of a normal, low-risk pregnancy that terminates in the un-complicated delivery of a single, term, nondefective, healthy infant, the new mother confronts numerous stressors. These stressors are related to physiologic, psychologic and interpersonal issues induced by the pregnancy, labor, and delivery, as well as the care requirements of the newborn infant. Physiologic events raise issues of body image, body integrity, physical trauma, and death. Psychologically, self-esteem is called into question by behavioral issues that arise during labor and delivery and by concerns about one's ability to bring forth a normal child and be a competent mother. Also, the perception of various events surrounding pregnancy and childbirth as losses is frequently an additional source of psychological stress. Interpersonally, the woman must reassess and redefine her relationship to others, especially to her own mother and to the father of the child. Dealing with the thoughts, feelings, and behaviors induced by the mother–infant interaction is an additional interpersonal demand. Deviations such as abortion, ectopic pregnancy, other complications of pregnancy, complications of labor, twins, a defective infant, or perinatal death tend to increase the intensity of the stressors. The pressures may also be increased by a strained interpersonal relationship, such as occurs with marital discord or a particularly irritable infant.

The effect of the stressors on behavior, psychological response, and interpersonal relationships is predicated on numerous variables. A particular untoward event that occurs in the course of pregnancy or birth may have special, symbolic significance for the individual. Some complication of these processes may rekindle an unresolved complex of thoughts and feelings surrounding a previous similar event. In any case, either emergent might tend to increase the stress. On the other hand, successful coping with a similar event in the past or the anticipation of and planning for a predicted complication may act to blunt the effect of a stressor. The usual coping mechanisms of the individual also influence the response to a stressful event. Environmental support, especially from physicians, nurses, spouse, and the woman's mother can exert positive influences and prevent pathologic responses.

The age of the woman is also of considerable significance. If all other conditions are equal, the reaction to an abortion or stillbirth on the part of a 40-year-old woman whose remaining reproductive years are limited may well be different from that of a 20-year-old who still has many years in which to conceive successfully. The woman who sees pregnancy only as a path to motherhood may react quite differently to a perinatal loss from the woman who plans pregnancy for very different reasons.

Early animal studies confirm that responses to a stressful event are nonspecific; indeed, a primary quality for perceiving an event as stressful is its novelty. In addition to the specifics of the stimulus, in and of itself, it is evident that responses to a stimulus are the result of its psychological meaning for the involved individual. These studies have relevance to pregnancy, labor, and delivery because it has been shown that there are endocrine responses to anticipation of surgery, admission to a hospital, and various examinations. Earlier studies used adrenal responses as the indicator of stress. However, more recent work has clearly demonstrated that adrenal response may be modified by endogenous opiates. Further, the endogenous opiates are themselves responsive to various situations, including childbirth. Growth hormone, prolactin, and catecholamine levels are also affected by stressful situations. Many of the usual events surrounding uncomplicated pregnancy, labor, and the puerperium may be psychologically stressful to the woman; complications obviously increase the stress. Further, the specific effect of the marked increases and rapid shifts in the levels of the reproductive hormones, estrogen and progesterone, on other biological systems, especially at birth, has yet to be systematically investigated.

The recent explosion in scientific discoveries has permitted some understanding of the relationship between various biological systems and the feelings and behaviors of humans. Even though many links are still missing, that a relationship exists is incontestable. Thus, it is necessary to recognize that psychological and behavioral responses associated with pregnancy, labor, delivery, and puerperium have a biological substrate. The exact nature of this substrate will, undoubtedly, be better understood as scientific frontiers advance.

To summarize, numerous stressors accompany normal pregnancy and early motherhood. Complications of pregnancy and unanticipated outcomes magnify these normal stressors and add new ones. Responses to the stressors may be exhibited biologically, psychologically, and/or behaviorally and depend on numerous factors related not only to the stressors themselves but also to multiple, additional variables. How stressful an event is for an individual is determined as much by how the event is perceived as by the characteristics of the situation itself. Further, the novelty of the situation is a significant variable that affects the individual's perception of an event as being stressful.

NORMAL PREGNANCY

Numerous psychological and behavioral tasks confront every pregnant woman: acceptance of the pregnancy; preparation for childbirth, acceptance of motherhood; changes in life style; and changes in relationships with husband, mother, and others. Even under optimal conditions, dealing with these tasks is a demanding requirement. When however, there are additional stressors such as illness of a child or of the husband, infidelity, interference with career goals, previous pregnancy complications, or fetal loss, the result may be a sequence of distressing psychological changes characterized by anxiety and/or depression, often accompanied by maladaptive behaviors. Persistent, repetitive, expressed concern about one's ability to maintain control during labor, about one's competency as a mother, about the normalcy of the fetus, and about the destructive effects of all this on future career goals are among the common indicators of stress. Physical complaints (especially those related to normal physiologic changes such as pelvic pressure) that are not relieved by reassurance and simple remedies are also indicative of stress. Lack of response to significant pregnancy events, such as quickening, may be a clue to nonacceptance of a pregnancy. Stress can also be assumed when there is undue concern with and continuing complaints about the usual bodily changes accompanying pregnancy.

Absence of preparation or difficulty in preparing for parenthood is evident when an expectant mother resists thinking about parenthood or changes in life-style and states, "No change is necessary." Parenthood may be seen as threatening and interfering with a gratifying way of life. In contrast to the usual initial doubts about maternal adequacy, severe self-criticism or excessive self-doubt may be present. In such cases, thoughts about doing something wrong, being a bad or poor mother, and having a disturbed or maladjusted child predominate. The appropriate preparations for childbirth and care of the child are avoided. Expectations regarding labor may be unrealistic and inappropriate. Thoughts about the baby are limited, negative, or hostile. The anticipated infant may be described as a "friend," or there is other evidence of role reversal or unrealistic expectations.

A better adaptation is likely to occur and pregnancy will tend to be less stressful if the mother of the pregnant woman is enthusiastic, supportive, and reassuring concerning childbearing, childbirth, and performance as a parent. Under such conditions, the childbearer's mother is acknowledged as a constructive role model, and the daughter wishes to emulate her. Mother and daughter are tolerant of each other's concerns and anxieties. They reminisce in significant and constructive ways about the past, so that role definition and role identification are enhanced. They inspire confidence and trust in one another. The daughter sees herself becoming an equal and, through the relationship, develops a workable, realistic model of child care. However, when past relationships have been poor and reconciliation has not been achieved, then the expectant mother is usually less trusting, less self-confident, and less prepared for the role of parent. In short, when she perceives her own mother as critical, unsupportive, disinterested, and unavailable, then a woman is more likely to have negative attitudes toward pregnancy and motherhood. This negative role model will generate hostile comments about the mother, and the pregnant woman will observe, "She wouldn't know about that; things were different in her time; she didn't care whether or not I conceived; I'm not sure she wants grandchildren;" and so on. Behaviorally, the pregnant woman who is locked into such a relationship tends, when she can, to separate herself from her mother, and, when she cannot, to provoke arguments when they are together.

A poor relationship with the husband adds to the stress of pregnancy and frequently precludes a smooth transition to the new roles dictated by pregnancy and parenthood. When the marital bond is weak and the relationship is strained, there is little sensitivity or responsiveness to the woman's needs; for the most part they are ignored or denied. Requests for help may be mocked or caustically criticized. When asked about what changes have occurred in the marital relationship since pregnancy, the answer is often, "None." The husband shows little interest in the pregnancy or in the necessary preparatory activities for childbirth or parenthood. If asked about perceived needs of the spouse, either parent may respond, "I don't know." The husband may enact his avoidance and widen his distance from his wife by increasing his time at work or giving himself over to leisure activities outside the home. Lack of mutual planning for childcare is another indication of a stressful marital relationship.

It is not unusual for complaints about sexual activity to become the focus of a strained relationship. In such a troubled relationship the husband frequently will not acknowledge the need for modification of previous sexual activity, and the wife does not acknowledge that her husband's needs remain unchanged. Thus, sexual activity becomes less satisfactory for each, which, in turn, leads to added stress for both.

NORMAL DELIVERY

Because of any of the various stressors referred to previously, uncomplicated labor and delivery frequently result in psychological symptoms and disordered behaviors. Many women feel depressed, describe a sense of loss, speak of not having done well in terms of their own expectations of their conduct in labor, and express their disappointment with the normal infant. The negative feelings about the infant are stated in ambivalent terms such as, "We really wanted a boy—but she's a darling little girl and we already love her very much" and "I always thought that newborn babies had more hair." These feelings result in bouts of crying; difficulty sleeping; irritability; hostility toward nurses, physicians, and the spouse; and minimal infant care. The rejection of the infant is a classic sign of postpartum stress. As soon as the infant stops feeding, whether bottle-fed or breast-fed, the stressed parturient rings for the nurse to return the infant to the nursery. On returning home, regardless of the reality, she complains that her husband is not attentive to the child and "expects me to do everything for it."

These feelings, attitudes, and behaviors (often called the "baby blues") are transient, develop about the 3rd day, and usually do not persist beyond 7 to 10 days. Because these signs and symptoms are common, biological correlates are hypothesized for their appearance. The precipitous changes in hormone levels following delivery support this hypothesis. This speculation is further reinforced by demonstrated cognitive deficits in many women during the early puerperium.

CESAREAN CHILDBIRTH

The confluence of stressors from three relatively independent sources produces a considerable level of stress in cesarean childbirth. First, there are the usual stressors of pregnancy. Second, there are the physical and psychological stressors of surgery. Third, as compared to the product of an uncomplicated delivery, the infant is more apt to be compromised and, therefore, perceived as defective. Parturient responses vary greatly and depend, in part, on whether the surgery was planned, as in many repeat cesarean sections, or unplanned, as the result of an emergency (e.g., prolapsed cord). Other factors influencing emotional and behavioral responses to cesarean section include, but are not limited to, past childbearing experiences, the ability to grieve, the attitude of the husband, the involvement of the husband in the labor and delivery, the time spent with the infant in the first 24 to 48 hours postpartum and the support provided by physicians and nurses.

Recent changes in birthing practices in the United States, especially among middle income, white women, may lead to cesarean sections being more stressful than in the past. The emphasis is now on prepared childbirth, on control in labor, on limiting analgesia, on avoiding anesthesia, and on very early mother–infant interaction. C-section, especially when unanticipated and unplanned, is prejudicial to these concerns because birth did not meet expectations; the surgery, therefore, leads to lowered self-esteem, anger, and guilt. Research data on the psychological responses to cesarean section are scant, and the few available studies involve small numbers and are descriptive with little significant data. However, when one interpolates data from other studies of pregnancy complications, the conclusion is almost certainly valid. Women feel less positively about the birth and describe it as a "shock," "a big disappointment," and as "totally different from what I planned."

TWINS

Twin pregnancy identifies the mother as being at high risk for complications of pregnancy, labor, delivery, and the puerperium. In addition, the infants are likely candidates for mortality and morbidity. Thus, the possibility of that mother being stressed is great. Unfortunately, there is very little data dealing specifically with the psychological or behavioral effects of a twin pregnancy on the mother. A wealth of data, however, describes the adverse physical effects of twinning on both the mother and fetus. Toxemia is three to five times more common in women with twins and occurs in 20% to 30% of all such pregnancies. Anemia is more common. Physical discomfort is increased. In order to reduce the incidence of prematurity and other complications, it is frequently recommended that physical activity be severely curtailed; indeed, prolonged bed rest may be indicated.

Due to overdistention of the uterus, uterine atony is not unusual. Malpresentations are frequent, especially of the second twin, requiring operative delivery. Postpartum hemorrhage is more likely, and, if there have been intrauterine manipulations, the incidence of pelvic infection is increased. More than 50% of all twins are premature, and a twin's risk of perinatal death is at least three times that of a singleton. This is due to not only the prematurity but also an increased incidence of severe congenital anomalies. Even though systematic studies are scarce, it seems reasonable to assume that the multiple complications will be a source of stress to the woman with twins. Because of easy fatiguability and admonishments to rest, the woman pregnant with twins cannot carry out her usual duties and responsibilities; for many, this results in guilt, depression, and anxiety. In addition, the wife's increased dependency on the husband and inability to shoulder her usual share of household chores may lead to marital discord. Sexual harmony is threatened not only by the change in interpersonal relations but also by the physical conditions attendant on the twin pregnancy.

The previous reference to concerns about one's competency as a mother as a significant source of postpartum stress is doubly applicable in the case of twins. This is especially true when twins are the products of the first pregnancy. There is evidence that the mother of twins spends one third more time attending to their physical needs than does the mother of a singleton; at the same time, however, she devotes half as much time to each infant. She may well be aware of not being able to respond as much as she would like, with resulting feelings of guilt, depression, and anxiety. In addition, as previously noted, twins are frequently premature, and there is substantial evidence that prematurity is a source of stress to the parent. The mother of a preemie is often shocked initially by the appearance of the infant; she is likely to perceive the baby as abnormal and to blame herself for delivering before term. The babies' small size magnifies the mother's fears of her inability to minister to their needs and leads to self-doubt and lowered self-esteem. Because the premature infants are frequently in an isolation nursery, the mother is not involved in the babies' care; this reinforces her sense of not being competent. It is not unusual for one twin to remain in the nursery after the other has been discharged. Thus, the mother will have an opportunity to establish routines of care only to have them abruptly interrupted by the arrival of the second twin. This requires another reorganization of her time and effort, and it, too, is disruptive and a source of stress. The physical efforts of caring for two newborns are considerable.

Caring for twins adversely affects patterns of sleep. Longer periods are required for night feeding and the infants may awaken at different times requiring additional care. Loss of sleep results in daytime fatigue and irritability, increasing parental stress. This, in turn, may lead to disruption of the relationship between new parents, especially if the marital bond was somewhat weak prior to delivery.

ABORTION

Abortion can be either spontaneous or induced; whether the psychological response to one differs from the psychological reaction to the other has not been systematically investigated. It can be speculated that competency and self-esteem play a more significant role in spontaneous abortion and issues of guilt come to the fore when the abortion is induced.

Because induced abortion may be perceived as the solution to an intolerable situation, it can give rise to an initial feeling of relief and lead to a sense of mastery and control that overshadows the guilt. In either case, the stresses surrounding abortion vary considerably depending on biologic, psychological, and social factors. The age, gravidity, and parity of the woman are significant. A 35-year-old woman who has had several successful pregnancies interspersed by one or two spontaneous abortions may not be at all stressed by another spontaneous abortion; a 35-year-old who has been involuntarily infertile, who has been exposed to numerous medical and surgical interventions in an effort to increase fertility, and who finally conceives may be psychologically devastated by a spontaneous abortion. In the latter instance the abortion may represent a loss of considerable significance and give rise to a marked grieving reaction.

The length of gestation and the woman's involvement with the pregnancy are other important variables. The woman whose menses are irregular with the interval varying from 28 to 40 days may become pregnant without ever suspecting it. She may then have a very early abortion that is diagnosed only with the onset of bleeding. She stands in marked contrast to the woman who has already become invested in the pregnancy and has begun planning for a child, and who then spontaneously aborts late in the first or early in the second trimester.

The need to be hospitalized for necessary surgical intervention adds to the stress of an abortion. Many patients who abort can be treated adequately as outpatients, but some require hospitalization for blood loss or surgical evacuation. As previously discussed, surgery itself is a challenge and adds to the other stresses of abortion, thereby increasing the emotional risk of the experience.

Since the legalization of abortion, there has been an increased interest in the psychological and social sequelae. Numerous studies have been reported but, unfortunately, findings are not consistent. The variation is in large part explainable by differences among the populations studied. The postabortal psychological situation of a mature woman who has had a stable marital relationship, becomes pregnant as a result of failed contraception, and, along with her husband, reaches a thoughtful decision to abort cannot be compared to that of the young teenager who conceives while testing her awakening sexuality and is coerced to abort by punitive parents. The varying methodologies employed for evaluating postabortal psychological states as well as the diverse lengths of follow-up also account for some of the differences in the findings from various studies. Because many abortions solve social dilemmas, the immediate response may be one of relief, which in turn can mask an underlying guilt. Indeed, such unresolved guilt may not surface until a later date in relation to other reproductive events.

Before legalization of abortion a limited number of studies had been carried out that found few negative psychological sequelae. Some studies demonstrated a small incidence of postabortal psychiatric disturbance in individuals with prior severe psychopathology; the postabortal difficulty appeared related to the extent of psychiatric disturbance rather than to the pregnancy loss. In several studies, psychiatric and psychological evaluations demonstrated an improvement in both attitudes and behaviors. In one study, patients who were denied an abortion because their psychiatric problems were insufficiently severe fared worse postdelivery than did disturbed individuals following abortion.

Since the legalization of abortion, investigators generally have found that psychiatric sequelae from abortion are rather rare. Relief and happiness have been the predominant moods, and significant postabortal feelings of guilt and depression have been relatively uncommon. Pregnancy termination has been viewed as an effective means of dealing with a personal crisis, with the women subsequently demonstrating increased autonomy and emotional maturation. When one views the issue of abortion in relation to adolescence, a number of studies have demonstrated a decrease in educational, social, and economic attainments for adolescents carrying to term, and marital instability for those who wed as a result of pregnancy. In contrast, data indicate that following the abortion, single, youthful women are more likely to use contraception effectively, to achieve more education, and to obtain more vocational career training than do those who carry to term.

Some women do experience transient difficulty related to abortion, and at times, adverse reactions are seen in clinical practice. There are patients who display a number of characteristics that appear to predict a greater likelihood of guilt or depression following abortion. These include a number of different groups: patients of young age, especially those who have been pressured by the family or sexual partner to have the abortion; patients who are aborted because of medical problems; patients who initially feel a great deal of conflict about the abortion and desire to have children in the future; patients who are having the abortion because of financial or social pressures; patients whose religion or morals are opposed to abortion; and patients with prior psychiatric difficulty. The degree of social support available to the patient also appears to be a predictor of difficulty with the abortion experience.

On the basis of current evidence, it may be concluded that most women deal adaptively with the stresses caused by abortion, and in time they are able to grieve effectively and to resolve any underlying guilt. Those who are unable to do so may become depressed and exhibit chronically troublesome guilt, especially at a later date.

STILLBIRTH

For statistical purposes stillbirth is defined as the birth of a dead fetus after 20 weeks of pregnancy. Obstetrically, stillbirth is usually considered as the birth of a dead fetus after the time of viability. This latter definition is less specific, especially in view of recent improvements in the care of low birth weight infants but, psychologically, it is more appropriate. When viability is a variable, psychological, emotional, and behavioral reactions can be differentiated from those following late second trimester abortions. As with other complications of pregnancy, anticipation of the untoward event modifies the ensuing stress. A diabetic woman who receives special care during pregnancy, who recognizes the possibility of the intrauterine demise of the fetus, and who then learns that this has happened can be assumed to be stressed in quite a different way from the woman who has had a completely normal, uncomplicated pregnancy but then delivers a stillborn because of a sudden, unanticipated, intrapartum catastrophe such as a prolapsed cord. In either event, the death of a fetus is a substantial loss that gives rise to grieving.

In other circumstances involving death, the griever is likely to receive support from family, friends, and health care workers, as well as society's cultural rituals. With a stillbirth those supports are frequently lacking and, when offered, may well be inappropriate and inadequate. Grieving is more difficult because so little is known of the dead fetus; it has no personal characteristics nor are there any associated memories to aid in dealing with the loss. Moreover, not only is there the loss of the fetus who was the "child inside," but there is the loss of the expected "outside child" for whom the woman is psychologically prepared.

The guilt that accompanies most losses is even greater with a stillbirth because of the intimate physical relationship of the fetus and mother. Because the cause of death is physically related to her, the mother blames herself for the loss. All too often, the father of the child is subject to the same stresses and may have similar feelings; he may therefore be unable to help the parturient grieve. On the other hand, if he does offer her support she may direct her anger at him for not being as distressed as she is by the loss. Women who have experienced a stillbirth often display anger toward pregnant women and toward women who have recently delivered; they also tend to be more aware of the presence of babies and young children. There is evidence that physicians, possibly because of their own guilt, tend to isolate themselves from women who have given birth to a dead fetus; thus, support from the health-care team is less available than when death comes in other situations. The patient's normal reactions of bereavement, such as crying, are upsetting to the staff; rather than being encouraged to express her grief, she is frequently sedated or inappropriately reassured that she can conceive again.

The inability to deal adaptively with the loss may result in an idealization of the lost baby plus rapid resort to another pregnancy in order to replace the lost child. Because in the nature of things this replacement child will fail to meet the unrealistic expectations for the stillborn, the new child may suffer abuse. The woman who has delivered a stillbirth may misdirect her anger toward her other children, blaming them for the stillbirth, isolating herself from them, and withdrawing.

The negative effect on the sense of competency and self-esteem that pervades all losses will be more fully explored when considering the birth of a defective infant.

DEFECTIVE CHILD

All pregnant women tend to create images and expectations of the unborn child that have been referred to as an "idealized image." These images range from gross characteristics, such as sex and amount of hair, to nuances and subtle qualities within the dyadic interaction. In reality, even a perfectly normal infant cannot totally conform to these expectations. Thus, the newborn is always defective in the psychological view of the parturient. This gives rise to grieving for the child who was not born and requires active attachment to the child who is born. When there is a significant defect of obvious kind, such as microcephaly or harelip, the task of adapting is all the more stressful. The mother and father's need to cope with the demands of new parenthood and the specific characteristics of the child expose the individuals, the marital relationship, and the infant's development to a great deal of stress.

Parental emotional responses to a defective child have been investigated; they include shock, guilt, denial, anger, sadness, and anxiety. Depressive symptoms are commonly seen and are indicative of grieving. Guilt is frequently present, and the mother may ask, "What did I do to cause this? What could I have done to prevent it? Is there something wrong with me?" A defective child is always a blow to self-esteem. It causes the mother to question her ability to produce a normal child and to fear for her competency as a caretaker of the defective child.

Numerous investigators have studied interactions between mothers and defective infants; a critical factor appears to be the behaviors and appearance of the child. Much of the work has been done with premature infants, a special category of defective infants. It has been found that premature infants elicit different caretaking interactions from those evoked by full-term infants. Caregivers are more active with preterm infants and more likely to elicit behavioral exchanges than are caregivers of full-term infants; this may be related to the passivity of the premature infant and the mother's feeling that she has to take more responsibility for establishing an interaction. It has been well established that premature infants are overrepresented among abused and neglected infants. It has been noted for example that mothers find the preemie's cry and facial movements more aversive than those of full-term infants. In a study of infants with cleft palates, mothers averted their gaze from the baby more often than did mothers with normal infants and, while hospitalized, discouraged visits from relatives. Clearly, there was a sense of shame, and a desire to hide the infant from the eyes of others.

Mothers of high-risk infants describe the child's cry as being distressing, sick sounding, and urgent. If, in addition, the baby's sensory capacity is reduced, the infant may appear unresponsive and thus reinforce the mother's sense of lack of competency.

Denial is a common method of dealing with the psychological impact of the defect. It is a common experience on obstetrical services that on one day a clear explanation of the defect and its implications is given to the mother, and on the next day, she will claim that she was "never told." The degree of denial may be so extreme that it extends to not giving consent for indicated medical and surgical procedures, and to not making adequate plans for care on leaving the hospital.

That the birth of a defective child exerts strain on the marital relationship seems self-evident. While each parent is dealing with his/her own grief, guilt, anger, and anxiety, it may be very difficult to be supportive of the other. Added to this is the absolute need to consider the reality of the newborn. Individuals are usually admonished not to make important decisions when psychologically stressed. Yet, in these instances, before they have had an opportunity to work through the psychological trauma and to deal cognitively with all the implications of this troubling newborn, the parents are pressured to make critical choices that might well prove decisive for the child's future. These decisions will also affect the marital relationship. One group of investigators found that the incidence of family disruption was related to specific characteristics of the defective child. Even when family intactness is not at issue, in many cases parents describe experiencing isolation, confinement, and fewer outside activities.

The effect of a defective child, expecially one who is premature, on mother–infant attachment has also been investigated. Numerous authors have studied factors that contribute to this bond and have concluded that there are both constitutional and experiential components. The mother's willingness and ability to subjugate her own interests to those of the child are affected not only by her own psychological and physiological makeup but also by the behaviors and appearance of the infant. A defective infant adds to the stress of establishing a healthy, normal relationship.

In summary, the birth of a defective infant can act as a specific stressor that gives rise to emotional distress for both parents and that can result in psychological and behavioral symptoms. Such an infant strains the marital relationship and may lead to marital discord; in addition, it stresses and affects the early mother–infant interactions.

OTHER DELIVERY TRAUMA

As noted earlier, normal pregnancy, cesarean section, twins, abortion, perinatal death, and the birth of a defective child can each give rise to an appreciable amount of psychological stress. The degree of tension is increased when other pregnancy, labor, and postpartum events involve additional medical and surgical complications. For example, the considerable blood loss that frequently accompanies ectopic pregnancy, placenta previa, and postpartum uterine atony is extremely stressful in and of itself; it gains special force, however, by the degree to which it adds to the existing stressors. Serious blood loss results in easy fatiguability, the need for frequent periods of rest, and a tendency toward more than the usual amount of sleep.

The complications of pregnancy may require emergency surgery. For many individuals surgery is at best a major stressor; when related to pregnancy however, it raises concerns about current and future reproductive capabilities. This serves as yet another source of tension and dread. Surgery, of course, adds to the anxiety surrounding bodily trauma, pain, and death. When late pregnancy complications are accompanied by the birth of a live infant, the mother's physical ability to render necessary care is prejudiced. This, in turn, may lead to a further decrease in self-esteem, an increase in guilt, and an inevitable burden of hostility toward the infant.

The current interest in "prepared childbirth" has conditioned some women to expect to have control not only over their own feelings and behaviors during labor but also over events surrounding labor, including where it takes place, who should deliver (physician or midwife), and the use of analgesia and anesthesia; an unexpected complication may shatter these expectations and increase the paturient's vulnerability.

SUMMARY

Normal pregnancy, labor, delivery, and the puerperium are potential stressors to the average woman. Some women react to these stresses with psychological symptoms and various maladaptive behaviors. When complications occur, stress is increased and the likelihood of maladaptation is greater.

Developmental Sources of Stress: The First through the Fifth Year of Life

MOLLIE M. WALLICK, PhD

INTRODUCTION

From the outset, stress is a necessary concomitant of development. Greenacre (1945) views birth as acutely traumatic and proposes it as the forerunner of anxiety; Rank (1952) expands on the analytically recognized significance of the birth trauma and humans' persistent attempts to overcome it. Similarly, Leboyer (1976) considers the neonatal period to be fraught with fear, pain, and anguish; he suggests patience and increased sensitivity, along with a variety of techniques, to eliminate or attenuate the deleterious components of this initial rite of passage.

Others (e.g., Murphy, 1962) have focused on the infant's and the young child's coping patterns. In evaluating the interactive behavior of neonates, Brazelton (1973) documented such coping responses as self-quieting after noxious stimuli, post-distress consolability (assessed by means of a series of graded procedures offered by the examiner), and self-control over interfering motor activity. In studying behavioral individuality in early childhood, Thomas and Chess (1977) were im-

189

pressed by their subjects' obvious temperamental differences as early as the first few weeks of life; responses to environmental stimuli and ease of modifiability proved remarkably consistent over time and were also predictive of later ability to deal with environmental demands and expectations.

Still others have studied the impact of environmental influences. Rank (1955) found that subsequent to specific traumatic events, most often involving separation from parents, many preschool children with severe psychopathology became symptomatic. Exploring the significance of life events as precipitating factors for both physical and mental illness in children of various ages, Coddington (1972) established the relative values and the rank order of a series of discrete stressful events, both desirable and undesirable. According to his research, the impact of specific experiences and the amount of readjustment that these events necessitate vary according to the age level of the child.

Benswanger (1982) proposes the use of an ecological approach in studying stressful events in early childhood:

> A complex interplay of forces influences the way a child reacts to stress, how he copes, makes use of available resources, recovers, or fails to recover. The forces involved in this interplay may be termed the "developmental-ecological context." ... This context consists of many interdependent elements including family history, prenatal conditions, constitutional and temperamental factors, family interactions, cultural, religious, and ethnic traditions, developmental process and physical health, as well as a variety of other social and environmental influences. (pp. 267–268)

The current consideration of developmental sources of stress in the first 5 years of life will be addressed from an ecological perspective. Implications of the various dimensions specified by Benswanger (1982) will be recognized—at times, implicitly—in the discussion of the relative stressfulness of various experiences.

EVENTS INVOLVING SEPARATION

Many stressful occurrences in early childhood involve separation from significant persons—most often, parents. Included among these are relatively minor as well as major losses: brief separations, separation for a sibling's birth, hospitalization, child-care arrangements, household moves, parental separation and divorce, and the ultimate separation, death.

Brief Separations

Neonatal Period. Concerning the earliest separation of all, professionals are indebted to Klaus and Kennell (1970, 1976, 1982; Klaus et al., 1972; Kennell et al., 1974; Kennell, Trause, & Klaus, 1975; Ringler, Kennell, Jarvella, Navojosky,

& Klaus, 1975; Ringler, Trause, Klaus, & Kennell, 1978) for their ground-breaking study of the effects on later mothering of a temporary separation in the period following delivery. In the late 1970s, both in this country and abroad, the value of early contact, as demonstrated by Klaus and Kennell, was supported by other research (Carlsson et al., 1979; de Chateau, 1980; Greenberg, Rosenberg, & Lind, 1973; Grossman, Thane, & Grossman, 1981; Hopkins & Vietze, 1977; Siegel, Bauman, Schaefer, Saunders, & Ingram, 1979; Sousa et al., 1974).

Recently, however, critical reviews of Klaus and Kennell's original work, and of their hypothesized sensitive period, have appeared in books and scientific journals (e.g., Chess & Thomas, 1982; Herbert, Sluckin, & Sluckin, 1982; Korsch, 1983; Lamb, 1982a, 1982b, 1982c; Lamb & Hwang, 1982; McCall, 1982; Rutter, 1983). Two frequently articulated shortcomings of the bonding phenomenon are the lack of evidence of any enduring effects on mothers and infants, and the virtual impossibility of finding comparable separation and nonseparation groups.

A recently reported study (Wallick, 1985) documents that, regrettably, it is still possible to find naturally occurring separation groups and that there may indeed be long-range sequelae of inadequate maternal–infant bonding (specifically, these sequelae include increased incidence of retention in grade, speech impairment, and slow learner/educationally handicapped status). Even the critics recognize the positive consequences of interaction in the period immediately after delivery. Although the issue of neonatal contact and its aftereffects is apparently unresolved, early and extended parent–infant contact should be made available to all parents who want it and for whom it is medically feasible.

Toddler Stage. During the second half of the first year of life, most children demonstrate an attachment to their caretaker. At that time they are not yet able to retain a stable mental image of the caretaker (this usually appears around 3 years of age), which makes this a period of increased vulnerability. During this period, regular physical contact with the caretaker is necessary to reassure the child that the caretaker has neither changed into a different person nor disappeared altogether (Yates, 1983).

When parents leave the home for an evening without telling their young child that a sitter will be there, they ignore the stress the youngster will experience should he or she awaken to find the parents missing; anxiety will be intensified if the sitter is a stranger. They also deny the child the opportunity to master the separation and, thereby, to cope with subsequent inevitable separations with increasing comfort.

Separation for a Sibling's Birth. Although most parents prepare a child thoughtfully for the birth of a sibling, they often neglect to prepare for the mother's disappearance of several days' duration—which may, itself, be more traumatic than incorporating a new family member. Mothers often leave hurriedly for the delivery, at times in the middle of the night, and in other subtle ways may be less sensitive than usual to the young child's needs.

In their study of preschool children's reaction to the birth of a sibling, Legg, Sherick, and Wadland (1974) found that the youngsters did best when cared for in their own homes by a person familiar to them and when permitted to visit in the hospital. Trause et al. (1981) studied 31 firstborn children, under 3½ years, who had been separated from their mothers during hospitalization for a sibling's birth; approximately half of the children were allowed to visit their mothers for 1 hour per day. Significant increases in temper tantrums, activity level, and sleep problems were reported in both groups, but it is also true that, initially, the children who visited were significantly more responsive to their mothers and to the new siblings. Sibling visitation was recommended as a ''potentially powerful way to help children cope with the stress of maternal separation'' (p. 38).

Still another report (Robertson & Robertson, 1971) describes the disruption caused by a separation of 10 to 27 days for childbirth, a more extended period than is currently customary in the United States. The Robertsons temporarily fostered four firstborn children, under 2½ years of age. They report variations in response, ''related to age, levels of ego maturity and object constancy, previous mother–child relationship, length of separation, and defense organization'' (p. 312). But even with optimally structured substitute care, the children's distress over separation was reflected in their lowered frustration tolerance, increased sadness, irritability, and clinging. After reunion, the children demonstrated more moodiness, defiance, and aggressive behaviors.

Heinicke and Westheimer (1965) studied 10 toddlers aged 13 to 32 months; they were separated from their families and brought to a residential nursery, where they remained from 12 to 148 days. In 7 of the 10 cases the separation was for childbirth. Although at the time of reunion the new sibling's presence did have an impact, the reason for the separation was not a major variable affecting the child's response to that separation. In comparison with their matched controls, upon reunion, all of the toddlers initially turned from their mothers and avoided contact as if in retaliation for the abandonment. In contrast, affectionate interaction was readily resumed with the fathers who had visited their youngsters in the nursery. The toddlers' initial avoidance of maternal contact was followed by ambivalence, with the children communicating a complex mixture of hostile defiance coupled with affection. Twenty weeks after reunion, disturbed behavior could be detected (for 2 additional weeks) only in the child who experienced the most extended separation. This is consistent with Ainsworth's observation (1966) that the longer the separation, the greater the likelihood of delayed reattachment toward the mother.

Hospitalization

The stress of illness not requiring hospitalization will be considered in a subsequent section. In considering the impact of hospitalization, one is faced with the difficult task of teasing out the effects of the precipitating illness or injury and its treatment.

Wolff (1973) lists three variables that contribute to the effects of hospitalization: the child's age; the child's personal adjustment and past experiences; and the actual hospital procedures.

The Child's Age. Schaffer and Callendar (1959) studied the reactions of 76 children under 1 year of age to short-term hospitalization (in most cases, less than 2 weeks); observations were made immediately following admission, shortly before discharge, and on return from the hospital. (Mothers were allowed contact only during a daily visiting hour.) The infants' behavior differed appreciably according to age: babies 7 months and older behaved much as toddlers and preschool children customarily do; they demonstrated much more disturbed behavior on admission and after discharge, apparently related to mother's absence and their need for her physical presence. In contrast to this, infants less than 7 months adjusted immediately to the new environment and to the people in it; on discharge, their disturbed behavior was less severe and of briefer duration than that of their older counterparts.

Prugh and colleagues studied the reactions to hospitalization of 200 children aged 2 to 12 years (Prugh, Staub, Sands, Kirschbaum, & Lenihan, 1953). Even with exemplary medical and nursing care, Prugh et al. found that children under 4 years of age evidenced a severely disturbed reaction, including panic attacks, angry outbursts on parents' departure, depression, withdrawal, occasional somatic concomitants of anxiety, and disturbances in their eating, toileting, and sleeping.

In reviewing his own extensive case records, Levy (1945) was impressed by the number of children in whom fears, night terrors, dependency, negativism, and other affective symptoms followed closely after the youngsters had undergone an operation. Of 124 behaviorally disordered children who had experienced a prior operative procedure, emotional sequelae were most prominent between the ages of 1 and 3 years (50%, compared with 11% of children from 3 to 6 years; 10%, from 6 to 9 years; and 8%, above 9 years).

Based on the Levy (1945), Prugh et al. (1953), and Schaffer and Callender (1959) findings, it appears that emotional sequelae of hospitalization are maximal in children between 7 months and 4 years of age: Apparently their adaptive resources are attenuated by their cognitive development and by their sharper responses to pain, greater dependency, and relatively limited experiences away from home.

Personality Factors and Past Experiences. The Prugh et al. study (1953) indicated more stressful reactions to hospitalization in children who had previously been exposed to traumatic experiences. This was true as well in children whose prior personality adjustment was inadequate and whose parental relationships were unsatisfying. It is likely that the poorly attached and insecure child lacks the reassurance of a stable mental image of loving and caring parents.

A study of young children's adjustment to tonsillectomy (Stacey, Dearden, Pill, & Robinson, 1970) demonstrated more disturbed reactions in a number of different circumstances. These included youngest children; only children; and youngsters who had responded negatively to strangers, had visited infrequently away from home, or had experienced a recent traumatic separation from their parents.

Hospital Procedures. In the Prugh et al. study (1953), specific diagnostic and therapeutic procedures were generally interpreted by the child according to his or her level of psychosexual development. Surgery requiring an anesthetic produced traumatic effects, both while the child was hospitalized and after discharge. Other variables affecting reaction included the following:

> The type of illness, the particular organ or organ system involved, the nature of the immediate handling by and relationship with the physician performing the procedure, the degree of support gained from parent-surrogate relationships with ward personnel [and] the child's previous experience with illness or pain (on his own part or that of the children observed on the ward). (p. 94)

Children aged 2 to 4 years often reacted to frightening procedures as hostile attacks and interpreted them as punishment; not uncharacteristically, they promised "to be good." Procedures necessitating movement away from the ward and the familiar personnel were especially upsetting, adding to the youngsters' fear of the unknown and apparently intensifying their discomfort at separation from parents. Although on the surface the reactions of children aged 4 to 6 years appeared similar to those of their younger counterparts, in fact, the aggression of the older children was more controlled and their fear of specific procedures was more realistic.

In his classic study of surgical procedures in childhood as the origin of psychic trauma, Levy (1945) found that in 1- to 3-year-olds the ensuing symptoms were especially severe when the surgery involved the genitalia, as, for example, in circumcision. Considering the preoccupation with body intactness and castration anxiety characteristic of the genital stage of development, this is not at all surprising. When the operation followed an earlier one, the later procedure exacerbated extant fears; if, however, the earlier fears had already subsided, no additional effect was noted.

In order to prevent postoperative fears, Levy (1945) advised postponing surgery, if possible, until after the age of 3 years, especially if the child appears anxious or unduly dependent on his or her mother. (Similarly, Wolff [1973] suggested postponement until after the age of 4 years.) Levy also recommended delaying additional surgery, if at all possible, until all emotional sequelae of earlier operative procedures become quiescent.

Child-Care Arrangements

There are 8½ million preschoolers in the United States whose mothers are employed, the majority because of economic necessity and others because of career orientation or preference for employment status. By 1990 the prediction is that half of all preschool children, approximately 11 million youngsters, will have mothers in the work force, often necessitating daily separation for 8 to 10 hours (the larger portion of the children's waking hours). In the past, the traditional solution was to find a surrogate mother—grandmother, aunt, ''nanny,'' or housekeeper—to provide the necessary long-term care, ideally in the child's home. Now an alternative solution is emerging for the care of preschool children of working mothers. The steady increase in the numbers of extended family in the work force coupled with geographic mobility and the rapidly decreasing availability of housekeepers/nannies has resulted in a major shift toward the use of group day care.

Currently there is a strong emphasis on early developmental education for all children; as a result, many youngsters whose mothers do *not* work also experience enforced separation from primary attachment figures in a preschool setting. Like day care, nursery school attendance, too, necessitates a reactive accommodation to sustained separation, albeit of shorter daily duration. Another significant difference is that nursery school customarily involves an adjustment to one set of caretakers, whereas, day care staffing patterns often require adjustment to as many as three shifts of caretakers each day.

Half-Day Nursery School. In exploring nursery school adjustment in 36 three-year-olds, Bloom-Feshbach (1981) found high levels of separation distress, in particular, during initial school entry. Limited distress at separation is predictable and healthy, and reflects a secure interpersonal bond (Bowlby, 1969); a prolonged problematic response, however, is generally indicative of more serious separation difficulty. In the Bloom-Feshbach study, children with fewer separation problems had no prior history of intense stranger anxiety and came from families with secure mother–child relationships and high paternal involvement. An ability on the part of the children to initiate early contact with teachers (in contrast with teacher-seeking after 2 months of school) was viewed as adaptive. The pupil:teacher ratio in the classroom was a significant predictor of separation difficulty, with more problems associated with larger classes.

Nursery school entrance generally occurs during the rapprochement phase of the separation–individuation process (Mahler, Pine, & Bergman, 1975), a time when tension is particularly high between dependency needs and strivings for autonomy. It may be that the child copes with the tension by recapitulating aspects of the separation–individuation sequence (Bloom-Feshbach, Bloom-Feshbach, & Gaughran, 1980). Although a traumatic coping experience may exacerbate existing psychological problems, successful adjustment may stimulate psychological growth (van Leeuwen & Pomer, 1969).

Full-Time Group Day Care. Of the 8½ million children under 6 years whose mothers were employed in 1980, 1.9 million were in day-care centers and more than 5 million were cared for privately in homes other than their own. The literature on the effects of day care contains many inconsistencies: Some studies report beneficial results in regard to social interaction (Schwarz, Krolick, & Strickland, 1973) and intellectual development (Falender & Heber, 1975), whereas others report such adverse effects as anxious attachment, defensive and avoidant reactions especially in younger children (Blehar, 1974; Moore, 1969), and fear of a stranger following the mother's departure (Ricciuti, 1974). Still others report no fear of strangers and no detrimental effects on attachment behaviors (Caldwell, Wright, Honig, & Tannenbaum, 1970; Doyle, 1975; Kearsley, Zelazo, Kagan, & Hartmann, 1975). Schiller (1978) found that with day-care entry within the first 2 years of life adaptability increased and separation stress was attenuated; Lahikainen and Sundquist (1979) report that children younger than 2 years protest their mother's departure most, whereas children older than 3 years "are most likely to show symptoms of fear" (p. 85); Guendelman (1980) found separation most stressful for children under 18 months.

It is possible that the variables offered by Rutter (1981) and by Kagan, Kearsley, and Zelazo (1978) may account for some of the reported inconsistencies. Rutter emphasized the significance of the quality of care, along with the characteristics of the child and of his family (including familial attitude toward both maternal employment and day care). He also reported the likelihood that children under 3 years would have more difficulty coping with a full day of care away from home; that firstborn children, unaccustomed to sharing their mother, may not adapt as easily to day care; that boys may be more affected by group care than girls; that the day-care adjustment of children with prior difficult separation experiences or known insecure attachments is likely to be at risk (as was true of half-day nursery school); and that day care is best delayed when there are major stresses or changes in family routine. Rutter reported that although day care "for very young children is not likely to result in serious emotional disturbance, it would be misleading to conclude that it is without risks or effects" (p. 4).

Kagan and his associates (1978) have found that attendance at a day-care center "staffed by conscientious and nurturant adults during the first 2½ years of life does not seem to produce a psychological profile very different from the one created by rearing totally in the home" (pp. 260–261). However, the Kagan group recommends that group care be initiated either when the infant is between 1 and 7 months or more than 15 to 18 months of age, that is, before attachments are beginning to be formed or after they are firmly established. For children under the age of 3 years, Kagan et al. recommended that a caretaker be responsible for no more than three children.

Although Clarke-Stewart (1982) agrees on the importance of the caretaker:child ratio, she considers the characteristics of the caregiver to be even more important. According to Clarke-Stewart, a caregiver who considers herself a professional, who has training in child development, who has at least 5 years' experience, and who is part of a training and support network of educationally oriented centers is most likely to give sensitive, involved care and to have a positive influence on the child's development.

In a critical review of more than 40 studies on the effects of day care, Belsky and Steinberg (1978) conclude that in respect to emotional development:

> The weight of the evidence indicates that daycare is not disruptive of the child's emotional bond with his mother, even when daycare is initiated in the first year of life. In addition, there is no indication that exposure to daycare decreases the child's preference for his mother in comparison with an alternative familiar caregiver. Finally, with respect to social development, the existing data indicate that daycare-reared children, when compared with age-mates reared at home, interact more with peers in both positive and negative ways. Some evidence does suggest that children enrolled in daycare for extended periods of time show increased aggression toward peers and adults and decreased cooperation with adults and involvement in educational activities once the child enters school, but these consequences are more likely to be functions of particular socialization values than of daycare in general. (p. 944)

The studies reported here must be interpreted with care, and extrapolations made with great caution. Systematic empirical investigation of day care and its effects is relatively recent, with that of Caldwell, Wright, Honig, and Tannenbaum (1970) being the earliest published. Most research has been restricted primarily to well-funded centers of relatively high quality: Often these are university-based or university-connected, with high staff:child ratios, and with programs thoughtfully designed to foster cognitive, social, and emotional development. Unfortunately, in terms of type or quality, these centers are not representative of most day care currently available to parents in the United States.

Household Moves

The impact on young children of moving to a different home is frequently overlooked. A move motivated by economic reverses or by separation/divorce is especially problematic, because such a move is burdensome on adults as well. But even in the absence of concomitant financial strain, Kliman (1968) reported that moving itself stresses "the child's concept of himself and the world" (p. 106). In the case of the child under 3 years of age, Kliman observed that the physical environment may incorporate features of a transitional object, as described by Winnicott (1953).

Although toddlers and younger children are invested less in their milieu than in family members, Kliman (1968) noted that following a move, the younger child is likely to regress developmentally. Moore (1969) considered that for the child less than 2 years of age, change of routine was the most frequent cause of distress.

Although all children suffer from maternal fatigue and parental dissatisfaction with the move, older children are more likely to miss friends, relatives, and familiar surroundings. Serious disturbance is most frequently reported among anxious children and in families with insecure relationships.

Parental Separation and Divorce

Because the divorce rate is highest early in marriage, many of its victims are young children, most of whom—because of the "tender years doctrine"*—are living with their mother. Indeed, 21% of the 5 million children living with a divorced mother are under 6 years of age (U.S. Bureau of the Census, 1983). It is difficult to tease out the effects of the legal event of divorce from those of the preceding "emotional divorce" (Despert, 1962), with its characteristic discordance and strain.

In most cases, the months before separation are disharmonious and the separation period itself is stormy. Most traumatic is the kind of situation in which there are changes of household locks, police involvement, grandparental intervention, forced entry and surreptitious removal of furnishings, and allegations by one parent concerning danger posed by the other. Both separation and divorce represent a disruption of regular contact with two parents and, often, an abrupt change in daily routine. For the preschool child, a concomitant move away from familiar surroundings may exacerbate the stress of divorce. As did Kliman (1968), Stirtzinger (1984), too, relates the family home to a transitional object: An analysis of drawings of preschool children of divorce suggests that the children's "mourning is fixated for a time at least around loss of the home and cannot proceed as quickly to the loss of the real parent objects or toward the process of seeing the parents as real people and adjusting to a new style of living" (p. 2).

Although theoretical proposals abound concerning the impact of divorce on the preschool child, pertinent research in this age group has been relatively limited. Preschool children are referred infrequently for psychiatric evaluation and are less accessible as research subjects than are older children. Then, too, the stress of divorce may be cumulative over time.

An early investigation of the impact of divorce on the preschool child was that of McDermott (1968), who reported on the experiences of 16 children, 10 of whom demonstrated acute behavioral changes presenting management problems:

> There is often an initial period of shock and acute depressive reactions. Clinically observed regressive phenomena were followed by restoration of previous skills and subsequent resolution and mastery both in play and verbally.

> Sex differences were noted, with boys demonstrating more dramatic changes in behavior, characterized by the abrupt release of aggressive and destructive feelings. Boys

---

*A number of colorful comments are found in the "tender years" cases. "There is but a twilight zone between a mother's love and the atmosphere of heaven, and all things being equal, no child should be deprived of that maternal influence unless it should be shown there are special or extraordinary reasons for so doing" (*Luter v. Luter*, 1938); "For a boy of such tenders years nothing can be an adequate substitute for mother love—for that constant ministration required during the period of nurture that only a mother can give because in her alone is duty swallowed up in desire, in her alone is service expressed in love" (*Jenkins v. Jenkins*, 1921).

seemed more vulnerable to gross disruption of identifications already in process than the girls. Some of the children, principally girls, seemed to show a tendency to identify with selected pathological features of the parent of the same sex. (p. 1431)

Hetherington, Cox, and Cox (1978) reported on a 2-year study of 24 boys and 24 girls of preschool age and 48 matched controls from intact families: Children in divorced families were "more dependent, disobedient, aggressive, whining, demanding, and unaffectionate than children in intact families" (p. 174). The effects were most prominent in mother–son interactions. One year after divorce, stress in parent–child interactions peaked, after which marked improvement occurred, especially in mother–child relations.

In a retrospective review of the records of 387 children referred for outpatient psychiatric evaluation, Kalter (1977) found twice as many children from divorced families as would be expected from their incidence in the general population. In the case of 91 children under 7 years, the proportion exhibiting aggression toward parents was more than twice as high in the divorced single-parent group as it was in children from intact families. For boys under 7 years, children of divorce had significantly fewer school problems than did children from intact homes.

Using parent report, teacher report, and direct observation, Hodges, Wechsler, and Ballantine (1979) studied 26 preschool children from divorced homes and 26 from intact families. Few statistically significant differences were noted: On observation in preschool and day-care centers, children of divorce were more withdrawn in structured situations than were children from intact families; the converse was true in unstructured situations. Children from intact families were viewed as more cooperative by their parents than were children from divorced families (as rated by their parents). Teachers did not rate the children differently on any of the measured dimensions. In relation to children of divorce, maladjustment was predicted by younger parents, limited financial resources, and geographic mobility, though these variables were unrelated to maladjustment in children from intact homes.

The longest ongoing inquiry into the effects of parental divorce on children is that of Wallerstein and Kelly (1975). Their sample includes 131 subjects who ranged from 2½ to 18 years of age in 1971. Of these, 34 preschool children were divided by age into three subgroups: 2½ to 3¼ years; 3¾ to 4¾ years; and 5 to 6 years.

In the youngest group, family disruption triggered regressions, fretfulness, cognitive bewilderment, heightened aggression, and neediness. . . . The more vulnerable children . . . showed depressive reactions and/or constriction and delays in development.

In the middle preschool group, divorce appeared to cogwheel with early superego development, specifically burdening the child's self-esteem and self-image. . . . Some children suffered with feelings of responsibility for driving the father away. Poor outcome here included signs of depressive illness and, again, developmental inhibitions.

In the oldest preschool children, it became possible for the first time for a child to experience family turbulence and divorce without breaking developmental stride. . . . In the vulnerable children, we saw particular difficulty in bringing resolution to oedipal conflicts, and consequent delay in beginning the tasks of latency. . . . Of particular concern is the early disruption in learning which may be difficult to reverse. (pp. 614–615)

One year later, at follow-up, 44% of the preschool children were considered to be in significantly worsened psychological condition, although none had had any prior history of psychological difficulty. Wallerstein and Kelly (1975) attributed the children's psychological deterioration to the diminished quality of the mother–child relationship during the year following divorce. In contrast to their peers who did less well, 42% of the preschool children seemed "to have weathered the initial postseparation period and to have resumed the developmental progress which had been briefly interrupted" (Wallerstein, 1977, p. 290). Wallerstein related their improvement

to the reestablishing of caretaking, reasonable routines, and adequate parenting by the custodial parent . . . ; the capacity of the divorcing parents to keep continuing angers and conflicts separate from their relationship with the children; . . . teachers with time and sensitivity to offer individual support and encouragement to the child; appropriate distancing from a pathological parent–child relationship, where this preceded the divorce; and the absence of overt rejection or desertion by either parent. (p. 290)

In accordance with other research (e.g., Hetherington et al., 1978), Wallerstein and Kelly (1980) found that after 18 months, many of the boys, whose adjustment at the time of the divorce was almost on a par with that of the girls, were significantly more distressed, whereas many of the girls seemed to have recovered. At 5-year follow-up, many of the preschool children were still moderately to severely depressed (Wallerstein & Kelly, 1980), irrespective of sex.

Recently, preliminary findings of a 10-year follow-up of the same longitudinal study were reported (Wallerstein, 1984). The preschool children who had been the most troubled at the time of their parents' divorce, "by virtue of their own immaturity at the time and the repressive processes at work, have emerged less consciously troubled than their older siblings, who had difficulty in mastering or erasing the memory of the family travail" (p. 458). Wallerstein recognizes that the attitudes expressed may reflect the youngsters' current adolescent stage and that future research is needed to validate the findings. Even if proven true that younger children are ultimately less scarred by divorce, their original disequilibrium and deteriorated functioning are nonetheless real and sobering. As one of the Wallerstein preschool children of divorce reported as an adolescent, "Divorce sure isn't easy on kids" (1984, p. 456).

Stepparenting

An offshoot of separation and divorce involves the stepparent family, sometimes called "recoupled," "reconstituted," or "blended." The death of a parent may also result in a stepparent situation, though, today, blended families more commonly represent an attempt to form a new marriage after one or both partners have had divorces (Jacobson, 1980). The likelihood that recoupled family members have experienced rejection and/or abandonment adds to the unique vulnerability of the marital arrangement.

The child in a blended family must accommodate to an expanded number of relationships, including a stepparent or two and, often, stepsiblings—not to mention additional "grandparents," "aunts," "uncles," and "cousins." The child must learn to share at least one biological parent with a new stepparent, while maintaining a new kind of relationship with the other biological parent and, possibly, with biological siblings who are no longer in the home.

There are no hard statistics as to the number of reconstituted families in the United States. Experts estimate that 6.6 million children under 18 years of age live full time with a stepparent; if part-time residents of a stepparent household were included, the figure would probably be closer to 15 million (Duffin, 1978). Much of what is known about the stepfamily phenomenon is due largely to the work of Emily and John Visher (1979, 1982), founders of the nationally acclaimed Stepfamily Association of America.

Young children and persons of adult age generally accept a stepparent with much greater ease than do teenage children (Duberman, 1973). In a 6-year follow-up of the Hetherington, Cox, and Cox study (1981), it was found that young boys often formed close attachments and positive relationships with their stepfathers; but even with a supportive stepfather, a continued positive relationship with the biological father was needed for the youngster to develop cognitive and social competence.

For girls living in a reconstituted family, the outcome in the Hetherington et al. study (1981) was not significantly different from that of girls of divorced or intact families (in the study). This finding contradicts that of Santrok, Warshak, Lindberg, and Meadows (1982), who reported unfavorable outcomes for girls in reconstituted families, possibly associated with the presence of a stepfather. Similarly, Kalter (1977) found that of the first 400 children referred to Youth Services, one fifth of all girls referred for psychiatric evaluation came from a blended family with divorce in its background; this represented approximately twice the rate for boys, leading Kalter to conclude that "living in a stepparent household, typically with a stepfather, subsequent to a divorce, constitutes an especially stressful circumstance for girls" (p. 44). It should be noted that Kalter's analysis is based on "all girls"; the small number of subjects under 7 years of age obviated statistically significant findings in the youngest subsample of both males and females.

Death

For all ages, death is the ultimate separation. In studying children's reactions to death, Anthony (1972) found that children less than 4 or 5 years old either ignored the phenomenon or responded to it with puzzlement or with detached and somewhat callous interest. Connell (1979) related this apparent lack of overt grief to bewilderment and fear of abandonment. Deutsch (1937) hypothesized that the inability of the immature ego to bear the strain of mourning precipitates narcissistic self-protective mechanisms, including the omission of affect; she assumed that the "general tendency to 'unmotivated' depressions is the subsequent expression of emotional reactions which were once withheld and have since remained in latent readiness for discharge" (p. 22).

Bowlby (1961) observed, in contrast, that, upon the loss of a loved object during the period roughly between 6 months and 6 years of age, young children, like adults, go through the sequence of responses characteristic of mourning—namely, protest, despair, and detachment. But Bowlby noted two significant differences in early childhood: (1) an abbreviated time period of mourning, and (2) premature development of the processes leading to detachment, because they "coincide with and mask strong residual yearning for and anger with the lost object, both of which persist, ready for expression, at an unconscious level" (p. 484). Bowlby attributed the precipitate onset of defensive processes (fixation, ego splitting, and repression) to subsequent psychopathology, in the form of "faulty personality development and proneness to psychiatric illness" (p. 487).

Indeed, many studies suggest the probable pathogenicity of childhood bereavement. Unfortunately, much of the research is difficult to interpret, in that the investigators lump together all losses occurring before a specified age in the late teens, thereby ignoring the critical variable of "level of libido development" (A. Freud, 1960, p. 61). However, several studies do analyze the data according to loss within discrete age periods and thereby shed light on the area of current interest.

In exploring the relationship between early bereavement and psychiatric disturbance in childhood, Rutter (1966) found that many of the youngsters who were observed to be more disturbed than the control subjects had lost a parent during the 3rd or 4th year of life; in the nature of things, this would have deprived the child at least of a model for identification. Referral for services was made most frequently around the age of puberty.

At least one elegant study involving adult psychiatric inpatients and outpatients (Beck, Sethi, & Tuthill, 1963) demonstrated a correlation between early childhood bereavement (before the age of 4) and subsequent depression. Munro (1966) reported no evidence that maternal loss in early childhood predisposes an individual to develop depressive illness; at the same time, he stated that in the case of severely depressed patients, there was a likelihood of early maternal death. Earle (1961), too, reported significantly more depression in persons separated from their mothers by death than in those separated for other reasons.

As with adult depressives, there is a tendency for sociopaths to have experienced early parental loss. In studying sociopaths, neurotic patients, and controls, Greer (1964) found that significantly more sociopaths than neurotics or controls had been parentally deprived before the age of 5 and had in fact lost *both* parents. In a later comparison of suicidal and nonsuicidal patients with sociopathic and neurotic disorders, Greer (1966) found that suicidal neurotics had a significantly higher incidence of parental loss, commonly of both parents, and, most often, before 5 years of age.

Kliman (1968) studied 18 "nonpatient" children within 15 months of their bereavement. The youngsters ranged from less than a year in age to 14 years. The 8 children with the poorest ratings of emotional health were the youngest children (under 4 years) who had suffered the loss of either parent, girls who had lost a mother before the age of 8 years, and adolescent boys whose fathers had died. As a potential prognostic sign Kliman offers persistent overt disbelief, which he distinguishes from "a treasured fantasy that the lost parent is still alive somewhere . . . [and from] the difficulty preschool children have in comprehending that death is permanent" (p. 81).

The preceding studies have documented the probable pathogenicity of early childhood bereavement. But the point should be made that many bereaved youngsters apparently escape subsequent psychopathology altogether. As is true in regard to other stressors in the first years of life, complex forces—many as yet unknown—act to mitigate the impact of early object loss.

EVENTS IN WHICH SEPARATION IS NOT AN ISSUE

In the stressors considered thus far, separation from caretakers has been of cardinal importance. However, within the first 5 years of life other events occur that are also sources of stress, although separation is not a central issue. Among these stressors are physical handicaps and illness not requiring hospitalization; child abuse and neglect; sibling rivalry; and overstimulating and/or frightening experiences.

Physical Handicaps and Illness Not Requiring Hospitalization

Physical Handicaps. In general, adaptation to physical handicaps—on the part of the child—is somewhat easier in childhood, especially when the handicap is present at birth or develops very early in life (Connell, 1979). Some handicaps (e.g., cerebral palsy and spina bifida) may involve disturbances in appearance, mobility, and control of bodily functions.

Wolff (1973) distinguished between *recognized* and *masked handicaps*. She proposed unrecognized handicaps as the more potent psychological hazard, and offered as examples undetected deafness, mild cerebral palsy, and petit mal. If a child is stressed by a recognized handicap, the stress is often compounded by parental overprotection or rejection (which in turn results from unconscious parental guilt).

Recently, the attitude of society has shifted in the direction of increased tolerance of handicaps. In the educational sphere, Public Law 94-142 became the law of the land in 1975, guaranteeing a free public education in the least restrictive environment for all children, regardless of handicap.

Childhood Illness. Being ill generally involves associated psychological difficulties. Anna Freud (1952) noted that some young children resist relinquishing— even temporarily—recently achieved skills in independent eating and toileting; when asked to behave as patients, they become difficult and even intractable. Other youngsters regress all too readily and may later need to relearn previously mastered abilities. In the case of a young child, Freud considered restraint of movement even more upsetting than temporarily relinquishing ego skills: "Young toddlers, who have only recently learned to walk, . . . stand up stubbornly in their beds for the whole course even of severe illnesses . . . until exhaustion forces them to adopt the lying position" (p. 72). Following a serious illness, even in the absence of hospitalization, Freud (1952) reported that "mood swings, changes in the relationship to parents and siblings, loss of self-confidence, temper tantrums often appear for the first time. . . . Symptoms, such as bed wetting, soiling, feeding and sleeping troubles . . . may reappear" (p. 70).

Chronic illnesses often necessitate dietetic restrictions that identify the child as "different"; at times these have pathologic sequelae. For example, Shirley (1963) reported that, for children with diabetes, a rigid dietary regimen often caused chronic emotional tension that, in turn, exacerbated regulation of blood sugar level. Some children responded with overdependence; others resorted to "anxious compulsiveness, passive resistance, or outright rebellion" (p. 531).

Wolff (1973) observed that children with diabetes often have "magical notions of why *they* were singled out by this disease" (p. 85) and guilt feelings in relation to their parents. Earlier, Langford (1948) had written of young children's animistic explanations of their illness and of their childish misconceptions and fears: To most children, all illness is at least partially caused by their own disobedience and misdeeds.

In analyzing variations in response to physical pain, Anna Freud (1952) emphasized the pain's psychic meaning:

According to the child's interpretation of the event, young children react to pain not only with anxiety but with other affects appropriate to the content of the unconscious fantasies, i.e., on the one hand with anger, rage and revenge feelings, on the other hand with masochistic submission, guilt or depression. (p. 76)

Freud also explained the child's characteristic devotion to the doctor in terms of the psychological meaning of pain: "The infliction of pain calls forth passive masochistic responses which hold an important place in the child's love life" (p. 77).

Child Abuse and Neglect

Although child maltreatment has been recorded for many years, it was not until 1962, with Kempe's seminal description of the battered child (Kempe, Silverman, Steele, Droegemueller, & Silver, 1962), that child abuse and neglect emerged as an area of professional interest. Recent dramatic increases in recorded abuse reflect more systematized reporting procedures, along with an exponential increase in the incidence of the phenomenon. Indeed, today, child maltreatment is not only a significant source of stress, but is also a foremost cause of serious injury and death in preschool children.

Legal definitions of child maltreatment vary from very specific descriptions to more general conceptualizations. In distinguishing between abuse and neglect, it is generally agreed that abuse implies an act of commission, in contrast to neglect, which signifies an act of omission. In most child abuse legislation, emotional abuse is also included as a reportable condition.

All abused and neglected children are at risk for developmental and emotional disorders. While being fed and dressed, neglected babies are deprived of tactile/ proprioceptive stimulation and pleasurable social interaction. Because their internal body processes are neither validated nor integrated by appropriate parental responses, the consequence according to Steele (1983) may well be the absence of an integrated sense of self. In addition, throughout life, this may also give rise to a tragically diminished sense of self-esteem.

When caretaking behavior is determined by the caretaker's convenience and not by the child's needs, and when early exploratory activities are thwarted, the child incorporates the caretaker's unempathic attitude. Deprived of mutually satisfying interactions, the child "is motivated more by the necessity to avoid pain than by pleasurable reward, thus throwing out of balance the normal regulatory function of the pleasure principle" (Steele, 1983, p. 238). Punitive attempts to control a child's behavior may take place during feeding, dressing, and sleeping activities, and are often observed during toilet training. With self-initiated activities prohibited, the child develops "a persistent, mild, pseudoparanoid attitude toward other people, particularly those in authority. . . . These features, plus a tendency toward a mild, chronic anaclitic type of depression, and persistent needy dependence continue on into adulthood" (p. 239).

In considering the effect of physical abuse on psychological development, Steele observed:

> The frequent bruises, lacerations, burns, and fractures which happen to nearly all children during childhood have relatively little untoward effect on the psyche if they are of accidental origin. It is the fact that the injury is inflicted by the person to whom the child must look for care and protection that is most traumatic. (p. 237)

Steele proposed that, under such circumstances, there is a possibility of distortion or disintegration of ego development. In the absence of any means of protection, the child's exposure to external pain may preclude the development of appropriate ways of dealing with anxiety. Instead, the child may respond with "either helpless, submissive withdrawal or excessive, aggressive discharge" (p. 240).

During extensive clinical work with abused children, Green (1982), too, observed that the children's overwhelming experiences often resulted in a paralysis of ego functioning and acute anxiety states. He also noted that "early and pervasive exposure to parental rejection, assault, and deprivation had an adverse effect on the development of subsequent object relationships. . . . Violence and rejection were regarded as the major ingredients of human encounters" (p. 253). Green reported further that abused children relied excessively on primitive defense mechanisms; that they frequently engaged in aggressive and destructive behavior; that they were often dejected and self-deprecatory; that they commonly exhibited masochistic and self-destructive behavior; and that they manifested difficulties in separation and in adjustment to school. Regardless of their innocence in the situation, young children generally considered themselves in some way responsible for—and, therefore, deserving of—parental punishment and threatened abandonment.

In a controlled study of toddlers who experienced abuse and neglect (George & Main, 1979), observations were made of interactions with caregivers and peers in a day care setting. The abused toddlers either ignored friendly overtures and caring approaches by adults or responded to them negatively. They expressed significantly more aggressive acts, including physical assault, toward both peers and caretakers.

Sexual Abuse and Misuse. Variants of child abuse are childhood sexual abuse and misuse. In child sexual abuse, a child is used for the sexual gratification of a person who is significantly older. The term "sexual misuse" was coined by Brant and Tisza (1977) to refer to the sexual stimulation of a child, to a degree which is inappropriate for his age and development. Because a large number of incidents are unreported, the actual extent of the problem is unknown. However, sexual abuse is considered the "most concealed, most distressing, and most controversial form of child abuse" (Summit & Kryso, 1978, p. 250).

Child sexual abuse is most frequently perpetrated by members of the immediate family (incest) or by neighbors or close acquaintances of the child; overall, girls are more frequently reported as sexually abused than are boys. Although documented most frequently in the age range of 11 to 14 years (DeFrancis, 1971), in recent years accounts of preschool children as targets of sexual abuse have increased markedly, at times such events occurring within the day-care setting itself. In 1979, Finkelhor observed that almost one fourth of reported cases involved children under the age of 6 years. Four years later, Khan and Sexton (1983) found that one half of reported cases of sexual abuse and gonorrhea in children under 12 involved youngsters less than 6 years of age.

Sexually abused and misused children present with both physical and behavioral signs and symptoms. On examination such infants may manifest reddened or traumatized genitalia or more generalized symptoms, such as disturbances in activity level, sleeping, and eating. Toddlers and preschool children may be brought in with genital irritation or injury, or with such physical complaints as stomachache, anxiety, insomnia, and attentional problems. As less specific symptoms of sexual abuse and misuse, Brant and Tisza (1977) indicated "enuresis, hyperactivity, altered sleeping patterns, fears, phobias, overly compulsive behavior, learning problems, compulsive masturbation, precocious 'sexual play,' excessive curiosity about sexual matters, and separation anxiety" (p. 84).

Being assaulted by a known and trusted person adds to the child's confusion and exacerbates the psychic trauma that the child sustains. Summit and Kryso's clinical experience (1978) reinforces the observation of Peters (1973) that preoedipal rape victims not only blame themselves but also take on the guilty reactions of their parents. The children feel undeserving of love and care, with their perceptions of heightened sexuality commingled with feelings of fear and guilt. "The child grows up expecting and deserving abuse, often searching endlessly and hopelessly for a redeeming experience with an older partner" (Summit & Kryso, 1978, p. 249). Given the rate of positive cultures for gonorrhea found in their very young pediatric group, Khan and Sexton (1983) added potential medical sequelae to these psychological consequences.

Sibling Rivalry

A well-recognized stressor in early childhood, and one with implications throughout the life cycle, relates to the status of sibling. Indeed, Sigmund Freud (1958) observed that children harbor death wishes toward new siblings, and Winnicott (1964) considered the stress arising from the birth of a sibling to be so commonplace as to be classified as "normal." In reviewing the literature on sibling birth, Legg, Sherick, & Wadland (1974) found the most frequently reported immediate reaction to a sibling's birth to be "direct aggression toward the baby, attention-seeking behavior, and varying degrees of regression, with the alternative of a move toward mastery and independence" (p. 4).

In his discussion of the stress associated with the birth of a sibling, Moore (1969) reported on a study by Henchie (1963) of the immediate reactions and subsequent relationships of 66 children to their next younger siblings. Initially, only 15%

showed marked displeasure and an additional 27%, slight displeasure. When the younger child became a play-disrupting toddler, there was a tendency for older siblings' attitudes to deteriorate; by the age of 8 years, however, disregarding normal squabbles, only 11% of the children had a strained relationship with their younger siblings.

At the time of their siblings' birth, Henchie (1963) found a greater probability of disturbance in 89% of children under 3 years (especially those separated for the first time) and in 11% of children older than 6 years. Although no overall difference was found between sexes, a male newborn produced somewhat more negative reactions in boys and more disturbance in the mother–child relationship in girls. Birth order had a limited impact on the older sibling, with the distress of firstborns only slightly more than that of later born children.

Thomas, Birch, Chess, and Robbins (1961) reported on the birth of a sibling in 18 families who participated in a large early childhood study. More than half of the older children showed aggressive behavior toward the new baby and marked regression in ego functioning. The researchers found ''a definite relationship between the characteristics of primary reactivity in the child and the type of response to the birth of a sibling'' (p. 800). Disturbances were nonexistent or minimal in children who, from birth on, had adapted easily to new stimuli.

In an earlier investigation of sibling rivalry, Levy (1938) found a positive relationship between closeness of the mother–child relationship and disturbance on the part of the child at the birth of a sibling. Levy found initial aggression most frequently directed toward the mother. Legg and associates (1974) found that when witnessing breast-feeding, children responded with jealousy and resentment. In their study of 21 families, they observed that on the occasion of a younger sibling's birth, active paternal involvement with the displaced child made the inevitable diminution of maternal attention more tolerable.

Overstimulating and/or Frightening Experiences

Reference has been made in earlier sections to experiences that might be classified as ''overstimulating and/or frightening.'' For example, although young children often react with jealousy when witnessing a new sibling nursing at the mother's breast, overstimulation, confusion, and fear may also be salient aspects of the experience. Legg and her colleagues (1974) told of a 15-month-old girl who on first witnessing breast-feeding had screamed ''Eat, eat!'' as if the infant were eating the mother. Some youngsters requested a turn at the breast, which—if granted— could arouse ''very exciting fantasies on the older child's part'' (p. 31).

Also previously noted was the horrifying experience of child abuse. In the section on sexual abuse and misuse, mention was made of sexual overstimulation, which may lead later to precocious seeking out of sexual stimulation or, conversely, to dread of sexual activity in adulthood. Other overstimulating and/or frightening experiences include observing the primal scene and witnessing crimes of violence.

Sibling presence at childbirth is at least potentially overstimulating and will be considered briefly.

Primal Scene. Kliman (1968) explained the trauma experienced in observation of the primal scene (parental coitus) in terms of the child's perceptual and cognitive framework. Because the young child's immature ego lacks a firm sense of reality, parental sexual behavior may be misunderstood and may stimulate sadistic and/or castration fantasies. Fraiberg (1952) reported the development of night terrors, daytime fearfulness, and interference with a sense of reality in a 2½-year-old girl who had observed her grandparents having intercourse.

Witnessing Crimes of Violence. Witnessing parental suicide or homicide, too, is deeply disturbing; it may interfere with the child's sense of reality and may impact negatively on subsequent emotional development. Loss of a significant love object, for whatever reason, may undermine later affective development, even in the absence of immediate evidence of psychological distress:

> Observing the violent ending of a loved person's life adds a crushing load of over-stimulating perceptions, plus conflict over the child's own homicidal impulses which have been excited by the real life example. When the murder of one love-object has been committed by another, the calamitous example of the latter's weakness in respect to homicidal impulses further undermines the child's ability to control similar impulses of his own. (Kliman, 1968, p. 119)

Sibling Presence at Childbirth. A recent study (Mehl, Brandsel, & Peterson, 1977) suggests that sibling presence at childbirth facilitates an open attitude toward birth as a ''natural'' process. Many hospitals now offer alternative birthing rooms, with an environment that simulates the home setting and affords an opportunity for participation by the entire family, including young children. Anderson (1979) studied 43 children who were present at the birth of a sibling; she found that, with anticipatory guidance during pregnancy and sensitive care during childbirth, children as young as 2 years had ''not only the ability, but the need and desire to participate as fully as possible in the birth of their siblings'' (p. 87). That the experience might be considered overstimulating for some children was indicated by anecdotal reports:

> One 2-year-old was awakened in the middle of the night for the birth, and cried softly for a brief period and clung to the father. . . . The second qualified positive experience involved a 3-year-old girl who was shocked at the blood, and decided the mother and baby were both dead. This naturally scared the child, but because of the discussions which followed, the parents considered it a positive learning experience for the child. (Anderson, 1979, p. 80)

Studies of the long-term sequelae of sibling presence at childbirth are clearly indicated.

CONCLUSION

Stressful Events Not Considered

The current consideration of developmental sources of stress has not been exhaustive. Not included in the discussion were several environmental stressors that impact negatively during the first 5 years of life.

The circumstance of illegitimate birth and subsequent rearing by an unmarried parent spawns even more complex problems than does living in a family made incomplete by death, divorce, or separation. Potent generalized stressors are often present that are not related exclusively to illegitimacy; these include chronic poverty and sociocultural deprivation. The confusing partial relationship to a father, the stressed responses of a mother seeking at once to prepare herself for a career, to have a social life, to make ends meet, and to rear her baby form a syndrome that is repeated throughout the culture.

Also conspicuously absent in the discussion were considerations of stress caused by parental mental illness, by adoption, by placement in foster home care, and by natural environmental calamity. In the latter category are disasters such as earthquake, tornado, and war. Preschool children exposed to such psychic trauma as wartime blackouts (Solomon, 1942) often display heightened activity and aggression, in sharp contrast to earlier behavior. Residual sequelae characteristically diminish the youngsters' ability to cope with even ordinary environmental demands.

Variations in Reaction to Stress

Many variables influence the degree of disequilibrium caused by the developmental stressors considered in this chapter. As indicated earlier, Benswanger's ecological approach (1982) is helpful in studying the impact of stressful events in early childhood. Yates (1983), too, proposes the use of a complex biopsychosocial matrix consisting of "the magnitude and duration of the stressful event; the reactions of significant adults to the stress; the ambiguity of circumstances; and the child's age, emotional well being, available defenses, temperament, personality traits, and attributes" (p. 131).

Yates (1983) observed that several variables "can be consciously altered to diminish the emotional morbidity which attends natural and man-made stress" (p. 131). Most often, the stressor itself cannot be eliminated; however, the reactions of significant persons can be altered, ambiguities clarified, the child's defenses supported, and his or her problem-solving ability and sense of mastery enhanced. Considering the multiplicity of developmental stressors to which a child is subject during the first 5 years of life, the need for stress management techniques becomes apparent.

REFERENCES

Ainsworth, M. (1966). The development of infant-mother attachment. In B. Caldwell & H. Riccuiti (Eds.), *Child Development and Social Policy* (pp. 1–94). Chicago: University of Chicago Press.

Anderson, S. V. D. (1979). Siblings at birth: A survey and a study. *Birth and the Family Journal, 6*, 80–87.

Anthony, S. (1972). *The discovery of death in childhood and after.* New York: Basic Books.

Beck, A. T., Sethi, B. B., & Tuthill, R. W. (1963). Childhood bereavement and adult depression. *Archives of General Psychiatry, 9*, 295–302.

Belsky, J., & Steinberg, L. D. (1978). The effects of day care: A critical review. *Child Development, 49*, 929–949.

Benswanger, E. G. (1982). Stressful events in childhood: An ecological approach. *Child Care Quarterly, 11*, 267–279.

Blehar, M. C. (1974). Anxious attachment and defensive reactions associated with day care. *Child Development, 45*, 683–692.

Bloom-Feshbach, S. (1981). Separation reactions and nursery school adjustment. *Dissertation Abstracts International, 41*, 4251–4252.

Bloom-Feshbach, S., Bloom-Feshbach, J., & Gaughran, J. (1980). The child's tie to both parents: Separation patterns and nursery school adjustment. *American Journal of Orthopsychiatry, 50*, 505–521.

Bowlby, J. (1961). Childhood mourning and its implications for psychiatry. *American Journal of Psychiatry, 118*, 481–498.

Bowlby, J. (1969). *Attachment and loss* (Vol. 1). New York: Basic Books.

Brant, R. S. T., & Tisza, V. B. (1977). The sexually misused child. *American Journal of Orthopsychiatry, 47*, 80–90.

Brazelton, T. B. (1973). *Neonatal behavioral assessment scale.* Philadelphia: Lippencott.

Caldwell, B. M., Wright, C., Honig, A., & Tannenbaum, J. (1970). Infant day care and attachment. *American Journal of Orthopsychiatry, 40*, 397–412.

Carlsson, S. G., Fagerberg, H., Horneman, G., Hwang, G. P., Larsson, K., Rodholm, M., Schaller, J., Danielson, B., & Gundewall, C. (1979). Effects of various amounts of contact between mother and child on the mother's nursing behavior. *Infant Behavior and Development, 2*, 209–214.

Chess, S., & Thomas, A. (1982). Infant bonding. *American Journal of Orthopsychiatry, 52*, 213–222.

Clarke-Stewart, A. (1982). *Daycare.* Cambridge: Harvard University Press.

Coddington, R. D. (1972). The significance of life events as etiologic factors in the diseases of children. *Journal of Psychosomatic Research, 16*, 7–18, 205–213.

Connell, H. M. (1979). *Essentials of child psychiatry.* London: Blackwell Scientific Publications.

de Chateau, P. (1980). Parent–neonate interaction and its long-term effects. In E. G. Simmel (Ed.), *Early experience and early behavior* (pp. 109–179). New York: Academic Press.

DeFrancis, V. (1971). Protecting the child victim of sex crimes committed by adults. *Federal Probation, 35*, 15–20.

Despert, J. (1962). *Children of divorce.* Garden City, NY: Dolphin Books.

Deutsch, H. (1937). Absence of grief. *Psychoanalytic Quarterly, 6*, 12–22.

Doyle, A. B. (1975). Infant development in day care. *Developmental Psychology, 11*, 655–656.

Duberman, L.: (1973). Step-kin relationships. *Journal of Marriage and the Family, 35*, 283–292.

Duffin, S. R. (1978). *Yours, mine, & ours: Tips for stepparents*. Washington, DC: National Institute of Mental Health.

Earle, A. M., & Earle, B. V. (1961). Early maternal deprivation and later psychiatric illness. *American Journal of Orthopsychiatry, 31*, 181–186.

Falender, C. A., & Heber, R. (1975). Mother-child interaction and participation in a longitudinal intervention program. *Developmental Psychology, 11*, 830–836.

Finkelhor, D. (1979). *Sexually victimized children*. New York: Free Press.

Fraiberg, S. (1952). A critical neurosis in a two-and-a-half year old girl. *Psychoanalytic Study of the Child, 7*, 173–215.

Freud, A. (1952). The role of bodily illness in the mental life of children. *Psychoanalytic Study of the Child, 7*, 69–82.

Freud, A. (1960). Discussion of Dr. John Bowlby's paper. *Psychoanalytic Study of the Child, 15*, 53–62.

Freud, S. (1958). Interpretation of dreams. In J. Strachey (Ed. and Trans.), The *standard edition of the complete psychological works of Sigmund Freud* (Vol. 4). London: Hogarth Press.

George, C., & Main, M. (1979). Social interactions of young abused children: Approach, avoidance, and aggression. *Child Development, 50*, 306–318.

Green, A. H. (1982). Child abuse. In J. R. Lachenmeyer & M. S. Gibbs (Eds.), *Psychopathology in childhood* (pp. 244–267). New York: Gardner Press.

Greenacre, P. (1945). The biological economy of birth. In A. Freud, H. Hartmann, & E. Kris (Eds.), *Psychoanalytic study of the child* (Vol. 1, pp. 31–51). New York: International Universities Press.

Greenberg, M., Rosenberg, I., & Lind, J. (1973). First mothers rooming-in with their newborns. *American Journal of Orthopsychiatry, 43*, 783–788.

Greer, S. (1964). Study of parental loss in neurotics and sociopaths. *Archives of General Psychiatry, 11*, 177–180.

Greer, S. (1966). Parental loss and attempted suicide: A further report. *British Journal of Psychiatry, 112*, 465–470.

Grossman, K., Thane, K., & Grossman, K. E. (1981). Maternal tactual contact of the newborn after various postpartum conditions of mother–infant contact. *Developmental Psychology, 17*, 158–169.

Guendelman, S. D. R. (1980). Children's readiness to separate from their parents. *Dissertation Abstracts International, 40*, 4260.

Heinicke, C., & Westheimer, I. (1965). *Brief separations*. New York: International Universities Press.

Henchie, V. (1963). *Children's reactions to the birth of a new baby*. Unpublished thesis in child development, University of London Institute of Education.

Herbert, M., Sluckin, W., & Sluckin, A. (1982). Mother-to-infant "bonding." *Journal of Child Psychology & Psychiatry, 23*, 205–221.

Hetherington, E. M., Cox, M., & Cox, R. (1978). The aftermath of divorce. In J. H. Stevens, Jr. & M. Matthews (Eds.), *Mother/child father/child relationships* (pp. 149–176). Washington, DC: National Association for the Education of Young Children.

Hetherington, E. M., Cox, M., & Cox, R. (1981). Effects of divorce on parents and children. In M. Lamb (Ed.), *Nontraditional families* (pp. 233–288). Hillsdale, NJ: Erlbaum.

Hodges, W. F., Wechsler, R. C., & Ballantine, C. (1979). Divorce and the preschool child: Cumulative stress. *Journal of Divorce, 3,* 55–67.

Hopkins, J. B., & Vietze, P. M. (1977, April). *Postpartum early and extended contact.* Paper presented at a meeting of the Society for Research in Child Development. New Orleans, LA.

Jacobson, D. S. (1980). Stepfamilies. *Child Today, 9,* 2–6.

Jenkins v. Jenkins, 173 Wis. 592, 181 N.W. 826, 827 (1921).

Kagan, J., Kearsley, R., & Zelazo, P. (1978). *Infancy: Its place in human development.* Cambridge, MA: Harvard University Press.

Kalter, N. (1977). Children of divorce in an outpatient psychiatric population. *American Journal of Orthopsychiatry, 47,* 40–51.

Kearsley, R. B., Zelazo, P. R., Kagan, J., & Hartmann, R. (1975). Separation protest in daycare and home-reared infants. *Pediatrics, 55,* 171–175.

Kempe, C. H., Silverman, F. N., Steele, B. F., Droegemueller, W., & Silver, H. K. (1962). The battered child syndrome. *Journal of American Medical Association, 181,* 17–24.

Kennell, J. H., Jerauld, R., Wolfe, H., Chesler, D., Kreger, N. C., McAlphine, W., Steffa, M., & Klaus, M. H. (1974). Maternal behavior one year after early and extended post-partum contact. *Developmental Medicine and Child Neurology, 16,* 172–179.

Kennell, J. H., Trause, M. A., & Klaus, M. H. (1975). Evidence for a sensitive period in the human mother. *Parent–infant interaction, Ciba Foundation Symposium, 33,* 87–101.

Khan, M., & Sexton, M. (1983). Sexual abuse of young children. *Clinical Pediatrics, 22,* 369–372.

Klaus, M. H., Jerauld, R., Kreger, N. C., McAlphine, W., Steffa, M., & Kennell, J. H. (1972). Maternal attachment. *New England Journal of Medicine, 286,* 460–463.

Klaus, M. H., & Kennell, J. H. (1970). Mothers separated from their newborn infants. *Pediatric Clinics of North America, 17,* 1015–1037.

Klaus, M. H., & Kennell, J. H. (1976). *Maternal–infant bonding.* St. Louis, MO: C. V. Mosby.

Klaus, M. H., & Kennell, J. H. (1982). *Parent–infant bonding* (2nd ed.). St. Louis, MO: C. V. Mosby.

Kliman, G. (1968). Psychological emergencies of childhood. New York: Grune & Stratton.

Korsch, B. M. (1983). More on parent–infant bonding. *Journal of Pediatrics, 102,* 249–250.

Lahikainen, A. R., & Sundquist, S. (1979). The reactions of children under four years to day nursery. *Psychiatria Fennica,* 73–86.

Lamb, M. E. (1982a). The bonding phenomenon. *Journal of Pediatrics, 101,* 555–557.

Lamb, M. E. (1982b). Early contact and maternal–infant bonding. *Pediatrics, 70,* 763–768.

Lamb, M. E. (1982c). Second thoughts on first touch. *Psychology Today, 16,* 9–11.

Lamb, M. E., & Hwang, C. P. (1982). Maternal attachment and mother–neonate bonding. In M. E. Lamb & A. L. Brown (Eds.), *Advances in developmental psychology* (Vol. 2, pp. 1–39). Hillsdale, NJ: Erlbaum.

Langford, W. S. (1948). Physical illness and convalescence: Their meaning to the child. *Journal of Pediatrics, 33,* 242–250.

Leboyer, R. (1976). *Birth without violence.* New York: Alfred Knopf.

Legg, C., Sherick, I., & Wadland, W. (1974). Reaction of preschool children to the birth of a sibling. *Child Psychiatry & Human Development, 5,* 3–39.

Levy, D. M. (1938). *Study in sibling rivalry.* Research monograph 2, American Orthopsychiatric Association.

Levy, D. M. (1945). Psychic trauma of operations in children and a note on combat neurosis. *American Journal of the Disabled Child, 69,* 7–25.

Luter v. Luter, 120 S.W.2d 203, 205 (Mo. Ct. App. 1938).

Mahler, M., Pine, F., & Bergman, A. (1975). *The psychological birth of the human infant.* New York: Basic Books.

McCall, R. B. (1982). A hard look at stimulating and predicting development. *Pediatrics in Review, 3,* 205–212.

McDermott, J. F. (1968). Parental divorce in early childhood. *American Journal of Psychiatry, 124,* 1424–1432.

Mehl, L. E., Brandsel, C., & Peterson, G. H. (1977). Children at birth: Effects and implications. *Journal of Sex and Marital Therapy, 3,* 274–279.

Moore, T. (1969). Stress in normal childhood. *Human Relations, 22,* 235–250.

Munro, A. (1966). Parental deprivation in depressive patients. *British Journal of Psychiatry, 112,* 443–457.

Murphy, L. B. (1962). *The widening world of childhood: Paths toward mastery.* New York: Basic Books.

Peters, J. J. (1973). Child rape: Defusing a psychological time bomb. *Hospital Physician, 9,* 46–49.

Prugh, D. G., Staub, E. M., Sands, H. H., Kirschbaum, R. M., & Lenihan, E. A. (1953). A study of the emotional reactions of children and families to hospitalization and illness. *American Journal of Orthopsychiatry, 23,* 70–106.

Rank, B. (1955). Intensive study and treatment of preschool children who show marked personality deviations, or "atypical development," and their parents. In G. Caplan (Ed.), *Emotional problems of early childhood* (pp. 491–501). London: Tavistock.

Rank, O. (1952). *The trauma of birth.* New York: Robert Brunner.

Ricciuti, H. (1974). Fear and the development of social attachments. In M. Lewis & L. A. Rosenblum (Eds.), *The origins of fear* (pp. 73–106). New York: Wiley.

Ringler, N. M., Kennell, J. H., Jarvella, R., Navojosky, B. J., & Klaus, M. H. (1975). Mother-to-child speech at 2 years. *Journal of Pediatrics, 86,* 141–144.

Ringler, N. M., Trause, M. A., Klaus, M., & Kennell, J. (1978). The effects of extra postpartum contact and maternal speech patterns on children's IQs, speech, and language comprehension at five. *Child Development, 49,* 862–865.

Robertson, J., & Robertson, J. (1971). Young children in brief separation: A fresh look. *Psychoanalytic Study of the Child, 26,* 264–315.

Rutter, M. (1966). *Children of sick parents* (Maudsley Monograph No. 16). London: Oxford University Press.

Rutter, M. (1981). Social-emotional consequences of day care for preschool children. *American Journal of Orthopsychiatry, 51,* 4–28.

Rutter, M. (1983). *Maternal deprivation reassessed* (2nd ed). New York: Penguin Books.

Santrock, J. W., Warshak, P., Lindberg, C., & Meadows, L. (1982). Children's and parents' observed social behavior in stepfather families. *Child Development, 53,* 472–480.

Schaffer, H. R., & Callender, W. M. (1959). Psychologic effects of hospitalization in infancy. *Pediatrics, 24,* 528–539.

Schiller, J. D. (1978). Child care arrangements and ego functioning: The effects of stability and entry age on young children. *Dissertation Abstracts International, 40,* 93–94.

Schwarz, J. C., Krolick, G., & Strickland, R. G. (1973). Effects of early day care experience on adjustment to a new environment. *American Journal of Orthopsychiatry, 43,* 340–346.

Shirley, H. F. (1963). The physically handicapped child. In *Pediatric psychiatry* (pp. 498–537). Cambridge, MA: Harvard University Press.

Siegel, E., Bauman, K. E., Schaefer, E. S., Saunders, M. M., & Ingram, D. D. (1979). Hospital and home support during infancy. *Pediatrics, 66,* 183–189.

Solomon, O. C. (1942). Reactions of children to black-outs. *American Journal of Orthopsychiatry, 12,* 361–362.

Sousa, P. L. R., Barros, F. C., Gazalle, R. V., Begeres, R. M., Pinheiro, G. N., Menezes, S. T., & Arruda, L. A. (1974, October). *Attachment and lactation.* Paper presented at the Fourteenth International Congress of Pediatrics, Buenos Aires. Argentina.

Stacey, M., Dearden, R., Pill, R., & Robinson, D. (1970). *Hospitals, children and their families.* London: Routledge & Kegan Paul.

Steele, B. F. (1983). The effect of abuse and neglect on psychological development. In J. D. Call, E. Galenson, & R. Tyson (Eds.), *The frontiers of infant psychiatry* (pp. 235–244). New York: Basic Books.

Stirtzinger, R. (1984, October). *"Where is my daddy's house?" Preschool-age children of divorce and transitional phenomena—A study.* Paper presented at the 31st Annual Meeting of the American Academy of Child Psychiatry, Toronto.

Summit, R., & Kryso, J. A. (1978). Sexual abuse of children: A clinical spectrum. *American Journal of Orthopsychiatry, 48,* 237–251.

Thomas, A., Birch, H. G., Chess, S., & Robbins, L. C. (1961). Individuality in responses of children to similar environmental situations. *American Journal of Psychiatry, 117,* 798–803.

Thomas, A., & Chess, S. (1977). *Temperament and development.* New York: Brunner/Mazel.

Trause, M. A., Voos, D., Rudd, C., Klaus, M., Kennell, J., & Boslett, M. (1981). Separation for childbirth: The effect on the sibling. *Child Psychiatry and Human Development, 12,* 32–39.

U.S. Bureau of the Census. (1983). *Statistical abstract of the United States:* 1984 (104th ed.). Washington, DC: Author.

van Leeuwen, K., & Pomer, S. (1969). The separation-adaptation response to temporary object loss. *Journal of the American Academy of Child Psychiatry, 8,* 711–733.

Visher, E. B., & Visher, J. S. (1979). *Stepfamilies. A guide to working with stepparents and stepchildren.* New York: Brunner/Mazel.

Visher, E. B., & Visher, J. S. (1982). *How to win as a stepfamily.* Chicago: Contemporary Books.

Wallerstein, J. S. (1977). Responses of the preschool child to divorce: Those who cope. In M. F. McMillan & S. Henao (Eds.), *Child psychiatry: Treatment and research* (pp. 269–292). New York: Brunner/Mazel.

Wallerstein, J. S. (1984). Children of divorce: Preliminary report of a ten-year follow-up of young children. *American Journal of Orthopsychiatry, 54,* 444–458.

Wallerstein, J. S., & Kelly, J. B. (1975). The effects of parental divorce: Experiences of the preschool child. *Journal of the American Academy of Child Psychiatry, 14,* 600–616.

Wallerstein, J., & Kelly, J. (1980). *Surviving the breakup: How children and parents cope with divorce.* New York: Basic Books.

Wallick, M. M. (1985). The effects of mother–infant bonding. *Journal of the Louisiana State Medical Society, 137,* 40–47.

Winnicott, D. W. (1953). Transitional objects and transitional phenomena: A study of the first not-me possession. *International Journal of Psycho-analysis, 34,* 89–97.

Winnicott, D. W. (1964). *The child, the family, and the outside world.* London: Penguin Books.

Wolff, S. (1973). *Children under stress.* Baltimore: Penguin Books.

Yates, A. (1983). Stress management in childhood. *Clinical Pediatrics, 22,* 131–135.

Developmental Sources of Stress: Latency

JOSEPH D. NOSHPITZ, MD

The latency period is roughly equivalent to the grade-school years. Dynamically, it is the interval that falls between the end of the oedipal period (with the accompanying formation of the superego) and the beginning of puberty (Freud, 1905/1953); chronologically, it subtends the era between the 6th and the 10th to 12th birthdays (Sarnoff, 1976).

DEVELOPMENTAL ASPECTS

The Adjustment Disorders of latency are dominated by the presence of a number of new developmental emergents. These include the consolidation of the superego, the transition from preoperational to concrete operational thinking, the reordering of object relations, and the beginning of school (Benson & Harrison, 1980). This may sound like a curious list. The first three items are all internal psychological categories, whereas the last is apparently a totally external ad hoc event characteristic of our particular culture. For the child, however, school is a psychological factor (or, more precisely, cluster of interrelated factors) of such magnitude that it must

217

be regarded as a major biopsychosocial event in and of itself. It offers the child a unique and powerful milieu whose structure and influence will persist throughout latency and dominate vital aspects of psychic life. School must therefore be included in the roster of major developmental shaping forces that come to bear on this epoch and, in particular, that affect the appearance of Adjustment Disorders.

A brief consideration of each of these areas will provide a useful introduction to this discussion. First, then, the superego (Freud, 1924/1961).

Consolidation of the Superego

This part of the psychic apparatus has no biologic referent, that is to say, no clear neuroanatomic locus of representation. Nonetheless, it is widely accepted that somewhere between the ages of 4 and 6, there emerges as part of normal development a well-recognized component of personality that serves as an inner regulator, or inner "voice," to guide behavior and responses to the world. This new-formed superego has two components, the conscience and the ego-ideal. Each of these plays a formidable role in both the formation of character and the unfolding of latency; accordingly, it will help to review them both:

Conscience. The conscience operates in several different ways. It is often experienced as a conscious inner moralist, a voice that speaks from within to forbid and to warn; it possesses an evident capacity to inhibit so that the individual is unable to carry out a forbidden intention (usually without conscious awareness of why it is impossible to act as desired at that moment); and finally, the conscience acts as internal punisher. The last function can be so potent that under extreme circumstances it can drive people quite literally to self-destruction; short of that it can beget a wide variety of inner sufferings and symptom formations.

Ego-ideal. The ego-ideal for its part sets model and goal for behavior. The person compares his or her self-perceived identity, actions, and appearance to other people with his or her idealized identity, actions, and appearance. There is an inner template of an ideal self that the child either approaches or fails to come near—and it is the extent of this gap between self-as-perceived and self-as-ideal that is the measure of one's self-esteem. This kind of self-feeling is a day-to-day, moment-to-moment aspect of experience, and it plays an active part in the everyday contentment and happiness—or dismay and unhappiness—of the latency child as he or she grows.

Within this context, then, what are some of the sources of stress that development thrusts to the fore? Clearly many kinds of behavior can bring about the sort of inner conflict implied by superego sanctions. These range all the way from extreme forms of aggressiveness to the mere thinking of irreligious thoughts; any such act can evoke a sense of guilt. Many children do not tolerate guilt very well and display an amazing array of symptoms when such inner pressures build up. Accordingly, any such intrapsychic conflict can precipitate considerable degrees of reaction among the more vulnerable latency children. Sometimes this takes form as a kind of expiation; the child complains of sleep disorder, stomachaches, headaches, fears, or inhibitions. Sometimes it finds expression as provocative behavior aimed as evoking punishment; not infrequently this overflows into some typical, albeit transient symptomatic behavior such as sibling battles, explosive rage, school avoidance, or fire setting.

Cognitive Transformation

The second latency emergent is the shift in cognitive style from the preoperational level to that of concrete operations (Piaget, 1936/1952). It is noteworthy that the chief problem-solving tactic of the preoperational epoch is the use of fantasy to address and resolve the important real-life issues. The 4-year-old is sure that wishing hard enough, or wishing in just the right way, will make desired events happen. Thoughts have power; words have power; they can affect the real world. As this preoperational mode is left behind, such a technique for coming to grips with life's difficulties becomes less and less feasible. For the 6-year-old, handling stressful issues by wishing and imagining is no longer as serviceable or as easily accomplished as it was at the age of 4. Once into latency, the pressure now is for a more mature— and more realistic—search for solutions. This in turn makes coping and dealing with life's demands a great deal more difficult, and the vulnerability for Adjustment Disorder is accordingly increased. Hence this is a transformation of considerable importance (Freud, 1911/1958).

Although in itself not usually a source of stress, this cognitive transformation has certain aspects that can color symptomatic behavior and lend themselves to troublesome forms of expression (Furman, 1980). In particular, concrete operational thinking implies the capacity for conservation, seriation, and classification. The latter two functions involve the ordering of items in sequence and the listing and naming of members of particular sets. These can be baseball cards, butterflies, bottle caps, or beer cans; the latency child begins to delight in the use of newly acquired intellectual capacities and is often vitally interested in collecting and classifying (Bornstein, 1951). The symptomatic aspects of this become evident when obsessive thoughts appear, when everything has to be counted, when one has to wash incessantly, or when it becomes necessary to carry out each detail of elaborate compulsive routines in a prescribed sequence. In certain instances one encounters involvement with excruciatingly precise calorie counting as accompaniment to a prepubertal anorexic syndrome. The initiation of such patterns can be specific to stress responses, and they can be transient (and thus Adjustment Disorders) or full blown, extended syndromes that dominate the child's (and family's) life for prolonged periods.

The shifts in interpersonal adaptation at this time are no less striking. Within psychoanalytic theory, the child who has closed out the oedipal situation now begins to abandon the bodies of the parents as targets of sexual and aggressive yearnings. Instead, the youngster begins to idealize the same-sex parent and to use him or her as an object of identification; in this way the child begins to learn how to handle life's challenges as a future man or woman. Clearly this is a complex requirement and it is not surprising that it is often incomplete or that it becomes entangled in some troublesome idiosyncratic pattern. Some of this can be quite normal; thus, the little girl's choice of a tomboyish stance during latency, with evident identification with father or older brother, is not ordinarily a cause for parental concern or professional involvement. (In the case of effeminacy in little boys, however, this is not true (Green, 1987). A son's preference for a feminine identity is usually considered problematic by parents and may indeed lead to early referral. This, however, need not take on the proportions of true gender identity disorder). In the face of the fair wear and tear of everyday experience, a child with strong residual oedipal attachments to his or her parent(s) (bonds that for whatever reason have never been relinquished) is likely to enter latency in a highly vulnerable state. Such a youngster can become prey to a wide variety of symptoms ranging from separation-anxiety reactions to depressive responses. In particular, the child will not respond well to stress. For example, such phenomena as the arrival of a new baby, the illness of a parent, or even the absence of a parent on a trip can have a catastrophic impact on the child's state of mind, and a flood of symptomatic behaviors follow.

The Impact of School

Finally, in the more vulnerable latency child, school is a classical begetter of symptoms. This can occur in any or all of four major provinces: school attendance, cognitive challenge, authority issues, and peer encounters.

School Attendance. To begin with, there are the issues implicit in the demand for school attendance as such. The child can challenge this requirement by posing difficulties in arising in the morning or in getting organized in time to catch the school bus; by avoiding school on grounds of anxiety or somatic symptoms; and by failing to stay in school on the basis of truancy (i.e., antisocial intent and action). Any of these patterns can appear as a transient reaction to various kinds of stress, such as a move to a new community, parental separation, surgery for a sibling, or a natural disaster that affects the community.

Cognitive Challenge. Next, there is the matter of cognitive mastery, the encounter with schoolwork as such. This is the realm of such basic skills as reading, writing, and arithmetic, learning, remembering facts (e.g., dates and personages in history or geographic names and relationships), test taking, studying, and, in short, overall academic performance. The many internal hazards and obstacles that may interfere with cognitive performance are well known, as are the effects on cognitive performance (attention, concentration, integration, cross modal representation, understanding, and recall) of a wide variety of external stressors. Failed school performance (where a child's capacities would seemingly have allowed for success) is perhaps the commonest reason for child psychiatric referral. When such failure appears in a previously well-functioning child, it indicates a serious kind of Adjustment Disorder.

Authority Issues. Special problems arise around the interaction with teacher and school administration in general. Here a number of fateful issues are joined, particularly in the realm of sorting out authority relationships and in respect to the acceptance of external social regulation of one's impulses. Where the groundwork has been poorly laid during the early years, various patterns of negativism, oppositionality, and rebelliousness are likely to become manifest. Provocative behavior, unruliness, disobedience, and defiance may occur, and major problems follow. Or refusal to do schoolwork on various levels (e.g., required classroom responses, homework, book reports, term papers, science projects) may be the overt way the child rebels against authority. Again, this kind of activity can occur as a transient phenomenon (as a true Adjustment Disorder), or it may become institutionalized as a chronically embattled state that persists throughout latency.

The opposite kind of disturbance around authority can also be present, where extreme anxiety about teacher's criticism and paralyzing fear of such encounter can dominate a given child's life for a while and give rise to anxiety states, various forms of depression, nightmares, somatic symptoms, and other forms of distress.

Peer Encounters. Finally, the matter of peer interaction is a central issue in the child's adjustment during latency. At this age the child first begins to enter into an individualized social pattern away from life with the family, and the conduct of this more independent component of existence normally takes place in the company of peers.

All through this interval, the wide range of interactions now available becomes a powerful conditioner of experience and self-esteem. A brief look at a number of the adaptive issues entailed in this encounter will give some sense of what is at stake. There is the matter of making friends at all, of being able to accept a bid for interaction, of knowing how to respond in a reasonably appropriate way when addressed, and of being able to engage in a comfortable exchange with another child—as opposed to remaining isolated and becoming a chronic (usually excluded) outsider. There is the keeping of friends—the so-called social skills, or competence at interaction that dictates the outcome of initial relationship bids. These skills allow individuals to approach each other, become interested in each other, and not drive each other away. There is the problem of entrance into the peer group, of finding a compatible group and of earning and maintaining a place within it. The establishment of a group role is normally part of such a process, as is the ability to attain one's level within the status hierarchy. A variety of social competencies are necessary for all this, including the ability to give and take within a teasing exchange; to be entertaining, a good listener, or helpful to others in some fashion; to face up to challenges to one's territory; to cope with enticements to do the forbidden; and thus on and on. Failure in these realms begets an enormous amount of suffering in latency children, with all the accompanying readiness for Adjustment Disorder.

These, then, are some of the tasks implicit in the latency experience. They do not include many special circumstances; for example, chronic illness; visible physical handicaps such as congenital spasticity; invisible physical handicaps such as diabetes; deficiencies in special senses, such as blindness or deafness; and special subcultural requirements dictating eating patterns or garments that differ from those of peers. The list of tasks referred to here speaks instead for the developmental problems implicit in the process of latency as such, because these problems may impinge on the average child or on the child with mild to moderate degrees of vulnerability.

COPING STYLES

In surveying some forms of adaptation and coping styles that latency children typically employ, as well as some of their response patterns to stress, it is important to note that the growing-up process in itself offers a common means for expressing disturbances of adjustment. Given a stressful course to run, some children will seek to advance the growth process by becoming premature junior adults, whereas others will strive to evade growing up and cling—or return—to more immature patterns. Thus either precocity or regression may be resorted to (or, in some instances, a combination of both so that the child's behavior displays features of each) in the service of coping. Such forms of adjustment can be transient, or they can accompany characterological disturbances; when relatively brief and passing in character, they may form typical Adjustment Disorders.

Regressive Style

An example of a regressive syndrome of this sort involves the appearance of whining, clinging behavior, along with a reappearance of thumb-sucking or bed-wetting. In addition, there may be difficulty with separation. When that is present, the commonest form it takes is school refusal; the youngster usually complains of being sick or of being afraid to leave home, either because of an expressed concern about what might happen to his or her parents or fear of someone or something at school (a strict teacher, a bullying peer). In any case, the central feature of the disorder is an expressed inability to cope at an age-appropriate level. This can be quite an ephemeral cluster of behaviors lasting hours or days. If it persists longer, it takes on the character of an Adjustment Disorder.

Anxiety Type. Sometimes the primary manifestation is in the form of anxiety as such. The child is frightened, perhaps phobic about specific items like dogs or people with umbrellas; sometimes the fear is more general and the panic is related to some vague unnameable source of danger or to the possibililty of war and atomic destruction. Where a strong obsessive tendency is present, this can serve to bind and contain the feelings of terror—but the child must then put up with the repeated washings, changes of underwear many times a day, or other ritualistic behaviors to which he or she is driven. Under such circumstances, the anxiety bursts out chiefly when the adult criticizes the compulsive routines or refuses to comply with the child's rituals.

Depressive Type. An alternative to feeling anxious is to feel depressed. Not uncommonly these occur together, but either affect may appear as the predominant mood accompanying a regressive episode. Where depression is paramount, the child is sad, cries frequently and all too readily, and speaks of feeling unhappy. At the same time, he or she is likely to seek close physical proximity to objects of attachment and often fails to function well in some important area, such as self-care or school performance. Not infrequently, anxious concerns are voiced about health or the future (Cytryn & McKnew, 1979).

Withdrawal Type. An even more disturbing kind of regressive behavior occurs when the predominant finding is withdrawal. Here the child displays no particular affect but instead conveys the chief impression of emptiness. One suspects that underneath the child's dulled and dispirited visage is a pool of profoundly stressful emotion. None of this is visible on the surface, however; the most prominent affective tone is one of distance, shallowness of feeling, constriction, and loss of interest. The child has apparently solved the problem of too much stress by becoming numb, turning away from the world into a state of apathetic distance. During an interview he or she seems more remote and empty than overtly distressed. Schoolwork often suffers, peer relations fall away, and the surrounding adults feel unable to reach the youngster. Such withdrawal often is transient; where it settles in as a prolonged pattern, it can presage very serious pathology indeed.

Somatizing Type. Another common regressive response to stress is found among that sizable population of children who seem to experience relatively little emotional response to stress as such. They don't get angry or frightened or sad; instead, they complain that something has gone wrong with their bodies (Kavanaugh & Mattson, 1979). They have a sort of somatic shunt mechanism that substitutes physical symptoms for psychic pain; in effect, a stress experience that might evoke depression or panic is diverted directly into the somatic realm. Thus, if something happens that could bring grief or fear into such a younster's life, he or she falls ill with fever or vomiting, complains of stomach pains or headaches for which no biological basis can be found, or develops a sleep disturbance. An allied adaptive device involves having an accident. There is no awareness that any of this is connected to the current state of personal or family disarray; it is something that just happens; it is simply there.

Learning Inhibition Type. There is a pattern of failed adaptation that takes form, not as a symptomatic emotional, behavioral, or somatic state, but rather as a disturbance of function. In adults, such a pattern is called work inhibition (a familiar version is writer's block); in childhood it means an inability to do academic work. The child simply cannot learn or perform at school. With school occupying so central a site in the geography of a child's mind, such an inhibition can be of catastrophic import. All of a sudden the able child is transformed into a dull, inept student, assignments are lost or ignored, homework isn't done, or the child spends hours over books and produces almost nothing—a sort of constipation of the mind takes place and learning activities stop. Like the other conditions described, it may persist a few months and then recede. This diminution of symptoms may come about through therapy, through a gradual spontaneous relaxation of the child's defensive posture, or through a change in the stressful circumstances that initiated this reaction (e.g., the child adapts to and makes friends with the new stepparent). In any case, when things go well, the burden of tension lightens, and the capacity to do academic work returns. Unfortunately things don't always go well, and the end result may be major educational deficits.

Precocious Type. The obverse of this, the precocious pattern, is less likely to be a passing phenomenon. Most children who take such a turn adopt this position as an enduring characterological attitude. Behaviorally it takes form as the child insists on making decisions about clothing, foods, bedtime, choice of TV programs, and the like from a very early age. Such a youngster will press his or her case strongly, even in the face of forceful parental disagreement. Sometimes the areas of decision making may go much further, such as determining what the family will eat that day, or which movie they will go out to see, or where they will go on vacation. This kind of precocity must be distinguished from the following type, oppositional behavior. The precocious child is not so much oppositional as self-assertive. Often enough such premature assumption of responsibility is a response to parental helplessness or depression; as the parent loses his or her ability to function (in the face of a serious loss, marital breakdown, or an endogenous illness), the child responds by taking over. This can be cut short by the parent's resumption of the parental role in an appropriate fashion (although there may be a period of stress during the changeover). Where the excessive precocity persists for a relatively brief interval (for months rather than years), it can be considered a true Adjustment Disorder.

Oppositional Type. The oppositional syndrome is probably the commonest form of behavior disorder (Finch & Green, 1979). Here the disturbance in adjustment takes the form of pitting oneself against parental authority. There is an element of clinging to the parents in all this; oppositional children get a great deal of parental attention; indeed, in some instances the interaction is almost continuous. But it is a sadomasochistic connectedness, with frustration and retaliation as the hallmarks of the engagement. The child deals with parental initiatives by negating, refusing, opposing, and denying; in effect, by a kind of willful negativism designed specifically to challenge the parents' authority. Any aspect of comportment may be involved, from chores and manners to schoolwork and observance of curfew. Again, there can be a short-lived flurry of oppositional activity that persists a few weeks or a few months, or the behavior can become part of a chronic, characterologically rooted pattern. It may become evident as early as the 2nd year of life, persist continuously throughout childhood, and extend on into adolescence.

Aggressive (Conduct Disorder) Type. A far more severe form of reactive disturbance occurs when aggressive behavior appears in a form that is more than merely oppositional. This can assume diverse configurations and includes overt behaviors such as bullying, cruelty to animals, sexual invasiveness, and wild tantrums, as well as covert acts such as firesetting, vandalism, stealing, cheating, and lying (Patterson, 1982). Running away and truancy are also common. Like oppositional behavior, this is typically a long-standing, characterological behavioral mode. However, outbreaks may occur in youngsters who encounter a disturbing confrontation in their lives. Thus, such behavior can be one of the manifestations of a child's reaction to loss, response to a move to new community, or way of dealing with parental separation or divorce. Indeed, it is particularly likely to occur in the face of some alteration in family circumstance, because familial perturbations evoke a state of menace, frustration, or rage in the latency child, and quite often a melange of all three. Precipitating circumstances can include a divorced primary caretaker's establishment of a new liaison with a potential marital partner or the entrance of a foster child into the existing family set. Any one of a wide variety of changes can be perceived as a disruptive challenge, and the youngster reacts accordingly. The response is often more complex than mere delinquent behavior; anxiety, depression, and sometimes a state of maintained excitement can accompany the deliberate misbehavior.

In evaluating youngsters with this picture, it is not unusual to find such factors as a heavy burden of guilt accompanying the misbehavior, so that in addition to the expression of rage and hurt, there is also an almost deliberate seeking of punishment. (The dynamics resemble Freud's designation of a "criminal from a sense of guilt," 1957). Or a strong masochistic trend may be found, and rather complex dynamic constellations come into view that take the treatment far beyond the mere management of disruptive behavior. Indeed, the basic characterological disorder is the factor setting the stage, so that the Adjustment Disorder occasioned by the stressor of the moment usually takes form as a mixture of emotional and conduct disorder.

COMMON SOURCES OF STRESS IN LATENCY

Relatively few factors commonly precipitate Adjustment Disorders in latency children. Many have been alluded to already. They follow the same general scheme as the emergents that accompany the onset of latency. They occur in each of three realms: school, home, and neighborhood.

School as Stress

The Break Away from Home. The first level of challenge that confronts the child in school is the need to adapt to a nonhome environment. The weeping of the nursery school child when his or her mother leaves is the archetype of this aspect of school; at whatever age it begins, school can be the first real break in the stable atmosphere of being a loved child in a caring home. Clearly this is a variable of sizable proportions. Many children spend large parts of each day away from home at day-care centers or with baby-sitters; for them school is not as novel. Nonetheless it is unique in the configuration it offers and the demands it makes on the child.

For it makes very considerable demands. There are levels of conformity imposed by the physical structure of the school building with its sometimes complex geography, multiple areas of specialized function, and permitted and forbidden sites for student entrance. There are social factors to be met and mastered, and there is the primary mission of school, to create a learning environment and to have children master the prescribed curriculum. The hazards are real and weighty.

Group Encounter and Its Complications. Once in school, the child faces requirements for group encounter and participation as well as for linking up with individuals at the peer level. All this is not without genuine dangers. During latency in particular the potential hazards can take the form of teasing, excluding, and victimizing. Each of these can be a major source of stress, sometimes of such intense character as never to be forgotten. They are two-sided affairs; the teasers—the individuals who have engaged in these practices and visited them on others—sometimes leave these experiences with a difficult-to-eradicate sense of guilt. The stricken look of a youngster who, because of race or a physical handicap, has been the butt of a group assault, even if it is primarily verbal, may remain in the memory of one of the assaulting rabble as a permanent accusing presence. However, at the time the position of the attacker is probably less likely to give rise to an Adjustment Disorder than the experience of the victim. Children so abused on the school yard, whether by being excluded from a longed-for group affiliation, menaced or maltreated by a bully, or converged on and harassed by an array of peers (or, sometimes, by a single high-status peer), will become depressed and school-avoidant, or will run away (albeit in latency rather briefly as a rule), withdraw, or do poorly at their schoolwork. The narcissistic wounds may evoke a state of inner rage, but the rage is blocked in its normal channel of discharge. The inimical group or the individual bully is experienced as unassailable, and the rage may be redirected to inappropriate figures at home (e.g., to a helpless younger sib); or, more commonly, the rage is turned inward and intense feelings of self-pity, self-hatred, or low self-esteem may ensue. Any or all of these can enter into a subsequent disturbance in adjustment. Sometimes, too, the rage turns outward, and in one way or another the abused child victimizes other smaller children at school or the school property itself. Under such circumstances, the Adjustment Disorder becomes complicated by and eventually blends into a Conduct Disorder.

Cognitive Issues. In the very nature of the academic enterprise, every school-child faces formidable cognitive challenges. For a rather small percentage of school attenders, the stature of their cognitive strengths towers over the demands made by the usual curriculum—and may indeed bypass it altogether. Thus, some children learn to read on their own during the preschool years and breeze through grade school and high school "without ever cracking a book." But these are rare cases. For the very large majority of youngsters, academic work is inherently stressful, testing their capacities and challenging their competence on many fronts. It requires attention, concentration, memory, and visual and auditory competence. Academic achievement implies as well the ability to recognize symbols as symbols, the ability to learn these symbols, and the ability to manipulate the symbols one has learned. It also demands the capacity to integrate new information with old, along with the associated capacity to bring old information to bear selectively on new situations. All of this depends on the acquisition of specific skills like the comprehension and manipulation of numbers and the mastery of elementary arithmetic concepts (e.g., carrying or subtraction). In addition, it mandates the presence of certain character traits like the patience to keep trying after an initial failure, the openness to learning through trial and error, the ability to accept criticism and to learn from it, and a host of other intellectual and personality requirements. Given the enormous variability of the human species, it is not altogether surprising that many children lag behind in some one or several of this extensive array. Often enough, skilled and creative teachers can figure out ways to help children past this weakness or that; in many instances, however, the weakness as such, or the weakness plus some complicating interpersonal hazard (e.g., fear of teacher) or intrapersonal vulnerability factor (e.g., narcissistic inability to tolerate criticism) is such that it becomes a major hazard and is identified as a "learning disability." This can become a stumbling block that can wreak havoc in a child's—and often enough in a family's—life. Whether it be an immigrant family looking toward education as the way up to a better life, or an upper-middle-class family with a long tradition of cognitive excellence and a high level of performance expectation, families can experience a child's inability to learn well at school as catastrophic. When the child's problem is first recognized, a sort of familywide Adjustment Disorder can ensue. For the involved child who faces all this, the tangle of guilt, helplessness, defensiveness, rage, and self-devaluation that presently appears can spill over into a symptomatic syndrome at any point.

Teacher-Related Issues. To shift now from cognitive to interpersonal sources of stress, the child also engages the matter of authority in school in a way far different from at home. To begin with, there is no enmeshed relationship between teacher or principal and student. There was no prior symbiotic episode; they did not share a rapprochement crisis; the teacher was never an oedipal object—in brief, there is a measure of distance and objectivity in the administration of discipline that can be appreciated by the prepared child. In contrast to this, the youngster who has never achieved a good symbiotic rapprochement or oedipal resolution may not be at all ready to accept such an external structure; he or she perceives whatever happens as filled with symbolic portents and personal threats or challenges. Discipline then becomes a matter that evokes either overwhelming guilt and anxiety or unbridled rage and aggression. Either response can make for Adjustment Disorder and threaten the capacity of the affected child to become integrated into the academic structure. Such an overanxious reaction or conduct disorder response style is not unheard of in the early adjustment to school. Indeed, so ubiquitous are some of these behaviors (children who do not speak at school for a while, children who steal chalk, boys who kick girls when no one is watching or who bully younger students, children who are tearful at the outset) that skilled teachers take the milder expressions of such tendencies for granted and develop great competence in their management. Indeed, in the early grades, good teachers probably treat more Adjustment Disorders than do members of any other discipline. The more severe manifestations, however, are quite another matter. Sometimes the violence, obsessiveness, anxiety, or sadness are present as intense and unrelenting aspects of comportment; under such circumstances parental consultation and the teacher's usual tactics for bringing children along are of no avail. The child may then be referred and another set of approaches essayed. When that happens, the attendance at school itself becomes problematic. School avoidance syndromes can appear in some instances, or truancy in others. Cutting classes comes into the picture or cutting school generally. Although less common in early latency, where conduct disorder is part of the picture, truancy can become an important issue as the grade-school years advance. It is as though the general stress and reactivity evoked by the authority problems cause the child to respond with ever more massive attempts at flight and avoidance. Sometimes this is a transient response to particular stressors; at such times, despite the presence of the already existing difficulties, an Adjustment Disorder is added as well. Ultimately, where the youngsters are sufficiently troubled and where the situation persists, special education, home-bound instruction, or residential placement may be necessary.

Home and Stress

Many aspects of life at home impinge on children as major sources of stress. Essentially, they are products of the rich mix of family life. Again, a large number of variables is involved along with a readiness to form resonating and mutually augmenting feedback loops. These can become stable foci or disturbance that serve as sites of sustained vulnerability; in the face of stress, the troubled relation with a peer, or the festering struggle between parent and child (be it father and son, mother and daughter, or any other pairing) can overflow into major symptomatic responses (flight, physical abuse, suicidal act, physical illness, etc.).

Direct Parent-Child Interaction

Separation Issues. A first level of stressors arises within the direct interaction between parent and child. Sometimes a parent who has been at home most of the time decides to go to work (whether because of economic necessity, boredom, recovery from a depression, ambition, or change in the sociopolitical climate). As a rule, some substitute parenting arrangement is devised: A baby-sitter is brought in; the child goes (or is taken) to a relative, neighbor, or professional caretaker who lives in the area; an after-school program is resorted to; or some other plan is worked out. In any case, someone else takes over while the parents are at work. For most latency children, this falls well within their capacity to cope. In certain instances, however, even if adequate substitute care is provided, children who are temperamentally more needy or who have already been stressed by prior events in their lives will experience such a change in available parenting as a disruptive and traumatic business. More serious still is the chain of events that begins when a parent goes to work without providing a pattern of substitute parenting. Under those circumstances, one consequence may be to convert a previously secure youngster into a lonely, frightened "latchkey" child; this, in turn, can initiate a whole new set of vulnerabilities and/or symptomatic responses (Garbarino, 1980).

Similarly, if a parent becomes depressed, withdraws, or experiences some other change in his or her life (e.g., learns that a child was fathered by someone else), that situation creates distance between self and child; the youngster will experience it as a direct challenge to his or her coping capacity.

Closeness Issues. But it is not only distance that can increase excessively; too much closeness can also be challenging. A parent can become anxious and preoccupied with fears about health, safety, or seduction and begin to hover over and excessively limit the child. The result is a sort of psychological stifling; youngsters may either rebel against it or accept the dangerousness of the world and become frightened in turn.

On a different level of closeness, a child's increased size and growth may kindle an erotic response in a fragile and immature parent, and active seductive behavior may ensue. Although the most likely time for the occurrence of incestuous advances of this sort is during puberty, such sexual acts can begin at any age in a child's life. There is now considerable literature on the impact of sex abuse on child development; many documented instances of serious long-term effects have been reported (Finkelhor, 1984). But here too a wide range of responses is possible, and some children show major evidences of stress around the time the incestuous events take place.

Exploitation. There are other dimensions of home-engendered stress. The demands made upon a child in a household can be unusual and severely burdensome. Quite young children become pressed into service as preparers of meals, housecleaners, or caretakers of infants or younger sibs. The stresses of poverty in particular can so disorganize the adults that the availability of the latency child as another pair of hands is too great a lure to ignore. Sometimes a child is simply exploited for a parent's convenience or financial gain. The usual case is that of a poorly educated single parent, who has several children and may be a substance abuser— and who just cannot cope. The parent needs help from somewhere. Someone must perform many of the necessary functions that would otherwise go untended and relieve the distraught parent from at least some of the massive burdens of a crisis-ridden existence. And so, willy-nilly, the child is thrust into a position of considerable responsibility. This is an annealing experience. To be sure, some children emerge from this kind of test by fire with a wisdom and maturity beyond their years. (Their symptoms may not appear for decades until, as adults, they look back in bitterness and tell their therapists of the rage they feel—and have always felt— because they were deprived of so much of their childhoods.) Many others become depressed, enraged, or distraught in turn. The Cinderella syndrome actually exists, except that no fairy godmother or Prince Charming comes to the rescue, except in fantasy.

Another aspect of the Cinderella story also exists and can produce quite serious reactions. It is no rare story to hear of a younger sib who becomes the target of an older sibling's hostility. Some wrangling between siblings is expectable under any circumstances, but extreme cases exist that involve one child tyrannizing another to the point of total frustration, self-hate, or panic. Usually this implies a failure in parental caretaking as well; the tenacity, the persistence and the implacable quality of the offending older child are too much for the parents; the orderliness of the relationships within the home and protection of the younger child (or children) simply fall by the wayside.

Physical Abuse. An even more sinister pattern involves parental psychological and physical violence, both between spouses and toward children.

Violence directed not toward the spouse but toward the child produces the phenomenon of child abuse. Much has been written about the psychological impact of the various forms of child abuse, in terms of both short-range and long-range effects. For all children, the impact of such events is fraught with much distressing meaning. As always, the critical aspect is the continuum of experience. A good case can be made that an occasional slap on a child's bottom may be a constructive act when administered by a loving parent as a way of driving home a lesson in deportment. Many cultures have not only tolerated but expected a certain level of violence between husband and wife and/or between parent and child. To illustrate this, one has only to consider the relevant values resident in our own culture over the span of the 20th century (e.g., songs that include such lines as "reading and writing and 'rithmetic taught to the tune of the hickory stick"). But very few cultures or family traditions will accept extreme degrees and forms of violence involving torture, mutilation, and simple cruelty. In terms of our values and mores, these behaviors are rejected with revulsion; in terms of hospital emergency room experience, they are nonetheless practiced daily in American society.

Child abuse is a predictable begetter of severe psychological responses on the part of the child, both immediately and over the long term. Children have been burned, crippled, or killed at the hands of their caretakers; even where lesser degrees of violence have been involved, the emotional consequences can be severe. Today, the police or other community agencies typically become involved. This often leads to the physical departure (and hence to the psychological loss) of an offending parent to whom the child may be intensely, albeit ambivalently, attached. As a result, the experience is doubly traumatic; the child has endured the emotional meaning of the physical assault and has added to it the loss of an important object of attachment. The impact is likely to be grievous, and symptoms often follow.

Psychological Abuse. In recent years, ever more attention has begun to be directed toward the phenomenon of psychological abuse of children. This has been difficult to define, and to date it is still an area of specialized interest. Because in fact so much that is considered Adjustment Disorder stems directly from such experiences, it is worth reviewing some of the thinking that has recently emerged.

Psychological abuse had been divided (Garbarino, Guttman, & Seeley, 1986) into five categories: rejecting, terrorizing, ignoring, isolating, and corrupting. Each has its own implications for development and takes different forms at different moments in the child's course of growing up. For the school-age child, it includes such parental behaviors as the following:

Rejecting. Labeling the child with disparaging and devaluing titles; scapegoating and belittling the child in the course of everyday family interactions. The target is the child's fragile sense of narcissism and self-valuation.

Terrorizing. Placing the child at the focus of inconsistent and impossible demands (the classical "double bind"); forcing the child to choose between opposing parents; criticizing the child for failing to meet impossible demands.

The goal is to set up a state of anxious and unresolvable dependency in the child that allows the caretaker to exercise a kind of absolute tyranny.

Ignoring. Failing to protect the child or to interfere on the child's behalf when he or she is attacked; failing to respond to requests for help; ignoring accomplishments or favorable school reports.

Isolating. Forbidding contacts with other children either in the family home or at the homes of others; withdrawing the child from school. This fosters a state of chronic maintained paranoia that leaves the child open to community censure and prone to intense feelings of resentment and panic.

Corrupting. Involving the child in sexual activity such as pornography or sex play (either with adults or with other children); teaching the child to steal or to participate in parental dishonesty; goading the child to bully or to assault others. The outcome is to teach the child that covert antisocial activity is a preferred way of life, thus launching the child on an antisocial career.

The items in this sad litany are all too common in the accounts of many children brought to professional attention. They are all products of family interaction; they are obvious sources of stress; and, albeit they do not bruise the skin, they manage nonetheless to leave jagged psychological scars in the psyches of vulnerable children.

Indirect Parent–Child Interaction. Moving from the stresses caused by actions that impinge directly on the child to the adjacent array of events that are likely to have indirect effects, a common and major site for such stress lies in the realm of changes, disturbances, or disruptions of family structure. These include parental differences, the leave-taking of a parent from the home, or the entrance of a new parent figure. It encompasses as well other children who enter or leave the home. Listing some of the details of such circumstances will illustrate the rich menu of possibilities associated with such events.

Parental Discord. Parents can challenge each other in many ways, overt and covert. They can engage in loud, demonstrative quarrels involving accusations, obscenities, and threats. Or they can resort to extended periods of frozen silence and ask the child to relay messages: "Please tell your mother to pass the salt," or "Tell your father to pay the utilities bill." The parents can engage in violent abusive behavior toward one another: They can throw things, destroy each other's property, or strike and beat each other (usually it is the physically stronger father who beats the mother). Any or all of these can be played out in front of the children, offering at once a terrifying experience of possible injury to primary objects of attachment, threatened dissolution of the family, and a model for hostile and disturbing adaptation as a constituent of adult intimacy.

The memory of interparental violence is clinically, for many adults, among the most frightening and distressing images to rise up in recollection. Where physical violence between the parents is involved, the impact can become nightmarish. For some children it is simply a terrifying and disruptive experience to see their mother and father fight, and once encountered, it echoes in the child's mind with long-lingering reverberations. Evidently, the effect on a given child varies enormously; subcultural realities, idiosyncratic temperamental factors, the moment in development at which the event occurs, the propinquity of other traumatic experiences, and the availability of reassuring and consoling others are among the variables mediating the impact and influencing the outcome. Nonetheless, the report of such deeply disturbing memories is not uncommon as part of the recall of many troubled adults. The most consistent finding running through the histories of juvenile delinquents is that of parental discord (Emery, 1982).

There is probably no single route by which parental strife leads to these deleterious outcomes. Basic to such etiologic formulations is the likelihood that children identify not only with the parents as individuals but with their relationship. For the child, the interaction between the parents is a palpable presence. Its quality, integrity, warmth, tensions, deviations, and pathology can all become incorporated into the elaborating personality configuration of the involved child. Thus, the youngster may regard the interparental violence as a model, feel responsible for keeping the peace, feel guilty for his/her real or fantasied role in causing the trouble, seek to ward off the anxiety aroused by the parental fighting through identification with the aggressor, develop ingenious ways of withdrawal, or find some other way to adapt to the quarreling. In any case, the difficulties that arise in this area are prime generators of Adjustment Disorders.

Parental Departure. Parents leave home for many reasons. A bout of illness, physical or mental, may require extended hospitalization. A parent may be sent to prison for a time; this is a surprisingly common experience in the life of many Americans. The marriage may drive one parent or the other to leave for a trial separation. The mother may take the children and move in with her own mother for a time, or with a sib, friend, or other relative. Or the father may move out and take a hotel room, move in with a girl friend, or find some other temporary alternative setting. Whatever the reason, the effect on the children is predictably disruptive, sometimes even catastrophic. The parent they live with is typically in a state of emotional disarray; the parent who has left is often more or less out of touch; and the involved youngsters must deal with a sense of fragmentation and abandonment that can be painful indeed (Rutter, 1971).

Parental Kidnapping. A particularly ferocious variety of parental departure occurs when the hostility of the one parent toward the other is so great that the noncustodial parent literally kidnaps the children. The kidnapper-parent's fantasy is almost always one of rescuing the youngsters from the evil impact of the spouse (or ex-spouse). The children typically go through a difficult adjustment period in the wake of such an experience.

Divorce. Separations can be brief, they can be recurrent, or they can become permanent. In the latter instance they are usually the prelude to divorce. Latency children become frequent spectators to and, often enough, active participants in divorce proceedings. Early in latency a typical reaction is to harbor the most intense fantasies of bringing the parents back together. Later in this period, a peculiar kind of judgmental reaction is seen; the child decides that one parent or the other is the truly guilty party and accordingly rushes to the defense of the other "innocent" and sinned-against parent (Gardner, 1987). In any divorce action the turmoil is great, and many children go through serious emotional stress as participants. Research indicates that all too often the initial Adjustment Disorder gives way to more chronic patterns of disturbance, and the continuing echoes of the experience can be detected years later (Wallerstein & Kelly, 1980).

The Encounter with an Alternative Parent. With the breakup of the nuclear family, the door is open for each parent to make new liaisons. Accordingly, new men or women may appear in the child's life and implicitly—often explicitly— demand a place of some kind. Mother may contract a new boyfriend, who becomes a fiancé, perhaps moves in, and presently becomes, formally, a stepfather. Father, who may have the children on weekend visits, has them meet his live-in girlfriend, who might, again, presently offer the children a relationship as stepmother. The alternative parents often have children of their own, so that a whole new family must be confronted. The possible permutations are considerable, and the emotional overtones are no less multiple and complex. If these encounters take place soon after the marital breakup, they will typically run athwart the child's desperate wish to have his or her parents reunite. The result is a state of enormous stress and distress, perhaps accompanied by protest, and sometimes by an outbreak of depressive, phobic, or aggressive symptoms.

But the family transformations need not be so overt; even more subtle changes can be disturbing. Thus for several years, an 8-year-old boy had sojourned in a household with his divorced mother and her boyfriend (whom the child called "Dad"). At one point, he heard his mother tell someone that she and the boyfriend planned to be married in a few months. Immediately the youngster's schoolwork fell off, and he started to play with fire. This underlines the general point that to the vulnerable child, almost any change in family structure can have considerable impact.

Other Children. A familiar source of stress in the preschool years is the arrival of a new baby. During latency, however, this is rarely so disturbing an event. On the other hand, what often proves difficult for the grade-school youngster is the baby's beginning ambulation. Once the toddler starts to crawl and then to walk, he or she is likely to be drawn to the territory and the possessions of the older sib, and to invade, manipulate, and appropriate whatever is to be found there. The stress, rage, and protest of the older sib are predictable; sometimes this may overflow into physical retaliation—whereupon the parents usually come down heavily on the latency youngster. With this, the sense of mistreatment becomes associated with a conviction of unfairness, and a real crisis can ensue.

Another difficult kind of encounter occurs when the parent takes in day-care or foster children. In our day-care hungry culture, this is a common presence in many homes. The result is that the latency child finds maternal attention fractionated into ever smaller dribs and drabs during the afternoon and early evening hours. For the more needy and vulnerable grade-school child, this can be a considerable challenge and evoke a great deal of reaction.

Family Moves

Americans are a most remarkably mobile people. Occupational pursuits cause many Americans to move, often over relatively wide expanses, in order to find a more remunerative or congenial livelihood. The result is that children are forever being pulled out of school and neighborhood, thrust into new and often challenging surroundings, and given the understanding that they are expected to adapt. For the most part they try their level best to do so, and for the most part they more or less succeed. On the other hand, the casualty rate is fairly high in terms of a persisting sense of dislocation, loneliness, and feelings of not fitting in. The many moves that families make, and the many kinds of moves (from one military base to another, from one overseas post to another, from one American city to another, from one ethnic environment to another, from a company branch in one state to a company headquarters in another, etc.) sometimes play havoc with a given child's sense of belongingness and security. It is a usual story for the child therapist to hear that the symptoms started after a particular change of family milieu. Sometimes this is felt very keenly by the child in terms of his or her room; features in the arrangement of the former room are different in the new environment, and the youngster misses the friendly containment that had gone along with a feeling of at homeness and security. Not all children are equally affected, and some youngsters thrive on the novelty of new environments. For the most part, however, sundering the established network of relationships, having to make new friends in a strange environment, learning the rules, requirements, and limits of a new school, and having to give up all the familiar terrain mastered slowly over years in order to come to grips with an entirely new locale can prove daunting to the more vulnerable child and beget untoward reactions.

SUMMARY

Latency is a period of special kinds of strength and particular varieties of vulnerability. The strengths derive from the youngster's increasing ability to think in concrete but empiric fashion, to follow rules, and to learn. The hazards come from the continuing need to be close to and relatively dependent on the parents, from the youngster's inability to solve the problems of his or her world including coping with the demands of school, and from the requirement that the child achieve a considerable measure of impulse control. Given the mobility of our population and the high rate of divorce, numerous stresses inherent in our culture affect large numbers of people and have a considerable impact on children. The variability in our educational system compounds these demands on children.

REFERENCES

Benson, R. M., & Harrison, S. I. (1980). The eye of the hurricane: From 7 to 10. In S. I. Greenspan & G. H. Pollock (Eds.); *The course of life* (Vol. 2, pp. 137–144). Washington, DC: U.S.D.H.H.S.

Bornstein, B. (1951). On latency. In R. Eissler, A. Freud, H. Hartmann, & E. Kris (Eds.), *The psychoanalytic study of the child* (Vol. 6, pp. 227–285). New York: International Universities Press.

Cytryn, L., & McKnew, D. H. (1979). Affective disorders. In: J. Noshpitz, (Ed.), *Basic handbook of child psychiatry* (pp. 321–341). New York: Basic Books.

Emery, R. E. (1982). Interparental conflict and the children of discord and divorce. *Psychological Bulletin, 92*(2), 310–330.

Finch, S. M., & Green, J. M. (1979). Personality disorders. In J. Noshpitz (Ed.), *Basic handbook of child psychiatry* (Vol. 2, pp. 235–249). New York: Basic Books.

Finkelhor, D. (1984). *Child sexual abuse*. New York: Free Press.

Freud, S. (1953). Three essays on the theory of sexuality. In J. Strachey (Ed. and Trans.), *The standard edition of the complete psychological works of Sigmund Freud* (Vol. 7). London: Hogarth Press. (Original work published 1905)

Freud, S. (1957). Some character types met with in psychoanalytic practice. In J. Strachey (Ed. and Trans.), *The standard edition of the complete psychological works of Sigmund Freud* (Vol. 14). London: Hogarth Press.

Freud, S. (1958). Formulation on the two principles of mental functioning. In J. Strachey (Ed. and Trans.). *The standard edition of the complete psychological works of Sigmund Freud* (Vol. 12). London: Hogarth Press. (Original work published 1911)

Freud, S. (1961). The dissolution of the Oedipus complex. In J. Strachey (Ed. and Trans.), *The standard edition of the complete psychological works of Sigmund Freud* (Vol. 19, pp. 173–179). London: Hogarth Press. (Original work published 1924)

Furman, E. (1980). Early latency—normal and pathological aspects. In S. I. Greenspan & G. H. Pollock (Eds.), *The course of life* (Vol. 2, pp. 1–32). Washington, DC: U.S.D.H.H.S.

Garbarino, J. (1980). Latchkey children. *Vital issues, 30*(3), 1–4.

Garbarino, J., Guttman, E., & Seeley, J. W. (1986). *The psychologically battered child.* San Francisco: Jossey-Bass.

Gardner, R. A. (1987). Child custody. In J. Noshpitz (Ed.), *Basic handbook of child psychiatry* (Vol. 5, pp. 637–646). New York: Basic Books.

Green, R. (1987). *The "Sissy Boy Syndrome" and the development of homosexuality.* New Haven: Yale University Press.

Kavanaugh, J., & Mattson, A. (1979). Psychophysiologic disorders. In J. Noshpitz (Ed.), *Basic handbook of child psychiatry.* New York: Basic Books.

Patterson, G. (1982). *Coercive family process.* Eugene, OR: Castalia.

Piaget, J. (1952). *The origins of intelligence in children.* New York: International Universities Press. (Original work published 1936)

Rutter, M. (1971). Parent–child separation: Psychological effects on the children. *Journal of Child Psychology and Psychiatry, 12,* 233–260.

Sarnoff, C. (1976). *Latency.* New York: Jason Aronson.

Wallerstein, J. S., & Kelly, J. B. (1980). *Surviving the breakup: How parents and children cope with divorce.* New York: Basic Books.

Developmental Sources of Stress: Puberty

BERTRAM SLAFF, MD

THE CRISIS OF PUBERTY

In the life experience of everyone, new steps in growth and development are periods of extraordinary stress; these are called "normative crises." Puberty is quintessentially such a crisis.

The Need to Accept Growth and Change

Eleven-year-old Marjorie suddenly developed a terror of going to school and absolutely refused to go. She was particularly alarmed about arithmetic, declaring she was stupid and couldn't understand anything at all about what was going on. Further questioning revealed that it was "addition" in arithmetic about which she felt particularly insecure.

What especially confused her parents was that previously Marjorie had been a reasonably bright student (although her grades were not as good as her 14-year-old sister's) and that arithmetic had been one of her better subjects.

She was referred to a therapist who determined that she had developed a school phobia and that its nature was such that it contraindicated employing those "first aid" supportive measures which might facilitate a rapid return to school. He recommended that she be withdrawn from school on a medical leave of absence and that she enter psychotherapy.

Marjorie reacted with great relief. She thanked the therapist for rescuing her and with great joy began to work as her father's assistant in the studio where he painted in oils.

The feeling of relief and gratitude ended swiftly when the therapist insisted that the anxieties about school be confronted and discussed. Marjorie then perceived him as an enemy, pushing her to face pain. She felt that she ought to leave psychotherapy, as it was making her feel worse. Nevertheless, she stayed in treatment.

One day Marjorie declared vehemently that she had heard psychiatrists were always looking for a sexual meaning in everything. She wanted it clearly understood that sex had nothing to do with her problem. In fact, she found the whole subject unattractive. Her periods had not started yet, and she was happy about this. She thought from the way her sister talked about them that they were a "messy business." All she wanted to do was to stay a little girl, be at home with her parents, help her father in his studio, and have fun. She denied fearing growing up; rather she declared herself not especially interested in it. She was reacting as though she had the choice of whether or not to permit growing up.

Gradually it became apparent to Marjorie that she was fighting off the acknowledgment of the imminent beginning of her periods. She likened the expectation of having periods to the child's game "Pin the Tail on the Donkey." She elaborated on this by saying it was like having something added to oneself that made one feel different, no longer like oneself.

It was pointed out to her that she had compared the anticipation of her period to having something "added" to her. Suddenly she broke into tears and rushed out of the therapist's office crying, "I hate you."

Although a period of resistance followed, an important clue had been elicited that contributed to the understanding of her school phobia. Marjorie was terrified of her expected periods, which she feared would be something "added" to her, changing her into something else, not herself. This included fear of the "addition" of breasts. Her defense was to try to go backward, to return to the security remembered from earlier years, to renounce school and learning, to stop time. Nevertheless, implicit in this apparent renunciation of adolescent sexuality was an unconscious return to oedipal sexuality in which, as a little girl, she could spend time assisting her beloved father in his studio, while her older sister was compelled to attend school.

As it became clearer to Marjorie that she was trying to do the impossible, to stop time and growth, she gradually began to prepare to accept the imminent pubertal changes. She agreed to cooperate with home instruction classes for the balance of the term and did return to school when the new term began. (Slaff, 1979, pp. 504–505)

EARLY CHILDHOOD ISSUES

In seeking to understand an individual going through the normative crisis of puberty, it is essential to review the adaptive successes and failures throughout his or her development. Blos (1962) states, ''The urgent necessity to cope with the novel condition of puberty evokes all the modes of excitation, tension, gratification and defense that ever played a role in previous years—that is, during the psychosexual development of infancy and early childhood'' (p. 11).

Piaget (1969) has described how at about 18 months of age the primitive (''sensorimotor'') thinking of infancy is gradually transformed into the egocentric (''preoperational'') thinking of early childhood; this in turn is followed by the ''concrete operational'' thinking in the 7- to 11-year-old and leads finally to the capacity for ''abstract operational'' thinking of the 11- to 15-year-old, the level that continues into adulthood.

It is hypothesized that derivatives of infantile, egocentric, and concrete operational thought continue to be influential during youth. These vestigial modes of thought and adaptation leave the young person highly vulnerable to illogical fears, primitively determined assumptions, and various conclusions that he or she may suspect are absurd but nonetheless may continue to feel as true. At the same time, the youth may be much too embarrassed to speak about such things.

BIOLOGICAL FACTORS

Katchadourian (1977) states, ''What makes the second decade particularly fascinating is the opportunity it offers for observing the interaction of biological and psychological processes. The biological changes of puberty, although variable, are universal and orderly'' (p. 17). The changing body elicits psychological reactions of enormous variety and unpredictability. More knowledge is needed concerning the behavioral manifestations of the biological changes and their underlying physiological processes.

Concerning the biological and psychosocial variables confronting the early adolescent, Hamburg (1974) has noted that in both of these arenas there is the sharpest possible discontinuity with the immediate past and that in almost no sphere is it possible to draw on analogous past experience as a support or guide.

She describes three sets of new preemptive demands for the early adolescent. The first are the responses to the biological changes of puberty. The body is undergoing changes that are surprising, unpredictable, and uncontrollable. The youth is likely to be unaware of the wide range of variation concerning these body changes. Concern over body image is extraordinarily intense.

The second are the challenges posed by entry into junior high school where the student leaves the security of a stable classroom community and moves into a new realm with many different teachers and changes of class during the course of a school day. Academic expectations are enlarged with attendant worries about achievement abilities. There is anxiety about the ability to make new friendships under these changing circumstances.

The third set of difficulties derives from entry into the new role status of adolescents, as participants in the "teen culture." In a dimly perceived way the early adolescent urgently feels in need of a new set of behaviors, values, and reference persons.

> The initiation of puberty occurs in response to maturational changes which begin in the central nervous system. More specifically, the hypothalamus must attain sufficient physiological maturity for puberty to begin. It, rather than the pituitary gland, is the prime mover of this process. The mechanism seems to be this: from infancy on, traces of sex hormones circulate in the blood. These function as inhibitors of the prepubertal hypothalamus. When the hypothalamic cells have matured sufficiently, a sensitization mechanism is set on a cellular level for the commencement of puberty. At that time, the hypothalamic cells become less sensitive to circulating sex hormones; they secrete "gonadotrophin releasers" which can now spring into action. Their site of action is the pituitary, which in turn releases gonadotrophins, along with other activating hormones such as TSH (thyroid stimulating hormone), ACTH (adrenocoricotrophic hormone), and growth hormone. The feedback circuit has then been established. (Malmquist, 1979, p. 206)

The gonads have a dual function: They produce germ cells (sperm and ova) and secrete hormones. The major ovarian hormones belong to two classes, estrogens and progestational compounds. The major hormones produced by the testes are called androgens, the main one being testosterone.

> Sex hormones are also produced in both sexes by the adrenal glands, which are located just above the kidneys. The cortex, or outer part of the adrenal, produces a number of steroid hormones in both sexes, including androgens and small amounts of estrogen. The other adrenocortical hormones (such as cortisone) are very important in stress reactions and in a number of other physiological functions. . . .

> Because testosterone, estrogen, and progesterone are produced mainly by the gonads and are responsible for the final maturation of the reproductive system and the development of secondary sexual characteristics, they are commonly referred to as the "sex hormones.". . . "Male" and "female" sex hormones exist in both sexes but in different concentrations. (Katchadourian, 1977, p. 91)

PSYCHOLOGICAL FACTORS

On a social level puberty may be said to begin in perhaps the fourth grade when the first girl, who may be 9 years old, begins to manifest early body changes and thus alerts her classmates to this phenomenon. The early breast changes may be dealt with first by denial or shame or efforts at concealment at what may be experienced as a "freakish" deviation from the norm of the other 9-year-olds.

> Whether the body changes come too fast or too slowly, too soon or too late, they can be a source of agonized self-consciousness. . . . Even the adolescent whose maturation

keeps pace with that of his contemporaries is likely to feel badly out of step with them. (Stone & Church, 1957, pp. 303, 304)

PHYSICAL CHANGES

Goldings (1979) has stated that girls, who from birth or even before, are developmentally more advanced than boys, have by the age of 13 consolidated a full 2-year lead, showing a physiological maturation consistently in advance of the boys who are chronologically their peers. There is variability in the rate of accomplishment of the pubertal changes so that at any one point in time some girls of 11, 12, and 13 years will have achieved their entire physiological adolescent development whereas others will not yet have begun to mature. The same is true for 13- through 15-year-old boys.

While the *onset* and *rate* of these changes is variable, the sequence of bodily changes is relatively fixed for girls and for boys. For girls, the budding of breasts and skeletal growth spurts begin around 9 or 10. During the ensuing years there is generally the appearance of pubic hair and a fiftyfold increase in estrogen secretion. Accompanying these endocrinological events is a remolding of the bony pelvis, and an enlargement of uterus and vagina as well as labia and clitoris. The spurt in skeletal growth reaches its peak shortly after the twelfth year. Axillary hair and menarche occur around age 13 and following this latter event the rate of skeletal growth declines rapidly. Although the menarche indicates mature uterine development, it does not generally indicate full reproductive capacity. Irregular and anovulatory menstrual cycles may occur for an additional 12 to 18 months.

For the boy, the growth events may be less obvious and dramatic during the 10-to-13 year period since the major spurt in skeletal growth occurs at age 15 years and the apex of the strength spurt is at 16 years. From 10 to 11 there is a slight increase in the size of the penis and testes and the appearance of downy pubic hair. This is followed by increased prostatic activity and excretion of urinary gonadotropins with attendant enlargement of the nipples and areolae. At 14 there is growth of the genitals with testicular enlargement proportionately greater than that of the penis. (Seminal ejaculation generally occurs one year after the maximal penis growth, and the breaking of the voice occurs quite late in adolescence.) Testicular enlargement is the greatest bodily change during the prepubertal period and includes changes in size. . . , in scrotal coloring, and in pain sensitivity.

The velocity of growth in both boys and girls doubles for a year or more, thereby achieving a rate of growth equivalent to that experienced by the child at age 2. (Goldings, 1979, p. 201)

Physically advanced and physically larger children as a group show improved intellectual performance (on IQ tests), social adaptation, and psychological health over the group of slower maturers and smaller sized children. For boys at least part of the height-IQ correlation demonstrated between those who mature early and those who mature late persists in adult form when both groups have become fully grown and show no differences in height.

> The boys' world at ages 10 to 13 (and in mid-adolescence, too) places a premium on bodily prowess as a social and personal tool—both socially and psychologically physical capabilities may resonate in the child with the issues of his endowments or deficiencies from earlier life. When these early anxieties receive a physical confirmation in the tempo of growth, important psychological dislocations can be precipitated or fixed. . . .

> The child is vitally aware of the changes occurring in children around him. He may express his mixed longing and apprehension in condensed and poignant ways. One 11½-year-old boy of slightly small stature complained to his parents that he had not yet had his "growth squirt." An 11-year-old girl returned from summer camp determined that she would not marry because the kind of boy she liked was strong and muscular and might "beat me up and make me bleed.". . .

> A careful tally may be kept as to who has and who has not had her period, what it was like, how you can tell. Emphasis on the future role of the menstrual period in terms of fertility is far overshadowed by the thoughts and fantasies of hurt, damage, and mess. (Goldings, 1979, pp. 201, 202, 203)

PUBERTAL MISCONCEPTIONS

Here it must be mentioned that no matter how appropriately the adult world seeks to explain menarche and help the young person to confront this without distress, profound misunderstandings are still frequent. A 12-year-old had been elaborately prepared for menarche and had been told that bleeding was a recognition of her biological maturation and fertility. When her first period began with a brownish discharge instead of the red blood she had anticipated, she became convinced that masturbation had permanently damaged her organs. Too ashamed to confide this worry to anyone, she suffered for many months until the establishment of regular periods with reddish flow corrected this misapprehension.

Another 12-year-old was the somewhat tomboyish daughter of divorced parents. Her mother had been an actress; she was generally assumed to be a curvaceous and attractive woman. Leora and her mother were in constant conflict and had been fighting for many years. As Leora began to develop, adults began to congratulate her on filling out, becoming a woman, and beginning more and more to resemble her beautiful mother. Leora reacted to this with a sense of horror. She bound her budding breasts and exercised furiously, trying to hold on to her tomboyish figure. She dieted vigorously, giving rise to the worry that she might be developing anorexia. In psychotherapy, it became apparent that Leora was responding to the remarks about her filling out, becoming a woman, and resembling her mother, as though she was at risk for losing her own personality and becoming someone else, her mother. This fear of being annihilated as herself drove her to these strenuous efforts to resist pubertal changes.

Christopher suffered from a quality for which he was much envied by his peers. He had had an early and powerful growth spurt, and, at the age of 14, was the tallest boy in his high school class. He was athletically skilled and was very good at basketball. Although he won praise for being tall, Christopher "felt small." He constantly was burdened with thoughts that his height was a mirage, a fantasy, and that he would be exposed in some way as a fake, a phony. He was aware of the unreality of these ruminations but was unable to shake himself free of them.

His body ego, the mental representation of his physical self, was fixated at the perception "small."

Christopher was the youngest of three sons. His loving mother had told him that, as her youngest, no matter how big he became, he would always be her baby. It appeared that Christopher had responded to this most concretely; if he would always be his mother's baby, he would therefore always be small, as babies are. That he had actually become tall could not be integrated into this fixed conviction of smallness. Afterward, when this had been brought to consciousness, he was able to perceive that his mother had been speaking metaphorically, not literally, and was gradually able to release himself from the strictures of smallness and acknowledge and enjoy his present body size.

Variations in growth may be the cause of severe anxiety in susceptible youth.

There is some breast growth in males which usually takes the form of a hard node, under the nipple and its surrounding area, the areola. In a study of a large number of 10 to 16-year-old boys, close to 40% (30% among blacks) showed breast enlargement. The peak incidence was in the fourteen to fourteen and a half year old group (65%). In many cases the enlargement disappeared within a year. Boys and their parents, if not aware of the normality and the transient nature of these changes may be concerned about its "feminizing" aspects. . . .

Because it is not unusual for one breast to develop faster than the other, an adolescent girl may worry about the asymmetry that results, especially if she does not know that the difference is usually corrected by the time development is completed. (Katchadourian, 1977, pp. 7, 56)

Youngsters who have been apparently well instructed in the anticipation of pubertal changes may still manifest severe embarrassment over the fantasies what may accompany these changes and make efforts somehow to deny, block, or camouflage body experiences expressing these developments. Thirteen-year-old Todd wrapped his penis in mounds of paper tissue each night to prevent evidence of nocturnal emissions being discovered by his mother on his pajamas or sheets. He was horrified that this might betray the kinds of thoughts he was having, which he felt were entirely incompatible with his reputation within the family of being a young gentleman.

Acne is a frequent source of anxiety for pubertal youngsters. Noncritical comments by friendly adults about the very common occurrence of acne as responses to the sudden hormonal changes taking place do not seem to relieve the troubled youth of the concerns, "What have I done to cause this? Am I eating too many sweets? Do I masturbate too often? Do I have bad thoughts? Am I being punished? Will these blemishes ruin me for life?"

Braces are another source of worry among these youngsters. Orthodontists are familiar with the many resistant youths who refuse to cooperate, because they feel their present social lives are being severely impaired by the presence of the hated braces.

In general, relief from individual anxieties may be gained to some extent from the support system of groups of friends. However, important divergencies from the group may themselves produce anxiety. The girl whose breasts are "too big" and the girl whose breasts are "too small" may each be suffering. So may the boy or girl who is small in stature.

Diabetic youngsters are prone to feel these differences acutely. They may be tempted to ignore the dietary requirements of their diabetes and order typical teenage fare in order to be "just like the others"; hospital emergency rooms are accustomed to seeing some of these youths in diabetic crises.

The fat or the skinny child may similarly be vulnerable as are youngsters with a chronic illness or a handicap.

> The wish for environmental mastery is a major issue of puberty. The physical changes of this age period, experienced as inexplicable, along with the internal fear of losing ground create a perpetual anxiety about loss of control. Environmental mastery is partially a reaction formation which assists the individual to deal with the helplessness produced by an upsurge of aggressive and sexual drives and with the body image distortion associated with the growth spurt and rapid change in body shape. Penile erections and nocturnal emissions in the boy and the onset of menarche in the girl, while gratifying, all indicate that the individual no longer has complete control of the body. An inevitable narcissistic involvement easily becomes narcissistic regression especially if the adolescent is without sociopsychological and cultural support. . . .
> In puberty . . . infantile drives may takes precedence over the mastery of current reality and appropriate adaptive responses. (Miller, 1978, p. 436)

Blos (1962) writes, "This infantile admixture is responsible for the bizarreness and regressive character of adolescent behavior; it is the typical expression of the adolescent struggle to regain or to retain a psychic equilibrium which has been jolted by the crisis of puberty" (p. 11).

This chapter on puberty began with the statement, "In the life experience of everyone, new steps in growth and development are periods of extraordinary stress;

these are called 'normative crises.' Puberty is essentially such a crisis.'' In concluding this presentation it is important to affirm the ''normative'' component and to emphasize that the stresses remarked upon here are among the adaptive challenges that everyone must face throughout the life cycle.

REFERENCES

Blos, P. (1962). *On adolescence*. New York: The Free Press.

Goldings, H. J. (1979). Development from ten to thirteen years. In J. D. Noshpitz (Ed.), *Basic handbook of child psychiatry* (Vol. 1, pp. 199–205). New York: Basic Books.

Hamburg, B. A. (1974). Early adolescence: A specific and stressful stage of the life cycle. In G. V. Coelho, D. A. Hamburg, & J. E. Adams (Eds.), *Coping and adaptation* (pp. 102–124). New York: Basic Books.

Katchadourian, H. (1977). *The biology of adolescence*. San Francisco: W. H. Freeman.

Malmquist, C. P. (1979). Development from thirteen to sixteen years. In J. D. Noshpitz (Ed.), *Basic handbook of child psychiatry* (Vol. 1, pp. 205–213). New York: Basic Books.

Miller, D. (1978). Early adolescence: Its psychology, psychopathology, and implications for therapy. In S. C. Feinstein & P. L. Giovacchini (Eds.), *Adolescent psychiatry* (Vol. 6, pp. 434–447). Chicago: University of Chicago Press.

Piaget, J. (1969). The intellectual development of the adolescent. In G. Caplan & S. Lebovici (Eds.), *Adolescence: Psychosocial perspectives* (pp. 22–26). New York: Basic Books.

Slaff, B. (1979). Adolescents. In J. D. Noshpitz (Ed.), *Basic handbook of child psychiatry* (Vol. 3, pp. 504–518). New York: Basic Books.

Stone, L. J. & Church, J. (1957). *Childhood and adolescence*. New York: Random House.

━ *CHAPTER 11* ━━━━━━━━━━━━━━━━━━

Flood, Tornado, and Hurricane

MARY LYSTAD, PhD

The mental health literature on human response to natural disasters has grown considerably in the past several years. This chapter analyzes that literature with regard to conceptualizations of stress, social supports and coping in disasters; disaster-related behaviors; disaster responses specific to floods, tornados, and hurricanes; and implications for research on and services to disaster victims.

CONCEPTUALIZATIONS OF STRESS, SOCIAL SUPPORTS, AND COPING IN DISASTERS

The key constructs in understanding individuals' response to disaster include stress resulting from the crisis, social supports at time of crisis, and coping skills of the individual victim.

Some of the most significant work related to individual response and disasters comes from theoretical formulations about stress. Dohrenwend and Dohrenwend (1981) link stressful life events, as they are affected by social situations and personal dispositions, to health and mental health consequences for individuals. The authors offer several hypotheses about these linkages. One is a hypothesis of straightforward cause and effect: Stressful life events result in adverse health changes. Two more hypotheses concern the exacerbation of stressful life events by social and personal dispositions; the combination of factors results in adverse health changes. A fourth hypothesis proposes that symptoms of adverse health changes lead to stressful life events, which, in turn, increase the degree of adverse health changes.

Research findings do not reveal consistent patterns of disaster-related behaviors that can be attributed solely to these variables. Lystad (1985) adds to the preceding paradigm the cultural definition of cause and effect, as perceived by the individual in his/her social milieu; it can increase stress, which then leads to adverse health changes. This cultural factor appears to be an important determinant in both the degree of psychological stress that ensues from an event and the receptivity of the individual victim to various prevention and intervention options.

Still further theoretical formulations about stress are disaster specific, focusing on the event itself and on individual, social, and cultural responses to such emergencies. Frederick (1980) and others have theorized that technological disasters create more mental stress than do natural disasters because they are defined, as originating from humans rather than from God. Still other theoreticians differentiate among phases of a disaster; Baker (1964) differentiates between more frequent immediate psychological effects of the disaster experience and less frequent long-term consequences of disaster for the individual. Others have looked at the magnitude of the disaster. Kastenbaum (1974), for example, hypothesizes a significant difference between those disasters that affect the individual's whole environment and those that affect only a part of it.

Human service workers have little control over factors in the environment that cause stress among clients. Their efforts thus are focused on increasing the social supports and coping skills of these persons so that they are better equipped to manage the stress and are less at risk for emotional problems. With regard to social supports, Taylor (1978) has constructed hypotheses regarding the importance of political, economic, and family interactions and supports in disasters. His variable, political supports, refers to functions served by public figures at disaster sites. Economic supports are defined as financial institutions that provide funds in aid of recovery of the community. Family supports refer to the functioning of family members in warning system evacuation and extended family assistance.

Barton (1969) points to the existence of a two-part emergency social system. Identification of the first part is based on exploring individual patterns of adaptive and nonadaptive reactions to stress, particularly the motivational basis for various types of helping behavior (e.g., altruism and close relationship to the victim). Barton concludes that discrete patterns of individual behavior can be conceptually aggregated to reflect the community's informal mass assault on disaster-generated needs. The second part of the system is the community's formal organization. Here Barton broadens his initial discussion of the individual basis of helping behavior by examining a community model of the same.

Quarantelli and Dynes (1977) have added an organizational level of study, looking at local disaster-relevant organizations and emergency groups with particular attention to emergency responses and planning for such responses. These authors emphasize a planning perspective, in order to determine what can and should be done in advance of disasters to deal with their occurrence. They have also attempted to correct what are seen as widely held misconceptions about postdisaster environments, particularly as related to the reactions of individuals in impact areas, such as assumptions of panic, looting, personal and social pathology, and helplessness. These assumptions are not borne out in fact.

Theoretical formulations that relate to individual coping responses to mass disaster events focus on perception, personality characteristics, and social behaviors. Slovic, Lichtenstein, and Fischoff (1979) look at the perception of risk in disaster situations. They hypothesize that those persons who perceive the risk as great are more likely to heed warnings and to take some individual action to avoid or ameliorate consequences than those who do not. In the case of technological risks, those who perceive the risk as great are also more likely to blame the government for policies that allow the risk to occur.

Cohen and Ahearn (1980) point out that coping is partially dependent on one's emotional or psychological tools, those personal characteristics of individual strengths and weaknesses. These individual resources include one's sense of self-esteem, ability to communicate, and capacity for bearing discomfort without either disorganization or despair.

Lystad (1985) looks at those aspects of coping that are dependent on social behaviors, ability to seek support, understanding, and aid in problem resolution. Her work shows that disaster victims are better able to handle the losses of loved ones and property if they are well integrated into a social matrix of family, friends, and neighbors who are able to provide immediate assistance of comfort, food, clothing, housing, and physical care at time of crisis.

DISASTER-RELATED BEHAVIORS

Mental health professionals experienced in disaster work usually define the postdisaster period in terms of several phases related to the emotional responses of disaster victims as they experience and cope with the crisis (see Cohen & Ahearn, 1980; Farberow, 1978).

The first phase usually occurs at time of impact and in the period immediately afterward. Emotions are strong and include fear, numbness, shock, and confusion. People find themselves being called upon and responding to demands for heroic action to save their own and others' lives and/or property. Altruism is prominent, and people cooperate well in helping others to survive and recover. The most important resources during this phase are the family, neighbors, and emergency service workers of various sorts.

The second phase of disaster generally extends from one week to several months after the disaster and is characterized by change in appetite, digestive problems, difficulties in sleeping, and headaches. Anger, suspicion, and irritability may surface. Apathy and depression may occur, as well as withdrawal from family and friends and heightened anxiety about the future. On the other hand, also found among survivors, even with loss of loved ones and possessions, is a strong sense of having shared with others a dangerous experience and having lived through it. During this phase, supported by the influx of local, state, and federal agencies who offer all kinds of help, the victims clear the debris and clean out their homes of mud and wreckage. They anticipate that there will soon be available considerable help in solving their multiple problems. And emergent community groups that develop from the specific needs caused by the disaster are especially important.

The third phase of the disaster, generally lasting up to a year, is notable for strong feelings of disappointment, resentment, and bitterness if delays occur and the hopes for, and promises of, governmental aid are not fulfilled. Outside agencies may pull out, and some of the indigenous community groups may weaken or disappear. During this phase there may be a gradual loss of the feeling of shared community as victims concentrate on solving their own problems.

The last phase, reconstruction, may last several years if not the remainder of the lives of some victims. During this time the victims of large-scale disasters realize that they will need to solve the problems of rebuilding their own homes, businesses, and lives largely by themselves, and they gradually assume responsibility for doing so. The appearance of new buildings to replace demolished ones and the development of new programs and plans can serve to reaffirm the victims' belief in their community and in their own capabilities. When such positive events are delayed, however, emotional problems that appear may be serious and intense. Community groups—political, economic, religious, fraternal—with a long-term investment in the community and its people become crucial elements to successful reconstruction.

Mental health disaster workers have noted age-specific reactions of children and adolescents to disaster (Farberow & Gordon, 1981; Lystad, 1989). These reactions to stress may appear immediately after the disaster or after the passage of days or weeks. The following composite list is not exhaustive:

Preschool Reactions	Latency Age Reactions	Preadolescent and Adolescent Reactions
Crying	Headaches, other physical complaints	Headaches, other physical complaints
Thumbsucking		
Loss of bowel/bladder control	Depression	Depression
Fear of being left alone, of strangers	Fears about weather, safety	Confusion
	Confusion	Poor performance
Irritability	Inability to concentrate	Aggressive behaviors
		Withdrawal and isolation

Preschool Reactions	Latency Age Reactions	**Preadolescent and Adolescent Reactions**
Confusion	Poor performance	
Clinging	Fighting	
Immobility	Withdrawal from peers	

DISASTER RESPONSES SPECIFIC TO FLOOD, TORNADO, AND HURRICANE

In the last 10 years numerous studies have focused on the short- and long-term consequences of varying types of disasters. Findings on common natural disasters of flood, tornado, and hurricane are presented here in terms of the nature of the event, individual and societal responses to the event, cultural interpretations of the event, and differential responses among more vulnerable groups.

The Nature of the Event

A number of researchers have looked at the mental health consequences of disaster in terms of the nature of the event; that is, was it accidental in nature or was it due to human indifference or greed? One disaster that has received considerable attention related to this question took place in Buffalo Creek, West Virginia, on February 26, 1972. On that day, a slag dam constructed by a mining company gave way, unleashing 132 million gallons of black slag, debris-filled mud, and water into the Buffalo Creek valley below, carrying with it bridges, houses, cars, trailers, and human bodies. Those individuals who had climbed up hillsides to safety watched helplessly as relatives, friends, and neighbors were propelled past them by the swirling black waters. Three hours later the last of the water emptied into the Guyandotte River, leaving 125 dead, hundreds injured, and thousands homeless.

The coal miners of Buffalo Creek and their families had a long history of disaster experiences. They argued that the disaster was not an act of God, as the coal company contended, but was the result of improper dam construction, deviance from federal regulations, and lack of proper maintenance, inspection, and warning systems. Lifton (1976) reports that the extraordinary number of clinical psychiatric symptoms, in 97% of the survivors, is tragic testimony to the origin of the disaster: the neglect of safety regulations by the mining company. In addition to the confusion and bitterness over their recognition that the disaster was caused by other people, over time the survivors have expressed their humiliation at the low value that the neglect seemed to place on their own lives. According to Nugent (1973), various investigations of the event produced even more stress because of the feelings of shame and whitewash involved.

In studying the long-term effects of the Buffalo Creek disaster on victims 2 years after the disaster, Titchener, Kapp, and Winget (1976) found persistence of symptoms and the appearance of actual change in character and life-style. Underlying the clinical picture were unresolved grief, survivor shame, and feelings of impotent rage and hopelessness. These clinical findings had persisted for the 2 years, and a definite symptom complex, labeled the "Buffalo Creek syndrome," was pervasive. The methods used by the survivors to cope with the overwhelming impact of the disaster—first-order defenses, undoing, psychological conservatism, and dehumanization—actually preserved their symptoms and caused disabling character changes.

Individual Responses to the Event

Individual responses have been looked at in terms of behavioral symptoms of stress. By means of survey research on Buffalo Creek flood survivors, Gleser, Green, and Winget (1981) found that grim emotional and psychological reminders were associated with the disaster 2 years after its occurrence. Similarly, they report that local mental health professionals in the area perceived a higher incidence of severe anxiety, depression, belligerence, and alcohol abuse associated with the event. The authors review the factors that affect the prevalence of long-term psychopathology among disaster victims. They include the following:

1. The extent to which the disaster poses a serious threat to the life of the individual
2. The prolongation of physical suffering and disruption of normal life occurrences
3. The extent of displacement or changes in the environment
4. The proportion of the community affected by the disaster

Miller, Turner, and Kimball (1981) studied two groups of victims of the 1976 Big Thompson Canyon flood, in which 139 persons were killed and another 681 were left homeless. They interviewed 65 elderly and 97 adults of child-rearing age 1 year later, in order to ascertain whether there had been any change in the incidence of drug use (including coffee, tea, and alcohol) and in the appearance of other psychophysiological symptoms of disturbance. Overall, drug abuse was not found to be a major problem, but among men alcohol consumption had increased slightly. Permanent relocation outside the canyon inhibited psychological recovery and yearnings for the old residence caused symptoms of depression. Of the adults of child-rearing age, 14% had considered suicide since the flood.

Logue, Hansen, and Struening (1981) looked at the long-range health effects of the 1972 Hurricane Agnes on a cross-section of female residents of the Wyoming Valley, Pennsylvania; the sample consisted of 396 flood group and 166 nonflood group respondents. Findings suggest that stress associated with disasters may be responsible for long-term morbidity. Property loss, financial difficulties, physical work, consumption of alcohol, and perceived distress, all resulting from the flood, could consistently be associated with the development of hypertension among 29 female victims in the recovery period. Husbands of flood victims were found to have experienced more long-term health problems than husbands of nonflood respondents. There also appears to be a likelihood that the Wyoming Valley population was less able to adapt to the flood and resulting changes because of the social and economic problems they experienced before the flood. The economic problems meant that fewer resources were available for recovery and reconstruction after the crisis.

Societal Responses to the Event

In addition to investigating the reactions to stress displayed by individuals, investigators have looked at those responses to stress that become evident within the social fabric, particularly in terms of the effects on family and community supports. Kai Erikson (1976) studied the survivors of the Buffalo Creek flood and found that they had suffered both individual and collective trauma, that is, damage to the integrity of their community. These effects were delayed until the rebuilding phase. The need for hasty resettlement involved the inevitable destruction of the survivors' social network; the victims suddenly had new neighbors whom they perceived as less moral than themselves. They fell into a state of apathy, and experienced spatial and temporal disorientation along with feelings of hopelessness and separation. They were unable to relate to their family members, much less make new relationships. The area's ethic of neighborliness and kinship had previously held community members together and served as a source of collective strength in time of need; as a result of the resettlement, this ethic fell apart; the victims felt isolated and were unable to substitute personal strengths for community strength in order to rebuild their own lives.

Church's study (1974) of relocation after the Buffalo Creek disaster shows that families were placed in overcrowded trailer parks that were set up without reference to natural community groupings and without victim participation in the planning. As a result, they became hostile, resentful, and depressed. Church suggests that in order to alleviate the emotional stress resulting from disasters, planning should include the attempt to maintain the natural grouping of survivors in shelters and/or temporary housing, the creation of mobile crisis intervention mental health teams for both consultation and implementation of prevention strategies, the use of ombudsmen, and continuation of in-service training.

Cultural Interpretations of the Event

Some studies of human responses to disaster have linked patterns of response to collective value orientations. Cross-cultural differences are more striking among nonindustrialized societies, but even within American society significant differences are readily identifiable. They relate not only to mental health consequences but also to the willingness of persons to accept prevention/intervention programs.

The approach of a tornado caused $2.5 million in destruction to property in a section of San Angelo, Texas, where only a year before (May 1953) a tornado had struck, killing 11, injuring 150, and destroying many homes. Moore (1958) utilized this unique opportunity to examine a twice-striken population. Using data from the town's previous disaster, Moore compiled a sample of 114 persons, comparable to the sample from the first disaster. Twenty-two additional intensive interviews were conducted. Moore found that victims often hid emotional damage by inaccurately stressing financial damage. When, under certain conditions, they admitted emotional damage, it was widespread. Endemic fear of weather was magnified. More storm cellars were built. Schoolchildren displayed uneasiness and restlessness, although discipline problems were reduced. A high value was placed on self-reliance. Survival and restoration of the city resulted in a feeling of collective confidence, but illness of emotional origin appeared. Religion became more important in daily practice, as a source of institutional aid and as a means of explaining the disaster's cause. The cultural resistence of residents to admitting emotions and accepting help nullified the utility of institutional sources of information on emotional needs.

Sims and Baumann (1977) studied the coping styles of tornado victims in one northern and one southern state in the 1970s. The number of deaths caused by tornado is strikingly higher in the South than in the rest of the United States. A sample of 57 females from Alabama and 24 females from Illinois allowed for a comparison of differences in response to the threat of tornados and the psychology affecting the nature of those differences. Sims found that personality, culture, physical environment, and feelings about that environment influence coping ability and the extent to which a person controls his or her own life. The data show that these southerners felt themselves to have little power over their future and assumed God to be a causal agent of their fate. They also identified luck as a major force in their lives, which further displayed a lessening in control of their future. Most northerners believed that success results from hard work. Only one third of the Alabama sample saw success as resulting from their own efforts. Finally, the northerners accepted technology and authority, whereas southerners ignored these functions to a large degree and watchfully yet passively awaited the catastrophe.

Differential Responses of Vulnerable Groups to the Event

Three groups have been singled out for special study in disaster situations: children and the elderly, because they may be less able to care for themselves; and disaster workers, because of the severe work stress they may face over long periods of time.

Children. Studies of children's reactions to a variety of disasters reveal certain patterns of response. With regard to natural disasters, Perry, Silber, and Bloch

(1956) studied the families of 62 primarily black children, victims of tornados that struck rural schoolhouses in Mississippi in 1955. These investigators found that the rural character of the communities was a positive factor in getting families to work together and to share the experience of the disaster openly with their children. Other factors were also found to minimize the effects of the disaster on the child, including the recognition of dependency needs, an extended family network for the social and psychological support of the children, and the children's having a role in the division of labor within their families' households.

Silber, Perry, and Bloch (1958) studied victims of a 1953 tornado in Vicksburg, Mississippi; it had destroyed a motion picture theater filled with children, several of whom were killed as they watched a late matinee. They found that the surviving children reacted to this traumatic life experience not as isolated individuals but within the context of their interaction with their parents at impact and subsequent to the disaster.

Five months after a severe winter storm, Burke and colleagues surveyed 64 children (Burke, Borus, Burns, Millstein, & Beasley (1982). It happened that 6 months before the disaster, their behavior had been assessed by means of a parent rating scale conducted during a Head Start program. Findings showed that after the storm, some problem behavior scores had increased significantly. The subgroups of children at high risk were boys, whose anxiety scale scores increased significantly, and children accepted for Head Start only because their parents said they had special needs, whose aggressive conduct scale scores increased significantly. A further finding was that when queried after the disaster, the parents of these children denied behavior changes; this finding supports previous impressions that after a natural disaster, self-blame and guilt lead parents to supress their own and their children's distress.

Newman (1976) initiated clinical observations of the emotional status of children who were survivor plantiffs of the Buffalo Creek dam disaster of 1972. A personal psychiatric assessment of 11 children under 12 years of age showed that all were emotionally impared by the experience. Fantasy-eliciting techniques (such as draw-ings and storytelling) and postflood behavior allowed for an estimate of the degree of impairment by comparison to preflood behavior and developmental norms. Im-pairment was a function of developmental level at the time of the disaster, percep-tions of the family's reactions, and amount of exposure to the disaster.

The Elderly. There have been comparatively few studies of responses of the elderly to disasters. One by Kilijanek and Drabek (1979) looked at the long-term effects of the 1966 Topeka tornado on the elderly. They found that older victims, when compared to younger victims, regarded the loss of exterior items (gardens and trees) and house-related damage as most important. The elderly received less aid from community resources and were less likely to use insurance and other economic resources in the service of recovery. Further, they were less likely to increase insurance coverage or to use credit after the disaster. In general they did not perceive any long-term negative consequences regarding their physical or mental health.

Disaster Workers. A number of studies have focused on the effects of disasters on disaster workers. These persons often are themselves personal victims of the disaster, who then proceed to work long hours at an intense pitch of activity.

Laube (1973) studied disaster workers who helped out after Hurricane Celia. This devastating storm hit Corpus Christi, Texas, in 1970, killing 30 people, injuring hundreds, and causing extensive property damage. The psychological responses of 27 nurses who worked during the disaster indicated that they suffered from severe stress caused by excessive physical demands and concern for their own safety. Most of the nurses (59%) coped adequately with their anxiety and were not aware of any decrease in efficiency. However, in the future, Laube writes, it would seem desirable to offer workshops on disasters for nurses.

Rayner (1958) also studied the responses of nurses in cases of disaster and states that they respond to disasters both emotionally and organizationally. Because of their training, a sense of urgency presses them toward immediate action. If action is inhibited, frustration levels rise. Nurses also identify with victims' predicaments in a way similar to a parent or spouse, which often affects the nurses' functioning. The nurses' role in a calamity may demand that they make decisions about issues that are usually within the domain of physicians. This, plus a natural anxiety about absent family members, leads to role conflict. Organizational problems may be avoided by taking time to plan and observe the whole situation, to recognize that normal procedures are inapplicable, and to adapt however one must to new needs. Again specific training is recommended to prepare nurses for the exigencies of disaster.

Cohen and Ahearn (1980) emphasize that helpers in catastrophes are a group who may suffer secondarily from the effects of death and destruction but who, in a sense, may also be another category of victims. These include individuals who provide safety and control functions, give medical assistance, facilitate information and communication, and deliver support services to the injured and their relatives. A major way of coming to terms with the experience is sharing with others through comprehensive programs of debriefing and, if further help is needed, referral to a mental health professional. These authors write that one of the most serious problems of disaster workers is overwork leading to fatigue and withdrawal. This is especially problematical in the first days after the disaster because workers toil long hours under stress and chaos. The outcome is frequently a burned-out feeling and a lowering of morale.

Cohen and Ahearn write that for the mental health disaster worker, psychological assistance to victims is one of the most challenging and most stressful of professional practices. The intense emotional climate in the disaster setting not only demands a repertoire of skills to meet needs, but also continuous attention and activity aimed at mitigating and managing all kinds of painful expressions due to stress.

IMPLICATIONS FOR RESEARCH AND SERVICES

The available research findings are largely complementary and lead to the conclusion that the nature of the event itself, as well as the individual, social, and cultural responses, are all critical in determining the mental health consequences of disasters. When the origin of the event is defined as willful aggression by other humans and when the magnitude of the event affects physical and social well-being over time, psychological stress is more likely to occur. When a person has limited coping strengths and limited ability to interrelate with others, possesses meager family and community support systems, and feels that crisis is punishment for his/her wrongdoings, considerable stress over time is more likely.

Obviously greater integration of theoretical constructs are needed, along with the development of more refined hypotheses. Also required are more stringent research designs including (1) standardization of measurement instruments, (2) pre- and postdisaster stress measurements, (3) control groups, and (4) investigation of the event right after its occurrence as well as long-term follow-up of victims. Moreover, a natural disaster cannot be looked at in isolation but must be fitted into the context of daily stressors impinging on both the individual and his or her society.

The available research findings confirm that natural disasters can result in severe mental health problems, and it is evident that such problems must be addressed on community, state, and national levels. Experienced mental health workers have discussed several principles to keep in mind when assisting the victim of a major natural disaster (Cohen and Ahearn, 1980; Farberow, 1978). The first principle is that the target population is primarily normal. Victims have been subjected to severe stress and may be showing various signs of emotional strain. This transitory disturbance is to be expected and does not necessarily imply mental illness. People do not disintegrate in response to disaster, and they do respond to active interest and concern.

Another principle is that disaster workers should avoid mental health labels. Many persons are unable to accept and will actively refuse help for ''emotional problems.'' The aim in most cases will be to provide human services for problems that are accompanied by emotional strain. It is important then not to use words that imply mental illness, such as *counseling, therapy, neurotic,* and *psychotic*.

A third principle is that workers must be innovative in offering help. Each disaster is unique and requires adaptive responses if help is to be most effective. Consequently workers should abandon the traditional approach and apply outreach procedures involving case finding in the community and at various disaster centers.

One more principle is to fit the mental health program into the community in order to have it accepted. The program director will want to plan neighborhood get-togethers and the like to discuss community concerns and to set priorities for recovery. For the local citizenry the sense of participation in decision making will be very useful. Selection of workers, both professional and nonprofessional, from within the disaster community has an additional advantage for the workers. When the victims of a disaster are able to participate fully in their reconstructive and rehabilitative activities, the recovery from the disaster may be much quicker and the long-term effects less serious.

These and other strategies are described in greater detail in three valuable training manuals for mental health workers dealing with disaster victims. The manuals are:

Handbook for Mental Health Care of Disaster Victims (Cohen & Ahearn, 1980)

Workers in Major Disasters (Farberow & Gordon, 1981)

Training Manual for Human Service Workers in Major Disasters (Farberow, 1978)

Innovations in Mental Health Services to Disaster Victims (Lystad, 1989)

Single copies of the Farberow, Farberow and Gordon, and Lystad manuscripts are available free of charge from the National Institute of Mental Health, 5600 Fishers Lane, Rockville, Maryland 20857.

REFERENCES

Baker, G. (1964). Comments on the present status and the future direction of disaster research. In G. Grosser, H. Wechsler, M. Greenblatt (Eds.), *The threat of impending disaster*. Cambridge: MIT Press.

Barton, A. (1969). *Communities in disaster*. Garden City: Doubleday.

Burke, J., Borus, J., Burns, B., Millstein, K., & Beasley, M. (1982). Changes in children's behavior after a natural disaster. *American Journal of Psychiatry, 139,* 1010–1014.

Church, J. (1974). The Buffalo Creek disaster: Extent and range of emotional and/or behavioral problems. *Omega, 5,* 61–63.

Cohen, R., & Ahearn, F. (1980). *Handbook for mental health care of disaster victims*. Baltimore: The Johns Hopkins University Press.

Dohrenwend, B., & Dohrenwend, B. (Eds.). (1981). *Stressful life events and their contents*. New York: Prodist.

Erikson, K. (1976). Loss of communality at Buffalo Creek. *American Journal of Psychiatry, 133,* 302–305.

Farberow, N. (1978). *Training manual for human service workers in major disasters* (DHEW Publication No. ADM 78-538). Washington, DC: U.S. Government Printing Office.

Farberow, N., & Gordon, N. (1981). *Manual for child health workers in major disasters* (DHHS Publication No. ADM 81-1071). Washington, DC: U.S. Government Printing Office.

Frederick, C. (1980). Effects of natural vs. human-induced violence upon victims. [Special issue]. *Evaluation and Change,* 71–75.

Gleser, G., Green, B., & Winget, C. (1981). *Prolonged psychosocial effects of disaster: A study of Buffalo Creek*. New York: Academic Press.

Kastenbaum, R. (1974). *Disaster, death and human ecology. Omega, 5,* 65–72.

Kilijanek, T., & Drabek, T. (1979). Assessing long-term impacts of a natural disaster: A focus on the elderly. *Gerontologist, 19*, 555–566.

Laube, J. (1973). Psychological reactions of nurses in disaster. *Nursing Research, 22*, 343–347.

Lifton, R., & Olson, E. (1976). Death imprint in Buffalo Creek. In H. J. Parad, H. L. P. Resnik, & L. G. Parad (Eds.), *Emergency and disaster management* (pp. 295–308). Bowie, MD: Charles Press.

Logue, J., Hansen, H., & Struening, E. (1981). Some indications of the long-term health effects of a natural disaster. *Public Health Reports, 96*, 67–79.

Lystad, M. (1985). Human response to mass emergencies: A review of mental health research. *Emotional First Aid, 2*, 5–18.

Lystad, M. (Ed.). (1989). *Innovations in mental health services to disaster victims* (DHHS Publication No. ADM 89-1390). Washington, DC: U.S. Government Printing Office.

Miller, J., Turner, J., & Kimball, E. (1981). Big Thompson flood victims: One year later. *Family Relations, 30*, 111–116.

Moore, H. (1958). *Tornadoes over Texas: A study of Waco and San Angelo in disaster.* Austin: University of Texas Press.

Newman, J. (1976). Children of disaster: Clinical observations at Buffalo Creek. *American Journal of Psychiatry, 133*, 306–312.

Nugent, T. (1973). *Death at Buffalo Creek: The 1972 West Virginia flood disaster.* New York: Norton.

Perry, S., Silber, E., & Bloch, D. (1956). *The child and his family in disaster: A study of the 1953 Vicksburg Tornado.* Washington, DC: National Academy of Sciences-National Research Council (Publication No. 394); Committee on Disaster Studies (Report No. 5).

Quarentelli, E., & Dynes, R. (1977). Response to social crisis and disaster. *Annual Review of Sociology, 3*, 23–49.

Rayner, J. (1958). How do nurses behave in disasters? *Nursing Outlook, 6*, 572–579.

Silber, E., Perry, S., & Bloch, D. (1958). Patterns of parent–child interaction in a disaster. *Psychiatry, 21*, 159–167.

Sims, J., & Baumann, D. (1977). The tornado threat: Coping styles of the North and South. *Science, 176*, 1386–1392.

Slovic, P., Lichtenstein, S., & Fischoff, B. (1979). Images of disaster: Perception and acceptance of risks from nuclear power. In G. Goodman & W. Rowe (Eds.), *Energy risk management* (pp. 223–245). London: Academic Press.

Taylor, V. (1978). Future directions for study. In E. Quarantelli (Ed.), *Disasters: Theory and research* (pp. 251–280). Beverly Hills, CA: Sage.

Titchener, J., Kapp, F., & Winget, C. (1976). The Buffalo Creek syndrome: Symptoms and character change after a major disaster. In H. Parad, H. Resnik, and L. Parad (Eds.), *Emergency and disaster management: A mental health sourcebook* (pp. 283–294). Bowie, MD: The Charles Press.

— CHAPTER 12 —

Fire

NORMAN R. BERNSTEIN, MD

Fire is the process by which elements combine and, when reduced to a gaseous condition, produce heat and flame; or fire is the phenomenon of combustion manifesting light, flames, and heat, and destroying materials. Because fire has so many types and contexts, it can be contrasted with floods and earthquakes, cyclones, hurricanes, and other natural disasters. It is coexistent with and needed by civilization. It is believed that humans have used fire for more than 500,000 years (*Encyclopaedia Britannica*, 1983). Throughout the history of civilization, people have struggled with fire. Mythology is tied to the use of fire. Freud (1950) spoke of the many myths and symbols that people have created about taking fire from the gods, the many forms of the myth of Prometheus, and the sexualization and fear of fire. There is hellfire, and there are people fired up with enthusiasm. Bachelard (1964) wrote:

Among all phenomena, it is really the only one to which there can be so definitely attributed the opposing values of good and evil. It shines in Paradise. It burns in Hell . . . it is cookery and it is apocalypse. It is a pleasure for the good child sitting prudently by the hearth; yet it punishes any disobedience when the child wishes to play too close to its flames . . . it is a tutelary and terrible divinity, both good and bad. . . . (p. 7)

Fire can come from many sources: It is used in industry as well as to heat home furnaces, to provide energy for society, and to keep people warm and cook food. There are fires of self-immolation and child abuse. At times, suicide by fire has attracted great political attention. Persons who are seriously ill also may commit suicide by fire. In warfare Napalm has been used for firebombing, and during World War II heavy explosive bombardment produced devastating fire storms in cities such as Dresden, Germany, and Tokyo, Japan.

The intentional fires of war without doubt stand out among the many forms of conflagration; but the others remain significant in terms of their toll of human life, property, and suffering. Arson is commonly committed for financial gain (Barracato & Michelmore, 1976), and "fire-for-profit" has become an epidemic in North America. Children who set fires ("firebugs") may be suffering from pyromania or incendiarism. Malfunctions in engines or fuel systems are responsible for airplane and ship fires and are all part of the broad spectrum of ignition.

There is a preponderant association of home fires and poverty. Electrical fires occur both accidentally and by intent in areas of old housing, old wiring, and poor insulation. Space heaters, which are easily toppled, are most common in poverty-level housing, where overcrowding, carelessness, and alcoholism increase the likelihood of accidents.

The context alters the conflagration. Forest fires started by lightning (Payne, 1982) help to achieve ecological balance. Fires also occur in combination with natural disasters, such as tornadoes and earthquakes; for example, the Tokyo earthquake of 1923 produced fires that destroyed 70% of the city (*Encyclopaedia Britannica*, 1983). Even religious use of fire can be dangerous. Torches used in worship have caused serious fires, and ritual candles sometimes ignite clothing and decorations.

As a final note, fireworks are incendiary, and tradition has it that Mrs. O'Leary's cow set fire to the city of Chicago in 1871, though bovine arson is rare.

PARADIGM OF THE HOUSE FIRE

The psychology of disasters has been studied in the relationship of individual and group collapse. The "protective barrier" described for the psyche by Winer and Pollack (1980) is demolished by fire. Large community fires demolish the structure of the town and produce the kind of social catastrophe found at Buffalo Creek, West Virginia, where a dam broke in 1972 (Stern, 1977). The pattern of the common house fire most clearly explicates the situation. For several reasons such fires are more common in the United States than in any other nation. One is the predominant use of wood in construction; another is the widespread deterioration of the inner cities, combined with aging houses and increased utilization of electrical appliances (such as television, irons, and heaters) that overload the circuitry. In contrast to the forest fires in vulnerable areas, the typical house fire tends to have an unexpected onset. California, for example, has a fire season; fires are watched and reported so that people know what is coming, even though they may suffer disaster. These brushfires differ dramatically from the situation in the northern and eastern parts of the country, where a home can change abruptly from a safe haven—peaceful, quiet, and protecting—to a terrifying trap—hot, smoky, and dangerous.

HOW FIRE KILLS

The terrifying images of fire's destructiveness arise from its actual devastating terror and damage. Quite frequently in house fires, the individual does not die of burn injury but is suffocated as the fire uses up the available oxygen. Burning plastics from housewares and furniture produce toxic gases (hydrochloric acid and cyanide, among them) plus other irritants, and they are being shown increasingly to produce fatalities. But if fire does burn the person, it may destroy the skin and any of the underlying tissues, including the muscle and bone. The protective cover of the body is charred, destroying the nerve endings that are sensitive to pain so that the person is no longer able to react and pull away from a dangerous situation. Bacteria can readily invade and grow in the layers below the skin. If more than 75% of the body area is burned, the outlook is desperate. This is true not only because of the danger of infection, but also because the loss of fluid containing protein and vital minerals occurs so rapidly that intravenous drip does not easily replace the loss. Shock ensues, leading to circulatory failure and an inability to maintain the supply of oxygen and food substances to the brain and other vital parts of the body. Death can follow quickly. In electrical injuries, the amount of fire may be quite small, and the extent of the burn injury may not immediately be clear, but within a week an affected limb can blacken and fall off. The normal protozoan flora on the body can infest and kill in ensuing weeks.

What a fire also produces is the abrupt alteration of a comfortable home to a ruin. This may simultaneously involve loss of property, security, money, and loved ones. Other members of the family may be hospitalized; some may be killed; and the patient will suffer the combined traumata of his or her own burns and multiple losses, the sudden veritable destruction of his or her normal life, and a host of ill effects that may never be fully undone. A person's mental health is as vulnerable to disaster as his or her home (McLeod, 1984).

IMMEDIATE REACTIONS

Crisis, by definition, is any situation that affects the emotional or mental equilibrium of the individual to the extent that intervention should be supplied in order to preclude possible damaging physical or psychological sequelae. In terms of time, it may extend from minutes to months, and it can readily develop into an emergency that necessitates immediate attention. It implies pressing, sudden, urgent need. In one case a married woman of 37 would not leave her burning home until she had put on her makeup; possessions were less important to her. Her crisis included the loss of her suitable appearance and self-respect. In some fires one of the psychological sequelae is hostility toward friends, family, and even the fire fighters, along with suspicion directed toward helping personnel, such as emergency staff. In the Dupont Plaza Hotel fire in San Juan, Puerto Rico, in 1986, the Spanish-speaking fire fighters increased distrust and anxiety for many trapped guests.

In fire disaster the period of maximal stress or direct stress can last from only a few minutes to hours. "Severity and totality of the stress (disaster) supersedes the intrapsychic predisposition as determinant of neurotic stress response" (Chamberlain, 1980, p. 240). Initially there is diminished responsiveness to the external world, called *psychic numbing* or *emotional anesthesia*. This usually begins soon after the traumatic event. Individuals may complain that they feel detached or estranged from other people, that they have lost the ability to be interested or to enjoy anything, or that they do not feel emotions of any type. Because traumatic events destroy the balance between the patient and his or her environment, they impair adaptive skills (Horowitz, 1986; Kardiner, 1959; van der Kolk, 1987; White, 1972). Smith (1982) noted that trauma ruptures the container of a person's life.

Lifton's (1964) descriptions of Hiroshima survivors have much in common with descriptions of people evicted from their homes by flames. He noted the striking psychological feature of a prompt individual shift to confrontation with extinction. An example of such a threat is Clause Bahnson's (1964) near death in Denmark at the hands of the Nazis, which he described as a contraction of his lifespace. In terms of dynamic theory, this phenomenon involves a redistribution of cathexis with withdrawal from peripheral objects and reinvestment in central or focal objects. In dangerous situations the field, both spatially and temporally, shrinks to very limited proportions. The previous few minutes and, especially, the next and decisive few minutes constitute the limits of awareness. Spatially, the world then consists of only the crucial immediate loci involved in the outcome of the problem situation. One man who escaped from a burning building recalled nothing except getting his new chain saw out of the inferno. He felt only mild fear. This experience with fire resembles the familiar regressive reaction of the somatically ill for whom the body itself and a few external relevant objects may constitute the total perceived universe. In both cases, perception is limited to those spatial and temporal cues that bear directly on overcoming the immediate danger; to describe it with more expressive color—the world constricts.

A total rearrangement takes place, thus constituting the new "essential" field. The crucial characteristics of this field are that it includes only a few significant items and that every one of these items is directly relevant to the danger situation.

According to Kurt Lewin's (1936) field theory, there is a continuous reorganization of more and less important parts of the individual's experiential field.

The essential feature of Posttraumatic Stress Disorder is a maladaptive reaction to an identifiable psychosocial stressor that occurs within 3 months after the onset of the stressor. Nagera (1966) stressed Freud's concepts of a "complemental series" of internal and external factors, including constitutional differences during childhood, in the development of later life disturbances. It remains difficult to dissect out which individuals will cope in a fire emergency, as the complemental series is not readily known.

The duration, timing, and context of a specific stressor within a person's life affects its severity. For example, the stress of losing a home is different for a child and an adult. The severity of the reaction is not completely predictable from the character of the stressor. Individuals who are particularly vulnerable may have a severe form of the disorder following only a mild or moderate stressor, whereas others may encounter a marked and continuing stressor and respond with only a mild form. For a fire catastrophe it is very difficult to predict from a general history who will become a hero and who will collapse (though past history of valor or paralysis under stress are obvious indicators). A home fire is a psychologically traumatic event that is outside the range of usual human experience. Individuals who endure such a catastrophe often show both short-term and long-term effects. In the short term, the characteristic symptoms involve the reexperiencing of the traumatic event; the numbing of responsiveness to, or reduced involvement with, the external world; and a variety of autonomic, dysphoric, or cognitive symptoms. Brittle control of emotions, apathy, raging, praying, or thrashing about all can occur. The disorder is apparently more severe and longer lasting when the stressor is of human design. Children and adults who have been victims of arson reflect on the event with bitterness for years afterward, even if they emerged physically unscathed. Terr (1985) noted how people can feel haunted by traumatic events for years. Commonly, the individual has recurrent painful, intrusive recollections of the event or reexperiences it in recurrent dreams or nightmares. Seeing a police car or parked fire engine or driving past a fire station can cause panicky feelings in adults and shrieking and wailing in preschool children. Diminished responsiveness to the external world—psychic numbing or emotional anesthesia—usually begins soon after the traumatic event. Intimacy, tenderness, and sexuality are markedly decreased; the fire survivors become obsessed with rummaging through the remains of their homes, seeking smoking remnants as if they could, in this fashion, recapture some elements of their previous existence. Conscious memories of flames may pursue adults and children to bed, producing hyperalertness, exaggerated startle-response, and insomnia. Survivors often describe painful guilt feelings about surviving when many others did not, or about the selfish things they had to do in order to survive. They may avoid activities that arouse recollections of the blaze, such as turning on a stove to cook.

FEAR OF FIRE

For people who have experienced a major home fire there are expectable residues of apprehension for months thereafter. This is shown in myriad accounts of how newspaper reports can rekindle panicky feelings and how survivors become cautious about fireplaces, lighters, and matches. These reactions are similar to the hyper-alertness of burn unit staffs to fire prevention; such people zealously buy extinguishers and rope ladders, check the working order of their smoke alarms, and sometimes have nightmares about fires. However, for most people who have been burned out of their homes, the pressures of everyday life—cooking, volatile cleaning agents, and the presence of people who smoke cigarettes and other forms of tobacco—force them to adjust. And many of them smoke as well. They are bothered by the lighter flames, but their tensions drive them paradoxically further toward "lighting up." Over the months, however, even this passes, and patients tend toward realistic acceptance of the ever-present occurrence of flames in society. Marijuana users follow the pattern of cigarette smokers.

Classical fire phobias do not commonly develop because emotional energies appear invested in the catastrophic realities. One patient remarked that she didn't like being near anyone lighting a cigarette, but as it was such a commonplace social event, she simply steeled herself and did not cringe or make any remarks. People who "light up" do not usually ask even obviously burn-scarred people if smoking bothers them.

YOUNG CHILDREN

Immediate Reactions

In World War II, Anna Freud and Dorothy Burlingham (1943) noted that the apprehensions of British children during bombings were related to their parents' response. This is very much the case in home fires. When parents are absent, as is tragically common, the children regress, become paralyzed, and seem to experience sustained terror. In multiproblem families, one or both parents are commonly absent and later can offer little reliable or consistent help in recovery from the situation. It is thus not feasible to dissect out this support feature from the overall family disorganization. Terr (1984) noted that there is little modification of reality in these disasters. She described what she calls "foreshortening of the future" (p. 114) in children after acute risk to life. Individuals may experience a sense of foreboding and perception of omens of trouble for years after a catastrophe. Anecdotally, this reaction is frequently reported after major fires.

Acute regressive behavior is common: Loss of bowel training, enuresis, night terrors, dreams of fire and disintegration, sleep disturbances, stammering, and intense nailbiting are all common, along with regressive play, clinging, and crying. These reactions may run their course in weeks or months, but evidence of increased anxiety can persist in drawings and themes of play around restitution and loss.

Young children can also have tantrums and expressions of rage, thereby showing their fury at "the bad man" who set the fire or whose carelessness caused it.

Self-Limited Responses

Case Illustrations

A 5-year-old girl lost her home in an electrical wiring blaze. For months afterward, she experienced nightmares; and for a year, there was a fear of being left alone, some irregular enuresis, and excessive clinging. She did not refer to the fire and refused to talk about it. She focused on having lost her favorite toys and fussed over this facet of the experience.

Three Vietnamese children of 5, 7, and 9 years who were brought to Boston for burn care after their home had been destroyed by firebombing were obedient and seemed to eat and sleep unremarkably. They did not verbalize fears through translators although they asked about their parents. They were more tolerant of pain than American children. For months in play therapy, however, they compulsively drew airplanes bombing villages and homes in flames, repetitively delineating their experience.

One midwestern 3-year-old child saw his home disappear in a winter fire. He was almost mute for months afterward, clinging closely to his mother and his teddy bear. The unfamiliar bed he moved into kept him awake for hours each night until spring, although he said little to his parents about the experience. He seemed to be going through a period of bereavement for a lost world, but ultimately he returned to his jolly, energetic way of relating.

Long-Term Registration of the Fire

Most noninjured children are lost to psychiatric follow-up. Anecdotal data accord with the general information about catastrophes, indicating that long-term school problems, emotional lability, and bad dreams may go on for months to years, even though general social conduct is unremarkable. The registration of the trauma is submerged but not strongly repressed, and probing can readily mobilize it. However, this probing does not serve an adaptive function. Most lives are reorganized normally. Terr (1985) noted how normal adults incorporate many of these traumata as weird feelings, omens, and concerns about the occult (p. 529).

SCHOOL-AGE CHILDREN

Immediate Reactions

Case Illustration

Jeffrey and Gary, ages 9 and 11 years, were brothers in a mining family in a small town in Missouri. They both sustained moderate burns; Jeffrey, of his legs, and Gary, of his chest and one upper arm. Gary showed initial indifference to his pain; for the first day both seemed shocked, apathetic, and still, later expressing feelings of fear and a sense of unreality. The younger boy showed increased irritability that persisted for at least a year. Neither brother wet or soiled but showed some sleep disorder. The event was recalled later, although this was forcibly evoked in a lawsuit that required depositions from the children. Six years later most of their spontaneous concerns were about the social embarrassment of showing their scars in public. The reorganization of their lives left them in the social mainstream and the fire was a bad memory.

Identification with nursing staff and doctors is common in burned children. Many school-age patients say they want to become physicians, a classic example of identification with the aggressor. For intact children the ambition to become a fireman or policeman is common but only occasionally lasting. The linkages to the family make children cling to each other in a state of wordless support. The parents who sanguinely plan for the future help everyone. Optimism can be soothing in a crisis.

Self-Limited Reactions

A home fire may force parents to change living arrangements; often they must separate the children and take the family through several moves prior to permanent resettlement. The arrival of fire marshals, police, and insurance agents makes some children feel guilty about what happened. This can be transformed into a sense of righteous victimization by tort lawyers who offer dazzling amounts of money as goals in lawsuits and often advance money to help the family get going as the suit unfolds. Because the attorneys often get 30% to 40% of the settlement, their enthusiasm is comprehensible without recourse to the unconscious. A lawsuit force-fully externalizes guilt, places blame on others, mobilizes energies, and provides clear goals and new allies. Loss of appetite, bowel and micturition disorders, tics, headaches, fear of leaving parents, and withdrawal from friends may all abate.

Conceptualizing the reactive process involves consideration of at least three variables: (1) predispositional factors, (2) precipitating or onset factors, and (3) perpetuating factors. The process involves a matter of configurational specificity

with variables such as genetic predisposition, personality organization, key relationships, defensive operations, and the social setting. Burn injury, family support,
litigation, and school help are all factors (Kris, 1956).

Sandler (1967) described retrospective trauma in which the perception of some
particular situation evokes the memory of an earlier experience that, under the
present conditions, becomes traumatic.

Case Illustration

Cesar, age 11 years, was in a house fire caused by defective wiring. In the course of this
fire, his sister was burned badly and disfigured. Cesar prayed incessantly for forgiveness,
and the nuns at his parochial school repeatedly reassured him that he had done no wrong.
Despite this, for the ensuing 14 months he continued to have nightmares of the fire, to
express compulsive requests for forgiveness, and to suffer from insomnia. Three years earlier
he had gone through a period of fire setting and playing with fire; although no injuries had
resulted, he had been punished for this behavior and had been very contrite. After the house
burned, he had a recrudescence of this earlier guilt. Ten years later, he married and then
divorced. His disfigured sister was the one he kept seeking out to forgive him for unrelated
marital conduct.

Long-Term Reactions

Some school-age children delay their grieving for months before showing the
fear and loss that the disaster has engendered; a significant increment of time must
pass before they show the effects of the overwhelming of their protective shield
and the flooding of their ego by stimulation, with the resultant loss of its capacity
to organize. It is strange but true that only retrospectively is it possible to know
whether some childhood experiences have been traumatic. When an Adjustment
Disorder develops, it means that a specific and meaningful stress has found the
point of vulnerability in a normal person. Such disorders generally fade, but the
incorporation of traumatic memories in fantasies—as in reveries, phobias about
fire, alarm reactions when conflagrations are shown on television, or bad dreams—
persist in diminishing intensity and parallel the younger child's pattern. Inattention
at school may last for months.

ADOLESCENCE

Immediate Reactions

Following an experience with fire, many adolescents manifest the behaviors
described by Armand M. Nicholi, Jr. (1988):

The reaction may cause impairment in academic or occupational functioning or in
relationships with others. The symptoms must persist for at least 1 week but not for

more than 6 months after the stressful condition has ceased. The disorder may be associated with depression, with anxiety, or with a mixture of both. It may also be associated with disturbances of conduct such as truancy, vandalism, or reckless driving. (p. 656)

Case Illustration

John, 15 years old, was smoking marijuana in his home when he heard his family returning. He stuffed the cigarette into the sofa where it seemed to be extinguished; in fact, however, it smoldered and when everyone had gone to bed, it set the home ablaze. The house was destroyed, and the boy's 11-year-old sister was badly burned. John reacted with outward cool and emotional containment but became truant, drove other people's cars without consent, and wrecked the family car. He reportedly gave up marijuana but without ever acknowledging guilt for the conflagration. He gambled recklessly and compulsively with his education and his life and did not settle down for the several years of his sister's treatment and incomplete rehabilitation. At no time would he come for counseling or evaluation. He denied concerns about the lost property and shared few of his feelings with his parents but he was moderately helpful to his sister in practical ways.

The adolescent may show apparent indifference in his or her initial response. Immediate reactions are often marked by more childlike regression but they are likely to be interspersed with greater outbursts of rage that coerce attention from relatives and friends.

Self-Limited Reactions

Self-limited reactions include the rages, snits, slamming of doors, hitting of audio equipment, tantrums, and anxiety attacks over weeks. The overt, long-term reactions are very much related to the environmental supports—getting into a new house and back to school, or replacing clothes and familiar furniture and reassuming activities with peers or getting back to sports.

Edwards (1976) reported that a married couple became engaged in a serious argument as to whether the pieces of material blowing past the window during a violent storm in Oregon were from the neighbor's fence or his roof. The latent emotion came to the surface when the neighbor's house collapsed. Other examples of emerging suppressed affect are seen in large fires.

MILITARY AND CIVILIAN DISASTERS

Fires in warfare with its intentional killing may be assumed to have their own dynamics: group forces, morale, and anticipation of death and training. Milgram and Hobfoll (1986) make the point that a military conflict is a very different kind of stressor than civilian disasters, and the fires produced by weaponry, such as phosphorous shells, Napalm, and the exocet missiles in the Falklands ship fires, are all different paradigms of psychologic set. During warfare, military personnel expect disaster or at least its threat. The soldiers aboard the ships hit by exocet missiles reported (Bernstein, personal communication, 1988) that although they had gone to the Falklands thinking it would be silly to fight over it, they soon learned to recognize the threat of combat; three hundred men were burned in the ship fires set by the enemy's exocet missiles. Because these soldiers were members of elite units with high morale, good training, and a clear mission, they did not show a high incidence of shock reactions overall. As an English medical officer remarked to me, of this volunteer force, "When you take the queen's shilling, you have to take what comes" (personal interview by Bernstein, 1990). These men did not have to deal with the destruction of their personal world as do many civilians facing fire; they had a continuing *community* to sustain them and share their fate, albeit with a tough-minded philosophy. Solnit and Priel (1975), reporting on burned Israeli soldiers, noted that some of the young men's concerns derived specifically from childhood experiences, not their recent combat. Trivial issues can be magnified.

Israeli soldiers caught in burning tanks know they have about thirty seconds to get out or be charred. Survivors harbor this intense flashback for years. British troops on the *Galahad* and the *Excalibur* in the Falklands, where 300 burn casualties were sustained, had vivid recall of what gear they wore because the equipment— helmets, hoods, packs, or gloves—determined whether they had minor or crippling burns when the ships were set afire. According to my interviews with these men, years later they still have flashbacks to the war. Tourists trapped in the Dupont Plaza Hotel fire in Puerto Rico remain obsessed years later about the ladder from the helicopter that rescued them (personal interview by Bernstein, 1990).

More than 40 years ago, the Coconut Grove fire occurred in a Boston nightclub where two thousand people were assembled; the conflagration is believed to have originated in a defective cooking range. Five hundred people were killed in the fire, and many news reports and later studies describe the considerable differences in reactions of various people who were present (Benzaquin, 1967; Keyes, 1984); the recollections of many of the surgeons and psychiatrists who treated victims have enhanced the fund of information. The event occurred during World War II, and many servicemen were present who behaved quite coolly, heroically seeking to get others out. Some people denied that anything serious was wrong until it was too late to save themselves. Other people were very ingenious about finding their way out of the building. The revolving doors at the entrances proved to be one of the major reasons for the great loss of life. In the ensuing panic many desperate people jammed adjacent panels of the revolving doors; this prevented the doors from turning and prevented any escape. For years afterward memories varied from amnesia to hypermnesia to recollections in dreams and nightmares and to specific surges of survivor guilt at anniversaries of birthdays of the dead. In 1943 Adler reported that 54% of Coconut Grove survivors interviewed were afflicted with posttraumatic neuroses. Lindeman (1967) found similar outcomes.

Michelle McBride (1977) wrote a book about her childhood trauma and burns in a 1958 parochial school conflagration in Chicago and called it *The Fire That Will Not Die*. She is still vividly involved with this experience and in helping others who have been in fires.

Guilt from never having installed or maintained their smoke or fire alarms is superadded and permanently embedded in the memory of parents who lose children in fires.

Anger may occur in individuals, or it may be collective and organized. Anger may be directed toward individuals or groups, such as a minority ethnic group. Catastrophes tend to evoke the phenomenon of scapegoating, and examples of this were described after the Coconut Grove nightclub fire and the Aberfan landslide disaster. Latent hostility against certain groups may be released. After the Coconut Grove fire, Jews were blamed. During wartime, anger is usually channeled toward the enemy. The "near miss" and "narrow escape" feeling of combat soldiers also affects fire survivors; it makes them feel vulnerable for months after the cataclysm. Some people feel guilty because they escaped death whereas others perished; survivors wonder if they could have done more in their efforts at rescue. Edwards (1976) cited an example of survivor guilt in a little boy who, in the course of the atomic bombing of Nagasaki, was caught beneath a fallen beam with a spike pressed on his chest. He felt sure that the spike was a punishment designed especially for him because he had collected butterflies and pinned them to a board.

SPECIAL REACTIONS

One young woman of 26 had been in a house fire when she was 4 years old. She reported that more than 20 years later, certain odors produced a recrudescence of terror, sometimes with palpitations and sweating or with the visual recall of her burning bedroom.

Some individuals recall images of heroic fire fighters, rushing police, and speeding ambulances. Still others retain the sense of altered mood in the emergency: "This couldn't really be happening to me," or "I could only think—so this is how I am going to die." Adler (1943), in her studies during the 1940s of burn patients, reported that survivors who were rendered unconscious from injuries and who had a complete loss of many of the traumatic memories seemed to fare better than survivors with more complete recall.

The symptoms of psychic damage were present, in varying degrees, in victims and their loved ones alike: grief, guilt, anxiety, depression, recurrent nightmares, either apathy or hyperactivity, withdrawal from or inability to resume normal activities, a sense of unreality, persistent resentment, and always the fear, reasoned or imagined, of a new disaster about to happen—fear of being in crowds, entering a restaurant, or sitting in a theater. For many the experience led to lives of restlessness or inconsistent behavior, indefinable dissatisfaction, or even complete incapacity.

LOOTING

A common example of the social breakdown that follows fires is the plundering and marauding so common after such disasters. The very word *loot* is derived from the Sanskrit word for booty obtained during community upheaval. After the Great Chicago Fire of 1871, looting was a significant problem. The Pinkerton police put up a sign stating:

THIEVES & BURGLARS

Orders are hereby given to captains, lieutenants, sergeants, and men of Pinkerton's preventive police that they are in charge of the burned district from Polk Street, from the river to the lake, and to the Chicago River. Any person stealing or seeking to steal any of the property in my charge, or attempt to break open the safes, as the men cannot make arrests to the present time they shall—KILL THE PERSONS BY MY ORDERS, NO MERCY SHALL WE ALLOW THEM, BUT DEATH SHALL BE THEIR FATE—

Allan Pinkerton

This epitomizes the great surge of destructive rage that occurs after large fires (Barr, 1984, p. 1).

PANIC

Immediate and Long-Term Responses

Panic is defined as an acute fear reaction, with overwhelming anxiety marked by loss of self-control, often followed by nonsensical and irrational flight behavior (Stone, 1988). It develops as a result of a feeling of entrapment, collective powerlessness, and individual isolation in a predisposing situation. Studies from numerous disasters have shown that, despite dramatic reports in the literature, panic is uncommon. It occurs only when there is an immediate threat of personal destruction, with escape believed to be possible at the moment but expected to become impossible in the immediate future. When panic does develop, it can be contagious and may lead to mass headlong flight. In theater fires, the risk of being crushed to death has not deterred people from stampeding a single exit, even though other exits were available.

John Keating (1983) reported on a study of 119 fire victims between 1980 and 1983, stating:

Most people don't panic in a fire, but react bravely . . . Panic generally occurs only where exits have been blocked and masses of people are jammed together. Males are more likely to fight a fire, while females more often try to warn others in the building, call a friend, or go for help. People who escape from fires often return quickly to retrieve mementos or pets which frequently have escaped on their own but not to get valuables . . . fire victims generally act neither irrationally nor selfishly. People don't abandon others but act very bravely, especially if it's a family member. In no instances were people simply abandoned. (p. 24)

In adults, the immediate and long-term responses tend to be less demarcated than in children but nonetheless persist underneath overt behavior.

Case Illustrations

A Massachusetts Institute of Technology student doing graduate work in physics was in his laboratory proceeding with some experiments when a bubble chamber in the laboratory next door exploded, setting fire to the building. The student first ran out of the building to save himself, but it was a Saturday afternoon and he recalled seeing the janitor there with very few other people. He thereupon went back into the burning building to get the janitor and pull him out of the fire. The student was severely burned and awarded a medal for his bravery in the situation, even though the janitor died in the fire. For years afterward the patient recalled the event and felt considerable guilt because he had not saved the other man. He expressed very little recrimination at having been injured trying to help someone else.

In contrast, a teenager from a somewhat spoiled background went to help another boy put out a blaze and was injured in the fire. He never overcame his bitterness at having received his injuries while performing a good deed. Talk of heroism embarrassed him.

Many patients express concern about why they are being punished, what they have done wrong, and whether their suffering is appropriate, although superficially they appear to conduct moral lives. Some patients feel ashamed of what has happened, and the public exposure of their lives and vulnerability bothers them. This compunds the guilty feeling of neglect, stupidity, and culpability concering the causes of the fire. Seeking a coherent meaning for a catastrophe is a very basic emotional issue.

Case Illustration

Mcdonald C., a 47-year-old businessman, was an alcoholic and had gone into the jewelry trade part-time. While making jewelry, after having had a few drinks, he knocked over a Bunsen burner and ignited volatile solvents that he used in his work. His synthetic shirt caught fire, causing extensive burns on his arms, chest, and chin. The patient was aware at the time that he had sustained a period of intense pain followed by an alteration of consciousness—a strange calm that permitted him to call his wife and tell her to get the police while he put out the flames. In the hospital he reverted to infantile and self-pitying demonstrations that persisted throughout the course of his hospitalization. He kept berating himself for the tipsy negligence that caused the injury, seeing it as a part of his lifelong self-damaging wasteful style. He felt his experience was condign punishment for his misspent life.

LOSS

For some burned people, the loss of their home is one of the most significant concomitants of the event. Their property, treasures, toys, clothes, and memorabilia are often destroyed, all at the same time. In such a situation people feel cut off from the network of normal living and from their relationships with others. Even if they move to another comfortable house and replace the needed material objects lost in the fire, they may mourn the loss of their possessions for a long time afterward. Nightmares may persist for years. Some individuals may experience a constriction of feeling and a downcast mood that also lasts for years. If there has been a loss of a sibling accompanied by a great deal of mourning, this deepens the dejection and prolongs it. Associated with the loss is often survivor guilt, even though there is nothing the individual could have done to prevent the injury to the other person. Neither actual bravery nor apathy correlates neatly with survivor guilt. People who have done heroic things frequently do not forgive themselves for not having done more, and people who have done nothing may seem overtly as guilty. If long hospitalization and disfigurement occur, then other issues supervene and transform the problem of recovery from a catastrophic episode of acute stress into the lengthy adjustment of learning to live along a deviant life trajectory as a handicapped and disfigured person. This life of handicaps overlies and complicates the other reactions, pressing them into memory but not eradicating them. Whole series of events may be hammered one upon the other: homelessness, change in health, loss of a spouse, living away from parents, drop in financial status, revision of personal habits—all can be abruptly altered. One Scottish soldier in the Falklands remained self-hating and unable to work for years afterward because he escaped with minor burns when a missile hit his frigate whereas "better men" were burned to death in the same incident (personal interview by Bernstein, 1990).

HUMOR

Fire survivors may suffer and struggle to assimilate their experience for a protracted period. Like war stories, the reports of the event get shaped over time, and wry jokes about the disaster are not uncommon. Such jokes occur at all ages. They may follow shortly after the event but are more likely to be part of the gallows humor about the fire in succeeding months. Few young children will joke about a fire, although they may excitedly replay the events with toys in order to master the anxiety. School-age children will occasionally make light of the disaster with jokes— sometimes in-family jibes—about what happened. Adolescents are more likely to show levity (albeit tinged with counterphobia) and to jest about all the clothes and gear they can now replace. Adults usually make frequent bitter comments, although a few can adopt a jocular tone in describing what happened. One depressed prostitute tried to kill herself by setting her Florida bungalow on fire, inadvertently causing a gas explosion that blasted her out the door to safety and life. She joked that she couldn't even kill herself effectively. She later came for therapy and called the suicide attempt her "Blast," deriding her own incompetence, even at suicide, and acknowledging that fate had spared her.

In comparison to the descriptions of patients who have survived cancer, there is little of the Lazarus syndrome in survivors of fires although they may feel as if they have returned from the fires of hell. The official organization of burned people is called The Phoenix Society, referring to the myth of the bird arising from the ashes after destroying itself by fire. Surgeons and some other medical personnel sometimes tag burn patients as "crispy critters," and neighbors may view them ambivalently as harbingers of doom and make Typhoid Mary jibes. Disfigured people can be derided with labels such as "Martian" and "Mummy." These reactions endure for years after the event.

ADULTS IN A HOTEL FIRE

Immediate and Long-Term Reactions

Ninety-eight people burned to death or were asphyxiated in the Dupont Plaza Hotel fire in Puerto Rico in 1986. Many of the survivors suffered from posttraumatic syndromes, but some did not. The following case illustrations are from survivors who were seen by me 3 years after the event.

Case Illustrations

Mrs. R. was a 50-year-old married woman who got up from a nap in her hotel room to find it filled with smoke. She awakened her husband and they went out into the corridors to join other terrified guests. They went down the stairs and up the stairs; in the elevators several people died of the fumes, and they were warned not to use them. Ultimately they went up to the roof and were rescued by helicopter. She found that thereafter she was always apprehensive about closed places; she no longer goes to movies. Inhaling anything that smells of smoke still upsets her, and she feels irritated for a long time afterward. She can't be around cigarette smoke; she feels that her voice becomes sore and croaking on any exposure of this kind. She is preoccupied with thinking about the *meaning* of the accident, the cause. She feels permanently diminished. She is no longer the same functional person she once was. Three years later she continues to persistently reexperience the fire in recurrent dreams and intrusive, distressing recollections. She states that everyone says she is nervous, hypervigilant, and easily startled. She has resumed her regular family activities.

Another guest, who was at the hotel with his wife and two adolescent children on a trip to reconcile his marriage, had an almost identical experience of wandering through the hotel for hours until rescued. He reported that after a few months of similar symptoms, the only remainders of distress were feelings of discomfort when in a large building like a railway station, airport, or courthouse.

Horowitz (1986) wrote of abreaction and catharsis as useful ways of "processing of incompletely integrated stress events" (p. 119). This was true for some victims, who could work off what had happened. Some remained permanently terrified of fire, and I interviewed one survivor who literally jumped backward when a waitress flinched from the hot plate she was holding; this reaction occurred even though he had done a lot of thinking and had been in therapy for his fears of fire following the disaster.

Little in the literature tells of the forging of stronger personalities through adversity and the stress of fire. All these patients seem to have cracks in their personality structure even when they have made excellent recoveries. An occasional one will say that he or she is a more complete and profound person following the brush with death and the fear of a fiery end, but it is not a positive change in overall adaptation. Most are diminished.

One couple who owned a shop in the hotel had settled in Puerto Rico after years of fleeing Hitler and moving through France, Italy, Spain, and Uruguay. Their shop was destroyed while they experienced the horror of watching the building go up in flames. After months of psychotherapy and relocation to another shop, they no longer experienced anxiety symptoms, but now in their late 60s, they felt exhausted about life and sad about the world, even while continuing to work. They had been diminished by the experience, and their final resources were depleted.

The stress of fire differs from the polarized images of fire mentioned at the outset of this chapter; it seems to bring out the negative aspects of what can happen and underscores none of the benefits of the controlled use of combustible energy for mastery of the world.

REFERENCES

Adler, A. (1943). Neuropsychiatric complication in victims of Boston Coconut Grove disaster. *Journal of the American Medical Association, 123,* 1089–1101.

Bachelard, G. (1964). *The psychoanalysis of fire.* Boston: Beacon Press.

Bahnson, C. B. (1964). Emotional reactions to internally and externally derived threat of annihilation. In G. H. Grosser & M. Greenblatt (Eds.), *The threat of impending disaster.* Cambridge, MA: MIT Press.

Barr, D. (1984, October 10). *Inside Lincoln Park* (p. 1). 2:45.

Barracatto, J., & Michelmore, P. (1976). *Arson.* New York: Avon.

Benzaquin, P. (1967). *Holocaust, fire in Boston's Coconut Grove* (in Foreword, unnumbered). Boston: Branden.

Chamberlain, B. (1980). The psychological aftermath of disasters. *Journal of Clinical Psychiatry, 41*(7), 238–244.

Edwards J. G. (1976). Psychiatric aspects of civilian disasters. *British Medical Journal, 32,* 944–947.

Encyclopaedia Britannica (1983). Fire (Vol. IV, p. 148). Chicago: Encyclopaedia Britannica.

Freud, A., & Burlingham, D. T. (1943). *War and children.* New York: Medical War Books.

Freud, S. (1950). The acquisition of power over fire. In E. Jones (Ed.), *Collected papers of Sigmund Freud* (Vol. 5). London: Hogarth.

Horowitz, M. J. (1986). *Stress response syndromes*. Northvale, NJ: Jason Aronson.

Kardiner, A. (1959). Traumatic neuroses of war. In S. Arieti (Ed.), *American handbook of psychiatry* (pp. 245–247). New York: Basic Books.

Keating, J. (1983, September 16). People do better under stress. *USA Today* (p. 24).

Keyes, E. (1984). *Coconut Grove*. New York: Athenaeum.

Kris, E. (1956). The recovery of childhood memories in psychoanalysis. *Psychoanalytic Study of the Child, 11,* 54.

Lewin, K. (1936). *Principles of topological psychology*. New York: McGraw Hill.

Lifton, R. J. (1964). Psychological effects of the atomic bomb in Hiroshima. In G. H. Grosser, H. Wechlser, & M. Greenblatt (Eds.), *The threat of impending disaster*. Cambridge: MIT Press.

Lindeman, E. (1967). A perspective on coping behavior. *Archives of General Psychiatry, 17,* 227–284.

McBride, M. (1970). *The fire that will not die*. Chicago: Chicago Review Press.

McLeod, B. (1984). In the wake of disaster. *Psychology Today, 18,* 54–57.

Milgram, N., & Hobfoll, S. (1986). Generalizations from theory and practice in war-related stress. In N. Milgram & S. Hobfoll (Eds.), *Stress and coping in time of war* (pp. 316–352). New York: Brunner/Mazel.

Nagera, H. (1966). *Early childhood disturbances, the infantile neurosis and the adult disturbances*. New York: International Universities Press.

Nicholi, A. (1988). The adolescent. In A. Nicoli (Ed.), *The new Harvard guide to psychiatry* (p. 656). Cambridge, MA: Harvard University Press.

Payne, S. J. (1982). *Fire in America*. Princeton, NJ: Princeton University Press.

Sandler, J. (1967). Trauma, strain and development. In S. S. Furst (Ed.), *Psychic trauma* (pp. 154–174). New York: Basic Books.

Smith, J. R. (1982). Personal responsibility in traumatic stress reactions. *Psychiatric Annual, 12,* 1021–1030.

Solnit, A., & Priel, B. (1975). Psychological reactions to facial and hand burns in young men. In R. S. Eissler, A. Freud, M. Kris, S. L. Lustman, & A. Solnit (Eds.), *The psychoanalytic study of the child* (Vol. 30). New Haven: Yale University Press.

Stern, G. M. (1977). *The Buffalo Creek disaster*. New York: Vintage.

Stone, E. M. (1988). *American psychiatric glossary*. Washington, DC: American Psychiatric Press.

Terr, L. (1984). Children at acute risk, psychic trauma. In L. Grinspoon (Ed.), *Psychiatry update* (p. 114). Washington, DC: American Psychiatric Press.

Terr, L. (1985). Remembered images and trauma: A psychology of the supernatural. In A. Solnit, R. Eissler, & P. Neubauer (Eds.), *The psychoanalytic study of the child* (Vol. 40, pp. 493–534). New Haven: Yale University Press.

van der Kolk, B. A. (1987). *Psychological trauma*. Washington, DC: American Psychiatric Press.

White, R. W. (1972). *The enterprise of living*. New York: Holt, Rinehart & Winston.

Winer, J. A., & Pollock, G. H. (1980). Adjustment and impulse control disorders. In A. M. Friedman, H. I. Kaplan, & B. Sadock (Eds.), *Comprehensive textbook of psychiatry* (pp. 1812–1829). Baltimore: Williams & Wilkins.

── CHAPTER 13 ──────────────────────────

Human-Engendered Bodily Trauma: Rape and Spouse Beating

CAROL C. NADELSON, MD
MALKAH T. NOTMAN, MD

PSYCHOLOGICAL RESPONSE TO EXTERNAL TRAUMA

Professionals in the field have debated the extent and nature of the psychological impact of externally distressing events for many years (Nadelson & Notman, 1979). Freud (1920/1964) stated: "Such an event as an external trauma is bound to provoke a disturbance on a large scale in the functioning of the organism's energy and to set in motion every possible defensive mechanism." The individual attempts to master the experience in a variety of ways, often involving repetition of the event, or portions of it. Freud understood the dreams of persons who had experienced severe trauma as attempts at mastery. Sometimes these dreams revived psychically traumatic memories from early childhood and were thus an exception to his proposition that dreams are wish fulfillments. Theoretical psychoanalytic attention, however, continued to focus on neurotic anxiety responses and was less specifically concerned with external trauma itself. The investigations of war neuroses seen during and after World War II provided an important window that stimulated further work on this subject (Grinker & Spiegel, 1945; Kardiner & Spiegel, 1941; Rado, 1942). A brief review of this area will provide a means of understanding how rape and abuse fit within this evolving conceptual framework.

Kardiner and Spiegel (1941) stated that when fear is directed inward by questioning the individual's ability to deal with danger—or directed toward the group, by questioning its ability to protect the individual—then a new and greater peril is created.

In extending these observations, Deutsch (1942) and Sutherland and Orbach (1953) reported that many medical and surgical patients manifested little concern about dying, but were more concerned about disruption of their daily patterns of living. The investigators postulated that these reactions were aspects of normal adaptation to fear-provoking circumstances, rather than evidence of pathological denial or symptoms of neurotic disorders. Fenichel (1945) suggested that differences in reactions to external events depended on differences in individual defensive patterns; Greenson (1949) stated that an overwhelmingly stressful event causes the victim to feel helpless and to resort to extreme defenses, including denial and identification with the aggressor, as a means of attempting to gain control.

In his early work, Janis (1954) indicated that the guilt often seen after trauma is related to the emergence of aggressive impulses. Because these may be experienced by the victim as a violation of superego requirements, they are likely to decrease self-esteem (Deutsch, 1942; Grinker & Spiegel, 1945; Strain & Grossman, 1974). Furthermore, Janis (1958) stated that threats that could not be influenced by the individual's own behavior were unconsciously perceived in the same way as threats of parental punishment for bad behavior in childhood. This perception resulted in attempts to control anger and aggression in order to ensure that there would be no further provocation. Such an unconscious distortion may, in part, explain the lack of overt expression of anger in so many rape and abuse victims, along with the overwhelming experience of shame and guilt.

Janis (1958) also described the exacerbation of past anxiety symptoms that may occur in persons who experience great stress. Optimistic fantasies about compensatory satisfaction in the future may be used to attenuate situational anxiety. Such fantasies derive from the ones that functioned as effective reassurances in childhood threat situations and may also contribute to understanding of the intrapsychic process in those who are abused, especially when the abuse has happened repeatedly.

Engel (1963) expanded the concept of trauma and included (1) loss or threat of loss of an object, body part, status, plans, way of life, ideals, and so on; (2) injury or threat of injury, infliction of pain, or mutilation; and (3) frustration of drives. He emphasized the interrelationship between experiences and the importance of individual variability.

Utilizing a broader concept of trauma, Furst (1967) described response mechanisms that were protective against further exposure to trauma, but that were psychologically costly because they resulted in loss of self-esteem. This is clearly applicable in considering situations of repeated abuse. Stresses involving a threat of body damage may reactivate previously repressed early memories of physical danger. Past helplessness and lack of control are evoked, and regression may occur. Strain and Grossman (1974) have emphasized the importance of guilt and fear of retaliation, reactivation of separation anxiety, and threat to narcissistic integrity as determinants of responses.

Titchener and Kapp (1976) provided further evidence that reactions to catastrophe "are not those of individuals with weak egos" but that the extent of a disaster may reawaken anxieties in most people, so that "all of us are susceptible to traumatic neuroses" (p. 299). From their work with survivors of the Buffalo Creek disaster, they also reported that they were able to be effective therapeutically by helping the victims link past and "previously worked through childhood anxieties with the overwhelming anxieties aroused by the disaster" (p. 299).

These descriptions are all applicable to rape and abuse victims who experience a threat of death or serious injury, are fearful of retaliation, and feel helpless. They tend to suppress any expression of aggression toward the perpetrator and feel guilty for their supposed role in the violence. This guilt is reinforced by social criticism. On the other hand, victims are disappointed with persons in authority who do not support them or give credence to their stories (Greer & Stuart, 1984).

Special conflicts regarding the expression of aggression in women bear on their responses to rape and abuse (Miller, Nadelson, Notman, & Zilbach, 1981). Because restrictions on the expression of aggression are more stringent for women than for men, women have difficulty acknowledging and accepting their own aggression or responding actively to their attackers.

The preservation or loss of self-esteem is an important component of the reaction to stress. Jacobsen (1975) has stated, "Self-esteem depends on the extent to which the individual can live up to the goals and standards of his ego ideal" (p. 22). In describing people's responses to war threats, Glover (1941) and Schmideberg (1942) indicated that the outstanding mediating factors were the individual's self-attitudes and the loss of previously effective self-assessments that had strengthened that person's sense of invulnerability. Thus, the individual's positive or negative view of his or her ability to cope may change the course of the resolution of that trauma and the future capacity to respond to trauma. A successful response enhances self-esteem; an ineffective one leaves a damaged self-esteem. Because rape and abuse victims are often blamed and sometimes accused of provoking or contributing to their victimization, they cannot feel successful. Further, because acknowledgment or outward expression of aggression violates the internal self-image of women, self-esteem can be damaged in confronting the feelings generated by the experience.

RAPE

Rape is one of the fastest growing violent crimes. Almost 92,500 rapes were reported in 1987, although it is estimated that at least half of all rapes are never reported (Federal Bureau of Investigation, 1988). Most rape victims are women. Male and homosexual rape are reported less frequently, and the actual incidence is not known. From 30% to 50% of female rape victims know their assailants (Rapkin, 1979; Solola, Scott, & Severs, 1983). It is possible that this factor, as well as the attendant fear of retaliation and embarrassment, inhibits reporting and leads to underrepresentation of those cases that do appear for prosecution (Rapkin, 1979). Further, most rapes appear to be planned; one study reported that only 16% could be considered impulsive (Amir, 1971).

Since consent is crucial to the definition of rape, the experiences that can be considered rape range from surprise attacks with threats of death or mutilation to an insistence on sexual intercourse in a social or family interaction where sexual contact is unexpected or not agreed upon.

Burgess and Holmstrom (1974) have divided rape victims into three groups: victims of forcible completed or attempted rape; victims who were an "accessory" (p. 981) due to their inability to consent; and victims of sexually stressful situations where the encounter went beyond the expectations and ability of the victim to exercise control. Despite the different circumstances, rape victims report similar experiences.

Characteristically, the experience is overwhelmingly terrifying, and the victim fears for her life. Rape engenders a sense of helplessness, intensifies conflicts about dependence and independence, and generates self-criticism, shame, and guilt. Difficulty handling anger and aggression and persistent feelings of vulnerability are among the repercussions. These are coped with and more or less mastered by the individual victims depending on age, life situation, the circumstances of the rape, specific personality attributes, and the responses of those encountered in the aftermath.

Rape is a crisis situation in which a traumatic external event disrupts the balance between internal ego adaptation and the environment. This extreme environmental stimulus produces a response similar to that which occurs in the face of other situations described in the literature on massive stress, including community disasters (Tyhurst, 1951), war (Glover, 1941, 1942; Kardiner, 1941; Kardiner & Spiegel, 1941; Rado, 1942; Schmideberg, and 1942), surgical procedures (Deutsch 1942). In rape, as in other crisis situations, the unexpected nature of the catastrophe and the resources available to the victim for coping with an encounter that she experiences as life threatening are critical factors (Notman & Nadelson, 1976).

The experience of rape is a violation of the self. In addition to the breach of physical integrity, there is an invasion of the inner and most private psychologic space of the individual, as well as a loss of autonomy and control (Nadelson, Notman, & (Hilberman) Carmen, 1986). For those rape victims who know their assailant, the feeling of betrayal adds to this sense of violation. In the face of severe trauma, the individual tends to feel alone, at the center of a disaster. The person who shares the experience with a group is less prone to subsequent self-blame than the victim of a solitary traumatic event. Because the rape victim is generally alone, she does not have the kind of group support that so often helps other disaster victims. In fact, the opposite usually is true. As described in other sections of this chapter, depending on the degree of trauma and the adaptive capacity of the individual, varying degrees of disintegration may occur in a previously well-adapted person. These include major physiological reactions such as vasomotor and sensorial shifts. Tyhurst (1951) reported on the extremes of reaction among victims of fires and floods. He described a range from those who are "cool and collected" to those who respond with "states of confusion, paralyzing anxiety, inability to move out of bed, hysterical crying or screaming" (p. 7). The majority of the victims, he indicated, showed variable responses. They were "stunned and bewildered," and demonstrated restricted attention and other fear responses such as automatic or stereotyped behavior. The rape trauma syndrome described by Burgess and Holmstrom (1974) delineates these aspects of response to rape.

Immediately after a traumatic event, the individual perceives adaptive and maladaptive self-responses and may question these reactions. A positive or negative view of one's ability to cope may affect the course of resolution of the trauma, as well as the capacity to manage future stress. During this phase, self-esteem may be either enhanced or damaged.

Group support enables the victim to feel less isolated and helpless. Obviously a victim who is alone (i.e., the rape victim) can only hope for support later and may be disappointed by the failure of the group, including family, friends, and the community, to validate her experiences. As an individual begins to recover, the responses of others are important. Thus, social variables are crucial determinants of the eventual response. At this time, the loss of those self-reassuring mechanisms that had fostered a sense of invulnerability may result in decreased self-esteem. The victim blames him/herself for lacking perception or ignoring danger.

The rape trauma syndrome defines a postimpact response that consists of two stages: an acute disorganizational phase with behavioral, somatic, and psychological manifestations; and a long-term reorganizational phase with variable components depending on the ego strengths, social networks, and specific experiences of the victim. Burgess and Holmstrom (1974) comment on two types of response: "the expressed style" in which the victim is emotional and visibly upset, and "the controlled style" in which denial and reaction-formation seem to be the most prominent defenses. In addition, they describe feelings of shock and disbelief in many victims, and they comment on the prevalence of guilt and self-blame in the initial phase. The reorganizational phase, they report, varies considerably for each individual; however, the patterns of response appear to be similar to those reported in the other types of stress reactions.

As part of the response to rape, Sutherland and Scherl (1970) discuss an early period of outward adjustment with an apparent temporary resolution of the immediate anxiety-provoking issues. During this phase the victim often returns to her usual life patterns and attempts to behave as if all is well. Denial of the reality of what has happened and suppression of affect are prominent. This is followed by an integration and resolution phase in which the victim integrates the experience with her self-image and attempts to restore her sense of competence.

Rape constitutes a stress to which all women are vulnerable. The helplessness of the victim reinforces feelings of powerlessness and vulnerability, and restitution may be hampered by lack of support. Condemnation reinforces guilt and lowers self-esteem (Notman & Nadelson, 1976). Despite varying circumstances and different degrees of surprise, violence, and degradation, the victim almost always experiences guilt and shame related to the perception of the rape as a sexual act for which she is responsible.

Concerns are frequently expressed about whether a different degree of activity or passivity might have prevented the attack. Passivity and compliance are internalized as appropriate feminine behavior; in this circumstance, however, the same compliance may be interpreted as inadequate resistance and therefore construed as willing participation.

In further considering the response to rape, there are important developmental and life-stage considerations. The single woman between the ages of 17 and 24 is the most frequently reported rape victim. She is often particularly vulnerable by virtue of being alone and inexperienced. Further, in this age group, the frequency with which rape victims report prior knowledge of the rapist is notable. For a young woman, the experience of rape may revive concerns about separation and independence, and her overall sense of adequacy is challenged. Another problem for the younger rape victim involves the ensuing gynecological examination; this may be perceived, especially by an inexperienced or severely traumatized woman, as another rape.

The woman with children must deal with the problem of what, how, and when to tell them about what happened to her, and she may become concerned regarding her ability to protect and care for them.

The divorced or separated woman is more likely to be blamed, and her lifestyle, morality, and character may be called into question. For her part, she may experience the rape as a confirmation of feelings of inadequacy.

For the middle-aged woman the issues of control and independence are particularly important. She is often in a period of critical reassessment of her life and may be experiencing menopause. The self-devaluation and accompanying feelings of worthlessness and shame can be particularly intense, especially if she has concerns about her sexual adequacy.

Therapy

Therapeutic intervention must address itself to facilitating return to the previous level of adaptation. In assessing rape victims, among the important considerations are previous adjustment (including stress tolerance), adaptive resources, environmental supports, and life stage.

Although the applicable therapeutic principles are similar to those for other types of crisis, particular attention must be directed to the specific nature of the rape trauma. The impact of the violence of the act is often neglected. The sexual nature of the experience arouses feelings and conflicts about sexuality. The victim may find it difficult to obtain help because to do so she must reveal herself and reexperience her humiliation. Many sexual abuse victims are reluctant to expose themselves to further violation, so they remain secretive and do not seek help.

A particularly important aim of therapy is the restoration of a sense of control. Because helplessness, fear, deception, and humiliation are so prominent, the therapeutic encounter must enable the victim to gain and maintain control and to attain restoration of her self-esteem and sense of competence. In the immediate posttraumatic period, regression is counterproductive, and efforts should be directed toward fostering mastery.

An issue to be addressed in the immediate crisis period is the effect of the rape on the victim's relationships. The ability of persons in her environment to support her will determine, in part, the extent to which continued therapy becomes necessary. With most personal crises, the therapist reinforces the importance of sharing feelings about the experience with significant others in the person's life. In contrast to this strategy, because of the real possibility that the revelation may disrupt the relationship, no clear guidelines exist about communicating the event of the sexual abuse. Thus, a husband may perceive the rape as an act of deception on the part of his wife, and the parents of an adolescent may project their own sense of guilt and become angry with the victim.

Family and friends must be sensitized to the meaning of the rape so that they are able to give support to the victim. The rape may intensify preexisting conflicts in relationships, and augment existing strains. If the victim chooses not to tell close friends or family members, guilt or estrangement may occur. If she is able to talk about the experience, mastery is facilitated. However, a friend or family member who is initially willing to listen may find the repetitive reworking of the experience difficult to tolerate and may need to be warned to expect this reaction.

Because the victim feels isolated, alienated, ashamed, and guilty, the initial response she receives from professionals, friends, and family is particularly important. Group and family support enables the victim to feel less isolated and helpless.

Women who have been raped are often reluctant to be labeled as patients, in the usual sense. The idea of being seen as psychologically "sick" may intensify lowered self-esteem. The victim needs as measure of respect and approval for the way that she handled the rape and for her subsequent efforts to cope. She needs support and reassurance about her intactness and her femininity. She may be sensitive, volatile, and somewhat disorganized. The victim may attempt to expiate her guilt by being compliant or suppressing negative or angry feelings and may even accept blame. At times she may displace her anger onto persons who are attempting to help, for example, friends, doctors, or the police.

It is useful to differentiate short-term crisis goals from long-term issues that require referral for psychotherapy. Individuals who will need therapy are more likely to be people who have a history of difficulty in resolving crises. Indications of this may be prior relationship difficulties, phobic reactions, sexual problems, anxiety and depression, or previous instability (of jobs or living situations) related to stress. The nature of the rape itself is important. It may have been more traumatic because it involved a considerable degree of violence, it may have been prolonged, and/or it may have been a group assault. It may also have been more closely related to underlying conflicts and previously stressful experiences, or the individual may have been undergoing an intercurrent life stress, for example, an impending divorce.

Although crisis-oriented therapy is aimed at restoration of the previous level of functioning, long-term effects of rape do occur and are not always readily apparent. Long-standing depression or recurrent depressive reactions may follow such an experience. The victim may also have difficulty with current and future sexual relationships. She may remain mistrustful of men and conflicted about sexuality (Nadelson, Notman, Zackson, & Gornick, 1982). Her sexual partner may, in turn, respond to this defensively, angrily, or critically, further contributing to her distress. Failure in this relationship then accentuates her sense of being helpless, damaged, and incompetent. It is possible to anticipate some of these longer term effects by means of careful evaluation. Counseling for the partner and family may be desirable to enable them to understand their responses (Silverman & Apfel, 1983). Criticizing or blaming the victim, or denying the degree of her distress, may protect the family from an awareness of their own vulnerability. This is particularly pertinent for the spouse or boyfriend.

One characteristic reaction to trauma is the tendency to repetition. As part of her response, the rape victim may have recurrent nightmares and phobic reactions, and may reexperience the rape in fantasy. On occasion, some women will unconsciously thrust themselves once again into vulnerable positions. The therapist must be aware of this possibility.

Treatment of the rape victim includes the components of short-term crisis-oriented therapy, along with the additional necessity of working with the impact of the external reality and its implications. As indicated, the self-esteem of the victim is threatened and is likely to be diminished. Any social condemnation and suspicion directed toward the victim enhance shame and guilt related to internalized sexual prohibitions; in such cases the therapeutic task is more difficult. The therapist must be able to see the complex interaction of all of these factors. A focus on any one of them that neglects the others is unlikely to come to grips with the difficulties in a way promoting eventual resolution.

Although it is difficult to predict the long-term needs of the rape victim, attention to persisting effects is important, because the working out of trauma proceeds in many different ways. Some issues that seem to reemerge at a later date are:

1. Mistrust of men with consequent avoidance of appropriate socialization
2. Sexual disturbances
3. Phobic reactions
4. Anxiety and depression often precipitated by seemingly unrelated events that refer to some detail of the original trauma

SPOUSE ABUSE

Violence has been estimated to occur in 50% of American families (Gelles, 1974; Gelles & Straus, 1975; Straus, 1977–1978; Walker, 1979), and its major manifestation appears to be spouse abuse. Although abuse of husbands has been reported, its incidence is estimated to represent only 7% of the total. In this chapter, then, spouse abuse refers to abuse against wives by their husbands.

The problem of spouse abuse is not limited to a particular social class or ethnic group; however, the highest reported incidence is among the poor, probably because they are more likely to come to the attention of public agencies. In a study of 600 couples who were in the process of divorce, 40% of lower-class women and 23% of middle-class women reported physical abuse by their spouses (Levinger, 1966).

The result of spouse abuse may be homicide. One study reported that 40% of the homicides in a major U.S. city involved spouses (Kansas City Police Department, 1973). The majority of male victims of homicide are killed by someone outside the family, but female victims are more often killed by a spouse. Further, wife beating is often accompanied by physical and/or sexual abuse of the children (Gayford, 1975; Hilberman & Munson, 1977–1978; Scott, 1974).

Most clinicians define an abused or battered wife as one who is subjected to serious and/or repeated physical injury as a result of deliberate assaults by her husband. The severity of such abuse has been graded along a continuum: (1) not requiring medical attention, (2) requiring outpatient attention, and (3) requiring hospitalization (Scott, 1974). Scott categorized the frequency of abuse as (1) regular, (2) episodic (situational), (3) increasing, and (4) terminal. As Hilberman (1980) notes, however, pushing and shoving may not constitute a threat to life and may even be considered permissible by a couple; but if the assailant were a stranger, the same behaviors would be considered violent acts.

Available data on wife abuse suggest that wives who are abused by their husbands were often abused by their parents when they were children (Gayford, 1975; Gelles, 1974; Hanks & Rosenbaum, 1977; Hilberman & Munson, 1977–1978; Parker & Schumacher, 1977; Pizzey, 1975; Rounsaville, 1978; Scott, 1974; Walker, 1979). Hilberman and Munson (1977–1978) studied the connection between reported violence between parents, alcoholism, and a history of physical and/or sexual abuse as children. Abusing husbands had early histories of emotional deprivation, lack of protection, violence (as witnesses and as objects of abuse), and alcoholism. Most abused women had married and left home at an early age in order to escape from violent and seductive fathers. Although future husbands often did not have histories of violent behavior until they were married, the women generally ignored evidence of the men's potential for violence because of the urgent need to marry in order to escape their home environment.

Authors (Gayford, 1975; Gelles, 1974; Hilberman & Munson, 1977–1978) have also reported an association between alcohol use and marital violence. Drinking accompanied by violence occurred in 22% to 100% of reported episodes. Many spouse abusers who were alcoholics, however, were also abusers when they were sober. Many women reported that the abuse increased during pregnancy (Hilberman & Munson, 1977–1978); this often led to abortions and premature births (Gayford, 1975; Gelles, 1974; Hilberman & Munson, 1977–1978; Walker, 1979).

Within those marriages in which violence occurred, the men were often characterized as immature and remorseful (Martin, 1976) when they were not violent. The women often felt sorry for their husbands because of their histories of deprivation and abuse. Battered women often have difficulty leaving their husbands; this is especially true if the battering is not very frequent, if the wife was battered by her parents when she was a child, or if she has few resources emotionally or economically (President's Commission, 1978). There have been reports that many women hope their husbands will change and stop abusing them; there is, however, little support for the idea that women remain in these relationships because of masochism (Gayford, 1975; Gelles, 1976; Martin, 1976; Rounsaville, 1978; Scott, 1974; Straus, 1977; Waites, 1977–1978; Walker, 1977–1978). Although many of the women in Martin's (1976) study did leave their marriages for brief periods, they returned because of economic and emotional dependence on their husbands, and threats of further violence from which they felt they had no protection. Fear, especially in the presence of continuing threats, appears to be a major deterrent to activity (Martin, 1976; Symonds, 1978). Another reason for the reluctance to leave may be "learned helplessness," the sense of inability to effect change, which has been described by many authors as a particular problem for women (Ball & Wyman, 1977–1978; Seligman, 1975; Waites, 1977–1978; Walker, 1977–1978). This phenomenon has been described in the "Stockholm syndrome" (Ochberg, 1980), where positive feelings, perhaps based on some mixture of terror, dependence, and gratitude, come to be expressed by captives and hostages toward persons who have terrorized them. The same dynamics may be operational in battered women.

Some women were assaulted daily, whereas others were beaten intermittently and lived in constant anticipatory terror (Dewsbury, 1975; Fonseka, 1974; Gayford, 1975; Gelles, 1974; Hilberman & Munson, 1977–1978; Martin, 1976; Scott, 1974; Walker, 1979). Some women sought recourse through the criminal justice system, but these attempts were often frustrated by the unresponsiveness of officials, as well as threats of retaliation by the husband (Chapman & Gates, 1978; Eisenberg & Micklow, 1976; Field & Field, 1973; Gates, 1977; Hilberman & Munson, 1977–1978; Walker, 1979). Although most women were passive and did not defend themselves, the few women who did so resorted to violence in desperation, and their behavior usually surprised them. They were often unaware of the extent of their rage and their capacity for violence (Hilberman & Munson, 1977–1978).

Extreme jealousy characterized many of the abusive husbands (Gayford, 1975; Gelles, 1974; Hilberman & Munson, 1977–1978; Scott, 1974). These men made active efforts to keep their wives isolated. If the women left the house for any reason, they were likely to be accused of infidelity and assaulted. Even medical appointments were often made in secrecy. Friendships with women were discouraged, and the husbands often embarrassed their wives in the presence of others by asserting that they were lesbians, prostitutes, or otherwise unacceptable.

Violence often erupted when a husband was not immediately gratified. A common pattern was for the husband to come home late after being with another woman and to provoke an argument that resulted in violence. The assaults usually occurred at night and on weekends, so children were witnesses and participants. Children also became involved when they attempted to defend or protect the mother.

Clinicians have been impressed by the frequency with which child abuse and spouse abuse occur together. Gayford (1975) reported that 37% of the women and 54% of the men beat their children, and Hilberman and Munson (1977–1978) identified physical and/or sexual abuse of children in one-third of the families they studied. Emotional neglect, abuse, and frequent separations were the norm, and in these violent homes the children were both witnesses and targets of abuse (Gayford, 1975; Gelles, 1974; Hilberman & Munson, 1977–1978; Scott, 1974; Walker, 1979).

Impact of Abuse

Among the battered women, Hilberman and Munson (1977–1978) have described a response pattern similar to the rape trauma syndrome. Terror was constant but because chronicity and unpredictability were also characteristic, severe agitation and anxiety with fears of imminent doom were typically present. These women were unable to relax or to sleep; during the daytime they were fatigued and lacked energy. Their lives were pervaded by an omnipresent sense of helplessness, incompetence, and despair. They often saw themselves as deserving abuse and as powerless to change their fate.

Somatic symptoms such as headaches, asthma, gastrointestinal symptoms, and pain were frequent. More than half of the women studied had prior psychiatric histories, with depression being the most frequent diagnosis. They had also been treated for drug overdoses and suicide attempts. Although over many years they had had multiple medical contacts, they often did not reveal the abuse to their physicians, nor were they asked (Dewsbury, 1975; Hilberman & Munson, 1977–1978).

A high incidence of somatic, psychological, and behavioral symptoms have been described in their children, including headaches, abdominal complaints, asthma, peptic ulcer, and rheumatoid arthritis. Depression, suicidal behavior, and overt psychosis were also seen (Gayford, 1975; Hilberman & Munson, 1977–1978). Among the preschool children and young schoolchildren, somatic complaints, stuttering, school phobias, enuresis, and insomnia were frequent. The insomnia was often accompanied by intense fear, screaming, and resistance against going to bed at night. Most children had impaired concentration and difficulty with schoolwork. Older children showed differential behavior patterns divided along gender lines. The most frequently reported cluster for boys included aggressive disruptive behavior, stealing, temper tantrums, truancy, and fighting with siblings and schoolmates. Girls were more likely to experience somatic symptoms.

Therapeutic Implications

As with rape victims, abused wives displayed inattention, self-blame, and disbelief. This is supported by the tendency of victims to deny violence. Thus, when taking a history, general questions about violence may be less productive than direct questions, for example, "Is anyone at home hitting you?" (Hilberman, 1980). Hilberman warns that once established, marital violence tends to escalate and the outcome may be fatal. Thus, she and others (Gayford, 1975; Hilberman & Munson, 1977–1978; Martin, 1976; Pizzey, 1975; President's Commission, 1978; Ridington, 1977–1978; Straus, 1977; U.S. Commission on Civil Rights, 1978; Vaughan, 1977; Walker, 1978, 1979) emphasize the need to attend to the realities of the lives of victims. It is essential to coordinate the provision of medical care, legal counseling, and social supports.

Those working with battered women often become frustrated and angry at the victims' passivity, fear, and failure to follow through on suggestions, as well as by the frequency with which they return to the abusive situation (Hilberman & Munson, 1977–1978; Walker, 1977–1978, 1979). Workers' attempts to rescue victims and overidentification with their helplessness and dependency may make it difficult for women to take action on their own behalf (Ball & Wyman, 1977–1978; Ridington, 1977–1978). Support and psychotherapeutic work must be directed at fostering autonomy, independence, and self-esteem.

Often the process is long and difficult. Because of their mistrust, fear, and low self-esteem, these women may be reluctant to reveal the extent of the abuse. Their history of lack of a trusting relationship early in life makes it difficult for them to establish a therapeutic alliance, even with those who promise help. Further, they often fear loss of control, especially of their rage.

Although involvement of the husband has often been seen as an important component of therapy, in some circumstances it may be counterproductive. Before couples therapy can be productive, the abused partner may require individual therapy and a chance to establish some control and autonomy (Pizzey, 1975; Straus, 1974).

The issues involved in human-engendered bodily trauma are complex and not easily summarized. The clinician must be aware of the multidetermined and multifaceted nature of any abusive situation as well as the patient's various responses to it. Effective intervention depends to a great extent on the sensitivity of the clinician to these various responses and his or her willingness to be flexible in working with the different reactions to this type of abuse.

REFERENCES

Amir, M. (1971). *Patterns of forcible rape*. Chicago, IL: University of Chicago Press.

Ball, P. G., & Wyman, E. (1977–1978). Battered wives and powerlessness: What can counselors do? *Victimology: An International Journal, 2,* 545–552.

Burgess, A., & Holmstrom, L. (1974). Rape trauma syndrome. *American Journal of Psychiatry, 131,* 981–986.

Chapman, J. R., & Gates, M. (Eds.). (1978). *The victimization of women*. Beverly Hills, CA: Sage.

Deutsch, H. (1942). Some psychoanalytic observations in surgery. *Psychosomatic Medicine, 4,* 105–115.

Dewsbury, A. (1975). Family violence seen in general practice. *Review of Social Health Journal, 95,* 290–294.

Eisenberg, S., & Micklow, P. (1976). The assaulted wife: Catch 22 revisited. *Women's Rights Law Reporter, 5,* 138.

Engel, G. (1963). *Psychological development in health and disease*. Philadelphia, PA: Saunders.

Federal Bureau of Investigation. (1988, November). *Uniform crime report. Preliminary annual release*. Washington, DC: U.S. Department of Justice.

Fenichel, O. (1945). *The psychoanalytic theory of neurosis*. New York: Norton.

Field, M., & Field, H. (1973). Marital violence and the criminal process: Neither justice nor peace. *Social Service Review, 47,* 221–240.

Fonseka, S. (1974). A study of wife beating in the Camberwall area. *British Journal of Clinical Practice, 28,* 400–402.

Freud, S. (1964). New introductory lectures on psychoanalysis. In J. Strachey (Ed. and Trans.), *The standard edition of the complete works of Sigmund Freud* (Vol. 22). London: Hogarth Press. (Original work published 1920)

Furst, S. S. (1967). Psychic trauma. In S. S. Furst (Ed.), *Psychic trauma*. New York: Basic Books.

Gates, M. J. (1977, May). *The battered woman: Criminal and civil remedies*. Paper presented at the 130th annual meeting of the American Psychiatric Association, Toronto, Ontario, Canada.

Gayford, J. J. (1975). Battered wives. *Medicine and Science Law, 15*, 237–245.

Gelles, R. J. (1974). *The violent home: A study of physical aggression between husbands and wives.* Beverly Hills, CA: Sage.

Gelles, R. J. (1976). Abused wives: Why do they stay? *Journal of Marriage and the Family, 38*, 659–666.

Gelles, R. J., & Straus, M. A. (1975). Family experience and public support of the death penalty. *American Journal of Orthopsychiatry, 45*, 596–613.

Glover, E. (1941). Notes on the psychological effects of war conditions on the civilian population. Part I: The Munich crisis. *International Journal of Psychoanalysis, 22*, 132–146.

Glover, E. (1942). Notes on the psychological effects of war conditions on the civilian population. Part III: The blitz. *International Journal of Psychoanalysis, 23*, 17–37.

Greenson, R. (1949). The psychology of apathy. *Psychoanalytic Quarterly, 18*, 290–303.

Greer, J., & Stuart, I. (Eds.). (1984). *Victims of sexual aggression: Treatment of children, women and men.* New York: Van Nostrand Reinhold.

Grinker, R., & Spiegel, H. (1945). *Men under stress.* Philadelphia, PA: Blakiston.

Hanks, S. E., & Rosenbaum, P. (1977). Battered women: A study of women who live with violent alcohol-abusing men. *American Journal of Orthopsychiatry, 47*, 291–306.

Hilberman, E. (1980). Overview: The ''wife beater's wife'' reconsidered. *American Journal of Psychiatry, 137*, 1336–1347.

Hilberman, E., & Munson, M. (1977–1978). Sixty battered women. *Victimology: An International Journal, 2*, 460–471.

Jacobsen, E. (1975). The regulation of self-esteem. In E. J. Anthony & T. Benedek (Eds.), *Depression and human existence.* Boston: Little, Brown.

Janis, I. L. (1954). Problems of theory in the analysis of stress behavior. *Journal of Social Issues, 10*, 12–25.

Janis, I. L. (1958). *Psychological stress.* New York: Wiley.

Kansas City Police Department. (1973). *Conflict management: Analysis/resolution.* Kansas City, MO: Author.

Kardiner, A. (1941). *The traumatic neuroses of war* (Medical Monograph II–III). New York: P. B. Hocher.

Kardiner, A., & Spiegel, H. (1941). *War stress and neurotic illness.* New York: P. B. Hocher.

Levinger, G. (1966). Sources of marital dissatisfaction among applicants for divorce. *American Journal of Orthopsychiatry, 36*, 803–807.

Martin, D. (1976). *Battered wives.* San Francisco, CA: Glide.

Miller, J., Nadelson, C. C., Notman, M. T., & Zilbach, J. (1981). Some considerations of self-esteem and aggression in women. In S. Klebanow (Ed.), *Changing concepts in psychoanalysis.* New York: Gardner Press.

Nadelson, C. C., & Notman, M. T. (1979). Psychoanalytic considerations of the response to rape. *International Review of Psychoanalysis, 6*, 97–104.

Nadelson, C. C., Notman, M. T., & (Hilberman) Carmen E. (1986). The rape victim and the rape experience. In W. Curran (Ed.), *Modern forensic psychiatry and psychology* (pp. 339–362) Philadelphia, PA: Davis.

Nadelson, C. C., Notman, M. T., Zackson, H., & Gornick, J. (1982, October). A follow-up study of rape victims. *American Journal of Psychiatry, 139*, 1266–1270.

Notman, M. T., & Nadelson, C. C. (1976, April). The rape victim: Psychodynamic considerations. *American Journal of Psychiatry, 133,* 408–413.

Ochberg, F. M. (1980). Victims of terrorism (Editorial). *Journal of Clinical Psychiatry, 41,* 73–74.

Parker, B., & Schumacher, D. (1977). The battered wife syndrome and violence in the nuclear family of origin. A controlled pilot study. *American Journal of Public Health, 67,* 760–761.

Pizzey, E. (1975). Chiswick women's aid: A refuge from violence. *Review of Social Health Journal, 75,* 297–298, 308.

President's Commission on Mental Health. (1978). *Report of the subpanel on women's mental health* (Vol. 3, Appendix). Washington, DC: U.S. Government Printing Office.

Rado, S. (1942). Pathodynamics—Treatment of traumatic war neurosis (traumatophobia). *Psychosomatic Medicine, 4,* 362–369.

Rapkin, J. (1979, October). The epidemiology of forcible rape. *American Journal of Orthopsychiatry, 49,* 634–647.

Ridington, J. (1977–1978). The transition process: A feminist environment as reconstitutive milieu. *Victimology: An International Journal, 2,* 563–575.

Rounsaville, B. (1978). Theories in marital violence: Evidence from a study of battered women. *Victimology: An International Journal, 3,* 11–29.

Schmideberg, M. (1942). Some observations on individual reactions to air raids. *International Journal of Psychoanalysis, 23,* 146–176.

Scott, P. D. (1974). Battered wives. *British Journal of Psychiatry, 125,* 433–441.

Seligman, M. E. (1975). Helplessness: *On depression, development and death.* San Francisco, CA: WH Freeman.

Silverman, D., & Apfel, R. (1983). Caring for victims of rape. In C. Nadelson & D. Marcotte (Eds.), *Treatment interventions in human sexuality* (pp. 195–213). New York: Plenum.

Solala, A., Scott, C., & Severs, H. (1983). Rape: Management in a non-institutional setting. *Obstetrics and Gynecology, 61,* 373–378.

Strain, J., & Grossman, S. (1974). *Psychological care of the medically ill.* New York: Appleton, Century, Crofts.

Straus, M. A. (1974). Leveling, civility and violence in the family. *Journal of Marriage and the Family, 36,* 13–29.

Straus, M. A. (1977). A sociological perspective on the prevention and treatment of wife beating. In M. Roy (Ed.), *Battered women.* New York: Van Nostrand Reinhold.

Straus, M. A. (1977–1978). Wife beating: How common and why? *Victimology: An International Journal, 2,* 443–458.

Sutherland, A. M., & Orbach, C. E. (1953). Psychological impact of cancer and cancer surgery: Depressive reactions associated with surgery for cancer. *Cancer, 6,* 958–962.

Sutherland, S., & Scherl, D. (1970, April). Patterns of response among victims of rape. *American Journal of Orthopsychiatry, 40,* 503–511.

Symonds, M. (1978). The psychodynamics of violence-prone marriages. *American Journal of Psychiatry, 38,* 213–222.

Titchener, J., & Kapp, T. (1976). Family and character change at Buffalo Creek. *American Journal of Psychiatry, 133,* 295–299.

Tyhurst, J. S. (1951). Individual reactions to community disaster: The habitual history of psychiatric phenomena. *American Journal of Psychiatry, 107,* 764–769.

United States Commission on Civil Rights. (1978). *Battered women: Issues of public policy.* Washington, DC: Author.

Vaughan, S. R. (1977, May). *The last refuge: Shelter for battered women.* Paper presented at the 130th annual meeting of the American Psychiatric Association, Toronto, Ontario, Canada.

Waites, E. A. (1977–1978). Female masochism and the enforced restriction of choice. *Victimology: An International Journal, 2,* 535–544.

Walker, L. E. (1977–1978). Battered women and learned helplessness. *Victimology: An International Journal, 2,* 525–534.

Walker, L. E. (1978). Treatment alternatives for battered women. In J. R. Chapman & M. Gates (Eds.), *The victimization of women.* Beverly Hills, CA: Sage.

Walker, L. E. (1979). *The battered woman.* New York: Harper & Row.

Stress Experienced by Robbery Victims, Hostages, Kidnapping Victims, and Prisoners of War

BRUCE L. DANTO, MD

STRESS-RELATED VIOLENCE

This chapter considers the human reaction to four major types of stress-related violence. Initially, it may appear that there is no relationship among these several forms of victimization because each seems unique; their differences emerge in the very names of the areas covered in this chapter: victims of armed robbery (along with unarmed robbery—frequently referred to as "mugging"), victims of kidnapping, hostages, and prisoners of war.

To some extent these forms of violence may be discussed elsewhere in this volume, but in this chapter, the spotlight falls on them in terms of their implications for the victims.

One needs to know the nature of the violence connected with the crime. Certain factors unite the victims of all these crimes, for example, in any of them, there may be no previous relationship between the victim and the offender. Where captivity is associated with the offense, which certainly is the case with the latter three, a relationship may indeed form between the victim and the perpetrator. The kind of stress connected with an armed robbery will also be influenced by the existence, or the degree, of any relationship between the victim and the offender.

Before examining these separate categories of victimization, it is important to consider the types of stress associated with any violent offense.

Reactions to Crimes

According to Barkas (1978), violent, and even nonviolent, crimes bring about four types of reactions in victims: physical, financial, social, and psychological. The first two reactions are readily visible because of the evidence of trauma as well as material loss; they are regularly described in newspapers and in the general media coverage of crime. The physical residua of violent crime elicit a great deal of public sympathy, depending on the visibility and painfulness of the wounds. If they result in major blemishes or incapacity, then others who are not even familiar with the facts of the robbery can see that something serious happened to the person.

Those who have studied robbery victims as well as survivors of kidnapping, hostage-taking, or prisoner-of-war camps are aware of both the physical injuries that occur under such circumstances and the resulting permanent psychological wounds. All these victims have in common the knowledge that their injuries were willfully inflicted by other human beings and cannot be attributed to vague concepts such as Fate or Mother Nature.

The psychological scars merit particular note. The kind of injury that causes psychosomatic symptoms is most often overlooked. Underlying many such symptoms are significant levels of both anxiety and depression. When combined with an incident of this type, the ensuing painful emotions constitute Posttraumatic Stress Disorder.

Victims who become physically handicapped as the result of a crime have great difficulty resolving their fears and anger about the crime. Their sense of loss is intensified.

The combination of emotional shock following the beginning of the incident of victimization, as well as the victim's disbelief during the crime, combine to produce an after-the-fact denial of its occurrence, and, more commonly, of its horror. Such victims frequently fear that during or after a crime they will feel completely helpless. The more prolonged the contact between the victim and perpetrator, the more the fear becomes enlarged or magnified to the point of actual terror. This reaction frequently produces submissive or clinging behavior that may later embarrass the victim and provoke a great deal of self-blame, leading to a crippling degree of guilt.

A crime victim's psychological reaction to the experience may be followed by apathy and anger. A delayed response of increased anger may lead in turn to an augmented feeling of fear that progressively restricts the victim's activities, culminating in considerable self-blame or even self-punishment.

Bard and Sangrey (1979) point out that in an essentially materialistic culture like American Society, people in general are not comfortable with abstractions. It seems that the more physical and concrete is the presentation of the reality, the more possible it is to measure the effect of an experience. Thus, most individuals can respond to a loss of property or to a physical injury because their bodies and material possessions generally consume their attention. On the other hand, the authors point out that when the self, a purely psychological entity, experiences damage, which cannot be seen or measured, most other persons are at a loss to sense the depth and the traumatic intensity of the experience. It is as if one were to say, "There isn't a mark on her. If I can't see it, I have trouble believing it."

In the face of being robbed, kidnapped, or taken as a hostage or a prisoner of war, an individual's response and survival as a victim will depend on many factors, despite the context in which the victimization occurs. Characteristically, such victims have no advance warning. They are unable to anticipate the effects of the stress or to gather their resources internally and externally in order to cope with these effects. Ultimately, their previous experiences determine how they adjust; individuals who have had to deal with much adversity in the past, are likely to fare better than persons without such a background. Failure to react appropriately, however, increases the ensuing sense of frustration and stress burden.

When property is taken in a robbery, its emotional value may be more significant than its monetary worth. The robbery victim may feel great sentimental attachment to a stolen object of little material value and experience a deeper sense of violation from its loss than would someone who loses but can replace even the most expensive items.

In addition to the degree of sentimental attachment or the symbolic meaning of the lost object to the victim, over a given period of time the capacity of the individual to respond to stress will fluctuate. At one point, a person may feel stronger and more capable of dealing with the stress of victimhood than at other times. Another factor that can influence the progress of a crisis reaction is the kind of help a victim receives in the moments and days immediately following the traumatic event. The more support available, the better the adjustment, as was evident during the release of hostages from the American Embassy in Iran in January 1981 (Bolz, 1987).

People caught up in this type of crisis feel off balance. They do strange things that later trouble them and their loved ones. For example, in one incident in Colombia in the early 1980s, an embassy was taken over by terrorists. One of the ambassadorial hostages who had been kept in the embassy for several days was observed gathering milk cartons around him, then sitting in a corner in a totally regressed position. Such aberrant behavior is remembered not only by persons who share the experience, but by the victims as well. When they reflect on their handling of that particular moment of stress, the memory adds measurably to their psychologic burdens.

It should be apparent that suffering the violent disruption of normalcy described in these four major areas of victimhood is in itself enough to cause an imbalance within the self.

Phases of Crisis Reaction

Bard and Sangrey (1979) observed that a crisis reaction develops in three stages. The initial stage is called *Impact* and occurs immediately after the violent event. During this phase victims become emotionally fragmented; their sense of personal security and integrity shatters; and they become disorganized. Many victims find themselves in a state of psychic shock; some become numb and disoriented and can be seen moving about aimlessly. Many feel a sense of disbelief, as though the experience is not happening to them.

During this phase, victims undergo marked feelings of vulnerability, helplessness, and isolation. As in the example of the embassy hostage in Colombia, they may become quite childlike and dependent, incapable of making even the simplest decision. They may seek help from persons around them, such as other hostages, to reassure them, offer help, and tell them what to do. This response is familiar to many a psychotherapist who has had a patient or client come for help and approach the situation as though the psychotherapist were going to take over management of the crisis.

Ego defenses become weakened, usually leaving victims open to the influence of others and submissive to individuals able to lead in a crisis. Such "crisis managers" become unusually powerful after the event. Depending on their objectives, crisis managers in this type of takeover can be either a danger or an asset.

No one can function for very long in such a state, and in one way or another many victims presently reconstruct their defenses. If this reconstruction takes place without satisfactory internal or external support during the Impact phase, the ego defenses reassemble in a dysfunctional way and ultimately produce additional sources of stress.

The second phase is called *Recoil*. The victims begin the struggle to adapt to the violation and to pull themselves together emotionally. During this recovery period, they have to deal with a number of distressing emotions such as fear, anger, sadness, self-pity, and guilt.

In this phase, many victims go through a period of direct denial and feel emotionally detached. They are unable to respond with much feeling to anything, almost as if they are not actually involved in the experience. To face such emotions, one must recall the events of the crime and reexperience the feelings aroused by these events, leading inevitably to the fact—and emotional reality—of victimhood. In the face of this, it may be very difficult for victims to relive the events of the crime.

Following the victims' release to safety, friends and relatives may not be able to offer the kind of support that makes it possible to share the reliving of those experiences.

Fear is one of the most difficult emotions with which victims must come to terms; they may not be emotionally capable of facing the intensity of the terror that was experienced until long after the event.

Many victims are afraid of encountering the criminal again. This is particularly true in cases of robbery, kidnapping, and hostage-taking. From my own experience of having been a hostage with three of my four children in 1975, I recall that following the end of the experience, my eldest daughter, for almost a week, continued to see a man walking down the street with a gun. Similarly, for other kinds of victims, because of the psychic trauma of the moment, memory of the crime recurs in repetitive dreams.

One response to internal efforts on the part of the victim to deal with anxiety is the development of a phobic reaction. In the mind of the victim, people come to represent the events. This is particularly likely if the perpetrator's ethnic or racial background is different from the victim's. Some victims may attempt to escape anxiety by avoiding persons of similar racial or ethnic identity to that of the perpetrator.

Common to almost all victims is the overwhelming feeling of anger toward the criminal or perpetrator of violence. Sometimes these feelings are expressed directly, sometimes in dreams, and sometimes through fantasy. When connected with dreams and fantasy, the feelings tend to carry with them the objective of revenge. It should be remembered that the wish for revenge is natural and can help relieve some of the anxiety that begins to collect around the feeling of anger.

On the other hand, some victims internalize their anger; they experience the self-directed rage as guilt feelings and accordingly may develop severe depression. They may become socially withdrawn and develop psychosomatic symptoms of distress, such as sleep disturbance, headaches, sweating, weight loss, tremors, and attacks of tachycardia. Many victims suffer a loss of sex drive; some males may experience total impotence for a period of time following the crisis.

The third phase outlined by Bard and Sangrey is called *Reorganization*. During this phase, the violated self becomes reorganized as the victim begins to put together or to assimilate the various elements in the painful experience. The more serious the violation, the longer it takes to complete this phase. Among the factors that influence how long it takes to reorganize is the basic nature of the violence itself. A victim of an unarmed robbery needs less time to reorganize than someone who has been assaulted or injured.

Most victims never entirely forget the crime. With proper support, their suffering is reduced over time but they are likely to find that the experience persists as part of themselves. The professionals who work with victims of violence have observed that the achievement of a successful reorganization depends on the kind of help the victim receives. Such support involves not only familial care and the kindly offerings of friends, but also whatever professional help is available when the crisis ends.

ROBBERY AND MUGGING

Robbery and mugging are those acts undertaken by one or more persons that deprive victims of their property. Regardless of whether the robber is armed or unarmed, in the very process of taking things by force, violence is always an implicit threat.

What makes armed robbery peculiarly significant to the victim is that prior to the holdup relatively few offenders have had any meaningful acquaintanceship or relationship with the victim. Notwithstanding their status as mutual strangers, it would be a mistake to assume that there is no psychological importance to the role of the perpetrator.

According to John M. MacDonald (1975), certain kinds of victims are particularly vulnerable. MacDonald indicates that the likeliest victims of armed robbery are as follows: drug pushers and users; customers of prostitutes; criminals; persons careless with money; hitchhikers and drivers; drunks; persons within high-crime areas; persons in high-risk occupations, and physically handicapped persons. Victims who are involved in illegal practices (e.g., the first three groups) rarely notify the police because in their social circumstance they prefer not to draw police attention to themselves. Indeed, such victims' understandable reluctance to contact the police makes them even more attractive targets; the robber is reasonably sure that they won't do anything to make his or her apprehension likely. On the other hand, going down the list, physically handicapped persons, very young children, or senior citizens are quite likely to turn to the police for help.

One factor frequently overlooked as a determinant of the stress reactions robbery victims may have is the significance of the kind of weapons used. In a fascinating discussion of weapons and their role in robbery, Skogan (1978) indicated that in almost any society a vast number of potentially destructive instruments are readily at hand that, because of this availability, constitute a causal force in the development of criminal careers. Robberies should be differentiated from purse snatchings and other personal property crimes, because robberies involve the use or threat of force. The data arising from various studies conducted by criminologists and crime-studying agencies show that in two thirds of the commercial robberies, the robber uses a firearm. Next in frequency after armed robbery is unarmed robbery. The use of knives and other weapons, such as clubs, rocks, and bottles occurs somewhere between the first and second types with knives being perhaps more common than the other modalities (excluding firearms).

From the point of view of dangerousness, firearms are the most lethal weapon, followed by knives. The robbery victim, however, is equally threatened by a rock, a piece of glass, or a club of some type (i.e., a baseball bat). According to Skogan (1978), other studies have shown that a robber who simply displays a gun reduces the need to use additional force, because a gun immobilizes victims, who are immediately paralyzed by fear. Thus, somewhat paradoxically, crimes involving guns tend to produce fewer injuries but more psychological trauma. The same may be said for brandishing a weapon such as a knife, because to the victim, it symbolizes lethality. Both kinds of weapons seem to be effective in forestalling precipitous victim-reactions to the robbery. In other words, once a weapon appears, the victims are less likely to take any positive action to thwart the intent of the robbers.

Skogan (1978) observed that firearms were more likely to be employed when larger groups or establishments were targeted for a robbery. In a one-to-one confrontation between robber and victim, the use of firearms may be unnecessary, particularly if the victim is small, physically impaired, or elderly and the robber is young, tall, and apparently strong. Despite this type of crowd- and size-connection with firearms, single-employee establishments are more commonly victimized by criminals bearing firearms than are groups of individuals.

The data seem to suggest that weapons of any kind are more likely to be used by robbers against men, and that adults between the ages of 17 and 39 are more likely than others to be accosted with a lethal weapon. Armed robbers are usually male.

HOSTAGES AND KIDNAP VICTIMS

Similarities and Differences of Hostage-Taking and Kidnapping

Hostage and kidnap victims will be discussed in the same section because they bear a marked resemblance to one another. Although kidnap victims are frequently taken as hostages, a basic difference exists between the perpetrators of the two types of offenses and, to some extent, also between their respective victims. Professional criminals usually employ kidnapping as a means of achieving financial gain. Terrorist groups employ kidnapping when they have targeted a particular person as either being wealthy or having political influence. The purpose of such a kidnapping is perhaps to gain money, political concessions, or the release of political prisoners, or the intent may be to weaken the government and challenge leadership within a particular country. In contrast to this, an individual criminal kidnapper is simply interested in ransom. The reason for the political terrorist and the civil criminal to kidnap a victim may be the same in terms of money, or different in terms of political uses, but they have in common that they deliberately choose the victim to meet a specific end.

A hostage, on the other hand, is not likely to be specifically targeted but is merely a person who happens to be readily available. Hostages are commonly chosen on the spur of the moment at the hands of a terrorist group, a criminal group, a mentally disturbed hostage-taker, or in the context of a jail or prison uprising where prisoners rebel and grab guards.

Probably the best-known of all kidnappings is that of Charles Lindbergh's son in 1932. Equally interesting to those concerned with criminal history is the record of the trial of the alleged kidnapper, murderer, and extortionist, Bruno Richard Hauptmann.

In an infamous example of hostage-taking, almost everyone in the world came to know about the survivors and hostages of the American Embassy in Iran. There was a great deal of sympathetic feeling as well for the families of the 52 hostages taken by the Iranian students.

Despite the widespread occurrence of hostage-taking and kidnapping, autobiographical material concerning kidnappers is sparse and of an anecdotal nature (Miller, 1971; Moorehead, 1980; Pepper, 1978). Similarly, there are few accounts regarding hostages, but those that have been written seem to involve people who became hostages in the latter part of the 1970s (Bucheli, 1982; Follet, 1983; Queen, 1981; Rosen, 1982).

Most professionals working in the field have observed, and I can confirm from my own work, that about 70% of kidnappers ask for payment within 30 minutes after making a demand. The amount of the demand varies from ridiculously small sums to fantastically large figures in the millions of dollars. When the demands are posed by terrorists, the amount will be large and the target will be a bank, a financially successful business, or a group of business people. Associated with this type of confrontation may be additional demands to release prisoners and distribute food to the poor. Sometimes the demands are vague but if the listener presses for more details, the kidnapper may become frustrated and vent anger on the victim. In contrast, the terrorist-kidnapper may simply hang up the telephone or make some comment about this type of behavior causing the victim's death.

Both kidnapping and hostage-taking are serious crimes and can be life threatening. Nor does this form of malfeasance claim any single victim; the family, friends, co-workers, and even a whole nation may be affected emotionally and share the stress experience, both during the time of detention and following the victim's release.

The Stockholm Syndrome

Law enforcement agencies, in particular, have made much of a phenomenon known as the "Stockholm Syndrome" (Crelinsten & Szabo, 1979), which involves hostages and, in some cases, kidnap victims. The term, coined by Conrad Hassle of the Federal Bureau of Investigation, applies to a curious kind of positive or even protective feeling that some hostages develop toward their captor(s). The event to which it refers occurred in 1974 when a young female employee of a Swedish bank engaged in sexual relations and fell in love with a bank robber who kept her hostage for several days. Following her release, she berated the prime minister for failing to understand her captor's point of view. In my experience, this type of identification with the aggressor does not happen only to individuals. It can also occur among groups of hostages, with turncoats in the military, and with concentration camp survivors. The phenomenon can actually enhance one's survival, if only because the victim then cooperates with and placates the captor and thus does not act in a provocative or threatening manner. However, this phenomenon did not happen in the case of the American Embassy hostages taken by the Iranians, and it rarely happens among prisoners of war who are ultimately released.

Other Common Reactions of Victims

A child kidnap victim is likely to engage in magical thinking and subsequently will view the world in terms of omens. Various objects may come to represent another kidnapping, for example, the sight of a car or bus like the one involved in the original event. Even the odor of gasoline fumes can sometimes activate old, painful memories of the traumatic experience. To be sure, the same type of subtle reminder might not cause flashbacks in the same way or to the same extent as it would with adults. Children, however, may become phobic about riding in a car, being in the dark, being near animals, or doing anything else that becomes a symbolic reminder of the crime. Adults fix more on realistic phobic objects, such as confronting strangers; being outside their homes and offices alone; being near people, even police officers, who carry firearms; or being anywhere without some armed protection, alarm or security system, or other protective measures.

Adults tend to develop amnesia for the kidnap event or hostage situation, whereas children maintain a fresh recall for details, even distorted ones, for some time. Obviously this depends in part on the age of the child; a child younger than 10 years at the time of the crime is likely to have a considerably blunted level of recall.

Hostages and kidnap victims may suffer greatly during the period of their captivity if they represent the targets toward whom their captors feel great animosity. In general, the more political the motives of the perpetrators, the worse the victim will be treated. This treatment may involve both actual brutality, such as keeping fluid and food intake at near-starvation levels, and emotional humiliation. Common to hostage-takers and kidnappers may be a pattern of keeping the victim in absolute isolation, withholding usual creature comforts, such as warm food, bedclothes, mattress, and clean living quarters, as well as forcing the bound victim to lie on the floor in the dark. In addition, noxious odors may impair ventilation because the victim is imprisoned in such a confined space. For example, in one case (Miller, 1971), the victim was kept in a packing crate for 83 hours. It was later learned that the battery and air condenser calculated by the kidnapper to have enough air supply for 7 days would in fact have stopped functioning just a few hours after the victim was actually released.

Being in a hostage situation may affect a victim's relationships with fellow victims in various ways. In a personal communication at a meeting, Moorehead

Kennedy revealed that during the Iranian crisis some of the victims developed concerns about a breakdown in sexual mores in terms of homosexual acting-out. They were afraid that the prolonged removal from family members and the stress and emotional deprivation of the hostage experience would cause some of them to seek support in this particular manner.

It is not uncommon initially for kidnap victims and hostages to become totally disoriented as to time, place, and person, depending on whether the perpetrators are wearing clever disguises. If the perpetrators' names are unknown to the victim, the victim may refer to them or think of them as "Mr. Thin," "Mr. Moustache," "Mrs. Glasses," "Mr. Fat," "Mr. Italian," and so on. Victims increase their ability to survive such stress if they mark off the passing days; if nothing else, these can be measured by counting shifts and noticing who comes to guard them. Victim-hostages count the number of people they see during a given period of time and use that as their frame of reference. This becomes particularly important as a survival technique if the victims are kept in a dark room and cannot gain access to natural lighting.

Even though most people have been exposed to firearms indirectly via the news media and television, the actual presence of real firearms while one is being held captive is enormously stressful and adds considerably to the sheer terror of the circumstance.

Being physically restrained adversely affects many persons who are accustomed to freedom of movement. Uncertainty about the future and fear of being killed become significant sources of personal stress. In my own situation, the saving grace during our hostage experience, which occurred in the course of a robbery, was that I felt myself to be the appointed leader of my three children and housekeeper. Because I felt responsible for the survival of the group, I was able to set aside my fears for personal safety. It is a matter of unpleasant speculation now whether the stressful circumstance would have been different had the gun been pointed directly at me. Having been a police officer, which provided experience in facing many people with guns, as well as having worked with dangerous persons in my capacity as a psychiatrist, I am unlikely to have met any threat greater than that which I had already experienced. In such circumstances, people tend to cope with their particular personal stress by using the experience and knowledge they have gained as well as with the skills they have acquired in basic survival.

Under favorable circumstances, the more a person is exposed to victimhood, the greater his or her ability to handle life-threatening circumstances, such as being kidnapped or taken hostage.

The inability to sleep is frequently the product not only of anxiety but also of pain. The pain is not necessarily a consequence of deliberate torture; it can arise because the kidnapper or hostage-taker is very anxious. As a result, the bonds or handcuffs, may be tightened to such an extent that pain is inevitable. Particularly for adults, weight loss is almost invariably a consequence of being a kidnap victim or hostage. Restlessness is often due to sheer boredom and can be dealt with only by fantasizing activity or by actually working productivity during confinement. The person who becomes an effective housekeeper of his or her own territory or prison cell has begun to combat some of the aspects of stress provoked by victim status. A person held in captivity either falls into a state of passive surrender or engages in a meaningful observation and assessment of the hostage-taker(s). The victim who begins to understand what is expected of him or her can manipulate the situation and feed the sought-after information in a way that minimizes the risk of torture, or even death. Such an outcome is ultimately in the hands of the kidnapper, who may be mentally disturbed, or terrorists, who may deal with their frustration at not obtaining their ends by ending the life of the victim.

PRISONERS OF WAR

Historical Background

Prisoners of war (POWS) constitute an area of particular interest that has intrigued me since I worked on assignment to Special Forces, Fort Bragg, North Carolina. Part of this assignment was to develop a bibliography regarding hostage and pris-oner-of-war survival, as well as to design programs that would make it possible for captives to survive the experience. Training programs have been planned and developed relative to this particular area.

For American military personnel especially, there has been a history of change in regard to treatment received by prisoners of war. One can see subtle changes for other Western countries as well, notably England. One of the first recorded incidents involving American prisoners of war has been described by H. B. Barnby (1966). This is an interesting chronicle of personnel from the U. S. naval vessel *Maria*, who were held as prisoners of war in the period from 1795 to 1797. It wasn't until 1797 that the last of the prisoners were released to return to the United States.

Despite long years of being away from their country and their families, and despite not having the same military benefits that veterans enjoy today, basically these prisoners received decent treatment. Many of them were permitted to work, have servants, and consort with women. They were more political prisoners than anything else.

However, following World War I, as American military personnel were drawn into conflicts beyond Europe, they confronted an Asiatic philosophy toward captured military personnel best reflected by the concept of *Bushido*, which means "no surrender." This term achieved significance during World War II when the Japanese captured large numbers of prisoners in the Philippines following the fall of Cor-regidor and Bataan. Those persons interested in military history as well as those of us who treat the by-products of military history—former prisoners of war—must consider the impact of Bushido on the prisoner-of-war experience for American and Allied personnel. The Asiatic perspective does not allow for honor in surrender. Thus, if military personnel are taken prisoner, they are not entitled to proper food or medical attention. The same experience was repeated in Korea and Vietnam.

This helps to explain the kinds of treatment reported in some anecdotal accounts of prisoner-of-war experience, as well as the findings of several studies (Engel, 1968; Garrett, 1981; Rowe, 1971). So extensive are these anecdotal and research accounts that it would not be possible to cover all that have been reported.

Reactions to Capture

Even to those who have not had military experience it should be apparent that once a soldier is captured on the battlefield, he is thrown into a different kind of military crisis circumstance. He not only fears for his life in terms of having been caught in combat, but he may be isolated from his fellows and deprived of information about what is happening as well as what his future will be. He is totally defenseless against any kind of torture or physical abuse imposed on him by the host enemy. He soon learns what he can expect in medical care, food, or basic human comforts. For enemy propaganda purposes, he may be exposed to humiliating treatment by being paraded through the town where he is held captive. In addition, he may be displayed on television in order for the enemy to gain prestige by showing a representative of a beaten foe. This was a common experience during the Vietnam War. As media coverage improves, one can anticipate this will happen with increasing frequency. It is apparent that war is no longer simply a matter of armed conflict between two enemies. It is also a competition for media coverage and political posturing.

It has been rather commonly reported that for almost all prisoners of war, depression is an initial or rapidly developing complication. This occurs not only as a result of the loss of freedom and fear for the future, but because of various kinds of physical complications, such as wounds, jaundice, infection, and dermatitis. In addition, there may be an almost obsessional level of preoccupation with life as a prisoner of war. During this experience, many prisoners report repetitive dreams about their captivity; it is apparent that anxiety generated by the captive state requires dream work and other kinds of psychic relief mechanisms to help dissipate it.

R. Garret (1981) stated, "A prisoner is a member of the losing side who does not run away fast enough." Although prisoners are not always members of the losing side, they sometimes absorb the loss until their side achieves victory or both sides simply stop fighting, such as happened in Iran and Iraq. They wanted to eliminate further loss.

In a very real way, at times food parcels from the Red Cross are the only touch of home available to prisoners (aside from letters, which may or may not be delivered). It would be impossible to determine how such parcels affect the basic nutritional status of prisoners of war who have been starved, but at the very least they are morale boosters, providing a taste of life that awakens memories of better days. During World War II the opportunities for receiving such parcels were much greater for prisoners of war in Europe than for prisoners in Asiatic countries.

Prisoners of War in Europe and Asia

One measure of the kind of psychic stress associated with being a prisoner of war is reflected in various studies, such as one in 1942 (Wolf and Ripley, 1947). This survey by Army psychiatrists showed that it was difficult for World War II prisoners to rehabilitate themselves. Those who returned to duty had a high rate of psychiatric breakdown and disability. It is notable that this occurred among prisoners with outstanding military records who previously had performed satisfactorily and had accommodated well to discipline.

Older prisoners of war were frequently more concerned about what was happening at home and, consequently, they suffered more. Younger men despised the older prisoners and considered themselves to be stronger characters than their melancholy elders. The politics of the region in which military personnel were taken prisoner also affected their prisoner-of-war experience. For example, in both World Wars I and II the Germans acted in a manner contrary to accepted Western behavior; the conduct of persons responsible for the camps was tantamount to acts of perversion. Nonetheless, prisoners of war were usually not isolated from one another and were permitted to form groups in the various stalags in which they were kept. There was some degree of medical care, and the food was infinitely better than that available to Allied personnel who were taken prisoner by the Japanese, the North Koreans and Chinese, and the Vietcong and North Vietnamese. On the other hand, the Japanese and other Asiatics were, at least, being true to their own culture. They beat up prisoners and, on many occasions, executed them; but it was not uncommon for them to thrash their own men and, under certain conditions, to sentence them to death as well. The camps were crowded in the Japanese internment areas, but so were the Japanese in their own quarters.

Vietnam prisoners of war were controlled by the Vietcong, who made a deliberate effort to cut off all communication. Prisoners were isolated, chained to stakes, and assigned to somebody who did not speak English. Unknown to many prisoners, fellow prisoners from the same army might be in cages on the other side of the hill.

The stress associated with being a prisoner of war was also reflected in the tendency of some prisoners to develop a degree of reaction so severe that they were unable to shake off the ensuing state of apathy. In Korea, young American prisoners died of what many of the troops referred to as ''giving-up-itis.'' They simply fell into a convenient hole or ditch and expired. Following the war, medical studies of such cases failed to reveal anything other than general cardiovascular collapse as a cause of death. This brings to mind the work of Avery Wiseman and Tom Hackett, who examined the phenomenon of patients with a prediliction for death. Prior to death such individuals apparently, withdrew socially and proceeded to die in association with an otherwise insignificant medical complication.

One of the most moving accounts of this kind of apathy and withdrawal from life is to be found in James Rowe's (1971) book, *Five Years to Freedom.*

RESEARCH ON STRESS-RELATED REACTIONS

Some meaningful research has demonstrated the body's response to stress because of terror, marked anxiety, or intense emotion.

In reviewing clinical material concerning persons who died following exposure to a situation of intense emotional impact—even one of joy—George Engle (1968) observed that there were changes in the environment of the deceased which he or she had felt powerless to change or control. (Engel offered examples of zoo animals who exhibited behaviors similar to human reactions in cases where cagemates were killed.)

In situations where the environment had changed, deaths resulted from the victims' perception of themselves as powerless and without social or psychological resources in terms of coping skills (Engel, 1968). In other words, the deceased had apparently reached an impasse in dealing with a significant change in how they saw themselves or their environment.

The clinical material led Engel (1968) to conclude that the giving-up given-up complex consisted of five characteristics:

1. Helplessness or hopelessness
2. A negative or reduced sense of worth
3. Loss of gratification or roles or relationships in life
4. Confusion or loss of continuity about past, present, and future
5. Recall and reactivation of earlier periods of giving up

Behaviors and feelings typical of these five characteristics are as follows:

1. The person might report being at the end of his or her rope, seem to be confused or at a loss, or might discuss previous efforts to reverse such feelings; in any case, he or she feels incapacitated.
2. The person no longer feels masterful, in command, and so on.
3. The person loses standing in the community, family, or among colleagues.
4. Old methods of coping are not working, and the person has difficulty visualizing the future.
5. Because the person recalls old failures while anxiety mounts, an unimportant

event may serve as the catalyst that creates or worsens existing feelings of total failure and inability to cope.

Because prompt resolution is not possible, the person may seesaw between giving up and struggling for mastery. When failure appears imminent and information cannot be handled effectively, an emergency biological defense system is triggered. In this "overload" state, neurohumeral mechanisms from the midbrain and forebrain areas of the limbic system are activated and send messages to the hypothalmus. The individual's emergency systems are thus mobilized to prepare the body to deal with or avoid damage.

Cannon (1957), in his classic publication, discussed voodoo deaths. Death can occur when one primitive simply "bones" another, that is, points a bone directly at him. Cannon felt that such deaths occurred because the body's response to overwhelming fear and terror produced shock; he postulated that adrenalin was activated and internal mechanisms were produced as a continuous outpouring. He predicted that before death, voodoo victims would breathe rapidly, have a rapid pulse, and show hemoconcentration from fluid loss from the tissues and blood, causing the heart to beat faster and faster, leading to a persistent contraction, and then to death in systole.

On the other hand, Richter's (1957) rat experiments were significant in terms of paralleling analagous situations terrifying to humans, which bring about a change of environment or the physical equipment of the body to normally deal with such pressures. While determining how a rat could swim and how it reacted to temperature changes, it was learned that shaving off its whiskers, or confining the animal in a bag, or holding it upright, or denying it any avenue of escape while threatening it with immediate drowning, all produced death quickly—even while the rat was being held or shortly after swimming began. Electrical contacts had been placed in the experimental rats to make EKG records. Such electrical cardiac tracings showed the opposite of what Cannon had predicted. The rats promptly died following a vagal effect on the heart—a slowing down rather than an acceleration. At the same time, breathing slowed and body temperature dropped. The heart finally stopped in diastole. The so-called vagal death was caused by parasympathetic system overstimulation rather than stimulation of the sympathicoadrenal system. Initial reaction to stress was an accelerated heart rate that improved when the stress was removed.

The results were confirmed by injecting the rats with sublethal amounts of cholinergic drugs such as morphine, physostigmine, and mecholyl. Even $\frac{1}{10}$th of the lethal dose of 50 miligrams of morphine produced the sudden death response of rats within a few minutes after they were placed in the swimming containers. The reaction of hopelessness and helplessness preceded the giving-up given-up.

Richter concluded that in human beings, as in rats, it is possibile that hopelessness and death may result from a combination of reactions, all of which can produce overstimulation of vagal tone, producing cardiac arrest.

These data show how emotional trauma and alteration of the environment, such as taking people hostage or prisoner of war, can affect the body and its neurohumeral defenses. When hope of a chance to escape is lost or group acceptance or approval are removed, severe damage to the body and/or death can occur. Such stress is significant and accounts for sudden death among prisoners, as in the Korean prisoner-of-war camps where young, otherwise healthy, soldiers lowered themselves into holes and died of "giving up-itis."

EFFECTS OF PRISONER-OF-WAR LIFE-STYLE

Irritability, the depression arising from the constant wearing of leg-irons, and the enforced boredom attendant on being a prisoner of war, are elements of this life-style that have a telling effect on prisoners of war. They are deprived of any opportunity to be productive and creative; among them, only those most determined to survive are able to overcome the profound limitations of their lives. Not the least of the stresses burdening the POWs are the marked feelings of abandonment they have in connection with the failure of their own side to rescue them. Similarly, when their efforts to escape have not met with success, some recaptured prisoners become crippled by a complete letdown. In some instances their physiologic condition becomes so overtaxed that they find themselves near collapse. Along with the defeat they feel in association with the failed escape effort is the punishment meted out by the host enemy. The latter further compromises an already deprived level of nutrition and applies physical punishment and increased restraint. In addition, the crushing depression and disappointment of having tried and failed is, for many brave soldiers, worse than the punishment that follows recapture.

Particularly in the course of the Vietnam experience, prior to becoming prisoners, American soldiers had had to adjust to dehumanization as a way of survival. Dehumanization results from fighting an enemy who cannot be seen in terms of a set-piece type of battle. Not being able to confront the enemy directly made soldiers feel helpless. There were also differences in race, language, culture, and the recurrent threat that the most gentle-looking person—even a child—could, in fact, be the enemy. Basic mistrust and insecurity was then aggravated by the circumstance of becoming a prisoner. Before they were taken prisoners of war, it had become apparent to many men that they were simply "bodies" to fight with. The moral and political reasons for the war became hazy and doubts arose for almost everyone involved in Vietnam. This was radically different from World War II, where both the military and civilians popularly endorsed the war. Being involved in a war that is generally unpopular produces additional stress in soldiers. The same type of experience was seen among the U. S. Marines in Lebanon; however, in that instance there was little contact between American troops and the warring Arab factions, and prisoners of war were not taken.

For POWs, faith and religion are of considerable significance in respect to both stress and survival. On the stress side is the slowly eroding confidence of faith, the feeling that God has failed to protect the soldier who has become a prisoner of war.

Perhaps the intensity of faith, as the prisoner defines it, may make the thought of joining God through death an inviting idea. By means of this fantasy, the POW not only attempts to achieve relief from pain and suffering, but also to acquire a rescue source of support by joining God.

On the positive side of the equation, faith has enabled many a prisoner to endure, and, when coupled with a good marriage and strong family ties, it enhances his basic potential for survival. In essence, trauma is the central issue for the prisoner of war. In one sense, everyone can understand the trauma of war, particularly those who have experienced it; at the same time, however, it is easy to overlook that persons who have suffered this experience are likely to have entered combat with certain narcissistic difficulties involving problems of self-esteem regulation, high ego ideals, and vulnerability. The traumatic experience of war, and especially of being a POW, can aggravate these underlying conditions and produce a regressive decompensation that can then become the nucleus of a traumatic experience. It should not be overlooked, however, that in some cases, a prisoner may become more functional and gain new strength and insight as a result of mastering this terrifying experience.

AFTEREFFECTS OF BEING A PRISONER OF WAR

For everyone, it is apparent that trauma can foster a general regressiveness, which may or may not become a permanent feature of ego functioning. This is a further reflection of the stress of being in combat and especially of being a prisoner of war. For the on-the-line combat veteran, three experiences tend to run counter to the magical thinking soldiers experience in battle. The magical feeling comes to awareness in terms of a kind of heightened adolescent sense of well-being and a feeling of protection from any and all sources of injury. This fantasy is dispelled by either being injured, having a buddy get injured or killed, or becoming a prisoner of war. All these traumatic experiences serve as their own sources of stress and trauma.

For these soldiers, as well as for those who have known other kinds of traumatic experience, the onset of symptoms may be delayed. In cases I have dealt with from World War II, survivors of concentration camps and combat soldiers, have had reactions that were delayed for as long as 17 to 20 years. They were then triggered by some remotely related event, such as a son or daughter entering the service, or the recurrence of another war far removed from the one the veteran originally experienced. This demonstrates that for decades to come, veterans may continue to have difficulties associated with that stress.

Survivor guilt is another source of stress, particularly for the veteran. It is not necessarily limited to those who have come home from the war. It can also be associated with guilt arising from having survived when other members of a prisoner-of-war camp died.

Nightmares offer further evidence of the traumatic quality of the experiences encountered by the combat soldier and the prisoner of war. Each may have different kinds of nightmares that not only help him, but cause him to relive the pain of the combat and captivity experiences. Such dreams reinforce the basic negative exposure to the experience itself and thus help keep the trauma alive.

Figley (1978) continues to point out that the usual signs of traumatic war neurosis are catastrophic dreams, general irritability, sensitivity to loud noises, and a tendency to be aggresive and even violent. These responses may be followed by periods of extreme tenderness. In general, there is a lessening of one's ability to function in most of the activities of daily life. Amnesia, other memory disturbances, and the psychosomatic symptoms seen in ordinary neuroses are conspicuously absent.

As an offshoot of traumatic neurosis, an exaggeration of existing character pathology may also be present. Some POWs may become very antisocial or unusually passive-dependent. Such responses are likely in persons who entered the military service with an existing predisposition or a preceding history.

A final group who display a variant form of traumatic stress are persons who present a symptom picture of disassociation, yet appear otherwise to be mentally healthy. They do not seek treatment for traumatic stress, but they may be referred for some coincidental problem such as marital conflict, sexual difficulties, and the like. They tend to deny, isolate, or dissociate from the traumatic experience. It is only when behavior occurs in its more florid form that it is likely to be recognized.

In comparison with the combat veteran, there were additional sources of burdening stress for the prisoners of war in Vietnam and Korea. Many of them were threatened with war crimes trials, with possible execution as the penalty. These pressures did not immediately threaten combat veterans who were not held captive. Secondly, about 40% of the veterans of Vietnam captivity spent 6 months in solitary confinement; about 20%, from 1 to 2 years, and about 10%, longer than 2 years. Four prisoners spent more than 4 years in solitary confinement.

MITIGATING EFFECTS ON IMPRISONMENT

The prisoners of war responded to captivity in different ways. Those who were able to exercise or to participate in any form of resistance to efforts to dehumanize and destroy them came out with less severe trauma. For all POWs their existence, at best, was lonely, monotonous, and boring. Prisoners who were exposed to a group atmosphere containing some elements of military structure showed a somewhat better ability to withstand the difficulties already described. The most psychologically devastating experience was solitary confinement. This was offset or contended with best if persons confined in this way were able to establish a wall-knocking system of communication with others who were being similarly treated. This was part and parcel not only of survival but of resistance to the efforts of the enemy to induce a devastating type of emotional surrender.

Similarly, those who were able to hold onto a sense of humor, work hard, keep themselves clean and active, and maintain some sense of physical well-being in terms of moderate exercise programs were able to contend with the stress of prisoner-of-war status more effectively.

The experience of solitary confinement had an impact that was not limited to psychological or physical symptoms but produced other changes as well. Prisoners looked older than the average population for their age group. They showed lower suggestibility, higher superego development, and a greater need for achievement. In terms of their basic personality structures, these men were in general more competitive.

Most of the Vietnam prisoners of war who were studied and who had the capacity to describe their experience reported that in the initial days of their captivity, they developed a hyperalertness and an intense interest in even the most trivial details of prison environment, including everything to do with their captors.

FAMILY-RELATED STRESSES

A particularly painful factor for the prisoner of war, as for the hostage and kidnap victim, is his concern about family and his realization that family members have no way of knowing whether he is alive. This area of concern produces a paradoxical phenomenon. On the one hand, worry about family either causes or aggravates stress, and on the other hand, worry may reduce stress by driving the individual to reminisce about all aspects of a happy marriage and happy family relationships. By the same token, if there is no meaningful family relationship or if there has been marital disharmony, the prisoner's adjustment to captivity is the more burdened. Not only is Posttraumatic Stress Disorder evident when the veteran comes home or returns to active duty—there are also other measurements of dysfunction. In about 30% of the families of prisoners of war, divorce occurs. Family integration is something that takes a long time. Even after reunion, the family that has lived for so long with the stress of uncertainty about the welfare of their loved one continues to experience stress. Children may have to become accustomed to the idea that they actually do have a father. In some instances, at the time he was captured, the children may not have been aware of their father's existence because they were too young. In general children cope with this phenomenon according to how successfully their mothers cope. Many children grow and develop well psychosexually while their father is held captive; once he returns home, however, their difficulties begin.

Both the returning prisoner and his family have to adjust to the reality of a family that heretofore has had a matriarchal structure. For many of these families a social-sexual role conflict ensues because the woman has discovered her own power and independence. The military man who is used to exercising command and giving orders, both in the military as well as in the family arena, is in for a shock. This difference may provoke an irreconcilable conflict.

Regarding parent–child relationships, it has been observed that the more stressful his captivity, the more difficult it appears to be for the father to establish close and satisfying relationships with his children after returning home. Similar problems have arisen between the POW and his wife.

CONCLUSIONS

Robbery victims, hostages, kidnap victims, and prisoners of war are exposed to nonfamilial forms of violence that, despite the differences in quality and setting of violence, share common stress factors. On the other hand, unique features accompany each kind of victimhood. The ripple effect draws the victim's family, friends, and those who are concerned about his or her welfare into a much broader array of covictims—an ever-widening ramification of targets for the act of violence itself. Unquestionably, within this spectrum of disorders, the family of the robbery victim, as well as the victim, suffer the least, depending on what type of scars—physical and psychological—were inflicted on the victim. The family of the kidnap victim suffers significantly more than the robbery victim, but not quite as much as the victim who has been taken hostage. The family of the kidnap victim can hope that unless they are dealing with a mentally disturbed offender, once a ransom has been paid, the victim will be returned. Hostage-taking for political purposes, as well as hostage-takings that occur in spontaneous prison riots cause greater stress because the penalty for failure to meet the demands of the captors may be death of the victim.

The most prolonged and intense type of stress for victims and their families occurs in the case of prisoners of war.

The circumstances that bear on these victims should cause professionals to reflect further about the unique characteristics and the kinds of support systems necessary to help such individuals over the long term once the immediate captivity crisis has been resolved. More than that, too little time and attention have been devoted to developing programs that help family members secondarily affected through their association with the primary victims of violence. Some significant work has been done regarding the families of prisoners of war, but not enough attention has been paid to the family members of victims of robbery, kidnapping, and hostage-taking.

REFERENCES

Bard, M., & Sangrey, D. (1979). *The crime victim's book*. New York: Basic Books.
Barkas, J. L. (1978). *Victims*. New York: Scribner's.
Barnby, H. G. (1966). *The prisoners of Algiers*. New York: Oxford University Press.
Bolz, F. A. (1987). *How to be a hostage and live*. Secaucus, NJ: Lyle Stuart.
Bucheli, F. (1982). *Hostage*. Grand Rapids, MI: Zondervan.

Cannon, W. B. (1957). "Voodoo" death. *Psychosomatic Medicine, 19,* 182–190.

Crelinsten, R. D., & Szaba, D. (1979). *Hostage-taking.* Toronto: Lexington Books.

Engel, G. L. (1968). A Life setting conducive to illness: The giving-up given-up complex. *Archives of Internal Medicine, 69,* 293–300.

Figley, C. R. (Ed.). (1978). *Stress disorders among Viet Nam veterans.* New York: Brunnel/Mazel.

Follet, K. (1983). *On wings of eagles.* New York: Morrow.

Garrett, R. (1981). *POW.* London: David & Charles.

MacDonald, J. M. (1975). *Armed robbery.* Springfield, IL: Charles C. Thomas.

Miller, B. (1971). *83 Hours till dawn.* Garden City, NY: Doubleday.

Moorehead, C. (1980). *Fortune's hostages.* London: Hamish Hamilton.

Pepper, C. B. (1978). *Kidnapped.* New York: Harmony Books.

Queen, R. (1981). *Inside and out.* New York: Putnam.

Richter, C. P. (1957). On the phenomenon of sudden death in animals and man. *Psychosomatic Medicine, 19,* 191–198.

Rosen, Barry, & Rosen, Barbara. (1982). *The destined hour.* Garden City, NY: Doubleday.

Rowe, J. N. (1971). *Five years to freedom.* Boston: Little, Brown.

Skogan, W. G. (1978). Weapon use in robbery. In J. A. Inciardi and A. E. Pottieger (Eds.), *Violent crime: Historical and contemporary issues* (Vol. 5, pp. 61–74). Beverly Hills, CA: Sage.

Wolf, S., & Ripley, H. S. (1947). Reactions among allied prisoners of war subjected to three years of imprisonment and torture by the Japanese. *American Journal of Psychiatry, 104,* 180–193.

Child Abuse: Its Nature and Treatment

BRANDT F. STEELE, MD

Child abuse is a pattern of human behavior that can be understood and treated in psychological terms, but it is not a "psychiatric" illness in the ordinary sense of the term. Maltreatment of children is defined as any nonaccidental events or experiences that interfere with the optimal physical, intellectual, emotional, or social development of the child. It includes physical abuse, various forms of neglect, emotional abuse, and sexual exploitation. Such deleterious interactions may be perpetrated by relatively healthy people or by persons with various mental disorders such as schizophrenia, affective disorders, personality disorders, sociopathy, or perversions. When present, these psychiatric illnesses need to be treated appropriately. The maltreatment syndromes, however, are not usually an integral part of such psychiatric illness and require more specific understanding and attention in treatment. At the same time, it is important to emphasize that the treatment of the various syndromes of child abuse and neglect is complex. Among the critical variables are the great variety of kinds of maltreatment, the many kinds of perpetrators involved, and the wide range of age and developmental stages of the child victims.

CAUSES OF CHILD ABUSE

An important characteristic of the maltreatment syndromes is the pattern of generational repetition. With rare exceptions, those parents who maltreat children were physically or emotionally abused, neglected, or sexually exploited in their own childhood. Adult perpetrators (as well as older children) tend to treat young children as they themselves were treated in their early years. Thus the therapy of abuse is concerned with psychological symptomatology and the release of behaviors related to traumatic events occurring in childhood. In the child victim, these are the acute recent effects of abuse. In the adult abuser they are the residual, long-lasting effects of the earlier abuse, now somewhat modified by time, experience, and the more mature capabilities and behavioral expressions of adulthood.

The growing infant or child has many needs associated with changing states and developmental stages. In all forms of abuse, the primary source of damage to the child's developing psyche is the lack of appropriate response by the caregiver. The use of the child for the satisfaction of the adult's needs and concerns (rather than the rendering of respect for the child's needs) results in psychological deficits, distortions, and fixations. These emerge in the form of a basic lack of trust, low self-esteem, poor sense of identity, delayed and distorted cognitive development, poor social relationships, and various sadomasochistic behaviors as well as distorted patterns of sexual expression and aggressive behavior. The child experiences vague anxieties; chronic, low-grade, unfocused depression; and difficulty in finding pleasure in life.

Manifestations of these basic psychological problems are extremely varied, depending on the child's temperament, the type of abuse, its frequency, and the general emotional climate in which the child has lived. Disturbances may occur in the routines of living, eating, sleeping, or toilet training, and later on in the form of preschool, kindergarten, and elementary school difficulties. These problems are expressed in learning difficulties, antisocial or withdrawn behaviors, or unusual aggression. Vague anxieties and nightmares are common. In adults the same basic psychological difficulties become manifest in isolated, withdrawn social behaviors; great difficulty in close intimate contacts; marital and sexual difficulties; problems with authority and employment; and often delinquent, antisocial, or criminal behavior. Both children and adults experience a pervasive difficulty in finding pleasure and satisfaction in their lives. Self-destructive and suicidal thoughts and behaviors are not infrequent.

It is obvious that these children and adults could well be classified as borderline or narcissistic personality disorder, posttraumatic stress syndrome, or sexual aberration (such as pedophilia). Treatment could be conducted within the framework of such diagnostic categories, but it is important to determine through careful history and evaluation whether these psychological difficulties stemmed from maltreatment in early life. Where this is the case, treatment must be carried out with full recognition of deeply distorted object relationships. During adulthood individuals experience many kinds of physical emotional, or sexual trauma. If, however, they have had adequate positive object relations and interpersonal experiences in their earliest years, they do not, as a rule, develop the serious, long-lasting symptoms described earlier. Maltreatment in childhood makes an individual much more vulnerable and susceptible to traumatic consequences from even relatively minor stress or trauma experienced later in life.

Inasmuch as the patient's difficulties have arisen from the caregivers' basic disregard, inconsistency in care (often accompanied by massive criticism), and physical attacks on the child during early life, the most basic ingredient of treatment is the provision of an alternative relationship that is reliable, empathic, nonjudgmental, patient, and understanding. This is the carrier wave upon which all treatment must be conducted whether the patient is a child victim or an adult perpetrator (who was once an abused child and who, behind his adult facade, is still a child). This requires more than an expression of sympathy for the patient's plight, an interest in his or her well-being, and good advice for better living. It necessitates careful, noncritical listening and understanding, along with appropriate interpretation of the feelings and thoughts that have been unconscious or denied. There must be full easy acceptance of the way the patient feels and thinks, with help in understanding why he or she has thought and felt in certain ways and what bearing this has had on interactions with other people (including, of course, the therapist). Formerly abused, neglected persons are exquisitely sensitive to rejection or abandonment. It is therefore necessary for the therapist to be especially careful to warn of expected absences or any changes in appointments as well as to be somewhat more open than usual in negotiating hours and fees. In sum, every effort should be made that the patient should not reexperience the dominating, controlling, disregarding behavior of the caregiving figures of early life.

THERAPEUTIC CONSIDERATIONS

Therapy is directed toward helping the patient develop a more adequate and cohesive sense of self with better self-esteem and a feeling of greater mastery over his or her own life and behavior; ultimately the patient should be more able to enjoy a successful life. This is conveyed essentially along two main channels: cognitive understanding, and affective or emotional development.

Development of Cognitive Understanding

Reconstruction of the distressing, disturbing, traumatic events of earlier life, especially with respect for the patient's own perceptions of the past, can bring a valuable degree of intellectual appreciation of what happened. The goal is to replace chaotic uncertainties and denials with a more orderly grasp of events. Very often, especially in cases of sexual abuse, children are confused because of having been told that events did not really happen the way they remember them—it was all imagination; or they have been warned that the abuse is a secret that must not be told; or they have been threatened by punishment, even death, if they tell anyone what has happened. In all cases of abuse or neglect, especially of a sexual nature, the child (or the later adult) must be helped to know that he or she can be believed and not be blamed. Even in cases where it is apparent that the child has been behaving in a way that would obviously cause trouble, it is necessary to reconstruct the previous life episodes leading to the development of such aberrant and self-defeating behaviors. Reconstruction of past events and development of a cognitive understanding of the family milieu in which the abuse and neglect occurred, along with an appreciation of time sequences and the relationship of events to each other, enable the patient to get a broader perspective on the past and enhance respect for his or her own reality testing. Only through establishing some validity for self-perceptions can the patient begin to develop a useful understanding of the complexity of his or her responses to these perceptions, and to improve self-esteem.

Emotional Catharsis

In addition to attaining a cognitive intellectual understanding, the patient must be helped to reexperience in some degree the more or less unconscious repressed affective states that accompanied the abuse and neglect. Apparently this can be accomplished only in an atmosphere of safety and with the help of an "auxiliary ego," a therapist who interprets reality and enables the patient to resolve and control disintegrating anxiety. Such emotional catharsis, coupled with increased cognitive understanding, enables the patient to gain increasing mastery over responses to life situations and gradually to relinquish the excessive use of defensive maneuvers such as denial, rationalization, masochistic behavior, overcompensation, and identification with the aggressor. Identifications that are formed with the caregiving figures of early life are deeply embedded and difficult to relinquish. Identification with the aggressor (or with aggression itself) and many of the other defense mechanisms can be relinquished or alleviated only through repeated therapeutic clarification and interpretation of transference reactions.

Most difficult of all for the patient to recognize and relinquish is the very intense and disturbing identification with the unempathic, uncaring authority figures of early months and years. This internal representation is destructive and distorting to both the patient's object relations and self-concept; unfortunately this representation is probably not sufficiently altered through the ordinary techniques of conveying cognitive understanding or through interpretations of transference and defenses. The ability to be empathic can be acquired only through being empathically cared for and cared about. Thus the patient's original identification with unempathic, uncaring figures of early years can be changed only through developing a new identification with an empathic caregiver, namely the therapist. It usually takes a long time for a patient who has been significantly neglected to become trusting and dependent enough to assume this new identification. Despite the patient's hostile, critical attacks, the therapist must maintain a stance of noncritical understanding before such trust can develop. It may often be necessary to readily acknowledge the inevitable empathic failures and mistakes that therapists make and then, in a non-critical way, to help the patient see how he or she responds to such events and how the disregard experienced in early life has been so sensitizing as to leave the patient exquisitely vulnerable to later external events of criticism or disregard.

Suicide Attempts

The most severe forms of self-critical and self-destructive behavior appear in the common thoughts of suicide as well as in the actual suicidal attempts. It is usually helpful to discuss such thoughts and actions very calmly, directly, and openly, particularly in relation to what has precipitated them. Two different patterns can be discerned that may be either quite separate or concurrent. One is the feeling of being bad, a sinner, an unacceptable person who should be dead. Not infrequently, this is an echo of actual verbal statements made by caregivers early in life, as well as an expression of feeling guilty for being and doing all sorts of things that were pictured as bad and deserving of punishment. A common variation is the patient's awareness of unconsciously identifying with and repeating the behavior of the past abusers. Since the patient is just as bad as the hated parent whom he or she wanted to kill, the patient also deserves to die. The other common theme is that life is unbearably painful and bleak; one is helplessly unable ever to make anything work out well; it is hopeless and too painful to try to seek success or love, or to keep anything going in life. The suicide then is simply an attempt to get away from the agonizing, futile process of trying to live. In this sense, it is not a punishment but rather a release from pain. Clarification and discussion of these patterns usually diminishes suicidal proclivities to a safe level. In severe cases protective hospitalization may be necessary.

MODES OF THERAPY

The preceding description of treatment has primarily related to long-term individual psychotherapy. This can be accomplished in many ways. The individual preferences and theoretical models of the therapist must, of course, be taken into consideration. The main themes of therapy can be worked out within the framework of various orientations, whether they are psychoanalytic, the object relationship framework of Mahler, the self-psychology of Kohut, or the theories and concepts of Kernberg, Masterson, Adler, and Buie. Frequently many adults who were abused and neglected in childhood later demonstrate forms of psychopathology that could be classified as borderline or narcissistic personality disorder. In fact, the psychopathology of persons so classified is often related to distorted psychic development associated with poor caretaking experiences in early life. To some extent, whether one diagnoses a case as a child abuser or victim of abuse on the one hand or as a borderline or narcissistic personality disorder on the other, depends on whether one is classifying according to etiology or to later expressions of psychopathology.

Other modes of treatment besides individual psychotherapy are commonly used to help the perpetrators of maltreatment. These include self-help groups such as Parents Anonymous, parenting education classes, courses in child development, group psychotherapy, family therapy, and marital therapy or counseling. Much group therapy is conducted by social workers and psychologists, but psychiatrists are also often involved as team members or consultants. Such group therapies enable patients to face problems with group support, to realize that they are not unique or abnormal, and to share their troubles with others who are similarly burdened. Often enough the lives of these adults are characterized by isolation, alienation, and general difficulties in social activities. Hence, in addition to the intellectual and emotional insights gained in group therapies, there is the direct effect of the new interpersonal relationships they are thus able to form. Group experience can also diminish the inevitable fear of exposure and pave the way for more intensive individual therapy. The usual problems of low self-esteem, poor identity, helplessness, and aggression are dealt with in groups, although usually on a less deep level than in individual therapy. The confrontational aspects of group dynamics are often helpful in getting patients to face the realities of what happened to them as child victims as well as to recognize their aberrant attitudes and behaviors as adults.

FAMILY ISSUES

In nearly all cases of maltreatment, in addition to the active role of the perpetrator of abuse or neglect, a significant part is played by the nonabusive spouse or live-in partner. To some degree this partner condones the abuse, subtly instigates it, or fails to intervene and protect the child victim. In the worst cases both parental figures may be equally active in the abuse in the same or different ways. Thus it is always advisable to have both caregivers involved in treatment, either individually or in some form of couples or group therapy.

In any form of therapy it is necessary to explore the meaning of each child to the caregiver, and the perceptions that the caregiver has of the child's abilities and intentions. These views are usually highly distorted in the direction of believing that the child has greater capacities to obey and please the caregiver than would be age-appropriate, and that the child deliberately fails to do so or purposefully causes trouble. Such misperceptions are potent stimuli to episodes of abuse and neglect; they are derivative of the abusers' own past that needs to be understood and relinquished.

As a long-term residue of early life deprivation, many perpetrators have a terrible sense of emptiness that neither spouse nor child has been able to assuage. This can emerge as a strong clinging dependency on the therapist with expressed desires to be hugged or held and rocked like a 2-year-old. Such needs must be acknowledged and accepted by the therapist, who cannot in reality fulfil them, but can help the patient feel safe enough to try to find satisfaction through interaction with other adults. It can be very growth promoting if the therapist is able to enlist the aid of a warm, sensitive social worker or paraprofessional who maintains frequent contact with the patient and provides practical help and counseling around the problems of daily living and child rearing. In addition to its obvious practical benefit, this can serve as well to dilute the intense dependency on the therapist and to enable the process of insight and change to proceed more quickly. One of the main goals of treatment is to enable the patient to break away from distrustful fear-driven isolation and thus to acquire freedom to find safety, help, and pleasure in many new contexts and relationships; in other words, to construct the kind of social network that healthy families employ when they raise their children.

ADDITIONAL THERAPEUTIC CONCERNS

Therapists need to be wary of pseudoimprovement in patients. After the establishment of an initial working alliance, these troubled adults may appear to be much better. This can occur both with patients who were initially very reluctant, untrusting, and negativistic as well as with those who were cooperative from the outset. As a survival technique, many of them learned early in life to hide their inner feelings and ideas, to be very sensitive to the expectations of others, and to behave in a way that would be pleasing and avoid trouble.

In all cases in which there is an accompanying or coexisting affective disorder or schizophrenia, appropriate pharmacotherapy should be instituted. For these illnesses such medication is as effective in abusers as it is in other patients; unfortunately, however, such treatment is not likely to benefit the psychological states associated with the maltreatment syndrome per se except to improve the general quality of the patient's life and to heighten the degree of availability for psychotherapy. It is the nonendogenous depressions that are so very common throughout the lives of formerly maltreated persons, and these conditions do not respond very well to the usual antidepressive medications. The origin of the biologic depression is quite different. In some patients, particularly those who have suffered significant sexual abuse, there are attacks of anxiety, flashbacks, and nightmares, as well as an element of depression. These symptoms are in many ways similar to the symptoms of post traumatic stress syndromes. These patients often respond to treatment with phenelzine, as do people who have such symptoms following other kinds of disasters or war experience. Although pharmacotherapy may alleviate the outward symptoms, the underlying psychological problems still exist and require psychotherapy.

SEXUAL ABUSE

Although the basic principles of treatment still apply, some of the late psycho-pathological derivatives of this form of maltreatment require more specific attention. This is particularly true of the later ramifications of sexual abuse in childhood. Sexual abuse is often accompanied by or even overshadowed by physical abuse and neglect, a combination that may affect the later derivatives. Adults who were sexually abused in childhood later demonstrate many varieties of sexual problems ranging from complete avoidance of sexual activity to impotence, frigidity, compulsive sexual activity, sadomasochism, promiscuity, prostitution in both males and females, pedophilia, incestuous behavior, and rape. Each such condition, of course, requires special individual consideration. It is not just the sexual nature per se of the maltreatment in childhood that accounts for the degree and character of the disturbances. The general emotional atmosphere within which the child developed before, during, and after the sexual exploitation is of equal or even greater importance and must be dealt with in treatment. The basic qualities that are present in many cases and are especially prominent in incest, pedophilia, and rape include the elements of aggression or violence combined with the exploitative character of the relationship. They are manifested by a high degree of unempathic lack of consideration for the victim. These factors are essentially related to the identification with the caregivers of early life, who were much more likely to be aggressive and who were also very unempathic and inconsiderate of the child's state and needs. Women who were former victims of incest seem to be much more damaged by their mothers' long-standing indifference and lack of care and protection than they were by the actual incestuous act. This again involves generational transmission. In a great majority of cases, mothers of girls who become incest victims were themselves victims of incest or of other forms of neglect and abuse. Much masochistic behavior in adults is a manifestation of primary attachments to sadistic love objects and can be traced back to maltreatment in the earliest years of life. A majority of women in shelters for battered wives give a history of maltreatment, including an account of having been victims of incest. To be effective, treatment eventually must deal with the low self-esteem and helpless, submissive attachments to as well as the identification with the uncaring authorities of early life.

Perpetrators of Sexual Abuse

Perpetrators of incest, or intrafamilial sexual abuse, are relatively responsive to treatment, especially when the abuse has involved only older children or adolescents. Individual psychotherapy alone can be successful, although it often helps to include group or family therapy or marital counseling either concurrently or sequentially. Inasmuch as incest is a symptom of serious general family dysfunction and marital breakdown, family therapy can be invaluable. The perpetrator must be helped to understand the whys and hows of his behavior, realize the nature of and accept full responsibility for his actions, and give up the rationalizing excuses of "I was drunk," or "the child wanted it" or "was seductive" or "enjoyed it." As part of this he must openly apologize and acknowledge to the child victim that he bears sole blame for the incest and that it is no way the child's fault. This must not be just a pro forma statement but one made openly with deep feeling and sincerity. The preceding remarks apply both to homosexual and heterosexual incest by fathers as well as to the equally serious but probably less common incestuous acts of mothers. Other close family members may be perpetrators. At the present time in American society it seems wise to have the backing of court-ordered long-term treatment. There is a powerful tendency on the part of perpetrators and society in general to deny or minimize the seriousness of sexually abusive behavior (i.e., "He promised not to do it again"). This makes judicial intervention a necessary adjunct to treatment. Most experienced clinicians find such controlling intervention can be managed, and that even if it is experienced as a repetition of early childhood disregard and control, it does not interfere seriously with the therapist–patient relationship. The delay or distortion of the therapeutic alliance is temporary.

Treatment of perpetrators of intrafamilial sexual abuse is much more difficult if the victims are infants or children under 4 or 5 years of age. Such abusers show little or no real empathy for the children, are apt to be more aggressive, have many characteristics of antisocial personality disorder, and are more likely to have complicating problems of alcoholism or other substance abuse. Commonly these adults have histories of being sexually abused, often with accompanying aggression, very early in their own lives. Some may show subtle signs of a psychotic disorder. Treatment must be individualized and carried out in any form that seems appropriate or possible. Court supervision is probably always essential, and, for the protection of the child, permanent legal separation of perpetrator and child is often necessary.

The treatment of the extrafamilial forms of sexual abuse, chronic pedophilia, and rape, is still problematical, especially when accompanied by high levels of aggression. Within the limitations of the present state of inadequate knowledge and limited experience of effective therapy for such conditions, the best that can be said is that long-term treatment is necessary. This may involve up to 3 years in a closed institution, or it may take the form of carefully monitored equally long therapy under strict probation in an outpatient setting. There is little evidence that psychotherapy alone can adequately help chronic, compulsive pedophilia and prevent recidivism. Hormonal treatment with depoprovera can diminish sexual drive and stop pedophilic activity while it is being used; after the hormone is discontinued, however, it has not been very successful in preventing recidivism. In some cases the diminution in sexual drive has allowed more effective psychotherapy to take place.

Behavior modification using aversive techniques, particularly with adolescent sex offenders, has apparently been effective, although these programs are of such recent development that long-term results are not yet known. In general, older pedophiles give a history of having started their activities in adolescence, whereas the adolescent offenders describe having themselves been victims of sexual molestation in earlier childhood. It is thus evident that the best chance for treatment and prevention of the repetitive cycles of sexual molestation is the availability of programs for adequate therapy of the child victims.

TREATMENT OF THE CHILD

Therapy of maltreated children must be highly individualized and linked to age, developmental status, and the particular kind of abuse that has occurred. The aims of treatment are similar to those set for adult perpetrators and include increasing the ability to trust by making dependency safe, improving self-image and identity formation, validating reality perceptions, stimulating emotional and cognitive development, supporting participation in normal pleasures, and normalizing social and sexual behaviors. Although infants may be subjected to all kinds of abuse either concurrently or at different times, usually one kind is predominant at the time that treatment is initiated. Common to all victims of abuse are deficits and distortions in psychic development related to the lack of empathy in caregivers, and these problems require different kinds of therapeutic address at different ages.

Infants

Infants with nonorganic failure to thrive due to maternal deprivation obviously need to be provided with an adequate, normal "good enough mother." When given such a warm, sensitive, appropriately responsive caregiver in the home, hospital, or foster care, these babies begin to thrive and blossom both physically and emotionally. In milder cases of shorter duration the biological mother may be helped by brief insight therapy plus much support from other sources, and the baby left in her care. In more severe cases, the mother's overwhelmed, depressive, helpless, isolated, angry state and her identifications with the unempathic care and deprivation suffered in her own childhood are too deeply embedded to be altered in a short time. Such character traits cannot be changed fast enough to help the infant, who is on an urgent time scale of rapid development. Accordingly, despite the problems of separation and attachment that may arise and that must be dealt with in both mother and baby, the infant must be given some kind of protective maternal care elsewhere. If possible reunion of the family is contemplated, contacts between mother and child should be maintained during the mother's therapy in order to minimize future difficulties. Careful follow-up is necessary to make sure the mother's improvement has not resulted primarily from the mother's not having had to care for the child.

Older Children

In the most severe cases, older, neglected, and physically abused children may also need protective custody and placement; even in mild cases, however, if they remain at home, they always require careful protective supervision. Even though parents may respond to treatment, their improvement rarely happens soon enough or adequately enough to correct the damage already inflicted on the child's psychic organization. Older children still need empathic mothering in their daily care and therapy in order to reopen the normal channels of development. Of course, just as in normal child care, the mothering functions of sensitivity and empathic appropriate response to the child's state and needs become increasingly less direct and concrete and gradually shift into more symbolic, verbal, intellectual expression. Thus by late childhood and adolescence it is increasingly inappropriate and unnecessary in therapy to use actual feeding, holding, comforting, play activity, and physical control of behavior. Insight and change are encouraged, and the intense dependency that has been a necessary prerequisite for therapeutic alliance is gradually replaced by separation, individuation, and independence.

Any therapy of abused children should always include contact with the child's caregivers, that is, either the biological parents or, if parental rights have been temporarily or permanently terminated, the parental surrogates. If the child remains in the family of origin or is to be returned there from foster care, there must be concomitant treatment of the caregivers who have perpetrated the abuse. For very young children a psychologically oriented day-care program may be helpful, particularly if it provides needed extra stimulation. Individual psychotherapy utilizing play techniques can be instituted early in the child's life, followed in later years by appropriate standard modes of individual child psychotherapy or child psychoanalysis. Attendance at therapeutic preschools and kindergartens where teachers are knowledgeable about child abuse can be extremely effective. Older children can be successfully treated in group situations, either as the sole therapeutic modality or as an accompaniment or precursor to individual psychotherapy. Present information suggests that it is best to arrange such groups according to the kind of abuse experienced; victims of sexual abuse should constitute a separate group. Groups should also be organized on the basis of age, with latency age children, pubertal children, and adolescents placed optimally with their own peers.

The earlier, the more severe and the more protracted the abuse in a child's life, the more serious and the more difficult to treat are the psychic sequelae. In like proportion the longer must treatment continue, whether it be for the recently traumatized child or for the adult whose psychic life and behavior are still being hampered by the unhappy childhood experience. It takes much time and new experience with empathic caregivers for the patient gradually to relinquish both the concentration on primitive submissive masochistic attachments to the early caregivers and the identification with their style of child care and their unempathic attitudes toward children. In addition to acknowledging and validating the reality of the patient's past deprivations and abuse, sooner or later it becomes useful to resurrect some memories of whatever better qualities the abusive parents may have shown even occasionally, as well as any memories of better care provided by some other more kindly persons during childhood. Such reconstructions plus current experience with the therapist and other empathic adults provide the patient with new role models, new self-objects with whom to identify. They thereby make possible the attainment of new self-esteem with better interpersonal relationships and a general sense of greater satisfaction with one's life. A total inability to recall any good empathic relationship during the patient's early years makes true rehabilitative therapy extremely problematic. Yet even in the most difficult cases children have the resiliency and developmental potential to use minimal amounts of empathic care in a constructive way.

Assault by Fellow Citizens

CHARLES KEITH, MD

    This chapter will discuss types of assaults arising at the hands of nonfamilial fellow citizens that come as a surprise to and that temporarily overwhelm the victim; such attacks often result in various manifestations of a postassault stress syndrome.

    In order for a society to achieve stability, the majority of its citizens must invest a leader or institutional authority with shared superego values. The resulting submission to the communal superego authority facilitates identification with fellow citizens and ensures that the majority obey the community's laws (Freud, 1955). This process buttresses the sustaining illusion of the invulnerability of one's body and private property against assault from fellow citizens (Titchener & Ross 1974; Weiss & Payson, 1967). This illusion must continually be reinforced by a particular version of reality. Most citizens must be able to feel that they can operate within society's framework of rule by law, that they can carry out their daily activities at home and at work, and that, as they do so, they are generally safe from assault.

    This illusion of invulnerability has genetic roots in infancy, when the caretakers are invested by the infant with the omnipotent power to provide absolute protection from the prototypical dangers of development. An example is the mother soothing her 8-month-old infant when the sudden approach of an unknown person momentarily overwhelms the baby with stranger anxiety.

    A sense of safety and invulnerability results from the confluence of these group

327

identificatory, societal, and developmental processes; thereafter it serves as a buffer and protective membrane against stress and supports the normal denial of danger (Lazarus, 1983). Thus, in everyday life one does not need to be in a state of constant psychophysiological "fight-flight" alert against assault by a fellow citizen.

There is a correlation between indices of stress and psychopathology, and geographical area. In particular, there are high-crime neighborhoods characterized by frequent assaults by fellow citizens (Dohrenwend, 1973; Husaini & Neff, 1980; Kessler, 1979; Rutter, 1973). In some of these neighborhoods as many as 23% of the citizens may be assaulted each year, versus 3.5% within the general population (U.S. Department of Justice, 1983).

The emerging field of victimology is concerned with the frequency, type, and quality of assault and victimization visited on various populations, and with the possible interactions between victim and victimizer (Ellenberger, 1955; Fattah, 1981; S. Schafer 1968; Von Hentig, 1948). Some have expressed concern that victimologists' investigations of the qualities making certain victims prone to victimization may unwittingly reinforce society's natural tendency to scapegoat victims, by appearing to suggest it was their fault that they were raped, robbed, and so on (Symonds, 1975). However, an increasing number of studies are emerging in this area, and it is evident that the nature and sequelae of being victimized and assaulted are becoming a focus of scientific study. Many disciplines (such as criminology, sociology, and psychology) are participating in these efforts, complementing the studies and observations that have emerged within psychiatry in recent decades. For instance, it has been documented that specific groups are particularly vulnerable to victimization (Huston, Geis, Wright, & Garrett, 1976): These include runaways (Justice & Duncan, 1976), elderly persons in low-income housing (Logan, 1979), street people (Silbert & Pines, 1982), and the deinstitutionalized mentally ill (Lehman & Linn, 1984). Of them all, the age and sex group most vulnerable to assault and victimization consists of 18 to 20-year-old males (M. J. McDermott, Stanley, & Zimmerman-McKinney, 1982).

A common observation emerging from the follow-up studies of individuals assaulted by fellow citizens is that the acute stress response originally thought to be self-limiting Adjustment Disorder turned out to develop into and merge with ongoing Posttraumatic Stress Disorder.

TYPES OF ASSAULTS

Verbal Threats

As with all stressors, the context of the verbal threat is crucial. Threatening phone calls or letters of unknown origin often come as a shock; they invade the private space of the home and may arouse considerable anxiety. Verbal threats erupting from a chronically angry fellow employee or mouthed by a distraught taxi driver during rush-hour traffic, however, may have little impact because such statements may be an anticipated, accepted aspect of the social surround.

Although the subject has been studied within the psychological laboratory (e.g., Orbach, 1978; Ramirez & Lasater, 1976), virtually no systematic clinical psychiatric literature concerns the impact of verbal threats by fellow citizens. In a detailed case history, Solnit & Kris (1967) described how a mother's verbal threat of abandonment of her 3-year-old daughter had multiple effects on the little girl's developing sense of self, body image, and ambivalent maternal ties. In general, a young child's magical thinking and concreteness of thought result in a greater vulnerability to verbal threats. Piaget told of a worrisome conviction sustained over years of childhood that he had been kidnapped as an infant. During his early adolescence, he learned that this frightening event had never in fact occurred; instead, it had been fabricated and told to him and his parents by his nanny as a threat (Piaget, 1962). Typical childhood fears, such as fear of the dark and of ghosts, have multiple genetic roots such as the child's magical projective thought processes and impulse life. One common source of such fears, however, is verbalized threats from babysitters, adult acquaintances, and peers. Such threats can become screen memories for conflicts involving immediate family members. Children undergoing sexual abuse are often verbally threatened to maintain secrecy. During latency, verbal threats of aggression are often made by peers, and such expressions become quite frequent in early adolescence, particularly in the junior high school setting. Ganging up on a student and cornering him/her in a bathroom can terrorize a pupil resulting, in some instances, in a refusal to attend school. Neighborhood and school racial tensions spawn frequent verbal threats of violence. In gang-prone areas such as large, urban, lower-class settings, many youngsters undergo verbal extortion and victimization when they encounter or are drawn into a gang culture (Friedman, Mann, & Adelman, 1976).

Physical Assault and Kidnapping

Agressive Behavior in Day-Care Settings. Assault by a fellow citizen, that is, interpeer aggression, is an important issue in early childhood (Parke & Slaby, 1983). Inadequate child-care settings may stimulate and allow excessive hostile aggressive encounters among children. In a film study of hitting among 1- to 3-year-old children in a low socioeconomic day-care program, it was found that each boy hit another child 6 times per hour (Brownlee & Bakeman, 1981). Thus, during a 10-hour day at the center, 10 boys would deliver 60 blows per hour or 600 hits a day to other children. One third of these blows were classified as "hard" with intent to hurt. Such high levels of peer aggression in many day-care settings are beginning to raise concerns. Children attending an adequately staffed research day-care setting were found, on entering public school, to have 15 times the frequency of aggressive behavior as that displayed by the control group of home-reared children (Finkelstein, 1982). This alarming finding resulted in immediate institution of teacher training and supervision in the day-care setting, geared toward explicit programmatic control of aggressive interactions. For the next several months the day-care teachers made intensive efforts to control and sublimate the children's aggression. As a result, on entering kindergarten the levels of aggression of the experimental children approached those of the home-reared control group. However, the vast majority of day-care settings do not have the resources to institute such teacher training and supervision. A serious question must therefore be raised about the sequelae of stress resulting from multiple daily assaults by children's peers in day-care settings. Levels of aggressive hitting among peers in schools remain high at least through puberty (Saint J. Neill, 1976).

Corporal punishment in schools has long been of considerable concern to educators but has received little systematic study from psychiatric observers. Although its practice is waning in the Western world, there are still many areas in the United States where physical punishment is an institutionalized, legal practice. Critics of corporal punishment are concerned that it amounts to assault by fellow citizens.

The Chowchilla School Bus Kidnapping. Terr (1979, 1981b, 1983a) intensively studied the reactions of 23 latency and early adolescent children to a bizarre assault. The incident involved kidnapping children on a school bus and imprisoning them in a buried truck for 36 hours. Although none of the children were physically harmed during the duration of the kidnapping, they were kept in darkness, were not given food, and were verbally threatened. Interviewing of the children and their parents began 5 months after the kidnapping. The children recalled fears of being separated from parents, of dying, and of being harmed by the kidnappers. Most of the children came to believe they could have predicted and/or prevented the kidnapping if they had paid more attention to "omens." These are reconstructions of events prior to the kidnapping that came to serve as explanations and attempts to master the unexplainable event (Bulman & Wortman, 1977; Lee & Rosenthal, 1983; Seligman, 1975). All of the children continued to experience persistent fears of being alone, confronting strangers, hearing loud noises, and being kidnapped again.

Many of the children reenacted the kidnapping with little symbolic disguise in their interpersonal and psychophysiological behaviors. Immediately following the trauma, repetitive terror dreams and nightmares depicting the actual kidnapping were present in all of the children. As the months passed, the dreams became less frightening and more disguised.

Nineteen of the 23 children appeared to develop personality changes, with the boys tending to become more aggressive and the girls more regressed and anxious.

Family instability, including physical moves and parental separations, seemed to increase in the postkidnapping period and could usually be connected with the stress, guilt, fear, and anger aroused by the assault. Parental anger was common and was typically directed toward the community and institutional authorities, such as mental health clinics and the police.

Four years after the kidnapping, follow-up studies replicated many of the findings from the immediate follow-up studies (Terr, 1983a). Many of the children and families were reluctant to participate in the follow-up interviews. Cash bribes were necessary for some to participate. (This reluctance to participate in follow-up interviews has also been noted in studies of disaster by Lindy, Grace, & Green, 1981; and Poulshock & Cohen, 1975.) Long-term sequelae were found in most of the children. Posttraumatic play of a repetitive, literal, nonmastering quality was present in 14 of the 23 children (Teer, 1981a). There was embarrassment and continuing guilt at having been a victim. All the children still had multiple fears and terror dreams, although in most cases the intensity and frequency of these experiences had lessened.

The children continued to have vivid recall of the details of the kidnapping. Terr raised the possibility that absence of denial and failure to repress the trauma may be a new finding specific for children. However, earlier authors (e.g., Lidz, 1946; Leopold & Dillon, 1963) had noted that many adults have painful, vivid detailed recall of trauma. Omens were still frequently used by the children as if personal responsibility and guilt for the kidnapping were preferable to helplessness and chance.

All the children expressed pessimism about their future and expected a shortened life. From her study of the Chowchilla kidnapping children and others who have undergone equally severe stress, Terr (1983c) postulated that for victims of severe trauma the belief in a personally foreshortened life may be a specific finding. The belief that one's life would be cut short by death or by another disaster appeared not to be an aspect of childhood depression, a condition not usually found in these children. Approximately 1 year after the kidnapping, psychophysiological symptoms involving urinary difficulties, stomach pains, and obesity appeared in 12 children.

Curiously, the signs of Posttraumatic Stress Disorder that occurred in all the children appeared to be quite similar in all age groups, ranging from early latency through early adolescence.

Though Terr's investigations were not a controlled study, it is one of the most intensive, dramatic accounts of children's reaction to stress to be found in the psychiatric literature. Her study dispels any remaining naive belief that children are "tough" and resistant to severe stress. Her work also buttresses the currently emerging child abuse literature, which amply demonstrates that children are quite vulnerable to the long-term sequelae of severe acute and chronic stress (Green, 1983).

Airplane Hijacking and Hostage-Taking. Analogous to the Chowchilla kidnapping is airplane hijacking and hostage-taking. Although hijackers have been studied in some detail, the victims of hijacking, all of whom have undergone severe life-threatening stress, have not been studied from a stress disorder standpoint. In

light of the dramatic Chowchilla findings, one would surmise that stress symptomatology is quite frequent in the victims of plane hijacking assaults (Ecclestone,
1980).

Other Forms of Physical Assault. There are few if any systematic psychiatric
studies of adult victims of physical assault per se. In most studies, physical assault
victims are lumped together with victims of rape, auto and occupational accidents,
and natural disasters (Krupnick, 1980). The assumption appears to be that for all
types of severe bodily and psychic assault (Sisler, 1978), the stress response syndrome is a basically similar final common pathway.

Krupnick and Horowitz (1981) presented a case vignette of a woman who had
been attacked by an unknown assailant. This woman entered psychotherapy in the
authors' stress response research study. Following the attack, she was immobilized
for a time by multiple fears and could not leave her house unaccompanied. She
felt enraged at the police for not helping her sufficiently. As the therapy progressed,
themes of guilt emerged as she wondered whether she had unwittingly provoked
the attack. She became frightened of her vulnerability and sense of weakness.

The authors noted the high frequency of anger and rage themes in victims'
therapeutic material in contrast to the anticipated themes of sadness and loss. Many
of these reactions appear in the form of intrusive, unwanted thoughts and preoccupations that interfere with daily activities and concentration. There is a reactivation
of latent preconscious and unconscious negative self-images mastered by the victims
prior to the assault. These negative self-images intertwined with rage at the assailant
and authorities are among the important factors that stimulate the surprisingly high
levels of guilt suffered by assault victims.

Physical assaults leading to death result in severe, reverberating stress reactions
within victims' families (Eth & Pynoos, 1984). Rynearson (1984) notes that the
22,500 homicides in the United States in 1981 probably resulted in approximately
100,000 immediate family survivors. These survivors have rarely been studied.
Rynearson described therapeutic interviews with 12 middle-class adults whose spouse
or child had been murdered by a nonfamily member, often completely unknown
to the victim and the family. All survivors suffered intrusive fantasies about the
murder and the psychically reconstructed murderer. Most had repetitive, conscious
wishes to murder the assailant. Though many of the crimes remain unsolved, trial
and punishment of the murderer appeared to reduce the preoccupation with revenge.
The need for retribution often blocked the mourning process, sometimes for years.
As long as 1 year after the murder most of the survivors continued to evidence
symptoms of Posttraumatic Stress Disorder. In a similar study, Burgess (1975)
described how the legal necessities of interrogation by prosecutors, identification
of the body, and participation in subsequent court proceedings complicated and
delayed the mourning process.

Burgess (1975), as well as other investigators, has noted that community support
systems avoid the victims of assault. The victim's tendency to blame him/herself
is counterpoised by the community's readiness to accuse and scapegoat the victim

and thus to reassure itself that there is an explanation for such crimes and that they could not occur by mere chance or because of a community's shortcomings.

Ethologists have long noted that injured animals, particularly of the pack variety, are often turned upon by fellow packmembers who exclude, further maim, or actually kill the injured pack member (Scott, 1975). Apparently the injured animal no longer can return the pack's social signals of acceptance and so becomes an outsider who responds with confusing signals, arousing aggressive and exclusionary urges from the rest of the pack. Complementing these group dynamics are the tendencies of individual members of society to identify with the aggressor (victimizer), to disavow the victim ("Thank goodness it happened to him and not me"), and to feel guilt over and subsequently deny one's own hostile, victimizing wishes to rob and rape ("I will not associate with anyone (victim) who engages in or thinks about such matters"). These defensive patterns counterbalance altruistic urges of members of society toward victims, as manifested by victim compensation programs, support groups for victims, and so on.

Vandalism

Destruction and theft of property by fellow citizens is the most common form of criminal assault, yet there is little if any psychiatric literature concerning its effect on victims. Perpetrators of vandalism have been studied in some detail (Ward, 1973). Victims of armed robbery and mugging have been studied (see Chapter 14), though mugging involves an attack on both the body and the belongings of the victim. Why might vandalism and robbery per se fall within the purview of the stress disorders? Its study from a stress viewpoint is justified because personal property, such as one's car, house, or purse, becomes a cathected substructure of the body ego and the self. A prologue to theft in adulthood can be observed in the nursery. Dawe (1934) found that the majority of aggressive behaviors in a nursery school setting involved children losing their possessions to another child. Everyday observations suggest that theft and destruction of one's property and physical attack on one's body result in similar sequelae. However, following vandalism and robbery, the symptoms of stress are attenuated and probably resolve more rapidly. Shock, guilt, the urge for revenge, and fears of further property assault and entry into one's home are similar to the findings following bodily assaults (Paap, 1981; Smale & Spickenheuer, 1979). The sparing of the body from both pain and the threat of direct injury and death may be the central factor in the reduced intensity of stress symptomatology. However, only a direct investigation of vandalism victims will clarify this issue.

Automobile Accidents

Most studies of stress following automobile accidents do not distinguish between perpetrators of accidents and victims who are struck by another vehicle (Bordow & Porritt, 1979; Denny-Brown, 1945; Modlin, 1967; Noyes, Hoenk, Kuperman,

& Slymen, 1977). It is usually assumed the stress symptomatology is the same in both groups. Those repeatedly perpetrating motor vehicle accidents may be more aggressive (Shere & Priel, 1972). It is surmised that as many as 10% of automobile fatalities, particularly single vehicle collisions, may be suicidal. This would suggest that at least prior to the event, those who perpetrate accidents and those who are victims may in fact not be similar groups (Tabachnick et al., 1966; Huffine, 1971; Smelzer & Vinokur, 1974).

The syndrome of compensation neurosis is usually connected with accidents; it has remained vague and ill-defined and has served to confuse the clinical perspectives and treatment of postaccident stress symptomatology. There appears to be a consensus now that only a small percentage of accidents result in litigation. Litigants are usually males (2:1), and their recovery from Posttraumatic Stress Disorder may be delayed by the litigation (Weighill, 1983).

Horowitz (1974) presented one of the few clinical vignettes in the literature concerning the reaction of a driver to an assault by another automobile. A trucker was forced off the road by a swerving vehicle, resulting in the death of a female hitchhiker (who had been picked up against company rules). After an initial state of shock and numbness lasting several weeks, the trucker developed nightmares of mangled bodies, daytime anxiety, fears of driving, irritable temper outbursts, drinking, difficulty concentrating, and guilt about the death of the hitchhiker. These reactions are the typical panoply of symptoms that characterize Posttraumatic Stress Disorder.

Three young women were reported to have developed full-blown anorexia nervosa for the first time following auto accidents in which they were struck and injured by other drivers (Damlouji & Ferguson, 1985). The stress of the accident and anxiety about the effect of the injuries on their body image as perceived by themselves and others appeared to be the key precipitants for the eruption of the anorexic symptoms.

It has been suggested that the enclosed space of the vehicle and the suddenness and force of high-speed impacts resulting in violent body movements and subsequent injuries combine to increase the sense of helpless vulnerability. These elements of violence, surprise, helplessness, and bodily injury all occurring in a brief time span can easily overwhelm the individual's stimulus regulatory system thus creating fertile grounds for Posttraumatic Stress Disorders.

Riots

Most assaults from fellow citizens occur in the context of general social stability (at least in the Western industrialized world) so that victims of assault can still believe and have hope that help is available. This help may be in the form of police protection of the victim and apprehension of the assaulter, or in the belief that one can find a safe haven in one's home, church, school, and other protective communal environments.

For varying lengths of time, riots may sweep away these protective, sheltering forces as homes are invaded, police become helpless, and the usual sanctuary of the church and similar institutions is voided by the mob psychology of the rioters.

In most of these situations, the unstable social fabric and more pressing needs (e.g., in some emerging Third World countries) make it difficult to study and learn about the sequelae of riots. The riots in the urban ghettos of the United States in the 1960s were an exception to this generalization. During these riots, general social stability held firm. A question that is perhaps worthy of study by social historians is why so surprisingly little study from a stress standpoint was carried out with the victims and participants in these riots (Caplan & Page, 1968).

However, systematic studies of stress reactions to riots in general are almost nonexistent. Several studies were conducted following the late-1960 surge of hostilities in Belfast, Ireland. The long-standing schism between the Catholic and Protestant communities in Northern Ireland could well raise doubts as to whether the riots involved "fellow citizens." The results of the studies have been mixed. Following the riots, an increase in tranquilizer prescriptions and admissions to psychiatric outpatient clinics were suggestive of increased stress symptomatology (Lyons, 1971; Fraser, 1971). One study asserts that in spite of years of communal strife there has been little psychological damage to children, citing as evidence a low rate of juvenile delinquency, high educational standards, and no increase in referral to child guidance clinics (Harbison, 1983).

Others are less sanguine as they detail the loss of morale in the Belfast schools, with decreased performance levels, pupil absenteeism, youth preoccupied with hatred and destruction, increased gang activity, and a widespread belief among children that violence is the only solution to intergroup conflicts (Fields, 1979; Fraser, 1973; Schwartz, 1982).

Studies of stress involving the Arab–Israeli conflict are probably more appropriately discussed under the heading of "war," yet the combatants are living side by side in a community setting (Freedman, 1980; Zuckerman-Bareli, 1979). Bombings and shellings seem to produce minimal stress symptoms, whereas terrorist attacks raising the specter of complete surprise at the entering of houses involved higher levels of anxiety and stress symptomatology. Observations of the Lebanon civil strife indicate an increase in alcoholism, addiction, suicide, and depression among the Moslem population (Pattison, 1984). During the Vietnam war a form of behavior called fragging, which involved the violent physical assault on a military officer by a dissatisfied soldier (thus representing an attack by a fellow citizen), was a surprisingly frequent occurrence. However, only those convicted of perpetrating the fragging have been studied (Bond, 1976).

A riot within a prison represents a breakdown of intense communal ties between guards and inmates. Hillman (1981) studied the emotional aftermath of one of the worst riots in U.S. prison history. Although 33 inmates died, none of the guard hostages were killed in spite of being held hostage for 36 hours. While being held hostage, the guards were in a totally helpless, terrified state and were constantly bombarded with a stimulus overload of nearby killings and destruction. One year after the riot, the guard hostages continued to be plagued by sleep disturbances, terrifying dreams, intrusive frightening memories, and the usual multiple daily fears experienced by most survivors of extreme stress. None of the guards felt that they had regained their preriot levels of personality functioning.

CONCLUSION

Assaults by fellow citizens are within the woof of the social fabric from earliest childhood through old age and occur across all social classes and within all ethnic, racial and geographic social groupings. So widespread have been these assaultive phenomena that in the past some of them may have been taken for granted as "just a part of life." This is probably one of the reasons the study of the impact of assaults is still in its infancy. However, the increasing awareness in recent years of the long-term sequelae of severe stress on both the developing child and the adult will most surely lead to further and more extensive clinical investigations. These studies should in turn have profound legal, social, and treatment implications concerning society's care and protection of its citizens, both young and old.

REFERENCES

Bond, T. C. (1976). The why of fragging. *American Journal of Psychiatry, 133,* 1328–1331.

Bordow, S., & Porritt, D. (1979). An experimental evaluation of crisis intervention. *Social Science Medicine,* 13A, 251–256.

Brownlee, J. R., & Bakeman, R. (1981). Hitting in toddler-peer interaction. *Child Development, 52,* 1076–1079.

Bulman, R. J., & Wortman, C. B. (1977). Attributions of blame and coping in the "Real World"—severe accident victims react to their lot. *Journal of Personality & Social Psychology, 35,* 351–363.

Burgess, A. (1975). Family reaction to homicide. *American Journal of Orthopsychiatry, 45,* 391–398.

Caplan, N. C., & Page, J. M. (1960). A study of ghetto riots. *Scientific American, 219,* 15–21.

Damlouji, N. F., & Ferguson, J. M. (1985). Three cases of posttraumatic anorexia nervosa. *American Journal of Psychiatry, 142,* 362–363.

Dawe, H. C. (1934). An analysis of two hundred quarrels of pre-school children. *Child Development, 5,* 139–157.

Denny-Brown, D. E. (1945). Disability arising from closed head injury. *Journal of the American Medical Association, 127,* 429.

Dohrenwend, B. S. (1973). Social status and stressful life events. *Journal of Personality and Social Psychology, 28,* 225–235.

Ecclestone, J. (1980). After-care important for hostages. *International Journal of Offender Therapy and Comparative Criminology, 24,* 85–86.

Ellenberger, H. (1955). Psychological relationships between criminal and victim. *Archives of Criminal Psychodynamics, 1,* 257–290.

Eth, S., & Pynoos, R. (1984, July 6). Trauma of child in parent death said neglected. *Psychiatry News* pp. 23, 27.

Fattah, E. A. (1981). Becoming a victim: The victimization experience and its aftermath. *Victimology, 6,* 29–47.

Fields, R. M. (1979). Child terror victims and adult terrorists. *Journal of Psychohistory, 7,* 71–75.

Finkelstein, N. W. (1982, September). Aggression: Is it stimulated by day care? *Young Children,* pp. 3–9.

Fraser, M. (1973). *Children in conflict.* New York: Basic Books.

Fraser, R. M. (1971). The cost of commotion: An analysis of the psychiatric sequelae of the 1969 Belfast riots. *British Journal of Psychiatry, 118,* 257–264.

Freedman, A. M. (1980). Children under fire: Israel. In E. F. Purcell (Ed.), *Psychopathology of children and youth: A cross-cultural perspective* (pp. 157–199). New York: Josiah Macy Jr. Foundation.

Freud, S. (1955). Group psychology and the analysis of the ego. In J. Strachey (Ed. and Trans.), *The standard edition of the complete psychological works of Sigmund Freud,* (Vol. 23, pp. 67–144). London: Hogarth Press.

Friedman, C. J., Mann, F., & Adelman, H. (1976). Juvenile street gangs: The victimization of youth. *Adolescence, 11,* 527-533.

Green, A. H. (1983). Dimension of psychological trauma in abused children. *Journal of the American Academy of Child Psychiatry, 22,* 231–237.

Harbison, J. (Ed.). (1983). *Children of the troubles.* Belfast, Stranmillis College Learning Resources Unit.

Hillman, R. G. (1981). The psychopathology of being held hostage. *American Journal of Psychiatry, 138,* 1193–1197.

Horowitz, M. (1974). Stress response syndrome: Character style & dynamic psychotherapy. *Archives of General Psychiatry, 31,* 768–781.

Huffine, C. L. (1971). Equivocal single-auto traffic fatalities. *Life-Threatening Behavior, 1,* 83–95.

Husaini, B. A., & Neff, J. A. (1980). Characteristics of life events and psychiatric impairment in rural communities. *Journal of Nervous & Mental Disease, 168,* 159–166.

Huston, T. L., Geis, G., Wright, R., & Garrett, T. (1976). Good samaritans as crime victims. *Victimology, 1,* 284–294.

Justice, B., & Duncan, D. F. (1976). Running away: An epidemic problem of adolescence. *Adolescence, 11,* 365–371.

Kessler, R. C. (1979). Stress, social status and psychological distress. *Journal of Health & Social Behavior, 20,* 259–272.

Krupnick, J. L. (1980). Brief psychotherapy with victims of violent crime. *Victimology, 5,* 347–354.

Krupnick, J. L., & Horowitz, M. J. (1981). Stress response syndromes. *Archives of General Psychiatry, 38,* 428–435.

Lazarus, R. S. (1983). The costs and benefits of denial. In S. Breznitz (Ed.), *The denial of stress* (pp. 1–33). New York: International Universities Press.

Lee, J. A. B., & Rosenthal, S. J. (1983). Working with victims of violent assault. *Social Casework, 64,* 593–601.

Lehman, A. F., & Linn, L. S. (1984). Crimes against discharged mental patients in board-and-care homes. *American Journal of Psychiatry, 141,* 271–274.

Leopold, R. L., & Dillon, H. (1963). Psychoanatomy of a disaster; A long term study of post traumatic neuroses in survivors of a marine explosion. *American Journal of Psychiatry, 119,* 913–921.

Lidz, T. (1946). Casualties from Guadalcanal: Study of reactions to extreme stress. *Psychiatry, 9,* 193–213.

Lindy, J. D., Grace, M. C., & Green, B. L. (1981). Survivors: Outreach to a reluctant population. *American Journal of Orthopsychiatry, 51,* 468–478.

Logan, M. N. (1979). Crime against the elderly: Cruel and unusual punishment. *Victimology, 4,* 129–131.

Lyons, H. A. (1971). Psychiatric sequelae of the Belfast riots. *British Journal of Psychiatry, 118,* 265–273.

McDermott, M. J., Stanley, J. E., & Zimmerman-McKinney, M. A. (1982). The victimization of children and youths. *Victimology, 7,* 162–177.

Modlin, H. C. (1967). The post accident anxiety syndrome: Psychosocial aspects. *American Journal of Psychiatry, 123,* 1008–1012.

Noyes, W., Jr., Hoenk, P. R., Kuperman, S., & Slymen, D. J. (1977). Depersonalization in accident victims and psychiatric patients. *Journal of Nervous & Mental Disease, 164,* 401–407.

Orbach, I. (1978). The victim's reaction to an attack as a function of his perception of the attacker following a verbal insult. *European Journal of Social Psychology, 8,* 453–465.

Paap, W. R. (1981). Being burglarized: An account of victimization. *Victimology, 6,* 297–305.

Parke, R. D., & Slaby, R. G. (1983). The development of aggression. In P. H. Mussen & E. M. Hetherington (Eds.), *Handbook of child psychology: Vol. 4. Socialization, personality, and social development* (4th ed., pp. 605–641). New York: Wiley.

Pattison, E. M. (1984). War and mental health in Lebanon. *Journal of Operational Psychiatry, 15,* 31–38.

Piaget, J. (1962). *Play, dreams and imitation in childhood.* New York: Norton.

Poulshock, S., & Cohen, E. (1975). The elderly in the aftermath of a disaster. *Gerontologist, 15,* 357–361.

Ramirez, A., & Lasater, T. (1976). Attitudinal and behavioral reactions to fear-arousing communications. *Psychological Reports, 38,* 811–818.

Rutter, M. (1973). Why are London children so disturbed? *Procedures of the Royal Society of Medicine, 66,* 1221–1225.

Rynearson, E. K. (1984). Bereavement after homicides: A descriptive study. *American Journal of Psychiatry, 141,* 1452–1454.

Saint J. Neill, S. R. (1976). Aggressive and non-aggressive fighting in twelve-to-thirteen year old preadolescent boys. *Journal of Child Psychology & Psychiatry, 17,* 213–220.

Schafer, S. (1968). *The victim and his criminal.* New York: Random House.

Schwartz, R. E. (1982). Children under fire: The role of the schools. *American Journal of Orthopsychiatry, 52,* 409–419.

Scott, J. P. (1975). *Aggression* (2nd ed.). Chicago: University of Chicago Press.

Seligman, M. E. P. (1975). *Helplessness: On depression, development and death.* San Francisco: Freeman.

Shere, E. S., & Priel, I. (1972). Psychological aspects of motor vehicle accidents. *Israel Annals of Psychiatry & Related Disciplines, 10,* 92–100.

Silbert, M. H., & Pines, A. M. (1982). Victimization of street prostitutes. *Victimology, 7,* 122–133.

Sisler, G. C. (1978). Psychiatric disorder associated with head injury. In *Brain disorders: Clinical diagnosis and management* (Vol. 1, pp. 137–152). Philadelphia: W. B. Saunders.

Smale, G. J. A., & Spickenheuer, H. L. P. (1979). Feelings of guilt and need for retaliation in victims of serious crimes against property and persons. *Victimology, 4,* 75–85.

Smelzer, M. L., & Vinokur, A. (1974). Life events, subjective stress and traffic accidents. *American Journal of Psychiatry, 131,* 903–906.

Solnit, A. J., & Kris, M. (1967). Trauma and infantile experiences: A longitudinal perspective. In S. S. Furst (Ed.), *Psychic Trauma* (pp. 175–220). New York: Basic Books.

Symonds, M. (1975). Victims of violence: Psychological effects and aftereffects. *American Journal of Psychoanalysis, 35,* 19–26.

Tabachnick, N., Litman, R. E., Osman, M., Jones, W. L., Cohn, J., Kasper, A., & Moffet, J. (1966). Comparative psychiatric study of accidental and suicidal death. *Archives of General Psychiatry, 14,* 60–68.

Terr, L. C. (1979). Children of Chowchilla: A study of psychic trauma. In A. J. Solnit, R. S. Eissler, A. Freud, M. Kris, & P. B. Neubauer (Eds.), *Psychoanalytic study of the child,* (Vol. 34, pp. 547–623. New Haven: Yale University Press.

Terr, L. C. (1981a). Forbidden games: Post-traumatic child play. *Journal of the American Academy of Child Psychiatry, 20,* 741–760.

Terr, L. C. (1981b). Psychic trauma in children: Observations following the Chowchilla school-bus kidnapping. *American Journal of Psychiatry, 138,* 14–19.

Terr, L. C. (1983a). Chowchilla revisited: The effects of psychic trauma four years after a school-bus kidnapping. *American Journal of Psychiatry, 140,* 1543–1550.

Terr, L. C. (1983b). Life attitudes, dreams and psychic trauma in a group of "normal children." *Journal of the American Academy of Child Psychiatry, 22,* 221–230.

Terr, L. C. (1983c). Time sense following psychic trauma. *American Journal of Orthopsychiatry, 53,* 244–261.

Titchener, J. L., & Ross, W. D. (1974). Acute or chronic stress as determinants of behavior, character and neurosis. In E. F. Brody & S. Arieti (Eds.), *American handbook of psychiatry,* (Vol. 3, pp. 39–60). New York: Basic Books.

U.S. Dept. of Justice. (1983). *Criminal victimization in the United States, 1981.* Washington, DC: Bureau of Justice Statistics.

Von Hentig, H. (1948). *The criminal and his victim.* New Haven: Yale University Press.

Ward, C. (1973). *Vandalism.* New York, Van Nostrand Reinhold.

Weighill, V. E. (1983). Compensation neurosis: A review of the literature. *Journal of Psychosomatic Research, 27,* 97–104.

Weiss, R. J., & Payson, H. E. (1967). Personality disorders IV: Gross stress reactions, In A. M. Friedman & H. I. Kaplan (Eds.), *Comprehensive textbook of psychiatry,* (pp. 1027–1031). Baltimore: Williams & Wilkins.

Zuckerman-Bareli, C. (1979). Effects of border tensions on residents of an Israeli town. *Journal of Human Stress, 5,* 29–40.

Stress Engendered by Military Action on Military and Civilian Populations

JON A. SHAW, MD

War is a constant of history. The annals of humans have been characterized by an endless series of warring conflicts between tribes, nations, and states. In the vastness of its potential destructiveness, war represents a stress of unusual dimensions.

It has been estimated that more than a hundred armed conflicts are presently being waged around the globe (Shawcross, 1984). The threat as well as the actual experience of loss, injury, and death characteristic of military action challenge the illusion of safety within which we live our lives. Emotionally, war affects military and civilian populations adversely, not only during exposure to actual military conflict, but also during prolonged periods of fearful anticipation as well as during the long days of its aftermath. Ultimately, the experiences of war have to be integrated into the lives of those individuals who endure it directly as well as borne by the families who are left with their grief. This chapter will focus on war as a stress and on its traumatic impact on military personnel as well as on the civilians caught up in the vortex of military action.

Psychic trauma has been defined as "a stimulus, arising from an external situation or from massive inner sexual and aggressive excitement, which is experienced as overwhelming the ego's capacity" (Moore & Fine, 1967, p. 91). This chapter will examine the notion of psychic trauma occurring as the consequence of overwhelming external circumstances. These circumstances may arise as a consequence of natural forces beyond human control (accidents, disasters of nature, illness), or they may be products of human intention in the form of assault, rape, or war. It is evident that war can serve as a vast laboratory that provides the opportunity to observe how individuals adapt to continuous threats of injury and death. Although war trauma could serve as a determinant of psychic trauma, Freud recognized that it was, nevertheless, the inner experience of distressing affects inherent in the traumatic situation and the unconscious meaning attributed to the trauma that overwhelmed the ego.

THE MILITARY EXPERIENCE IN WAR

Men who engage in war frequently experience stress reactions of a magnitude sufficient to render them unable to function effectively in combat. In modern warfare, psychiatric casualties represent a major source of disability and consequent loss of manpower. The manifestations of combat stress reactions are diffuse and may involve both the psychic and somatic spheres. Glass (1951) noted:

> The signs and symptoms are quite variable. The clinical findings may change in a matter of hours or from day to day. In many patients they are mild, as exemplified by those persons who only verbalize the subjective sensations of fear in battle, with no objective evidence of anxiety. In others tearfulness, depression, gross tremulousness, hysterical blindness or paralysis may occur. A smaller group of patients exhibit such a severe disruption of personality functions that they are out of contact with their environment and represent a transient psychotic syndrome. (p. 471)

From his experiences in the Korean conflict Glass (1957) delineated less overt but clearly allied psychiatric problems, that is, self-inflicted wounds, accidental injuries, avoidance of combat by desertion, refusal to obey orders, and passive nonparticipation by individuals, who in battle contributed little firepower or aggressive activity.

More recent experiences in war have revealed variations on the same theme. The nature of the low intensity warfare characteristic of the later stages of the Korean and Vietnamese conflicts revealed the capacity of people with character and behavior disorders to disrupt effective performance through insubordination, disciplinary problems, and substance abuse (Jones & Johnson, 1975). The Israeli Defense Forces noted that after the Peace of Galilee war in Lebanon in 1982, 90% of the psychiatric casualties who required further institutional treatment were suffering from some form of character disorder (Belenky, Tyner, & Sodetz, 1983).

Probably the most striking variation on the psychiatric experience in modern warfare occurred in the 1973 Arab–Israeli war; this may indeed represent a harbinger of things to come. This war lasted approximately 4 weeks and was characterized by unrelenting and sustained combat, unusual ferocity, fluidity of battle, and the use of massive firepower. Battles were fought day and night with continuous deployment of armor, artillery, and air power consuming vast material resources.

Psychiatric casualties accumulated rapidly; for every 100 soldiers wounded in action there were approximately 30 psychiatric casualties (Belenky et al., 1983). In contrast to the combat exhaustion described in World War II, these soldiers were not suffering from sustained fatigue subsequent to the gradual wearing down of biological resilience; on the contrary, the intensity of battle was found to be a more important variable than its duration. These casualties were diagnosed as suffering from "battle shock," an intense emotional reaction to the stress of battle. This condition was characterized by fear, anxiety, depression, and sleep disturbance.

The modern battlefield confronts its participants with a nuclear-biological-chemical configuration, a "star wars" electronification of battle along with the high lethality of modern weaponry. Moreover, all this is experienced in a context of intense and sustained combat operations without rear areas of refuge and clear air superiority. Together these factors make for an enormous acceleration of the intensity of combat stress. The magnitude of this experience, characterized as it is by sudden catastrophic violence and devastation, acts to nullify the preparedness of the soldier. This milieu diminishes the relevance of warrior virtues and personal initiative, and there emerges a new awareness of the individual's helplessness before random death. In such a battle situation, it is likely that psychiatric casualties will exceed "wounded in action" casualties, and a more intense and pervasive stress response will then become prominent. The anticipated responses may be similar to the disaster shock syndrome described by Tyhurst (Tyhurst, 1951). He noted that approximately 75% of the participants are rendered stunned, bewildered, and anxiety ridden; moreover, they exhibit physiological concomitants of fear. A small proportion (10%–25%) display manifestly inappropriate responses such as paralyzing anxiety, confusion, and hysterical screaming.

One of the puzzling questions regarding modern warfare is: How can any individual adapt to a situation where there is so little opportunity for survival? What enables a man to risk his life, to bear the tension, to endure the fear of death, and to observe his friends fall by his side? As Grinker and Spiegel (1945) ask, what possesses a rational man to act so irrationally? The forces are complex, multilayered, and not easily discernable. Certainly with the increasing complexity of war and the sophisticated technology of modern weaponry, the individual has little autonomous capacity to ensure his survival by means of his own warrior skills. Yet in spite of the horrors of war, men adapt to the stresses of combat with varying degrees of success and purpose.

Combat imposes unique mental and physical hardships on its participants. A spectrum of stressors derive from military action. Laufer, Brett, and Gallops (1984) have described five specific stressors associated with war that seem particularly traumatogenic:

1. Combat, with its exposure to injury and death
2. Abusive violence, particularly the witnessing of cruelty, unnecessary violence, and the destructive impact of modern weaponry
3. The death or wounding of friends
4. Isolation from peers
5. Contact with death and dying outside of combat, a common experience for individuals who have the task of triaging the wounded or bagging the dead

The uniformity of the traumatic experiences of war allows exploration of those processes that determine the soldier's capacity to sustain himself in combat. In the wake of military action, the continuum of combat stress reactions ranges from those who are able to function and adapt to combat to those who represent combat failures. An individual able to function effectively in a combat situation would represent a successful adaptation. An unsuccessful adaptation is characterized by a psychological failure on the part of the soldier to function effectively in combat.

The stressful experience can best be defined as a process of encounter and adaptation; a dynamic interaction between the individual, his biological resilience, and his repertoire of defenses and coping behaviors on the one hand, and the specific environmental stress on the other. Particularly important are the individual's definition or subjective interpretation of the stressor and the nature of the stressful experience. Another important variable is the time pattern of the encounter, that is, whether it is sudden and unexpected or the result of prolonged and cumulative exposure to the stressor. Every soldier has a breaking point—a point of heightened vulnerability beyond which there is a decrement in combat effectiveness.

Combat stress reactions are inversely related to the phenomenon of successful adaptation to combat (Swank & Marchand, 1946). The chronology of breakdown in combat indicates that there is a bimodal distribution over time. Initially it is the inexperienced troops who are vulnerable; indeed Jones (1981) has suggested that breakdowns among "green troops" account for 75% of psychiatric casualties. With increasing exposure to combat, psychiatric casualty rates decrease, only once again to increase gradually with continued and prolonged exposure to combat.

Certainly in the first week of combat, the sudden awareness of the violence of war, the frequency of random death, the inability to evaluate risks realistically, and the tenuousness of group cohesion and group solidarity contribute to early failures in combat. With increasing experience in war, however, the soldier begins to appraise the combat situation realistically, to sort out the various dangers, and to make the appropriate response with a sense of mastery and control. He develops "battle wiseness" (Swank & Marchand, 1946). The importance of the first battle experience, "the bloodying of the troops," and its role in promoting successful adaptation were recounted by Dr. J. Thomas Calhoun, Surgeon-in-Chief of the second Division, U.S. Army during the American Civil war (Deutsch, 1944). He noted, "When men have passed through the baptism of fire together, they feel they have something in common. They have a common interest which diverts their thoughts away from home" (p. 376). The commonly shared dangers and hardships impel individuals to move closer together, promoting group identification and group cohesion. The men forge new relationships that increase their capacity to tolerate the stress of combat. They become a band of brothers united against adversity.

The power of the group to enhance the individual soldier's resistance to stress is determined by a number of factors. The group provides the individual with the assurance that he does not fight alone. An emotional bond mitigates the aloneness of the battlefield, facilitating a sense of succor among comrades. Individual needs and values are subordinated to the group's needs and standards of conduct.

Even the successful adaptation to combat is associated with the experience of stress. It is a rare individual who does not manifest some of the normal psycho-physiological reactions to stress; these include fearfulness, startle reactions, hypervigilance, sleep disturbances, nightmares, emotionality, irritability, somatic complaints, cold sweats, fatigue, tremors, and enduring tension. Menninger (1948) reported on a survey of infantry soldiers experiencing combat in World War II, noting that approximately 70% described a pounding heart; 45%, a sinking feeling in the stomach; 30%, cold sweats; 25%, nausea; 25%, shakiness and tremulousness; 25%, stiff muscles; 20%, vomiting; 20%, general weakness; 10%, involuntary bowel movement; and 6%, involuntary urination.

There is evidence that, with prolonged exposure to combat, individual vulnerability to stress progressively increases. Swank and Marchand (1946) observed that after approximately 30 days of battle there is a slow but definite decline in combat performance. In the Mediterranean theater in World War II, Appel and Beebe (1946) noted that approximately 90 days of exposure to combat was the average length of endurance before noneffective behavior became frequent. Such prolonged exposure to combat is associated with a gradual loss of biological resilience. Chronic fatigue, sleep deprivation, enduring battle tension, and marginal sustenance with food and water begin to take their toll. The participants in battle easily observe that with continuing exposure to combat there is a diminishing chance of survival. Of paramount importance is the increasing loss of comrades through wounds and death, which gradually undermines group cohesion and group solidarity, the most important factors contributing to the capacity to resist stress.

Combat Stress Reactions

The responses to the stress of battle fall along a continuum ranging from anticipatory feelings of anxiety associated with the unknown to states of complete exhaustion. In anticipation of battle, the individual mobilizes characterological and defense constellations. Deeply engrained patterns of behavior for coping with impending feelings of helplessness are utilized to confront both internal and external fears.

In the days before battle the individual may experience the *precombat syndrome,* usually associated with irritability, anxiety, and functional complaints such as weakness, palpitations, dyspnea, and abdominal pains (Swank & Marchand, 1946). Upon entry onto the battlefield, the soldier struggles to keep stress within tolerable limits. With exposure to combat there are transient fear reactions, particularly in the face of unknown situations or, sudden and unexpected danger. Preexisting psychiatric disorders may render the individual vulnerable to sudden and intense experiences of stress. If the intensity of battle is sustained, unrelenting, and associated with massive destruction, the individual may manifest battle shock, an intense emotional reaction characterized by fear, anxiety, depression and sleep disturbance.

Conversion Disorders and dissociative reactions usually occur in the early stages of combat in concert with the proclivities of the individual's defenses and coping style. Depressive disorders may occur at any time reflecting the various exigencies of loss in all its myriad forms.

Frequently the prolonged exposure to stress results in an incipient failure to contain the stress. There is a disruption in the individual's emotional equilibrium. One begins to see the psychophysiological responses associated with the gradual wearing down of the biological reserves: tremulousness, startle reactions, fatigue, somatic complaints, and sleep and appetite dysfunctions. Concurrently there are disturbances in emotionality manifested by tension, irritability, and impaired cognition (which is in turn associated with worry, difficulties in concentrating, and distractibility).

The struggle for self-preservation may lead individuals to develop an evacuation syndrome as a way to escape combat. In every war there are medically acceptable avenues for evacuation. In World War I, it was the "soldier's heart" or "shell shock." In World War II, initially, soldiers with "war neurosis" were evacuated. It was only when General Omar Bradley issued a directive on April 26, 1943, stating that psychiatric casualties would be diagnosed as combat exhaustion, with its implication of tiredness and treatability, that evacuation rates were controlled (Department of the Army, 1966).

The *old sergeant syndrome* refers to an individual with combat exhaustion. His defenses have been compromised. He exhibits mental and physical sluggishness, apathy, confusion, tremulousness, startle reactions, and fear. Too many of his comrades and buddies have been lost and he stands alone before his fears.

Defenses against Stress

Grinker and Spiegel (1945) have stated:

The basic problem in all cases of war neurosis is anxiety and its management. Whatever the dynamic source of anxiety, it is brought out by the battle situation, and no matter how strong or weak a person may be in his relationship to his fellow man he becomes ill from his incapacity to handle this emotion. (p. 129)

When discussing combat stress reactions it is important to distinguish between fear and anxiety. Fear refers to an external stimulus or danger that is experienced as a threat to the self. Anxiety refers to a signal alerting the individual to an inner danger, to the emerging presence of an emotion or affect that has to be managed or warded off. It plays a preparatory role in evoking defensive and coping behavior. Shaw (1983) has suggested that the sine qua non of the combat stress reaction is that when an individual confronts the threat—and the consequent fear—of injury and death (external danger), there ensues a threatened intrusion into conscious awareness of the feelings of helplessness (internal danger). The experience of unwanted thoughts and feelings of helplessness and inability to cope destabilizes the existing equilibrium; it mobilizes defenses and coping behavior to promote adaptation. Successful adaptation to combat involves the warding off of intrusive affects of helplessness.

In the face of battle fear, both extrinsic and intrinsic mechanisms, rational and irrational processes enable the individual to ward off the feelings of helplessness and inability to cope. The most powerful of all the extrinsic variables is that associated with a sense of group cohesion, the feeling of belonging to a powerful group. Some other factors that play a major role in allowing the individual soldier to achieve mastery over his fears include his biological resilience, the way he defines the situation, his character structure, and his defensive constellations.

The Traumatic Situation

When the individual soldier begins to experience self-doubt, to question both his own capacity to cope and the ability of his leaders and his comrades to protect him, the matrix is formed that "germinates the seeds of the traumatic situation" (Kardiner & Spiegel, 1947, p. 37). Freud (1926 & 1955a) noted that the essence of the traumatic situation is the experience of helplessness (p. 166).

In some situations, a sudden and unexpected danger may overwhelm the individual leaving him helpless before his fears. In other instances, however, the prolonged and cumulative exposure to the stressors of war may undermine the processes of adaptation; for example, the loss of comrades diminishes group cohesion. The "wear and tear" of battle may then compromise biological resilience. The failure of defenses is associated with increasing disruption in physical, emotional, cognitive, and psychomotor functioning. The soldier may turn inward in a state of brooding self-absorption, with a concomitant loss of emotional investment in his comrades. Paralyzed by both real and imaginary threats to the self, he loses his capacity to adapt to the changing conditions.

The point beyond which the individual no longer retains his capacity to adapt and to remobilize defenses may be called the "traumatic breaking point." Once this point is passed, the person is inundated by feelings of helplessness, inability to cope, terror, and panic. The traumatic situation is characterized by the collapse of all effective coping behavior. Even perceptions become inaccurate, distorted by imagination and fear. Judgment and discrimination fail. The executive apparatuses become unfocused and disorganized (Kardiner & Spiegel, 1947).

The Posttraumatic Stress Reactions

It is out of the failure of adaptation to the traumatic situation that the posttraumatic syndrome emerges. The individual begins to perceive the losses he has sustained. In response to the traumatic situation, he comes to utilize a variety of defense and characterological strategies in an attempt to integrate the overwhelming experience. The traumatic situation is evaluated in terms of its impact on the individual's life, vis-à-vis standards of conduct, ego-ideal, and the expectations of others. The person has to come to terms with a new awareness of his own vulnerability.

The soldier who has failed (or who feels he has failed) his comrades faces issues of self-reproach. Depression, guilt, and self-recrimination may collect around the nidus of the traumatic experience, giving rise to an incapacitating neurosis.

Freud (1939 & 1955c) described two patterns of response to a traumatic situation, which he called the positive and negative effects. The positive effect is characterized by attempts once again to make the trauma come alive. The impetus is to remember the experience and to repeat it, with the intent this time of achieving the sense of mastery that was denied the individual on his first exposure. (This particular component of the response is usually associated with such concepts as "fixation to the trauma" and the "compulsion to repeat.")

The negative response to the trauma, Freud's "negative effect," is characterized by the need to distance oneself from the painful experience. The traumatic events are repressed (forgotten). The principal expressions of this form of adaptation are avoidance, inhibition, and phobic behavior. This mode of response to the stress of war, although no less frequent, has generally not received much attention in the literature.

Kardiner & Spiegal (1947) described the following as the constant features of the posttraumatic stress response:

1. *Fixation on the Trauma.* A proclivity to recall or reexperience the traumatic memory in a multiplicity of different ways
2. *Altered Dream Life.* The experience of helplessness, often in association with disorganized aggression reproduced through dream images
3. *Irritability.* Characterized by startle reaction, lower thresholds of responsiveness, disturbance of sleep, fright reactions, and hyper-sensitivity
4. *Aggression and Violence.* Identification with the role of the aggressor as a defense against feelings of helplessness
5. *Inhibitory Phenomena.* Associated with fatigue, loss of interest in work, and psychic numbness

A subgroup of combat veterans has been described as exhibiting a rather specific form of posttraumatic syndrome, characterized by a conditioned response to any external stimuli reminiscent of battle-field experiences. This pattern is manifested in the form of physiological responses of arousal such as startle reactions along with elevated pulse rate, blood pressure, and muscle tension (Kolb, 1984).

Studies of the posttraumatic syndromes have proliferated subsequent to the Vietnam conflict. Smptom patterns have been shown to include anxiety-depressive manifestations, flashbacks (intrusive memories and emotions reminiscent of the traumatic situation), repetitive nightmares, irritability, startle reactions, a proclivity to aggressive-violent behaviors, emotional numbness, cognitive constriction, psychosomatic features, and a generally lower level of adaptive functioning (Figley, 1978, Schwartz, 1984, Van Der Kolk, 1984).

A study of 382 soldiers who experienced combat stress reactions during the Peace of Galilee War showed that one year after their experiences in the war, 59% manifested Posttraumatic Stress Disorder (PTSD). This compares to 16% of 334 soldiers who were matched on sociodemographic variables and who had fought in the same battles but who did not have a combat stress reaction (Solomon, Schwarzwald, & Weisenberg, 1985). The authors made several interesting observations.

1. Soldiers treated in forward echelons and subsequently returned to their combat units suffered less PTSD, indeed, approximately 50% as much as their counterparts who were transferred to rear echelon units.

2. For both the index group and control group, the cases of PTSD that did occur were predominantly chronic in nature (in the control group a small percentage were classified as delayed).

3. As noted, soldiers who had suffered front combat stress during the war and were thereupon sent to rear units reported a higher level of war-related stress than those who were returned to their combat units.

4. PTSD represents a failure of adaptation to trauma characterized by wide ranging dysfunctions in the biological, psychological, and social spheres.

THE CIVILIAN EXPERIENCE

The effects of military action on the civilian population are less well known. Shawcross (1984) has stated that between 1979 and 1982, 4 million people and 45 nations were engaged in combat that killed unnumbered millions. For example, it is estimated that in the course of a 5-year period, 320,000 children died in Mozambique as a result of war (Dyregrov, Raundelin, Lwanga, & Mugisha, 1987).

What is perhaps most surprising is how frequently the civilian population is reported to adapt to the stressors of war with a sense of equanimity. Gillespie (1942) noted, "One of the most striking things about the effects of war [World War II] on the civilian population has been the relative rarity of pathological mental disturbances among the civilians exposed to air raids (p. 23).

Ziv and Israeli (1973) compared the effects of shelling on the manifest anxiety level of children living in kibbutzim. They found no differences between those who did experience bombardment and those who did not. In a second study Ziv, Kruglanski, and Shulman (1974) noted that the children under fire exhibited greater patriotism, more covert aggression, and greater appreciation of courage as a valued personality trait. A study was conducted of the effects of a war environment on the dreams and sleep habits of a particular group of Israeli youth. These youngsters lived in a northern border town that was frequently subjected to terrorist activities. The findings demonstrated a proclivity on the part of these boys and girls to repress the horrors of military activity. The youths slept longer and their dreams showed fewer horror, sexual, and aggressive themes than did those of their counterparts in a nonborder town (Rofe & Lewin, 1982). Zuckerman-Bareli (1982) studied the effects of shelling and terrorist attacks on six Israeli settlements along the northern border, comparing three kibbutzim and three moshav noncommunal settlements housing nonwestern immigrants. Moshav members experienced a higher frequency of emotional and social disturbances than did the kibbutz members. The communal life of the kibbutz contributed to a higher level of satisfaction and group identification. This difference highlights the complexity of the processes influencing the resistance to stress, particularly the importance of a sense of belongingness, group cohesion, shared values, and common purpose among the participants in war, both civilian and military. A study of coping mechanisms of Israeli women during wartime revealed that 70% of the upper class and 50% of the lower class were categorized as effective copers. This was related to differences in education, socialization, and the person's sense of self-confidence and independence (Breznitz-Svidousky, 1982).

CIVILIAN STRESS REACTIONS TO MILITARY ACTION

There are relatively few studies of the effects of military action on individual civilian participants in war. Individual psychological responses to traumatic events may be categorized phenomenologically as immediate or delayed stress reactions. Immediate responses may include transient fear reactions, acute panic states, psychophysiological manifestations of anxiety, passive reactions, states of frozen immobility, disorientation, confusion, and amnesia.

The delayed stress reactions may on the other hand be associated with fixation to the trauma, psychic numbness interfering with resumption of one's life tasks, residual symptoms of guilt, self-reproach, pessimism, apathy, emotional lability, episodic aggressiveness, and depression.

Thus, among survivors of the Holocaust, the long-term psychological effects include an unrelenting and enduring sense of guilt, loss, grief, and rage woven into a conspiracy of silence, denial, and avoidance. This pattern is known to have even been passed on to the children of such families (Danieli, 1982). The children are reported to grow up with a sense of painful bewilderment, not understanding the inexplicable torment within the family and their own sense of guilt. The home atmosphere of such families has been characterized by "pervasive depression, worry, symbiotic clinging within the family, and mistrust and fear of the outside world" (Danieli, 1982, p. 408).

More recently the psychological state of refugees fleeing from the war-torn areas of the world has received increasing attention and study. In recent years refugees have taken flight from Palestine, Hungry, Poland, Czechoslovakia, Vietnam, Cambodia, Cuba, Afghanistan, El Salvador, Nicaragua, Lebanon, Ethiopia, Uganda, Mozambique, and so on. The massive uprooting and resettlement of refugees with their well-documented medical and emotional problems has become a world health problem. For Americans, the influx of 1 million Cuban exiles, 500,000 Indochinese refugees, and approximately 500,000 refugees from Central America into this country has brought the plight of these individuals into national awareness.

The extensive health problems of war refugees associated with the conditions of flight and the problems of adaptation to a new culture have been described. Carlin has recounted the acute and enduring traumatic effects of perilous escape, exposure to violence, mutilation, violence, rape, and starvation (Carlin, 1979; personal communication, 1984). Patterns of bereavement associated with the loss of loved ones and the associated loss of language and customs are evident. Entrance into the new culture confronts the already traumatized refugee with personal and ethnic identity conflicts and changing social expectations. Studies have demonstrated that these individuals display progressive adaptive capacities permitting their gradual assimilation into the United States; at the same time, however, the residual effects of trauma continue long after their flight. For example, a longitudinal study of the adaptational problems of Vietnamese refugees during their first 3 years in the United States revealed a progressive reduction in their rates of unemployment and welfare utilization; nevertheless, this cohort was reported to continue to exhibit compromised physical and mental health (Lin, Masuda, & Tazuma, 1984).

Bereavement

Many stressors have an impact on a civilian population suddenly caught up in the midst of war. Of them all, however, the most grievous is the loss of loved ones. Gleser, Green, & Winget (1981) noted that in the Buffalo Creek disaster, bereavement and the threat to life served as the predominant stressors giving rise to the subsequent prolonged pathology. Civilians suffer not only as the innocent victims of war but also as the bereaved of those lost in battle and through cruel mischance. The suffering of those whose most crucial relationships are severed in battle was poignantly stated by the Greek tragedian, Aeschylus, in Clytemnestra's description of the capture of a Grecian city and how the vanquished "women have flung themselves on lifeless bodies, husbands, brothers—little children are clinging to the old dead that gave them life, sobbing from throats no longer free" (Hamilton, 1942, p. 241). Grief and mourning bring with them an attendant guilt, side by side with fantasies of responsibility through acts of omission and commission. These resonate with underlying contradictory wishes; they are all too frequent presences among the survivors of war.

The capacity to mourn has its own developmental line. The circumstances of loss, the nature of the prior relationship, and the degree of ambivalence all influence the process of mourning. Children and adolescents who experience early object loss suffer the consequences of defensive splitting with its peculiar acceptance and denial of the loss (Blum, 1984). The lost object is idealized, and hateful affects are withdrawn and redirected either toward the self or toward others in the world at large. The predominant affect of children experiencing early object loss is rage rather than grief (Wolfenstein, 1969). Fantasies of reunion, identification with the lost object, and ego restrictions are common psychological sequelae. The capacity for interpersonal relationships becomes compromised, frozen in time, and encumbered by guilt and self-reproach. Long after the military action has ceased, the bereaved continue to suffer.

A study of war widows in Israel revealed a high incidence of loneliness, emptiness, and feeling that part of the self was missing (Kirschner, 1982). Many complained of guilt, spoke of wanting to die, feared a nervous breakdown. Anger was a common experience as the widows directed their rage toward the army, the family, and the husband who had abandoned them. There was a struggle to determine if the husband's death had value or was a useless sacrifice.

In addition to the losses associated with death, there are other losses as well: separations from loved ones, the loss of homeland, the loss of ideals, the loss of protective security (shelter, food, and confidence regarding one's well-being), and the losses associated with bodily injury. There is a new awareness of biological vulnerability and of the limited capacity of others to protect the self. The premature exposure to death, injury, and the limitations of the parents to protect the self poses a specially grievous stress to children; unable to ensure their own survival, the youngsters find themselves suddenly exposed and afraid in a hostile world.

War and Children

In his monograph, *Children of War,* Rosenblatt (1983) states:

There are places in the world like Northern Ireland, Israel, Lebanon, Cambodia and Vietnam that have been at war for the past twenty years or more . . . the children living in these places have known nothing but war in their experience. The elements of war, explosions, destructions, dismemberments, eruptions, noises, fire, death, separation, torture, grief, which ought to be extraordinary and temporary for any life are for these children normal and constant. (p. 15)

He relates his conversations with the children of these war-torn lands. A 15-year-old Palestinian girl notes, "I would not bring children into this world" (p. 93); speaking of the Arabs an Israeli girl comments, "I hate them without reason" (p. 67); and a Cambodian child relates, "Peace is worth more than gold" (p. 137). Overall the effects of war on children vary with the nature and intensity of military action, the degree of exposure to violence and brutality, the character of separation experiences, psychological development, personality structure, and the pattern of family and social adaptation.

Greenacre (1943 & 1971) has defined trauma as "any condition which seems definitely unfavorable, noxious, or drastically injurious to the development of children" (p. 277). The exposure to war represents a gross interference with the developmental rights of the child. Yet the cognitive immaturity, plasticity, and adaptive capacities of the child have often veiled the effects of war in a certain obscurity.

Anna Freud and Burlingham (1943) described a large number of children who had witnessed air raids; some of them had seen their houses destroyed. The authors noted that all the children over 2 years of age had acquired an understanding of the significance of the air raids. These children could vaguely distinguish between falling bombs and anti-aircraft weaponry, knew the importance of taking shelter, and were well aware that fire could be started by incendiaries. These authors described the children's adjustment, noting that after 3 years of war the idea of fighting, killing, and bombing had ceased to be extraordinary. These activities were accepted by the children as a part of their world. Gillespie (1942) described as a remarkable feature of the home front, the low incidence of child psychiatric casualties compared to the number anticipated. The response of children to military action is greatly influenced by the behavior of the adults around them. Freud and Burlingham (1943) observed that if the bombing occurred when the small children were in the care of their mothers or familiar surrogates, the little ones did not seem particularly affected by the air raids. The presence of loving and protective parents was enough to provide the necessary illusion of safety.

Children lack the cognitive capacities of the adult. Their theories of causality are egocentric. Children are rarely able to talk about their frightening experiences. Unable to transform their internal conflicts and feelings into words, children utilize action, play, aggressive and regressive activities, and other behavioral states. Some children may turn passive reactions into active ones and play out the traumatic experiences in war games. Others may exhibit regressive behaviors associated with bed-wetting, insatiable demands, thumb-sucking, or tension discharge. Still others withdraw their emotional interest from the outside world.

It is apparent that exposure to the sudden realities of mutilation and death, encounter with the realistic limitations of the protective power of loving parents, and the abrupt and unexpected impact of violence and brutality may undermine a child's illusion of safety. The reaction of children to the traumatic situation is greatly influenced by their underlying fantasy life and interpretation of events. Greenacre (1945/1971) has observed that in contrast to traumatic experiences that are interpreted as incidental, overt traumatic experiences that resonate with an underlying fantasy cause more intense memory traces and may lead to a fixation on the trauma. This fixation may in turn lead to a compelling need to repeat the traumatic experience in a continuing effort to achieve mastery over the traumatic situation.

Children struggle to achieve mastery over their own aggressive and destructive impulses. These attempts at control take form as the result of both conscious and unconscious self-regulation, neutralization, and the internalization of parental standards. The youngster who experiences sudden and unexpected exposure to violence at a time when he or she is in the midst of establishing controls is likely to have the entire structuralization of the control apparatus undermined. It is well known that children severely traumatized by child abuse have a tendency to identify with the role of aggressor.

Terr (1983) described a number of posttraumatic responses in children 4 years after a school bus kidnapping: These included thought suppression of the traumatic experience, disturbances in time sequence, omen formation, repetitive nightmares, recurring fears, a readiness to condensation of disparate experiences, and a sense of pessimism about future possibilities.

Several observers have studied children as war refugees (Arroya & Eth, 1985; Carlin, 1979, 1980; Dyregrov et al., 1987; Lin et al., 1984; Sack, Angell, & Kinzie, 1986). There is considerable evidence that the posttraumatic effects are serious and enduring. Sack et al. (1986) noted that 50% of the Cambodian war refugee children had a diagnosis of PTSD. There was considerable comorbidity. Other prominent diagnoses were Major Depressive Disorder, Generalized Anxiety Disorder, and Intermittent Depressive Disorder. Arroya and Eth (1985) studied 30 youngsters, 17 years of age or less, who had taken flight from Central America and who were later referred to a mental health clinic. Many had been separated from their families. Often the parents had preceded the child to this country, leaving the child behind with relatives and with a perception of having been abandoned to the repeated violence of war. The investigator noted that approximately 33% of these youngsters exhibited Posttraumatic Stress Disorders. Other diagnostic categories included Adjustment Disorders, Separation-anxiety Disorder, Somatoform Disorders, and Major Depressive Disorder and Dysthymia.

Carlin (personal communication, 1984) has estimated that 50% of the refugees from Indochina are children. She divided them into three categories: (1) babylift orphans; (2) unaccompanied minors without family members in the USA (foster children); and (3) children arriving with their refugee families. It was evident that for these children, the experiences of war and flight resulted not infrequently in learning delays, personal and ethnic identity problems, culture shock, and regressive behaviors. Among the younger arrivals, interruptions in preverbal and verbal development were common.

Follow-up studies have indicated that physically, emotionally, and socially, child refugees from Indochina, especially the younger adoptees, have fared extremely well in this country. Developmental progress has been restored, and most of the physical and emotional handicaps associated with their poor environmental background have been surmounted (Carlin, personal communication, 1984).

Studying the effects of war in Uganda on a cohort of adolescents, Dyregrov et al. (1987) noted the youngster's resiliency in the face of extreme stress. There was a proclivity for these adolescents to identify with the helper professions and to prepare in an hopeful, anticipatory way for future positions in a society without war or violence. The youngsters exhibited little evidence of identification with the aggressor. The authors add a word of caution, however; beneath the manifest coping and adaptive strivings of these youth were discernible themes of uncertainty and anxiety.

The tragedy of war is nowhere more evident than in Mozambique, where it is estimated that there are 4.6 million refugees, the great majority of whom are reported to be children. Fifty percent of the population is under 15 years of age. The peculiar brutality of the *bandidos* is evident in their kidnapping of 6- to 16-year-old children from local villages, coercing them into military training, and forcing them to fight against their own villagers and families. The child's failure to comply may result in the cutting off of an ear, the fingers of a hand, or even death. The *bandidos* appear motivated by a wish to destabilize and spread terror among Mozambicans without any interest in winning the hearts of the people or acquiring territory for the establishment of an alternative government. A recent opportunity to evaluate 12 of these children (who had been recaptured by government forces) revealed a high incidence of PTSD and depressive symptomatology (Shaw & Harris, 1988). There was a proclivity for these children to see themselves as victims of war, and, as Dyregrov et al. (1987) had observed, rather than identifying with the aggressor, the children tended to identify with future career patterns where they would be helpers of other victims. Without exception the children indicated they did not want to be soldiers and yearned for peace and freedom from war. Although separated from their families, who lived in the country controlled by the *bandidos,* the majority asked to remain in Maputo, the capital of Mozambique, where they would be free from the risk of recapture. There was also considerable variation in the way each child responded to the trauma, contingent on a number of variables, including the intensity, type, and duration of the traumatic experience; participation in forced military activities; the killing of innocent villagers; victimization by mutilation; the witnessing of the killing of parents, family members, and other villagers; the child's age; previous experiences of loss; and the youngster's basic adaptive/coping style.

ADAPTATION TO STRESS

Whether disasters occur in war or in peacetime events such as the Buffalo Creek flood, the Kansas City Hyatt-Regency Skyway collapse, or the USS *Belknap*–USS *Kennedy* collision in the Mediterranean Sea, a central motif winds its way through the traumatic situation. The experience of psychic trauma is associated with a sudden and unexpected realization of a new and overwhelming reality, a sense of helplessness and inability to cope, and a feeling of vulnerability. The illusion of safety has been unmasked (Shaw, 1985).

The capacity to tolerate stress, whether inherent in the soldier in combat or in the civilian suddenly surrounded by military action, is influenced by a number of factors. The biological resilience of the individual is of paramount importance. The diminishing capacities of advancing age, intercurrent illness, fatigue, chronic battle tension, the continuous exposure to the elements, or the deprivation of rest, sleep and food, all serve to lessen the individual's physical powers and to increase vulnerability to stress. Prolonged exposure to stress is associated with depletion of the biological reserves. Experiences in war have documented the importance of physical conditioning and physical fitness as a bulwark against the stress of combat.

Another factor that contributes enormously to the process of adaptation to the stress of military action is the individual's definition of the situation. A person's affective response to a situation is a direct expression of how he or she defines it. Individuals most resistant to stress often exhibit a cognitive flexibility that enables them to cope with change. They experience stress not as a threat but as a challenge to be mastered. They maintain a sense of having control of their fate.

Santayana observed, "A lion must have more confidence that God is on his side than the gazelle" (Becker, 1973, p. 21). Soldiers materially enhance their sense of mastery, not only over the enemy but over their fears as well, when they have confidence in their physical and emotional capacities, realistically appraise their weaponry, trust their leaders, and prepare for battle through realistic training. It is not happenstance that in combat, elite military units, superbly trained and knowledgeable, have a lower incidence of psychiatric casualties than do conventional units.

Another important element in the adaptation to military action is character structure. Subsequent to his experiences in the Korean conflict, Glass (1953) noted, "A basic component of the psychosomatic resistance against combat failure is the role played by individual personality structure" (p. 93). Because of the inherent proclivity to utilize passive modes as a way of coping with external and internal stress, the passive personality is particularly vulnerable to fear. These individuals are unable to discharge tension through action. Again, soldiers with a highly developed sense of conscience often appear to be more resistent to combat stress; their internalized rules and standards impel them to do their duty. By the same token, the self-absorbed (narcissistic) soldier, preoccupied with self-worth and survival, is uniquely vulnerable to the stress of combat.

One of the most important determinants affecting the individual's response to the stress of military action is the capacity for identification with the group. The group takes on a meaning and validity that transcends individual life. The individual soldier fights bravely out of both a sense of honor and a need to avoid appearing unsoldierly in the eyes of his comrades. The degree of identification and satisfaction with Israeli communal life was found to be an important variable mitigating the stress of border incidents (Zuckerman-Bareli, 1982).

One of the most intriguing aspects of the soldier's adaptation to combat is the contribution of the processes of denial and wishful thinking to the individual's capacity to master the stress of battle. There is evidence that in response to the threat of injury and death, almost everyone tends to employ universal psychological defense constellations. The denial of one's vulnerability in the face of death is well known. Few people go to war with any realistic notion of what it is all about. Bond (1953) has written, "They go with the very unrealistic view that states, it is going to be the other man that is killed, not myself" (p. 143).

Ernest Becker (1973) has noted that one of the "great rediscoveries of modern thought is that of all things that move man, one of the principal ones is his terror of death" (p. 11). Death is a complex presence with rich symbolic meaning that is multidetermined through cultural and personal experiences. People yearn for a fate that transcends the reality of human biological limitations. The individual employs a number of mechanisms to deny helplessness before the laws of biology, thus preserving an excessively idealized self-image that will, in the unconscious, last forever. Military action, by its very violence, challenges these intrinsic belief systems.

Masserman wrote that three basic psychological defenses are essential to a sense of mental health or psychological well-being (1955). Shaw has referred to these as the narcissistically vital defenses that allow the individual to keep biological vulnerability out of conscious awareness (1983). The effectiveness of the individual soldier is partially contingent on the maintenance of those processes; as long as they operate, he is able to keep out of conscious awareness the emerging sense of helplessness before the fear of death.

The first narcissistic defense is *the myth of personal invulnerability*. In spite of rational awareness to the contrary, each one of us cherishes an irrational belief that enables us to deny our biological fragility and the threat of individual death. The heroic soldier whose deeds of valor may have earned him countless honors not infrequently cherishes the magical belief that nothing can hurt him.

The second narcissistic defense is *the delusion of the omnipotent leader*. Just as children imagine their all-powerful and knowledgeable parents will always be there to protect and guide them, so the soldier often turns to his leaders as omnipotent officers who will in some magical way be able to assure his survival.

The third narcissistic defense is, *I am a part of an all-powerful group that will protect me*. The importance of group cohesion and the attribution of meaning to the group is nowhere more eloquently stated than in *Goodbye Darkness*, the memoirs of William Manchester (1979), who served as a marine in the Pacific in World War II. He writes:

It was an act of love. Those men on the line were my family, my home. They were closer to me than I can say, closer than any friends had been or ever would be. They had never let me down and I wouldn't do it to them. I had to be with them rather than let them die and me live with the knowledge that I might have saved them. Men I now know do not fight for flag or country, for the marine corps or the glory or any other abstractions. They fought for one another. (p. 391)

These narcissistically vital defenses allow the individual to keep out of awareness both biological vulnerability and the threatened emergence of a sense of helplessness and inability to cope before the fear of injury and death. The effect of these defenses is to provide an illusion of safety. In this context, psychic trauma can be understood as the sudden and unexpected discovery that one's sense of safety is illusory. The individual is left alone and afraid, overwhelmed with feelings of helplessness.

In this sense too, the concept of psychic trauma is explicable within the current understanding of developmental processes. The child enters the world wrapped about by the protective configuration of the parental milieu. There is a sense of being shielded from danger by omnipotent and omniscient parents. The young child has no awareness of his or her parents' vulnerability to injury and death. There is no understanding of the limitations of the self and the object. To allow development to proceed optimally, the child's limited cognitive capacities automatically weave an illusion of safety about the self and the immediate family.

It is only with further psychological development that the infantile omnipotence with its protective shell of narcissistic invulnerability are slowly eroded away by doses of painful reality. If the child is fortunate, the dawning awareness of reality will be imposed in small enough quantities to assimilate piecemeal with some sense of mastery.

Only gradually does the child become aware of the inevitability of his or her death. Many of our cultural values, religious beliefs, and behavior are orchestrated for the purpose of obscuring and denying this aspect of the human condition.

Hence, with powerful cultural support, the child evolves a defense constellation that allows putting the reality of mortality out of awareness. A residue of magical omnipotence, industriousness, and proven capacities enables the individual who has been well-nurtured and well-loved to repress the fear of death, awareness of transience, and his or her own biological fragility.

To be sure, as the developmental experience accumulates, the child's illusion of safety is modified by an ever greater appreciation of reality. Nevertheless, by means of the narcissistically vital defenses, other defense constellations, characterological structures, and adaptive coping mechanisms, a magical sense of safety is at least partially maintained.

Individual and developmental experiences add immeasurably to one's sense of confidence and to the feeling that one can always overcome adversity. Freud (1900 & 1955b) wrote:

I have found that people who know that they are the preferred or favored by their mother give evidence in their lives of a peculiar self-reliance and an unshakable optimism which often seem like heroic attributes and bring actual success to their possessor. (p. 398)

Realistic capacities also contribute to the illusion of safety. The individual soldier whose sense of assurance is built on his training, superb physical conditioning, familiarity with weaponry, and group cohesion often has the kind of conviction that enables him to achieve triumph over adversity. The individual is most capable of resisting stress whose biological resiliency, definition of the situation, characterological structure and narcissistically vital defenses support a sense of being in control, of being able actively to master obstacles, and of having the capacity to resolve any adverse situation to his own advantage.

SUMMARY

Military action threatens all of its participants—soldier, family unit, spouse, and child. The trauma of war is associated with the threatened emergence into conscious awareness of feelings of helplessness and inability to cope. Characterological and defense constellations are mobilized to promote cognitive integration, to ward off feelings of helplessness, and to facilitate adaptation. The continuum of stress responses varies from successful adaptation with the individual's restoration of trust in coping ability to a sense of being overwhelmed by the traumatic situation. There are intrinsic and extrinsic mechanisms, rational and irrational processes by which the individual attempts to contain the feelings of helplessness and to promote effective coping behavior. A number of critical processes enable a person to maintain a sense of being in control and to preserve a sense of safety; these include biological resilience, self-confidence in adaptive skills, cognitive flexibility, realistic capacity to appraise danger, mature defense constellations, adaptive characterological structures, and narcissistically vital defenses. The spectrum of stress-related disorders emerges out of the failure of adaptation to the traumatic situation.

REFERENCES

Appel, J. W., & Beebe, G. W. (1946). Preventive psychiatry. *Journal of the American Medical Association, 131,* 1469–1476.

Arroyo, W. & Eth, S. (1985). Children traumatized by Central American warfare. In S. Eth & R. Pynoos (Eds.), *Post-traumatic stress disorder in children* (pp. 103–120). Washington, DC: American Psychiatric Press.

Becker, E. (1973). *Denial of death.* New York: The Free Press.

Belenky, G., Tyner, F. G., & Sodetz, F. J. (1983). *Israeli battle shock casualties, 1973 and 1982.* Washington, DC: Walter Reed Army Institute of Research.

Blum, H. (1984). Splitting of the ego and its relation to parent loss. *Journal of the American Psychiatric Association, 32,* 301–324.

Bond, D. D. (1953). The common psychological defense to stressful situations and the patterns of breakdown when they fail. In *Symposium on Stress* (pp. 142–152). Walter Reed Army Medical Center. Washington DC: U.S. Government Printing Office.

Breznitz-Svidovsky, T. (1982). Israeli women on the home front. In C. D. Spielberger & N. A. Milgram (Eds.), *Stress and anxiety* (Vol. 8, pp. 117–122). New York: Hemisphere Publishing.

Carlin, J. E. (1979). Southeast Asian refugee children. In J. Noshpitz (Ed.), *Basic handbook of child psychiatry: Vol. 1. Development* (pp. 290–300). New York: Basic Books.

Carlin, J. E. (1980, May). *Boat and land refugees: Mental health implications, for the recent arrival compared with earlier arrivals.* Paper presented at the meeting of the American Psychiatric Association, San Francisco.

Danieli, Y. (1982). Families of survivors of the Nazi Holocaust: Some short and long-term effects. In C. D. Spielberger & N. A. Milgram (Eds.), *Stress and anxiety* (Vol. 8, pp. 405–422). New York: Hemisphere Publishing.

Department of the Army. (1966). *Neuropsychiatry in World War II* (Vol. 1). Zone of interior, office of the surgeon general. Washington, DC: Author.

Deutsch, A. (1944). Military psychiatry: The Civil War, 1861–1865. In *American psychiatry 1844-1944* (p. 376). New York: Columbia University Press.

Dyregrov, A., Raundalen, M., Lwanga, J., & Mugisha, C. (1987, October). *Children and war.* Paper presented at the annual meeting of the Society for Traumatic Stress Studies, Baltimore.

Figley, C. (Ed.). (1978). *Stress disorders among Vietnam veterans.* New York: Brunner Mazel.

Freud, A., & Burlingham, D. T. (1943). *War and children* (Medical War Books). New York: Ernst Willard.

Freud, S. (1955a). *Inhibitions, symptoms, and anxiety.* In J. Strachey (Ed.), *The standard edition of the complete works of Sigmund Freud* (Vol. XX). London, Hogarth Press. (Original work published 1926)

Freud, S. (1955b). Interpretation of dreams. In J. Strachey (Ed.), *The standard edition of the complete works of Sigmund Freud* (Vol. 4). London: Hogarth Press. (Original work published 1900)

Freud, S. (1955c). Moses and monotheism. In J. Strachey (Ed.), *The standard edition of the complete works of Sigmund Freud* (Vol. 23). London: Hogarth Press. (Original work published 1955)

Gillespie, R. D. (1942). *Psychological effects of war on citizen and soldier.* New York: Norton.

Glass, A. J. (1951). Combat exhaustion. *U.S. Armed Forces Medical Journal, 2,* 1, 471.

Glass, A. J. (1953). The problem of stress in the combat zone. In *Symposium on Stress* (pp. 90–102). Walter Reed Army Medical Center. Washington DC: U.S. Government Printing Office.

Glass, A. J. (1957). Observations upon the epidemiology of mental illness, in troops during warfare. In *Symposium on preventive and social psychiatry* (pp. 185–198). Walter Reed Army Institute of Research, Walter Reed Army Medical Center. Washington DC: U.S. Government Printing Office.

Gleser, G. C., Green, B. L., & Winget, C. N. (1981). *Prolonged psychosocial effects of disaster: A study of Buffalo Creek.* New York: Academic Press.

Greenacre, P. (1971). The Influence of infantile trauma on genetic patterns. In *Emotional growth* (Vol. 1, pp. 260–299). New York: International Universities Press. (Original work published 1945)

Grinker, R., & Spiegel, J. (1945). *Men under stress.* New York: McGraw Hill.

Hamilton, E. (1942). *The Greek way.* New York: Modern Library.

Jones, F. D. (1981). Combat stress: Tripartite model. *International Review of the Army, Navy and Air Force Medical Services, 54,* 247–254.

Kardiner, A., & Spiegel, H. (1947). *War stress and neurotic illness.* New York: Paul B. Hoeber.

Kirschner, E. (1982). Data on bereavement and rehabilitation of war widows. In C. A. Spielberger & N. A. Milgram (Eds.), *Stress and anxiety* (Vol. 8, pp. 219–224). New York: Hemisphere Publishing.

Kolb, L. A. (1984). The post-traumatic stress disorders of combat: A subgroup with a conditioned emotional response. *Military Medicine, 149,* 237–243.

Laufer, R. S., Brett, E., & Gallops, M. S. (1984). Post-traumatic stress disorder (PTSD) reconsidered: PTSD among Vietnam veterans. In B. A. Van Der Kolk (Ed.), *Post-traumatic stress disorder: Psychological and biological sequelae.* Washington DC: American Psychiatric Press.

Lin, K., Masuda, M., & Tazuma, L. (1984). Problems of Eastern refugees and immigrants: Adaptational problems of Vietnamese refugees, Part IV. *Psychiatric Journal of the University of Ottawa, 9,* 79–84.

Manchester, W. (1979). *Goodbye darkness: A memoir of the Pacific war.* Boston: Little, Brown.

Masserman, J. (1955). *The practice of dynamic psychiatry.* Philadelphia: Saunders.

Menninger, W. C. (1948). *Psychiatry in a troubled world.* New York: Macmillan.

Moore, B. E., & Fine, B. D. (Eds.). (1967). *A glossary of psychoanalytic terms and concepts.* New York: American Psychoanalytic Association.

Rofe, Y., & Lewin, I. (1982). *The effect of the war environment on dream and sleep habits.* In C. D. Spielberger & N. A. Milgram (Eds.), *Stress and anxiety* (Vol. 8, pp. 67–80). New York: Hemisphere Publishing.

Rosenblatt, R. (1983). *Children of war.* Garden City, NJ: Anchor Press/Doubleday.

Sack, W. H., Angell, R. H., & Kinzie, J. D. (1986). The psychiatric effects of massive trauma on Cambodian children: II. The family, the home, and the school. *Journal of the American Academy of Child & Adolescent Psychiatry, 25,* 377–383.

Schwartz, H. (Ed.). (1984). *Psychotherapy of the combat veteran.* New York: Spectrum Publications.

Shaw, J. A. (1983). Comments on the individual psychology of combat exhaustion. *Military Medicine, 148,* 223–231.

Shaw, J. A. (1987). Psychodynamic considerations in the adaptation to combat. In G. Belenky (Ed.), *Contemporary studies in combat psychiatry* (pp. 117–132). New York: Greenwood Press.

Shaw, J. A. (1985, May). *The traumatic situation and psychic truama.* Paper presented at the meeting of the American Psychiatric Association, Dallas, TX.

Shaw, J., & Harris, J. (1988). *Children of war in Mozambique.* Unpublished manuscript.

Shawcross, W. (1984, September 2). Too many Holocausts have made mankind numb (Editorial). *Washington Post.*

Solomon, Z., Schwarzwald, J., & Weisenberg, M. (1985, June). *Mental health sequelae along Israeli soldiers, in the 1982 Lebanon War.* Medical Corps Department of Mental Health. Tel-Aviv: The Israel Defense Forces.

Swank, R. L., & Marchand, F. (1946). Combat neuroses: Development of combat exhaustion. *Archives of Neurology and Psychiatry, 55,* 236–247.

Terr, L. (1983). Chowchilla revisited: The effects of psychic trauma four years after a school bus kidnapping. *American Journal of Psychiatry, 140,* 1543–1550.

Tyhurst, J. S. (1951). Individual reactions to community disaster, The natural history of psychiatric phenomena. *American Journal of Psychiatry, 107,* 764–769.

Van Der Kolk, B. A. (Ed.). (1984). *Post-traumatic stress disorder: Psychological and biological sequelae.* Washington DC: American Psychiatric Association.

Wolfenstein, M. (1969). Loss, rage, and repetition. *Psychoanalytic Study of the Child, 24,* 432–462.

Ziv, A., & Israeli, R. (1973). Effects of bombardment on the manifest anxiety level of children living in kibbutzim. *Journal of Counseling & Clinical Psychology, 40,* 287–291.

Ziv, A., Kruglanski, A., & Shulman, S. (1974). Children's psychological reactions to wartime stress. *Journal of Personality & Social Psychology, 30,* 24–30.

Zuckerman-Bareli, C. (1982). Effects of border tension on the adjustment of kibbutzim and moshavim on the northern border of Israel: A path analysis. In C. D. Spielberger & N. A. Milgram (Eds.), *Stress and anxiety* (Vol. 8, pp. 81–91). New York: Hemisphere Publishing.

── CHAPTER 18 ──────────────────────────

Prejudice and Exclusion as Social Traumata

PAUL L. ADAMS, MD

Among the social traumata in the current societal scene, exclusion and prejudice, having structural as well as mentalistic aspects, are high in both prevalence and pathogenicity. Exclusion and prejudice take many forms. Prejudice and discrimination are usually based on ethnicity and so are designated as racism, but a broader application includes classism, sexism, and ageism (or "childism," which is ageism mobilized against young people). Many rhetoricians have designated antiblack racism to be the paradigmatic expression of discrimination and in an effort to validate their claims, have compared every oppressed group to blacks, thus describing women (or members of the lower class, children, or the elderly) as "niggers." Pierce and Allen (1975), however, have viewed childism as the prototypic form of oppression, the model and precursor of all others. Their logic is arresting and persuasive.

Prejudice and exclusion have come to be regarded as social traumata by American psychiatry. This chapter first considers changing styles of conceptualizing racism; then discusses an epidemiologic approach to racism, with some examples of individualized and institutionalized racism; and concludes with a look at racism in DSM-III diagnoses, in psychiatric services, and in recent literature.

CHANGES IN RESEARCH FOCUSES

Research into discrimination and prejudice surged to the forefront of investigative efforts between 1940 and 1970 and abated to some extent thereafter. This does not mean that discrimination has vanished, but only that it currently is not a well-funded, hot topic for study; it is not a topic for which leading politicians are amenable or "ready." The National Institute of Mental Health (NIMH) reduced support of scholarly or service projects aimed at easing discrimination. The NIMH-funded Epidemiologic Catchment Area studies in five centers (1979–1985) gave no direct heed to racism, Adjustment Disorders, or even generalized anxiety.

Not being well-funded and therefore not fiscally encouraged, discrimination research is rather sparse on the contemporary scene; accordingly, earlier decades provide the most substantial contributions. From 1940 through 1970, research—even when anecdotal, impressionistic, and inductive—was powerful in consequence. The ruling in *Brown vs. The Board of Education of Topeka, Kansas* (1954) and related cases showed how potent the scholarly work of social psychologists could become. In that instance, it made an impact on amenable Supreme Court justices.

The tenor of the times was markedly different in the 1940s, 1950s, and 1960s than in succeeding years; it is exemplified by books such as *Patterns of Negro Segregation* (Johnson, 1943), *An American Dilemma* (Myrdal, 1944), or *The Nature of Prejudice* (Allport, 1954). Other notable works of the period are *Black Skin, White Masks* (Fanon, 1967) and *The Wretched of the Earth* (Fanon, 1966) or the more encyclopedic *American Negro Reference Book* (Davis, 1966). The Johnson (1943) work cited four main patterns of blacks' responses to racial segregation: acceptance, avoidance, direct hostility and aggression, and indirect or deflected hostility. By the 1960s, many participants in black liberation struggles refuted the idea that discrimination could be accepted by even a few individuals, because to accept it required a profound self-hatred. However, by 1980, although government leaders would not say openly that discriminated people *accepted* their oppression, as policy-makers they counted on this acceptance and were pleased to observe that minority groups had declined in open militancy.

Prejudicial exclusion is, even if neglected, a potent psychosocial stressor impinging on the daily lives of many Americans and interfering with their mental and social adaptation and adjustment. This is clear in Powell, Yamamoto, Romero, and Morales (1983). Racism has two forms: attitudinal (Grossack, 1954; McConahay & Hough, 1976) and structural (Kluegel & Smith, 1983). Attitudinal racism is evidenced in prejudicial ideologies, contempt, insults, jokes, hatred, and the belief that ethnic minorities are a sinister detriment to the fabric of good American culture. Structural racism exists whenever the ethnic or racial minority is unable to attain equal survival chances within the society. Structural racism can best be documented by differential statistics in the economic realm, including health statistics, but attitudinal racism requires documentation by public opinion polls and related kinds

of attitudinal interviews or surveys. The practicing psychiatrist with social sophis-
tication knows how to discern both types of racist oppression in patients. Perhaps
there has been no fuller explication than by Pinderhughes (1968, 1969, 1970, 1971,
1976), of the ways in which dominant groups utilize projections and other distortions
when encountering groups and individuals with "stranger" characteristics. Projective identification, splitting, denial, identification with the aggressor, role reversal,
repression, narcissistic identification, isolation of affect, displacement, renunciation, intellectualization with illusions, delusions, and stereotypic self-fulfilling
prophecies—all come into play when racism in either attitudinal or structural forms
enters to buttress oppression. Pinderhughes (1976) noted:

> We can observe similar dynamics in the interactions between men and women, rich
> and poor, management and labor, college administrators and students, whites and
> blacks, colonial powers and their colonies, and adults and children. (p. 153)

Any groups of people who are vulnerable to discrimination could be suitable
subjects for discussion here—women, the chronic poor, children, the elderly, and
Hispanic- or Asian- or Jewish-Americans. But because the "best case" (and the
case most often considered in mental health journals) is that of the black- or African-
American, this discussion will consider blacks first and Jews second, with American
Indians, Japanese-Americans, and Hispanic-Americans tying for a close third. (See
Table 18.1, later in this chapter for a frequency count of 70 articles concerning
varied ethnic groups published from 1969–1984 in mental health journals.)

By the late 1980s, fashions in terminology had shifted so that preferred usage
had come to be "African-American," "black, " "Black," or "Afro-American"
rather than "Negro," (with "colored" stricken from most lists of acceptable no-
menclature). This trend was discovered early in the 1970s when the Phelps-Stokes
Fund surveyed 46 publications aimed at "persons of African descent" (Smythe,
1976). The literature in the medical, psychiatric, and behavioral science world
paralleled the terms used in popular black publications. By 1968, two black American psychiatrists published *Black Rage* (Grier & Cobbs, 1968). Simultaneously,
while the publications of mainstream psychiatry adopted black as their most commonly used appellation for "persons of African descent," a reaction arose within
professional associations, so that efforts were now directed to curb and contain the
vociferousness of black caucuses, Hispanic psychiatrists, radical caucuses, and gay
and lesbian groups, and to return psychiatry to the medical mainstream, thereby
minimizing emphasis on societal and psychosocial factors.

More and more often, by the 1970s, it was said that psychiatry could not change
the world, despite child advocacy's having been the summary challenge of efforts
like the Joint Commission on the Mental Health of Children late in the 1960s.
Combining an emphasis on biological and empirically based psychiatry with a
diminution of psychosocial emphases, the American Psychiatric Association and
other professional groups nonetheless condemned racial prejudice and made active
attempts to integrate groups of ethnic minority psychiatrists into regular Committee

status within their organizations. Yet, oddly, by 1985, the officers and trustees of the American Psychiatric Association were conspicuously lacking in black faces and Hispanic intonations.

Academic psychiatry departments are always more sensitive to granted funds than are professional associations whose membership is composed of many clinical practitioners. The departments quickly reshaped themselves into biologically geared entities, boosting work in consultation and liaison with other specialty departments, and recruiting the available biochemical or psychopharmacological workers who could be wooed into academic psychiatry. Such academic departments often persisted in giving verbal encomiums for the "biopsychosocial model," but insiders as well as independent observers acknowledged that their deepest commitment was only for the "bio" part of the term. In rare instances, some biologically strong departments did not feel driven to confine their reverence to chemical efforts. They began to build sound programs in behavioral sciences, psychotherapies, and pathogenesis and thus to move toward realizing the promise of truly eclectic and broad-based departments of psychiatry. Through epidemiology, "all was not lost."

FOCUS ON EPIDEMIOLOGY

In all of these events and trends of the 1970s and 1980s, discrimination research diminished. It lost status and it lost funding. Instead, psychiatry began to foster the epidemiologic approach to mental disorders; this had been established during the 1950s and 1960s but began its true ascendancy during the 1970s and 1980s. A major text by Schwab and Schwab (1976), entitled *Sociocultural Roots of Mental Illness: An Epidemiologic Survey,* reviewed the recent history of social psychiatry within the more generic field of psychiatry and used the epidemiologic approach as the now-preferred route for linking social to individual pathology. The last president of the American Psychiatric Association to state any preferences for the social model of psychiatry was Alan Stone (1980). Stone characterized the dynamic, biologic, behavioral, and social models and declared that the social was the more fruitful. But for the most part, psychiatric officials today contend that psychiatry cannot offer solutions for the vast social ills afflicting our nation. In 1973, Ransom Arthur had predicted a parting of the ways for the social model and biological psychiatry, asserting that a new, nonmedical specialty would emerge with its own approaches to the solution of mental health problems and leave psychiatry to become a firmer biomedical specialty. What Arthur did not foresee was the capability for expedient adaptability to market conditions, especially within academic departments, that has enabled epidemiologists and social scientists to enter these services, to take up work hand-in-glove with their more biologically oriented colleagues, and to make salutary contributions and modifications to the ongoing efforts.

Discrimination research may owe its future achievements to psychiatric epidemiology and the related disciplines. Likewise, past discrimination research may be faulted on conceptual, axiomatic, methodologic, and technologic grounds whereas future investigative undertakings will be regarded as credible, even praiseworthy, only to the extent that they employ all the terms and metaphors of the epidemiologic approach.

Epidemiology, with its focus on cases of disease and disorder, may be another instance of medicalizing deviance. However, it does hold out the promise of helping to provide a broad perspective on sociocultural (not just ''biosocial'' or ''psycho-social'') causes and correlates of human agony and suffering. Therefore, in what follows I shall attempt to use epidemiologic terminology. In any case, this has long been held to be the only safe and respectable way to sneak social criticism into medicine.

Social Stressors and Psychopathology

Victimization by racism, whether in its institutionalized or individualized forms, is expressed in a contemporary vocabulary as *living with psychosocial stress* (Axis IV in the *Diagnostic and Statistical Manual of Mental Disorders,* 3rd ed.-revised [DSM-III-R] (American Psychiatric Association, 1987).

In DSM-III-R (American Psychiatric Association, 1987) psychiatric imputation of causes to psychosocial stressors is spelled out most fully in ''Reactive Attachment Disorder of Infancy,'' where the etiologic stressors are *not* spelled out on Axis IV but are made integral to the Axis I diagnostic criteria themselves. That inclusion of known causes or provocations may be surprising in a taxonomy, but in a clinical diagnostic manual the specification of known precipitating stress (in this instance, neglect and rejection with failure in attachment and bonding) promises to clarify and to assist clinical workers. Racism, being diffused into institutional life, may be harder to grasp in the particular case of Adjustment Disorders and reactive disorders. However, if psychiatrists inquire, they will learn that racism is a potent stressor in individuals' disorders. Certainly, the clinical child psychiatrist cannot escape racism's pertinence in black and Hispanic children who are excluded so frequently from schools, suspended, assigned to special education and discipline programs, and regarded as stupid, slow learners in a self-fulfilling prophecy. At times, actual reactive disorders of fear, anger, and perplexity, with sudden losses of self-esteem, are seen in children from ethnic minorities who are subjected to prejudices and discrimination (Powell, Yamamoto, Romero, & Morales, 1983). For some groups of people, psychosocial stresses become so regular, chronic, and additively severe that they are said to make such people more vulnerable to psychopathology and to place them at significantly greater risk. *Vulnerability, at risk,* and other items in the epidemiologic lexicon need to be explained briefly.

Terminology for Psychosocial Noxae

The general term for normlessness, lack of social norms, lack of integration, and conflicting and equally potent alternative forms of institutional life remains *anomia* or *anomy,* derived from the French *anomie* made so popular by Emile Durkheim in his classic study, *Le Suicide* (1897/1951).

From the perspective of the individual, anomia is *alienation,* a term whose contemporary meaning is derived from the writings of the young Karl Marx (1961). Alienation denotes feelings of estrangement from oneself, intimacy with others, natural surroundings, and vocation (the work a person has sought out). Fromm (1962) stated that Freud's "transference" content was explicable by the nature of one's infantile life; but for its intensity the transference depended on the extent of one's alienation in all spheres of living, not on infancy alone. Hence, the alienating traumata for infancy and the alienation of subsequent life would together, but neither alone, account for the establishment of and final intensity of transference distortions that are seen in psychoanalysis. The analyst makes a comprehensive assessment of the patient's estrangement in work, self-regard, intimate relationships, and the natural world in order to account more fully for the transference reactions presented in treatment. Racism, plausibly, can pervade each of these parameters of the patient's life.

Marginality is one recurrent form of alienation that the psychiatrist who studies racial, sexual, and age discrimination finds of interest. Marginality first assumed its current referents in the work of Park (1926) and Davis and Barnes (1927). Although these writers used "marginal" to describe an *area* in which cultural traits from adjacent areas meet and produce a "mixed type of culture at the margins," their successors were quick to point out that people who were not typical of either of the two mixed cultures—and who had part of both but not all of either—were "marginal" men and women. Recently immigrated ethnic groups, yuppies, the black bourgeoisie, adolescents, Americans for whom English is a second language, all have been so characterized, neither fish nor fowl, but marginal and alienated (see *The Marginal Man,* Stonequist, 1937, for the classic presentation of both racial and cultural marginality). Some form of marginality is apparent in the demoralization of almost every "ethnic" patient described in the book *Psychotherapy and Culture Conflict* (Seward, 1956). Being marginally placed adds precariousness to each such patient's mental health: the Jew who is a closet Nazi, the woman longing to be male, the black who dreams of being white. Racism has been incorporated, abetted by marginal status.

Morbidity risk is the epidemiologic term for the chances that individuals or groups (host) will become ill when they contact environmental noxae (disease agents in the environment). Hence, it is a calculation reflecting the strengths and protections built up within the host (host resistance) as well as the virulence or pathogenicity (toxicity) of the disease agents in both treated and untreated cases. Because both host and disease agent interact with their respective or shared surroundings (environment), the characteristics of milieus must enter into the calculus to give the famous epidemiologic triad of host-agent-environment (Cassel, 1976), that must be considered in any disorder. Morbidity risk may or may not be more general than *caseness,* that is, becoming an identified case of a host who succumbed to the disease and met most of the generally agreed-on criteria for such disease or disorder. Examples of prejudice and exclusion adding to morbidity risk will be given later.

Vulnerability has some of the same reference points as morbidity risk (being at risk), but, in most literature, it connotes an increment of precariousness and endangerment. Yet, caseness and morbidity rates are the ultimate quantitative indices for vulnerability. Morbidity risk varies according to certain host, agent, and environment conditions. On the basis of morbidity expectations for their age group, economic class, skin color, urban center-city residence, and so on, some black children, for example, eventually contribute to the expected statistical norm of delinquency and are called vulnerable, whereas others do not live up to and, indeed, defy the predictors of pathology—and consequently are called invulnerable.

Vulnerability appraised throughout the life cycle of humans may manifest alternating patterns of crises and challenge. The so-called signposts, or landmarks, of vulnerability are nothing more than the hazardous crises and transitions in the various developmental phases—birth and separation from the mother; stranger anxiety; language development; toilet training; perennial encounters with irrational authority; the birth of a sibling; phallic oedipal strivings; school experiences; the forming of non-blood-related acquaintanceships, associations, and chumships; accidents; family conflict and parental divorce; solitude or loneliness; adolescence and identity crises, the experiences of getting a job and leaving home, development of intimate and loving relationships, parenthood, loss of one's parents, children leaving home, threats of job loss, menopause, retirement, dying. Small wonder that the life cycle has been compared, rakishly, to a fatal illness full of intercurrent horrors, or that developmental psychiatry has come to be problem oriented, stressing danger and disorder. Undoubtedly, psychiatry has been prompted to consider childism, classism, racism, and sexism as environmental conditions that hammer at their victims so fiercely that only relatively invulnerable persons can make it through life crises without serious morbidity.

Life events and weighted events called *life crisis units* (LCUs) are ways of quantifying many of the traumatic episodes that beset the human life cycle (Rahe, 1975). Simply put, LCUs can be added up as a metric for the total stress an individual has sustained during the past year or month. *Stress,* then, is the concept that explains how sociocultural conditions drive people mad. Psychosocial stress is almost a catchphrase today for all the sociogenic or nonphysical sources of human suffering. Is racism a psychosocial stress? is a question needing to be addressed in clinical psychiatry.

True to the physicist's analogy, stresses from the environment are said, in the parlance of epidemiology, to lead to *strains* (or the more medical cognates of *disability, deficit, impairment,* or *deformation*) when the affected person is harmed by the given stresses. In a more subjective vein, it is often said that the stressed individual, in the process of becoming strained, feels *distress* or *dysphoria.*

Hassles are the minor annoyances and burdens that beset daily life. When they are numerous, they have been reported to lead to even greater strain and disability than do LCUs or stresses (Kanner, Coyne, Schaefer, & Lazarus, 1981).

Protection against Stress and Disease

The epidemiologic lexicon contains many terms for the factors that reinforce host resistance to environmental noxae. Margaret Morgan Lawrence in her book, *Young Inner City Families: Development of Ego Strength under Stress* (1975), showed how urban black families under the most deprived circumstances can encircle their members protectively and sustain their mental health. This section, will offer some examples of these protectors of young minority group members from stress and disorder, ranging from very general to specific conditions.

The best general protective condition to stave off anomia is its opposite, *the rule of norms*. Whether religiously or secularly cast, a sense of tradition has served as a bulwark for many discriminated youths in a derogating and persecuting world. A sense of tribal pride from belonging to an ancient tradition has been salutary to many young black, Jewish, and Hispanic patients buffeted by racism. Similarly, the Asian-American who can claim and embrace a civilization or religion that predated the Western ones has been imbued with a protective identity that both defends and enables positive growth. When the "Tex-Mex" male child who is short of stature and loses fist fights at school looks beyond his Hispanic roots to state philosophically, "Not all the Aztecs were big and tall," he has penetrated to a heritage-norm that will be beneficial for his future. The black woman who can attest to the following form of ethnic pride is advantaged psychologically (Gwaltney, 1980):

I have always been conscious of a kind of pride—not this kind of pride they got in the streets now. It was that real pride from knowing who you were. My grandfather made me feel that way before I was a teenager. It had something to do with knowing where you had come from and knowing your family's history. He made me conscious of the fact that I was black and that I had a history like everybody else. That was something different than the garbage they handed out in school that kept telling us how much we owed Lincoln. (pp. 237–238)

Acceptance by others in an atmosphere of pluralism and equality leads to self-acceptance and to feelings of belonging. Ideally, a society characterized by an absence of racism would grant equality to both black and Jew. Such, however, is not the case in late 20th-century America, and the social fact is that this mode of strengthening host resistance is not accessible. The issue in prejudice and discrimination is precisely that the critical element of acceptance is lacking. Fortunately, acceptance by one's own ethnic group may offer at least partial compensation.

Personal traits of the host can contribute to some resistance to stress and strain. *Resiliency* or invulnerability is a summation of all those personal attributes that enable the black, the Jew, and other discriminated groups to achieve some degree of mental health. To whatever degree a minority patient's personal integration and self-acceptance exist, the individual's resources and adaptive assets, such as coping strategies and ego strengths, are enhanced. In poetry, Gwendolyn Brooks (1949) perceived this relative invulnerability of Chicago's black and poor, when she wrote:

His lesions are legion,
But reaching is his rule.

In clinical psychiatry, the existence of a relatively adaptive premorbid personality is assumed to aid the individual recovering from a state of severe disturbance to return to his or her former level of coping and stronger ego functioning.

But some very important mediators or buffers that aid and protect the victims of discrimination do not always reside in the individual. An array of supportive interpersonal networks is also a very strong buffer, especially against racism. These support systems are vital for the psychiatric rehabilitation of the mentally disordered, in crisis interventions, and in immunizing the individual against future morbidity. They are often thought to account for blacks' high first, but low subsequent, admission rates to mental hospitals. Supportive networks for black individuals and families have received continuing attention (Lindblad-Goldberg & Dukes, 1985).

The lack of a socially supportive floor under them has been invoked as one of the conditions accounting for the greater incidence of adjustment and other mental disorders among the more than 100,000 Cuban refugees who came after 1979 to the United States. They were the youngest wave of Cubans ever to seek refuge, but they also were more often black. Even if they had been castigated in Cuba as maladjusted, discontented, incompetent *Lumpenproletarians*—some of them from mental hospitals and correctional facilities—they discovered, on arrival in the United States that governmental subsidies here for Cuban refugees were paltry or absent, in contrast to the munificence that greeted the first wave of mainly affluent, white Cubans in the 1950s. The *Marielitos* (itself a derogatory term) had mostly grown up under a regime that had provided for the basic economic wants of all, with little discrimination against youths, blacks, and integrated members of the lower class. Their culture shock on arriving here was compounded by racism and a lack of social supports (Bernal, 1982). They were reviled and rejected by Cubans, U.S. blacks and Anglos, and Jews. Endowed with resiliency by their youth and aspirations, without social supports and few opportunities for employment, they drifted after arriving in the United States, unable to enculturate and to survive through the aboveground labor market. Mental disorders recurred because of their stressful encounters with societal conditions.

Sociocultural Resources Support Host Resistance

As later vignettes will exemplify, even under a regime of exclusion and prejudice, sociocultural advantages and supplies can mitigate noxae to some degree. Both the noxious agent and the supportive network derive from the sociocultural environment, which is in turn the very source from which the host originates. So psychiatric epidemiology is a little more complex than infectious disease epidemiology, and linear cause-to-effect explanations are too simplistic to be useful in accounting for psychiatric disturbances. Wade Hampton Frost (cited by Cassel, 1976) believed:

Epidemiology at any given time is something more than the total of its established facts. It includes their orderly arrangement into chains of inference which extend beyond the bounds of direct observation. (p. 107)

Cassel (1976) agreed with Frost and averred that these chains of inference separate "creative epidemiologic studies from studies which may display considerable rigor in their methods but which are essentially pedestrian" (p. 107).

Etiologic discourse about mental disorders reflects some of the complexity of its subject matter: A complete dynamic assessment of causation requires consideration of background circumstances that may predispose the host to become a case of disorder when certain triggering or precipitating conditions are met. Clear delineation of proximate and remote causes, as well as necessary and sufficient conditions, and the invoking of an ecological approach often make it indispensable for the psychiatric epidemiologist to adopt systems as a frame of reference. Otherwise a search for causes or even for relatively invariant correlates is fraught with logical and empirical hazards.

RACISM EXEMPLIFIES PSYCHOSOCIAL NOXAE

Institutionalized Racism: Indices and Markers

No discrete line demarcates individualized racism from the institutionalized form because, by definition, an institution consists of recurrent and predictable behavior of individuals carrying out preset roles in interaction with one another. Institutionalized racism ceases to be a matter of mental prejudice and becomes a patterned routine of exclusionary and exploitative behavior, a part of the structured social system with an ideology and physical apparatus to support the racist institution.

Institutionalized racism oppresses its victims by curbing that victim's survival chances in a variety of ways: first, to prosper economically; second, to be treated with the esteem and honor of someone fully and unquestionably human; and, finally, to exercise power and influence on a basis of equality with the ruling majority. According to Weber (1964) any analysis of hierarchy or stratification must attend to these three forms of opportunity separately—*economic life chances, honor chances,* and *power chances;* this distribution of advantages is often dispensed in modern societies according to class, status, and party. The psychiatrist usually neglects the study of socioculturally structured patterns of discrimination because of greater interest in individualized racism.

Individualized Racism: Indices and Markers

Because novels and other forms of popular literature and entertainment have addressed the individualized forms of racist prejudice and exclusion, such writings will be cited in some of the discussion that follows. Generally speaking, moving personalized statements on racism have appeared in the instruments of mass culture before such topics were mentioned in the psychiatric literature. Hence, it seems fair to say that psychiatry's concern for racism's impact on the individual has not been early to appear or avant-garde in thrust; if anything, it was voiced late and was given to understatement. The principal mechanisms whereby individualized racism operates are splitting, denial, projective identification, role reversal, identification with the aggressor, and narcissistic identification. These defensive mechanisms appear throughout the following examples of individualized racism.

Teasing, Belittling, Ridiculing, Disparaging. Ethnic teasing presupposes stereotyping and familiarity with the stereotype; thus some sharing of knowledge about prejudice is a necessity before teasing occurs between victimizer and victim. Racial jokes too are predicated on rigid stereotypes; by the same token, black or Jewish humor utilizes the racist stereotypes but often gives them a twist that surprisingly and comically elevates or adds to the status of the black or Jew.

In *Black Boy* Richard Wright (1945) summed up the unfunny sting of being teased in this way:

> "Nigger, do you think you'll ever amount to anything?" he asked in a slow, sadistic voice.
> "I don't know, sir," I answered, turning my head away.
> "What do niggers think about?" he asked.
> "I don't know, sir," I said, my head still averted.
> "If I was a nigger, I'd kill myself," he said. I said nothing. I was angry. (pp. 164–165)

This form of teasing and disparaging can take flight only from a springboard of racist ideology. Both in slavery and in the Reagan era, blacks and Jews have been held, by racist criteria, to be inferior, and their exploitation by superiors to be appropriate and acceptable. Oddly, the black slavery in which 75% of white Southerners took no part disappeared, but its racist ideology and practices have persisted (Gaertner & McLaughlin, 1983).

Labeling, Stereotyping, Stigmatizing, Derogating. Even though the children's taunting retort contends "Names will never hurt me," the appellation of "nigger" or "kike"—or "brat," "cunt," "trash," "dago," "mick," "hunkie," "spick," "squarehead," "wop," "kraut," "limey," "chink," and "Jap"—is insulting and offensive to the individual so designated. The word "damn" placed before the ethnically disparaging name compounds the injury.

A psychiatrist who grew up in a Jewish family, within a working-class, largely Polish Catholic neighborhood in a large eastern industrial city, recalls being routinely called "sheeny," as well as "kike," "Christ-killer," and "jewboy." The name-calling started when, at the age of 4 years, he began to appear in the streets alone. Moreover, he recalled that a store, dubbed "the candy store" by his family, was known to their non-Jewish neighbors as "the Jew store." For a person to be labeled inferior thoughout the life cycle can create stress and, often, pathology. As an adult, that psychiatrist, although religiously pallid, was pro-Zionist and feared at times a resurgence of antisemitic holocausts. Some ingredients of a partial Post-traumatic Stress Disorder lingered.

Scapegoating, Dehumanizing. Benjamin Kaplan (1967) stated succinctly how scapegoating emerges:

> Prejudice is the tendency to transfer guilt and blame from person to person and from group to group. The causes of prejudice are frustration, guilt, fear, anxiety and need for self-glorification. When we persecute a minority group we project on them the burden of our own sins and by punishing them we hope to expiate our own guilt. (p. 73)

Adorno and colleagues (1950) also depicted scapegoating as a person's alienated response to frustration—usually of economic wants:

> . . . and then, being unable due to intellectual confusion to tell the real causes of his difficulty, he lashes out about him, as it were, venting his fury upon whatever object is available and not too likely to strike back. (p. 233)

Jews are said by Noshpitz (1979) and Allport (1954) to have originated the term *scapegoat* and to have employed a goat literally as a bearer of the sins of the populace. Subsequently, however, Jews have sometimes contended that they are the scapegoat for all humanity, the victims of oppression by projection and displacement. Allport acknowledged, "Psychological theory alone will not tell us why certain groups are scapegoated more than others" (p. 244), so sociocultural constructs must be invoked. Patterns of immigration, for example, help explain nationality-based prejudice, and the historical fact that Jews have fared worse at the hands of Christians than at the hands of Moslems or other religious communities contributes to understanding why Jews have been almost the all-purpose scapegoats for antisemitic Christians.

Dehumanizing of victims of racial and religious hatred, as a cognitive-affective-behavioral device, has been described in relation to class and national enemies by Adams (1972), Bernard, Ottenberg, and Redl (1963), and Buber (1952). Buber articulated the viewpoint that dehumanization, the conversion of a fellow human being into a nonhuman thing, is a delusional transformation that has to be made by any potential killer. Thus it was that Trotsky advised the Bolshevik soldiers to fire on their comrades, the sailors who staged the Kronstadt rebellion, *thinking of them not as rebellious former comrades but as partridges.* Conceived as dehumanized beings, the sailors could be murdered with dispatch, and it was easy to quell the rebellion. But as Bernard and her coauthors knew, those individuals who

can by a willful delusion convert other human beings into things can come presently
to perceive themselves too as dehumanized things. Other-directed dehumanization
facilitates self-directed dehumanization. They are two forms of alienation, at times
bordering on madness within the perpetrator.

The victim too is stressed, made vulnerable, by an episode of dehumanization.
In 1845 Frederick Douglass (cited in Davis & Walden, 1970) wrote of the numbing
from chronic dehumanizing stress in his enslavement by one Mr. Covey:

> I was somewhat unmanageable when I first went there, but a few months of this
> discipline tamed me. Mr. Covey succeeded in breaking me. I was broken in body,
> soul, and spirit. My natural elasticity was crushed, my intellect languished, the dis-
> position to read departed, the cheerful spark that lingered about my eye died; the dark
> night of slavery closed in upon me; and behold a man transformed into a brute! (pp.
> 49–50)

Dehumanization for being a black child, oppressed on both counts, traumatized
this young adult male informant whose father was white (Gwaltney, 1980):

> Things hardly ever happened in a clear-cut way so that I could say, "Oh, that's what
> is happening" or "That's what I am doing!" . . . Things just happened to you and
> you didn't know how important they were. . . . When I was a child and an adult
> molested me, sexually or in hundreds of other ways, I never resisted because I didn't
> have any idea that I had some rights over my own body . . . people were handling
> my *mind* without my permission! Not only without my permission! The worst thing
> was that they were manipulating me without my *knowledge*. . . . My father never
> talked to me without trying to manipulate me. . . . My father regarded my mind as
> an enemy and he had to suppress it to assure himself that he was in control of my
> body. In that respect he was like all white men I have ever known. (pp. 44–45)

Ignoring, Neglecting, Looking Away. In *Invisible Man,* Ralph Ellison (1952/1953)
depicted the plight of the black person who is invisible to whites and whom whites
"look through":

> I am an invisible man. . . . I am invisible, understand, simply because people refuse
> to see me. . . . When they approach me they see only my surroundings, themselves,
> or figments of their imagination—indeed, everything and anything except me. . . . you
> often doubt if you really exist. You wonder whether you aren't simply a phantom in
> other people's minds. (p. 7)

Ellison's broadened metaphor of being invisible encompassed more than being
ignored or neglected. It became indicative of all the aspects of being an outcast:
feeling rejected, derogated, mistrusted, and a butt of superstition and of all types
of distortion—the receptacle for the other group's projections, unconscious wishes,
rage, grandiosity, and self-contempt.

The Latin word *negligere* means "not to pick up," hence a neglected child is one whose care is shunned by the putative caretaker. In the human community, whenever an exploited group's needs are ignored by the exploiting majority, neglect occurs. Rather like the "neglect" of a stroke patient who denies a body part that has been rendered substandard, within recent history certain white politicians have opted to practice benign neglect toward black, poor, child, and female groups, thereby permitting discrimination to follow the open market processes, and to wax, even if *prejudice* wanes.

Denying Opportunity and Equal Rights. Turner Brown's book *Black Is* (1969), reflected the 1960s type of frustration and moral indignation that occurs when equal opportunity and results are denied on racist grounds.

> Black is being given special vocational training for the jobs that will have disappeared before you learn how to do them.
>
> Black is having your paratrooper son return to the neighborhood when he's on duty.
>
> Black is being told you ran down a neighborhood that was fifty years old when you finally got to move in.

Doctrines such as "relative deprivation" have been put forward more to blur than to illuminate the overall failure to move blacks as an ethnic minority toward equality in the United States. The doctrine that rising expectations, higher aspirations, and greater discontent will occur whenever relative advantage accrues to any blacks has a very old history and a continuing standing among the racist ideologies proclaimed in white America: "Let any succeed and they'll all get restless." In 1880 Ray Stannard Raker recorded the expression of that selfsame neoconservative idea by a white attorney in Alabama:

> If you educate the Negroes they won't stay where they belong; and you must consider them as a race, because if you let a few rise it makes the others discontented. (Cited in Willhelm, *Who Needs the Negro?* 1971, pp. 145–146)

A similarly frustrating logic of shutout and denial of opportunity was everywhere when Michael Gold (1930), of impoverished immigrant Jewish derivation, completed eighth grade at age 12 years and sought a job in New York City.

> I found a job as errand boy in a silk house. But it was temporary. The very first morning the shipping clerk, a refined Nordic, suddenly realized I was a Jew. He politely fired me. They wanted no Jews. In this city of a million Jews, there was much antisemitism among business firms. Many of the ads would read: Gentile Only. . . . How often did I slink out of factory or office where a foreman said Jews were not wanted. How often was I made to remember I belonged to the accursed race, the race whose chief misfortune it is to have produced a Christ. (p. 306)

Excluding and Segregating. Although by July 1967 some 75% of white Americans (in a Gallup poll) believed "Negroes are treated the same as whites," and many white social scientists and politicians, even in the 1960s but dramatically more so in the 1970s and 1980s, put forth the ideology of relative deprivation to buttress that misinformed public opinion, blacks, in actuality, fell ever farther behind the economic gains made by whites. If black liberationists—from Martin Luther King to the present—call out for justice, while denying the beneficence of legislation that favors equal opportunity but obtains ever more unequal American results, liberal whites flinch at the blacks' ingratitude and conservative whites mouth relative deprivation to gloss over the facts. Willhelm (1971) explained it thus:

> [White America] shifts from racial hostility to racial exclusion not only because the price is cheaper, but also because the nature of economic change permits indifference to Negroes. (p. 154)

Willhelm noted how prejudice was discarded but inequality and injustice deepened in America after 1954—in hiring, employment (or structural unemployment), automation, education, the expanding military establishment, housing, and health. For each area, prejudice has lessened but exclusion has grown; so Willhelm asks "Why discriminate when one can eliminate?"

Since 1960, with the dissolution of some racial barriers, a secure black middle class, indisputably, has emerged, and this affluent group now gets blamed for rising expectations. But it is generally conceded that working-class and lower-class blacks are materially no better off. This led Wilson (1980) to conclude that, originally pushed aside by racism, the black worker today is being finished off by economic and technologic circumstances. In 1930, 84% of black males participated in the labor force but by 1983 only 56% participated, with tens of thousands finding themselves ground into chronic "structural" unemployment. The overall black unemployment rate hovered close to 17% with black teenage unemployment at 45% in May of 1985 (Hill, 1985).

Many fear a future for the American black group that may not be altogether dissimilar from genocide (Farrell, Dawkins, & Oliver, 1983). As American Indians can attest, being a redundant ethnic group among white Americans, and becoming economically irrelevant and ignored, may foretell the annihilation of that ethnic group.

Imposing Concentration Camp Internment. Not only American Indians have been concentrated into special encampments and reservations, so have Japanese-Americans and European Jews. Only the Holocaust has received considerable attention in psychiatric literature. Millions of human beings were exterminated by a "Christian" regime that ran the Nazi concentration camps; hence, it is no wonder that the horrors of antisemitism have been studied, documented, and interpreted by psychiatrists. It is hoped that this attention will continue.

What of the Japanese-Americans' concentration camp experience? Accompanied by objections from only the National Association for the Advancement of Colored People (NAACP), the Quakers and other pacifists, and the Socialist Party—groups whose objections were barely audible in wartime America—117,999 persons of Japanese ancestry were "relocated," under Roosevelt's Executive Order 9066 in February 1942, from the Pacific Coast to 10 "relocation centers" in the interior of continental United States. Two thirds of those interned were U.S. citizens but all were confined in the concentration camps. It was a surprising and odd precedent for a multiethnic nation to adopt, but it was fired by war-fevered patriotism, with fear and vindictiveness linked to racist prejudice about the Yellow Peril, and it was justified by "military necessity." (Not then but today, even the "surprise" attack of Pearl Harbor is questioned.) The internees lived in tar-papered barracks heated by coal stoves and were guarded against escaping by military police; they lost 400 million dollars of West Coast property (less than 10% of which was repaid by U.S. government reparations in the mid-1950s). It was the first mass exodus or forced internment of an ethnic minority in the United States since President Andrew Jackson signed the 1830 Indian Removal Act, requiring American Indians' general displacement to lands west of the Mississippi River.

During the 1830s, thousands of Indians were displaced and murdered: Choctaw, Creek, Seminole, Sauk, Fox, Chicasaw, Cherokee, Sioux, and others. Of the 14,000 Cherokees forced onto the Trail of Tears in 1838, over 4,000 died en route to Indian Territory, west of the Mississippi. By 1860, from nearly a million in 1607, the U.S. Indian population had been reduced to 300,000. And by 1983, excluding 65,000 Alaskans and 160,000 Indians in Oklahoma, there were about 530,000 American Indians living on Federal Indian Reservations (Bureau of Indian Affairs, 1983). Still fewer than a million. Their unemployment rate averages about 50%, and alcoholism and depression are prevalent among them.

The Nazi concentration camps are a special example of racist exclusion, internment, terror, and murder. The numbers are numbing: Over 6 million Jews were exterminated, and of these, up to 4 million were killed in Auschwitz camp alone. Those who were slaughtered, and those who survived were subjected to massive and catastrophic stresses and traumata. Studies of survivors have revealed vital data about both the noxae and the protectors against stress of such unbearable magnitude.

Among survivors the direct sequelae are startle reactions, anxiety and nightmares, insomnia, depression, social withdrawal, irritability, dizziness, and headache (Haefner, 1969), all signs and symptoms often included under the rubric of Posttraumatic Stress Disorder. Individual coping patterns to surmount the trauma have included psychic withdrawal, the desire to survive and wreak revenge, a drive to find meaning in what happened, a compulsion to be a witness, religious and political commitments, fantasy formation (Klein, 1974), hope, the will to live, and mastery through constructive activity (such as Bettelheim's, 1943, studying "behavior in extreme situations"). Eitinger (1964), a Norwegian psychiatrist, as well as Frankl (1963) the Viennese Adlerian-existentialist, Niederland (1961), Chodoff (1970), Cath (1981),

Heller (1982), Klein (1974), Ehrentheil (1978), Luchterhand (1971), and Krystal (1968) have added to our understanding of both risk factors and protective factors among those who survived German concentration camps.

Dor-Shav (1978) studied 42 Israeli Holocaust survivors and 20 controls in a double-blind procedure and demonstrated that survivors did show greater personality constriction and impoverishment 25 years later; they were "less accessible, less connected, and more labile," and "would appear to fear close emotional contact" (p. 1). Their prolonged, severe stress led to impoverished, more primitive, and dedifferentiated egos. Eddy de Wind (1971), reporting findings from analyses of 22 Holocaust survivors, declared their psychic position to be much like that of damaged, severely traumatized preoedipal children. Shamai Davidson (1979) from Tel Aviv reported a study of social supports of the Holocaust survivors when (1) they were within the death camps, (2) they had just been liberated and returned to a "normal society," (3) they lived out the subsequent years of their lives. Davidson's emphasis on social bonds and the support derived from networks of fellowship and comradeship seems particularly valuable. Naturally, human connectedness is what masters of terror and brainwashing, such as the Nazis, are determined to inhibit— therefore, the practice of good sociability by interned minority group members would not be as salutary as prior steps to prevent the institution of terror against ethnic minorities or to prevent their ever getting placed in concentration camps. The easy next step after "concentration" has occurred is "liquidation"—*die Loesung*—the imposition of systematic annihilation. Life after concentration camp is not easy for the survivors either.

One little emphasized sequel to Nazi antisemitism was the more typical antisemitism of the pogrom on July 14, 1946, against Polish Jews who had survived the Holocaust. They were killed at Kielce on that date in an act that will memorialize for a long time to come that murderous antisemitism neither began nor ended with the Nazis. Antisemitism too has been institutionalized, as well as individualized; in millions of snickers and gentlemen's agreements, antisemitic prejudices pave the way to riot and murder.

Imposing Violence and Murder. When the dominant group kills the victims of oppression and discrimination, the spectrum of prejudice and exclusion has reached its most extreme form. That is not to say that prejudiced groups move in stepwise fashion—from teasing and disparaging to labeling to neglecting to depriving to scapegoating to locking up in concentration camp to murder, or that they only commit violence and murder after a lengthy prehistory. In fact, in the minds and hearts of the prejudiced the ghost of murder has been present from the earliest formulations onward. Long before they were relocated, Jews, American Indians, and Japanese-Americans had often been killed in murderous breakthroughs of the always implicit "ultimate solution." Murder and violence reinforce, inspire, and pattern every lesser form of prejudice. The American blacks' experience assuredly has not been devoid of murder and violence. Violence has appeared directly in the form of flogging, tar-and-feathering, and lynching; somewhat less directly in being sent in disproportionate numbers to Vietnam; and implicitly in being deprived of justice in the allocation of survival chances, with higher infant mortality, inaccessibility of health services, and so on. When a militant black sees violence to be inextricably woven into the fabric of American racism, he or she speaks that same truth uttered by psychiatry. For to be the object of prejudice and exclusion is to see oneself always as a prospective victim of murder, becoming edgy, vigilant, careful—living in terror. To be powerless and to feel "played cheap" is to be at risk of individual pathology—Adjustment Disorder, depression, anxiety disorders, and others—in the shadow of threats to survival itself.

RACISM IN PSYCHIATRY

Racism and DSM-III Diagnoses

Psychosocial stressors are now known to weigh heavily on several population groups. These are the groups with a known heightened risk or vulnerability:

1. Females
2. Discrimination-oppressed minority groups
3. Lower-class persons
4. Separated and divorced persons
5. Those with few social skills
6. Those with low self-esteem
7. Those with external locus of control or low sense of self-direction
8. Those with fewer social supports (although some evidence on this is contradictory) (Eron & Peterson, 1982)

Those with genetic vulnerability (alcholism, mood disorder, sociopathy, etc.) should be added to the other 8 biopsychosocial risk groups. Indeed, a tangle of vulnerability promises to replace the former conception of a tangle of pathology. The tangle refers to the complex interactions among class, ethnicity, gender, social supports, and coping skills whenever a psychosocial stress such as racism is selected for scrutiny.

DSM-III-R permits diagnosticians at least to guess about the severity of any psychosocial stressor, such as being the victim of discrimination, and to record that guess on Axis IV. If this can be spelled out, documented carefully, and quantified in terms of life events or life change units, all the better. Apparently, few clinical psychiatrists use Axis IV very extensively. Hence, in their net effect, American psychiatrists are very like those Russians who objected to the inclusion of any social stresses in the multiaxial diagnostic approach on grounds of the nonexistence of these stresses in socialist nations. Even in a capitalist nation, many psychiatrists beg off, claiming ignorance about, or proclaiming a desire to ignore, social stressors.

DSM-III-R gives special consideration to stress in a few groups of conditions, namely, Reactive Attachment Disorder of Infancy, Posttraumatic Stress Disorders, Adjustment Disorders, and "brief reactive psychosis." Anxiety Disorders and social phobia, as well as numerous others, might be added to that listing.

In the Adjustment Disorders, however, an odd logic characterizes psychiatric thinking. On the one hand, whenever the symptoms are only transient, say, reflecting a developmental crisis or transition, psychiatrists suspect only a stress response or a reactive disorder and not an endogenous disorder. On the other hand, however, they regard permanence and severity of symptoms as in some way a gauge of stress severity (Axis IV). As a result, Stress Disorders and Anxiety Disorders, on Axis I, are viewed by many as if they comprise rather benign conditions, whereas malignant and perennial stressors noted on Axis IV are viewed as more severe and more potent in sustaining and aggravating Axis I psychopathology. That is having it both ways, for Axis IV does and does not govern severity of pathology on Axis I.

The undocumented Mexican woman, who lives in a Los Angeles slum and derives income as a pieceworker in a garment factory, lives in a state of chronic tension (insomnia, fear, loneliness, longing for absent family, suspicion, palpitations) that could make her fully eligible for several diagnostic appellations. However, many psychiatrists would minimize her psychosocial noxae and place their greatest emphasis on her "objective," overt Axis I phenomenology. As a result, she may wind up with a recorded diagnosis of one or more of the following:

1. Posttraumatic Stress Disorder (because she escaped in the nick of time from a traumatic experience, a raid by the Immigration and Naturalization Service)

2. Generalized Anxiety Disorder (because she works despite her level of jitteriness and apprehension)

3. Social phobia (if she remains stuck at home, fearing even to attend Mass because she might be picked up and deported, going to or coming back from the church)

4. Conversion Disorder (because she has fainted in public three times when she felt impending panic; besides, the psychiatrist thinks expressive and dramatic Latinas are hysterical anyway)

5. Agoraphobia (if she has had several episodes of panic when going out alone)

6. Adjustment Disorder (because the psychiatrist has not assessed the true magnitude of her psychosocial stressors)

7. Brief reactive psychosis (if she had a good remission in less than 2 weeks of stuporous psychosis)

8. Depressive Disorder (if other signs and symptoms became superadded to her insomnia, anxiety, and loneliness)

9. Separation Anxiety Disorder (when the psychiatrist identifies the homesickness of almost hallucinatory proportions, the feelings of estrangement, and a history of having had school phobia as a 6-year-old and of never having spent a night away from her mother until she illegally crossed the Mexican border into California

Clearly, the elicitation and coding of psychopathology interrelated with stress has not become highly developed in American psychiatry. The following case vignette gives an indication of the benefits accruing from greater specificity and clarity in psychiatric historiography and diagnosis.

A 28-year-old Burmese woman completed her medical training in Chicago, where she had shared an apartment with her sister (a primary care physician) and her sister's husband (a general psychiatrist). Moving to a small rural community in central Tennessee, she set up a solo practice. By the end of the first month she became fidgety and edgy, but this quickly escalated to stark paranoid delusions and hallucinations. Her voices said, "What are you doing here, 70 miles from nowhere? Watch out for these rednecks. Your office is bugged. You are doomed to fail professionally." She could not work and, on the advice of her brother-in-law in Chicago, went the 70 miles mentioned by her voices to see a psychiatrist. The psychiatrist hospitalized her, talked with her about her stresses and lack of a supportive family and city, and gave 5 mg of haloperidol daily. Within 5 days she was completely recovered, ate the ward food without discomfort, and decided to wrap up her practice and return to Chicago within a month or two. She was seen 2 months exactly from the date of onset of her disorder and was normal, disclaiming any memory for the psychotic episode and stating that she could not remember it but had a faint recall of being in a state of "nervous exhaustion but it seems more like a dream than anything that really occurred."

Her psychiatrist had taken pains to be open-minded, explore her good premorbid adjustment, including her ability to leave her home country and to move to America by retaining her original culture, religion, and warm relations with a part of her original family. He had empathy for her estranged situation, felt no unhinging by her paranoid delusions and voices, and was reluctant to make a quick diagnosis of paranoid schizophrenia without substantiation. He attempted to learn from the patient and to elicit a careful story of her infancy and childhood, her chumships during preadolescence, her sexual history, her adolescence and young adulthood struggles to be a physician, her emigration from Burma and immigration to the United States, her residency stresses and coping devices, and the details of her stresses on entering rural Tennessee. He learned of her Eastern viewpoint that one's family are not "outgrown" and that fierce adult independence is not a personal goal, only dependability. He learned about her intensified culture shock in rural Tennessee where she was regarded as an extremely different and peculiar specimen of a derogated ethnic group. As a Buddhist she had been considered a pagan, of course. As a Burmese she was one body in a Yellow Peril.

The important fact remains that, if psychiatry wishes to devote its energies and resources to racism, it is necessary to develop an ever-improving conceptual, theoretical, methodologic, and technical repertoire for doing so. That would include better use of Axis IV especially. The way is available if the will can only be developed.

Discrimination in Psychiatric Service: Recent Reports

Psychiatry has a less-than-ideal record in respect to the handling of racial prejudice and exclusion, in society and in clinical practice. That record was reviewed and documented by Thomas and Sillen in *Racism and Psychiatry* (1974), which remains a sourcebook and classic compilation of how racism has permeated psychiatry as a part of ethnocentric white attitudes and institutions. All the *J'accuse* literature about psychiatric racism makes informative reading. Jones, Lightfoot, Palmer, Wilkerson, and Williams (1970) even presented a description of difficulties encountered by five black physicians who had completed their psychiatric residencies in a white training center. Nevertheless, in this section, a narrower current-practice topic will be examined: recent reports of racial discrimination in psychiatric clinical services.

Since 1969, psychiatric literature has used the racism-as-stressor model extensively, as shown in Table 18.1 (Baker, 1984; Christmas, 1973; Dohrenwend & Dohrenwend, 1974; Eron & Peterson, 1982; Flaherty & Meagher, 1980; King, 1978; Lewis, Shanok, Cohen, Kligfeld, & Frisone, 1980; Sandler, 1980; Schwab, McGinnis, & Warheit, 1973) to account for differential rates of psychopathology or of physical disorders among distinct ethnic groups (see Back, Wilson, Bogdonoff, & Troyer, 1969; Blumberg, 1983; Culpepper & Froom, 1980; Harburg, Erfurt, Chape, et al., 1973; Harburg, Erfurt, Hauenstein, et al., 1973; Harburg, Gleibermann, Ozgoren, et al., 1978; Harburg, Gleibermann, Roeper, et al., 1978; James & Kleinbaum, 1976; Schwab et al., 1973).

More pointedly, several authors have discussed and documented current clinical practices that discriminate against minority patients, usually blacks, who constitute the largest documented American ethnic minority. Blank and Silk (1979) described an instance of scapegoating black patients on the occasion of transforming a psychiatric ward into a clinical service for teaching residents. June Jackson Christmas (1973) detailed the stresses of racism, segregation, discrimination, and poverty, and she described the features of broadened sociopsychiatric services required to aid the mental health of black people living in inner cities in the United States. Flaherty and Meagher (1980) compared the case records of 66 black patients and 35 white patients with schizophrenia and reported that the two groups, although demographically similar and also alike on extent, chronicity, and severity of their pathology, differed in respect to length of stay in hospital (shorter for blacks); use of medication, seclusion, and restraints (more for blacks); and referral to recreational or occupational therapy (lower for blacks). There was little room left to doubt that racism remained integral to psychiatric hospital practice in the United States.

Lewis E. King (1978) aptly reviewed all the diagnostic and methodologic snarls that confront anyone who studies race, gender, or class in relation to mental disorder and warned against assumptions and paradigms that "perpetuate oppression." Dorothy O. Lewis et al. (1980) issued a similar message, that is, the race of the delinquent youth determines his or her management, for the black adolescents go preponderantly to correctional facilities whereas white adolescents with equivalent

Table 18.1. Literature on Ethnic Groups, 1969–1984

Ethnic Group	Number of Articles	Author and Date
Africans	2	Blumberg (1983); Ramasuvha (1982)
Alaskans	1	Popkin et al. (1976)
African-Americans	23	Allen et al. (1977); Back et al. (1969); Baker (1984); Blank & Silk (1979); Bowman (1980); Christmas (1973); Culpepper & Froom (1980); Faulkner et al. (1975); Flaherty & Meagher (1980); Forrest (1980); Harburg, Erfurt, Chape, et al. (1973); Harburg, Erfurt, Hauenstein, et al. (1973); Harburg, Gleibermann, Dzgoren, et al. (1978); Harburg, Gleibermann, Roeper, et al. (1978); Holmes & Heckel (1970); James & Kleinbaum (1976); Lewis et al. (1980); McAdoo (1977); Rahe et al. (1972); Sandler (1980); Schwab et al. (1973); Silver et al. (1984); Vander Kolk (1978)
Cambodians	1	Kinzie et al. (1984)
Chinese Americans	2	Kuo et al. (1979); Sue & Chin (1983)
Minority Student Counselors	1	Casas et al. (1980)
Hispanic Americans	13	Burnam et al. (1984); Cohen & Fernandez (1974); Dressler & Bernal (1982); Gaitz & Scott (1974); Mirowsky & Ross (1984); Olivares et al. (1973); Roberts (1980); Ross et al. (1983); Ross & Mirowsky (1984); Ruiz & Padilla (1977); Sandler (1980); Timmreck & Stratton (1981); Vander Kolk (1978)
Indians (East)	1	Nichter (1981)
Italian Americans	1	Bruhn et al. (1972)
Japanese	2	Lazarus et al. (1966); Yamamoto & Davis (1982)
Japanese Americans	2	Heller (1982); Sata (1983)
Jews	13	Cath (1981); Chodoff (1970); Davidson (1979); de Wind (1971); Dor-Shav (1978); Eaton et al. (1979); Ehrentheil (1978); Gay & Shulman (1978); Haefner (1969); Heller (1982); Klein (1974); Luchterhand (1971); Palgi (1978)
Liberians	1	Wintrob (1967)
Peruvian Indians	1	Stevenson (1977)
Turkish *Gastarbeiter*	1	Suzuki (1981)
Vietnamese Americans	2	Harding & Looney (1977); Vignes & Hall (1979)
West Indians	1	Burke (1980)

symptoms are ushered into psychiatric facilities. Similarly, Sandler (1980), studied a sample of adjustment problems that included 51% black children and 46% Chicanos. All had been referred by their teachers as maladjusted, and these evaluations had been confirmed by a life event scale (Coddington, 1972) and the Louisville Behavior Checklist (Miller, 1967), a parent rating instrument. Sandler found that ethnic incongruence of neighborhood, presence of only one parent, and lack of an older sib deprived children of social support and all added to certain types of maladjustments in the children studied. Although lacking in punch, the Sandler report and study suggest the problems and promises that inhere in research on ethnic stresses and psychopathology. Both individualized and institutionalized racism remain pervasive challenges to psychiatry.

Since 1969, biracial or biethnic psychotherapy has been described in some detail. Examples are to be found in Adams (1970, 1977), Allen, Brown, Jackson, and Lewis (1977), Forrest (1980), and Holmes and Heckel (1970); it is noteworthy that, nationwide, white–black interaction is still likely to be the most frequent form of biethnic encounter. Even the raters of stress and psychopathology show ethnic bias differences. This finding has been documented by Askenasy, Dohrenwend, and Dohrenwend (1977), Dohrenwend and Dohrenwend (1974), Langner, Gersten, and Eisenberg (1974), and Rosenberg and Dohrenwend (1975), all of whom issue strong cautions about survey instruments that use raters without control for bias and ethnic differences.

CONCLUSION

The study of racism as a complex of psychosocial stressors is in its infancy, especially for those who prefer understatement and the exercise of great caution about any and every expression of social criticism. The format of a *Handbook of Stress* (Goldberger & Breznitz, 1982) may have suggested a tentative understatement when it devoted only 1 of its 46 chapters to "The Social Contexts of Stress" (Pearlin, 1982). In that chapter scarcely any allusion was made to ethnic discrimination, and that only in the most general terms. Pearlin concluded the chapter, however, with a declaration that appears to be an apt description of the current scene and Zeitgeist:

> There is little reason to rest with the present state of our knowledge about the social origins of stress . . . (for) some of the knowledge is more putative than convincingly documented. . . . I would emphasize in particular *the need to move away from attempts to identify separate sources of stress* [italics added] to the specification of the process leading to stress . . . [of] the confluence of life events, chronic strains and self-concept in producing stress. (p. 378)

If future professionals seek diffuseness and shy away from identifying "separate sources of distress'' like those contained in racism, knowledge of racism as stressor will surely be impeded.

REFERENCES

Adams, P. L. (1970). Dealing with racism in biracial psychiatry. *Journal of the American Academy of Child Psychiatry, 9,* 33–43.

Adams, P. L. (1972). Dehumanization and the legitimation of violence. In J. H. Masserman & J. J. Schwab (Eds.), *Man for humanity* (pp. 148–180). Springfield: Charles C. Thomas.

Adams, P. L. (1977). Black patients and white doctors. *Urban Health, 6,* 21–33.

Adorno, T. W., Frenkel-Brunswik, E., Levinson, D. J., & Sanford, R. N. (1950). *The authoritarian personality.* New York: Harper.

Allen, I. M., Brown, J. L., Jackson, J., & Lewis, R. (1977). Psychological stress of young black children as a result of school desegregation. *Journal of the American Academy of Child Psychiatry, 16,* 739–747.

Allport, G. W. (1954). *The nature of prejudice.* Cambridge: Addison-Wesley.

American Psychiatric Association. (1987). *Diagnostic and statistical manual of mental disorders* (3rd ed.-revised; DSM-3-R). Washington, DC: Author.

Arthur, R. J. (1973). Social psychiatry: An overview. *American Journal of Psychiatry, 130,* 841–849.

Askenasy, A. R., Dohrenwend, B. P., & Dohrenwend, B. S. (1977). Some effects of social class and ethnic group membership on judgments of the magnitude of stressful life events: A research note. *Journal of Health and Social Behavior, 18,* 432–439.

Back, K. W., Wilson, S. R., Bogdonoff, M. D., & Troyer, W. G. (1969). Racial environment, cohesion, conformity and stress. *Journal of Psychosomatic Research, 13,* 27–36.

Baker, F. M. (1984). Black suicide attempters in 1980: A preventive focus. *General Hospital Psychiatry, 6,* 131–137.

Bernal, G. (1982). Cuban families. In M. McGoldrich, J. K. Pearce, & J. Giordano (Eds.), *Ethnicity & family therapy* (pp. 187–207). New York: Guilford Press.

Bernard, V. W., Ottenberg, P., & Redl, F. (1963, March). *Dehumanization: A barrier to reducing international tensions.* Paper presented at the annual meeting of the American Orthopsychiatric Association, Washington, DC.

Bettelheim, B. (1943). Individual and mass behavior in extreme situations. *Journal of Abnormal & Social Psychology, 38,* 417–452.

Blank, R. J., & Silk, K. R. (1979). Racism as a response to change: The introduction of residents onto a psychiatry ward. *Journal of Nervous and Mental Disease, 167,* 416–421.

Blumberg, L. (1983). Duodenal ulcer, urban stress and the concept of ''marginal man.'' *South African Medical Journal, 64,* 630–632.

Bowman, P. J. (1980). Toward a dual labor-market approach to black-on-black homicide. *Public Health Report, 95,* 555–556.

Brooks, G. (1949). The children of the poor. In *Selected poems.* New York: Harper & Row.

Brown v. The Board of Education of Topeka, Kansas, 347 U.S. 483 (1954).

Brown, T. (1969). *Black is.* New York: Grove Press.

Bruhn, J. G., Philips, R. U., & Wolf, S. (1972). Social readjustment and illness patterns: Comparisons between first, second and third generation Italian-Americans living in the same community. *Journal of Psychosomatic Research, 16,* 387–394.

Buber, M. (1952). *Good and evil*. New York: Scribner's.

Bureau of Indian Affairs. (1983). *Federal Indian Reservations*. Washington, DC: U.S. Department of the Interior.

Burke, A. W. (1980). Family stress and the precipitation of psychiatric disorder. *International Journal of Social Psychiatry, 26*, 35–40.

Burnam, M. A., Timbers, D. M., & Hough, R. L. (1984). Two measures of psychological distress among Mexican Americans, Mexicans and Anglos. *Journal of Health and Social Behavior, 25*, 24–33.

Casas, J. M., Furlong, M. J., & Castillo, S. (1980). Stress and coping among university counselors: A minority perspective. *Journal of Counseling Psychology, 27*, 364–373.

Cassel, J. (1976). The contribution of the social environment to host resistance: The fourth Wade Hampton Frost Lecture. *American Journal of Epidemiology, 104, 2*, 107–123.

Cath, S. H. (1981). The aging survivor of the Holocaust. Discussion: The effects of the Holocaust on life-cycle experiences: The creation and recreation of families. *Journal of Geriatric Psychiatry, 14*, 155–163.

Chodoff, P. (1970). The German concentration camp. *Archives of General Psychiatry, 22*, 78–87.

Christmas, J. J. (1973). Psychological stresses of urban living: New directions for mental health services in the inner city. *Journal of National Medical Association, 65*, 483–511.

Coddington, R. D. (1972). The significance of life events as etiologic factors in the disease of children, I: A survey of professional workers. *Journal of Psychosomatic Research, 16*, 17–18.

Cohen, L. M., & Fernandez, C. L. (1974). Ethnic identity and psychocultural adaptation of Spanish-speaking families. *Child Welfare, 53*, 413–421.

Culpepper, L., & Froom, J. (1980). Incarceration and blood pressure. *Social Science & Medicine, 14S*, 571–574.

Davidson, S. (1979). Massive psychic traumatization and social support. *Journal of Psychosomatic Research, 23*, 395–402.

Davis, C. T., & Walden, D. (Eds.). (1970). *On being black: Writings by Afro-Americans from Frederic Douglass to the present*. New York: Fawcett World Library.

Davis, J., & Barnes, H. E. (1927). *Introduction to sociology*. New York: DC Heath.

Davis, J. P. (1966). *The American Negro reference book*. Englewood Cliffs, NJ: Prentice-Hall.

de Wind, E. (1971). Psychotherapy after traumatization caused by persecution. *International Psychiatry Clinic, 8*, 93–114.

Dohrenwend, B. P., & Dohrenwend, B. S. (1974). Social and cultural influences on psychopathology. *Annual Review of Psychology, 25*, 417–452.

Dor-Shav, N. K. (1978). On the long-range effects of concentration camp internment on Nazi victims: 25 years later. *Journal of Consulting & Clinical Psychology, 46*, 1–11.

Douglass, F. (1970). Narrative of the life of Frederick Douglass. In C. T. Davis, & D. Walden (Eds.), *On being black: Writings by Afro-Americans from Frederick Douglass to the present* (pp. 49–50). New York: Fawcett World Library. (Original work published 1845)

Dressler, W. W., & Bernal, H. (1982). Acculturation and stress in a low-income Puerto Rican community. *Journal of Human Stress, 8*, 32–38.

Durkheim, E. (1951). *Suicide*. New York: The Free Press. (Original work published 1897)

Eaton, W. W., Lasry, J. C., & Sigal, J. (1979). Ethnic relations and community mental health among Israeli Jews. *Israeli Annals of Psychiatry and Related Disciplines, 17,* 155–174.

Ehrentheil, O. F. (1978). The effects of various degrees of social pressure. *Mental Health & Society, 5,* 141–150.

Eitinger, L. (1964). *Concentration camp survivors in Norway & Israel.* London: Allen & W. Unwin.

Ellison, R. (1953). *Invisible man.* New York: New American Library (Paper). (Original work published 1952)

Eron, L. D., & Peterson, R. A. (1982). Abnormal behavior: Social approaches. *Annual Review of Psychology, 22,* 231–264.

Fanon, F. (1966). *The wretched of the earth* (C. Farrington, Trans.). New York: Grove Press.

Fanon, F. (1967). *Black skin, white masks* (C. L. Markmann, Trans.). New York: Grove Press.

Farrell, W. C., Dawkins, M. P., & Oliver, J. (1983). Genocide fears in a rural black community: An empirical examination. *Journal of Black Studies, 14,* 49–67.

Faulkner, A. O., Heisel, M. A., & Simms, P. (1975). Life strengths and life stresses: Explorations in the measurement of the mental health of the black aged. *American Journal of Orthopsychiatry, 45,* 102–110.

Flaherty, J. A., & Meagher, R. (1980). Measuring racial bias in inpatient treatment. *American Journal of Psychiatry, 137,* 679–682.

Forrest, L. (1980). Get your black hands off me! *RN, 43,* 54–55.

Frankl, V. (1963). *Man's search for meaning.* New York: Washington Square Press.

Fromm, E. (1962). *Beyond the chains of illusions: My encounter with Marx and Freud.* New York: Simon and Schuster.

Gaertner, S. L., & McLaughlin, J. P. (1983). Racial stereotypes: Associations and ascriptions of positive and negative characteristics. *Social Psychology Quarterly, 46,* 23–30.

Gaitz, C. M., & Scott, J. (1974). Mental health of Mexican-Americans: Do ethnic factors make a difference? *Geriatrics, 29,* 103–110.

Gay, M., & Shulman, S. (1978). Comparison of children of Holocaust survivors with children of the general population in Israel. *Mental Health Society, 5,* 252–256.

Gold, M. (1930). *Jews without money.* New York: Liveright.

Goldberger, L., & Breznitz, S., (Eds.). (1982). *Handbook of stress: Theoretical and clinical aspects.* New York: The Free Press.

Grier, W. H., & Cobbs, P. M. (1968). *Black rage.* New York: Basic Books.

Grossack, M. M. (1954). Perceived Negro group belongingness and social rejection. *Journal of Psychology, 38,* 127–130.

Gwaltney, J. L. (1980). *Drylongso.* New York: Random House.

Haefner, H. (1969). Psychosocial changes following racial and political persecution. *Research Publications of the Association for Research in Nervous & Mental Disease, 47,* 101–117.

Harburg, E. H., Erfurt, J. C., Chape, C., Hauenstein, L. S., Schull, W. J., & Schork, M. A. (1973a). Socioecological stressor areas and black-white blood pressure: Detroit. *Journal of Chronic Disease, 26,* 595–611.

Harburg, E. H., Erfurt, J. C., Hauenstein, L. S., Chape, C., Schull, W. J., & Schork, M. A. (1973b). Socioecological stress, suppressed hostility, skin color, and black-white male blood pressure: Detroit. *Psychosomatic Medicine, 35,* 276–296.

Harburg, E. H., Gleibermann, L., Ozgoren, F., Roeper, P., & Schork, M. A. (1978). Skin color, ethnicity, and blood pressure, II: Detroit whites. *American Journal of Public Health, 68*, 1184–1188.

Harburg, E. H., Gleibermann, L., Roeper, P., Schork, M. A., & Schull, M. J. (1978). Skin color, ethnicity, and blood pressure, I: Detroit blacks. *American Journal of Public Health, 68*, 1177–1183.

Harding, R. K., & Looney, J. G. (1977). Problems of Southeast Asian children in a refugee camp. *American Journal of Psychiatry, 134*, 407–411.

Heller, D. (1982). Themes of culture and ancestry among children of concentration camp survivors. *Psychiatry, 45*, 247–261.

Hill, N. (1985, May 3). Black workers and the minimum wage. *Texas Observer*, p. 18.

Holmes, G. R., & Heckel, R. V. (1970). Psychotherapy with the first negro male on one southern university campus: A case study. *Journal of Consulting & Clinical Psychology, 34*, 297–301.

James, S. A., & Kleinbaum, D. G. (1976). Socioecologic stress and hypertension related mortality rates in North Carolina. *American Journal of Public Health, 65*, 354–358.

Johnson, C. S. (1943). *Patterns of Negro segregation*. New York: Harper.

Jones, B. E., Lightfoot, O. B., Palmer, D., Wilkerson, R. G., & Williams, D. H. (1970). Problems of black psychiatric residents in white training institutes. *American Journal of Psychiatry, 127*, 798–803.

Kanner, D. A., Coyne, J. C., Schaefer, C., & Lazarus, R. S. (1981). Comparison of two modes of stress measurement: Daily hassles and uplifts versus major life events. *Journal of Behavioral Medicine, 4*, 1–39.

Kaplan, B. (1967). *The Jew and his family*. Baton Rouge: Louisiana State University Press.

King, L. M. (1978). Social and cultural influences on psychopathology. *Annual Review of Psychology, 29*, 405–433.

Kinzie, J. D., Frederickson, R. H., Ben, R., Fleck, J., & Karls, W. (1984). Post-traumatic stress disorder among survivors of Cambodian concentration camps. *American Journal of Psychiatry, 141*, 645–650.

Klein, H. (1974). Delayed affects and after-effects of severe traumatisation. *Israeli Annals of Psychiatry, 12*, 293–303.

Kluegel, J. R., & Smith, E. R. (1983). Affirmative action attitudes: Effects of self-interest, racial affect, and stratification beliefs on whites' views. *Social Forces, 61*(3), 797–824.

Krystal, H. (1968). *Massive psychic trauma*. New York: International Universities Press.

Kuo, W. H., Gray, R., & Lin, N. (1979). Locus of control and symptoms of psychological distress among Chinese-Americans. *International Journal of Social Psychiatry, 25*, 176–187.

Langner, T. S., Gersten, J. C., & Eisenberg, J. G. (1974). Approaches to measurement and definition in the epidemiology of behavior disorders: Ethnic background and child behavior. *International Journal of Health Services, 4*, 483–501.

Lawrence, M. M. (1975). *Young inner city families: Development of ego strength under stress*. New York: Behavioral Publications.

Lazarus, R. S., Opton, E., Tomita, M., & Kodama, M. (1966). A cross-cultural study of stress-reaction patterns in Japan. *Journal of Personality & Social Psychology, 4*, 622–633.

Lewis, D. O., Shanok, S. S., Cohen, R. J., Kligfeld, M., & Frisone, G. (1980). Race bias in the diagnosis and disposition of violent adolescents. *American Journal of Psychiatry, 137*, 1211–1216.

Lindblad-Goldberg, M., & Dukes, J. L. (1985). Social support in black low-income single parent families: Normative and dysfunctional patterns. *American Journal of Orthopsychiatry, 55*(1), 42–58.

Luchterhand, E. G. (1971). Sociological approaches to massive stress in natural and manmade disasters. *International Psychiatry Clinic, 8,* 29–53.

Marx, K. (1961). Economic and philosophical manuscripts. In E. Fromm (Ed., T. B. Bottomore, Trans.), *Marx's concept of man.* New York: Frederick Ungar.

McAdoo, H. (1977). Family therapy in the black community. *American Journal of Orthopsychiatry, 47,* 75–79.

McConahay, J. B., & Hough, J. C. (1976). Symbolic racism. *Journal of Social Issues, 32,* 23–45.

Miller, L. (1967). Louisville behavior checklist for males 6–12 years of age. *Psychological Reports, 21,* 885–896.

Miller, L. (1972). Social behavior checklist: An inventory of deviant behavior for elementary school children. *Journal of Consulting and Clinical Psychology, 22,* 134–144.

Mirowsky, J., & Ross, C. E. (1984). Mexican culture and its emotional contradiction. *Journal of Health and Social Behavior, 25,* 2–13.

Myrdal, G., Sterner, R., & Rose, A. (1944). *An American dilemma.* New York: Harper.

Nichter, M. (1981). Idioms of distress: Alternatives in the expression of psychosocial distress: A case study from South India. *Cultural and Medical Psychiatry, 5,* 379–408.

Niederland, W. G. (1961). The problem of the survivor. *Journal of Hillside Hospital, 10,* 233.

Noshpitz, J. D. (1979). The Jewish child. In J. D. Noshpitz (Ed.), *Basic handbook of child psychiatry: Vol. 1. Development* (pp. 276–282). New York: Basic Books.

Olivares, L., Castaneda, E., Grife, A., & Alter, M. (1973). Risk factors in stroke: A clinical study in Mexican patients. *Stroke, 4,* 773, 781.

Palgi, P. (1978). Persistent traditional Yemenite ways of dealing with stress in Israel. *Mental Health Society, 5,* 113–140.

Park, R. E. (1926, May 1). Behind our masks. *The Survey, 56,* 136.

Pearlin, L. I. (1982). The social contexts of stress. In L. Goldberger, & S. Breznitz (Eds.), *Handbook of stress: Theoretical and clinical aspects* (pp. 367–379). New York: The Free Press.

Pierce, C. M., & Allen, G. R. (1975). Childism. *Psychiatric Annals, 5,* 15, 18–19, 23–24.

Pinderhughes, C. (1968). The psychodynamics of dissent. In J. Masserman (Ed.), *The dynamics of dissent* (pp. 56–81). New York: Grune & Stratton.

Pinderhughes, C. (1969). Understanding black power: Processes and proposals. *American Journal of Psychiatry, 125,* 11.

Pinderhughes, C. (1970). The universal resolution of ambivalence by paranoia with an example in black and white. *American Journal of Psychotherapy, 24,* 597–610.

Pinderhughes, C. (1971). Somatic, psychic, and social sequelae of loss. *Journal of American Psycho-Analytic Association, 19,* 670–696.

Pinderhughes, C. (1976). Black personality in American society. In M. M. Smythe (Ed.), *The Black American reference book* (pp. 128–158). Englewood Cliffs, NJ: Prentice-Hall.

Popkin, M. K., Stillner, V., Pierce, C. M., Williams, M., & Gregory, P. (1976). Recent life changes and outcome of prolonged competitive stress. *Journal of Nervous and Mental Disease, 163,* 302–306.

Powell, G. J., Yamamoto, J., Romero, A., & Morales, A. (Eds.), (1983). *The psychosocial development of minority group children.* New York: Brunner/Mazel.

Rahe, R. H. (1975). Epidemiological studies of life changes and illness. *International Journal of Psychiatry in Medicine, 6,* 133–146.

Rahe, R. H., Gunderson, E. K. E., Pugh, W. M., Rubin, R. T., & Arthur, R. J. (1972). Illness prediction studies. *Archives of Environmental Health, 25,* 192–197.

Ramasuvha, V. S. (1982). Aspects of stress among traditionally living people in a developing country. *South African Medical Journal, 61,* 879–880.

Roberts, R. E. (1980). Prevalence of psychological distress among Mexican-Americans. *Journal of Health and Social Behavior, 21,* 134–145.

Rosenberg, E. J., & Dohrenwend, B. S. (1975). Effects of experience and ethnicity on ratings of life events as stressors. *Journal of Health & Social Behavior, 16,* 127–129.

Ross, C. E., & Mirowsky, J. (1984). Socially-desirable response and acquiescence in a cross-cultural survey of mental health. *Journal of Health and Social Behavior, 25,* 189–197.

Ross, C. E., Mirowsky, J., & Cockerham, W. C. (1983). Social class, Mexican culture, and fatalism: Their effects on psychological distress. *American Journal of Community Psychology, 11,* 383–399.

Ruiz, R. A., & Padilla, A. M. (1977). Counseling Latinos. *Personnel & Guidance Journal, 55,* 401–408.

Sandler, I. N. (1980). Social support resources, stress, and maladjustment of poor children. *American Journal of Community Psychology, 8,* 41–52.

Sata, L. S. (1983). Mental health issues of Japanese-American children. In G. J. Powell, J. Yamamoto, A. Romero, & A. Morales (Eds.), *The psychosocial development of minority group children* (pp. 362–372). New York: Brunner/Mazel.

Schwab, J. J., McGinnis, N. H., & Warheit, G. L. (1973). Social psychiatric impairment: Racial comparisons. *American Journal of Psychiatry, 130,* 183–187.

Schwab, J. J., & Schwab, M. E. (1976). Sociocultural roots of mental illness: An epidemiological survey. New York: Plenum.

Seward, G. H. (1956). *Psychotherapy and culture conflict.* New York: Ronald.

Silver, B. J., Goldston, S. E., & Silver, L. B. (1984). The 1990 objectives for the nation for control of stress and violent behavior: Progress report. *Public Health Reports, 99,* 374–384.

Smythe, M. M. (1976). The Black American reference book. Englewood Cliffs, NJ: Prentice-Hall.

Stevenson, I. N. (1977). Colerina: Reactions to emotional stress in the Peruvian Andes. *Social Science & Medicine, 11,* 303–307.

Stone, A. (1980). Presidential address: Conceptual ambiguity and morality in modern psychiatry. *American Journal of Psychiatry, 137,* 887–891.

Stonequist, E. V. (1937). *The marginal man.* New York: Scribner & Sons.

Sue S., & Chin R. (1983). The mental health of Chinese-American children: Stressors and resources. In G. J. Powell, J. Yamamoto, A. Romero, & A. Morales (Eds.), *The psychosocial development of minority group children* (pp. 385–397). New York: Brunner/Mazel.

Suzuki, P. T. (1981). Psychological problems of Turkish migrants in West Germany. *American Journal of Psychotherapy, 35,* 187–194.

Thomas, A., & Sillen, S. (1974). *Racism and psychiatry.* Secaucus, NJ: Citadel Press.

Timmreck, T. C., & Stratton, L. H. (1981). The health opinion survey translated into Spanish as a measure of stress for Hispanic cultures. *Journal of Psychiatric Nursing and Mental Health Services, 19,* 9–13.

Vander Kolk, C. J. (1978). Physiological reactions of black, Puerto Rican, and white students in suggested ethnic encounters. *Journal of Social Psychology, 104,* 107–114.

Vignes, A. J., & Hall, R. C. W. (1979). Adjustment of a group of Vietnamese people to the United States. *American Journal of Psychiatry, 136,* 442–444.

Weber, M. (1964). *The theory of social and economic organization* (T. Parsons, Trans.). New York: Free Press.

Willhelm, S. M. (1971). *Who needs the Negro?* Garden City: Doubleday.

Wilson, W. J. (1980). *The declining significance of race* (2nd ed.). Chicago: University of Chicago Press.

Wintrob, R. M. (1967). A study of disillusionment: Depressive reactions of Liberian students returning from advanced training abroad. *American Journal of Psychiatry, 123,* 1593–1598.

Wright, R. (1945). *Black boy.* New York: Harper & Row.

Yamamoto, K., & Davis, O. L. (1982). Views of Japanese and American children concerning stressful experiences. *Journal of Social Psychiatry, 116,* 163–171.

The Psychological Impact of Being Accused of, Investigated for, or Tried for Malfeasance

SEYMOUR L. HALLECK, MD

The term *malfeasance* describes conduct believed to be evil or harmful to a specific individual or to society in general. Although such conduct is usually condemned by the community, it does not always elicit an adverse community response. An individual who is unaware of having committed a harmful act or who has committed it under duress is usually not blamed or punished. Other harmful acts may be justified by the particular circumstances in which they occurred (for example, injuring another person in self-defense). Ordinarily blame is not assessed unless the harmful conduct was done intentionally, knowingly (knowing that it could cause harm but not intending to cause harm), recklessly, or negligently. Both in criminal and in civil law, these states of mind or patterns of conduct on the part of the malfeasor are necessary for the establishment of liability (Kadish & Paulsen, 1975).

The psychological impact of being labeled as a person who has done harm (whether to specific individuals or to society) is rarely discussed in legal or in medical textbooks. Most of the writing available on this subject is fictional. Here, however, the literature is rich, often depicting the painful, even agonizing suffering of persons labeled as wrongdoers. The fictional as well as the occasional verbal accounts of the experience of being accused of or investigated for malfeasance suggest that the stresses are severe enough to be of concern to behavioral scientists and physicians (Charles, Wilbur, & Frane, 1985; Perr, 1988). Unfortunately, discussion of this issue must rely heavily on anecdotes, introspection, and opinion. The following material is based on many interviews with defendants and attorneys involved in both civil and criminal processes as well as on my own experiences as a defendant in a malpractice suit.

THE SOURCES OF STRESS

The stressful aspect of being accused of or investigated for malfeasance is generated by a community response that invokes blame. Often, aversive consequences may be imposed on the wrongdoer without resorting to actual litigation. Violations of social values or social rules may result in punishment that results from changed attitudes or practices on the part of the community or its organizations. In many societies a person accused of adultery, for example, will be exposed to significant aversive consequences initiated by family, friends, and others in the community. Organizations such as the church may punish individuals who violate its precepts by denying them sacraments. In other instances, wrongdoers may be denied economic privileges that are freely granted to others. A bad credit record, for example, with the implied accusation of being a poor financial risk, can be a very substantial handicap in our society. Loss of esteem, intimacy, spiritual relief, or economic opportunity are formidable stresses that can be heaped on those accused of malfeasance even if no formal legal action is taken against them.

In the civil courts, malfeasors are accused of inflicting specific harms on individuals. Here, the wrongdoer is sued by the individual who is harmed (a plantiff) who seeks a remedy in the form of money. Such civil litigation may result in the wrongdoer losing both public esteem and wealth. In criminal litigation, on the other hand, the harms that must be remedied are presumed to be against the community. Here, the malfeasor is at risk of punishment (loss of freedom or money) that is felt to be morally deserved (he must pay his debt to society) or that meets some utilitarian need of the society (such as deterrence or restraint).

Accusations of malfeasance may, indeed, result in community sanctions such as public censure or denial of privileges; however, they may also lead to no further action at all. An accusation may simply be made and not be taken seriously enough by others in the community to bring about adverse consequences. If accusations are taken seriously, they lead to a process of investigation into the charges usually conducted through some legal means. Once individuals are subject to such investigation, they must, within the legal process, be responsive to many inquiries concerning their alleged wrongful conduct. They may have to appear for depositions or other court procedures. They will spend many hours discussing their situation with their attorneys and will also spend a great deal of time searching for witnesses, records, or documents that might verify their defensive position. All of these activities are burdensome (Halleck, 1980). They disrupt the alleged wrongdoer's life and encourage a position of chronic defensiveness. Once the investigation begins, the defendant lives under a cloud of preoccupation concerning possible consequences and need for vindication that dominates a great deal of his or her life (Charles, Wilbert, & Kennedy, 1984).

Under certain conditions, individuals can be investigated without being accused of anything. This is a relatively common event, and it is worth noting because it provides at least a general insight into how stressful even the threat of accusation can be. Individuals whose tax returns are audited by the Internal Revenue Service (IRS) are really not being accused of wrongdoing. Nevertheless, the tax audit process is highly stressful for many people, whether they are innocent or guilty of violating IRS regulations. Even individuals who keep unusually precise records and adhere to the letter of the law may still worry that they have made mistakes and will be punished. Those who are less careful about filling out their returns or keeping careful records are likely to suffer considerable anxiety and to spend to great deal of time searching for documents with which to verify their returns.

In civil or criminal litigation, once an investigation has produced sufficient evidence to go ahead with the process of litigation, the defendant's stresses tend to escalate. Most civil and criminal cases are settled one way or another long before they reach the trial stage, but, if there is a trial, it is an especially formidable stress for the defendant. At this point there may be a great deal of publicity and public condemnation by adversaries and unfriendly witnesses. To most individuals, the courtroom itself is a strange and frightening place, in which there is the constant risk of performing poorly or of making a damaging mistake. Defendants must remain calm as the adverse parties present their cases. It is not easy to sit quietly while being publicly condemned. When defendants have a chance to set out their own side of the issue, they are under extraordinary pressure to perform well; as a result, they may experience overwhelming anxiety when called to testify. The most stressful moment in the process of litigation perhaps occurs when the judge or jury announces the verdict. Unless one has observed or participated in trials it is difficult to appreciate the degree of tension, excitement, and fear that pervades the courtroom at this moment.

The Nature of Stress

The stresses of being accused of, investigated for, or tried for malfeasance are best conceptualized as losses. The most serious of these is the possible loss of freedom. Given current correctional practice, this loss is complicated even further when inmates are deprived of freedom under relatively brutal conditions. Prisons these days are more than just places where people go *as* punishment. To the extent that they go beyond the deprivation of freedom and impose severe conditions upon inmates, for example, putting them at constant risk of assault, they are also places where people go *for* punishment (Silberman, 1978).

In civil litigation there is a potential loss of money, opportunities, and social status. There is also a substantial loss of time. Even persons who are heavily insured for claims of personal injury or malpractice have no remedy for the amount of time they must spend away from work or pleasurable activities in order to be involved with their case.

Another potential loss is of reputation or self-esteem. Being a defendant in either civil or criminal litigation is almost always a humiliating experience. A person who has enjoyed a good community reputation risks its loss in the process of litigation. The defendant's own favorable self-view is also threatened. In court it is difficult to face accusations of wrongdoing without at some point wondering about self-worth. This is an especially painful phenomenon if the accusations are partially correct, but even if the accusations are wholly incorrect, the power of the court makes the defendant who does not have a stable self-concept worry about his or her validity as a person (Brown, 1987).

The defendant also experiences a powerful sense of loss of personal control over the course of life events. Choices become limited and autonomy is compromised as one is forced to participate in a process of litigation and can do little to alter it.

Finally, litigation confronts people with their vulnerability. Persons who have previously led stable and protected lives can find it to be an extremely disruptive and disorienting experience. Most people read about civil or criminal trials and assume that this is something that happens to others. Being a defendant reminds the individual of the realistic dangers of everyday living and the precarious nature of "normal" existence. It is a little bit like being in a major accident; and, indeed, for some individuals, it is followed by symptomatology similar to that seen in posttraumatic stress reactions (Halleck, 1986).

RESPONSES TO STRESS

The emotional responses to litigation vary with the individual and with the circumstances of accusation and litigation, but certain general responses usually appear. Ordinarily, the defendant feels unjustly accused and may feel a great deal of animosity, indeed even of rage toward the accusers. This response often occurs even when the defendant recognizes that the accusation is warranted. Almost all defendants also experience some intrapunitive responses and blame themselves for real or imagined misconduct. Individuals who are innocent may blame themselves for not having been more careful, believing they should have avoided the possibility of litigation. There is also a powerful tendency to catastrophize and exaggerate the consequences of losing the legal battle. This is particularly true in civil suits where the actual consequences of loss are rarely as catastrophic as imagined (Wykoff, 1961).

The degree to which the individual suffers or becomes incapacitated by the process of litigation is largely influenced by his or her existing personality makeup. Ego and superego strengths are important here. Defendants who can use the defense mechanism of denial are at some advantage, particularly if, at critical moments of litigation, they can switch back to a more realistic appraisal of the situation. It also helps to be able to intellectualize and thus to isolate the content of what is happening from one's feelings. Rationalization may help preserve self-esteem. To a certain extent, projection may help to retain comfort, but this is at best a risky defense mechanism if it results in a failure to assess the power of an adversary or in inappropriate behavior that compromises a person's legal defense. Individuals whose superego structures are highly intrapunitive are likely to suffer greatly during the litigation process. On the other hand, people with psychopathic tendencies may well endure the process with greater ease.

The strength of family support is a critical issue. Defendants are likely to be exceptionally demanding and needy at this time. Marriages that are not particularly strong are at some risk of dissolving during litigation because defendants make more demands on spouses and are unlikely to be responsive to their needs (Eisenberg, 1987). Sometimes weak marriages hold together only until the end of litigation. Following the ordeal of litigation, during the ensuing period of relative calm and contemplation, both partners may come to appreciate that they were unable to help one another in this critical time and that they do not wish to remain together.

Those defendants who have an opportunity to enjoy other activities are more likely to go through litigation without undue distress or disruption of their lives. Certainly, criminal defendants who are out on bail have a much easier time of it than those who remain in prison. In general, defendants who are active and involved in work or recreational activities where they can gain a certain amount of self-esteem and other types of reinforcement do much better.

Having sufficient financial resources to be unworried by cost is a major factor in easing the stress of litigation. Even persons who are insured against liability suits sometimes wonder whether their insurance is adequate and if a successful lawsuit will result in bankruptcy. Having other sources of revenue serves in part to alleviate this concern. When criminal charges are involved, the quality of legal counsel often determines the outcome. Good attorneys are expensive, and defendants who can afford them are in an advantageous position.

A strong religious faith may also help many individuals to survive the distress of litigation. It is especially helpful in coping with the existential problems of personal vulnerability and helplessness.

The guilt or innocence of the defendant may make some difference in his or her response to litigation. Persons who acknowledge some guilt but try to defend themselves may be subject to many intrapunitive feelings. The defendant's position of belief in innocence, however, also risks making the litigation more stressful. The individual who feels falsely accused is driven to self-defense, and this usually means a prolonged exposure to uncertainty and the stresses of litigation. There is a powerful tendency among persons accused of wrongdoing to minimize the harms they have caused or to insist they are totally innocent. This is not a matter of outright dishonesty. Rather, most defendants probably distort the facts in a manner that supports their self-concept and self-esteem, and serves their interests. This is particularly likely when the litigation process is prolonged and the events that are being discussed happened many years previously. In this situation, memory for the individual under attack tends to be self-serving.

POSSIBLE REMEDIES

The person accused of wrongdoing can initiate certain responses to make the processes of accusation, investigation, and trial less stressful. First of all, discussing the issue with other individuals, though perhaps somewhat embarrassing, is an important way to receive the counsel and support of others. When I was being sued for malpractice, I made it a point to be very open about the suit and to discuss it in any situation that seemed appropriate. I almost always received very helpful and supportive responses.

The defendant also benefits by performing a kind of cognitive self-therapy. It is important for the person to stress the realities of what can happen in the course of litigation and to measure them against fantasies. Usually the fantasies turn out to be catastrophic in character and much worse than the realities. Cognitive messages of optimism and reinforcement of self-image are also helpful.

Persons who are intellectually inclined can alleviate anxiety and achieve some mastery of the situation by becoming heavily and productively involved in the case. This may include studying the legal issues or other technical aspects of the situation. Albeit a painful experience, being a defendant can also be an educational one.

It is also important that the defendant not give up other aspects of life that are positively reinforcing. With the exception of the time that must be spent in efforts to deal with the case successfully, the defendant should remain heavily involved in meeting everyday obligations and enjoying the usual pleasures in other aspects of life.

Finally, all means of tension reduction including meditation, self-hypnosis, deep muscle relaxation, or vigorous athletic activity can be very helpful. Reliance on alcohol or drugs is, of course, ill-advised.

The stresses of being accused of, investigated for, and tried for wrongdoing bear some resemblance to the stresses of going off to war. The alleged malfeasor is exposed to a significant disruption of life-style and to a certain amount of danger. He or she encounters a wealth of new experiences that take on powerful meaning against the background of excitement and tension pervading any conflict with high stakes. The defendant meets new people, makes new friends and, perhaps, new enemies. For some, being accused of or tried for malfeasance can be a traumatic encounter with society that leaves indelible scars. For others, it is a maturing experience that, like going off to war, may be remembered with mixed feelings of bitterness and warmth. Even when the experience results in emotional growth, however, it is painful. There are easier ways of seeking growth.

REFERENCES

Brown, S. (1987). The doctor who chose death over a malpractice trial. *Medical Economica*, *6*, 22–57.

Charles, S. C., Wilbert, J. R., & Kennedy, E. C. (1984). Physicians' self reports of reactions to malpractice litigation. *American Journal of Psychiatry*, *141*, 563–565.

Charles, S. C., Wilbur, J. R., & Frane, K. J. (1985). Sued and non sued physicians' self reported reactions to malpractice litigation. *American Journal of Psychiatry*, *142*, 437–440.

Eisenberg, N. (1987). Malpractice suits are a family affair. *Medical Economics*, *4*, 27, 138.

Halleck, S. L. (1980). *Law in the practice of psychiatry*. New York: Plenum.

Halleck, S. L. (1986). Doctors as defendants: Are we too "precious"? *Contemporary Psychiatry*, *5*, 1–4.

Kadish, S., & Paulsen, M. (1975). *Criminal law and its processes*. Boston: Little, Brown.

Perr, I. (1988). Claims of psychiatric injury after alleged false arrest. *Journal of Forensic Sciences*, *33*(1), 21–34.

Silberman, C. E. (1978). *Criminal violence, criminal justice*. New York: Random House.

Wykoff, R. L. (1961). The effects of malpractice suits upon physicians in Connecticut. *Journal of the American Medical Association*, *176*, 1098–1101.

— CHAPTER 20

Forced Displacement to a New Environment

PETER STEINGLASS, MD
ELLEN GERRITY, PhD

This chapter will review available data regarding the relationship between a specific type of stressful life event—a forced displacement to a new environment—and the subsequent incidence of mental health problems. In examining this question, we will integrate research findings from four major sources: (1) studies of involuntary relocation necessitated by natural and/or human-made disasters; (2) studies of politically motivated relocations (e.g. urban renewal, migration); (3) studies of institutional relocation (especially of the aged); and (4) the research on job-related relocation. This last group of studies will include some data on voluntary relocation. They are included because they provide a valuable baseline regarding the mental health impact of relocation itself (as opposed to forced displacement) as a potential stressor.

This literature must still be viewed as preliminary, even at times as speculative, rather than as substantive. It is not surprising, therefore, that thus far few consistent findings have emerged from these studies. Instead, results often seem idiosyncratic and limited to the particular situation being studied. For this reason, we will include in our chapter not only a review of the major findings of research in these four areas (disaster studies, politically motivated relocation, institutional relocation, and job-related displacement), but also a review of various stress models in which the association between forced displacement and stress-induced psychiatric disorders is examined.

LITERATURE ON NATURAL AND HUMAN-CAUSED DISASTERS

From 1971 to 1980, under the guidelines of the Disaster Relief Act 326 separate events were declared by the President to be "federal major disasters" (Melick, Logue, & Frederick, 1982). The vast majority of these events were natural disasters necessitating relief and/or rehabilitation for substantial numbers of people living in the communities. Although occasionally a disaster was a delimited one, primarily affecting the commercial areas of a community, the more typical situation was one in which both residential and commercial areas were damaged or destroyed. Hence high on the list of necessary relief efforts was often a need for temporary shelter followed by relocation to new housing.

It has long been assumed that such disaster-precipitated, involuntary relocations would be associated with substantial short- and long-term evidence of psychosocial maladjustment, if not major psychopathology (Logue, Melick, & Hansen, 1981). Many of the early clinically oriented disaster studies certainly suggested that this was the case. The best example of this kind is the extensive study of the Buffalo Creek, West Virginia, flood carried out by a team of mental health professionals under the overall direction of the Department of Psychiatry of the University of Cincinnati Medical School (Glesser, Green, & Winget, 1981). The details were as follows: Following the sudden bursting of an earthen dam, a mass of water rushed through Buffalo Creek Valley destroying numerous small communities dotting the valley for several miles downstream from the dam. Property loss was massive, loss of life was substantial, and community integrity was virtually destroyed. Survivors were relocated in multiple makeshift trailer communities sited considerably downstream from the original communities. For most of the survivors, relocation sites that had originally been designed as temporary housing became quasi-permanent residences. Little effort was made to relocate survivors on the basis of prior communal ties or extended family relationships.

A class-action suit was subsequently initiated by a group of survivors against the coal-mining company whose alleged negligence had led to the dam's bursting and the subsequent flood. In connection with this, an extensive study of the psychiatric status of survivors was undertaken. The findings of the study are conditioned by the fact that only plaintiff families in the law suit were studied. But keeping this in mind, the findings can be divided into two parts—those related to individual psychodynamics and those thought to emanate from individual/community interactions. Regarding psychological response patterns, the psychiatric team reported both short-term and long-term (2 years postdisaster) sequelae in over 80% of adults and 90% of children interviewed. Short-term responses in adults took the form of psychic numbing, sluggishness in both thinking and decision making, anxiety, grief and despair, and severe sleep disturbances. Long-term responses included depressive symptoms, somatic complaints, and survivor guilt, plus characterological changes in the direction of listlessness, apathy, decreased social interaction, and chronic depression. Children experienced similar symptoms but were subject to developmental problems as well.

Thus the findings suggested almost uniform short-term and long-term psychopathology in both adults and children. The research team members, who were primarily psychoanalytically oriented, suggested that the symptom complex (which they dubbed the "Buffalo Creek Syndrome") resulted from the activation of intense affects; these overwhelmed the ego's capacity to integrate the traumatic experience and to control and discharge these affects. As a consequence, ego collapse occurred and required fully 6 to 24 months to reorganize.

The impression left by these clinical findings was that a disaster like Buffalo Creek leads to widespread and lasting psychopathology. Previously healthy individuals were as vulnerable to these effects as were previously compromised individuals. At the same time, however, it should be clear that the scientific rigor of the study is suspect. No comparison group was used in the research design, the subjects were plaintiffs in a law suit, the investigators were sympathetic to these victims of industrial negligence, and the interview data were largely clinical (not based on research instruments of established reliability and validity).

Moreover, an objective review of the empirically based disaster literature of the past two decades leads to a somewhat different conclusion (Quarantelli, 1979). Although the prevailing opinion still suggests that long-term psychological consequences are profound and negative (Bennet, 1970; Gleser et al., 1981; Melick, 1976; Moore, 1958), this conclusion is far from universal. Other studies have suggested that changes in psychological status are at most mildly negative (Bromet, 1980; Dohrenwend, Dohrenwend, Kasl, & Warheit, 1979; Logue, 1978) or insignificant (Bates, Fogelman, Parentin, Pittman, & Tracey, 1968; Hall & Landreth, 1975; Sterling, Drabek, & Key, 1975). Indeed, such events may actually lead to improved functioning especially in relation to family life (Bolin, 1976; Drabek, Erickson, & Crowe, 1975) and neighborhood relations (Moore, 1958).

How might these seemingly contradictory findings be interpreted? One possible contributory factor is a methological issue—the difficulty in dealing with the disaster variable. That is, the comparability of psychological impairment findings across disaster studies may not have surfaced because as generic phenomena disasters are simply not interchangeable. Attempts to deal with this problem via the development of disaster typologies have not yet yielded a sophisticated, reliable, and consistently meaningful product (i.e., the identification of specific disaster-related dimensions that are predictably associated with differential mental health outcomes) (Green, 1982). In sum, there is so little agreement about how to structure the disaster variable in a research design that a "disaster differences" hypothesis cannot yet be critically examined.

A different approach has been proposed by a growing number of reviewers of this literature; they are attempting to look more carefully at the dominant theoretical models that underpin this work in order to seek out more satisfying alternative models (Kinston & Rosser, 1974; Perry & Lindell, 1978; Tierney & Baisden, 1979). In particular, the "breakdown model" suggests that negative psychological outcomes are the inevitable result of exposure to the extreme and prolonged stress associated with natural disasters; this is now being criticized on the grounds that it does not adequately explain the seemingly contradictory findings from different studies regarding mental health consequences. Interest has turned instead to multidimensional interactional models that attempt to consider both social context and personal attributes (e.g. family and social community) as well as characteristics of the disaster in explaining outcomes regarding psychological and social functioning.

A study of the long-term effects of Cyclone Tracy was carried out by Milne (1977). It provides one of the most interesting studies of the mental health impact of relocation to appear in the disaster literature. This storm was of almost unprecedented intensity; it struck the Australian community of Darwin on Christmas Day 1974, totally destroying an estimated 5,000 of the 8,000 homes in the community and leaving only about 500 in continuously habitable shape. A massive airlift was necessary to transport people vast distances to other communities capable of providing medical assistance and emergency shelter. As a result, during the ensuing 6 days through New Year's Eve, the community population was reduced from 45,000 to 10,500 people.

Milne attempted to focus specifically on the postdisaster adjustment of three different groups of subjects: those who remained in Darwin because they either refused to be evacuated or were never placed on the evacuation list; those who were initially evacuated, but had returned to Darwin by the time the study was carried out approximately 1 year postdisaster; and those who were evacuated and never returned to Darwin. Utilizing a structured symptom checklist designed to measure pre- versus postdisaster psychosocial functioning, the most interesting analyses dealt with comparisons among the three different samples of Darwin people. Basically, the findings indicated those respondents who had stayed in Darwin fared best; nonreturned evacuees fared worst. This group experienced a significantly greater degree of "worry and depression," "lack of confidence," and psychosomatic disturbances. Perhaps most interesting of all, in their postdisaster adjustment patterns the returnees were closer to the stayers than to the nonreturned evacuees.

Milne's interpretation of his findings echoed a theme found repeatedly in the disaster literature. It suggests that, in the long run, victims who remain within the community and its natural social support network fare much better than do evacuees, (Crabbs & Heffron, 1981; Poulshock & Cohen, 1975). Milne likens the postdisaster reactions of a community like Darwin to a "therapeutic community"; he cites Fritz (1961) and Dynes & Quarantelli (1975) as other authors who have emphasized that in postdisaster communities group process variables serve to strengthen the adaptive capacities of community residents.

POLITICALLY MOTIVATED RELOCATION

Forced displacement can occur as a result of many things. It may come about because of political changes or as a by-product of industrialization: the construction of dams; urban renewal; development of new road systems; expanding industry; or the closing of nonprofitable businesses (Shumaker & Conti, 1985). Such politically caused migrations can simulate the disaster setting in three important ways: (1) Homes are destroyed by an "outside" force; (2) affected individuals are forced to relocate; and (3) neighborhood and other ties are disrupted as a consequence of the event. Under these circumstances, certain disaster-impact stresses are, of course, missing: death, injury, loss of some types of personal possessions, and the intervention of nature as the "causal-blame" factor. Despite these differences, urban renewal and other such activities provide a real-life experimental setting for the study of the mental health consequences of forced displacement and disruption of neighborhood ties and support systems.

A now-classic study of this type of forced displacement was carried out by Marc Fried and his colleagues in the early 1960s (Fried, 1963). More than 500 residents of Boston's West End were interviewed both before and after they had been relocated to make room for urban renewal. Fried had anticipated that residents would report short-term psychological discomfort in response to the crisis of being forced to move. He discovered instead that they experienced a severe grief reaction. Rather than being transitory, this grief reaction persisted for a long time after these residents had resettled in a new neighborhood. In fact, up to a year after the move almost 50% of respondents reported feeling sadness or depression, and 2 years after relocation 25% of residents still felt sad or depressed.

Fried interpreted this grief reaction as a response to the loss of stable neighborhood social networks that had been a central ingredient in community life. Dislocation from the old neighborhood had fragmented the established networks of easily accessible and familiar interpersonal contacts that were essential to the social life of the West End. Fried found that the severe grief reactions were commonest among residents who had held the most positive feelings about their West End neighbors, and most pronounced among persons who reported that their five closest friends had lived in the West End. When asked how they felt about being forced to leave the West End, typical resident responses were: "I lost all the friends I knew"; "I felt like my heart was taken out of me"; "I felt as though I had lost everything."

These data led Fried to postulate that feelings of home are integrally tied to a specific place, a phenomenon he called "sense of spatial identity." He defined "spatial identity" as an aspect of personal identity that derives from a sense of connectedness to a home. Fried also invoked Erik Erikson's concept of group identity, which refers to the individual's sense of belonging, of being a part of larger human and social entities.

Because Fried's study was based on extensive interview data and included pre-relocation as well as post-relocation measures, his findings have been widely cited as a reference point for understanding the mental health consequences of involuntary relocation. Further, by analogizing relocation reactions to the already familiar process of bereavement, Fried placed the data within a familiar and comprehensible framework. At the same time, however, it must be pointed out that no formal clinical evaluations of the subjects were carried out. Hence the extent of diagnosable psychopathology in the sample attributable to the forced relocation remains unclear. Nevertheless, Fried's descriptions of subject reactions suggest that a sizable number would have met DSM-III criteria for Major Depressive Disorder and/or Adjustment Disorder.

Fried's conclusions have received additional support from more recent research focusing on forced displacement due to urban renewal. Two main findings emerge from these studies: (1) Forced relocation is associated with some type of maladjustment (variously defined) among some proportion of relocated individuals (Brand & Smith, 1974; Joyce & Nenno, 1966; Kasl & Rosenfield, 1980; Mogey, Donahue, & Wiersma, 1971; Thursz, 1964); and (2) this impact on psychological adjustment is most likely secondary to the major disruptions in social ties and support systems associated with the forced relocation.

In contrast to the substantial body of research on the psychological consequences of urban renewal, research studies of politically caused *migrations* are relatively rare. By and large, these studies have been able to examine parameters of coping and adjustment to forced displacement only after the stressful event has occurred. Because of the degree of disruption usually associated with such migrations (e.g., displacement secondary to war), systematic study of their psychiatric consequences has proven extremely difficult to carry out.

One notable exception is a longitudinal study of the evacuation of residents of the Israeli community of Ophira, a small town at the southern tip of the Sinai peninsula, which had to be totally evacuated in March 1982 as a consequence of the Camp David agreement with Egypt (Steinglass, De-Nour, & Shye, 1985). During the month immediately preceeding evacuation and relocation, information was systematically collected from a subsample of 66 married adults. This data collection focused on demographic variables, coping styles, perceived social network characteristics, and psychosocial functioning. Two years post-relocation in Israel proper, a second panel of data collection was then carried out on a subgroup of these subjects. Thus the investigators were able to examine not only the cross-sectional relationships among coping styles, social network characteristics, and psychosocial adjustment, but were also able to compare pre-relocation response patterns with long-term adjustment postdisplacement.

The unique characteristics of the Ophira community—especially its small size, its relative geographical isolation from Israel proper, and the fixed membership of the community—made it an ideal "natural experiment" for examining the psychosocial consequences of a politically motivated forced displacement. Not only was the displacement event "standardized," but even more importantly, the characteristics of the community meant that key environmental variables were also strikingly similar for all members of the community. What individuals made of these environmental resources obviously differed, but the potential availability of resources was remarkably standardized for all subjects studied.

The main findings from this study can be summarized as follows:

(1) Cross-sectional pre-relocation analyses indicated clear-cut and powerful relationships between (a) selected dimensions of individual coping style (active coping and self-image) and psychological adjustment; (b) perceived personal network size and social adjustment; and (c) specific sociodemographic variables (ethnic origin and educational level) and adjustment.

(2) At the same time, measures of individual coping style and personal network characteristics were not significantly correlated, suggesting that these two domains reflect different types of resource variables.

(3) Post-relocation assessments of psychosocial functioning carried out 2 years after the evacuation indicated that levels of distress remained high. But more importantly, these assessments indicated that level of pre-relocation distress was a highly accurate predictor of subsequent adjustment post-relocation.

(4) Pre-relocation assessments of coping style and personal network characteristics were *better* predictors of long-term post-relocation adjustment (at 2-year follow-up) than were repeat measures of these characteristics ascertained at the time of follow-up (this last set of findings are unpublished data). In particular, cross-lagged correlational findings indicated the following sequence as the most plausible one in determining long-term adjustment: Pre-relocation coping styles, especially the degree to which the individual was manifesting active coping strategies, appeared to determine the level of psychological demoralization present at the time of the evacuation; this level of demoralization was in turn the best predictor of long-term adjustment.

Based on these findings, Steinglass and his colleagues argued that both the indices of individual coping style and personal network characteristics utilized in the study were reflective of underlying personal constructs subjects held about the nature of their environment. The coping style indices were thought to reflect the subject's perception of the environment as choate, comprehensible and masterable. The perceived size of the subjects' personal networks, on the other hand, reflected a personal construct about the extent to which they felt embedded in an extensive and stable social network. To the extent that subjects felt themselves to be part of a choate and masterable environment (despite the disruption of the forced relocation about to be experienced), and embedded in a stable and substantive personal network, the proximal negative implications of the forced displacement seemed to be significantly attenuated. Steinglass and his colleagues further argue that this ability of personal constructs to attenuate proximal distress (especially degree of demoralization) is in turn one of the major mediators of the differential long-term psychological impact of the relocation as well.

Prior studies of psychological distress in response to involuntary relocation have differed in their conclusions about the level of distress experienced by the populations studied. In particular, the extent to which proximal distress is sustained over longer periods of time is unclear. The picture that seems to be emerging, however, is that the characteristics of the stressor event itself play a large role in the subsequent level and persistence of psychological distress. Relocations secondary to stressful events that (1) are human-caused rather than natural occurrences, and (2) affect whole communities appear to have more profound and perhaps more long-lasting effects. Follow-up data currently being analyzed in the Ophira study may also shed further light on this question.

INSTITUTIONAL RELOCATION

Institutional relocation represents a different type of forced displacement. In general, residents of institutions can be viewed as a more vulnerable population and at greater risk for relocation actions that are beyond their control. The research in this area focuses on three types of populations: (1) elderly residents of nursing homes and other institutions; (2) psychiatric inpatients; and (3) mentally retarded inpatients. Conceptually, the notion is that the displacement of such potentially vulnerable populations might place them at risk for substantial post-relocation psychopathology.

The Elderly

Studies of the mental health effects of relocation on the elderly have been numerous but unfortunately subject to many design flaws. A numer of solid reviews of this literature are available (Carp, 1976; Lawton, 1977; Kasl & Rosenfield, 1980); they repeatedly make the same points in calling the various studies of the elderly to task. For example, Kasl and Rosenfield characterize the literature on the effects of residential environment on the aged as "significantly flawed." They ascribe this to the quasi-experimental character of these studies and to the almost uniform tendency to speculate about cause and effect between environmental and mental health outcome variables without postulating or studying possible intervening variables.

The various reviews of the literature suggest that studies of relocation and the elderly can be divided into four major groups: (1) the impact on the aged of new or planned housing, with attention paid to environmental characteristics such as location, available services, and architectural structure; (2) the impact of institutionalization and institutional environments; (3) the consequences of relocation or forced residential moves; and (4) the impact of special residential settings, particularly retirement communities. For our purposes, the studies of relevance are those that examine forced displacement of elderly persons living in or relocated to institutions.

Studies of the impact of institutionalization and institutional transfer on the aged have documented far more profound negative effects than those examining the effects of home-to-home relocation. Prominent here is the strikingly higher mortality rate of aged subjects within the first year of hospitalization or institutionalization (Pastalan, 1980; Rowland, 1977). However, as Kasl and Rosenfield (1980) have pointed out, these data should not be used to infer that the specific stress associated with environmental change produces this higher mortality rate. A plausible alternative hypothesis is that the condition of the aged in these studies is such that institutionalization occurs at times of significant deterioration or debilitation. Moreover, rather than stress being caused by the relocation itself, other major contributing factors might bring this about, such as specific physical attributes of the institution, including diet, sensory deprivation, and decreased social contact.

It might seem that studies of individuals transferred from one institution to another would provide a better model for the examination of the impact of relocation. Here too, however, the characteristics of the two residential environments involved, as well as variations in the relocation process or the decision to transfer, can clearly influence outcome findings. A study by Jasnau (1967) illustrates this point nicely. Jasnau observed that for the transferred group, overall group means for mortality rates were higher compared to pretransfer rates or to controls. However, within-group analyses suggested that this finding held only for subjects who were part of a mass move carried out with no individual preparation. In particular, he demonstrated that following the move, subjects who received individualized attention (casework service, psychological support, etc.) actually showed a lower-than-expected death rate.

Similar findings emerged from a study by Bourestom and Tars (1974) that attempted specifically to tease out two variables—whether the move was voluntary or involuntary, and the degree of environmental change involved—and to examine the contribution of these variables to differential post-relocation adjustment. Their study compared adjustment in three different groups: (1) a "radical change" group, in which individuals were being moved from a county nursing home facility to a new and much larger proprietary home in a nearby community; (2) a "moderate move" group, in which a nursing home population was being moved to a new building located several hundred yards away, with staff, patient groups, and the nature and structure of the program remaining basically intact; and (3) a "control" group of nursing home residents who were not relocated. The major dependent measure was mortality rate. The "radical change" group had a significantly higher mortality rate (43% died during the period of 6 months preceding relocation through the year following relocation compared to a rate of 21% for controls). The "moderate change" group, although experiencing a higher death rate than controls, did not have a statistically significant difference in mortality rates.

Schulz and Brenner (1977) have conducted an extensive review of research on relocation of the elderly. They conclude that findings are consistent with the hypothesis that an individual's response to the stress of relocation is determined largely by the "perceived controllability and predictability of the event surrounding the move, and differences in environmental controllability between pre- and post-relocation environments" (p. 33). However, they also point out that thus far no studies available in the literature have been specifically designed to test critically the relevance of controllability and predictability as mediators of stress response.

Psychiatric Inpatients

The effect of relocation on psychiatric inpatients seems to depend on the type and number of transfers. Studies of patients transferred to another institution only once report no significant adverse effects from the move (Barrington, Burke, & La Faue, 1962; Smith, Oswald, & Farucki, 1976). Repeated transfers, however, result in an increased incidence of psychiatric symptoms, for example, social withdrawal and decreased self-care (Lentz & Paul, 1971; Zlotowski & Cohen, 1968). A short distance relocation (e.g., within the same complex) seems to have an opposite effect; that is, patients may actually show a slight improvement in overt behavioral symptomatology (DeVries, 1968; DiScipio & Wolf, 1974).

Heller (1982) suggested that the lack of adverse effects from single transfers may be because this patient population tends to withdraw from their social environment and to have little attachment to peers and staff. DeVries (1968) attributed the improvement associated with short-distance transfers to the increased level of social interaction that occurs when these normally withdrawn patients begin to cope with the disruption and uncertainty of the move.

Mentally Retarded Inpatients

Only a few studies have been done on the impact of institutional transfer on mentally retarded inpatients. The few findings related to the profoundly retarded are conflicting. In this group, following transfer, Carsrud, Carsrud, Henderson, Alisch, and Fowler (1979) reported a decrease in overall activity whereas Cohen, Conroy, Fraser, Snelbecker, and Spreat (1977) reported an increase in activity. On the other hand, in Cohen's study the *severely* retarded inpatients became more withdrawn and showed decreases in language functioning after institutional transfer. Another study (Rago, 1976) involved 342 transferred mentally retarded persons; it found their mortality rate to be twice that of the residents who remained in the institution from which the study patients had been moved.

Environmental change was also examined by Martindale and Kilby (1982); they conducted a study of the short- and long-term effects on mentally retarded residents of transfer from a public residential facility. The general finding was that multiple transfers tended to lead to more deterioration in behavior than to improvements.

Coffman and Harris (1980) attributed these kinds of behavior problems to "transition shock" and compared relocation difficulties to transitional adjustments made by nonretarded persons, for example, divorce aftermath, release from prison, and culture shock.

As with the elderly and the psychiatric inpatients, mentally retarded persons appear to experience more difficulty with the characteristics surrounding a relocation (e.g. timing, frequency, type of new environment, amount of preparations for the move) than with the displacement itself. This suggests that future research should focus on the context of the entire displacement rather than exclusively on the postdisplacement adjustment period.

JOB-RELATED DISPLACEMENT

Research interest in the effects of displacement on physical and mental health has been stimulated by the perception of American society as a highly mobile one. Census figures suggest that 20% of the population relocate each year and that the typical American moves 14 times in his or her lifetime. Within a 5-year period, almost 50% of the U.S. population relocate at least once (Long & Boertlein, 1976). Several good review articles are available dealing with this literature (Brett, 1980; Heller, 1982; Shumaker & Conti, 1985; Stokols & Shumaker, 1982).

In her review of this literature, Brett (1980) contends that popular interest in the psychological consequences of relocation has resulted in the creation of a series of "folklore"-induced myths about the stresses related to job transfer. Her review is organized around a comparison of each of these myths with the formal research data available regarding that particular area. The popular perception of relocation regards it as highly stressful and associated with negative mental health outcomes; her conclusion is that the research literature does not uniformly substantiate this. At the same time, however, Brett offers the following general comment about the empirical literature on job transfer: "None of these studies delves deeply into the reasons why a job transfer is disruptive, what stimulates coping, or why poor mental or physical health may result from a transfer" (page 104).

The author claims that (as of 1980) she was unable to find any studies that specifically attempted to relate job transfer with degree of employee mental health. That is, no study was designed to address magnitude and type of mental disorders specifically and critically as dependent variables. Thus, mental health status as an outcome variable must be largely inferred from other measures, such as job satisfaction, social adjustment, or level of nonspecific distress.

Nevertheless, this literature is of interest in that unanticipated and mandated relocation secondary to job transfer may be the best analogy available to a relocation event occurring in a context that has potentially positive, as well as negative attributes. Presumably this type of relocation is both personally meaningful, as well as a product of the dictates and needs of the larger business or corporation. In this sense, it provides a sharp contrast to the relative absence of choice and meaning that occurs during redevelopment (slum clearance, highway construction, etc.) or disaster-instigated displacement.

The most important conclusion to be drawn from this kind of general mobility research is that relocation per se does not appear to be consistently associated with negative health outcomes. In general, when carefully designed surveys of large-scale samples are performed, the impact of residential mobility is far less severe than is commonly hypothesized (e.g., Brett & Werbel, 1978; Butler, McAllister, & Kaiser, 1973). This is true even when it is involuntary in nature.

At the same time, however, these studies have made clear that job relocation is not a uniformly benign experience. For example, McKain's (1973) study of military family relocation demonstrated strong correlations between feelings of alienation from the community (in this case expressed by the wife-mother in the family) and postrelocation reports of multiple family problems. These findings provide a significant conformation of the importance of connectedness to the community as a mediator of the stresses associated with involuntary relocation. But the findings also make clear that some people, if subjected to relocations (even anticipated relocations), are surely at risk for mental health problems.

The challenge, therefore, is to develop more sophisticated research models of this stressor, which pay attention not only to multifaceted assessments of subjects experiencing the stressor, but which propose equally detailed descriptions of the critical environmental and stressor-related variables that contributed to outcome variance. In this sense, this research literature in its current state has many of the same methodological and conceptual difficulties noted in the disaster research literature (Green, 1982).

Thus, although very little hard evidence is available from these mobility studies, hypotheses regarding sources of potential disruption are both of interest and clearly applicable to disaster-initiated relocations. Basically, what has been suggested by authors like Brett is that emphasis should be placed on the subject's ability to maintain role-directed social routines as the central determinant of adequacy of adjustment to relocation. Even though direct testing of such hypotheses has not yet been done, indirect evidence supportive of their validity can be inferred from available literature. Hence, at the very least, these are interesting working hypotheses worthy of more focused research. Increasingly sophisticated stress and coping models have evolved in recent years. Promising future studies are likely to emerge from the application of these new tactics to the problem of relocation.

STRESSES ASSOCIATED WITH FORCED DISPLACEMENT

The early studies of the effects of displacement secondary to urban renewal (Fellman & Brandt, 1970; Fried, 1963) suggested that the stress of relocation produces profound psychological consequences; however, subsequent studies have suggested precisely the opposite. This is especially true when destruction of whole communities is not the precipitant for the relocation (Brett, 1980; Kasl & Rosenfield, 1980; Schulz & Brenner, 1977). In fact, there are even suggestions in the literature that, on balance, relocation may be associated with positive mental health outcomes (Barrett & Noble, 1973; Hendrick, Wells, & Faletti, 1982).

Thus, it seems clear that it is necessary to look beyond the independent variable alone—forced displacement—to obtain a better understanding of the differential mental health outcomes of people exposed to these stressors. In particular, researchers need to identify the person-related and environment-related mediator variables that play a role in this developing and complex model.

Some examples of how such models might evolve can be found in writings of authors like Brett (1980) and Stokols and Shumaker (1982). In Brett's discussion, the primary concept is that of personal identity, an underlying personality construct that is enacted in the social roles a person plays while, at the same time, being shaped and formed as a function of these roles. These roles, in turn, consist of a set of routines—in essence, a series of behavioral programs—consisting of predictable sequences of behaviors and their outcomes connected to the person's role in various social settings. Insofar as moving and/or relocation has the potential of disrupting these routines, it can also threaten the underlying identity or sense of self. This is especially likely if such a disruption interferes with the attainment of valued outcomes or leads to a sense of uncertainty or lack of control over the environment.

Within this model, it is assumed that a person experiencing such stress will seek to establish similar routines in a new setting in order to replace valued outcomes, reduce uncertainty, and reassert control. If blocked in this process and if repeated efforts lead to increasing feelings of hopelessness in achieving or accomplishing this goal, symptoms of helplessness, depression, and withdrawal will inevitably arise. Finally, within this model, adjustment can be seen as the successful reestablishment of routines that provide valued outcomes and feelings of control. Presumably, the greater the perceived disruption of routines, the more difficult the adjustment is likely to be. This then is the assumed theoretical connection between relocation as a stressor and adverse mental health outcome.

One interesting aspect of the proposed model is its conceptualization as a cyclical model. As summarized by Brett (1980), the model "consists of three parameters that cycle: a cognitive appraisal that an event will disrupt routines, and evaluation of the likelihood that those routines can be re-established (hope), and a behavioral response, then a cognitive re-appraisal of the event, a re-evaluation of the likelihood that routines can be re-established, another behavioral response, and so on" (p. 102). Brett's model is therefore based solely on individual psychological parameters. Personality factors determine coping styles, and these styles, in turn, determine the magnitude of anxiety, depression, and so on associated with relocations or displacements.

Stokols and Shumaker (1982) take a very different position, emphasizing instead the interaction of individual and environmental variables as critical to mental health outcome. The individual variables on which they focus are the dimensions of "predictability" and "perceived control." These two psychological elements are factors that have been identified in the stress literature as major mediating variables of the impact of a stressful life event. However, Stokols and Shumaker argue that the focus on environmental predictability and controllability is far too narrow a conceptualization of the psychological meaning of mobility. Instead, they suggest a conceptualization that emphasizes the "context" of mobility, in particular the spatial and temporal components of relocation. Subjectivity rather than objectivity is emphasized as the crucial theoretical frame for the model.

In this model, major distinctions are made between (1) "place specificity," defined as the regular and observable association between a person's activities and certain locations (basically an objective assessment of environmental context); (2) "place dependence," which denotes the individual's perceptions of being strongly attached to places (a subjective assessment); and (3) "person-environment congruence," defined as "the belief that one's important goals and activities are accommodated by existing environmental conditions" (p. 158). Low person–environment congruence might occur either when people are separated from places to which they feel strong personal or cultural ties (a separation that might be voluntary or involuntary), or when people remain for long periods of time in undesirable places. Either of these situations would presumably lead to chronic life stress and negative mental and physical health outcomes. This model suggests that an assessment of the impact of relocation can be meaningful only if the person–environment congruence of the prior living situation is adequately determined.

Empirical evidence supporting this model derives from a longitudinal survey of 242 employed male and female adults carried out by Stokols and Shumaker. Comparisons were made between measures of environmental experience, dispositional factors, and health indices of emotional and physical well-being assessed at the time of relocation and then again 3 months later. Multivariate analyses of covariance and discriminate function analyses supported, in a general way, key hypotheses suggested by the authors' model.

The stress and coping models suggested by authors like Brett, and Stokols and Shumaker have obvious relevance for forced displacements caused by natural disasters. For example, discussions about which dimensions should be included in a typology of disasters often are centered on the concepts of predictability and controllability. These concepts are especially relevant when distinguishing human-made from natural disasters, or communitywide disasters from smaller, more personalized disaster experiences. Presumably, these would therefore predict such dependent outcomes measures as health status (both mental and physical).

CONCLUSION

In this chapter we have examined the evidence, pro and con, for possible links between forced displacement and negative mental health consequences. Toward this goal, we have looked at both the disaster-instigated displacement literature and the literature dealing more generally with relocation. What are the major conclusions to be drawn from these studies?

Regarding specific mental health consequences, on balance it appears that some displacement situations clearly lead to major negative mental health consequences. Studies reviewed here indicate that in some circumstances individuals may experience adjustment difficulties, depression, anxiety, feelings of alienation, social withdrawal, or various somatic problems (such as loss of appetite or sleeping disturbances) as a result of forced displacement. However, the overall picture is still so unclear as to provide little support for a conclusion that *most* individuals who undergo forced relocation should be considered at risk to develop serious mental health problems.

Nevertheless, we have also pointed to a number of problems inherent in this body of research that make the task of isolating the specific impact of forced displacement/relocation a difficult one and obviate against clear-cut conclusions. These difficulties may be summarized as follows:

1. The literature examining the mental health effects of forced displacement is a very small one and is, on balance, methodologically flawed.
2. With every stressful event necessitating relocation other losses are suffered secondary to the primary displacement. No study done to date has been specifically designed to look at the impact of forced displacement independent of these consequent traumata. For example, no studies are available that covary the effect of financial loss, death of family members or friends, or even such basic variables as socioeconomic status (SES) in the statistical analyses of their data. Thus, it can only be assumed that the reported relationships between forced displacement and mental health status are not attributable instead to some confounding variable.
3. Many disaster-instigated displacement studies (the largest group of studies we reviewed) deal with unique situations—especially with isolated communities unrepresentative of the general populations. Further, the applicability of the findings from these studies to other populations has rarely been systematically explored; as a result, the validity of generalizations based on these findings cannot be assumed.
4. The vast bulk of studies from the nondisaster displacement literature deals either with relocation of the elderly or with relocation secondary to job transfer. The first topic—the elderly—is devoted to an often compromised, high-risk population (e.g., nursing home residents) and may therefore be similarly misleading. The second topic—job transfer—combines examples of mandated relocation (e.g., studies of military families) along with self-motivated relocation; their findings may therefore be confusing and seemingly contradictory because the stressful situations are so different.
5. The general relocation literature, although far more voluminous than its di-

saster-related counterpart, is no less flawed regarding design issues, size and representativeness of subject samples, lack of clarity of definition of outcome variables, and sensitivity to statistical error.

Yet despite these many methodological problems, it is also the case that a number of consistent findings are beginning to emerge from this work. Of perhaps greatest import at this point is that these results seem consistent with already established findings in the stress and coping literature. For example, one relatively consistent finding in the stress and coping literature indicates that the negative mental health consequences of a particular stressor event are related directly to the degree to which the event is perceived as unpredictable and uncontrollable (Averill, 1973). This suggests that a focus on these variables would be profitable for the study of the consequences of forced displacement. Our review of the impact of forced displacement secondary to disasters or political upheavals certainly suggests that a comparable principle holds here as well.

Further, unpredictability is most likely a primary characteristic of the stressor (forced displacement) itself. However, individual perceptions regarding uncontrollability may well be a product of the impact of the external stressor on the two primary social organizations in which a person lives—the family and the community. This interpretation certainly is consistent with findings from relocation studies that have looked at breakdown in community coherence (Erikson, 1981) or family integrity (Bolin, 1982) as primary variables. Thus in seeking to determine the ultimate magnitude of mental health consequences of displacement, we might propose the following sequence as critical: a forced relocation can precipitate a set of family and community responses that the individual perceives as evidence of organizational disintegration. To the extent that relocation does have this effect, the tendency to experience the event as uncontrollable is heightened, and the ensuing mental health consequences are likely to be far more negative. On the other hand, insofar as the family and community are able to maintain their organizational integrity, the impact of the displacement on individuals is likely to be minimized.

REFERENCES

Averill, J. (1973). Personal control over adverse stimuli and its relationship to stress. *Psychiatric Bulletin, 80,* 286–303.

Barrett, C. L., & Noble H. (1973). Mother's anxieties versus the effects of long distance move on children. *Journal of Marriage and the Family, 35,* 181–188.

Barrington, L., Burke, J. L., La Faue, H. G. (1962). Mass transfer of two wards of chronic mental patients. *Psychiatric Quarterly, 36,* 286–295.

Bates, F., Fogelman, C., Parentin, V., Pittman, R. H., & Tracey, G. S. (1968). *The social and psychological consequences of natural disaster.* Washington, DC: National Academy of Sciences, National Research Council.

Bennet, G. (1970). Bristol Floods, 1968. *British Medical Journal, 3,* 454–458.

Bolin, R. C. (1976). Family recovery from natural disasters: A preliminary model. *Mass Emergency, 1,* 267–277.

Bolin, R. C. (1982). *Long-term family recovery from disasters.* Boulder: University of Colorado.

Bourestrom, N., & Tars, S. (1974). Alterations in life patterns following nursing home relocations. *Gerontology, 14,* 506–510.

Brand F., & Smith, R. (1974). Life adjustment and relocation of the elderly. *Journal of Gerontology, 29,* 336–340.

Brett, J. M. (1980). The effect of job transfer on employees and their families. In C. L. Cooper & P. Payne (Eds.), *Current concerns in occupational stress* (pp. 99–136).

Brett, J. M., & Werbel, J. D. (1978). *The effect of job transfer on employees and their families: Baseline survey report.* Washington DC: Employee Relocation Council.

Bromet, E. (1980). *Three Mile Island: Mental health findings.* Pittsburgh: University of Pittsburgh Western Psychiatric Institute.

Butler, E. W., McAllister, R. J., & Kaiser, E. J. (1973). Effects of voluntary and involuntary residential mobility on females and males. *Journal of Marriage and the Family, 35,* 219–227.

Carp, F. M. (1976). Housing and living environments of older people. In R. H. Binstock & F. Shanas (Eds.), *Handbook of aging and the social sciences* (pp. 244–271). New York: Van Nostrand Reinhold.

Carsrud A. L., Carsrud, K. B., Henderson, C. J., Alisch, C. J., & Fowler, A. V. (1979). Effects of social and environmental change on institutionalized mentally retarded persons: The relocation syndrome reconsidered. *American Journal of Mental Deficiency, 84,* 266–272.

Coffman, T. L., & Harris, M. C. (1980). Transition shock and adjustments of mentally retarded persons. *Mental Retardation, 18,* 308.

Cohen, H., Conroy, J. Q., Fraser, D. W., Snelbecker, G. E., & Spreat, S. (1977). Behavioral effects of interinstitutional relocation of mentally retarded residents. *American Journal of Mental Deficiency, 82,* 12–18.

Crabbs, M. A., & Heffron, E. (1981). Loss associated with a natural disaster. *Personnel and Guidance Journal, 59*(6), 378–382.

DeVries, D. L. (1968). Effects of environmental change and of participation on the behavior of mental patients. *Journal of Consulting and Clinical Psychiatry, 32,* 532–536.

DiScipio, W. J., & Wolf, S. (1974). Clinical and discharge status as a function of transfer from chronic to acute wards. *Journal of Community Psychiatry, 2,* 144–147.

Dohrenwend, B. P., Dohrenwend, B. S., Kasl, S. V., & Warheit, G. T. (1979, October 31). *Technical analysis report on behavioral effects to the president's commission on the accident at Three Mile Island* (Advance copy).

Drabek, T., Key, W., Erickson, P., & Crowe, J. (1975). The impact of disaster on kin relationships. *Journal of Marriage and the Family, 37,* 481–494.

Dynes, R. R., & Quarantelli, E. L. (1975). *Community conflict: Its absence and its presence in natural disasters.* Preliminary paper, The Ohio State University Disaster Research Center.

Erikson, K. T. (1981). *Everything in its path: Destruction of comunity in the Buffalo Creek flood.* New York: Academic Press.

Fellman, G., & Brandt, B. (1970). *Neighborhood a highway would destroy. Environment & Behavior, 2,* 281–301.

Fried, M. (1963). Grieving for a lost home. In L. Duhl (Ed.), *The urban condition: People and policy in the metropolis* (pp. 151–171). New York: Simon & Schuster.

Fritz, C. E. (1961). Disaster. In R. K. Merton & R. A. Nisbet (Eds.), *Contemporary social problems*. New York: Harcourt.

Gleser, G. C., Green, B. L., & Winget, C. (1981). *Prolonged psychosocial effect of disaster: A study of Buffalo Creek*. New York: Academic Press.

Green, B. L. (1982). Assessing levels of psychological impairment following disaster: Consideration of actual and methodological dimensions. *Journal of Nervous and Mental Disease, 170,* 544–552.

Hall, P. S., & Landreth, P. W. (1975). Assessing some long-term consequences of a natural disaster. *Mass Emergencies, 1,* 55–61.

Heller, T. (1982). The effects of involuntary residential relocation: A review. *American Journal of Community Psychiatry, 10,* 471–492.

Hendrick, C., Wells, K. S., & Faletti, M. V. (1982). Social and emotional effects of geographical relocation on elderly retirees. *Journal of Personal and Social Psychiatry, 42,* 951–962.

Jasnau, K. F. (1967). Individualized versus mass transfer for nonpsychotic geriatric patients from mental hospitals to nursing homes, with special reference to death rate. *Journal of the American Geriatrics Society, 15,* 280–284.

Joyce, D., & Nenno, M. (1966, December). *The social functioning of the dislodged elderly: A study of post relocation assistance*. Institute of Environment Studies, University of Pennsylvania.

Kasl, S. V., & Rosenfield, S. (1980). The residential environment and its impact on the mental health of the aged. In J. E. Birren & R. B. Sloane (Eds.), *Handbook of mental health and aging* (pp. 468–498). Englewood Cliffs, NJ: Prentice-Hall.

Kinston, W., & Rosser, R. (1974). Disaster, effects on mental and physical state. *Journal of Psychosomatic Research, 18,* 437–456.

Lawton, M. P. (1977). The impact of the environment on aging and behavior. In J. E. Birren & K. W. Schaic (Eds.), *Handbook of the psychology of aging.* (pp. 276–301). New York: Van Nostrand Reinhold.

Lentz, R. J., & Paul, G. L. (1971). Routine vs therapeutic transfer of chronic mental patients. *Archives of General Psychiatry, 25,* 187–191.

Logue, J. N. (1978). *Long-term effects of a major natural disaster: The Hurricane Agnes flood in the Wyoming Valley of Pennsylvania, June 1972.* Unpublished doctoral dissertation, Columbia University.

Logue, J. N., Melick, M. E., & Hansen, H. (1981). Research issues and directions in the epidemiology of health effects of disasters. *Epidemiology Review, 3,* 140–162.

Long, L. H., & Boertlein, C. G. (1976). The geographical mobility of Americans. In *Current population reports* (Special Studies Series P-23, No. 64). Washington, DC: U.S. Department of Commerce, Bureau of the Census.

Martindale, A., & Kilby, C. A. (1982). Symposium on changes of environment: Personal and social consequences. *British Journal of Mental Subnormality, 28,* 3–12.

McKain, J. L. (1973). Relocation in the military: Alienation and family problems. *Journal of Marriage and the Family, 35,* 205–209.

Melick, M. E. (1976). *Social, psychological and medical aspects of stress-related illness in the recovery period of a natural disaster.* Unpublished doctoral dissertation, State University of New York at Albany.

Melick, M. E., Logue, J. N., & Frederick, C. J. (1982). Stress and disaster. In L. Goldberger & S. Breznity (Eds.), *Handbook of stress: Theoretical and clinical aspects* (pp. 613–630). New York: Free Press.

Milne, G. (1977). Cyclone Tracy: I. Some consequences of the evacuation for adult victims. *Australian Psychologist, 12,* 39–54.

Mogey, J., Donahue, M., & Wiersma, E. (1971, December 3). Social effects of eminent domain: Changes on households after involuntary relocation for Southwest Expressway (I-95) Boston, 1968–1970—Final report. (A research project funded by Commonwealth of Massachusetts Department of Public Works and the U.S. Department of Transportation, Federal Highway Administration).

Moore, H. E. (1958). Some emotional concomitants of disaster. *Mental Hygiene, 42,* 45–50.

Pastalan, L. A. (1980). *Relocation, mortality, and intervention.* Paper presented at the annual meeting of the American Psychological Association, Montreal.

Perry, R. W., & Lindell, M. (1978). The psychological consequences of natural disaster: A review of research on American communities. *Mass Emergencies, 3,* 105–115.

Poulshock, S. W., & Cohen, E. S. (1975). The elderly in the aftermath of a disaster. *Gerontology, 15,* 357–361.

Quarantelli, E. L. (1979), The consequences of disaster for mental health: Conflicting views. Columbus: Ohio State University.

Rago, W. V. (1976). On the transfer of the profoundly mentally retarded. *Mental Retardation, 14,* 27.

Rowland, K. F. (1977). Environmental events predicting death for the elderly. *Psychiatric Bulletin, 84,* 349–372.

Schulz, R., & Brenner, G. (1977). Relocation of the aged: A review and theoretical analysis. *Journal of Gerontology, 32,* 323–333.

Shumaker, S. A., & Conti, G. J. (1985). Understanding mobility in America. In I. Altman & D. M. Werner (Eds.), *Home Environments* (pp. 237–253). New York: Plenum.

Smith, J. M., Oswald, W. Y., & Farucki, G. Y. (1976). Effects of relocation on the satisfaction of psychiatric inpatients. *Journal of Clinical Psychiatry, 32,* 845–848.

Steinglass, P., De-Nour, A. K., & Shye, S. (1985). Factors influencing psychosocial adjustment to forced geographical relocation. *American Journal of Orthopsychiatry, 55*(4), 513–529.

Sterling, J., Drabek, T., & Key, W. (1975). The long-term impact of disaster on the health self-perceptions of victims. Paper presented at the meeting of the American Sociological Association, Chicago.

Stokols, D., & Shumaker, S. A. (1982). Psychological context of residential mobility and well-being. *Journal of Social Issues, 38,* 149–171.

Thursz, D. (1964). *Where are they now? A study of the impact of relocation on former residents of southwest Washington who were served in an HWC demonstration project.* Washington, DC: District of Columbia Redevelopment Land Agency.

Tierney, K. J., & Baisden, B. (1979). Crises intervention programs for disaster victims: A source book and manual for smaller communities. Washington, DC: DHEW publication No. (ADM) 79-675.

Zlotowski, M., & Cohen, D. (1968). Effects of environmental change upon behavior of hospitalized schizophrenic patients. *Journal of Clinical Psychiatry, 24,* 470–475.

Geographic Change as a Stressor: Developmental Perspectives

GORDON K. FARLEY, MD
SIDNEY WERKMAN, MD

Changes of residence, often to other cities and countries, characterize the contemporary world. Until recently, Americans were far more mobile than people of other nations, but for positive and negative reasons—better transportation and communications, economic incentives, a decline in nationalism, and forced migrations—other countries are fast catching up with us.

In many cities of the United States, the great wave of south Asian immigration coming in the wake of the Vietnam War has increased the burden of mental health problems (Looney, 1979). The millions of guest workers who have moved to northern European countries and the Middle East, as well as the immense dislocations in Africa motivated by politics and hunger have made migration an increasingly significant source of stress.

Even so, the United States remains the most mobile country in the world. In the course of his or her life, the average person in Japan moves 5 times, and in England

7 times, but, in the United States, 14 moves will occur in the course of an average lifetime. Twenty percent of the population in the United States changes residences each year.

Geographic change thrusts the entire family, from young child to parents to grandparents, into a state of uncertainty. The loss of the basic support network, mounting anxiety, frequent presence of physical threat, and need to adapt to rapid change can easily engender troubling characterological patterns and in many cases, overt psychopathology. However, there is another side to it as well. Geographic change can also be helpful in personal and family development and is often a necessary accompaniment to certain nodal points in development. For example, the need for specialized schooling, choice of career, marriage, changing careers, and even retirement may suggest or necessitate a geographic move. Such moves can offer exhilaration and an opportunity to start anew with a clean slate, which can be most beneficial. Typically, psychiatric tradition has emphasized the negative aspects of moves, suggesting that they merely postpone the resolution of family, career, and, in some cases, psychopathological tensions. Moves, however, may offer the opportunity for the development of new skills, new identity configurations, and the possibilities for considerable growth at small psychological cost. Where a move is effective, the burdens of old obligations, entanglements, and identities can be shed, and the person may then be able to develop more adaptive ways. For example, one father overseas said, "I like to be able to shut the desk on my mistakes every 3 years and start over again in a new place."

THE STRUCTURE OF MOVING

A series of regular, predictable stages and events gets set in motion by a move (see Table 21.1). Obviously, not all stages will occur in every move in the same sequence. However, both research and clinical experience suggest the importance of the recurrent issues involved in separation from accustomed surroundings, familiar people, typical activities, and a sense of belonging (Paykel, 1978; Paykel et al., 1969; Paykel, Prusoff, & Uhlenhuth, 1971). Before a move a family has a sense of place and status in its community. Healthy families and individuals experience intimacy and a sense of belonging and permanence. Families live within an ambience composed of the history, activities, recurrent recreations, amusements, and celebrations that characterize their home and neighborhood. From these they develop a sense of belonging, of status or role. Their lives have a quality of permanence, of living in the present with plans for the future.

Leaving or Separation

Once the decision to move has been made, the actual moving time tends to be taken up with the physical and practical aspects of packing, loading the moving

Table 21.1. Stages of Geographic Moves

Engagement	Separation	Transition	Entering	Reengagement
Status (Role)	Celebration (Parties; gifts)	Statuslessness ("Becoming")	Vulnerability (Risk-taking)	Transformed status
Intimacy	Loss	Chaos, anxiety	Extensive involvements	Commitment (Intensive, limited)
		Access to symbols Death—rebirth "Sacred" knowledge		
Present time (Permanent)	Future (Temporary)	Timeless	Now (Temporary)	Present (Permanent)
		———————— Grieving[a] ————————		
		———————— Mentors[a] ————————		

[a]Grieving and mentors are particularly important during these stages (separation, transition, entering).

vans, finding a new place to live. The celebrations that occur typically hide the necessary grieving and sadness. Very often a move is decided on by a single family member, usually the primary breadwinner, without considering the feelings and the wishes of the rest of the family. However, this very omission sets a family up for psychological and emotional stresses and conflicts that can have far-reaching psychiatric consequences. For all, there is a shift in the temporal focus of their lives. For those who are nostalgic and unwilling to move, life is no longer lived in the present but rather in the past; and for those who deny the pain of the moving and look forward to their next residence, the focus shifts to the future. In any case, it is a phase that carries with it built-in loss and tension.

The Phase of Transition

This very experience in time is the one most often neglected by people who move. It is not only a temporal but a psychological event. The family has neither settled into the new home nor totally given up the old one. The phase may continue intrapsychically long after a move has been completed. When this phase of transition or statuslessness is exaggerated, odd thoughts and fears can develop; it is then that anxiety and panic typically occur. There is no definite sense of identity but rather an experience of a loss of the old and uncertainty about the new.

In fortunate cases it is a time when new visions and dreams can occur, and new ideas, new directions, new symbols, and new views of life can emerge. It is a time in which it is most important to have guides, helpers, even mentors to assist the person's move into the novel situation. A teacher, minister, or fellow worker can be most useful at this time. Ceremonies and regular activities, family meetings, and family outings on a regularly scheduled basis can help an individual or family both to profit from the phase of transition and to move on to a permanent sense of reengagement.

Entering

Moving to a new environment does not guarantee that the person will feel a sense of belonging. Instead, whether one is entering a new job, neighborhood, or school, there is an extended period when uncertainty and a sense of vulnerability are likely to be experienced. This may result in superficial, extensive, and exaggerated involvements. The mover may make extravagant commitments, become involved in antisocial groups, or turn away from his or her usual modes of action. This can be observed in microcosm on the part of anyone who is on a vacation trip; on such occasions, drinking, sexual, or gambling activities that are not at all the usual pattern of a person's life may well appear. At this time a person makes decisions based on gratifying immediate wishes and enjoying present pleasures, as opposed to exercising judgment about the long-term effects of such decisions. During this period there is no sense of permanence, historic story, or narrative to a person's life to call on. Decisions are made without any background, support, or depth of consideration.

Reengagement

This stage has been reached when a renewed sense of role and status become established in a new neighborhood, school, or job. Recommitments of the family to its characteristic, comfortable ways become evident. The individual and family begin to settle down once again into a life of psychological orderliness, direction, and satisfaction.

Obviously, the major symptoms that develop in periods of moving occur during separation, transition, and entering. During the celebrations of separating or leaving, these symptoms often go unrecognized and may be rationalized, but it is well to pay attention to them.

Increasingly, research has emphasized that the actual move is of less importance than the meaning assigned by the individual or family to the event. The ability of the family to know the structure of moves and ways of adapting to them is also of high importance. As Rutter (1981) has pointed out, "A person's cognitive appraisal of a life event involves not only perception of the meaning of the event but also a cognitive set reflecting the anticipation of what can be done about it" (p. 350).

Because moves are so frequent in contemporary society it is well to know how to make them effectively. Moves, whether of school or residence, can be assimilated well if there is a foreknowledge of their structure and of the expected stresses. Considerable research emphasizes that the anxiety, uncertainty, and anticipation that attend a move are more important physiological stressors than is the life event itself (Frankenhaeuser, 1979, 1980).

It must be mentioned that moves to another country have unique stresses built into them and, inevitably, result in psychological tension. Strange foods, noises, smells, and jarring cultural customs are likely to give rise to a sense of discord.

DEVELOPMENTAL ASPECTS OF MOVES

As with many other life events, children are affected more by the meaning of the move to their parents or to themselves than by the actual move itself. That is, if the parents are comfortable about a move, the children will be supported in their ability to make that move. If, however, the parents disagree, and become depressed or dysfunctional over a move to a new neighborhood or a new city, the children, so dependent on parents, will experience an acute sense of anxiety and vulnerability (Werkman, 1977, 1979).

The infant lives in a world shaped almost totally by the mood of parents. Parents who communicate a sense of calm, optimism, and pleasure at the prospect of a move will give the infant a sense of confidence about what is happening. The alternative state of mind may well translate into psychophysiological symptoms— sleep disturbance, crying, eating disturbances, and so on—on the part of the infant.

The energetic toddler who moves about actively needs parents who have time both to allow freedom of action and exploration, to seek actively for playgrounds, to find appropriate playmates for the child, and simultaneously to remain alert to the dangers from accidents in a novel environment.

The curious, vulnerable young school-age child needs parents who can help organize that curiosity and who are particularly alive to the dangers of sexual, violent, and neglectful kinds of child abuse at the hands of caretakers or others in a new and strange environment.

There are differential sensitivities to environmental change present in boys and girls; these differences must be taken into account in the assessment of the effects of moves on both sexes.

Because of the extraordinary physical, psychological, social, and educational changes taking place in their lives, adolescents have the greatest difficulty in moving to a new environment. In high school the social network is a rigid affair, hard to leave and even harder to enter. Boy–girl relationships become important in adolescence as do career molding expectations and the development of self-identity. These are complex issues and intimately interwoven with the englobing milieu. It is not surprising that few teenagers want to move from or are able quickly to reconnect with a new social system (Werkman, Farley, Butler, & Quayhagen, 1981).

Suggestions for Parents

Children deserve the opportunity to participate in family discussions about a move. Parents do well to speak frankly about their motivations for the move. Even when the parents believe the child should be delighted by a move to a larger house or a more financially stable career, they should allow children an opportunity to express anger, disappointment, or grief. Parents must learn to tolerate disagreements and disappointments on the part of the teenager rather than to stifle them. This is a time to allow for unusually wide limits in the child's behavior and to maintain a tolerant attitude toward lapses in manners or relationships with adults. Children will naturally cry, fuss, and complain. They will make unusual demands for time with parents and show their tension in bodily reactions such as sleep, eating, and bowel disturbances and often in the form of transient behavioral symptoms (Coelho & Ahmed, 1980).

Safety and Accidents

It is important to study the limits of safety in a new house or neighborhood, and to offer simple, definite rules about how far a child can go from the front door, when he or she must return home, and how to get in touch with parents. Crossing the street, going to movies alone, going across town alone, and choosing new friends must all be discussed.

Adults

The aftermath of a move—to a college, to a new town for a career step, even into a marriage—produces a great increase in overt psychiatric symptoms. A considerable part of psychiatric practice consists of single adults who have made moves and find themselves anxious, depressed, or involved in substance abuse. The ecology of the single adult involves many of the issues described in the structure of geographic moves. In addition, the single adult is at particular risk for feeling loneliness, making poor decisions about relationships, turning to cults and other dysfunctional support systems, or falling into depression.

CHANGING FAMILY RELATIONSHIPS

Any move will involve changes in how parents relate to each other, to their children, to other relatives and to their jobs. If a move has been made for career advancement, the breadwinner might invest totally in the new career demands and spend no time with the family. Social and recreational activities change. Consider a family in which the father is absent all day at work in a glass-sheathed building. He returns home at night to play with his children and do household chores. Weekends may be taken up with mowing the lawn, watching television, painting furniture, and playing golf. Mothers become used to the pattern of school, carpools, music lessons, and community activities. Children spend many hours in their schools and the rest of their time in well-known parts of their community.

Any change can result in extraordinary tensions in all of these relationships. The father may immerse himself in a new career and the extra work demands; he may become inordinately busy and lose contact with his family. Parents may have to entertain much more at home or away from home, leaving their children feeling abandoned and lost, even though there is no overt wish to neglect them.

Relatives who are left behind may complicate a move. Sick grandparents, alcoholic uncles, and shared property arrangements with family members may cause continued concern. Although the family members who move shed painful burdens, they may also lose their sense of participation in decisions affecting close relatives and may experience guilt over this. Previously submerged ambitions and marital problems may surface at this juncture. When a move is made with the implicit thought of giving a marriage one more chance in new surroundings, it carries with it an almost built-in self-destruct factor. As parents become busy in a new community, the change in family organization may leave children feeling abandoned, anxious, and depressed—particularly if parents neither recognize their changed investments nor wish to acknowledge them.

MOTIVATIONS FOR MOVING

The positive ones—better pay, career advancement, closeness to valued relatives or friends, climate—need little discussion. However, even these motivations need to be considered in terms of the interests of the entire family. Negative, conflicted motivations can produce considerable problems within a family resulting in anger, depression, and acting out. Unrealistic dreams for greater excitement, fulfillment, or financial rewards may motivate the move. Fantasy draws families to the Sunbelt, to LasVegas, in a way reminiscent of the people who were drawn to the California Gold Rush more than a century ago. When fantasies cannot be realized or have not been assessed in a realistic way, the move can result in disappointment, conflict, and disaster. Some families may wish to return to a childhood home and to take up the "simple life" that existed several decades ago. Often a family will move because of a dimly conscious longing for a sense of community, small-town life, or a sense of effectance in changing and interacting with "the system." Others may move because of an unconscious wish to regulate interpersonal distance through geographic mobility. Sometimes a wish to deny the reality of a low-paying job or an unhappy marriage may impel a move that is guaranteed to be destructive. Obviously, psychiatrically disturbed people, manic patients, and rootless schizophrenic people move from one place to another in response to their psychopathology. Such moves inevitably result in frustration and further symptoms.

The important considerations in motivations are whether there has been thought about a move, whether a healthy dose of reality has been added to whatever other motivations may be present, and what kinds of coping and adaptational strategies the individual and family may possess to help them master a change of residence.

Individuals and families construct views or fantasies about moves, in effect, a "myth" about a move, which can have great psychic utility. They are likely to fantasize that in the new setting, life will be better, more exciting, or ideal; in fact, this prophecy may be self-fulfilling.

MOVE TO A NEW SCHOOL

Such a move is expected and necessary for all children growing up in the United States. It offers an opportunity for learning and using greater independence and flexibility. Thus, it has many positive aspects. However, a fair amount of literature points out that moves, particularly when they are too frequent and badly spaced, can have serious consequences for the child and may result in school failure (Holland, Kaplan, & Davis, 1974). In many cases, a school move may result in a "watershed phenomenon" with better students being academically enhanced by the experience and the less successful students being negatively influenced (Whalen & Fried, 1973).

An 8-year-old boy was found by his teacher to be failing several subjects in a small-town elementary school. The father, a high school teacher, had previously been unemployed for nearly 1 year and prior to that had been employed in a large city school system. Because of the difficulty in obtaining employment, the father felt that he had to take this offer of a position in a semirural school system. In addition, both mother and father had the fantasy that "Things will be better for us in the country." They had met during a vacation in the mountains and thought that a return to that setting might rescue a failing marriage. The family was very religiously oriented, and the 8-year-old boy had been an outstanding student in his previous parochial school. The family had not yet found a congregation in the new town and there was no parochial school.

MOVE TO A NEW RESIDENCE

In order to develop a sense of comfort in a new community, each person needs a group of supports for defining and solving problems (see Table 21.2). However, a number of recurring psychological issues need to be faced in order to arrive at such a positive state.

Social Acquaintances and Activities

Although it may seem obvious, people need to cultivate new friends who share hobby and craft interests, church activities, boy and girl scout groups, passionately felt causes, political groups, recreational and athletic activities. The most transportable positive quality a person may possess is a narrow, definable interest such

Table 21.2. *Useful Support Systems*

Problems	Type of Support Needed	Solution
Social isolation	Social activities Group identity	Social integration
Loneliness	Close friends	Intimacy Caring
Vulnerability in emergencies	Helpers for crisis	Assistance
Resources not known	Referral agents	Connection with resources
Confusion about future	Models Mentors Goal setting	Clarity
Low self-esteem	Respectors of competence, potential	Higher self-esteem
Boredom, isolation, stimulus deprivation	Challenges New information	Perspective, energy

as a musical, literary, intellectual, artistic, or athletic skill. This is particularly true for adolescents and preadolescents. For many, finding people just to visit with helps to develop a sense of personal comfort and identity.

A 15-year-old boy sought psychiatric consultation because of declining school grades, loss of appetite, and depression. The family had recently moved from Ohio to Denver, Colorado, because of an exceptional executive job opportunity for the father. The son was resentful about the move and angrily stated that he had neither been consulted or listened to regarding this family change. Both mother and father thought that the boy should be happy about the move because it represented an advancement for his father that would benefit the entire family. After living in Denver for nearly 6 months, the family had not yet become involved in a church although they had been very active in their previous hometown. The son had been interested in cross-country running and music but had not pursued these interests in his new school. Identification of these issues in family and individual psychotherapy led to a resolution and better family functioning within 3 months.

Intimate Friends and Relatives

Friends and relatives are needed in order to combat the feelings of emotional isolation, that is, the sense of not being known or understood in a new place. Most people need at least one close friend with whom to share complaints about a job or interest, to boast about life's triumphs, to gossip with. A child needs a friend who will listen and not judge, who will continue to care about him or her no matter what happens.

One of the considerable problems in moving is the loss of relatives. Children thrive on having grandparents, aunts, and uncles who will come to Christmas pageants and dance recitals, who are available to take them to the zoo on the weekend, and who are there on holidays and birthdays. After a move, these presences become telephone voices and notes on a card. It is not the same.

Resources in the New Community

It is necessary to find the hardware stores, record shops, automobile mechanics, furniture stores, and places to buy kitchen utensils or painting materials in the new community. When such resources cannot be found, a kind of environmental isolation occurs, often without the person or family being aware of what is missing. Parents of children with special needs face unusual stresses. In some cases a move may be motivated by the needs of the child for specialized and scarce services.

Help in Emergencies

A family needs the names of doctors, insurance agents, lawyers, and plumbers to contact when trouble occurs. A family needs to know what special resources are available in the new community; otherwise, when acute problems surface, a sense of panic may develop. If not well handled, any emergency may disturb the entire family adaptation to a new community.

Respect for Competence

Young or old, each person needs someone who can recognize that what he or she is doing is significant. Otherwise, a loss of self-esteem or self-confidence may occur. For many people, their competence in noncareer activities—gardening, rug weaving, involvement in social or political organizations—is what matters most. A little league baseball player needs to get connected with a new team; a singer needs to join a church choir.

A Sense of Meaning

Children must be integrated effectively into their schoolwork and into the changed family interests that occur in the wake of a family move; if they feel left out, anxiety will surface. A sense of the significance of one's work assures comfort in life (Erikson, 1964; White, 1963).

Table 21.2 (Useful Support Systems) summarizes ways of achieving a sense of comfort and effectiveness in a new home or community.

MOVING FOR THE DISADVANTAGED FAMILY

For the disadvantaged or poor family, a move is usually quite difficult. Often enough the change of residence is brought about for reasons quite out of the control of the family. Instead of a move to a better job, a better city, or a position of more responsibility, the move is likely to be caused by the loss of a job, an eviction from rented quarters, legal problems, or flight from an abusing spouse. Instead of a change of residence that has been planned, well thought out, eagerly looked forward to, and extensively discussed, the move is likely to be sudden, impulsive, and undiscussed with no definite geographic target in mind at the beginning. On arriving in the new city, the family has nowhere to go; until a shelter can be found, they may live in their car for a few days, or even weeks. If the move is across state lines, there is a delay before eligibility for welfare assistance can be established. All of these concomitant events disrupt regular family activities, roles, and expectations. At such times families are unusually vulnerable to a variety of stressors, and both child and spouse abuse are likely to occur. Children who are separated from familiar surroundings, routines, supports, and playmates tend to become irritable and cranky and thus are more likely to provoke or contribute to abuse through noncompliance. The concerns of these families are much more apt to revolve around the primal necessities of life such as food, shelter, and health than around the somewhat more subtle dimensions of social support, role, position, personal validation, recognition, and alienation.

A 37-year-old mother, a single parent was turned in to the child protection service by a neighbor because the mother had locked her 8-year-old daughter out of the house for 2 hours when the outside temperature was only 8°F. Authorities came to investigate and learned from the mother that although the daughter was rebellious, noncompliant, and undisciplined, there had never before been an incident of abuse or suspected abuse. The mother and daughter had moved from Chicago to Denver 5 months previously and had lived in their car for 6 days before finding temporary housing in a church-run shelter. Although mother and daughter had argued many times before, fighting had intensified markedly after the move. The daughter had missed nearly half of the days she should have attended school because of real and feigned illness; school personnel thought that an unusually tight bond existed between mother and daughter because the mother often seemed to keep the girl home for company. The daughter had had severe academic problems since changing schools, had stolen things from fellow students, and at other times had stolen money from her mother and had given money or candy to friends at school. The mother had not yet become eligible for aid to dependent children and had not yet found employment.

CHILDREN'S ANXIETIES IN A MOVE TO A NEW RESIDENCE

Children fret most about leaving friends; they have become attached to their current playmates and cannot conceive building new friendships. A child who has had difficulty in making friends in the past will carry to a new residence the implicit burden: ''Will anybody like me where I am going?'' Such children need assurances that their parents will help them achieve integration in a new community, that the parents will not, themselves, rush quickly into their careers and social activities, psychologically abandoning the children.

One crucial aspect of a move may have to do with the family pet. These pets function almost as a transitional object giving the child a sense of familiarity and continuity with the past. Can the pet be tolerated in the new environment? Do parents decide to move to an apartment where a Great Dane would be unacceptable? Do they move to a central city heedless that a child who has grown up with a pony can no longer keep that animal or have any place to ride?

OVERSEAS AND A NEW CULTURE

Approximately 230,000 American children attend school overseas each year, and 5 million Americans work overseas (Luebke, 1976). Many of these are military families (Frank, Shanfield, & Evans, 1981; Shaw & Pangman, 1975). Families and single adults who live overseas confront a unique set of psychological and developmental challenges. Frequent travel and geographic mobility make it necessary to adapt to a variety of friends and neighborhoods, schools, and social activities. There is little opportunity for transient families to set down deep roots in a community. Instead, people overseas become adept at developing short-term friendships and fitting into different sets of local athletic and recreational activities. Adjustment to the language and culture of a new country and ultimately, readjustment to the culture of the United States are important.

Increasingly, it is also important to take into account the possibilities of terrorism and armed conflict in various areas of the world as well as the longer term issues of unusual physical illnesses and differing cultural and sexual mores. Drug use, patterns of sexuality, changing values, and cultural expectations in a new country may conflict with the experience and preferences of the individual.

Many of the social and cultural expectations of the United States must be altered and adapted to the ways of a new country.

A 14-year-old girl sought help because of difficulty sleeping, failure in all school subjects, and difficulty in making or keeping friends. On interview, she said that other children teased her and were mean and that the teachers were all inadequate. Her father was an oil person, and the family had moved from Colombia to Tunis and most recently to France. The patient rebelled at the prospect of learning French and said she wanted to return to the United States and live with her grandparents. She said that after many attempts, she had given up trying to invest in a new place and a new culture.

PREVENTIVE AND THERAPEUTIC ASPECTS OF A MOVE

Awareness and Rehearsal

It is important to discuss a move, to consider the reality of the future home, and to negotiate and resolve differences about the move within a family beforehand. Once a family has decided to move, a certain amount of conflict must be submerged and put out of consciousness in order for anxiety to be bound and realistic action and planning to occur. Any discrepancy between fantasy and reality must be resolved in favor of the reality of the move, or a new reality may be constructed. It is important to listen to children and respond to their concerns with seriousness even though what they have to say may not affect the outcome or decision.

Individual and Family Counseling

When important symptoms appear either before or after a move (psychophysiological symptoms in children; sexual acting out, fighting, school performance decrements, accident proneness in adolescents; anxiety, depression, fatigue, and physical symptoms in adults), these can best be handled through counseling or psychiatric treatment.

Short-Term Use of Medication

When states of considerable anxiety arise, the short-term use of hypnotics and benzodiazepines can be considered. The treatment of transient phobic responses— agoraphobia, school phobia, and adult dirt and disease phobias in a new country— may optimally be handled by a combination of counseling and benzodiazepines.

REFERENCES

Coelho G. Z., & Ahmed, P. I. (Eds.). (1980). *Uprooting and development*. New York: Plenum.

Erikson, E. H. (1964). *Insight and responsibility*. New York: Norton.

Frank, M., Shanfield, S. B., & Evans, H. E. (1981). The in-and-out parent: Strategies for managing re-entry stress. *Military Medicine, 146,* 846–849.

Frankenhaeuser, M. (1979). Psychoendocrine approaches to the study of emotion as related to stress and coping. In H. E. Howe & R. A. Dienstbier (Eds.), *Nebraska symposium on motivation, 1978* (pp. 123–161). Lincoln: University of Nebraska.

Frankenhaeuser, M. (1980). Psychoendocrine approaches to the study of stressful person-environment transactions. In H. Selye (Ed.), *Selye's guide to stress research* (Vol. 1, pp. 46–70). New York: Van Nostrand.

Holland, J. V., Kaplan, D. M., & Davis, S. D. (1974). Interschool transfers: A mental health challenge. *Journal of School Health, 44,* 74–79.

Looney, J. G. (1979). Adolescents as refugees. In S. C. Feinstein & P. L. Giovacchini (Eds.), *Adolescent psychiatry* (Vol. 7, pp. 199–208). Chicago: University of Chicago Press.

Luebke, P. T. (1976). *American elementary and secondary community schools abroad.* Washington, DC: American Association of School Administration.

Paykel, E. S. (1978). Contribution of life events to causation of psychiatric illness. *Psychological Medicine, 8,* 245–254.

Paykel, E. S., Myers, J. K., Dienelt, M. N., Klerman, G. L., Lindenthal, J. J., & Pepper, M. P. (1969). Life events and depression: A controlled study. *Archives of General Psychiatry, 21,* 753–760.

Paykel, E. S., Prusoff, B. A., & Uhlenhuth, E. H. (1971). Scaling of life events. *Archives of General Psychiatry, 25,* 340–347.

Rutter, M. (1981). Stress, coping, & development: Some issues and some questions. *Journal of Child Psychology and Psychiatry, 22,* 323–356.

Shaw, J. A., & Pangman, J. (1975). Geographic mobility and the military child. *Military Medicine, 140,* 413–416.

Werkman, S. (1977). *Bringing up children overseas.* New York: Basic Books.

Werkman, S. (1979). Coming home. In S. C. Feinstein & P. L. Giovacchini (Eds.), *Adolescent psychiatry* (Vol. 7, pp. 178–190). Chicago: University of Chicago Press.

Werkman, S., Farley, G. K., Butler, C., Quayhagen, M. (1981). The psychological effects of moving and living overseas. *Journal of the American Academy of Child Psychiatry, 20,* 645–657.

Whalen, T. E., & Fried, M. A. (1973). Geographic mobility and its effect on student achievement. *Journal of Educational Research, 67,* 163–165.

White, R. W. (1963). Ego and reality in psychoanalytic theory. *Psychological Issues* (Monograph No. 11). New York: International Universities Press.

— CHAPTER 22 ————————————

Loss of an Ideal

MICHAEL H. STONE, MD

The phrase "loss of an ideal" is semantically imprecise, admitting of such possibilities as loss of access to someone who had served as an "ideal" (through death or family breakup) or loss via disillusionment with someone who was still available, but whose ability to serve as an ideal has become drastically diminished. This chapter will consider the latter phenomenon.

Idealization is a process evident at very early stages of development. The infant's global pleasure in the mother is soon accompanied by, or transformed into, the more specific emotion of adoration. The parent of either sex becomes idealized as soon as the infant can begin to form a separate mental image of the parent, not only visually (which occurs within the first weeks or months) but psychologically (a process already in high gear, presumably, by the time attachment and separation anxiety manifest themselves in the second half of the first year). For a parent to become an ideal in any meaningful sense of the term, a child's ego boundaries need to develop to the stage where there are separate inner representations of "me" and the parent, and enough language skills and vocabulary must be available to express explicit value sentiments, such as "I want to be like Mama" or "I want to be like Daddy." Needless to add, it helps if the parents are "good-enough" in Winnicott's sense (1965)—reasonably warm, tender, caring, and soothing—to foster idealization without requiring the child's denial of a dreadful reality to maintain this vital positive attitude toward the caretakers. From the standpoint of survival needs, the child's tendency to idealize his or her caretakers is natural and necessary. If, however, this inclination must sit side by side with an awareness of their hostility or exploitativeness, the child will be in jeopardy. The situation will then be rather like that of the Graf Zeppelin, technically capable of getting to where it has to go but also quite capable of blowing up unexpectedly.

The child's expanding world embraces first the wider family and then the school, with its new set of authority figures and potential friends. The possibilities for hero worship are then no longer confined to the immediate caretakers, and new horizons open. The parents or their surrogates, nevertheless, usually retain primacy in the child's pantheon of ideal types, if for no other reason than that the memory traces used to build up these object representations are earlier and therefore etched more deeply into the neurophysiological clay that forms the child's inner life. Hence, when the hero no longer worthy of worship is a parent, rather than, say, a once-revered teacher or an athletic star, young people become particularly vulnerable to disillusionment and to its adverse psychological sequelae.

The loss of an ideal can occur in a number of special contexts. The short-range and long-range effects will differ in accordance with that context and also in accordance with the abruptness and severity of the disillusionment. Severity alludes not only to the intensity of the disillusioning experience; it refers as well to the extent of the area on the child's inner map of crucial relationships that is affected after the fall from grace. An idol may have a clay foot, for example, and still retain most of its aura. But if the idol has been smashed to shards, no reconstruction is possible; and the loss of that ideal will be permanent.

These processes of idealization and disillusionment, it should be emphasized, are phenomena of normal development. Under optimal circumstances, the good-enough parent provides enough compassion, understanding, reliability, and fairness to warrant the child's idealization. As children mature, this need for an all-powerful and all-loving adult gradually lessens, permitting them to see the parents in more realistic terms. This process proceeds with (and actually requires) minor disillusionments (Mama sometimes yells at me when it was my brother's fault; Daddy doesn't catch a football as well as Mr. So-n-So. . .), none of which is devastating. Although the norms for idealization and disappointment appropriate to each stage of development are not easy to establish, clinicians can agree with acceptable reliability as to when these norms have been grossly exceeded. Disillusionment itself represents an end point on a continuum pertaining to disappointment. The material that follows highlights the pathological rather than normal phenomena pertinent to the loss of an ideal.

CONTEXTS: THE AREAS OF LIFE WHERE DISILLUSIONMENT IS APT TO OCCUR

Children need ideal figures with whom to identify and from whom to gain the reassurance and strength necessary to progress comfortably to the next stages of life. This idealization will be well placed if the parent (or other relative, or extrafamilial hero) embodies such qualities as successfulness, integrity, and morality, including respect for interpersonal, and especially sexual, boundaries. Unlike famous athletes, actors, scientists, and the like whom people worship from afar and scarcely expect ever to meet, family figures must also bestow genuine love and warm concern if they are to remain ideal. It may be fair to say, in fact, that the child expects a different set of ideal qualities from family figures than he or she expects from people in the larger world. Certainly normal adolescents realize, with only transitory and minor disillusionment, that their mother or father cannot be all-knowing, as wise as Einstein, as endurably powerful in the batter's box as Don Mattingly, or as popular and glamorous as Raquel Welch. Only a few young people have parents who are the best at what they do. But all children rightfully expect the love and nurture that only their parents can (potentially) provide. The ideal parents give love, nurture, and a general outline for how to live life; parents present a general array of possible roles and occupations that might be appropriate for and within reach of each particular child. During latency and adolescence, fortified (under ideal circumstances) by this nurture and guidance, children identifies with a number of "best" persons from the world at large, whom they then strive to emulate.

Some of the intrafamilial situations leading to severe disillusionment include the following areas (there will necessarily be some overlap in the various categories):

1. *Occupation*. A parent who may have been an adequate provider for the family is fired or declines in ability in an increasingly noticeable way, or invests heavily in some project that fails completely and engenders a catastrophic loss of income for the family, and so on.

2. *General Competence*. A parent is recognized as unable to handle ordinary stresses adequately, to come up with a correct appraisal of other people, or to have the right answers to various everyday conflicts. At the extreme, the parent may be mentally incompetent, grossly psychotic, and episodically hospitalized.

3. *Assertiveness*. A parent may be seen as generally correct in judgment, and adequate in caring and compassion, yet woefully lacking in courage, drive, perseverance, or will, to the extent that the family fortunes suffer. The family (or the parent) comes to be regarded as weak and ineffectual.

4. *Trustworthiness*. A parent may come to be recognized as deceitful, unfaithful, or "crooked" in dealings with the outside world. Such discoveries will be all the more devastating if the parent has been glaringly hypocritical in professing to have virtues that are diametrically opposite to the traits he or she manifests—a condition that becomes more and more apparent to the child—or if the parent turns out to be a criminal, capable of violence and so on.

5. *Sex.* A parent who exploits a child sexually imposes on the victim the simultaneous burdens of premature introduction into a sphere of activity for which the child is emotionally unprepared and of disillusionment from realizing the parent's abject failure to protect and respect the child's boundaries as well as to maintain major social standards.

6. *Character.* There are parents who respect boundaries, move competently in the world, do their duty in the performance of various parental obligations (to feed, clothe, shelter, etc.), yet who demonstrate such degrees of meanness, spitefulness, intolerance, or vengefulness as to force on the child an awareness of being inextricably bound for life to someone the younster is unable to love or respect and would not at all want to resemble. In the more extreme instances, a child may be subjected to humiliation (verbal or physical) so profound as to evoke hatred, including the impulse to murder the offending parent. Disillusionment is a part of the child's experience in this situation, but one that would take second place to the more immediate responses of pain and shame. The more the parent concentrates his fire on a particular child whom he consciously wishes to hurt, the more the child is in the presence of genuine malice (as opposed to a general pettiness the child could learn not to take personally). Here, one would anticipate maximal disillusionment.

Loss of an ideal may be precipitated by behavior (on the part of a parent or other important figure) confined to one of the preceding areas or by behavior that touches on several areas at once. In order to illustrate some of the more typical situations, as we encounter them in our clinical work with psychiatric patients (especially with children and adolescents), I have selected a number of vignettes, some from private practice, and others from hospital work. The latter include some of the 550 patients treated on the long-term psychotherapy unit at New York State Psychiatric Institute between 1963 and 1976, 80% of whom I have traced in a follow-up study (Stone, 1986; Stone, Stone, & Hurt, 1987). Among these hundred of borderline and psychotic patients were many disillusioned adolescents, whose fate I have been able to document 10 to 20 years later.

CLINICAL VIGNETTES

Case A

A 20-year-old woman was admitted to a psychiatric facility because of a suicide gesture with sleeping pills. Because of her mutism, at first it was difficult to establish her diagnosis. It was not even clear whether this was elective on her part, or a manifestation or catatonia. Three months passed before she spoke audibly enough to be heard, but she gave so sparse and fragmented a story that the events leading up to her admission could still not be pieced together. Although she had been living with them at the time, her parents professed no clear knowledge of her immediate past history. During the ensuing 9 months in the hospital, although cooperative and superficially affable, she was noted to be depressed, sullen, and withdrawn. After a year had passed, she finally summoned the courage to reveal a 10-year story of sadistic incestuous relations with her father; he was an executive in a large company who had threatened to kill her if she ever revealed what took place. The year before her hospitalization he had gotten her pregnant. He and the mother drove her to an abortion clinic, leaving her to get back home on her own as best she could. She became acutely psychotic and made the suicide gesture mentioned earlier. Her disillusionment with her father as a model of how a man should behave was an intense as her loss of respect for her mother, who acted as though ignorant of what had gone on and did nothing to shield her daughter. The patient was also aware that her father was now having sexual relations with her next-younger sister, and she felt powerless to intervene.

This patient ultimately emerged as "borderline" rather than schizophrenic. She was fortunate in having an unusually sensitive female therapist (it is doubtful she could ever have told her story to a man) who worked with her over a 4-year period. The first few years after leaving the hospital were rocky: She was able to work, but tended to avoid close contacts with anyone. She was fearful of men and was unable to shake off her earlier impression of sex as something dirty and disgusting. The consistent protectiveness of her obviously competent therapist helped undo her image of women (herself included) as inept and indifferent. Eventually, she entered into a stormy affair with a man who had some of the exploitative qualities of the father. After this ended, she met a more suitable man and married him. As of this writing, 8 years after her hospitalization and 2 years after her marriage, she is reasonably content and is functioning well.

Comment. This case illustrates the difficulty in making neat correlations between the severity of an adolescent's disillusionment with a parent, and the young person's eventual adaptational level. The sordid details of her latency and adolescent years are omitted here, both for lack of space and to protect her confidentiality; in any case their character would seem to preclude the possibility of a normal life. What seems to emerge from such constellations is that prognosis depends not only on symptoms, family influences, and negative constitutional factors (viz., risk genes for a psychosis, low birth weight, physical deformity) but also on such assets as courage, perseverance, self-discipline (cf. Kolb, 1982), attractiveness, intelligence, and a number of other attributes not often mentioned in the standard catalogue of ego strengths and defenses. Fortunately this patient possessed enough of these nonspecific assets to permit the development of trust and to render her appealing enough to win the love of a man of similarly good character.

Case B

An 18-year-old girl was admitted to a psychiatric hospital after a long history of running away from home, drug abuse, truancy, and promiscuity. Her hospitalization occurred when she took an overdose of tranquilizers after having been deserted by a man on whom she had become dependent.

When she was 5 years old, her father left the home under mysterious circumstances. For a long time she believed that he had died, having been told by her mother that he had been killed in an accident. Later, she overheard conversations to the effect that he was very much alive and had made efforts to contact her, only to have these efforts thwarted by the mother. This led to disillusionment with her mother, as though somewhere out there was a nice daddy whose potential relationship with her was being spoiled by his spiteful ex-wife. When confronted, the mother admitted that the father was indeed alive, but had been kept away on purpose, because of having repeatedly beaten the mother and molested the patient sexually. The girl's feeling of disillusionment persisted, however, shifting its focus now onto the sociopathic father. The mother could henceforth be regarded as protective, although peculiarly secretive: If this was all there was to the story, why the need to dissimulate? Plagued by doubts and crestfallen about the revelations, the patient ran away at 13 and began to lead a dissolute life.

The patient spent 2 years on a unit devoted to long-term psychotherapy. By DSM-III criteria, she would have been considered a "borderline personality." Because of the antisocial features (truancy, running away, etc.) the prognosis seemed ominous. Happily, at follow-up 20 years later, the story turned out much better. As with the patient from the preceding vignette, after 7 or 8 years of hard work and disappointments in her personal life, there were enough positive factors within her personality and in her external life to permit an excellent recovery, especially in the occupational sphere.

Case C

A 20-year-old college sophomore was admitted to a psychiatric hospital following a near-fatal suicide attempt with carbon monoxide.

Because of his arrogance, he had made himself unpopular with his fellow students. Although this led to ostracism and a sense of loneliness, the more direct precipitant of the suicide attempt was his poor performance on his most recent exams. His bad grades exposed him as far less successful than he liked to envision himself. He feared humiliating scenes in his family toward whom he was outwardly contemptuous but inwardly fearful of having disgraced.

He came from a family of extraordinary wealth and prominence in Saudi Arabia, where his father had been a self-made tycoon. Two years before the patient's hospitalization, the father, under the impact of public revelations about his shady business manipulations, had jumped off a roof and died. The patient's reaction was one of bland indifference. Their relationship had always been distant and strained: The father was away on business more than half the year and, when home, was hypercritical of the patient, whom he saw as an undisciplined and ambitionless playboy.

Throughout his adolescence, the patient's attitude toward his father had been sharply contradictory: "I idol-worshipped him, because he was a VIP and made it big all on his own, but I hated him because he never had a kind word for me and never spent any time with me.'' When the patient was 8, he had had to show his father a mediocre report card, whereupon his father beat him continuously for an hour.

In the 2 years between his father's suicide and his hospitalization, his behavior had taken an antisocial turn: He stole money from his mother, he drove recklessly, stayed out at bars until the small hours, neglected his studies, and abused alcohol (something particularly frowned upon in his religion).

I saw the patient in two separate consultations in the hospital, 5 months apart. During the first he was markedly circumstantial, barely allowing one to get a word in edgewise. Though his affect was bland and his personality mainly narcissistic (contemptuous and superior, in particular), he nevertheless talked of suicide as something he was "determined" to do as soon as he was discharged, defiantly stating that we "couldn't stop him."

Five months later, a transformation had taken place. This patient was much more candid about the humiliations he had experienced, both directly (from his father's rejecting attitude) and indirectly (from having to realize with the abruptness of the suicide itself, that his father was a "fake"). He had begun to make his peace with his disillusionment, and he felt more distant from the affairs of the family and more able to contemplate making his own way in the world.

Case D

A 17-year-old girl of Italin-American extraction was admitted to a psychiatric hospital because of a suicide gesture with pills and an episode of wrist cutting. An attractive and personable young woman who had been a consistent "A" student in her high school, she was viewed by her peers as having everything. Her suicidal impulses and deepening depression (the latter beginning around 15 years) seemed inexplicable to her schoolmates and friends, the more so as her parents were well-to-do and lavished every attention on her.

Behind this rosy exterior was quite a different picture. The males in her family were involved in organized crime. Beginning around the time she was 14, both her father and her uncle made sexual overtures toward her. When she was 16, her uncle was killed in a gangland "rubout"—an event that received much publicity in the tabloids. As a result she became aware of the sharp discrepancy between her original image of the family and the low esteem in which it was now held in the surrounding community. She suffered some ostracism at school.

There was no one, within the family or outside of it, that she could turn to for support about either issue (the incest or the scandal): Both parents pooh-poohed the newspaper accounts; she was warned to say nothing about the incestuous advances "if she knew what was good for her." The uncle had been a favorite of hers when she was younger; the disillusionment she experienced in relation to this man was particularly keen. All at once the revered male figures in her life became despicable: Men who were supposed to protect her were using her; men she once saw as pillars of the community were criminals. Yet she still loved them both; her uncle and her father had been (mostly) good to her, led exciting lives (before she realized what the excitement was all about), and were charming. This confrontation with their social status was more than she could assimilate, and she became anxious and distraught.

She not only suffered the loss of an ideal, but had to grapple with the worry, however ambivalent her feelings toward her father had become, that he could easily meet with the same fate as her uncle.

Comment. The young woman in this clinical example suffered disillusionment in two major areas at once: public disgrace of a parent and the infraction of the sexual boundary between parent and child. Few adolescents have the objectivity and independence to shrug off the taunts of school acquaintances concerning a scandal in the family. This patient was no exception. Forced to make a sweeping reversal of all her previous assumptions about her father's goodness, she had now to choose between reality (and the need to distance herself from him) versus loyalty (at the cost of wholesale denial of reality). With her idol shattered, she became despondent and suicidal.

Case E

An 18-year-old college freshman was referred for psychotherapy because of depression and anxiety concerning a crisis in her family.

Her father, whom she had always looked up to because of his high standing in the community, became exposed as a homosexual who suddenly found himself under indictment for molesting some of the boys at the private school where he was headmaster.

Her disillusionment was compounded by a profound mistrust concerning the stability of relationships (her parents' marriage seemed a fraud now). Nothing was secure anymore, not even her own identity: If her father "came out of the closet" in his 40s, how could she be sure of what she was, or of how long her presumably heterosexual orientation would remain in force? Several years of therapy were needed before she regained any measure of self-confidence in her relationship with men, and even then her mistrust of men and her general air of bitterness were not much diminished.

Case F

A 19-year-old woman was admitted to a psychiatric hospital after she had cut her wrists during the breakup of a romantic relationship. In order to escape an intolerable family situation, she had dropped out of high school shortly before graduation and had now been on her own for 3 years. As a child she had lived on a huge estate and in lavish circumstances. Her father was head of a prominent business firm; the family's name was recognized by everyone in the city. When she was 14 years old, her three brothers had forced themselves on her sexually in a kind of gang-rape; shortly thereafter her father, a chronic alcoholic, made similar advances toward her that she repulsed. Her self-image was no less shattered by these experiences than were her images of the males in her family. She ran away, supported herself with menial work, and became habituated to a variety of street drugs.

After spending 7 months in the hospital, she appeared less depressed and less ashamed about the events occurring in her family. She was able to obtain work as a model and within several years had become much sought after and highly paid. Her fortunes reversed when she was 25; another woman usurped her high standing in the agency, and she was no longer given the most favorable jobs. She made another suicide gesture and was briefly hospitalized. Two years later she became engaged to a man from an old and respected family. Once again, however, her feelings of unworthiness (on account of her past) reasserted themselves and became unbearably intense; finally, 3 weeks after the wedding ceremony, she committed suicide with barbiturates.

Case G

Because of conflicting loyalties in a custody battle, a 16-year-old girl sought counseling. Her parents had divorced when she was 7. Her father, a politician who was well thought of in their community, remarried soon afterward; her mother, several years later. Her mother was originally to have retained custody, but her father was a man of considerable vengefulness who was determined to have his own way. He threatened his ex-wife that he would ruin her if she attempted to hold on to their daughter. When she would not yield, he accused the mother of being crazy, mounted extensive litigation in family court, and coached his 7-year-old daughter (whom he now retained, after refusing to return her from a visit) in reciting complaints about the mother ("She's crazy"; "She hates me"). The court awarded the father custody. This decision pleased the girl, who idealized her father and was charmed by his new wife.

For the next 8 years the girl rarely saw her mother; she was never permitted to speak to her by phone unless her father or stepmother was standing close by. After a while the mother called only infrequently. This was interpreted as proof of her mother's indifference. Because of this interference, for a long time the girl remained unaware of her mother's feelings. The stepmother insisted that the girl not address her mother by that title, telling her repeatedly, "She never took care of you; *I'm* your real mother!" The stepmother was prone to outbursts of rage and tantrums of jealousy, provoked by the most trifling incidents. The girl was not permitted to see friends in their homes and was made to do most of the household work.

When she was 16, during one of her rare visits with her mother, she began to mention a few of the scenes that occurred at home with her stepmother. The fears instilled in her about her mother's craziness and indifference began to seem exaggerated. These attributes were more applicable, as she could now understand, to her stepmother. In contrast, her mother was calm and did not force her daughter to take sides. At the end of a long conversation, the first one in which either spoke from the heart about what had gone on over the years, the daughter was considerably shaken. Her world was upside down. Everyone had qualities opposite to the ones she had been taught to assign them. Her mother's indifference was revealed as the self-sacrifice of the "Solomon's baby" story in the Bible, where, rather than permit her child to be cut in half by the king's guards, the real mother lets the other woman keep the infant.

As the daughter became aware of her father's vengefulness, whose effect was to deny her access to her quite normal mother throughout the whole of her adolescence, she experienced a total disillusionment. The good guys turned out to be the bad guys and vice versa. At first she scarcely knew whom to believe and spent a number of sessions with a therapist. With the help of this neutral observer, the girl, who was psychologically much healthier than the patients of the preceding examples, decided to remain with her mother. Because, as it turned out, her once idealized father and stepmother had betrayed her, it was a long time before she could relate to them with civility.

DISCUSSION

In his monograph on tripartite theory (1923/1961) Freud spoke of the ego-ideal as one of the two important compartments of *Superego*, the other being the repository of internalized prohibitions. Given that human beings are social creatures, what Freud was at pains to deal with here was the inevitable interplay between the needs of the individual and the needs of the group. The child must learn to restrain certain impulses and, simultaneously, to emulate the most adaptive and successful members of his or her immediate family and of the larger human family. Many psychoanalytic writers have described the process of internalization that creates the mental structures subserving these prohibitions and ideal formation; among them Jacobson (1964) is of particular importance.

In normal family life the formation of the ego-ideal is not always easy to follow; indeed, its importance may not be fully recognized. Everything proceeds in an integrated, slowly evolving and harmonious fashion, as the child, later the adolescent, gradually transforms the ideal, out of which the fantasy-self is created, into the real self of adult life. This transformation takes place through hard work (the "industry" of which Erikson, 1956, spoke)—it is necessary in order to become whatever it was that seemed most appealing and appropriate during the earlier stage of identification and mimicry.

Only when adolescents can begin to perform adequately the tasks that embody their ego-ideal can they develop solidity in the sense of self. Their identity is inchoate, tentative, fragile. Quite literally, the ego-ideal is the spine that holds them upright. Adolescents have a "self" still in quotation marks, kept going by a gossamer but nonetheless vital illusion: their *ideal*. The fragility of this illusion (at least in young people) has been addressed recently by Chassequet-Smirgel (1985, p. 194).

Those whose ideal types, especially within the family, maintain their integrity year after year, never causing a major disappointment are a privileged group indeed, for they are able to develop a sense of conviction about how life should be led, within an atmosphere of durability and security. Mother and father are good persons who stand up for what is right and can always be counted on. Children who trust the steadfastness of their parents' love can endure small signs of weakness in parental behavior, with only minor and transient disillusionment. Circumscribed weakness of this sort may inspire the resolve to behave with greater courage during their own adult life. Perhaps this is what happened with Freud when, still in his boyhood, he learned from his father about the latter's obsequiousness before an antisemitic bully.

As in the clinical illustrations in this chapter, the disillusionments suffered by those who become our patients are generally quite severe and are often qualitatively different as well. For Jacob Freud to have stepped into the street at the bully's command is one thing; had Jacob carried on a secret affair with his son's fiancée— that would have been another! That would have been betrayal.

Years ago, the mother of one of my patients sabotaged her daughter's engagement by telling her fiancée's draft board that he really shouldn't be "4-F" (physically ineligible) because his back was "not injured" (even though it actually was). That was malice. Malice ruins a relationship permanently. Malice on the part of one's ideal shatters that ideal. Only slightly less shattering are the instances, such as those depicted in most of the vignettes, of betrayal, humiliation, hypocrisy, corruption, public disgrace, or abject social failure. A common example of such failure would be a father whose alcoholism causes him to lose his job, social standing, and position of authority in the family. All these examples will strain a young person's capacity for denial to the utmost, or else overwhelm it—but not to the point of irreversible loss of the ideal, as occurs in reaction to parental malice. Even incest need not shatter the ideal, unless, as in the first vignette, it is admixed with malice.

The effects of disillusionment are not easily assessed because they depend only partly on the root causes of the loss-of-ideal; for the rest, one must take into account the individual's genetic loading. Thus, there may be an inherited risk factor for functional psychosis or for a borderline variant thereof in the person suffering the disillusionment. Other constitutional factors enter in as well: Is the person resilient, attractive, bright? If so, the loss may be easier to compensate for. Or, the person may be lacking in these qualities, in which case a loss of the same dimensions may be devastating. Do other members of the family come to the rescue? Or do they take the side of the offending parent (or other idealized figure), leaving the child with no one to support his or her growing awareness of the hero's shortcomings?

Before considering the therapeutic possibilities for undoing the effects of serious disillusionment, it is worth mentioning that the theme under discussion is a common one both in literature and in the biographies of well-known people. It can be instructive to learn how certain celebrated figures, real and imaginary, dealt with this aspect of their own personal histories.

The theme of disillusionment is central, for example, to Arthur Miller's *Death of a Salesman*. The hero fails to flesh out the illusion of goodness and adequacy that is so important to the development of his two sons. For the boys, the sudden discovery that their father is a washed-up and pathetic cheat is crushing. The sons, especially Biff, feel despair—as they, too, are doomed to failure. Their only solution is itself born of despair: a refusal to compete. This tendency toward giving up is apparent in many narcissistic adolescents. Once they have suffered a profound disillusionment, few young people dare to expose themselves again to possible failure; even the extraordinarily talented remain crippled in some area of their lives. Beethoven made his way in the world despite his father's being loutish, brutal, and drunk—but at the price of bitterness and of alienation from conventional society (poignantly expressed in his "Testament"). Tennessee Williams was witness to his father's mediocrity in business, his alcoholism, and his incestuous overtures to his daughter (which seemed to have precipitated her psychosis). Williams became a great playwright—but one whose personal life was scarcely more gratifying than Beethoven's. The important plays, incidentally, all deal with the theme of disillusionment: In *The Glass Menagerie* it is Laura's and Amanda's, with each other and with the dead father's lack of success; in *A Streetcar Named Desire,* it is Blanche's disillusionment with the loss of antebellum status and elegance (she loses her sense of identity, becoming aimless and promiscuous, as a result); in *Cat on a Hot Tin Roof* everyone, in effect, becomes disillusioned with everyone else—there is the hero's homosexuality, the cancer of "Big Daddy," which threatens his powerful position in the family, and the mendacity of the rest of the family.

Comparable to the early environment of Tennessee Williams was that of Henry Roth, whose autobiographical novel *Call It Sleep* also depicts mental illness in a family member (the father, in this instance) and its bewildering, disillusioning effects on the child. The same may be said for Eugene O'Neill, witness to his mother's morphinism (cf. *Long Day's Journey into Night*) and his father's alcoholism (cf. *The Iceman Cometh*). The theme of disillusionment and loss of an ideal is particularly strong both in *The Iceman Cometh* and in *Desire under the Elms,* a story that centers around the sons' disillusionment with their irascible father. Thomas Wolfe's family seems to have been less disturbed than those of the aforementioned writers, although his bombastic, largely ineffectual father and penny-pinching mother were enough to make him feel *You Can't Go Home Again* (the title of the sequel to *Look Homeward Angel,* where the disillusionment with both parents is spelled out in remarkable detail).

Not many generalizations can be made about optimal therapy for those who have suffered the kinds of disillusionment alluded to in this chapter. Much depends on when, in a young person's life, the loss of an ideal occurs. The clinical vignettes show a range of severity and abruptness (in the way an individual loses the ability to continue looking up to a once-idealized figure) and a range of ego strength in the patients. There may be critical periods when a particular type of loss would exert maximal stress. Mothers are supposed to be pillars of strength and models for identification, particularly for their pubescent daughters; fathers play similar roles in the lives of their 14- or 15-year-old sons. The daughter 12 years of age whose mother suffers a mental breakdown or the 14-year-old boy whose alcoholic father gets in trouble with the law may be more vulnerable than if similar crises had occurred when they were 4 years younger. A therapist, preferably of the same sex, may be of great help to such an adolescent, serving simultaneously as a sympathetic listener and counselor, and also as a figure worthy of idealization. The therapist, for these reasons, can help compensate for the no-longer-idealized figure within the family.

Well-integrated persons, such as the young woman in Case G show greater resiliency and require much less treatment than someone with a borderline condition or a full-blown psychosis. The therapist's role as potential confidante should not be minimized as mere support. Evidence has begun to accumulate to the effect that having even *one* person to share one's most painful secrets can spell the difference between survival and suicide (Friedman & Corn, 1985). The girl in Case D faced a sweeping disillusionment with her entire family: father, mother (to whom she could say nothing about the incest), uncle. The tie to her therapist first guaranteed her survival and later, by affirming her values and offering her continued support, gave her, in effect, safe conduct between the family of origin and the life that lay beyond.

As patients approach the age of 20, the sex of the therapist begins to make little difference; support and ideal replacement are still crucial elements in the treatment, but in suitable cases, the greater objectivity and distance from the lost ideal permits analytic exploration. This in turn should foster solidification of the defenses and ego assets, minimizing the need for reliance on the once-idealized parents.

A patient I contacted in connection with a follow-up study (some 15 years after her discharge from a psychiatric facility specializing in analytically oriented psychotherapy) illustrates this point. This woman, now in her mid-30s, a successful artist and the mother of two children, described her (male) therapist at the hospital:

> Dr. L. helped me more than any person in my life. My first therapist was more conventional but I didn't like him. I never felt the kind of sincerity and love for him as I did from Dr. L. L. was like the mother I wished I had but never did: My real mother was preoccupied and cold; L. was more maternal, even though he was a man. He became my model for what a person could be like, ought to be like. Later, I found another ideal person in an older woman who was the leader of the religious organization I joined. Because she was my mother's age and sex, I felt, even more than I had with Dr. L., that I at last had a mother. As a result, I'm less resentful of my own mother and get along better with her than I did when I was growing up.

This kind of identification, at once restorative and growth-promoting, has sometimes gone by the name of *transference-cure*. Another example of how this may unfold within the context of long-term intensive therapy may be gleaned from a final vignette.

Case H

Because of a suicide gesture made in response to a romantic disappointment, an adolescent girl of 17 years was hospitalized on the long-term unit of a psychiatric hospital. The relationship had been turbulent. Her boyfriend had often failed to show up, leaving her stranded for hours; at other times he had excited her jealousy by taunting her about interest in other girls. Her homelife had been characterized by serious neglect on the part of otherwise well-meaning parents, who were both immature and given to constant quarreling. The father, outwardly successful, became more and more alcoholic; her mother diverted most of her attention away from the patient and focused it on her difficult and demanding husband. The father ultimately lost his job. By the time the patient had left the hospital and entered college, the family could scarcely afford tuition and were often tardy about this and all other obligations that concerned her day-to-day support. The patient, now a young woman of 20, filled most of her thrice-weekly sessions with tales of the family crises from the week before. She felt completely disillusioned in both her once-effective father and her distracted and scatterbrained mother. The rest of her family was indifferent or unsympathetic. There was no one to turn to but her therapist.

Treatment focused, of necessity, on the practical issues of how to keep her going, both at school and in her social life, despite the lack of emotional or financial support from her parents. Once in a great while her situation was calm enough to permit exploration of a dream or some other manifestation of her unconscious life. Often the focus was on the minutiae of her schoolwork. Despite the apparent superficiality of the therapy and its crisis-intervention atmosphere, she made great strides. Initially diagnosed borderline, she was presently free of any impulsivity or self-damaging acts and was no longer panicky when alone. She more resembled the average neurotic patient. In the 2nd and 3rd year of posthospital therapy, the sessions were devoted largely to discussions about her disillusionment with both parents. She had begun to idealize and to identify with her current therapist. At age 23, this process led her to want to pursue a career in one of the helping professions. She enrolled in postgraduate courses to help her meet the requirements for an eventual doctoral degree. Thanks to her determination and self-discipline, she was able to actualize her plans.

CONCLUSIONS

The disillusionment that follows the loss of an ideal will vary in its deleterious effects on development according to such factors as (1) the nature of the negative experiences, (2) the age at which they are suffered, (3) whether one was directly victimized by the once-idealized person or was merely the involuntary witness of that person's failure, (4) one's genetic and constitutional vulnerability, (5) one's ego strength and personal assets (viz., self-reliance, perseverance).

In the therapeutic encounter with the patient who has lost an ideal, the therapist must provide the proper balance of supportive and exploratory interventions; in addition, however, it may be necessary to serve as a replacement for the lost ideal, a role in which the therapist must be worthy, not merely willing, to serve. So long as the disillusionment is not too severe and far-reaching, the continuity of the treatment often serves as an effective antidote, if this is fortified by the most important ingredient of all: the therapist's integrity.

REFERENCES

Chassequet-Smirgel, J. (1985). *The ego ideal*. New York: Norton.
Erikson, E. H. (1956). The problem of ego-identity. *Journal of the American Psychoanalytic Association, 2*, 56–121.

Freud, S. (1961). The ego and the id. In J. Strachey (Ed. and Trans.), *The standard edition of the complete psychological works of Sigmund Freud* (Vol. 19, pp. 3–66). London: Hogarth Press. (Original work published 1923)

Friedman, R. C., & Corn, R. (1985). Follow-up five years after attempted suicide at age seven. *American Journal of Psychotherapy, 39,* 108–113.

Jacobson, E. (1964). *The self and the object world.* New York: International Universities Press, pp. 89–155.

Kolb, L. C. (1982). Assertive traits fostering social adaptation and creativity. *Psychiatric Journal of the University of Ottawa, 7,* 217–225.

Stone, M. H. (1986). Exploratory psychotherapy in schizophrenia-spectrum patients: A reevaluation in the light of long term follow up of schizophrenic and borderline patients. *Bulletin of the Menninger Clinic, 50,* 287–306.

Stone, M. H., Stone, D. K., & Hurt, S. (1987). Natural history of borderline patients treated by intensive hospitalization. *Psychiatric Clinics of North America, 10,* 185–206.

Winnicott, D. W. (1965). *The maturational processes and the facilitating environment.* New York: International Universities Press.

Economic Trauma: A Public Health Problem

JOSEPH H. HERZBERG, MD

During recent years, environmental concerns about many different potential health hazards have claimed increasing attention. Americans have become alerted to the hazards of air, water, and noise pollution; more recently, the carcinogenic threat posed by the leakage of toxic waste dumps has caught the headlines. Although these environmental concerns are serious, the number one health problem in the United States has, in fact, been at the workplace, with costs to industry estimated at $75 billion to $100 billion a year. Expenses come from absenteeism, diminished productivity, increased health insurance charges, and direct and indirect health-related expenses.

THE EXPERIENCE OF ECONOMIC STRESS

Ecological stressors like water, air, and noise pollution are everywhere in the environment, a constant background factor of everyday life. But economic stresses are equally ubiquitous and offer a particularly dangerous and intrusive presence in daily experience because of the immediacy of their stress effect. It is generally true that the impact of any stress is related directly to the way the individual perceives it, and economic stresses are perceived as quickly and as intensely as having to pay the next bill. In addition, economic stresses resonate powerfully with former experiences of loss of control stemming from earlier life events, especially those occurring during childhood and young adulthood. One way to construe the emotional impact of the growth process on children under ordinary circumstances is to regard it as a series of deprivations as, bit by bit, the child has to relinquish childhood perogatives. But less attention is given to the emotional impact on children of having to live under circumstances of actual poverty or marked economic insecurity. Children account for an increasing percentage (30%) of all persons in America living in poverty. More will be said about this later in discussing the impact of poverty and economic insecurity on the family.

Evidence is mounting that economic stresses must be regarded as part of the main burden of public health concerns. A study for the Joint Economic Committee of Congress was conducted at the Johns Hopkins School of Public Health (Brenner, 1984). It found that changes in national employment had dramatic effects on the nation's health. Brenner's report includes estimates that the direct effect of a 10% decrease in employment on a variety of health and social conditions included a 1.2% increase in total mortality, or 24,450 additional deaths; a 1.7% increase in cardiovascular mortality, or 17,392 deaths; a 4.2% increase in the population of mental hospitals, or 5,885 persons hospitalized; and a 1.3% increase in cirrhosis mortality, or 401 deaths.

In addition, the study indicates that the effects of a 10% decline in per capita income include a 1% increase in total mortality, a 1.5% increase in cardiovascular mortality, a 3.7% increase in suicides, and a 2.6% increase in imprisonments.

Furthermore, Brenner (1984, estimated that a 10% rise in the rate of business failures results in a 0.3% increase in cardiovascular deaths.

The evidence is that the unemployment rate (see Table 23.1) is significantly related to increases in cigarette consumption and the proportion of the population living alone, and that the business failure rate is significantly related to increases in cigarette smoking and alcohol consumption. According to Brenner, alcohol consumption and the percentage of the population living alone were linked to suicide rates that are 11 times the national average. These effects can be directly attributed to the unemployment rate.

As the country experiences a recovery period, persons employed in businesses that were seriously damaged by the recession but that are not participating in the national recovery, experience maximum psychological deprivation stress. After a severe recession, employment-related indices may not return to prerecession levels for 4 or 5 years.

The report concludes by noting that between 1950 and 1980 (the period covered by the study) chronic diseases and external causes such as suicide, homicide and accidents replaced infectious disease as the major cause of deaths and illness.

Table 23.1. Latent Data: Unemployment Rates (Seasonally Adjusted), July 1985

Labor Force[a] (age in years)	Percentage Unemployed	Number of Workers
Total	7.2	9,052,000
Men (16+)	7.0	4,644,000
Women (16+)	7.4	3,807,000
White	6.4	6,362,000
Men (20+)	5.6	2,944,000
Women (20+)	5.7	2,299,000
Teens (16–19)	16.3	1,119,000
Black	15.0	1,854,000
Men (20+)	12.6	726,000
Women (20+ yrs)	13.2	750,000
Teens (16–19)	41.3	378,000
Hispanic (16+)	11.2	836,000

[a]Average duration = 15.4 weeks; median duration = 7.2 weeks. Of all unemployed, 27.8% were unemployed 15 weeks or longer (14.9% for 27+ weeks). In number of workers, 2,349,400 were unemployed 15+ weeks (1,259,200 for 27+ weeks).

Source: From Bureau of Labor Statistics Release USDL 85-304 (1985).

FACTORS CONTRIBUTING TO JOB-RELATED STRESS

A Blue Cross–Blue Shield survey of a broad cross-section of workers in two midwestern states illustrates the widespread effects of job-related stress. According to the survey, five out of six workers at all levels of employment—from the executive suite to the assembly line—complained that job stress was a major factor in generating anxiety, depression, a poor self-image, colds, asthma, chest pains, and difficulty in breathing. Although job stress is generally thought of in terms of the harried, frenetic Type A executive driving to get to the top, dull, dead-end, assembly-line work patterns can pose equal health hazards.

Lack of satisfaction with the job, loss of control over time to complete the job, absence of recognition, loss of control over potential merger or acquisition, loss of control over environmental conditions, and the absence of empathic responses from superiors and subordinates can all increase occupational stress. More than that, a failure to be promoted or the experience of being fired can be the ultimate economic and financial trauma and is experienced on a highly personal basis. According to S. Martin Nemirow (personal communication, 1985), policy analyst for the U.S. Labor Department, studies done during the Great Depression of the 1930s, when the unemployment rate was 25%, showed that people blamed themselves for being unemployed. Nemirow further observed that this is a remarkable testimony to the human capacity for guilt. This displaced, self-directed anger may be at the root of the rage that gets further displaced onto an unemployed worker's wife and children in the form of physical abuse. Alcoholism, too, is often a part of the unemployed or unpromoted worker's characteristically displaced anger and demoralization.

Case Study

Jim had worked 15 years as a body frame inspector on an automobile assembly line and had gained the respect of his peers and supervisors. He worked overtime and often encouraged his peers to do the same. With the economic recession of the 1970s and 1980s, Jim was threatened by cutbacks and layoffs, but, by means of his seniority and good performance, he managed to retain his job. However, as the years passed, Jim received smaller and less frequent wage increases. Moreover, with the passage of time, the auto frame company for which he worked became more automated and less labor intensive. In the face of these changes, Jim displayed less and less interest in attending employee training sessions covering advanced high-tech assembly techniques. He ignored the growing evidence that more of the recently hired employees, including those recently promoted to supervisory levels, had strong technical backgrounds.

A crushing disappointment for Jim occurred when he was not selected to participate in the company supervisory program. Indeed, this was the second time that Jim had been passed over for promotion to supervisor.

Three months later, the plant manager noted a trend of complaints from the supervisors who worked with Jim. They remarked that Jim was not his old self, his productivity had decreased, he would talk compulsively and pessimistically about his future at the company, he would come to work later and leave earlier, and he would miss days at work because of illness. He was noted to have become less friendly and sociable, eating lunch alone and talking in an openly angry and defensive manner.

Jim's supervisor found two approaches for dealing with the problem. First, he recommended that Jim take a 3-week vacation, without pay, with his wife; second, he noted that Jim was already increasing his alcohol consumption seriously, and he recommended that Jim attend the plant employee assistance program (EAP). His few beers with the boys after work had grown in amount and frequency so that he would appear for work obviously hung over. The EAP counselor considered Jim suicidal and believed his recent accidents on the job to be motivated by self-destructive and self-punitive impulses.

Comment. An analysis of the economic stresses on Jim reveals many contributing factors threatening workers today. First, a deep background problem of insecurity emanates from the nation's troubled economy. The threat of job loss with cutbacks or layoffs, some related to mergers and acquisitions, is often ominously present. Second, a special kind of threat arises from the introduction of technological labor-saving and labor-displacing machinery and instruments. Economic insecurity from this quarter can pose very serious threats to pride and autonomy. Failure to keep up with new advances through vocational growth threatens loss of control in the face of the march of younger "baby boomer" workers, who have been raised with computers and other high technology. Displacement involves loss of the primary support group of fellow workers, who, along with the family, form the linchpin of an individual's feeling of emotional security. Threats of unemployment can lead to self-blame. This had been the case with Jim, even where he had not been at fault initially.

CHANGES IN EMPLOYMENT PATTERNS

The growth of the two-spouse worker family has had notable impact on the male worker. Between 1972 and 1984, 60% of new jobs were taken by women; this was due at least in part to the expansion of the service sector (*e.g.,* retail, fast food, insurance) and slow growth of the manufacturing sector, the latter being traditionally male, the former traditionally female. This can add to the demoralized, and even emasculated, feeling experienced by men like Jim or, indeed, by unemployed males in general.

The meaning of unemployment for women and minority ghetto residents is likely to be different than it is for men in general. Women often have traditional maternal and household roles to fall back upon, and historically, their identity has not been so linked to their paying job. When men become unemployed, they do not know what to do with themselves. Among unemployed men, 80% are bluecollar workers with few educational, cultural, or leisure-time interests. Women's unemployment is more likely to result from voluntary movement in and out of the labor force. The service sector is not as vulnerable to cyclical layoffs as is the manufacturing sector.

The hard-core ghetto unemployed do not suddenly set aside a work identity they have had for years. If the male unemployed worker reverts to a life of criminal self-employment in the ghetto, at least he feels like his own boss. This role gives him a defensive macho feeling to compensate for feelings of worthlessness related to having had poor male models. Most legitimate job openings are for traditionally female service and retail jobs, driving the ghetto male further underground and onto the streets to earn money. The vicious cycle continues because a worker needs an extended duration of unemployment, for example, 9 months, to qualify for unemployment insurance; this, in turn, encourages increased illegal activity. An increasing number of black women, like white women, are working outside the home; moreover, they also collect welfare, which further adds to the masculinity problem of the males. Under affirmative action, black women have the double advantage of being both black and female, even though the job market is already in their favor compared to black men.

For the unemployed male, the decline of the extended family and the diminished community role in extending aid to persons facing personal crises further exacerbate the problem of demoralization. Relatives are not there to give him a job or to help tide him over. The Labor Department has cut back funding to mutually supportive job search groups; indeed, the federal government has turned over most of its responsibility for the unemployed to the states. Furthermore, adding to the frustration of the unemployed male vis-à-vis the government is a bifurcation between a training bureaucracy and a benefits bureaucracy. To retain benefits the unemployed worker is legally obligated to be ready to take a job at a moment's notice, which interferes with getting more job-related education and training.

Unions represent only the employed, not the unemployed, and, in the nature of things, they concern themselves chiefly with higher seniority workers. Historically, unions have pushed for higher wages, even at the expense of laying off lower seniority workers. An interesting finding related to the 8.5 million unemployed is that almost two thirds of this group receive no unemployment compensation benefits. This is true largely because the unemployed have exhausted their 26-week allotment or because of federal and state cutbacks in the 1980s.

The implications of unemployment are particularly grievous for the workers' families because the unemployed may lose their homes and their cars. When they use up their resources, they go onto welfare. Many of the unemployed drift into the underground economy. They do odd jobs and sometimes set up small businesses that usually go bankrupt. Follow-up on these persons to determine if they regain employment is difficult because their telephone service is often cut off, and many of them move frequently. Thus, the theory of some administration policy analysts that stricter federal and state unemployment benefits create greater incentives to seek employment elsewhere is often untestable.

THE WELFARE TRAP

Welfare itself has been the target of tightening restraints and has contributed to an increase of poverty and hunger in the United States. From 1978 to 1984, the number of poor people in America increased by about 10 million. In 1980 the poverty line was calculated by the Census Bureau to be $10,610 for a family of four. Several million people were cut off the food stamp programs in the 1980s. According to a study done by the House Ways and Means Committee, between 1980–1984, in real terms, the combined value of food stamps and welfare payments declined by 8% to 9.7%. Their value in 18 states, for families with no other income was only two thirds of the poverty threshold—or less.

As of 1983 children accounted for 39% of all Americans living in poverty. That figure represented 22.2% of all children and 46.7% of all black children. According to these figures, the younger the child, the more likely he or she was to be living in poverty, with many at nutritional risk if not frankly hungry, especially late in the month as the food stamps run out.

In a typical situation a welfare mother of five, who became a mother at 16, may now, at 32, have become a grandmother. Such a woman can often give only limited love and affection as well as food. Humiliation, long waiting lines, rudeness, and indifference often await her at public assistance offices. Some teenage mothers, demoralized by premature responsibility of their own after years of being neglected themselves, see pregnancy as a way out. The more babies they have, the more money they get from Aid to Families with Dependent Children, which is one of the major welfare programs. Many of these single heads of households want to get out of the vicious poverty–hunger cycle but are trapped by political and economic obstacles.

ECONOMIC STRESSES: OTHER TYPES, OTHER SETTINGS

Though the initial discussion emphasized the more traditional industrial setting with its attendant economic insecurities, many other types of economic stress both at the workplace and in the family threaten physical and mental health.

First, the following stresses may be found within the workplace milieu: demotion, compulsory relocation, travel demands, overwork, family separation, fatigue, high-risk work (nuclear repair, toxic substances, explosives, carcinogenic chemicals, etc.), lack of proper job safety, loss of retirement benefits, fear of foreign competition, erosion of unions, early retirement, forced retirement, integration with minorities and opposite-sex workers, competition with colleagues, and plant closings. And, of course, success can bring stress. Promotion, for example, can lead a person to fear the increased expectations on his or her performance.

At home, the family is always affected by economic threats, both directly and indirectly. Higher rates of marital separation and divorce are well-known accompaniments of economic stresses at work. Indeed, it is the family that most acutely experiences actual or threatened loss of income, with such chilling possibilities as loss of housing, educational deprivation for children and adults, and other threats to securitty.

The increasing prevalence of the two-worker family leads to its own problems in respect to marital satisfaction and involvement with children, not to mention the stresses relating to proper child care and the inherent added expenses. Sociological and longitudinal studies of children from two-career parents should be helpful in the future.

On a spiritual level, and in the realm of personal satisfaction, the profound impact of the ubiquitous marketing and packaging culture has taken its toll. We are surrounded by increasingly clever and sophisiticated market segmenting and targeting, and by computer-driven mass appeals couched in the form of electronic and print media and correspondence. Some cultural critics and social observers have talked about the marketing or packaging personality as most characteristic of our age. As people are increasingly more image conscious, this has the effect of decreasing the depth of interpersonal satisfaction in everyday relationships.

Finally, poverty studies have shown that a higher incidence of mental and physical illness occurs in the lower classes and among the frankly impoverished. Every recognized study has come to the same conclusion about the rate of mental illness and poverty. The only exception appears to be the affective disorders, whose prevalence and incidence seem to be independent of financial security. What happened to Jim can happen to anyone in any socioeconomic class, as economic stresses threaten basic self-esteem and lead to demoralization and depression.

REFERENCES

Brenner, M. H. (1984, June). *Estimating the effects of economic change on national health and social well-being* (Joint Economic Committee of the U.S. Congress). Washington, DC: U.S. Government Printing Office.

U.S. Department of Labor. (1985). *Bureau of Labor Statistics Release* (USDL 85-304). Washington, DC: U.S. Government Printing Office.

Vulnerabilities

One of the main currents in modern psychiatric research is the attempt to understand the factors that make some individuals prone to react to challenges in disturbed fashion whereas others, exposed to the same stress, seem to cope without undue difficulty. The focus in recent years has fallen ever more on the matter of vulnerabilities on the one hand, and supports or protective factors on the other. This is indeed, a hopeful arena of study; if we become able to discern what makes a given individual vulnerable or what protects someone who might otherwise have been vulnerable, then we can develop techniques and approaches to serve both the single patient who faces serious dilemmas as well as whole classes of potentially traumatized individuals, who can be spared enormous amounts of pain. One of the most important advances in this area has been the research in temperament. Once an objective and verifiable account of infant temperament can be established, it should have a direct impact on the tactics of child rearing, education, and mental health management in general. In a sense such a profile states whether special vulnerabilities are present and what kind of problems they presage; it also catalogs any special competencies that have been identified, as well as the best ways to maximize them.

The realm of neuroendocrinology presents another approach that is bearing prime fruit. We are now beginning to unravel the biological codes that underlie health and illness, and that bind together the concepts of mind and body in a functional unit. In particular, this work is opening up the heretofore obscure pathways between the experience of a psychological stress and the resultant appearance of medical and psychological disabilities. Some fascinating possibilities are becoming apparent, and the emerging findings are enormously suggestive.

Pathogenesis of the Adjustment Disorders: Vulnerabilities due to Temperamental Factors

STELLA CHESS, MD

For the purpose of categorizing temperament and studying its functional significance for normal and deviant psychological development, it is useful to divide behavior into the *what*, the *why*, and the *how*. The what of behavior comprises abilities and talents, the why indicates motivations and goals, and the how represents behavioral style or temperament. A similar formal analysis of behavior into these three types has been utilized by several developmental psychologists in the past (Cattell, 1950; Guilford, 1959). Two children may dress themselves with equal skillfulness and ride a bicycle with the same dexterity and have the same motives for engaging in these activities. Two adolescents may display similar learning ability and intellectual interests, and their academic goals may coincide. Two adults may show the same technical expertness in their work and have the same reason for devoting themselves to their jobs. Yet these two children, adolescents, or adults may differ significantly with regard to the quickness with which they move, the ease with which they approach a new physical environment, social situation, or task, the intensity and character of their mood expression, and the effort required by others to distract them when they are absorbed in an activity. In other words, they may differ in their temperamental characteristics.

IDENTIFICATION OF TEMPERAMENT

In this definition, temperament is a conceptual term that categorizes a functionally significant component of an individual's psychological structure.

The temperamental factor in any item or sequence of behavior or adaptive pattern can be identified by several characteristics:

1. Temperament is not immutable, but it shows some consistency over time. In some individuals, temperament may change over a period of months or several years; in others, consistency may be evident over extended periods, even many years. The characteristics of a transient adaptive pattern may be influenced by temperament, but the transient nature of the behavior will suggest that it is not primarily determined by temperament. Thus, for example, a child may show an avoidance withdrawal reaction to a new school situation. If he or she has consistently shown this type of behavior to previous new school experiences and to other new situations in the past, then the current reaction is most probably due to a temperamental characteristic. If, on the other hand, the child has previously shown positive responses to new school settings and other new situations, with quick and even immediate adaptation, then the current avoidance reaction is not temperamentally based, but must have some other origin. In this latter case, the manner of avoidance may be influenced by temperament, such as whether the withdrawal is expressed quietly or by a loud tantrum, but it would not be caused by temperament.

2. Temperament shows a significant degree of cross-situational consistency. Temperamentally persistent children will show this characteristic in most, though not necessarily in all their activities. Youngsters with quiet mood expression, whether it be of pleasure or displeasure, will respond in this fashion to family, to peers, to teachers, and to strangers. But special factors in one or another specific life experience may alter this cross-situational consistency. Thus, children who have low persistence temperamentally may stick doggedly to one specific task if they happen to be highly motivated for that particular activity. Or youngsters who temperamentally have a high energy level of mood expression may be quiet and subdued in a setting in which they feel intimidated and afraid to express themselves. But history from parents and/or teachers will indicate which is the typical cross-situational temperamental pattern for any given child.

3. Temperamental characteristics will be evident in situations where they are clearly not the result of motivational factors, such as goals or defense mechanisms.

Thus, temperamentally distractible children may have their attention diverted even from an activity they wish to pursue. Such a child may be on his way home from school to meet his friends for a ball game he would enjoy, be distracted by a passing parade, and forget the ball game. In this regard temperament can be regarded as a nonmotivational influence on behavior, as contrasted to values, goals, and defense mechanisms.

These characteristics are the basis on which the temperamental component of a behavioral pattern can be identified. Temperament will comprise those aspects of behavior that show some significant degree of consistency over time and from one life situation to another, and that are expressed even in settings where they serve no motivational goals. To identify temperament, therefore, the clinician will require data on the details of the individual's behavior in a number of different situations and over at least a time span of several months.

In this definition, temperament is a categorical term and has no implications as to etiology or immutability. Like any other characteristics of the individual, its features can undergo a developmental course that will be significantly affected by environmental circumstances. In this respect it is no different from height, weight, intellectual competence, perceptual skills, or motivational patterns. As is the case for all such physical or psychological characteristics, the young child's temperament may be relatively unchanged by subsequent environmental influences, or it may be reinforced and heightened, diminished, or otherwise modified during the developmental course. Other definitions of temperament have been proposed that narrow the range of the concept, such as a primary emphasis on the affective component, or that make an assumption as to etiology, such as a genetic basis for temperament. However, such alternative formulations make assumptions for which there is inadequate empirical evidence and restrict the usefulness of the concept of temperament, especially for clinical use.

BACKGROUND AND METHODOLOGY

Until the 1950s, relatively little attention had been paid by psychiatric theory or practice to the functional significance of temperament in the child's developmental course. Freud had asserted that "each individual ego is endowed from the beginning with its own peculiar dispositions and tendencies" (1950, p. 316). Pavlov and his followers had postulated the existence of congenitally determined types of nervous systems as basic to the course of subsequent behavioral development (Pavlov, 1927). However, both psychoanalysis and behaviorism, the latter being the outgrowth of Pavlov's work, concentrated on the motivational, goal-directed aspects of behavior and on the decision experiences of early life (Freud, 1949; Watson, 1928). A number of investigators from the 1930s through the 1950s had reported observations of individual behavioral stylistic differences in young children (see Thomas & Chess,

1977, for summaries of these studies), but no systematic, comprehensive studies of temperamental attributes and their significance for later psychological development had been reported.

My colleague's and my own clinical experience and review of the literature of the 1950s led us to question the adequacy of the prevalent theories of the pathogenesis and evaluation of behavior disorders in children that ignored the active role of the child in interaction with environmental influences (Thomas & Chess, 1977). We decided to test our hypothesis that the child's temperament characteristics could, under certain circumstances, contribute to a vulnerability to the development of behavior disorder. To do this we launched the New York Longitudinal Study (NYLS) in 1956. The NYLS families are a relatively homogeneous native-born, middle-class group. To date, 133 subjects have been followed from the first few months of life into early adulthood. Originally, we explored the possibility of obtaining data from the neonatal period onward. A pilot study showed that the newborn infant's behavior varied significantly from day to day, even from hour to hour, and that data collection and analysis would be an exceedingly demanding and complex procedure. Further exploration indicated that, in general, the infant's behavioral characteristics usually began to show definiteness and consistency of patterning between the 4th and 8th weeks of life. Hence came the decision to start data collection at 2 to 3 months of age. Data-gathering procedures in the first 3 years of life relied primarily on semistructured interviews with the parents at regular intervals, which concentrated on obtaining detailed, factual accounts of the child's behavior in the various routines of daily life. These descriptions were linked at all times to the environmental context in which they occurred. Special attention was paid to any new situations or changes in routine, and details of the child's reactions were obtained and traced until an adaptation to the new situation had been accomplished. The accuracy of the parents' reports for this type of objective, factual, and nonjudgmental descriptions of their children's behavior was confirmed by comparison with direct observations of 18 infants made by two separate observers at different but closely timed interviews (Thomas, Chess, & Birch, 1968). As the children grew older, other data-gathering procedures were added, including psychometric testing, nursery school, kindergarten and lower-grade teacher interviews, classroom observations, and a special interview for parental practices and attitudes. A full clinical workup was done on any child who showed any significant degree of deviant behavior, and regular clinical follow-ups obtained. In addition to the parent interviews, direct semistructured interviews were done with the subjects when they reached adolescence and early adulthood (Chess & Thomas, 1984).

CATEGORIES OF TEMPERAMENT

An inductive content analysis was carved out of the parent interview protocols for the infancy period in the first 22 children enlisted in the NYLS. As a result, nine categories of temperament were established. Item scoring was used, a 3-point scale was established for each category (in our later rating procedures, and those of other workers, a 7-point scale has been used), and the item scores transformed into a weighted score for each category on each record. High intra- and interscores reliability, at the 90% level of agreement, was achieved.

The nine categories of temperament and their definitions follow:

1. *Activity Level.* The motor component present in a given child's functioning and the diurnal proportion of active and inactive periods

2. *Rhythmicity (Regularity).* The predictability and regularity of biologic functions such as sleep-wake cycle, hunger, feeding pattern, and elimination

3. *Approach or Withdrawal.* The nature of the initial response to a new stimulus, such as a new food, new person, new toy, or new place. Approach responses are positive, withdrawal ones negative, whether displayed by mood expression and/or motor activity

4. *Adaptability.* Responses to new or altered situations. Here one is not concerned with the nature of the initial responses (that is, approach or withdrawal), but with the ease with which they can be modified in desired directions

5. *Threshold of Responsiveness.* The intensity level of stimulation that is necessary to evoke a discernible response, irrespective of the specific form that the response may take, or the sensory modality involved

6. *Intensity of Reaction.* The energy level of response, irrespective of its quality or direction

7. *Quality of Mood.* The amount of pleasant, joyful, and friendly behavior, as contrasted with unpleasant, crying, and unfriendly behavior

8. *Distractibility.* The effectiveness of extraneous environmental stimuli in interfering with or altering the direction of the ongoing behavior

9. *Attention Span and Persistence.* Two categories that are related and rated together. Attention span concerns the length of time a particular activity is pursued. Persistence refers to the continuation of an activity in the face of obstacles to the maintenance of the direction of the activity

THREE TEMPERAMENTAL CONSTELLATIONS

Three temperamental constellations of functional significance have been defined by qualitative analysis and factor analysis of the NYLS data. The youngsters in the first group are characterized by regularity, positive approach responses to most new stimuli, high adaptability to change, and mild or moderately intense mood that is preponderantly positive. These children quickly develop regular sleep and feeding schedules, take to most new foods easily, smile at strangers, adapt easily to a new school, accept most frustrations with little fuss, and conform to the rules of new games with no trouble. Such a youngster, whom we have chosen to call the easy child, is usually a joy to parents, pediatricians, and teachers. This group comprises about 40% of the NYLS sample.

At the opposite end of the temperamental spectrum is the group characterized by irregularity in their biological functions, negative withdrawal responses to many if not most new stimuli, nonadaptability or slow adaptability to change, and intense mood expressions that are often negative. These children show irregular sleep and feeding schedules, slow acceptance of new foods, prolonged adjustment periods to new routines, people, or situations, and relatively frequent and loud periods of crying. Their laughter is also characteristically loud. Frustration typically produces an intense tantrum. This is the temperamentally difficult child, and parents, pediatricians, and teachers find such youngsters to be very problematic indeed. This group comprises about 10% of our NYLS sample.

The third noteworthy temperamental constellation is marked by a combination of negative responses of mild intensity to new stimuli, with slow adaptability after repeated contact. In contrast to the difficult children, these youngsters are characterized by mild intensity of reactions, whether positive or negative, and by less of a tendency to show irregularity of biological functions. The negative mild responses to new stimuli can be seen in the first encounter with the bath, a new food, a stranger, a new place, or a new school situation. If given the opportunity to reexperience such new situations over time and without pressure, such a child gradually comes to show quiet and positive interest and involvement. A youngster with this characteristic sequence of response we have aptly if inelegantly called the slow-to-warm-up child. About 15% of our NYLS sample fall into this pattern.

As can be seen from the preceding percentages, not all children fit into one of these three temperamental constellations. This results from the varying and different combinations of temperamental attributes that are manifested by individual children. More than that, among the children who do fit one of these patterns, there is a wide range in the degree of expression of any given trait. Some are extremely easy children in practically all situations, others are relatively easy although not always so. A few children are extremely difficult with all new situations and demands, others show only some of those characteristics, and those to a relatively mild extent. For some children it is highly predictable that they will warm up slowly in any new situation, others warm up slowly with certain types of new stimuli or demands, but quickly with others.

It should be emphasized that the various temperamental characteristics and constellations all represent variations within normal limits. Thus, for example, high activity as a temperamental attribute is qualitatively different in its behavioral manifestations and consequences from the pathological syndrome of hyperactivity. Within a sample of children studied for a specific temperamental attribute any given child may be easy, difficult, or slow-to-warm-up temperamentally, have a high or low activity level, be distractible with low persistence, or the opposite, or show any other relatively extreme rating score. However, such a difference from the average rating of a group is not a criterion of psychopathology; it is rather an indication of the wide range of behavioral styles exhibited by normal children—or by normal adults for that matter.

A detailed exposition of the various temperamental categories and constellations can be found in our recent volume (Chess & Thomas, 1986). This volume also spells out the different ways in which temperament is expressed and influences the course of psychological development at sequential developmental periods (infancy, toddler stage, middle childhood, adolescence, and adult life).

GENERALIZATION OF TEMPERAMENT CATEGORIES

It has been possible to rate each of the nine categories of temperament, as well as the three constellations (easy, difficult, and slow-to-warm-up) in each NYLS subject at different age levels into early adulthood (Chess & Thomas, 1984). The same has been true of three other populations we have followed: a Puerto Rican working-class sample residing in New York, a group of mildly retarded children living at home, and a large sample of children suffering from physical handicaps resulting from congenital rubella. These same temperamental categories and constellations have also been identified in a large number of studies from many centers in this country, as well as in various European and Asian countries, Canada, Australia, and Kenya (Ciba Foundation Symposium, 1982; de Vries, 1984; Hsu, Soong, Stigler, Hong, & Liang, 1981; Maziade et al., 1985). Other categories and constellations of temperament have been suggested by other workers, but their functional significance has yet to be demonstrated. A number of questionnaires have now been developed which are designed to rate temperament in the various age-periods of childhood, adolescence, and early adult life (see Chess & Thomas, 1984, p. 45, for references). A protocol for obtaining temperamental data in clinical practice has also been developed (Thomas & Chess, 1977, Appendix D), and is elaborated in detail in our recent volume (Chess & Thomas, 1986).

ORIGINS OF TEMPERAMENT

Temperament is an empirical categorical term, without any implications as to etiology. Several studies have indicated an appreciable, but by no means exclusive genetic role in the determination of temperamental individuality in the infant (Buss & Plomin, 1975; Torgersen & Kringlen, 1978). Prenatal or perinatal brain damage does not appear to influence temperament in any striking fashion. Thus far, the available data indicate that parental attitudes and functioning have at the most a modest etiological influence, and that sociocultural factors may help to shape temperament in the infant. Maternal anxiety preceding or at least starting in pregnancy may be a significant factor (Thomas & Chess, 1977; Thomas, Chess, & Korn,

1982). Kagan (1982) has recently reported an association between a temperamental attribute of behavioral inhibition to unfamiliar events (similar to our approach–withdrawal category) in 2-year-olds and a higher and less variable heart rate. This finding suggests a promising direction for research into the relationships between temperamental and psychophysiological characteristics. Prenatal variations in hormonal activity or other chemical or physiological influences on the developing brain may also play a significant role in the origin of temperamental individuality. This hypothesis still remains to be tested.

CONSISTENCY OF TEMPERAMENT OVER TIME

Temperamental characteristics of the young infant are not immutable. Like all other psychological phenomena, such as intellectual competence, coping mechanisms, adaptive patterns, and value systems, temperamental attributes are affected by continued genetic and maturational factors, as well as by a host of environmental influences. In our NYLS subjects, various patterns of consistency and/or change have been evident: (1) clear-cut consistency; (2) consistency in some aspects of temperament at one period and in other aspects at other times; (3) distortion of the expression of temperament by other factors, such as psychodynamic patterns; and (4) change in a conspicuous temperamental trait. Some subjects showed a combination of several of these possibilities, that is, consistency over time with one or several temperamental attributes, along with distortion in another, plus change in several others, and so on (Thomas & Chess, 1977).

In many NYLS subjects continuity throughout childhood, and even into adult life, has been typical of one or more temperamental characteristics or constellations. In a number of subjects this has been strikingly evident. This, however, should not be interpreted as evidence of some fixed immutable intrapsychic process. It indicates rather that over time, there had been stability in the dynamics of interplay between the person and the environment. Without this stability, all types of change and discontinuity, whether in temperament or in any other psychological phenomenon, may develop.

For the research workers in developmental psychiatry or psychology, the study of the dynamic processes involved in changes in temperament is as fruitful—or even more productive—an area of investigation as is the study of continuity. Actually, inasmuch as behavioral development at all ages reflects the constant interplay of both phenomena, the explorations into each issue—continuity and change—go hand in hand.

For the clinician dealing with a child with an Adjustment Disorder, the possibility of tracing the developmental course of a particular temperamental attribute or pattern may be quite useful. Such information serves as one aspect of the analysis of the origin and evaluation of the disorder. Where accurate historical data are available, this can be done, though the clinician should always be aware of the distortions of memory that can occur with retrospective recall (Chess & Thomas, 1984, pp. 6–7). However, whether the past history is clear, confused, or ambiguous, the clinician's diagnostic evaluation and therapeutic strategies still rest basically on how he or she assesses the current status of the child, the parents, and any other pertinent environmental influences.

VULNERABILITY AND GOODNESS OF FIT

The research studies of recent years have identified temperament as a major etiological factor in the development of Adjustment Disorders in children. As Michael Rutter put it:

> The last decade has seen a burgeoning of interest in temperament. There has been an accompanying substantial growth in our knowledge and understanding of the importance of temperamental differences. Temperament constitutes a variable of considerable predictive power in developmental psychopathology, a power with both practical and theoretical implications. (Ciba Foundation Symposium, 1982, p. 14).

This does not mean that temperament plays an important role in *all* cases of Adjustment Disorders in children. But it does so frequently enough that the clinician who ignores the possibility in differential diagnostic procedures will inevitably be led astray. This we have seen happen repeatedly in our consultative clinical practice, where parents have consulted us after unsatisfactory experiences with other psychiatrists.

To emphasize the importance of temperament in developmental psychopathology does not mean that any particular temperamental attribute or pattern, even an extreme one, is *ipso facto* pathological. To the contrary, as emphasized earlier, all temperamental attributes and constellations are normal aspects of the child's psychological functioning. For a given child, however, a temperamental characteristic can become a source of vulnerability and a significant factor in the development of an Adjustment Disorder. This occurs when the demands and expectations of the parents and/or other significant individuals in the child's life are very difficult or impossible for the child to meet because of that temperamental factor. This formulation we have conceptualized in what we have called the ''goodness of fit'' model of development. When the child's (or adult's) capacities, motivations, and temperament and the demands and expectations of the environment are in accord, then goodness of fit results. Such consonance between child and environment potentiates optimal positive development. Should there be dissonance between the capacities and characteristics of the child (or adult) on the one hand and the environmental opportunities and demands on the other, a state of poorness of fit ensues that leads to maladaptive functioning and distorted development. Goodness of fit and consonance, poorness of fit and dissonance are not abstractions; they are the concrete consequences of specific matchings. Here the model is useful only when applied to an individual person at a particular developmental level within the context of his or her actual family, who express the specific values and demands of a given socioeconomic group and culture.

Poorness of fit and psychosocial stressors. The *Diagnostic and Statistical Manual of Mental Disorders,* Third Edition, Revised (DSM III-R; American Psychiatric Association, 1987) defines the essential feature of an Adjustment Disorder as "a maladaptive reaction to an identifiable psychosocial stressor, that occurs within three months after the onset of the stressor. . . . The stressors may be single . . . or multiple . . . they may be recurrent . . . or continuous" (p. 329). Poorness of fit, as we have formulated it, in effect represents a psychosocial stressor. The environmental demands or expectations that are dissonant with the child's characteristics and capacities represent a psychosocial stressor for that child, even though this may not be the case with another child with different characteristics.

The goodness of fit model can be applied not only to temperament, but to other issues as well. For example, if a child is having difficulties in functioning at school, this may reflect a poorness of fit involving a temperamental factor, but it may also be the result of parents' and teachers' demands for a level of academic functioning that is beyond the child's cognitive capacities. In recent years, whether they use the term as such, a number of developmental psychologists and psychiatrists have begun to use the goodness of fit model to analyze the nature of the child's interaction with parents, peers and teachers (see Chess & Thomas, 1984, pp. 22–23, for references).

The present discussion is, however, confined to the way in which vulnerability and poorness of fit that involve temperamental factors can in childhood lead to Adjustment Disorders. It is understood that vulnerability may also arise from a poorness of fit in which temperament may play only a minor or an insignificant role.

STRESS AND VULNERABILITY

There is no implication that goodness of fit requires the absence of stress and conflict for the child. Quite the opposite is true. Stress and conflict are essential aspects of the developmental process in which new demands and expectations for enhanced levels of functioning occur continuously, keeping step with the ever-increasing capacities of the growing child. When these enlarging stresses, demands, and conflicts are in harmony with the rate of growth of the developmental capacities and potentials, then the consequences of such stress are constructive, rather than harbingers of behavioral disturbance. Actually, if parents attempt to shelter their children from stress, the consequences can be the development of a child tyrant or a child whose self-image crystallizes as inadequate to master the opportunities and demands of growing up in the same way that other children do. This we have seen repeatedly in our NYLS group. For example, if the parents of a temperamentally difficult child attempt to appease his loud tantrums when denied something he wants by giving in to him, this will only reinforce the occurrence of such tantrums. Presently such parents have a child tyrant on their hands, one who must be granted every wish and whim. Or, a slow-to-warm-up child may appear uncomfortable in every new social situation. If the parents try to shield her from this discomfort by avoiding such exposure whenever they can, then the youngster may never develop a sense of social ease, competence, and the capacity to develop new friendships in unfamiliar settings. What is required, rather, is that quietly, patiently, and consistently, the parents and others demand that the child become an active member of new groups. At first this may be difficult for the youngster but ultimately, this can be mastered with considerable profit. It is also possible to identify the kinds of situations that are likely to be stressful for a particular child because of temperament, and to map procedures and schedules calculated to make the child's adaptation positive. For example, if a high activity child is taken on a long automobile ride, the parents can make regular stops to allow the youngster to run around for a few minutes. Experienced and sensitive teachers, who identify such a child in their classroom, can help by assigning various active tasks, such as erasing the blackboard or taking messages and papers to the principal's office, so that the child is not forced to sit immobile for hours at a time. These may seem like very prosaic and superficial preventive strategies, but their implementation may have profound positive psychological effects for a youngster in whom one or another extreme, albeit normal, temperamental factor is at work.

It is therefore not stress as such, but the excess of stress due to poorness of fit that results in behavior problems. Such excessive stress occurs, for example, if parents demand that a child with withdrawal tendencies make a speedy and even immediate positive adjustment on first being entered into nursery school or into any other strange and unfamiliar situation, or if teachers expect a high activity child to sit quietly in his or her seat without fidgeting for long periods of time, or if a youngster with temperamentally low persistence and short attention span is required to concentrate at length without a break on some specific assignment.

PARENTAL ATTITUDES AND PRACTICES

Parents may place excessive and unreasonable demands on their child, or may make irrational judgments on the meaning of the child's behavior. Excess stress or demands can be equated with the formulation of "psychosocial stressor" (American Psychiatric Association, 1987, p. 329). But it should not be assumed that such undesirable or even pathogenic parental attitudes and practices necessarily reflect fixed unhealthy intrapsychic constellations. This may be true in some cases, but the great majority of parents are truly committed to doing whatever they can to help their children grow up to be self-confident adults who are physically and psychologically healthy. However, parents may become confused as to the proper course of action if their child's temperament and behavior differs from that of their relatives' and friends' offspring of the same age. Or they may blame themselves if their child is temperamentally difficult, and their guilt and anxiety may distort their judgment and their way of handling the child. Or they may be pressured by the overt or unspoken criticism of other parents if their child shows behavior that is deviant from the cultural norm. For example, one set of intelligent, thoughtful parents who were eager to have children had a first boy who was a typical temperamentally difficult child. The parents were bewildered when their tender loving care and their attention to the child's needs did not result in a smooth, easy development for the youngster. In their confusion and despair, they tried one approach after another, trying a new approach when each strategy did not bring quick results. They consulted several psychiatrists, from whom they got conflicting evaluations and advice. Neither the parents nor the psychiatrists identified the difficult temperament, nor the role it played in the child's behavior. When the child was 10 years old (he was not an NYLS subject), and the parents finally consulted one of us, the boy already had severe social and academic problems, and had truly become a child tyrant in the family. By that time the parents had two other young children, both of easy temperament, who were flourishing impressively in terms of their psychological development.

In contrast to this situation, one of our NYLS mothers had a slow-to-warm-up daughter, which the mother recognized. The girl made a slow but eventually positive adjustment to the first year of nursery school. At the end of the year, the school arranged an evening affair in which the children were to perform and to which the parents were invited. When this mother came in with her daughter, the child took one look at the strange auditorium and the mass of strange adults, climbed up on her mother's lap and remained there all evening, refusing to participate in the performance. When the mother reported the incident to us, she explained that she had noticed other parents casting glances at her and her daughter, and making all kinds of critical judgments about this mother and her child. Her inferences as to the other parents' reactions were undoubtedly correct. She related the incident to us with amusement, which reflected her accurate understanding of what had happened. One can see how another mother, however, without insight, might very well have accepted the other parents' judgments as valid, become convinced that either she was a bad mother or that her child had some peculiar psychological problems, or both. Such a derogation of herself and her child could only have led her to put excessive pressure on the girl, to try to shield her from strange settings, or to vacillate between the two approaches, with predictably unfavorable and even pathogenic consequences for the youngster.

Where a parent or parents misinterpret the meaning of the child's behavior, this may lead them into irrational responses that will further exacerbate the youngster's undesirable behavior; this in turn will intensify the parent's reactions, and so on. The escalating poorness of fit interaction may end in one or another type of behavioral disorder. A striking example was evident in one of the NYLS families. The youngster, Roy, was highly distractible from infancy onward. This, in his first few years of life was not a problem; and indeed in many ways this temperamental quality made his management easier as it was simple to distract him from an annoying or dangerous activity, such as poking at electrical outlets. But as Roy grew older, this pattern became not only undesirable, but even infuriating to his mother. Roy would forget dental and other after-school appointments, would start chores his mother requested and then go off in another direction, or be late getting off to school, in spite of reminders, because he became distracted while dressing. His mother perceived this behavior as deliberately oppositional to her wishes, based on the interpretation, in her own words, that "He does everything he can to make my life miserable." Constant badgering on her part was completely counterproductive, as Roy responded by tuning out his mother's voice. In effect, by her own responses to him, her initial misjudgment that Roy was deliberately ignoring and opposing her was transformed into a self-fulfilling prophecy. The father was a rather passive figure in the household, who detached himself from this escalating antagonistic mother–child interaction. Parent counseling with the mother was a complete failure. The evidence was clear that the mother's interpretation was distorted and that Roy was basically a cooperative, cheerful youngster. The mother herself reported many instances where he had forgotten a date he had made with a friend for some pleasurable activity. The mother, however, refused to accept the implications of these data and clung to her position that Roy was deliberately oppositional to her. The harmful effects of this maternal attitude and behavior were ameliorated only when Roy reached older adolescence and could make his life increasingly independent of his mother.

SIMILARITY OF PARENT AND CHILD TEMPERAMENT

Does goodness of fit mean that similarity of parent and child temperament is always desirable? A parent and child with similarly intense negative temperamental reactions are all too likely to end up screaming at each other repeatedly over even minor disagreements. On the other hand, one set of NYLS parents who were both quick-moving and intensely expressive individuals, were confused and exasperated at their daughter's slow-moving and mildly expressive behavior. They found her hard to understand and compared her unfavorably to her younger sister, whose temperament was similar to theirs. As could be expected, this had unfavorable consequences for the older girl's development. But, in another family, where the son was one of the most extreme members of the NYLS temperamentally difficult group, the story was different. The father was of opposite temperament—quiet and mild in his responses. Rather than this difference assuming a pathogenic character, the father was pleased at his young son's loud reactions, whether positive or negative, calling him "lusty." He was also supportive of his wife, who tended to worry that the child's difficult pattern was somehow her fault. As a result, even though his adaptation to new situations and demands was typically stormy, this youngster never developed an Adjustment Disorder, and he has functioned well into his middle 20s (our last follow-up with him).

All possible combinations exist. Sometimes, similar parent and child temperaments contribute to a goodness of fit, and sometimes to a poorness of fit. The same variability occurs with differences in parent and child temperament. The issue of child vulnerability due to temperamental factors is determined by the goodness or poorness of fit between parental demands and expectations and the child's temperament, and not by similarity or dissimilarity of temperament.

SOCIOCULTURAL INFLUENCES

The goodness of fit model requires a consideration of the specific values, demands, and opportunities of a given socioeconomic group and culture. To illustrate, in the middle-class subjects of NYLS subjects, high activity level was typically not a source of vulnerability, whereas in the working-class Puerto Rican families it was. The middle-class NYLS families lived in large apartments or private homes, and in areas where the streets were safe and ample outdoor play areas were available. The high activity youngsters, therefore, had many opportunities to satisfy their high motor activity needs constructively. The opposite was true of the high activity Puerto Rican youngsters. Their families lived in small apartments in an area of the city where the streets were unsafe and outdoor playgrounds were inadequate. Restricted to their cramped apartments, these youngsters' motor activity was inhibited or became destructive, and led, in a number of cases, to Adjustment Disorders.

By contrast, irregular sleep patterns were sometimes a source of vulnerability for the NYLS children, but not for the Puerto Rican youngsters. For the most part the NYLS parents demanded a regular bedtime for their children, retaining the rest of the evening for themselves, undisturbed by their young children. For the child with an irregular sleep pattern, this was a difficult or impossible expectation. Some parents accepted the disruptions of their evening schedules with little annoyance. Others, however, reacted with marked irritation and repeatedly exploded at the child, setting the stage for a sleep adjustment disorder. The Puerto Rican parents, on the other hand, were typically unconcerned whether their young children went to bed early or late, or continued to interact with them socially until their own bedtime.

SPECIFIC TEMPERAMENT FACTORS
AND VULNERABILITY

Children with the difficult temperament pattern are the most vulnerable to the development of Adjustment Disorders in early and middle childhood. This has been evident not only in the NYLS sample (Chess & Thomas, 1984), but also in reports from other centers (Thomas et al., 1982; Maziade et al., 1985). They display intense negative withdrawal reactions in the face of new experiences, and they adapt slowly to such novel encounters. These, together with biological irregularity, burden these children with high levels of stress as they try to respond to both the early and later childhood demands for socialization—regular sleep and feeding schedules, toilet training, peer relationships, adaptation to school, and mastery of unanticipated new situations and expectations. However, an Adjustment Disorder can develop with any temperamental attribute or constellation if the expectations for change and adaptation are overly dissonant to the particular child's characteristics. The distractible child with low persistence is put under excessive stress if expected to concentrate without interruption for long periods of time; the persistent child reacts similarly if his or her absorption in an activity is too often prematurely and abruptly terminated; the high activity child responds poorly if restricted in possibilities for constructive motor activity; the low activity child suffers if mislabeled as intellectually slow or reluctant to comply with parental or teachers' requests; and the slow-to-warm-up youngster fails if pressured into a speed of adaptation to the new beyond his or her capacities. Even the easy child may become vulnerable. This can occur especially if such a child has adapted behaviorally to idiosyncratic parental standards and demands and is then confronted outside the home, especially at the hands of peers or teachers, with such contradictory expectations that it is impossible for the child to reshape behaviors to fit these new environmental requirements (see Chess & Thomas, 1986; Thomas et al., 1968, for detailed discussion with clinical examples of the various ways in which specific temperament factors become sources of vulnerability to Adjustment Disorder development). No temperamental pattern is fated to create psychopathology, nor can any confer an immunity to the development of an Adjustment Disorder.

SYMPTOM CHOICE

We analyzed the origins of the Adjustment Disorders that occurred within the NYLS sample and found that these reactions derived from a poorness of fit between the goals, abilities, and temperament of the child, and the expectations of the environment. (To be sure, the more severe syndromes involve other factors, such as childhood psychosis, recurrent major depression, or organic brain syndrome.) On the other hand the type of symptom that the child developed was shaped by a number of factors: the child's developmental stage; the specific areas in which excessive demands were made by parents, teachers or peers; temperamental factors; and sociocultural influences (Chess & Thomas, 1984).

INTERVENTION BY THE MENTAL HEALTH PROFESSIONAL

In the previous sections of this chapter, the various specific examples and case vignettes have indicated many of the possibilities for effective intervention. These possibilities exist both for prevention and treatment and can be utilized not only by mental health professionals, but also by pediatricians, and, in many instances, by teachers and nurses as well. The basic approach in intervention involves parent education and guidance, though, in some cases, direct treatment of the child may be necessary. In addition to the guidance provided to the parents directly, the mental health professional may also have many opportunities to act as a consultant to pediatricians, nurses, or teachers.

Prevention

The mental health professional is often consulted by parents who are concerned that their child's behavior differs from the expected norm of their sociocultural group. The parents may have tried to change this behavior, only to find that they have either been ineffective, or even made matters worse. They come for professional advice with the anxious question, "What is wrong with my child?" or "What is wrong with me?" or both.

In such cases, if the professional finds that the child is essentially healthy psychologically and that the behavior of concern reflects of the child's temperament, then effective preventive intervention is most promising. This involves educating the parents to a number of key facts:

1. Babies are born with different styles of behavior, just as they are born with different physical characteristics.
2. These different styles are all normal, even though some may make for easier management of the child's daily routines, whereas others make for more difficult management.
3. The parents should not try to change their child's typical style of behavior to one that they might consider to be more desirable. Such pressure can succeed only in putting the youngster under great stress. However, as the child grows older, he or she can learn progressively to understand his or her

own temperament; to appreciate in what situations it is an asset and when it has consequences that are undesirable. As this insight develops, the child will be able, independently, to modify behavior to fit the necessities of specific situations.

4. Parents should not expect to find one simple set of rules that will work best for all children.

5. Above all, parents should learn that if they are having difficulties with their caretaking activities, this does not necessarily mean that they are either incompetent or psychologically disturbed.

The mental health professional can educate the parents to these facts, and can teach them how to apply such an approach specifically to their own child's behavior. The caretaking strategy that is optimal for their particular child can then be detailed. Some parents can grasp the essence of such a discussion in one session; others may require several. Most parents will respond favorably to such an educational process and make the changes necessary to prevent the development of an Adjustment Disorder.

From numerous anecdotal personal communications, it is clear that an increasing number of mental health professionals are using such a preventive approach. Also, a number of pediatricians are giving parents this kind of educational orientation regarding temperament, as a routine part of well-baby care.

Parent Guidance

In other cases, the mental health professional will be consulted with regard to a child who has already developed a clear-cut Adjustment Disorder. If the clinical evaluation indicates that this problem is the result of a poorness of fit between parental expectations and demands on the one hand and the child's temperament on the other, then parent guidance is the treatment of choice. This procedure includes the formulation of a program of altered functioning by the parents that can ameliorate the excessive and harmful stress for the child. Whenever indicated, guidance of the parents can also include recommendations for other appropriate environmental changes that the parents can implement, such as a change in school placement or alteration of living arrangements for the child.

Parent guidance can also be a valuable treatment technique in cases of Adjustment Disorder in which temperament is not a major issue. Thus, this approach may be useful if a poorness of fit results from parental demands and expectations that are excessive for a child's cognitive capacities or motor skills.

Parent guidance is not a form of family therapy or parent therapy. The basic emphasis in parent guidance is on the effort to bring about change in the parents' *behavior* and *overtly expressed* attitudes, and not on the attempt to identify and treat any underlying parental conflicts, anxieties, or pathological defenses. Such an approach assumes that a child's Adjustment Disorder does not necessarily reflect the existence of deep-seated anxieties, conflicts, or maladaptive conditioned reflex patterns in either parent or child or both, conditions that must be eliminated for treatment to be successful. It also assumes that if the parent does have some significant degree of psychopathology, this does not prevent her or him or both from making changes in the specific behaviors that are proving detrimental to the child. Anna Freud put it well. She "[refuses] to believe that mothers need to change their personalities before they can change the handling of their child" (1960, p. 37).

Parent guidance has the great virtue of enlisting the parents as direct allies in the therapeutic process, allies whose influence on the child is continuous and intimate from day to day. It is the rare parent who does not really wish his or her child a healthy, happy, and productive future, no matter whether the parent's own behavior is serving to promote or undermine this goal. It is this consonance in the values of the mental health professional and parent and their mutual concern for the child's welfare that make this therapeutic alliance possible. When effective, this approach avoids the necessity for long and expensive direct treatment of the child. In some cases, where direct psychotherapy of the child is required, simultaneous parent guidance may significantly expedite the course of the child's treatment (see Chess & Thomas, 1984, Ch. 20, for details of the parent guidance process).

In approximately 50% of the NYLS childhood Adjustment Disorder cases in whom a temperamental factor was a significant influence in the development of the problem behavior, parent guidance was evaluated by qualitative clinical judgment as successful. In any given instance an average of only 2 to 3 guidance sessions was required for this successful outcome.

In a child psychiatric practice extending over many years, one of us (S.C.) has found the therapeutic procedure of parent guidance to be as valuable as with the NYLS families. In these cases the number of sessions required was often longer than in the NYLS group. The study group children almost always came to our clinical attention shortly after the onset of symptoms, whereas in clinical practice the disorder had existed for months or, even in some cases, for several years before the parents sought professional help.

Parent guidance may also be utilized effectively in group sessions. The advantage of this approach is that the different parents in the group can compare notes with one another and receive reassurance that their child's apparently deviant behavioral style is not unique. Several centers are currently utilizing parent guidance in groups for temperament-related issues, but reports of their therapeutic effectiveness have not yet been reported in the literature.

Parent guidance fails when the parent refuses to consider that his or her functioning with the child is undesirable and requires change. There are various reasons for such rigidity (Chess & Thomas, 1984), but when this occurs, direct treatment of the child becomes necessary. Direct treatment may also be indicated if the parent is unavailable or the symptoms of the disorder are severe.

Direct Treatment

Direct treatment of the young child relies heavily on play therapy. No matter how effective this treatment may be, one cannot expect the youngster to gain insight into the nature of his or her temperament and why it has certain consequences in particular situations and with specific people. As the child grows older, capacity to conceptualize a self-image begins to develop, permitting verbal discussions in which the clinician defines temperamental attributes and their consequences in various life situations. The clinician can also define the kinds of situations in which a temperamental factor is creating difficulties for the child; with this, the therapeutic goal of self-monitoring and modification of behavior in such situations becomes feasible. With the adolescent patient, the achievement of such insight and the attainment of this therapeutic goal become progressively more possible, and with the adult even more so.

CONCLUSION

As emphasized throughout this chapter, temperamental characteristics as such are a normal aspect of a child's psychological structure. They become a source of vulnerability to Adjustment Disorders only when there is poorness of fit with environmental demands and expectations, which thus become psychosocial stressors. On the other hand, throughout the life cycle each temperamental attribute or pattern can be an asset in the mastery of the many constructive stresses and challenges. For example, the child who adapts slowly to the new is not likely to make hasty judgments and impulsive commitments. The highly distractible youngster is easily responsive and alert to the feelings of others, as he catches cues and nuances even when they are peripheral to his central task of the moment. The high activity child has an abundance of energy that can be exceedingly productive when utilized in the pursuit of organized structured goals.

Similarly, the goodness of fit model is useful not only in the prevention and treatment of behavior disorders. This model also gives the parent and any professional adviser to the family a strategy for the optimal development of each child by shaping adaptive opportunities and demands so that they are consonant with the child's temperament.

Finally, in no way do we advocate a temperamental theory of personality or psychopathology. To do so would be to revert to one or the other discredited constitutionalist theories of the past. On the other hand, to overlook the functional significance of temperament can serve only to ignore one important aspect of a child's psychological identity.

REFERENCES

American Psychiatric Association. (1987). *Diagnostic and statistical manual of mental disorders*, (3rd ed., rev.). Washington, DC: Author.

Buss, A. H., & Plomin, R. (1975). *A Temperament theory of personality development*. New York: Wiley.

Cattell, R. B. (1950). *Personality: A systematic and factual study*. New York: McGraw-Hill.

Chess, S. & Thomas, A. (1984). *Origins and evolution of behavior disorders*. New York: Brunner/Mazel.

Chess, S., & Thomas, A. (1986). *Temperament in clinical practice*. New York: Guilford Press.

Ciba Foundation Symposium 89. (1982). *Temperamental differences in infants and young children*. London: Pitman.

de Vries, M. W. (1984). Temperament and infant mortality among the Masai of East Africa. *The American Journal of Psychiatry, 141*, 1189–1194.

Freud, A. (1960). *The child guidance clinical as a center for prophylaxis and enlightenment. Recent developments in psychoanalytic child therapy*. New York: International Universities Press.

Freud, S. (1949). *An outline of psychoanalysis*. New York: Norton.

Freud, S. (1950). *Collected papers* (Vol. 5). London: Hogarth Press.

Guilford, J. P. (1959). *Personality*. New York: McGraw-Hill.

Hsu, C., Soong, W., Stigler, J. W., Hong, C., & Liang, C. (1981). The temperamental characteristics of Chinese babies. *Child Development, 32*, 1337–1340.

Kagan, J. (1982). *Psychological research on the human infant*. (1982). An evaluative summary (p. 32). New York: William T. Grant Foundation.

Maziade, M., Capèraá, P., Laplante, B., Boudreault, M., Thivierge, J., Côté, R., & Boutin, P. (1985). Value of difficult temperament among 7 year olds in the general population for predicting psychiatric diagnoses at age 12. *American Journal of Psychiatry, 142*, 943–946.

Pavlov, I. P. (1927), *Conditioned reflexes: An investigation of the physiological activity of the cerebral cortex* (G. V. Anrep, Trans. and ed.). London: Oxford University Press.

Thomas, A., Chess, S., & Birch, H. G. (1968). *Temperament and behavior disorders in children*. New York: New York University Press.

Thomas, A., & Chess, S. (1977). *Temperament and development*. New York: Brunner/Mazel.

Thomas, A., Chess, S., & Korn, S. J. (1982). The reality of difficult temperament. *Merrill-Palmer Quarterly, 28*, 1–20.

Torgersen, A. M., & Kringlen, E. (1978). Genetic aspects of temperamental differences in infants. *Journal of American Academy of Child Psychiatry, 17*, 433–444.

Watson, J. (1928). *Psychological care of infant and child*. New York: Norton.

Stress, Neuroendocrine Patterns, and Emotional Response

JAMES P. HENRY, MD, PhD

NEUROENDOCRINE RESPONSES ACCOMPANYING THE EMOTIONS OF FEAR, ANGER, DEPRESSION, AND THEIR POLAR OPPOSITES

Differentiation of Anger, Fear and Depression

Recently Panksepp described four anatomically distinct neural circuits in the limbic system of the brain. He regarded these as facilitating various kinds of adaptive, behavioral, and physiological responses to stimuli and stresses coming from the environment. In particular, these structures modulate such states as expectance, rage, fear, and panic (where the usual sense of the term *panic* is to designate the response of the subject to separation and object loss) (Panksepp, 1982). These emotions are considered the basic responses that arise in the life of

Parts of this chapter have appeared in different form in "Neuroendocrine Patterns of Emotional Response," by J. P. Henry, 1986, in *Emotion: Theory, Research, and Experience* (Vol. 3, pp. 37–60), R. Plutchik and H. Kellerman (Eds.), San Diego: Academic Press. Copyright 1986 by Academic Press, Inc. Adapted with permission of the publisher.

any mammal faced with challenges to territoriality or to attachment. In humans, subjective reports indicate that such emotions are changed by the neocortex into subtle "feelings." The formulation of the many different qualities of feelings out of raw emotions has been compared to the process of mixing primary colors to create various composite hues (Plutchik, 1984).

Methodologically, it has been difficult to separate out anger, fear, and despair in terms of the different cardiovascular reactions with which they are associated. Various techniques have been developed to cope with this issue: Drama students have been asked to simulate different emotional states by imagining themselves in particular kinds of scenes, and professional actors have been studied in a similar fashion. It has been observed that when anger or fear was generated, they could be distinguished in that anger produced much greater increases in blood pressure and pulse rate than did fear (Schwartz, Weinberger, & Singer, 1981; Weerts & Roberts, 1976). Finger temperature was more elevated among the professional actors when they were enacting anger than when dramatizing fear (Ekman, Levenson, & Fresen, 1983). In addition to simulated emotions, studies have been carried on with people of various temperaments. Catecholamine measurements were made on individuals who were later found to be violent, aggressive, and irritable: The ratio of norepinephrine to epinephrine was especially high in those in whom aggressiveness was particularly notable (Kadish, 1983). These subjects were filled with feelings of chronic rage, diffuse anger, and continuing resentment; they were irritable and reactive in everyday exchanges and were often in serious difficulties. Their resting sympathetic tone was quite elevated. In contrast to this relatively dominant norepinephrine profile, other individuals tested out to be fearful, passive, suggestive, and frequently in a state of chronic doubt. These people showed relatively high epinephrine excretion.

In another study, subjects were culled from people who were suffering stage fright or facing situations that stressed their sense of adequacy. The stage fright cases showed a slowing of the heart (a parasympathetic response) when they had to get up to speak (Dimberg, Fredrikson, & Lundquist, 1986). When interns at a medical school had to present material before very senior and critical audiences, a similar reaction was found, that is, adrenaline was released. This appears to be characteristic of the response to circumstances that bring about a fear of failure or a question of one's own adequacy.

Yet another population subjected to study was a group of actively competing ice hockey players. This is a rather special collection of people (the old joke is, I went to a fight and a hockey game broke out) characterized by intense competitiveness and occasional rather violent aggressive outbursts. Within this population, during the contests a sharp rise of noradrenaline was found in the player's urine (Elmadjian, Hope, & Lamson, 1958).

In the course of experimental work with animals, one of the goals has been more precise understanding of the various brain loci involved in these several emotional states. Ethologists recognize in cats, certain patterns of behavior as typical of a defensive stance (flattening the ears, retracting the head, and hissing). In contrast to this, preparation for attack involves holding the ears erect and assuming a different body posture. Within the framework of these observations, electrodes were implanted into the brains of cats so that with the animals fully conscious and unrestrained, various nuclei could be stimulated at will. It has thus been determined that separate brain mechanisms underlie the fight and the flight responses, and that accordingly, fear and anger are associated with different physical locations in the brain. In particular, when the basal portion of the amygdalar nuclei was stimulated, the defensive posture immediately appeared. A cholinergic pattern ensued that included vasodilation and a mild increase in blood pressure and heart rate. In contrast to this, when the central portion of the amygdala was stimulated, the cats prepared to attack. Under these conditions, there was a sharp increase at once in heart rate, blood pressure, and peripheral resistance characteristic of the response to norepinephrine.

There are thus different neuroendocrine sequences of fight, flight, and distress responses (Henry, 1982; Henry & Stephens, 1977). Clearly, the response evoked will be a function of the cognitive evaluation of the nature of the stimulus pattern confronting the organism. One kind of environmental situation may arouse fear, another anger and attack, and yet another helplessness or dismay. Presumably various neocortical areas make a primary evaluation at the cognitive level of response. The emotions, however, arise from a deeper stratum, in paticular, the limbic system. It is here that the amygdalar nuclei come into action and play a critical role in determining the character of the emotional reaction that will arise (Rolls, 1975).

However, even deeper strata underlie the limbic responses; these are found in the brain stem. It has been suggested (Aston-Jones, Foote, & Bloom, 1983) that the important decisions about turning to deal with outer stimuli as against switching back to respond to inner stimuli, that is, extraversion as against intraversion, are modulated through the locus coeruleus. This is an important pair of midline nuclei located within the pontine region. In a different context, these two tendencies, extraversion or the inclination toward active coping can be attributed to the left hemisphere; whereas depressive imagery and the introversion of dreams are thought to be associated with the right hemisphere (Ley, 1984; Sackeim et al., 1982).

Of special interest have been the studies of the responses that animals will show in the face of defeat, a possible analog of the depressive reaction in humans. It has been determined that when an animal recognizes it is up against too powerful an opponent and it has lost control of a contested situation, then the raphe nuclei (which are particularly rich in serotonin) become involved. This phenomenon has been studied in the case of the tree shrew, a small but very aggressive animal. Cells in the raphe nuclei were monitored, and it was observed that when an animal faced defeat, there was a marked increase in the activity of this group of cells. In contrast to this finding, the victorious animal showed something of a falling off of the discharge from this area (Walletschek & Raab, 1982). Related observations have been made through studies of the serotonin level in the blood of monkeys, where a dominant monkey manifests an increase in plasma serotonin (McGuire, Raleigh, & Johnson, 1983).

Thus, the sources of the limbic system's capacity to initiate the emotions of fear, anger, and depression are located deep in the brain stem. Dealing as it does with choice of inward- or outward-directed action, the locus coeruleus is linked to the amygdala through sympathetic fibers. The raphe nuclei, concerned with responses to loss of control and defeat, rely on serotonin pathways to link them to the hippocampus.

In general, where an animal feels it can cope with a challenge, it becomes angry and fights. The result is an activation of the amygdalar systems and the hypothalamic controls of the autonomic system; norepinephrine is then the typical transmitter that begins to rise. This is accompanied by an increase in blood pressure and pulse rate; at the same time, the urinary ratio of norepinephrine to epinephrine goes up.

Other aspects of the neuroendocrine system are involved as well. The pituitary increases its outflow of gonadotropic hormone so that testosterone begins to rise, and there is an increased sympathetic discharge to the kidneys and the adrenal medulla. In particular, the level of tyrosine hydroxylase increases, which means that there will be greater synthesis of norepinephrine.

When, instead of anger, the fear-anxiety emotion is dominant, then epinephrine becomes the neurotransmitter that rises, and the basal amygdalar nuclei become activated. The pulse and blood pressure rise somewhat but not as much as with anger (Stock, Schlör, Heidt, & Buss, 1978). The cholinergic system tends to be particularly active so that there is vasodilation in readiness for the explosive expression of flight behavior. Such activity demands intense exertion, and glucose levels increase as well as other adaptations necessary for the "getaway."

A somewhat different pattern of response comes about when the organism is not so much in a state of flight as in a condition of helplessness. This is accompanied by a high level of anxiety with its own neurohormonal profile. In particular, it is associated with a rise of adrenocorticotropic hormone (ACTH), the "distress" hormone that tends to make an organism more open to learning new patterns of behavior (DeWeid et al., 1972). Being overcome and dominated requires mastering a whole new repertoire of social behaviors (Kinsbourne, 1981). For when one social mammal defeats another, the victor will commonly require the defeated one to behave in a supportive way as a demonstration of subordination. In contrast to the active flight type of behavior, which is dominated by fear, the animal under these conditions demonstrates the conservation-withdrawal response, involving a more passive fearful stance and conveying elements of depression. With the distress of the frustration, the adrenal-cortical axis is aroused, releasing the cortical activating hormone (Henry & Stephens, 1977).

In birds and reptiles the adrenal medullary chromaffin cells and the steroidogenic adrenal cortical tissues are intermingled in islets throughout the gland. But in the mammals the medulla nests within the enwrapping and enveloping cell mass of the cortex. It appears that the evolutionarily advanced emotion of anxiety, which involves looking ahead with a curious blending of fear and helplessness, required the development of this particular merger of sympathetic adrenal medullary and adrenal cortical function. The cortex and medulla of the suprarenal gland have quite different nervous and hormonal drive mechanisms (Axelrod & Weinshilboum, 1972). The medulla produces norepinephrine because of the activity of the enzyme tyrosine hydroxylase, whose activity is determined by sympathetic stimulation. In order for it to produce large quantities of epinephrine, the blood from the adrenal cortex must carry to the medulla supplies of an enzyme produced in the cortex under the influence of the pituitary's adrenal corticotrophic hormone. So it appears that the peculiar intimate anatomic relation of the adrenal's two components in the mammal contributes to its more efficient expression of the forward-looking emotion of anxiety.

The Role of the Hippocampus in Stress Responses

A new group of studies has recently emerged (Wilson, 1985) suggesting that the hippocampus controls the pituitary-adrenal cortical response to stress. Many experiments have contributed to this point of view. Various investigations have involved excision of the hippocampus, electrical stimulation of this region, and other interventions. Taken together, they suggest that the hippocampus acts to inhibit the stress response of the adrenal cortex. Thus, if the hippocampus of mice is removed, and they are subjected to stress, then their blood pressure will rise and the level of plasma corticosterone will be considerably higher than in nonstressed controls (Ely, Greene, & Henry, 1977). In effect, the hippocampus acts as a kind of brake to protect the pituitary-adrenal-cortical system from excessive arousal.

The role of the hippocampus in central functioning has also come under continuing study (O'Keefe & Nadel, 1978). It turns out that the hippocampus plays a central role in memory; indeed, it serves as an exchange for the entire neural memory system and receives data from all the different sensory inputs. The information so garnered is then compared with a stable cognitive map of the normal environment, based on the organism's previous experience. When a mismatch occurs, for example, if an important attachment figure is missing (a parent frantically searching for a lost child; a child seeking his or her parent), this brain region matches the memory of that figure and the percepts indicating that the figure is present or absent. When a mismatch occurs, there will be both a sense of distress and a sense of uncertainty. The hippocampal outflow can travel along the cortico-hypothalamic tract and result in initiating the inhibitory action of the hypothalamic-pituitary-adrenal axis. In effect, some of the emotional responses to social stimuli are mediated through this channel.

It is important to recognize that the biological substrate of depression differs from that of the fight or flight responses. Instead of fight or flight, an animal can despair and collapse into a state of submission (Henry & Meehan, 1981; Henry, 1983). Among the basic mechanisms operating in depression is the release of ACTH and the accompanying inhibition of prior behavioral patterns and general attempts to achieve (DeWeid et al., 1972). It is the first link in a sequence of ACTH-corticosterone-endorphin release and signals a withdrawal from competition. The endorphins are part of the distress reaction, and the defeated animal then is numbered as a result of the simultaneous action of the corticosterone and the internal opiate (Miczek, Thompson, & Shuster, 1982).

The corticoids have a number of effects such as the release of glucose and increased blood volume. They also affect the immune system and influence T and B cell activity (Riley, 1975; McClelland, Floor, Davidson, & Saron, 1980). It is evident that the defeat response and the accompanying suppression and inhibition can affect the capacity of the immune system to protect the organism (Visitainer, Volpicelli, & Seligman, 1982). More than that, the defeat reaction results in a parasympathetic (the trophotrophic vagal response) outflow, which has a number of consequences. The heart rate slows, the walls of the blood vessels relax, and antidiuretic hormone is released (Henry, 1984).

As noted, this kind of pulse slowing was observed in phobic public speakers (Dimberg et al., 1986). When fainting or vasovagal syncope actually occurs, it is a short-term response that does not involve the fight or flight reaction; instead it allows the individual to survive by simulating death. It appears to be triggered by afferent impulses from the left ventricle as it beats vigorously in a poorly filled condition. The impulses lead to sudden slowing of the heart and decrease in peripheral resistance in the muscles. The ensuing temporary cardiovascular collapse provides a dramatic alternative to the fight or flight dilemma.

The hippocampal-adrenocortical response is not involved in fainting. Rather this style of reaction involves a relearning of former patterns of response as well as mustering of all of one's resources in order to deal with such events as the experience of being wounded, of losing blood, and of other threats to physical integrity. The subordination of activity to the victor's demands gives the social mammal a chance to survive as a member of a group; an option that a more aggressive response would not offer (DeWeid et al., 1972).

Neuroendocrine Patterns of Elation and Relaxation

In contrast to the fight, flight, and depression responses, a mechanism is also available in the brain and endocrine system for serenity and relaxation. In lower mammals the associated behavior is calmness and grooming; in humans it may be such a pattern as meditation or casual, comfortable social exchange. The classical opposite to depression is elation, which presumably arises when the individual feels in control, nurtured, attached, and comfortably together with the significant other. When a person feels positive social support, the frontotemporal association cortex is grooming and being groomed (Kling, Steklis, & Deutsch, 1979). Nursing, too, may fit into this sequence. Light, friendly chatting and exchange with others in a sociable fashion may be the human equivalent of grooming. The current research on meditation and relaxation indicates that a reduction of sympathetic outflow, fall of plasma renin, lowered blood pressure and slowed pulse rate accompany these practices (Patel, Marmot, & Terry, 1981). The experienced practitioner can achieve quite marked changes in metabolic functioning. Indeed, these behaviors can be utilized either alternatively to or as a support for drug usage (Luborsky et al., 1982). The study of elation is still relatively undeveloped but a few experiments suggest that the tethering of such animals as swine so that they cannot move unhindered will result in raising their plasma corticosterone, whereas allowing them some measure of freedom to pull on straps will relieve this process (Dantzer & Mormede, 1981). Another study with suggestive findings involved the hormonal responses of medics assigned to the helicopter rescue of downed pilots in Vietnam. The command was as happy with the retrieval of valuable personnel as the pilots were to escape the threat of capture: Thus the whole operation was emotionally highly rewarding to the medics. Their positive feelings found expression not only in euphoria but also in a sharp reduction of urinary corticoids. A similar fall in corticoid level has been recorded in successful flight crews in space as well as in hypnotized people who are in a pleasant state of trance (Bourne, 1970; Lutwak, Whedon, Lachance, Reid, & Lipscomb, 1969; Sachar, Fishman, & Mason, 1965).

But corticosterone is not the only hormone affected by success. Those who take part in contests and who win show an elevation in the level of circulating testosterone (Mazur & Lamb, 1980). More than that, during the period of elation when the individual feels he or she has gained much positive social regard, the adrenocorticotropic stress hormones and the endorphin numbing hormones are lowered; at the same time, however, in the male, the testosterone level rises. In the female there is probably an increase in both the testosterone and the estrogen and progesterone group (Levine, Coe, Smotherman, & Kaplan, 1978; Mazur & Lamb, 1980; Thompson & Wright, 1979).

Evidence for Specificity: Independence of Catecholamine and Corticoid Systems

The question has arisen whether the controls of the level of corticoids and the degree of activation of the catecholamine system work independently or are inversely related. Levine's studies of primates going through a depressive reaction to separation have established that grief increases the levels of corticoids (Levine et al., 1978). Recent work shows that the degree of catecholamine activation is not necessarily decreased at such a time. Indeed the two levels can rise together (Jimerson et al., 1983), demonstrating that the hypothalamic-pituitary-adrenal axis and the adrenergic responses can react independently. Other investigators (Barnes et al., 1983; Schatzberg et al., 1983) have made related observations of concurrent elevation of plasma norepinephrine and epinephrine as well as MAO activity in depressed patients.

Ultimately, through a number of investigations, it has been possible to conclude that the physiology of defeat and subordination differs from that of aggression and victory. In the face of defeat the hippocampal-septal mechanism is activated, which in turn leads to a hypothalamic discharge of adrenocorticotropic hormone. On the other hand, victory involves direct stimulation of the adrenal, which causes a rise in the several adrenal catecholamines and the associated enzymes, in particular, tyrosine hydroxylase. As the individual continues to strive to maintain control, there is a release of norepinephrine into the plasma. In humans it has been observed (Lundberg & Frankenhaeuser, 1980) that when subjects enjoyed effective control without at the same time experiencing distress, catecholamines were released, but cortisol actually diminished. This stood in contrast to the plight of the subjects who lost their sense of mastery and experienced distress; under those conditions the release of catecholamines persisted, but the plasma cortisol levels increased. Once again the two processes were shown to be independent of one another. Animal work has confirmed these findings. Chronic experiments carried out with societies of mice and acute studies with pairs of fighting mice and pairs of fighting tree shrews (Ely & Henry, 1978; Hucklebridge, Gamal-El-Din, & Brain, 1981; Von Holst, Fuchs, & Stöhr, 1983) have all demonstrated that the experience of aggression and achievement of social control or dominance differs physiologically from that of defeat and subordination.

Attention has been drawn (Henry, 1982; Henry, 1983) to the specific and different neuroendocrine patterns that are elicited with various emotions. This work has been summarized in Figure 25.1 (Berkenbosch, 1983). Essentially the animal's cognitive perception of whether a situation requires aggression, submission, or escape is determined by the sense of control that it perceives within the context of the particular social interaction.

Each of these choices leads to quite a different sequence of neuroendocrine events. Where the overall state is one of successful aggression, then the noradrenaline and plasma testosterone rise sharply. On the other hand, where there is a

	Challenge to Control (Positive)	Threat to Control (Ambivalent)	Loss of Control (Negative)
Behavioral response (coping style)	Display Achievement Aggression	Withdrawal Avoidance Escape	Surrender Submission Helplessness
Result	Control of situation	Removal of situation	Victim of situation
Emotional state	Assertive, low anxiety	Apprehensive, tense, fearful	Depressed High anxiety
Hormonal levels	Noradrenaline, testosterone high	Adrenaline high	Cortisol high Testosterone low

Figure 25.1. The neuroendocrine response to challenge varies according to the perception of control.

distinct experience of threats to control, with an associated activity directed toward flight, adrenaline rises. And finally, when the experience is one of loss of control, with associated depression, then the profile is one of high cortisol and low testosterone.

HORMONAL SHIFTS AND EMOTIONAL STATES

Recent studies have shown that a number of different hormonal measures are associated specifically with different emotional states. Hormonal shifts not only occur in response to such physical stressors as changes of temperature but also rise and fall in reaction to emotional states. For example, a monkey fed a pleasant-tasting but calorie-free diet will starve. Yet, despite hunger and lack of nourishment, its corticosterone level will not be affected. Deny that same animal the food being handed out daily to its cagemates and its raised corticosterone levels will bear witness to the monkey's furious distress. It is thus becoming clear that in addition to being a controlled and self-regulatory mechanism that responds to physiological feedback, the endocrine system is also involved in the systemic response to many sociopsychological influences (Mason, 1975). These can effect the balance of hormones in a major way, both over the short term and for extended periods of time. In particular, the rage, fear, and submissive responses all have specific hormonal accompaniments. The altered hormonal levels will change physiological states, which in turn can bring about irreversible biologic changes. One example is the case of arteriosclerosis where long-lasting endocrine disturbance involving sympathetic arousal causes the smooth muscles of the vascular bed to hypertrophy; as time goes on the vessels ultimately become diseased (Henry & Stephens, 1977).

As shown in Figure 25.2, when the cortisol levels (along the x-axis) are low, the emotional state involves togetherness, attachment, and elation. Then, as the cortisol rises, the emotional state shifts to one of object loss, helplessness, and depression. The y-axis here measures the degree of activation of the amygdalar-sympathetic-adrenal medullary axis. The medullary and cortical axes in the normal range, are in the midrange of the diagram. Elevation of the fight, the flight, or the catecholamine axis is noted in conditions of high demand and arousal (as occurs in borderline hypertension). Both the sympathetic and the pituitary-adrenal cortical systems may be aroused in cases of coronary heart disease (Henry & Meehan, 1981); whereas in autoimmune disease, the adrenal-cortical axis is now considered the likely candidate (Henry & Meehan, 1981; Henry, 1983).

NEUROENDOCRINE PATTERNS OF EMOTION EXPRESSED IN INSTINCT-DRIVEN ARCHETYPES

There is now considerable evidence that much of the structuring of emotions and self- (and species-) preservative behavior arises within subcortical regions and

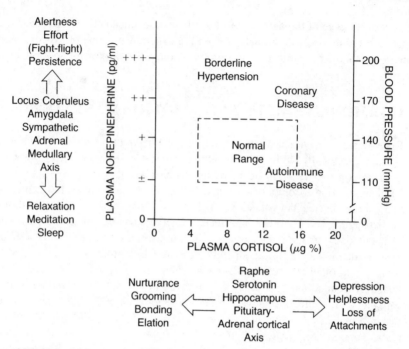

Figure 25.2. Contrasting axes of neuroendocrine response.

is mediated by hormone-driven neuronal complexes (MacLean, 1975). In animal experiments, after their cerebral cortex has been destroyed, hamsters will still attempt to control their environments. They can engaged in such activities as maternal behavior and play (Murphy, MacLean, & Hamilton, 1981). Birds are particularly good examples of such patterning because their neocortex is at best rudimentary. Nonetheless, even when they are brought up in isolation with no models from which to learn, their behavior is very adaptive. It has a strong element of determined goal-directedness and involves such varied patterns as protecting territory by song or display, building nests, brooding eggs, and feeding and raising chicks. As these various behaviors succeed one another, each is preceded by the release of a particular hormone (Hinde, 1982).

Perhaps the most striking example of instinctual or archetypal behavior is found in the conduct of the beaver. Beavers, coming to maturity, need only the raw materials—running water, mud, sticks, and twigs—in order to start the complex engineering of dam construction. The final outcome is a system of lodges and canals as well as the dam, all of which intercommunicate and support one another (Willson, 1968).

Studies with the sex hormones have been particularly productive of examples of this type. In mammals, testosterone seems to be basic to the kind of continuing effort that results in the achievement of status (Purifoy & Koopmans, 1979). In male mammals including man, the achievement of success in the course of competition brings about a rise in the testosterone level; lacking testosterone, the male rodent will not persist in attempts at solving problems (Thompson & Wright, 1979). Maternal behavior in the rodent, on the other hand, requires two hormones, progesterone and estrogen (Bridges, 1984).

It seems likely that the patterns of neuronal development that are specific for each sex depend on the levels of sex hormones affecting very specific parts of the brain; this is true both in rodents and, most likely, in humans (Hines, 1982). Thus, for the maternal behavior noted earlier, the region at the front end of the hypothalamus is critical. New data speak for the possible existence of some kind of sexually differentiated instinctual or archetypal behavior patterns in humans (Durden-Smith & deSimone, 1983). Changes in the brain at puberty are being studied, and there is some evidence indicating that high levels of androgen must be present for normal males to develop competent spatial abilities (as measured by the capacity to locate camouflaged designs) (Hier & Crawley, 1982).

The influence of these sex hormones is especially critical prenatally. It is essential that a brain be masculinized during fetal development in order for the later expression of normal male sexual behavior to take place; this masculinization must occur during a limited and critical perinatal stage (Ward & Weisz, 1980). In the rat fetus a testosterone surge must occur on Days 18 and 19 of intrauterine growth; if lacking, then the adult male rat will later be unable to respond appropriately to a female in heat. This occurs despite normal levels of circulating androgen in adulthood. It is of considerable interest that the factor of psychological stress can enter into this process in a critical fashion. If a rat mother is subjected to such stress during the vulnerable interval, then the necessary surge of testosterone will not occur because the stress has induced high ACTH levels, which prevent it (Warren, Schmidt, & Franzino, 1984). In effect, as a result of a social stress impinging on the parent, the offspring develops as a sexual deviate.

Observations on homosexual men in Germany suggest this same event may occur in humans. Reasoning that during World War II unusual stress was experienced by the German population at large, a survey of 800 homosexual men in East Germany was conducted to determine their year of birth. It turned out that a great many more homosexual had been born born during those late years of the war when events were particularly disturbing (Dörner et al., 1980). A detailed further study compared the mothers of a group of homosexuals and a matched control group of heterosexuals. In particular, the state of the mothers during their pregnancy was explored. It developed that fear of bombings, loss of a partner, or other severe loss of attachment occurred much more frequently among the mothers of the homosexual men than among the mothers of the control group of heterosexual subjects (Dörner, 1981).

Women, too, have been studied from the point of view of the effects of sex hormones on behavior (Dalton, 1977). The investigator sought to correlate certain special behavioral aspects of women with the days of the menstrual cycle. She studied a population of schoolgirls and noted that offenses against discipline occurred much more often during the premenstrual period than during other days in the cycle. A similar finding obtained in a survey of imprisoned women, regarding when they originally committed their crimes and when they subsequently got in trouble for negativistic behavior within the prison. In each case the eruptions of disturbing activity tended to occur close to the onset of the menstrual flow. The investigator concluded that the shifts in the balance of hormones produced intervals during which these women were less able to tolerate discipline and were more easily provoked.

It was commented that approximately 40% of women show an alteration in their behavior in response to the cyclical hormonal swings of their monthly rhythms. This could be observed in such activities as driving, conduct at work, the readiness to make irrational decisions, and overall level of impatience. Indeed, on two occasions in the 1980s, women who had been found guilty of murder in British courts had their sentences commuted to manslaughter on the grounds of being in a state of lesser responsibility because of premenstrual tension. Two separate judges accepted this view and neither one imposed a prison sentence (Brahams, 1983). In brief, aspects of human behavior that have powerful social meaning, such as sexual preference or homicidal acts, are now considered to be affected by naturally occurring hormonal stimulation in the brain.

There are other moments in the life cycle when the effects of hormones appear preeminent. Thus, in sheep, the way mothers attach to their newborn infants is apparently very sensitive to the existing hormonal patterns. The formation of attachment can be interrupted in a variety of ways; on the other hand, once it occurs, it will persist for an extended period. In humans, the concept of bonding has been introduced to suggest that the mother's postpartum hormonal state makes her especially available for intense attachment to the newborn baby (Klaus & Kennell, 1982). Interruptions in early contact with the baby are thought to interfere with the bonding process. Conditions like prematurity that isolate the infant from the mother for weeks after delivery may interfere seriously with subsequent bonding (Klaus, 1970). In fact, a rich pattern of exchange on both a verbal and a much more subtle nonverbal level plays back and forth between the mother and the young infant and has a significant role in the type and depth of attachment that presently develops (Trevarthan, 1983). When a primate loses primary partner, a severe behavioral depression ensues, accompanied by an intense pituitary-adrenal cortical response (Coe, Mendoza, Smotherman, & Levine, 1978).

The effect of early social experience on lifelong patterns of attachment behavior can be demonstrated in other ways. Children in the Israeli kibbutzim are reared together in cohorts from shortly after birth. One study found that there were neither love affairs nor marriages among members of the same cohort, in later years; this proved true for 125 separate marriages of such young people. This situation occurred despite the existence of close and affectionate relationships among peers within the same group (Fox, 1980). A more extensive study looked at the records of thousands of kibbutz-reared young people and found not a single marriage between children who had been reared together from birth to the age of 6 years (Sheper, 1971). Very intense familiarity apparently created a type of sibling bond that prevented post-pubescent attachment.

Instinctual or Archetypal Behavior

To return to the theme of instinctual behavior or innate archetypal machinery, another possible example may be the transmission of phobias from one generation to another. When phobic individuals were exposed to pictures of blood, body mutilation, or snakes and spiders, it was possible to demonstrate a marked rise in their excretion of adrenal cortical hormone. In effect, it was as though these individuals carried within them a specific neuroendocrine distress response; it is important to note that this mechanism was not found in normals, that is, nonphobic subjects (Fredrikson, Sundin, & Frankenhaeuser, 1985). This kind of finding was substantiated by a twin study that displayed similar genetic tendencies (Torgersen, 1979). A host of such phobic stimuli are known: being crowded or locked into a small space; being watched; having to eat with strangers; being concerned with illness and fears of death; being afraid of blood or body injury; fearing thunder and lightning; and reacting excessively to spiders, snakes, rats, mice, and heights (Melville, 1977). Such psychological presences may have played a role in the survival of human beings during the millenia when they were hunter-gatherers, thus causing evolvement of inherited transmission patterns. In primates, it has been demonstrated that subjects that have never seen a snake will show intense fear if a snake crawls in front of them on the floor (Torgersen, 1979).

In a different but parallel area, the basis of speech and the capacity for receiving and comprehending speech are related to very specialized anatomy within the brain. Centers such as Broca's and Wernicke's areas are critical to speech and its perception. Again these evolutionary emergents have come into being to allow speech to occur as a part of normal development. In particular, the ability to master syntax appears to be based on inherited brain structures so that regardless of the language to be learned, a child will develop the capacity to speak in syntactically specific and, ultimately, in grammatically correct fashion, both rapidly and fluently (Chomsky, 1972). For example, children may grow up in an environment where many adults make grammatical errors; nonetheless the children may use pronouns correctly. In a review of Chomsky's proposals another investigator (Eimas, 1985) commented that children are innately endowed with perceptual mechanisms that enhance the acquiring of human speech. The effectiveness of these mechanisms permits the child to achieve quick mastery of language.

Yet another inherited behavioral capacity is associated with expressing emotion. One group has studied the nature of the facial changes that accompany particular emotions. Happiness, surprise, sadness, fear, anger, and disgust each mobilize rather specific facial expressions (Ekman, 1971). Thus, for example, peoples in New Guinea who lived remote from Western culture and who had had no contact with it, when experiencing anger or grief, used exactly the same facial movements as seen in the West. It is in fact possible to make a great many different facial configurations; yet only a very few are ubiquitous expressions of particular emotions. The conclusion is that despite differences in social organization, culture, or language, the particular forms of facial expression associated with the individual affects are universal.

Indeed, in many ways, this universality extends beyond facial expression to include bodily gestures, such as displays of threat, forms of expressing respect or at least indicating subordination to another, and many means of demonstrating affection between adult mates (Eibl-Eibesfeldt, 1983). Numerous observations have been made of the patterns of mothers interacting with their newborn infants. A lively smile is universally present, and a rather characteristic dance of head and face involves head nodding, eyebrows going up and then the head being lowered toward the baby while the mother talks and continues to smile. This sequence is repeated over and over again in regular fashion; it is, in effect, a form of instinctive ritual dance, unlearned and untaught but accompanied by intense emotions. It is undoubtedly one of the organizing bases of the mother–child attachment pattern (Trevarthan, 1983).

Other such motoric expressions of emotion have been observed among nursery school children. Using a method developed for ethological investigations, a French behavioral psychologist, Hubert Montagner, studied the way 2- and 3-year olds interact behaviorally. He observed that a child would initiate a leadership pattern by getting others to follow whatever he or she began (Pines, 1984). This is not a matter of aggressive behavior; instead it is a variety of attractive behavior that has a pacifying quality. Montagner's observations have allowed for a very fine breakdown of the elements involved: For example, he described gestures of begging with the hand or taking the chin of the other child in the hand and/or tipping one's head over the shoulder to look back. Such actions offer a marked contrast to children's behavior if they threaten or want to initiate a fight; under such conditions, the body leans forward or the head tips forward, fists ball up, and teeth are clenched. It differs again from flight patterns that would be accompanied by turning the eyes away and moving the head or the entire body backward. In effect, the behavioral expression of the emotional component of the fight or flight pattern is inborn and universal. The same may be said for the expression of depression. In that case, the child will be isolated and will assume a sitting or standing position apart from the others, or will be curled up in the fetal position, lying on the floor and crying. Hence, whether one studies facial expression or the larger body postures, the innate components are there for happiness, anger, fear, or sadness and are already demonstrable in the social behavior of very young children. More than that, these particular modes of configuring the face or gesturing with the body can be shown to develop in children who are born deaf or blind (Eibl-Eibesfeldt, 1973).

When in need of a feeling of protection, of security, and of being loved, adult behavior tends to take the form of wanting to be held or cuddled (Hollender & McGehee, 1974). This wish to be held is intensified during pregnancy, and it stands in sharp contrast to the almost regular decrease in the desire for sexual intercourse as pregnancy proceeds. Thus it seems that the sexual yearnings are separate from the need for being held and hugged, and for having close body contact.

The desire to have a baby is similar in its universality and intensity (Davitz, 1984). This has been called "baby hunger," and some women, for a period of time, may show an almost obsessive involvement with young infants. It is assumed that a maternal yearning arises from biological promptings. Subcortical mechanisms present in the hamster mediate such behavior, and presumably similar structures are present in the human brain. This desire may prepare a woman psychologically for the actual behavioral and cognitive elements of mothering. As is true for all the powerful instinctual patterns, the yearning involved may transcend and, indeed, completely overwhelm rational considerations; this tendency is commonly seen in relationship to sexual drives and may very well characterize the emotional address toward having an infant. Presumably, again, baby hunger is connected with the functioning of the estrogen and progesterone mechanisms. The young adolescent male with his high testosterone level may be very sexually driven but apparently does not experience this craving to care for a baby. According to Davitz, the powerful biological forces that underlie baby hunger are specific to women.

Despite romantic protestations as to its inherent inscrutability and incomprehensibility, romantic love too has come under study. The rapid and sometimes frequent shifts between emotional highs and lows of the love-struck person, varying as they do from the shattering of separation to the elation of reconciliation, are usual vicissitudes in a courtship. It has now been suggested (Liebowitz, 1983) that these sequences involve hormones such as the endorphins and the catecholamines are engaged causing rapid changes in the brain's limbic centers. In a sense the same basic attachment impulse is operative as in baby hunger (Tennov, 1979). During such intense love interactions, the person is literally obsessed with the object of his or her affections; what ultimately emerges is a lasting attachment that in many ways resembles the mother–infant bond. It may well be that similar neuroendocrine mechanisms are functional.

Both the right hemisphere and the limbic system seem to be activated. The intense and high level of emotion, the role of dreams, and the ready resort to poetry, metaphors, and symbols are evidence of the contribution from these areas. Again inherited or archetypal patterns may be involved.

SUMMARY

An array of inherent mechanisms based on patterns of organization within the structures of the brain activate changes in the level of the catecholamine and corticoid hormones. These mechanisms find external expression in the form of gestures, facial expression, and bodily posture, and they portray the elementary emotions: sadness, happiness, rage, and fear. Still more complex behaviors rely on this inner structuring and involve instinctual patterns such as attachment to the young and other aspects of maternal behavior. These behaviors rely on a type of biological grammar that is facilitated by appropriate hormonal levels. Where maternal behavior is concerned, the female gonadal hormones, estrogen and progesterone, dominate. Such behavior is not learned. Indeed, the neocortex has been excised from rodents and it continues unimpeded (MacLean, 1975). In fact, many such species-specific behaviors appear to be unlearned and simply to express the way brain stem structures, the limbic system, and the striatal complex were laid down during the development of the species. In humans, a number of such patterns have now been identified or are coming to be recognized by means of continuing studies; they include mother–infant interaction, the social gesturings by which young children indicate various mood states, and the universal patterns observed for making threats or offering welcome. All give evidence of built-in physiological mechanisms involving hormonally facilitated patterns. In the same vein, various forms of love or attachment behavior seem to be expressions of inherited response patterns, for example, the intensity of a woman's yearning for an infant or the romantic love of individuals for one another. Within the framework of Jungian psychology, such patterns of behavior and the associated effects would be considered as "archetypes of the collective unconscious" (Jung, 1972).

REFERENCES

Aston-Jones, G., Foote, S. L., & Bloom, F. E. (1983). Anatomy and physiology of locus coeruleus neurons: Functional implications. In M. B. Ziegler & R. C. Lake (Eds.), *Frontiers of clinical neuroscience: Vol. 2. Norepinephrine* (pp. 92–116). Baltimore: Williams-Wilkins.

Axelrod, J., & Weinshilboum, R. (1972). Catecholamines. *New England Journal of Medicine, 287*, 237–242.

Barnes, R. F., Veith, R. C., Borson, S., Verbey, J., Raskind, M. A., & Halter, J. B. (1983). High levels of plasma catecholamines in dexamethasone-resistant depressed patients. *American Journal of Psychiatry, 140*, 1623–1625.

Berkenbosch, R. (1983). *The role of catecholamines in the control of the secretion of proopiomelanocortin derived peptides from the rat pituitary gland and its implications in the response to stress.* Unpublished doctoral dissertation, University of Amsterdam, Amsterdam.

Bourne, P. G. (1970). *Men, stress, and Vietnam.* Boston: Little, Brown.

Brahams, D. (1983). Premenstrual tension and criminal responsibility. *Practitioner, 227*, 807–813.

Bridges, R. S. (1984). A quantitative analysis of the roles of dosage sequence and duration of estradiol and progesterone exposure in the regulation of maternal behavior in the rat. *Endocrinology, 114*, 930–940.

Chomsky, N. (1972). *Language and mind*. New York: Harcourt.

Coe, C., Mendoza, S. P., Smotherman, W. P., & Levine, S. (1978). Mother–infant attachment in the squirrel monkey: Adrenal response to separation. *Behavioral Biology, 22*, 256–263.

Dalton, K. (1977). The sociological significance of the premenstrual syndrome. In *The premenstrual syndrome and progesterone therapy* (Chapter 19, pp. 140–149). Chicago: Yearbook Medical Publisher.

Dantzer, R., & Mormede, P. (1981). Pituitary adrenal consequences of adjunctive activities in pigs. *Hormones and Behavior, 15*, 386–395.

Davitz, L. L. (1984). *Baby hunger: Every woman's longing for a baby*. Minneapolis: Winston Press.

DeWeid, D., Van Delft, A. M. L., Gispen, W. H., Weijnen, J. A. W. M., Van Wimersma, Greidanus, T. J. B. (1972). The role of pituitary-adrenal system hormones in active avoidance conditioning. In S. Levine (Ed.), *Hormones and behavior* (pp. 135–171). New York: Academic Press.

Dimberg, U., Fredrikson, M., & Lundquist, O. (1986). Autonomic reactions to social and neutral stimuli in subjects high and low in public speaking fear. *Biology & Psychology, 23*, 223–233.

Dörner, G. (1981). Sex hormones and neurotransmitters as mediators for sexual differentiation of the brain. *Endokrinologie, 78*, 129–138.

Dörner, G., Geier, T., Ahrens, L., Krell, L., Münx, G., Sieler, H., Kittner, E., & Müller, H. (1980). Prenatal stress as possible aetiogenic factor of homosexuality in human males. *Endocrinology, 75*, 365–368.

Durden-Smith, J., & deSimone, D. (1983). *Sex and the brain*. New York: Arbor House.

Eibl-Eibesfeldt, I. (1973). The expressive behavior of the deaf- and blind-born. In M. V. Cranach & I. Vino (Eds.), *Social communication and movement* (pp. 163–194). London: Academic Press.

Eibl-Eibesfeldt, I. (1983). Patterns of parent–child interaction in a cross-cultural perspective. In A. Olivero & A. Zapella (Eds.), *The behavior of human infants*. New York: Plenum.

Eimas, P. D. (1985). The perception of speech in early infancy. *Scientific American, 252*, 46–52.

Ekman, P. (1971). Universal and cultural differences in facial expressions of emotion. In J. K. Cole (Ed.), *Nebraska symposium on motivation* (pp. 207–283). Lincoln: University of Nebraska Press.

Ekman, P., Levenson, R. W., & Friesen, W. V. (1983). Autonomic nervous system activity distinguishes among emotions. *Science, 221*, 1208–1210.

Elmadjian, F., Hope, J. M., & Lamson, E. T. (1958). Excretion of epinephrine and norepinephrine under stress. In G. Pincus (Ed.), *Recent progress in hormone research proceedings of the Laurentian Hormone Conference 1957* (Vol. 14, pp. 513–553). New York: Academic Press.

Ely, D. L., Greene, E. G., & Henry, J. P. (1977). Effect of hippocampal lesion on cardiovascular, adrenocortical and behavioral response patterns in mice. *Physiology and Behavior, 18*, 1075–1083.

Ely, D. L., & Henry, J. P. (1978). Neuroendocrine response patterns in dominant and subordinate mice. *Hormones and Behavior, 10*, 156–169.

Fox, R. (1980). *The red lamp of incest: An inquiry into the origins of mind and society*. Notre Dame, IN: University of Notre Dame Press.

```

Fredrikson, M., Sundin, O., & Frankenhaeuser, M. (1985). Cortisol excretion during the defense reaction in humans. *Psychosomatic Medicine, 47*, 313–319.

Henry, J. P. (1982). The relation of social to biological processes in disease. *Social Science and Medicine, 16*, 369–380.

Henry, J. P. (1983). Coronary heart disease and arousal of the adrenal cortical axis. In T. M. Dembrowski, T. Schmidt, & G. Blümschen (Eds.), *Biobehavioral bases of coronary-prone behavior*. New York: S. Karger.

Henry, J. P. (1984). On the triggering mechanism of vasovagal syncope. *Psychosomatic Medicine, 46*, 91–93.

Henry, J. P., & Meehan, J. P. (1981). Psychosocial stimuli, physiological specificity and cardiovascular disease. In H. Weiner, M. A. Hofer, & A. J. Stunkard (Eds.), *Brain, behavior and bodily disease*. New York: Raven Press.

Henry, J. P., & Stephens, P. M. (1977). *Stress, health and the social environment. A sociobiologic approach to medicine*. New York: Springer Verlag.

Hier, D. B., & Crawley, W. E. (1982). Spatial ability in androgen deficient men. *New England Journal of Medicine, 306*, 1202–1205.

Hinde, R. A. (1982). Endocrine behavior–environment interaction. In *Ethology* (pp. 162–166). A Fontana Paperback Masterguide.

Hines, M. (1982). Prenatal, gonadal hormones and sex differences in human behavior. *Psychological Bulletin, 92*, 56–58.

Hollender, M. H., & McGehee, J. B. (1974). The wish to be held during pregnancy. *Journal of Psychosomatic Research, 18*, 193–197.

Jimerson, D. C., Insel, T. R., Reus, V., & Kopin, I. (1983). Increased plasma MHPG in dexamethasone resistant, depressed patients. *Archives of General Psychiatry, 40*, 173–176.

Jung, C. G. (1972). *Two essays on analytical psychology*. Princeton, NJ: First Princeton Bollingen Paperback Printing.

Kadish, W. (1983). Personality traits and the norepinephrine to epinephrine ratio. Unpublished masters thesis, Yale University, New Haven, CT.

Kinsbourne, M. (1981, May). Sad hemisphere, happy hemisphere. *Psychology Today*, p. 92.

Klaus, M. H. (1970). Mothers separated from their newborn infants. *Pediatric Clinics of North America, 17*, 1015–1037.

Klaus, M. H., & Kennell, J. H. (1982). *Parent–infant bonding*. St. Louis: C. V. Mosby.

Kling, A., Steklis, H. D., & Deutsch, S. (1979). Radiotelemetered activity from the amygdala during social interactions in the monkey. *Experimental Neurology, 66*, 88–96.

Levine, S., Coe, C. L., Smotherman, W. P., & Kaplan, J. N. (1978). Prolonged cortisol elevation in the infant squirrel monkey after reunion with mother. *Physiology and Behavior, 20*, 7–10.

Ley, R. G. (1984). Cerebral laterality and imagery. In A. Sheckh Anees (Ed.), *Imagery— Current theory, research, and application*. New York: Wiley.

Liebowitz, M. (1983). *The chemistry of love*. Boston: Little, Brown.

Luborsky, L., Crits-Cristoph, P., Brady, J. P., Kron, R. E., Weiss, T., Cohen, M., & Levy, L. (1982). Behavioral versus pharmacological treatments for essential hypertension—a needed comparison. *Psychosomatic Medicine, 44*, 201–213.

Lundberg, U., & Frankenhaeuser, M. (1980). Pituitary-adrenal and sympathetic-adrenal correlates of distress and effort. *Journal of Psychosomatic Research, 24*, 125–130.

Lutwak, L., Whedon, G. D., Lachance, P. A., Reid, J. M., & Lipscomb, H. S. (1969).
```

Mineral electrolyte and nitrogen balance studies of Gemini VII fourteen day orbital space flight. *Journal of Clinical Endocrinology and Metabolism, 29*, 1140–1156.

MacLean, P. D. (1975). Sensory and perceptive factors in emotional function of the triune brain. In R. G. Grenell & S. Gabay (Eds.), *Biological foundations of psychiatry* (Vol. 1, pp. 177–198). New York: Raven Press.

Mason, J. W. (1975). Emotion as reflected in patterns of endocrine regulation. In L. Levi (Ed.), *Emotions: Their parameters and measurement* (p. 143). New York: Raven Press.

Mazur, A., & Lamb, T. A. (1980). Testosterone, status and mood in human males. *Hormones and Behavior, 14*, 236–246.

McClelland, D. C., Floor, E., Davidson, R. J., & Saron, C. (1980). Stressed power motivation, sympathetic activation, immune function and illness. *Journal of Human Stress, 6*, 16–19.

McGuire, M. T., Raleigh, M. J., & Johnson, C. (1983). Social dominance in adult male *vervet* monkeys: Behavior—biochemical relationships. *Social Science Information, 2*, 311–328.

Melville, J. (1977). *Phobias and obsessions*. New York: Coward, McCann, & Geoghegan.

Miczek, K. A., Thompson, M. L., & Shuster, L. (1982). Opioid-like analgesia in defeated mice. *Science, 215*, 1520–1523.

Murphy, M. R., MacLean, P. D., & Hamilton, S. C. (1981, July 24). Species-typical behavior of hamsters deprived from birth of the neocortex. *Science, 213*, 459–461.

O'Keefe, J., & Nadel, L. (1978). *The hippocampus as a cognitive map*. Oxford: Oxford University Press.

Panksepp, J. (1982). Toward a general psychological theory of emotions. *Behavior and Brain Science, 5*, 407–467.

Patel, C., Marmot, M. G., & Terry, D. J. (1981). Controlled trial of biofeedback-aided behavioral methods in reducing mild hypertension. *British Medical Journal, 282*, 2005–2008.

Pines, M. (1984, December). Children's winning ways. *Psychology Today, 18*, pp. 59–65.

Plutchik, R. (1984). Emotions: A general psychoevolutionary theory. In K. R. Scherer & P. Ekman (Eds.), *Approaches to emotion*. Hillsdale, NJ: Lawrence Earlbaum.

Purifoy, F. E., & Koopmans, L. H. (1979). Androstenedione, testosterone, and free testosterone concentration in women of various occupations. *Soc. Biol. 26*(3), 179–188.

Riley, V. (1975). Mouse mammary tumors: Alterations of incidence as apparent function of stress. *Science, 189*, 465–467.

Rolls, E. T. (1975). *The brain and reward*. Oxford & New York: Pergamon Press.

Sachar, E. J., Fishman, J. R., & Mason, J. W. (1965). Influence of the hyponotic trance on plasma 17 hydroxycorticosterone concentrations. *Psychosomatic Medicine, 27*, 330–341.

Sackeim, H. A., Greenberg, M. S., Weiman, A. L., Gur, R. C., Hungerbuhler, J. P., & Geschwind, N. (1982). Hemispheric assymetry in the expression of positive and negative emotions. *Archives of Neurology, 39*, 210–218.

Schatzberg, A. F., Orsulak, P. J., Rothschild, A. J., Salomon, M. S., Lerbinger, J., Kizuka, P. P., Cole, J. O., & Schildkraut, J. J. (1983). Platelet MAO activity and the dexamethasone suppression test in depressed patients. *American Journal of Psychiatry, 140*, 1231–1233.

Schwartz, G. E., Weinberger, D. A., & Singer, J. A. (1981). Cardiovascular differentiation of happiness, sadness, anger and fear following imagery and exercise. *Psychosomatic Medicine, 43*, 343–364.

Sheper, J. (1971). Self-imposed incest avoidance and exogamy in second generation Kibbutz adults. Unpublished doctoral Dissertation, Rutgers University, The State University of New Jersey, Newark.

Stock, G., Schlör, K. H., Heidt, H., & Buss, J. (1978). Psychomotor behavior and cardiovascular patterns during stimulation of the amygdala. *Pfluegers Archives, 376*, 177–184.

Tennov, D. (1979). *Love and limerance: The experience of being in love*. New York: Stein & Day.

Thompson, W. R., & Wright, J. S. (1979). "Persistence" in rats: Effects of testosterone. *Physiological Psychology, 7*, 291–294.

Torgersen, S. (1979). The nature and origin of common phobic fears. *British Journal of Psychiatry, 134*, 343–351.

Trevarthan, C. (1983). Interpersonal abilities of infants as generators for transmission of language and culture. In A. Oliverio & M. Zapella (Eds.), *The behavior of human infants* (pp. 145–176). New York: Plenum.

Visitainer, M. A., Volpicelli, J. R., & Seligman, M. F. P. (1982). Tumor rejection in rats after inescapable or escapable shock. *Science, 216*, 437–439.

Walletschek, H., & Raab, A. (1982). Spontaneous activity of dorsal raphe neurons during defensive and offensive encounters in the tree shrew. *Physiology and Behavior, 28*, 697–705.

Ward, I. L., & Weisz, J. (1980). Maternal stress alters plasma testosterone in fetal males. *Science, 207*, 328–329.

Warren, D. W., Schmidt, C. A., & Franzino, S. J. (1984). Adrenocorticotropin stimulates testosterone production by fetal rat testes. *Annals New York Academy of Sciences, 438*, 677–680.

Weerts, T. C., & Roberts, B. (1976). The physiological effects of imagining anger-provoking and fear-provoking scenes. (abstract). *Psychophysiology, 13*, 174.

Wilson, M. M. (1985). Hippocampal inhibition of the pituitary adrenalcortical response to stress. In Susan B. Burchfield (Ed.), *Stress: Psychological and physiological interactions* (pp. 163–183). New York: Hemisphere Publishing.

Wilsson, L. (1968). *My beaver colony*. Garden City, NY: Doubleday.

Protective Factors: Ego Strengths

Just as vulnerabilities tell of the proneness of individuals to be overwhelmed, so do ego strengths and supports describe those positive factors that protect the individual from the potential inroads of stressful experiences. Ego strengths are less studied by a discipline that concerns itself with the remediation of ego failure; the concerns of the psychiatrist must in the nature of things turn to those factors that cause pain and breakdown. But shoring up the defendable areas of personality is as much a part of treatment as repairing the breaches that are so obvious and cry out so loudly for succor and relief. Hence, the following material explicates some of the means to keep an ego from failing, give it additional structure, prop it up in the face of threats and challenges, and help it over otherwise insurmountable obstacles.

Where does ego strength come from? To be sure, there are always the innate factors, which are perhaps best summed up by the term *temperament*. But several external circumstances make all the difference in the face of adversity. First, the supportive role of the family can never be overestimated in times of crisis. Then the presence of friends and a circle of well-wishers, such as neighbors or fellow members of social groups, offer a source of essential resilience. Beyond that, the factor of religion is probably the modality most often resorted to by people in pain, and the one least likely to be incorporated into the work of the mental health professional. Finally, a large group connection, be it subculture, community, ethnic group, or political party, can offer a variety of opportunities to seek companionship and obtain support in the face of stress and adversity.

All in all, the bridges to help many suffering people find relief and comfort can be constructed of social building blocks from a variety of human sources. For more vulnerable patients, direct professional help may be essential, but even then it is generally true that such individuals need to strengthen their egos before they can tolerate any exploration into the nature of their problems or the causes of their distress. The presence of supportive and protective factors may head off many troublesome disorders and cushion those exposed individuals against the stresses that confront them. Hence, both preventively and therapeutically, strengthening the patient's ego should be of central interest to the psychiatrist.

— CHAPTER 26 ———————————

Family and Extended Family as Ego Supports

LILLIAN H. ROBINSON, MD
RICHARD F. DALTON, MD

DEVELOPMENT OF EGO SUPPORTS

Infancy and Early Childhood

Throughout the life cycle, ego support by one's family and extended family is important, but it is especially so for the helpless infant whose ego is not yet fully formed. The helplessness itself is potentially traumatic, a "crisis" according to Erikson's (1965) formulation, and it requires the total support of loving parents or other nurturing caretakers. Considerable emphasis has been placed on experiential components, particularly deficient nurturing, as primary factors in pathogenesis. Temperament, constitutional dimensions, and inner conflict are sometimes ignored. In order for individuals to form intimate relationships, they must have experienced some positive nurturance during their formative years. When there is early, repeated, or continuing trauma due to seductive, sadistic, and unnurturing caregivers, an imbalance is developed between drive and ego control with resulting conflicts and disharmony within the ego. According to Anna Freud (1983) deficit, conflict, and

499

trauma all have potential for interfering with normal development and producing psychopathology. Identification with parents' unhealthy defenses can also contribute to pathogenesis. Ritvo cites examples of patients with phobic parents and states:

> Early histories of such patients indicate some of the ways in which early experience, in the total sense of the interaction of constitution and environment, may prepare the way for future pathogenic internal conflict in interaction with external events which have specific points of connection with internal conflicts and their derivative fantasies. (Freud, 1982, p. 89)

It is clear that the caregiver of a young child can contribute to pathology or can help normal development in a variety of ways. It is important to recognize, however, that pathology tends to be multidetermined and should not be attributed to unitary causes. Freud (1983) has cautioned that ignoring the general complexities of development can lead to inadequate, simplistic theories of pathogenesis and has warned against assuming that the main pathogenic agent is invariably the "unempathic mother." She points out that a good first year is no guarantee of future mental health and states that her observations of children show that neurosis or a developmental defect can result from subsequent traumas, including the loss of the mother via a sibling's birth or the mother's premature return to work outside the home. Also, if either the mother or the child has trouble giving up the symbiotic unity of a good first year, psychopathology may result. Without minimizing the importance of the first year, Freud reminds us that, despite inadequate early care, in later life some children show healthy adaptation. Arlow (1981) has suggested that some therapists' eagerness to embrace the "unempathic mother" theory of pathogenesis may stem from their rescue fantasies, together with the notion that cure can come from a kind of replacement therapy in which the therapist becomes the empathic mother, theoretically allowing the patient to resume healthy development.

Regarding pathogenesis, it is not entirely clear how temporary separations in childhood later affect the individual. Hinde (1981) has shown that repeated and prolonged removal of the child from the home is associated with behavioral disturbances in adolescence. He has also shown, however, that some children are at greater risk than others, suggesting that factors within the home (e.g., the child's level of dependence on mother) might be more important than the actual separation as contributors to subsequent problems. He states:

> The general conclusions to be drawn here are that repeated or prolonged separations are most likely to be associated with long-term sequelae if accompanied by a disturbed family background, and that the precise nature of the consequence depends on the sex of the child and a considerable number of other variables. (p. 53)

Thus, depending on preseparation conditions, children respond variously to separation. Although the effect is generally negative (especially with prolonged separation), some children who are not particularly vulnerable or needy might conclude on the basis of their early separation experiences that reunion predictably follows separation, in which case later separations might not be disturbing.

What remains unclear is how recent changes within the social structure have affected the early relationship between the young child and the primary caregiver. The question, ''Have the increased divorce rate and shifting geographical patterns and smaller families changed the way primary caregivers relate to infants?'' remains, at this time, unanswered.

Adolescence

As infants grow up and progress through childhood and adolescence, they need different kinds of ego support from families. If family members infantalize children by helping too much with things that they need to learn to manage themselves, excessive dependency and feelings of incapability may result. Many well-meaning parents become overly involved in their children's schoolwork, sometimes assuming responsibility for their academic success; their misconception is that this is helpful, supportive parental behavior. Sometimes parents intrude into their children's relationships with peers, feeling that they must choose their youngsters' friends and settle their quarrels. Such intrusive parental behavior deprives the child of the opportunity to master important age-appropriate tasks. Truly supportive families convey their interest, empathy, and understanding to their children along with their confidence that the young people can learn to manage their own responsibilities. Some parents regard discipline to be incompatible with support and accordingly withhold empathy and understanding when it is most needed by the child who is in disgrace.

HUMAN NEEDS FOR FAMILY SUPPORT SYSTEMS

A large body of research has demonstrated the health promoting benefits of appropriate, supportive interaction among family members. The existence of a suitable family support system has been shown to buffer psychological stress, thus helping to prevent physical and mental illness (Greenblatt, Becerra, & Serafetinides, 1982; Kaplan, Cassel, & Gore, 1977; Nuckolls, Cassel, & Kaplan, 1972). Caplan (1974) has emphasized the basic human need for close interdependent relationships that provide a sense of belonging, enhance feelings of self-worth, and promote healthy adaptation. On the other hand the absence of an effective social support system has been shown to increase susceptibility to disease (Chan, 1977). Isolated humans and other social animals are more vulnerable to stress. Spitz (1965) discovered that severe depression and arrest in development of all sectors of the personality result from early loss of the primary caretaker (with no adequate replacement of the mothering person). Workers in social psychiatry have repeatedly demonstrated the adverse effects on older individuals when loss of family support occurs through death, separation, illness, or emotional unavailability of family members (Nuckolls et al., 1972).

Mental Illness

Several workers have demonstrated the specific relationship between family support and the development of mental illness. Warheit (1979) found that patients who had suffered serious losses tended to have more severe bouts of depression and use the services of physicians and clinics more than patients who had not experienced equivalent losses. He showed that the presence of a spouse correlated significantly with lower depression scores. Statistical regression equations also demonstrated that when used to predict high depression scores, losses and the absence of resources were significant variables.

Flaherty and co-workers studied 44 outpatients with unipolar depression in order to determine the association among social support systems, life events, social adjustment, and depressive symptoms (Flaherty, Gaviria, Black, Altman, & Mitchell, 1983). Their work showed that depressed individuals with higher social support enjoyed better social adjustment and had fewer depressive symptoms than did individuals with low support. The work confirmed the findings of other researchers who had shown that social support accounts for a greater amount of variance in depression than do life events. They studied a depressed population and found that the effects of social support do not serve merely to buffer deleterious effects of life events but are in fact more directly related to outcome.

Mishler and Scotch (1963) investigated the sociocultural factors related to the development of schizophrenia. The authors discussed the problems regarding epidemiology at some length and concluded that schizophrenia occurred more frequently in people who were isolated from family and friends as well as in people who were not part of an intimate, sharing social group.

Accident-Proneness

In a study of accident-proneness in automobile drivers, Tillman and Hobbs (1949) demonstrated that accident-prone drivers did indeed exist. The investigators reviewed the records of accidents from a bus company extending over a 6-year period and on the basis of their data, were able to differentiate high and low accident-prone groups and to describe certain personality traits that distinguished them. In contradistinction to individuals who were in the low accident-prone group, members of the high accident-prone group had life histories that evidenced social disregard as well as isolation from family and friends. The backgrounds of the two groups were also distinctly different in that the high accident-prone drivers came more frequently from unstable homes, often with divorced parents.

Pregnancy

Nuckolls et al. (1972) studied the relationships between psychosocial assets, social stress (as measured by Cumulative Life Change Score), and the prognosis of pregnancy. Psychosocial assets were measured early in pregnancy by questionnaire (the Adaptive Potential for Pregnancy). At 32 weeks, subjects completed the Schedule of Recent Experience, from which scores were calculated for life change both during pregnancy and for the 2 preceding years. Following delivery, the medical record was used to score each pregnancy as "normal" or "complicated." Complete data were obtained on 170 subjects. The findings showed that women with high cumulative life changes before and during pregnancy who also had favorable psychosocial assets had a complication rate that was only one third the rate of women who had comparable high cumulative life changes but accompanying low psychosocial assets. Their study also showed that in the absence of high cumulative life change, there was no significant relationship between psychosocial assets and complications.

Stress Response

Animal studies reviewed by Kaplan et al. (1977) have provided evidence of the protective effect of the presence of family members and a close social network for individuals undergoing some form of stress. Among other experiments they discussed Conger, Sawrey, and Turrel's (1958) study about the effects of isolation on stress response. Conger et al. had demonstrated that the efficacy with which an unanticipated series of electric shocks (given to animals previously conditioned to avoid them) can produce peptic ulcers is determined, among other things, by whether the animals are shocked in isolation, which produces high ulcer rates, or in the presence of mates, which produces low ulcer rates. They also quoted Henry, Meehan, and Stephens (1967), who showed that persistent hypertension can be produced in mice when they are placed in an overcrowded living situation. These investigators determined, however, that the hypertension was produced only when the mice were "strangers," that is, not littermates. Finally, they quoted Liddell (1950) who had demonstrated that when a young goat was isolated from its mother and subjected to a monotonous stimulus, it would develop signs of a traumatic experimental neurosis. On the other hand, when subjected to the same stimulus in the presence of its mother, the goat's twin showed no such disturbance.

These human and animal studies strongly imply a relationship between the development of certain illnesses and diseases and an individual's connectedness with family members and friends. The issue, however, is not simply the relationship between social connectedness and the development of illness. Kaplan et al. (1977) underscored the notion that social supports are likely to be protective during stressful times. They quoted Holmes who showed that a high rate of tuberculosis in Seattle occurred in individuals who were isolated within the neighborhoods in which they lived. A high incidence of tuberculosis also occurred in people who were living alone in one room, in those who had multiple occupational and residential moves, and in those who were either single or divorced. The point that Kaplan makes is that isolation from family members or from an intimate group leaves the individual in a vulnerable state.

STUDIES OF SOCIAL RELATIONSHIPS

The specific qualities of intimate relationships that render an individual less vulnerable to illness are not well understood. What it is about relationships that helps to mitigate illness also remains a mystery. Porritt (1979) stressed the necessity for empathy, respect, and genuineness in relationships if they are to provide effective stress-buffering support. The quantity of relationships is also important. Pattison, Llamas, and Hard (1979) found that healthy individuals list twice as many important others as do mentally ill persons. Despite the intense ambivalence that schizophrenic individuals typically felt for their family members, two thirds of their important others were close relatives.

House, Robbins, and Metzner (1982) studied the prospective association of social relationships and activity with mortality over a 12-year period. They interviewed and examined a cohort of 2754 adult men and women and found that those men who reported a higher level of social relationships and activities between 1967 and 1969 were significantly less likely to die during the follow-up period than those who reported a lower level of social relationships. The findings for women were similar, although when age and other risk factors were controlled, they were not statistically significant. An important finding was that no association could be discerned between mortality and satisfaction with social relationships. The authors offered three possible reasons for this: (1) The report of satisfaction with a relationship may be less stable over time than the report of intensity of the relationship, and thus the satisfaction measures might be very unreliable; (2) people may be satisfied with relationships for many different reasons that may not have been captured by the measures; (3) the maintenance of a relationship may somehow be more important to well-being than the quality of that relationship.

Although House and co-workers were not able to answer fully the question of how and why social relationships are predictive of mortality, their data showed that mere diversion from work and the routines of daily living was not the effective component that reduced the risk of death. They intimated that to have positive effects, a relationship must require greater active effort by the individual and some contact with other people. The question that remains, "How does this intimate contact reduce the vulnerability to illness?" has been approached by many theorists. It is evident that an individual's self-esteem and sense of security are crucial. Anyone confronted by a stressful situation will respond by attempting to adapt in a fashion that reduces the stress. If, however, over a period of time the individual's attempts to reduce the stress are not effective, the persistent stress comes to be experienced as internally threatening and insecurity results. If the insecurity and the threatening feelings continue unabated, the individual maintains a hypervigilent, on-guard position accompanied by either a conscious or unconscious wariness. Feelings of inadequacy make it impossible to return to the previous homeostatic baseline. The individual who perceives family and social supports to be inadequate will then turn to others, either directly or indirectly, for help. Although family members are not always able to reduce the individual's external pressures, they do provide support and intimacy and offer the opportunity for the individual to "bounce off" someone else. This mitigates and, at times externalizes, the feelings of insecurity and low self-esteem.

The mechanism for the positive effects of family support can be understood through infant studies. Very early in life, the infant's tension is relieved through the ministrations of a caretaker who feeds, diapers, and shields the baby from extraneous stimuli. The growing child learns to trust the primary caregiver's vigilance regarding needs and helpfulness with tension. A pattern is set up so that by 3 to 5 years of age the child learns self-soothing by remembering the caregiver's soothing words and gentle comforting. Perhaps this is encoded neurologically. The child, as well as the later adult, learns to turn to other members of the species for the kind of interactions that maintain homeostasis. When an individual is confronted with a major change (e.g., death of a spouse, change in physical location, change in job), the resulting insecurity is a product of the fear that previous means for tension release will be disrupted and will no longer be available. Thus, in the face of strong family and social supports, life changes are less stressful because the individual's means of tension release are not threatened.

In explaining how these psychological variables are translated physiologically, Kaplan et al. (1977) quoted Bovard (1962), who had postulated a biological theory. His formulation suggested that stressful psychological stimuli are mediated through the posterior and medial hypothalamus; this arousal leads to the release of a neurotransmitter, which in turn acts on the anterior pituitary. Bovard had further postulated that a second center was located in the anterior and lateral hypothalamus and could be stimulated by a positive supportive relationship. When this happened, it called forth a "competing response" that would inhibit the stress stimulus and minimize its effects. All of these theories are a matter of conjecture, awaiting the epidemiological research necessary to determine the specific components of relationships that help decrease vulnerability to illness and death. Furthermore, Morgane and Stern (1972) have noted that basic needs activate drive mechanisms in the brain that are established by natural selection. Wishes and desires might then be thought of as subjective experiences of behavioral drives. They emphasized the role of the limbic forebrain-hypothalamic-limbic mid-brain formation in the mechanism by which the organism reacts to desire and motivation.

They also implicated the importance of the hippocampal formation, the fornix system, the mammilary body, the mammillo-thalamic bundle, the thalamus, the cingulate gyrus, and other cortical areas, and finally the entorhinal area and hip-pocampal formation in this process. Morgane and Stern emphasized that early in development, as the child is learning to relate to the primary caregiver, the immature neurological system develops a means of discharging energy. The child learns that the primary caregiver is a resource for the discharge.

CHANGING PATTERNS IN CONTEMPORARY SOCIETY

Contemporary changes in society make it more difficult for families to continue to be supportive. Among those changes is the increasing divorce rate. In the period from 1960 to 1975 the annual number of divorces rose by 80%. Although divorce is traumatic for all parties involved, evidence attests that it is most traumatic for children. Bohannan (1975) found that children of divorced families have difficulty with a particular area of learning, the understanding of ambivalence. Because the child lives in a single-parent family and does not experience the give and take of a marriage, one parent may be perceived as being right and the other parent as being wrong. Often the child never gets to experience the reality that each parent is right on some occasions and at other times wrong. Because the hallmark of any enduring relationship is the ability to tolerate the coexistence of positive and negative feelings, this lack of experience with ambivalence may interfere with future rela-tionships.

Another factor influencing the support that individuals get from families is the so-called decline of the extended family in America. Many theorists point to the urbanization of the United States as a condition that has led to isolation as opposed to interdependence within families. Pilisuk and Froland (1978) affirmed the view of the isolated, middle-class, suburban family. They stated that because of the lack of ties with extended family members or with larger social groups urban families place intense emotional expectations on the four or five members residing within the immediate family. There are sociologists, however, who feel that in fact the extended family is not breaking down in the face of social change. Sussman (1965) showed that the extended family continues to provide certain types of assistance for members. In addition to financial support, social interactions, including rec-reational and ceremonial activities, are still enjoyed by members of extended fam-ilies. Sussman stated that although urbanization certainly produced some disruptions in family relationships, the extended family network has accommodated to these early changes. His view is that as a unit, the extended family has survived the changing sociological trends by adapting.

The importance of grandparents to their grandchildren has received modest at-tention. Kellum, Ensminger, and Turner (1977) found that in a poor, urban, black community, grandmother-mother families had the same low risk for developmental problems as the nuclear mother-father families. Indeed the mother-grandmother families were more successful with their children than mother-stepfather families. Benedek (1970) described the special benefits that grandparents and grandchildren can give to each other:

> The love of grandparents gives the child a sense of security in being loved without always deserving it. Thus the undemanding love of the grandparents preserves for the child a piece of the self-indulgent sense of omnipotence experienced unconsciously during infancy. (p. 201)

Grandparents who live near their grandchildren often act as surrogate parents, providing the parents some relief from burdensome feelings that accompany constant responsibility for young children. Grandparents also benefit from a relationship with their grandchildren through which they can feel needed and loved. Adolescents often become protective of grandparents. Benedek stated:

> Their attitude toward their grandparents appears to reach that post ambivalent phase of object relationship which Karl Abraham described as characteristic of maturity . . . The grandparents respond to the manifestations of the protective, even if somehow condescending, love of their grandchildren as balm for whatever wounds old age inflicts upon them. (p. 202)

Although it is clear that the extended family, as an institution, has not disappeared in the face of urban change, it is also evident that it does not provide the same level of support that it once did when generations of large families lived close to one another. Financial support and the sharing of ceremonies and recreational activities continue within extended families; however, geographical distance affects the immediate support and tension release that family members can get from one another.

Although most individuals maintain ties to members of their extended families, there is a tendency in Western society to underestimate the positive value of these relationships. In fact, these ties can provide mutual help and support for family members. Uzoka (1979) attributed this undervaluation to the prevalent idealization of the nuclear family as an optimal functioning unit and the denial that most families function as extended families. He suggested that the myth of the intact nuclear family served as a defense against the painful feelings of separation and loss in the early industrial period when individuals were often uprooted and separated from their families. He pointed out that modern transportation and communication have rendered this defense obsolete. The assumption that the nuclear family is the only desirable form of family organization sometimes leads to an erosion of bonds with grandparents, aunts, uncles, and cousins and is reflected in the way our society cares for its aged, sick, and impoverished members. Mental health professionals who overvalue the nuclear family model have sometimes promoted isolation of individuals from their extended families, insisting that overcloseness will lead to excessive dependency.

Uzoka questioned the validity of making distinctions between nuclear and extended family systems and suggested that helping professionals should, instead, encourage people to face family obligations and to feel free to acknowledge emotional ties and needs without guilt.

SUMMARY

An abundance of information shows that family support and intimacy help the individual to cope with adversity and to be less vulnerable to certain illnesses and accidents. It is likely that this effect is mediated through both psychological and physiological means. Whether changing contemporary social patterns will adversely affect the ability of family and extended family to function as ego supports is yet to be determined.

REFERENCES

Arlow, J. (1981). Theories of pathogenesis. *Psychoanalytic Quarterly, 50,* 488–514.
Benedek, T. (1970). Parenthood during the life cycle. In E. J. Anthony & T. Benedek (Eds.), *Parenthood: Its psychology and psychopathology* (pp. 185–206). Boston: Little, Brown.
Bohannan, P. (1975). Marriage and divorce. In A. Freedman & H. Kaplan (Eds.), *The comprehensive testbook of psychiatry* (pp. 3258–3267). Baltimore: Williams & Wilkins.
Bovard, E. (1962). The balance between negative and positive brain system activity. *Perspectives in Biology & Medicine, 6,* 116–127.
Caplan, G. (1974). *Support systems and community mental health.* New York: Behavioral Publications.
Chan, K. B. (1977). Individual differences in reactions to stress and their personality and situational determinants: Some implications for community mental health. *Social Science and Medicine, 11,* 89–103.
Conger, J., Sawrey, W., & Turrel, E. (1958). The role of social experience in the production of gastric ulcers in hooded rats placed in a conflict situation. *American Journal of Abnormal Psychology, 57,* 214–220.
Erikson, E. H. (1965). *Childhood and society.* New York: Norton.
Flaherty, J., Gaviria, F., Black, E., Altman, E., & Mitchell, T. (1983). The role of social support in the functioning of patients with unipolar depression. *American Journal of Psychiatry, 140,* 473–476.
Freud, A. (1982). Scientific forum on the psychoanalytic approach to the nature and location of pathogenesis. *The Bulletin of the Hampstead Clinic, 5,* 87–152.
Freud, A. (1983). Problems in pathogenesis. *Psychoanalytic Study of the Child, 38,* 383–388.
Greenblatt, M., Becerra, R. M., & Serafetinides, E. A. (1982). Social networks and mental health: An overview. *American Journal of Psychiatry, 139,* 977–984.
Henry, J., Meehan, J., & Stephens, P. (1967). The use of psychosocial stimuli to induce prolonged systolic hypertension in mice. *Psychosomatic Medicine, 29,* 408–432.

Hinde, R. A. (1981). Family influences. In M. Rutter, (Ed.), *Scientific foundations of developmental psychiatry* (pp. 47–66). Baltimore: University Park Press.

House, J., Robbins, C., & Metzner, H. (1982). The association of social relationships and activities with mortality: Prospective evidence from the Tecumseh Community Health Study. *American Journal of Epidemiology, 116,* 123–140.

Kaplan, B., Cassel, J., & Gore, S. (1977). Social support and health. *Medical Care (Supplement), 15*(5), 47–58.

Kellum, S. G., Ensminger, M. E., & Turner, R. J. (1977). Family structure and the mental health of children. *Archives of General Psychiatry, 34,* 1012–1022.

Liddell, H. (1950). Some specific factors that modify tolerance for environmental stress. In H. Wolff, S. Wolff, & C. Hare (Eds.), *Life stress and bodily disease* (pp. 155–171). Baltimore: Williams & Wilkins.

Mishler, E., & Scotch, N. (1963). Sociocultural factors in the epidemiology of schizophrenia: A review. *Psychiatry, 26,* 315–351.

Morgane, P. J., & Stern, W. C. (1972). Relationship of sleep to neuroanatomical circuits, biochemistry, and behavior. *Annals of the New York Academy of Sciences, 193,* 95–111.

Nuckolls, B., Cassel, J., & Kaplan, B. (1972). Psychosocial assets, life crisis and the prognosis of pregnancy. *American Journal of Epidemiology, 95,* 431–441.

Pattison, E. M., Llamas, R., & Hard, G. (1979). Social network mediation of anxiety. *Psychiatric Annals, 9*(9), 56–67.

Pilisuk, M., & Froland, C. (1978). Kinship: Social networks, social support and health. *Social Science and Medicine, 12B–13B,* 273–280.

Porritt, D. (1979). Social support in crisis: Quantity or quality? *Social Science and Medicine, 13,* 715–721.

Spitz, R. (1965). *The first year of life.* New York: International Universities Press.

Sussman, M. (1965). Relationships of adult children with their parents in the United States. In T. Shanas & T. Streib (Eds.), *Social structure and the family: Generational relations* (pp. 62–92). Englewood Cliffs, NJ: Prentice-Hall.

Tillman, W., & Hobbs, G. (1949). The accident prone automobile driver: A study of the psychiatric and social background. *American Journal of Psychiatry, 106,* 321–331.

Uzoka, A. F. (1979). The myth of the nuclear family. *American Psychologist, 34,* 1095–1106.

Warheit, G. (1979). Life events, coping, stress, and depressive symptomatology. *American Journal of Psychiatry, 136,* 502–507.

Ego Strength and Coping Capacity: Friend and Social Group Affiliation

WILLIAM C. SZE, PhD

Throughout history, human beings have always preferred aggregated living, no matter how small the size of the aggregation. In the beginning, this preference may have reflected biological factors, because human growth is rather a slow process in comparison to that of other animals. Even in primitive times human infants had to be cared for by others for several years before becoming self-sufficient. As a rule, the mother's importance is paramount because she not only gives birth to the child, but also provides the care that ensures survival. The infant otherwise has a minimal survivorship; without protracted care of the young, the human race would not be able to continue. In some instances, because a mother is unable to fulfill her mothering responsibilities, they may fall in the hands of other people. Preserving the human species thus becomes a communal responsibility.

Besides the physical needs for survival, a person needs to reckon with the idea or awareness of self, or individuality. The concept of identity, or self, is not framed in isolation, but requires some reference point. A 10-year-old boy, for example, in defining his own strength, utilizes the other boys in his class or social network as the basis for comparison. Without such a reference point, the concept of strength would have no meaning. By the same token, individuals without a firm reference point are often easily influenced by others. The classic study on autokinetic phenomenon by Sherif (1935) supports this general contention.

George H. Mead has discussed this relationship of group and individual self-definition. According to Mead (1962):

> Selves can only exist in relationship to other selves. No hard-and-fast line can be drawn between our own selves and the selves of others, since our own selves exist as such in our experience only in so far as the selves of others exist and enter as such into our experience also. (p. 168)

For Harry Stack Sullivan (1953b), "Personality is the relatively enduring pattern of recurrent interpersonal situations which characterize a human life" (pp. 110–111).

Overall, the interactionalists have created excitement in the behavioral sciences by focusing on the transactional level of human behavior between humans, as well as between humans and their environment. By the 1940s small group theory and field theory emerged as conceptual frameworks for studying behavior. Freud (1955) had theorized about the implications of groups in relationship to ego function as early as 1921, although his major concern was with ego defenses and transference. Kurt Lewin's (1951) work in field theory contributed to both practical research and theory in the area of group dynamics, and the groundwork was discussed in terms of clinical applications by Redl and Wineman (1951), Slavson (1950), Bion (1947–1950), and Moreno (1934). The new knowledge of behavioral sciences has led researchers further down the path from the discovery of the significance of friendships and peer relations to the formulation of group dynamics, and finally to the function of social networks as viable theoretical constructs for the application of the clinical work.

This chapter will examine two social relationships—friendship and social group affiliation—as vital psychosocial instruments in the development of self (ego) and the resolution of coping measures.

FRIENDSHIPS AND PEER RELATIONSHIPS

Friendships and peer relationships occupy a unique position among social groups in the development of the self. Grunebaum and Solomon (1982) described different stages of the development of peer relationships from infancy to adolescence in terms of their various impacts on the needs of the ego. Selman (1980) focused on how the child structures peer relations. He proposed a conceptual framework for charting the growth in interpersonal awareness and conceptions of friendship as an ontogenic sequence of hierarchical stages. Sullivan (1953a), focusing on the stage of preadolescence, stated that peer relationships correct autistic or fantastic self-images and that such self-evaluations lead to social accommodation and adaptation.

Hamburg and Adams (1967) discussed the relationship between the ability to become engaged in significant friendships and successful adjustment to college campus life. They identified the functions of friendship at this life stage:

1. Clarification of new self-definitions and career possibilities
2. Intellectual stimulation through informal discussion groups
3. Learning experiences through pooled information and use of coping skills
4. Learning experiences through role complementarity
5. Support in time of crisis
6. Provision of a sounding board for alternate points of view

Rubin (1974) conceptualized social interaction in terms of five patterns:

> We join each other in pairs, groups, and organizations. We mold one another's behavior through subtle and not so subtle messages. We conform to the opinions and demands of others. We help one another in times of need. We experience and express love for one another. (p. 1)

The opposite of these five patterns are separating, asocializing (although Rubin thought that there was no simple term for the opposite of molding, I believe "asocializing" conveys that meaning), resisting, hurting, and hating.

Joining seems to be the most pivotal of the five positive modes of interaction. Schachter (1959), in an empirical study, noted that people, like other animals, draw close to each other when they are afraid or anxious as a mode of reducing the perception or experience of threat.

The reaching-out process, however, might also be part of an effort to enhance the individual's sense of well-being. To establish friendship or to join a group is indicative of the desire to expand one's social environment and is an attempt on the part of the individual to enhance self-worth. The characteristics of the self's well-being are part of the psychoemotional needs of the individual. As Hamburg and Adams (1967) observed, "In general, individuals cope more effectively with disability problems when they have a firm sense of belonging in high valued groups" (pp. 281–282). Kaplan, Cassel, and Gore (1977) listed nine emotional needs that can be derived from some social support mechanisms: security, affection, trust, intimacy, nurturance, succorance, belongingness, affiliation, and approval. Others (French, Rogers, & Cobb, 1974; Gruenberg, 1967; Leighton, 1959; Parkes, Benjamin, & Fitzgerald, 1969; Segal, Weiss, & Sokol, 1965), also documented, with numerous research findings, the notion of the importance of social support mechanisms in the individual's health.

For example, Kaplan and his associates (1977) focused on nine specific characteristics of social support that reinforce the individual's self-assessment, adaptation, and modulation. The specific characteristics are:

1. *Appraisal Opportunities.* The evaluation of what is happening, reality reassurances
2. *Persuasion.* Opportunity to tell the other that inconsistent or dissonant cognitions can be made consistent
3. *Normative Fit.* The comfort, consensus, and complementarity an individual feels in shared supportive norms ("us" versus "them")
4. *Group Solidarity.* The feeling of "we-ness"
5. *Intimacy Opportunities.* Opportunities for intimacy and the sharing of personal thoughts
6. *Role-Self Rewards/Approval.* Self-esteem from approval for roles that are well performed
7. *Dependable Social Networks.* Support in normal and crisis situations and provision of reliable norms
8. *Tangible Support.* Concrete events that provide social reinforcement
9. *Love of Significant Others.* Love of spouse, friends, and so on

In light of this discussion, it appears that the self is not just a human entity; it is the social self that determines one's selfness. Hence, the ego might also be viewed as the individual's sensorium, through which the sense of reality of the social world and of the self are being integrated.

Once the social self is established, one can then feel much safer expanding the psychosocial horizon into a more mature ego state. Otherwise, the individual is easily threatened and frustrated by the inability to control impulses or excitement in a large social context. Redl and Wineman (1951) for example, in their study of wayward youth, discussed the phenomenon of "group psychological intoxication"—inability of an ego to stand up under the impact of excitement.

A number of studies (Cowen, Pederson, Babigian, Izzo, & Trost, 1973; Kohn & Clausen, 1955; Roff, Sells, & Golden, 1972) have pointed out the relationship between unpopularity among peers and adult psychological disturbances. The lack of peer-group interaction leads to psychopathology, for Caplan (1974), because:

. . . relevant messages about expectations and evaluations of an individual's behavior are not being constantly communicated, or else that the individual is unfamiliar with expectations and the evaluative clues of those around him. . . . He is consequently never able to feel safe and valued, and his autonomic nervous system and hormonal mechanisms are continually in a state of emergency arousal, so that the resulting

physiological depletion and fatigue increase his susceptibility to a wide range of
physical and mental disorders. (pp. 1–2)

Failure to establish a stable social self might cause a person to have difficulties
in expanding psychosocial horizons. Friendship and peer group relations offer a
middle ground between isolation and the greater social context—a direction, reference point, emotional nourishment, and buffering mechanism—allowing the individual to adapt or modulate the psyche into a well-integrated psychosocial self.

It is known that a major part of learning is smooth and ego enhancing and yet,
at times, can also be distressing. For example, a mother with a 5-year-old daughter,
Pat, invites a neighbor's daughter, Jackie, the same age, to play with her daughter.
In the beginning, the mother simply wants to find a playmate for her daughter, but
she ends up finding a peer. Afterward, Pat tells her mother that she was able to
play some games much better than Jackie. Pat also says with great pleasure that
she taught Jackie to play with some of her toys. Here is a vivid example of the
self consciously sizing another up in terms of "Am I ok?" or "Am I better than
others?" Such play sessions seem to provide an opportunity for the two girls to
establish a reference point. Although the "Who am I" question is frequently associated with the adolescent stage, it is a subject of concern at a much earlier age.
The reference point gives either some ego-enhancing pleasure or ego-distress signals
depending on the reflection the person sees from the scale of the reference point.
In this scenario, Jackie seems to make the best of the situation by not showing her
inability to challenge Pat; she, in turn, learns from Pat to improve her game skills.
This takes the edge of the competitiveness away. Both of them seem to relate with
each other on the basis of helping, loving, and having fun together. This is then a
mixed scenario or two-staged relationship: a competitiveness in order to discern the
peerness, and a graceful acceptance of Pat's superiority with emphasis on the girls'
friendship. In everyday life there are, perhaps, more mixed-type scenarios than
either pure peer-type or friend-type.

The freedom-from-stress situation does not necessarily last very long. To continue this example, the mother invites another girl, Nancy, who is also 5 years old
and who has just moved into the neighborhood, to play with Pat and Jackie. Now
there are three girls of the same age in the social group. Nancy appears to be pretty,
sweet, and good in creating play-themes. Pat and Jackie both want to be close to
Nancy. Yet they are afraid to betray their loyalty to their old friendship and also
fear retaliation from each other by making a first move. This possessive phenomenon
and the pressure to loyalty have created a great tension in the group. As a result,
Nancy is temporarily being isolated without knowing why. She becomes uncomfortable, feeling that no one wants to be close to her. All in all, the triad complication
results in a stressful situation. This illustration underscores the need for careful
attention to size, structure, and dynamics of interplay among the members in a
social group.

SOCIAL GROUP (SOCIAL NETWORK) AFFILIATION AND SOCIAL SUPPORT

The need for "social group" affiliation has long been an interesting subject for social scientists, whereas the need for a "social network" is a relatively recent social concept promulgated by many sectors of helping professionals. Distinction between the terms is frequently not clear, and at best, there seems to be a large overlap. Of the two terms, *social group* seems more generalized, referring usually to primary relationships that are close, frequent, face to face, and accompanied by warmth and commitment. *Social network* is generally used to focus on the fulfilling of specific human needs. Pattison and Pattison (1981), however, in discussing social network, viewed it as a "social construct" of the links between ego and salient significant others. The interactions in a therapeutic social network should possess the characteristics of frequent interaction, positive affect, a strong instrument component of assistance, and balanced reciprocity of affective and instrumental exchange between ego and other.

Tolsdorf (1976), in discussing the scope of the social network analysis, focused on 12 content areas: primary kin; secondary kin; primary friend; secondary friend; economic, recreational, political, religious, sexual, fraternal, and mutual aid; and service associates. The categories are not mutually exclusive and may occur in any combination in any given relationship. In each case, however, the focus is on support, advice, and feedback.

Tolsdorf (1976), noted that the social network may also be a source of stress. He noted the relationship between the individual's perception of his or her social network and coping ability, and the differences in perception of the structure, content, and function of networks among individual network members. In fact, the individual and the network are in a constant interaction, and they shape and maintain (or undercut) each other. In other words, an individual's network is shaped and maintained by his or her use of and attitude toward it.

Weiss (1974) attempted to classify the type of human need with the type of relational provisions found in specialized social groupings. He labeled six types of relational provisions—attachment, social integration, opportunity for nurturance, reassurance of warmth, sense of reliable alliance, and guidance—each of which has variable levels of importance in different individuals in different life phases or with different immediate or long-range concerns of different character or taste. Weiss's idea provides a focus on the often loosely defined concept of social network as a helping model and leads to further examination of the individual's "person–environment fit" as a model for intervention by the helping professional. To use this model, the helping professional has to consider the "best fit" concept.

For instance, a teenage girl escaping from an unhappy family life into an early and unprepared marital relationship in order to acquire a reassurance of worth, might discover that a person–environment is "unfit" if she equates attachment or dependency with reassurance of worth. Such selection of inappropriate social networks are common in our society and may lead to disastrous psychological consequences. Manipulation of the person–environment fit, on the other hand, becomes a crucial consideration in the therapy process.

When an appropriately selected social network is functioning well, the clinical value can then be noted. Gourash (1978) cited four such therapeutic functions of the social network:

1. To buffer the experience of stress
2. To provide instrumental and affective support
3. To screen and refer to professional services
4. To transmit attitudes, values, and norms about help seeking

The first two functions tend to eliminate or delay the need for seeking outside help; the second two facilitate the search for professional intervention when the limits of the social network to deal with a problem become clear.

On the societal level, the social network provides a linkage between the individual and a service delivery system. It creates a social resource in supplementing existing service gaps or in linking formal care to informal care, such as discharging an alcoholic patient from a substance abuse clinic with a referral to an AA group for further help. Volunteer or support groups thus might supplement, complement, or follow formal care in an inpatient or outpatient facility, aiding the transition from mental disturbance to coping in a given social context.

SOCIAL SUPPORT

Some writers make no distinction between the terms *social network* and *social support* in the helping process. Others focus on the latter term as a direct, concrete expression of the potential for help in a social network. Social support has been a major focus in those writers interested in the impact of life event changes on depression. Cassel (1974) contended that social supports serve as "protective factors buffering or cushioning the individual from the physiologic or psychologic consequences of exposure to the stressor situation" (p. 478). D'Augelli (1983) likewise emphasized that social support is an important factor in mediating stressful life events.

Barrera (1981), reviewing the literature on the function of social support, listed six such areas—material aid, physical assistance, intimate interaction, guidance, feedback, and social participation. He found that among pregnant teenagers, for example, supportive network members helped buffer stressful events that accompanied the pregnancy. Not all measures of support were of equal impact. According to Barrera, the subjective perception of the individual or method utilized in the offer of support might produce negative consequences such as overprotectiveness, interference, and invasion of privacy. The negative impact of some forms of intervention have also been noted by Colletta (1979), Raschke (1977), and Weiss (1979).

Self-help groups usually influence members by the activities of the group. Lenrow and Burch (1981) identified four broad functions of such support systems:

1. They help individuals to control problem behaviors (e.g., child abuse, drinking, overeating).
2. They help individuals cope with stressful conditions they do not expect to change (e.g., handicaps, terminal illness, divorce, grief).
3. They help individuals cope with crisis-of-life transitions (e.g., career change, first baby, retirement).
4. They help individuals explore new interests and learn to take charge of their lives in more fulfilling ways (e.g., assertiveness training).

In everyday life, support is part of normal social intercourse and is often taken for granted. A visit, call or letter to express condolence may buffer or cushion painful feelings; overcome the sense of isolation, helplessness, and despair; and might prevent grief from becoming a disability. This preventive function has been largely overlooked in the literature, because of the difficulty of studying something that has not yet come into being. The multiferous functions of support in quotidien social interaction, according to Gottlieb (1981), provide people with:

> Another means of gaining a richer, contextual understanding of coping behavior and human development, since its study requires consideration of the complex interplay between attributes of individuals, attributes of social aggregates in which they are embedded, and attributes of the situational and socio-cultural environment influencing the structure and the behavioral patterns of these social aggregates. (p. 28)

CONCEPTS THAT ENHANCE EGO GROWTH AND COPING STRATEGIES

Friendship, peer relationship, and social group affiliation are all concepts that have the quality of alleviating human distress and enhancing the well-being of self. They possess common instrumental values for the service of human desire or needs such as socializing, security, affection, intimacy, helping, loving, and others. They elicit altruistic behavior, a necessary element in helping human growth and social cohesion.

Reifying these concepts makes it possible to examine their common property and their function or dysfunction in modulating psychosocial life. Strictly speaking, friend and peer are not identical, but both serve a useful purpose in psychosocial life. *Friend* implies one who gives a supportive or kindly relationship to another.

Peer implies an equal quality in respective social demographical areas such as age, sex, profession, or rank. Friends do not necessarily have to possess equality, but it is helpful if two friends have a close background so that they can share their common interests or life experiences.

Anyone living in a socially, politically, and economically complex society has one time or another become affiliated with some social group(s). Despite the difference of the purpose or nature of the various groups, they all share at least three characteristics: membership requirement (formal or informal), face-to-face interaction, and common goal or purpose. Without these basic characteristics, the group would instead be merely a collection of individuals.

A group that is used appropriately usually expands a person's social network or social support system; it can sometimes take the form of a mutual-aid or self-help group. Such groups are inevitable results of movements toward a service society and consumerism; they embody democratic ideals of participation, alternative caregiving systems, and so on (Katz, 1977).

This new caregiving system in part certainly has shifted the focus from traditional licensed professional help to newly formed people–people help. This people–people approach is extremely utilitarian in the quest for self and personal growth through friendship and peer relationship, which enhance the individual's capacity to develop coping mechanisms. At the other end of the spectrum, an individual might join a group to legitimize his or her deviant behavior, "by reforming the norms of society, by reducing the sanctions against his behavior; that is, by changing, not himself, but the rule-making others" (Sagarin, 1969, p. 21). An example would be homosexuals who join gay liberation groups for the purpose of reframing the individual stigma into a social or political issue. This type of group participation generates some social sympathy, which, in turn, dilutes the individual stigma and subsequently mitigates social pressures or individual stresses.

In summary, these concepts appear to have an important place in enhancement of ego growth and coping strategies. However, there has not been much progress in making those concepts more specific in ways that could generate more applied research. Much work, therefore, remains to be done to transform these concepts into verifiable terms, a truism that, unfortunately, often mires behavioral studies.

REFERENCES

Barrera, M., Jr. (1981). Social support in the adjustment of pregnant adolescents: Assessment issues. In B. H. Gottlieb (Ed.), *Social networks and social support* (pp. 75, 84, 86). London: Sage.

Bion, W. R. (1947–1950). Experiences in groups: Parts I–V. *Human Relations, 1,* 314–320, 487–496; *2,* 13–22, 295–304; *3,* 3–14.

Caplan, G. (1974). *Support systems and community mental health* (pp. 1–2). New York: Behavioral Publications.

Cassel, J. (1974). Psychosocial processes and stress: Theoretical formulations. *International Journal of Health Services, 6,* 471–482.

Colletta, N. D. (1979). Support systems after divorce: Incidence and impact. *Journal of Marriage and the Family, 41,* 837–846.

Cowen, E. L., Pederson, A., Babigian, H., Izzo, L. D., & Trost, M. A. (1973). Long-term follow-up of early detected vulnerable children. *Journal of Consulting and Clinical Psychology, 41,* 438–446.

D'Augelli, A. (1983). Social support networks in mental health. In J. K. Whittaker, J. Garbarino & Associates (Eds.), *Social support networks* (pp. 90–91). New York: Aldine.

French, J. R. P., Jr., Rogers, W., & Cobb, S. (1974). Adjustment as person-environment fit. In G. V. Coelho, D. A. Hamburg, & J. Adams (Eds.), *Coping* (pp. 316–333). New York: Basic Books.

Freud, S. (1955). Group psychology and the analysis of the ego. In J. Strachey (Ed. and Trans.), *The standard edition of the complete psychological works of Sigmund Freud* (Vol. 18, pp. 69–134). London: Hogarth Press.

Gottlieb, B. H. (1981). Social network and social support in community mental health. In B. H. Gottlieb (Ed.), *Social network and social support* (pp. 11–42). London: Sage.

Gourash, N. (1978). Help-seeking: A review of the literature, *American Journal of Community Psychology, 6,* 499–517.

Gruenberg, C. (1967). The social breakdown syndrome, some observations. *American Journal of Psychiatry, 123,* 12.

Grunebaum, H., & Solomon, L. (1982). Toward a theory of peer relationship II: On the stages of social development and their relationship to group psychotherapy. *International Journal of Group Psychotherapy, 32,* 283–307.

Hamburg, D. A., & Adams, J. E. (1967). A perspective on coping behavior. *Archives of General Psychiatry, 17,* 279, 281–282.

Kaplan, B. H., Cassel, J. C., & Gore, S. (1977). Social support and health. *Medical Care* [Supplement], *15*(5), 47–58.

Katz, A. H. (1977). Self-help groups. In *Encyclopedia of social work,* (Vol. 2, 17th Issue, p. 1257). Washington, DC: National Association of Social Workers.

Kohn, M., & Clausen, J. (1955). Social isolation and schizophrenia. *American Sociological Review, 20,* 265–273.

Leighton, A. (1959). *My name is legion.* New York: Basic Books.

Lenrow, P. B., & Burch, R. W. (1981). Mutual aid and professional services: Opposing or complementary. In B. H. Gottlieb (Ed.), *Social network and social support* (p. 233). London: Sage.

Lewin, K. (1951). *Field theory in social science.* New York: Harper.

Mead, G. H. (1962). The I and the Me. In T. Parsons (Ed.), *Theories of Society* (p. 168). New York: The Free Press of Glencoe.

Moreno, J. L. (1934). *Who shall survive?* Washington, DC: Nervous and Mental Disorders Publishing.

Parkes, N., Benjamin, B., & Fitzgerald, R. E. (1969). Broken heart: A study of increased mortality among widowers. *British Medical Journal, 1,* 740–743.

Pattison, E. M., & Pattison, M. L. (1981). Analysis of a schizophrenic psychosocial network. *Schizophrenic Bulletin, 7,* 135–142.

Raschke, H. J. (1977). The role of social participation in postseparation and postdivorce adjustment. *Journal of Divorce, 1,* 129–140.

Redl, F., & Wineman, D. (1951). *Children who hate.* Glencoe, IL: Free Press.

Roff, M., Sells, B., & Golden, M. M. (1972). *Social adjustment and personality development in children.* Minneapolis: University of Minnesota Press.

Rubin, Z. (Ed.). (1974). *Doing unto others.* Englewood Cliffs, NJ: Prentice-Hall.

Sagarin, E. (1969). *Odd man in: Societies of deviants in America.* Chicago: Quadrangle Books.

Schachter, S. (1959). *The psychology of affiliation.* Palo Alto, CA: Stanford University Press.

Segal, B., Weiss, E., & Sokol, R. (1965). Emotional adjustments, social organization, and psychiatric treatment. *American Sociological Review, 30,* 548–555.

Selman, R. (1980). *The growth of interpersonal understanding: Developmental and clinical analysis.* New York: Academic Press.

Sherif, M. (1935). A study of some social factors in perception. *Archives of Psychology, 187,* 5–60.

Slavson, S. R. (1950). *Analytic group psychotherapy.* New York: Columbia University Press.

Sullivan, H. S. (1953a). In H. S. Perry & M. L. Gavel (Eds.), *The collected works of Harry Stack Sullivan* (Vol. 1, p. 245). New York: Norton.

Sullivan, H. S. (1953b). *The interpersonal theory of psychiatry.* New York: Norton.

Tolsdorf, C. C. (1976). Social networks, support, and coping: An exploratory study. *Family Process, 15,* 409–410, 416.

Weiss, R. S. (1974). The provisions of social relationships. In Z. Rubin (Ed.), *Doing unto others* (pp. 24–25). Englewood Cliffs, NJ: Prentice-Hall.

Weiss, R. S. (1979). *Going it alone.* New York: Basic Books.

Ego Strength and Coping Capacity: Large Group Affiliation

WILLIAM C. SZE, PhD
BARRY IVKER, PhD

Group membership and group identity serve many functions for the individual. This chapter will consider the relationship of individualism and group membership as an aspect of cultural development in a given society, the range of functions of group membership in contemporary society, the range of interactive relationships possible between an individual and the groups with which he or she is identified and/or chooses to identify with, and the implications of group membership and/or identity in the interaction between therapist and client.

INDIVIDUALISM AND GROUP MEMBERSHIP IN CULTURAL HISTORY

The 20th century is the age of mass identity and of the isolated individual. Television and the movies provide images of thousands of individuals blending into

521

one voice, screaming allegiance to a führer, raising their hands in identical salutes or their legs in identical goosesteps; it is a way of using technology to turn other less desirable individuals into passive, pliable masses. It is also an age characterized by the desire to "do my own thing," that is, by the individual drive toward existential authenticity and Rogerian self-realization.

In traditional or primitive societies the group or groups take precedence over the individual. Identity is defined in terms of place or station, status, and role rather than some notion of unique psychological personality. A woman might identify herself as the mother of her eldest son, third wife of a chief, one of a set of twins, someone's daughter, or member of a given age group. She might, in fact, have several names, each used in its appropriate time and circumstance. Upon the birth or initiation of a grandchild, she might be eligible to join a council of female elders or become a midwife or the symbolic mother of the clan. Individual temperament does not go unnoticed in such societies, but those individual characteristics that make it more difficult to fulfill assigned roles are viewed as impediments with potentially tragic consequences. Such idiosyncrasies might be tolerated in carefully circumscribed circumstances. In Nigeria, for example, a main function of Mbari houses seems to be to provide opportunities for individual artistic expression outside of prescribed ritualistic modes. Idiosyncrasies might be ridiculed in traditional societies, as in the case where husband and wife don't observe traditional sex roles in the division of labor. Or there might be fear that they will lead to tragic consequences, with potential disaster for the collective (Oedipus's acts of incest bring famine and infertility to his realm). Any unusual circumstances—such as the birth of twins or left-handedness—might be viewed as a sign of magical powers conferred by the gods, or a sign of some secret sin that would have to be atoned for in a prescribed manner. Because social station is determined by what is considered to be the normal and required performance at a given life stage, it is possible to understand how, for example, the failure of a woman to conceive a child could affect that individual and her ability to feel at home in her culture. A reader of the biblical narrative of Sarah can begin to comprehend her bitterness as she faces the ridicule of the fertile concubine Hagar and refuses to be consoled by Abraham's profession of love for her. In such an integral society, the change of a single custom, such as the missionaries' prohibition of male and/or female circumcision rites at puberty—requirements for being initiated into tribal lore, entering adulthood, and becoming eligible for marriage—could rend the fabric of tradition and tribal unity.

Some provision is made for adjusting the society to the bent of the individual. If, in a primitive society, the disharmony in a marriage exceeds the efforts of the two involved families to resolve the spouses' conflicts (because marriage is more a question of uniting families than individuals), a reluctant divorce can be arranged. But if a person breaks taboos, or even seems by nature to adhere too perfectly to social norms or standards, the price of individual impulse, exceptionality, or non-compliance is extensive expiation, death, or banishment (excommunication); and an individual without a social place—without people to mourn for him or her properly after death—is doomed to isolation and restless wandering for eternity.

In traditional African society, individualism is associated with sorcery—the selling of magical devices and the working of spells for any individual who can pay the price, regardless of the social consequences. Such sorcerers live alone, as contrasted to medicine men who help members of a specific society and live in honored status in its midst. Where a sorcerer is a woman, the symbol of such a lust for power is frequently associated with a voluntary giving up of fertility. If a woman refuses to marry an appropriate partner and waits for someone "special," the mate who finally appears usually turns out to be a forbidden match or a demon lover—a universal theme in folklore. Both she and the lover are "too good to be true." Once the penalty has been paid, ordinary mortals reaffirm the social value of conformity to group norms and consensus.

There appears to be a point in most civilizations where individualism gains ascendance and demands recognition. Plato was aware of such a stage in Greek society and feared its consequences. In *The Republic* his vision of utopia reaffirms the value of collective authority. The idiosyncrasies of parental care were to be abolished, and children were to be raised in societally run children's homes. Artists were to be respected for their individual genius, but if their productions were judged to raise the passions of society beyond acceptable levels, they were to be politely escorted out of the city. The root *idio* (*idiot, idio*syncratic) is derived from the notion of excessive individuality—the refusal of the individual to become involved in sociopolitical activities—to accept Aristotle's definition of man as a political animal. Excessive emphasis on individualism was associated with social decline and the ultimate decadence of the culture.

In Europe, the importance of individualism grew with the Renaissance and, as in ancient Greece and Rome, was reflected in the desire of wealthy and powerful nobles to commemorate their own existence in portraits of themselves and their families. By the end of the 17th century, the clear social class structure began to break down (as it did in major African cities in the 1950s and 1960s). The rising middle classes married their sons to the dowerless daughters of impoverished noblemen. The literature of the time is filled with *parvenus,* individuals who were able to work themselves into society above their assigned social station. The Age of Reason that extolled common sense and cosmic and sociopolitical order became increasingly fascinated with the weird and the exotic in fauna and flora and with excesses in human behavior like sexual perversity, madness, criminality, and unusual customs of ancient and primitive societies. Edward Gibbon, sensing the ripeness of the age and parallels with Roman society, wrote his classic work, *The History of the Decline and Fall of the Roman Empire.*

By the Romantic period the role of the artist (the *poète maudit*) epitomized the tension between the remarkable individual and the by-then largely bourgeois society that valued stability over progress in the arts and brilliant, unpredictable displays of genius. The heroes of Romantic works become Satan, Cain, robbers, unwitting perpetrators of incest, political rebels, and so on. Stendhal's hero in *Le Rouge et le Noir* rejects the two socially accepted roles for a person of his station (the military and the priesthood) and in being true to himself finds his existential freedom in prison, awaiting execution. By the end of the century, the heroes of novels become examples of decadence; Wagner wrote of the *Götterdämmerung;* and Spengler wrote of the decline of the West.

As the inheritors of this current development of the ethos of individualism, young people today are urged to "do their own thing." They are encouraged to define their financial and emotional readiness for marriage by moving out of their familial context into a frequently distant apartment where they can determine their own values unhampered by parental influence. In such a society, progress, change, and novelty are valued over stability; and the opinions, ideas and innovations of the young take precedence over the mature reflections of the elderly. Instead of careful inspection of new ideas, as by the protectors of orthodoxy in the case of Galileo, the ideas of the young Einstein have helped rather quickly to overthrow the traditional ideas of the Newtonian universe. Popular moral standards challenge the right of society to interfere with the individual's right to do anything that does not clearly infringe on the rights of others or endanger society at large. The message of existential philosophy is that people are isolates obligated to work out individual "authentic" solutions to the pain of human existence and that adherence to collective norms, whether religious, political, or cultural, represents bad faith, or in more popular language—"copping out." Sartre's analysis of Jewish identity as a response to antisemitism and negritude as a response to colonialism points to a transcendence of this temporary collective consciousness once the individual is truly liberated.

Encounter groups are based on the notion of "finding the self." Therapists face the challenge of defining their craft not in terms of fitting the individual back into the very neurotic collectivity that helped produce the need for therapy, but of fitting therapeutic goals into the value structure and unfolding character of the individual.

Given freedom of religion, mobility of class structure, and freedom of association, the individual has both the liberty of self and the burden and perplexity of translating this sense of self-awareness into the avenues of group identification that are most useful in unfolding his or her personality. With the decline of the greater family and traditional role identity, modern industrial society risks the formation of a large cadre within its population who experience feelings of rootlessness, isolation, normlessness, loss of identity, and loss of purpose. In Sartre's terms, the freedom from traditional constraints has not yet been translated into a freedom to do anything purposeful and meaningful. Dostoyevski envisioned such a state in his portrayal of the "underground man," whose isolation is associated with his feeling of the tyranny of norms—his need at all costs to declare that $2 + 2$ can equal 5 if and when he wishes it to. In Dostoyevski's *The Brothers Karamazov,* Ivan declares that in a universe where God is dead, all individual acts, no matter how terrifying and repulsive, are permissible. In "The Legend of the Grand Inquisitor," from the same book, the Inquisitor confronts the risen Christ over the issue of the burden of individual freedom, and insists that Jesus has expected too much from men in requiring each of them to seek spiritual bread—men will willingly follow anyone who offers them material bread in exchange for their freedom. Twentieth-century fascists, following the works of Pareto and others, made a science of manipulating mass insecurity by using food, national prestige, and collective answers as the price of removing this burden of individual freedom.

But even in our world of lonely crowds or crowds of lonely people, group formation is a ubiquitous phenomenon and not just representative of "other-directed" or tradition-bound individuals. Given the freedom to choose group affiliation, it is thus appropriate to study the function of membership of a given individual in any particular group.

THE FUNCTIONS OF MEMBERSHIP IN THE GROUP

Anxiety Reduction

Membership in a group can serve to reduce the anxiety of being alone in the modern world. In the face of complex sociopolitical issues it can offer clear-cut solutions or function like a superego, defining standards, and appropriate beliefs and actions. In the face of suffering and death it may offer the security of a relationship with a divine being or force, rewards and punishments for human behavior, and the assurance of salvation and an afterlife. In and of itself religion usually does not ask for complete dissolution of the ego as a price for membership in the group. Most religions require individual choice and conscience even while emphasizing the ideal of submission to the will of God.

But one of the anomalies of modern life is the ability of cults and their charismatic leaders to win over the minds particularly of young adherents so that they turn their backs on their families and traditional values and totally devote their energy, possessions, and loyalty to single individuals who speak for the entire group. Attribution Theory states, "There is a tendency of individuals to unconsciously seek plausible explanation for their feelings among whatever explanations are available in the environment, that is, to attribute causation based on the available cognitive input (Galanter, Babkin, Babkin, & Deutsch, 1979). Ungerleider and Wellisch (1979), utilizing the MMPI, found that individuals remaining in cults had superego deficits compared with those who had left their cults. The cult uses pressure, anxiety, and intense guilt at levels that induce mental and emotional disorders even in relatively well-adjusted youths (Delgado, 1980). To prevent defection while prolonging commitment, the cults isolate their members from contact with groups espousing competing ideologies and sources of information that would discredit their doctrines. They set up a life-style that encompasses every moment of the waking day and every facet of daily activity. They also set up strong affective bonds with cult members and act to sever preexisting emotional bonds with nonmembers (Bittner, 1963; Hargrove, 1980). Ungerleider and Wellisch (1979, p. 279), discussing Chinese modes of "thought reform," isolate eight techniques for attracting and keeping new adherents to the group:

1. Milieu control
2. Mystical manipulation
3. Demands for political and/or ideological purity
4. Personal confession
5. Acceptance of basic group dogma as sacred
6. Constriction or "loading" of language into polarizing terms
7. Subordination of person to doctrine
8. Dispensation of existence

Not all those who go through ideological or religious conversion are emotionally weak individuals who are brainwashed into accepting the group as their superego. Many converts are attracted to the spiritual life offered by a religious group as part of a new learning experience. But the tragedy in Jonestown, Guyana, indicated the ultimate danger of the submission of the individual ego to the will of the group and its leader. And in somewhat milder form, this submission of the individual ego to the collective in terms of codes of uniform dress, behavior, and values is apparent in college fraternities and political splinter groups, among many others.

Affection and Acceptance

The group can provide a basis for affection and acceptance of the individual—at times unquestioned acceptance. In a religious group this affection may include not only the love of other members, but of a divine power. The group of adherents may symbolize mutual affection by physical signs, such as hugging or the kiss of peace; in a few 19th-century American utopian communities, by nonorgastic sexual intercourse; or among homosexuals, by a selection of sexual partners. Such affection is notable in members of an athletic team or a performing troupe when things go well or poorly. The affection can be generated by direct interaction or by a more intangible sharing of beliefs that is evident even on a first meeting—a feeling of kinship, affection, and acceptance when someone introduces him- or herself as an Elk, a Mormon, a Mason, a player of dulcimers, an owner of Edsels, a pedophile, a hang-glider enthusiast, a closet poet, and so on. The group can provide the individual with a source of potential partners or mates with an assurance of similarity of important interests, values, and concerns.

The Search for Identity and Self-Definition

The group may provide a basis for self-evaluation, identity, self-definition, place, role, and status. Self-evaluation is accomplished by means of comparison with other persons. The subjective feelings of correctness in one's opinions and the subjective evaluation of the adequacy of one's performance on important abilities and skills are part of the satisfaction of group membership (Festinger, 1954). Particularly among people of low social esteem, task contributions to the group lead to increases in status, either in homogeneous groups of the disadvantaged or the discriminated against, or in mixed groups where the disadvantaged can demonstrate competencies that they have no opportunities to utilize in the larger society (Ridgeway, 1982). The disproportionate number of blacks in the U.S. military attests to the perceived ability to advance according to merit at a pace not possible in civilian life. When there is a promise of such participation, the more valued the position, the greater the commitment to the group and the greater psychological impact of its loss or gain.

Primary and Reference Groups

A distinction here is in order between primary and reference groups. Primary membership requires face-to-face contact. Reference groups involve self-proclaimed membership in a group that may be vaguely defined and spread out all over the world.

Etzioni (1968) states that collectivity facilitates the movement from a set of macroscopic normative values either declared by the group or imagined by the individual into a potential capacity for action. One can have an anticipatory affiliation. As he further states: "Man as an active creature has a capacity to project himself into the future by projecting a future and pulling himself toward it. In the process, he changes both his environment and himself" (Etzioni, 1968, pp. 32, 98). An individual, for example, might aspire to achieve middle-class status. Such an affiliation might channel the individual's energy to pursue a higher education and work longer hours than individuals without such goals. The middle class for such an aspirant might be considered an "abstract" or "illusional" collective, because it may not involve actual interactions with other individuals. But membership in a reference group may involve substantive activities—ritual observance with others, choice of mate, way of life, choice of number of children, sexual behavior, even potential martyrdom—or just a sense of symbolic commonality with others with whom one may have no contact but who share a commitment.

Increase in Knowledge Base, Competency, and Status

The function of the group—primary or reference—might serve to enhance the individual's knowledge base or professional status. A community of scholars, professionals, or even hobbyists or enthusiasts might meet to share ideas or might publish their ideas and argue over points of controversy in letters to the editor. They might enhance their careers by publishing a set number of papers and achieving recognition in the field, or they might lose status if their findings were discredited or dismissed by persons whose ideas were accepted as current wisdom or who controlled research funding.

The Group as a Power Base

Any reference or primary group could also decide that its ideas were important enough to influence others outside the group. Ludwig Gumplowicz (in Timasheff, 1961) viewed social and cultural evolution as a product of the struggle between social groups, with the individual being a product of the group with which he or she identified. In a sense, the founders of the American Constitution and the writers of *The Federalist Papers* envisioned such a situation when they diverged from the current European political theories with regard to ideal forms of government and political parties. European theorists had stated that a republican form of a government was suitable only for small states, whereas large nations were best governed by monarchies. Political and religious factions were considered devisive, symbolic of disunity, and therefore not tolerable. Voltaire, for example, no friend of the Catholic Church, still felt that it should be retained as the sole religious institution in France in order to satisfy the people's religious needs without any squabbling between sects. Jefferson and Adams, on the other hand, felt that the power of the executive and the regime could be held in check by balancing it with the selfish interests of those with different regional, religious, economic, and political ideologies, to the benefit of the entire populace. The American people have seen an open avowal of the importance of block voting, especially since the civil rights movement in the 1960s, with political analysts assessing the impact on any given issue or election of the Jewish, black, yuppie, women's, Hispanic, and homosexual vote on the local, state, and national level. It is rare that an individual can get into a position where he/she can have an impact by the force of position or influence alone. But as part of a political action group, such persons can feel that their interests are being served and furthered and that they can have an impact on the kind of environment their children will live in. To quote Gumplowicz (in Timasheff, 1961):

> Society was the sum total of conflicting groups, each group being centered around one or more common interests. Everywhere men feeling themselves closely bound by common interests endeavor to function together as units in the struggle for domination. (p. 62)

According to Spencer's view of social Darwinism, society is a rather vague universe of social groups in conflict (in Timasheff, 1961). Radical feminists have attempted to raise awareness of the link between individual problems and societal inequities by coining the phrase "The personal is political" and writing books like *Sexual Politics* (in Baker, 1982, p. 324). In similar fashion, black poets like Gwendolyn Brooks raised the eyebrows of some more radical writers and critics by writing poetry about nature and reflecting on personal feelings in a time of revolution.

Survival Issues

Group involvement may go beyond power and influence and may include survival issues as well. Jewish efforts to ransom fellow Jews throughout the ages or to find countries of refuge for those fleeing the Holocaust; the involvement of blacks with the Underground Railroad; Indians' unification of one-time warring clans into defensive confederations in the 19th century; underground resistance efforts throughout Europe during the Third Reich were all concerned with physical survival as well as with the quality of existence. What the individual was not able to do alone or in small groups, he or she could sometimes accomplish in larger groups. Often there was a sense of individual sacrifice for the continued survival of the group. Ironically, there is a commonality of guilt feelings among survivors of natural and human catastrophes—survivors of Hiroshima and Nagasaki, of the Holocaust, and even among blacks who made it out of the ghetto and achieved some level of prosperity (Devore, 1983), which has also at times provided a meaningful basis for group formation.

The Relationship between Individual and Group

We have discussed the difference between primary and reference groups in terms of the degree of contact of the membership. In fact, a whole range of relationships are possible between the individual and the group.

The individual may be part of a group by birth. Such an identity may be welcomed, passively accepted, ignored, hated, or eschewed. By and large people are born into a certain gender, nation, region, race, religion, socioeconomic class, ethnic group, and family. Certain of these labels are more stubbornly intrinsic than others, and, depending on the society, their impact is variously felt. Relatively few people change their gender or are born with ambiguous gender, but individuals can variously celebrate, accept, or struggle against biological and social sex roles. Currently in the United States the overlap of sex roles is increasing, and men and women feel more comfortable in roles previously reserved for the opposite sex. Serious female writers like George Eliot or George Sand often used a male pseudonym or an outrageous masculine bearing to win acceptance in the 19th century; such ploys are now unnecessary. Among the Apache, the trials of manhood were so difficult that males who felt sure of failure withdrew into the women's houses. Currently it is considered neither unmasculine to be nurturing nor unfeminine to enter the world of the professions or even of hard physical labor, or to run a marathon.

People can leave a country of origin and repatriot themselves. But some countries (like Greece and certain Eastern bloc nations) will not recognize repatriation and will lay claims on their exiles should they return for a visit. On the other hand people may choose to keep alive their national origins by forming groups of ex-patriots to maintain language, culture, or even political aims. In spite of the efforts of some immigrants to melt into the mainstream and become indistinguishable from all other Americans, ethnics in this country increasingly feel comfortable with hyphenated labels of identification. Estonian-Americans meet in New Jersey every 2 years to celebrate their culinary, musical, and linguistic heritage. Second and third generation Serbian-Americans choose to congregate every month, reserving a whole floor of a hotel where they sing ethnic songs and dance late into the night; for years they segregated themselves into two distinct groups reflecting a split in the Serbian church that had occurred years ago in their country of origin, where this schism is no longer of any significance. Jewish and Moslem Syrian-Americans, by no means numerous in this country, join together in social clubs to celebrate Syrian culture and even invite each other to weddings in spite of political and religious animosities present in their country of origin. Some Cubans in Florida meet to plot the overthrow of Castro and communism and dream of returning to their native land. People may leave the region of their birth, but still retain an accent, a pace of walking and working, a way of interacting with people, a cuisine, even a nostalgia for the natural cycle of the year somewhere else in the world (e.g., a remembrance, in a subtropical climate, of four distinct seasons).

People are born a certain race. Blacks, for example, may celebrate or accept features like skin color and kinky hair or may resort to physical or chemical means of relaxing or "conking" their hair or lightening skin color. If light enough in skin color, they may choose to pass as whites. They may studiously adopt dress, linguistics, housing, and occupational characteristics of the mainstream. Or they may celebrate their origins or attempt to eradicate the pain or shame of slavery by adopting new names, studying old languages, wearing distinctive dress, organizing for political purposes, engaging in artistic interaction and cultural enrichment, and developing new modes of religious expression (e.g., the use of the term *Muslim,* as opposed to *Moslem*). In some areas of the world, like Hawaii, racial and ethnic mixing may be the dominant pattern, whereas in countries like South Africa every effort is made by law to keep not only the "pure races" genetically distinct, but the mixed groups as well.

Individuals may leave one religion for another, though at some periods of European history and in some countries proselytizing individuals for the dominant faith may have been or may currently be a punishable or even a capital offense. The Third Reich demonstrated a willingness to go back five generations in defining Jewishness, even among third- and fourth-generation converts to Christianity (in ironic parallel to definitions of race in this country that labeled 1/32 "black blood" as sufficient lineage to define blackness). Even after conversion, proselytes might still long nostalgically for childhood rituals that they continue to follow in modified form. In many countries the Catholic Church utilized many reframed pagan elements of native religions to bridge the gap between faiths. The similarities of pagan gods and Christian saints allowed native populations to feel at home in their new faith.

Schematizing the relationship of individual and group demonstrates that both elements openly or covertly help to determine the criteria and the consequences of membership. The group can require submergence of the individual ego, as in certain cults, and can enforce conformity on a wide scale or just selectively. Eighteenth-century France, for example, had little tolerance for heterodoxy of political and religious ideas but did not seem to mind rather wild expressions of eroticism. Antiabortion advocates in this country might not be interested in any other issues but abortion in defining the basis for their political affiliation.

The group can demand exclusivity of membership. Most Western religions, for example, view membership in several religions as problematic whereas Oriental religions, like Hinduism and Buddhism, do not. The group could even encourage membership in a wide variety of other groups and/or tolerate and encourage a wide divergence of opinion and behavior (e.g., The League of Women Voters).

The individual may welcome the submergence of ego and conformity with group norms or may pretend to conform and secretly follow his or her own path. Such a stance is particularly common in cases where open adherence to a forbidden group would be met with discrimination, persecution, or death, such as with Maranos and Moriscos of 15th- through 17th-century Spain and Portugal and their territories, or with the Masons in 18th-century Europe.

The individual may follow a mode of passive resistance, either subtly going against group norms or turning the aggression inwardly in a mode of self-hatred or self-destruction. He or she may assertively try to change the system from within (e.g., recent radical Dutch Catholic theologians, members of the charismatic movement, or members of the National Association for the Advancement of Colored People) or may accept exile or willingly leave the group to start a reform movement. Or the individual can remain peripheral to the group (such as in the Spanish literary character of the picaro) or accept the role of nonconformist, loner, or even pariah.

What complicates this analysis is that the individual holds membership, inescapably and by choice, in a variety of primary and reference groups, each providing a different relationship, which is frequently dynamic rather than static in nature. Even a single term, such as *homosexual,* is deceptively complex. Greek culture distinguishes several types of single-sex erotic affiliations, each having a separate name. A recent American study (Bell & Weinberg, 1978) defined several varieties of homosexuality—for example, in terms of polygamous or monogamous life-style—with overlapping memberships. Historically, male and female homosexuality have not received the same kind of treatment. Biblically, male homosexuality was ostensibly a capital offense, whereas female homosexuality was not even mentioned; nor, for example, in contemporary America do gay men and women behave identically. Jewish and Catholic homosexuals might have different interests depending on their backgrounds and their degree of identification with their religions of origin. At certain life-stages American Catholic homosexuals who are native-born function in ways that are psychologically different from the patterns of Catholic homosexuals from areas in Latin America or the Mediterranean basin, where, for example, the unavailability of women during early adulthood makes homosexual behavior at this life-stage more often the norm than the exception. Yet all these diverse homosexual elements might join together politically in a given local or even a national campaign to win rights for themselves and other groups and/or to elect candidates sympathetic to their cause. A homosexual political conservative might be viewed as a traitor to the cause or a welcome sign of the diversity of the group and the transcendence of stereotyping.

INDIVIDUALISM, UNIVERSALITY, AND GROUP IDENTITY AND THERAPY IN THEORY AND PRACTICE

How therapy should deal with this complexity is a difficult subject, but worthy of consideration. Freud chose Oedipus as a paradigm for what he felt was a universal aspect of human behavior. Diderot in 18th-century France, in *Le Rêve d'Alembert* had one of his characters note that it was common knowledge that if a boy of 6 had the strength of a man of 30, he would kill his father and marry his mother. In the Bible, one of Jacob's sons and one of David's sons seduced the concubines of their respective fathers. Jung spoke of the collective unconscious as a universal substratum of individual consciousness, and Frazer and later Stith Thompson among many others noted similarities of folk themes in peoples around the world. Authors ranging from William Butler Yeats to D. H. Lawrence to T. S. Eliot to James Joyce used such images in efforts to raise their works to a level that could be appreciated by all people. Whether of a Freudian or Jungian bent, similarities of dream content seemed to reinforce these universalist notions. Given the devastating impact of chauvinism and religious intolerance in world history, nationalism and ethnicity could be viewed as devisive forces in the world, motivating human catastrophes like World Wars I and II. Oriental philosophies tended to diminish the importance of individual peculiarities of birth and acculturation in favor of an intellectual process of spiritual liberation. Similar efforts were undertaken in encounter groups. Utopian ideals of peace and brotherhood were embodied in the notion of "citizens of the world." The political cartoonist Herblock epitomized this ideal in his acknowledgment of the stature of Albert Einstein, upon the latter's death. He portrayed the earth set in the heavens with a sign on it covering many nations—"Albert Einstein lived here."

Even so, Einstein inescapably came from a given background that influenced his writings in specific ethnic, political, and social issues. Freud's works are currently being challenged in part for their insensitivity to or vagueness on issues involving women and/or for being culture-bound responses to Austrian Victorian society and its sexually repressed, male-dominated nuclear family structure. Moreover, in nations all over the world, individuals are seeking a divergence of group identity to answer particular needs. The unit of politics that seems to function well for most people is the nation-state. Yet nations group themselves in alliances that have psychological as well as political significance (e.g., The Third World, The

Organization of African States, the European Common Market, The Warsaw Pact). Within nations there has been a resurgence of interest in cultural and religious and sometimes in political ethnicity that was first met with hostility and now is accepted with tolerance (at least on the cultural and religious level) in countries as diverse as the United States, Poland, Turkey, Israel, and Ghana. An individual in such a country might become involved predominantly in progress and well-being for self and family; for an ethnic, religious, or political group; or for his or her nation or association of nations; and the person might get along variously well or be in conflict with other apparently similar individuals who place their emphasis on a different level of individual or group affiliation.

There has been a rapid increase in the number of articles written on the demands of doing therapy with ethnic minorities, as well as with women, particularly during certain times of stress (e.g., after rape, mastectomy, or gynecological surgery), and with homosexuals. Therapy groups are organized according to the homogeneity of certain key experiences or backgrounds of their members to underscore the importance of this commonality in the interaction process. The self-help movement recognizes the importance of such commonality in the manner that individuals in the group progress being recipients of help to becoming helpers and leaders of new members. An individual may confront a therapist with the statement: "You don't know what I feel, you've never been [raped, black, poor, divorced, etc.]," as a resistance maneuver or as a test of a therapist's sympathy or mettle. There is a value in allowing abusive parents to meet with each other so that they can recognize each other's difficulties and support each other's progress in parenting skills. Likewise, the parents of murder victims, the mothers of children killed by drunk drivers, or the children of Holocaust survivors can benefit from getting together to discuss similarities of feeling.

Clinicians have to recognize that individual clients come from a variety of contexts with levels of importance unique to each person. A systems approach sensitizes the professional to such contexts, for example, the possibility that Costa Rican machismo might allow for a man to cook a meal for his family whereas Mexican machismo might not; or that a hysterectomy may evoke different responses from white and black males or from blacks of different classes.

CONCLUSION

What this chapter may imply then is that in accepting a given client's individuality, the clinician must become sensitized to the impact of group identity and membership as the client perceives it. In the era of social change in the late 1950s and the 1960s, it became fashionable to emphasize humanness and universality and to discount the impact of particularisms as being superficial and nonessential to character. A person might have said, "In our conversation I was so impressed with your political views [or the oedipal basis for your neuroses], that I didn't notice that you were a [woman, black, amputee, etc.].'' It might be possible now, without losing this vision of the universal in the individual, to put his or her group membership into a perspective that enriches the notion of the complex human personality and thereby facilitates the therapy process.

REFERENCES

Baker, A. J. (1982). The problem of authority in radical movement groups: A case study of lesbian-feminine movements. *Journal of Applied Behavioral Science, 18,* 323–341.

Bell, A. P., & Weinberg, M. S. (1978). *Homosexualities: A study of diversity among men and women.* New York: Simon & Schuster.

Bittner, E. (1963). Radicalism and the organization of social movements. *American Sociological Review, 28,* 28–40.

Delgado, R. (1980). Limits of prosletyzing. *Society, 17,* 25–33.

Devore, W. (1983). Ethnic reality: The life model and work with black families. *Social Casework, 64,* 525–531.

Etzioni, A. (1968). *The active society.* New York: The Free Press. 32, 98.

Festinger, L. (1954). A theory of social comparison processes. *Human Relations, 7,* 117–140.

Galanter, M., Babkin, R., Babkin, J., & Deutsch, A. (1979). The moonies: A psychological study of conversion and membership in a contemporary religious sect. *American Journal of Psychiatry, 136,* 165–170.

Hargrove, B. (1980). Evil eyes and religious choices. *Society, 17,* 20–24.

Ridgeway, L. C. (1982). Status in groups: The importance of motivation. *American Sociological Review, 47,* 76–88.

Timasheff, N. S. (1961). *Sociological theory* (pp. 62, 70). New York: Random House.

Ungerleider, J. T., & Wellisch, D. K. (1979). Coercive persuasion (brainwashing), religious cults and deprogramming. *American Journal of Psychiatry, 136,* 279, 281.

The Adjustment Disorder Syndrome

The previous sections of this book were devoted largely to an account of the varieties of stressors and to a description of the vulnerabilities and ego strengths associated with these stressors. It seems appropriate to follow this with a review of what is known about the Adjustment Disorders. Oddly enough, these illnesses are among the most commonly diagnosed within the practice of psychiatry and are among the most effectively treated. Many people come for professional attention in the wake of some highly disturbing and stressful experience, and the sequence that follows is not unfamiliar. The doctor quite correctly diagnoses an Adjustment Disorder of some type: The patient attends a few sessions, feels better, and withdraws from treatment. That is a usual profile of events.

Yet despite the frequency with which they are diagnosed and treated, very little has been written about these disorders. We became all too aware of that aspect of the field when one potential author after another was unable to accept an assignment to write about some aspect of Adjustment Disorder. The explanation offered was always the same, namely, that there was so little literature about the syndrome. So we offer a less than complete account of the condition and some of its variants as they occur in childhood and adulthood; we are by no means content with this state of affairs, but until additional literature develops, we must confine ourselves to what is available.

— CHAPTER 29 —

Disturbances of Conduct Following Stress

CHARLES KEITH, MD

AGGRESSIVE RESPONSES TO STRESS

Aggressiveness that may lead to hostile, antisocial behavior appears to be a frequent, if not universal, reaction to severe stress. Follow-up studies of human reactions to a wide range of severe stressors indicate that aggressive hostile urges, wishes, fantasies, and behavior are basic organismic responses to high levels of acute and chronic stress (Silver & Wortman, 1980; Weiss & Payson, 1967). Though this spectrum of hostile aggressiveness did not become one of the DSM-III criteria for the diagnosis of Posttraumatic Stress Disorder, some of the symptoms that were included, such as startle reactions, are probably nascent aggressive responses (American Psychiatric Association, 1980).

One explanation for this almost universal hostile-aggressive response to stress is that it represents a derivative of a basic biological defense whereby cells and organisms attack and protect themselves in the face of assaults by stimuli. The sequence of stress and excessive stimuli → unpleasure → hostile destructiveness has been observed repeatedly in ethological and laboratory studies of animals. Parens (1979) has used this sequence in his reformulation of psychoanalytic aggressive drive theory to account for much of the hostile destructiveness that appears in the human over and above the personal symbolic meanings of a given stress (such as that exemplified by survivor guilt). The frequency and surprisingly high levels of guilt suffered by stress victims can in part be explained by this surge of hostile aggression.

In fact, arousal itself with little discernible unpleasure has been shown to increase aggressive behavior (Harris & Siebel, 1975). Such diverse situations as riots following athletic contests on the one hand, and bites by household pets following playful roughhousing on the other, attest to the tendency of aggressive-destructive behavior to flow out of increased stimulation.

As noted, stimulation-unpleasure can induce aggressive destructiveness. During human development, anxiety and dread regularly accompany this surge of aggressive destructiveness flowing out of painful excessive stimulation. These affects and urges, in turn, take on symbolic meaning and become integrated into the evolving characterological, defensive, and adaptive personality structure. Subsequent stress tends to dissolve these more abstract, complex defensive and coping mechanisms, resulting in the release of anxiety and a propensity toward more primitive acting (Bellak, 1963; Caplan, 1981; Kinston & Rosser, 1974). The younger the child, the less solidified his or her character structure and hence the greater the proclivity for aggressive acting and conduct disturbance under stress.

Case Vignette

When it became necessary for his mother to enter full-time employment, a 4-year-old boy without previous behavioral problems was placed by his parents in a day-care center. Within a few weeks of entering the new setting, the staff asked for consultation with a therapeutic preschool program because Billy had begun repeatedly striking other children, was angry with the staff, and was refusing to follow rules. The consultant found the day-care setting to be understaffed, with a low teacher-child ratio. The harried teachers could not meet the demands of the many children and morale among the staff was low. Because it was unclear how much of Billy's conduct disturbance was due to the deleterious day-care setting or to his own psychopathology, it was recommended that he enter a therapeutic day school for further evaluation.

On the first day in the therapeutic school, Billy's conduct disturbance did not appear. His angry expressions quickly abated as he began to enjoy working with his teachers and peers. Further evaluation revealed no significant psychopathology. At the conclusion of the study, Billy's parents placed him in an adequately staffed, well-run day-care center. At one year follow-up there had been no recurrence of the conduct disturbance.

Thus, it appears that Billy struck out aggressively because of stress resulting from a lack of appropriate need satisfaction for a child his age. Billy's striking out brought him needed attention; this may confirm Winnicot's suggestion that children who strike out repeatedly against the environment are still actively seeking help, whereas those who have given up and fallen into a state of helplessness may not come to the attention of adults and hence may go untreated (Seligman, 1979).

Aggressive Behaviors in Adolescence

As with younger children, adolescents are prone to utilize aggressive behaviors as sequelae of stress reactions (Andreason & Hoenck, 1982; Andreason & Wasek, 1980). The majority of studies of poststress reactions in adults show that only a small minority develop conduct disturbances. It is a reasonable conclusion that most of the adults investigated in poststress studies appear able to inhibit the behavioral expression of the aggressive response. Lazarus (1983) suggests that with increasing age there is a lessened hostile response to severe stressors.

Life event research suggests that there is an increase in the frequency of stressful life events prior to the onset of conduct disturbances, such as delinquency (Gersten, Langner, Eisenberg, & Orzeck, 1974) and drug abuse in adolescence (Duncan, 1977). Though life event research has been thoroughly critiqued and often criticized (Brown, 1974; Kessler, 1983; Monroe, 1982), clinical experience does support the notion that a cascading of stressors and mounting anxiety lead to a release of latent, more primitive patterns of behavioral discharge.

In an epidemiological survey of young children, Richman (1977) found that behavior disorders increase in direct proportion to the number of stressful life events. Wolfgang and Feriacuti (1967) suggest that in violent urban subcultures the multiplicity of developmental stressors leads to institutionalized patterns of aggression. It is well established that acute and chronic stresses in early childhood due to familial, parental, developmental, genetic, and socioeconomic disturbances result in increased risk (particularly in males) of chronic aggressive behavior and persistent conduct disturbances. This leads into the topic of early-onset conduct disorders which is beyond the scope of this chapter.

STUDIES OF CONDUCT DISTURBANCE FOLLOWING STRESS

To my knowledge, there has been no study of conduct disturbances per se following acutely stressful events. In almost all studies, conduct disturbance is included as one of the panoply of poststress symptomatology. In a study of individuals with Posttraumatic Stress Disorder (PTSD) caused by a variety of stressors, Horowitz, Wilner, Kaltreider, & Alvarez (1980) found the following derivatives of aggression: 80% were easily annoyed; 40% had temper outbursts; 40% complained of frequent arguments and strong urges to break things; and 20% had conscious urges to injure someone. In the following review, conduct disturbance will be regarded in broad perspective with manifestations ranging from hostile wishes and feelings to overt antisocial behavior of a singular, episodic, or continuing nature.

Most investigators believe that poststress conduct disturbances are usually not a simple extension of a previously established Conduct Disorder but may appear de novo following acute stress. Case studies that explore the connection between prestress character structure and poststress symptomatology are infrequent (Furst, 1967; Hendin, Pollinger, Singer, & Ullman, 1981; Krystal, 1968); when the focus is narrowed down to pre- and poststress conduct disturbance, clinical accounts are almost nonexistent. All investigators emphasize that the general, universalistic effects of stress are always expressed within the context of an individual's unique psychobiological response patterns (Ochberg, 1978).

During childhood and adolescence separation pressures are often accompanied by conduct disturbances (Feinstein, 1980). Norwegian boys whose sailor fathers left for extended periods demonstrated more aggressive, disturbed peer interactions than did a father-present control group of boys (Lynn & Sawrey, 1959). Hetherington and Dew (1970) found that adolescent girls from father-absent homes tended to be inappropriately assertive and promiscuous. Rapaport (1984) presented a vignette of a 14-year-old boy who was sent away to school so as not to be in the way while the father remarried. In response to the separation-rejection, the boy began persistently to break school rules and to fight with peers. Winer & Pollock (1980) told of a security guard who repeatedly vandalized cars after he learned that his wife was having an affair and threatened to leave him.

Aftereffects of the Holocaust

Among the multigenerational effects of the Holocaust are conduct disturbances in the children of survivors. In part these are caused by the separation trauma (Sterba, 1968) and the stress symptomatology and guilt of the surviving parents, who, as a result, have difficulty setting appropriate behavioral limits for their children (Sigal, Silver, Rakoff, & Ellin, 1973).

War Combat

The numerous studies of PTSD resulting from war combat emphasize irritability, aggressive-hostile urges, angry outbursts, homicidal urges, and impulsivity as frequent symptoms that often persist for years following combat (Archibald, 1963, 1965; Futterman, 1951; Lidz, 1946). A recent study of Vietnam veterans with PTSD suggest that as many as 25% experienced severe impulsivity often leading to incarceration (Atkinson, 1984). In a way similar to combat soldiers, other victims of war such as children (Fraser, 1973; Schwartz, 1982), military nurses (Smith, 1982), refugees (Kinzie, 1984), and even families of hostages (McCubbin, 1983), experience long-term sequelae of hostile-aggressive urges and behavioral outbursts.

Physical Illness and Trauma

Children of physically ill parents experience high levels of latent aggression (Arnaud, 1959; Friedlander & Viederman, 1982) and may have an increased risk for behavioral disorders (Bonnard, 1964; Rutter, 1966).

As part of the general regression secondary to illness, physically ill children may manifest demanding aggressive behavior (Prugh, 1967). Chronically physically ill children, as a group, have an increased risk of psychiatric disturbance (particularly involving social isolation); despite this, however, they have lower than average levels of behavioral disorder (Breslau, 1985). On the other hand, children who came close to death but survived may have an increased risk of conduct problems due to overprotective, guilty parenting. Hospitalization under 1 year of age appears to have few long-term emotional sequelae. However, hospitalization during the ages of 2 to 4 leads to an increase in conduct disturbances suggesting persistent struggles over autonomy, passivity, and individuation as well as the direct effects of the hospitalization and illness stress (Sigal, 1974). Bradford & Balamaceda (1983) present a case vignette of a 38-year-old woman who for the first time shoplifted and was arrested following her husband's myocardial infarction and her own job layoff. Chronic reactive aggression sometimes results from bodily trauma (Denny-Brown, 1945; Titchener & Ross, 1974). Psychosocial stressors may fuel persistent irritable, aggressive behavior released via disinhibition, as a result of damage to the frontal and temporal brain lobes (Kwentus, Peck, Hart, & Kornstein, 1985).

Psychiatrically Disturbed Parents

Children with a parent who commits suicide are vulnerable to the onset of conduct disturbance following the suicide (Cain & Fast, 1972). However, children of a psychotic parent show surprisingly few conduct disturbances, at least in their earlier years (Sussex, 1963; Sameroff, Barocas, & Seifer, 1984). As the children of a severely mentally ill parent move through the school years, however, the risk of conduct disturbance increases (Rolf, Crowther, Teri, & Bond, 1984; Rosenheck, 1984).

Kidnapping

Terr (1979, 1981) found that 6 of the 23 children in the Chowchilla kidnapping became "mean" and persistently irritable.

Community Disasters

Studies of survivors of floods (Gleser, Green, & Winget, 1981; Newman, 1976; Titchener & Ross, 1976), fires (Lindemann, 1944), tornadoes (Bloch, 1956) and explosions (Leopold & Dillon, 1963; Ploeger, 1972), indicate that common sequelae are persistent irritability, anger, explosive outbursts, and occasional physical violence and delinquency. Several authors suggest that disasters caused primarily by human negligence or error rather than by a natural event such as a flood or earthquake, intensify the poststress rage (Wilkinson, 1983).

Following community disasters, looting is one of the most common conduct disturbances. Although there are no systematic studies of looters, Wolfenstein (1957) suggested the following motivations: the need to replenish emptiness and loss; destruction of social bonds and absence of usual police protection; the belief that fate or God has broken a promise of protection so that the individual is freed from his/her social contract and can break promises to fellow citizens. Survival makes certain individuals, feel absolved of guilt in contrast to experiencing the more common survivor guilt. However, some people who are usually delinquent or irresponsible may become prosocial in the aftermath of a disaster and assist enthusiastically in rescue work (Hill & Hansen, 1962).

Physical Stressors

Several laboratory studies have attempted to show that heat, crowding, and noise increase aggressive behavior in the human. Although results have been mixed, the trend of the findings is to suggest that these physical stressors do increase aggressive tendencies (Parke & Slaby, 1983; Rule & Nesdale, 1975).

CONCLUSION

Because a uniform response to severe stress is aggressive destructiveness, at times resulting in overt conduct disturbance, basic psychobiologic principles are most likely operating. Further understanding of this phenomenon must include consideration of brain physiology and structure involved in aggressive behavior; mediating variables (e.g., affects of anxiety, fear, and rage); general developmental factors (e.g., the timing of stress, levels of cognitive understanding of stressful events, and the ability to tame affects); the individual's unique defensive and coping strategies involving the mastery of stress and hostile aggression; and the meaning, intensity, and duration of the stress in its familial and social context. Although these variables are part of any general discussion of stress-response syndromes, this chapter has attempted to tease out and focus on the destructive aggressive responses as a particularly fruitful avenue for further study.

REFERENCES

Andreasen, N. C., & Hoenk, P. R. (1982). The predictive value of adjustment disorders: A follow-up study. *American Journal of Psychiatry, 139*, 584–590.

Andreasen, N. C., & Wasek, P. (1980). Adjustment disorders in adolescents and adults. *Archives of General Psychiatry, 37*, 1166–1170.

Archibald, H. C., Long, D. M., Miller, C., & Tuddenham, R. D. (1963). Gross stress reaction in combat—A 15-year follow-up. *American Journal of Psychiatry, 119*, 317–322.

Archibald, H. C., & Tuddenham, R. D. (1965). Persistent stress reaction after combat. *Archives of General Psychiatry, 12*, 475–481.

Arnaud, S. H. (1959). Some psychological characteristics of children of multiple sclerotics. *Psychosomatic Medicine, 21,* 8–22.

Atkinson, R. M., Sparr, L. F., Sheff, A. G., White, R. A. F., & Fitzsimmins, J. T. (1984). Diagnosis of posttraumatic stress disorder in Vietnam veterans: Preliminary findings. *American Journal of Psychiatry, 141,* 694–696.

Bellak, L. (1963). Acting out: Some conceptual & therapeutic considerations. *American Journal of Psychotherapy, 17,* 375–389.

Bloch, D. A., Silber, E., & Perry, S. E. (1956). Some factors in the emotional reaction of children in disaster. *American Journal of Psychiatry, 113,* 416–422.

Bonnard, A. (1964). Truancy and pilfering associated with bereavement. In S. Lorand & H. I. Schneer (Eds.), *Adolescents: Psychoanalytic approach to problems and therapy* (pp. 152–179). New York: Harper & Row.

Bradford, J., & Balmaceda, R. (1983). Shoplifting: Is there a specific psychiatric syndrome? *Canadian Journal of Psychiatry, 28,* 248–254.

Breslau, N. (1985). Psychiatric disorder in children with physical disabilities. *Journal of the American Academy of Child Psychiatry, 24,* 87–94.

Brown, G. W. (1974). Meaning, measurement and stress of life events. In B. S. Dohrenwend & B. P. Dohrenwend (Eds.), *Stressful life events: Their nature and effects* (pp. 217–243). New York: Wiley.

Cain, A. C., & Fast, I. (1972). Children's disturbed reactions to parent suicides. In A. C. Cain (Ed.), *Survivors of suicide* (pp. 93–111). Springfield: Charles C. Thomas.

Caplan, G. (1981). The mastery of stress: Psychosocial aspects. *American Journal of Psychiatry, 138,* 413–425.

Denny-Brown, D. E. (1945). Disability arising from closed head injury. *Journal of the American Medical Association, 127,* 429–436.

Duncan, D. F. (1977). Life stress as a precursor to adolescent drug dependence. *International Journal of Addictions, 12,* 1047–1056.

Feinstein, S. C. (1980). Identity and adjustment disorders of adolescence. In H. I. Kaplan, A. M. Freedman, & B. J. Sadock (Eds.), *Comprehensive textbook of psychiatry* (3rd ed., Vol. 3, pp. 2640–2646). Baltimore: Williams & Wilkins.

Fraser, M. (1973). *Children in conflict.* New York: Basic Books.

Friedlander, R. J., & Viederman, M. (1982). Children of dialysis patients. *American Journal of Psychiatry, 139,* 100–103.

Furst, S. S. (1967). *Psychic trauma.* New York: Basic Books.

Futterman, S., & Pumpian-Mindlin, E. (1951). Traumatic war neuroses five years later. *American Journal of Psychiatry, 108,* 401–408.

Gersten, J. C., Langner, T. S., Eisenberg, J. G., & Orzeck, L. (1974). Child behavior and life events. In B. S. Dohrenwend & B. P. Dohrenwend (Eds.), *Stressful life events: Their nature and effects* (pp. 159–170). New York: Wiley.

Gleser, G. C., Green, B. L., & Winget, C. (1981). *Prolonged psychosocial effects of disaster: A study of Buffalo Creek.* New York: Academic Press.

Harris, M. B., & Siebel, C. E. (1975). Affect, aggression and altruism. *Developmental Psychology, 11,* 623–627.

Hendin, H., Pollinger, A., Singer, P., & Ulman, R. B. (1981). Meanings of combat and the development of posttraumatic stress disorder. *American Journal of Psychiatry, 138,* 1490–1493.

Hetherington, E. M., & Dew, J. (1970). Unpublished manuscript, University of Wisconsin.

Hill, R., & Hansen, D. A. (1962). Families in disaster. In G. W. Baker & D. W. Chapman (Eds.), *Man and society in disaster* (pp. 185–221). New York: Basic Books.

Horowitz, M. J., Wilner, N., Kaltreider, N., & Alvarez, W. (1980). Signs and symptoms of posttraumatic stress syndrome. *Archives of General Psychiatry, 37,* 85–92.

Kessler, R. C. (1983). Methodological issues in the study of psychosocial stress. In H. B. Kaplan (Ed.), *Psychosocial stress: Trends in theory and research* (pp. 267–342). New York: Academic Press.

Kinston, W., & Rosser, R. (1974). Disaster effects on mental and physical state. *Journal of Psychosomatic Research, 18,* 437–456.

Kinzie, J. D., Frederickson, R. H., Ben, R., Fleck, J., & Karls, W. (1984). Posttraumatic stress disorder among survivors of Cambodian concentration camps. *American Journal of Psychiatry, 141,* 645–650.

Krystal, H. (1968). *Massive psychic trauma.* New York: International University Press.

Kwentus, J. A., Peck, E. T., Hart, R. P., & Kornstein, S. (1985). Closed head trauma: Psychiatric complications. *Psychosomatics, 26,* 8–17.

Lazarus, R. S., & DeLongis, A. (1983). Psychological stress and coping in aging. *American Psychologist, 38,* 245–254.

Leopold, R. L., & Dillon, H. (1963). Psychoanatomy of a disaster: A long term study of posttraumatic neuroses in survivors of a marine explosion. *American Journal of Psychiatry, 119,* 913–921.

Lidz, T. (1946). Casualties from Guadalcanal: Study of reactions to extreme stress. *Psychiatry, 9,* 193–213.

Lindemann, E. (1944). Symptomatology and management of acute grief. *American Journal of Psychiatry, 101,* 141–148.

Lynn, D. B., & Sawrey, W. L. (1959). The effects of father absence on Norwegian boys and girls. *Journal of Abnormal Social Psychology, 59,* 258–262.

McCubbin, H., & Figley, C. R. (1983). Bridging normative and catastrophic stress. In H. I. McCubbin & C. R. Figley (Eds.), *Stress and the family: Vol. 1. Coping with normative transitions* (pp. 218–228). New York: Brunner/Mazel.

Monroe, S. M. (1982). Assessment of life events: Retrospective vs concurrent strategies. *Archives of General Psychiatry, 39,* 606–610.

Newman, C. J. (1976). Children of disaster: Clinical observations at Buffalo Creek. *American Journal of Psychiatry, 133,* 306–312.

Ochberg, F. (1978). The victim of terrorism: Psychiatric considerations. *Terrorism, 1,* 147–168.

Parke, R. D., & Slaby, R. G. (1983). The development of aggression. In E. M. Hetherington & P. Mussen (Eds.), *Handbook of child psychology* (4th ed., Vol. 4, pp. 547–641). New York: Wiley.

Ploeger, A. (1972). A 10-year followup of miners trapped for two weeks under threatening circumstances. In C. Spielberger & J. Sarason (Eds.), *Stress and anxiety* (pp. 23–28). Washington, DC: Hemisphere Publishing.

Prugh, D. (1967). Children's reactions to illness, hospitalization and surgery. In A. M. Freedman & H. I. Kaplan (Eds.), *Comprehensive textbook of psychiatry* (pp. 1369–1376). Baltimore: Williams & Wilkins.

Rapaport, J. L., & Ismond, D. R. (1984). *DSM III training guide for diagnosis of childhood disorders.* New York: Brunner/Mazel.

Richman, N. (1977). Behavior problems in preschool children: Family and social factors. *British Journal of Psychiatry, 131,* 523–527.

Rolf, J. E., Crowther, J., Teri, L., & Bond, L. (1984). Contrasting developmental risks in preschool children of psychiatrically hospitalized parents. In N. F. Watt, E. J. Anthony, L. C. Wynne, & J. E. Rolf (Eds.), *Children at risk for schizophrenia* (pp. 526–534). New York: Cambridge Press.

Rosenheck, R., & Nathan, P. (1984). Treatment for children of volatile psychotic adults in the adult psychiatric setting. *American Journal of Psychiatry, 141,* 1555–1559.

Rule, B. G., & Nesdale, A. R. (1975). Environmental stressors, emotional arousal & aggression. In I. G. Sarason & C. D. Spielberger (Eds.), *Stress and anxiety* (Vol. 3, pp. 87–103). New York: Wiley.

Rutter, M. (1966). Children of sick parents. *Institute of Psychiatry, Maudsley Monographs No. 16.* London: Oxford University Press.

Sameroff, A. J., Barocas, R., & Seifer, R. (1984). The early development of children born to mentally ill women. In N. F. Watt, E. J. Anthony, L. C. Wynne, & J. E. Rolf (Eds.), *Children at risk for schizophrenia* (pp. 482–514). New York: Cambridge University Press.

Schwartz, R. E. (1982). Children under fire: The role of the schools. *American Journal of Orthopsychiatry, 52,* 409–419.

Seligman, M. (1979). *Helplessness: On depression, development & death.* San Francisco: Freeman Press.

Sigal, J. J. (1974). Enduring disturbances in behavior following acute illness in early childhood: Consistencies in four independent follow-up studies. In E. J. Anthony & C. Koupernik (Eds.), *The child in his family* (Vol. 3, pp. 415–424). New York: Wiley.

Sigal, J. J., Silver, D., Rakoff, V., & Ellin, B. (1973). Some second generation effects of survival of the Nazi persecution. *American Journal of Orthopsychiatry, 43,* 320–327.

Silver, R. L., & Wortman, C. B. (1980). Coping with undesirable life events. In J. Garber & M. Seligman (Eds.), *Human helplessness: Theory & applications* (pp. 279–340). New York: Academic Press.

Smith, J. R. (1982). Personal responsibility in traumatic stress reactions. *Psychiatric Annals, 12,* 1021–1030.

Sterba, E. (1968). Psychotherapy with survivors of Nazi persecution (Discussion of Chapter 8). In H. Krystal (Ed.), *Massive psychic trauma* (pp. 261–263). New York: International Universities Press.

Sussex, J. N., Cassman, F., & Raffel, S. C. (1963). Adjustment of children with psychotic mothers in the home. *American Journal of Orthopsychiatry, 33,* 849–854.

Terr, L. C. (1979). Children of Chowchilla: A study of psychic trauma. *Psychoanalytic study of the child, 28,* 547–623. New Haven: Yale University Press.

Terr, L. C. (1981). Psychic trauma in children: Observations following the Chowchilla school bus kidnapping. *American Journal of Psychiatry, 138,* 14–19.

Titchener, J. L., & Kapp, F. T. (1976). Family & character change at Buffalo Creek. *American Journal of Psychiatry, 133,* 295–299.

Titchener, J. L., & Ross, W. D. (1974). Acute or chronic stress as determinants of behavior, character & neurosis. In S. Arieti & E. B. Brody (Eds.), *American handbook of psychiatry* (Vol. 3, pp. 39–60). New York: Basic Books.

Weiss, R. J., & Payson, H. E. (1967). Personality disorders IV: Gross stress reaction I. In

A. M. Freedman & H. I. Kaplan (Eds.), *Comprehensive textbook of psychiatry* (pp. 1027–1031). Baltimore: Williams & Wilkins.

Wilkinson, C. B. (1983). Aftermath of a disaster: The collapse of the Hyatt Regency Hotel skywalks. *American Journal of Psychiatry, 140,* 1134–1139.

Winer, J. A., & Pollock, G. H. (1980). Adjustment disorders. In H. I. Kaplan, A. M. Freedman, & B. J. Sadock (Eds.), *Comprehensive textbook of psychiatry* (Vol. 2, pp. 1812–1817). Baltimore: Williams & Wilkins.

Wolfenstein, M. (1957). *Disaster.* London: Routledge & Kegan Paul.

Wolfgang, M., & Feriacuti, F. (1967). *The subculture of violence: Toward an integrated theory of criminology.* London: Tavistock.

Psychological Responses to Stress: Work and Academic Inhibition and Withdrawal

JERRY W. JOHNSON, MPA
GLENN SWOGGER, JR., MD

The psychological reactions to stress included under the heading "adjustment disorders"* run the gamut of idiosyncratic behaviors, which vary from individual to individual. They are determined by things such as ego strength, life-cycle considerations, the subject's personal history of coping, and personal life losses.

Adjustment reactions occur in otherwise healthy individuals, including children (Harrison & McDermott, 1980; Quay & Werry, 1972) who are under stress. Such individuals do not have psychopathology. They tend to regress to the general adaptive behaviors classified as neurotic or immature (Campbell, 1981). The psychological responses of withdrawal and inhibition fall into these general categories (Vaillant, 1977). They represent unconscious behaviors that are usually of a temporary nature but that may require professional diagnosis and treatment.

---

*Also called "adjustment disorders" or "transient situational personality disorders" (Campbell, 1981, p. 14). The term "adjustment reactions" will be used in this chapter.

Stress coping possibilities can be viewed in a flight-fight paradigm (see Figure 30.1), they can be analyzed in a psychological defense mechanisms (or adaptive mechanisms) model (Vaillant, 1977) (see Figure 30.2), or they can be shown in a stress response syndrome model (Horowitz, 1985) (see Figure 30.3).

This chapter concerns itself specifically with work and academic inhibition and/or withdrawal.

Fight

Adaptive						Maladaptive
Works	Works excessively	Argues (writes aggressive memos or deflects anger onto family)	Complains excessively	Fights constantly	Causes accidents	Attacks others physically
Sleeps	Sleeps excessively (spends weekends watching TV or sleeping)	Feels hopeless, withdrawn, and inhibited	Avoids work (spends time pursuing other interests)	Quits trying and plateaus out	Is prone to accidents	Experiences physical immobilization due to ill health

Flight

Figure 30.1. Fight/flight responses to stress. Copyright 1989 by The Menninger Foundation. Reprinted by permission.

WORK AND ACADEMIC WITHDRAWAL

The person experiencing withdrawal may present himself as "aloof, detached, disinterested, removed, and apart; he has difficulty in spontaneously initiating or planning with other people. He is unable to mingle freely and communication with others is an effort. He cannot share his experiences with others and even in a group appears to work independently rather than cooperatively" (Campbell, 1981, p. 689).

If the initial stressor is an isolated situation, such as a change in supervisors that causes the individual to feel threatened on the job, withdrawal may be limited to the work environment. The person's behavior outside the work setting may manifest stress in other ways, for example, overprotection and concern about his/her children and their well-being.

Where the stressor is more deep-seated or complex, as may be experienced in dealing with early childhood losses during the mid-life transition, a subject's withdrawal will generally pervade all spheres of life, such as avoidance of meaningful

Level I   Psychotic mechanisms (common in psychosis, dreams, and childhood)
Denial (of external reality)
Distortion
Delusional projection

Level II   Immature mechanisms (common in severe depression, personality
disorders, and adolescence)
Fantasy (schizoid withdrawal, denial through fantasy)
Projection
Hypochondriasis
Passive-aggressive behavior (masochism, turning against the self)
Acting out (compulsive delinquency, perversion)

Level III Neurotic mechanisms (common in everyone)
Intellectualization (isolation, obsessive behavior, undoing, rationalization)
Repression
Reaction formation
Displacement (conversion, phobias, wit)
Dissociation (neurotic denial)

Level IV   Mature mechanisms (common in "healthy" adults)
Sublimation
Altruism
Suppression
Anticipation
Humor

Figure 30.2. Schematic table of adaptive mechanisms. *Source: Adaptation to Life* by George E. Vaillant, 1977, Boston: Little, Brown and Co. Copyright 1977 by George E. Vaillant. Reprinted by permission.

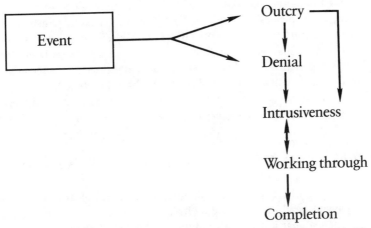

Figure 30.3. Phases of responses after a stressful event. *Source:* "Disasters and Psychological Responses to Stress" by Mardi J. Horowitz, *Psychiatric Annals,* 15(3). Copyright 1985 by SLACK Inc. Reprinted by permission.

relationships, extreme depression, increased use of alcohol or drugs, daydreaming, or excessive sleep. For example, one otherwise successful individual ran marathon distances each and every day. When asked what he was running away from, he said that he and his wife had disagreed about how they should discipline their children. At work, he just wanted to be left alone.

Withdrawal, in the context of an adjustment reaction, will "typically remit when the stressor ceases, or when a new level of adaptation is reached" (Campbell, 1981, p. 14). The manifest reaction to the initial stressor or combination of stressors (such as divorce, marriage, illness or injury, retirement, natural disaster, death of a parent, or a child leaving home) may be subtle or dramatic and pronounced.

Early signs of withdrawal may take on the appearance of healthy adaptation, such as a student's closing the dormitory room door "to get things done." This apparently normal behavior may develop into skipping classes because of tiredness and the need for more sleep.

WORK AND ACADEMIC INHIBITION

Work or academic inhibition may be the result of unresolved superego–id conflict, that is, the individual unconsciously reprocesses the conflict when later situations rekindle the original, repressed feelings. The person experiencing inhibition will exhibit restraint or will lack spontaneity in normal behavioral patterns or activities. The inhibited behavior "is evidence of an *unconscious* defense against forbidden *instinctual* drives" (American Psychiatric Association, 1984, p. 52). Such behavior may be manifested as sexual dysfunction if the person has had prior unsatisfactory sexual experiences, or it may be manifested as fear of public speaking if the inhibited individual is criticized after a speech by a supervisor or teacher.

For example, a sales executive in his late 30s, who spoke regularly to his sales force and to a committee of superiors, was criticized during a group presentation by his new boss, a man about his father's age, whom he saw as being "like my father." This experience brought back strong and painful memories about his father and the manner in which his father used to criticize him. In subsequent presentations, this sales executive became much more formal in his speaking style and less spontaneous during the question-and-answer periods.

COPING AND PROFESSIONAL INTERVENTIONS

The individual who experiences inhibition or withdrawal as a maladaptive response to psychosocial stressors will return to more normal behavior as the stressor remits or when a new level of adaptation is achieved (American Psychiatric Association, 1987). In the example of the student, the individual may adapt by mastering a school subject, thus gaining enthusiasm and confidence to try a different

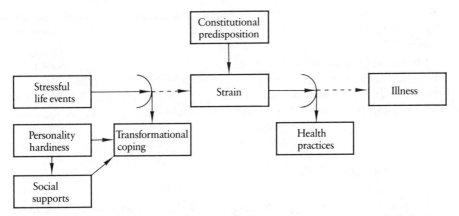

Figure 30.4. Factors affecting health/illness status. *Source: The Hardy Executive: Health Under Stress* by Salvatore R. Maddi and Suzanne C. Kobasa. Copyright 1984 by Dow Jones-Irwin. Reprinted by permission of Brooks/Cole Publishing Co., Pacific Grove, CA 93950.

approach in other classes and with other teachers. In the case of the sales executive, the individual may experience relief from symptoms if he begins to work for a more relaxed and less fatherlike supervisor with a more collegial supervisory style.

The severity and the duration of the reaction is not completely predictable from the severity of the stressor. Individuals who are particularly vulnerable may react with a more severe form of the disorder after only a mild or moderate stressor, whereas others may have only a mild form of the disorder in response to a marked and continuing stressor (American Psychiatric Association, 1987).

Individuals who are experiencing severe or chronic reactions to the stressor may require immediate professional intervention until they can achieve a higher level of adaptation. Treatment possibilities will be discussed in later sections.

Preventing recurrences of episodic stress reactions of inhibition and/or withdrawal should be a goal that is set early in the course of professional intervention. As the stress reaction subsides, the individual can be made more aware of conscious choices for future coping. Maddi and Kobasa (1984) have suggested a model of coping that emphasizes the personal benefits of transformational coping. Exercise and social supports seem to have an especial efficacy in the coping process (Maddi & Kobasa, 1984) (see Figure 30.4).

The mature adaptive mechanisms of Vaillant (1977) (see Figure 30.2) should be considered as another model.* Also included in this group are exercise, team sports, and social group activities (Maddi & Kobasa, 1984). Other adaptive mech-

---

*Each of us has a "profile" of more and less effective adaptive mechanisms which we unconsciously and habitually use in response to stressful situations. This "profile" defines the style and range of an individual's coping capacities.

anisms would be volunteer activities, consciousness-raising readings and seminars, self-relaxation and visualization techniques, technical skills, and stress management training.

Clinical judgment will be needed to determine the severity of the stressor and the extent of the maladaptive response of the individual to the event. Severe or chronic reactions, such as anxiety or depression, to a single stressful event may indicate consideration of a differential diagnosis (American Psychiatric Association, 1987).

DIAGNOSIS

Because work inhibition and withdrawal may be associated with a wide range of syndromes and many etiological factors, diagnosis is always a primary consideration. The nature of stress response disorders is such that a careful diagnostic workup will correspond to a primary mode of therapy: Taking a thorough history will allow for the ventilation of many feelings and for the development of a supportive relationship; these in turn will promote more active and effective coping efforts.

In making a diagnosis of work inhibition or withdrawal due to psychosocial stressors, it is important to consider biological factors, other psychiatric conditions, significant familial events, and the social and cultural context. Even if the necessary diagnostic criteria are present, such as an identifiable psychosocial stressor arising within the past 3 months, followed by the subsequent onset of the work inhibition or withdrawal, the symptoms may nonetheless have other causes. For example, a deterioration in school functioning and/or the appearance of withdrawal in a young student, after a disappointment in love, may in fact represent the onset of a schizophrenic process. Thus, although work inhibition and withdrawal are not entirely diagnoses of exclusion, the astute clinician may be more helpful to the patient and may ultimately prevent a great deal of unnecessary grief by taking a thorough and detailed history and doing a complete diagnostic workup. In addition to having specific psychodynamic roots, work inhibition and withdrawal can also constitute nonspecific responses to a wide variety of medical and psychiatric conditions. In such instances they may function as coping efforts in reaction to the primary illness.

Table 30.1 represents a biopsychosocial perspective on mental health and disease, in which persons are seen as living systems composed of more or less integrated and well-functioning syntheses of elements at several levels. This table serves as a framework for diagnostic thinking, and a checklist for differential diagnosis. The following diagnostic considerations occur at various systems levels.

In general, any sort of impairment of functioning at the biological level, especially if insidious in onset, may first be manifested by behavioral symptoms such as work inhibition or withdrawal. Thus a person may react to the onset of an organically determined impairment of functioning, such as Alzheimer's disease or Huntington's

Table 30.1. Systems Levels Relevant to Differential Diagnosis

Individual	Interpersonal
Genetic	Family
Pathophysiological	Group
Intrapsychic	Organizational
	Sociocultural

chorea, by defensively avoiding tasks, withdrawing from social contact, appearing to be disinterested, or rationalizing a lack of activity. An admixture of depression may be apparent and in some instances the person may appear to be lazy or malingering.

Such a pattern of defensive withdrawal may reflect an unconscious awareness of disability or may result from an effort at conscious concealment. Sometimes these motivations are difficult to untangle, especially if the examiner is perceived as a threat—as someone who will discover and reveal the disability or who will define the social, organizational, legal, or financial response to it. Genetic and other "constitutional" factors, such as temperament, also play a role in determining the suitability of a person for various tasks or roles. If the mismatch is too great, inhibition or withdrawal are possible coping responses.

Other disease entities that involve fatigue and diminution of energy, such as malignancies, unrecognized diabetes, and hypothyroidism, may also provoke concern because of changes in work or social functioning. Many disorders of brain and body functioning may be easily differentiated in their later stages. During the onset or early manifestations of the condition, it may be quite a different matter. It therefore behooves the psychiatric diagnostician to take a careful history, to order appropriate laboratory tests, and to maintain a certain index of suspicion. Only in this way can he or she hope to tease out these problems on the basis of whatever coping behaviors they elicit.

Drug abuse, particularly the continuous use of drugs, may also be associated with work inhibition or withdrawal. Many business organizations are facing the problem of employee drug use during the working day or poor performance as a result of hangover or other aftereffects. So-called amotivational syndromes may appear, in which a complex mixture of drug effects and resocialization into a counterculture may lead to a lack of investment and interest in work or in previously valued social relationships.

In respect to psychiatric syndromes, work inhibition or withdrawal may be an early symptom of a schizophrenic process. Major depressive episodes are often accompanied by disturbances in work and social functioning. In these instances the primary diagnosis is obviously some form of depressive disorder. More subtle and more difficult to diagnose are certain chronic depressive disorders, where constriction of interest, lack of energy, and loss of capacity for enjoyment may first be observed in the form of work inhibition, decrease in previously adequate performance, or social withdrawal. Obsessional disorders may also decompensate into increasing degrees of rumination and passive-aggressive behavior; these too can appear as disturbances in work functioning. Here the chronicity and obsessional quality of the symptoms are distinctive; such decompensation may occur in a person of chronic obsessional character structure in response to a recent stressor or life event.

Episodes of work inhibition and withdrawal that are associated with a recent stressor and thus fit this diagnostic category may be associated with specific psychodynamic conflicts. These conflicts often involve issues of aggression, performance anxiety, and fears of autonomy. Success at work may be experienced as though it were a vengeful triumph over a parent or sibling, associated with feelings of guilt and anxiety; such a constellation will then lead to inhibition or avoidance of work. Real engagement with a significant task, especially a task open to public scrutiny and possible criticism, may be dreaded and avoided because it provokes fears of being put to the test and failing.

Persons affected by such conflict are often enormously energetic at accomplishing trivial tasks that are in some sense ''off-the-record'' or do not lead to any tangible end point. Completing work tasks is a different matter; it may lead to a change in status. Gaining a degree catapults the student out of the university into a new world; receiving a promotion leads to new challenges, and perhaps to relocation. These supposedly desired results may come to be feared because they could lead to a disruption of social ties and dependent relationships. Some of these fears may be quite realistic, since a change in status can indeed lead to altered social support relationships and the disruption of institutional and organizational ties. In other instances, fears of autonomy and aloneness relate more to fantasies (sometimes of grandiose character) of independence and lack of need for others. The following case vignette illustrates some of these psychodynamics, along with their relationship to family dynamics.

A freshman college student was hospitalized because his academic functioning had collapsed, he had become diffusely anxious and panicky, and he had appealed to his family for help. In high school he had been an outstanding student and the apple of his father's eye. His father had encouraged the young man to feel superior to all his friends and had organized much of his own social life around his son. Moreover, the father had expressed grave doubts about how he himself would manage when his son left home for college. The parents' marriage was bleak and beset with long-standing conflicts. At the large college that the student entered, far from being in the limelight, he was merely one among many. In contrast to his easy course through high school, he actually did poorly on his first tests. He became increasingly anxious in test situations and presently developed the additional symptoms that led to his hospital admission.

In this example, there was evidence of more severe psychopathology than could be subsumed under a diagnosis of work inhibition. However, as in cases of work inhibition, fears of autonomy and performance anxiety were clearly apparent. Also apparent was the way in which the student's own psychopathology was nurtured and reinforced by the nature of the family context, in particular by his symbiotic relationship with his father and his concerns about what would happen to his parents if he were to leave home successfully.

Another important dynamic that may underlie instances of work inhibition and especially withdrawal has to do with mourning processes. Uncomplicated, normal grieving is frequently accompanied by some degree of disinterest in the person's surroundings and/or a diminished level of functioning at usual tasks; nonetheless it is considered a separate diagnostic entity. In many cases where work inhibition or withdrawal has been followed by a psychosocial stressor, there is a more subtle experience of loss and mourning.

As Horowitz (1976) has so clearly demonstrated in his work on the stress response syndrome, acute traumata and stressors exert part of their intermediate and long-term impact by depriving people of their sense of self as it existed before the event. Persons who have been robbed and mugged may no longer experience themselves as strong and in control; instead they now feel weak and vulnerable. A driver who has been in an automobile accident may feel guilty and careless, and may no longer be able to maintain his or her previous self-image as skilled and careful. Once criticized, the salesman mentioned earlier felt unaccepted and resentful, rather than confident and friendly, as he had formerly seen himself.

All of these incidents represent losses or gaps in the self-concept, necessitating a process of mourning, repair, and reintegration. This element of mourning and reintegration should always be looked for when a psychosocial stressor leads to work inhibition or withdrawal: These symptoms may be the overt behavioral manifestations of the underlying psychological work that is going on. Although the mourning process is likely to be very clear in response to a major stressor, under many circumstances it may not be obvious. For example, a divorce is often associated with significant disruption in work functioning (mixed at times with compulsive overwork), along with social withdrawal (mixed with social hyperactivity), and all these reactions may be accompanied by episodes of depression and other symptoms.

As exemplified in the brief case described earlier, family dynamics often play a crucial role in intensifying reactions to relatively minor stressors. This fact has important diagnostic and therapeutic implications. A consideration of family dynamics may help the therapist understand the development of work inhibition or withdrawal. Sessions in which the patient sits together with other family members may be of great diagnostic aid in understanding the psychodynamics and family dynamics. Even if for some reason the family cannot be seen, and diagnosis and treatment are to be carried out on an individual basis, an awareness of the family system is usually essential. It provides the framework for therapeutic interventions.

The person's organizational context, the milieu within which he or she works, also deserves attention. What is the prevailing level of morale in the workplace? Is the employer organization undergoing rapid change? Are there any threats of job loss? How clearly defined is the person's task? In our consultation programs for executives and managers, we sometimes see poorly functioning individuals whose work roles are unclear. In these situations of "role conflict" or "role ambiguity," as they are called, the organization may manifest a considerable degree of ambivalence about whether it really wants the task done as stated; this ambivalence may in turn be internalized by the affected employees, thus forming the basis of work inhibition or withdrawal.

A manager was seen in consultation because of his poor performance and lack of engagement with his work tasks. He was the quality control manager in his organization, but he had been moved to a small office in a building separate from the production facility. His employer was a company that was primarily engaged in producing large quantities of a product in a competitive market. The organization seemed to be giving him two contradictory messages: "Do your job as directed, but don't interfere with production or deadlines!" The manager had difficulty challenging this implicit directive, getting clarification of his role, and recognizing the implications of the treatment he received. He responded by functioning poorly.

In other instances, group dynamic processes within a work group may paralyze an individual who acts as the container for a significant conflict within the group.

In exploring work inhibition and withdrawal, clinicians must take into account the person's identity and role expectations as a member of other social groups. Gender, race, ethnicity, religion, peer group membership, and generational cohort may all involve role expectations that conflict with those in the work setting. Values, attitudes toward authority, expectations about interpersonal closeness or distance, patterns of communication, and work ethic may vary. Work inhibition or social withdrawal may reflect confusion, embarrassment, uncertainty, value conflicts, or lack of understanding of what roles are appropriate or of the competency needed to exercise those roles. Withdrawal or apparent disinterest represents flight from the work role and/or its concomitant social relationships.

There are also changes over time in the social and cultural meanings of work and sociability. Work is imbued with values and meanings that may be valid at one time and place, but that may subsequently change. Attitudes toward the future, and the meaning of one's own work in relation to what one can expect of the future, may also change. The present degree of social change and turbulence and the diffuse sense of threat in our society may have led some people to withdraw from commitments or to experience conflicts about full involvement in future-oriented work activities. Such conflicts would manifest themselves as work inhibition or diffuse withdrawal.

THERAPY

As stated before, the diagnostic process also initiates therapy. Appropriate therapy depends on understanding the significant elements at various systems levels and the ways in which they are intertwined. In the course of a diagnostic process, conditions other than work inhibition or withdrawal will sometimes be discovered; their treatment will not be discussed here. The emphasis here will be on intervention at the level of individual and family psychodynamics, and the ways in which intervention at these levels can take into account organizational and sociocultural factors.

The basic process in work inhibition and withdrawal involves disruption of a previous level of functioning, often with some degree of regression in the overall level of adaptation accompanied by elements of mourning and reintegration. Therefore, the basic orientation of therapeutic endeavors should be toward interventions that will assist the inherent processes of reintegration and make for a resumption of higher level functioning. We suggest the following:

1. Brief individual or family therapy should be instituted, with an orientation toward those issues involved in the immediate problem.

2. A primary focus should be placed on improving the person's efforts to deal with the original stressor, through ventilation of feelings regarding the experience, clarification of its meaning, impact on the self-concept, identification of adaptive styles that have been brought into play as well as possible alternatives, and promotion of the mourning/reintegration process.

3. To the extent that the stressor and subsequent reactions have disrupted supportive social networks, efforts to repair or replace them must be promoted. The relationship with the therapist itself provides extremely valuable support. Usually, however, the development of social supports should not end there. The therapist may want to help the patient work out breaches in family or marital relationships, and resume or develop relationships with allies, peers, mentors, or teachers in work or school settings. In situations where a person is a member of a group facing a common problem, such as a woman in a management setting, contact with other women in similar roles from the same or other companies may be extremely useful. In some instances, the therapist may need to help the patient overcome inner resistances and a reluctance to engage in such contacts.

4. If the systems approach as outlined here is valid, then the value of cognitive reappraisal of the work-inhibited or withdrawn person's situation should not be underestimated. Exploration of the organizational context with the help of the therapist, for example, not only allows assessment of organizational realities and pressures, but also gives the patient a chance to disentangle the web of his or her own contributions to the problem from the labyrinth of organizational realities. This learning experience is crucial and necessary in such psychotherapy, because there is often a "fit" or "valence," as Bion put it (Rioch, 1970), between individual characteristics and group and organizational pressures. An improved assessment of the mix of individual and organizational contributions to the problems at hand may then be used to

plan further steps. Should a person leave a work or school setting because it is inappropriate for his or her needs? Should the patient confront an authority within the organization with the problems as he or she understands them and discuss the situation with a view to making some appropriate change? Does the person need to change his or her own behavior in some way or to take some other action? These questions require an accurate assessment of organizational and sociocultural as well as individual and family dynamics.

REFERENCES

American Psychiatric Association. (1984). *Psychiatric glossary*. Washington, DC: Author.
American Psychiatric Association. (1987). *Diagnostic and statistical manual of mental disorders* (3rd ed.-Rev.; DSM-III-R). Washington, DC: Author.
Brown, M. (1977). *Psycho-diagnosis in brief*. Dexter, MI: Huron Valley Institute.
Campbell, R. J. (1981). *Psychiatric dictionary* (5th ed.). New York: Oxford University Press.
Harrison, S. I., & McDermott, J. F., Jr. (Eds.). (1980). *New directions in childhood psychopathology: Vol. 1. Developmental considerations*. New York: International Universities Press.
Horowitz, M. J. (1976). *Stress response syndromes*. New York: Aronson.
Horowitz, M. J. (1985). Disasters and psychological responses to stress. *Psychiatric Annals* (Vol. 15, No. 3). Thorofare, NJ: Slack.
Maddi, S. R., & Kobasa, S. C. (1984). *The hardy executive: Health under stress*. Homewood, IL: Dow Jones-Irwin.
Quay, H. C., & Werry, J. S. (Eds.). (1972). *Psychopathological disorders of childhood*. New York: Wiley.
Rioch, M. J. (1970). The work of Wilfred Bion on groups. *Psychiatry, 33,* 56–66.
Vaillant, G. E. (1977). *Adaptation to life*. Boston, MA: Little, Brown.

Adjustment Reactions: The Psychotic Syndrome

SHERMAN C. FEINSTEIN, MD
RANDY KETTERING, PhD
MARTIN HARROW, PhD

Psychological response forms to life stressors include neurosis, conduct disturbance, work or academic inhibition, behavioral withdrawal, and psychosis. Just as the term *stress* has come to take on manifold meanings since Selye's (1956) study, so too the term *psychosis* has led to much confusion among mental health professionals. Menninger, Mayman, and Pruyser (1963) have warned that the use of the term may incorrectly imply a specific disease rather than a description of various forms of the "penultimate stage of organismic disequilibration and disorganization" (p. 260). In this chapter we consider an acute psychotic reaction to be an altered state of consciousness involving gross reality distortions, with marked regression in object relations, fragmentation of the self experience, dissolution of executive functions of the ego accompanied by a disorder of thinking and feeling, and a response to the demand for coping with a large variety of stressors.

An individual's ability to cope with a stressful life event or internal psychic conflict depends on the vulnerability of the personality in the face of the intensity of perceived stress. Perception of an event can be modified by neurophysiological processes as well as by ego defenses. Psychoses, therefore, may occur as the result of (1) an aberrant neuroendocrinological response produced by genetic abnormality; (2) drug toxicity, due to mind-distorting drugs; (3) physical illness, including brain tumor; (4) developmental stresses occurring in psychologically vulnerable individuals; or (5) conflicting life situations. Psychosis can be characterized as an extreme state of personality disorganization with organic and emotional components, in which the individual's ability to interpret reality in a comprehensible manner and behave adaptively is impaired. The altered state of consciousness that accompanies the personality disorganization may last a variable period of time, and sometimes its expression may be consciously controlled.

Bleuler (1950) defined psychosis as a complicated structure that can manifest itself in different states at different times. These states and behavioral presentations were formerly taken to be the disease process itself, presupposing different etiologies for different components of psychotic disorganization: impaired emotional relationships characterized by aloofness or preoccupation and exaggeration; pervasive affectively charged states; disturbances in sensory perception; bizarre, incomprehensible behavior and mobility patterns; autistic resistance to change; outbursts of intense anxiety and panic; impairment in the sense of identity; interferences with intellectual development; and delusional preoccupations, hallucinations, and acute discharge of sexual and aggressive impulses.

LITERATURE REVIEW

Two major conceptualizations of psychosis as a syndrome manifesting cognitive, behavioral, and emotional dysfunction are emphasized in the literature (Oltmanns & Maher, 1988; Strauss, 1969). The *categorical* conceptualization regards alterations of consciousness to be phenomena that are qualitatively distinct from the ideational products and perceptual phenomena of normal experience (Jaspers, 1963; Kraepelin, 1919/1968; Mayer-Gross, Slater, & Roth, 1950). For example, Jaspers distinguished three categories of psychopathologic phenomena within the realm of ideation: delusions, delusionlike ideas, and overvalued ideas. The latter two were considered to be comprehensible extensions of more normal ideas that arose out of a state of exaggerated affect. Delusions were considered to be constructions that attempted to describe a fundamental, pathological, subjective experience.

The *continuum* view considers delusions and hallucinations to be only quantitatively exaggerated forms of normal phenomena, and not based on some experience that is consensually incomprehensible (Arlow & Brenner, 1964; Bleuler, 1974; Menninger et al., 1963; Sullivan, 1953; Schafer, 1968). Cross-sectional investigation of beliefs and sensory experiences in psychotic patients (Strauss, 1969) and college students (Bowers, 1974; Chapman & Chapman, 1980) support the continuum notion of psychotic phenomena. Recent studies involving detailed analysis of major dimensions of delusions also provide general support of a continuum viewpoint (Harrow, Rattenbury, & Stoll, 1988; Hole, Rush, & Beck, 1979; Kendler, Glazer, & Morgenstern, 1983; Kettering, 1984; Rudden, Gilmore, & Frances, 1982). Longitudinal studies of delusions, and research on the onset of delusions and recovery from them, can be interpreted from several viewpoints. However, they best fit in with a continuum viewpoint (Bowers, 1974; Carr, 1983; Docherty, Van Kammen, Siris, & Marder, 1978; Harrow, Carone, & Westermeyer, 1985; Harrow & Silverstein, 1977; McGlashan, Levy, & Carpenter, 1975; Sacks, Carpenter, & Strauss, 1974).

In the Chapman (1980) study, the judgment by college students about the degree of psychosis attributable to a variety of experiences reported by subjects, identified for universal ideas, beliefs, and experiences, varied reliably according to changes in both the qualitative content of the idea (bizarreness) and the individual's commitment to the idea. In earlier but complimentary studies concerning the onset of psychosis, J. Chapman (1966) and Bowers (1974) observed that alterations in visual perception occurred prior to the onset of a psychotic experience. Chapman (1966) noted that as various perceptual phenomena were continuously experienced by patients, they developed less rational and eventually unrealistic or bizarre explanations for them. This formulation has become an important one in the field, although it can be questioned by data showing similar attentional and perceptual difficulties in disturbed patients who did not develop psychotic activity (Freedman & Chapman, 1973; Harrow, Tucker, & Shield, 1972).

More recently, the continuum conceptualization of psychotic phenomena has been advanced with respect to disordered thinking considered from a longitudinal and developmental frame of reference (Harrow, Lanin-Kettering, Prosen, & Miller, 1983; Harrow & Prosen, 1979). Feinstein and Miller (1979) used this model to discuss psychotic reactions in adolescence, differentiating between stress-induced transitional psychotic states and schizophrenia.

PSYCHOTIC PROCESS

An individual possessing either fragile character defenses or a neuroendocrinological vulnerability can respond to the configuration of forces experienced as stress in a manner that precipitates a psychotic reaction. The development and maintenance of psychotic symptoms is a result of the variability in the integrative functions of the ego as it attempts to master this configuration of forces.

The vulnerability can be demarcated into a number of steps. The first involves the reemergence of intrapsychic conflicts concerning the expression of erotic or aggressive impulses that have been previously managed and maintained in psychic equilibrium. This rekindled conflict precipitates a profoundly disturbing "organismic panic" that characterizes the subjective experience of anxiety that emerges. As a consequence of this intense panic, a transient paralysis of the integrative, executive functions of the ego occurs, resulting in a loss of the subjective experience of self-continuity and sameness. This panic gradually diminishes as the ego struggles to construct a best possible solution for resolving the encountered conflict. This solution may serve both as an explanation of the disruption in self-continuity and as a prophylaxis against the recurrence of a similar conflictual crisis situation. The final stage of the psychotic process occurs as a consequence of the person's having undergone numerous disorganizing experiences of ego paralysis and reorganization. In this stage, the previously held explanations become more cognitively refined, crystallized, and integrated into the reorganization of the self as a psychotic self-identity.

Psychotic symptoms are observed to wax and wane during an acute psychotic reaction as both the internal and external adaptive situations change. This situational change modifies the information that must necessarily be integrated into the "best possible solution" of the conflict. The resulting symptoms may include pervasive feelings of sadness, bizarre or excessive overactivity, autistic regression, extreme self-absorption, delusional preoccupation, hallucinations, and the acute discharge of sexual and aggressive impulses in an inappropriate manner. These symptomatic reactions occur because the perceived stressor causes the individual to experience actual or potentially intolerable episodes of helpless self-disintegration. The ensuing behaviors become adaptive attempts to reconstitute the personality and represent strategies for coping with a specific stressful event or situation. Each person, however, may tend to assume a certain characteristic symptom picture (hebephrenic, catatonic, paranoid, simple) from one episode of disturbance to the next, which reflects the person's premorbid character organization and strategies for adaptation.

STRESS AND THE COURSE OF PSYCHOSIS

With regard to the course of psychosis and psychotic symptoms, the subjective experience of delusional belief or hallucinatory perception varies during the numerous phases of the illness. During the acute phase, the experience is primarily one of disorganizing panic, a dreamlike state of consciousness during which the person's capability of recognizing the deviant nature of the psychotic symptoms is diminished because of the intensity of the emotional upheaval.

This causes the sense of self-continuity to be less frequently disrupted, and permits the opportunity for a "new self" to be experientially constructed, integrating the delusional material into the old self-identity, and thereby diminishing the ego-dystonic nature of the experience. Yet, because the ego functions have not regained their equilibrium, increases in either internal or external stress can transiently disrupt the stability of the newly established sense of self. The repeated disorganization forces the person to retrench and reconsider the preformed delusional ideas, increasing the fixity and conviction about symptoms beyond that provided by the "historical truth" (Freud, 1938/1964; Frosch, 1967) of the thematic content and the experience of earlier ego states. The chronic phase of the illness is a time when the belief about the psychotic idea or experience is no longer amenable to change. By this time, ego functions have stabilized and the experience of organismic panic has subsided.

THERAPEUTIC APPROACHES

General Considerations

Adequate treatment of the psychotic syndrome consists of (1) reducing stress; (2) altering perception of stress by providing emotional support so that the stress, although still perceived, is not felt to be persecutory; and (3) providing a biochemical dampener to the stress response. Furthermore, because the symptomatic responses of the patient evoke more stress-producing environmental reactions, interruption of this feedback mechanism becomes necessary, or the resulting emotional surrender may leave the patient totally helpless.

Any treatment approach to the psychotic disorders depends on various genetic factors that influence the process and course of the illness. The prepsychotic personality with its developmental experiences and deficits, both emotional and neurobiological, demands a frame of reference related to the idiosyncrasies of the patient and his or her social environment. Various life-stages present certain specific stresses and require particular therapeutic approaches appropriate to the individual, familial, peer, vocational, and/or educational needs of the person. Pubescence, separation from or loss of meaningful others, and sexual experimentation can all contribute to the onset of the process. Separately or together, they serve as major adoptive contexts that must be mastered and that may require enormous modifications in intrapersonal and interpersonal operations. Finally, the altered state of consciousness brings with it a degree of destructuring. A typical clinical pattern of central nervous system malfunction follows, which requires supportive and pharmacological care related to the protection of the individual's psychic and physical function.

When psychosis appears during puberty, specific therapeutic problems must be considered. One of these is aberrant response to tranquilizers. Puberty produces significant endocrinological and biochemical changes that are at their maximum for a period of some 3 years. During this interval, adolescents appear to react differently from adults to a variety of psychopharmacotherapeutic agents, particularly phenothiazines, amphetamines, and antidepressants (Feinstein & Miller, 1979).

For example, over a 2-year period, a 15-year-old schizophrenic girl, who was also diabetic, was treated in the same clinical setting on three separate occasions with adult-adequate doses of phenothiazine. The first two attempts at treatment produced no remission of her psychosis. The first course of treatment was administered when she was 13; the next, 1 year later; and the final course, 9 months later. The last dosage schedule, begun when it was apparent that she was approaching psychological maturity, resulted in remission 6 weeks later.

Hospitalization

Disturbed patients are often psychiatrically hospitalized because of the social problems observed or deduced by others. There are two additional indications for hospital treatment of acute psychotic reactions: a pathological intrafamilial home environment that inhibits all potentiality for growth and emotional support; and serious problems created by the disturbed behavior of the person that results in danger to the self or to others.

The duration of hospital treatment depends on three factors: its quality, the program's ability to meet the treatment needs of the patient, and the intensity of the personality distortion created by the illness. The therapeutic approach to acute psychotic reactions then demands a proper integration of a sophisticated social systems approach into the individual that meets both specific and nonspecific needs, the efficient use of neuroleptics, and adequate psychotherapy.

Studies of good outcomes of psychotic reactions indicate that a positive therapeutic relationship is an important factor in achieving a favorable result. In addition, such a relationship can aid in the formation of a more favorable convalescent environment and presents the possibility of altering the reorganized psychotic identity. These two factors are crucial in long-term recovery, because, beyond the remission of the acute psychosis process, there must be a resolution of a postpsychotic regressive state that occurs in a social context (Kayton, Beck, & Koh, 1976).

In the early stages of the psychotic process, the therapeutic management may allow only for sensitive management of the milieu in order to reduce episodes of "organismic panic." The establishment and development of a trusting, supportive relationship may also begin at this time. More formal insight-oriented psychotherapy is not usually possible until the psychotic state is in remission and the regressive phase has been terminated (Kayton, 1973).

Although it remains pertinent to inquire whether individual psychotherapy is indicated, Dyrud and Holzman (1973) conclude that a plurality of treatment techniques is necessary. These techniques may be employed simultaneously or sequentially; they range from behavioral approaches that reduce the ambiguity of the environment to individual psychotherapeutic efforts that place additional stress on the patient.

Certain therapeutic attitudes for the therapist are particularly helpful in facilitating the treatment program. Patients should be assured that, as far as possible, their therapist will be available to them as long as is necessary. If hospitalization is implemented, a therapeutic continuity of care should be established during the inpatient phase and carried forward during outpatient treatment. Kayton's study showed that a well-treated schizophrenic episode permitted the patient to continue individuation even after the termination of psychotherapy. Psychotherapy, however, should continue for at least a year following a breakdown and remission.

It is all too easy for treatment programs to encourage continued helplessness and to fail to discourage passivity and withdrawal. For example, the separation from significant others is a major stress for all individuals and is often destructive for those who have experienced a psychotic reaction, because they may find it virtually impossible to work through the object loss. Complicating matters further is that psychotic adolescents also find it difficult to make new object attachments. Yet, it is possible to dilute the intensity of the primitive involvement with others that can characterize these adolescents by supplying a network of relationships through which a variety of people provide a supportive, accepting environment. This promotes a feeling of safety without interfering with the individuality of the patient, and maximizes the opportunity for influencing outcome (Kayton, Beck, & Koh, 1976).

It does not generally help to offer schizophrenic patients an infinite amount of love. This usually arouses rage. Therapeutic interpretations are often met with blank denial, and reality confrontations tend to produce paranoid ideation. A more appropriate therapeutic approach is one in which the patient's perception of the self is accepted and understood. The therapist attempts to understand the psychotic experience as part of a current phenomenological stress. To some extent the therapist also assumes the harsh self-criticism of the patient, modifying it to a degree while making certain it is not denied. The therapeutic stance that communicates to the patient "I accept your hallucinatory or confused experiences" basically reassures the patient that his or her aggression will not overwhelm the therapist. Additionally, short, supportive sessions are advised until sufficient remission and resolution of the postpsychotic regression have occurred, allowing more intrusive and potentially disruptive explorations.

Family and group approaches to the posttherapeutic treatment of psychotic reactions and schizophrenia are valuable ancillary supports. Characteristic disturbances of communication may be identified, which are adaptive responses to the presence of a highly pathological individual in the group or family. These double-bind communications occur in pseudomutual family structures and function to keep the pathological defense systems operating. Group and family therapeutic approaches should be considered as part of the overall effort to deal with these serious disorders.

Psychopharmacological Approaches

Treatment of psychotic disorders has been revolutionized by the introduction of psychotropic drugs. Although the discovery of the effectiveness of chlorpromazine led to the development of an entirely new approach, with extensive scientific expansion of psychopharmacology, unrealistic hopes for the cure of serious mental illness have not been realized (World Health Organization, 1976). However, as part of a total approach to the treatment of psychotic reactions, the use of neurotropic drugs is essential.

Phenothiazines. Phenothiazines are the most common drugs in the treatment of schizophrenia. They include aliphatics (chlorpromazine, promazine, triflupromazine); and piperidines (thioridazine, piperacetazine, mesoridazine). Chlorpromazine (Thorazine) was the first drug used in the treatment of schizophrenia in adolescents, and reports of its use have appeared in the literature for over 30 years. Outside of the United States, it remains one of the most common drugs used in this age group.

The piperadines, and especially thioridazine (Mellaril), are particularly effective for agitation, hallucinations, and delusions. They also are useful in treating those adolescents who show obvious signs of depression in association with the schizophrenic process.

Side effects with the phenothiazines are common. With chlorpromazine and thioridazine, drowsiness, apathy, lethargy, or somnolence are frequent, even in low doses. Individuals should be warned about the possible side effects as well as the possibility of allergic reactions, which are not uncommon. Benign side effects include fatigue and dry mouth. More serious side effects include leucopenia, jaundice, and dystonia. There is, however, a lack of information about the appearance of side effects, as to how much is a result of dose, age, and sex. In general, the side effects do not appear related to dosage or age. The dosage must be carefully regulated so that a therapeutic result is achieved, while minimizing the inhibition of the learning processes. Daily interviews to determine the dosage effect, answer questions, and allay anxiety are particularly necessary in treatment of the patient.

Piperazines (flupherazine, perphenazine, trifluphenazine, acetophenazine, proclorperazine, carphenazine, butaperazine) are useful. The most commonly used piperazine is trifluopherazine (Stelazine). This drug seldom produces drowsiness or motor inhibition and only in isolated instances has it been reported to induce seizures. However, although dystonic reactions are rare with high doses, extrapyramidal symptoms are noted. These include oculogyric crisis, akathisia, and head and neck dystonias. These quickly respond to antiparkinsonian drugs (benztropine). These agents should not be continued indefinitely, but the dosage of the tranquilizer should be reduced.

Butyrophenones. Haloperidol and triperidol are among the butyrophenones most commonly used. Haloperidol (Haldol) is a potent antipsychotic agent with a low incidence of side effects (dystonia). It is particularly useful in the treatment of adolescent psychoses, especially in those young people who show excessive hyperactivity. There are some reports that haloperidol is better than chlorpromazine in reducing impulsiveness, hostility, and aggressiveness. It is said not to produce the drowsiness and lethargy that interfere with learning, but high doses may result in side effects that include drowsiness, dystonic reactions, and muscle spasm.

Thioxanthenes (chlorprothixene, thiothixene) are reported to be useful in those who show signs of psychomotor retardation, by providing stimulation along with antipsychotic properties. They are less likely to produce hematopoetic liver damage, or photosensitivity reactions.

Dihydroindolone (Molindone) is a psychotropic with some characteristics of an antidepressant. Campbell (1977) reports that with the exception of extrapyramidal side effects, it has fewer untoward reactions than aliphatic and piperidine phenothiazines.

CONCLUSION

Reintegration after a psychotic episode is a variable process; its speed depends on the extent of psychotic regression and the intactness of the personality. A wide range of therapeutic approaches have been discussed, including the use of hospitalization, antipsychotic medication, and various forms of psychotherapy. It must always be remembered, however, that the humanizing approach is critical in the final synthesis.

REFERENCES

Arlow, J. A., & Brenner, C. (1964). *Psychoanalytic concepts and the structural theory.* New York: International Universities Press.

Bleuler, E. (1950). *Dementia praecox or the group of schizophrenias.* New York: International Universities Press. (Original work published 1924)

Bleuler, M. (1974). The long-term course of the schizophrenic psychoses. *Psychological Medicine, 4,* 244–254.

Bowers, M. B., Jr. (1974). *Retreat from sanity: The structure of emerging psychosis.* New York: Human Sciences Press.

Campbell, M. (1977). Treatment of childhood and adolescent schizophrenia. In J. M. Weiner (Ed.), *Psychopharmacology in childhood and adolescence* (pp. 101–118). New York: Basic Books.

Carr, V. J. (1983). Recovery from schizophrenia: A review of patterns of psychosis. *Schizophrenia Bulletin, 9,* 95–125.

Chapman, J. (1966). The early symptoms of schizophrenia. *British Journal of Psychiatry, 112,* 225–251.

Chapman, L., & Chapman, J. (1980). Scales for rating psychotic and psychotic like experiences as continua. *Schizophrenia Bulletin, 6,* 476–480.

Docherty, J. P., Van Kammen, D. P., Siris, S. G., & Marder, S. R. (1978). Stages of onset of schizophrenic psychosis. *American Journal of Psychiatry, 135,* 420–426.

Dyrud, J. E., & Holzman, P. S. (1973). The psychotherapy of schizophrenia: Does it work? *American Journal of Psychiatry, 130,* 670–673.

Feinstein, S. C., & Miller, D. (1979). Psychoses of adolescence. In J. D. Noshpitz (Ed.), *Basic handbook of child psychiatry* (pp. 708–722). New York: Basic Books.

Freedman, B., & Chapman, L. (1973). Early subjective experience in schizophrenic episodes. *Journal of Abnormal Psychology, 82,* 46–54.

Freud, S. (1964). Splitting of the ego in the process of defence. In J. Strachey (Ed. and Trans.), *The standard edition of the complete psychological works of Sigmund Freud* (Vol. 23, pp. 275–278). London: Hogarth Press. (Original work published 1938)

Frosch, J. (1967). Delusional fixity, sense of conviction, and the psychotic conflict. *International Journal of Psychoanalysis, 48,* 475–495.

Harrow, M., Carone, B. J., & Westermeyer, J. (1985). The course of psychosis in early phases of schizophrenia. *American Journal of Psychiatry, 142,* 702–707.

Harrow, M., Lanin-Kettering, I., Prosen, M., & Miller, J. G. (1983). Disordered thinking in schizophrenia: Intermingling and loss of set. *Schizophrenia Bulletin, 9*, 354–367.

Harrow, M., & Prosen, M. (1979). Schizophrenic thought disorders: Bizarre associations and intermingling. *American Journal of Psychiatry, 136*, 293–296.

Harrow, M., Rattenbury, F., & Stoll, F. (1988). Schizophrenic delusions: An analysis of their persistence, of related premorbid ideas, and of three major dimensions. In T. Oltmanns & B. Maher (Eds.), *Delusional beliefs* (pp. 184–211). New York: Wiley.

Harrow, M., & Silverstein, M. (1977). Psychotic symptoms in schizophrenia after the acute phase. *Schizophrenia Bulletin, 3*, 608–616.

Harrow, M., Tucker, G. J., & Shield, P. (1972). Stimulus overinclusion in schizophrenic disorders. *Archives of General Psychiatry, 27*, 40–45.

Hole, R. W., Rush, A. J., & Beck, A. T. (1979). A cognitive investigation of schizophrenic delusions. *Psychiatry, 42*, 312–319.

Jaspers, K. (1963). *General psychopathology* (J. Hoenig (Ed.) & M. Hamilton (Trans.). Chicago: University of Chicago Press. (Original work published 1923)

Kayton, L. (1973). Good outcome in young adult schizophrenia. *Archives of General Psychiatry, 129*, 103–110.

Kayton, L., Beck, J., & Koh, S. D. (1976). Postpsychotic state, convalescent environment, and therapeutic relationships in schizophrenic outcome. *American Journal of Psychiatry, 133*, 1269–1274.

Kendler, K. S., Glazer, W., & Morgenstern, H. (1983). Dimensions of delusional experience. *American Journal of Psychiatry, 140*, 466–469.

Kettering, R. L. (1984). An investigation of some aspects of delusional ideation: The exploration of their interrelationship and modification during psychiatric hospitalization. Unpublished doctoral dissertation, The University of Chicago.

Kraepelin, E. (1968). *Lectures on clinical psychiatry*. New York: Hafner. (Original work published 1919)

Mayer-Gross, W., Slater, E., & Roth, M. (1969). *Clinical psychiatry*. Baltimore: Williams and Wilkins.

McGlashan, T. H., Levy, S. T., & Carpenter, W. T. (1975). Integration and sealing over: Clinically distinct recovery styles from schizophrenia. *Archives of General Psychiatry, 32*, 1269–1272.

Menninger, K., Mayman, M., & Pruyser, P. (1963). *The vital balance*. New York: Viking Press.

Oltmanns, T., & Maher, B. (1988). *Delusional beliefs*. New York: Wiley.

Rudden, M., Gilmore, M., & Frances, A. (1982). Delusions: When to confront the facts of life. *American Journal of Psychiatry, 139*, 929–932.

Sacks, M. H., Carpenter, W. T., & Strauss, J. S. (1974). Recovery from delusions. *Archives of General Psychiatry, 30*, 117–120.

Schafer, R. (1968). The mechanisms of defense. *International Journal of Psychoanalysis, 49*, 49–62.

Selye, H. (1956). *The stress of life*. New York: McGraw-Hill.

World Health Organization. (1976). Psychotropic drugs and mental illness. *WHO Chronicle, 30*, 420–424.

Stress, Adjustment Disorders, and Treatment Interventions in Mental Retardation

THOMAS G. WEBSTER, MD

Mentally retarded persons are subject to many of the same stresses and stress reactions as the population at large. Thus, the same principles are generally applicable for the prevention and treatment of Adjustment Disorders. This chapter will clarify what is different in mental retardation. That is, it will highlight those stresses, reactions, and interventions that are more unique to, more common among, or more severe in mentally retarded persons.

The mixture of similarities and differences in the way retarded people adjust as compared to nonretarded persons is often a source of confusion and stereotypes. Attitudes that exaggerate the differences can lead caretakers to experience a sense of helplessness and the retarded to encounter neglect. However, denial or avoidance of the very real distinctions that do exist may lead to additional stress; ultimately, such denial could also lead to neglect.

When working with patients with mental retardation, the psychiatrist's clinical approach to Adjustment Disorders should begin with an awareness and clarification of the stereotypes, biases, and adverse attitudes one finds in oneself, in one's colleagues, the public, the family and in the retarded people themselves. Stereotypes may add significantly to the stress; avoiding or correcting such preformed attitudes can help significantly with the Adjustment Disorders. Furthermore, biased attitudes about mental retardation may interweave with biased attitudes about emotions, mental illness, and psychiatry. Misconceptions are common and may strongly affect the thinking of psychiatrists when they encounter and treat retarded patients with Adjustment Disorders.

Most cases of Adjustment Disorder in mentally retarded persons involve primarily the same factors found in the general population. However, mentally retarded persons tend to be more vulnerable in certain respects and are apt to experience more stress than does the nonretarded population. At the same time, the retarded are also apt to be less vulnerable. For example, a retarded person may be protected from a particular stress either by internal biopsychological limitations or by external psychosocial supports.

Much remains to be clarified about the overall impact of mental retardation in producing differences in the incidence, nature, and treatment of Adjustment Disorders. More adequate epidemiologic studies of large populations in the community—including better definition and identification of Adjustment Disorders—would be necessary. Available statistical studies report a higher incidence of serious mental disorders in the mentally retarded as compared to nonretarded populations, both within institutions and in the community.

The basic psychiatric skills that would be deployed in the assessment and treatment of mentally retarded persons are more similar to than different from the relevant psychiatric skills for nonretarded persons and their families. In any event, in dealing with persons who happen to be mentally retarded, psychiatrists have every reason to feel confident that their clinical skills are very relevant for the management of Adjustment Disorders.

Stereotypes, biases, and myths about mentally retarded persons are common, even among professional workers. These stereotyped views tend to attribute stress reactions and psychopathology to mental retardation per se. The biases are compounded by the stigma of mental illness, avoidance of psychiatry, and lack of adequate health insurance coverage. Moreover (and most unfortunately), such influence may be accompanied by a hopeless attitude or may serve as a rationalization for not intervening as actively as in cases of nonretarded persons. The usefulness of psychiatric assessment and intervention may be overlooked by other caretakers because the person is retarded, and relatively fewer cases are brought to psychiatric attention. Parents of retarded children may experience unresolved guilt, they may erect strong defenses, and they can maintain firm stereotypes about emotional disturbances. These stand in contrast to their views about the more concrete biological and intellectual elements they attribute to the retarded child (whom they may regard as being simply "retarded").

The limitations in psychiatric manpower and available financing for psychiatric care are very real, especially for many families in which mental retardation is present. However, psychiatrists should not participate in the form of neglect based on stereotypes of mental retardation. From the standpoint of effective intervention and overall cost efficiencies—and not solely on humanitarian grounds—the Adjustment Disorders and other psychiatric syndromes that afflict retarded persons merit at least the same active prevention and treatment interventions as do those that affect the population at large.

Similarly, because the retarded have handicaps and coping mechanisms similar to those of other handicapped persons, they are subject to parallel stresses, have equivalent reactions, and require interventions comparable to those that apply to more visible or physical handicaps. These interventions include all the usual biological, psychological, and social modalities that bring help, relief, and healing.

Mentally retarded persons are often underrepresented in psychiatric case loads, psychiatric research, and psychiatric training. By the same token psychiatrists are generally underrepresented in both the research and training programs and the clinical assessment and treatment teams addressing mental retardation. Psychiatrists should be as active in assuring equal treatment for persons with retardation as they have been in championing equal treatment of mental illness (as compared to other medical and surgical illness).

DEFINITIONS—DSM-III-R CONSIDERATIONS

The Diagnostic and Statistical Manual of Mental Disorders (DSM-III-R) (American Psychiatric Association, 1987) and, indeed, all technical or official definitions of mental retardation include the presence of both significantly subaverage general intellectual functioning (IQ of 70 or below) and concurrent deficits or impairments in age-appropriate adaptive behavior.

Mental retardation is a clinical developmental syndrome, not an etiological disease entity. It includes a slow rate of biopsychosocial development, a tendency to fixation in comparatively immature patterns of personality structure and adaptation plus other psychosocial features. It should be noted that even though it presents a real limitation, immaturity is not necessarily pathology. For example, compared to an adult, a normal child's immaturity has definite adaptive limitations, but it also has adaptive advantages, such as greater flexibility. A relatively dependent mentally retarded person who is easily led has evident adaptive disadvantages; but, given guidance and support in mobilizing his or her unique adaptive advantages, this condition offers coping capacities as well. From the standpoint of reactions to stress, mentally retarded persons are in some ways "different." However, in terms of their adaptive potential, to regard them primarily as mentally defective can be both inaccurate and misleading.

DSM-III-R (American Psychiatric Association, 1987) diagnostic criteria for Adjustment Disorder include (in part):

A maladaptive reaction to an identifiable psychosocial stressor or stressors, that occurs within three months of the onset of the stressor. . . . The maladaptive nature of the reaction is indicated either by impairment in *occupational (including school)* functioning or in usual *social* activities or relationships with others or by symptoms that are in excess of a *normal and expectable* reaction to the stressor [italics added]. (p. 329)

For purposes of the mentally retarded, when classifying the Adjustment Disorders, biological stressors, biological and psychological functioning, and "different" normal and expectable reactions should also be considered. All these should also be weighed when assessing and intervening in Adjustment Disorders. The DSM-III-R descriptions of Adjustment Disorders have a blind spot for biological stressors; consideration of the mental retardation helps correct that oversight.

STRESSORS, ADJUSTMENT DISORDERS, AND INTERVENTIONS SPECIFIC TO MENTAL RETARDATION

What stresses, reactions, and interventions are more specific to mental retardation? It is important to note that the necessary generalizations will sometimes obscure the tremendous variety of conditions associated with mental retardation, the uniqueness of individual cases, and the specificity of clinical judgment by the psychiatrist clinician. Bearing this in mind, the following sections provide suggested guidelines.

Stressors

Compared to the general population mentally retarded persons are subject to a wider range of stresses, biological as well as psychosocial.

Biological Factors. Examples of potential stresses from *biological* factors include:

1. Physical anomalies and handicaps may be present, such as the stigmata and cardiac impairment in Down's syndrome, disfigurements and other visible stigmata, blindness, and lameness.
2. Neurological complications, such as seizures and impaired motor coordination, are common. These are more likely to be present in cases of moderate to severe mental retardation.
3. More frequent illnesses and hospitalizations can often be expected.
4. In some cases, reduced sensory perception of external stimuli on a neurological and end-organ basis may be present (e.g. reduced vision, hearing or

tactile perception), and this may include relative sensory deprivation during formative years (e.g., deprivation associated with impaired sucking reflex or weak crying during infancy). This in turn can make for subsequent impairment in the intensity and quality of mother–infant and interpersonal relations. In such instances, complications in ego development are likely to ensue as well as increased vulnerability to later psychosocial stressors.

5. "Supposed biological stress" may occur. Sometimes the symptoms of psychosocial Adjustment Disorders lead to uncertainties, anxieties, and projections on the part of parents, peers, or caretakers, who begin to fear (understandably but erroneously) that the symptoms are due to a progression of the physical or neurological conditions or are simply part of being retarded.

6. Other sources of biological stress are not unique to the retarded person's physical state; they do, however, increase the degree of stress. For the retarded (as against nonretarded persons) the physical changes of puberty and other maturational milestones occur both emotionally and socially at a less mature stage of personality development. Mentally retarded adolescents are less prepared to cope with puberty and other milestones of biological maturation; hence they may find the biological changes of puberty more stressful.

7. A similar state of affairs prevails in later maturational stages. For a variety of biological reasons, the complications of mid-life and old age occur earlier and/or more severely for the retarded. Evidence of the histopathological similarities of Alzheimer's disease and Down's syndrome point to one of many biological factors that bring added stress for adjustment to later life. All too frequently these changes end in premature death.

8. In some instances, the impact of biological stresses can also be less for the retarded, in part because of the protectiveness of others. This protective factor is already active before the stress of biological change occurs.

Psychosocial Stressors Directly Related to the Mental Retardation. Stressors to which mentally retarded individuals are especially vulnerable include the following:

1. Individuals who are mentally retarded are likely to experience traumatic rejections, failures, losses, and/or dislocations; the associated reduction in self-esteem further increases their vulnerability.

2. Overstimulation is also commonly experienced. Retarded persons, especially children but adults as well, wear "the hidden cap of invisibility," because others often assume that they "won't understand anyway." This can result in sexual abuse, exploitation, or exposure to situations (in home, institution, or community) from which children or handicapped persons are usually— and appropriately—protected.

3. Mentally retarded persons may be easily led into experiences that they are

not prepared to handle. Whether they are held back by overprotectiveness or thrust prematurely into facing excessive expectations, there tends frequently to be a dysynchrony in the readiness of the retarded to face more demanding requirements or new challenges.

4. Fresh and recurrent traumatic encounters never end, because mentally retarded persons repeatedly and perpetually encounter the traumata of social stigma. The recurrent sorrow of parents of a mentally retarded child has a corollary in this recurrent opening of old wounds for the retarded person.

5. Greater vulnerability to stress may also be based on the reactions of parents and other primary caretakers. The retarded are more dependent in many concrete ways and hence more vulnerable as well. Again and again they encounter the impersonal stress arising from the unaware and insensitive behavior of primary support persons. Such impersonal stressful behavior is often not intentionally aimed at the retarded person; it occurs occasionally (perhaps inevitably) from even the most attentive and concerned support persons and families.

Psychosocial Stressors Not Directly Related to Mental Retardation. Usual stresses for which mentally retarded persons may be *less* vulnerable than nonretarded persons include the following:

1. Their relative dependence and the protective environment within which they often live tend to decrease or delay their exposure to some of the stresses that nonretarded persons encounter routinely. Thus, because of the handicap and prior vulnerabilities, a protective support system is likely to be mobilized and accessible. Hence there is less exposure to some of the usual stresses that come with greater autonomy.

2. There is less awareness of complex psychosocial stresses whose threatening implications require more conceptual grasp to appreciate, including some commonly imagined threats that never materialize. Examples include fear of divorce when parents argue, fear of sex when touched, or fear of mistreatment when detecting subtle social signs of prejudice. It comes down to a kind of complacent naiveté: "What you don't know won't hurt you." Along with this there is sometimes a less personalized depth to the personal relations of mentally retarded persons in that they establish more concrete or superficial relations, in this sense there is less vulnerability to deep personal wounds. Naturally, these protections from immediate stresses may also leave blind spots that increase their vulnerability to future complications and unforeseen stresses. Generally, research and clinical experience support the belief that lack of support from close friends leads to much greater pain in the face of common stressors.

3. A similarly mixed blessing of reduced vulnerability may result from the more concrete or superficial nature of their relationships. Retarded children, as

compared to nonretarded children, are sometimes more easily led, more trusting, and more readily accepting of home-to-school or family-to-friends transitions. To some degree this is proportional to the degree of retardation. For example, the mildly retarded child demonstrates more expected childhood separation anxieties and makes more emotionally significant distinctions between family and friends (i.e., distinctions that resemble those of nonretarded children) than do moderately or severely retarded children.

Adjustment Disorders

The Adjustment Disorders of mentally retarded persons, like the stressors, include factors that are rather specific to the primary condition; an example would be the typical biopsychosocial factors in Down's syndrome (the characteristic facies, congenital anomalies, etc.). Adjustment Disorders obviously also include factors that are only indirectly related to or are quite independent of the mental retardation.

The psychiatric assessment of an Adjustment Disorder in a person with mental retardation can make a significant contribution by making clear the interplay of different factors and avoiding the temptation to explain the reaction too readily on the basis of stereotypes.

Clinical Assessment. The psychiatrist should assess relatively independently the medical (physical or specific etiological), neurological, intellectual, psychiatric (emotional and psychodynamic), social and family components of both the patient's chronic condition and the more acute Adjustment Disorder. In each of these dimensions the psychiatrist will need to assess both the assets and limitations. Careful attention to each such parameter will help the psychiatrist avoid the common tendency of overattribution of the Adjustment Disorder to whichever is the most prominent or visible problem (e.g., Down's syndrome, moderate mental retardation, schizophrenia, or a social event such as job failure).

For example, despite the more commonly shared features of Down's syndrome, and whether the person is a 4-year-old, an adolescent, or an adult, individuals with that condition will also have different degrees and types of neurological deficits, physical stigmata, associated anomalies, intellectual levels, emotional development, personality traits, family and social stresses, and Adjustment Disorders.

Table 32.1 illustrates the lack of strong correlations among such factors as the relative severity of (1) intellectual impairment; (2) brain disease, if evident; and (3) emotional disturbance, if present, according to different medical diagnostic categories. In cases involving mental retardation, a psychiatric diagnostic assessment of Adjustment Disorder necessitates a similar level of diagnostic specificity of unique individual variables. The psychiatrist should assess and intervene (or withhold intervention) for each dimension rather than overly attribute the Adjustment Disorder to any one dimension (such as Down's syndrome, mental retardation, or a given social stressor).

Table 32.1. Distribution of the Severity of Three Handicaps According to Medical Diagnosis

		Degree of Retardation	Severity of Brain Disease	Severity of Emotional Disturbance
Down's syndrome	+	4 (borderline)	8 (mild)	29 (mild)
(N = 39)	++	24 (IQ 50–69)	31 (moderate)	10 (moderate)
	+++	11 (IQ 20–49)	0 (severe)	0 (severe)
Metabolic disorder	+	0	0	2
(Cretinism and	++	2	3	2
phenylketonuria)	+++	2	1	0
(N = 4)				
Organic brain disorder, other types:				
Prenatal with skull	+	2	9	7
anomaly (N = 24)	++	11	11	15
	+++	11	4	2
Prenatal, other	+	1	2	2
(N = 8)	++	2	5	5
	+++	5	1	1
Perinatal (N = 14)	+	0	3	5
	++	6	6	7
	+++	8	5	2
Postnatal (N = 9)	+	2	1	1
	++	3	5	7
	+++	4	3	1
Undetermined origin	+	3	15	4
(N = 22)	++	13	7	15
	+++	6	0	3
Familial (N = 6)	0	—	3	—
Mental retardation	+	1	3	1
	++	3	0	4
	+++	2	0	1
Childhood psychosis,	0	—	14	—
functional (N = 16)	+	4	2	0
With mental retardation	++	8	0	2
	+++	4	0	14
Etiology undetermined	0	—	10	—
(N = 17)	+	4	7	5
Mental retardation	++	8	0	9
	+++	5	0	3

Table 32.1. Continued

	Degree of Retardation		Severity of Brain Disease	Severity of Emotional Disturbance
	0	—	27	—
	+	21	50	56
Totals	+ +	80	68	76
(*N* = 159)	+ + +	58	14	27
		159	159	159

Source: Statistics were obtained in a study series of 159 retarded children, Greater Boston Preschool Program (community nursery schools) for Retarded Children. From "Unique Aspects of Emotional Development in Mentally Retarded Children," by T. G. Webster, in *New Directions in Childhood Psychopathology: Vol. 2. Deviations in Development* (Chapter 38, p. 945), S. I. Harrison and J. F. McDermoth (Eds.), 1982, New York: International Universities Press. First published in *Psychiatric Approaches to Mental Retardation,* edited by F. J. Menaloscino, pp. 3–54, 1970, New York: Basic Books. Reprinted by permission.

Significance of the Mental Retardation Syndrome. In any individual Adjustment Disorder, the primary aspects of the mental retardation syndrome such as intellectual limitation or personality immaturity may or may not come significantly into play. For example, for the mentally retarded as compared to nonretarded persons, their limited capacity for imaginary play or their tendency to concrete thinking may serve either to enhance or to minimize the severity of an Adjustment Disorder arising from a given stressor.

Adjustment Disorders Directly Related to the Mentally Retarded Condition

1. Exaggerated dependency or regression may occur in the face of new challenges.
2. Mentally retarded persons tend to exhibit exaggerated repetitiveness, perseveration, or compulsive traits in the face of frustrations or a struggle for control.
3. If the mentally retarded individual is "led by the hand," smoother transitions in separation and loss reactions occur in areas such as school versus home behavior or family versus stranger transitions. A "trust of strangers" may be present, based on the relatively more superficial quality of personal relations. In other Adjustment Disorders, this may be overridden by the need to repeat or find the familiar (persons, places, things, or rituals) in concrete ways while coping with the anxiety of a new venture.
4. Reversible accentuation of some aspects of the retardation may exist, such as transient pseudoretardation or regression in respect to previously acquired intellectual functions.

Adjustment Disorders Secondary to but Related to the Mentally Retarded Condition

1. These take form as personality states involving exaggerated expectations of failure and vulnerable self-esteem.
2. There is less vulnerability to some conditions related to Adjustment Disorders, such as less boredom with the kinds of monotonous tasks that might throw other people into secondary behavioral complications. For example, a bright child who is bored and insufficiently challenged in a classroom may act up and get into trouble; whereas a retarded child is more apt to pursue repetitive chore-tasks, especially when easily led and pleasing the teacher.

Adjustment Disorders Relatively Unrelated to the Mentally Retarded Condition. A given stress such as a death in the family may evoke a response that is entirely unrelated to the mental retardation. However, the ensuing Adjustment Disorder practically always brings into play individual, physical, and psychosocial traits that have at least an indirect relation to the retardation. Even if the stressor and the psychodynamic reactions are more closely related to the mental retardation, the Adjustment Disorder may nonetheless comprise of predominantly unrelated symptoms, such as stomach complaints or other psychosomatic symptoms.

Age and Stage Adjustment Disorders. The mental retardation syndrome may be a primary consideration or may be a negligible factor in specific Adjustment Disorders related to developmental or age-specific reactions. For example:

1. Home-to-school and home-to-hospital transitions
2. Deinstitutionalization transitions
3. Adjustment Disorders in response to developmental aspects of adolescence
4. Adjustment Disorders in response to occupational stress
5. Sex, marriage, and/or independent living of young adulthood
6. Middle age, aging, loss of parents or other primary caretaker

Coping Mechanisms—Interventions

As described in the preceding sections, the choice of intervention must be based on an accurate assessment of multiple diagnostic and situational factors. In addressing these conditions, the increased role of the supporting cast (in addition to the patient and the psychiatrist) is a definite consideration. However, the patient's amenability to the usual one-to-one psychotherapeutic intervention by a psychiatrist is commonly overlooked or minimized. Psychiatrists share in this problem (Group for the Advancement of Psychiatry, 1979). In combination with a psychiatrist's basic clinical skills, relatively little additional training in the special problems of mental retardation can often carry the professional a long way.

Primary Prevention. It is important to eliminate or reduce known potential sources of stress. In addition to measures that apply to the general population, one must address those hazards and vulnerabilities that are more specific to mental retardation (as described earlier). The mentally retarded person must receive more protection, education, training, and preparation for experiences that are not usually as stressful for nonretarded persons. Students must be guided repeatedly through simulations in preparation for a new and predictably stressful experience. Similarly, in the face of an unpredicted but preventable failure, the retarded person should be helped to review the situation repeatedly and to practice the necessary coping behavior until achieving success (GAP, 1979; Menaloscino, 1977; Webster, 1982).

Early Intervention

Psychiatric Consultation. Timely consultation to mentally retarded individuals, and to their families, schools, and pediatricians can provide early access and facilitate necessary interventions by professionals. This is especially true of *regular* psychiatric consultation to settings where mentally retarded persons live, train, play, or work. Routine visits and familiarity with clients, families, and staff can often facilitate early intervention and preventive measures. Intervention is more apt to be delayed where one deals only with casualties that first appear for consultation or office visits after a crisis has produced major symptoms. Crisis intervention may be headed off by earlier minicrisis intervention (GAP, 1979; Menaloscino, 1977; Webster, 1982).

Several excellent examples of psychiatric consultation in mental retardation (including Case Vignettes 1–3 in this chapter) are described in a report of the Group for the Advancement of Psychiatry (GAP, 1979), of which I was a coauthor.

Case Vignette 1

John, a 13-year-old mentally retarded and neurologically impaired student, was on the verge of school expulsion for poor school performance and increasingly disruptive behavior. The parents strongly opposed "giving up" by the school or by John. Psychiatric intervention helped the family and school personnel to understand John's specific physical and mental handicaps; his turbulent adjustment anxiety, both conscious and unconscious; and his sense of failure, defectiveness, and personal rejection. The intervention helped to modify conflictual attitudes on the part of the parents and the school personnel. The psychiatric consultation favorably interrupted a vicious cycle of rejecting behavior which had escalated despite valid and plausible concerns from the perspective of each participant. (GAP, 1979, pp. 656–657)

Medical Complications. Psychiatric assessment and intervention in Adjustment Disorders can make sure that any medical complications have early or regular attention. This is essential in order to determine the relevance of such medical difficulties to the particular psychosocial reaction and thus be able to prescribe the optimal intervention (American Psychiatric Association (APA) Commission on Psychiatric Therapies, 1984. GAP, 1979; Higgs, 1983; Kornfeld & Finkel, 1982; Lurie, 1982; Menaloscino, 1977; Singh & Winton, 1984; Webster, 1982).

Behavioral Conditioning. This is often a significant factor in stress. Despite their learning handicap, mentally retarded persons have an asset that may at times be overlooked: If a relatively simple experience is repeated over and over again, they can learn it as well or better than nonretarded persons. Many frustrations and failures are inevitably part of being retarded, and they in turn impair the individual's motivation for more adaptive learning (APA Commission on Psychiatric Therapies, 1984; Bernstein, 1979; Fellner, Laroche, & Sulzer-Azaroff, 1984; Menaloscino, 1977). In order to counteract the cumulative impact of such experiences, it is important to assure positive and successful new ventures and conditioned learning.

For example, when a mentally retarded adolescent is starting a job placement in a new setting, the stakes are high. The new job can be an opportunity to reinforce successful adjustment, or it can serve to reinforce the experience of failure and a sense of hopelessness. A premium should be placed on repeated simulations and on the learning of rudiments through successful small steps. Risks and uncertainties about details should be minimized. The successful teacher focuses the retarded person's attention on the known and on making confident small steps of learning and accomplishment, while minimizing the new and potentially overwhelming "big picture" and the associated mass of uncertainties.

Individual Psychotherapy and Counseling. These therapeutic services are crucial for early assessment and intervention. Expert individualized attention is often necessary in order to achieve a more successful adjustment reaction with the specific assets and limitations associated with a given type of mental retardation (APA Commission on Psychiatric Therapies, 1979; Bernstein, 1979; GAP, 1979; Higgs, 1983; Levine, 1984; Matson, 1984; Reid, 1980; Webster, 1982).

Case Vignette 2

Mary, a 15-year-old retarded girl with epilepsy, became disruptive, silly, and demanding at home but not at school. Periodically she would alternate this home pattern with sudden lapses into withdrawn and unresponsive behavior. Although she had moderate breast development and other secondary sex characteristics, she maintained her simple, childlike expectations of affection from her father. The father's discomfort with her changing teenage sexuality and his impatience with her exaggerated, silly, inappropriate, and regressive behavior contributed to a vicious circle. Mary sensed her father's rejection and tried harder in ever more ineffective ways to capture his attention. Alternately, she had moments of withdrawal into a depressive state that included a foggy and confused demeanor. Her antiepileptic medication had required adjustment to reduce the mental clouding; but, with her advancing age, it apparently also reduced her seizure threshold, hence the sudden lapses of unresponsiveness. Psychotherapy helped Mary integrate a more accurate perception of the changes in her own body, mind, and family reactions. Consultation with the father reinforced more favorable reactions for both of them and led to a reversal of Mary's disruptive Adjustment Disorder. (GAP, 1979, p. 658)

Family Therapy. The presence of a built-in support system is an asset that is more likely to be present in cases of Adjustment Disorder with accompanying mental retardation than in Adjustment Disorder without mental retardation. Intervention should be carried out within the framework of that support system and should not undermine effective supporting family members or prior professional workers. On the other hand, if the support system for a retarded individual is inadequate, then such family intervention and therapy are apt to be more difficult to accomplish than would be true with nonretarded cases. That is, if the family—which may be a single parent—has been overwhelmed and/or has not mobilized successfully in response to the mentally retarded condition, it may be less responsive to the additional burden of an Adjustment Disorder. The presence of such a support network distinguishes the family in which the deviance of the retarded person is prominent (a state of affairs which is more common in cases seen in private psychiatric practice) as compared to families with multiple handicaps and numerous limitations affecting multiple family members (APA Commission on Psychiatric Therapies, 1984; Bernstein, 1979; Gallagher, 1983; GAP, 1979; Higgs, 1983; Kornblatt & Heinrich, 1985; Levine, 1984; Matson, 1984; Menaloscino, 1977; Webster, 1982).

Case Vignette 3

Jeff, a 6-year-old boy with Hurler's disease (gargoylism) became depressed and apathetic in nursery school and was more tearful, demanding, and unruly at home. The well-educated and attentive parents thought that Jeff's Hurler's disease, which at the time had only mildly visible stigmata, may have begun a more rapid progression, or that perhaps Jeff needed stronger disciplining. Reexamination by the pediatrician and neurologist revealed no change in the child's neurologic condition. Interviews with the parents, however, disclosed they had visited another family with a 12-year-old child with much more advanced Hurler's disease. Jeff's parents were greatly shocked and dismayed when the other mother told them that her son, at the age of 6 years, had looked just like Jeff.

In the family sessions the parents came to realize that their own reaction had led them unwittingly to "give up" on Jeff, to withdraw, and to become more impatient with his behavior. In the wake of several psychiatric sessions with the parents and meetings with the nursery teacher, Jeff's depressive grief and difficult behavior improved. The parents' own grief had been accentuated by the confrontation with more advanced Hurler's disease. Only after they had been helped to deal more directly with this was Jeff able to improve. In spite of their educated knowledge about Jeff's condition, the parents had previously maintained a state of successful emotional denial. (GAP, 1979, pp. 607–609)

Group Therapy. Formal and informal group psychotherapy, such as that available within some school or residential settings for mentally retarded persons, may both be helpful. This often involves a greater use of natural groupings and self-help groups with the psychiatrist functioning as consultant. Frequently the groups have the character of an informal social or work activity group (APA Commission on Psychiatric Therapies, 1984; Bernstein, 1979; GAP, 1979; Webster, 1982).

Pharmacotherapy. Benzodiazepines, neuroleptics, antidepressants, lithium, and other psychoactive medications are generally used in the same manner as for the nonretarded. This applies as well to medication for attention deficit disorder with hyperactivity, most notably amphetamines and methylphenidate. Related stimulant drugs, such as magnesium pemoline and more recent experimental substances, have appeared periodically to be greeted as "breakthroughs" for improved cognitive learning. To date, however, their success has been transient.

In some cases of mental retardation, disruptive behavior and impulsive tendencies with secondary complications may, at times, require tranquilizers. Major tranquilizers can be useful for psychotic or extremely disruptive behavior; they may, however, be overused as a behavioral suppressant. The criteria for the use of minor tranquilizers should be the same as for anxiety and psychosomatic symptoms in nonretarded patients.

Because seizures are more common among the mentally retarded, antiepileptic medications are commonly employed. Stress and crises of adjustment may sometimes be ameliorated by adjusting antiepileptic medications.

Drug abuse is found among mentally retarded patients. Drug misuse or overuse by families and caretakers, particularly in institutional settings, is not uncommon.

Compliance issues include work with the family or caretakers as well as with the retarded patients themselves. Collaboration with pediatricians, family physicians, school physicians, nurses, and other health professionals is clearly essential (Aman, Field, & Bridgman, 1985; APA Commission on Psychiatric Therapies, 1984; Bernstein, 1979; Matson, 1984; Reid, 1980; Schalock, Foley, Toulouse, & Stark, 1985; Tyrer, Walsh, Edwards, Berney, & Stephens, 1984).

Special Education, Rehabilitation, and Work-Related Staff. In crisis intervention or early prevention of Adjustment Disorders in the mentally retarded, the psychiatrist is more apt to find useful support colleagues than are encountered in treating equivalent conditions in the nonretarded. Because prior working relations often have already been established with the patient and family, a little psychiatric intervention and collaboration may go a long way. Such interventions are likely to be more successfully collaborative and less competitive if the psychiatrist has had other working contacts with such colleagues in their mutual community (APA Commission on Psychiatric Therapies, 1984; Anderson & Allen, 1985; Bernstein, 1979; GAP, 1979; Menaloscino, 1977; Reid, 1980; Webster, 1982).

Self-Help and Community Groups. Families of the mentally retarded often have active and established community contacts. In the face of Adjustment Disorders, these can then function as resources for intervention. By the time the psychiatrist is contacted, however, sometimes these supports have worn thin. This in itself can be part of the problem contributing to the Adjustment Disorder. This may also prove to be one of the most readily repaired factors in the sequence of stress, Adjustment Disorder, and psychiatric intervention (Kornblatt & Heinrich, 1985; Menaloscino, 1977; Schalock et al., 1985; Singh & Winton, 1984; Webster, 1982).

Continuing Psychiatric Consultation. As secondary and tertiary prevention, the crisis that brings a case with mental retardation and Adjustment Disorder to a psychiatrist may also serve as an effective entry for continuing psychiatric consultation. This may provide a heretofor neglected professional function, involving integrative assessment and orchestration of the previously fragmented multiple factors and personnel. For patients and families with mental retardation, this is often the most useful aspect of psychiatric intervention.

With the mentally retarded in particular, the psychiatrist is apt to find gaps and overlaps in professional services. Often a great premium must be placed on simple concrete guidance, more so than is appropriate in the psychiatric consultation and psychotherapy for Adjustment Disorders in nonretarded persons.

SUMMARY

There is a special competence needed by and a special role for the psychiatrist in conducting Adjustment Disorder interventions with mentally retarded persons. Such a professional must be able to integrate and weigh the relevance of multiple biopsychosocial factors; the professional must understand and must be equipped to orchestrate a variety of influences. The psychiatrist can thus focus interventions toward achieving optimal feasible adjustment. This stands in contrast to the all too frequent failures that come from relying excessively on resources (inside and outside the mentally retarded person) that have tended to be overworked in the past.

Such an approach brings new light and hope—not rosy platitudes—based on a realistic assessment of assets and limitations. The psychiatrist must, however, be appropriately open to learning, for he or she is likely to encounter many capable persons in the case who have had more experience with the particular patient and family or with mental retardation in general. Optimally, stressful crises and Adjustment Disorders can turn into new growth and learning experiences for both the patient and family. Based on the effective rapport that has been established with the patient, family, pediatricians, and agencies, there should be appropriate follow-up after the crisis.

Given psychiatric training in biological medicine, psychotherapy, pharmacotherapy, and social systems experience with serious mental disorders, the psychiatrist is apt to feel less pressured to provide miracles and yet less inclined toward despair because of the inherent limitations in cases of mental retardation. A psychiatrist is apt to know that when working with retarded patients and their families, providing accurate empathy and emotional rapport is sometimes a more crucial ingredient than other technical procedures. The psychiatrist is prepared by training and experience to address the developmental, psychodynamic, and biopsychosocial context of emotional disorders. Such a professional is therefore more apt to regard the Adjustment Disorder and the necessary interventions as an opportunity for help within a longer range context. When dealing with Adjustment Disorders, there is often an even greater premium on such an orientation in cases involving mental retardation as compared to managing parallel conditions within the general population.

REFERENCES

Aman, M. G., Field, C. J., & Bridgman, G. D. (1985). City-wide survey of drug patterns among non-institutionalized mentally retarded persons. *Applied Research in Mental Retardation, 6,* 159–171.

American Psychiatric Association (APA) Commission on Psychiatric Therapies. (1984). *The psychiatric therapies: Pt I. The somatic therapies: Pt II. The psychosocial therapies* (pp. 17–18, 202–203, 502–508, 629–636, 817–829). Washington, DC: American Psychiatric Association.

American Psychiatric Association (APA). (1987). *Diagnostic and statistical manual of mental disorders* (DSM-III-R; 3rd ed.-rev.). Washington, DC: Author.

Anderson, S. C., & Allen, L. R. (1985). Effects of a recreation therapy program on activity involvement and social interaction of mentally retarded persons. *Behaviour Research and Therapy, 23,* 473–477.

Bernstein, N. R. (1979). Mental retardation. In J. D. Noshpitz & S. I. Harrison (Eds.), *Basic handbook of child psychiatry: Vol. 3. Therapeutic interventions* (pp. iii, 628–641). New York: Basic Books.

Fellner, D. J., Laroche, M., & Sulzer-Azaroff, B. (1984). The effects of adding interruption to differential reinforcement on targeted and novel self-stimulatory behaviors. *Journal of Behavioral Therapy and Experimental Psychiatry, 15,* 315–321.

Gallagher, J. J. (1983). Families of handicapped children: Sources of stress and its amelioration. *Exceptional Child, 50,* 10–19.

Group for the Advancement of Psychiatry (GAP). (1979). *Psychiatric consultation in mental retardation* (GAP Publication No. 104, pp. 600–691). New York: Group for the Advancement of Psychiatry.

Higgs, R. (1983). Making up her mind: Consent, pregnancy and mental handicaps. *Journal of Medical Ethics, 9*(4), 219–226.

Kornblatt, E. S., & Heinrich, J. (1985). Needs and coping abilities in families of children with developmental disabilities. *Mental Retardation, 23,* 13–19.

Kornfeld, D. S., & Finkel, J. B. (1982). *Psychiatric management for medical practitioners* (pp. 109, 227–235). New York: Grune & Stratton.

Levine, H. G. (1984). Situational anxiety and everyday life experiences of mildly mentally retarded adults. *American Journal of Mental Deficiency, 90,* 27–33.

Lurie, H. J. (1982). *Practical management of emotional problems in medicine* (rev. ed., pp. 19, 43, 161). New York: Raven Press.

Matson, J. L. (1984). Psychotherapy with persons who are mentally retarded. *Mental Retardation, 22*(4), 170–175.

Matson, J. L., Kazdin, A. E., & Senatore, V. (1984). Diagnosis and drug use in mentally retarded emotionally disturbed adults. *Applied Research in Mental Retardation, 5,* 513–519.

Menaloscino, F. J. (1977). *Challenges in mental retardation: Progressive ideology and services.* New York: Human Sciences Press.

Reid, A. H. (1980). Psychiatric disorders in mentally handicapped children: A clinical and follow-up study (including adjustment disorder and mental retardation). *Journal of Mental Deficiency Research, 24,* 287–298.

Schalock, R. L., Foley, J. W., Toulouse, A. & Stark, J. A. (1985). Medication and programming in controlling the behavior of mentally retarded individuals in community settings. *American Journal of Mental Deficiency, 89,* 503–509.

Singh, N. W., & Winton, A. S. (1984). Increasing physicians' awareness and use of community resources for mentally retarded persons. *Journal of Mental Deficiency Research, 28,* 199–205.

Tyrer, S. P., Walsh, A., Edwards, D. E., Berney, T. P., & Stephens, D. A. (1984). Factors associated with a good response to lithium in aggressive mentally handicapped subjects. *Progress in Neuropsychopharmacological and Biological Psychiatry, 8,* 751–755.

Webster, T. G. (1982). Unique aspects of emotional development in mentally retarded children. In S. I. Harrison & J. F. McDermott Jr. (Eds.), *New directions in childhood psychopathology: Vol. 2. Deviations in development.* (pp. 929–978). New York: International Universities Press. (First published 1970, in F. J. Menaloscino, Ed., *Psychiatric approaches to mental retardation,* pp. 3–54. New York: Basic Books).

Prevention and Intervention

———————————————————

This, the final section of the book, contains the material we have been able to assemble on patterns of prevention and techniques of intervention. It is important to state at the outset that there is no unique treatment for the Adjustment Disorders. All the usual psychiatric modalities, the various psychotherapies, pharmacotherapy, and the behavioral methods are appropriate and are best used in combined form. An additional element, however, is often present with these disorders: Because they arise so regularly in the face of a stressor that simultaneously affects or is shared by many people, the use of self-help groups is especially appropriate.

These disorders often respond well to treatment. If, however, they are left untreated—and this is a common state of affairs (e.g., someone suffers a posttraumatic phobic reaction but goes without help because he insists on "toughing it out," or a victim of rape wants to avoid facing again what she thought and felt at the time of the trauma)—such conditions can have a highly uncertain outcome. Many patients undergo a reaction of greater or lesser severity but then achieve a spontaneous recovery. Others do not recover but succeed in masking their disability while the symptoms go underground, leaving a residuum of vulnerability and important but covert limitations. Some of these reactions remain overt but the individual does not seek help, and the symptoms presently become set into personality or become progressively more severe. When that happens, the long-range consequences may include a great deal of suffering and disability. It appears eminently sensible to get the message across to the public that these conditions merit attention and are treatable. This would seem to be a public health issue of major proportions.

Toward Preventive Interventions in Early Childhood Object Loss

GILBERT W. KLIMAN, MD

DEATH OF A PARENT VERSUS OTHER LOSSES

At one time (Kliman, 1968) psychiatric investigators believed that by studying the phenomena attending a loss of human relationships (as in childhood death of a parent), they would be inspecting a cauldron in which mental illnesses were brewed. However, the evidence did not bear out their expectations in quite the way they had anticipated. The data assembled to date (Gregory, 1965, 1966; Osterweis, Solomon, & Green, 1984) do suggest that the long-term effects of death of a parent include detriments to emotional well-being, school performance, and social behavior. The most definitive study of psychopathology among bereaved children is Gregory's. It shows that compared to children from intact families who were also studied over a period of more than 5 years, those Minnesota schoolchildren who were orphaned of one or both parents experienced more school grade failures, more failures to complete school, more truancy, and more multiple arrests. However, when considering children of separation and divorce, the distinction between intact family and subject children was much greater (Gregory, 1965).

Bereavement may increase the risk of mental illness later in life as well as suicide (Osterweis, 1984), but from a statistical point of view, the effects are not profound, and the experience is not necessarily or inevitably traumatic. In contrast, all too often children caught up in situations of object loss because of divorce or foster care do seem to be in a cauldron that brews psychopathology (Kliman, Schaeffer, & Friedman, 1982; Offord, Abrams, & Allen, 1979). Maternal depression is also a loss experience for children that deprives many of them of necessary parental functions and interactions. These lost parental services range from reflected joy to simple attentiveness. Children of psychiatrically disturbed parents in general have losses that are often continuing, persistent, perplexing, depleting, and ultimately catastrophic (Goodman & Isaacs, 1984).

No comparison of various bereaved groups with children of mentally ill parents has ever been conducted. But it is suspected that children of parents with major psychiatric disorders have greater losses of developmentally vital services than do the majority of children who lose one parent by death. And because the children are also probably genetically loaded for psychiatric disorder, this form of loss of object relationships is especially likely to be damaging.

Bereaved children usually have a surviving parent and retain most of their environmental supports and familiar human objects. The finding that less impairment was present among bereaved than among divorced children can also be explained on another basis: In the case of the bereaved child, a firm attachment and developmentally useful relationship to the parent had usually been formed, which permitted many developmental tasks to be well launched or even completed.

Many other factors are at work that may differentiate among the outcomes of various forms of early childhood object loss. For one thing, there is the factor of timing, which can allow completion of developmental tasks and may indeed allow preparations for stress. But even prior to an acute stress, too long a period of strain can be debilitating. Death of a young child's parent is usually a rather sudden stress. Major causes of early parental death include accidents and abrupt cardiac insults. Thus, many childhood bereavements occur with little time for preparation. In contrast, separated, divorced, and foster-placing families will often go through stressful upheavals for several years before the object loss situation occurs. Thus, during the prodromal stages, the involved children may lose emotional supplies and parental services for years—in the course of which they are passing developmental phases whose successful outcome depends on parental participation.

Other relative advantages accrue to children bereaved by death. They are at least free to mourn and are often socially and ritually supported in doing so. Few such arrangements within the structure of the social network encourage the mourning of object loss in divorce and foster placements. In the discontinuous and discordant relationships that surround and precede such nonbereavement losses, children are often not free to mourn losses and may never allow themselves to perceive realistically what is going on around them. Their self-concept often develops with insufficient assistance from their caregivers and they lack a valid grasp of their own personal history. Moreover, if they are still in a stage of magical thinking, their efforts to attribute responsibility for the loss to their own behavior are all too likely to jeopardize self-esteem.

Hypothetically, a still more malignant outcome is likely when the situation of object loss is complicated by psychopathology on the part of the remaining caregiver. This is particularly serious if that psychopathology involves depression and/or substance abuse. Such pathologic parenting may involve chronic loss of developmentally needed caretaking. There are often harmful oscillations in the degree of parental investment in the child, oscillating qualities in the kinds of affect displayed, oscillating attention and inattentiveness, physical and psychological absence, negligence, and severe discord or violence within the household. These depleting experiences are in and of themselves wounding; more than that, however, such wounds may be contaminated by such psychological toxins as development interferences through abuse. For these reasons the sharp discontinuities of permanent object loss through death may be far less detrimental.

TOWARD A CLASSIFICATION OF OBJECT LOSS EXPERIENCE

Various classifications of childhood pathogenic experiences have been proposed for application to object loss situations (Ainsworth, 1962; Kliman, 1968; Spitz, 1946; Yarrow, 1961). In keeping with both modern psychoanalytic thinking and modern concepts of treatment planning, a classification of object loss experiences and the surrounding situations might include such categories as "depleting," "understimulating," "overstimulating," "toxic," and "conflictual" loss situations, along with various combinations.

Definitions

Within such a proposed classification, a number of definitions can be offered along with illustrative but by no means exhaustive examples and some associated planning for preventive and therapeutic maneuvers. Some of these categories are:

1. A "depleting" loss experience

Definition. The term "depleting" refers to a child's experience of chronic loss, arising because of insufficient narcissistically supportive parental services, such as attentiveness. Established psychological functions then are eroded.

Example. A preschool child raised by a sole caregiver who becomes basically inattentive may have little or no support for already established executive functions such as toilet training and early reading efforts. These functions then regress. Under such circumstances, efforts at prevention would involve good day care. Treatment would require therapeutic education for the child accompanied by supportive counseling for the mother/caretaker.

2. An "understimulating" loss experience

Definition. The chronic absence of average expectable degrees of input, dialogue, and interaction with adult human objects during childhood, with the consequent loss of critical developmental ingredients. It is similar to a "depleting" loss, but interferes more with psychological structures not yet up and running.

Example. An infant is raised by a self-absorbed, depressed sole caregiver, who cannot maintain a sufficient dialogue between self and infant. Speech is slow to develop. Prevention involves the diagnosis of maternal depression during pregnancy and the early postpartum period. Therapy involves prescribing antidepressant medication for mother and providing supplementary caregiving for both the mother and infant during the infant's first year.

3. An "overstimulating" loss experience

Definition. This is a paradoxical situation that arises when the absence of one human object causes a disinhibition of the input from a surviving human object. Rather than an insufficiency of input, the result is an overload of the child's adaptive abilities.

Example. An oedipal-phase child loses the same-sex parent by death or divorce. This leads to a mutually compensatory but excessive intimacy with the remaining opposite-sex parent. In the case of divorce, prevention involves marital counseling. Where therapy is indicated, parent counseling should include such topics as appropriate independence for the one-parent child and increased awareness of the need for reduced stimulation.

4. A "toxic" loss experience

Definition. This is a variety of overstimulating experience, in which the loss experience is accompanied by a specific kind of psychopathologic input rather than simply by an excessive quantity of stimulation.

Example. A child of any age loses one parent and is left with a psychotic or substance-abusing surviving parent. This adult then proceeds to involve the child in efforts to share delusional or substance-abusing practices. For a delusional or substance-abusing patient who has children, any effort at prevention must involve a family component as part of the treatment plan. In the case of hospitalized, psychotic patients, evaluation of their children should be routine, although in fact it is not. Therapy involves including the child in the treatment of the patient and including the child's at-home caregiver. Treatment may also include physical separation and, if necessary, foster placement.

5. A "conflictual" loss experience

Definition. A situation of loss heightens the antagonism between two agencies of the mental apparatus, such as the child's impulses (id) and the child's moral controls (superego).

Example. A 6-year-old child experiences loss of the caregiver from whom the youngster had acquired moral and ethical standards. In terms of the child's previous understanding of morality, the remaining or the new caregiver is experienced as seductive or demands behavior of very different moral and ethical character, precipitating conflict and resultant anxiety in the child. As a rule, prevention is not possible. Treatment can be undertaken through caregiver guidance as well as by means of psychoanalytically oriented interpretation of the child's conflicts. This would include not only conflicts between impulses and impulse-controls, but also the loyalty conflict of the child caught between diverse standards of impulse-control.

IDENTIFYING THE CHILD WHO IS AT RISK OF DAMAGE BECAUSE OF OBJECT LOSS EXPERIENCE

Simple Developmental Considerations

Example A. The infant is faced with complete loss of caregiver. Here, Spitz's (1946) model can be useful. The infant at risk for anaclitic depression because of object loss is characterized by the following situational and personal factors:

1. Age is at least 4 months and probably less than 18 months.
2. There has been a continuous caregiving experience by a sole caregiver.
3. Caregiving by that sole caregiver has been abruptly terminated.

Example B. The toddler and young child in any loss situation is affected by the following factors:

1. The child is cared for by a single parent or sole caregiver.
2. The family is set within a small or very unsupportive social network.
3. A handicapping or cosmetically disfiguring physical condition or mental retardation is present.
4. The child has sustained toxic, depleting, or understimulating prior experiences.

Example C. The adolescent is faced with death of or loss of the same-sex parent. The following factors are likely:

1. Role-model behavior previously stimulated by the deceased parent has diminished, and school performance has declined, with accompanying attendance difficulties and early antisocial signs.
2. Other factors are not clear, but healthy adolescents are capable of full adult mourning following the death or prolonged loss of a parent. Hence, failure to mourn should be suspect, particularly when accompanied by prolonged affect reversal or an absence of sad affect.

SCREENING PROCEDURES—EMPHASIS ON FOSTER CARE

During any one year, 500,000 children are in foster care, each of whom has experienced an object loss. Placement in foster care, even if very brief, is associated with a high incidence of current psychopathology and a high incidence of later sociopathy (Kliman et al., 1982; Wolkind, 1973). Therefore, the very fact of a child's being placed is a public health marker. It is important for the child psychiatrist to realize that the experiences of the child are likely to be beneficial after being in placement. The experiences that occur prior to placement account for the high incidence of current psychopathology and are, accordingly, a proper subject for concern, screening, and treatment.

A lesson from schizophrenia research is applicable here. A prospective study of children of schizophrenic mothers was conducted by Sameroff, Barocas, and Seifer (1984). It dealt with adopted or foster-placed children of psychotic mothers, and it indicated that it is difficult to attribute their psychopathology to the experience of foster care. Rather, what emerged was that among the child-surrendering mothers, the severity of psychopathology was higher than among other schizophrenic mothers. A related phenomenon was also reported by Wender, Rosenthal, Kety, Schulsinger and Welner (1974). In a retrospective study he found a far higher degree of psychopathology among schizophrenic mothers giving up their children for adoption than among mothers in general.

Women who place their children in foster care also differ from those who do not on the dimension of depression (Wender, 1974). Substance abuse is also a common reason for foster care placement (Kliman, 1982). Substance-abusing women who place their babies are likely to seriously neglect the infants; in a series of 200 such families studied by Black and Mayer (1980), 30% of the mothers behaved in this way. Further, the substance-abusing mothers who do place their babies are significantly more depressed (on Beck Depression Inventory scores) than are their child-caring peers (Finnegan, Oehlberg, Regan, & Rudrauff, 1981).

Many children of both schizophrenic and depressed mothers share a characteristic preplacement history. Inconstancy of parental attitude and style in the infant's care or even extremes of discontinuity of attention to the infant may be present. It certainly characterized the care of children studied by Tizard (1977); he made his observations in modern residential nurseries where the children had little opportunity to develop continuous attachments to adult caregivers. Such infants, by the time they reached the age of 8 years, had become markedly attention seeking, restless, disobedient, and unpopular among peers.

At the point of entry into foster care, good selection of foster parents and psychiatric screening of foster children are both valuable mental health measures. Proper placement within foster care will in itself account for major and measurable advantages. Among children placed in intellectually stimulating homes (Freeman, 1928; Kliman, 1982), a rise in IQ occurs as well as a rise in Wide Range Achievement Test Scores (Kliman, 1982). The child psychiatrist consulting with a foster care agency should determine which children have entered foster care with disparities between chronological age and grade placement and which children have the lowest Wide Range Achievement Test Scores (as administered by the schools). Ideally, such children should be placed with foster parents of higher than average educational status.

Each foster child should be screened by a behavioral inventory such as the Achenbach Child Behavior Inventory. The latter has been widely used to assess foster children (Olmstead, 1980); I recommend it for completion by foster parents in the first month of placement. The inventory should be reviewed by a child psychiatrist acting as consultant to the foster care agency. Children with Achenbach scores over 80 should be considered for more in-depth clinical evaluations and treatment.

There is a practical implication to screening in foster care. By detecting the most disturbed children at time of entry, the psychiatrist can attach a clinical marker to a child who is likely to become an administrative burden to the social service system. Disturbed children will more often "bounce" among foster homes than children who are not already psychiatrically disordered (Kliman & Schaeffer, 1990) and tend to become increasingly costly to the social service system. Early treatment has been demonstrated to reduce the bouncing rate (Kliman, 1982).

Screening is not so clearly indicated in bereavement by death, nor has it been widely applied in divorce and separation. However, it should be considered as a voluntary procedure (with parental consent) to be administered in schools with a high incidence of separated and divorced families.

Beyond screening, every child in a contested custody situation is entitled to an evaluation (Wallerstein & Kelly, 1980); where the parents do not seek it, this should be recommended by the school psychiatrist. In this situation of impending object loss, the school psychiatrist is also in a good position to request a full evaluation so that he or she can provide an impartial opinion about the child's best interests.

GENERAL PRINCIPLES OF PREVENTIVE MANAGEMENT IN EARLY OBJECT LOSS

1. There should be continuity both of caregiving and of associated narcissistic supplies for all children. This is one reason why foster care is usually (but not always) beneficial.—In 75% of foster families, the child's need for stability of placement is met in the first 12 months (Kliman, 1982).
2. The child's sense of personal history should be reinforced by discussion. This should be guided by the remaining caregivers and by the network of persons familiar with the child's past.
3. The child's personal locus of control has been placed in question by events over which he or she has had little power; accordingly, his or her sense of influence over events should be enhanced through encouragement and prescription of age-appropriate self-conducted activities. If a geographic change followed the loss, the activities should include letter writing or visits with old neighbors and phone calls to old friends.
4. If the child is over 3 years old, the work of mourning should be facilitated (Furman, 1974; Kliman, 1968, 1974, 1975, 1977, 1979a, 1979b, 1980; Kliman & Rosenfeld, 1980). The best facilitator is usually a familiar adult. Following a death, the surviving parent can help the child do the work of remembering with associated affect. This involves working over the memories repeatedly, gradually accepting the painful reality of loss of person and situation, and developing more available relationships and activities (Kliman, 1982). The surviving parent should be encouraged to participate in the community's grief as well as to allow the child to be part of religious and social rituals connected with the death. If a supportive adult is available to assist the surviving parent, the child will often benefit from being brought to the funeral and the graveside and from taking part in religious events. Children need help in clarifying cognitive ambiguities surrounding any loss or death, and they need respect for their developmental difficulties in attaining the same degree of sadness and the same rapidity of closure of mourning as do the adults and adolescents around them.
5. The intergenerational lack of emotional synchrony in reaction to any object loss needs recognition and acceptance, which is best accomplished through guidance of the caregivers (Kliman, 1979b; Kliman & Rosenfeld, 1980).

A PARTICULAR APPROACH TO PREVENTION— THE PERSONAL LIFE HISTORY BOOK METHOD

The Personal Life History Book Method (Kliman, 1990) is a form of situational crisis intervention. Technically, it is a variety of focused psychotherapy that is designed for use in cases of childhood bereavement, divorce, or placement in a foster family.

As part of this method, 15 or 20 sessions are spent with a child and up to 10 with the adult caregivers. Some of the sessions are conducted jointly with the child and caregivers. From the outset, the technique should be explained as preventive. Where foster placement is involved, the foster parents and biological family should both be helped to understand that the child will be reacting to passively experienced loss with possible active efforts to create a new rejection and resulting loss. In case of bereavement by death, the rationale will be to prevent pathologic reactions such as failure to mourn, new symptom formation, or constriction of emotional life.

The narrow task that focuses the therapy is the construction of a consensually created and validated personal life history book for the child. The child's history is written and illustrated by the therapist together with and, in part, by the child; the therapist will seek the child's assistance according to the youngster's developmental status and abilities. In the course of this process, the child acquires a concrete product—the original copy of the book—along with a framework for the discussion of loss experiences. In therapy sessions, the child is provided a perspective on how feelings of loss can complicate the ability to accept the good things about his or her surviving family or foster family, siblings, school, possessions, and friends. The child is encouraged to write chapters about the here and now as well as about the past, with interpretation of any tendency to active self-rejection. This is usually understood as an effort to avoid feeling like a passive victim of abandonment and loss. All available adults are enlisted to assist this endeavor, concretely providing photos and facts.

Even a single placement in foster care for a brief period is associated with increased incidence of sociopathy (Wolkind, 1973), due to prior adversities. Thus, special preventive efforts should be made to have foster children verbalize rather than *behave* as if they feel "robbed" by life. Their early antisocial impulses should be interpreted as maladaptive efforts to control the situation actively, to be robbers instead of robbed, assaulters instead of assaulted, victimizers instead of victims. Healthy forms of psychological activity can be fostered by the therapist and caregiver, particularly through encouraging the child to seek telephone contacts, to make visits, and to form compensatory new relationships. Recently my preventive use of the personal life history book with individual children has been replicated with small groups of foster children (Bondy, D., Davis, D., Hagen, S., Spiritos, A., Winnick, A., and Wright, C., 1990). In itself, foster care is a good preventive measure (Kliman, Schaeffer, & Friedman, 1982). Compared to what happens to so many of the children who return home to disturbed biological families, it is effective in reducing sociopathic behavior (Bohman, 1980).

REFERENCES

Ainsworth, M. D. S. (1962). The effects of maternal deprivation: A review of findings and controversy in the context of research strategy. In *Deprivation of maternal care: A reassessment of its effects*. (Public Health Papers No. 14). Geneva: World Health Organization.

Black, R., & Mayer, J. (1980). Parents with special problems: Alcoholism and opiate addiction. In C. H. Kempe & R. E. Helfer (Eds.), *The battered child*. Chicago: The University of Chicago Press.

Bohman, M., & Sigvardsson, S. (1980). Adoption and fostering as preventive measures: A prospective and longitudinal study of boys of negative social heritage. *Association of British Adoption and Fostering Agencies, 101*, 3, 25–36.

Bondy, D., Davis, D., Hagen, S., Spiritos, A., Winnick, A., & Wright, C. (1990). Brief, focused preventive group psychotherapy: A preliminary report on the use of the personal life history method with groups of foster children. I: Method and behavioral/social outcomes. *Journal of Preventive Psychiatry, 5*, 1.

Finnegan, L. P., Oehlberg, S., Regan, D., & Rudrauff, M. (1981). Evaluation of parenting, depression and violence profiles in methadone-maintained women. *Child Abuse and Neglect, 5*, 267–273.

Freeman, F. N., Holzinger, K. J., & Mitchel, B. C. (1928). The influence of environment on the intelligence, school achievement and conduct of foster children. *Twenty-seventh yearbook of the National Society for the Study of Education* (Part I, pp. 103–217). New York: National Society for the Study of Education Press.

Furman, E. (1974). *When a child's parent dies*. New Haven: Yale University Press.

Goodman, H., & Isaacs, L. D. (1984). Primary prevention with children of severely disturbed mothers. *Journal of Preventive Psychiatry, 2*, 3, 4.

Gregory, I. (1965). Anterospective study following childhood loss of a parent. *Archives of General Psychiatry, 13*, 94.

Kliman, G. (1968). *Psychological emergencies of childhood*. New York: Grune and Stratton.

Kliman, G. (1974). Death of a parent occurring during a child's analysis. In *Trauma: Monograph V of the Monograph Series of the Ernst Kris Study Group*. New York Psychoanalytic Institute, New York: International Universities Press.

Kliman, G. (1975). Analyst in the nursery: Application of child analytic techniques in a therapeutic nursery. *The psychoanalytic study of the child* (Vol. 30). New York: New York Times Publishing.

Kliman, G. (1977). Preventive measures in childhood bereavement. In N. Linzer (Ed.), *Understanding bereavement and grief*. New York: Yeshiva University Press.

Kliman, G. (1979a). Childhood mourning: A taboo within a taboo. In I. Gerber, A. Wiener, & A. Kutscher (Eds.), *Perspectives on bereavement*. New York: MSS Information Corporation.

Kliman, G. (1979b). Facilitation of mourning during childhood. In I. Gerber, A. Wiener, & A. Kutxcher (Eds.), *Perspectives on bereavement*. New York: MSS Information Corporation.

Kliman, G. (1980). Death: Some implications in child development and child analysis. In *Advances in thanatology* (Vol. 4, No. 2). New York: Arno Press.

Kliman, G., & Rosenfeld, A. (1980). Parents as preventive psychiatrists. In G. Kliman & A. Rosenfeld (Eds.), *Responsible parenthood*. New York: Holt, Rinehart & Winston.

Kliman, G., Schaeffer, M., & Friedman, M. (1982). *Preventive interventions with children entering foster family care: An assessment*. White Plains, NY: The Center for Preventive Psychiatry.

Kliman, G., & Schaeffer, M. (1990). Prediction and prevention with foster children. *Journal of Preventive Psychiatry, 5*, 1.

Offord, D. R., Abrams, N., Allen, N., & Poushinsky, B. A. (1979). Broken homes, parental psychiatric illness and female delinquency. *American Journal of Orthopsychiatry, 49*(2), 252–264.

Olmstead, J. (1980). *Children's service needs assessment: Family foster care survey*. Office of Research, Analysis and Information Services Division, Dept. of Social and Health Services, Olympia, WA.

Osterweis, M., Solomon, F., & Green, M. (Eds.). (1984). *Bereavement: Reactions, consequences, and care*. Washington, DC: National Academy Press.

Rutter, M. (1977). Sociocultural influences. In M. Rutter & L. Hersor (Eds.), *Child psychiatry: Modern approaches*. Oxford, England: Blackwell Publications.

Sameroff, A. J., Barocas, R., & Seifer, R. (1974). The early development of children born to mentally ill women. In N. Watt (Ed.), *Children at risk for schizophrenia: A longitudinal perspective*. Cambridge, England: Cambridge University Press.

Spitz, R. (1946). Hospitalism: A follow-up report. In *The psychoanalytic study of the child* (Vol. 2, pp. 113–117). New York: International Universities Press.

Tizard, B. (1977). *Adoption: A second chance*. London: Open Books.

Tizard, B., & Hodges, J. (1978). The effect of early institutional rearing on the development of eight-year-old children. *Journal of Child Psychology and Psychiatry, 19*, 99–118.

Wallerstein, J. S., & Kelly, J. B. (1980). *Surviving the breakup: How children and parents cope with divorce*. New York: Basic Books.

Wender, P. H., Rosenthal, D., & Kety, S. S. (1968). A psychiatric assessment of the adoptive parents of schizophrenics. In D. Rosenthal & S. S. Kety (Eds.), *The transmission of schizophrenia*. Oxford, England: Pergamon Press.

Wender, P. H., Rosenthal, D., Kety, S. S., Schulsinger, F., & Welner, J. (1974). *Cross-fostering: A research strategy for clarifying the role of genetic and experiential factors in the etiology of schizophrenia*. Oxford, England: Pergamon Press.

Wolkind, S., & Rutter, M. (1973). Children who have been "in care": An epidemiological study. *Journal of Child Psychology and Psychiatry, 14*, 97–105.

Yarrow, L. (1961). Maternal deprivation: Toward an empirical and conceptual re-evaluation. *Psychological Bulletin, 58*, 459–490.

— CHAPTER 34 ———————————————————

The Impact of Life Stress in Infancy, Childhood, and Adolescence

IRVING N. BERLIN, MD

Life stresses are either acute, single events or chronic, ongoing constellations of forces that impinge on the life of the individual for variable lengths of time and with varying intensity. In infancy, childhood, and adolescence these events may bear primarily on the family or parents and, because of the inherent quality of the relationships, may thus secondarily stress a particularly vulnerable infant, child, or adolescent.

The effects of any stressor may vary depending on the developmental maturity of the individual. Special vulnerabilities resulting from hereditary factors, pre- and perinatal traumata, special environmental factors, and particular invulnerabilities possessed by a specific infant act to alter the effects of a stressor (Askenasy, Dohrenwend, & Dohrenwend, 1977).

Most stress research has been done on adults. Holmes, Rahe, and their collaborators (Casey, Masuda, & Holmes, 1967; Holmes & Holmes, 1970; Holmes & Masuda, 1973; Holmes & Rahe, 1967; Rahe, 1968) are among the most respected researchers in this area; their scales for measuring stress have shown great reliability.

However, Spitz (1953), Bowlby (1977), and others have described the serious stressors in infancy. Subsequently, Coddington developed stress scales for children and Teicher and co-workers studied the stressors that were related to suicide and suicide attempts in adolescents. The Coddington (1972a, 1972b) scale and Teicher's (1979) hierarchy of stresses are remarkably congruent. They identify those stressors that most seriously affect the psychological adjustment of children and adolescents. A study of major factors etiologic to suicide in American Indians by Dizmang, Watson, May, and Bopp (1974) reaffirms the Teicher hierarchy of stressors.

GENERAL HIERARCHY OF STRESSORS IN TERMS OF SEVERITY OF IMPACT

Throughout any individual's preadult life, the most powerful stressor likely to be encountered is the total loss of or prolonged separation from the nurturant parent.

Divorce has a particularly severe impact on the preschool and school-age child; it is less disturbing to development during infancy or adolescence.

Severe maternal depression has its most noxious effect on the infant and young child.

At all ages, abuse, both violent and sexual, acts as a major source of stress.

In infancy and early childhood, acute illness that leads to hospitalization and separation is a major stressor; this circumstance has a severe impact in adolescence as well.

Throughout the life cycle, chronic illness and/or developmental disability also serve as severe stressors.

Hereditary or congenital structural developmental problems of an orthopedic nature, such as club foot and spinal bifida, require repeated painful surgery; other congenital defects, such as cardiac anomalies, also require uncomfortable procedures or surgeries. Such conditions may be both life threatening and very painful. These issues will be described in greater detail in connection with each developmental stage.

Acute and serious illnesses of parents, including mental illness, cause separations and/or interfere with the parents' ability to attend to the developmental needs and relationship requirements of the infant, child, or adolescent. In the nature of things, parental mental illness is a powerful stressor of children.

Family moves that separate the young adolescent from a peer group may offer the youngster's development a serious challenge. Other stressors important to adolescents will be discussed subsequently.

Factors that have an impact on family homeostasis may be important sources of stress. Among these are severe and chronic illness of a sibling, unemployment of the father, and family moves that are seriously disturbing to parents or siblings (Andrews, Tennant, Hewson, & Valliant, 1978; Tennant & Andrews, 1976).

For the purpose of this chapter Erikson's (1950) developmental stages and the tasks that need to be mastered at each stage will be used to describe the effect of stress on development.

INFANCY: BASIC TRUST VERSUS MISTRUST

The process of attachment described by Bowlby (1977) and others builds on the infant's increasing capacity to trust adults. This in turn is fostered by the parent's ability to be responsive to the infant's cues and needs. However, the entire process may be seriously interfered with by separations from the nurturant parent. Spitz (1953) described anaclitic depression occurring during the first year of life due to separation from the mother. He documented that separations of 3 months or more in the second half of the first year of life, where no nurturing person is provided for the infant, result in severe depression, complete refusal to accept nourishment, and often death due to intercurrent infections. If the mother (or other consistent nurturing person) is made available in less than 3 months, recovery from the depression occurs. Although some researchers believe such a severe depression may not occur, data from recent studies confirms the serious impact of early separation from a nurturing person.

Studies in both adolescent suicide and borderline personalities by Teicher (1979), Dizmang et al. (1974), Masterson (1981), and Nielson (1983) indicate that separation of 6 months' duration during the first year of life leads to later severe depression and feelings of distrust of adults and interferes with the normal development of relationships important at all ages.

Severe neglect or abuse of an infant by a depressed or alcoholic mother seriously interferes with the infant's anticipation of having needs met promptly. This leads to problems of trust, first with the caretaking adults and later with everyone, and tends to interfere with productive living throughout the subsequent developmental stages. The conflicts engendered at each stage prevent thorough integration of the functions inherent in that stage and may affect later development.

Researchers have now documented the infant's early awareness of the immediate environment (Brazelton, Scholl, & Robey, 1966) and ability to express anxiety in situations where there is little ongoing support by the nurturant person. The behavioral manifestations that may ensue in the face of such deprivation are colic, motor restlessness, problems in sleeping, and constant crying or wailing. In severe instances there are interferences with weight gain, body growth, and maturation of sensory-motor capacities.

In addition, a number of other emergent developmental capacities fail to occur. These include enjoyment of the practicing phase, the establishment of object constancy (the internalization of the reassuring presence of the mother so that there is an awareness of the mother's presence even when she is out of sight), and the working through of the separation-individuation process. This failure of development in infancy and early childhood has been thought to be an important etiologic factor in ''borderline'' children, adolescents, and adults and is related to interference with the developmental tasks of the next period (Rinsley, 1982).

PRESCHOOL CHILD: AUTONOMY VERSUS SHAME AND DOUBT (AGES 2–3); INITIATIVE VERSUS GUILT (AGES 4–6)

The developmental tasks of the preschool child involve the use of the new-found capacities of walking, talking, and skillful eye–hand coordination in order to explore the world and gain some independence from the mother.

Acquisition of Autonomy versus Shame and Doubt

From 1½ to 2½ years of age the child begins to develop a healthy autonomy from his or her mother. If the mother is unable to let the child go, some deviation of the earlier symbiotic relationship will persist, and the child may well continue to have doubts about being competent to survive alone. The symbiotic parent often uses shaming of the child in order to stifle normal bids for separation. Some mothers become angry at the child's attempt at autonomy and push the child away, producing a feeling of shame, anxiety, and fearfulness along with a sense that the rejection is due to the child's badness. In addition, sphincter control over bowel and bladder is developed at this stage. Failure to achieve such control because of the ambivalence of parents may lead to retention of body excreta; this in turn begets shame about not achieving the milestones mastered by other children. This sense of shame is especially stimulated when the child enters preschool and is teased both by adults and by other children (Kliman & Rosenfeld, 1980; Mahler, 1972).

Acquisition of Initiative versus Guilt

The 2- to 4-year-old is engaged in very active exploration of the world, taking great pleasure in each newly initiated activity and in practicing it until it is mastered. Simultaneously, the child deals with oedipal conflicts, without the intrusion, it is hoped, of destructive or oppressive measures by parents. Thus, the parent of the same sex becomes the object of identification and imitation. Where guilt does arise, it comes both from the rejection of active exploration (as if such activities were bad) and from the expression of harsh attitudes by the parent of the same sex (which prevents the resolution of the oedipal struggle and produces massive guilt in the child about feelings and desires toward the parent of the opposite sex).

The most important stressor of all is likely to be the death of one or both parents, an event that deprives the child of major support and sustenance. Usually the death of one parent results in major depression in the other parent, leaving the child with no one available to meet needs. The child looks sad, despondent, depressed, weepy, and manifests all the characteristics of a grief reaction. He or she experiences a need for comfort and for the reassurance that care and affection will still be available. There is often a loss of bladder and/or bowel control, use of baby talk, and regression in socialization marked by clinging to an adult and difficulty in separating. The degree of disturbance is related to earlier developmental vicissitudes as well as to the sex of the parent who dies. Where oedipal conflicts are severe, the death of the same-sex parent tends to increase guilt and depression. Usually, however, the mother's death is more traumatic.

For the preschool child, divorce may be bewildering, but if he or she remains with a capable nurturant parent, it is usually not terribly stressful. However, if custody is given to a parent who cannot spend much time with the child or who is not very nurturant, and the child is placed in the hands of inadequate caretakers, divorce may be extremely stressful for the child. Also, inappropriately long visitations with the noncustodial parent along with concurrent separation from the nurturant parent may arouse anxieties in the child. The child's sense of time is undeveloped, and a long absence from the custodial parent may feel like a permanent loss. The questions of custody and visitation must be thought out with great care in order to facilitate meeting the needs of the child at this developmental stage.

Another important stress for the preschool child is separation from the family because of the need for medical or surgical care. Hospitalization may produce massive anxiety. In many hospitals, parents are encouraged to remain with the child for as long as possible each day to allay the anxiety, fear, and pain, and to help the healing process.

Although the substitute caretakers may be other familiar family members, such as grandparents, when the child is separated from the parents for as long as several months because of prolonged vacations or parental illness, the resulting sense of loss may produce massive withdrawal and regression.

The onset of a severe acute or chronic illness, such as asthma or rheumatic fever, or the repair of congenital defects (like orthopedic or cardiac anomalies) requiring surgery, produces overwhelming stress in the child for several reasons: the great pain involved, the helplessness of the child to deal with the pain, and the child's frightening recognition that the all-powerful parents are unable to reduce the pain. Because the "good," uncomplaining child is the one desired by physicians, parents, and hospital personnel, children are encouraged to deny the hurt, the chronic pain, and their fear of the procedures. They learn to be brave to the detriment of their personality development. Because they are not encouraged to talk about the fears and pain they may experience, many of these youngsters become withdrawn and shy. They also have difficulty putting their feelings into words. They have a distorted image of themselves as damaged and bad; otherwise, it seems to them, they would not be afflicted with this problem. In many instances, these children will retain this self-image of an imperfect, damaged person all their lives.

Clearly, in the face of separations, the healing intervention requires the presence of caretakers who can supply the necessary physical and psychological comfort. The stress of pain during physical illness or in the course of correction of congenital defects requires parents and health professionals to encourage the child to acknowledge pain. This can be done by open and frequent verbalization by adults of how much it hurts and by providing opportunities to play out the procedures, thus allowing the child to release pent-up feelings. The drawings by 4- and 5-year-olds of the monsters who surround them, and the children's glee when Play Ladies allow them to give make-believe shots to the doctor dolls demonstrate the need children have for permission to feel their anger. By giving shots to the people who produce the pain, the children feel a little more in control and to some extent less helpless (Cassel, 1974).

The other major stress at this age is child abuse, which is often discovered in children who appear either withdrawn and depressed or overly aggressive. Their stress arises from the unpredictable nature of the abusing parent's behavior; these children signal what has happened by their distrust of all adults, by severe startle reactions to sudden movements around them, or by teasing, provocative behavior that elicits anger and predictable violence from others. They may also appear either withdrawn and depressed or very aggressive toward other children.

Abused children require opportunities to play out their fearfulness, anger, and distrustful hatred toward the adults they depend on either in groups or in individual sessions (Fried, 1982).

Case Vignette

Four-year-old Tommy was covered with bruises and cigarette burns and had been hospitalized three times with broken limbs. It took him 3 months of cautious play with toy cars in the playroom before he could imitate his therapist's continual demonstrations of horrendous car crashes with accompanying vocal noises. Finally, he could smash cars into each other, first whispering and at last yelling "Smash bang!" He then put dolls in the cars, and they were constantly run over; the ambulances would turn over on their way to the hospital, and the dolls were pronounced "All dead." At first these actions were carried out with anxious glances at the therapist, who encouraged the play. During this phase, Tommy began to be less aggressive and provocative in the foster home. When, after 5 months of once-a-week play therapy, he could rescue the dolls and make them all well, he could let himself receive and return affection from his foster parents.

Abused children need a secure, predictable environment in which to grow and many opportunities, such as play groups or individual therapy, to redevelop trust in adults. Recent efforts to reeducate abusing parents and to help them develop a new relationship with their child have had some success.

STRESS IN THE SCHOOL-AGE CHILD:
INDUSTRY VERSUS INFERIORITY

The developmental tasks of the grade-school child are to use increased cognitive capacities and to invest the self in learning and in socialization with peers (mostly of the same sex).

Industry typifies the school-age child's investment of energies in learning and in the peer relationships. With children of this age, the great pleasure that emanates from the effective learner along with the incessant questions and delight in new learning are all common experiences. If feelings of inferiority arise, they stem from both failure in the mastery of learning as well as the lack of rewarding peer relations (because of inappropriate behavior and lack of interest in mutual learning and sharing).

At this age, parental loss by death or secondarily by divorce can also be serious stresses. The school-age child can usually understand cognitively that death is a permanent loss, whereas divorce means partial loss of a parent. However, the cognitive awareness is very concrete; the child's understanding of the causes of death is fragmentary and may require simple explanations. Yet, one has to be aware of oversimplification: Telling a child that death is like going to sleep can make a child afraid to go to bed at night. Visitations after divorce are important, and stress usually occurs only if children are used by the parents in a continuing battle against each other. As is to be expected, parental loss may lead to regression, that is, depression and inability to learn and to interact with friends (Finch & Saylor, 1984). To encourage their expression of feelings, school-age children characteristically require open discussion of events and freely offered comments by understanding adults. They also need to have permission to seek out a particular adult for physical and psychological comfort (Cobb, 1976; Gersten, Langner, Eisenberg, & Orzek, 1974).

The death of a brother or sister or a sibling's severe illness has a major impact. The child needs to share grief with the grieving parents and needs to be able to be open about some of the guilt feelings aroused by the rivalries and jealousies common to all children. A sibling's death or serious illness brings the child's own mortality into sharp focus, these fears need to be discussed, with reassurance about his or her own expected longevity.

The impact of severe or chronic illness on children at this age is a major life stress. The hospital experience itself is frightening, and the child must be prepared for it by discussion with the parents and with the physician and, when possible, by visiting the hospital ahead of time so it is not altogether strange and unfamiliar. If surgery is contemplated, visits to an operating room to become acquainted with it are helpful. Frequent discussions about what will be done and the expected results are important. Because children's ideas of their body parts are fragmentary, it helps considerably if they learn about their bodies and how they work. Parents need to be at the child's bedside as much as possible.

There are many fears about the effects of chronic disease on children, as well as its impact on activities. It is critical that the physician realize how little the child or parents actually understand and absorb during the first shock of hearing a diagnosis of diabetes, hemophilia, seizure disorder, asthma, and so on. The more the child and family understand about the illness and its effects, the better. One of the main tasks is to help the parents not to overprotect the child. Many children may try to use the illness to avoid the tasks of learning or to neglect the developmentally necessary responsibilities that are important to family life such as participation in household chores. Alertness to any signs of the child's anxiety and to the youngster's tendency to manipulate the family will enable the physician to be of considerable help. He or she can then communicate to the family that they need to help the child continue to function as normally as possible. The physician can also encourage firmness in the parents to prevent or reduce emotional problems for both child and family.

Because of the cognitive readiness of the school-age child to use such techniques, varieties of role-playing and drama may enhance the youngster's efforts to master very frightening situations and may thus be very helpful in dealing with stress.

Case Vignette

Brad, an 11-year-old, has congenital heart disease that has led to numerous invasive diagnostic procedures and cardiac surgery to repair a defective heart valve. When he was started in treatment, however, he found himself unable to talk in therapy. He could only say in emotionless tones that he was scared with each procedure. However, he began to show some feeling and involvement when the therapist built a clay figure and invited Brad to show him the operations that help heart disease.

Brad first used broomstraws to demonstrate how the cardiac catheterizations are done. Taking the role of the pediatric surgeon, he uttered reassuring phrases "It won't hurt," "We just have a little further to go." He listened to the heart with a stethoscope while beatiing out a heart rhythm on the table, emphasizing the irregular heart beats. As surgeon he exclaimed, "My that boy is blue, quick the oxygen!" With the therapist's help Brad built a large heart with four chambers. He then proceeded to do surgery. He corrected a septal defect announcing with satisfaction, "I'm done, it's OK, good as new." He and the therapist read a high school anatomy section of a biology book. He imitated a murmur with a squishing sound as he listened to the heart.

Just prior to another operation to correct some leakage not controlled in the previous one, he and the therapist performed five mock operations. The first three were failures, and they talked together about what was wrong. Brad's excellent memory of conversations held at his bedside contributed a tense but accurate description of what needed to be done. The fourth heart was repaired but, as had occurred in his own case, a scar gave way. The fifth heart was successfully repaired. Subsequently, during the actual surgery, the therapist was at Brad's bedside and stayed in the recovery room until he awakened. This was the first time Brad had had anyone with him during these frightening experiences. This surgery was successful. During the four subsequent sessions therapist and patient continued their mastery of heart surgery, and then Brad began to talk of his fear that his health problems would kill his fragile, very neurotic mother. He also worked through his father's absences from home on army overseas duty, and his younger siblings' anger at him because he was the center of attention at home and did not have to do chores, go to school, and so on.

His mastery of the heart surgery plus his better understanding of heart physiology and structure through reading with the therapist all contributed to his feeling more competent and eager to learn in other areas.

In considering interventions, the first step is to become aware of the problem. It is important for teachers and school counselors who are working with a child of this age to be alert to behavioral changes, especially from learning to nonlearning. A cheerful child who suddenly becomes depressed or who begins to behave in a stubborn way in class may be involved in conflict at home or could be experiencing overwhelming stress. School personnel who invite the child to talk, express their concern, and lend a listening ear can provide an important escape valve for the child's feelings of anxiety, hurt, fear, and anger. The school staff may also be able to help the parents recognize the need to be open with the youngster and to invite discussion of fears and anxieties. Parents and other adults who understand the limitations of their child's grasp on his or her own anatomy and physiology can find simple ways to share such information.

Thus, a girl of 7 or 8 who draws a picture of herself as an elipse inside of which are teeth biting on organs is describing her view of what her insides are like and how she construes the pain she has experienced.

ROLE OF DEPRESSION AND MASTERY OF STRESS

One indicator of continuing stress in childhood and early adolescence is the presence of chronic depression. Currently, many studies are being conducted on major chronic depression in childhood. Numerous investigations reveal that most of these young people have evidenced such depression for years. They tend to be loners, they do not learn well, and 80% to 90% have been—or are being—physically and sexually abused by their parents or close relatives. Thus, the failure to recognize the signs of chronic stress precludes early intervention. These young people are often very suspicious and mistrustful of adults; at the same time, however, they are also very hungry for a supportive and understanding relationship. It is of interest that in individual treatment, they enjoy playing childlike games such as dominoes, with ever-increasing expressions of feelings about their need to win. Given the opportunity to use finger paints, especially if the therapist introduces such activity as fun, some youngsters will begin drawing stilted figures, houses, and so on, and after a while may experiment with smearing. Others may use dolls and a dollhouse to act out aggressive, punitive fantasies, usually involving adult doll figures who are run over, thrown from rooftops, or buried under a mound of blocks.

In a few school settings, several such youngsters have been brought together in a play group. At first there was structured play in the form of active games as well as more passive activities such as drawing a mural together. The peer groups began over time to play more spontaneously, and, in one group, to play out science fiction TV and movie stories.

A number of studies reveal that by the third grade, chronic depression can often be identified in the school-age child. The most obvious sign is failure to get involved in the excitement of learning. These youngsters seek to avoid school, and, once in school, they do very little work. They have problems in attending to lessons and in concentrating on reading. When questioned or reprimanded, they offer a blank look of nonunderstanding. They are loners, and some of them seek to escape the depression by solvent sniffing, mostly of glue, paint, and gasoline. Inquiries at home reveal that these youngsters have no friends, sleep and eat poorly, and are not involved with their families.

As noted, the prior stress of physical abuse or continued stress of physical and/or sexual abuse produces distrust of adults and inability to relate to peers.

When teachers and other school personnel become aware of the presence of depression, their efforts to teach these children and to facilitate group interchange of experiences and feelings have been very helpful. The major modalities employed have been group therapy with a large cognitive component, that is, discussion of depression, the underlying anger, and so on.

Because alienation from noncaring adults is almost universal, initially the child often distrusts the caring expressed by adults; after a time, however, it becomes very important.

Some mildly depressed youngsters try to deny the previous or ongoing trauma in their lives by studying hard. Although they enjoy their teachers' praise and the relationships offered them, they do so without the spontaneity and fun characterized by their age group (Finch & Saylor, 1984).

STRESS IN EARLY AND MIDDLE ADOLESCENCE— DEVELOPMENTAL TASKS: IDENTITY VERSUS ROLE CONFUSION

Erikson describes the developmental tasks of adolescence as first the establishment of an identity. Where this process is unsuccessful, the youngster faces the risk of suffering role confusion. In effect, the adolescent must establish who he or she is in the views of others, especially peers. The ability to use formal operational thinking means that the youth can now present ideas more clearly using inductive logic. The young person understands a good deal more about his or her world.

During this period the need arises to establish a work role or to determine a direction in studying for a profession or preparing for a job. Adolescents also begin to separate from their families and more and more to become their own person. They start to develop their own ideas about the world and their own mores (sometimes different from those of their families). Their closeness with peers and beginning intimacy with persons of the opposite sex also help to establish their independence and identity (Burke & Weir, 1978; Pasley, 1969).

When adolescents cannot take these steps, they remain confused about who they are. In many ways they continue to be dependent on their family; they are unable to find a future role for themselves in life; and, over time, they become more distant from peers of both sexes.

In later adolescence the developmental tasks include the achievement of intimacy where intimacy means the capacity to commit oneself to another in the form of a stable affiliation. Failing that, young people feel isolated. Intimacy occurs primarily with persons of the other sex, and when this task is not mastered, the individual can only become distanced from others. He or she dares not risk close friendships or sexual relationships in which both closeness and responsibility to others would be experienced. Such capacities as the pleasures of intellectual challenge and the ability to call on inner resources and to depend on intuitions are not present, because they depend upon long-standing reliable trusting experiences with age-mates.

In summary, the goals of early adolescence are to deal with the altered body structure produced by the hormonal changes, to become part of a close-knit same-sex peer group, to begin to utilize recently acquired formal operational thinking capacities (i.e., to think in abstract terms about mathematics, science, history, philosophy), to become creative and enthusiastic about changing the world, and to become gradually more independent of parents.

In mid-adolescence the tasks are to begin a separation process from the family, without sliding over into alienation. The adolescent uses the peer group to develop close feelings and begins to explore a sense of intimacy with friends of the same sex and attachments to the opposite sex. The preparation for work or professions begins during this period (Klos & Peddock, 1978).

Stress research in this age group lists many events as sources of trauma. In order of importance, these include death of a parent, death of a sibling (especially by suicide), and acute severe illness. Chronic illness that alters one's self-image as a desirable friend and potential spouse is especially important. The factors that lead to depression in the school-age child continue to play a similar role in adolescence.

Adolescent depression is now very commonly recognized; its effect seems to be that of a very important stressor leading to or exacerbating various psychophysiological conditions such as diabetes, asthma, ulcerative colitis, anorexia nervosa, and bulimia (Graham & Stevenson, 1963; Hoteling, Atwell, & Linsky, 1978; Kaplan, Landa, Weinhold, & Shenko, 1984; Wyler, Masuda, & Holmes, 1971).

In its chronic form, adolescent depression seems to result from previous serious stresses especially parental loss, that have inhibited functioning.

Acute depression often appears as a result of severe stresses that the adolescent seems unable to share with anyone (Valliant, 1977). Depression and the usual effect of stress alter the adolescents' capacity for maintaining identity. Ultimately, in this situation teenagers feel and behave as if they were alone, isolated, and confused about their capabilities as persons.

It is important to recognize that in early adolescence, family moves from one part of the country to another are serious disruptions. It is extraordinarily difficult to replicate the closeness attained with one's initial peer group in any subsequent peer interactions. The first close heterosexual relationship reaffirms one's identity as a valued person. Hence the loss of a first girlfriend or boyfriend is of critical importance because it ruptures the intimacy and excitement of this encounter.

Another source of serious stress is loss of parental support through loss of a job by a parent, divorce, or alienation of a parent because of his/her competitive feelings. Some parents may envy the possibilities of the new, intimate, rewarding and sexually satisfying experiences that are open to the adolescent. This kind of alienation may occur when a parent of the same sex feels that he or she has missed out on these experiences, or when a parent of the opposite sex feels jealousy of adolescent rivals (Berlin, 1979; Sarason, Johnson, & Siegel, 1978).

DEPRESSION—ADOLESCENT SUICIDE

Teicher's (1979) research validated by recent data from the Southwestern American Indian Adolescent Suicide studies (Berlin, 1985), indicates that the most common and significant event connected to suicide by an adolescent is the recent death of a parent or important supportive adult. Other important factors are loss of peer support and loss of a sweetheart, through breaking off or moving away. It is particularly important to note that in both these studies, early loss of a parent (during the first 2 years of life) followed by the loss of an important adult during adolescence seems in the first instance to be etiologic, and in the second instance to act as a precipitating factor in 70% of adolescent suicides.

Another important precipitant of suicide attempts is losing face or letting parents and family down by failing in the first semester of college (Harris, 1972). In many American Indian tribes, being jailed for a minor crime and/or intoxication is felt as a terrible blow to one's dignity and a serious offense against the family, clan, and tribe (Berlin, 1985).

Divorce seems less of a stressor at this age, particularly if both parents remain available.

The physician needs to be aware of the vulnerabilities of adolescents who have suffered severe trauma in early childhood. He or she must be attuned as well to the importance of the peer group and especially of the first heterosexual relationships, and to the overriding need at this age for an adult who will listen and provide opportunities for the adolescent to talk, feel understood, and ventilate worries and hurts without being lectured to or advised. The adult must communicate empathy for the pain of the adolescent and confidence in the adolescent's ability to work out his or her destiny and to cope with problems effectively. These are important ways of preventing serious consequences to life stresses for adolescents (Cobb, 1976; Heller, 1979).

GENERAL PRINCIPLES OF STRESS MANAGEMENT

At any age after infancy, a key factor in stress management is the ability of adults to anticipate the young person's pain in difficult situations and to provide an atmosphere conducive to free expression of concerns and feelings.

As part of effective parenting for children facing painful procedures or life events, adults need to provide a consistently available parental presence.

Of utmost importance also are parental attitudes that give the child or adolescent permission to talk with them openly, as well as to turn to teachers, counselors, and others, about their concerns. This freedom permits sharing the stressful events with potentially helpful adults, who in turn enable the child or adolescent to master the life stress more successfully and to develop a sense of competence and control.

SUMMARY AND CONCLUSIONS

Severe stress at every developmental stage interferes to some degree with the mastery of developmental tasks and the achievement of the goals appropriate to that stage.

In infancy and early childhood, the capacity to trust and depend on adults is disrupted. Without intervention the most serious consequences can result, with ultimate failures in attachment and in the capacity to make relationships.

In the preschool and school-age years, an encounter with excessive stress may seriously hamper the initiatives that result from both maturation and development. This can lead to overdependence and guilt and an inability to realize the need for independent ventures and activities; eventually the individual may become tied to the parent in a very ambivalent relationship. The helplessness resulting from stress interferes with separation-individuation and the experiencing of object constancy.

Because stress reduces industry, that is, the use by a person of energies to learn and to form relationships and friendships, the child may feel inferior and not as lovable as his or her peers.

Stress in early and middle adolescence will also impede the critical working through of developmental tasks. It will interfere with the person's establishing a stamp on the world, enjoying the mastery of abstract thought, and better understanding the world and believing in the possibility that it can be changed. Stress also interferes with both close peer relationships and the beginning of intimate and responsible attachments to members of the opposite sex. The confusion about identity and the loneliness and hunger for relationships that result from stress may seriously skew a youngster's outlook and capacity to become independent of his or her family.

The major factors that reduce the impact of stress are the concerns and attention of adults who, by their continued involvement, can provide many kinds of assistance. Help can range from supplying nurturance, to enabling the youngster to free himself or herself from the stifling dependence on a nurturant adult, to providing the inspiration and the concrete aid that allow a child to continue to learn and grow despite the stress. In adolescence, it can mean assistance in finding models who can in turn help the young person discover, identify, and gradually venture into a variety of relationships with increasing responsibility in these efforts.

REFERENCES

Andrews, G., Tennant, C., Hewson, D. M., & Valliant, G. E. (1978). Life event stress, social support, coping style, and risk of psychological impairment. *Journal of Nervous and Mental Disease, 166,* 307–316.

Askenasy, A. R., Dohrenwend, B. P., & Dohrenwend, B. S. (1977). Some effects of social class and ethnic group membership on judgments of the magnitude of stressful life events: A research note. *Journal of Health and Social Behavior, 18,* 432–439.

Berlin, I. N. (1979). Some implications of the developmental processes for treatment of depression in adolescence. In French & Berlin (Eds.). *Depression and children and adolescents* (pp. 66–76). New York: Human Science Press.

Berlin, I. N. (1985). Prevention of adolescent suicide among some native American tribes. In S. Feinstein, M. Sugar, A. Esman, J. Looney, A. Schwartzberg, & A. Sorosky (Eds.). *Adolescent psychiatry: Developmental and clinical studies* (pp. 77–93). Chicago: University of Chicago Press.

Bowlby, J. (1977). The making and breaking of affectional bonds, I, II. *British Journal of Psychiatry, 130,* 201–210, 421–431.

Brazelton, T. B., Scholl, M. L., & Robey, J. S. (1966). Visual responses in the newborn. *Pediatrics, 37,* 284–290.

Burke, R. J., & Weir, T. (1978). Sex differences in adolescent life stress, social support and well-being. *Journal of Psychology, 98,* 277–288.

Casey, R. L., Masuda, M., & Holmes, T. H. (1967). Quantitative study of recall of life events. *Journal of Psychosomatic Research, 11,* 239–247.

Cassel, J. (1974). Psychosocial process and "stress." *Social Psychiatry, 6,* 186–193.

Cobb, S. (1976). Social support as a moderator of life stress. *Psychosomatic Medicine, 38,* 300–313.

Coddington, R. D. (1972a). The significance of life events as etiologic factors in the diseases of children. I. A survey of professional workers. *Journal of Psychosomatic Research, 16,* 7–18.

Coddington, R. D. (1972b). The significance of life events as etiologic factors in the diseases of children. II. A study of a normal population. *Journal of Psychosomatic Research, 16,* 205–213.

Dizmang, L. J., Watson, J., May, P. A., & Bopp, J. (1974). Adolescent suicide at an Indian Reservation. *American Journal of Orthopsychiatry, 44,* 43–49.

Erikson, E. H. (1950). *Childhood and society.* New York: Norton.

Finch, A., & Saylor, C. (1984). An overview of childhood depression. In P. Burns & G. Lavigne (Eds.), *Progress in pediatric psychology* (pp. 138–147). New York: Grune & Stratton.

Fried, M. (1982). Endemic stress: The psychology of resignation and the policy of scarcity. *American Journal of Orthopsychiatry, 52,* 4–19.

Gersten, J. C., Langner, T. S., Eisenberg, J. G., & Orzek, L. (1974). Child behavior and life events: Undesirable change or change per se? In B. S. Dohrenwend & B. P. Dohrenwend (Eds.), *Stressful life events: Their nature and effects* (pp. 159–170). New York: Wiley.

Graham, D. T., & Stevenson, I. (1963). Disease as response to life stress. I. The nature of the evidence. In H. I. Lief, V. F. Lief, & N. R. Lief (Eds.), *The psychological basis of medical practice* (pp. 115–136). New York: Harper & Row.

Harris, P. W. (1972). *The relationship of life change to academic performance among selected college freshmen at varying levels of college readiness.* Unpublished doctoral dissertation, East Texas State University, Commerce, TX.

Heller, K. (1979). The effects of social support: Prevention and treatment implications. In A. P. Goldstein & F. H. Kanfer (Eds.), *Maximizing treatment gains: Transfer enhancement in psychotherapy* (pp. 201–228). New York: Academic Press.

Holmes, T. S., & Holmes, T. H. (1970). Short-term intrusions into the life style routine. *Journal of Psychosomatic Research, 14,* 121–132.

Holmes, T. H., & Masuda, M. (1973). Life change and illness susceptibility. In P. H. Abelson (Ed.), *Separation and depression. Science, 82,* 161–186.

Holmes, T. H., & Rahe, R. H. (1967). The social readjustment rating scale. *Journal of Psychosomatic Research, 11,* 213–218.

Hoteling, G., Atwell, S., & Linsky, A. (1978). Adolescent life changes and illness: A comparison of three models. *Journal of Youth and Adolescence, 7,* 393–403.

Kaplan, S. L., Landa, B., Weinhold, C., & Shenko, R. (1984). Adverse health behaviors and depressive symptomology in adolescents. *Journal of the Academy of Child Psychiatry, 23,* 595–601.

Kliman, G. W., & Rosenfeld, A. (1980). *Reponsible parenthood: The child psyche through the six-year pregnancy.* New York: Holt, Reinhart & Winston.

Klos, D., & Peddock, J. (1978). Relationship status: Scale for assessing the vitality of late adolescents' relationships with their parents. *Journal of Youth and Adolescence, 7,* 353–369.

Mahler, M. (1972). On the first three subphases of the separation individuation processes. *International Journal of Psychoanalysis, 53,* 333–338.

Masterson, J. F. (1981). *The narcissistic and borderline disorders: An integrated developmental approach.* New York: Brunner/Mazel.

Nielsen, G. (1983). *Borderline and acting-out adolescents: A developmental approach.* New York: Human Science Press.

Pasley, S. (1969). *The social readjustment rating scale: A study of the significance of life events in age groups ranging from college freshman to seventh grade.* Psychology tutorial thesis, Chatham College, Pittsburgh, PA.

Rahe, R. H. (1968). Life-change measurement as a predictor of illness. *Proceedings of the Royal Society of Medicine, 61,* 1124–1126.

Rinsley, D. (1982). Object relations theory and psychotherapy with particular reference to the self-disordered patient. In P. Giovacchini & L. B. Boyer (Eds.), *Treatment of the severely disturbed patient* (pp. 134–143). New York: Aronson.

Sarason, I. G., Johnson, J. H., & Siegel, J. M. (1978). Assessing the impact of life changes: Development of the life experiences survey. *Journal of Consulting and Clinical Psychology, 46,* 932–946.

Spitz, R. A. (1953). The psychogenic diseases in infancy: An attempt at their etiologic classification. *Psychoanalytic Study of the Child, 8,* 65–78.

Teicher, J. D. (1979). Suicide and suicide attempts. In J. D. Noshpitz (Ed.), *Basic handbook of child psychiatry* (Vol. 2, pp. 685–697). New York: Basic Books.

Tennant, C., & Andrews, G. (1976). A single scale to measure the stress of life events. *Australian and New Zealand Journal of Psychiatry, 10,* 27–32.

Valliant, G. (1977). *Adaptation to life.* Boston: Little, Brown.

Wyler, A. R., Masuda, M., & Holmes, T. H. (1971). Magnitude of life events and seriousness of illness. *Psychosomatic Medicine, 33,* 115–122.

— CHAPTER 35 ——————————————

Stress Prevention in Adults

GERALD J. McKENNA, MD
RANSOM J. ARTHUR, MD

This chapter will examine some areas of stress affecting the lives of individuals in our society, the impact of stress on our lives, particularly in the areas of health, and some theories on the ways to decrease the harmful effects of stressful events. A review of the history of human development through the ages indicates that stress has always been with us. The struggles of nations to provide the necessities of life and to deal with inter- and intrapersonal relationships, disasters, wars, and plagues provide evidence of a continual struggle with stressful events as well as with the effects of these events on the human organism.

The Industrial Revolution, with its rapid progression of historic changes up to the present time, has created new stressors that, though recognizable, remain poorly understood in terms of their microeffects on society. Behavior patterns have changed. Certainly, industrial societies of today bear little resemblance to societies of 200 years ago; a host of new disorders, both physical and mental, now plague humankind. External change may well be occurring so fast that the human organism is unable to keep pace. In his book, *Future Shock,* Alvin Toffler (1970), described this phenomenon and speculated on its human impact. Though stress appears to be a common daily occurrence, the psychiatric literature has given surprisingly little attention to its effects. Other medical specialties have attended to the effects of

616

stress on the body (hypertension, heart disease, trauma), but the emphasis has been more on the secondary effects of changes brought about by modern living (sedentary lifestyle, increased use of drugs) rather than on the primary effects of living in a stress-filled world.

Psychiatric literature has focused on the intrapersonal effects of interpersonal events such as separation, loss, impaired parent–child relationships, and affective restrictions. The focus on the biological aspects of mental disorders and on the treatment effects of psychopharmacology has been more recent. The psychology literature has given more attention to the effects of social supports on physical and mental health and has provided cognitive approaches to handling problems with behavior and affect management. Learning theory, behavior therapy, and techniques such as Stress Inoculation, have attempted to examine the relationship between stressful events and human reactions to them.

This chapter will review some of the relevant literature in both psychiatry and psychology to see how the problems of stress and stress prevention have been approached, in order to draw some conclusions about current understanding in this area.

LITERATURE REVIEW

Psychiatric literature on stress, prior to 1960, focused largely on major events (stressors) and individual reactions to them. Not surprisingly, war and its effects led to new descriptions and observations on reaction to major and continuous stressors. Southard (1919) described the phenomenon of shell shock among World War I combatants. Archibald & Tuddenham (1965), Brill & Beebe (1956), and many others (Dobbs & Wilson, 1960; Futterman & Pumpian-Mindlin, 1951; Kalinowsky, 1950; Lewis & Engle, 1954), described the stresses sustained by combatants during World War II, and the term *combat fatigue* appeared in the literature. Similar stress syndromes were described in concentration camp survivors and those interned as prisoners of war (Arthur, 1974; Arthur & McKenna, 1989; Chodoff, 1963; Friedman, 1949; Krystal, 1968; Nardini, 1952; Strom, 1968; Wolf & Ripley, 1947). This syndrome is now known as PostTraumatic Stress Disorder (PTSD) and is recognized to be the result of massive psychic trauma occurring in a variety of natural and human-made disasters and stressors (war, torture, rape, earthquakes, floods, fires, major transportation accidents) (Frederick, 1985; McKenna & Arthur, 1989). Attempts are being directed at early intervention to minimize the psychic effects of these tragedies. This intervention may minimize the long-term effects of PTSD by providing services such as rape counseling and postdisaster intervention. These interventions, however, take place after the stressor has occurred. The military has made some attempts to study the stressors that are presumed to cause Posttraumatic Stress Disorder. Policies can then be instituted to minimize the incidence of Posttraumatic Stress Disorder among combatants of future wars.

Stress Inoculation

In the psychiatric literature a number of authors discussed the cognitive and affective aspects of dealing with common stressors and their relationship with psychopathology (Beck, 1967, 1971; Chodoff, Friedman, & Hamburg, 1964; Menninger, 1938). Egbert, Battit, Welch, & Bartlett (1964) discussed the reduction of postoperative pain by the encouragement of instruction. Meichenbaum (1975) first discussed and developed the Stress Inoculation model, which was further developed by others.

Novaco (1977a) presented a behavioral cognitive therapy approach using Stress Inoculation in anger management. The treatment approach followed the Stress Inoculation procedure.

Stress Inoculation as described by Novaco consists of cognitive preparation, skill acquisition and rehearsal, and an application practice phase. In their treatment case, a patient with depression who was hospitalized had a 43-point drop in anger inventory from 301 to 258, which is greater than one standard deviation, accompanied by clinical improvement. The treatment procedure in this case consisted of educating the patient regarding the functions of anger and his personal anger patterns. A second cognitive preparation phase involved a number of factors. At first the patient was encouraged to identify persons and situations that triggered anger. There was a fostering of recognition of the difference between anger and aggression followed by an understanding of the cognitive somatic behavioral determinants of anger with the emphasis on anger-instigating self-statements. The patient was taught to self-discriminate justified from unnecessary anger and then to organize the signs of tension and arousal early in a particular provocation sequence followed by anger management concepts as coping strategies.

The skill acquisition and rehearsal phase involved familiarization with three sets of coping techniques, modeling of the techniques by the therapist, and then rehearsal by the patient. This skill acquisition and rehearsal phase involved both cognitive and affective levels. In the cognitive phase, two devices for anger regulation consisted of a task orientation to prevention and coping self-statements. This cognitive phase included preparation for a provocation, coping with arousal, and subsequent reflection in which the conflict was or was not resolved. The affective level, which is very important to Stress Inoculation, involved relaxation skills and maintenance of a sense of humor as a response that competed with the anger.

The behavior goals, according to Novaco, were to (1) promote effective communication of feelings, (2) learn assertive behaviors, and (3) implement task-oriented problem-solving action. In the application practice, the patient was exposed to doses of anger stimuli arranged according to a hierarchy of real-life anger situations that the patient might experience, but that were done in role-play and through imagery. In this way the patient increased anger management skills that were subsequently rehearsed with the therapist. In the discussion, it is noted that Bandura showed how cognitive processes function in stimulus control, guidance of behavior, representation of reinforcement contingencies, and as problem-solving operations that interfere with the occurrence of aggression.

Several other authors also described ways in which cognitive processes function and the relationship between depression, anger, stress, and sensitivity to aversive stimuli (Beck, 1971; Lazarus, 1968; Lewinsohn, Lobitz, & Wilson, 1973; Weissman, Klerman, & Paykel, 1971). The behavior therapy literature documents the precursors of the Stress Inoculation method (Wolpe & Lazarus, 1966). Novaco (1976) reviewed the functions and regulation of anger in an article describing some earlier conceptualizations of anger management in a positive manner. He described the various functions of anger and its regulation. He described the task orientation as having an adaptive effect in the face of provocation. This concept can, perhaps, be applied to stress prevention in other areas that create anxiety, as well as to the various dysfunctional and physiological responses to anger. It is this possible application, which will be described in this chapter, that makes the concept of Stress Inoculation so promising, because it provides the patient with a means of diminishing the effects of future stressful situations. In this sense it is the first true technique for psychological stress prevention.

Novaco (1976) emphasized the important function of remaining task oriented in anger-provoking situations. The situation was defined in terms of a problem calling for a solution rather than as a threat calling for attack. The individual thus avoids a response that escalates the anger sequence that has been destructive in the past. The task focusing directs the patient away from attention to internal stimuli, which are the physiological concomitants of anger. These physiological concomitants, in both anger and other strong emotional responses, often cause the individual to take actions that are dysfunctional rather than coping.

Novaco (1977) presented the application of Stress Inoculation procedures with regard to anger regulation and law enforcement training. The importance of these procedures for professional law enforcement personnel becomes obvious, but this is the first time that Stress Inoculation as a particular technique was provided as part of standard crisis intervention training. He emphasized the usefulness of the Stress Inoculation technique in improving intrapersonal rather than interpersonal conflict management, which had been most often presented in crisis intervention training. He also pointed out the need for application practice rather than rehearsal only of the cognitive self-control skills. This maxim was also confirmed by D'Zurilla and Goldfried (1971).

Meichenbaum, Turk, and Burstein (1975) described Stress Inoculation training in greater detail. The article details each phase of the Stress Inoculation package.

Phase 1, the educational phase, provides the subject with a plausible conceptual framework to understand the response to stressful events. Cognitive and behavioral coping techniques are then practiced. An example is provided of the cognitive aspect of the Stress Inoculation of multiphobic clients. The therapist suggests and reflects that the fear reactions involve two major elements: (1) the physiological response to heightened arousal, and (2) the patient's anxiety-engendering avoidant thoughts, images, and self-statements. The therapist then directs by both suggestion and actions to help the patient control physiological responses and to substitute positive coping self-statements for negative ones.

Phase 2 is the rehearsal phase. In this phase the therapist provides the patient with a variety of coping techniques to use at each phase of the coping process. The techniques include direct action in cognitive coping modes. Coping self-statements are encouraged and enable the patient to assess the reality of the situation, control negative thoughts and self-statements, acknowledge the use of the arousal being experienced, confront the phobic situations, and deal with the intense fear that is often present. The patient is also taught self-reinforcement for coping success.

Phase 3 of the Stress Inoculation involves the application of training. This allows for the rehearsal and implementation of the skills acquired during Phases 1 and 2 by either a laboratory or real-life exposure to the stressors. The article (Meichenbaum et al., 1975) discusses the application of Stress Inoculation training to experimentally induced pain. The pain in this situation consisted of three different components: sensory discriminative, motivational affective, and cognitive evaluative.

The sensory discriminative phase can be controlled by the physical and mental relaxation techniques accompanied by slow deep breathing. It was pointed out that an individual's expectations regarding pain increase anxiety, which subsequently leads to muscle tension, then to more pain and more anxiety, forming a circle that can become paralyzing. The relaxation procedures can interrupt this cycle.

The motivational affective phase includes feelings the patient has while experiencing pain, such as helplessness and absence of control, which can lead to exacerbation of the painful experience. The treatment strategies include attention diversion (focusing attention on something other than the pain); somatization in which the attention is focused on bodily processes and sensations, even including the pain; and imagery manipulations that change or transform the experience of pain by means of fantasy.

The results in this particular experiment of eight male volunteer college students, prepared with 1 hour of Stress Inoculation training, showed a dramatic objective and subjective difference on pre- and posttesting. In the pretest phase the mean was 17 minutes of pain tolerance; this was increased in the posttest measurements to 32 minutes (T .002). The article notes the complexity of Stress Inoculation training and that more research is necessary to adequately determine the necessary and sufficient treatment elements. Stress Inoculation training, according to this article, does have a significant potential as a prophylactic measure, especially in high-risk groups. Other authors who preceded Meichenbaum (1975) in this area, but did not fully develop the concepts of Stress Inoculation, include Chodoff et al. (1964) and Cohen and Lazarus (1973).

Meichenbaum (1977) discussed changes in behavior therapy and cognitive treatment that led to the development of Stress Inoculation training. He described how learning theory was being replaced by a cognitive orientation. The result has been a shift in emphasis from treatment-specific procedures for discrete situations, to a concern with general coping skills that can be applied across various response modalities, situations, and problems.

Various forms of treatment procedures have been developed that are concerned with skills training. Goldfried (1971), Goldfried, Decenteceo, and Weinberg (1974) and Goldfried and Trier (1974) emphasized four elements in the cognitive orientation: (1) describing the treatment rationale to the patient in terms of skills training; (2) using relaxation techniques as a generalized coping strategy; (3) using multiple theme hierarchies in the desensitization process; and (4) training the patient to decrease scene-induced anxiety, with accompanying use of stimulus learning and self-instructional training. They termed this technique systematic rational restructuring, which incorporates the rational emotive therapy that had been developed by Ellis (1973). Meichenbaum (1977) reviewed various approaches and the temporal development of skills training approaches in behavior therapy, with the various names that have been given to these approaches over the years. He described the gradual change in theoretical thinking in behavior therapy and finally recapitulated the various phases of Stress Inoculation training and its more general application to various clinical problems.

Jaremko (1979) reviewed the literature on Stress Inoculation, including a component analysis of Stress Inoculation and pointed out that Stress Inoculation has been successfully used to control laboratory-induced pain, multiphobias, interpersonal anxiety, anger, test anxiety, and speech anxiety. Jaremko also suggested a procedural model to better accommodate the variations in Stress Inoculation that would both increase and enhance procedural specification and maintain clinical flexibility in approaching the various syndromes. On the whole, the literature suggests that Stress Inoculation is a promising technique that might be enhanced by procedural uniformity.

Hussian and Lawrence (1978) and Fremouw and Zitter (1978) attempted to refute Stress Inoculations applicability to multiple stressors.

Meichenbaum and Turk (1976) and Meichenbaum and Asarnow (1979) described the Stress Inoculation package that is used in anger anxiety, and pain control.

Worthington and Shumate (1981) investigated the interactive influence of the three elements of Stress Inoculation training on pain control. The experiment involved tolerance to pain using the cold pressor task, and the results showed that subjects who used pleasant imagery were able to control their pain better than those who did not use the imagery. This replicated the finding of others in the use of imagery as a psychoanalgesic technique (Chaves & Barber, 1984, Grimm & Canfer, 1976, Worthington, 1978).

The imagery and conceptualization findings of Worthington, viewing pain as a multistage process, showed that imagery and conceptualization, as techniques to increase pain tolerance, were synergistic when together and were beneficial separately. The conceptualization aspect was postulated to affect the cognitive value of component or pain as described by Melzack (1973). The self-instructional training did not help in pain management and was often ignored by the subjects. This observation was noted as well by others (Hackett & Horan, 1980).

Schuler, Gilner, Austrin, and Davenport (1982) investigated the education phase in the overall Stress Inoculation training. Their findings indicate that the conceptualization phase is both important and effective. They noted that the full Stress Inoculation training decreased speech anxiety significantly when compared with a control group receiving only the rehearsal and application phases of Stress Inoculation training.

Spirito, Finch, Smith, and Cooley (1981) described the use of Stress Inoculation for anger and anxiety control, with an example of Stress Inoculation training to aid a hospitalized boy in managing anxiety and anger related to classroom assignments. The article concludes that Stress Inoculation training may be an effective approach in the management of these two clinical problems.

Social Supports

The next area of investigation in stress reduction or stress prevention, particularly as it relates to physical and mental health, is social supports. It has long been hypothesized that individuals with adequate social supports will be less likely to develop either physical or mental health problems. A number of investigators have examined this hypothesis to determine if, in fact, this is the case. Much of the earlier work in this area was hampered because a good scale or test to measure social support systems in a standard manner was lacking. McFarlane, Neale, Norman, Roy, and Steiner (1981) discussed the methodological issues important in developing such a scale. They noted that the theory that social supports are an important preventive against disease has been described by a number of authors (Antonovsky, 1974; Caplan, 1974; Henderson, 1977).

The authors developed a social support scale that they have used in subsequent studies and that is now in more general use. McFarlane, Norman, Streiner, Roy, and Scott (1980) began a longitudinal study to determine the influence of psychosocial supports on health. They discussed locus of control, first described by Rotter, Seeman, and Liverant (1962), as indicating a cognitive style by which individuals feel they exert control over events that influence them. The work by Rotter et al. defined external locus of control as a situation in which the individual feels controlled by external events and powers. Internal locus of control, on the other hand, indicated an individual's belief in his or her ability to exercise primary control over the environment. Since 1962, internal locus of control has been hypothesized to relate to decreased demoralization as a stressful situation mounts, and, concomitantly, with decreased symptoms of illness.

Lefcourt (1976), Rotter et al. (1962), and Johnson and Sarason (1978), also studied the effects of locus of control as a determinant in future health problems.

The article by McFarlane et al. (1980) finds that undesirable life events, as indicated by the subjects, correlated more strongly with measure of strain. External locus of control increased the impact of undesirable events and strengthened the disruptive influence of even desirable events. This conclusion agrees with the work of other investigators (Engle, 1971; Schmale, 1973; Vinokur & Selzer, 1975; Weiss, 1970). In the McFarlane study the authors used the SRS (Social Relationship Scale), which measures both the quantity and quality of an individual's social supporting network and its supposed helpfulness.

McFarlane, Norman, Streiner, and Roy (1984) reviewed the area of social supports as developed in the literature. They described the confusion in the literature regarding the relationship of social supports, life stressors, and health. The results of the various previous studies were mixed. They noted that the hypothesis that adequate social supports moderate the influence of stressful events and thus have an impact on physical and mental health is not always supported in the literature, and somewhat depends on the methodology involved (e.g., prospective vs. retrospective studies). Some articles would indicate that social supports act independently of stressful events in maintaining health (Andrews, Tennant, Hewson, & Vaillant, 1978), and others would indicate that good social supports act to prevent stressful events from occurring in the first place. The above articles support the hypothesis that social supports play a protective role in decreasing the number of stressful events, but the supports per se showed no mean effect on the interaction between social supports and health. The quality of social supports is more important than the quantity (as might be expected), but there was some evidence that the more extensive the social support network, the greater the number of stressful events. Those who felt least helped by their social support network did not feel helped by all of their relationships, but rather often felt unsuccessful in seeking help from the inner core of their social support network, particularly the spouse. They also reported more stressful events in their current life, during the preceding 5 years, and during their childhood. This supports the theory of Bowlby (1980) that there is a strong causal relationship between an individual's attachment experience with parents and a later capacity to form affectional bonds. The article also gives several references that review the literature on the relationship between social supports, health, and problems (Andrews et al., 1978; Broadhead et al., 1983; Thoits, 1982; Wallston, Alagna, Devellis, & Devellis, 1982).

McFarlane, Norman, Streiner, and Roy (1983) reviewed the results of the prospective study, which had been begun earlier. The previously held assumptions and beliefs in the areas of social supports and health were reviewed. They attempted to tease out the impact of the variables of the social support network, stressful events, and locus of control, on health. The results showed that prior distress was the strongest predictor of distress; the perception of the nature of change of events was more important than the actual life events, and there is a significant but weak correlation between demographic variables in measures of stress mediators and health. There was little evidence found for a mediating or buffering effect for a locus of control or for the helpfulness of extent of social network in predicting distress.

The authors emphasized the need for continuing research in this area. Caplan (1981) and Grant, Sweetwood, Yager, and Gerst (1981) also approached the issues of psychosocial aspects and quality-of-life events in relation to stress and psychiatric symptoms.

STRESS REDUCTION PROGRAMS

Stress has been recognized as a major factor in both physical and mental illness. Hospital programs, particularly in surgery, have successfully prepared patients to cope with the stress of major surgery. Programs to prepare patients for cardiac surgery, for instance, diminish the patient's anxiety by providing information and techniques to aid coping with the postsurgery routine. They may also be effective by their implicit assumption that there will be life after surgery and by allowing patients to participate actively in their recovery. These programs can be considered stress prevention techniques in that they accurately predict physiological stress (surgery), prepare patients to deal with the accompanying pain, and demystify the frightening process of major surgery.

Other medically oriented programs prepare patients to deal with the stress of chronic illness and may also be effective in engaging the patient in active management of the illness. Psychiatry has been slow to adopt similar programs to aid patients in the management of major mental disorders, although such training programs are recently receiving more attention.

Popular programs aimed at stress reduction abound, but no scientific follow-up on their results is evident. Programs of meditation, education, and exercise probably are helpful in overall stress reduction and prevention, but only anecdotal evidence supports this contention.

Behavioral techniques for stress prevention have been extant for the past 20 years but have remained at the fringes of psychiatric treatment until recently. The psychiatric/psychological literature on stress prevention includes that on behavior therapy, cognitive therapy, and the combination of these into Stress Inoculation. This latter technique represents a true attempt to aid patients in preventing the adverse effects of stress, both psychological and physiological. The term is borrowed from medicine and is somewhat of a misnomer because it does not involve introducing the causative agent of a disease into the body. It is meant, however, to provide the individual with a mechanism to better handle noxious stimuli. Stress Inoculation often involves three cognitive and behavioral steps: cognitive preparation, skill acquisition and rehearsal, and application of the techniques to real-life situations. When successful, it does provide an individual with a means of diminishing the toxic effects of future stressful situations.

Stress Inoculation has been used for a variety of purposes, including affect management, pain management, and relaxation skills training. Though also applied to interpersonal issues, the technique is primarily aimed at the management of intrapersonal problems.

Stress Inoculation has similarities to other forms of training geared toward handling potential and actual very stressful situations that normally involve anxiety and fear (psychological responses), plus the intense physiological responses that include increased heart rate, blood pressure, other autonomic nervous system discharge, and release of hormonal compounds such as epinephrine and norepinephrine. Examples of this would include military training and aircraft pilot training. The training aims at providing skills to handle stressful situations such as combat or, in the case of pilot training, the loss of engine power. The goal is to ensure that the individual's behavioral response is adaptive rather than dysfunctional. That is, the trainee learns increased alertness and physiological dexterity in the potentially stressful situation rather than, for example, becoming paralyzed by fear.

It appears likely that cognitive/behavioral techniques such as Stress Inoculation will have a positive impact on the treatment of a variety of conditions such as anxiety, phobias, and stress disorders. Training, and the techniques employed, may well be applicable over a variety of stressors, so that additional or unique training should not be needed for each discrete situation. The field of cognitive/behavior therapy should be able to provide treatment techniques that are useful in stress management and that preclude the use of psychopharmacological agents in the treatment of common stress disorders. Treatment techniques and appropriate medication should be used together in the treatment of more severe stress disorders with disabling symptoms.

CONCLUSION

The field of stress prevention in adults has received much popular attention. Attention by behavioral scientists has been more recent and much scientific inquiry needs to be done in this important area that affects everyone. Stress Inoculation is one cognitive/behavioral technique that provides promise in the treatment of a variety of stress-related disorders. The integration of cognitive/behavioral approaches with psychopharmacological techniques can be promising in the treatment of more severe stress disorders. Stress Inoculation, by itself, offers a technique for preventing the adverse effects of stress.

REFERENCES

Andrews, G., Tennant, C., Hewson, D., & Vaillant, G. (1978). Life event stress, social support, coping style, and risk of psychological impairment. *Journal of Nervous and Mental Diseases, 166,* 307–316.

Antonovsky, A. (1974). Conceptual and methodological problems in the study of resistance resources and stressful life events. In B. S. Dohrenwend & B. P. Dohrenwend (Eds.), *Stressful life events: Their nature and effects* (pp. 245–259). New York: Wiley.

Archibald, H. C., & Tuddenham, R. D. (1965). Persistent stress reaction after combat: A twenty year follow up. *Archives of General Psychiatry, 2,* 2475–2481.

Arthur, R. J. (1974). Psychiatric syndromes in prisoners of war and concentration camp survivors. In E. E. K. Gunderson & R. H. Rahe (Eds.), *Life stress and illness* (p. 49). Springfield, IL: Charles C. Thomas.

Arthur, R. J., & McKenna, G. J. (1989). Survival under conditions of extreme stress. In F. Flach (Ed.), *Stress and its management* (pp. 15–25). New York: Norton.

Bandura, A. (1973). *Aggression: A social learning analysis.* Englewood Cliffs, NJ: Prentice-Hall.

Beck, A. T. (1967). *Depression: Clinical, experimental, and theoretical aspects.* New York: Harper and Row.

Beck, A. T. (1971). Cognition, affect, and psychopathology. *Archives of General Psychiatry, 24,* 475–500.

Bowlby, J. (1980). *Attachment and loss.* New York: Basic Books.

Brill, N. Q., & Beebe, G. W. (1956). Follow-up study of war neurosis. *VA Medical Monograph.* Washington, DC: U.S. Government Printing Office.

Broadhead, W. E., Kaplan, B. H., James, S. A., Wagner, E. H., Schoenback, V. J., Gunson, R., Heyden, S., Tibblin, G., & Gehlback, S. H. (1983). The epidemiological evidence for a relationship between social support and health. *American Journal of Epidemiology, 5,* 521–537.

Caplan, G. (1974). *Support systems and community mental health: Lectures on concept development.* New York: Behavioral Publications.

Caplan, G. (1981). Mastery of stress: Psychosocial aspects. *American Journal of Psychiatry, 138,* 413–420.

Chaves, J. F., & Barber, T. X. (1984). Cognitive strategies, experimental modeling, and expectation in the attentuation of pain. *Journal of Abnormal Psychology, 83,* 356–363.

Chodoff, P. (1963). Late effects of the concentration camp syndrome. *Archives of General Psychiatry, 8,* 323.

Chodoff, P., Friedman, S., & Hamburg, D. (1964). Stress, defenses, and coping behavior: Observations in parents of children with malignant disease. *American Journal of Psychiatry, 120,* 743–749.

Cohen, F., & Lazarus, R. (1973). Active coping processes, coping disposition, and recovery from surgery. *Psychosomatic Medicine, 35,* 375–389.

Dobbs, D., & Wilson, W. P. (1960). Observations on persistence of war neuroses. *Diseases of the Nervous System, 21,* 686–691.

D'Zurilla, T. & Goldfried, M. (1971). Problem solving and behavior modification. *Journal of Abnormal Psychology, 78,* 107–126.

Egbert, L., Battit, G., Welch, C., & Bartlett, M. (1964). Reduction of post-operative pain by encouragement and instruction. *New England Journal of Medicine, 270,* 825–827.

Ellis, A. (1973). *Humanistic psychology: The rational-emotive support approach.* New York: Julian Press.

Engel, G. L. (1971). Sudden and rapid death during psychological stress: Folklore or folk wisdom? *Annals of Internal Medicine, 74,* 771–782.

Frederick, C. J. (1985). Selected foci in the spectrum of posttraumatic stress disorders. In

J. L. Laube & S. A. Murphy (Eds.), *Perspectives on disaster recovery,* (pp. 110–129). Norwalk, CT: Appleton–Century–Crofts.

Fremouw, W. J., & Zitter, R. E. (1978). A comparison of skills training and cognitive restructuring-relaxation for the treatment of speech anxiety. *Behavior Therapy, 9,* 238–249.

Friedman, P. (1949). Some aspects of concentration camp psychology. *American Journal of Psychiatry, 105,* 601–605.

Futterman, S., & Pumpian-Mindlin, E. (1951). Traumatic war neurosis five years later. *American Journal of Psychiatry, 108,* 401.

Goldfried, M. (1971). Systematic desensitization as training in self control. *Journal of Consulting and Clinical Psychology, 37,* 228–325.

Golfried, M. R., Decenteceo, E. T., & Weinberg, L. (1974). Systematic rational restructuring as a self control technique. *Behavior Therapy, 5,* 247–254.

Goldfried, M. R., & Trier, C. (1974). Effectiveness of relaxation as an active coping skill. *Journal of Abnormal Psychology, 83,* 348–355.

Grant, I., Sweetwood, J., Yager, J., & Gerst, M. (1981). Quality of life events in relation to psychiatric symptoms. *Archives of General Psychiatry, 38,* 335–339.

Grimm, L., & Kanfer, F. H. (1976). Tolerance of aversive stimulation. *Behavior Therapy, 7,* 593–601.

Hackett, G., & Horan, J. J. (1980). Stress inoculation for pain: What's really going on? *Journal of Counseling Psychology, 27,* 107–116.

Henderson, S. (1977). The social network, support and neurosis: The function of attachment in adult life. *British Journal of Psychiatry, 131,* 185–191.

Horan, J. J., Hackett, G., Buchanan, J. D., Stone, G. I., & Demchik-Stone, D. (1977). Coping with pain: A component analysis of stress inoculation. *Cognitive Therapy and Research, 1,* 211–221.

Hussian, R. A., & Lawrence, P. S. (1978). The reduction of test, state, and trait anxiety by test specific and generalized stress inoculation training. *Cognitive Therapy and Research, 2,* 25–38.

Jaremko, M. E. (1979). A component analysis of stress inoculation: Review and prospectus. *Cognitive Therapy and Research, 3,* 35–48.

Johnson, J. H., & Sarason, I. G. (1978). Life stress, depression, and anxiety: Internal-external control as a moderator variable. *Journal of Psychosomatic Research, 22,* 205–208.

Kalinowsky, L. B. (1950). Problems of war neurosis in light of experiences in other countries. *American Journal of Psychiatry, 107,* 340–346.

Krystal, H. (Ed.). (1968). *Massive psychic trauma.* New York: International Universities Press.

Lazarus, A. (1968). Learning theory and the treatment of depression. *Behavior Research and Therapy, 6,* 83–89.

Lefcourt, H. M. (1976). *Locus of control: Current trends in theory and research.* Hillsdale, NJ: Erlbaum.

Lewinsohn, P. M., Lobitz, W. C., & Wilson, S. (1973). Sensitivity of depressed individuals to aversive stimuli. *Journal of Abnormal Psychology, 81,* 259–263.

Lewis, N., & Engle, B. (1954). *Wartime psychiatry.* New York: Oxford University Press.

McFarlane, A. H., Neale, K. A., Norman, G. R., Roy, R. G., & Steiner, D. L. (1981). Methodological issues in developing a scale to measure social support. *Schizophrenia Bulletin, 7,* 90–100.

McFarlane, A. H., Norman, G. R., Streiner, D. R., & Roy, R. G. (1983). The process of social stress: Stable, reciprocal, and mediating relationships. *Journal of Health and Social Behavior, 24,* 160–173.

McFarlane, A. H., Norman, G. R., Streiner, D. L., & Roy, R. G. (1984). Characteristics and correlates of effective and ineffective social supports. *Journal of Psychosomatic Research, 28,* 501–510.

McFarlane, A. H., Norman, G. R., Streiner, D. L., Roy, R. G., & Scott, D. H. (1980). A longitudinal study of the influence of the psychosocial environment as health status: A preliminary report. *Journal of Health and Social Behavior, 21,* 124–133.

McKenna, G. J., & Arthur, R. J. (1989). Survival under adverse conditions. In F. Flach (Ed.), *Stress and its management* (pp. 26–36). New York: Norton.

Meichenbaum, D. (1975). A self-instructional approach to stress management: A proposal for stress inoculation training. In C. Spielberger & I. Sarason (Eds.), *Stress and anxiety* (Vol. 2). New York: Wiley.

Meichenbaum, D. (1977). Stress inoculation training. In *Cognitive behavior modification: An integrative approach* (pp. 143–182). New York: Plenum.

Meichenbaum, D., & Asarnow, J. (1979). Cognitive-behavior modification and metacognitive development: Implications for the classroom. In P. Kendall and S. Hollon (Eds.), *Cognitive behavioral intervention: Theory, research, and procedures.* New York: Academic Press.

Meichenbaum, D., & Turk, D. (1976). The cognitive behavior modification of anxiety, anger, and pain. In P. Davidson (Ed.), *Behavioral management of anxiety, depression, and pain.* New York: Brunner/Mazel.

Meichenbaum, D., Turk, D., & Burstein, S. (1975). The nature of coping and stress. In I. Sarason & C. D. Spielberger (Eds.), *Stress and anxiety* (Vol. 2, pp. 349–360). New York: Wiley.

Melzack, R. (1973). *The puzzle of pain.* New York: Basic Books.

Menninger, K. (1938). *Man against himself.* New York: Harcourt, Brace & World.

Nardini, J. E. (1952). Survival factors in American prisoners of war of the Japanese. *American Journal of Psychiatry, 109*(4), 241–248.

Novaco, R. W. (1976). The functions and regulation of the arousal of anger. *American Journal of Psychiatry, 133,* 10.

Novaco, R. W. (1977a). Stress inoculation: A cognitive therapy for anger and its application to a case of depression. *Journal of Consulting and Clinical Psychology, 45,* 600–608.

Novaco, R. W. (1977b). A stress inoculation approach to anger management in the training of law enforcement officers. *American Journal of Community Psychology, 5,* 327–347.

Rotter, J. B., Seeman, M., & Liverant, S. (1962). Internal versus external control of reinforcement: A major variable in behavior therapy. In N. F. Washburne (Ed.), *Decisions, values, and groups* (pp. 473–516). Oxford: Pergamon Press.

Schmale, A. H., Jr. (1973). Relationship of separation and depression to disease: A report on a hospitalized medical population. In M. Zax & G. Stricker (Eds.), *The study of abnormal behavior* (pp. 286–303). New York: Macmillan.

Schuler, K., Gilner, F., Austrin, H., & Davenport, D. G. (1982). Contribution of the education phase to stress inoculation training. *Psychological Reports, 51,* 611–617.

Southard, E. E. (1919). Shell shock and other neuropsychiatric problems. In *Five hundred and eighty nine case histories from the war literature, 1914–1918.* Boston, MA: W. M. Leonard. (Reprinted as *Mental illness and society policy: The American experience.* New York: Arno Press, 1973)

Spirito, A., Finch, A. J., Smith, T. L., & Cooley, W. H. (1981, winter). Stress Inoculation for anger and anxiety control: A case study with an emotionally disturbed boy. *Journal of Clinical Child Psychology,* pp. 67–70.

Strom, A. (1968). *Norwegian concentration camp survivors, Universitetsforlaget.* New York: Oslo/Humanities Press.

Thoits, P. A. (1982). Conceptual, methodological, and theoretical problems in studying social support as a buffer against life stress. *Journal of Health and Social Behavior, 23,* 145–149.

Toffler, A. (1970). *Future shock.* New York: Random House.

Vinokur, A., & Selzer, M. C. (1975). Desirable versus undesirable life events: Their relationship to stress and mental disease. *Journal of Personality and Social Psychology, 32,* 329–337.

Wallston, B. S., Alagna, S. W., Devellis, B. M., & Devellis, R. F. (1982). Social support and physical health. *Health Psychology, 2,* 367–391.

Weiss, J. M. (1970). Somatic effects of predictable and impredictable shock. *Psychosomatic Medicine, 32,* 397–409.

Weissman, M. M., Klerman, G. L., & Paykel, E. S. (1971). Clinical evaluation of hostility in depression. *American Journal of Psychiatry, 128,* 261–266.

Wolf, M. C., & Ripley, H. S. (1947). Reactions among allied prisoners of war subjected to three years of imprisonment and torture by the Japanese. *American Journal of Psychiatry, 104–180.*

Wolpe, J., & Lazarus, A. (1966). *Behavior Therapy Techniques.* Oxford: Pergamon Press.

Worthington, E. L., Jr. (1978). The effects of imagery content, choice of imagery content and self-verbalization on the self-control of pain. *Cognitive Therapy and Research, 2,* 225–240.

Worthington, E. L., Jr., & Shumate, M. (1981). Imagery and verbal counseling methods in stress inoculation training for pain control. *Journal of Counseling Psychology, 28,* 1–6.

Treatment for Stress-Related Disorders

JOSEPH D. NOSHPITZ, MD

The treatment of Adjustment Disorders is as varied as their form. Indeed, so common are these disorders and so manifold the fashions of their expression that practically every therapeutic modality has been invoked in an effort to help sufferers of their effects.

THE FIRST LEVEL OF COPING

Most people who face the impact of acute stress and who seek help turn first to family and friends and then to such usual sources of support as their family doctor and clergyman. Most Adjustment Disorders are managed on this level; The family member or friend may support, console, and spend a great deal of time with the afflicted person, or may even move in with the sufferer for a time. Sometimes the help is extended from a distance by frequent lengthy phone calls and sometimes by an emergency visit followed by active phone contacts. Physicians and clergymen, when called upon, offer the help traditional to their disciplines. They prescribe palliatives, pray with the sufferer, and lend a compassionate ear to the accounts of distress. Religion in particular has been a source of comfort and hope to many beleaguered people (Whitehead & Stout, 1989). It offers a supportive belief system; a set of ritual practices that reinforce the sense of linkage to a tradition and an ongoing community of believers; and the presence of an authoritative leader who can give guidance, ease guilt, and allow for the unburdening of inner feelings in a confidential atmosphere. In most instances, it also makes available supportive interactions with a well-disposed community whose linkage via religion evokes high levels of altruism. Collectively these can go far to improve the outlook of traumatized individuals who are reacting adversely to experienced stress.

THE SECOND LEVEL OF COPING: SELF-HELP GROUPS

A second level of intervention available to many people is the self-help group (Borman, 1989). Historically, such groups have always been present in our society in one form or another; in recent years, however, they have burgeoned and increased in numbers by leaps and bounds. Some of them are familiar, for example, Alcoholics Anonymous (AA); many are relatively obscure, such as groups to help recent widows and widowers, groups of parents who have lost children, or groups associated with specific medical conditions. The increasing number of these groups probably reflects a self-healing attempt on the part of a society where family breakdown, isolation, and alienation are an ever-increasing presence. The groups also represent an effort to deal with issues that organized helping professions have failed to come to grips with or have not dealt with adequately. Thus, AA was formed when medicine had little to offer the alcoholic.

Technically, these organizations can be categorized as follows:

1. *Self-Help Groups.* Activities like yoga or biofeedback that are dedicated to self-improvement
2. *Mutual-Help Groups.* Organizations such as AA, or associations formed by parents of handicapped children
3. *Peer-Help Groups.* Trained peers who work with identified target populations undergoing travail (e.g., hot lines where peers make themselves available to respond to suicidal adolescents)

In this chapter, for purposes of economy, they will all be referred to as self-help groups.

Not all such groups are built around specific difficulties, but the majority are so dedicated (e.g., people who have experienced recent heart surgery or who have been accused of sex abuse). All of them, however, are in some measure designed to help individuals or families cope with the moments of acute stress that so typically arise in the course of chronic conditions. Alcoholics Anonymous assumes that its members will have periodic crises of one sort or another and assigns an individual resource person to each member, who can then be contacted to offer support at moments of need.

The means by which such self-help groups are therapeutic has been the subject of considerable research. Several mechanisms appear to be at work:

1. The shared identity with others in like circumstances is a powerful buffer against the self-devaluation, social isolation, and sense of alienation that follow in the wake of many human vicissitudes. Within the group, instead of being a social reject, one acquires a sense of belonging. The former feeling of being different and alone is transformed into an experience of communication, mutual understanding, and sharing.

2. The sufferer is given a chance to help others with similar difficulties; this is often enormously rewarding and converts a state of passive vulnerability to one of active effectiveness.

3. A group ideology that amounts to a belief system often emerges; this functions as an effective rallying point and instills a sense of mission and positive goal-seeking that does much to dissipate anxiety and depression.

4. The sufferer characteristically finds an immediate place within a social network of people who may interact supportively and remain in contact between group meetings. Newsletters, parties, informal social visits, and numerous phone calls serve to enhance the sense of connectedness and participation; fairs or annual conventions extend the reach of the network enormously.

5. Many projects, often in the form of public relations or educational efforts, bring people together in common participation, with old-timers setting the tone and newcomers offering to help any way they can.

6. Within the group the characteristic emphasis is usually one of overcoming obstacles, achieving mastery, or, at any rate, keeping a positive outlook. Collectively, these factors make for hope and lessen the helplessness/hopelessness component of the Adjustment Disorder.

7. There is an associated active cognitive component to the group experience. Where applicable, the members often feed the latest scientific information into the pattern of group exchange, and in any case, they can always share individual experiences and coping efforts to enhance their array of adaptive possibilities. The bibliographies and the collations of data assembled by such groups often help professionals as well.

Self-Help Groups for Adolescents

Although fewer in number than the groups for adults, a number of self-help organizations for adolescents have also appeared (Shore & Mannino, 1989). The best known, Al-Teen, serves the children of alcoholics and operates in a manner parallel to that of AA. Other groups have been organized around specific syndromes, such as hemophilia, or around problem behaviors, such as drug addiction or drunk driving. Occasionally, urban gangs will transiently take on self-help features. On occasion such peer-oriented organizations, however, have provided negative as well as positive influences; that is, within the ambience of the group, antisocial leaders can sway youngsters or draw them into aberrant patterns that are at odds with the larger culture.

The notion of young people helping one another has intrigued many would-be helpers, and in recent years has taken form as hot lines, rap centers, runaway houses, and the like. As is true for most self-help groups, these are either divorced entirely from professional supervision or maintain only indirect connections of this kind via training programs, ad hoc consultation, sites for occasional referral, and so on. Within these programs, the emphasis is always on informality and accessibility; not infrequently the youths who participate in these services undergo meaningful increments of personal growth. As the work proceeds, they find themselves able to help others and able to cope with a variety of stresses, with all the learning, mastery, and reward that accompany such efforts. Nor are their efforts in vain; many young people who use these services indicate significant benefits from such contacts.

MENTAL HEALTH INTERVENTION

In addition to the nonpsychiatric modes of intervention, a number of formal therapeutic approaches are available for treating stress-related disorders. These include a variety of modalities: brief individual psychotherapy for adults and children, crisis intervention, family therapy, group therapy, behavioral therapy and psychopharmacology. This list is by no means exhaustive; a separate chapter on individual psychotherapy appears elsewhere in this volume. Moreover many different forms of therapy are currently employed within the confines of our culture. Nonetheless, this chapter will offer a representative sample of some of the more widely practiced approaches now in use.

Crisis Intervention

This kind of treatment (Swanson & Carbon, 1989) is designed to engage a patient who has been subjected to acute stress and is emotionally overwhelmed. The goal of the work is to address the person in a manner that brings about immediate symptom reduction and helps the patient cope more successfully with future crises. The underlying theory assumes that the individual strives always to maintain a homeostatic balance; under normal circumstances this results in a steady state. To be sure, disturbances arise, but when they do extra effort is exerted, the disruption is compensated for, and homeostasis is regained. When the stress is exceptional, however, either because it is inherently catastrophic (a rape experience or a natural disaster) or because it continues to mount over time to the point of becoming unendurable, at some point the efforts at maintaining homeostasis threaten to fail, and the person enters a state of enormous tension. This precarious, over-stressed state is the initial element in the crisis sequence. The individual perceives the sense of failing regulatory capacity as a major threat and typically strives to cope with all problem-solving capacities, but to no avail. He or she begins to feel a sense of things breaking up, sliding out from under, becoming desperate. In fact, as this advances, the person enters a condition of precrisis. It is still possible to cope, but only barely; he or she doesn't know what will happen next. Signs of emotional tension appear, and irritability mounts. Not infrequently these painful inner configurations will begin to resonate with vulnerabilities from earlier in the life cycle; memories are evoked of previous experiences of failure or emotional trauma; and the ensuing upheaval of remembered pain and danger adds to the current stress.

With this, the person experiences an urgent need for relief; it is precisely these excruciating emotional pangs that cause the individual to seek help. This can be done adaptively through some of the means referred to earlier, by turning to family, friends, physician, clergyman, self-help group, or mental health professional. Or it can be done maladaptively through substance abuse, suicide, flight, or some form of emotional breakdown. When a therapist *is* consulted, the existence of the state of acute pain often makes the individual peculiarly available for treatment.

In any case, with or without help, after the crisis has run its course, a postcrisis state ensues and a new homeostasis is established. If helped by formal or informal treatment, the new level should be at least as successful as the previous state. Indeed, optimally it should be more successful, because not only has the individual achieved mastery over the current challenge, but he or she may have, to some extent, also resolved the earlier traumatic emotions that were stirred up by the event. In effect, the person is now better prepared for future challenges.

Crisis intervention as a form of treatment has a number of specific characteristics that set it apart from the usual kinds of therapy. For one thing, it tends to be brief and intensive. For another, it involves clearly formulated goals aimed at resolving the present crisis. As a result, the focus is not on the past or on basic character issues; these may both come up but they are not the stated goals.

Instead, the therapist builds on the realities of the present situation with particular attention to the strengths the patient brings to the problem. The patient is invited, encouraged, or directed (as the therapist deems clinically wise) to mobilize these strengths in order to address the pain; the therapist specifies that one can only help a person help him- or herself. The patient's support system is reviewed, strengthened where possible, built up where lacking, and resorted to actively as necessary.

As they begin to work, the therapist confronts the patient actively in terms of unrealistic expectations, distorted perceptions, or excessive goals, in particular, challenging maladaptive behavior such as substance abuse. By and large the work is goal oriented, and its form is dictated by the nature of the crisis and the immediate goals. Flexibility is key, however, and the therapist has to make numerous adaptations to accommodate the individual variations in patient need.

The therapy can be divided into four stages. The first and second generally flow together and are accomplished during the first hour; nonetheless, it helps to view them separately. To begin with, the therapist reviews what brought the patient into crisis, what the person has done up to this point in trying to cope, what social resources are avilable to draw upon, and whether there is any danger of suicide or violence (i.e., any indication for immediate hospitalization). The therapist offers both help and hope but underlines the necessity for the patient to work to accomplish recovery. The therapist recapitulates in capsule form what the crisis seems to be and invites the patient to share in stating what they should strive for together. This brings the work to the next stage.

The second stage is essentially that of setting goals. Here, magical solutions are divorced from realistic possiblities, and specific attainable targets are set that will bring relief. The therapist stipulates that when these are arrived at, treatment will end. Formally or informally, the patient and the therapist enter into a contract.

The third stage may be a more extended one. The therapist begins to set tasks for the patient to perform. They may involve learning relaxation techniques, practicing certain kinds of thought sequences, or working on the management of specific feelings; in any case, they have to be attainable achievements whose mastery will at once strengthen the patient in the face of the present crisis and serve as well for later adaptation. At the same time, the therapist must always be ready to confront and discuss any hint of negative transference and to interpret the magical themes that tend to appear (magical causes or expectations of magical cure).

During this stage, the therapist should bring in members of the patient's family or support network and should try to connect the patient with self-help groups or other available sources of support within the community (including, when appropriate, emergency food and shelter, legal aid, and medical care).

The final stage brings the work to an end. It is hoped that the patient will have regained his or her precrisis state. Either or both participants may experience a strong inclination to continue, but the counsel of wisdom is to interrupt at this point. In the course of termination, the therapist should go over the history of the crisis, what the patient was like at the outset, what methods were used, and what problem-solving techniques were acquired. It is important that there be a formal closing to the crisis work even if the patient continues in therapy.

Behavioral Techniques

A wide variety of behavioral methods are now available, and part of the work of initiating treatment is to select the approach best fitted to the symptoms the patient is experiencing (Suinn, 1989). (An alternative approach is to seek to discern the patient's characteristic way of coping and to design the treatment in keeping with that. Although currently being explored, this method is not yet adequately developed.) Some of the more widely used approaches follow.

Affective/Autonomic Therapies. These behavioral methods are directed toward the patient's state of autonomic arousal. It takes the form of anxiety or anger that either accompanies other symptoms, begets other difficulties, or is itself the syndrome to be addressed. The following techniques seek to relieve the symptoms.

Relaxation Training. A number of general techniques exist to achieve relaxation; prominent among them are biofeedback and progressive relaxation.

In *biofeedback,* the therapist attaches a meter that records blood pressure or muscle tension and can then seek to lower the reading on the dial by conscious acts of relaxation. With practice, patients learn that they can control their autonomic processes by concentrating on their state of inner being, which offers many people a considerable measure of reassurance and a sense of mastery.

In *progressive relaxation,* the patient is taught to relax successive groups of muscles in a systematic fashion: first the feet, then the legs, then the knees, then the thighs, and so on up to the trunk, the upper extremities, and the face and brow. The patient then learns to maintain the relaxed state for specified periods of time. In effect, the person seeks here to undo in overall fashion the tension induced by the stress, regardless of its origin.

There are various possible ways of augmenting the degree of relaxation. Cue-controlled efforts add reinforcers, such as silently repeating words like "calm" or "easy," or taking slow deep breaths while doing the relaxation exercise. The patient can initiate these tactics whenever tension builds up or a known, stress-producing experience reoccurs.

A more specific use of this technique is to seek to pair the relaxation effort with one of the stimuli known to initiate stress. Thus, a woman who has been subjected to an episode of violent rape may subsequently suffer from panicky responses whenever she contemplates intimacy. In therapy, she may be asked to fantasize a beginning approach to physical closeness and then to initiate a pattern of relaxation. The goal is to pair the desired behavior with a relaxation response and thus to displace the existing fear response. In this way a pattern of systematic desensitization can ensue.

Anxiety Induction. In contrast to relaxation, some techniques are based on confronting the patient with anxiety under controlled conditions. These anxiety-induction methods involve such strategies as implosion and flooding. The therapist guides the patient in recreating the traumatic event in imagination. All sorts of sensory and cognitive cues are recalled (the sounds, sights, smells, and thoughts associated with the trauma), with the patient blocked from any escape or avoidance throughout. The underlying theory is that reexposure to these stimuli without any possibility of evasion will act to extinguish the emotional response. A number of such reexposure sessions are usually necessary in order to extinguish all the elements in the pattern. To say the least, the therapist must be cautious in using such methods; improper application may, heighten the anxiety and make the patient worse. Suinn (1989) has accordingly developed a method that uses guided imagery to evoke anxiety, but that then invokes relaxation training to teach the patient how to cope with the distressing emotions. In effect, the patient gains control over the symptoms by learning to initiate them and then to employ tactics that make them abate. Theoretically, this concept could be extended to all arousal type conditions such as states of rage, impulsivity, and so on.

Somatic/Behavioral Therapies

1. *Stimulus Control.* This method is designed for patients whose symptom picture includes chronic worry. At the outset, the patient embarks on a period of self-observation in order to identify when the worrying is most likely to appear. Once this is accomplished, the therapist helps the patient set up a worry period, a half-hour sequence to which he or she relegates all further worrying. If worrying appears at any other time, the patient learns to arrest the process and to confine it to the allotted span.

2. *Learned Coping Behavior.* The patient recalls events during which he or she coped successfully with some aspect of the current stress (e.g., if the therapist dealing with exam anxiety, the patient would have to think of an exam that was handled well). The person then couples this thought with the current flare of fears and conscientiously and actively repeats the process until a true counterconditioning takes place. An alternative method directs the person to engage in patterns of behavior that provide some reward, by opening up his or her life and breaking down the restrictions imposed by the primary condition. The point is to give the patient a sense of success and control in the troublesome areas. This can be accomplished in many ways: biofeedback, guided imagery, self-statements, examination of the successes of others, and so on. Thus, viewing a film that shows someone approaching surgery, dentistry, or combat in a hesitant, guarded way and then gradually gaining confidence and mastery can be a meaningful learning experience. Watching a live model and then practicing the behavior oneself can be specially effective.

Cognitive Behavior Therapies. An individual's prior experience may have led to conscious or unconscious learning of deviant character. This in turn predisposes that person to misinterpret the world and to regard certain environmental stimuli as threatening. The following methods address this problem.

1. *Cognitive Restructuring.* This method includes such techniques as Rational Emotive Therapy (RET) and Systematic Rational Restructuring (SRR). In both therapies, the patients monitor and report their thoughts around the time of an anxiety episode. The patients then examine these thoughts with an eye to the degree of irrationality that may be present. There are likely to be many such, for example, the conviction that something catastrophic will ensue, or that there is a single proper way to act lacking which all is lost. Beck's triad—the pessimistic view by a person of the world, self, and future—is likely to be present. In any case, the validity of such mental sets is forcefully challenged (in RET) or carefully explored (in SRR).

The awareness of the negative and unrealistic quality of irrational thoughts and the sensitization to their presence lead the patient to try to set them aside and to substitute more wholesome and realistic viewpoints. Much rehearsal and practice at restructuring thoughts occupies the therapy time.

2. *Stress Inoculation Training*. Here again the patients are trained to regard their thought processes during episodes of upset. They then learn a variety of coping skills such as moving from unrealistic to more appropriate thinking and offering themselves praise. In addition, they consider the advent of a stressor (the feared situation), learn to relax, and study different ways of dealing with that particular set of circumstances. In the final stages of the work, the therapist might provide some video or concrete experience calculated to induce tension, so that the patients can rehearse and then try out their coping skills.

As with all therapy, it takes careful sorting out of the coping styles and the overall cognitive/emotional states of the given patient to discern which behavioral method is most appropriate for that person's particular personality profile.

Family Therapy Approaches

It is characteristic of all family work to regard the family as the preferred site of therapeutic address (Beal, 1989). To this end, the family is construed as a stable dynamic configuration with set, predictable relationship patterns from whose matrix the children must presently emerge as individuals in their own right.

Just as the individual is assumed to be in a state of actively maintained homeostasis, so too families are regarded as working constantly to keep a certain steady state. Within such a framework, the family member would react to stress according to his or her position within the family. The family members form a reciprocating network where what affects any one member impinges on—and is in turn affected by—every other member. In effect, the reaction of the individual is actually a function of the way the family works. Hence, in order to understand the response to a given event, the therapist needs to study the characteristics of that particular family organization. From this perspective it follows that to change the response of a given individual, the therapist needs to alter the family's structure.

Family relationships are essentially triadic, with shifting affiliations sought for or spontaneously arising within twosomes in order to ward off, exclude, or align against the third member. All sorts of permutations are possible, but when one family member is thus designated as the scapegoat, that one is likely to become the index patient. This is a typical outcome of family stress. The ensuing syndromes can vary from school phobia in children to alcoholism in adults. In any case, the emergence of the illness becomes part of the homeostatic, self-regulating system of that family. Accordingly, the therapist who addresses the sick individual as the focus of treatment without seeking to affect the family structure is likely to intensify this defensive process.

When confronted with a stress, families can respond in different ways with their coping efforts. The family members can turn against one another; they can take flight from one another and seek to distance themselves; one member can take up the burden and develop symptoms in order to maintain a relative stability; or people can come together and share a common worry. To some extent, within any given family context, many of these mechanisms may be at work. It is when a family resorts to one of these patterns exclusively that dysfunction and symptoms are likely to ensue. People can achieve a stable (albeit unhappy) state of chronic bickering, one individual may constantly give way in order to preserve a measure of harmony, or one individual may fall ill and involve the others in a consistent way around the ensuing symptoms, or someone can withdraw and allow the others to mesh closely— any or all of these involve some loss of good function in the service of preserving a state of stability. This is the key phenomenon that makes for illness on the one hand and a family approach to treatment on the other.

One of the commonest patterns is for parents to concentrate on a child in order to avoid direct confrontation with their own differences. The parents' worries concerning the child and the child's emotional focus on the parents create a pattern of great emotional intensity. If it persists, such a pattern is ultimately destructive to the child's developmental freedom. Under such conditions, the child is unable to differentiate from the parental nexus, and numerous difficulties ensue.

One factor that strongly influences stress responses is the degree to which individual family members are immersed in each others' lives, as against the degree to which they function as autonomous, self-regulating, and self-directing individuals. In general, where the degrees of autonomy are greater, coping will be more successful. Where fusion, enmeshment, and attachment pressures predominate, the response to stress is likely to be impaired. This comes into particular prominence where the nature of the stress involves the loss (through death, illness, or abandonment) of a key family member.

For families, as for individuals, the nature of the stress experience and the compensatory adjustments it evokes depend on the meaning of that stress to the particular family. Thus, to have the family name besmirched might have no meaning to some families and catastrophic meaning to others.

When symptoms do appear in a family member, the therapist regards them as expressing disturbances in the family's relationship pattern. The direction of treatment must, therefore, be toward altering the different attachment-sets within the family.

The therapist begins by seeking to identify the significant emotional links within the family. Along with this the therapist assesses the role that the index patient's dysfunction plays within the family context. As the work proceeds, the therapist tries to illuminate for the family the role of these symptoms in maintaining family equilibrium. The interactions of the various individuals, their strife, their withdrawal, and the kind and quality of their emotional involvement with one another come under review. Intergenerational issues are highlighted.

A major therapeutic tactic is to shift the emphasis from the difficulties occasioned by the index patient to the interplay of emotions within the family proper. Where emotional intensity is high, this becomes particularly difficult. For highly enmeshed families, helping the individual members sort out their own lives and achieve a measure of autonomy becomes a central aspect of therapy.

Group Therapy

One of the characteristics of late 20th-century American culture has been an ever-increasing resort to groups and group techniques for troubled people (Weiner, 1989). This has involved such large-group tactics as the self-help groups noted earlier, but many small-group measures are now employed as well. Physicians and hospitals organize groups of patients with similar conditions to allow for mutual support, lessening of the sense of aloneness, sharing and exploring of feelings engendered by the illness, and mutual education. Employers have introduced group methods to help with burnout and other job-related stresses. Psychiatric centers employ groups routinely as part of the therapeutic milieu.

One area of special importance in this connection is coping with stress. A shared stress (be it a common illness, a handicap, or a catastrophe of some sort) offers an immediate focus for the group effort. From the outset, a readiness for sharing and for belonging is likely to pervade the atmosphere. The participants feel open both to express their reactions and to learn from one another in terms of new social skills and coping tactics.

In working with such stress-related groups, a key principle is to avoid blaming or allowing participants to blame themselves for their misfortunes. Their responsibility begins with how they react to the event (or condition) and what they do with the feelings it evokes. A strong reality emphasis has to be present, and it helps to offer concrete suggestions for improved ways of dealing with the problem. At the least, it is always possible to teach relaxation techniques or exercises.

Self-help groups employ a number of basic principles. The leader seeks to create an atmosphere of hope that something can be done and of optimism: If we work together, we can help one another. An educational quality is essential; regardless of the nature of the stress, there are likely to be points of effective environmental change that can be discerned and clarified. Emergency money or equipment might be obtainable, or a job can be restructured, or some novel technique can be learned to help deal with a handicap.

The leader can reframe the stress experience itself for the group members by redefining the difficulties as challenges. They are an opportunity for the person to master a variety of painful issues, discover his or her own unrecognized resources, and sort out his or her life in terms of what really counts. Often the group members need active support and direction in order to confront painful issues. Where there is a bereavement, where a part of the body is lost, where the person's work involves dealing with death and dying, there is ample cause for pain and emotional defensiveness. The issue of "Why me?" is of burning importance. The sense of being punished or targeted for affliction often bears heavily on people in such circumstances. The encouragement to face such feelings, express them, and hear from others in similar circumstances can be extremely important for some group members.

Once the feelings can be worked with, the factor of catharsis comes into play. Some of this will take the form of blaming and accusation, but ultimately the inner wounds will find expression and description, and this is likely to ease some of the pain. Such experiences have powerful interactive effects because they allow group members to share in one another's resonance to these affective expressions. Sometimes, when the emotion threatens to boil over into action, the therapist needs to apply corrective measures and to draw appropriate distinctions between what a person thinks and feels, and what he or she does.

Yet another mechanism that plays a role in group process is desensitization. The repeated exposure from engaging in painful topics, if properly titrated, tends to make the group members better able to endure facing issues that they might initially have avoided.

The factor of group identification plays a considerable role in easing the distress occasioned by the precipitating stress. The individual is not the only sufferer, the only one chosen (by God, by fate, by whatever malign force it may be). His or her reactions are not aberrant of disquieting; they are the typical, and indeed, the predictable responses to this kind of stress. The person is, in short, an average member of this particular set of people. This can afford enormous relief and act as a source of real comfort.

In this connection it is possible to allay many of the fears that people bring to the group, such as of being mentally ill, falling apart, or having a nervous breakdown. By looking at the reactions in terms of stress and stress responses, the person need no longer fear for inner integrity. What he or she is going through is after all a normal response to an abnormal burden.

The structure of such stress-related groups is highly variable. It can take the form of a class (for preoperative patients or newly diagnosed diabetics, etc.); it can be defined as group therapy but be limited to two, or three, or six sessions (or to some other brief, time-limited arrangement); or it can be open-ended with no prestructured termination date. It can include formal instructional components (e.g., lectures, slide shows, videos) followed by a question-and-answer period, or it can seek to involve the persons attending in an active and open exchange. Regardless of the design, the aforementioned elements are all likely to come into play. Not infrequently a veteran patient is present who by now is well past the initial stress response, and who serves as model and guide for the others.

As in all therapy, the process of termination is important and plays a key role in the long-term effectiveness of the process. Where the structure is time-limited, the awareness of the approaching end point can intensify the ongoing effort. By referring to the limited time available, the therapist can motivate patients to overcome defensiveness and inhibition and to bring forward important issues. Not infrequently group members establish meaningful bonds with one another and use termination as a stimulus to reach out to others socially. In long-term groups, members who make enough progress to leave the group and continue on their own have considerable impact on the remaining group members; there is often a sense of loss coupled with the reassurance that with time and work, they, too, can recover from the stress-related disorder.

Technically, the essential work of the group therapist who is dealing with Adjustment Disorders is to apply crisis techniques. This involves looking at the nature of the stress, building on the available strengths in the group, and helping with the mastery of the intense affects produced by the crisis. As a rule, if psychiatric disorders other than the adjustment problem are present, these will usually manifest themselves in the course of the group exchange, and the therapist can then consider separate referral.

Again, as with any therapy, countertransference problems can be intrusive and can distort the nature of the work. The group members may be in the grip of serious disruptions in their lives, and the therapist must resist the tendency to overidentify with their pain or to take their side against some authority with whom they disagree (employer, ward doctor, parent, etc.). Under such circumstances it is all too easy to be overwhelmed by suffering or to become party to "splitting" behavior. Group acting-out can also be a problem, and it is vital to keep the issues raised (such as indignation about the out-of-group experiences described by some one group member) confined to the group context. Again, as in any therapy, careful attention to the degree of affect released in therapy is always necessary. Although appropriate affective expression is therapeutic and valuable, the experience of being overwhelmed during a session usually has an adverse effect, both on the individual and the group.

Pharmacotherapy

Few substantial studies would fit any type of psychopharmacological regimen to the stress-related disorders. At this point, treatment of these conditions should be essentially psychological, and the use of psychotropic agents must be regarded as supportive and symptom focused (Kelly & Frosch, 1989).

Whether the therapist uses medication is a function of the nature of the symptoms and their severity. Severe depression, for example, merits the use of antidepressants whether the condition is reactive or endogenous. Similar considerations hold true for anxiety. Generally speaking, the use of medication should facilitate psychotherapy rather than impair it; there is certainly no contradiction in their mutual use.

In the case of normal grief it is probably better not to medicate the patient, and, instead, to allow the process to go forward as it must. Where pathological grief is present, however, the reverse is true, and appropriate psychopharmacological treatment should be prescribed.

There are many ways of using medication. A common practice with acutely stressed patients is to give tiny doses of some active pharmacological agent for the placebo effect. Sometimes, merely having medication at hand, without ever using it, offers the patient helpful reassurance. Although the use of placebo is not in itself undesirable, it is important to distinguish between placebo effects and the active impact of a chosen drug.

A general principle to observe is always to give medications in the smallest dose possible and for the shortest possible intervals. The therapist should be concerned as well about the possible misuse of these powerful agents for the purpose of self-destruction. The presence of suicidal tendencies in the index patient or in anyone who is part of the patient's immediate environment should be an important factor in determining whether to offer such treatment, how to arrange for its management, and how much to make available.

A number of specific symptoms require consideration. Insomnia can be troublesome during an episode of severe stress response; a moderate dose of an anxiolytic taken at bedtime (usually a benzodiazepine given in half to one third of the usual daily dose) will probably offer relief. If severe depressive symptoms predominate, an antidepressant may best serve to ease the symptom. On the other hand, where outbursts of panic dominate the clinical picture, the potent short-acting benzodiazepines (like alprazolam) may be helpful.

Some bereaved patients are unable to mourn; instead they withdraw into a state of blocked emotional rigidity and keep their feelings tightly in check. Under such circumstances, small doses of anxiolytics can reduce the patient's anxiety about the warded-off feelings and facilitate mourning.

Where depressive symptoms appear as a direct response to stress, it is better to hold off on medication and allow the psychological work to run its course. If 2 months go by without the symptoms easing, then medication can be initiated. This assumes that the patient has never had such symptoms or medication before; where the patient is known to be vulnerable to depression, pharmacological treatment should be instituted from the outset.

Where Posttraumatic Stress Disorder is present, tricyclic antidepressants are indicated, or, in refractory cases, phenelzine, 45–75 mg/day, may be of help.

Brief reactive psychotic syndromes are known to arise in the face of stress. These are not unusual in patients with known major disorders, but may occur as well in individuals who are otherwise free of serious psychopathology. Treatment should include the use of an antipsychotic agent for as long as symptoms persist. As a rule, this condition clears within a few days, and in such instances, drug therapy should be interrupted by tapering off over a week or two.

Finally, beta-blockers like propranolol have been helpful with certain kinds of acute reactive anxiety states such as stage fright. Hence, under such conditions, their use should be seriously considered.

Brief Psychotherapy

As with all treatment for Adjustment Disorders, the goal of psychotherapy is to relieve symptoms by improving the patient's adaptation (Horowitz, 1989). Globally speaking, adaptation is presumed to have failed because the individual could not cope with change. In such a situation, the person's characteristic manner of structuring reality has encountered a series of changes in the external world that are incompatible with the person's mind-set. For example, the sense of self as secure and inviolate encounters the fact of the rapist; the sense of one's body as whole and enduring encounters the diagnosis of cancer. The inner reality and the changed outer circumstances cannot coexist, and an Adjustment Disorder appears. It is this disparity that brief therapy seeks to address. The therapist undertakes first a review of the changes that have come about; then attempts to study them within the context of the current pattern of adjustment; and finally, tries to help the patient distinguish reality from fantasy.

Structurally, one of the distinguishing characteristics of brief therapy is that it is time-limited. At the outset, the therapist specifies a certain period of time or a specific number of hours (typically such a course will run for 12 hours) during which the therapeutic work will continue—and at the end of which it is over. This sets the basic tone of the work and colors its unfolding thereafter.

In the address to the patient, the therapist assumes that stress-filled change evokes painful emotions, which, in their turn, are so disturbing that they are often warded off. The therapist seeks to bring the patient to face these feelings. By pointing out the presence of the defense and shedding light on why that defense has been instituted. Ultimately (where possible), the therapist helps the patient find better ways of coping.

In the wake of the trauma recurring or intrusive thoughts often torment the patient. These give some hint of the fearsome affects and ideation that the patient is keeping at bay. As these are worked with, they lose some of their mystique and a less panicky state of mind ensues. Along with this, it becomes possible to encounter and explore the more covert themes that have been fueling the disorder. The patient thus gradually becomes able to face the issues that he or she had been so sedulously avoiding. These issues are often derived from long-standing attitudes that existed well before the patient encountered the traumatic circumstances. The therapist must examine such fantasy elements with a critical eye in order to help the patient sort out the past. At the same time, the therapist should encourage the patient to try to face some of the reality situations that he or she has been avoiding and to keep track of inner experiences (perhaps through a diary or by means of dictated notes), so that these can be reviewed in therapy.

More specifically, in opening the therapeutic work, the therapist encourages the patient to tell the story of the recentt past and to describe, as spontaneously as possible, the disturbing event(s) that precipitated the reaction. The empathic bond established by this kind of gentle but attentive interest, plus the therapist's responsiveness to the affective components of the recital will go far toward building a therapeutic alliance. The patient must describe his or her various states of mind—both the positive, pleasurable, creative states, and the morbid, angry, anxious, troubled states. The traumatic events must be seen in connection with these several states. This allows more ready access to the affective components of the patient's experience and, by giving language to these subtle inner processes, makes for both improved communication and greater mastery. Presently it will emerge that given states, disturbing though they may be, are in fact protecting the patient from even more dangerous and incapacitating psychological experiences (e.g., rage outbursts may ward off guilty self-recriminations of suicidal degree). Moreover, the several states of mind are connected with ways of relating, both to self and to others.

Much of the early work involves an exploration of significant relationship patterns, especially those that color the interaction with the therapist. Early recognition of transference (and countertransference) phenomena and attention to the meaning of shifts of attitude from hour to hour will move the work forward rapidly. The patient may reenact the recent trauma within the therapist–patient context and may seek unconsciously to create in the therapist some of the same disturbing affects, so recently experienced and still being worked through by the patient. Clarification of such transactions is of signal importance for the work.

The patient entering the midphase of the process will often bring up material from early in life. The effect of prior traumatic events that resonate with the current experience begins to emerge, and the fantasy-shrouded quality of the patient's present perception becomes ever more evident. This is often accompanied by flashes of negative transference as the patient relives earlier painful experiences within the framework of the therapeutic interaction. Active interpretation of these feelings will help link together present and past experiences, increase the patient's sense of continuity and inner coherence, and convert a fantasy menace of overwhelming character into a reality stress that can be dealt with in practical terms.

In order to initiate the termination phase of brief therapy, somewhere in midcourse the therapist should reintroduce the fact of the time-limited structure and draw attention to the forthcoming end of the work. Sometimes the patient is surprised that the therapist actually meant it (when saying that termination would come at a certain date or at a specific hour); in any case it tends to focus attention on the therapist–patient connection and to bring this into the context of the patient's crisis response. Termination themes are likely to emerge thereafter, both overtly and symbolically. It is necessary to systematically work through unrealistic expectations and fantasy distortions of the therapist's role. In some instances, problems will come to light that the patient can continue to work on independently, or that indicate the need for more traditional (non-time-limited) therapy. Such matters should be clarified toward the closing hours. The real working through of the separation tends to occur close to–but not during–the final hour. That hour is often one where the patient seeks to demonstrate his or her controls and ability to operate without the therapist's help. It may therefore seem to be superficial in terms of the themes addressed, or the patient may appear nonchalant in respect to the ending of the relationship.

Child Psychotherapy for Adjustment Disorders

With traumatized children, highly flexible and diverse approaches are necessary (Carek, 1989). Among the array of possible interventions, individual psychotherapy will play a central role in some instances and a secondary role in others. Because it seeks to help the child cope successfully and develop appropriately, such psychotherapy has to deal with those aspects of the provocative stress that the child finds difficult to assimilate and that act to impede subsequent personality growth.

Just as with adults, child psychotherapy for stress-related disorders differs from conventional therapy in a number of respects. For one thing, it is time limited; a typical arrangement would be to set up somewhere between 6 and 12 sessions for the treatment at intervals of once a week to once a month. Some therapists use as few as 1 or 2 sessions; not infrequently at a second session a child will be concerned that he or she "talked too much" in the first.

Short-term therapy is not merely a briefer version of long-term work. The setting of goals, the limited time frame, the continual refocusing by the therapist, and the emphasis on the individual strengths and coping capacities of the patient serve to define such short-term intervention and to give it its unique quality.

For the child, the short-term nature of the process emphasizes separation-individuation; where there is at least some budding sense of autonomy, the statement of a time limit lends a curiously supportive quality to a youngster who feels so helpless and overwhelmed. It is a declaration of confidence by the therapist that there is something to be done, and it can be done without great delay. On the other hand, limiting the extent of the relationship is not always a desirable element to build in at the outset. For example, where the stress reaction is too catastrophic, or where the patient's developmental conflicts have frozen any autonomous strivings into a state of immobility, such an approach will not be productive.

Where the therapist deems it best not to focus on a fixed time frame, he or she can direct the emphasis toward attaining specific goals (such as resolving particular conflicts or relieving given symptoms). This usually shortens the time of therapy considerably.

On the other hand, brief therapy shares a number of characteristics in common with conventional child therapy. There is a primary need to establish a special kind of interpersonal relationship with the child that encourages opening up to a concerned, communicative, skilled, helpful adult. By means of therapeutic clarification and interpretation, the therapist asks the child to become more aware of his or her own motives and inner processes, more alive to the meaning of the precipitating stress, and more sensitive to his or her effects on the inner feelings of the surrounding people. In addition, a number of other therapeutic elements may come into play. One is the evocation and the mobilization of affect. Children defend themselves against their own feelings because they fear that their emotions will become over- whelming and uncontrollable; this is one reason many children are so vulnerable to stress. This walling off of disturbing emotion can become so central to a child's psychic economy that a fixation occurs, and little energy is left for wholesome developmental progress. Sometimes children can tell the therapist all about the event that precipitated their disability, but the account is lifeless and intellectual. It is only when the child can be helped to express the fear, jealousy, embarrassment, rage and/or pain engendered by the traumatic event that the sought-for relief is likely to follow. A characteristic example of this process is the child who can describe the experience of battering in a matter-of-fact way, but who cannot give up his or her symptoms (e.g., bullying other children) until remembering and reexperiencing the feelings evoked by the battering.

Some of the most useful elements that can be part of a course of therapy are catharsis and corrective emotional experience. Catharsis involves the discharge of pent-up affects as direct expression of emotion; when this occurs duirng the treatment of Adjustment Disorders, it often signals a turning point in the therapy. Corrective emotional experience entails a reliving with the therapist of a prior circumstance (e.g., a challenge to a parent), but with a radically different outcome. Thus, instead of counterattack, rejection, and humiliation, there is a readiness to consider what is said, to explore, and to understand it.

Three tenets should guide the therapist who works with children who have stress-related disorders.

1. *Focal Inquiry.* It can be assumed that underlying every Adjustment Disorder is a single primary issue that requires resolution. This becomes the central point throughout the therapy. It can often be discerned during the initial assessment, and it is the continuing focus thereafter.

2. *Dealing with Resistance.*The therapist must initiate work of mobilizing affect from the outset. The child is often more available during the first interview, and the beginning address to the defenses must be undertaken then. The identifying and the exploring (working through) of these psychic barriers will ultimately allow for the critical affective discharge.

3. *Bridging the Developmental Deficiency.* The relationship that develops when the patient allows the therapist to sense the patient's needs and struggles in an empathic way permits the therapist to step in adroitly with support, explanation, and suggestions. These will give the patient the necessary coping tools to attempt adjustment.

Technically, the tools available to the psychotherapist are; empathic mirroring, clarification, confrontation, and interpretation. The counselor's tools—suggestion, admonition, advising, and counseling—are probably best omitted from the psychotherapist's armamentarium, or at any rate used sparingly and with great discretion.

In the course of brief therapy, the therapist is likely to be far more verbal, ready to interrupt, directive, and, active than with other psychotherapeutic approaches. Among the means at the therapist's disposal, resort to confrontation and clarification will tend to predominate. At the same time, empathic mirroring is the prime relationship-building tool in the therapist's hands. This involves the therapist's opening him- or herself up emotionally, resonating with the patient's affective state, and finding ways to put into words what the patient is feeling. Where the therapist strategically selects and empathically expresses the points of resonance, the patient has a deep sense of being understood and "felt with." This tends, as a result, to open a channel between the participants. The therapist directs clarification primarily toward getting the patient to verbalize a variety of ideas and affects that are vaguely and globally experienced but are not clearly formulated or precisely identified. Much muddy thinking of this sort lies behind the frequent resort to "you know," so often interspersed among a teenager's remarks (as though the patient wished for the listener to understand—to "know"—without the communicant needing to clarify or to have self-knowledge of just what he or she has in mind). The therapist's pressure for the patient to find the necessary words and to be lucid and clear in exposition is a powerful force that dispels magical, ambiguous, and defensively screened ideation and flushes out hidden and incompletely realized inner meanings. Confrontation follows from this, because the themes that emerge when the therapist requests clarification are often magical explanations, contradictions, or unreal assumptions; the therapist then confronts the patient with these items. In effect, confrontation is the therapist's means of invoking the patient's reality-testing capacity and good judgment to challenge the patient's own motives and inner processes (as well as behavior). It usually involves bringing the patient face to face with something that he or she is avoiding—contradiction or an illogical position. In practice, the therapist can achieve confrontation with logical reasoning, humor, irony, or *gentle* sarcasm. It can never be done with hostility or with revenge as the predominant quality. At least, it can never be done therapeutically in that way. It is the appeal to reason par excellence and is effective only to the extent that the therapist can recruit the patient's own ego functions to help deal with the irrational aspects of the patient's behavior. Otherwise the patient experiences the challenge merely as criticism and rejection, which weakens the therapeutic alliance.

Finally, interpretation is the therapist's ultimate technique. The essential nature of interpretation is to create awareness where formerly there was none; in the nature of things this is hazardous and invites denial and rejection. The therapist must therefore handle interpretation with delicacy, finesse, and clinical sensitivity. It is a trenchant tool and can cause injury if not wielded well.

To repeat, then, interpretation is a means of making a patient aware. There is a potential for creating awareness about numerous things. The classic use of interpretation is to make repressed (i.e., unconscious) mental contents conscious. (In psychoanalytic theory this formulation held particularly for oedipal memories. It was posited that for a certain time during development, the child had held in mind a set of strongly felto edipal wishes; as development advanced, however, the child repressed these ideas—along with the associated feelings. Albeit unconscious, however, these now-forbidden wishes continue to function as active shaping forces on behavior. As a consequence, the adult later enacts these yearnings without knowing what drives him or her, and symptoms appear. During the course of treatment the therapist makes the unconscious conscious, and the oedipal memories return. But it is not just the memories of the events that are crucial; in fact, it is the oedipal affects that are the significant factors; to recapture the memories as such has little power as long as the affects (erotic yearnings, intense jealousies, death wishes, fears of dreadful retaliation) remain unconscious. Thus, it is necessary to recapture both sides of the repressed experience, the ideation as well as the emotion. But the essential act is to interpret the unconscious).

A second kind of interpretation is to make the patient aware of defenses. These unconscious mechanisms are universal presences both in sickness and health; they are basic to the regulation of both fantasies and emotions. They function entirely outside of awareness and need recognition and specification only when their activity results in distorting the patient's outlook and impeding adjustment. As an illustration, that a patient automatically blames others for his or her own unacceptable urges. The therapist points out the mechanism at work, saying in effect: When jealousy rises up in you, you project it out on others and experience these others as jealous and hence malevolent. That way you don't have to face the reality that the jealousy has arisen in you, that you yourself are feeling envious and acting accordingly.

If properly timed and given within a context of acceptance and warm support, such an interpretation can be a powerful illumination. Many mental mechanisms of various kinds are always at work and always unconscious; they can therefore be usefully interpreted.

A third use of interpretation is to bring together parts of the patient's experience that he or she has kept apart. Thus in a given hour, a man talks of impending prostate surgery without evident anxiety and then refers to work in his garden pond where he fears a repair may break down and leak. he sees no connection between the two until the therapist interprets this for him.

Because a large part of mentation is in fact unconscious, interpretation can operate on many levels and deal with a wide variety of issues. Of them all, the interpretation of transference, the relationship between what the patient says and does on the one hand, and what the patient feels toward the therapist on the other, is of key importance. It is the most effective means available to the psychotherapist to help the patient understand relationship issues. It is in the course of unraveling such interpersonal themes that the patient is likely to achieve the most rapid therapeutic gains. Thus, to return to the former example, if the patient begins to feel that the therapist is jealous, and the interpretation can be made within the transference (it is easier to think that I envy you than to face that the envy arises within you), the effect of the interpretation is likely to be maximal.

Taken together and properly and skillfully employed, these several mechanisms can go far toward relieving inner pain by giving the patient increased mastery over many vital psychic processes.

REFERENCES

Beal, E. M. (1989). Family therapy. In *Treatment of psychiatric disorders: A task force report of the American Psychiatric Association* (Vol. 3, pp. 2566–2577). Washington, DC: American Psychiatric Association.

Borman, L. D. (1989). Self-help and mutual aid groups for adults. In *Treatment of psychiatric disorders: A task force report of the American Psychiatric Association* (Vol. 3, pp. 2596–2606). Washington, DC: American Psychiatric Association.

Carek, D. J. (1989). Individual child psychotherapy. In *Treatment of psychiatric disorders: A task force report of the American Psychiatric Association*. (Vol. 3, pp. 2557–2565). Washington, DC: American Psychiatric Association.

Horowitz, M. J. (1989). Brief dynamic psychotherapy. In *Treatment of psychiatric disorders: A task force report of the American Psychiatric Association* (Vol. 3, pp. 2548–2556). Washington DC: American Psychiatric Association.

Kelly, K. V., & Frosch, W. A. (1989). Pharmacoptherapy. In *Treatment of psychiatric disorders: A task force report of the American Psychiatric Association* (Vol. 3, pp. 2585–2589). Washington, DC: American Psychiatric Association.

Shore, M. F., & Mannino, F. V. (1989). Self-help, mutual-help, and peer-helping services for youth. In *Treatment of psychiatric disorders: A task force report of the American Psychiatric Association* (Vol. 3, pp. 2607-2616). Washington, DC: American Psychiatric Association.

Suinn, R. M. (1989). Stress management by behavioral methods. In *Treatment of psychiatric disorders: A task force report of the American Psychiatric Association* (Vol. 3, pp. 2532–2547). Washington, DC: American Psychiatric Association.

Swanson, W. C., & Carbon, J. B. (1989). Crisis intervention: Theory and technique. In *Treatment of psychiatric disorders: A task force report of the American Psychiatric Association* (Vol. 3, pp. 2520–2531). Washington, DC: American Psychiatric Association.

Weiner, M. F. (1989). Group therapy. In *Treatment of psychiatric disorders: A task force report of the American Psychiatric Association* (Vol. 3, pp. 2578–2584). Washington, DC: American Psychiatric Association.

Whitehead, P. L., & Stout, R. J. (1989). Religion as ego support. In *Treatment of psychiatric disorders: A task force report of the American Psychiatric Association* (Vol. 3, pp. 2590–2595). Washington, DC: American Psychiatric Association.

Individual Psychotherapy in Adjustment Disorders

CARL P. ADATTO, MD

Individual psychotherapy for patients with Adjustment Disorders presents therapists with the challenge of a patient in a state of psychic disequilibrium. This results in a double demand: not only must the therapist cope with the appearance of affects related to the current psychosocial stress, but invariably one must address the mobilization of old intrapsychic conflicts that have been in a state of relative homeostasis. In an Adjustment Disorder, the aim of therapy is at once to restore the preexisting psychic balance and to assist the patient in gaining new insight as a result of the upheaval. Developmental changes or other forms of stress can stimulate the widening of psychic functioning. In individuals who have the ego capacity to reintegrate, such changes can then lead to an awareness of the newly opened psychic workings.

In some instances, only a restoration of psychic equilibrium and relief of symptoms are indicated. To achieve such an outcome, a variety of therapies may be used; among them, individual psychotherapy is one modality that can offer a good deal of help. Once these goals are reached, however, this therapy may terminate without the patient achieving any apparent degree of insight. It is in the nature of Adjustment Disorder that the diagnosis can be confirmed only after a period of time. Psychotherapy, like any treatment, seeks to relieve suffering; more than that, however, it offers the advantage of exploring the actual nature of the patient's problem. Thus, in addition to treating the disorder, it can also set the stage for more extensive therapeutic work.

THEORY AND TECHNIQUE

The application of psychoanalytic theory along with appropriate modifications of technique provides the basis for the concepts presented here. Among other important aspects, psychoanalytic theory regards intrapsychic workings along with unconscious conflicts and defenses as the critical determinants of symptoms and behavior. To be sure, patients may not have any interest beyond the relief of their immediate distress. The therapist, however, is oriented to look for a number of factors beyond the immediate issues presented by the patient; these factors include the patient's development (starting with infancy), object relationships, and the form taken by the structure and nature of the inner conflicts. If one uses psychoanalytic theory as a basis for psychotherapy, then one cannot be limited to the current problems and must tune in to the totality of the mental apparatus. From such a standpoint, psychosocial stress cannot be regarded in isolation; in addition to its direct impact, it functions as an awakener of preexisting unconscious psychic activity. By thus viewing the mind, the therapist can get to the effects of stress more accurately than if the inner workings are ignored.

There is a significant difference between the techniques of psychoanalysis and psychotherapy. Nonetheless, the basic tools of psychoanalytic technique can be adapted to psychotherapy. Employment of free association and the interpretation of transference and of defense are fundamental to psychoanalytic technique. Free association by the patient—the patient is asked to say whatever comes to mind— is used in psychoanalysis with the long-term aims of revealing the derivatives of unconscious conflicts and achieving the recovery of memories. Once obtained, these data can then be subjected to analysis. On the other hand, in individual psychotherapy, the associative process is used both to understand how the patient is currently affected by the stress, as well as to assess what conflicts have been mobilized. The associative process keeps the therapist from making assumptions that are not based firmly on patient data; in this way the therapist does not preempt the patient. The focus remains on the patient and on the patient's inner capacities to overcome the disorder. In using this kind of associative technique, it is important for the therapist to be quite active in terms of seeking clarification and elaboration of the patient's concerns as well as offering tentative interpretations. In this way the therapist can get an ever more comprehensive picture of the patient's defenses and psychological awareness.

It is important to consider the nature of interpretation. An interpretation can be viewed as a hypothesis that the therapist submits to the patient. It is a formulation that attempts to establish new connections among the patient's verbal, emotional, and behavioral productions; more than that, it has the aim of stimulating new understanding and, indeed, of changing the nature of the patient's psychic functioning. In effect, interpretations are explanatory concepts that attempt to lead the patient to fresh insights.

In addition to interpretation, other important forms of interventions are clarification and elaboration; these seek to expand and clarify what the patient has said, and they indicate the therapist's interest in a particular area. However, they do not assert the therapist's views as to what is going on in the patient's mind.

Interpretations that are not based on the patient's own productions and that arise only from the therapist's concepts about the patient are usually ineffective. Moreover, they can be counterproductive. A clarification could be phrased: "Can you tell me more about what you just said?" An interpretation, "You have said a and b, and expressed c. If we put these together could it mean that x is what you are experiencing?" Based on the effect on the patient, there are times when the differences between these interventions are not clear. Indeed, a clarification may sometimes have an interpretive effect and create new understanding in the patient, whereas an interpretation may simply evoke new associations.

The clinical material to follow will illustrate the importance of and differences between these forms of intervention. This psychoanalytically oriented technique achieves support and reassurance by helping the patient expand and regain use of mental activity, rather than by relying solely on the therapist's empathy and understanding.

Another important aspect of technique is the management of transference. Transference is a phenomenon observed when the patient unconsciously attributes to the therapist attitudes, feelings, and behavior that were originally experienced in the patient's early relationships with parents and other important figures. There are some transferences that exist at the outset of therapy (in the form of preset attitudes to people of a given age, a given gender, a given way of speaking, etc.). They have usually been set in motion prior to the time the patient first sees the therapist. One facet of the transference centers around the expectations patients have of the therapist at the outset of the work. To begin with, patients want relief from their symptoms. In addition, their stress sets in motion infertile expectations (regressive transference needs) that should be understood as part of the treatment. These transferences may be object related as defined earlier, such as an unconscious wish for a parent to give relief. In another sense transferences can be viewed as externalizations of the patient's psychic functioning onto the therapist. For example, patients may turn over to the therapist their ego functions, such as judgment or memory. Thus, a patient might ask the therapist: "What was I talking about when I left your office yesterday?" In essence the patient is asking the therapist to serve as an external memory. How the therapist handles the matter technically depends on many factors; however, it must be viewed, in addition to other determinants, as the patient's transferring part of the self—one's memory function—at that moment.

Or, patients may externalize their superego functions and expect the therapist to be punitive or to give praise. To be sure, it is sometimes difficult to separate transferences from other phenomena; nonetheless, the process of such explorations can often yield important therapeutic results. Examining the transference is an essential part of technique; it keeps the course of therapy oriented toward the patient's relationship life, and the focus of the work on the patient's mind.

An adolescent girl was in acute distress because of a failure in a love relationship; in the course of the initial interview she told the therapist: "You must think that I am weak for wanting to call my boyfriend and apologize for what I said. That's what my mother and father both told me." The transference onto the therapist was of two kinds: her self-criticism, and the parental attitudes. Clarification could have been attempted by asking the patient what prompted her to make the remark, or by asking for further details about the apology. In this instance, the therapist elected to interpret the remark (coming in sequence with other related associations) by posing the question: "You assume that I am like your parents in believing that you are weak; is it possible that you also are referring to your own self-criticism for being weak?" The patient veered away from talking about her parents and the therapist, and began, carefully and productively, to examine herself and her own actions.

There are many defenses (for instance, a stabilizing obsessive defense) that are useful to the patient in the fair wear and tear of everyday coping. In the face of stress, however, these defenses can be overwhelmed, which in turn sets in motion intense affects or changes in behavior. Ultimately it is these stress-related patterns that bring the patient to therapy. It is important to attempt to identify these defenses in order to help the patient understand what is happening psychologically. This can be done, however, without the therapist necessarily either encouraging the defense or attempting to analyze its relationship to unconscious derivatives.

The therapist can utilize these basic theories to help organize the data, while setting in motion a therapeutic process predicated on understanding the patient's psychic functioning. Because mental activity and behavior have multiple determinants, the therapist's task is to discover which of these determinants is the immediate issue. Basically, such an approach centers on therapeutic activity that stimulates the patient's reintegrative (healing) functioning.

CLINICAL EXAMPLES

Case 1

Following a serious automobile accident from which everyone had escaped with only minor injuries, a 35-year-old man came to therapy because of intense anxiety and concern about his safety and well-being. Although responsibility for the accident was charged to the other driver, he presently realized that the accident had occurred in part because of his own inattentiveness to the road. He had in fact been preoccupied with thoughts about his marital separation. Following a marriage of 10 years, a month previously his wife had asked for and he had consented to a separation. Although in some ways he welcomed the move, he simultaneously felt like a failure. He especially missed living with his three young children to whom he was devoted.

This accident had occurred 2 days prior to consulting the therapist. Following the accident, he had been overcome with feelings of remorse for recently ignoring his wife and children. He had discussed his problems with his father, but on realizing that the father could do little to help him, he had felt considerable restlessness. His father had recommended that he consult the therapist; the patient wryly said: "My father is turning me over to you." After a pause, the therapist asked what the patient wanted of him. The patient laughed and said that he wanted comfort and relief, something that no one could really give him. (Asking the patient what is wanted of the therapist can yield important data that might be crucial to the conduct of the treatment.)

The patient proceeded to say that he had always been an independent person, had been successful in his work of running a small business, and had never experienced the kind of emotional upheaval he was now encountering. It puzzled him not only that he acted recklessly, but also that he had turned to his father in the same way that he would once have turned to both parents (until his early adolescence). His mother had died 5 years previously following a protracted illness. This led quickly to thoughts that for the first years of his marriage he had turned to his wife for encouragement. This was a form of support that he had received in ever-lessening degree as the children came to occupy more of their time, and as he had less need for it.

These first associations led him to see that when he was in distress, he had a lifelong pattern of turning to someone for support and encouragement. Although he recognized that this was not unusual, it nonetheless stood in contrast to his established view of himself as a fairly independent person. The visit with his father, and the consultation with the therapist revived his awareness of this trait. Then he commented that he felt somewhat disgusted with himself, not only for looking for help that did not come but for not really wanting it. This opened up a flood of anger directed first toward his wife and then toward himself for turning to her at times instead of using his own resources. The therapist interpreted that the separation and accident appeared to have mobilized an old and troublesome problem that seemed connected to his current distress. He agreed and declared that he had better look into the matter.

During the next several appointments he came in feeling considerably improved. At the same time he expressed concern about what he called putting himself in other people's hands. Because he saw the therapeutic process as another sign of his dependency, he felt uneasy talking about himself. When asked to clarify this statement, he quickly discarded that issue and proceeded to talk about his sexual impotence of about 2 years' duration (there had been no previous indication of this problem). This led to his discussing his sexual history and, with considerable hesitancy, he related a homosexual experience he had had in college. He said that he was getting "into deep water," but it was a relief to stand back and look at these unexplored areas in perspective. It surprised him that he could talk about matters that were painfully embarrassing. The patient commented that he thought the therapist would be critical of him for what he had done. The therapist replied that perhaps it was also difficult for the patient to deal with self-criticism. The patient recalled several events in recent years in which he had created problems for himself by ignoring his own perceptions and judgment. At first he had blamed others, but then he had felt much better on realizing that it was he who had to be accountable. Being in charge of his own destiny was important to him.

During therapy there were instances in which he would wander off into details that the therapist considered to be defensive. For example, at one point the patient spoke in what seemed excessive detail about a movie he had seen; the therapist shared his observation about the wealth of detail with the patient and asked if something was being avoided that might be painful. After a studied pause, the patient said that he was depressed. He continued by revealing that he often went to movies when he was depressed. When asked to elaborate about his movie-unresolved issues, he felt that he now could deal with these without therapy. (It is important that the therapist not take the patient's decision to terminate at face value. Like any other association, it must be explored so that the patient can understand the conditions under which he is leaving therapy and can thus widen his self-understanding).

Another aspect of his decision not to pursue therapy was his fear of and wish for dependency within the therapeutic relationship. From the outset he had quickly grasped the related transference meanings when these were interpreted. The interpretive act of connecting some of his character traits and old anxieties with his current concerns about his marriage and the accident seemed again to turn the balance of forces toward active solution of his problem. The patient had no desire to explore further the issues raised by the upheaval, for example, the origins of his dependency conflict; his sexual problems, which he now considered manageable; or the problems of his marriage. It was evident that he had regained his previous equilibrium, and the new awareness of himself that he had achieved was sufficient to allow him to carry on without psychotherapy.

Treatment had the effect of at once expediting the return to his use of his perceptions, both internal and external, as well as of activating his memory; both served as important tools in the resolution of his acute conflict. There is no doubt that the stresses had set in motion the turmoil that had brought him to therapy. Until the patient began associating and engaging himself in the therapeutic situation, however, neither patient nor therapist could have predicted what it was that the stress had in fact precipitated.

Case 2

A 61-year-old woman came to therapy because of insomnia and feelings of depression that were noted over the previous several weeks. When her symptoms increased, she turned to her internist; when she failed to respond to his treatment, he referred her for psychotherapy. She said she was troubled by the knowledge that her symptoms were creating difficulties for her husband. Two months previously he had retired from his professional career at the age of 70; since then he seemed to be at a loss as to what to do with himself. Five years previously he had suffered a myocardial infarct from which he recovered; after that, both the patient and her husband had changed their life-style and had become less active. The patient said she was not sure who should be coming for help—herself or her husband, because neither of them was doing too well. Prior to her husband's retirement, and for a short while afterward, she had continued to pursue her usual activities; then she began to feel guilty for neglecting him. She had always been an active person and still was, nor had she ever had any serious physical problems. In the past she would occasionally become mildly depressed, but she always got prompt relief by keeping busy. Her four children (who were all married) and her five grandchildren were sources of continuing joy and companionship for her; she had many friends, was an avid reader, and regularly painted with a group of friends.

After relating her initial story, she seemed to have little more to say. When asked to speak more about herself, after some hesitation, she talked about her relationship with her husband. From the beginning of their marriage, they had spent little time together; for the most part her husband had tended to be occupied with his profession and his hunting and fishing expeditions. At first she had protested about his neglect; later she came to ignore it. Their sexual life had ceased some 15 years previously, and, with some embarrassment, she revealed sexual fantasies toward certain male friends. Suddenly, with a burst of contempt, she said that her husband had not been the successful man he appeared on the surface, but had in fact capitalized on her assets. After some uneasy silence, she declared that despite what she had just said, she did indeed love him.

When she returned the second time, she had already decided to enter therapy, telling the therapist, "I don't want to be psychoanalyzed, but I do want to clear up a few things in my life." She feared that if she examined herself too carefully, she might leave her husband, and this was something she had no desire to do. Yet she did want to look at herself, at her frustrations, and at her disappointment with what she termed, "dishonesty with myself." When the therapist asked her what she meant by being "psychoanalyzed," she promptly responded, "criticized," and soberly added, "Criticism shatters me."

She reported that on making the decision to enter therapy, her depression had lifted and she had slept well. Her sharp wit came through when she told the therapist: "With my help, you performed a miracle cure." A brief poem she had written that night referred to a painting that she had admired in the therapist's office. Her associations made it clear that, although somewhat aware of transference feelings to the therapist, her poem reflected a wish to paint like the artist whom she admired. Later she likened the therapeutic experience to her painting lessons where the instructors had encouraged her to develop her own style.

Because the patient had made it clear in many ways that she wanted to do her own work with minimal help, the therapist's interventions with this patient were parsimonious. It is important to note that from the outset the patient had given frequent associations about her narcissism, similar to those about being shattered by criticism. However, there were numerous occasions when the therapist asked for clarification. In one instance, the patient had switched associations from rageful fantasies about her husband to a description of a portrait that she was currently painting. When she said nothing further about the painting, the therapist asked her about it. In a sheepish way she revealed that she was painting a photograph of herself as a beautiful, 3-year-old child. This led her to explore her mingled shame and pride about her interest in her own appearance.

Toward the latter part of therapy she had, with many gestures and little emotion, described how she would like literally to dismember a woman who had flirted with her husband. Among the many available options, the therapist elected to point out the lack of emotion in the description she gave of using a hatchet to mutilate someone. At first she laughed, then began to cry. Her associations led to a recollection of being punished for dismembering an insect when she was young. She realized that she was afraid that the therapist might punish her for her fantasied thoughts. This interpretation opened up previously unexplored areas about her destructive fantasies, and how these were connected with the problem with her husband.

The treatment lasted about 18 months and covered many areas, especially her creativity and its link with her sexuality and aggression. Her contempt for her husband had antecedents in a relationship with an older brother favored by the father; her fantasies revealed considerable sadism and narcissistic interests. This was an aspect that had been well defended and with which she dealt gingerly in therapy.

In retrospect, it seemed that this woman had functioned adequately and had kept her conflicts in check by means of her creativity and her ability to use various defenses. Her problem also involved a developmental upheaval that had been brought to the surface by the stress of her husband's retirement. She was struggling with the fact of getting old and reintegrating her mind in a new way. The husband's continuous presence in the house provoked her Adjustment Disorder; it forced her to reexamine her own life and bring it up to date.

Upon reconstruction of her original problem, it was evident that the depression and insomnia related in part to her disappointment with herself for not being more open with her husband. The anger she felt toward him was difficult for her to integrate. His retirement catalyzed a problem that had been in the wings for some time, without requiring immediate attention. Despite progress during therapy, the husband's presence at home was a source of continued stress. About 2 months prior to terminating her therapy, her husband became bored with retirement and resumed work. With that stress removed and her symptoms relieved, the patient felt no further need for therapy. The therapist wondered whether she might be pushing aside other important problems; these were enumerated from her recent associations. She responded in a teasing way, "I'll do my own painting, doctor." Over the next few years she came in for occasional visits to check out issues raised in her self-therapy.

THERAPEUTIC CONSIDERATIONS

The two cases illustrate the process of therapy: By no means do they cover the full range of indications for individual psychotherapy in Adjustment Disorders. Patients with prolonged trauma or illness must deal with the immediacy of their stress reaction; some may have little interest or energy in pursuing the underlying problems mobilized by that stress. They might use the therapeutic situation to abreact the traumatic event with variations on the theme of the immediate situation. Such patients bring up few or no associations that lead to other areas; once symptoms have diminished, they leave therapy.

Some patients prefer to remain silent and withdrawn; attempts to encourage them to associate can be futile or, worse yet, tactless. Problems of transference and defense become obvious to the experienced therapist, but the patient may be more interested in reintegrating than exploring. Yet, even patients experiencing severe stress should be given the opportunity to deal with the current derivatives of the underlying conflicts. Such an approach often leads to expediting the resolution of their symptoms. For instance, some adolescents exhibit severe behavioral problems as a result of stress. Once they are given a chance to examine the scope of the problem and its relationship to their developmental changes, they can often return to more age appropriate functioning. If nothing else, such a procedure gives the therapist helpful diagnostic information about the psychic capacities of the patient; this in turn can be used in recommending effective therapeutic measures.

The duration of therapy is determined by many factors. The first patient presented is typical of many individuals who come for psychotherapy. Often the therapy is as brief as one or two sessions, following which the patient regains his or her usual level of functioning, and has neither the need nor the desire for further help. In these cases therapists must use their skill and clinical judgment about how best to make it clear to the patient that it is possible that some issues might not have been explored, and how best to convey that the patient might want to consider getting more therapy at a later date. There is a delicate therapeutic balance to be struck between being too assertive and authoritarian with the patient on the one hand, and being too unintrusive and self-effacing on the other. The former might keep some patients from revealing problems that need attention; the latter might result in a failure to clarify and address important problems.

The diagnosis of Adjustment Disorder can in itself be difficult. In the second patient, the diagnosis could not be made definitively until she had terminated therapy. Although she revealed and dealt with many neurotic conflicts during treatment, once the acute stress was removed, she had no need for further therapy. As a result of the knowledge gained about her during therapy, it was felt that the stress had created a disequilibrium; this in turn had evoked her latent neurosis. She had functioned adequately throughout her life; as a result of dealing with her stress and neurosis during treatment, she was able to resume functioning at an even higher level.

This patient illustrates how stress can set in motion certain stabilized problems that the patient may not have fully recognized and that in any case, she may previously have had no pressing need to pursue. It also illustrates the need for the therapist carefully to assess the mind and character of the patient. Her narcissistic orientation was not pathological, and indeed, served her well; recognizing its presence gave the therapist information about how to phrase interventions. It was important not to be active in a way that would be experienced as tactless, or that would allow the necessary interventions to be regarded as intrusions or criticism. In the case of the first patient, it was important for the therapist to pay heed to the patient's autonomy and to the man's sense of being proper. This information was used to construct interventions that could be usefully phrased and timed.

In some instances even mild stress can trigger the need for therapy. In others, the need to remain well defended, even in the face of severe stress, presents both patient and therapist with major issues. These may then require several periods of exploration before therapy is successful. For instance, following the death of his child, one patient came for therapy in clusters of a number of sessions at a time over a span of several years. During this interval, he was facing certain disappointments in his functioning at work, and he could deal only with bits and pieces of his injured self-esteem. Grief over the loss of his child was confluent with turmoil related to inner conflicts.

At times what appears at the outset to be an Adjustment Disorder turns out to be a more chronic type of problem. In such instances, the stress brings to the fore a problem with which the patient has been suffering for a long time. Relief of the immediate stress does little to alter the symptomatic or behavioral difficulties. In general, the greater the degree to which the stress or trauma provides the major etiological basis of the disorder, the more favorable the prognosis for prompt response to therapy. By the same token, failure to respond may indicate the presence of a more severe or chronic problem. A careful history might reveal the prior existence of frequent periods of dysfunction—and perhaps of previous therapy. It therefore becomes important for the therapist to give patients a full opportunity to present themselves. When associative technique and appropriate interventions are combined, they become diagnostic tools as well as a means of treatment. Through this method patients tend to reveal themselves more fully than they are likely to do if subject only to direct questioning.

From the first interview, the important issue is to assess the patient's problem and to set the stage for offering the amount and kind of therapy needed by that individual. This kind of individual psychotherapy takes into account the complexities of the mind, and the realization that overcoming a stressful reaction entails going beyond the obvious and being on the lookout for preexisting problems that have now been stirred up and are contributing significantly to the stress reaction. The assessment of the associative data, the defenses, and the transference permits the therapist to view the patient in totality, rather than from the limited vantage point of surface phenomena.

Author Index

Abeloff, M. D., 95, 127
Ablin, A. R., 35, 40, 95, 125
Abram, H. S., 112, 113, 124
Abramowitz, S. I., 165, 174
Abrams, N., 590, 599
Ack, M., 70, 124
Adams, A. B., 99, 124
Adams, J. E., 512, 519
Adams, M. A., 94, 95, 97, 124
Adams, P. L., 362, 373, 384, 385
Adatto, C. P., 651
Adelman, H., 329, 337
Adler, A., 276
Adler, R., 167, 172
Adorno, T. W., 373, 385
Agle, D. P., 93, 124
Ahearn, F., 249, 256, 257, 258
Ahmadian, S. Y., 114, 132
Ahmed, P. I., 423, 430
Ahrens, L., 493
Ainsworth, M., 192, 211, 591, 598
Alagna, S. W., 623, 629
Aldrete, J. A., 106, 130
Alexander, F., 146, 156
Alisch, C. J., 408, 415
Ali Taha, S., 150, 157
Alkov, R. A., 140, 156
Allain, A. M., 107, 133

Allen, G. R., 362, 389
Allen, I. M., 383, 384, 385
Allen, L. R., 582, 584
Allen, N., 590, 599
Allport, G. W., 363, 373, 385
Al Rifai, M. R., 150, 157
Alter, M., 389
Altman, E., 502, 508
Alvarez, W., 539, 544
Aman, M. G., 582, 584
American Academy of Pediatrics, 86, 119, 124
American Cancer Society, 96, 124
American Psychiatric Association, 3, 6, 7, 8,
    18, 58, 59, 124, 366, 385, 467, 476, 537,
    550, 551, 552, 558, 571, 579, 580, 582,
    584
Amir, M., 281, 290
Amshin, J., 103, 137
Anderse, C. D., 166, 172
Anderson, B., 89, 133
Anderson, D. L., 170, 175
Anderson, S. C., 582, 584
Anderson, S. V. D., 209, 211
Andreasen, N., 115, 124, 539, 542
Andrew, J. M., 108, 124
Andrews, G., 16, 18, 20, 601, 613, 615, 623,
    625
Ange, C., 67, 71, 85, 135

661

Angell, R. H., 353, 360
Angle, C. R., 150, 157
Anisman, H., 96, 140, 163, 174
Anthony, E. J., 61, 124
Anthony, S., 202, 211
Antonovsky, A., 61, 124, 622, 626
Apfel, R., 285, 292
Appel, J. W., 344, 358
Archibald, H. C., 540, 542, 617, 626
Arlow, J., 500, 508, 560, 567
Arnaud, S. H., 540, 543
Arnold, L. E., 70, 131
Arnstein, H. S., 26, 40
Arroyo, W., 353, 358
Arruda, L. A., 215
Arthur, R. J., 365, 385, 390, 616, 617, 626,
    628
Artusio, J. F., 105, 140
Asarnow, J., 621, 628
Asken, M. J., 116, 124
Askenasy, A., 6, 19, 384, 385, 600, 613
Aston-Jones, G., 479, 492
Atkins, A., 105, 133
Atkinson, R. M., 540, 543
Atlee, E., 100, 126
Atwell, S., 610, 614
Austrin, H., 622, 628
Averill, J., 61, 134, 414
Axelrod, J., 481, 492
Azarnoff, P., 69, 70, 109, 124, 125

Babigian, H., 513, 519
Babkin, J., 525, 534
Babkin, R., 525, 534
Bachelard, G., 260, 276
Back, K. W., 382, 383, 385
Baekeland, F., 92, 125
Bahnson, C. B., 263, 276
Baisden, B., 402, 417
Bakeman, R., 329, 336
Baker, A. J., 528, 534
Baker, F. M., 382, 383, 385
Baker, G., 248, 258
Bakst, H., 107, 132
Ball, P. G., 289, 290
Ballantine, C., 199, 213
Balmaceda, R., 541, 543
Bandura, A., 626
Barber, T. X., 621, 626
Barchas, J. D., 173
Bard, M., 296, 297, 313
Barkas, J. L., 295, 313
Barnby, H. G., 304, 313
Barnes, C., 107, 112, 138
Barnes, H. E., 367, 386
Barnes, R. F., 483, 492

Barocas, R., 541, 545, 594, 599
Barr, D., 272, 276
Barracatto, J., 261, 276
Barrera, M., Jr., 516, 518
Barrett, C. L., 411, 414
Barrington, L., 408, 414
Barros, F. C., 215
Barsch, R., 90, 125
Bartlett, G. S., 156
Bartlett, M. K., 110, 128, 626
Barton, A., 248, 258
Basbaum, A. I., 161, 172
Bashir, M. R., 5, 19
Baskiewicz, A., 75, 128
Bassett, D. L., 68, 136, 168, 174
Batchelor, W. F., 103, 135
Bates, F., 401, 414
Battit, G. E., 110, 128, 626
Baudry, F. D., 105, 106, 107, 111, 125
Baum, G. L., 93, 124
Bauman, K. E., 191, 215
Baumann, D., 254, 259
Bayer, M. J., 150, 156
Beal, E. M., 638, 650
Beardslee, W. R., 69, 70, 93, 125
Beasley, M., 255, 258
Beavers, W. R., 61, 73, 74, 84, 134
Bebbington, P., 10, 16, 20
Becerra, R. M., 501, 508
Beck, A. T., 202, 211, 561, 568, 618, 619, 626
Beck, J., 564, 565, 568
Beck, N. C., 172
Becker, E., 355, 356, 358
Beebe, G. W., 344, 358, 617, 626
Begg, M. W., 68, 136
Belenky, G., 341, 342, 358
Belfer, M., 106, 116, 125
Bell, A. P., 531, 534
Bellak, L., 538, 543
Bell-Isle, J., 99, 138
Belsky, J., 197, 211
Ben, R., 388, 544
Benedek, T., 507, 508
Benjamin, B., 512, 519
Bennet, G., 401, 415
Bennett, D. L., 127
Benson, R. M., 217, 236
Benswanger, E. G., 190, 210, 211
Benzaquin, P., 276
Bergeres, R. M., 215
Bergman, A., 99, 125, 158, 195, 214
Berkenbosch, R., 484, 492
Berlin, I. N., 600, 611, 613
Berman, E., 113, 132
Bernal, G., 370, 385
Bernal, H., 383, 386

Bernard, V. W., 373, 385
Berney, T. P., 582, 585
Bernstein, N. R., 115, 116, 125, 260, 580, 581, 582, 584
Berseth, C. L., 86, 125
Bettelheim, B., 377, 385
Bibring, G. L., 72, 77, 110, 132
Bieber, M. I., 146, 148, 156
Bieliauskas, L. A., 165, 173
Bilodeau, C. P., 83, 125
Binger, C. M., 35, 40, 95, 125
Bion, W. R., 511, 518
Birch, H. G., 208, 215, 476
Birtchnell, J., 33, 40
Bishry, Z., 158
Bittner, E., 525, 534
Black, E., 502, 508
Black, R., 594, 598
Blackwell, S., 166, 174
Blagg, C., 113, 125
Blakeman, R., 336
Blank, R. J., 382, 383, 385
Bleecker, M. L., 151, 156
Blehar, M. C., 196, 211
Bleuler, E., 560, 567
Bleuler, M., 560, 567
Bloch, D., 139, 254, 255, 259, 543
Block, A., 80, 82, 83, 125, 167, 171, 172, 173
Blom, G. E., 105, 132
Bloom, F. E., 479, 492
Bloom, J. R., 94, 97, 98, 110, 125, 126, 140
Bloom-Feshbach, J., 195, 211
Bloom-Feshbach, S., 195, 211
Blos, P., 240, 245, 246
Blum, H., 351, 358
Blum, R., 89, 125
Blumberg, L., 382, 383, 385
Blumenfield, M., 77, 106, 125
Boertlein, C. G., 409, 416
Bogdanoff, M. D., 92, 126, 382, 385
Bohannan, P., 506, 508
Bohman, M., 597, 598
Bolin, R. C., 401, 414, 415
Bolz, F. A., 296, 313
Bommelaera, K., 97, 131
Bond, D. D., 356, 358
Bond, L., 541, 545
Bond, T. C., 335, 336
Bondy, D., 597, 598
Bongar, B., 167, 172
Bonnard, A., 540, 543
Bopp, J., 601, 614
Bordow, S., 333, 336
Borman, L. D., 631, 650
Bornstein, B., 219, 236
Borowsky, M. S., 146, 156

Borson, S., 492
Borus, J., 255, 258
Boshes, B., 108, 126
Boslett, M., 215
Boston Collaborative Drug Surveillance Program, 126
Bothe, A., 105, 126
Boudreault, M., 476
Bourestrom, N., 407, 415
Bourne, P. G., 483, 492
Boutin, P., 476
Bouvier, L., 100, 126
Bovard, E., 505, 508
Boverman, H., 92, 138
Bowers, M. B., Jr., 560, 561, 567
Bowlby, J., 34, 40, 195, 202, 211, 601, 602, 613, 623, 626
Bowman, P. J., 383, 385
Boyer, S. L., 80, 125
Bradford, J., 541, 543
Brady, J. P., 494
Brahams, D., 488, 492
Brain, D., 69, 109, 126
Brand, F., 404, 415
Brandsel, C., 209, 214
Brandt, B., 410, 415
Brant, R. S. T., 206, 207, 211
Brazelton, T. B., 189, 211, 602, 613
Brenner, C., 560, 567
Brenner, G., 408, 411, 417
Brenner, M. H., 448, 454
Breslau, N., 89, 90, 126, 541, 543
Breslow, D. M., 99, 137
Brett, E., 342, 360
Brett, J. M., 409, 410, 411, 415
Breznitz, S., 384, 387
Breznitz-Svidovsky, T., 349, 358
Bridges, R. S., 487, 492
Bridgman, G. D., 582, 584
Brill, N. Q., 617, 626
Broadhead, W. E., 623, 626
Brodsky, A., 85, 128
Bromet, E., 401, 415
Brooks, G., 369, 385
Brown, B. M., 144, 147, 158
Brown, E., 94, 126
Brown, F., 28, 40
Brown, G., 10, 16, 18, 147, 156, 539, 543
Brown, J. L., 384, 385
Brown, M., 558
Brown, S., 395, 398
Brown, T., 375, 385
Brownlee, J. R., 329, 336
Bruce, T. A., 81, 126
Bruhn, J. G., 80, 81, 90, 126, 383, 385
Buber, M., 373, 386

Buchanan, J. D., 627
Bucheli, F., 301, 313
Buletti, J., 85, 139
Bulman, R. J., 330, 336
Burch, R. W., 517, 519
Bureau of Indian Affairs, 377, 386
Burgess, A., 281, 282, 290, 332, 336
Burke, A. W., 383, 386
Burke, F., 92, 126
Burke, J., 255, 258, 408, 414
Burke, R. J., 610, 613
Burlingham, D. T., 265, 276, 352, 359
Burnam, M. A., 383, 386
Burne, S. R., 99, 126
Burnell, G. M., 110, 125
Burns, B., 255, 258
Burstein, S., 619, 628
Burton, L., 98, 126
Bush, M., 90, 128
Buss, A. H., 463, 476
Buss, J., 480, 496
Busse, E. W., 100, 102, 126
Butler, C., 422, 431
Butler, E. W., 410, 415

Cain, A. C., 95, 99, 126, 541, 543
Cairns, N., 95, 134
Calahan, D., 156
Calcagno, P. L., 90, 135
Caldwell, B. M., 196, 197, 211
Caldwell, B. S., 69, 126
Calhoun, T. C., 174
Callender, W. M., 193, 214
Calnan. M. W., 156
Cameron, G. S., 109, 138
Camitta, B. M., 93, 99, 134
Campbell, A. G. M., 85, 128
Campbell, M., 566, 567
Campbell, R. J., 547, 548, 558
Cannon, W. B., 308, 314
Canter, A., 64, 131, 132
Cantwell, D. P., 5, 19
Caperaa, P., 476
Caplan, G., 60, 88, 93, 126, 508, 513, 518, 538, 543, 622, 624, 626
Caplan, N. C., 335, 336
Carbon, J. B., 633, 650
Carek, D. J., 646, 650
Carey, R. G., 97, 98, 126
Carlin, J. E., 350, 353, 354, 359
Carlsson, S. G., 191, 211
Carmen, E., 282, 291
Carone, B. J., 561, 567
Carp, F. M., 406, 415
Carpenter, W. T., 561, 568
Carr, V. J., 561, 567

Carron, H., 171, 172
Carsrud, A. L., 408, 415
Carsrud, K. B., 408, 415
Casas, J. M., 383, 386
Casey, R. L., 600, 613
Cassel, J., 367, 370, 371, 386, 501, 509, 512, 516, 519, 605, 613
Cassel, S., 69, 126
Cassem, N., 75, 78, 80, 81, 82, 83, 108, 110, 111, 115, 116, 127, 130, 131
Cassman, F., 545
Castelnuovo-Tedesco, P., 113, 127
Casteneda, E., 389
Castillo, S., 386
Catchlove, R., 171, 172
Cath, S. H., 377, 383, 386
Cattell, R. B., 457, 476
Cayner, J. J., 170, 174
Chad, Z., 132
Chamberlain, B., 263, 276
Chambers, W. M., 65, 127
Chan, K. B., 501, 508
Chandler, B. C., 80, 81, 126
Chape, C., 382, 383, 387
Chapman, J., 290, 560, 561, 567
Chapman, L., 560, 567
Chapman, R. C., 170, 175
Charles, S. C., 393, 394, 398
Chassequet-Smirgel, J., 441, 445
Chaves, J. F., 621, 626
Chesler, D., 213
Chess, S., 189, 191, 208, 211, 215, 457, 459, 460, 463, 464, 465, 466, 471, 472, 476
Chester, E. H., 93, 124
Chethik, M., 26, 40
Chia, J. N., 170, 175
Chin, R., 383, 390
Chintz, S. P., 127
Chodoff, P., 99, 130, 377, 383, 386, 617, 618, 620, 626
Chomsky, N., 489, 493
Christensen, M. F., 167, 172
Christmas, J. J., 382, 383, 386
Church, J., 242, 246, 253, 258
Ciba Foundation Symposium, 463, 465, 476
Cinciripini, P. M., 172
Cisin, I. H., 156
Clarke-Stewart, A., 196, 211
Clausen, J., 513, 519
Cleary, P. D., 151, 156
Cluff, L. E., 64, 131, 132
Coates, T. J., 104, 127
Cobb, B., 39, 40
Cobb, S., 75, 127, 512, 519, 606, 612, 613
Cobbs, P. M., 364, 387
Cockerham, W. C., 390

Coddington, R. D., 190, 211, 384, 386, 601, 613, 614
Coe, C., 483, 488, 493, 494
Coelho, G. Z., 423, 430
Coffman, G. A., 5, 6, 19
Coffman, T. L., 409, 415
Cohen, D., 408, 417
Cohen, E. S., 331, 338, 402, 417
Cohen, F., 620, 626
Cohen, H., 408, 415
Cohen, K., 171, 172
Cohen, L. M., 92, 136, 383, 386
Cohen, M., 96, 127, 494
Cohen, R., 249, 256, 257, 258, 382, 388
Cohn, F. W., 36, 40
Cohn, H. L., 39, 41
Cohn, J., 158, 339
Cole, J. O., 495
Colletta, N. D., 517, 519
Conger, J., 146, 147, 156, 503, 508
Connecticut Department of Motor Vehicles, 145, 156
Connell, H. M., 202, 203, 211
Conradt, B., 99, 138
Conroy, J. Q., 408, 415
Conti, G. J., 403, 409, 417
Cooke, R. E., 127
Cooley, W. H., 622, 629
Cooper, A. M., 5, 19
Cooper, J., 81, 134
Cooper, R., 136
Cope, D. N., 167, 175
Coppolillo, H. P., 113, 132
Corbett, J., 92, 127
Corn, R., 444, 446
Coryell, W., 6, 20
Cote, R., 476
Cowen, E. L., 513, 519
Cox, M., 199, 201, 212, 213
Cox, R., 199, 201, 212, 213
Cox, T., 166, 172
Coyne, J. C., 368, 388
Crabbs, M. A., 402, 415
Craig, T. J., 95, 127
Crain, A., 90, 127
Crane, L. A., 99, 137
Crawford, P., 90, 128
Crawley, W. E., 487, 494
Crelinsten, R. D., 301, 314
Crits-Cristoph, P., 494
Crossley, H. M., 156
Crowe, J., 401, 415
Crowther, J., 541, 545
Cuerdon, C., 120, 136
Culpepper, L., 382, 383, 386
Curran, W. J., 86, 127

Cytryn, L., 223, 236
Czaczkes, J. W., 113, 127

Dahlem, N. W., 74, 133
Dale, J. W., 150, 156
Dalton, K., 148, 156, 488, 493
Dalton, R., 67, 127, 499
Damlouji, N. F., 334, 336
Daniel, W. A., Jr., 127
Danieli, Y., 350, 359
Danielson, B., 211
Danilowicz, D. A., 108, 127
Danto, B. L., 294
Dantzer, R., 493
D'Augelli, A., 516, 519
Davenport, D. G., 622, 628
Davidson, H., 99, 127
Davidson, R. J., 482, 495
Davidson, S., 147, 156, 378, 383, 386
Davies, S., 173
Davis. C. T., 374, 386
Davis, D., 597, 598
Davis, J., 363, 367, 386
Davis, O. L., 383, 391
Davis, S. D., 425, 431
Davitz, L. L., 491, 493
Dawe, H. C., 333, 336
Dawkins, M. P., 376, 387
Dawson, R. B., 69, 131
Dean, A., 133
Dean, D., 131
Dearden, R., 193, 215
Deasy-Spinetta, P., 95, 140
Decenteceo, E. T., 621, 627
DeChateau, P., 191, 211
Deeter, W. R., 162, 173
DeFigueiredo, J. M., 9, 18
DeFonseka, C. P., 150, 156
DeFrancis, V., 207, 211
DeGoza, S., 75, 131
Delage, G., 132
Delaney, J. F., 168, 172
Delgado, R., 525, 534
DeLongis, A., 544
DeMaso, D. R., 69, 70, 93, 125
Demchik-Stone, D., 627
Denny-Brown, D. E., 333, 336, 541, 543
De-Nour, A. K., 113, 127, 404, 417
Department of the Army, 345, 359
Derdeyn, A. P., 47, 59
Derogatis, L. R., 95, 127
DeSimone, D., 487, 493
Despert, J., 198, 211
Deutsch, A., 344, 359, 525, 534
Deutsch, H., 202, 211, 279, 281, 290
Deutsch, S., 482, 494

Devellis, B. M., 623, 629
Devellis, R. F., 623, 629
Devore, W., 529, 534
DeVries, D. L., 408, 415
DeVries, M. W., 463, 476
Dew, J., 540, 543
DeWeid, D., 480, 482, 493
DeWind, E., 378, 383, 386
Dewsbury, A., 288, 289, 290
Diamond, E. F., 86, 128
Dienelt, M. N., 431
Dilley, J. W., 103, 128
Dillon, H., 331, 338, 541, 544
Dimberg, U., 478, 482, 493
Dimsdale, J. E., 80, 128
DiScipio, W. J., 408, 415
Dizmang, L. J., 601, 602, 614
Dobbs, D., 617, 626
Docherty, J. P., 561, 567
Doehrman, S. R., 81, 128
Doerfler, L. A., 165, 172
Dohrenwend, B. P., 6, 9, 10, 13, 14, 15, 18,
    19, 20, 151, 156, 247, 258, 382, 384, 385,
    386, 401, 415, 600, 613
Dohrenwend, B. S., 6, 12, 15, 18, 19, 151,
    156, 247, 258, 328, 336, 382, 384, 385,
    386, 390, 401, 415, 600, 613
Donahue, M., 404, 417
Dorman, J., 85, 138
Dorner, G., 487, 493
Dorsett, P., 114, 141
Dor-Shav, N. K., 378, 383, 386
Douglas, J. W. B., 68, 128
Douglass, F., 386
Dowling, J., 168, 173
Doyle, A. B., 196, 212
Drabek, T., 255, 259, 401, 415, 417
Dressler, W. W., 383, 386
Droegemueller, W., 205, 213
Drotar, D., 75, 85, 90, 92, 128
Drugan, R. C., 163, 174
Duberman, L., 201, 212
Dubin, W., 110, 128
Dubner, R., 162, 173
Dubovsky, S. L., 74, 81, 82, 92, 128
Duff, R. S., 85, 86, 128
Duffin, S. R., 201, 212
Dukes, J. L., 370, 389
Dumas, R., 110, 128
Dumont, M., 93, 128
Dunbar, F., 146, 156
Duncan, D. F., 328, 337, 543
Dunn, G. L., 109, 138
Durden-Smith, J., 487, 493
Durkheim, E., 367, 386
Dynes, R., 249, 259, 402, 415

Dyregrov, A., 348, 353, 354, 359
Dyrud, J. E., 564, 567
D'Zurilla, T., 619, 626

Eagle, C. J., 105, 133
Earle, A. M., 202, 212
Earle, B. V., 202, 212
Earle, E., 116, 128
Eaton, W. W., 383, 386
Eccles, D., 98, 134
Ecclestone, J., 332, 336
Eckhardt, L. O., 63, 64, 69, 77, 128, 137
Edelvich, J., 85, 128
Edwards, D. E., 582, 585
Edwards, E. T., 148, 158
Edwards, J. G., 269, 276
Egbert, L. W., 110, 128, 626
Egerton, N., 105, 129
Egri, G., 13, 15, 18
Ehrentheil, O. F., 378, 383, 387
Eibl-Eibesfeldt, I., 490, 493
Eiler, J. M., 100, 102, 103, 138
Eimas, P. D., 493
Eisenberg, J. G., 16, 19, 384, 388, 539, 543,
    606, 614
Eisenberg, M. G., 87, 89, 91, 129
Eisenberg, N., 396, 398
Eisenberg, S., 290
Eisendrath, S., 75, 93, 129
Eisenthal, S., 166, 173
Eitinger, L., 377, 387
Ekman, P., 478, 490, 493
Ellenberger, H., 328, 337
Ellin, B., 540, 545
Ellis, A., 621, 626
Ellis, G. L., 85, 141
Ellison, R., 374, 387
Elmadjian, F., 478, 493
Ely, D. L., 481, 484, 493
Emde, R. N., 117, 129
Emery, R. E., 233, 236
Encyclopedia Britannica, 260, 261, 276
Engel, G., 61, 66, 72, 78, 79, 81, 114, 129,
    279, 290, 305, 307, 314, 626
Engle, B., 617, 623, 627
Ensminger, M. E., 506, 509
Erfurt, J. C., 382, 383, 387
Erickson, M. E., 95, 126
Erickson, P., 401, 415
Erikson, E. H., 49, 59, 62, 87, 129, 427, 430,
    441, 445, 499, 508, 601, 614
Erikson, K., 253, 258, 415
Eron, L. D., 379, 382, 387
Ertel, I., 97, 132
Eshback, J., 113, 125
Eth, S., 332, 337, 353, 358

Etzioni, A., 527, 534
Evanczuk, K. J., 6, 19
Evans, H. E., 429, 430

Fagerberg, H., 211
Fagin, C. M., 69, 129
Falender, C. A., 196, 212
Faletti, M. V., 411, 416
Fanon, F., 363, 387
Farberow, N., 249, 250, 257, 258
Farley, G. K., 418, 422, 431
Farrell, W. C., 376, 387
Farucki, G. Y., 408, 417
Fast, I., 541, 543
Fast, J., 95, 126
Fattah, E. A., 328, 337
Faulkner, A. O., 383, 387
Fawzy, F., 96, 141
Fazan, L. E., 90, 141
Federal Bureau of Investigation, 281, 290
Feinberg, E. A., 93, 129
Feinstein, S. C., 540, 543, 559, 563, 567
Feldman, D. J., 93, 129
Feldman, J. G., 131
Fellman, G., 410, 415
Fellner, D. J., 580, 584
Fenichel, O., 279, 290
Ferguson, J. M., 334, 336
Feriacuti, F., 539, 546
Fernandez, C. L., 383, 386
Ferris, S. H., 101, 139
Festinger, L., 526, 534
Fetting, J., 95, 127
Feuerstein, R. C., 95, 125
Field, C. J., 582, 584
Field, H., 110, 128, 290
Field, M., 290
Fields, H. L., 161, 172
Fields, R. M., 335, 337
Figley, C. R., 311, 314, 348, 359, 544
Finch, A., 606, 609, 614, 622, 629
Finch, J., 148, 157
Finch, S. M., 224, 236
Fine, B. D., 341, 360
Fine, R., 112, 114, 133
Finesilver, C., 74, 129
Fink, P. J., 123, 131
Finkel, J. B., 580, 584
Finkelhor, D., 212, 230, 236
Finkelstein, N. W., 330, 337
Finnegan, L. P., 594, 598
Firestone, P., 167, 174
Fischoff, B., 249, 259
Fishman, J. R., 483, 495
Fishman, S., 95, 132
Fitzgerald, R. E., 512, 519

Fitzsimmins, J. T., 543
Flaherty, J., 382, 383, 387, 502, 508
Fleck, J., 388, 544
Flegal, S., 69, 125
Fleiss, J. L., 97, 129
Floor, E., 482, 495
Floreen, A., 172
Florian, V., 149, 157
Fogelman, C., 401, 414
Foley, J., 67, 109, 139, 141, 582, 585
Follet, K., 301, 314
Fonseka, S., 288, 290
Fontana, A. F., 19
Foote, S. L., 479, 492
Forbes, T. W., 147, 157
Ford, R., 69, 139
Fordyce, W. E., 161, 166, 167, 169, 170, 172
Forester, B., 97, 98, 129
Forman, J. B. W., 5, 20
Forrest, L., 384, 387
Foster, D. J., 94, 96, 97, 136, 140
Foster, S. B., 85, 130
Fowler, A. V., 408, 415
Fox, E. J., 170, 174
Fox, R., 61, 73, 83, 129, 136, 489, 493
Frader, J. E., 83, 85, 86, 129
Fraiberg, S., 24, 40, 209, 212
Frances, A., 5, 19, 561, 568
Francis, V., 112, 114, 133
Frane, K. J., 393, 398
Frank, H. A., 139
Frank, J., 69, 129
Frank, M., 429, 430
Frankenburg, W. K., 94, 129
Frankenhaeuser, M., 421, 430, 484, 489, 494
Frankl, V., 377, 387
Franzino, S. J., 487, 496
Fraser, D. W., 408, 415
Fraser, M., 335, 337, 540, 543
Fraser, R. M., 335, 337
Frederick, C., 248, 258, 400, 417, 617, 626
Frederickson, R. H., 388, 544
Fredin, H., 148, 157
Fredrikson, M., 478, 489, 493, 494
Freedman, A. M., 2, 335, 337
Freedman, B., 561, 567
Freeman, F. N., 595, 598
Fremouw, W. J., 621, 627
French, J. R. P., Jr., 512, 519
Frenkel-Brunswik, E., 385
Freud, A., 24, 40, 67, 104, 129, 202, 204, 212, 265, 276, 352, 359, 476, 499, 500, 508
Freud, S., 24, 30, 31, 40, 75, 129, 147, 157, 207, 212, 217, 218, 219, 236, 260, 277, 278, 290, 327, 337, 346, 347, 357, 359, 441, 446, 459, 476, 511, 519, 562, 567

Fried, M., 403, 410, 416, 425, 431, 605, 614
Friedlander, R. J., 540, 543
Friedman, C. J., 329, 337
Friedman, M., 590, 597, 599
Friedman, P., 617, 627
Friedman, R. C., 444, 446
Friedman, S., 98-99, 130, 618, 626
Friesen, W. V., 478, 493
Frisone, G., 382, 388
Fritz, C. E., 416
Froehling, S., 85, 130
Froland, C., 506, 509
Fromm, E., 367, 387
Froom, J., 382, 383, 386
Frosch, J., 562, 567
Frosch, W. A., 642, 650
Fruchter, H. J., 165, 175
Fuller, R., 104, 130
Furlong, M. J., 386
Furman, E., 23, 24, 26, 31, 40, 99, 130, 236, 596, 598
Furst, S. S., 280, 290, 540, 543
Futterman, S., 540, 543, 617, 627

Gaarder, K. L., 173
Gabriel, H. F., 108, 127
Gaertner, S. L., 372, 387
Gaitz, C. M., 100, 130, 383, 387
Galanter, M., 525, 534
Galdston, R., 105, 126
Gallagher, J. J., 581, 584
Gallops, M. S., 342, 360
Ganz, P. A., 99, 137
Garbarino, J., 231, 236, 237
Gardner, G. G., 98, 130
Gardner, R. A., 23, 24, 26, 27, 30, 31, 37, 38, 40, 41, 43, 45, 46, 48, 54, 56, 57, 58, 59, 234, 237
Garfield, R., 173
Garlington, B., 170, 174
Garrett, R., 305, 314
Garrett, T., 328, 337
Garrity, T. F., 80, 130
Garron, D. C., 165, 173
Garrow, D. H., 69, 94, 130
Gartner, A., 93, 130
Gaskill, H., 156
Gates, M., 290
Gaughran, J., 195, 211
Gaviria, F., 502, 508
Gay, M., 383, 387
Gayford, J. J., 286, 287, 288, 289, 291
Gaylor, M. S., 167, 171, 172, 173
Gaynor, J. A., 146, 156
Gazalle, R. V., 215
Geer, J., 162, 175

Gehlback, S. H., 626
Geier, T., 493
Geis, G., 328, 337
Geis, S., 104, 130
Geist, R., 92, 130
Gelles, R. J., 286, 287, 288, 291
Gentry, W. D., 85, 130
George, C., 206, 212
Gerdman, P., 148, 157
Gerrity, E., 399
Gerst, M., 10, 19, 624, 627
Gersten, J. C., 16, 19, 384, 388, 539, 543, 606, 614
Geschwind, N., 495
Getto, C. J., 81, 82, 128
Gieser, G. C., 416
Gillespie, R. D., 352, 359
Gilmore, M., 561, 568
Gilner, F., 622, 628
Gispen, W. H., 493
Glad, D., 156
Glass, A. J., 341, 355, 359
Glass, G. S., 151, 157
Glass, G. V., 81, 120, 136
Glazer, W., 561, 568
Gleibermann, L., 382, 383, 388
Gleser, G. C., 252, 258, 350, 359, 400, 401, 416, 541, 543
Glover, E., 280, 281, 291
Goetz, C., 10, 20
Gold, M., 375, 387
Goldberg, R. T., 171, 172
Goldberger, L., 384, 387
Golden, M. M., 513, 520
Goldfried, M., 619, 621, 626, 627
Goldings, H. J., 242, 243, 246
Goldsteen, K., 156
Goldsteen, R. L., 156
Goldstein, A., 162, 172
Goldstein, K., 79, 130
Goldston, S. E., 390
Good, R. S., 176
Goodman, H., 590, 598
Goodman, J. T., 167, 174
Goodwin, R., 70, 140
Gordon, K. K., 6, 19
Gordon, M., 6, 20
Gordon, N., 250, 258
Gordon, R. E., 6, 19
Gore, S., 501, 509, 512, 519
Gornick, J., 285, 291
Gossett, J. T., 61, 134
Gottlieb, B. H., 517, 519
Gottlieb, H., 171, 172
Gould, M., 18
Gourash, N., 516, 519

Grace, M. C., 331, 338
Gracely, R. H., 162, 173
Graham, D. T., 610, 614
Graham, P., 89, 138
Grant, I., 10, 19, 624, 627
Grau, J. W., 163, 173, 174
Gray, R., 388
Great Britain Ministry of Health, 70, 130
Greaves, G., 98, 142
Green, A. H., 212, 331, 337
Green, B. L., 252, 258, 331, 338, 350, 359,
    400, 401, 410, 416, 541, 543
Green, J. M., 224, 236
Green, L. C., 139
Green, M., 68, 70, 98, 130, 589, 599
Green, R., 220, 237
Green, W., 130
Greenacre, P., 189, 212, 352, 359
Greenberg, M., 191, 212, 495
Greenblatt, M., 501, 508
Greene, E. G., 481, 493
Greene, P. E., 99, 130
Greenson, R., 279, 291
Greenwood, M., 146, 157
Greer, J., 280, 291
Greer, S., 212
Gregg, J. M., 170, 175
Gregory, I., 589, 598
Gregory, P., 389
Greidanus, T. J. B., 493
Grier, W. H., 364, 387
Grife, A., 389
Grimm, L., 621, 627
Grinker, R., 279, 291, 342, 345, 359
Grobstein, R., 95, 132
Gross, S. A., 81, 82, 128
Grossack, M. M., 363, 387
Grosser, G., 70, 140
Grossman, B., 92, 138
Grossman, K., 191, 212
Grossman, K. E., 191, 212
Grossman, S., 71, 72, 75, 78, 79, 80, 82, 101,
    140, 279, 280, 292
Group for the Advancement of Psychiatry
    (GAP), 578, 579, 580, 581, 584
Gruenberg, C., 512, 519
Grunebaum, H., 511, 519
Guendelman, S. D. R., 196, 212
Guerra, F., 106, 130
Guidera, K., 96, 141
Guilford, J. P., 457, 476
Guise, B. J., 164, 175
Gunderson, E. K. E., 390
Gundewall, C., 211
Gunson, R., 626
Gur, R. C., 495

Guttman, E., 231, 237
Gwaltney, J. L., 369, 374, 387

Hackett, G., 622, 627
Hackett, T. P., 75, 78, 80, 81, 82, 83, 108,
    110, 111, 112, 115, 116, 125, 127, 128,
    130, 131, 141
Hackinski, V. C., 101, 130
Haefner, H., 383, 387
Hagan, S., 82, 137
Hageberg, K., 93, 131
Hagen, S., 598
Hagens, J. H., 110, 134
Haggerty, R. J., 89, 92, 117, 131
Hales, R., 123, 131
Hall, P. S., 401, 416
Hall, R. C. W., 383, 391
Hall, W., 166, 171, 173
Halleck, S. L., 392, 395, 398
Hallett, E. C., 168, 174
Hallin, R. G., 163, 175
Halter, J. B., 492
Hamburg, B., 75, 94, 131, 141, 240, 246
Hamburg, D., 75, 99, 115, 130, 131, 512, 519,
    618, 626
Hamilton, E., 351, 359
Hamilton, S. C., 486, 495
Hanks, S. E., 287, 291
Hansen, D. A., 542, 544
Hansen, H., 116, 131, 252, 259, 400, 416
Harbison, J., 335, 337
Harburg, E. H., 382, 383, 387, 388
Harcourt, R., 6, 20
Hard, G., 504, 509
Hardgrove, C., 69, 70, 125, 131
Harding, R. K., 383, 388
Hargrove, B., 525, 534
Harmon, R., 117, 129
Harris, J., 354, 360
Harris, M. B., 538, 543
Harris, M. C., 409, 415
Harris, P. W., 611, 614
Harris, T., 10, 16, 18
Harrison, A., 106, 125
Harrison, S. I., 217, 236, 547, 558
Harrow, M., 559, 561, 567, 568
Hart, R. P., 541, 544
Hartford, C. E., 115, 124
Hartmann, R., 196, 213
Hassanein, R., 95, 134
Hassell, L., 156
Hauenstein, L. S., 382, 383, 387
Hauge, G., 168, 173
Hay, D., 85, 131
Hazel, B., 85, 139
Healy, M. H., 116, 131

Heber, R., 196, 212
Heckel, R. V., 383, 384, 388
Heffron, E., 402, 415
Heffron, W., 97, 131
Heidt, H., 480, 496
Heiman, E. M., 167, 175
Heinicke, C., 192, 212
Heinrich, J., 581, 583, 584
Heisel, M. A., 387
Heller, D., 378, 383, 388
Heller, K., 612, 614
Heller, T., 408, 409, 416
Henchie, V., 207, 208, 212
Henderson, C. J., 408, 415
Henderson, S., 622, 627
Hendin, H., 540, 543
Hendren, R., 173
Hendrick, C., 411, 416
Henry, J., 503, 508
Henry, J. L., 163, 173
Henry, J. P., 477, 479, 480, 481, 482, 483,
    485, 493, 494
Herbert, M., 191, 212
Herndon, C. H., 114, 132
Hershman, J. M., 173
Hertzman, M., 160, 167, 173
Hervey, R. F., 170, 174
Herzberg, J. H., 447
Hetherington, E. M., 49, 59, 199, 200, 201,
    212, 213, 540, 543
Hewett, J. E., 165, 172
Hewson, D. M., 16, 18, 601, 613, 623, 625
Heyden, S., 626
Hickman, R., 113, 125
Hier, D. B., 487, 494
Higgins, M. D., 107, 133
Higgs, R., 580, 581, 584
Hilberman, E., 282, 286, 287, 288, 289, 291
Hilgard, J., 98, 131
Hill, N., 376, 388
Hill, R., 542, 544
Hillman, R. G., 335, 337
Hinde, R. A., 486, 494, 500, 509
Hines, M., 487, 494
Hinton, R. M., 98, 130
Hirsch, S. R., 155, 158
Hobbs, G. E., 146, 158, 502, 509
Hobfoll, S., 269, 277
Hodges, J., 599
Hodges, W. F., 199, 213
Hoenk, P. R., 333, 338, 539, 542
Hofer, M. A., 81, 134
Hole, R. W., 561, 568
Holland, J., 96, 97, 131, 137, 425, 431
Hollender, M. H., 494
Hollerstein, D., 103, 137

Hollingsworth, C. E., 99, 131
Holmes, G. R., 383, 384, 388
Holmes, T. H., 10, 11, 19, 143, 148, 157, 165,
    173, 600, 610, 613, 614, 615
Holmes, T. S., 600, 614
Holmstrom, L., 281, 282, 290
Holt, P. L., 146, 147, 157
Holton, C., 98, 134
Holzinger, K. J., 598
Holzman, P. S., 564, 567
Hong, C., 463, 476
Honig, A., 196, 197, 211
Hope, J. M., 478, 493
Hopkins, J. B., 191, 213
Horan, J. J., 622, 627
Horneman, G., 211
Horowitz, M. J., 144, 157, 263, 276, 277, 332,
    334, 337, 539, 544, 548, 549, 555, 558,
    644, 650
Horwood, C., 116, 136
Hosobuchi, Y., 163, 173
Hoteling, G., 610, 614
Hough, J. C., 363, 389
Hough, R. L., 386
House, J., 504, 509
Houts, C. B., 70, 131
Howell, D. A., 98, 131
Howell, M. C., 85, 141
Howell, M. D., 85, 138
Howells, J. G., 112, 131
Hsu, C., 463, 476
Huffine, C. L., 334, 337
Hughes, M. C., 92, 93, 131, 167, 173
Hungerbuhler, J. P., 495
Hurry, J., 10, 20
Hurt, S., 435, 446
Husaini, B. A., 328, 337
Husband, P., 147, 157
Hussian, R. A., 621, 627
Huston, T. L., 328, 337
Hutcherson, R. R., 147, 157
Hwang, C. P., 191, 213
Hwang, G. P., 211

Ibrahim, M. A., 83, 131
Imboden, J. B., 64, 131, 132
Imes, C., 80, 125
Ingram, D. D., 191, 215
Insel, T. R., 494
Irvin, N., 75, 128
Isaacs, L. D., 590, 598
Ismond, D. R., 544
Israeli, R., 349, 361
Ivker, B., 521
Izzo, L. D., 513, 519

Jackson, B., 64, 132
Jackson, J., 384, 385
Jackson, K., 109, 132
Jackson, R. L., 163, 173, 174
Jacobsen, E., 280, 291
Jacobson, D. S., 213
Jacobson, E., 441, 446
James, S. A., 382, 383, 388, 626
Janis, I. L., 279, 291
Janis, J. L., 111, 132
Jansen, M. A., 87, 129
Jardiolin, P., 6, 19
Jaremko, M. E., 621, 627
Jarvella, R., 190, 214
Jasnau, K. F., 407, 416
Jaspers, K., 560, 568
Jenkins, R. L., 173
Jerauld, R., 213
Jessner, L., 67, 104, 105, 117, 132
Jessop, D. J., 93, 140, 166, 175
Jimerson, D. C., 483, 494
Johnson, C., 480, 495
Johnson, C. S., 363, 388
Johnson, D. E., 86, 132
Johnson, J. H., 611, 615, 622, 627
Johnson, J. W., 547
Joint Commission on Mental Health of Children, 118, 132, 364
Joneas, J. H., 132
Jones, B. E., 382, 388
Jones, F. D., 341, 342, 359
Jones, J. C., 146, 150, 157
Jones, J. R., 167, 175
Jones, W. L., 158, 339
Jordan, K., 70, 78, 113, 137
Joseph, E. D., 145, 157
Joyce, D., 404, 416
Juliano, M. A., 116, 140
Jung, C. G., 492, 494
Justice, B., 328, 337

Kadish, S., 392, 398
Kadish, W., 478, 494
Kagan, J., 196, 213, 464, 476
Kahan, R. B., 78, 140
Kahana, R. J., 72, 77, 110, 132
Kaiser, E. J., 410, 415
Kalinowsky, L. B., 617, 627
Kalter, N., 199, 201, 213
Kaltreider, N., 539, 544
Kamel, M., 151, 158
Kanfer, F. H., 621, 627
Kanner, D. A., 368, 388
Kansas City Police Department, 286, 291
Kaplan, B., 373, 388, 501, 503, 505, 509, 512, 513, 519, 626

Kaplan, D. M., 95, 132, 425, 431
Kaplan, J. N., 483, 494
Kaplan, J. Z., 115, 141
Kaplan, S. L., 610, 614
Kapp, F., 251, 259, 545
Kapp, T., 280, 292
Karasu, T. B., 74, 132
Kardiner, A., 263, 277, 279, 281, 291, 346, 347, 360
Karls, W., 388, 544
Karon, M., 98, 141
Kartha, M., 97, 132
Kasl, S. V., 401, 404, 406, 407, 411, 415, 416
Kasman, C., 85, 135
Kasper, A., 158, 339
Kastenbaum, R., 248, 258
Katayama, Y., 163, 173
Katchadourian, H., 240, 241, 244, 246
Katz, A. H., 518, 519
Katz, E. R., 167, 172, 173
Katz, S., 149, 157
Kaufman, R., 68, 132
Kavanaugh, J., 223, 237
Kavenaugh, C., 115, 132
Kay, J. H., 105, 129
Kayton, L., 564, 565, 568
Kazdin, A. E., 585
Kearsley, R., 196, 213
Keating, J., 272, 277
Keefe, F. J., 170, 173
Keeler, E. C., 175
Keith, C., 327, 537
Kellerman, J., 173
Kellerman, V., 95, 132
Kellum, S. G., 506, 509
Kelly, J. B., 51, 52, 59, 199, 200, 215, 216, 234, 237, 595, 599
Kelly, K. V., 642, 650
Kempe, C. H., 205, 213
Kemper, J. T., 174
Kemph, J. P., 113, 132
Kendell, R. E., 5, 19
Kendler, K. S., 68, 5561
Kennedy, E. C., 394, 398
Kennedy, J. A., 107, 132
Kennell, J., 68, 75, 88, 128, 133, 190, 191, 213, 214, 215, 488, 494
Kern, R., 18
Kessler, R. C., 328, 337, 539, 544
Kettering, R. L., 561, 568
Kety, S. S., 594, 599
Key, W., 401, 415, 417
Keyes, E., 277
Khan, A. O., 114, 132
Khan, M., 207, 213
Khatami, M., 170, 173

Kiely, W. F., 83, 132
Kilby, C. A., 408, 416
Kilijanek, T., 255, 259
Killilea, M., 93, 126
Kiloh, L. G., 101, 132
Kilpatrick, D. G., 107, 133
Kimball, C. P., 79, 83, 84, 107, 110, 113, 133, 137
Kimball, E., 252, 259
King, L. M., 382, 388
Kinsbourne, M., 480, 494
Kinsman, R. A., 74, 133
Kinston, W., 402, 416, 538, 544
Kinzie, J. D., 353, 360, 383, 388, 540, 544
Kirschbaum, R. M., 69, 137, 193, 214
Kirschner, E., 351, 360
Kittner, E., 493
Kizuka, P. P., 495
Klaus, M., 68, 75, 88, 128, 133, 190, 191, 213, 214, 215, 488, 494
Klein, H., 377, 378, 383, 388
Klein, R. F., 80, 81, 82, 84, 130, 133
Kleinbaum, D. G., 382, 383, 388
Klepac, R. K., 168, 173
Klerman, G. L., 431, 619, 629
Kligfeld, M., 382, 388
Kliman, G., 23, 27, 28, 32, 34, 41, 197, 198, 203, 209, 213, 589, 590, 591, 594, 595, 596, 597, 598, 599, 603, 614
Kliner, V. A., 81, 133
Kling, A., 482, 494
Klos, D., 610, 614
Kluegel, J. R., 363, 388
Knight, R. B., 105, 133
Knudson, A., 98, 133
Knudson-Cooper, M. S., 146, 147, 157
Kobasa, S. C., 551, 558
Kodama, M., 388
Koenig, K., 117, 129
Koh, S. D., 564, 565, 568
Kohn, M., 513, 519
Kolb, L. A., 348, 360
Kolb, L. C., 436, 446
Koocher, G. P., 90, 94, 95, 96, 97, 133, 136, 140
Koopman, C., 166, 173
Koopmans, L. H., 487, 495
Koos, E. L., 61, 74, 133
Kopin, I., 494
Korn, S. J., 463, 476
Kornblatt, E. S., 582, 583, 584
Kornblum, H., 82, 133
Kornfeld, D. S., 81, 84, 97, 112, 123, 129, 133, 134, 580, 584
Kornstein, S., 541, 544
Korsch, B. M., 92, 112, 113, 114, 133, 191, 213

Kraepelin, E., 560, 568
Kramlinger, K. G., 165, 168, 173
Krant, M. J., 99, 133
Krasnoff, L., 6, 19
Kreger, N. C., 213
Krell, L., 493
Krell, R., 39, 41
Kremer, E. F., 167, 171, 172, 173
Kringlen, E., 463, 476
Kris, E., 268, 277
Kris, M., 329, 339
Krolick, G., 196, 215
Kron, R. E., 494
Krueger, D. W., 147, 157
Kruglanski, A., 349, 361
Krupnick, J. L., 332, 337
Kruse, E., 70, 131
Kryso, J. A., 206, 207, 215
Krystal, H., 75, 133, 378, 388, 540, 544, 617, 627
Kubie, L., 53, 59
Kubler-Ross, E., 35, 41, 75, 95, 97, 133
Kuo, W. H., 383, 388
Kuperman, S., 333, 338
Kushner, J. H., 35, 40
Kwentus, J. A., 541, 544

LaBaw, W. L., 98, 115, 134
Lachance, P. A., 483, 494
La Faue, H. G., 408, 414
Lahikainen, A. R., 196, 213
Lamb, M. E., 191, 213
Lamb, T. A., 483, 495
Lamson, E. T., 478, 493
Landa, B., 610, 614
Landreth, P. W., 401, 416
Landsverk, J., 96, 141
Lange, P., 113, 135
Langford, W. S., 204, 213
Langner, T. S., 16, 19, 384, 388, 539, 543, 606, 614
Lanin-Kettering, I., 561, 568
Lansky, S. B., 95, 97, 134
LaPlante, B., 476
Laroche, M., 580, 584
Larsson, K., 211
Lasater, T., 329, 338
Lasry, J. C., 386
Lassen, N. A., 101, 130
Laube, J., 256, 259
Lauer, M. E., 93, 99, 134
Laufer, R. S., 342, 360
Lawrence, M. M., 369, 388
Lawrence, P. S., 621, 627
Lawrie, J. H., 115, 135
Lawrie, R., 105, 134
Lawton, M. P., 406, 416

Lazarus, A., 619, 627, 629
Lazarus, H. R., 61, 110, 134
Lazarus, R., 328, 337, 368, 383, 388, 539, 544, 619, 620, 626
Leavitt, F., 165, 173
LeBaron, S., 131, 198
Leboyer, R., 189, 213
Lederman, R. P., 176
Lee, J. A. B., 330, 337
Lefcourt, H. M., 622, 627
Lefebvre, R. C., 170, 173
Legg, C., 99, 134, 192, 207, 208, 214
Lehman, A. F., 328, 338
Leigh, H., 81, 84, 134, 143
Leighton, A., 512, 519
Lenihan, E. A., 69, 103, 137, 214
Lenrow, P. B., 517, 519
Lentz, R. J., 408, 416
Leonard, R., 109, 110, 128, 140
Leopold, R. L., 331, 338, 541, 544
Lerbinger, J., 495
LeShan, L., 146, 147, 157
Leuchtag, A. K., 147, 157
Levenson, R. W., 478, 493
Leventhal, H., 167, 174
Leventhal, J. M., 90, 138
Levine, H. G., 580, 581, 584
Levine, M., 110, 112, 141
Levine, P. M., 95, 98, 134, 139
Levine, S., 483, 488, 493, 494
Levinger, G., 286, 291
Levinson, D. J., 385
Levitan, S. J., 112, 123, 134
Levy, D. M., 117, 134, 193, 194, 208, 214
Levy, L., 494
Levy, N. B., 114, 134
Levy, S. T., 561, 568
Lewin, I., 349, 360
Lewin, K., 264, 277, 511, 519
Lewinsohn, P. M., 619, 627
Lewis, D. O., 38, 41, 382, 388
Lewis, J. M., 61, 73, 84, 134
Lewis, M., 38, 41
Lewis, N., 617, 627
Lewis, R., 384, 385
Ley, R. G., 479, 494
Liang, C., 463, 476
Lichtenstein, S., 249, 259
Liddell, H., 503, 509
Lidz, T., 331, 338, 540, 544
Lieberman, M., 99, 141
Liebowitz, M., 491, 494
Lifton, R., 251, 259, 263, 277
Lightfoot, O. B., 382, 388
Lin, K., 350, 353, 360
Lin, N., 388
Lind, J., 191, 212

Lindberg, C., 201, 214
Lindblad-Goldberg, M., 370, 389
Lindell, M., 402, 417
Lindeman, E., 270, 277
Lindemann, E., 75, 127, 134, 541, 544
Lindenthal, J. J., 431
Lindy, J. D., 331, 338
Link, B. G., 3, 14, 18, 20
Linn, L., 110, 134, 328, 338
Linsky, A., 610, 614
Linton, S. J., 170, 173
Lipowski, Z., 74, 78, 95, 134
Lipscomb, H. S., 483, 494
Lipton, J. A., 167, 174
Litman, R. E., 158, 339
Litovitz, T. L., 150, 158
Liverant, S., 622, 628
Llamas, R., 504, 509
Lloyd, K., 93, 129
Lobitz, W. C., 619, 627
Logan, M. N., 328, 338
Logue, J., 252, 259, 400, 401, 416, 417
Long, D. M., 542
Long, L. H., 409, 416
Loomis, W. G., 115, 135
Looney, J. G., 383, 388, 418, 431
Love, R. R., 167, 174
Lowman, J. T., 95, 134
Lubchenko, L., 117
Luborsky, L., 494
Luchterhand, E. G., 378, 383, 389
Luebke, P. T., 429, 431
Lundberg, U., 484, 494
Lundquist, O., 478, 493
Lundwell, L., 92, 125
Lurie, H. J., 580, 585
Lutwak, L., 483, 494
Lwanga, J., 348, 359
Lynn, D. B., 540, 544
Lyons, H. A., 335, 338
Lystad, M., 247, 248, 249, 250, 259

MacDonald, J. M., 299, 314
Mace, N. L., 103, 135
MacGregor, F. M., 116, 135
Maclay, I., 69, 109, 126
MacLean, P. D., 486, 492, 495
Madden, J., 173
Maddi, S. R., 551, 558
Magrab, P. R., 90, 135
Mah, C., 163, 174
Mahaffy, P., 69, 109, 135
Mahdi, A. H., 150, 157
Maher, B., 560, 568
Mahler, M., 195, 214, 603, 614
Maier, S. F., 162, 163, 173, 174, 175
Main, M., 206, 212

Malec, J., 2, 170, 174
Maler, L., 69, 135
Malin, R. M., 139
Malkin, S., 99, 135
Malm, J. R., 84, 133
Malmquist, C. P., 241, 246
Maloney, M. J., 69, 71, 85, 135
Manchester, W., 356, 360
Mandel, J., 104, 127
Mann, F., 329, 337
Mann. M. M., 112, 139
Mannino, F. V., 632, 650
Mao, W., 170, 175
Marbach, J. J., 167, 174
Marchand, F., 343, 344, 345, 360
Marcus, J. L., 16, 19
Marder, S. R., 561, 567
Margolis, J. A., 151, 158
Markowitz, J., 18
Marks, R. M., 98, 135
Marmot, M. G., 483, 495
Marshall, C. L., 146, 150, 157
Marshall, J., 101, 130
Marshall, R. E., 85, 135
Marston, A. R., 173
Martin, D., 287, 288, 289, 291
Martin, H. L., 115, 135
Martin, J., 14, 18, 156
Martin, M. J., 166, 174
Martindale, A., 408, 416
Maruta, T., 165, 168, 170, 173, 174
Marx, K., 367, 389
Mason, D. J., 166, 174
Mason, J., 99, 106, 130, 137, 483, 485, 495
Mason, R. C., 64, 135
Massachusetts Consumer Directory, 109, 135
Masserman, J., 360
Masters, R., 97, 131
Masterson, J. F., 602, 614
Masuda, M., 350, 360, 600, 610, 613, 614, 615
Mathias, R. J., 5, 19
Matson, J. L., 580, 581, 582, 585
Mattison, R., 5, 19
Mattson, A., 88, 89, 135, 223, 237
Matzek, M. J., 117, 127
May, J. G., 84, 135
May, P. A., 601, 614
Mayer, J., 594, 598
Mayer-Gross, W., 560, 568
Maylew, J. F., 109, 135
Mayman, M., 559, 568
Maziade, M., 463, 471, 476
Mazur, A., 483, 495
McAdoo, H., 383, 389
McAllister, R. J., 410, 415
McAlphine, W., 213
McBride, M., 271, 277

McCall, R. B., 191, 214
McCaul, K. D., 164, 174
McClelland, D. C., 482, 495
McConahay, J. B., 363, 389
McCubbin, H., 540, 544
McDermott, J. F., 197, 214, 547, 558
McDermott, M. J., 328, 338
McFadd, A., 139
McFarland, R. A., 145, 157
McFarlane, A. H., 622, 623, 627, 628
McGehee, J. B., 491, 494
McGinnis, N. H., 382, 390
McGlashan, T. H., 561, 568
McGrath, P. J., 167, 174
McGuire, F. L., 147, 157
McGuire, M. T., 480, 495
McIntire, M. S., 150, 157
McKain, J. L., 410, 416
McKeaver, P., 90, 135
McKegney, F. P., 84, 113, 135
McKenna, G. J., 616, 617, 626, 628
McKnew, D. H., 223, 236
McLaughlin, J. F., 86, 135
McLaughlin, J. P., 372, 387
McLeod, B., 262, 277
McVeigh, F., 100, 126
Mead, G. H., 511, 519
Meadows, L., 201, 214
Meagher, R., 382, 383, 387
Meehan, J. P., 481, 494, 503, 508
Mehl, L. E., 209, 214
Meichenbaum, D., 618, 619, 620, 621, 628
Melick, M. E., 400, 401, 416, 417
Melville, J., 489, 495
Melzack, R., 160, 161, 165, 170, 174, 622,
    628
Menaloscino, F. J., 577, 579, 580, 581, 582,
    583, 585
Mendels, J., 10, 20
Mendoza, S. P., 488, 493
Menezes, S. T., 215
Menninger, K., 147, 158, 559, 560, 568, 618,
    628
Menninger, W. C., 360
Mersky, H., 166, 174
Messenger, K., 90, 126
Metcalf, D., 78, 113, 117, 129, 137
Metzner, H., 504, 509
Meyer, R. J., 115, 135
Mezzich, A. C., 5, 19
Mezzich, J. E., 5, 6, 19
Michelmore, P., 261, 276
Micklow, P., 290
Miczek, K. A., 482, 495
Milgram, N., 269, 277
Miller, B., 301, 302, 314
Miller, C., 542

Miller, D., 245, 246, 561, 563, 567
Miller, J., 252, 259, 280, 291, 561, 568
Miller, L., 384, 389
Miller, W. C., 107, 133
Millstein, K., 255, 258
Milne, G., 402, 417
Minde, K., 69, 135
Minnefor, A., 136
Minuchin, S., 90, 135
Mirotznik, J., 13, 20
Mirowsky, J., 383, 389, 390
Mishler, E., 502, 509
Mitchel, B. C., 598
Mitchell, T., 502, 508
Modlin, H. C., 333, 338
Moffat, J., 158, 339
Mogey, J., 404, 417
Monroe, S. M., 539, 544
Moody, P. M., 167, 174
Moore, B. E., 341, 360
Moore, G. L., 113, 124
Moore, H., 254, 259, 401, 417
Moore, R. C., 145, 157
Moore, T., 196, 197, 207, 214
Moorehead, C., 301, 314
Morales, A., 363, 366, 390
Moreno, J. L., 511, 519
Morgane, P. J., 505, 506, 509
Morgenstern, H., 561, 568
Morin, S. F., 103, 135
Mormede, P., 493
Morrell, C., 97-98, 135
Morris, J. L., 139
Morrison, D. H., 173
Morrow, G. R., 96, 97, 98, 127, 135, 138
Morse, J., 114, 141
Morse, R. M., 110, 111, 135
Mortensen, O., 167, 172
Moye, T., 173
Mrazek, D. A., 68, 135
Mugisha, C., 348, 359
Mulhern, R. K., 93, 134
Muller, H., 493
Mumford, E., 81, 111, 120, 136
Munro, A., 214
Munson, M., 286, 287, 288, 289, 291
Munx, G., 493
Murphy, L. B., 189, 214
Murphy, M. L., 97, 136
Murphy, M. R., 486, 495
Murray, J., 106, 125
Myers, J. K., 431
Myrdal, G., 363, 389

Nadel, L., 481, 495
Nadelson, C. C., 278, 280, 281, 282, 283, 285, 291, 292

Naftulin, D. H., 150, 158
Nagera, H., 41, 241, 264, 277
Naiman, J., 105, 139
Nardini, J. E., 617, 628
Nathan, P., 545
Natterson, J., 98, 133
Navojosky, B. J., 190, 214
Neale, K. A., 622, 627
Neff, J. A., 328, 337
Nemiah, J. C., 74, 92, 136, 148, 158
Nenno, M., 404, 416
Nerenz, D. R., 167, 174
Nesdale, A. R., 542, 545
Newcombe, R. G., 151, 158
Newman, C. J., 541, 544
Newman, J., 255, 259
Newman, R. I., 170, 174
Newson-Smith, J. G. B., 155, 158
Nichol, T. C., 92, 127
Nicholi, A., 268, 277
Nichols, S. E., 103, 104, 136
Nichter, M., 383, 389
Niederland, W. G., 377, 389
Nielsen, G., 602, 614
Nixon, J., 149, 158
Noble, H., 411, 414
Noel, B., 16, 19
Norman, G. R., 622, 623, 627, 628
North, R. A., 163, 173
Norton, J., 98, 136
Noshpitz, J. D., 217, 373, 389, 630
Notman, M. T., 278, 280, 281, 282, 283, 285, 291, 292
Novaco, R. W., 618, 619, 628
Noyes, R., 98, 115, 124, 136
Noyes, W., Jr., 333, 338
Nuckolls, B., 501, 502, 503, 509
Nugent, T., 251, 259

Ochberg, F. M., 287, 292, 540, 544
Ochitill, H. N., 103, 128
Oehlberg, S., 594, 598
Offord, D. R., 590, 599
Okasha, B., 151, 158
O'Keefe, J., 481, 495
Oken, D., 85, 97, 131, 136
Okeson, J. P., 174
Oleske, J., 136
Olivares, L., 383, 389
Oliver, J., 376, 387
Olmstead, J., 599
Olson, E., 259
Oltmanns, T., 560, 568
O'Malley, J., 90, 94, 95, 96, 97, 133, 136, 140
O'Neal, T., 82, 137
Opton, E., 61, 134, 388
Orbach, C. E., 279, 292

Orbach, I., 329, 338
Ordonez-Plaza, A., 92, 136
Orsulak, P. J., 495
Orzeck, L., 539, 543
Orzek, L., 16, 19, 606, 614
Osborne, F., 79, 110, 137
Osman, M., 151, 158, 339
Osofsky, H. J., 176
Osterweis, M., 589, 590, 599
Ostfeld, A. M., 108, 141
Ostrow, D. G., 103, 104, 136
Oswald, W. Y., 408, 417
Ottenberg, P., 373, 385
Ozgoren, F., 388
Ozoa, N., 92, 138

Paap, W. R., 333, 338
Padilla, A. M., 383, 390
Padilla, E. R., 147, 158
Page, J. M., 335, 336
Pakes, E. H., 34, 41
Paley, J. A., 81, 82, 128
Palgi, P., 383, 389
Palmer, D., 382, 388
Pangman, J., 429, 431
Panksepp, J., 477, 495
Parducci, A., 164, 175
Parentin, V., 401, 414
Park, R. E., 367, 389
Parke, R. D., 329, 338, 542, 544
Parker, B., 287, 292
Parkes, C. M., 116, 136
Parkes, N., 512, 519
Parsons, T., 61, 73, 136
Pasley, S., 610, 614
Pasnau, R. B., 96, 141
Pasnau, R. O., 99, 123, 131, 136
Pastalan, L. A., 407, 417
Patel, C., 483, 495
Paton, A., 114, 136
Patrick, C., 120, 136
Patterson, G., 225, 237
Pattison, E. M., 335, 338, 509, 515, 519
Pattison, M. L., 515, 519
Paul, G. L., 408, 416
Paul, M. H., 69, 126
Paulsen, M., 392, 398
Pavlov, I. P., 459, 476
Paykel, E. S., 419, 431, 619, 629
Payne, S. J., 261, 277
Payson, H. E., 327, 339, 537, 545
Pearlin, L. I., 384, 389
Pearn, J., 149, 158
Peck, E. T., 541, 544
Peddock, J., 610, 614
Pederson, A., 513, 519
Penhall, R. K., 168, 174

Pepper, C. B., 301, 314
Pepper, M. P., 431
Perhott, J. B., 112, 139
Perin, G. A., 35, 40
Perl, M., 103, 128
Perr, I., 392, 398
Perry, R. W., 402, 417
Perry, S., 139, 254, 255, 259
Perry, S. E., 543
Pesch, R. N., 175
Peters, J. J., 207, 214
Peters, S., 167, 174
Peterson, G. H., 209, 214
Peterson, R. A., 379, 382, 387
Petrillo, M., 67, 136
Pfeiffer, E., 102, 126
Pfohl, B., 6, 20
Philibert, D., 98, 139
Philips, R. U., 385
Phillips, V. A., 61, 134
Piaget, J., 29, 41, 219, 237, 240, 246, 329, 338
Pierce, C. M., 362, 389
Pilisuk, M., 506, 509
Pill, R., 193, 215
Pillemer, E., 106, 125
Pilowsky, I., 68, 136, 168, 174
Pinderhughes, C., 364, 389
Pine, F., 195, 214
Pines, A. M., 328, 339
Pines, M., 490, 495
Pinheiro, G. N., 215
Pinkerton, P., 89, 136
Pittman, R. H., 401, 414
Pizzey, E., 287, 289, 290, 292
Plank, E. N., 69, 116, 136
Plapp, J. M., 5, 9, 19
Pless, I. B., 87, 89, 90, 136, 141
Ploeger, A., 541, 544
Plomin, R., 463, 476
Plumb, M., 96, 137
Plutchik, R., 477, 495
Polan, H. J., 103, 137
Pollinger, A., 540, 543
Pollock, G. H., 261, 277, 540, 546
Pomer, S., 195, 215
Popkin, M. K., 383, 389
Porritt, D., 333, 336, 504, 509
Poteet, J. R., 98, 137
Poulshock, S. W., 331, 338, 402, 417
Poushinsky, B. A., 599
Powell, G., 94, 141, 363, 366, 390
Poznanski, E. O., 99, 137
President's Commission on Mental Health, 118,
    137, 287, 289, 292
Price, D., 106, 137
Price, K. P., 166, 174
Priel, B., 277

Priel, I., 334, 339
Prosen, M., 561, 568
Prugh, D. G., 60, 61, 62, 63, 64, 65, 66, 67, 68, 69, 70, 75, 76, 77, 78, 79, 80, 84, 87, 88, 89, 90, 94, 97, 98, 99, 104, 105, 108, 112, 113, 114, 115, 116, 117, 128, 137, 193, 194, 214, 541, 544
Prusoff, B. A., 419, 431
Pruyser, P., 559, 568
Pugh, W. M., 390
Pumpian-Mindlin, E., 543, 617, 627
Purifoy, F. E., 487, 495
Pynoos, R., 332, 337

Quarantelli, E. L., 249, 259, 401, 415, 417
Quay, H. C., 547, 558
Quayhagen, M., 422, 431
Queen, R., 301, 314
Quinlan, D. M., 79, 110, 111, 137
Quinton, D. M., 68, 137

Raab, A., 479, 496
Rabins, P. V., 103, 135
Rabkin, J., 9, 19
Rabkin, L., 39, 41
Rado, S., 279, 281, 292
Raffel, S. C., 545
Rago, W. V., 408, 417
Rahe, R. H., 10, 11, 19, 82, 137, 143, 148, 157, 165, 173, 368, 383, 390, 600, 614, 615
Rainey, L. C., 99, 100, 137
Rainey, R., 156
Rakoff, V., 540, 545
Rakusin, J. M., 16, 19
Raleigh, M. J., 480, 495
Ramasuvha, V. S., 383, 390
Ramirez, A., 329, 338
Ramos, S., 47, 59
Rank, B., 190, 214
Rank, O., 189, 214
Rapaport, J. L., 540, 544
Raphael, B., 117, 137
Rapkin, J., 281, 292
Raschke, H. J., 517, 520
Raskind, M., 101, 137, 492
Rattenbury, F., 561, 568
Raundalen, M., 348, 359
Ravenscroft, K., 75, 78, 115, 138
Rayner, J., 256, 259
Razin, A. M., 81, 82, 83, 84, 138
Redl, F., 373, 385, 511, 513, 520
Redmond, S., 115, 135
Regan, D., 594, 598
Reich, J., 165, 168, 174
Reich, P., 98, 137
Reichdahl, R. J., 147, 158

Reid, A. H., 580, 582, 585
Reid, J. M., 483, 494
Reinhart, J. B., 107, 112, 138
Reisberg, B., 101, 139
Reiser, D. E., 61, 92, 138
Reiser, M. F., 61, 92, 127, 134
Reus, V., 494
Rey, J. M., 5, 8, 9, 19
Rhymes, J., 109, 140
Ricciuti, H., 194, 214
Richards, I. N., 5, 19
Richlin, D. M., 167, 174
Richman, N., 539, 545
Richmond, J. B., 76, 138
Richter, C. P., 308, 314
Ridgeway, L. C., 527, 534
Ridington, J., 289, 292
Rie, H., 92, 138
Rigg, J. R. A., 109, 138
Riley, V., 482, 495
Ringler, N. M., 190, 191, 214
Rinsley, D., 603, 615
Rioch, M. J., 557, 558
Ripley, H. S., 306, 314, 617, 629
Robbins, C., 504, 509
Robbins, L. C., 208, 215
Roberts, B., 478, 496
Roberts, R. E., 383, 390
Robertson, J., 67, 138, 192, 214
Robey, J. S., 602, 613
Robinson, D., 193, 215
Robinson, L. H., 499
Rodholm, M., 211
Roeper, P., 382, 383, 388
Rofe, Y., 349, 360
Roff, M., 513, 520
Rogentine, G. N., 96, 138
Rogers, J., 146, 158
Rogers, R., 36, 41
Rogers, W., 512, 519
Roghmann, K. J., 87, 136
Roghmann, K. L., 92, 131
Rohsenow, D. J., 158
Rolf, J. E., 541, 545
Rolls, E. T., 479, 495
Rolsky, J. T., 35, 41
Romano, J., 78, 79, 129
Romero, A., 363, 366, 390
Rook, J. C., 175
Rose, A., 389
Rosen, B., 301, 314
Rosen, H., 35, 37, 38, 39, 40, 41
Rosenbaum, P., 287, 291
Rosenberg, E. J., 384, 390
Rosenberg, I., 191, 212
Rosenblatt, B., 36, 41
Rosenblatt, R., 351, 360

Rosenfeld, A., 596, 598, 603, 614
Rosenfield, S., 404, 406, 407, 411, 416
Rosenheck, R., 541, 545
Rosenthal, D., 594, 599
Rosenthal, S. J., 330, 337
Rosini, L. A., 85, 138
Ross, C. E., 383, 389, 390
Ross, R. D., 110, 125
Ross, W. D., 327, 339, 541, 545
Rossberg, R. H., 93, 138
Rosser, R., 402, 416, 538, 544
Rossman, I., 99, 138
Roth, M., 5, 19, 560, 568
Rothney, W., 70, 140
Rothschild, A. J., 495
Rothschild, C. S., 149, 158
Rotter, J. B., 622, 628
Rounsaville, B., 287, 292
Rousseau, O., 109, 138
Rowe, J. N., 305, 307, 314
Rowland, K. F., 407, 417
Roy, R., 164, 171, 175, 622, 623, 627, 628
Rubin, R. T., 390
Rubin, Z., 512, 520
Rudd, C., 215
Rudden, M., 383, 561, 568
Rudrauff, M., 542, 594, 598
Ruiz, R. A., 383, 390
Rule, B. G., 542, 545
Rumack, B. H., 150, 156
Rush, A. J., 170, 173, 561, 568
Rush, H. A., 93, 129
Rusk, H., 93, 102, 138
Russell, A. T., 5, 19
Rutter, M., 5, 20, 68, 87, 89, 137, 138, 191,
    196, 202, 214, 233, 237, 328, 338, 421,
    431, 465, 545, 599
Rynearson, E. K., 332, 338

Sabbeth, B. F., 90, 138
Sachar, E. J., 98, 135, 483, 495
Sack, W. H., 353, 360
Sackeim, H. A., 479, 495
Sacks, M. H., 561, 568
Sagarin, E., 518, 520
Saint J. Neill, S. R., 330, 338
Salomon, M. S., 495, 541
Sameroff, A. J., 545, 594, 599
Samora, J., 92, 136
Sandler, I. N., 382, 383, 384, 390
Sandler, J., 268, 277
Sands, H. H., 69, 137, 193, 214
Sanford, R. N., 385
Sanger, S., 67, 136
Sangrey, D., 296, 297, 313
Santrock, J. W., 201, 214
Sarason, I. G., 611, 615, 622, 627

Sarnoff, C., 237
Saron, C., 482, 495
Sata, L. S., 383, 390
Satterwhite, B., 90, 99, 136, 138, 141
Saunders, C. M., 99, 138
Saunders, M. M., 191, 215
Sawrcz, W., 156
Sawrey, W., 503, 508, 540, 544
Saylor, C., 606, 609, 614
Schachter, S., 512, 520
Schaefer, C., 368, 388
Schaefer, E. S., 191, 215
Schaeffer, M., 590, 595, 597, 599
Schafer, D. W., 115, 138
Schafer, R., 560, 568
Schafer, S., 328, 338
Schaffer, H. R., 90, 138, 193, 214
Schaller, J., 211
Schalock, R. L., 582, 583, 585
Scharl, A. E., 26, 41
Schatzberg, A. F., 483, 495
Schechter, J. O., 143
Scher, C. A., 105, 140
Scherl, D., 283, 292
Scherzer, A., 152, 158
Schienle, D. R., 100, 102, 103, 138
Schiff, H., 99, 138
Schildkraut, J. J., 495
Schiller, J. D., 196, 215
Schlesinger, H. J., 81, 120, 136
Schless, A. P., 10, 20
Schlor, K. H., 480, 496
Schmale, A., 96, 114, 129, 138, 623, 628
Schmideberg, M., 280, 281, 292
Schmidt, C., 139, 487, 496
Schmitt, F. E., 111, 139
Schmitt, M. H., 96, 138
Schneck, M. K., 101, 102, 139
Schoenback, V. J., 626
Scholl, M. L., 602, 613
Schork, M. A., 387, 388
Schowalter, J. E., 68, 69, 112, 139
Schrader, G., 6, 20
Schribner, B., 113, 125
Schuler, K., 622, 628
Schull, M. J., 388
Schull, W. J., 387
Schulman, J., 67, 109, 139, 141
Schulsinger, F., 594, 599
Schulz, R., 408, 411, 417
Schumacher, D., 287, 292
Schwab, F., 94, 139
Schwab, J. J., 365, 382, 390
Schwab, M. E., 365, 390
Schwartz, A. H., 145, 157
Schwartz, G. E., 478, 495
Schwartz, G. R., 85, 139

Schwartz, H., 348, 360
Schwartz, L., 10, 20
Schwartz, R. E., 335, 338, 540, 545
Schwarz, J. C., 196, 215
Schwarzwald, J., 348, 360
Schweiger, A., 164, 175
Scotch, N., 502, 509
Scott, C., 281, 292
Scott, D. H., 622, 628
Scott, D. L., 110, 139
Scott, J., 333, 338, 383, 387
Scott, P. D., 286, 287, 288, 292
Seeley, J. W., 231, 237
Seeman, M., 622, 628
Segal, B., 512, 520
Seifer, R., 541, 545, 594, 599
Seligman, M. E. P., 162, 163, 175, 287, 292, 330, 338, 482, 496, 538, 545
Seligman, R., 116, 139
Sells, B., 513, 520
Selman, R., 511, 520
Selye, H., 559, 568
Selzer, M. C., 623, 629
Selzer, M. L., 146, 147, 148, 158
Senatore, V., 585
Senn, M. J. E., 139
Serafetinides, E. A., 501, 508
Seres, J. L., 170, 174
Sethi, B. B., 202, 211
Severs, H., 281, 292
Seward, G. H., 367, 390
Sexton, M., 207, 213
Seyle, H., 143, 158
Shaffer, D., 5, 20, 94, 141
Shagass, C., 105, 139
Shambaugh, B., 29, 41
Shands, H., 75, 139
Shanfield, S. B., 167, 175, 429, 430
Shannon, D. C., 85, 141
Shanok, S. S., 382, 388
Sharp, B., 173
Shaw, A., 86, 139
Shaw, J. A., 340, 346, 354, 355, 360, 429, 431
Shawcross, W., 340, 348, 360
Sheff, A. G., 543
Shenko, R., 610, 614
Sheper, J., 489, 495
Shere, E. S., 334, 339
Sherick, I., 99, 134, 192, 207, 214
Sherif, M., 511, 520
Shield, P., 561, 568
Shipman, R., 167, 174
Shirley, H. F., 204, 215
Shore, M. F., 70, 139, 632, 650
Shrand, H., 70, 139
Shrout, P. E., 3, 6, 8, 13, 14, 18, 20
Shulman, S., 349, 361, 383, 387

Shumaker, S. A., 403, 409, 411, 417
Shumate, M., 621, 629
Shurka, E., 149, 157
Shuster, L., 482, 495
Shye, S., 404, 417
Sibert, J. R., 151, 158
Siebel, C. E., 538, 543
Siegel, E., 191, 215
Siegel, J. M., 613, 615
Siegel, L. G., 172
Siegel, S. E., 173
Sieler, H., 493
Sigafoos, A., 173
Sigal, J., 386, 540, 541, 545
Sigvardsson, S., 598
Silber, E., 75, 116, 139, 254, 255, 259, 543
Silberfarb, P. M., 95, 98, 134, 139
Silberman, C. E., 395, 398
Silbert, M. H., 328, 339
Silk, K. R., 382, 383, 385
Sillen, S., 382, 390
Siller, J., 139
Silver, B. J., 390
Silver, D., 537, 540, 545
Silver, H. K., 205, 213
Silver, L. B., 390
Silver, R. L., 545
Silverman, D., 285, 292
Silverman, F. N., 205, 213
Silverstein, M., 561, 568
Sime, A. M., 108, 139
Simmons, R. D., 115, 139
Simmons, R. G., 114, 139
Simms, P., 387
Simon, A., 78, 140
Simon, I. V., 85, 140
Sims, J., 254, 259
Singer, J. A., 495, 498
Singer, P., 540, 543
Singh, N. W., 580, 583, 585
Sipowitz, R. R., 67, 141
Siris, S. G., 561, 567
Sisler, G. C., 332, 339
Skipper, J. K., 109, 140
Sklar, L. S., 96, 140
Skodol, A. E., 3, 6, 8, 13, 14, 18, 20
Skogan, W. G., 299, 300, 314
Slaby, R. G., 329, 338, 542, 544
Slaff, B., 238, 239, 246
Slater, E., 560, 568
Slavin, L. A., 97, 140
Slavin, L. S., 94, 96, 136
Slavson, S. R., 511, 520
Slovic, P., 249, 259
Sluckin, A., 191, 212
Sluckin, W., 191, 212
Slymen, D. J., 334, 338

Smale, G. J. A., 333, 339
Smelzer, M. L., 334, 339
Smessaert, A., 105, 140
Smith, A., 110, 20, 95, 132
Smith, B. R., 64, 135
Smith, E. R., 363, 388
Smith, J., 148, 157
Smith, J. M., 408, 417
Smith, J. R., 263, 277, 540, 545
Smith, R., 404, 415
Smith, T. L., 622, 629
Smotherman, W. P., 483, 488, 493, 494
Smythe, M. M., 364, 390
Snelbecker, G. E., 408, 415
Sobel, R., 151, 158
Sodetz, F. J., 341, 358
Sokol, R., 512, 520
Solala, A., 281, 292
Solnit, A., 75, 88, 130, 140, 277, 329, 339
Soloff, P., 140
Solomon, F., 589, 599
Solomon, G. F., 114, 140
Solomon, K., 102, 140
Solomon, L., 511, 519
Solomon, O. C., 210, 215
Solomon, S. L., 103, 140
Solomon, Z., 348, 360
Soong, W., 463, 476
Sousa, P. L. R., 191, 215
Southard, E. E., 617, 628
Sparr, L. F., 543
Spector, S. L., 74, 133
Spickenheuer, H. L. P., 333, 339
Spiegel, D., 97, 98, 140
Spiegel, H., 279, 281, 291, 346, 347, 360
Spiegel, J., 342, 345, 359
Spinetta, J., 95, 140
Spirito, A., 597, 598, 622, 629
Spitz, R., 67, 140, 501, 509, 591, 593, 599,
   601, 602, 615
Spitzer, R. L., 5, 20
Spreat, S., 408, 415
Spring, B., 16, 20
Stacey, M., 193, 215
Staimen, M. G., 131
Stanford, G., 69, 141
Stangl, D., 6, 20
Stanley, J. E., 328, 338
Stark, J. A., 582, 585
Stark, M. H., 75, 88, 140
Staub, E. M., 69, 137, 193, 214
Steele, B. F., 205, 213, 215, 315
Steffa, M., 213
Steger, J. C., 161, 169, 172
Stein, N., 165, 175
Stein, R. E., 93, 140, 166, 175
Steinberg, L. D., 197, 211

Steinberg, M. D., 116, 140
Steiner, D. L., 622, 627
Steinglass, P., 399, 404, 417
Steklis, H. D., 482, 494
Stephens, D. A., 582, 585
Stephens, P. M., 479, 480, 485, 494, 503, 508
Sterba, E., 540, 545
Sterling, J., 401, 417
Stern, G. M., 261, 277
Stern, W. C., 505, 506, 509
Sternbach, R. A., 166, 175
Sterner, R., 389
Stevenson, I., 383, 390, 610, 614
Stewart, G. W., 5, 9, 19
Stewart, T. D., 149, 158
Stigler, J. W., 463, 476
Stillner, V., 389
Stillwell, D. M., 170, 174
Stirtzinger, R., 197, 215
Stock, G., 480, 496
Stocking, M., 70, 140
Stoddard, F., 115, 140
Stoeckle, J. D., 166, 173
Stokols, D., 409, 411, 417
Stoll, F., 561, 568
Stoll, J. R., 147, 158
Stone, A., 365, 390
Stone, D. K., 435, 446
Stone, E. M., 272, 277
Stone, G. I., 627
Stone, L. J., 242, 246
Stone, M. H., 432, 435, 446
Stonequist, E. V., 367, 390
Stout, R. J., 631, 650
Stoyva, J. M., 166, 172
Strain, J. J., 71, 72, 75, 78, 80, 82, 89, 101,
   140, 165, 175, 279, 280, 292
Stratton, L. H., 383, 391
Straus, M. A., 286, 287, 289, 290, 292
Strauss, J. S., 560, 561, 568
Streiner, D. L., 622, 623, 628
Streiner, D. R., 623, 627
Strickland, R. G., 196, 215
Strom, A., 617, 629
Struening, E., 9, 19, 252, 259
Stuart, I., 280, 291
Stuart, J. C., 144, 147, 158
Stueve, A., 13, 20
Suchman, E., 152, 158
Sue, S., 383, 390
Suinn, R. M., 635, 650
Suissa, A., 163, 174
Sullivan, H. S., 511, 520
Sultz, H. A., 131
Sulzer-Azaroff, B., 580, 584
Summit, R., 206, 207, 215
Sundin, O., 489, 494

Sundquist, S., 196, 213
Sussex, J. N., 541, 545
Sussman, M., 90, 127, 506, 509
Sutherland, A. M., 279, 283, 292
Sutherland, S., 292
Sutkin, L. C., 87, 129
Suzuki, P. T., 383, 390
Swank, R. L., 343, 344, 345, 360
Swanson, D. W., 170, 174
Swanson, S. W., 165, 168, 173
Swanson, W. C., 633, 650
Swartz, D. R., 140
Sweetwood, J., 624, 627
Swenson, W. M., 170, 174
Swogger, G., Jr., 547
Symonds, M., 287, 292, 328, 339
Szaba, D., 301, 314
Sze, W. C., 510, 521

Tabachnick, N., 147, 148, 158, 334, 339
Tagiuri, C. K., 75, 76, 137
Tanguay, P. E., 94, 141
Tannenbaum, J., 196, 197, 211
Tars, S., 407, 415
Tatten, H. A., 165, 172
Taylor, V., 248, 259
Tazuma, L., 350, 360
Teicher, J. D., 601, 602, 611, 615
Temoshok, L., 104, 127
Tennant, C., 10, 16, 18, 20, 601, 613, 615, 623, 625
Tennov, D., 491, 496
Teri, L., 541, 545
Terr, L. C., 264, 265, 266, 277, 330, 331, 339, 353, 360, 541, 545
Terry, D. J., 483, 495
Tewell, K., 98, 134
Thaler, M., 106, 137
Thane, K., 191, 212
Theorell, T., 10, 20
Thivierge, J., 476
Thoits, P. A., 623, 629
Thomas, A., 189, 191, 208, 211, 215, 382, 390, 459, 460, 463, 464, 465, 466, 471, 472, 476
Thomas, P. G., 68, 136, 168, 174
Thompson, M. L., 482, 495
Thompson, R., 69, 141
Thompson, T. L., 60, 77, 106, 125
Thompson, T. R., 86, 132
Thompson, W. R., 483, 487, 496
Thoroughman, J. C., 108, 141
Thorson, J., 148, 157
Thurman, A. E., 81, 126
Thursz, D., 404, 417
Tibblin, G., 626
Tierney, K. J., 402, 417

Tillman, A. W., 146, 158, 502, 509
Timasheff, N. S., 528, 534
Timbers, D. M., 386
Timmreck, T. C., 383, 391
Tisza, V. B., 114, 141, 206, 207, 211
Titchener, J. L., 110, 112, 141, 251, 259, 280, 292, 327, 339, 541, 545
Tizard, B., 595, 599
Tizard, J., 87, 138
Todres, I. D., 85, 141
Todres, J. D., 85, 138
Toffler, A., 616, 629
Toker, E., 112, 141
Tolsdorf, C. C., 515, 520
Tomita, M., 388
Toole, A., 93, 129
Toomey, T. C., 170, 175
Torda, C., 162, 175
Torgersen, A. M., 463, 476
Torgersen, S., 489, 496
Torgerson, W. S., 160, 174
Toulouse, A., 582, 585
Tracey, G. S., 401, 414
Trause, M. A., 190, 191, 192, 213, 214, 215
Travell, J. G., 170, 175
Trevarthan, C., 488, 490, 496
Trief, P., 165, 175
Trier, C., 621, 627
Trimble, M. R., 92, 127
Trost, M. A., 513, 519
Troyer, W. G., 81, 133, 382, 385
Tucker, G. J., 561, 568
Tuddenham, R. D., 542, 617, 626
Tufo, H. M., 108, 141
Tupin, J. P., 165, 174
Turbett, J. A., 70, 131
Turk, D., 619, 621, 628
Turkat, I. D., 164, 175
Turner, J., 170, 175, 252, 259
Turner, R. J., 506, 509
Turrel, E., 503, 508
Tuthill, R. W., 202, 211
Tyhurst, J. S., 281, 282, 292, 342, 361
Tyner, F. G., 341, 358
Tyre, T. E., 170, 175
Tyrer, S. P., 582, 585

Uhlenhuth, E. H., 419, 431
Ulman, R. B., 540, 543
Ungerleider, J. T., 525, 534
U. S. Bureau of the Census, 198, 215
U. S. Commission on Civil Rights, 289, 293
U. S. Department of Labor, 449, 454
U. S. Department of Justice, 328, 339
Unterecher, J., 93, 129
Uzoka, A. F., 507, 509

Vaillant, G. E., 16, 18, 547, 548, 549, 551, 558, 601, 610, 613, 615, 623, 625
Vance, J. C., 90, 141
Van Delft, A. M. L., 493
Van Der Kolk, B. A., 263, 277, 348, 361
Van Der Kolk, C. J., 383, 391
Van Kammen, D. P., 561, 567
Van Leeuwen, K., 195, 215
Van Wimersma, W. M., 493
Varner, R. V., 101, 130
Vaughan, S. R., 289, 293
Vaughn, G. F., 108, 141
Vaughn, L. F., 166, 172
Veith, R. C., 492
Veltri, J. C., 150, 158
Verbey, J., 492
Vernick, J., 97, 98, 141
Vernon, D., 67, 68, 109, 139, 141
Videka-Sherman, L., 99, 141
Viederman, M., 540, 543
Vietze, P. M., 191, 213
Vignes, A. J., 383, 391
Vinokur, A., 146, 147, 148, 158, 334, 339, 623, 629
Visher, E. B., 201, 215
Visher, J. S., 201, 215
Visintainer, J. A., 109, 142
Visitainer, M. A., 482, 496
Volberding, P. A., 103, 128
Volpicelli, J. R., 482, 496
Von Hentig, H., 328, 339
Voos, D., 215
Vreeland, R., 85, 141

Wadland, W., 192, 214
Wagner, E. H., 207, 626
Wagonfeld, S., 78, 113, 117, 129, 137
Waites, E. A., 287, 292
Wakeman, R. J., 115, 141
Wakerman, E., 33, 42
Walden, D., 374, 386
Waldfogel, S., 105, 132
Walker, L. E., 286, 287, 289, 293
Wall, P. D., 161, 174
Wallace, A. G., 81, 133
Wallerstein, J. S., 51, 52, 59, 199, 200, 215, 216, 234, 237, 595, 599
Walletschek, H., 479, 496
Wallick, M. M., 189, 191, 216
Wallinga, J., 70, 141
Wallskog, J. M., 93, 134
Wallston, B. S., 623, 629
Walsh, A., 582, 585
Ward, C., 333, 339
Ward, I. L., 487, 496
Ward, M. S., 117, 127
Warheit, G., 502, 509

Warheit, G. J., 156
Warheit, G. L., 382, 390
Warheit, G. T., 401, 415
Warren, D. W., 487, 496
Warshak, P., 201, 214
Wasek, P., 539, 542
Watkins, J. T., 98, 142
Watson, J., 459, 476, 601, 614
Weber, M., 371, 391
Webster, T. G., 569, 577, 579, 580, 581, 582, 583, 585
Wechsler, R. C., 199, 213
Weerts, T. C., 478, 496
Wehr, J., 95, 134
Weighill, V. E., 339
Weijnen, J. A., 493
Weil, W., Jr., 90, 127
Weiman, A. L., 495
Weinberg, L., 621, 627
Weinberg, M. S., 531, 534
Weinberger, D. A., 478, 495
Weiner, H., 61, 141
Weiner, M. F., 640, 650
Weinhold, C., 610, 614
Weinshilboum, R., 481, 492
Weir, T., 610, 613
Weisenberg, M., 161, 175, 348, 360
Weiss, E., 512, 520
Weiss, J. M., 623, 629
Weiss, R. J., 327, 339, 537, 545
Weiss, R. S., 515, 517, 520
Weiss, T., 494
Weissberg, M. P., 74, 92, 128
Weissman, A. D., 97, 100, 111, 112, 131, 141
Weissman, M., 150, 158, 619, 629
Weisz, J., 487, 496
Weitzman, M., 90, 126
Welch, C. E., 110, 128, 626
Wellisch, D., 96, 127, 141, 525, 534
Wells, K. S., 411, 416
Welner, J., 594, 599
Wender, P. H., 594, 599
Wennberg, J. E., 117, 142
Werbel, J. D., 410, 415
Werkman, S., 418, 422, 431
Werry, J. S., 547, 558
Wessel, M., 99142
Wesseling, E., 116, 142
West, N. D., 83, 142
Westermeyer, J., 561, 567
Westervelt, F. B., Jr., 113, 124
Westheimer, I., 192, 212
Whalen, T. E., 425, 431
Whedon, G. D., 483, 494
White, L. P., 85, 142
White, R. A. F., 543
White, R. K., 148, 150, 158

White, R. W., 263, 277, 427, 431
Whitehead, P. L., 631, 650
Whiteley, S., 85, 140
Whitlemore, K., 87, 138
Whitlock, F. A., 147, 148, 158
Wiener, A., 105, 106, 107, 111, 125
Wiersma, E., 404, 417
Wiesenfeld, Z., 163, 175
Wilbert, J. R., 394, 398
Wilder, C. S., 100, 142
Wilkerson, R. G., 382, 388
Wilkinson, A. H., 115, 135
Wilkinson, C. B., 541, 546
Will, L., 5, 19
Willer, J. C., 163, 175
Willhelm, S. M., 375, 376, 391
Williams, D. H., 382, 388
Williams, J., 5, 7, 8, 20, 173
Williams, L. H., 107, 133
Williams, M., 389
Willson, M., 82, 133
Wilner, N., 539, 544
Wilson, M. M., 481, 496
Wilson, S., 382, 385, 619, 627
Wilson, W. J., 376, 391
Wilson, W. P., 617, 626
Wilsson, L., 486, 496
Wineman, D., 511, 513, 520
Winer, J. A., 261, 277, 540, 546
Winget, C. N., 251, 252, 258, 259, 350, 359, 400, 416, 541, 543
Winnick, A., 597, 598
Winnicott, D. W., 216, 446, 583
Winton, A. S., 580, 583, 585
Wintrob, R. M., 383, 391
Wise, L., 116, 140
Wishnie, H. A., 81, 131
Wittkower, E., 75, 142
Wolf, M. C., 617, 629
Wolf, S., 80, 126, 306, 314, 385, 408, 415
Wolfe, H., 213
Wolfenstein, M., 42, 351, 361, 546
Wolfer, J. A., 109, 142
Wolff, S., 193, 194, 204, 216
Wolfgang, M., 539, 546
Wolkind, S., 594, 597, 599
Wolpe, J., 619, 629

Wolskee, P. J., 162, 173
Woods, H., 146, 157
Woolridge, P. J., 111, 139
World Health Organization, 565, 568
Worthington, E. L., Jr., 621, 629
Wortman, C. B., 330, 336, 537, 545
Wright, B. A., 149, 158
Wright, C., 196, 197, 211, 597, 598
Wright, G. N., 93, 142
Wright, J. S., 483, 487, 496
Wright, R., 328, 337, 372, 391
Wunsch-Hitzig, R., 18
Wykoff, R. L., 396, 398
Wyler, A. R., 396, 615
Wyman, E., 290, 610

Yager, J., 19, 289, 627
Yalom, I. D., 10, 142, 624
Yamamoto, J., 98, 390
Yamamoto, K., 363, 366, 391
Yanowitch, R. E., 145, 158
Yarrow, L., 591, 599
Yates, A., 191, 210, 216
Yospe, L. P., 170, 174
Young, L. V., 131
Youngs, D. D., 176
Yule, W., 89, 138

Zackson, H., 285, 291
Zarit, J. M., 102, 103, 142
Zarit, S. H., 102, 103, 142
Zborowski, M., 61, 62, 142, 166, 175
Zelazo, P., 196, 213
Zeligs, R., 99, 142
Ziegler, D. K., 166, 175
Zilbach, J., 280, 291
Zimberg, S., 84, 133
Zimmerman, M., 6, 20
Zimmerman-McKinney, M. A., 328, 338
Zipes, D. P., 81, 133
Zitter, R. E., 621, 627
Ziv, A., 349, 361
Zlotowski, M., 408, 417
Zola, I. K., 166, 175
Zubin, J., 16, 20
Zuckerman-Bareli, C., 335, 339, 349, 355, 361
Zuehlke, T. E., 98, 142

Subject Index

Abortion, 182–184
Abuse:
  child, 205–207, 208, 230–232, 315–326, 605
  spouse, 280, 286–290
Accident-proneness, 502
Accidents, 145–146, 152–157. *See also* Toxic
    ingestion
  automobile, 333–334, 502
  biopsychosocial reponse to, 148–150
  etiologic factors in, 146–148
Acquired immune deficiency syndrome (AIDS),
    103–104
Acute illness, 63–64
  catastrophic, 75–78, 80–83
  delirium in, 78–80
  direct effects of, 64–75
  ICUs, 83–87
  myocardial infarction, 80–83
  reactions of adults to, 71–75
  reactions of children to, 65–71, 604–605,
    606–608
Adaptive mechanisms, 548, 549, 551–552
Additive burden hypothesis, 15, 16, 17
Adjustment Disorders, 1, 3–4, 380, 535–536
  conduct disturbances as, 534–542
  DSM-III definition of, 3–4, 466, 571–572
  measuring psychosocial stressors in, 3–8

  in mentally retarded persons, 569–572
  and psychoses, 559–567
  temperament as factor in, 465–466, 471
  treatment for, 630–650, 651–660
  work withdrawal and inhibition as, 547–558
Adjustment Reactions, 1. *See also* Adjustment
    Disorders
Adolescents:
  depression in, 610, 611–612
  hostile-aggressive responses in, 539
  need for ego support, 501
  psychoses in, 563
  reactions to acute illness, 65–71
  reactions to chronic illness, 88–90
  reactions to fire, 268–269
  reactions to hospitalization, 66–71
  reactions to parental divorce, 52–53
  self-help groups for, 632–633
  stress in, 609–611
  suicide in, 611–612
Adrenaline, 478
Adults:
  reactions to acute illness, 71–75
  reactions to chronic illness, 90–94, 112–113
  reactions to hospitalization, 71–75
  stress reduction programs for, 616–625
  and surgery:

preparing for, 107–108, 111–112
reactions to, 105–107, 109–111
Affective/autonomic behavior therapies,
636–637
Aggressiveness, 225, 537–539
AIDS, *see* Acquired immune deficiency
syndrome
Airplane hijacking, 331–332
Alcoholics Anonymous, 631
Alienation, 367
Aliphatics, 565
Alprazolam, 643
Al-Teen, 632–633
Alzheimer's disease, 100–103
Amputation, 116
Anger. *See also* Aggressiveness
neuroendocrinology of, 477–480
as reaction to fire, 271
as reaction to parental death, 26
as reaction to parental divorce, 52, 55
Anomia, 367, 369–370
Anomy, *see* Anomia
Anticipatory mourning, 24
Antipsychotic medication, 565–566
Anxiety:
inducing, 636–637
neuroendocrinology of, 480–481
reducing, 525–526
Anxiolytics, 643
Arab–Israeli conflict, 335, 342
Archetypal behavior, 485–491
Assaults, 327–328. *See also* Crimes of violence
physical, 329–333
types of, 328–336
verbal, 328–329
Automobile accidents, 333–334, 502
Axis IV, *see* DSM-III, Axis IV ratings in

"Baby hunger," 491
Battered wives, 280, 286–290
Behavior, 457–458
archetypal, 485–491
Behavioral techniques, 624, 635–636
affective/autonomic, 636–637
anxiety induction, 636–637
cognitive restructuring, 637–638
learned coping, 637
relaxation, 636
somatic, 637
stimulus control, 637
stress inoculation, 618–622, 625, 638
Benzodiazepines, 643
Bereavement:
by children, 24–25, 26, 589–591
failure to mourn, 27–31, 643
in wartime, 350–351

Beta-blockers, 643–644
Biethnic psychotherapy, 384
Big Thompson Canyon flood, 252
Biofeedback, 636
Biracial psychotherapy, 384
Birth, 176–178
cesarean, 180–181
complications in, 184–188, 503
normal, 178–180
sibling presence at, 209
Brain stem, 479–480
Brief psychotherapy, 644–646
for children, 646–650
Brief separations, 190–192
*Brown v. The Board of Education of Topeka,
Kansas,* 363, 385
Buffalo Creek disaster, 251–252
bereavement in, 350
individual responses to, 252
psychopathology resulting from, 400–401
societal reponse to, 253
Burns, 115–116
Butyrophenones, 566

Cancer, 94–100
Catastrophic illness, 75–78, 80–83
Catecholamines, 478, 483–485
Catharsis, 318–319, 647
Cesarean childbirth, 180–181
Child abuse, 205–207, 208, 230–232, 315–326,
605
causes of, 316–317
and chronic childhood depression, 608–609
family issues in, 320–321
sexual, 206–207, 322–324
therapy for, 317
cognitive, 317–318
emotional, 318–319
family, 320–321
group, 320
individual, 317–319
treating infants, 324
treating older children, 325–326
Childbirth:
cesarean, 180–181
complications in, 184–188, 503
normal, 178–180
sibling presence at, 209
Child care:
aggressive behavior during, 329–330
in child's own home, 235
effect on preschool children, 194–197
Children. *See also* Adolescents; Infants
abuse of, 205–207, 208, 230–232, 315–326,
605
assaults on, 329–332

Children (*continued*)
  bereavement of, 24–25, 26, 589–591
  chronic depression in, 608–609
  common surgical procedures for, 117
  and custody litigation, 47–48
  defective, 185–187
  desire of, for parental reconciliation, 46–47
  and disillusionment, 434–435, 442–444
  effect of hospitalization on, 66–71, 192–194
  effect of household moving on, 197,
      422–423, 425–427, 428–429
  exploitation of, 230
  expression of feelings, 46
  failed mourning in, 27–31
  and family support, 499–501
  in foster care, 594–595
  "goodness of fit" development model for,
      465–466
  grade-school-age, 217–236, 606–608
    cognitive transformation in, 219–220
    coping styles of, 222–225
    developmental aspects of, 217–222
    home life as source of stress for, 229–235
    impact of school on, 220–222, 226–228
    parent–child interactions of, 229–235
    reactions to fire, 267–268
    reactions to parental divorce, 51–52
    regressive coping style of, 222–225
    superego in, 218–219
  hostile-aggressive reponses in, 538–542
  and idealization, 432–433, 441–444
  kidnapping of, 302, 330–332, 541
    by parent, 233–234
  mourning process in, 24–25, 26, 589–591
  moving to new school, 425
  neglect of, *see* Child abuse
  newborn, defective, 185–187
  and object loss, 589–594
  and parental divorce:
    reactions to, 49–57
    sources of stress in, 43–48
  and peer relationships, 511–512, 514
  and personal life history book, 596–597
  physical assaults on, 329–332
  physical handicaps in, 203–204
  preparing for sibling death, 34–35
  preparing for surgery, 108–109
  preschool, 189–210, 603–605
    child care and, 194–197
    and death of parent, 589–591
    effect of death on, 202–203
    frightening experiences of, 208–209
    illness in, 204–205
    need for ego support, 499–501
    and object loss, 589–597
    overstimulation of, 208–209

  reactions to fire, 265–266
  reactions to parental divorce, 50–51
  and separations, 190–192
  sexual abuse of, 206–207
  sibling rivalry among, 207–208
  and stepparents, 201
  psychotherapy for, 646–650
  reactions to acute illness, 65–71
  reactions to amputation, 116
  reactions to burns, 115–116
  reactions to chronic illness, 88–90, 112
  reactions to disasters, 250–251, 254–255
  reactions to fire, 265–269
  reactions to hospitalization, 66–71, 192–194
  reactions to parental death, 23–34, 589–591,
      604, 606
  reactions to parental divorce, 49–57, 198–200
  reactions to sibling death, 36–40
  reactions to surgery, 104–105, 108
  self-help groups for, 632–633
  sexual abuse of, 206–207
  and sibling death, 34–40
  sibling rivalry among, 207–208
  similarity of temperament with parents,
      469–470
  stress management for, 612
  temperament in, 458–467
  treatment of, 472–475, 646–650
    for child abuse, 324–326
  verbal assaults on, 329
  and war, 351–354
Chloropromazine, 565–566
Chowchilla school bus kidnapping, 330–331,
    541
Chronic burden hypethesis, 15, 16, 17
Chronic illness, 87
  Alzheimer's desease, 100–104
  cancer, 94–100
  reaction of adults to, 90–94
  reaction of children to, 88–90
Chronic pain, 168–169
  medication for, 168–169
  psychiatric treatment for, 169–171
Circumcision, 117
Clarification, 647, 648, 653
Coconut Grove fire, 270
Cognitive behavior therapies, 637–638
Cognitive restructuring, 637–638
Combat, 341–348. *See also* Warfare
Concentration camp internment, 376–378
Conduct disturbances, 225, 537–542
Confrontation, 647, 648
Coping styles of school-age children, 222–225
Coronary care units (CCUs), 80–82
Corticoids, 482, 483–485
Corticosterone, 483, 485

Countertransference, 642, 645
Crimes of violence, 278–280, 294–295. *See
        also* Assaults
    hostage-taking, 300–304
    kidnapping, 300–304, 330–332, 541
    muggings, 299–300
    rape, 281–286
    reactions to, 209, 295–299
    robbery, 299–300
    spouse abuse, 286–290
Crisis, definition of, 262–263
Crisis intervention, 633–635
Crisis reaction, 297–299
Cuban refugees, 370
Cults, 525–526
Custody litigation, 47–48
Cyclone Tracy, 402

Day care:
    aggressive behavior during, 329–330
    in child's own home, 235
    effect on preschool children, 194–197
Death. *See also* Parental death; Sibling death
    effect on young children, 202–203
    by fire, 262
Defective child, birth of, 185–187
Defense mechanisms, *see* Adaptive mechanisms
Delirium, 78–80
    postoperative, 110–111
Delivery:
    cesarean, 180–181
    complications in, 184–188
    normal, 180
Depression:
    in adolescents, 610, 611–612
    chronic, in children, 608–609
    diagnosing, 553–554
    following parental death, 30–31
    medication for, 642, 643
    neuroendocrinology of, 479–480, 481–482,
        490
    in those with low social support, 502
Developmental stressors:
    in adolescence, 238–246, 609–612
    in grade-school-age children, 217–236,
        606–608
    in preschool children, 189–210, 603–605
Dihydroindolone, 566
Disasters, 257–258. *See also* Fires
    community response to, 248–249, 253
    cultural interpretations of, 253–254
    dislocations caused by, 400–403
    explosions, 541
    floods, 251–252, 541
    hostile-aggressive response to, 541–542
    hurricanes, 252–253, 255, 256
    individual reactions to, 249–251, 252–253

    nature of, 251–252
    problems in studying, 401–402
    reactions of children to, 254–255
    reactions of disaster workers to, 256
    reactions of the elderly to, 255–256
    tornados, 254, 255, 541
Discrimination, 362
    and DSM-III diagnosis, 379–381
    epidemiology of, 365–371
    individual, 371–379
    institutionalized, 371
    in psychiatric services, 382–384
    research on, 363–366
Disillusionment, 433, 434–435, 442–445
Displacement, 399–400
    caused by disasters, 400–403
    institutional, 406–409
    job-related, 409–410
    politically motivated, 403–406
    stresses associated with, 410–412
Divorce, *see* Parental divorce
Drugs, 642–644
    for treating chronic pain, 168–169
    for treating mentally retarded, 582
    for treating psychoses, 565–566
DSM-III:
    Axis IV ratings in, 4–9
    definitions in, 3–4, 466, 571–572
    and racism, 379–381
Dupont Plaza Hotel fire, 275–276

Economic stresses, 447–454
Ego support:
    development of, 499–501
    from family, 499–508
    from friendships, 510–518
    from large-group affiliations, 521–534
Elation, 482–483
Elderly:
    institutional relocation of, 406–408
    reactions to disasters, 255–256
Empathic mirroring, 647, 648
Employment patterns, 451–452
Epidemiology, 365–371
Epinephrine, 478, 480, 481, 483
Exclusion, 362, 363, 376. *See also*
        Discrimination
Explosions, 541
Extended families, 506–508
External trauma, 278–280
    rape, 281–286
    spouse abuse, 286–290

Families:
    changing patterns in, 506–508
    as ego support, 499–508
    therapy for, 320–321, 638–640

Fight or flight response, 479, 480, 481, 490, 548
Fires, 260–262, 541
  civilian disasters, 270–271
  Dupont Plaza Hotel fire, 275–276
  fear of, 265
  how they kill, 262
  looting in, 272
  loss from, 274
  panic in, 272–273
  reactions to, 262–264
    in adolescents, 268–269
    in children, 265–268
  survivors of, 274–275
  in warfare, 269–270
Floods, 251–252, 541
Forced displacement, 399–400
  caused by disasters, 400–403
  institutional, 406–409
  politically motivated, 403–406
  stresses associated with, 410–412
Foster care, 594–595, 597
Friendships, 511–514, 517

Geographic change, 418–430. *See also* Forced displacement
"Goodness of fit" development model, 465–466, 467, 469–470
Grade-school-age children, 217–236, 606–608
  cognitive transformation in, 219–220
  coping styles of, 222–225
  developmental aspects of, 217–222
  home life as source of stress for, 229–235
  impact of school on, 220–222, 226–228
  parent–child interactions of, 229–235
  reactions to fire, 267–268
  reactions to parental divorce, 51–53
  regressive coping style of, 222–225
  superego in, 218–219
Grandparents, 506–507
Grieving, *see* mourning
Groups, 515–518. *See also* Self-help groups
  in cultural history, 521–525
  functions of, 525–532
  as power bases, 528
  primary, 527–532
  for reducing anxiety, 525–526
  reference, 527–532
  relationships between individuals and, 529–532
  therapy in, 532–533, 640–642
Guilt, 271, 603
  as reaction to parental death, 29–30
  as reaction to parental divorce, 55–56
  as reaction to sibling death, 36–37

Haldol, 566
Haloperidol, 566
Hassles, 368
Hemodialysis, 112–113
Hippocampus, 481–482
Holocaust, 540
Hormones, 485–491
Hospitalization:
  for psychosis, 564–565
  reactions of adults to, 71–75
  reactions of children to, 66–71, 192–194
Hostages, 300–304
Hostile-aggressive response to stress, 539–542
Household moves, 235, 418–419
  and disadvantaged families, 427–428
  effects of:
    on children, 197, 422–423, 425–427, 428–429
    on family relationships, 423–424
  motivations for, 424–425
  to new residence, 425–427
  overseas, 429
  stages in, 419–422
Humor, in fire survivors, 274–275
Hurricane Agnes, 252–253
Hurricane Celia, 256
Hurricanes, 252–253, 255, 256

Idealization and disillusionment, 432–445
Illness:
  acute, 63–87
  catastrophic, 75–78, 80–83
  chronic, 87–104
  reactions of adults to, 71–75, 90–94
  reactions of children to, 65–71, 88–90, 204–205, 604–608
  as source of stress, 60–63
Individualism:
  in cultural history, 521–525
  and therapy, 532–533
Infants:
  and brief separations, 190–192
  need for ego support, 499–501
  reactions to acute illness, 65–71
  reactions to chronic illness, 88–90
  reactions to hospitalization, 66–71
  reactions to parental divorce, 49–50
  stress in, 602–603
  treatment for abuse, 324
Inhibition, work, 550–551
  diagnosing, 552–556
  therapy for, 556–558
Inpatients, institutional relocation of, 408–409
Insomnia, 643
Instinctual behavior, 485–491

Institutional relocation, 406
  of elderly, 406–408
  of mentally retarded inpatients, 408–409
  of psychiatric inpatients, 408
Intensive care units (ICUs), 83–87
Internment, 376–378
Interpretation, 645, 648–650, 652–653
Intervention, 472–475, 633
  behavioral techniques, 635–638
  crisis intervention, 633–635
  family therapy, 638–640
  group therapy, 640–642
  individual psychotherapy, 644–646, 651–660
  in mental retardation, 578–583
  pharmacotherapy, 642–643
  preventive, 472–473, 589–597
  in rape trauma, 284–286
Intimate relationships and illness, 504–506
Isolation, 503–504
Israeli kibbutzim, 488–489. See also
        Arab–Israeli conflict

Jenkins v. Jenkins, 198, 213
Job-related displacement, 409–410
Job stress, 449–451
Jonestown, Guyana, 526

Kidnapping, 300–304, 329–332, 541
Kidney transplantation, 112–114

LCUs, see Life crisis units
Learned coping behavior therapy, 637
Life crisis units (LCUs), 368
Life event stress, 600–602. See also Stressors
  components of, 15–17
  measuring, 9–17
Limbic system, 477, 479–480
Litigation:
  custody, 47–48
  malfeasance, 395–397
Looting, 272, 541–542
Loss. See also Object loss
  in accusation of malfeasance, 394–395
  from fire, 274
  of an ideal, 432–445
Love, 491
Luter v. Luter, 198, 214

Malfeasance accusation, 392–398
  mitigating, 397–398
  reactions to stress of, 395–397
  sources of stress in, 393–395

Marginality, 367
Mastectomy, 116–117
Medication, 642–644
  for chronic pain, 168–169
  for treating mentally retarded, 582
  for treating psychoses, 565–566
Meditation, 482–483
Medulla, 480–481
Mellaril, 566
Membership groups, 532–533
  as power bases, 528
  relationships between individuals and,
        529–532
Mentally retarded inpatients, institutional
        relocation of, 408–409
Mental retardation, 569–571
  Adjustment Disorders specific to, 575–583
  DSM-III definition of, 571–572
Military conflict, see Warfare
Minority psychiatric patients, 382
Molindone, 566
Morbidity risk, 367–368
Mourning:
  by children, 24–25, 26, 589–591
  failure in, 27–31
Moving of household, 235, 418–419. See also
        Forced displacement
  and disadvantaged families, 427–428
  effects of:
    on children, 197, 422–423, 425–427,
        428–429
    on family relationships, 423–424
  motivations for, 424–425
  to new residence, 425–427
  overseas, 429
  stages in, 419–422
Muggings, 299–300
Mutual-help groups, see Self-help groups
Myocardial infarction, 80–83

Natural disasters, see Disasters
Neonatal separations, 190–191
Neuroendocrinology, 455–456
  and emotions, 477–481, 485–491
New York Longitudinal Study (NYLS),
        460–464, 467, 468–471, 474
Noradrenaline, 478
Norepinephrine, 478, 480, 481, 483, 484
Normal delivery, 180
Normal pregnancy, 176–177, 178–179
Norms, rule of, 369
Northern Ireland, 335
Nursery school, 195
NYLS, see New York Longitudinal Study

Object loss experience:
  in early childhood, 589–597
  managing, 596
  types of, 591–593
Ophira community, 404–406
Organ transplantation, *see* Kidney
  transplantation

Pain, 160–161, 171
  chronic, 168–169
  definition of, 161–162
  psychiatric treatment for, 169–171
  relationship to stress, 162–168
Panic, 272–273, 477, 561–562, 564, 643
Parental death, 23–34, 589–591, 604, 606
Parental discord, 232–233
Parental divorce, 234
  children's coping resources for, 54
  children's reactions to, 49–53, 55–57,
    198–200
  effects in adult life, 53
  sources of stress in, 43–48
Parents:
  absence of one, 43–44
  alternative, 234. *See also* Stepparents
  illness in, response of children to, 540, 541
  interacting with school-age children, 229–235
  of mentally retarded children, 570
  responses to child's temperament, 467–469
  role of, 473–475, 612
  similarity of temperament with child, 469–470
Peer-help groups, *see* Self-help groups
Peer relationships, 511–514, 518
Personal Life History Book, 596–597
Pharmacotherapy, 642–644
  for chronic pain, 168–169
  for mental retardation, 582
  for psychoses, 565–566
Phenothiazines, 565–566
Physical assaults, 329–333
Physical handicaps in young children, 203–204
Piperadines, 566
Poisoning, 150–157
  biopsychosocial reponse to, 151–152
  etiologic factors in, 151
Postoperative delirium, 110–111
Posttraumatic Stress Disorder (PTSD), 380,
  539–540, 643
  research on, 617
  in soldiers, 347–348
Precipitants *vs.* stressors, 1
Pregnancy:
  complications in, 184–188
  normal, 176–177, 178–179
  tendency for complications in, 503

  terminating, 182–184
  with twins, 181
Prejudice, *see* Discrimination
Preschool children, 189–210, 603–605
  child care and, 194–197
  and death of parent, 589–591
  effect of death on, 202–203
  frightening experiences of, 208–209
  illness in, 204–205
  need for ego support, 499–501
  and object loss, 589–597
  overstimulation of, 208–209
  reactions to fire, 265–266
  reactions to parental divorce, 50–51
  and separations, 190–192
  sexual abuse of, 206–207
  sibling rivalry among, 207–208
  and stepparents, 201
Preventive intervention, 472–473, 589–597
Primal scenes, 208, 209
Primary groups, 527–532
Prison, threat of, 394–395
Prisoners of war:
  aftereffects of, 310–311
  effects of life-style, 309–310, 311–312
  family-related stresses, 312–313
  reactions to capture, 305–306
Prison riots, 335–336
Proneness hypothesis, 15, 16, 17
Propranolol, 643–644
Psychiatric epidemiology, 365–371
Psychiatry, discrimination in, 382–384
Psychic trauma, 346–348, 354–358
Psychoanalysis *vs.* psychotherapy, 652
Psychopharmacology, 642–644
  for chronic pain, 168–169
  for mental retardation, 582
  for psychoses, 565–566
Psychosis, 559–560
  hospitalization for, 564–565
  literature review of, 560–561
  phases of, 562–563
  process of, 561–562
  psychopharmacological approach to, 565–566
  in puberty, 563
  symptoms of, 562
  therapeutic approaches to, 563–566
Psychosocial stress:
  groups with heightened vulnerability to,
    379–381
  measuring, 3–8, 11–17
  protection against, 368–371
  racism as, 366–368
Psychotherapy:
  biracial, 384
  brief, 644–650

for children, 646–650
individual, 644–646, 651–660
vs. psychoanalysis, 652
Puberty, 238–239, 243–246
  biological factors in, 240–241
  effect of earlier development on, 239–240
  physical changes in, 242–243
  psychological factors in, 241–242
  psychosis in, 563

Racism, 362
  and DSM-III diagnosis, 379–381
  epidemiology of, 365–371
  individual, 371–379
  institutionalized, 371
  in psychiatric services, 382–384
  research on, 363–366
Rape, 280, 281–286
Rational Emotive Therapy (RET), 637–638
Reference groups, 527–532
Regressive coping style, 222–225
Relationships:
  and illness, 504–506
  with peers, 511–514, 518
Relaxation, 482–483, 636
Religion, 525–526, 630–631
Relocation. *See also* Moving of household
  institutional, 406–409
  job-related, 409–410
  politically motivated, 403–406
  reactions to, 410–412
  resulting from disasters, 400–403
Renal transplantation, 112–114
Research:
  on conduct disturbance, 539–542
  on disaster psychopathology, 400–403
  on discrimination, 363–366
  on forced displacement, 412–414
  on psychoses, 560–561
  on social support, 622–624
  on temperament, 459–460
Resiliency, 369–370
Riots, 334–336
Robbery, 299–300
Rule of norms, 369

San Angelo, Texas, tornados, 254
School:
  impact of, 220–222
  moving to new, 425
School-age children, *see* Adolescents; Grade-
    school-age children
Self-help groups, 517, 518, 631–633, 640–641
  for adolescents, 632–633

Senile dementia, 100–103
Separations, 540
  brief, 190–192
  caused by death, 202–203
  caused by hospitalization, 192–194
  caused by household move, 197
  caused by parental divorce, 198–200, 201
  child-care, 194–197
  in neonatal period, 190–191
  between parent and preschool child, 191–203,
    500–501, 604–605
  between parent and school-age child, 229,
    540
Sex hormones, 487–488
Sexual abuse, 206–207, 322–324
Siblings, 234–235
  birth of:
    child presence at, 209
    parental separation for, 191–192
  death of, 34–40, 606
    guilt reactions in, 36–37
  rivalry among, 207–208
Social networks, 515–516, 518
Social support, 518
  from friendships, 511–514
  research on, 622–624
  from social networks, 515–516
  for victims of discrimination, 370
Somatic behavior therapies, 637
Spatial identity, 403
Spouse abuse, 280, 286–290
Stelazine, 566
Stepparenting, 201
Stillbirth, 184–185
Stimulus control therapy, 637
Stockholm Syndrome, 301–302
Stress:
  adaptation to, 354–358
  aggressive responses to, 537–539
  conduct disturbances following, 537–542
  developmental sources of:
    in puberty, 238–246, 609–612
    in school-age children, 217–236, 606–608
    in small children, 189–210, 603–605
  economic, 447–454
  job-related, 449–451
  measuring, 9–17
  programs for reduction of, 624–625
  psychiatric literature on, 617–624
  relationship to psychopathology, 15–17
  research on reactions to, 307–309
Stress Inoculation procedure, 618–622, 625, 638
Stress management:
  for adults, 616–625
  for children, 612
  literature review of, 617–624

Stressors:
  acute illness, 63–87
  child abuse, 205–207, 208, 230–232,
      315–326, 605
  chronic illness, 87–104
  crime, 278–313
  death of parent, 23–34, 604, 606
  death of sibling, 34–40, 606
  developmental:
    in grade-school children, 217–236,
        606–608
    in preschool children, 189–210, 603–605
    in puberty, 238–246, 609–612
  disasters, 247–277, 541–542
  discrimination, 362–358
  disillusionment, 433, 434–435, 442–445
  economic, 447–454
  fire, 260–276
  floods, 251–252, 541
  forced displacement, 399–414
  hospitalization, 66–75
  household moving, 235, 418–430
  hurricanes, 252–253, 255–256
  kidnapping, 300–304, 330–332, 541
  military combat, 341–358
  mugging, 299–300
  pain, 160–172
  physical, 542
  pregnancy, 184–188, 503
  rape, 280, 281–286
  robbery, 299–300
  separation, 190–203, 500–501, 604–605
  specific to mental retardation:
    biological, 572–573
    psychosocial, 573–575
  spouse abuse, 280, 286–290
  types of, 21–22
  vs. precipatants, 1
Stress reduction programs, 624–625
Suicide, 319
  in adolescence, 611–612
Superego, 218–219, 441
Supporting forces, 455
Surgery, 104–117
Systematic Rational Restructuring (SRR),
    637–638

Temperament, 455, 457
  categories of, 460–461, 463
  consistency of, 464–465
  constellations of, 461–463
  as factor in Adjustment Disorders, 465–466
  identification of, 458–459
  origins of, 463–464
  parental responses to, 467–469
  research on, 459–460
  similarity between parent and child, 469–470

Termination:
  of brief therapy, 645–646
  in group therapy, 642
Therapy:
  behavioral, 624, 635–638
  biracial, 384
  brief, 644–650
  for children, 57–58, 646–650
  for chronic pain, 169–171
  forms of, 633–650
  individual, 644–646, 651–660
  for psychoses, 563–566
Thioridazine, 566
Thioxanthenes, 566
Thorazine, 565–566
Tonsillectomies, 117
Topeka, Kansas, hurricane, 255
Tornados, 254, 255, 541
Toxic ingestion, 150–157
Transference, 642, 645, 653–654
Transient situational personality disorders, 547.
    See also Adjustment
    Disorders
Trauma, external, 278–280
  rape, 281–286
  spouse abuse, 286–290
Trifluopherazine, 566
Tripartite theory, 441
Triperidol, 566
Twins, 181–182
Two-worker families, 451, 453

Unemployment, 451–452
Urban renewal, forced displacement caused by,
    403–404

Vandalism, 333
Verbal threats, 328–329
Vicksburg, Mississippi, tornados, 255
Victimization hypothesis, 15, 16, 17
Violence, see Assaults; Crimes of violence
Vulnerability, 15, 16, 17, 368, 455
  and psychosis, 559, 561–562
  temperamental characteristics as sources of,
      465–466, 471

Warfare. See also Prisoners of war
  adaptation to stress in, 354–358
  aggressive-hostile response to, 540
  and children, 351–354
  civilian stress reactions to, 349–354
  fires in, 269–270
  low-intensity, 341
  research on stress in, 617
  stress of, 340–341
    on civilians, 348–354
    on servicemen, 341–348

Welfare, 452–453
Wife abuse, 280, 286–290
Withdrawal, 548–551
  diagnosing, 552–556
  therapy for, 556–558
Work inhibition, 550–551

diagnosing, 552–556
therapy for, 556–558
Work withdrawal, 548–551
  diagnosing, 552–556
  therapy for, 556–558